Rick

BEST OF EUROPE

2012

Germany, Austria, Switzerland & Czech Republic

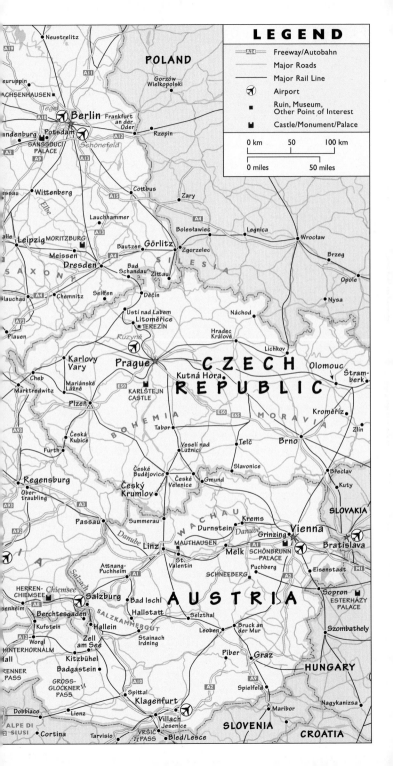

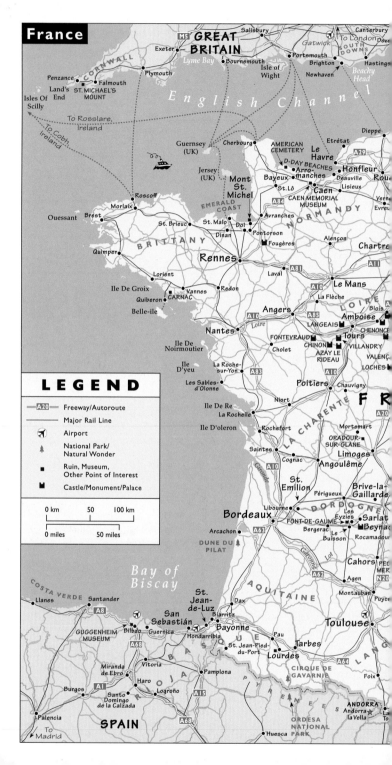

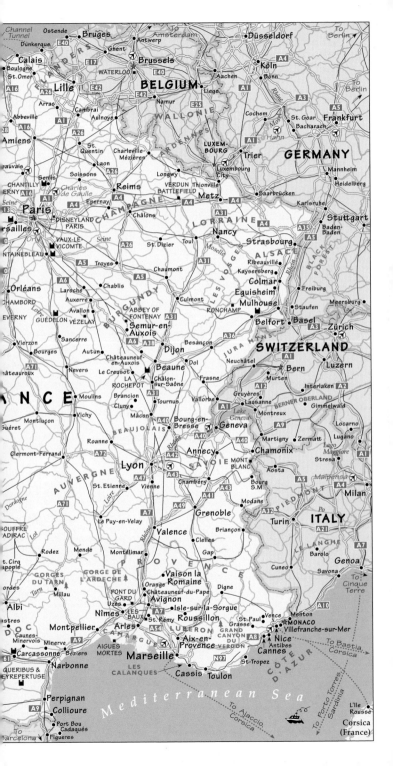

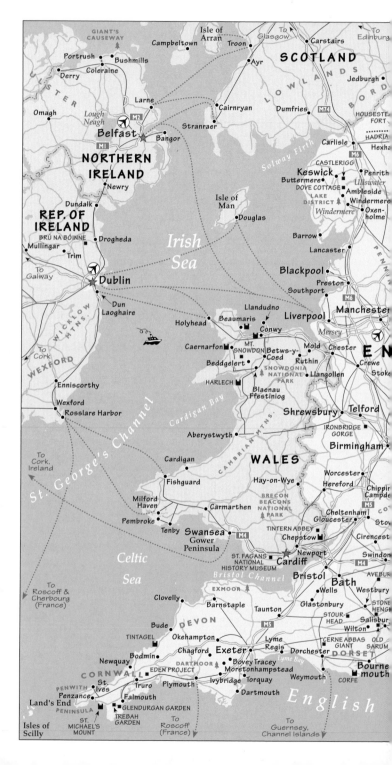

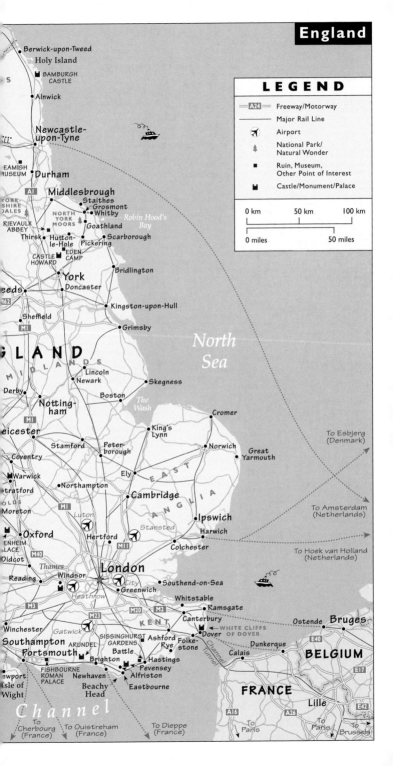

England

LEGEND

══A24══	Freeway/Motorway
——————	Major Rail Line
✈	Airport
⚇	National Park/ Natural Wonder
▪	Ruin, Museum, Other Point of Interest
⬛	Castle/Monument/Palace

0 km   50 km   100 km

0 miles   50 miles

Berwick-upon-Tweed
Holy Island
■ BAMBURGH CASTLE
• Alnwick

• Newcastle-upon-Tyne

EAMISH MUSEUM • Durham

A1

• Middlesbrough
Staithes
Grosmont
•Whitby
Robin Hood's Bay

YORK-SHIRE DALES
NORTH YORK MOORS
RIEVAULX ABBEY
Thirsk• Hutton-le-Hole Goathland
EDEN CAMP
CASTLE HOWARD Pickering • Scarborough

• York
• Doncaster
• Bridlington

eeds•
462

• Sheffield
M1

• Kingston-upon-Hull

NG L A N D

• Grimsby

MIDLANDS

• Lincoln
Derby• Newark
Notting-ham
M1
Boston
•Skegness

North Sea

The Wash

• Cromer

eicester
• Stamford
Peter-borough
• Norwich
Great Yarmouth

Coventry
• Ely
E A S T

■Warwick
•Northampton
• Cambridge

tratford
OLDS
Moreton
A N G L I A

• Ipswich

Oxford
Luton ✈
Stansted ✈
• Harwich

ENHEIM LACE
Didcot
M40
Hertford
M11
• Colchester

Reading •
Thames
•Windsor
London
• City
• Southend-on-Sea

M3
Heathrow
•Greenwich
• Whitstable

• Ramsgate

M23
M20 M2
• Canterbury

Winchester
Gatwick ✈
K E N T
Ostende Bruges

Southampton
SISSINGHURST GARDENS Ashford Folke-stone
■ WHITE CLIFFS OF DOVER
Portsmouth
ARUNDEL
Battle Rye
• Dover
Dunkerque
BELGIUM
E40

•Brighton
• Hastings
•Pevensey
• Calais

FISHBOURNE ROMAN PALACE
Newhaven Alfriston
Channel Tunnel

ewport sle of Wight
Beachy Head
• Eastbourne
FRANCE
E17

C h a n n e l
• Lille

To Cherbourg (France)
To Ouistreham (France)
To Dieppe (France)
A16
To Paris
A26
To Paris
To Brussels

To Esbjerg (Denmark)

To Amsterdam (Netherlands)

To Hoek van Holland (Netherlands)

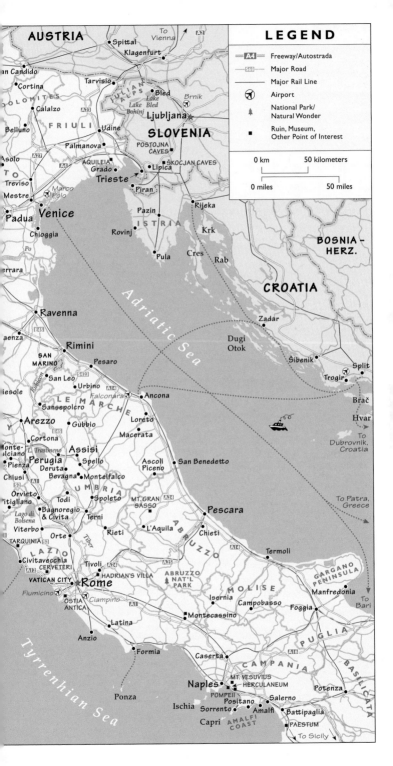

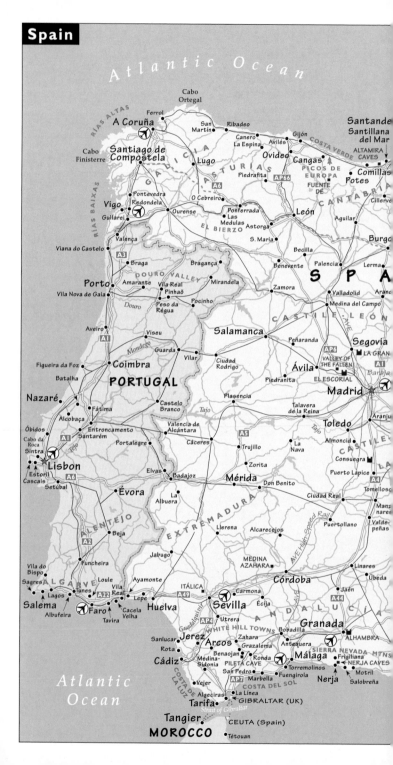

Rick Steves'®

BEST OF EUROPE

2012

CONTENTS

INTRODUCTION

Big Ben, the Eiffel Tower, and the Roman Colosseum. Yodeling in the Alps, biking down cobblestone paths, and taking a canal ride under the stars. Michelangelo's *David* and "Mad" King Ludwig's castles. Sunny Riviera beaches, medieval German towns, and Spanish streets that teem with people at night. Pasta and bratwurst, strudel and scones, Parisian crêpes and Tuscan grapes....

Europe offers a rich smorgasbord of cultures. To wrestle it down to a manageable size, this book breaks Europe into its top destinations. It then gives you all the information and opinions necessary to wring the maximum value out of your limited time and money in each location. If you plan to stay for two months or less in Europe, this book is all you need for a blitz trip.

Experiencing Europe's culture, people, and natural wonders economically and hassle-free has been my goal for more than 30 years of traveling, tour guiding, and travel writing. With this book, I pass on to you the lessons I've learned, updated for 2012.

Rick Steves' Best of Europe is the crème de la crème of places featured in my country guidebooks. It's balanced to include a comfortable mix of exciting cities and cozy towns: from Paris, London, and Rome to traffic-free Italian Riviera ports, alpine villages, and mom-and-pop châteaux. It covers the predictable biggies and mixes in a healthy dose of Back Door intimacy. Along with Leonardo in the Louvre, you'll enjoy Caterina in her cantina. I've been selective. For example, rather than listing countless medieval towns, I recommend only the best.

The best is, of course, only my opinion. But after three decades of travel research, I've developed a sixth sense for what travelers enjoy.

Key to This Book

Updates

This book is updated every year, but things change. For the latest, visit www.ricksteves.com/update, and for a valuable list of reports and experiences—good and bad—from fellow travelers, check www.ricksteves.com/feedback.

Abbreviations and Times

I use the following symbols and abbreviations in this book:

Sights are rated:

▲▲▲	**Don't miss**
▲▲	**Try hard to see**
▲	**Worthwhile if you can make it**
No rating	Worth knowing about

Tourist information offices are abbreviated as **TI,** and bathrooms are **WC**s. To categorize accommodations, I use a **Sleep Code** (described on page 14).

Like Europe, this book uses the **24-hour clock** for schedules. It's the same through 12:00 noon, then keep going: 13:00, 14:00, and so on. For anything over 12, subtract 12 and add p.m. (14:00 is 2:00 p.m.).

When giving **opening times,** I include both peak season and off-season hours if they differ. So, if a museum is listed as "May-Oct daily 9:00-16:00," it should be open from 9 a.m. until 4 p.m. from the first day of May until the last day of October (but expect exceptions).

For **transit** or **tour departures,** I first list the frequency, then the duration. So, a train connection listed as "2/hour, 1.5 hours" departs twice each hour, and the journey lasts an hour and a half.

About This Book

The book is organized by destinations, each one a mini-vacation on its own—filled with exciting sights, strollable neighborhoods, memorable restaurants, and homey, affordable accommodations.

In each chapter, you'll find these sections:

Planning Your Time contains a suggested schedule, with thoughts on how to best use your limited time.

Orientation includes specifics on public transportation, helpful hints, local tour options, easy-to-read maps, and tourist information.

Sights describes the top attractions and includes their cost and hours.

Sleeping describes my favorite hotels, from good-value deals to cushy splurges.

Eating serves up a range of options, from inexpensive pubs to fancy restaurants.

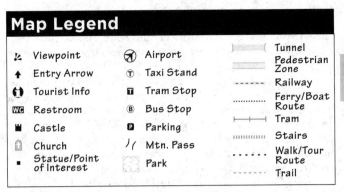

Use this legend to help you navigate the maps in this book.

Connections outlines your options for traveling to destinations by train, bus, and plane.

The **appendix** has transportation basics, a calling chart, a climate chart, a hotel reservation form, and information on US embassies for the countries in this book.

Browse through this book, choose your favorite destinations, and create your own itinerary. Then have a great trip! Traveling like a temporary local and taking advantage of the information here, you'll get the absolute most out of every mile, minute, and euro. I'm happy you'll be visiting places I know and love, and meeting some of my favorite people.

Planning

This section will help you get started on planning your trip—with advice on trip costs, when to go, and what you should know before you take off.

Travel Smart

Your trip to Europe is like a complex play—easier to follow and really appreciate on a second viewing. While no one does the same trip twice to gain that advantage, reading this book's chapters on your intended destinations before your trip accomplishes much the same thing.

Design an itinerary that enables you to visit the various sights at the best possible times. Note holidays, festivals, and days when sights are closed. For example, many sights in Florence are closed on Mondays; Tuesdays are bad in Paris. Museums and sights, especially large ones, usually stop admitting people 30-60 minutes before closing time.

Sundays have the same pros and cons as they do for travelers in the US (special events, limited hours, banks and many shops closed, limited public transportation, no rush hour). Saturdays are virtually weekdays, with earlier closing hours and no rush hour. Popular destinations are even more popular on weekends; book ahead for Fridays and Saturdays.

Mix intense and relaxed periods in your itinerary. To maximize rootedness, minimize one-night stands. It's worth a long drive after dinner to be settled into a town for two nights. Hotels are also more likely to give a good price to someone staying more than one night. Every trip (and every traveler) needs at least a few slack days (for picnics, laundry, people-watching, and so on). Pace yourself. Assume you will return.

Reread this book as you travel, and visit local TIs. While traveling, take advantage of the Internet and phones to make your trip run smoothly. By going online (at Internet cafés or your hotel), buying a phone card, or carrying a mobile phone, you can get tourist information, learn the latest on sights (special events, tour schedules, etc.), book tickets and tours, make reservations, reconfirm hotels, research transportation connections, and keep in touch with loved ones.

Enjoy the friendliness of the local people. Slow down and ask questions—most locals are eager to point you in their idea of the right direction. Keep a notepad in your pocket for organizing your thoughts. Wear your money belt, and figure out how to estimate prices in dollars. Those who expect to travel smart, do.

Trip Costs

Five components make up your trip cost: airfare, surface transportation, room and board, sightseeing and entertainment, and shopping and miscellany.

Airfare: A basic round-trip US-to-Europe flight costs around $700-1,500, depending on where you fly from and when (prices cheaper in winter), plus another $300-500 in taxes, fuel surcharges, and other fees. Consider saving time and money in Europe by flying "open jaw"—into one city and out of another—for example, into London and out of Rome.

Surface Transportation: Your best mode of travel depends on the time you have and the scope of your trip. For many, the best option is a Eurailpass. Note that train passes are generally only available outside of Europe. You may save money by simply buying tickets as you go (for more information, see page 1438 of the appendix).

Drivers can figure about $375 per person per week (based on two people splitting the cost of the car, tolls, gas, and insurance). Car rental is cheapest to arrange from the US; for trips over three weeks, look into leasing.

European Almanac

Population: The European Union (EU) has 492 million (the US has 313 million, and all of Europe, including the non-EU countries, numbers 731 million).

Area: The EU countries measure 1.7 million square miles (roughly half of the continental US).

Languages: Three main groups: Romance (Italian, Spanish, French), Slavic (Eastern Europe and Russia), and Germanic (German, Dutch, Scandinavian...and English). Most popular second languages are English and French.

Climate: Moderate, warmed by prevailing westerly sea winds. Average of about 65°F in summer, 40°F in winter.

Vegetation: In the north, a mix of conifers (pine and fir) and deciduous trees (oak, elm, and maple). Along the Mediterranean, there are olives, figs, and grapes.

Major Rivers: Danube, Rhine, Rhône, Po, and Seine.

Life Expectancy: About 77 years, among the highest in the world.

Religion: Largely Protestant in the North, Catholic in the South. Many Europeans claim no church affiliation.

Government: The EU is a federation of independent nations. Formed as an economic trade bloc, it is increasingly a political body with elected representatives.

Gross Domestic Product: The EU's nominal GDP is $15.9 trillion (a little more than the US).

Room and Board: You can easily manage in Europe in 2012 on an overall average of $120 a day per person for room and board (more for cities, less for towns). A $120-a-day budget allows an average of $15 for lunch, $5 for a snack, $25 for dinner, and $75 for lodging (based on two people splitting the cost of a $150 double room that includes breakfast). That's doable. Students and tightwads can enjoy Europe for as little as $60 a day ($30 per hostel bed, $30 for groceries).

Sightseeing and Entertainment: In big cities, figure $10-20 per major sight, $5-10 for minor ones, and $30 for splurge experiences (e.g., tours, concerts, gelato binges). An overall average of $30 a day works for most. Don't skimp here. After all, this category is the driving force behind your trip—you came to sightsee, enjoy, and experience Europe.

Shopping and Miscellany: Figure $2 per postcard, $3 per coffee and ice-cream cone, and $6 per beer. Shopping can vary in cost from nearly nothing to a small fortune. Good budget travelers find that this category has little to do with assembling a trip full of lifelong and wonderful memories.

Best of Europe Itinerary

Sightseeing Priorities

Only have a week to "see" Europe? You can't, of course, but if you're organized and energetic, you can see the two art-filled cultural capitals of London and Paris plus Europe's most magnificent landscape—the Swiss Alps.

Whether you have just a week, or longer, here are my recommended priorities. These itineraries are fast-paced, but doable by car or train, and each allows about two nights in each spot (I've taken geographical proximity into account). Most work best if you fly "open jaw."

If you have...

5 days:	Paris, Swiss Alps
7 days, add:	London
10 days, add:	Rome
14 days, add:	Rhine, Amsterdam, Haarlem
18 days, add:	Venice, Florence
24 days, add:	Cinque Terre, Rothenburg, Bavaria
31 days, add:	Bath, Salzburg, Hallstatt, Nice
37 days, add:	Provence, Barcelona, Madrid
43 days, add:	Vienna, Prague, Berlin
45 days, add:	Bruges

When to Go

May, June, September, and October are the best travel months. Peak season, July and August, offers the sunniest weather and the most exciting slate of activities—but the worst crowds. During this busy time, it's best to reserve rooms well in advance, particularly in big cities.

During the off-season, October through April, expect generally shorter hours at attractions, more closures for lunchtime (especially at smaller sights), fewer activities, and fewer—if any—guided tours in English. Especially off-season, be sure to confirm opening hours for sights at local tourist information offices.

As a general rule any time of year, the climate north of the Alps is mild (like Seattle), while south of the Alps it's like Arizona. For specifics, see the climate chart in the appendix. If you wilt in the heat, avoid the Mediterranean in summer. If you want blue skies in the Alps, Britain, and Scandinavia, travel during the height of summer.

Plan your itinerary to meet your needs. To beat the heat, start in the south in the spring and work your way north. To moderate culture shock, start in Britain and travel south and east.

Know Before You Go

Your trip is more likely to go smoothly if you plan ahead. Check this list of things to arrange while you're still at home.

You need a **passport**—but no visa or shots—to travel to any of the countries in this book. You may be denied entry into certain European countries if your passport is due to expire within three to six months of your ticketed date of return. Get it renewed if you'll be cutting it close. It can take up to six weeks to get or renew a passport (for more on passports, see www.travel.state.gov). Pack a photocopy of your passport in your luggage in case the original is lost or stolen.

Book your rooms well in advance if you'll be traveling during peak season or any major **holidays.**

Call your **debit- and credit-card companies** to let them know the countries you'll be visiting, so that they won't deny your international charges (see "Money," later).

If you're bringing a mobile device, you can download free information from **Rick Steves Audio Europe,** featuring hours of travel interviews; audio tours of major sights in London, Paris, Florence, Rome, and Venice; and more (at www.ricksteves.com /audioeurope, iTunes, or through the Rick Steves Audio Europe smartphone app; for details, see page 1444).

If you're interested in **travel insurance,** do your homework before you buy. Compare the cost of the insurance to the likelihood of your using it and your potential loss if something goes

INTRODUCTION

> ## Additional Online Resources
>
> Go online for more information on the following topics:
>
> **Phoning**
> www.ricksteves.com/phoning
>
> **VAT Refunds**
> www.ricksteves.com/plan/tips/vat.htm
>
> **Customs Rules and Duty Rates**
> www.cbp.gov (click on "Travel," then "Know Before You Go")
>
> **Sightseeing**
> www.ricksteves.com/plan/tips/museum.htm
>
> **Car Rental Insurance**
> www.ricksteves.com/cdw

wrong. For details on the many kinds of travel insurance, see www
.ricksteves.com/plan/tips/insurance.htm.

If you'll be **renting a car** in Europe, you'll need your driver's license, and in some countries (including Austria, Italy, and Spain), an International Driving Permit (IDP), available at your local AAA office ($15 plus the cost of two passport-type photos, see www.aaa.com). In other countries, it's recommended that you carry an IDP. Confirm pick-up hours—many car-rental offices close Saturday afternoon and all day Sunday.

Because **airline carry-on restrictions** are always changing, visit the Transportation Security Administration's website (www .tsa.gov/travelers) for an up-to-date list of what you can bring on the plane with you...and what you have to check. Some airlines may restrict you to only one carry-on (no extras like a purse or daypack); check with your airline.

Practicalities

Emergency and Medical Help: If you get sick, do as many Europeans do and go to a pharmacist for advice. Or ask at your hotel for help—they'll know the nearest medical and emergency services.

Lost or Stolen Passport: To replace a passport, you'll need to go in person to a US embassy (see page 1435). While not required, having a backup form of ID—ideally a photocopy of your passport and driver's license—speeds up a replacement. For more information, see www.ricksteves.com/help.

Time: European schedules—and this book—use the 24-hour clock. It's the same through 12:00 noon, then keep going: 13:00, 14:00, and so on. For anything over 12, subtract 12 and add p.m. (14:00 is 2:00 p.m.).

Most of continental Europe is generally six/nine hours ahead of the East/West Coasts of the US. The exceptions are the beginning and end of Daylight Saving Time: Europe "springs forward" the last Sunday in March (two weeks after most of North America), and "falls back" the last Sunday in October (one week before North America). For a handy online time converter, try www.timeanddate.com/worldclock.

Watt's Up? Europe's electrical system is different from North America's in two ways: the shape of the plug (two round prongs) and the voltage of the current (220 volts instead of 110 volts). For your North American plug to work in Europe, you'll need an adapter, sold inexpensively at travel stores in the US. As for the voltage, most newer electronics or travel appliances (such as hair dryers, laptops, and battery chargers) automatically convert the voltage—if you see a range of voltages printed on the item or its plug (such as "110-220"), it'll work in Europe. Otherwise, you can buy a converter separately in the US (about $20).

Discounts: While discounts are not listed in this book, seniors (age 60 and over), students with International Student Identification Cards, teachers with proper identification, and youths under 18 often get discounts—but you have to ask. To get a teacher or student ID card, visit www.statravel.com or www.isic.org.

Money

This section offers advice on how to pay for purchases on your trip (including getting cash from ATMs and paying with plastic), dealing with lost or stolen cards, and tipping.

What to Bring

Bring both a credit card and a debit card. You'll use the debit card at cash machines (ATMs) to withdraw cash for most purchases, and the credit card to pay for larger items.

As an emergency backup, bring several hundred dollars in hard cash (in easy-to-exchange $20 bills). Avoid using currency exchange booths (lousy rates and/or outrageous fees); if you have foreign currency to exchange, take it to a bank. Don't use traveler's checks—they're a waste of time (long waits at slow banks) and a waste of money in fees.

Cash

Cash is just as desirable in Europe as it is at home. Small businesses (hotels, restaurants, and shops) prefer that you pay your bills with cash. Some vendors will charge you extra for using a credit card, and some won't take credit cards at all.

Exchange Rates

1 euro (€) = about $1.40. To roughly convert prices in euros to dollars, add 40 percent: €20 is about $28.

1 British pound (£1) = about $1.60. To easily convert prices in pounds to dollars, add 60 percent.

1 Swiss franc (SF) = about $1. The Swiss franc is approximately equivalent to the dollar.

20 Czech crowns (*koruna*, Kč) = about $1. To estimate prices in dollars, drop the last digit and divide in half (e.g., 1,000 Kč = about $50).

Throughout Europe, cash machines (ATMs) are the standard way for travelers to get local currency. To withdraw money from an ATM, you'll need a debit card (ideally with a Visa or MasterCard logo for maximum usability), plus a PIN code. Know your PIN code in numbers because there are no letters on European keypads. You could use a credit card for ATM transactions, but it's generally more expensive (since it's considered a "cash advance" rather than a "withdrawal"). For security, it's best to shield the keypad when entering your PIN at the ATM.

When using an ATM, taking out large sums of money can reduce the number of per-transaction bank fees you'll pay. If the machine refuses your request, try again and select a smaller amount (some cash machines limit the amount you can withdraw—don't take it personally). If that doesn't work, try a different machine.

Many ATMs in Europe are located outside of a bank. Try to use the ATM when the branch is open; if your card is eaten by a machine, you can immediately go inside for help. If the ATM dispenses big bills, try to break them at a bank or larger store, since it's easier to pay for purchases at small businesses using smaller bills.

Even in Europe, you'll need to keep your cash safe. Use a money belt—a pouch with a strap that you buckle around your waist like a belt and wear under your clothes. Pickpockets target tourists. A money belt provides peace of mind, allowing you to carry lots of cash safely. Don't waste time every few days tracking down a cash machine—withdraw a week's worth of money, stuff it in your money belt, and travel!

Credit and Debit Cards

Visa and MasterCard are more commonly accepted than American Express. While you can use either a credit or a debit card for most transactions, using a credit card offers a greater degree of fraud protection (since debit cards draw funds directly from your account).

Just like at home, credit or debit cards work easily at larger hotels, restaurants, and shops. I typically use my credit card only in a few specific situations: to book hotel reservations by phone, to make major purchases (such as car rentals, plane tickets, and long hotel stays), and to pay for things near the end of my trip (to avoid another visit to the ATM).

Ask Your Credit- or Debit-Card Company: Before your trip, contact the company that issued your debit or credit cards.

• Confirm your card will work overseas, and alert them that you'll be using it in Europe; otherwise, they may deny transactions if they perceive unusual spending patterns.

• Ask for the specifics on transaction **fees.** When you use your credit or debit card—either for purchases or ATM withdrawals—you'll often be charged additional "international transaction" fees of up to 3 percent (1 percent is normal) plus $5 per transaction. If your fees are too high, consider getting a card just for your trip: Capital One (www.capitalone.com) and most credit unions have low-to-no international fees.

• If you plan to withdraw cash from ATMs, confirm your daily **withdrawal limit** (usually a maximum of €300 in the Eurozone and £300 in the UK). Some travelers prefer a high limit that allows them to take out more cash at each ATM stop, while others prefer to set a lower limit in case their card is stolen.

• Ask for your credit card's **PIN** in case you encounter Europe's chip-and-PIN system.

Other Fees: If merchants offer to convert your purchase price into dollars (called dynamic currency conversion, or "DCC"), refuse this "service." You'll pay even more in fees for the expensive convenience of seeing your charge in dollars.

Chip and PIN: If your card is declined for a purchase in Europe, it may be because of chip and PIN, which requires card-holders to punch in a PIN instead of signing a receipt. Much of Europe, including Great Britain, Ireland, France, the Netherlands, and Scandinavia, is adopting this system. Chip and PIN is used by some merchants and also at automated payment machines—such as those at train stations, parking garages, luggage lockers, and self-serve pumps at gas stations. If you're prompted to enter your PIN (but don't know it), ask if the cashier can print a receipt for you to sign instead, or just pay cash. If you're dealing with an auto-mated machine that won't take your card, look for a cashier nearby who can make your card work.

Travelex offers US travelers a chip-and-PIN card, called "Cash Passport," preloaded with euros or British pounds (www.travelex .com)—but you must load at least €150 (or £125) at an exorbitant exchange rate. The easiest solution is to carry sufficient cash.

Damage Control for Lost Cards

If you lose your credit, debit, or ATM card, you can stop people from using it by reporting the loss immediately to the respective global customer-assistance centers. Call these 24-hour US numbers collect: Visa (410/581-9994), MasterCard (636/722-7111), and American Express (623/492-8427).

At a minimum, you'll need to know the name of the financial institution that issued you the card, along with the type of card (classic, platinum, or whatever). Providing the following information will allow for a quicker cancellation of your missing card: full card number, whether you are the primary or secondary cardholder, the cardholder's name exactly as printed on the card, billing address, home phone number, circumstances of the loss or theft, and identification verification (your birth date, your mother's maiden name, or your Social Security number—memorize this, don't carry a copy). If you are the secondary cardholder, you'll also need to provide the primary cardholder's identification-verification details. You can generally receive a temporary card within two or three business days in Europe.

If you promptly report your card lost or stolen, you typically won't be responsible for any unauthorized transactions on your account, although many banks charge a liability fee of $50.

Tips on Tipping

Tipping in Europe isn't as automatic and generous as it is in the US—but for special service, tips are appreciated, if not expected. Here are some general guidelines.

Restaurants: Virtually anywhere in Europe, you can do as the Europeans do, and if you're pleased with the service, round up a euro or two. In most places, 5 percent is adequate and 10 percent is considered a big tip. Please believe me—tipping 15-20 percent in Europe is unnecessary, if not culturally insensitive. Tipping is only expected at restaurants with waiters and waitresses; skip the tip if you order food at a counter (in a pub, for example). Servers prefer to be tipped in cash even if you pay with your credit card (otherwise the tip may never reach your server).

Taxis: For a typical ride, round up about 5-10 percent (to pay a €4.50 fare, give €5; for a €28 fare, give €30). If the cabbie hauls your bags and zips you to the airport to help you catch your flight, you might want to toss in a little more. But if you feel like you're being driven in circles or otherwise ripped off, skip the tip.

Special Services: Tour guides at public sights often hold out their hands for tips after they give their spiel. If I've already paid for the tour, I don't tip extra unless they've really impressed me. At hotels, if you let porters carry your luggage, it's polite to give them a euro per bag (another reason to pack light). I don't tip the maid, but if you do, you can leave a euro per overnight at the end of your stay.

In general, if someone in the service industry does a super job for you, a tip of a couple of euros is appropriate...but not required. If you're not sure whether (or how much) to tip for a service, ask your hotelier or the TI; they'll fill you in on how it's done on their turf.

Sleeping

I favor accommodations (and restaurants) that are handy to your sightseeing activities. Rather than list lodgings scattered through-out a city, I choose two or three favorite neighborhoods and rec-ommend the best accommodations values in each, from $30 bunk beds to fancy-for-my-book $300 doubles.

Types of Accommodations

Hotels

Double rooms in hotels listed in this book will range from about $50 (very simple, toilet and shower down the hall) to $450 (maxi-mum plumbing and more), with most clustering at about $150 (with private bathrooms). Prices are higher in big cities and heavily touristed cities, and lower off the beaten path. Three or four people economize by requesting larger rooms.

During these times of economic uncertainty, many hotels will likely discount deeply to snare what customers they can. If you email several places and ask for their best prices, you'll find some eager to discount and others more passive. This can save you big bucks—with prices potentially far below those listed in this guide-book.

Prices at nearly any hotel can get soft if you book direct (without using a pricey middleman like the TI or a Web booking service), travel off-season, and/or pay cash (cash payment gets you an additional 5-10 percent discount at many hotels—ask when you check in). Assume that breakfast is included in the prices I've listed, unless otherwise noted. If breakfast costs extra and is optional, you may want to skip it. While convenient, it's often a poor value.

Hoteliers can be a great help and source of advice. Most know their city well and can assist you with everything from public tran-sit and airport connections to finding a good restaurant, the near-est Internet café, or launderette.

Even at the best places, mechanical breakdowns occur: Air-conditioning malfunctions, sinks leak, hot water turns cold, and toilets gurgle and smell. Report your concerns clearly and calmly at the front desk. For more complicated problems, don't expect instant results.

Sleep Code

To help you sort easily through the listings, I've divided the rooms into three categories based on the price for a standard double room with bath:

$$$ Higher Priced
$$ Moderately Priced
$ Lower Priced

To give maximum information in a minimum of space, I use the following code to describe the accommodations. Prices in this book are listed per room, not per person.

When a price range is given for a type of room, it means the price fluctuates with the season, size of room, or length of stay.

- **S** = Single room (or price for one person in a double).
- **D** = Double or twin. Double beds are usually big enough for nonromantic couples.
- **T** = Triple (generally a double bed with a single).
- **Q** = Quad (usually two double beds).
- **b** = Private bathroom with toilet and shower or tub.
- **s** = Private shower or tub only (the toilet is down the hall).

According to this code, a couple staying at a "Db-€140" hotel would pay a total of €140 (about $200) for a double room with a private bathroom. Unless otherwise noted, breakfast is included, hotel staff speak basic English, and credit cards are accepted.

If I mention "Internet access" in a listing, there's a public terminal in the lobby for guests to use. If I include "Wi-Fi," you can generally access it in your room (usually for free), but only if you have your own laptop or mobile device.

If you suspect night noise will be a problem, ask for a quiet room in the back or on an upper floor. To guard against theft in your room, keep valuables out of sight. Some rooms come with a safe, and others have safes at the front desk. Use them if you're concerned.

Checkout can pose problems if surprise charges pop up on your bill. If you settle up your bill the day before you leave, you'll have time to discuss and address any points of contention (before 19:00, when the night shift usually arrives).

If you're traveling beyond my recommended destinations, you'll find accommodations where you need them. Any town with tourists has a TI that books rooms or can give you a list and point you in the right direction. In the absence of a TI, ask people on the street or in pubs or restaurants for help.

Bed-and-Breakfasts and Pensions

Between hotels and hostels in price and style is a special class of accommodations: bed-and-breakfasts (B&Bs) and pensions. These are small, warm, and family-run, and offer a personal touch at a budget price—about $40-60 per person. Each country has these friendly accommodations in varying degrees of abundance, facilities, and service. Some include breakfast; some don't. They have different names from country to country—they're called *Gasthäuser* in Germany, *chambre d'hôte* in France, *affitta camere* in Italy, and *casa particulare* in Spain—but all have one thing in common: They satisfy the need for a place to stay that gives you the privacy of a hotel and the comforts of home at an affordable price.

Hostels

You'll pay about $25-30 per bed to stay at a hostel. Travelers of any age are welcome if they don't mind dorm-style accommodations or meeting other travelers. Cheap meals are sometimes available, and kitchen facilities are usually provided. Expect youth groups in spring, crowds in the summer, snoring, and great variability in quality from one hostel to the next. Family and private rooms are sometimes available on request, but it's basically boys' dorms and girls' dorms. You usually can't check in before 17:00 and must be out by 10:00. There is often a late-night curfew.

Making Reservations

Given the quality of the B&Bs and hotels I've found for this book, I'd recommend that you reserve your rooms in advance, particularly if you'll be traveling during peak season. Book several weeks ahead, or as soon as you've pinned down your travel dates. Note that some national holidays jam things up and merit your making reservations far in advance (see www.ricksteves.com/festivals, and tourist board websites per country—listed at www.towd.com). Just like at home, holidays that fall on a Monday, Thursday, or Friday can turn the weekend into a long holiday, so book the entire weekend well ahead of time.

Requesting a Reservation: To make a reservation, contact hotels and B&Bs directly by email, phone, or fax. Email is the clearest and most economical way to make a reservation. Or you can go straight to the hotel website; many have secure online reservation forms and can instantly inform you of availability and any special deals. But be sure you use the hotel's official site and not a booking agency's site—otherwise you may pay higher rates than you should. If phoning from the US, be mindful of time zones. Most hoteliers listed are accustomed to English-only speakers.

The hotelier wants to know these key pieces of information

(also included in the sample request form in the appendix):
- number and type of rooms
- number of nights
- date of arrival
- date of departure
- any special needs (e.g., bathroom in the room or down the hall, twin beds vs. double bed, air-conditioning, quiet, view, ground floor, etc.)

When you request a room, use the European style for writing dates: day/month/year. For example, for a two-night stay in July, I would request "2 nights, arrive 16/07/12, depart 18/07/12." (Consider in advance how long you'll stay; don't just assume you can tack on extra days once you arrive.) Mention any discounts offered—for Rick Steves readers or otherwise—when you make the reservation.

If you don't get a reply to your email or fax, it usually means the hotel is already fully booked (but you can try sending the message again, or call to follow up).

Confirming a Reservation: If the hotel's response includes its room availability and rates, it's not a confirmation. You must tell them that you want that room at the given rate. Many hoteliers will request your credit-card number for a one-night deposit to hold the room. While you can email your credit-card information (I do), it's safer to share that personal info via phone call, fax, two successive emails, or secure online reservation form (if the hotel has one on its website).

Canceling a Reservation: If you must cancel your reservation, it's courteous to do so with as much advance notice as possible—at least three days. Simply make a quick phone call or send an email. Family-run hotels and B&Bs lose money if they turn away customers while holding a room for someone who doesn't show up. Understandably, many hotels bill no-shows for one night.

Hotels in larger cities such as London sometimes have strict cancellation policies. For example, you might lose a deposit if you cancel within two weeks of your reserved stay, or you might be billed for the entire visit if you leave early. Internet deals may require prepayment, with no refunds for cancellations. If concerned, ask about cancellation policies before you book.

If canceling via email, request confirmation that your message was received to avoid being accidentally billed.

Reconfirm Your Reservation: Always call to reconfirm your room reservation a day or two in advance from the road. Smaller hotels and pensions appreciate knowing your time of arrival. If you'll be arriving after 17:00, be sure to let your hotelier know. On the small chance that a hotel loses track of your reservation, bring along a hard copy of your emailed or faxed confirmation. Don't

How Was Your Trip?

Were your travels fun, smooth, and meaningful? If you'd like to share your tips, concerns, and discoveries, please fill out the survey at www.ricksteves.com/feedback. I value your feedback. Thanks in advance—it helps a lot.

have the TI reconfirm rooms for you; they'll take a commission.

Reserving Rooms as You Travel: If you enjoy having a flexible itinerary, you can make reservations as you travel, calling hotels or B&Bs a few days to a week before your visit. If you prefer the flexibility of traveling without any reservations at all, you'll have greater success snaring rooms if you arrive at your destination early in the day. When you anticipate crowds (weekends are worst), call hotels at about 9:00 or 10:00 on the day you plan to arrive, when the hotel clerk knows who'll be checking out and just which rooms will be available.

Traveling as a Temporary Local

We travel all the way to Europe to enjoy differences—to become temporary locals. You'll experience frustrations. Certain truths that we find "God-given" or "self-evident," like cold beer, ice in drinks, bottomless cups of coffee, hot showers, and bigger being better, are suddenly not so true. One of the benefits of travel is the eye-opening realization that there are logical, civil, and even better alternatives.

Americans are enjoying a surge in popularity in Europe these days. But if there is a negative aspect to the image Europeans have of Americans, it's that we are big, loud, aggressive, impolite, rich, superficially friendly, and a bit naive.

Americans tend to be noisy in public places, such as restaurants and trains. My European friends place a high value on speaking quietly in these same places. Listen while on the bus or in a restaurant—the place can be packed, but the decibel level is low. Try to remember this nuance, and soften your speaking voice as a way of respecting their culture. While Europeans look bemusedly at some of our Yankee excesses—and worriedly at others—they nearly always afford us individual travelers all the warmth we deserve.

Judging from all the positive comments I receive from travelers who have used this book, it's safe to assume you'll enjoy a great, affordable vacation—with the finesse of an experienced, independent traveler. Thanks, and happy travels!

Back Door Travel Philosophy
From *Rick Steves' Europe Through the Back Door*

Travel is intensified living—maximum thrills per minute and one of the last great sources of legal adventure. Travel is freedom. It's recess, and we need it.

Experiencing the real Europe requires catching it by surprise, going casual..."Through the Back Door."

Affording travel is a matter of priorities. (Make do with the old car.) You can eat and sleep—simply, safely, and enjoyably—anywhere in Europe for $120 a day plus transportation costs. In many ways, spending more money only builds a thicker wall between you and what you traveled so far to see. Europe is a cultural carnival, and time after time, you'll find that its best acts are free and the best seats are the cheap ones.

A tight budget forces you to travel close to the ground, meeting and communicating with the people. Never sacrifice sleep, nutrition, safety, or cleanliness to save money. Simply enjoy the local-style alternatives to expensive hotels and restaurants.

Connecting with people carbonates your experience. Extroverts have more fun. If your trip is low on magic moments, kick yourself and make things happen. If you don't enjoy a place, maybe you don't know enough about it. Seek the truth. Recognize tourist traps. Give a culture the benefit of your open mind. See things as different, but not better or worse. Any culture has plenty to share.

Of course, travel, like the world, is a series of hills and valleys. Be fanatically positive and militantly optimistic. If something's not to your liking, change your liking.

Travel can make you a happier American, as well as a citizen of the world. Our Earth is home to six and a half billion equally precious people. It's humbling to travel and find that other people don't have the "American Dream"—they have their own dreams. Europeans like us, but with all due respect, they wouldn't trade passports.

Thoughtful travel engages us with the world. In tough economic times, it reminds us what is truly important. By broadening perspectives, travel teaches new ways to measure quality of life.

Globetrotting destroys ethnocentricity, helping us understand and appreciate other cultures. Rather than fear the diversity on this planet, celebrate it. Among your most prized souvenirs will be the strands of different cultures you choose to knit into your own character. The world is a cultural yarn shop, and Back Door travelers are weaving the ultimate tapestry. Join in!

AUSTRIA

VIENNA

Wien

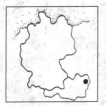

Vienna is the capital of Austria, the cradle of classical music, the home of the rich Habsburg heritage, and one of Europe's most livable cities. The city center is skyscraper-free, pedestrian-friendly, dotted with quiet parks, and traversed by electric trams. Many buildings still reflect 18th- and 19th-century elegance, when the city was at the forefront of the arts and sciences. Compared with most modern European urban centers, the pace of life is slow.

Vienna (*Wien* in German—pronounced "veen") has always been considered the easternmost city of the West. For 640 years, Vienna was the capital of the enormous Austrian Empire, a.k.a. the Austro-Hungarian Empire, a.k.a. the Habsburg Empire (after the dynasty that controlled this area, and at times much of the rest of Europe, for centuries). Stretching from the Alps of northern Italy to the rugged Carpathians of Romania, and from the banks of the Danube to sunny Dubrovnik, this multiethnic empire was arguably the most powerful European entity since Rome. And yet, of its 60 million people, only eight million were Austrian; Vienna was a kind of Eastern European melting pot. Today, the truly Viennese person is not Austrian, but a second-generation Habsburg cocktail, with grandparents from the distant corners of the old empire—Hungary, the Czech Republic, Slovakia, Poland, Slovenia, Croatia, Bosnia-Herzegovina, Serbia, Romania, and Italy.

Vienna reached its peak in the 19th century. Politically, it hosted European diplomats at the 1814 Congress of Vienna, which reaffirmed Europe's conservative monarchy after the French Revolution and Napoleon. Vienna became one of Europe's cultural

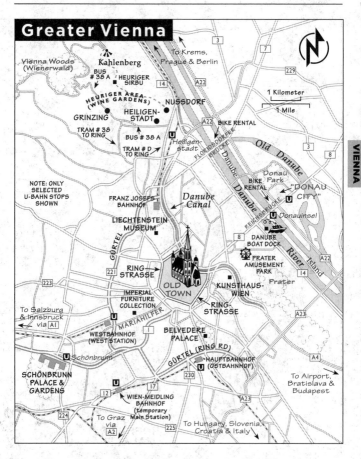

Greater Vienna

capitals, home to groundbreaking composers (Beethoven, Mozart, Brahms, Strauss), scientists (Doppler, Boltzmann), philosophers (Freud, Husserl, Schlick, Gödel, Steiner), architects (Wagner, Loos), and painters (Klimt, Schiele, Kokoschka). In 1900, Vienna's 2.2 million inhabitants made it the world's fifth-largest city—after New York, London, Paris, and Berlin. By the turn of the 20th century, Vienna sat on the cusp between stuffy Old World monarchy and subversive modern trends.

However, after starting and losing World War I, the Habsburgs lost their far-flung holdings. Then came World War II: While Vienna's old walls had long held out would-be invaders—Germanic barbarians (in Roman times), marauding Magyars (today's Hungarians, 10th century), Mongol hordes (13th century), Ottoman Turks (the sieges of 1529 and 1683)—they were no match for WWII bombs, which destroyed nearly a quarter of the city's buildings. In the Cold War, neutral Austria took a big bite out of

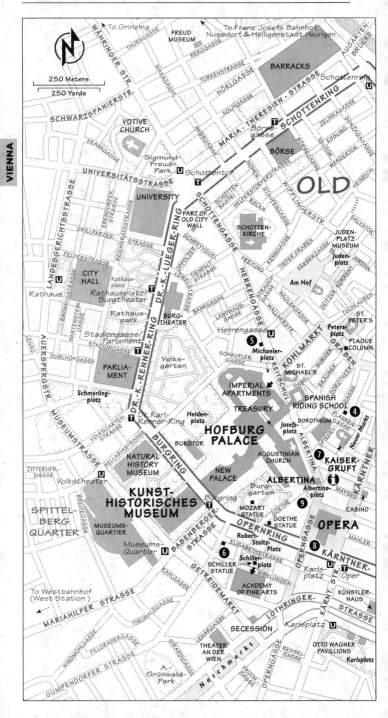

VIENNA

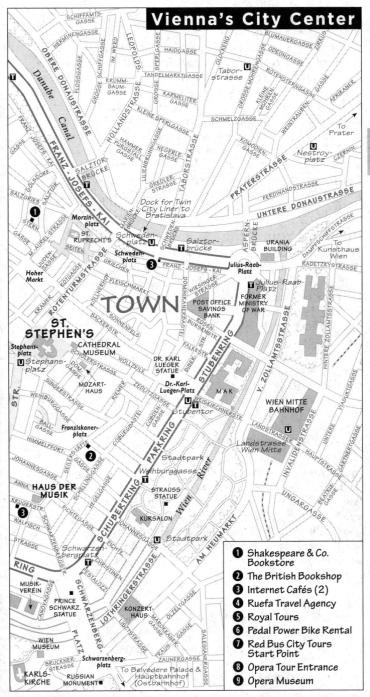

Vienna's City Center

1 Shakespeare & Co. Bookstore
2 The British Bookshop
3 Internet Cafés (2)
4 Ruefa Travel Agency
5 Royal Tours
6 Pedal Power Bike Rental
7 Red Bus City Tours Start Point
8 Opera Tour Entrance
9 Opera Museum

the USSR's Warsaw Pact buffer zone—and Vienna became, for a time, a den of spies.

Today Vienna has settled down into a somewhat sleepy, pleasant place where culture is still king. Classical music is everywhere. People nurse a pastry and coffee over the daily paper at small cafés. It's a city of world-class museums, big and small. Anyone with an interest in painting, music, architecture, beautiful objects, or Sacher-Torte with whipped cream will feel right at home.

From a practical standpoint, Vienna serves as a prime "gateway" city. The location is central and convenient to most major Eastern European destinations. Actually farther east than Prague, Ljubljana, and Zagreb, and just upstream on the Danube from Budapest and Bratislava, Vienna is an ideal launchpad for a journey into the East.

Planning Your Time

For a big city, Vienna is pleasant and laid-back. Packed with sights, it's worth two days and two nights on even the speediest trip. To be grand-tour efficient, you could sleep on the train on your way in and out—Prague, Berlin, Venice, Rome, the Swiss Alps (via Zürich), Paris, the Rhine Valley, Warsaw, and Kraków are each handy night trains away.

Palace Choices: The Hofburg and Schönbrunn are both world-class palaces, but seeing both is redundant—with limited time or money, I'd choose just one. The Hofburg comes with the popular Sisi Museum and is right in the town center, making for an easy visit. With more time, a visit to Schönbrunn—set outside town amid a grand and regal garden—is also a great experience.

Vienna in One to Four Days

Below is a suggested itinerary for how to spend your time. I've left the **evenings** open for your choice of activities. The best options are taking in a concert, opera, or other musical event; enjoying a leisurely dinner (and people-watching) in the stately old town or atmospheric Spittelberg Quarter; heading out to the *Heuriger* wine pubs in the foothills of the Vienna Woods; or touring the Haus der Musik interactive music museum (open nightly until 22:00). Plan your evenings based on the schedule of musical events while you're in town.

Day 1

    9:00   Take the 1.5-hour Red Bus City Tour, or circle the Ringstrasse by tram, to get your bearings.

 10:30   Drop by the TI for planning and ticket needs.

 11:00   Enjoy the Albertina Museum.

 13:00   Take the Opera tour (buy tickets at 12:40).

14:00   Follow my Vienna City Walk, including Kaisergruft visit and St. Stephen's Cathedral Tour (nave closes at 16:30, or 17:30 June-Aug).

Day 2

9:00   Browse the colorful Naschmarkt, or shop along Mariahilfer Strasse.

11:00   Tour the Kunsthistorisches Museum.

14:00   After a short break (and maybe a picnic) in the Burggarten, tour the Hofburg Palace Imperial Apartments and Treasury; if time, interest, and energy hold out, dip into the New Palace museums.

Day 3

Choose from among the following sights: Belvedere Palace, with its fine collection of Viennese art and great city views; the engaging Karlsplatz sights (Karlskirche, Wien Museum, Academy of Fine Arts, and The Secession); or a wide range of honorable mentions (Natural History Museum, Liechtenstein Museum, KunstHausWien and Hundertwasserhaus, Museum of Applied Art, Imperial Furniture Collection, Sigmund Freud Museum, Jewish sights, and so on).

If you need a break, linger in a classic Viennese café.

Or, to get out of town, tromp through the Vienna Woods, ending at the *Heuriger* wine pubs for dinner.

Day 4

9:00   Head out to Schönbrunn Palace to enjoy the royal apartments and grounds.

12:00   If the weather's good, picnic at Schönbrunn (on the lawn in front of the Gloriette), then return to downtown.

13:00   Rent a bike and head out to the modern Danube City "downtown" sector, Danube Island (for fun people-watching), and the Prater amusement park.

Orientation to Vienna

(area code: 01)

Vienna sits between the Vienna Woods (Wienerwald) and the Danube (Donau). To the southeast is industrial sprawl. The Alps, which arc across Europe from Marseille, end at Vienna's wooded hills, providing a popular playground for walking and sipping new wine. This greenery's momentum carries on into the city. More than half of Vienna is parkland, filled with ponds, gardens, trees, and statue-maker memories of Austria's glory days.

Think of the city map as a target with concentric sections: The bull's-eye is St. Stephen's Cathedral, the towering cathedral south of the Danube. Surrounding that is the old town, bound tightly by the circular road known as the Ringstrasse, marking what used to be the city wall. The Gürtel, a broader ring road, contains the rest of downtown. Outside the Gürtel lies the uninteresting sprawl of modern Vienna.

Addresses start with the *Bezirk* (district), followed by the street and building number. The Ringstrasse (a.k.a. the Ring) circles the first *Bezirk*. Any address higher than the ninth *Bezirk* is beyond the Gürtel, far from the center.

Much of Vienna's sightseeing—and most of my recommended restaurants—are located in the old town (inside the Ringstrasse). Walking across this circular district takes about 30 minutes. St. Stephen's Cathedral sits in the center, at the intersection of the two main (pedestrian-only) streets: Kärntner Strasse runs north-south and Graben runs east-west. To the northwest of the cathedral is the "Bermuda Triangle" of pubs and cafés for nightlife.

Several sights sit along, or just beyond, the Ringstrasse: to the southwest are the Hofburg and related Habsburg sights, and the Kunsthistorisches Museum; to the south is a cluster of intriguing sights near Karlsplatz; to the southeast is Belvedere Palace. A branch of the Danube River (*Donau* in German, DOH-now) borders the Ring to the north. As a tourist, concern yourself only with this compact old center. When you do, sprawling Vienna suddenly becomes manageable.

Arrival in Vienna
By Train
Vienna's train stations will be in disarray for the next few years, as they build a central train station (Hauptbahnhof) in the former Südbahnhof location to handle most traffic. Until this is done (likely in 2013), trains to different destinations depart from three stations around the city. As these departure points are prone to change, confirm carefully which station your train uses. As the stations themselves are also in flux (the main ones are all being renovated), the details I've listed below for each one are also subject to change. From most stations, the handiest connection to the center is usually the U-Bahn (subway) system; line numbers and stop names are noted below. The latter two stations also have a handy tram connection.

Westbahnhof (West Station): In the midst of a massive renovation, this station (at the west end of Mariahilfer Strasse, on the U-3 and U-6 lines) serves trains to/from many points in **Austria** (including Hallstatt and Salzburg), as well as **Germany,**

Switzerland, and **Hungary.** The Reisebüro am Bahnhof office sells maps, books hotels (for a pricey fee), and answers questions (Mon-Fri 8:00-19:00, Sat 8:00-13:00, closed Sun). During the ongoing construction, this station's many services are scattered throughout a provisional hall—including a train ticket office (daily 5:30-22:45), grocery store (daily 5:30-23:00), ATMs, change offices, a post office, and luggage lockers (€2-3.50). To reach airport buses and taxis, from the platforms, head outside and to the left. For the city center, ride the U-3 line (buy your ticket or transit pass from a machine, then follow *U-3* signs to the tracks; direction: Simmering). If your hotel is along Mariahilfer Strasse, your stop is on this line. If you're sleeping in the center—or just can't wait to start sightseeing—ride five stops to Stephansplatz, at the very center of town. From there, the TI is a five-minute stroll down pedestrian Kärntner Strasse.

Wien-Meidling Bahnhof: This temporary "main station" (a mile and a half southeast of Schönbrunn Palace, at the Philadelphiabrücke stop on the U-6 subway line and tram #62) serves most international trains, including southbound trains to/from **Italy, Slovenia,** and **Croatia,** as well as northbound trains to/from the **Czech Republic** and **Poland.** The once-small suburban station has been souped up to accommodate the traffic that formerly passed through the Südbahnhof. It has a train info desk (near track 1 and underground, near track 4), ATMs (near tracks 1 and 6), luggage lockers (underground, near track 7), and airport bus services. To reach the hotels on Mariahilfer Strasse, or to head to Stephansplatz, take the U-Bahn on the U-6 line (direction: Floridsdorf) to the Westbahnhof, then change to the U-3 line (see "Westbahnhof," above). If you're staying near the Opera, catch the direct tram #62 (direction: Karlsplatz). For Schwedenplatz, take the U-6 (direction: Floridsdorf) two stops to Längenfeldgasse, then change to the U-4 (direction: Heiligenstadt).

Ostbahnhof (East Station), a.k.a. Südbahnhof (South Station): The temporary Ostbahnhof (just south of Belvedere Palace) is near the former Südbahnhof, and is in the midst of the massive construction zone for the brand-new Hauptbahnhof (Main Station)—so, confusingly, it goes by any of these three names. For now, this station serves trains to/from **Bratislava,** Slovakia. To reach the city center, take tram #D to the Ring; to reach Mariahilfer Strasse, hop on bus #13A (U-1: Südtiroler Platz is also nearby).

By Plane

For information on nearby airports, see "Vienna Connections," at the end of this chapter.

Tourist Information

Vienna's one real TI is a block behind the Opera at Albertinaplatz (daily 9:00-19:00, tel. 01/211-140, www.vienna.info). At the TI, confirm your sightseeing plans, and pick up the free and essential city map with a list of museums and hours (also available at most hotels), the monthly program of concerts (called *Wien-Programm*) and the *Vienna from A to Z* booklet (both described below), and the annual city guide (called *Vienna Journal*). Ask about their program of guided walks (€14 each). The TI also books rooms for a €3 fee. While hotel and ticket-booking agencies at the train station and airport can answer questions and give out maps and brochures, I'd rely on the official TI.

Wien-Programm: This monthly entertainment guide is particularly important, listing all of the events, including music, walks, expositions, and evening museum hours. Note the key for abbreviations on the inside cover, which helps make this dense booklet useful even for non-German speakers.

Vienna from A to Z: Consider this handy booklet, sold by TIs for €3.60. Every major building in Vienna sports a numbered flag banner that keys into this booklet and into the TI's city map—useful for finding your way if you get turned around.

Vienna Card: The much-promoted €18.50 Vienna Card is not worth the mental overhead for most travelers. It gives you a 72-hour transit pass (worth €13.60) and discounts of 10-40 percent at the city's museums. It might save the busy sightseer a few euros (though seniors and students will do better with their own discounts).

Helpful Hints

Sisi Ticket: This €23.50 ticket covers the Royal Imperial Apartments at the Hofburg (including the Sisi Museum and Imperial Porcelain and Silver Collection—but *not* the Hofburg Treasury), Schönbrunn Palace's Grand Tour, and the Imperial Furniture Collection; the ticket saves €0.50 off the combined cost of the Hofburg apartments and Schönbrunn, making the good Furniture Collection effectively free (sold at any participating sight).

Teens Sightsee Free: Those under 19 get in free to state-run museums and sights.

Music Sightseeing Priorities: Be wary of Vienna's various music sights. Many "homes of composers" are pretty disappointing. My advice to music-lovers is to concentrate on these activities: Take in a concert, tour the Opera house, snare cheap standing-room tickets to see an opera there (even just part of a performance), enjoy the Haus der Musik, and scour the wonderful Collection of Ancient Musical Instruments in the

Hofburg's New Palace. If in town on a Sunday, don't miss the glorious music at the Augustinian Church Mass (see page 58).

Internet Access: The TI has a list of Internet cafés. **Netcafe** is near the Danube Canal (€4/hour with drink, daily 9:00-23:00, Schwedenplatz 3); **Surfland Internet Café** is near the Opera (€6/hour, daily 10:00-23:00, Krugerstrasse 10, tel. 01/512-7701); and **Netcafe-Refill** is close to many of my recommended hotels (€4/hour, daily 9:00-22:00, Mariahilfer Strasse 103, tel. 01/595-5558).

Post Offices: The main post office is near Schwedenplatz at Fleischmarkt 19 (Mon-Fri 7:00-22:00, Sat-Sun 9:00-22:00). Branch offices are at the Westbahnhof (Mon-Fri 7:00-22:00, Sat-Sun 9:00-20:00), near the Opera (Mon-Fri 7:00-19:00, closed Sat-Sun, Krugerstrasse 13), and scattered throughout town.

English Bookstore: Stop by the woody and cool **Shakespeare & Co.** (Mon-Sat 9:00-19:00 and sometimes later, generally closed Sun, north of Hoher Markt at Sterngasse 2, tel. 01/535-5053). Also inside the Ring is **The British Bookshop** (Mon-Fri 9:30-18:30, Sat 9:30-18:00, closed Sun, between Franziskaner Platz and the Ring at Weihburggasse 24, tel. 01/512-194-522).

Keeping Up with the News: Don't buy newspapers. Read them for free in Vienna's marvelous coffeehouses. It's much classier.

Travel Agency: Conveniently located just off the Graben, **Ruefa** sells tickets for flights, trains, and boats to Bratislava. They'll waive the service charge for train tickets for my readers (Mon-Fri 9:00-18:00, Sat 10:00-13:00, closed Sun, Spiegelgasse 15, tel. 01/513-4000).

Getting Around Vienna

By Public Transportation: Take full advantage of Vienna's simple, cheap, and super-efficient transit system, which includes trams (a.k.a. streetcars), buses, U-Bahn (subway), and S-Bahn (faster suburban trains). The smooth, modern trams are Porsche-designed, with "backpack technology" that locates the engines and mechanical hardware on the roofs for a lower ride and easier entry. I generally stick to the tram to zip around the Ring and take the U-Bahn to outlying sights or hotels. Trams #1, #2, and #D all travel partway around the Ring.

The free Vienna map, available at TIs and hotels, includes a smaller schematic map of the major public transit lines, making the too-big €2.50 transit map unnecessary. (Transit maps are also posted conveniently on U-Bahn station walls.) As you study the map, note that tram lines are marked with numbers or letters (such as #38 or #D). Buses have numbers followed by an *A* or *B* (such as

#38A); three-digit numbers are for buses into the outskirts. Night buses, which start with *N* (such as #N38), run after other public transit stops running. U-Bahn lines begin with U (e.g., U-1), and the directions are designated by the end-of-the-line stops. Blue lines are the speedier S-Bahns. Transit info: tel. 01/790-9100, www.wienerlinien.at.

Trams, buses, the U-Bahn, and the S-Bahn all use the same tickets. Buy tickets from *Tabak-Trafik* shops, station machines, marked *Vorverkauf* offices in the station, or—for trams or buses only—on board (tickets only, more expensive). You have lots of choices:

- Single tickets (€1.80, €2.20 if bought on tram or bus, good for one journey with necessary transfers)
- 24-hour transit pass (€5.70)
- 48-hour transit pass (€10)
- 72-hour transit pass (€13.60)
- 7-day transit pass (*Wochenkarte*, €14—but the catch is that it must start on Monday)
- 8-day "Climate Ticket" (*Acht-Tage-Klimakarte*, €28.80, can be shared—for example, 4 people for 2 days each). With a per-person cost of €3.60/day (compared to €5.70/day for a 24-hour pass), this can be a real saver for groups.

Kids under 15 travel free on Sundays and holidays; kids under 6 always travel free.

Stamp a time on your ticket as you enter the Metro system, tram, or bus (stamp it only the first time for a multiple-use pass). Cheaters pay a stiff €70 fine, plus the cost of the ticket. Rookies miss stops because they fail to open the door. Push buttons, pull latches—do whatever it takes. Before you exit an U-Bahn station, study the wall-mounted street map. Choosing the right exit—signposted from the moment you step off the train—saves lots of walking.

Cute little electric buses wind through the tangled old center. Bus #1A is best for a joyride—hop on and see where it takes you.

By Car: Vienna's comfortable, civilized, and easy-to-flag-down **taxis** start at €2.50. You'll pay about €10 to go from the Opera to the Westbahnhof. Pay only what's on the meter—any surcharges (other than the €2 fee for calling a cab or €10 fee for the airport) are just crude cabbie rip-offs. Rates are legitimately higher at night.

Consider the luxury of having your own **car and driver.** Johann (a.k.a. John) Lichtl is a kind, honest, English-speaking cabbie who can take up to four passengers in his car (€27/1 hour, €22/hour for 2 hours or more, €27 to or from airport, mobile 0676-670-6750). Consider hiring gentle Johann for a day trip to the Danube Valley (€160, up to 8 hours) or to drive you to Salzburg while sightseeing en route (€350, up to 14 hours; other trips can be arranged). These special prices are valid with this book in 2012.

By Bike: Vienna is a great city for biking. The bike path along the Ring is wonderfully entertaining. Your best sightseeing by bike is around the Ring, through the City Park, across the Danube Island, and out to the modern "Donau City" business district and nearby beach.

Borrowing a Free/Cheap Bike: Citybike Wien lets you borrow bikes from public racks all over town (toll tel. 0810-500-500, www.citybikewien.at). The bikes are heavy, clunky, and difficult to maneuver—with a solid wheel, single gear, basket, built-in lock, and ads on the side—but they're perfect for a short, practical joyride in the center (such as around the Ringstrasse).

While bike programs in other European cities are difficult for tourists to take advantage of, Vienna's system is easy to use. Bikes are locked into more than 50 stalls scattered through the city center. To borrow a bike, use the computer terminal at any rack to register: Press the credit card button, insert and pull out your card, register your name and address, and select a username and password for future rentals (you can also register online at www.citybikewien.at). Then punch in the number of the bike that you want to use to unlock it. Registration costs €1 (first time only), and they'll place a refundable €20 hold on your card while you're using the bike (only one bike per credit card—couples must use two different cards). Since the bikes are designed for short-term use, it costs more per hour the longer you keep it (first hour free, second hour €1, third hour €2, €4/hour after that). To avoid registering at a machine, you can also get a Citybike Tourist Card (sold for €2/day at Royal Tours, near the Hofburg at Herrengasse 1-3)—but this extra step isn't worth the trouble. When you're done, drop off your bike at any stall, and make sure it's fully locked into the rack to avoid getting charged for more time.

Renting a Higher-Quality Bike: If you want to ride beyond the town center—or you simply want a better set of wheels—check out **Pedal Power,** with a handy central location near the Opera house. The local authority on bike touring both in town and from here to points along the Danube, Pedal Power rents bikes and provides good biking info (€5/hour, €17/4 hours, €27/24 hours, daily 8:30-18:00, Elisabethstrasse 13 at the corner of Eschenbachgasse). They can also deliver a bike to your hotel and pick it up when you're done (€32/day including delivery, tel. 01/729-7234, www.pedalpower.at), and they organize bike tours (described later). **Crazy Chicken** bike rental, a short tram ride from the Westbahnhof, is less convenient but a lot cheaper (€3/hour, €12/day, daily 8:30-19:00, near recommended Pension Fünfhaus at Sperrgasse 12—see page 98 for directions, tel. 01/892-2134, mobile 0664-421-4789, www.crazychicken.at).

Tours in Vienna

Walking Tours—The TI's *Walks in Vienna* brochure describes the city's many guided walks. The basic 1.5-hour "Vienna at First Glance" introductory walk is offered daily throughout the summer (€14, leaves at 14:00 from near the Opera, in both English and German, just show up, tel. 01/876-7111, mobile 0664-260-4388, www.wienguide.at). Various specialized tours go once a week and are listed on their website.

Bike Tours—Several companies offer city tours. **Pedal Power** runs two different three-hour tours daily from May to September (€26/tour includes bike, €44 for both tours, €14 extra to keep the bike for the day, departs at 9:45 and 14:15 in front of Opera at corner of Operngasse and the Kärntner Ring, also rents bikes, tel. 01/729-7234, www.pedalpower.at). **Wolfgang Höfler** leads bike tours as well as walking tours (€140/2 hours, mobile 0676-304-4940, www.vienna-aktivtours.com, office@vienna-aktivtours.com; also listed later, under "Local Guides").

Bus Tours—**Red Bus City Tours'** convertible buses do a 1.5-hour loop, hitting the highlights of the city with a 20-minute shopping break in the middle. It covers the main first-district attractions as well as a big bus can, along with the entire Ringstrasse. But the most interesting part of the tour is outside the center—zipping through Prater Park, over the Danube for a glimpse of the city's Danube Island playground, and into the "Donau City" skyscraper zone. If the weather's good, the bus goes topless and offers great opportunities for photos (€14, departs hourly April-Oct 10:00-18:00, less frequently off-season, tours start one block behind the Opera at Lobkowitzplatz 1, pretty good recorded narration in any language, your own earbuds are better than the beat-up headphones they provide, tel. 01/512-4030, www.redbuscitytours.at). The boss, Gabriel, gives those with this book a free cold drink from the shop where you buy your tickets.

Vienna Sightseeing offers a longer, three-hour city tour, including a tour of Schönbrunn Palace (€39, 3/day April-Oct, 2/day Nov-March). They also run hop-on, hop-off bus tours with recorded commentary. The schedule is posted curbside (three different routes, €13/1 hour, €16/2 hours, €20/all day, departs from the Opera 4/hour July-Aug 10:00-20:00, runs less frequently and stops earlier off-season, tel. 01/7124-6830, www.viennasightseeing.at). Given the city's excellent public transportation and this outfit's meager frequency, I'd skip this tour; if you just want a quick guided city tour, take the Red Bus tours recommended above.

Ring Tram Tour—The **Vienna Ring Tram**, a made-for-tourists streetcar, runs clockwise along the entire Ringstrasse (€6 for one 30-minute loop, €9 for 24-hour hop-on, hop-off privileges, 2/hour 10:00-18:00, July-Aug until 19:00, recorded narration). The tour starts at the top and bottom of each hour on the Opera side of the Ring at Kärntner Ring. At each stop, you'll see an ad for this tram tour (look for *VRT Ring-Rund Sightseeing*). The schedule clearly notes the next departure time.

Horse-and-Buggy Tour—These traditional horse-and-buggies, called *Fiakers*, take rich romantics on clip-clop tours lasting 20 minutes (€40-old town), 40 minutes (€65-old town and the Ring), or one hour (€95-all of the above, but more thorough). You can share the ride and cost with up to five people. Because it's a kind of guided tour, talk to a few drivers before choosing a carriage, and pick someone who's fun and speaks English (tel. 01/401-060).

Local Guides—You'll pay about €140 for two hours. Get a group of six or more together and call it a party. The tourist board's website (www.vienna.info) has a long list of local guides with their specialties and contact information. **Lisa Zeiler** is an excellent guide (tel. 01/402-3688, lisa.zeiler@gmx.at). **Wolfgang Höfler,** a generalist with a knack for having psychoanalytical fun with history, enjoys the big changes of the 19th and 20th centuries (€135/2 hours, mobile 0676-304-4940, www.vienna-aktivtours.com, office@vienna-aktivtours.com, also leads bike tours—described earlier). If Lisa and Wolfgang are booked, they can set you up with other good guides.

Self-Guided Walk

Vienna City Walk

This walk connects the top three sights in Vienna's old center: the Opera, St. Stephen's Cathedral, and the Hofburg Palace. Along the way, you'll see sights covered elsewhere in this chapter (to find the full descriptions, flip to "Sights in Vienna," later), and get an overview of Vienna's past and present. Allow one hour, and more time if you plan to stop into any of the major sights along the way.

• *Begin at the square outside Vienna's landmark Opera house. (The Opera's entrance faces the Ringstrasse; we're starting at the busy pedestrian square that's to the right of the entrance as you're facing it.)*

Opera

If Vienna is the world capital of classical music, this building is its throne room, one of the planet's premier houses of music. It's typical of Vienna's 19th-century buildings in that it features a revival style—Neo-Renaissance—with arched windows, half-columns, and the sloping, copper mansard roof typical of French Renaissance

VIENNA

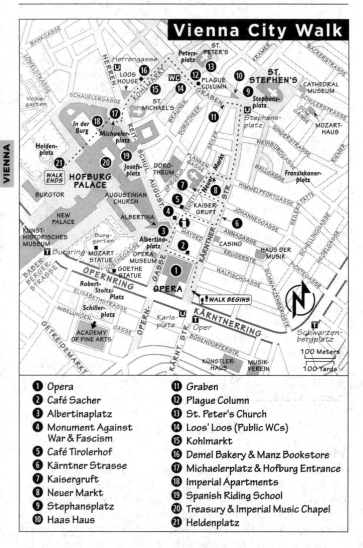

Vienna City Walk

1. Opera
2. Café Sacher
3. Albertinaplatz
4. Monument Against War & Fascism
5. Café Tirolerhof
6. Kärntner Strasse
7. Kaisergruft
8. Neuer Markt
9. Stephansplatz
10. Haas Haus
11. Graben
12. Plague Column
13. St. Peter's Church
14. Loos' Loos (Public WCs)
15. Kohlmarkt
16. Demel Bakery & Manz Bookstore
17. Michaelerplatz & Hofburg Entrance
18. Imperial Apartments
19. Spanish Riding School
20. Treasury & Imperial Music Chapel
21. Heldenplatz

châteaux. Since the structure was built in 1869, almost all of the opera world's luminaries have passed through here. Its former musical directors include Gustav Mahler, Herbert von Karajan, and Richard Strauss. Luciano Pavarotti, Maria Callas, Placido Domingo, and many other greats have sung from its stage.

In the pavement along the side of the Opera (and all along Kärntner Strasse, the bustling shopping street we'll visit shortly), you'll find star plaques forming a Hollywood-style walk of fame. These represent the stars of classical music—famous composers, singers, musicians, and conductors.

Looking up at the Opera, notice the giant outdoor screen onto which some live performances are projected (as noted in the posted schedules).

If you're a fan, take a guided tour of the Opera. If you're not, you still might consider springing for an evening performance (standing-room tickets are surprisingly cheap; see page 85). Regular opera tickets are sold at various points near here: The closest one is the small ticket office just below the screen, while the main one is across from the opposite side of the Opera, on Operngasse. For information about other entertainment options during your visit, check in at the Wien Ticket kiosk in the booth on this square.

The Opera marks a busy intersection in Vienna, where Kärntner Strasse meets the Ring. The Karlsplatz U-Bahn station in front of the Opera is an underground shopping mall with fast food, newsstands, lots of pickpockets, and even a Vienna Opera Toilet experience (€0.60, *mit Musik*).

• *Walk behind the Opera and across the street toward the dark-red awning to find the famous...*

Café Sacher

This is the home of the world's classiest chocolate cake, the Sacher-Torte: two layers of cake separated by apricot jam and covered in dark-chocolate icing, usually served with whipped cream. It was invented in a fit of improvisation in 1832 by Franz Sacher, dessert chef to Prince Metternich (the mastermind diplomat who redrew the map of post-Napoleon Europe). The cake became world-famous when the inventor's son served it next door at his hotel (you may have noticed the fancy doormen). Many locals complain that the cakes here have gone downhill, and many tourists are surprised by how dry they are—you really need that dollop of *Schlagobers*. Still, coffee and a slice of cake here can be €8 well invested for the historic ambience alone. While the café itself is grotesquely touristy, the adjacent Sacher Stube has ambience and natives to spare (same prices). For maximum elegance, sit inside.

• *Continue past Hotel Sacher. At the end of the street is a small, triangular, cobbled square adorned with modern sculptures.*

Albertinaplatz

As you enter the square, to the right you'll find the **TI**. On your left, the tan-and-white Neoclassical building with the statue alcoves marks the tip of the Hofburg Palace—the sprawling complex of buildings that was long the seat of Habsburg power (we'll end this walk at the palace's center). The balustraded terrace up top was originally part of Vienna's defensive rampart. Later, it was the balcony of Empress Maria Theresa's daughter Maria Christina, who lived at this end of the palace. Today, her home houses the **Albertina Museum,** topped by a sleek, controversial titanium canopy (called the "diving board" by critics). The museum's plush, 19th-century rooms are hung with facsimiles of its graphic collection, and an entire floor is dedicated to the Batliner collection, covering each artistic stage from Impressionism to the present day.

Albertinaplatz itself is filled with statues that make up the powerful, thought-provoking **Monument Against War and Fascism,** which commemorates the dark years when Austria came under Nazi rule (1938-1945).

The statue group has four parts. The split white monument, *The Gates of Violence,* remembers victims of all wars and violence. Standing directly in front of it, you're at the gates of a concentration camp. Then, as you explore the statues, you step into a montage of wartime images: clubs and WWI gas masks, a dying woman birthing a future soldier, and chained slave laborers sitting on a pedestal of granite cut from the infamous quarry at Mauthausen concentration camp, not far up the Danube from here. The hunched-over figure on the ground behind is a Jew forced to scrub anti-Nazi graffiti off a street with a toothbrush. Of Vienna's 200,000 Jews, more than 65,000 died in Nazi concentration camps. The statue with its head buried in the stone is Orpheus entering the underworld, meant to remind Austrians (and the rest of us) of the victims of Nazism...and the consequences of not keeping our governments on track. Behind that, the 1945 declaration that established Austria's second republic—and enshrined human rights—is cut into the stone.

Viewing this monument gains even more emotional impact when you realize what happened on this spot: During a WWII bombing attack, several hundred people were buried alive when the cellar they were using as shelter was demolished.

Austria was led into World War II by Germany, which annexed the country in 1938, saying Austrians were wannabe Germans anyway. But Austrians are not Germans—never were, never will be. They're quick to proudly tell you that Austria was founded in the 10th century, whereas Germany wasn't born until 1870. For seven years just before and during World War II (1938-1945), there was no Austria. In 1955, after 10 years of joint occupation by the victorious Allies, Austria regained total independence on the condition that it would be forever neutral (and never join NATO or the Warsaw Pact). To this day, Austria is outside of NATO (and Germany).

Behind the monument is **Café Tirolerhof,** a classic Viennese café full of things that time has passed by: chandeliers, marble tables, upholstered booths, waiters in tuxes, and newspapers. For more on Vienna's cafés, see page 79.

Often parked on the same square are the Red Bus City Tour buses, offering a handy way to get a quick overview of the city (see "Tours in Vienna," earlier).

• *From the café, turn right on Führichsgasse, passing the recommended cafeteria-style Rosenberger Markt Restaurant. Walk one block until you hit...*

Kärntner Strasse

This grand, mall-like street (traffic-free since 1974) is the people-watching delight of this in-love-with-life city. Today's Kärntner Strasse (KAYRNT-ner SHTRAH-seh) is mostly a crass commercial pedestrian mall—its famed elegant shops long gone. But locals know it's the same road Crusaders marched down as they headed off from St. Stephen's Cathedral for the Holy Land in the 12th century. Its name indicates that it leads south, toward the region of Kärnten (Carinthia, a province divided between Austria and Slovenia). Today it's full of shoppers and street musicians.

Where Führichsgasse meets Kärntner Strasse, note the city **Casino** (across the street and a half-block to your right, at #41)—once venerable, now tacky, it exemplifies the worst of the street's evolution. Turn left to head up Kärntner Strasse, going away from the Opera. As you walk along, be sure to look up, above the modern storefronts, for glimpses of the street's former glory. Near the end of the block, on the left at #26, **J & L Lobmeyr Crystal** ("Founded in 1823") still has its impressive brown storefront with gold trim, statues, and the Habsburg double-eagle. In the market for some $400 napkin rings? Lobmeyr's your place. Inside, breathe in the classic Old World ambience as you climb up to the glass museum (free entry, Mon-Fri 10:00-19:00, Sat 10:00-18:00, closed Sun).

• *At the end of the block, turn left on Marco d'Aviano Gasse (passing the fragrant flower stall) to make a short detour to the square called Neuer Markt. Straight ahead is an orange-ish church with a triangular roof and cross, the Capuchin Church. In its basement is the...*

Kaisergruft

Under the church sits the Imperial Crypt, filled with what's left of Austria's emperors, empresses, and other Habsburg royalty. For centuries, Vienna was the heart of a vast empire ruled by the Habsburg family, and here is where they lie buried in their fancy pewter coffins. You'll find all the Habsburg greats, including Maria Theresa, her son Josef II (Mozart's patron), Franz Josef, and Empress Sisi. Before moving on, consider paying your respects here (see listing on page 59).

• *Stretching north from the Kaisergruft is the square called...*

Neuer Markt

A block farther down, in the center of Neuer Markt, is the **four rivers fountain** showing Lady Providence surrounded by figures symbolizing the rivers that flow into the Danube. The sexy statues offended Empress Maria Theresa, who actually organized "Chastity Commissions" to defend her capital city's moral standards. The modern buildings around you were rebuilt after World War II. Half of the city's inner center was intentionally destroyed by Churchill to demoralize the Viennese, who were disconcertingly enthusiastic about the Nazis.

• Lady Providence's one bare breast points back to Kärntner Strasse (50 yards away). Before you head back to the busy shopping street, you could stop for a sweet treat at the heavenly, recommended Kurkonditorei Oberlaa (to get there, disobey the McDonald's arrows—it's at the far-left corner of the square).

Leave the square and return to Kärntner Strasse. Turn left and continue down Kärntner Strasse. As you approach the cathedral, you're likely to first see it as a reflection in the round-glass windows of the modern Haas Haus. Pass the U-Bahn station (which has WCs) where the street spills into Vienna's main square...

Stephansplatz

The cathedral's frilly spire looms overhead, worshippers and tourists pour inside the church, and shoppers and top-notch street entertainers buzz around the outside. You're at the center of Vienna.

The Gothic **St. Stephen's Cathedral** (c. 1300-1450) is known for its 450-foot south tower, its colorful roof, and its place in Viennese history. When it was built, it was a huge church for what was then a tiny town, and it helped put the fledgling city on the map. At this point, you may want to take a break from the walk to tour the church (see my self-guided tour on page 46).

Where Kärntner Strasse hits Stephansplatz, the grand, soot-covered building with red columns is the **Equitable Building** (filled with lawyers, bankers, and insurance brokers). It's a fine example of Neoclassicism from the turn of the 20th century—look up and imagine how slick Vienna must have felt in 1900.

Facing St. Stephen's is the sleek concrete-and-glass **Haas Haus,** a postmodern building by noted Austrian architect Hans Hollein (finished in 1990). The curved facade is supposed to echo the Roman fortress of Vindobona (its ruins were found near here). Although the Viennese initially protested having this stark modern tower right next to their beloved cathedral, since then, it's become a fixture of Vienna's main square. Notice how the smooth, rounded glass reflects St. Stephen's pointy architecture, providing a great photo opportunity—especially at twilight.

• *Exit the square with your back to the cathedral. Walk past the Haas Haus, and bear right down the street called...*

Graben

This was once a *Graben*, or ditch—originally the moat for the Roman military camp. Back during Vienna's 19th-century heyday, there were nearly 200,000 people packed into the city's inner center (inside the Ringstrasse), walking through dirt streets. Today this area houses 20,000. Graben was a busy street with three lanes of traffic until the 1970s, when it was turned into one of Europe's first pedestrian-only zones. Take a moment to absorb the scene— you're standing in an area surrounded by history, post-war rebuilding, grand architecture, fine cafés, and people enjoying life...for me, quintessential Europe.

Two blocks after leaving Stephansplatz, you reach Dorotheergasse, on your left, which leads (after two more long blocks) to the **Dorotheum** auction house. Consider poking your nose in here later for some fancy window-shopping. Also along this street are two recommended eateries: the sandwich shop Buffet Trześniewski—one of my favorite places for lunch (described on page 102)—and the classic Café Hawelka (described on page 79).

In the middle of this pedestrian zone is the extravagantly blobby **Holy Trinity plague column** *(Pestsäule)*. The 60-foot pillar of clouds sprouts angels and cherubs, with the wonderfully gilded Father, Son, and Holy Ghost at the top (all protected by an anti-pigeon net).

In 1679, Vienna was hit by a massive epidemic of bubonic plague. Around 75,000 Viennese died—about a third of the city. Emperor Leopold I dropped to his knees (something emperors never did in public) and begged God to save the city. (Find Leopold about a quarter of the way up the monument, just above the brown banner. Hint: The typical inbreeding of royal families left him with a gaping underbite.) His prayer was heard by Lady Faith (the statue below Leopold, carrying a cross). With the help of a heartless little cupid, she tosses an old naked woman—symbolizing the plague—into the abyss and saves the city. In gratitude, Leopold vowed to erect this monument, which became a model for other cities ravaged by the same plague.

• *Thirty yards past the plague monument, look down the short street to the right, which frames a Baroque church with a stately green dome.*

St. Peter's Church

Leopold I ordered this church to be built as a thank-you for surviving the 1679 plague. The church stands on the site of a much older church that may have been Vienna's first (or second) Christian church. Inside, St. Peter's shows Vienna at its Baroque best. Note

VIENNA

that the church offers free organ concerts (Mon-Fri at 15:00, Sat-Sun at 20:00).

• *Continue west on Graben, where you'll immediately find some stairs leading underground to...*

Loos' Loos

In about 1900, a local chemical-maker needed a publicity stunt to prove that his chemicals really got things clean. He purchased two wine cellars under Graben and had them turned into classy WCs in the Modernist style (designed by Adolf Loos, Vienna's answer to Frank Lloyd Wright), complete with chandeliers and finely crafted mahogany. While the chandeliers are gone, the restrooms remain a relatively appealing place to do your business—in fact, they're so inviting that they're used for poetry readings. Locals and tourists happily pay €0.50 for a quick visit.

• *Graben dead-ends at the aristocratic supermarket Julius Meinl am Graben. From here, turn left. In the distance is the big green and gold dome of the Hofburg, where we'll end this walk. The street leading up to the Hofburg is...*

Kohlmarkt

This is Vienna's most elegant and unaffordable shopping street, lined with Cartier, Armani, Gucci, Tiffany, and the emperor's palace at the end. Strolling Kohlmarkt, daydream about the edible window displays at **Demel,** the ultimate Viennese chocolate shop (#14, daily 10:00-19:00). The room is filled with Art Nouveau boxes of Empress Sisi's choco-dreams come true: *Kandierte Veilchen* (candied violet petals), *Katzenzungen* (cats' tongues), and so on. The cakes here are moist (compared to the dry Sacher-Tortes). The enticing window displays change monthly, reflecting current happenings in Vienna. Inside, there's an impressive cancan of Vienna's most beloved cakes—displayed to tempt visitors into springing for the €10 cake-and-coffee deal (point to the cake you want). You can sit inside, with a view of the cake-making, or outside, with the street action (upstairs is less crowded). Shops like this boast "K.u.K."—signifying that during the Habsburgs' heyday, it was patronized by the *König und Kaiser* (king and emperor—same guy). If you happen to be looking through Demel's window at exactly 19:01, just after closing, you can witness one of the great tragedies of modern Europe: the daily dumping of its unsold cakes.

Next to Demel, the **Manz Bookstore** has a Loos-designed facade.

• *Kohlmarkt ends at the square called...*

Michaelerplatz

This square is dominated by the **Hofburg Palace.** Study the grand

Neo-Baroque facade, dating from about 1900. The four heroic giants illustrate Hercules wrestling with his great challenges (Emperor Franz Josef, who commissioned the gate, felt he could relate).

In the center of this square, a scant bit of **Roman Vienna** lies exposed just beneath street level.

Do a slow, clockwise pan to get your bearings, starting (over your left shoulder as you face the Hofburg) with **St. Michael's Church,** which offers fascinating tours of its crypt. To the right of that is the fancy **Loden-Plankl shop,** with traditional Austrian formalwear, including dirndls. Farther to the right, across Augustinerstrasse, is the wing of the palace that houses the **Spanish Riding School** and its famous white Lipizzaner stallions. Farther down this street lies **Josefsplatz,** with the Augustinian Church, and the Dorotheum auction house. At the end of the street are Albertinaplatz and the Opera (where we started this walk).

Continue your spin: Two buildings over from the Hofburg (to the right), the modern **Loos House** (now a bank) has a facade featuring a perfectly geometrical grid of square columns and windows. Although the Loos House might seem boring today, in its time, it was considered to be Vienna's first "modern" building—with a trapezoidal footprint that makes no attempt to hide the awkwardly shaped street corner it stands on. Windows lack the customary cornice framing the top—a "house without eyebrows." Compared to the Neo-Rococo facade of the Hofburg, the stern Modernism of the Loos House appears to be from an entirely different age. And yet, both of these—as well as the Eiffel Tower and Mad Ludwig's fairy-tale Neuschwanstein Castle—were built in the same generation, roughly around 1900. In many ways, this jarring juxtaposition exemplifies the architectural turmoil of the turn of the 20th century, and represents the passing of the torch from Europe's age of divine monarchs to the modern era.

• *We'll finish up our tour where Austria's glorious history began—at the...*

Hofburg

This is the complex of palaces where the Habsburg emperors lived (except in summer, when they lived out at Schönbrunn Palace). Enter the Hofburg through the gate, where you immediately find yourself beneath a big rotunda (the netting is there to keep birds from perching). The doorway on the right is the entrance to the **Imperial Apartments,** where the Habsburg emperors once lived in chandeliered elegance. Today you can tour its lavish rooms, as well as a museum on Empress Sisi, and a porcelain and silver collection. To the left is the ticket office for the **Spanish Riding School.**

Continuing on, you emerge from the rotunda into the main courtyard of the Hofburg, called **In der Burg.** The Caesar-like statue is of Habsburg Emperor Franz II (1768-1835), grandson of Maria Theresa, grandfather of Franz Josef, and father-in-law of Napoleon. Behind him is a tower with three kinds of clocks (the yellow disc shows the phase of the moon tonight). To the right of Franz are the Imperial Apartments, and to the left are the offices of Austria's mostly ceremonial president (the more powerful chancellor lives in a building just behind this courtyard).

Franz Josef faces the oldest part of the palace. The colorful red, black, and gold gateway (behind you), which used to have a drawbridge, leads over the moat and into the 13th-century Swiss Court (Schweizerhof), named for the Swiss mercenary guards once stationed there. As you enter, you're passing into the historic core of the palace, the site of the first fortress, and, historically, the place of last refuge. Here you'll find the **Treasury** (Schatzkammer) and the **Imperial Music Chapel** (Hofmusikkapelle), where the Boys' Choir sings the Mass.

Back at In der Burg, face Franz and turn left, passing through the **tunnel,** with a few tourist shops and restaurants.

The tunnel spills out into spacious **Heldenplatz** (Heroes' Square). On the left is the impressive curved facade of the **New Palace** (Neue Burg). This vast wing was built in the early 1900s to be the new Habsburg living quarters (and was meant to have a matching building facing it). But in 1914, the heir-to-the-throne, Archduke Franz Ferdinand—while waiting politely for his long-lived uncle, Emperor Franz Josef, to die—was assassinated in Sarajevo. The archduke's death sparked World War I and the eventual end of eight centuries of Habsburg rule.

This impressive building saw even sadder days a few decades later, when Adolf Hitler addressed adoring throngs from the New Palace balcony in 1938, after Austria had been annexed.

Today the building houses the **New Palace museums,** an eclectic collection of weaponry, suits of armor, musical instruments, and ancient Greek statues. The two equestrian statues depict Prince Eugene of Savoy (1663-1736), who battled the Ottoman Turks, and Archduke Charles (1771-1847), who battled Napoleon. Eugene gazes toward the far distance at the prickly spires of Vienna's City Hall.

The Hofburg's **Burggarten** (with its much-photographed Mozart statue) is not visible from here, but it's just behind the New Palace. If you continued on through the Greek-columned passageway (the Äussere Burgtor), you'd reach the Ringstrasse, the Kunsthistorisches Museum, and the MuseumsQuartier.

• *Our walk is finished. You're in the heart of Viennese sightseeing. The Hofburg contains some of Vienna's best sights and museums. From the*

Opera to the Hofburg, from chocolate to churches, from St. Stephen's to Sacher-Tortes—Vienna waits for you.

Sights in Vienna

In the Old Town, Within the Ring

These sights are listed roughly from south to north. For a self-guided walk connecting many of central Vienna's top sights—including some of the ones below—see "Vienna City Walk," earlier.

▲▲▲**Opera (Staatsoper)**—The Opera, facing the Ring and near the TI, is a central point for any visitor. Vienna remains one of the world's great cities for classical music, and this building still belts out some of the finest opera, both classic and cutting-edge. While the critical reception of the building 130 years ago led the architect to commit suicide, and though it's been rebuilt since its destruction by WWII bombs, it's still a sumptuous place. The interior has a chandeliered lobby and carpeted staircases perfect for making the scene. The theater itself features five wrap-around balconies, gold and red decor, and a bracelet-like chandelier.

Depending on your level of tolerance for opera, you can simply admire the Neo-Renaissance building from the outside, take a guided tour of the lavish interior, visit the Opera Museum, or attend a performance.

Performances: For information on buying tickets and attending a performance, see page 85.

Tours: You can only enter the Opera if you're attending a performance or if you join a guided 45-minute tour in English (€6.50, ticket covers modest Opera Museum, described below; tours run July-Aug generally daily at the top of each hour 10:00-16:00; Sept-June fewer tours, afternoons only, and none on Sun; buy tickets 20 minutes before tour departs—ticket office is around the left side, as you face the main entrance; tel. 01/514-442-606). Tour times are often changed or cancelled due to rehearsals and performances. Schedules with daily listings for each month (including tour times) are posted all around the building; you can also pick up the monthly *Prolog* program, which includes the schedule for tours.

Opera Museum: Included in your opera tour ticket (whether you like it or not), this museum is a let-down. The permanent exhibit chronologically traces the illustrious history of the Vienna State Opera, highlighting the most famous singers, directors (including Gustav Mahler and Herbert von Karajan), and performances. It also features old posters, costumes, and lots of photographs (main topics in English, but most descriptions in German only). With some luck, you may find something more interesting amid the special exhibits (€3, or included in the Opera tour ticket; Tue-Sun 10:00-18:00, closed Mon; across the street and a block away from the Opera toward the Hofburg, tucked down a courtyard at Hanuschgasse 3, near Albertina Museum, tel. 01/514-442-100).

▲▲**Haus der Musik**—Vienna's "House of Music" is a high-tech experience that celebrates this hometown specialty. The museum is unique for its effective use of interactive touch-screen computers and headphones to explore the physics of sound. Really experiencing the place takes time. It's open late and makes a good evening activity. The first floor features a small exhibit on the Vienna Philharmonic Orchestra, including the batons of prominent conductors and Leonard Bernstein's tux. On the second floor, wander through the "sonosphere" and marvel at the amazing acoustics. Spend some time at the well-presented, interactive headphone stations to learn about the nature of sound and music; I could actually hear what I thought only a piano tuner could discern. The third floor features fine audiovisual exhibits on each of the famous hometown boys (Haydn, Mozart, Beethoven, Schubert, Strauss, and Mahler). Before leaving, pick up a virtual baton to conduct the Vienna Philharmonic. Each time you screw up, the musicians put their instruments down and ridicule you; make it through the piece, and you'll get a rousing round of applause.

Cost and Hours: €10, includes audioguide for third floor only, half-price Tue after 17:30, €15 combo-ticket with Mozarthaus, daily 10:00-22:00, last entry one hour before closing, 2 blocks from the Opera at Seilerstätte 30, tel. 01/513-4850, www.hdm.at.

▲**The Dorotheum: Vienna's Auction House**—For an aristocrat's flea market, drop by Austria's answer to Sotheby's. The ground floor has shops, an info desk with a schedule of upcoming auctions, and a few auction items. Some items are available for immediate sale (marked *VKP*, for *Verkaufpreis*—"sales price"), while others are up for auction (marked *DIFF. RUF*). Labels on each item predict the auction value.

The three upstairs floors have antique furniture and fancy knickknacks (some for immediate sale, others for auction), many brought in by people who've inherited old things and don't have room. Wandering through here, you feel like you're touring a museum with exhibits you can buy (Mon-Fri 10:00-18:00, Sat 9:00-17:00, closed Sun, classy little café on second floor, between the Graben pedestrian street and Hofburg at Dorotheergasse 17, tel. 01/51560, www.dorotheum.com).

Afterward, you can continue your hunt for the perfect curio on the streets around the Dorotheum, lined with many fine antique shops.

▲**St. Peter's Church (Peterskirche)**—Baroque Vienna is at its best in this gem, tucked away a few steps from the Graben.

Admire the rose-and-gold, oval-shaped Baroque interior, topped with a ceiling fresco of Mary kneeling to be crowned by Jesus and the Father, while the dove of the Holy Spirit floats way up in the lantern. Taken together, the church's elements—especially the organ, altar painting, pulpit, and coat of arms (in the base of the dome) of church founder Leopold I—make St. Peter's one of the city's most beautiful and ornate churches.

To the right of the altar, a dramatic golden statue shows the martyrdom of St. John Nepomuk (c. 1340-1393). The Czech saint defied the heretical King Wenceslas, so he was tossed to his death off the Charles Bridge in Prague (for the story, see page 234). In true Baroque style, we see the dramatic peak of his fall, when John has just passed the point of no return. The Virgin Mary floats overhead in a silver cloud.

The present church (from 1733) stands atop earlier churches dating back 1,600 years. On either side of the nave are glass cases containing skeletons of Christian martyrs from Roman times. Above the relic on the left is a painting of the modern saint Josemaría Escrivá, founder of the conservative Catholic organization Opus Dei, of *Da Vinci Code* notoriety.

Cost and Hours: Free, Mon-Fri 7:00-19:00, Sat-Sun 9:00-19:00; free organ concerts Mon-Fri at 15:00, Sat-Sun at 20:00; just off the Graben between the Plague Monument and Kohlmarkt, tel. 01/533-6433.

Mozarthaus Vienna—Opened in 2006 to commemorate Wolfgang's 250th birthday, this museum is easy to get excited about, but it disappoints. Exhibits fill the only surviving Mozart residence in Vienna, where he lived from 1784 to 1787, when he had lots of money (and produced some of his most famous works, including *The Marriage of Figaro* and *Don Giovanni*). While the museum might be worth the time and money for enthusiasts, I much prefer the Haus der Musik (described earlier).

Cost and Hours: €9, includes audioguide, €15 combo-ticket with Haus der Musik, daily 10:00-19:00, last entry 30 minutes before closing, a block behind the cathedral, go through arcade at #5a and walk 50 yards to Domgasse 5, tel. 01/512-1791, www.mozarthausvienna.at.

Judenplatz Memorial and Museum—The classy square called Judenplatz marks the location of Vienna's 15th-century Jewish community, one of Europe's largest at the time. Once filled with a long-gone synagogue, the square is now dominated by a blocky **memorial** to the 65,000 Viennese Jews killed by the Nazis. The memorial—a library turned inside out—invokes Jews' identity as "people of the book" and asks viewers to ponder the huge loss of culture, knowledge, and humanity that took place between 1938 and 1945.

The **Judenplatz Museum,** while sparse, has displays on medieval Jewish life and a well-done video re-creating the ghetto as it looked five centuries ago. Wander the scant remains of the medieval synagogue below street level—discovered during the construction of the Holocaust memorial. This was the scene of a medieval massacre. Since Christians weren't allowed to lend money, Jews were Europe's moneylenders. As so often happened in Europe, when Viennese Christians fell too deeply into debt, they found a convenient excuse to wipe out the local ghetto—and their debts at the same time. In 1421, 200 of Vienna's Jews were burned at the stake. Others who refused a forced conversion committed mass suicide in the synagogue (€2.50, Sun-Thu 10:00-18:00, Fri 10:00-14:00, closed Sat, Judenplatz 8, tel. 01/535-0431, www.jmw.at).

▲▲▲St. Stephen's Cathedral (Stephansdom)

This massive church is the Gothic needle around which Vienna spins. According to the medieval vision of its creators, it stands like a giant jeweled reliquary, offering praise to God from the center of the city. The church and its towers, especially the 450-foot south tower, give the city its most iconic image. (Check your pockets for €0.10 coins; ones minted in Austria feature the south tower on the back.) The cathedral has survived Vienna's many wars and today symbolizes the city's spirit and love of freedom.

Cost: It's free to enter the back part and north aisle of the church, but it costs €3.50 to get into the main nave, where most of the interesting items are located (more for special exhibits). Going up the towers costs €3.50 (by stairs, south tower) or €4.50 (by elevator, north tower). The €14.50 combo-ticket—covering entry, audioguide, both towers, and the catacombs tour—is overkill for most visitors.

Hours: The church doors are open daily 6:00-22:00, but the main nave is open for tourists Mon-Sat 9:00-11:30 & 13:30-16:30, Sun 13:30-16:30, until 17:30 June-Aug. During services, you can't enter the main nave (unless you're attending Mass) or access the north tower elevator or catacombs, but you can go into the back of the church.

Information: Tel. 01/515-523-526, www.stephanskirche.at.

Tours: The €4.50 tours in English are entertaining (daily at 15:45, check information board inside entry to confirm schedule, price includes main nave entry). The €1 audioguide is helpful.

❍ Self-Guided Tour: This tour will give you a good look at the cathedral, inside and out.

Cathedral Exterior: Before we go inside, let's circle around the cathedral for a look at its impressive exterior.

• *As you face the church's main entry, go to the right across the little*

square, and find the old-time photos next to the door marked 3a
Stephansplatz. *From here, you can take in the sheer magnitude of this
massive church, with its skyscraping spire.*

The church we see today is the third one on this spot. It dates
mainly from 1300-1450, when builders expanded on an earlier
structure and added two huge **towers** at the end of each transept.
The impressive 450-foot south tower—capped with a golden orb
and cross—took two generations to build (65 years) and was finished in 1433. The tower is a rarity among medieval churches in
that it was completed before the Gothic style—and the age of
faith—petered out. The half-size north tower (223 feet), around
the other side of the church, was meant to be a matching steeple.
But around 1500, it was abandoned in mid-construction, when the
money was used to defend the country against the Ottomans rather
than to build church towers. You can ascend both towers (stairs to
the south tower, an elevator to the north tower); for details, see the
end of this tour.

The cathedral was heavily damaged at the end of World
War II. Near where you are standing are **old photos** showing the
destruction. In 1945, Vienna was caught in the chaos between
the occupying Nazis and the approaching Soviets. Allied bombs
sparked fires in nearby buildings, and the embers leapt to the
cathedral rooftop. The original timbered Gothic roof burned, the
cathedral's huge bell crashed to the ground, and the fire raged for
two days. Civic pride prompted a financial outpouring, and the
roof was rebuilt to its original splendor by 1952—doubly impressive considering the bombed-out state of the country at that time.

• *Circle the church exterior counterclockwise, passing the entrance to the
south tower. If you're up for climbing the 343 stairs to the top, you could
do it now, but it's better to wait until the end of this tour (tower climb
described at the end of this tour).*

*As you hook around behind the church, look for the cathedral book-
shop (Dombuchhandlung) at the end of the block. Pause in front of that
shop and look toward the cathedral.*

Just above street level, notice the marble **pulpit** under the
golden starburst. The priest would stand here, stoking public opinion against the Ottomans to crowds far bigger than could fit into
the church. Above the pulpit (in a scene from around 1700), a saint
stands victoriously atop a vanquished Turk.

To your right, notice the entrance to the forlorn **Cathedral
Museum.** This pricey, skippable sight provides a close-up look at
piles of religious paintings, statues, stained-glass windows, illuminated manuscripts, and a treasury (€7, Tue-Sat 10:00-17:00, closed
Sun-Mon, Stephansplatz 6, tel. 01/515-523-689).

• *Continue circling the church, passing a line of horse carriages waiting
to take tourists for a ride. Go all the way around to the west facade.*

The Romanesque-style **main entrance** is the oldest part of the church (c. 1240—part of a church that stood here before). Right behind you is the site of Vindobona, a Roman garrison town. Before the Romans converted to Christianity, there was a pagan temple here, and this entrance pays homage to that ancient heritage. Roman-era statues are embedded in the facade, and the two **octagonal towers** flanking the main doorway are dubbed the "heathen towers" because they're built with a few recycled Roman stones (flipped over to hide the pagan inscriptions and expose the smooth sides).

• *Step inside.*

Cathedral Interior: Find a spot to peer through the gate down the immense **nave**—more than a football field long and nine stories tall. Stylistically, the nave is Gothic with a Baroque overlay. The nave's columns are richly populated with 77 life-size stone statues, making a saintly parade to the high altar.

To the right as you enter, in a gold-and-silver sunburst frame, is a crude Byzantine-style **Maria Pócs Icon** (Pötscher Madonna), brought here from a humble Hungarian village church. The picture of Mary and Child is said to have wept real tears in 1697, as Central Europe was once again being threatened by the Turks.

Along the left side of the nave is the **gift shop.** Step in to marvel at the 14th-century statuary decorating its wall—some of the finest carvings in the church.

To the left of the gift shop is the gated entrance to the **Chapel of Prince Eugene of Savoy.** Prince Eugene (1663-1736), a teenage seminary student from France, arrived in Vienna in 1683 as the city was about to be overrun by the Ottoman Turks. He volunteered for the army and helped save the city, launching a brilliant career as a military man for the Habsburgs. His specialty was conquering the Ottomans. When he died, the grateful Austrians buried him here, under this chapel, marked by a tomb hatch in the floor.

• *To access the main nave of the church, you'll have to pay admission. Once through the ticket line, start down the nave toward the altar.*

At the second pillar on the left is the Gothic sandstone **pulpit** (c. 1500), a masterpiece carved from three separate blocks (see if you can find the seams). A spiral stairway winds up to the lectern, surrounded and supported by the four church "fathers," whose writings influenced early Catholic dogma. The pulpit is as crammed with religious meaning as it is with beautifully realistic carvings. The top of the stairway's railing swarms with lizards (animals of light), and toads (animals of darkness). The "Dog of the Lord" stands at the top, making sure none of those toads pollutes the sermon. Below the toads, wheels with three parts (the Trinity) roll up, while wheels with four spokes (the four seasons and the four cardinal directions, symbolizing mortal life) roll down.

Find the guy peeking out from under the stairs. This may be a **self-portrait** of the sculptor. In medieval times, art was done for the glory of God, and artists worked anonymously. But this pulpit was carved as humanist Renaissance ideals were creeping in from Italy—and individual artists were becoming famous. So the artist included what may be a rare self-portrait bust in his work.

• *Continue up to the main altar.*

During World War II, many of the city's top art treasures were stowed safely in cellars and salt mines—hidden by both the Nazi occupiers (to protect against war damage) and by citizens (to protect against Nazi looters). The **stained-glass windows** behind the high altar were meticulously dismantled and packed away. The pulpit was encased in a shell of brick. As the war was drawing to a close, it appeared St. Stephen's would escape major damage. But as the Nazis were fleeing, the bitter Nazi commander in charge of the city ordered that the church be destroyed. Fortunately, his underlings disobeyed. Unfortunately, the church accidentally caught fire during Allied bombing shortly thereafter, and the wooden roof collapsed onto the stone vaults of the ceiling. The Tupperware-colored glass on either side of the nave dates from the 1950s. Before the fire, the church was lit mostly with clear Baroque-era windows.

To the right of the main altar is the **tomb of Frederick III.** This imposing, red-marble tomb is like a big king-size-bed coffin with an effigy of Frederick lying on top (not visible—but there's a photo of the effigy on the left). The top of the tomb is decorated with his coats of arms, representing the many territories he ruled over. Frederick III (1415-1493) is considered the "father" of Vienna for turning the small village into a royal town with a cosmopolitan feel.

• *After exploring the nave, consider three more church-related sights: touring the catacombs, and ascending either one of the two towers.*

Catacombs (Katakomben): The catacombs (viewable by guided tour only) hold the bodies—or at least the innards—of 72 Habsburgs, including that of Rudolf IV, the man who began building the south tower. This is where Austria's rulers were buried before the Kaisergruft was built (see page 59), and where later Habsburgs' entrails were entombed. The copper urns preserve the imperial organs in alcohol. I touched Maria Theresa's urn...and it wobbled (€4.50, daily 10:00-11:30 & 13:30-16:30, until 17:30 June-Aug, tours depart about every 30 minutes and are in German and English). Just be at the stairs in the left/north transept to meet the guide.

Ascending the North Tower: This tower, reached from inside the church (look for the *Aufzug zur Pummerin* sign), holds the famous "Pummerin" bell—cast from captured Ottoman cannons, this bell rings in the New Year. This tower is easier to ascend than the south tower (described next), but it's much shorter and not as exciting, with lesser views (€4.50, daily 9:00-11:30 & 13:30-16:30, until 17:30 in June-Aug, entrance inside the church on the left/north side of the nave; you can access this elevator without buying a ticket for the main nave).

Climbing the South Tower: The iconic south tower offers a far better view than the north one, but you'll earn it by climbing 343 tightly wound steps up the spiral staircase (€3.50, daily 9:00-17:30; this hike burns about one Sacher-Torte of calories). To reach the entrance, exit the church and make a U-turn to the left. This tower, once key to the city's defense as a lookout point, is still dear to Viennese hearts. (It's long been affectionately nicknamed "Steffl," Viennese for "Stevie.") No church spire in (what was) the Austro-Hungarian Empire is taller—by Habsburg decree. From the top, use your city map to locate the famous sights.

The Hofburg Palace

The complex, confusing, and imposing Imperial Palace, with 640 years of architecture, demands your attention. This first Habsburg residence grew with the family empire from the 13th century until 1913, when the last "new wing" opened. The winter residence of the Habsburg rulers until 1918, it's still the home of the Austrian president's office, 5,000 government workers, and several important museums. For an overview of the palace layout, see the facing page.

Planning Your Time: Don't get confused by the Hofburg's myriad courtyards and many museums. Focus on three sights: the Imperial Apartments, Treasury, and the museums at the New Palace (Neue Burg). With more time, consider the Hofburg's many other sights, covering virtually all facets of the imperial lifestyle.

Eating at the Hofburg: Down the tunnel to Heroes' Square is a tiny but handy sandwich bar called **Hofburg Stüberl.** It's ideal for a cool, quiet sit and a drink or snack (same €3 sandwich price whether you sit or go, Mon-Fri 7:00-18:00, Sat-Sun 10:00-16:00). For a cheap, quick meal, duck into the mod and efficient, cafeteria-style **Restaurant zum Alten Hofkeller** in a cellar under the palace (€5 plates, Mon-Fri 7:30-13:30, closed Sat-Sun and in Aug, on the street that runs along the right side of the Hofburg as you face the main entry, on the left-hand side at Schauflergasse 7). The **Soho Kantine,** in the basement of the National Library, is a cheap-but-not-cheery option (described on page 106).

▲▲▲Hofburg Imperial Apartments (Kaiserappartements)

These lavish, Versailles-type, "wish-I-were-God" royal rooms are

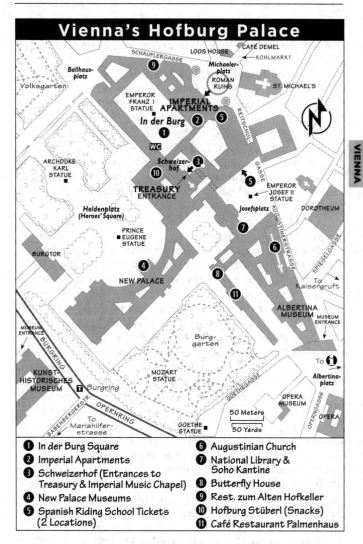

Vienna's Hofburg Palace

- ① In der Burg Square
- ② Imperial Apartments
- ③ Schweizerhof (Entrances to Treasury & Imperial Music Chapel)
- ④ New Palace Museums
- ⑤ Spanish Riding School Tickets (2 Locations)
- ⑥ Augustinian Church
- ⑦ National Library & Soho Kantine
- ⑧ Butterfly House
- ⑨ Rest. zum Alten Hofkeller
- ⑩ Hofburg Stüberl (Snacks)
- ⑪ Café Restaurant Palmenhaus

the downtown version of the grander Schönbrunn Palace. If you're rushed and have time for only one palace, make it this one. Palace visits are a one-way romp through three separate exhibits: a porcelain and silver collection, a museum dedicated to the enigmatic and troubled Empress Sisi, and the luxurious apartments themselves.

The Imperial Apartments are a mix of Old World luxury and modern 19th-century conveniences. Here, Emperor Franz Josef I lived and worked along with his wife Elisabeth, known as Sisi. The Sisi Museum traces the development of her legend, analyzing how her fabulous but tragic life created a 19th-century Princess

Diana. You'll read bits of her poetic writing, see exact copies of her now-lost jewelry, and learn about her escapes, dieting mania, and chocolate bills.

Cost and Hours: €10.50, includes well-done audioguide, also covered by €23.50 Sisi Ticket (see page 28), daily July-Aug 9:00-18:00, Sept-June 9:00-17:30, last entry one hour before closing, enter from courtyard through St. Michael's Gate—just off Michaelerplatz, tel. 01/533-7570, www.hofburg-wien.at.

Information: With the included audioguide and the self-guided tour below, you won't need the €8 *Imperial Apartments/Sisi Museum/Silver Collection* guidebook. If you listen to the entire audioguide, allow 40 minutes for the silver collection, 30 minutes for the Sisi Museum, and 40 minutes for the apartments.

➋ Self-Guided Tour: Your visit (and the excellent audioguide) starts on the ground floor.

Imperial Porcelain and Silver Collection: Here you'll see the Habsburg court's vast tableware collection, which the audioguide actually manages to make fairly interesting. Browse the collection to gawk at the opulence and to take in some colorful Habsburg trivia. (Who'd have thunk that the court had an official way to fold a napkin—and that the technique remains a closely guarded secret?)

Once you're through all those rooms of dishes, climb the stairs—the same staircase used by the emperors and empresses who lived here. At the top is a timeline of Sisi's life. Swipe your ticket to pass through the turnstile, consider the WC, and enter the room with the **Model of the Hofburg.** Circle to the far side to find where you're standing right now, near the smallest of the Hofburg's three domes. The Hofburg was the epicenter of one of Europe's great political powers—600 years of Habsburgs lived here. The Hofburg started as a 13th-century medieval castle (near where you are right now) and expanded over the centuries to today's 240,000-square-meter (60-acre) complex, now owned by the state. To the left of the dome (as you face the facade) is the steeple of the Augustinian Church. It was there, in 1854, that Franz Josef married 16-year-old Elisabeth of Bavaria, and their story began.

Sisi Museum: Empress Elisabeth (1837-1898)—a.k.a. "Sisi" (SEE-see)—was Franz Josef's mysterious, beautiful, and narcissistic wife. This museum traces her fabulous but tragic life. The exhibit starts where her life ended and her legend began (see her death mask and pictures of her funeral procession). You'll read bits of her poetic writing, see exact copies of her now-lost jewelry, and learn about her escapes, dieting mania, and chocolate bills. Admire Sisi's hard-earned thin waist (20 inches at age 16, 21 inches at age 50...after giving birth to four children). The black statue in the dark room represents the empress after the suicide of her son—aloof, thin, in black, with her back to the world. At the end, ponder the crude, knife-like file that killed Sisi. (In 1898, while visiting Geneva, she was murdered by an Italian anarchist.)

Imperial Apartments: After the Sisi Museum, a one-way route takes you through a series of royal rooms. The first room—as if to make clear that there was more to the Habsburgs than Sisi—shows a family tree tracing the Habsburgs from 1273 to their messy WWI demise. From here, enter the private apartments of the royal family (Franz Josef's first, then Sisi's).

Franz Josef's apartments illustrate the lifestyle of the last great Habsburg ruler. In these rooms, he presided over defeats and liberal inroads as the world was changing and the monarchy becoming obsolete. Here he met with advisors and welcomed foreign dignitaries, hosted lavish, white-gloved balls and stuffy formal dinners, and raised three children. He slept (alone) on his austere bed while his beloved wife Sisi retreated to her own rooms. He suffered through the assassination of his brother, the suicide of his son and heir, the murder of his wife, and the assassination of his nephew, Archduke Ferdinand, which sparked World War I and spelled the end of the Habsburg monarchy.

Among the Franz Josef rooms you'll see is the **audience room**, where Franz Josef received commoners from around the empire. They came from far and wide to show gratitude or to make a request. Imagine you've traveled for days to have your say before the emperor. You're wearing your new fancy suit—Franz Josef required that men coming before him wear a tailcoat, women a black gown with a train. You've rehearsed what you want to say. You hope your hair looks good. Suddenly, you're face-to-face with the emp himself. (The portrait on the easel shows Franz Josef in 1915, when he was more than 80 years old.) Despite your efforts, you probably weren't in this room long. He'd stand at the high table (far left) as the visiting commoners had their say. (Standing kept things moving.) You'd hear a brief response from him (quite likely the same he'd given all day), and then you'd back out of the room while bowing (also required). On the table is a partial list of 56 appointments he had on January 3, 1910 (three columns: family name, meeting topic, and *Anmerkung*—the emperor's "action log").

Franz Josef's **bedroom** shows off his spartan lifestyle. Notice his no-frills iron bed. He typically rose at 3:30 and started his day in prayer, kneeling at the prayer stool against the far wall. While he had a typical emperor's share of mistresses, his dresser was always well-stocked with photos of Sisi.

Sisi's Rooms include her exercise/dressing room, where servants worked three hours a day on the empress' famous hair. She'd exercise on the wooden structure and on the rings suspended from the doorway to the left. Afterward, she'd get a massage on the red-covered bed. In Sisi's main bathroom, you'll see her huge copper tub (with the original wall coverings behind it), where servants washed her hair—an all-day affair. Sisi was the first Habsburg to have running water in her bathroom (notice the hot and cold faucets). In the small salon, the portrait is of Crown Prince Rudolf, Franz Josef and Sisi's only son. On the morning of January 30, 1889, the 30-year-old Rudolf and a beautiful baroness were found shot dead in an apparent murder-suicide in his hunting lodge in Mayerling. The scandal shocked the empire and tainted the Habsburgs; Sisi retreated further into her fantasy world, and Franz Josef carried on stoically with a broken heart.

The tour ends in the **dining room.** It's dinnertime, and Franz Josef has called his extended family together. The settings are modest...just silver. Gold was saved for formal state dinners. Next to each name card was a menu listing the chef responsible for each dish. (Talk about pressure.) While the Hofburg had tableware for 4,000, feeding 3,000 was a typical day. The cellar was stocked with 60,000 bottles of wine. The kitchen was huge—50 birds could be roasted at once on the hand-driven spits. Franz Josef enforced strict protocol at mealtime: No one could speak without being spoken to by the emperor, and no one could eat after he was done. While the rest of Europe was growing democracy and expanding personal freedoms, the Habsburgs preserved their ossified worldview to the bitter end.

In 1918, World War I ended, Austria was created as a modern nation-state, the Habsburgs were tossed out...and Hofburg Palace was destined to become a museum.

▲▲▲Hofburg Treasury
(Weltliche und Geistliche Schatzkammer)

One of the world's most stunning collections of royal regalia, the Hofburg Treasury shows off sparkling crowns, jewels, gowns, and assorted Habsburg bling in 21 darkened rooms. The treasures, well-explained by an audioguide, include the crown of the Holy Roman Emperor, Charlemagne's saber, a unicorn horn, and more precious gems than you can shake a scepter at.

Cost and Hours: €12, €18 combo-ticket with Kunsthistorisches Museum and New Palace museums, Wed-Mon 10:00-18:00, closed Tue; from the Hofburg's central courtyard pass through the black, red, and gold gate, then follow *Schatzkammer* signs to the Schweizerhof; tel. 01/525-240, www.khm.at.

Audioguide Tours: A basic audioguide covering the top 11 jewels is included with your ticket. Or, for €2, you can rent an audioguide programmed to describe the top 100 stops—well worth it to get the most out of this dazzling collection.

❸ Self-Guided Tour: Here's a rundown of the highlights (the audioguide is much more complete).

Room 2: The personal crown of Rudolf II has survived since 1602—it was considered too well-crafted to cannibalize for other crowns. It's a big deal because it's the adopted crown of the Austrian Empire, established in 1806 after Napoleon dissolved the Holy Roman Empire (an alliance of Germanic kingdoms so named because it wanted to be considered the continuation of the Roman Empire). Pressured by Napoleon, the Austrian Francis II—who had been Holy Roman Emperor—became Francis I, Emperor of Austria (the stern guy on the wall, near where you entered). Look at the crown. Its design symbolically merges a bishop's miter ("Holy"), the arch across the top of a Roman emperor's helmet ("Roman"), and the typical medieval king's crown ("Emperor").

Rooms 3 and 4: These rooms contain some of the **coronation vestments and regalia** needed for the new Austrian (not Holy Roman) Emperor. There was a different one for each of the emperor's subsidiary titles, e.g., King of Hungary or King of Lombardy. So many crowns and kingdoms in the Habsburgs' vast empire!

Room 5: Ponder the **Cradle of the King of Rome,** once occupied by Napoleon's son, who was born in 1811 and made King of Rome. While pledging allegiance to democracy, Napoleon in fact crowned himself Emperor of France and hobnobbed with Europe's royalty. When his wife, Josephine, could not bear him a male heir, Napoleon divorced her and married into the Habsburg family. With the birth of the baby King of Rome, Napoleon and his new wife, Marie Louise, were poised to start a new dynasty of European rulers...but then Napoleon met his Waterloo, and the Habsburgs remained in power.

Room 6: For Divine Right kings, even child-rearing was a sacred ritual that needed elaborate regalia for public ceremonies. The 23-pound **gold basin and pitcher** were used to baptize noble children, who were dressed in the **hooded baptismal dresses** displayed nearby.

Room 7: These jewels are the true "treasures," a cabinet of wonders used by Habsburgs to impress their relatives (or to hock when funds got low).

Room 8: The eight-foot-tall, 500-year-old **"unicorn horn"** (a narwhal tusk), was considered to have magical healing powers bestowed from on high. This one was owned by the Holy Roman Emperor—clearly a divine monarch.

Religious Rooms: The next several rooms contain **religious objects**—crucifixes, chalices, mini-altarpieces, reliquaries, and bishops' vestments. Habsburg rulers mixed the institutions of church and state, so these precious religious accoutrements were also part of their display of secular power.

Room 10: The big red-silk and gold-thread **mantle,** nearly

900 years old, was worn by Holy Roman Emperors at their coronation.

Room 11: The collection's highlight is the 10th-century **crown of the Holy Roman Emperor.** It was probably made for Otto I (c. 960), the first king to call himself Holy Roman Emperor. The Imperial Crown swirls with symbolism "proving" that the emperor was both holy and Roman: The cross on top says the HRE ruled as Christ's representative on earth, and the jeweled arch over the top is reminiscent of the parade helmet of ancient Romans. The jewels themselves allude to the wearer's kinghood in the here and now. Imagine the impression this priceless, glittering crown must have made on the emperor's medieval subjects.

Nearby is the 11th-century **Imperial Cross** that preceded the emperor in ceremonies. Encrusted with jewels, it had a hollow compartment (its core is wood) that carried substantial chunks thought to be from *the* **cross** on which Jesus was crucified and *the* **Holy Lance** used to pierce his side (both pieces are displayed in the same glass case). Holy Roman Emperors actually carried the lance into battle in the 10th century. Look behind the cross to see how it was a box that could be clipped open and shut, used for holding holy relics. You can see bits of the "true cross" anywhere, but this is a prime piece—with the actual nail hole.

Room 12: Now picture all this regalia used together. The **painting** shows the coronation of Maria Theresa's son Josef II as Holy Roman Emperor in 1764. Set in a church in Frankfurt (filled with the bigwigs—literally—of the day), Josef is wearing the same crown and royal garb that you've just seen.

Room 12 also displays the **leather cases** used to store and transport the crowns, crosses, and other objects. Another glass case contains **relics**—such as a fragment of Jesus' manger, a piece of Christ's loincloth, and a shred of the Last Supper tablecloth.

The Rest of the Treasury: Rooms 13-15 have (among other things) **portraits of important Habsburgs,** such as Maximilian I and Mary of Burgundy. Room 16 contains the **royal vestments** (15th century), which display perhaps the most exquisite workmanship in the entire Treasury. Look closely—they're "painted" with gold and silver threads. But after seeing so much bling, by the time you view these vestments, they can seem downright understated— just another example of the pomp and circumstance of the majestic Habsburgs.

More Hofburg Sights
▲▲**Hofburg New Palace Museums**—The New Palace (Neue Burg) houses three separate collections (covered by a single ticket): The **Arms and Armor Collection** displays weaponry and body armor from all over the vast Habsburg Empire, including

exotic Turkish suits of armor. The **Ancient Musical Instruments Collection** shows instruments through the ages, especially the rapid evolution from harpsichord to piano. Admire Beethoven's (supposed) clarinet, Leopold Mozart's violin, a keyboard perhaps played by Wolfgang Mozart, and Brahms' piano. The **Ephesus Museum** has artifacts from the bustling ancient Roman city of 300,000 people (located in modern-day Turkey, near Kuşadası on the southwestern coast). The *Bronze Statue of an Athlete* is a jigsaw of 234 shattered pieces meticulously put back together. The *Statue of Artemis*, representing a pagan fertility goddess, is draped with sexy round objects—which may have symbolized breasts, eggs, or bulls' testicles. The included audioguide brings the exhibits to life and lets you hear the collection's fascinating old instruments being played. An added bonus is the chance to wander alone among the royal Habsburg halls, stairways, and painted ceilings.

Cost and Hours: €12, ticket covers all three collections and the Kunsthistorisches Museum across the Ring, €18 combo-ticket also includes the Hofburg Treasury, Wed-Sun 10:00-18:00, closed Mon-Tue, last entry 30 minutes before closing, almost no tourists, tel. 01/525-240, www.khm.at.

▲**Spanish Riding School**—This stately 300-year-old Baroque Hall at the Hofburg Palace is the home of the renowned Lipizzaner stallions. The magnificent building was an impressive expanse in its day. Built without pillars, it offers clear views of the prancing horses under lavish chandeliers, with a grand statue of Emperor Charles VI on horseback at the head of the hall.

Lipizzaner stallions were a creation of horse-loving Habsburg Archduke Charles, who wanted to breed the perfect animal. He imported Andalusian horses from his homeland of Spain, then mated them with a local line to produce an extremely intelligent and easily trainable breed. Italian and Arabian bloodlines were later added to tweak various characteristics. Lipizzaner stallions are known for their noble gait and Baroque profile. These regal horses have changed shape with the tenor of the times: They were bred strong and stout during wars, and frilly and slender in more cultured eras. But they're always born black, fade to gray, and turn a distinctive white in adulthood.

The school offers three options for seeing the horses:

Performances: The Lipizzaner stallions put on great 80-minute shows in spring and fall (March-June and Sept-Dec Sun at 11:00 and either Sat at 11:00 or Fri at 19:00, fewer shows in Jan, none in Feb or July-Aug, tel. 01/533-9031, www.srs.at). The formal emcee thoughtfully introduces each number in German and English as horses do their choreographed moves to jaunty recorded Viennese classical music (in 4:4 meter rather than 3:4—I guess horses can't waltz). The pricey seats book up months in advance, but standing room is usually available the same day, and there's not a bad view in the house (seats: €47-173, standing room: €23-31; box office opens at 9:00 and is located inside the Hofburg—go through the main Hofburg entryway from Michaelerplatz, then turn left into the first passage).

Training Sessions: Luckily for the masses, training sessions with music take place in the same hall and are open to the public. Don't have high expectations, as the horses often do little more than trot and warm up (€12 at the door, roughly March-June and mid-Aug-Dec Tue-Fri 10:00-12:00—but only when the horses are in town). Tourists line up early at Josefsplatz (the large courtyard between Michaelerplatz and Albertinaplatz), at the door marked *Spanische Hofreitschule*. But there's no need to show up when the doors open at 10:00, since tickets never really "sell out." Only the horses stay for the full two hours. As people leave, new tickets are printed, so you can just prance in with no wait at all. You can also buy tickets for the training sessions at the box office.

Stables: Any time of day, you can see the horses in their stalls and view videos of them prancing in the Reitschulgasse corridor. Guided one-hour tours of stalls are given daily (€16; tours at 14:00, 15:00, and 16:00; in English and German, reserve by calling 01/533-9031).

▲**Augustinian Church (Augustinerkirche)**—This is the Gothic and Neo-Gothic church where the Habsburgs got latched (weddings took place here), then dispatched (the royal hearts are in the vault—not open to the public). Don't miss the exquisite, tomb-like Canova memorial (Neoclassical, 1805) to Maria Theresa's favorite daughter, Maria Christina, with its incredibly sad white-marble procession. The church's 11:00 Sunday Mass is a hit with music-lovers—both a Mass and a concert, often with an orchestra accompanying the choir (acoustics are best in front). Pay by contributing to the offering plate and buying a CD afterwards. Programs are posted by the entry (church open long hours daily, Augustinerstrasse 3—facing Josefsplatz, with its statue of the great reform emperor Josef II and the imperial library next door).

Austrian National Library—Next to the Augustinian Church, this was once the library of the Habsburgs. Wandering through this impressive temple of learning—with a statue of Charles VI in the center—you find yourself whispering. The setting takes you back to 1730 and gives you the sense that, in imperial times, knowledge of the world was for the elite—and with that knowledge, the elite had power (€7, Tue-Sun 10:00-18:00, Thu until 21:00, closed Mon, recommended Soho Kantine in the basement good for a cheap lunch).

Burggarten (Palace Garden) and Butterfly House—This greenbelt, once the backyard of the Hofburg and now a people's park, welcomes visitors to loiter on the grass. On nice days, it's lively with office workers enjoying a break. The statue of Mozart facing the Ringstrasse is popular. The iron-and-glass pavilion now houses the recommended Café Restaurant Palmenhaus and a small but fluttery butterfly exhibit (€5.50; April-Oct Mon-Fri 10:00-16:45, Sat-Sun 10:00-18:15; Nov-March daily 10:00-15:45).

▲▲**Albertina Museum**—This building, at the southern tip of the Hofburg complex (near the Opera), was the residence of Maria Theresa's favorite daughter, Maria Christina, who was the only one allowed to marry for love rather than political strategy. Her many sisters were jealous. (Marie-Antoinette had to marry the French king...and lost her head over it.)

Maria Christina's husband, Albert of Saxony, was a great collector of original drawings and amassed an enormous assortment of works by Dürer, Rembrandt, Rubens, Schiele, and others. Today, reproductions of some of these works hang in the Albertina's elegant French-Classicist–style **state rooms** *(Prunkräume)*. Head to these rooms first for a great opportunity to wander freely under the chandeliers of a Habsburg palace, with its pure 19th-century imperial splendor unconstrained by velvet ropes.

Then follow signs for *Meisterwerke der Moderne* (*Die Sammlung Batliner,* on the top floor). These modern galleries hold a wonderful rotating exhibit from the museum's **Batliner collection** of modern art (from Impressionism to Abstract Expressionism, with minor works by major artists—Monet, Picasso, Chagall, Matisse), along with temporary exhibits.

To understand both the imperial apartments and the wonderful Batliner works, invest in the **audioguide,** which makes this collection a luxurious lesson in modern art appreciation—from Monet to today.

Cost and Hours: €9.50, generally meaningless without €4 audioguide, daily 10:00-18:00, Wed until 21:00, overlooking Albertinaplatz across from the TI and Opera, tel. 01/534-830, www.albertina.at.

Church Crypts near the Hofburg

Two churches near the Hofburg offer starkly different looks at dearly departed Viennese: the Habsburg coffins in the Kaisergruft, and the commoners' graves in St. Michael's Church.

▲▲**Kaisergruft: The Remains of the Habsburgs**—Visiting the imperial remains is not as easy as you might imagine. These original organ donors left their bodies—about 150 in all—in the unassuming Kaisergruft (the Imperial Crypt at the Capuchin Church), their hearts in the Augustinian Church (vaults closed to public), and their entrails in the catacombs below St. Stephen's Cathedral (described on page 49). Don't tripe.

Cost and Hours: €5, daily 10:00-18:00, last entry at 17:40, behind the Opera on Neuer Markt, tel. 01/512-6853.

Highlights: As you enter, be sure to buy the €0.50 map with a Habsburg family tree and a chart locating each coffin.

Find the pewter double-coffin under the dome. This tomb of **Maria Theresa** (1717-1780) and her husband, **Franz I** (1708-1765), is worth a close look for its artwork. Maria Theresa outlived her husband by 15 years—which she spent in mourning. Old and fat, she installed a special lift enabling her to get down into the crypt to be with her dear, departed Franz (even though he had been far from faithful). The couple recline—Etruscan-style—atop their fancy lead coffin. At each corner are the crowns of the Habsburgs—the Holy Roman Empire, Hungary, Bohemia, and Jerusalem. Notice the contrast between the Rococo splendor of Maria Theresa's tomb and the simple box holding her more modest son, **Josef II** (at his parents' feet). This understated tomb is in keeping with his enlightened politics.

Nearby, find the appropriately austere military tomb of **Franz Josef** (1830-1916) in the more brightly lit modern section. Flanking Franz Josef are the tombs of his son, the archduke **Rudolf,** and Empress Elisabeth. Rudolf and his teenage mistress supposedly committed suicide together in 1889 at Mayerling hunting lodge and—since the Church figured he forced her to take her own life and was therefore a murderer—it took considerable legal hair-splitting to win Rudolf this spot (after examining his brain, it was determined that he was mentally disabled and therefore incapable of knowingly killing himself and his girl). *Kaiserin* Elisabeth (1837-1898), a.k.a. **Sisi,** always gets the "Most Flowers" award.

In front of those three are the two most recent Habsburg tombs. **Empress Zita** was laid to rest here in 1989, followed by her son, **Karl Ludwig,** in 2007. The funeral procession for Karl, the fourth son of the last Austrian emperor, was probably the last such Old Regime event in European history. The monarchy died hard in Austria. Today there are about 700 living Habsburg royals, mostly living in exile. When they die, they get buried in their countries of exile.

Body parts and ornate tombs aside, the real legacy of the Habsburgs is the magnificence of this city. Step outside. Pan up. Watch the clouds glide by the ornate gables of Vienna.

▲**St. Michael's Church Crypt**—St. Michael's Church, which faces the Hofburg on Michaelerplatz, offers a striking contrast to the imperial crypt. Regular tours take visitors underground to see a typical church crypt—filled with the rotting wooden coffins of well-to-do commoners.

Climbing below the church, you'll see about a hundred 18th-century coffins and stand on three feet of debris, surrounded by niches filled with stacked lumber from decayed coffins and count-less bones. You'll meet a 1769 mummy in lederhosen and a wig, along with a woman clutching a cross with flowers painted on her high heels. You'll learn about death in those times—from how the wealthy didn't want to end up in standard shallow graves, instead paying to be laid to rest below the church, to how, in 1780, the enlightened emperor Josef II ended the practice of cemetery buri-als in cities but allowed the rich to become the stinking rich in crypts under churches. You'll also discover why many were buried with their chin strapped shut (because when the muscles rot, your jaw falls open and you get that ghostly skeleton look that nobody wants).

Cost and Hours: €5 for 45-minute tour, Mon-Sat at 11:00 and 13:30, mostly in German but with enough English, wait at the sign that advertises the tour at the church entrance and pay the guide directly.

Kunsthistorisches Museum and Nearby

▲▲▲**Kunsthistorisches Museum**—This exciting museum, across the Ring from the Hofburg Palace, showcases the gran-deur and opulence of the Habsburgs' collected artwork in a grand building (purpose-built in 1888 to display these works). While there's little Viennese art here, you will find world-class European masterpieces galore (including canvases by Raphael, Caravaggio, Velázquez, Dürer, Rubens, Vermeer, Rembrandt, and a particu-larly exquisite roomful of Bruegels), all well-hung on one glorious floor, plus a fine display of Egyptian, classical, and applied arts.

Cost and Hours: €12, also includes New Palace museums across the Ring; free for kids under 18, €18 combo-ticket also includes the Hofburg Treasury, Tue-Sun 10:00-18:00, Thu until 21:00, closed Mon, on the Ringstrasse at Maria-Theresien-Platz, U-2 or U-3: Volkstheater/Museumsplatz (exit toward *Burgring*), tel. 01/525-240, www.khm.at.

Audioguide Tours: You can rent an audioguide at the desk in the atrium. The free "Highlights" audioguide covers a selection of 20 pieces (including just 13 paintings). The €3 "Total" audioguide is far more comprehensive, covering 560 items (worth it if you want an in-depth tour).

◗ **Self-Guided Tour:** The Kunsthistorwhateveritis Mus-eum—let's just say "Koonst"—houses some of the most beautiful, sexy, and fun art from two centuries (c. 1450-1650). The collection reflects the joie de vivre of Austria's luxury-loving Habsburg rulers. At their peak of power in the 1500s, the Habsburgs ruled Austria, Germany, northern Italy, the Netherlands, and Spain—and you'll see a wide variety of art from all these places and beyond.

If you're short on time, focus on the Painting Gallery

Kunsthistorisches Museum

VAN DER WEYDEN & VAN EYCK

COREGGIO & PARMIGIANINO

To Opera   DÜRER   BOSCH

EARLY NORTHERN ART

MANTEGNA

RAPHAEL

17 ····· 16 ····· 14

RAPHAEL 1 ···· 2 ···· 3 ···· 4

Saal XI   Saal X   Saal IX

WC   WC

TITIAN Saal I

VERONESE Saal II   TINTO-RETTO

HOLBEIN   SNYDERS   BRUEGEL

THESEUS STATUE

Saal III

NORTHERN EUROPEAN ART

TOUR BEGINS

ITALIAN, SPANISH & FRENCH ART

ARCIMBOLDO   MORE ITALIAN ART

MAIN STAIRCASE

RINGSTRASSE   MORE NORTHERN ART

CAFÉ

7

RUBENS

Saal XIII   Saal XIV   Saal XV

CANALETTO Saal VII   BAROQUE Saal VI   CARA-VAGGIO Saal V

21   22   VERMEER   23

VELÁZQUEZ 10

TOUR ENDS

REMBRANDT

Not to Scale

↑ **ENTRANCE** (on ground level)

MARIA-THERESIEN-PLATZ

VIENNA

(Gemäldegalerie) on the first floor. Climb the main staircase, featuring Antonio Canova's statue of *Theseus Clubbing the Centaur.* Italian, Spanish, and French art is in the right half of the building (as you face Theseus), and Northern European art to the left. Notice that the museum labels the largest rooms with Roman numerals (Saal I, II, III), and the smaller rooms around the perimeter with Arabic (Rooms 1, 2, 3).

Italian, Spanish, and French Art: Saals I-III cover the Venetian renaissance. The first spans the long career of **Titian,** who painted portraits, Christian Madonnas, and sexy Venuses with equal ease. Next comes Paolo **Veronese,** whose colorful works reflect the wealth of Venice, the funnel through which luxury goods from the exotic East flowed into northern Europe. And **Tintoretto**'s many portraits give us a peek at the movers and shakers of the Venetian Empire.

Rooms 1-4 hold some of the museum's most important works: **Mantegna**'s *St. Sebastian,* **Correggio**'s *Jupiter and Io,* and **Raphael**'s *Madonna of the Meadow (Die Madonna im Grünen),* a geometrically perfect masterpiece of the High Renaissance, painted when Raphael was just 22.

Farther along, through the small rooms along the far end of this wing (likely Room 7, or possibly out on loan), find the cleverly deceptive portraits by Giuseppe **Arcimboldo.** His *Summer—* a.k.a "Fruit Face"—is one of four paintings the Habsburg court painter did showing the seasons (and elements) as people. With a pickle nose, pear chin, and corn-husk ears, this guy literally is what he eats.

Caravaggio (in Saal V) shocked the art world with brutally honest reality. Compared with Raphael's super-sweet *Madonna of the Meadow*, Caravaggio's *Madonna of the Rosary* (*Die Rosenkranzmadonna*, the biggest canvas in the room) looks perfectly ordinary, and the saints kneeling around her have dirty feet. In *David with the Head of Goliath (David mit dem Haupt des Goliath)* Caravaggio turns a third-degree-interrogation light on a familiar Bible story. David shoves the dripping head of the slain giant—the artist's self portrait—right in our noses.

When the Habsburgs ruled both Austria and Spain, cousins kept in touch through portraits of themselves and their kids. Diego **Velázquez** (in Room 10) was the greatest of Spain's "photo-journalist" painters: heavily influenced by Caravaggio's realism, capturing his subjects without passing judgment, flattering, or glorifying them.

Northern European Art: The other half of this floor features works of the "Northern Renaissance," which was more secular and Protestant than Catholic-funded Italian art (that means fewer Madonnas, saints, and Greek gods and more peasants, landscapes, and food). Paintings are smaller and darker, full of down-to-earth objects. Northern artists sweated the details, encouraging the patient viewer to appreciate the beauty in everyday things.

The undisputed master of the slice-of-life village scene was Pieter **Bruegel** the Elder—the Norman Rockwell of the 16th century. Saal X contains the largest collection of Bruegels in captivity. Despite his many rural paintings, Bruegel was actually a cultivated urbanite who liked to wear peasants' clothing to observe country folk at play (a trans-fest-ite?). He celebrated their simple life, but he also skewered their weaknesses—not to single them out as hicks, but as universal examples of human folly. *The Peasant Wedding (Bauernhochzeit)*, Bruegel's most famous work, is less about the wedding than the food. It's a farmers' feeding frenzy, as the barnful of wedding guests scrambles to get their share of free eats. *Bruegel's Peasant Dance (Bauerntanz)* shows a celebration at the consecration of a village church. The three Bruegel landscape paintings are part of an original series of six "calendar" paintings, depicting the seasons of the year.

Also in this section, don't miss **Rubens**' large, lush canvases (including *The Little Fur/Das Pelzchen*, depicting his much younger, dimpled bride); **Vermeer**'s *The Art of Painting (Die Malkunst)*, showing the painter at work in his studio, with a painstaking attention to detail; and **Rembrandt**'s frank self-portraits—one as a defiant young artist, the other as a broken old man.

▲**Natural History Museum**—In the twin building facing the Kunsthistorisches Museum, you'll find moon rocks, dinosaur stuff, and the fist-sized *Venus of Willendorf*—at 25,000 years old, the world's oldest sex symbol. This four-inch-tall, chubby stone statuette, found in the Danube Valley, is a generic female (no face or feet) resting her hands on her ample breasts. The statue's purpose is unknown, but she may have been a symbol of fertility for our mammoth-hunting ancestors. Even though the museum is not glitzy or high-tech, it's a hit with children and scientifically curious grown-ups. Of the museum's 20 million objects, you're sure to find something interesting.

Cost and Hours: €10, Wed-Mon 9:00-18:30, Wed until 21:00, closed Tue, on the Ringstrasse at Maria-Theresien-Platz, U-2 or U-3: Volkstheater/Museumsplatz, tel. 01/521-770, www.nhm-wien.ac.at.

MuseumsQuartier—The vast grounds of the former imperial stables now corral a cutting-edge cultural center for contemporary arts and design, including several impressive museums; the best are the Leopold Museum and the Museum of Modern Art.

Walk into the complex from the Hofburg side, where the main entrance (with visitors center, shop, and ticket office) leads to a big courtyard with cafés, fountains, and ever-changing "installation lounge furniture," all surrounded by the quarter's various museums. At the visitors center, various **combo-tickets** are available for those interested in more than just the Leopold and Modern Art museums. You can also rent a €4 **audioguide** that explains the complex (behind Kunsthistorisches Museum, U-2 or U-3: Volkstheater/Museumsplatz, tel. 01/525-5881, www.mqw.at).

The **Leopold Museum** features several temporary exhibits of modern Austrian art. The top floor holds the largest collection of works by Egon Schiele (1890-1918; these works make some people uncomfortable—Schiele's nudes are *really* nude) and a few paintings by Gustav Klimt, Kolo Moser, and Oskar Kokoschka. While this is a great collection, you can see even better works from these artists in the Belvedere Palace, described later (€11, €3 audioguide—worth it only for enthusiasts; June-Aug daily 10:00-18:00, Thu until 21:00; Sept-May Wed-Mon 10:00-18:00, Thu until 21:00, closed Tue; tel. 01/525-700, www.leopoldmuseum.org).

The **Museum of Modern Art** (Museum Moderner Kunst Stiftung Ludwig, a.k.a. "MUMOK") is Austria's leading gallery for international modern and contemporary art. It's the striking lava-paneled building—three stories tall and four stories deep, offering seven floors of far-out art that's hard for most visitors to appreciate. This huge, state-of-the-art museum owns works by "classical" modernists (Paul Klee, Pablo Picasso, Pop artists) and shows off up-to-the-minute contemporary art in revolving exhibits

(€9, €3 audioguide has more than you probably want to hear, daily 10:00-18:00, Thu until 21:00, tel. 01/52500, www.mumok.at).

Rounding out the sprawling MuseumsQuartier are an architecture center, Electronic Avenue, design forum, children's museum, "Quartier 21" (with gallery space and shops), and the **Kunsthalle Wien**—an exhibition center for contemporary art (two halls with different exhibitions, €8.50 for one, €7 for the other, €11.50 for both; daily 10:00-19:00, Thu until 22:00, tel. 01/521-8933, www.kunsthallewien.at).

Karlsplatz and Nearby

These sights cluster around Karlsplatz, just southeast of the Ringstrasse (U-1, U-2, or U-4: Karlsplatz). From the U-Bahn station's passageway, it's a 30-minute walk around the sights on Karlsplatz: the Karlskirche, Secession, and Naschmarkt (allow more time to actually visit these sights).

Karlsplatz—This picnic-friendly square, with its Henry Moore sculpture in the pond, is ringed with sights. The massive, domed Karlskirche and its twin spiral columns dominate the square. The small green, white, and gold pavilions that line the street across the square from the church are from the late 19th-century municipal train system *(Stadtbahn)*. One of Europe's first subway systems, this precursor to today's U-Bahn was built with a military purpose in mind: to move troops quickly in time of civil unrest—specifically, out to Schönbrunn Palace. With curvy iron frames, decorative marble slabs, and painted gold trim, these are pioneering works in the *Jugendstil* (Art Nouveau) style, designed by Otto Wagner, who influenced Klimt and the Secessionists. One of the pavilions has an exhibit on **Otto Wagner** (€2, April-Oct Tue-Sun 10:00-18:00, closed Mon and Nov-March, near the Ringstrasse, tel. 01/5058-7478-5173).

▲**Karlskirche (St. Charles' Church)**—Charles Borromeo, a 16th-century bishop from Milan, was an inspiration during plague times. This "votive church" was dedicated to him in 1713, when an epidemic spared Vienna. The church offers the best Baroque in Vienna, with a unique combination of columns (showing scenes from the life of Charles Borromeo, à la Trajan's Column in Rome), a classic pediment, and an elliptical dome. The dome's colorful 13,500-square-foot fresco—painted in the 1730s by Johann Michael Rottmayr—shows Signor Borromeo (in red-and-white bishops' robes) gazing up into heaven, spreading his arms wide, and pleading with Christ to spare Vienna from the plague.

The church is especially worthwhile for the chance to ride an **elevator** (installed for renovation work) up into the cupola. While the restoration of the interior is complete, work on the exterior will likely continue through 2012; when it's finished, the scaffolding and elevator will likely be taken down. Until that happens, the industrial lift takes you to a platform at the base of the 235-foot dome (if you're even slightly afraid of heights, skip this trip). Consider that the church was built and decorated with a scaffolding system essentially the same as this one. Once up top, you'll climb stairs to the steamy lantern at the extreme top of the church. At that dizzying height, you're in the clouds with cupids and angels. Many details that appear smooth and beautiful from ground level—such as gold leaf, paintings, and fake marble—look rough and sloppy up close. It's surreal to observe the 3-D figures from an unintended angle—check out Christ's leg, which looks dwarf-sized up close. Give yourself a minute to take it in: Faith, Hope, and Charity triumph and inspire. Borromeo lobbies heaven for plague relief. Meanwhile, a Protestant's Lutheran Bible is put to the torch by angels. At the very top, you'll see the tiny dove representing the Holy Ghost, surrounded by a cheering squad of nipple-lipped cupids.

Cost and Hours: €6, ticket covers church interior, elevator ride, and skippable one-room museum; audioguide-€2; Mon-Sat 9:00-18:00, Sun 13:00-18:00, last entry 30 minutes before closing; elevator runs until 17:30, last ascent at 17:00. The entry fee may seem steep, but remember that it funds the restoration.

Wien Museum Karlsplatz—This underappreciated city history museum, worth ▲ for those intrigued by Vienna's illustrious past, walks you through the story of Vienna with well-presented artifacts. Work your way up chronologically. The ground floor exhibits prehistoric and Roman fragments, along with some original statues from St. Stephen's Cathedral (c. 1350). The first floor focuses on the Renaissance and Baroque eras, including suits of armor, old city maps, booty from an Ottoman siege, and an 1850 city model showing the town just before the wall was replaced by the Ring. Finally, the second floor displays a city model from 1898 (with the new Ringstrasse), sentimental Biedermeier paintings and objets d'art, and early 20th-century paintings (including four by Klimt, as well as works by Schiele, Kokoschka, and other Secessionists).

Cost and Hours: €6, free first Sun of the month, open Tue-Sun 10:00-18:00, closed Mon, tel. 01/505-8747, www.wien museum.at.

▲Academy of Fine Arts (Akademie der Bildenden Künste)—Recently refurbished, this museum features a small but impressive collection of works by big-name artists, including quick, sketchy cartoons Rubens used to create his giant canvases; a Venice series by Guardi; a self-portrait by a 15-year-old Van Dyck; and a round Botticelli canvas, recently cleaned to show off its vivid colors, depicting the Madonna tenderly embracing the

Baby Jesus. The collection's highlight is the captivating, harrowing *Last Judgment* triptych by Hieronymus Bosch (c. 1482, with some details added by Lucas Cranach). Read the altarpiece from left to right, following the pessimistically medieval narrative about humankind's fall from God's graces: In the left panel, at the bottom, God pulls Eve from Adam's rib in the Garden of Eden. Just above that, we see a female representing the serpent hold out the forbidden fruit to tempt Eve. Above that, Adam and Eve are being shooed away by an angel. At the top of this panel, God sits on his cloud, evicting the fallen angels (who turn into insect-like monsters). In the middle panel, Christ holds court over the living and the dead. Notice the jarring contrast between Christ's serene expression and the grotesque scene playing out beneath him. These disturbing images crescendo in the final (right) panel, showing an unspeakably horrific vision of hell that few artists have managed to top in the more than half-millennium since Bosch.

The collection is magnificently lit and well-described by the €2 audioguide, and comes with comfy chairs. The fact that it's housed upstairs in a working art academy gives it a certain realness. As you wander the halls of the academy, ponder how history might have been different if Hitler—who applied to study architecture here but was rejected—had been accepted as a student. Before leaving, peek into the ground floor's central hall—textbook Historicism, the Ringstrasse style of the late 1800s.

Cost and Hours: €8, audioguide-€2; Tue-Sun 10:00-18:00, closed Mon, 3 blocks from the Opera at Schillerplatz 3; once inside, go up two floors, following signs for *Gemäldegalerie;* tel. 01/588-162-201, www.akademiegalerie.at.

▲**The Secession**—This little building, strategically located behind the Academy of Fine Arts, was created by the Vienna Secession movement, a group of nonconformist artists led by Gustav Klimt, Otto Wagner, and friends.

The young trees carved into the walls and the building's bushy "golden cabbage" rooftop are symbolic of a renewal cycle. The Secessionist motto, under the cabbage, reads: "To each age its art, and to art its liberty." Today, the Secession continues to showcase cutting-edge art, as well as one of Gustav Klimt's most famous works.

While the staff hopes you take a look at the temporary exhibits (and they're included in the ticket price whether you like it or not), most tourists head directly for the basement, home to the museum's highlight: Klimt's classic *Beethoven Frieze* (a.k.a. the "Searching Souls"). One of the masterpieces of Viennese Art Nouveau, this 105-foot-long fresco was the multimedia centerpiece of a 1902 exhibition honoring Ludwig van Beethoven. Read the free flier, which explains Klimt's still-powerful work, inspired by

VIENNA

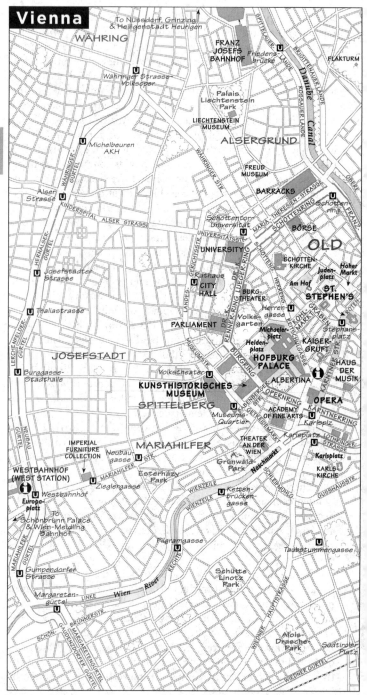

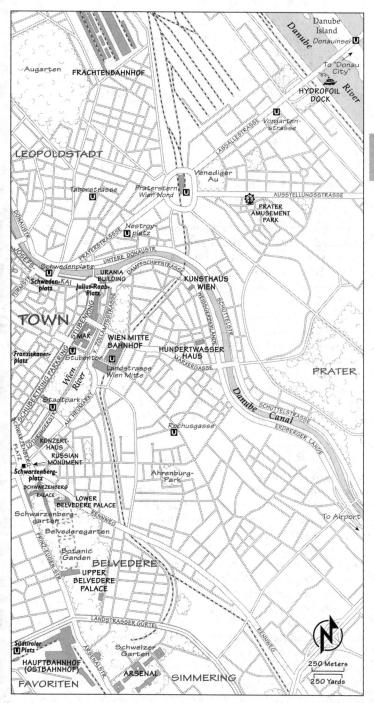

Beethoven's Ninth Symphony. Klimt embellished the work with painted-on gold (his brother, and colleague, was a goldsmith), and by gluing on reflecting glass and mother-of-pearl for the ladies' dresses and jewelry.

Cost and Hours: €5, as high as €8.50 during special exhibits, Tue-Sun 10:00-18:00, closed Mon, Friedrichstrasse 12, tel. 01/587-5307, www.secession.at.

▲**Naschmarkt**—In 1898, the city decided to cover up its Vienna River. The long, wide square they created was filled with a lively produce market that still bustles most days (closed Sun). It's long been known as *the* place to get exotic faraway foods. In fact, locals say, "From here start the Balkans."

From near the Opera, the Naschmarkt (roughly, "Munchies Market") stretches along Wienzeile street. This "Belly of Vienna" comes with two parallel lanes—one lined with fun and reasonable eateries, and the other featuring the town's top-end produce and gourmet goodies. This is where top chefs like to get their ingredients. At the gourmet vinegar stall, you sample the vinegar-like perfume—with a drop on your wrist. Farther from the center, the Naschmarkt becomes likeably seedy and surrounded by sausage stands, Turkish *Döner Kebab* stalls, cafés, and theaters. At the market's far end is a line of buildings with fine Art Nouveau facades. Each Saturday, the Naschmarkt is infested by a huge flea market where, in olden days, locals would come to hire a monkey to pick little critters out of their hair.

Hours and Location: Mon-Fri 6:00-18:30, Sat 6:00-17:00, closed Sun, closes earlier in winter; U-1, U-2, or U-4: Karlsplatz. For a picnic in the park, pick up your grub here and walk over to Karlsplatz (described earlier).

More Sights Beyond the Ring
South of the Ring
▲▲**Belvedere Palace (Schloss Belvedere)**—This is the elegant palace of Prince Eugene of Savoy (1663-1736), the still-much-appreciated conqueror of the Ottomans. Today you can tour Eugene's lavish palace, see sweeping views of the gardens and the Vienna skyline, and enjoy world-class art starring Gustav Klimt, French Impressionism, and a grab-bag of other 19th- and early-20th-century artists. While Vienna's other art collections show off works by masters from around Europe, this has the city's best collection of homegrown artists.

Cost and Hours: €9.50 for Upper Belvedere Palace only, €14 for Upper and Lower palaces—generally not worth it, gardens are free except for privy garden—included in big ticket, audioguide-€4 or €6/2 people, daily 10:00-18:00, Lower Palace only open Wed until 21:00, grounds open until dusk, no photos allowed inside, entrance at Prinz-Eugen-Strasse 27, tel. 01/7955-7134, www .belvedere.at.

Getting There: The palace is a 15-minute walk south of the Ring. To get there from the center, catch tram #D at the Opera (direction: Südbahnhof). Get off at the Schloss Belvedere stop (just below the Upper Palace gate), cross the street, walk uphill one block, and look for the gate on your right.

○ Self-Guided Tour: The Belvedere Palace is actually two grand buildings—the Upper Palace and Lower Palace—separated by a fine garden. For our purposes, the Upper Palace is what matters. Buy your ticket at the office behind the palace, then go around to the front to enter. Once inside, the palace's eclectic collection is tailor-made for browsing. It's organized roughly chronologically as you go up.

Ground Floor: The main floor displays a collection of Austrian Baroque (on the left) and medieval art (on the right). The Baroque section includes a fascinating room of grotesquely grimacing heads by **Franz Xaver Messerschmidt** (1736-1783), a quirky 18th-century Habsburg court sculptor who left the imperial life to follow his own, somewhat deranged muse. After his promising career was cut short by mental illness, Messerschmidt relocated to Bratislava and spent the rest of his days sculpting a series of eerily lifelike "character heads" *(Kopfstücke)*. Their most unusual faces are contorted by extreme emotions.

• *From the entrance, climb the staircase to the first floor and enter the grand red-and-gold, chandeliered...*

Marble Hall (First Floor): This was Prince Eugene's party room. *Belvedere* means "beautiful view," and the view from the Marble Hall is especially spectacular.

• *To the right is the...*

East Wing (First Floor): Alongside Renoir's ladies, Monet's landscapes, and Van Gogh's rough brushstrokes are similar works by their lesser-known Austrian counterparts. Around 1900, Austrian artists come to the fore, soaking up Symbolism, Expressionism, and other Modernist trends.

In the two rooms full of sumptuous paintings by **Gustav Klimt,** you can get caught up in his fascination with the beauty and danger he saw in women. To Klimt, all art was erotic art. He painted during the turn of the century, when Vienna was a splendid laboratory of hedonism. The famous painting of *Judith I* (1901) shows no biblical heroine—Klimt paints her as a high-society Vienna woman with an ostentatious dog-collar necklace. With half-closed eyes and slightly parted lips, she's dismissive... yet mysterious and bewitching. Holding the head of her biblical victim, she's the modern femme fatale. In what is perhaps Klimt's best-known painting, *The Kiss,* two lovers are wrapped up in the colorful gold-and-jeweled cloak of bliss. Klimt's woman is no longer dominating, but submissive, abandoning herself to her man in a fertile field and a vast universe. In a glow emanating from a radiance of desire, the body she presses against is a self-portrait of the artist himself.

Klimt nurtured the next generation of artists, especially **Egon Schiele.** While Klimt's works are mystical and otherworldly, Schiele's tend to be darker and gloomier. One of Schiele's most recognizable works, *The Embrace,* shows a couple engaged in an erotically charged, rippling moment of passion. Striking a darker tone is *The Family,* which depicts a crouching couple. This family portrait from 1918 is especially poignant because his wife died while he was still working on it.

The Rest of the Upper Palace: The Belvedere's collection goes through the whole range of 19th- and 20th-century art: Historicism, Romanticism, Impressionism, Realism, tired tourism, Expressionism, Art Nouveau, and early Modernism.

Grounds and Gardens: The delightfully manicured grounds are free and fun to explore. The only area with an entry fee is the **privy garden,** along the left side of the Lower Palace (and accessed through that palace).

Lower Palace: Covered by a separate ticket, this is the home where Prince Eugene actually hung his helmet. Today it contains a small stretch of three of his private apartments (relatively uninteresting compared to the sumptuous Habsburg apartments elsewhere in town). The Lower Palace also houses some generally good special exhibits, as well as the entrance to the privy garden, orangerie, and stables (until 12:00). If the special exhibits intrigue you, it's worth buying the combo-ticket to get in here; otherwise, I wouldn't bother to visit.

East of the Ring
Museum of Applied Art (Österreichisches Museum für Angewandte Kunst)—Facing the old town from across the Ring, the MAK, as it's called, is Vienna's answer to London's Victoria and Albert Museum. The MAK is more than just another grand building on the Ringstrasse. It was built to provide models of historic design for Ringstrasse architects and is a delightful space in itself (many locals stop in to enjoy a coffee on the plush couches in the main lobby). The relatively sparse collection shows off the fancies of local aristocratic society, including fine *Jugendstil* pieces (among them Klimt designs for a palace in Brussels). Each wing is dedicated to a different era. Exhibits, well-described in English (borrow the captions in each room), come with a playful modern flair—notable modern designers were assigned various spaces. The unique gift shop also makes for a fun diversion.

Cost and Hours: €8, €10 includes a hefty English guidebook, free on Sat, open Tue-Sun 10:00-18:00, Tue until 24:00, closed Mon, Stubenring 5, tel. 01/711-360, www.mak.at.

Eating at the MAK: The beautiful lobby hosts an inviting **café**. The **Restaurant Österreicher im MAK,** in the same building, is named for Chef Helmut Österreicher, who's renowned for his classic and modern Viennese cuisine. Classy and mod, it's trendy for locals (€9-23 plates, daily 8:30-1:00 in the morning, reserve for evening, tel. 01/714-0121).

▲**KunstHausWien: Hundertwasser Museum**—This "make yourself at home" museum and nearby apartment complex are a hit with lovers of modern art, mixing the work and philosophy of local painter/environmentalist Friedensreich Hundertwasser (1928-2000). Stand in front of the colorful checkerboard building and consider Hundertwasser's style. He was against "window racism": Neighboring houses allow only one kind of window, but $100H_2O$'s windows are each different—and he encouraged residents in the Hundertwasserhaus (a 5-10 minute walk away, described below) to personalize them. He recognized "tree tenants" as well as human tenants. His buildings are spritzed with a forest and topped with dirt and grassy little parks—close to nature and good for the soul.

Floors and sidewalks are irregular—to "stimulate the brain" (although current residents complain it just causes wobbly furniture and sprained ankles). Thus $100H_2O$ waged a one-man fight—during the 1950s and 1960s, when concrete and glass ruled—to save the human soul from the city. (Hundertwasser claimed that "straight lines are godless.")

Inside the museum, start with his interesting biography. His fun paintings are half psychedelic *Jugendstil* and half just kids' stuff. Notice the photographs from his 1950s days as part of Vienna's bohemian scene. Throughout the museum, keep an eye out for the fun philosophical quotes from an artist who believed, "If man is creative, he comes nearer to his creator."

Cost and Hours: €9 for Hundertwasser Museum, €12 combo-ticket includes special exhibitions, half-price on Mon, open daily 10:00-19:00, extremely fragrant and colorful garden café, tel. 01/712-0491, www.kunsthauswien.com.

Getting There: It's located at Untere Weissgerberstrasse 13 (tram #1: Radetzkyplatz or U-3: Landstrasse). Note that the tram stop is much closer than the U-Bahn stop. From the Landstrasse U-Bahn stop, walk 10 minutes downhill (north) along Untere Viaduktgasse (a block east of the station), or ride tram #0 three stops to Radetzkyplatz; from there signs point to the museum.

Hundertwasserhaus: The KunstHausWien provides by far the best look at Hundertwasser, but for an actual lived-in apartment complex by the green master, walk five minutes to the one-with-nature Hundertwasserhaus (at Löwengasse and Kegel-gasse). This complex of 50 apartments, subsidized by the government to provide affordable housing, was built in the 1980s as a breath of architectural fresh air in a city of boring, blocky apartment complexes. While not open to visitors, it's worth visiting for its fun and colorful patchwork exterior and the Hundertwasser festival of shops across the street. Don't miss the view from Kegelgasse to see the "tree tenants" and the internal winter garden that residents enjoy.

Hundertwasser detractors—of which there are many—remind visitors that $100H_2O$ was a painter, not an architect. They describe the Hundertwasserhaus as a "1950s house built in the 1980s" that was colorfully painted with no real concern for the environment, communal living, or even practical comfort. Almost all of the original inhabitants got fed up with the novelty and moved out.

North of the Ring

▲**Liechtenstein Museum**—The noble Liechtenstein family (who own only a pint-size country, but whose friendship with the Habsburgs goes back generations) amassed an incredible private art collection. Their palace was long a treasure for Vienna art-lovers. Then, in 1938—knowing Hitler was intent on plundering artwork to create an immense "Führer Museum"—the family fled to their tiny homeland with their best art. Since the museum reopened in 2004, attendance has been disappointing, but the problem is its location (and perhaps its steep price)...not its worthiness. The Liechtensteins' "world of Baroque pleasures" includes the family's rare "Golden Carriage," which was used for their grand entry into Paris in 1738. It was carted to the edge of town and assembled there. It's a rare example of the French Rococo style, as nearly all such carriages were destroyed in the French Revolution. The museum also has a plush Baroque library, an inviting English Garden, and an impressive collection of paintings, including a complete cycle of early Rubens.

Cost and Hours: €10 on Fri-Sat and Mon-Tue, more for temporary exhibits; €30 on Sun—when ticket includes permanent and temporary exhibits, lunch, and concerts at 11:00 and 15:00; gardens are free but aren't worth the trip on their own; audioguide-€1; Fri-Tue 10:00-17:00, last entry 30 minutes before closing, closed Wed-Thu, gardens open until 20:30; Fürstengasse 1—take tram #D to Bauernfeldplatz/Porzellangasse, tel. 01/319-5767-252, www.liechtensteinmuseum.at.

Sigmund Freud Museum—Freud enthusiasts enjoy seeing the humble apartment and workplace of the man who fundamentally changed our understanding of the human psyche. Dr. Sigmund Freud (1856-1939), a graduate of Vienna University, established his practice here in 1891. For the next 47 years, he received troubled patients who hoped to find peace by telling him their dreams, life traumas, and secret urges. It was here that he wrote his influential works, including the landmark *Interpretation of Dreams* (1899). Today, you can walk through his three-room office (but not the apartments next door, where Freud lived with his large family). The rooms are tiny and disappointingly bare. Freud, who was Jewish, fled Vienna when the Nazis came to power. He took most of his furniture with him, including the famous couch that patients reclined on (now in a London museum). All in all, the museum is quite old-fashioned—tediously described in a three-ring binder loaned to visitors, which complements the more general audioguide.

Cost and Hours: €7, audioguide-€2, daily July-Sept 9:00-18:00, Oct-June 9:00-17:00, cool shop, half a block downhill from the Schlickgasse tram #D stop, Berggasse 19, tel. 01/319-1596, www.freud-museum.at.

West of the Ring, on Mariahilfer Strasse

▲Imperial Furniture Collection (Hofmobiliendepot)— Bizarre, sensuous, eccentric, or precious, this collection is your peek at the Habsburgs' furniture—from grandma's wheelchair to the emperor's spittoon—all thoughtfully described in English. The Habsburgs had many palaces, but only the Hofburg was permanently furnished. The rest were done on the fly—set up and taken down by a gang of royal roadies called the "Depot of Court Movables" (Hofmobiliendepot). When the monarchy was dissolved in 1918, the state of Austria took possession of the Hofmobiliendepot's inventory—165,000 items. Now this royal storehouse is open to the public in a fine and sprawling museum. Don't go here for the *Jugendstil* furnishings. The older Baroque, Rococo, and Biedermeier pieces are the most impressive and tied most intimately to the royals. Combine a visit to this museum with a stroll down the lively shopping boulevard, Mariahilfer Strasse.

Cost and Hours: €7.90, covered by €23.50 Sisi Ticket (see page 28), Tue-Sun 10:00-18:00, closed Mon, Mariahilfer Strasse 88, main entrance around the corner at Andreasgasse 7, U-3: Zieglergasse, tel. 01/5243-3570, www.hofmobiliendepot.at.

▲▲▲Schönbrunn Palace (Schloss Schönbrunn)

Among Europe's palaces, only Schönbrunn rivals Versailles. This former summer residence of the Habsburgs is big, with 1,441 rooms. But don't worry—only 40 rooms are shown to the public. Of the plethora of sights at the palace, the highlight is a tour of the Royal Apartments—the chandeliered rooms where the Habsburg nobles lived. You can also stroll the gardens, tour the coach museum, and visit a handful of lesser sights nearby.

Getting There: While on the outskirts of Vienna, Schönbrunn is an easy 10-minute subway ride from downtown. Take U-4 to Schönbrunn and follow signs for *Schloss Schönbrunn*. Exit bearing right, then cross the busy road and continue to the right along the yellow building to the main entry courtyard, which will be on your left.

▲▲▲Royal Apartments—While the palace's exterior is Baroque, the interior was finished under Maria Theresa in let-them-eat-cake Rococo. As with the similar apartments at the Hofburg (the Habsburgs' winter home), these apartments give you a sense of the quirky, larger-than-life personalities who lived here—especially Franz Josef (r. 1848-1916) and Sisi. Your tour of the apartments, accompanied by an audioguide, covers one small section of the palace's grand interior on a clearly signed route. You have two tour options: Imperial (shorter and cheaper) or Grand (longer and more expensive). Both follow the same route at first, but after a certain point the Imperial group is politely excused while the Grand gang continues on to see a few more rooms.

Moving from room to room, you're immersed in imperial splendor. The chandeliers are made either of Bohemian crystal or hand-carved wood with gold-leaf gilding. Highlights include Franz Josef's study and bedroom (and the bed he actually died in). The Mirrored Room was where six-year-old Wolfie Mozart performed his first concert. The opulent, chandeliered Great Gallery—with its mirrored walls and dramatically frescoed ceilings—was the site of a famous 1961 summit between John F. Kennedy and Nikita Khrushchev.

Fortunately, the palace managed to escape destruction when WWII bombs rained on the city and the palace grounds. The palace itself took only one direct hit. Thankfully, that bomb, which crashed through three floors—including the sumptuous central ballroom—was a dud. Most of the public rooms are decorated in Neo-Baroque, as they were under Franz Josef and Sisi. The rest of the palace was converted to simple apartments and rented to the families of 260 civil servants, who enjoy rent control and governmental protections so they can't be evicted.

Cost: The 22-room **Imperial Tour** (€10.50, 35 minutes, Grand Palace rooms plus apartments of Franz Josef and Sisi—mostly 19th-century and therefore least interesting) or the 40-room **Grand Tour** (€13.50, one hour, includes Imperial Tour plus Maria Theresa's apartments—18th-century Rococo). If venturing beyond the apartments, consider one of two combo-tickets: The **Schönbrunn Classic Pass Light** includes the Grand Tour, as well as other sights on the grounds—the Gloriette viewing terrace, maze, and privy garden (€16.50, available April-Oct only).

The **Schönbrunn Classic Pass** includes all of the above, plus the court bakery (complete with *Apfelstrudel* demo and tasting; €19.50). However, none of these extra sights is really worth the cost of entry, so I'd skip them and just do the Grand Tour, followed by a mosey through the impressive grounds (which are free).

Hours: Daily July-Aug 8:30-18:00, April-June and Sept-Oct 8:30-17:00, Nov-March 8:30-16:30.

Crowd-Beating Tips: Schönbrunn suffers from crowds. It can be a jam-packed sauna in the summer. It's busiest from 9:30 to 11:30, especially on weekends and in July and August; it's least crowded after 14:00, when there are no groups. To avoid the long delays in summer, make a reservation by telephone for no extra charge a few days in advance (tel. 01/8111-3239, answered daily 8:00-17:00, wait through the long message for the operator). You can also book online with a credit card at www.schoenbrunn .at. You'll get an appointment time and a ticket number. Check in at least 30 minutes early. Upon arrival, go to the "Group and Reservations" desk (immediately inside the gate on the left at the gate house—long before the actual palace), give your number, pick up your ticket, and jump in ahead of the masses. If you have time to kill, spend it exploring the gardens or Coach Museum.

▲▲**Palace Gardens**—Unlike the gardens of Versailles, meant to shut out the real world, Schönbrunn's park was opened to the public in 1779 while the monarchy was in full swing. It was part of Maria Theresa's reform policy, making the garden a celebration of the evolution of civilization from autocracy into real democracy. Today it's a delightful, sprawling place to wander—especially on a sunny day. You can spend hours here, enjoying the views and the people-watching. And most of the park is free, as it has been for more than two centuries (open daily sunrise to dusk, entrance on either side of the palace).

The large, manicured grounds are laid out on angled, tree-lined axes that gradually incline, offering dramatic views back to the palace. The small side gardens flanking the palace are the most elaborate. As you face the back of the palace, to the right is the **privy garden** (*Kronprinzengarten*, €2); to the left are the free **Sisi Gardens.** Better yet, just explore, using a map (pick one up at the palace) to locate several whimsical **fountains;** a kid-friendly **maze** *(Irrgarten)* and playground area (€2.90); and the **Gloriette,** a purely decorative monument celebrating an obscure Austrian military victory and offering a fine city view (pay for a pricey drink in the café or shell out €2 to hike up to the viewing terrace—or skip the whole thing, as views are about as good from the lawn in front; included in Schönbrunn Passes described earlier, daily April-Sept 9:00-18:00, July-Aug until 19:00, Oct 9:00-17:00, closed Nov-March).

At the west end of the grounds is Europe's oldest **zoo** (*Tiergarten*), built by Maria Theresa's husband for the entertainment and education of the court in 1752 (€14, €20 combo-ticket with desert and palm house, daily April-Sept 9:00-18:30, closes earlier off-season, tel. 01/877-9294). Nearby are two skippable sights: The **palm house** (*Palmenhaus*; €4, €6 combo-ticket with desert house, €20 combo-ticket also includes zoo, daily May-Sept 9:30-18:00, Oct-April 9:30-17:00, last entry 30 minutes before closing) and the **Desert Experience House** (*Wüstenhaus*; €4, same combo-tickets and hours as palm house).

A **tourist train** makes the rounds all day, connecting Schönbrunn's many attractions (€6, 2/hour in peak season, none Nov-mid-March, one-hour circuit). Unfortunately, there's no bike rental nearby.

▲**Coach Museum Wagenburg**—The Schönbrunn coach museum is a 19th-century traffic jam of 50 impressive royal carriages and sleighs. Highlights include silly sedan chairs, the death-black hearse carriage (used for Franz Josef in 1916, and most recently for Empress Zita in 1989), and an extravagantly gilded imperial carriage pulled by eight Cinderella horses. This was rarely used other than for the coronation of Holy Roman Emperors, when it was disassembled and taken to Frankfurt for the big event. You'll also get a look at one of Sisi's impossibly narrow-waisted gowns, and (upstairs) Sisi's "Riding Chapel," with portraits of her 25 favorite horses.

Cost and Hours: €6, audioguide-€2, daily April-Oct 9:00-18:00, Nov-March 10:00-16:00, last entry 15 minutes before closing, 200 yards from palace, walk through right arch as you face palace, tel. 01/525-24-3470.

East of the Danube Canal

▲**Prater**—Since the 1780s, when the reformist Emperor Josef II gave his hunting grounds to the people of Vienna as a public park, this place has been Vienna's playground. While tired and a bit run-down these days, Vienna's sprawling amusement park still tempts visitors with its huge 220-foot-tall, famous, and lazy Ferris wheel (*Riesenrad*), roller coaster, bumper cars, Lilliputian railroad, and endless eateries. Especially if you're traveling with kids, this is a fun, goofy place to share the evening with thousands of Viennese (rides run May-Sept 9:00-24:00—but quiet after 22:00, March-April and Oct 10:00-22:00, Nov-Dec 10:00-20:00, grounds always open, U-1: Praterstern, www.prater.at). For a local-style family dinner, eat at Schweizerhaus (good food, great Czech Budvar—the original "Budweiser"—beer, classic conviviality).

Donauinsel (Danube Island)—In the 1970s, the city dug a canal parallel to the mighty Danube River, creating both a flood barrier and a much-loved island escape from the city (easy U-Bahn access on U-1 to Donauinsel). This skinny, 12-mile-long island provides a natural wonderland. All along the traffic-free, grassy park, you'll find locals—both Viennese, and especially immigrants and those who can't afford their own cabin or fancy vacation—at play. The swimming comes tough, though, with rocky entries rather than sand. The best activity here is a bike ride. If you venture far from the crowds, you're likely to encounter nudists on inline skates.

"Donau City"—This modern part of town, just beyond the Donauinsel, is the skyscraping "Manhattan" of Austria. A business, residential, and shopping zone surrounded by inviting parkland, this corner of the city is likely to grow as Vienna expands. Its centerpiece is the futuristic UNO City, a major outpost of offices for the United Nations. While it lacks the Old World character, charm, and elegance of the rest of Vienna, Donau City may interest travelers who are into contemporary glass-and-steel architecture (U-1: Kaisermühlen VIC).

Experiences in Vienna

Vienna's Café Culture

In Vienna, the living room is down the street at the neighborhood coffeehouse. This tradition is just another example of Viennese expertise in good living. Each of Vienna's many long-established (and sometimes even legendary) coffeehouses has its individual character (and characters). These classic cafés can be a bit tired, with a shabby patina and famously grumpy waiters who treat you like an uninvited guest invading their living room. Yet these spaces somehow also feel welcoming, offering newspapers, pastries, sofas, quick and light workers' lunches, elegant ambience, and "take all the time you want" charm for the price of a cup of coffee. Rather than buy the *International Herald Tribune* ahead of time, spend the money on a cup of coffee and read the paper for free, Vienna-style, in a café.

As in Italy and France, Viennese coffee drinks are espresso-based. Obviously, *Kaffee* means coffee and *Milch* is milk; *Obers* is cream, while *Schlagobers* is whipped cream. Americans who ask for a "latte" are mistaken for Italians and given a cup of hot milk.

Cafés

These are some of my favorite Viennese cafés. All of them, except for Café Sperl, are located inside the Ring (see map on pages 100-101).

Café Hawelka has a dark, "brooding Trotsky" atmosphere, paintings by struggling artists who couldn't pay for coffee, a saloon-wood flavor, chalkboard menu, smoked velvet couches, an international selection of newspapers, and a phone that rings for regulars. Frau Hawelka died just a couple weeks after Pope John Paul II. Locals suspect the pontiff wanted her much-loved *Buchteln* (marmalade-filled doughnuts) in heaven. Herr Hawelka, now alone and understandably a bit forlorn, still oversees the action (Wed-Mon 8:00-2:00 in the morning, Sun from 10:00, closed Tue, just off the Graben, Dorotheergasse 6, U-1 or U-3: Stephansplatz, tel. 01/512-8230).

Café Central, while a bit touristy, remains a classic place, lavish under Neo-Gothic columns. They serve fancy coffees (€4-6) and two-course lunches (€10), as well as entertain guests with live piano each evening from 17:00-22:00 (daily 7:30-22:00, corner of Herrengasse and Strauchgasse, U-3: Herrengasse, tel. 01/533-3764).

Café Sperl dates from 1880 and is still furnished identically to the day it opened—from the coat tree to the chairs (Mon-Sat 7:00-23:00, Sun 11:00-20:00 except closed Sun July-Aug, just off Naschmarkt near Mariahilfer Strasse, Gumpendorfer 11, U-2: Museumsquartier, tel. 01/586-4158; see map on pages 94-95).

Café Bräunerhof, between the Hofburg and the Graben, offers classic ambience with no tourists and live music on weekends (light classics, no cover, Sat-Sun 15:00-18:00), along with a practical menu with daily specials (open long hours daily, Stallburgasse 2, U-1 or U-3: Stephansplatz, tel. 01/512-3893).

Other Classics in the Old Center: All of these places are open long hours daily: **Café Pruckel** (at Dr.-Karl-Lueger-Platz, across from Stadtpark at Stubenring 24); **Café Tirolerhof** (2 blocks from the Opera, behind the TI on Tegetthoffstrasse, at Führichgasse 8); and **Café Landtmann** (directly across from the City Hall on the Ringstrasse at Dr.-Karl-Lueger-Ring 4). The Landtmann is unique, as it's the only grand café built along the Ring with all the other grand buildings. **Café Sacher** (see page 35) and **Demel** (see page 40) are famous for their cakes, but they also serve good coffee drinks.

Wein in Wien: Vienna's Wine Gardens

The *Heuriger* (HOY-rih-gur) is a uniquely Viennese institution. When the Habsburgs let Vienna's vintners sell their own new wine (called *Sturm*) tax-free, several hundred families opened *Heurigen* (HOY-rih-gehn)—wine-garden restaurants clustered around the edge of town. A tradition was born. Today, they do their best to maintain the old-village atmosphere, serving their homemade wine (the most recent vintage, until November 11, when a new vintage year begins) with small meals and strolling musicians. Most *Heurigen* are decorated with enormous antique presses from their vineyards. Wine gardens might be closed on any given day; call ahead to confirm if you have your heart set on a particular place.

(For a near-*Heuriger* experience in downtown Vienna, drop by Gigerl Stadtheuriger—see page 102.)

I've listed three good *Heuriger* neighborhoods—all on the outskirts of Vienna (see the map on page 21). I've listed them in order from east to west, and from least to most touristy. To reach the neighborhoods from downtown Vienna, it's best to use public transportation (cheap, 30 minutes, runs late in the evening, directions given per listing below), or you can take a 15-minute taxi ride from the Ring (about €15-20).

Planning Your Time: While there are some "destination" *Heurigen,* it can be disappointing to seek out a particular place, as the ambience can change depending on that evening's clientele (i.e., locals vs. tour groups). I've described a few neighborhoods that are worth exploring; wander around one or two of them, then choose the *Heuriger* with the best atmosphere. It's easiest to stick to one *Heuriger* neighborhood, though it's potentially more fun to hop from area to area; the handy bus #38A (described below) connects Heiligenstadt, Grinzing, and (with a transfer to tram #D) Nussdorf.

Getting Around the *Heurigen:* The three neighborhoods I list are relatively close to each other—within a few minutes' bus ride or about a half-hour walk. The handiest public-transit connections are these:

Tram #D runs from the Ring to Nussdorf, the least touristy *Heuriger* neighborhood. On the way, it passes the Grinzinger Strasse stop, where you can catch bus #38A (toward the other two neighborhoods). Tram #D runs every 5-10 minutes (fewer trams after 23:00, last tram around 24:30).

Bus #38A connects the Heiligenstadt U-Bahn station (U-4 line) with the *Heurigen* in Heiligenstadt (Fernsprechamt/Heiligenstadt stop), and then Grinzing (Grinzing or Himmelstrasse stops). Bus #38A runs frequently into the evening (8/hour until 19:00, then 6/hour until 22:00, then 4/hour until 24:00; last bus around midnight).

Tram #38 starts on the Ring at the Schottentor stop and goes to Grinzing (roughly the same hours as Tram #D).

Taxis stand by in touristy Grinzing; from the other places, you might need to ask the *Heuriger* to call one for you (figure about €15-20 between the *Heurigen* and the Ring or any hotel I list).

Nussdorf—An untouristy district, characteristic and popular with the Viennese, Nussdorf has plenty of *Heuriger* ambience. This area feels more real than the other two—with a working-class vibe, streets lined with local shops, and characteristic *Heuriger* that feel a little bit rougher around the edges. Right at the last stop on tram #D's route (Beethovengang), you'll find three long and skinny places side by side. Of these, **Schübel-Auer Heuriger** is my favorite—bigger, classier, and with the most user-friendly buffet (many dishes are labeled, and the patient staff speaks English). Its rustic ambience can be enjoyed indoors or out (Tue-Sat 16:00-24:00, closed Sun-Mon, Kahlenberger Strasse 22, tel. 01/370-2222). The other two are also worth considering: **Heuriger Kierlinger** has a particularly rollicking, woody room around its buffet (daily 15:30-24:00, Kahlenberger Strasse 20, tel. 01/370-2264). **Steinschaden** feels a bit more like a traditional restaurant. Though it has a typical *Heuriger* buffet, it also has menus and table service (daily 15:00-24:00, Kahlenberger Strasse 18, tel. 01/370-1375).

Getting to the Nussdorf *Heurigen:* Take tram #D from the Ringstrasse (stops include the Opera, Hofburg/Kunsthistorisches Museum, and City Hall) to its endpoint (the stop labeled *Nussdorf* isn't the end—stay on for one more stop to Beethovengang). Exit the tram, cross the tracks, bear right down the street, and look for the *Heurigen* on your left.

Heiligenstadt (Pfarrplatz)—Between Nussdorf and Grinzing, hiding just above the unappealing main road, is Pfarrplatz, which feels like a charming village square watched over by a church. Beethoven lived—and began work on his Ninth Symphony—here in 1817; he'd previously written his Sixth Symphony *(Pastorale)* while staying in this then-rural district. He hoped the local spa would cure his worsening deafness. (Confusingly, the name "Heiligenstadt" is used for two different locations: this little neighborhood, and the big train and U-Bahn station near the river.) Right next to the church, **Mayer am Pfarrplatz** (a.k.a. Beethovenhaus) is famous, touristy, and feels more polished—almost trendy—compared to the other *Heurigen* I list. This place has a charming inner courtyard under cozy vines with an accordion player, along with a sprawling backyard with a big children's play zone (Mon-Fri 16:00-24:00, Sat-Sun 11:00-24:00, Pfarrplatz 2, tel. 01/370-1287). **Weingut and Heuriger Werner Welser** is a block uphill (go up Probusgasse). It's big (serving large tour groups) and traditional, with dirndled waitresses and lederhosened waiters. It feels a bit crank-'em-out, but it's still lots of fun, with music nightly from 19:00 (open daily 15:30-24:00, Probusgasse 12, tel. 01/318-9797).

Getting to the Heiligenstadt *Heurigen:* Take the U-4 line to its last station, Heiligenstadt, then transfer to bus #38A. Get off at Fernsprechamt/Heiligenstadt, walk uphill, and take the first right onto Nestelbachgasse, which leads to Pfarrplatz and the Beethovenhaus. Bus #38A also runs uphill from here, past the Grinzing *Heurigen*, to the Kahlenberg viewpoint (described later).

Grinzing—Of the many *Heuriger* suburbs, Grinzing is the most famous, lively...and touristy. If you're looking to avoid tour groups, head elsewhere. But it's the easiest, most accessible zone that I list. You can't walk down the street without stumbling over great, interchangeably touristy options—so much so, in fact, that I won't bother pointing you to a specific place. Just find your favorite ambience. (Since this isn't exactly fine wine anyway, the difference in quality is negligible.) The district is also simply pretty. Like the other two, it feels like a charming town all its own, with an onion-domed church and carefully manicured streetscape.

Getting to the Grinzing *Heurigen:* Take tram #38 from the Schottentor stop on the Ring to its endpoint. If you are coming from the other *Heurigen* neighborhoods, take bus #38A, which makes two stops in this district: The Grinzing stop is at the bottom of town (and just across the street from the stop for tram #38); the next stop is Himmelstrasse, a bit uphill (and easier for strolling down past your options). If you get off at the Grinzing stop, follow Himmelgasse uphill toward the green onion-top dome. You'll pass plenty of wine gardens—and tour buses—on your way up. Just past the dome, you'll find the heart of the *Heurigen.*

Entertainment in Vienna

Vienna—the birthplace of what we call classical music—still thrives as Europe's music capital. On any given evening, you'll have your choice of opera, Strauss waltzes, Mozart chamber concerts, and lighthearted musicals. The Vienna Boys' Choir lives up to its worldwide reputation. If techno or rock are more your scene, you'll find plenty in the pubs and clubs of the "Bermuda Triangle" neighborhood near St. Stephen's Cathedral and along the Gürtel.

Besides music, you can spend an evening enjoying art, watching a classic film, or sipping Viennese wine in a village wine garden. Save some energy for Vienna after dark.

Music

As far back as the 12th century, Vienna was a mecca for musicians—both sacred and secular (troubadours). The Habsburg emperors of the 17th and 18th centuries were not only generous supporters of music, but fine musicians and composers themselves. (Maria Theresa played a mean double bass.) Composers such as Haydn, Mozart, Beethoven, Schubert, Brahms, and Mahler gravitated to this music-friendly environment. They taught each other, jammed together, and spent a lot of time in Habsburg palaces. Beethoven was a famous figure, walking—lost in musical thought—through the Vienna Woods. In the city's 19th-century belle époque, "Waltz King" Johann Strauss and his brothers kept Vienna's 300 ballrooms spinning.

This musical tradition continues into modern times, leaving some prestigious Viennese institutions for today's tourists to enjoy: the Opera, the Boys' Choir, and the great Baroque halls and churches, all busy with classical and waltz concerts. As you poke into churches and palaces, you may hear groups practicing. You're welcome to sit and listen.

The best-known entertainment venues are the Staatsoper (a.k.a., "the Opera"), the Volksoper (for musicals and operettas), the Theater an der Wien (newly reopened, opera and other performances), the Wiener Musikverein (home of the Vienna Philharmonic Orchestra), and the Wiener Konzerthaus (various events). These events are listed in the monthly *Wien-Programm* (available at TI).

In Vienna, it's music *con brio* from October through June, reaching a symphonic climax during the Vienna Festival each May and June. Sadly, in summer (generally July and August), the Boys' Choir, Opera, and many other serious music companies are—like you—on vacation. But Vienna hums year-round with live classical music; touristy, crowd-pleasing shows are always available.

Buying Tickets: Most tickets run from €40 to €55 (plus a stiff booking fee when booked in advance or through a box office like the one at the TI). A few venues charge as little as €25; look around if you're not set on any particular concert. While it's easy to book tickets online long in advance, spontaneity is also workable, as there are invariably people selling their extra tickets at face value or less outside the door before concert time. If you call a concert hall directly, they can advise you on the availability of (cheaper) tickets at the door. Vienna takes care of its starving artists (and tourists) by offering cheap standing-room tickets to top-notch music and opera (generally an hour before each performance).

Vienna Boys' Choir (Wiener Sängerknaben)—The boys sing (from a high balcony, heard but not seen) at the 9:15 Sunday Mass from September through June in the Hofburg's Imperial Music Chapel (Hofmusikkapelle). The entrance is at Schweizerhof; you can get there from In der Burg square or go through the tunnel from Josefsplatz.

Reserved seats must be booked two months in advance (€5-29; reserve by fax, email, or mail: fax from the US 011-431-533-992-775, whmk@chello.at, or write Hofmusikkapelle, Hofburg-Schweizerhof, 1010 Wien; call 01/533-9927 for information only—they can't book tickets at this number).

Much easier, standing room inside is free and open to the first 60 who line up. Even better, rather than line up early, you can simply swing by and stand in the narthex just outside, where you can hear the boys and see the Mass on a TV monitor.

Boys' Choir concerts are also given Fridays at 16:00 in late April, May, June, September, and October on stage at the Musikverein, near the Opera and Karlsplatz (€36-56, around 30 standing-room tickets go on sale at 15:30 for €15, Karlsplatz 6; U-1, U-2, or U-4: Karlsplatz; tel. 01/5880-4173).

They're talented kids, but, for my taste, not worth all the commotion. Remember, many churches have great music during Sunday Mass. Just 200 yards from the Boys' Choir chapel, the Augustinian Church has a glorious 11:00 service each Sunday (see page 58).

The Opera—The Vienna State Opera (Staatsoper), featuring Vienna Philharmonic Orchestra musicians in the pit, is one of the world's top opera houses. They put on 300 performances a year, but in July and August the singers rest their voices (or go on tour). Since there are different operas nearly nightly, you'll see big trucks out back and constant action backstage—all the sets need to be switched each day. Even though the expensive seats normally sell out long in advance, the opera is perpetually in the red and subsidized by the state. The excellent "electronic libretto" translation screens help make the experience worthwhile for opera newbies. (Press the button to turn yours on; press again for English.)

Opera Tickets: Seats range from €8 to €168. You can book tickets in advance by phone (tel. 01/513-1513, phone answered daily 10:00-21:00) or online (www.wiener-staatsoper.at); you'll give them your credit-card number, then pick up your tickets at the box office just before show time. If you want to inquire about tickets in person, head to the theater's box office, which is open from 9:00 until one hour before each performance. The Opera has two ticket offices. The main one is on the west side of the building, across Operngasse and facing the Opera. A smaller one is just under the big screen on the east side of the Opera (facing Kärntner Strasse).

Unless Placido Domingo is in town, it's easy to get one of 567 **standing-room tickets** (*Stehplätze*, €3 up top or €4 downstairs). While the front doors open one hour before the show starts, a side door (middle of building, on the Operngasse side) opens 80 minutes before curtain time, giving those in the know an early grab at standing-room tickets (tickets sold until 20 minutes after curtain time). Just walk straight in, then head right until you see the ticket booth marked *Stehplätze*. If fewer than 567 people are in line, there's no need to line up early. If you're one of the first 160 in line, try for the "Parterre" section and you'll end up dead-center at stage level, directly under the Emperor's Box (otherwise, you can choose between the third floor—*Balkon*, or the fourth floor—*Galerie*). Dress is casual (but do your best) at the standing-room bar. Locals save their spot along the rail by tying a scarf to it.

Rick's Crude Tips: For me, three hours is a lot of opera. But just to see and hear the Opera in action for half an hour is a treat. You can buy a standing-room spot and just drop in for part of the show. Ending time is posted in the lobby—you could stop by for just the finale. If you go at the start or finish, you'll get the added entertainment of seeing Vienna all dressed up. Of the 567 people with cheap standing-room tickets, invariably many will not stand through the entire performance. If you drop by after showtime, you can wait for people to leave and bum their tickets off them—be sure to ask them for clear directions to your spot. (While it's perfectly legal to swap standing-room spots, be discreet if finding your spot mid-performance—try to look like you know where you're going.) Even those with standing-room tickets are considered "ticket-holders," and are welcome to explore the building. As you leave, wander around the first floor (fun if skipping out early, when halls are empty) to enjoy the sumptuous halls (with prints of famous stage sets and performers) and the grand entry staircase. The last resort (and worst option) is to drop into the Café Oper Vienna and watch the performance live on TV screens (inside the Opera, reasonable menu and drinks).

"Live Opera on the Square": Demonstrating its commitment to bringing opera to the masses, each summer the Vienna Opera projects several performances live on a huge screen on its building, and even puts out chairs for the public to enjoy...and it's all free (these projected performances are noted as *Oper live am Platz* in the official Opera schedule—posted all around the Opera building; they are also listed in the *Wien-Programm* brochure).

Vienna Volksoper—For less-serious operettas and musicals, try Vienna's other opera house, located along the Gürtel, west of the city center (see *Wien-Programm* brochure or ask at TI for schedule, Währinger Strasse 78, tel. 01/5144-4360, www.volksoper.at).

Theater an der Wien—Considered the oldest theater in Vienna, this venue was designed in 1801 for Mozart operas—intimate, with just a thousand seats. Reopened in 2006 for Mozart's 250th birthday, it treats Vienna's music-lovers to a different opera every month—generally Mozart with a contemporary setting and modern interpretation—with the excellent Vienna Radio Orchestra in the pit. With the reopening of Theater an der Wien, Vienna now supports three opera companies; this one is the only company playing through the summer. They also feature occasional ballet, operetta, and other performances (facing the Naschmarkt at Linke Wienzeile 6, tel. 01/5883-0660 for information, tickets available at www.theater-wien.at).

Touristy Mozart and Strauss Concerts—If the music comes to you, it's touristy—designed for flash-in-the-pan Mozart fans. Powdered-wig orchestra performances are given almost nightly in grand traditional settings (€25-50). Pesky wigged-and-powdered Mozarts peddle tickets in the streets. They rave about the quality of the musicians, but you'll get second-rate chamber orchestras, clad in historic costumes, performing the greatest hits of Mozart and Strauss. These are casual, easygoing concerts with lots of tour groups. While there's not a Viennese person in the audience, the tourists generally enjoy the evening.

To sort through your options, check with the ticket office in the TI (same price as on the street, but with all venues to choose from). Savvy locals suggest getting the cheapest tickets, as no one seems to care if cheapskates move up to fill unsold pricier seats. Critics explain that the musicians are actually very good (often Hungarians, Poles, and Russians working a season here to fund an entire year of music studies back home), but that they haven't performed much together so aren't "tight."

Of the many fine venues, the **Mozarthaus** might be my favorite. Intimate chamber-music concerts take place in a small room richly decorated in Venetian Renaissance style (€35-42, Thu-Fri at 19:30, Sat at 18:00, near St. Stephen's Cathedral at Singerstrasse 7, tel. 01/911-9077).

Strauss Concerts in the Kursalon—For years, Strauss concerts have been held in the Kursalon, where the "Waltz King" himself directed wildly popular concerts 100 years ago (€39-56, concerts nightly generally at 20:15, tel. 01/512-5790 to reserve). Shows last two hours and are a mix of ballet, waltzes, and a 15-piece orchestra. It's touristy—tour guides holding up banners with group numbers wait out front after the show. Even so, the performance is playful, visually fun, fine quality for most, and with a tried-and-tested, crowd-pleasing format. The conductor welcomes the crowd in German (with a wink) and English; after that...it's English only.

Musicals—The Wien Ticket pavilion next to the Opera (near Kärntner Strasse) sells tickets to contemporary American and British musicals performed in German (€10-109). Same-day tickets are available at a 24 percent discount from 14:00 until 18:00 (ticket pavilion open daily 10:00-19:00). Or you can reserve (full-price) tickets for the musicals by phone (call Wien Ticket at tel. 01/58885).

Films of Concerts—To see free films of great concerts in a lively, outdoor setting near City Hall, see "Nightlife in Vienna," next.

Ballroom Dancing—If you like to dance (waltz and ballroom), or watch people who are really good at it, consider the Dance Evening at the Tanz Café in the Volksgarten (€5-6, May-Aug Sun from 18:00, www.volksgarten.at).

Organ Concerts—St. Peter's Church puts on free organ concerts weekdays at 15:00 and weekends at 20:00 (see page 44).

Classical Music to Go—To bring home Beethoven, Strauss, or the Wiener Philharmonic on a top-quality CD, shop at Gramola on the Graben or EMI on Kärntner Strasse.

Nightlife in Vienna

If powdered wigs and opera singers in Viking helmets aren't your thing, Vienna has plenty of alternatives. For an up-to-date rundown on fun after dark, check www.viennahype.at.

City Hall Open-Air Classical-Music Cinema and Food Circus—A thriving people scene erupts each evening in summer (mid-July–mid-Sept) at the park in front of City Hall (Rathaus, on the Ringstrasse). Thousands of people keep a food circus of 24 simple stalls busy. There's not a plastic cup anywhere, just real plates and glasses—Vienna wants the quality of eating to be as high as the music that's about to begin. About 3,000 folding chairs face a 60-foot-wide screen up against the City Hall's Neo-Gothic facade. When darkness falls, an announcer explains the program, and then the music starts. The program is different every night—mostly movies of opera and classical concerts, with some films. The TI has the schedule (programs generally last about 2 hours, starting when it's dark—between 21:30 in July and 20:30 in Aug and early Sept).

Since 1991, the city has paid for 60 of these summer event nights each year. Why? To promote culture. Officials know that the City Hall Music Festival is mostly a "meat market" where young people come to hook up. But they believe many of these people will develop a little appreciation of classical music and high culture on the side.

Bermuda Triangle (Bermuda Dreieck)—The area known as the "Bermuda Triangle"—north of St. Stephen's Cathedral, between Rotenturmstrasse and Judengasse—is the hot nightspot in the old town. You'll find lots of music clubs and classy pubs, or *Beisl* (such as Krah Krah, Salzamt, Bermuda Bräu, and First Floor—for cocktails with a view of live fish). The serious-looking guards have nothing to do with the bar scene—they're guarding the synagogue nearby.

Gürtel—The Gürtel is Vienna's outer ring road. The arches of a lumbering viaduct (which carries a train track) are now filled with trendy bars, sports bars, dance clubs, strip clubs, antique shops, and restaurants. To experience—or simply see—the latest scene in town, head out here. The people-watching—the trendiest kids on the block—makes the trip fun even if you're looking for exercise rather than a drink. Ride U-6 to Nussdorfer Strasse or Thaliastrasse and hike along the viaduct.

English Cinema—Several great theaters offer three or four screens of English movies nightly (€6-9): **Burg Kino,** a block from the Opera, facing the Ring (see below); **English Cinema Haydn,** near my recommended hotels on Mariahilfer Strasse (Mariahilfer Strasse 57, tel. 01/587-2262, www.haydnkino.at); and **Artis**

International Cinema, right in the town center a few minutes from the cathedral (Schultergasse 5, tel. 01/535-6570).

The Third Man at Burg Kino—This movie, voted the best British film ever by the British Film Institute, takes place in 1949 Vienna—when it was divided, like Berlin, between the four victorious Allies. With a dramatic Vienna cemetery scene, coffeehouse culture surviving amid the rubble, and Orson Welles being chased through the sewers, the tale of a divided city about to fall under Soviet rule and rife with smuggling is an enjoyable two-hour experience while in Vienna (€8, in English; 3-4 showings weekly—usually Friday evening, Sunday afternoon, and Tuesday early evening; Opernring 19, tel. 01/587-8406, www.burgkino.at).

Sleeping in Vienna

As you move out from the center, hotel prices drop. My listings are in the old center (figure at least €100 for a decent double), along the likeable Mariahilfer Strasse (about €90), and near the Westbahnhof (about €70).

Book ahead for Vienna if you can, particularly for holidays. Business hotels have their highest rates in September and October, when it's peak convention time. Prices are also high right around New Year's Eve. Steer clear of Internet booking sites—hotels lose big and you pay more. Book direct by phone, fax, or email.

While few accommodations in Vienna are air-conditioned, you can generally get fans on request. Places with elevators often have a few stairs to climb, too. Viennese elevators can be confusing: In most of Europe, 0 is the ground floor, and 1 is the first floor up (our "second floor"). But in Vienna, elevators can also have floors P, U, M, and A before getting to 1—so floor 1 can actually be what we'd call the fifth floor.

For tips on reaching your hotel upon arrival in Vienna, see "Vienna Connections" at the end of this chapter.

Within the Ring, in the Old City Center

You'll pay extra to sleep in the atmospheric old center, but if you can afford it, staying here gives you the best classy Vienna experience.

$$$ Hotel am Stephansplatz is a four-star business hotel with 56 rooms. It's plush but not over-the-top, and reasonably priced for its sleek comfort and incredible location facing the cathedral. Every detail is modern and quality; breakfast is superb, with a view of the city waking up around the cathedral; and the staff is always ready with a friendly welcome (Sb-€160-180, Db-€210-250, prices vary with season and room size, prices shoot up during conventions—most often in Sept-Oct; generally less Fri-Sun, July-Aug, and in winter; extra bed-€50, children stay for

Sleep Code

(€1 = about $1.40, country code: 43, area code: 01)
S = Single, **D** = Double/Twin, **T** = Triple, **Q** = Quad, **b** = bathroom,
s = shower only. English is spoken at each place. Unless other-wise noted, credit cards are accepted, rooms have no air con-ditioning, and breakfast is included.

To help you sort easily through these listings, I've divided the rooms into three categories, based on the price for a standard double room with bath:

$$$ Higher Priced—Most rooms €120 or more.
$$ Moderately Priced—Most rooms between €75-120.
$ Lower Priced—Most rooms €75 or less.

Prices can change without notice; verify the hotel's current rates online or by email. For other updates, see www.ricksteves.com/update.

free or very cheap, air-con, free Internet access and Wi-Fi, gym and sauna, elevator, Stephansplatz 9, U-1 or U-3: Stephansplatz, tel. 01/534-050, fax 01/5340-5710, www.hotelamstephansplatz.at, office@hotelamstephansplatz.at).

$$$ Hotel Pertschy, circling an old courtyard, is big and hotelesque. Its 56 huge rooms are elegantly creaky, with chandeliers and Baroque touches. Those on the courtyard are quietest (Sb-€95-114, Db-€139-169 depending on room size, €20-30 cheaper off-season, extra bed-€36, non-smoking rooms, free Internet access and Wi-Fi, elevator, Habsburgergasse 5, U-1 or U-3: Stephansplatz, tel. 01/534-490, fax 01/534-4949, www.pertschy.com, pertschy @pertschy.com).

$$$ Pension Aviano is another peaceful, family-run place. It has 17 comfortable rooms with flowery carpet and other Baroque frills, all on the fourth floor above lots of old-center action (Sb-€104, Db-€148-169 depending on size, roughly €20-30 cheaper per room in July-Aug and Nov-March, 5 percent discount if you book direct and mention Rick Steves, extra bed-€25-33, non-smoking, fans, free Internet access and Wi-Fi, elevator, between Neuer Markt and Kärntner Strasse at Marco d'Avianogasse 1, tel. 01/512-8330, fax 01/5128-3306, www.secrethomes.at, aviano @secrethomes.at).

$$$ Hotel Schweizerhof is classy, with 55 big rooms, all the comforts, shiny public spaces, and a formal ambience. It's centrally located midway between St. Stephen's Cathedral and the Danube Canal (Sb-€85-95, Db-€120-140, low prices are for July-Aug and slow times, with cash and this book get your best price and then

VIENNA

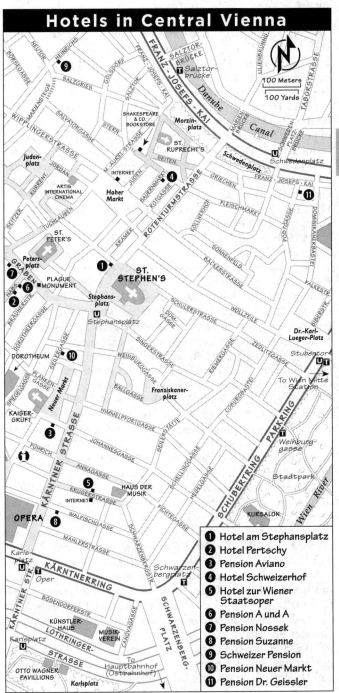

Hotels in Central Vienna

1. Hotel am Stephansplatz
2. Hotel Pertschy
3. Pension Aviano
4. Hotel Schweizerhof
5. Hotel zur Wiener Staatsoper
6. Pension A und A
7. Pension Nossek
8. Pension Suzanne
9. Schweizer Pension
10. Pension Neuer Markt
11. Pension Dr. Geissler

claim a discount, extra bed-€35, grand breakfast, free Wi-Fi, elevator, Bauernmarkt 22, U-1 or U-3: Stephansplatz, tel. 01/533-1931, fax 01/533-0214, www.schweizerhof.at, office@schweizerhof .at). Since this is in the "Bermuda Triangle" nightclub area, it can be noisy on weekends (Thu-Sat). If you'll be here then, ask for a quiet room when you reserve.

$$$ Hotel zur Wiener Staatsoper, the Schweizerhof's sister hotel, is quiet, with a more traditional elegance. Its 22 tidy rooms come with high ceilings, chandeliers, and fancy carpets on parquet floors (tiny Sb-€80-100, Db-€115-150, Tb-€135-175, rates depend on demand, cheaper prices are for July-Aug and Dec-March, extra bed-€22, fans on request, elevator, free Wi-Fi, a block from the Opera at Krugerstrasse 11; U-1, U-2, or U-4: Karlsplatz; tel. 01/513-1274, fax 01/513-127-415, www.zurwienerstaatsoper.at, office @zurwienerstaatsoper.at, manager Claudia).

$$$ Pension A und A, a friendly eight-room B&B run by Andreas and Andrea, offers a sleek, mod break from crusty old Vienna. This pricey place, wonderfully located just off the Graben, replaces Baroque doilies with contemporary style and blinding-white minimalist public spaces (Sb-€98-128 depending on season; Db-€149 in May-Aug, €179 in Sept-Oct, €129 in Nov-Feb; includes breakfast, air-con, free Wi-Fi, Habsburgergasse 3, floor M, tel. 01/890-5128, www.aunda.at, office@aunda.at).

$$ At Pension Nossek, an elevator takes you above any street noise into Frau Bernad and Frau Gundolf's world, where the children seem to be placed among the lace and flowers by an interior designer. With 32 rooms right on the wonderful Graben, this is a particularly good value (S-€52-60, Ss-€62, Sb-€76-80, Db-€120, €30 extra for sprawling suites, extra bed-€35, cash only, air-con, elevator, pay Internet access and Wi-Fi, Graben 17, U-1 or U-3: Stephansplatz, tel. 01/5337-0410, fax 01/535-3646, www.pension -nossek.at, reservation@pension-nossek.at).

$$ Pension Suzanne, as Baroque and doily as you'll find in this price range, is wonderfully located a few yards from the Opera. It's small, but run with the class of a bigger hotel. The 25 rooms are packed with properly Viennese antique furnishings and paintings (Sb-€82, Db-€106-127 depending on size, small discount with this book and cash, extra bed-€25, spacious apartment for up to 6 also available, discounts in winter, fans on request, elevator, free Internet access and Wi-Fi, Walfischgasse 4; U-1, U-2, or U-4: Karlsplatz and follow signs for Opera exit; tel. 01/513-2507, fax 01/513-2500, www.pension-suzanne.at, info@pension-suzanne.at, manager Michael).

$$ Schweizer Pension has been family-owned for four generations. Anita and her son Gerald offer lots of tourist info and 11 homey rooms for a great price, with parquet floors. True to its name, it feels very Swiss—tidy and well-run (S-€46-55, big Sb-€68-81, D-€68-79, Db-€89-98, Tb-€109-125, prices depend on season and room size, cash only, entirely non-smoking, elevator, free Wi-Fi, laundry-€18/load, Heinrichsgasse 2, U-2 or U-4: Schottenring, tel. 01/533-8156, fax 01/535-6469, www.schweizer pension.com, schweizer.pension@chello.at). They also rent a quad with bath (€129-139—too small for 4 adults but great for a family of 2 adults/2 kids under age 15).

$$ Pension Neuer Markt is family-run, with 37 comfy but faded rooms in a perfectly central locale. Its hallways have the ambience of a cheap cruise ship (Ss-€70-80, Sb-€90-110, smaller Ds-€80-90, Db-€90-135, prices vary with season and room size, extra bed-€20, request a quiet room when you reserve, fans, elevator, free Internet access and Wi-Fi, Seilergasse 9, tel. 01/512-2316, fax 01/513-9105, www.hotelpension.at/neuermarkt, neuermarkt @hotelpension.at).

$$ Pension Dr. Geissler has 23 plain-but-comfortable rooms in a modern, nondescript apartment building about 10 blocks northeast of St. Stephen's, near the canal (S-€48, Ss-€68, Sb-€76, D-€65, Ds-€77, Db-€95, 20 percent less in winter, elevator, Postgasse 14, U-1 or U-4: Schwedenplatz—Postgasse is to the left as you face Hotel Capricorno, tel. 01/533-2803, fax 01/533-2635, www.hotelpension.at/dr-geissler, dr.geissler@hotelpension.at).

On or near Mariahilfer Strasse

Lively Mariahilfer Strasse connects the Westbahnhof (West Station) and the city center. The U-3 line, starting at the Westbahnhof, goes down Mariahilfer Strasse to the cathedral. This tourist-friendly, vibrant area is filled with shopping malls, simpler storefronts, and cafés. Its smaller hotels and private rooms are generally run by people from the non-German-speaking part of the former Habsburg Empire (i.e., Eastern Europe). Most hotels are within a few steps of an U-Bahn stop, just one or two stops from the Westbahnhof (direction from the station: Simmering). The nearest place to do laundry is **Schnell & Sauber Waschcenter** (wash-€4.50 for small load or €9 for large load, plus a few euros to dry, daily 6:00-23:00, a few blocks north of Westbahnhof on the east side of Urban-Loritz-Platz).

$$$ NH Hotels, a Spanish chain, runs two stern, stylish-but-passionless business hotels a few blocks apart on Mariahilfer Strasse. Both rent ideal-for-families suites, each with a living room, two TVs, bathroom, desk, and kitchenette (rack rate: Db suite-€99-200, going rate usually closer to €110-125, €17/person for optional breakfast, apartments for 2-3 adults, 1 kid under 12 free, non-smoking rooms, elevator, pay Wi-Fi). The 73-room **NH Atterseehaus** is at Mariahilfer Strasse 78 (U-3: Zieglergasse,

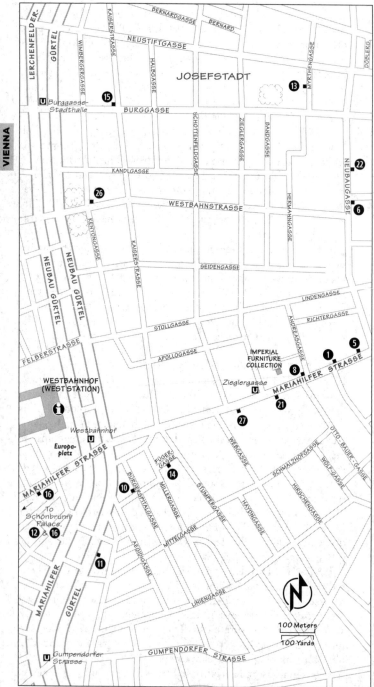

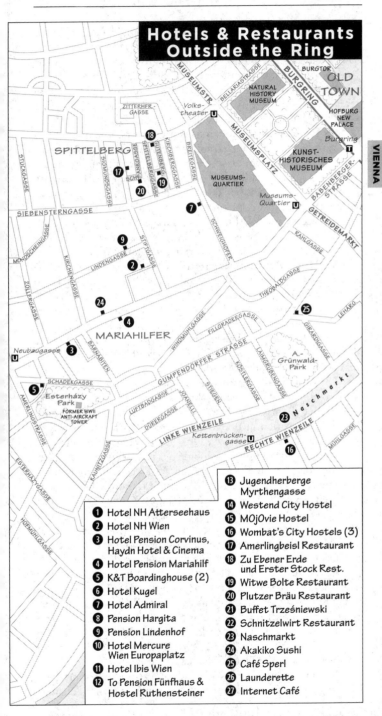

Hotels & Restaurants Outside the Ring

1. Hotel NH Atterseehaus
2. Hotel NH Wien
3. Hotel Pension Corvinus, Haydn Hotel & Cinema
4. Hotel Pension Mariahilf
5. K&T Boardinghouse (2)
6. Hotel Kugel
7. Hotel Admiral
8. Pension Hargita
9. Pension Lindenhof
10. Hotel Mercure Wien Europaplatz
11. Hotel Ibis Wien
12. To Pension Fünfhaus & Hostel Ruthensteiner
13. Jugendherberge Myrthengasse
14. Westend City Hostel
15. MOjOvie Hostel
16. Wombat's City Hostels (3)
17. Amerlingbeisl Restaurant
18. Zu Ebener Erde und Erster Stock Rest.
19. Witwe Bolte Restaurant
20. Plutzer Bräu Restaurant
21. Buffet Trześniewski
22. Schnitzelwirt Restaurant
23. Naschmarkt
24. Akakiko Sushi
25. Café Sperl
26. Launderette
27. Internet Café

VIENNA

tel. 01/524-5600, fax 01/524-560-015, nhatterseehaus@nh-hotels .com), and **NH Wien** has 105 rooms at Mariahilfer Strasse 32 (U-3: Neubaugasse—follow *Stiftgasse* signs to exit and turn left from top of escalator; from Mariahilfer Strasse, enter through shop passageway between Nordsee and Tchibo—or from Lindengasse 9, tel. 01/521-720, fax 01/521-7215, nhwien@nh-hotels.com). The website for both is www.nh-hotels.com.

$$ Hotel Pension Corvinus is bright, modern, and proudly and warmly run by a Hungarian family: Miklós, Judit, Anthony, and Zoltan. Its 12 comfortable rooms are spacious, and some are downright sumptuous (Sb-€69-79, Db-€99-109, Tb-€119-129, ask for best price with this book, extra bed-€26, also has apartments with kitchens, most rooms non-smoking, air-con, elevator, free Internet access and Wi-Fi, parking garage-€17/day, on the third floor at Mariahilfer Strasse 57-59, U-3: Neubaugasse, tel. 01/587-7239, fax 01/587-723-920, www.corvinus.at, hotel@corvinus.at).

$$ Hotel Pension Mariahilf's 12 rooms are clean, well-priced, and good-sized (if outmoded), with a slight Art Deco flair (Sb-€60-75, twin Db-€78-98, Db-€88-109, Tb-€99-139, 5-6-person apartment with kitchen-€129-169, lower prices are for Nov-Feb or longer stays, book direct and ask about a Rick Steves discount, elevator, free Wi-Fi, parking-€18, Mariahilfer Strasse 49, U-3: Neubaugasse, tel. 01/586-1781, fax 01/586-178-122, www .mariahilf-hotel.at, office@mariahilf-hotel.at).

$$ K&T Boardinghouse rents spacious, comfortable, good-value rooms in two locations. The first has three bright and airy rooms three flights above lively Mariahilfer Strasse (no elevator). The second location, just across the street, has five units on the first floor (Db-€79, Tb-€99, Qb-€119, 2-night minimum, no breakfast, air-con-€10/day, cash only but reserve with credit card, non-smoking, free Internet access and Wi-Fi, coffee in rooms; first location: Mariahilfer Strasse 72, second location: Chwallagasse 2; for either, get off at U-3: Neubaugasse; tel. 01/523-2989, mobile 0676-553-6063, fax 01/522-0345, www.ktboardinghouse .at, k.t@chello.at, Tina). To reach the Chwallagasse location from Mariahilfer Strasse, turn left at Café Ritter and walk down Schadekgasse one short block; tiny Chwallagasse is the first right.

$$ Haydn Hotel is big and formal, with masculine public spaces and 50 spacious rooms (Sb-€80-90, Db-€110-120, suites and family apartments, ask about 10 percent Rick Steves discount, extra bed-€30, all rooms non-smoking, air-con, elevator, free Internet access, pay Wi-Fi, parking-€15/day, Mariahilfer Strasse 57-59, U-3: Neubaugasse, tel. 01/5874-4140, fax 01/586-1950, www .haydn-hotel.at, info@haydn-hotel.at, Nouri).

$$ Hotel Kugel is run with pride and attitude. "Simple quality and good value" is the motto of the hands-on owner, Johannes

Roller. It's a big 32-room hotel with simple Old World charm, offering a fine value (Db-€85, supreme Db with canopy beds-€105-115, cash only, completely non-smoking, free Internet access, free cable Internet in some rooms, some tram noise, Siebensterngasse 43, at corner with Neubaugasse, U-3: Neubaugasse, tel. 01/523-3355, fax 01/5233-3555, www.hotelkugel.at, office@hotelkugel.at). Herr Roller also offers several cheaper basic rooms for backpackers.

$$ Hotel Admiral is huge and practical, with 80 large, workable rooms. This last resort is on a dreary street across from a rowdy nightclub (request a quiet room), and lacks the charm and personality of my other listings (Sb-€70, Db-€94, mention this book and ask for best Rick Steves price, cheaper in winter, extra bed-€25, breakfast-€6/person, free Internet access and Wi-Fi; limited free parking is first-come, first-served—otherwise €10/day; a block off Mariahilfer Strasse at Karl-Schweighofer-Gasse 7, U-2 or U-3: Volkstheater, tel. 01/521-410, fax 01/521-4116, www.admiral.co.at, hotel@admiral.co.at).

$ Pension Hargita rents 19 generally small, bright, and tidy rooms (mostly twins) with Hungarian woody-village decor. While the pension is directly on bustling Mariahilfer Strasse, its windows block noise well. This spick-and-span, well-located place is a great value (S-€40, Ss-€47, Sb-€57, D-€54, Ds-€60, tiny Db-€65, Db-€68, Ts-€75, Tb-€82, Qb-€112, reserve with credit card but pay with cash to get these rates, extra bed-€12, breakfast-€5, completely non-smoking, lots of stairs and no elevator, free Internet access, pay Wi-Fi in some rooms, corner of Mariahilfer Strasse and Andreasgasse, Andreasgasse 1, U-3: Zieglergasse, tel. 01/526-1928, fax 01/526-0492, www.hargita.at, pension@hargita.at, Erika and Tibor).

$ Pension Lindenhof rents 19 very basic, very worn but clean rooms. It's a dark and mysteriously dated time warp filled with plants (and a fun guest-generated postcard wall); the stark rooms have outrageously high ceilings and teeny bathrooms (S-€32, Sb-€40, D-€54, Db-€72, T-€81, Tb-€108, Q-€108, Qb-€144, cheaper during slow times, hall shower-€2, cash only, elevator, next door to a harmless strip bar at Lindengasse 4, U-3: Neubaugasse, tel. 01/523-0498, fax 01/523-7362, www.pensionlindenhof.at, pensionlindenhof@yahoo.com, run by Gebrael family; Zara, Keram, and his father George speak English).

Near the Westbahnhof (West Station)

$$$ Hotel Mercure Wien Europaplatz offers high-rise modern efficiency and comfort in 211 air-conditioned rooms, directly across from the Westbahnhof (Db-€130-170 depending on season, online deals as cheap as Db-€69 if you book well in advance, breakfast-€15, free Internet access and Wi-Fi in lobby, pay Wi-Fi in rooms, elevator, parking-€15/day, Matrosengasse 6, U-3: Westbahnhof, tel. 01/5990-1181, fax 01/597-6900, www.mercure .com, h1707@accor.com).

$$ Hotel Ibis Wien, a modern high-rise hotel with American charm, is ideal for anyone tired of quaint old Europe. Its 340 cookie-cutter rooms are bright, comfortable, and modern, with all the conveniences (Sb-€69-75, Db-€87-93, Tb-€106, breakfast-€10, air-con, elevator, free Internet access and Wi-Fi in lobby, parking garage-€12/day; exit Westbahnhof to the right and walk 400 yards, Mariahilfer Gürtel 22-24, U-3: Westbahnhof; tel. 01/59998, fax 01/597-9090, www.ibishotel.com, h0796@accor.com).

$ Pension Fünfhaus is big, plain, clean, and bare-bones— almost institutional—with tile floors. The neighborhood is run-down (with a few ladies loitering late at night), but this 47-room pension offers the best doubles you'll find for under €60 (S-€34, Sb-€43, D-€49, Db-€58, Tb-€84-92, 4-person apartment-€98-104, cash only, closed mid-Nov-Feb, includes basic breakfast, Sperrgasse 12, U-3: Westbahnhof, tel. 01/892-3545 or 01/892-0286, fax 01/892-0460, www.pension5haus.at, vienna@pension5haus.at, Frau Susi Tersch). Half the rooms are in the main building and half are in the annex, which has good rooms but is near the train tracks and a bit scary on the street at night. From the station, ride tram #52 or #58 two stops down Mariahilfer Strasse away from center, and ask for Sperrgasse. Crazy Chicken bike rental, listed on page 31, is just a block farther down Sperrgasse.

Cheap Dorms and Hostels near Mariahilfer Strasse

$ Jugendherberge Myrthengasse is your classic huge and well-run HI youth hostel, with 280 beds (€17-21/person in 2- to 6-bed rooms, price depends on season, includes sheets and breakfast, non-members pay €3.50 extra, pay Internet access, free Wi-Fi in lobby, always open, no curfew, lockers and lots of facilities, coin-op laundry, Myrthengasse 7, tel. 01/523-6316, fax 01/523-5849, hostel@chello.at).

$ Westend City Hostel, just a block from the Westbahnhof and Mariahilfer Strasse, is well-run and well-located, with 180 beds in 4- to 12-bed dorms (€22-29/person depending on how many in the room, Db-€66-92, rates vary by season, cheaper Nov-mid-March—except around New Year's; includes sheets, breakfast, and locker; cash only, pay Internet access, free Wi-Fi, laundry-€7, Fügergasse 3, tel. 01/597-6729, fax 01/597-672-927, www.westend hostel.at, info@westendhostel.at).

$ MOjOvie is a creative "little neighbourette," combining a residential apartment feel with a hostel vibe. This network of apartments offers dorm beds as well as private units sleeping two to four (dorm bed–€20, €23-26/person in a private room with shared bathroom, €35-45/person for apartment with private bathroom, includes sheets and towels, cash only for charges under €100, free Wi-Fi, laundry service, shared kitchen, reception open 8:00-23:00, Kaiserstrasse 77, tram #5 or a 10-minute walk from Westbahnhof, mobile 0699-1155-5505, www.mymojovie.at, accommodation@my mojovie.at).

$ More Hostels: Other hostels with €17-20 beds and €50 doubles near Mariahilfer Strasse are **Wombat's City Hostel** (3 locations: one near tracks behind the station at Grangasse 6, another even closer to station at Mariahilfer Strasse 137, and a new one near the Naschmarkt at Rechte Wienzeile 35; tel. 01/897-2336, www.wombats-hostels.com, office@wombats-vienna.at) and **Hostel Ruthensteiner** (smoke-free; leave the Westbahnhof to the right and follow Mariahilfer Strasse behind the station, then left on Haidmannsgasse for a block, then turn right and find Robert-Hamerling-Gasse 24; tel. 01/893-4202, www.hostelruthensteiner .com, info@hostelruthensteiner.com).

Eating in Vienna

The Viennese appreciate the fine points of life, and right up there with waltzing is eating. The city has many atmospheric restaurants. As you ponder the Eastern European specialties on menus, remember that Vienna's diverse empire may be no more, but its flavors linger.

While cuisines are routinely named for countries, Vienna claims to be the only *city* with a cuisine of its own: Vienna soups come with fillings (semolina dumpling, liver dumpling, or pancake slices). *Gulasch* is a beef ragout based on a traditional Hungarian shepherd's soup (spiced with onion and paprika). Of course, Wiener schnitzel is traditionally a breaded and fried veal cutlet (though pork is more common these days). Another meat specialty is boiled beef *(Tafelspitz)*. While you're sure to have *Apfelstrudel*, try *Topfenstrudel*, too (wafer-thin strudel pastry filled with sweet cheese and raisins). The *dag* you see in some prices stands for "dekagram" (10 grams). Therefore, *10 dag* is 100 grams, or about a quarter-pound.

On nearly every corner, you can find a colorful *Beisl* (BYE-zul). These uniquely Viennese taverns are a characteristic cross between an English pub and a French brasserie—filled with poetry teachers and their students, couples loving without touching, housewives on their way home from cello lessons, and waiters who enjoy serving hearty food and drinks at an affordable price. Ask at your hotel for a good *Beisl*. (Beware: Despite non-smoking laws, *Beisls* may

VIENNA

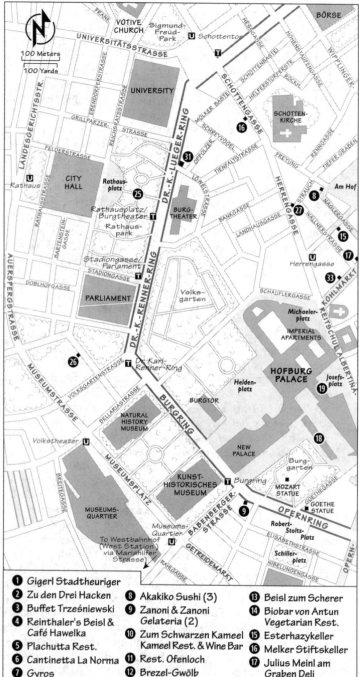

1. Gigerl Stadtheuriger
2. Zu den Drei Hacken
3. Buffet Trześniewski
4. Reinthaler's Beisl & Café Hawelka
5. Plachutta Rest.
6. Cantinetta La Norma
7. Gyros
8. Akakiko Sushi (3)
9. Zanoni & Zanoni Gelateria (2)
10. Zum Schwarzen Kameel Kameel Rest. & Wine Bar
11. Rest. Ofenloch
12. Brezel-Gwölb
13. Beisl zum Scherer
14. Biobar von Antun Vegetarian Rest.
15. Esterhazykeller
16. Melker Stiftskeller
17. Julius Meinl am Graben Deli

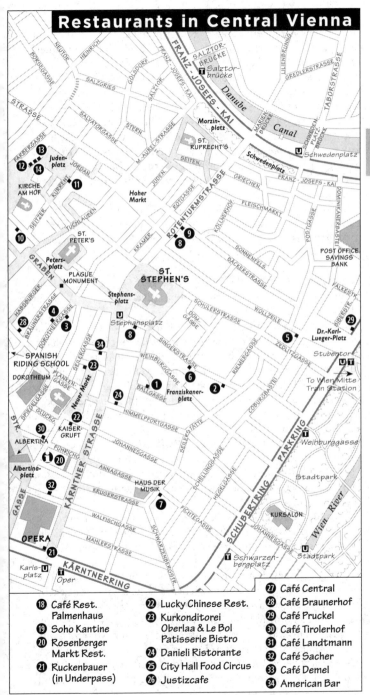

Restaurants in Central Vienna

18 Café Rest. Palmenhaus
19 Soho Kantine
20 Rosenberger Markt Rest.
21 Ruckenbauer (in Underpass)
22 Lucky Chinese Rest.
23 Kurkonditorei Oberlaa & Le Bol Patisserie Bistro
24 Danieli Ristorante
25 City Hall Food Circus
26 Justizcafe
27 Café Central
28 Café Braunerhof
29 Café Pruckel
30 Café Tirolerhof
31 Café Landtmann
32 Café Sacher
33 Café Demel
34 American Bar

still be quite smoky; fortunately, most have outdoor seating.

For hardcore Viennese cuisine, drop by a *Würstelstand*. The local hot-dog stand is a fixture on city squares throughout the old center, serving a variety of hot dogs and pickled side dishes with a warm corner-meeting-place atmosphere. Be adventurous: Generally, the darker the weenie, the spicier it is. Key words: *Weisswurst*—boiled white sausage; *Bosna*—with onions and curry; *Käsekrainer*—with melted cheese inside; *Debreziner*—spicy Hungarian; *Frankfurter*—our weenie; *frische*—fresh; *Kren*—horseradish; and *Senf*—mustard (ask for *süss*—sweet, or *scharf*—sharp). Only a tourist puts the sausage in a bun like a hot dog. Munch alternately between the meat and the bread ("that's why you have two hands"), and you'll look like a native.

Two other don't-miss Viennese institutions, its cafés and wine gardens, are covered under "Experiences in Vienna" on page 79.

Many restaurants offer a "*menu*," a fixed-price bargain meal, at lunchtime.

Near St. Stephen's Cathedral

Each of these eateries is within about a five-minute walk of the cathedral (U-1 or U-3: Stephansplatz).

Gigerl Stadtheuriger offers a fun, near-*Heuriger* wine cellar experience (described on page 80), without leaving the city center. Just point to what looks good. Food is sold by the piece or weight; 100 grams *(10 dag)* is about a quarter-pound (cheese and cold meats cost about €3 per 100 grams, salads are about €2 per 100 grams; price sheet posted on wall to right of buffet line). The *Karree* pork with herbs is particularly tasty and tender. They also have menu entrées, spinach strudel, quiche, *Apfelstrudel,* and, of course, casks of new and local wines (sold by the *Achtel,* about 4 oz). Meals run €7-12, and there's often accordion or live music on weekends (daily 15:00-24:00, indoor/outdoor seating, behind cathedral, a block off Kärntner Strasse, a few cobbles off Rauhensteingasse on Blumenstock, tel. 01/513-4431).

Zu den Drei Hacken, another fun and typical *Weinstube,* is famous for its local specialties (€10 plates, Mon-Sat 11:00-23:00, closed Sun, indoor/outdoor seating, Singerstrasse 28, tel. 01/512-5895).

Buffet Trześniewski is an institution—justly famous for its elegant and cheap finger sandwiches and small beers (€1 each). Three different sandwiches and a *kleines Bier (Pfiff)* make a fun, light lunch. Point to whichever delights look tasty (or grab the English translation sheet and take time to study your 22 sandwich options). The classic favorites are *Geflügelleber* (chicken liver), *Matjes mit Zwiebel* (herring with onions), and *Speck mit Ei* (bacon and eggs). Pay for your sandwiches and a drink. Take your drink tokens to the lady on the right. Sit on the bench and scoot over to a tiny table when a spot opens up. Trześniewski has been a Vienna favorite for more than a century...and many of its regulars seem to have been here for the grand opening (Mon-Fri 8:30-19:30, Sat 9:00-17:00, closed Sun; 50 yards off the Graben, nearly across from brooding Café Hawelka, Dorotheergasse 2; tel. 01/512-3291). In the fall, this is a good opportunity to try the fancy grape juices—*Most* or *Traubenmost*. Their other location, at Mariahilfer Strasse 95 (near many recommended hotels), serves the same sandwiches with the same menu in the same ambience (Mon-Fri 8:30-19:00, Sat 9:00-18:00, closed Sun, U-3: Zieglergasse, tel. 01/596-4291).

Reinthaler's Beisl is a time warp that serves simple, traditional *Beisl* fare all day. It's handy for its location (a block off the Graben, across the street from Buffet Trześniewski) and because it's a rare restaurant in the center that's open on Sunday. Its fun, classic interior winds way back (use the handwritten daily menu rather than the printed English one, €6-12 plates, daily 11:00-22:30, at Dorotheergasse 4, tel. 01/513-1249).

Plachutta Restaurant, with a stylish green-and-cream, elegant-but-comfy interior and breezy covered terrace, is famous for the best beef in town. You'll find an enticing menu with all the classic Viennese beef dishes, fine desserts, attentive service, and an enthusiastic and sophisticated local clientele. They've developed the art of beef to the point of producing popular cookbooks. Their specialty is a page-long list of *Tafelspitz*—a traditional copper pot of boiled beef with broth and vegetables. Treat the broth as your soup course. A chart on the menu lets you choose your favorite cut. Make a reservation for this high-energy Vienna favorite (€16-21/pot, daily 12:00-22:30, 10-minute walk from St. Stephen's Cathedral to Wollzeile 38, U-3: Stubentor, tel. 01/512-1577).

Cantinetta La Norma, a short walk from the cathedral, serves fresh, excellent Italian dishes amid a cozy, yet energetic ambience. Even on weeknights the small dining area is abuzz with friendly chatter among its multinational, loyal regulars (€8 pizzas and pastas, €7-18 entrées, lunch specials, daily 11:00-24:00, outdoor seating, Franziskaner Platz 3, tel. 01/512-8665, run by friendly Paco).

Gyros is a humble little Greek/Turkish joint run by Yilmaz, a fun-loving Turk from Izmir. He simply loves to feed people—the food is great, the prices are decent, and you almost feel like you took a quick trip to Istanbul (€8-12 plates, Mon-Sat 10:00-24:00, Sun 10:00-18:00, a long block off Kärntner Strasse at corner of Fichtegasse and Seilerstätte, mobile 0699-1016-3726).

Akakiko Sushi is a small chain of Japanese restaurants with an easy pan-Asian menu that's worth considering if you're just schnitzeled out. They serve sushi, of course, but also noodles, stir-fry, and other meals. The €11 bento box meals are a decent value.

VIENNA

There are several convenient locations: Singerstrasse 4 (a block off Kärntner Strasse near the cathedral), Rotenturmgasse 6 (also near the cathedral), Heidenschuss 3 (near other recommended eateries just off Am Hof, U-3: Herrengasse), and Mariahilfer Strasse 42-48 (fifth floor of Kaufhaus Gerngross, near many recommended hotels, U-3: Neubaugasse). Though they lack charm, these are fast and reasonable (€8-11 meals, all open daily 10:30-23:30).

Ice Cream!: **Zanoni & Zanoni** is a very Italian *gelateria* run by an Italian family. They're mobbed by happy Viennese hungry for their huge €2 cones to go. Or, to relax and watch the thriving people scene, lick your gelato in their fun outdoor area (daily 7:00-24:00, 2 blocks up Rotenturmstrasse from cathedral at Lugeck 7, tel. 01/512-7979). There's another location behind the Kunsthistorisches Museum, facing the Ring (at Burgring 1, U-2 or U-3: Volkstheater/Museumsplatz).

Near Am Hof Square

The square called Am Hof (U-3: Herrengasse) is surrounded by a maze of atmospheric medieval lanes; the following eateries are all within a block of the square.

Zum Schwarzen Kameel Wine Bar ("The Black Camel") is filled with a professional local crowd enjoying small plates from the same kitchen as their fancy restaurant, but at a better price. This is *the* place for horseradish and thin-sliced ham (*Beinschinken mit Kren,* €8.50 a plate, *Achtung*—the horseradish is *hot*). I'd order their *Vorspeisenteller* (a great *antipasti* dish that comes with ham and horseradish) or *Tafelspitz* (€16). Stand, grab a stool, find a table on the street, or sit anywhere you can—it's customary to share tables in the wine-bar section. Fine Austrian wines are sold by the *Achtel* (eighth-liter glass) and listed on the board; Aussie bartender Karl can help you choose. They also have a buffet of tiny €1-2 sandwiches. For a splurge, the **Zum Schwarzen Kameel Restaurant** is a tiny, elegant alternative. The dark-wood, 12-table, Art Nouveau restaurant serves fine gourmet Viennese cuisine (three-course lunch-€40, three-course dinner-€65 plus pricey wine, both open Mon-Sat 8:30-24:00, closed Sun, Bognergasse 5, tel. 01/533-8125).

Restaurant Ofenloch serves good, old-fashioned Viennese cuisine with formal service, both indoors and out. This 300-year-old eatery, with great traditional ambience, is dressy (with white tablecloths) but intimate and woodsy (€10 lunch specials, €13-19 main courses, Mon-Sat 11:00-22:30, closed Sun, Kurrentgasse 8, tel. 01/533-8844).

Brezel-Gwölb, a Tolkienesque wine cellar with outdoor dining on a quiet square, serves forgettable food in an unforgettable atmosphere. It's ideal for a romantic late-night glass of wine (daily 11:30-23:30; leave Am Hof on Drahtgasse, then take first left to

Ledererhof 9; tel. 01/533-8811).

Beisl zum Scherer, around the corner, is untouristy and serves traditional plates for €8-15. Sitting outside, you'll face a stern Holocaust memorial. Inside comes with a soothing woody atmosphere and intriguing decor. Let friendly Sakis explain the daily specials—which don't show up on the English menu (Mon-Sat 11:30-22:00, closed Sun, Judenplatz 7, tel. 01/533-5164).

Biobar von Antun Vegetarian Restaurant is a cheery and earthy little place with a €7 lunch special and hearty €10 salads, plenty of vegan options, and the fancy juices you'd expect (daily 12:00-23:00, on Judenplatz at Drahtgasse 3, tel. 01/968-9351).

Esterhazykeller, both ancient and popular, has traditional fare deep underground. For a cheap and sloppy buffet, climb down to the lowest cellar. For table service on a pleasant square, sit outside (Mon-Sat 11:00-23:00, Sun 16:00-23:00, may close for lunch in Aug-Sept and/or in bad weather, just below Am Hof at Haarhof 1, tel. 01/533-3482).

Melker Stiftskeller is an untouristy *Stadtheuriger* in a deep and rustic circa-1626 cellar with hearty, inexpensive meals and new wine. Avoid this place when it's hot out, as there's no outdoor seating (Tue-Sat 17:00-24:00, closed Sun-Mon and mid-July-mid-Aug, between Am Hof Square and Schottentor U-Bahn stop at Schottengasse 3, tel. 01/533-5530).

Julius Meinl am Graben, a posh supermarket with two floors of temptations right on the Graben, has been famous since 1862 as a top-end delicatessen with all the gourmet fancies. Assemble a meal from the picnic fixings on the shelves. There's also a café, with light meals and great outdoor seating; a stuffy and pricey restaurant upstairs; and a take-away counter with good benches for people-watching while you munch (shop open Mon-Fri 8:00-19:30, Sat 9:00-18:00, closed Sun; restaurant open Mon-Sat until 24:00, closed Sun; Am Graben 19, tel. 01/532-3334).

Near the Opera

These eateries are within easy walking distance of the Opera (U-1, U-2, or U-4: Karlsplatz).

Café Restaurant Palmenhaus overlooks the Palace Garden (Burggarten—see page 58). Tucked away in a green and peaceful corner two blocks behind the Opera in the Hofburg's backyard, this is a world apart. If you want to eat modern Austrian cuisine surrounded by palm trees rather than tourists, this is the place. And, since it's at the edge of a huge park, it's great for families. Their fresh fish with generous vegetables specials are on the board (€8.50 lunch plates available Mon-Fri, €15-18 entrées, open daily 10:00-24:00, serious vegetarian dishes, fish, extensive wine list, indoors in greenhouse or outdoors, Burggarten 1, tel. 01/533-1033).

Soho Kantine is a grim, government-subsidized cantina serving the National Library and offering the best cheap, sit-down lunches in the Hofburg. Pay for your meal—your choice of bland meat or bland vegetarian—and a drink at the bar, take your token to the kitchen, and then sit down and eat with the locals (€6 two-course lunch, Mon-Fri 11:30-15:00, closed Sat-Sun and Aug, hard to find on ground floor of library—opposite the butterflies in a forlorn little square with no sign, Burggarten, Josefsplatz 1, tel. 01/532-8566, mobile 0676-309-5161).

Rosenberger Markt Restaurant is mobbed with tour groups. Still, if you don't mind a freeway-cafeteria ambience in the center of the German-speaking world's classiest city, this self-service eatery is fast and easy. It's just a block toward the cathedral from the Opera. The best cheap meal here is a small salad or veggie plate stacked high (daily 10:30-23:00, lots of fruits, veggies, fresh-squeezed juices, addictive banana milk, ride the glass elevator downstairs, Maysedergasse 2, tel. 01/512-3458).

Ruckenbauer, a favorite for a quick bite, is a fast-food kiosk in a transit underpass under the street in front of the Opera, between the entryways marked *U2/U4* and *U1*. Their €1.60 *Tramezzini* sandwiches and fine pastries make a classy, quick picnic lunch or dinner before the Opera, just 100 yards away (Mon-Fri 6:00-20:00, Sat-Sun 9:00-20:00).

Lucky Chinese Restaurant is simply a good, modern, and well-located option for Chinese food. The inside is fresh and air-conditioned, the outside seating is on a great square, and the service is friendly (€10-15 plates, daily 11:30-23:00, Neuer Markt 8, tel. 01/512-3428).

Kurkonditorei Oberlaa may not have the royal and plush fame of Demel (see page 40), but this is where Viennese connoisseurs serious about the quality of their pastries go to get fat. With outdoor seating on Neuer Markt, it's particularly nice on a hot summer day. Upstairs has more temptations and good seating (€10 daily three-course lunches, great selection of cakes, daily 8:00-20:00, Neuer Markt 16, other locations about town, including the Naschmarkt, tel. 01/5132-9360).

Le Bol Patisserie Bistro (next to Oberlaa) satisfies your need for something French. The staff speaks to you in French, serving fine €8 salads, baguette sandwiches, and fresh croissants (Mon-Sat 8:00-22:00, Sun 10:00-20:00, Neuer Markt 14).

Danieli Ristorante is your best classy Italian bet in the old town. White-tablecloth dressy, but not stuffy, it has reasonable prices. Dine in their elegant back room or on the street (€13-18 pizzas and pastas, €18-25 main courses, fresh fish specialties, daily 10:00-24:00, 30 yards off Kärntner Strasse opposite Neuer Markt at Himmelpfortgasse 3, tel. 01/513-7913).

City Hall Food Circus

During the summer, scores of outdoor food stands and hundreds of picnic tables are set up in the park in front of the City Hall (Rathausplatz). Local mobs enjoy mostly ethnic meals for decent-but-not-cheap prices and classical entertainment on a big screen. The fun thing here is the energy of the crowd and a feeling that you're truly eating as the Viennese do...not schnitzel and quaint traditions, but trendy "world food" with young people out having fun in a fine Vienna park setting (mid-July-mid-Sept daily from 11:00 until late, in front of City Hall on the Ringstrasse, U-2: Rathaus).

Just West of the Ring

Justizcafe, the cafeteria serving Austria's Supreme Court of Justice, offers a fine view, great prices, and a memorable lunchtime experience—even if the food is somewhat bland. Enter the Palace of Justice through its grand front door, pass through tight security, say "wow" to the Historicist architecture in the courtyard, and ride the elevator to the rooftop. You can sit behind the windows inside or dine outside on the roof, enjoying one of the best views of Vienna while surrounded by legal beagles (€8-12 main dishes, Mon-Fri 11:00-14:30, closed Sat-Sun, Schmerlingplatz 10, U-2 or U-3: Volkstheater/Museumsplatz, mobile 0676-755-6100).

Spittelberg Quarter

A charming cobbled grid of traffic-free lanes and Biedermeier apartments has become a favorite neighborhood for Viennese wanting a little dining charm between the MuseumsQuartier and Mariahilfer Strasse (handy to many recommended hotels; take Stiftgasse from Mariahilfer Strasse, or wander over here after you close down the Kunsthistorisches Museum; U-2 or U-3: Volkstheater/Museumsplatz). Tables tumble down sidewalks and into breezy courtyards filled with appreciative natives enjoying dinner or a relaxing drink. It's only worth the trip on a balmy summer evening, as it's dead in bad weather. Stroll Spittelberggasse, Schrankgasse, and Gutenberggasse, then pick your favorite. Don't miss the vine-strewn wine garden at Schrankgasse 1. To locate these restaurants, see the map on pages 94-95.

Amerlingbeisl, with a charming, casual atmosphere both on the cobbled street and in its vine-covered courtyard, is a great value, serving a mix of traditional Austrian and international dishes (always a €5 vegetarian daily special, other specials for €6-10, €9-14 dinners, daily 9:00-2:00 in the morning, Stiftgasse 8, tel. 01/526-1660).

Zu Ebener Erde und Erster Stock ("Downstairs, Upstairs") is a charming little restaurant with a near-gourmet menu. True to its name, it has two distinct eating zones (with the same menu): a casual, woody bistro downstairs (traditionally the quarters of the poor); and a fancy Biedermeier-style dining room with red-velvet chairs and violet tablecloths upstairs (where the wealthy convened). There are also a few al fresco tables out front. Reservations are smart (€10-19 main dishes, €25 traditional three-course fixed-price meal, seasonal specials, Mon-Fri 7:30-21:30, last seating at 20:00, closed Sat-Sun, Burggasse 13, tel. 01/523-6254).

Witwe Bolte is classy and a good choice for uninspired Viennese cuisine with tablecloths. The interior is tight, but its tiny square has wonderful leafy ambience (€11-17 main dishes, daily 11:30-23:30 except closed 15:00-17:30 mid-Jan-mid-March, Gutenberggasse 13, tel. 01/523-1450).

Plutzer Bräu, next door to Amerlingbeisl, feels a bit more touristy. It's a big, sprawling, impersonal brewpub serving stick-to-your-ribs pub grub (€7-9 vegetarian dishes, €9-20 meals, ribs, burgers, traditional dishes, Tirolean beer from the keg, also brew their own, daily 11:00-2:00 in the morning, food until 24:00, Schrankgasse 4, tel. 01/526-1215).

Near Mariahilfer Strasse

Mariahilfer Strasse (see map on pages 94-95) is filled with reasonable cafés serving all types of cuisine. For a quick yet traditional bite, consider the venerable **Buffet Trześniewski** sandwich bar at Mariahilfer Strasse 95 (see page 102).

Schnitzelwirt is an old classic with a 1950s patina and a clientele to match. In this smoky, working-class place, no one finishes their schnitzel ("to-go" for the dog is wrapped in newspaper, "to-go" for you is wrapped in foil). You'll find no tourists, just cheap €6-11 schnitzel meals (Mon-Sat 10:00-23:00, closed Sun, Neubaugasse 52, U-3: Neubaugasse, tel. 01/523-3771).

The **Naschmarkt** (described on page 70) is Vienna's best Old World market, with plenty of fresh produce, cheap local-style eateries, cafés, *Döner Kebab* and sausage stands, and the best-value sushi in town (Mon-Fri 6:00-18:30, Sat 6:00-17:00, closed Sun, closes earlier in winter; U-1, U-2, or U-4: Karlsplatz, follow *Karlsplatz* signs out of the station). Survey the lane of eateries at the end of the market nearest the Opera. The circa-1900 pub is inviting. Picnickers can buy supplies at the market and eat on nearby Karlsplatz (plenty of chairs facing the Karlskirche).

Vienna Connections

By Train

Remember, Vienna has several train stations, the biggest of which are undergoing an extensive renovation. Be sure you know which station your train departs from; see page 26 for the basic run-down, but always confirm locally. For general train information in Austria, call 051-717 (to get an operator, dial 2, then 2).

From Vienna by Train to: Salzburg (almost hourly, 2.5-3 hours), **Hallstatt** (hourly, 4 hours, change in Attnang-Puchheim), **Munich** (6/day direct, 4.25 hours; otherwise about hourly, 5-5.75 hours, transfer in Salzburg), **Berlin** (8/day, most with 1 change, 9.5 hours, some via Czech Republic; longer on night train), **Zürich** (nearly hourly, 9-10 hours, 1 with changes in Innsbruck and Feldkirch, night train), **Rome** (3/day, 12-13 hours, plus several overnight options), **Venice** (3/day, 8-9.5 hours with changes—some may involve bus connection; plus 1 direct night train, 12 hours), **Frankfurt** (6/day direct, 7 hours; plus 1 direct night train, 10 hours), **Paris** (7/day, 12-17 hours, 1-3 changes, night train), **Amsterdam** (3/day, 11.5-12.5 hours, 1-2 changes, longer night-train options involve change in Germany), **Budapest** (every 2 hours direct, 3 hours; more with transfers), **Prague** (5/day direct, 4.75 hours; more with 1 change, 5-6 hours; 1 night train, 8 hours), **Kraków** (3 decent daytime options, 6.25 hours direct or 7-8.5 hours with 1-3 changes, plus a night train), **Ljubljana** (1 convenient early-morning direct train, 6 hours; otherwise 6/day with change in Villach, Maribor, or Graz, 6-7 hours).

By Plane
Vienna International Airport
This airport, 12 miles from the center, has easy connections to Vienna's various train stations (airport tel. 01/700-722-233, www .viennaairport.com).

The 30-minute ride into town by **taxi** costs about €35-40 (including the €11 airport surcharge).

The cheapest way into the city center is by **S-Bahn** train (€3.60, 2/hour, 24 minutes, buy 2-zone ticket from machines on the platform, price includes any bus or S- or U-Bahn transfers). The fast **CAT** (City Airport Train) takes a third less time but costs nearly triple (€10, €11.50 includes a ride to your final destination on Vienna's transit system, 2/hour, usually departs at :05 and :35, 16 minutes, www.cityairporttrain.com). Both land you at the Wien-Mitte Bahnhof, an easy U-Bahn ride from all my recommended hotels.

If you're staying near Schwedenplatz or the Westbahnhof, consider one of the convenient express **buses** (note destination and times on curbside TV monitors; €6, 2-3/hour, generally 20-30 minutes, buy ticket from driver, tel. 0810-222-333 for timetable info, www.postbus.at).

Bratislava Airport (Letisko Bratislava)
Bratislava Airport is six miles northeast of downtown Bratislava.

The airport offers budget flights on low-cost carriers Ryanair (www.ryanair.com) and Danube Wings (www.danubewings.eu). Some airlines market it as "Vienna-Bratislava," thanks to its proximity to both capitals. To reach Vienna, you can take a Eurolines bus to the Erdberg stop of Vienna's U-3 subway line. A taxi directly to Vienna costs €60-90 (depending on whether you use a cheaper Slovak or more expensive Austrian cab).

SALZBURG

Salzburg and its residents—or at least its tourism industry—are forever smiling to the tunes of Mozart and *The Sound of Music*. Thanks to its charmingly preserved old town, splendid gardens, Baroque churches, and Europe's largest intact medieval fortress, Salzburg feels made for visitors. As a musical mecca, the city puts on a huge annual festival, as well as constant concerts. It's a city with class. Vagabonds wish they had nicer clothes.

Even without Mozart and the von Trapps, Salzburg is steeped in history. In about A.D. 700, Bavaria gave Salzburg to Bishop Rupert in return for his promise to Christianize the area. Salzburg remained an independent city (belonging to no state) until Napoleon came in the early 1800s. Thanks in part to its formidable fortress, Salzburg managed to avoid the ravages of war for 1,200 years...until World War II. Much of the city was destroyed by WWII bombs (mostly around the train station), but the historic old town survived.

Eight million tourists crawl its cobbles each year. That's a lot of Mozart balls—and all that popularity has led to a glut of businesses hoping to catch the tourist dollar. Still, Salzburg is both a must and a joy.

Planning Your Time

While Salzburg's sights are mediocre, the town itself is a Baroque museum of cobbled streets and elegant buildings—simply a touristy stroller's delight. Even if your time is short, consider allowing half a day for the *Sound of Music* tour. The *S.O.M.* tour kills a nest of sightseeing birds with one ticket (city overview, *S.O.M.* sights,

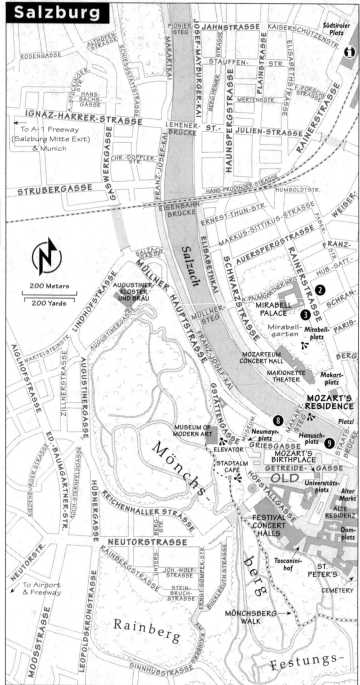

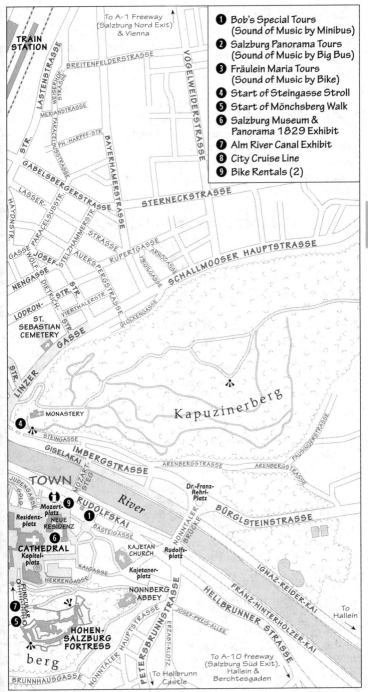

1 Bob's Special Tours
(Sound of Music by Minibus)

2 Salzburg Panorama Tours
(Sound of Music by Big Bus)

3 Fräulein Maria Tours
(Sound of Music by Bike)

4 Start of Steingasse Stroll

5 Start of Mönchsberg Walk

6 Salzburg Museum &
Panorama 1829 Exhibit

7 Alm River Canal Exhibit

8 City Cruise Line

9 Bike Rentals (2)

and a fine drive by the lakes).

You'd probably enjoy at least two nights in Salzburg—nights are important for swilling beer in atmospheric local gardens and attending concerts in Baroque halls and chapels. Seriously consider one of Salzburg's many evening musical events (a few are free, some are as cheap as €12, and most average €30-40). To get away from it all, bike down the river or hike across the Mönchsberg cliffs that rise directly from the middle of town.

A day trip from Salzburg to Hallstatt (the small-town highlight of the Salzkammergut Lake District—see next chapter) is doable, but involves about five hours for the round-trip transportation alone and makes for a very long day. An overnight in Hallstatt is better.

Orientation to Salzburg

(area code: 0662)

Salzburg, a city of 150,000 (Austria's fourth-largest), is divided into old and new. The old town, sitting between the Salzach River and its mini-mountain (Mönchsberg), holds nearly all the charm and most of the tourists. The new town, across the river, has its own share of sights and museums, plus some good accommodations.

Tourist Information

Salzburg has three helpful TIs (main tel. 0662/889-870, www .salzburg.info): at the **train station** (daily June-Aug 8:15-19:30, Sept-May 8:45-18:00, tel. 0662/8898-7340); on **Mozartplatz** in the old center (daily 9:00-18:00, July-mid-Sept until 19:00, closed Sun mid-Jan-Easter and Oct-mid-Nov, tel. 0662/889-870); and at the **Salzburg Süd park-and-ride** (generally open daily July-Aug 10:00-16:30 but sometimes longer hours, May-June Thu-Sat 10:00-16:30, Sept Mon-Sat 10:00-16:30, closed in winter, tel. 0662/8898-7360).

At any TI, you can pick up a free city-center map (the €0.70 map has a broader coverage and more information on sights, but probably isn't necessary), the Salzburg Card brochure (listing sights with current hours and prices), and a bimonthly schedule of events. Book a concert upon arrival. The TIs also book rooms (€2.20 fee and 10 percent deposit).

Salzburg Card: The TIs sell the Salzburg Card, which covers all your public transportation (including Mönchsberg elevator and funicular to the fortress) and admission to all the city sights (including Hellbrunn Castle and a river cruise). The card is pricey, but if you'd like to pop into all the sights, it can save money and enhance your experience (€25/24 hours, €33/48 hours, €38/72 hours, €3 cheaper Nov-April). To analyze your potential savings, here are the major sights and what you'd pay without the card: Hohensalzburg Fortress and funicular-€10.50; Mozart's Birthplace and Residence-€12; Hellbrunn Castle-€9.50; Salzburg Panorama 1829-€2; Salzach River cruise-€13; 24-hour transit pass-€4.20. Busy sightseers can save plenty. Get this card, feel the financial pain once, and the city will be all yours.

Arrival in Salzburg

By Train: The Salzburg station is undergoing a huge renovation, so for the next several years its services will be operating out of temporary structures in the parking lot. Still, you'll find it all here: train information, tourist information, luggage lockers, and so on.

Getting downtown couldn't be easier, as immediately in front of the station a bus stop labeled *Zentrum-Altstadt* has **buses** lined up and leaving every two minutes. Buses #1, #3, #5, #6, and #25 all do the same route into the city center before diverging at the far end of town. For most sights and city-center hotels, get off just after the bridge. For my recommended hotels in the new town, get off at Makartplatz, just before the bridge. (Buses to and from the airport use the *Flughafen* stop in front of the train station.) **Taxis** charge about €8 (plus €1 for your bag) to take you to your hotel.

To **walk** downtown (15 minutes), turn left as you leave the station, and walk straight down Rainerstrasse, which leads under the tracks past Mirabellplatz, turning into Dreifaltigkeitsgasse. From here, you can turn left onto Linzergasse for many of my recommended hotels, or cross the Staatsbrücke bridge for the old town (and more hotels). For a slightly longer but more dramatic approach, leave the station the same way but follow the tracks to the river, turn left, and walk the riverside path toward the fortress.

By Car: Coming on A-1 from Vienna or Munich, take A-10 toward Hallein, and then take the next exit (Salzburg Süd) in the direction of Anif. First, you'll pass the recommended Hellbrunn Castle (and zoo), then the Salzburg Süd TI and a park-and-ride service—a smart place to park while visiting Salzburg. Park your car (€5/24 hours), get sightseeing information and transit tickets from the TI, and catch the shuttle bus into town (€1.90 for a single ticket, or covered by €4.20 *Tageskarte* day pass, both sold at the TI, more expensive if you buy tickets on board, every 5 minutes, bus #3, #8, or #28). If traveling with more than one other person, take advantage of a park-and-ride combo-ticket: For €13 (€10 in July-Aug), you get 24 hours of parking and a round-trip on the shuttle bus for up to five people.

Mozart never drove in the old town, and neither should you. But if you don't believe in park-and-rides, the easiest, cheapest, most central parking lot is the 1,500-car Altstadt lot in the tunnel under the Mönchsberg (€14/day, note your slot number and which

SALZBURG

of the twin lots you're in, tel. 0662/846-434). Your hotel may provide discounted parking passes.

Helpful Hints

Don't Trust Hotelier Recommendations: Salzburg is addicted to the tourist dollar, and it can never get enough. Virtually all hotels are on the take when it comes to concert and tour recommendations, influenced more by their potential kickback than by what's best for you. Take their advice with a grain of salt.

Internet Access: The Internet kiosk a few doors down from the Mozartplatz TI is well-located, but too expensive (€2/10 minutes). Two Internet cafés at the bottom of the cliff, between Getreidegasse and the Mönchsberg lift, have good prices and hours (€2/hour, daily 10:00-22:00). Across the river, there's a big, handy Internet café on Theatergasse (near Mozart's Residence, €2/hour, daily 9:00-23:00). Travelers with this book can get online free for a few minutes (long enough to check email) at the Panorama Tours terminal on Mirabellplatz (daily 8:00-18:00).

Post Office: A full-service post office is located in the heart of town, in the Neue Residenz (Mon-Fri 7:00-18:30, Sat 8:00-10:00, closed Sun).

Laundry: The launderette at the corner of Paris-Lodron-Strasse and Wolf-Dietrich-Strasse, near my recommended Linzergasse hotels, is handy (€10 self-service, €15 same-day full-service, Mon-Fri 7:30-18:00, Sat 8:00-12:00, closed Sun, tel. 0662/876-381).

Cinema: Das Kino is an art-house movie theater that plays films in their original language (a block off the river and Linzergasse on Steingasse, tel. 0662/873-100).

Getting Around Salzburg

By Bus: Single-ride tickets for central Salzburg *(Einzelkarte-Kernzone)* are sold on the bus for €2.10. At machines and *Tabak/Trafik* shops, you can buy €1.90 single-ride tickets or a €4.20 day pass *(Tageskarte,* good for 24 hours; €5 if you buy it on the bus). To get from the old town to the station, catch bus #1 from Hanuschplatz; or, from the other side of the river, catch #1, #3, #5, or #6 at Theatergasse, near Mirabell Gardens. Bus info: tel. 800-660-660.

By Bike: Salzburg is great fun for cyclists. The following two bike-rental shops offer a discount to anyone with this book—ask for it. **Top Bike** rents bikes on the river next to the Staatsbrücke (€6/2 hours, €10/4 hours, €15/24 hours, usually daily April-June and Sept-Oct 10:00-17:00, July-Aug 9:00-19:00, closed Nov-

March, free helmets with this book, tel. 06272/4656, mobile 0676-476-7259, www.topbike.at, Sabine). **A'Velo Radladen** rents bikes in the old town, just outside the TI on Mozartplatz (€4.50/1 hour, €7/2 hours, €16/24 hours; mountain bikes-€6/hour, €18/24 hours; electric bikes available for those who want less exercise, daily 9:00-18:00, until 19:00 July-Aug, but hours unreliable, shorter hours off-season and in bad weather, passport number for security deposit, mobile 0676-435-5950). Some of my recommended hotels and pensions also rent bikes, and several of the B&Bs on Moosstrasse let guests use them for free.

By Funicular and Elevator: The old town is connected to the top of the Mönchsberg mountain (and great views) via funicular and elevator. The **funicular** *(Festungsbahn)* whisks you up to the imposing Hohensalzburg Fortress (included in castle admission, goes every few minutes—for details, see page 130). The **elevator** *(MönchsbergAufzug)* on the east side of the old town propels you to the recommended Gasthaus Stadtalm café and hostel, the Museum of Modern Art, wooded paths, and more great views (€2 one-way, €3 round-trip, daily 8:30-19:00, Wed until 21:00; July-Aug daily until 1:00 in the morning, May-Sept starts running at 8:00).

By Taxi: Meters start at about €3 (from train station to your hotel, allow about €8). Small groups can taxi for about the same price as riding the bus.

By Buggy: The horse buggies *(Fiaker)* that congregate at Residenzplatz charge €36 for a 25-minute trot around the old town (www.fiaker-salzburg.at).

Tours in Salzburg

Walking Tours—On any day of the week, you can take a two-language, one-hour guided walk of the old town without a reservation—just show up at the TI on Mozartplatz and pay the guide. The tours are informative, but you'll likely be listening to everything in both German and English (€9, daily at 12:15 and 14:00, tours split into two single-language groups when turnout is sufficiently high, tel. 0662/8898-7330). To save money (and avoid all that German), you can easily do it on your own using this chapter's self-guided walk.

Local Guides—Salzburg is home to over a hundred licensed guides. I recommend two hardworking young guides in particular. **Christiana Schneeweiss** ("Snow White") has been instrumental in both my guidebook research and my TV production in Salzburg (€135/2 hours, €150/3 hours, tel. 0664/340-1757, www.kultur -tourismus.com, info@kultur-tourismus.com); check her website for bike tours, private minibus tours, and more. **Sabine Rath** also knows her city well, and is a joy to learn from (€135/2 hours,

€175/4 hours, €265/8 hours, tel. 0664/201-6492, www.tourguide
-salzburg.com, info@tourguide-salzburg.com). Salzburg has many
other good guides (to book, call 0662/840-406).

Boat Tours—City Cruise Line (a.k.a. Stadt Schiff-Fahrt) runs a
basic 40-minute round-trip river cruise with recorded commentary
(€13, 9/day July-Aug, 7/day in June, fewer Sept-Oct and April-May,
no boats Nov-March). For a longer cruise, ride to Hellbrunn and
return by bus (€16, 1-2/day April-Oct). Boats leave from the old-
town side of the river just downstream of the Makartsteg bridge
(tel. 0662/8257-6912). While views can be cramped, passengers are
treated to a fun finale just before docking, when the captain twirls
a fun "waltz."

▲▲***The Sound of Music* Tour**—I took this tour skeptically (as
part of my research)—and liked it. It includes a quick but good
general city tour, hits the *S.O.M.* spots (including the stately home
used in the movie, flirtatious gazebo, and grand wedding church),
and shows you a lovely stretch of the Salzkammergut Lake
District. This is worthwhile for *S.O.M.* fans and those who won't
otherwise be going into the Salzkammergut. Warning: Many
think rolling through the Austrian countryside with 30 Americans
singing "Doe, a deer..." is pretty schmaltzy. Local Austrians don't
understand all the commotion, and the audience is mostly native
English speakers.

Of the many companies doing the tour, consider Bob's Special
Tours (usually uses a minibus) and Panorama Tours (more typical
and professional, big 50-seat bus). Each one provides essentially
the same tour (in English with a live guide, 4 hours) for essentially the same price: €37 for Panorama, €40 for Bob's. You'll get
a discount from either if you book direct, mention Rick Steves,
pay cash, and bring this book along (you'll need to actually show
them this book to get the deal). Getting a spot is simple—just call
and make a reservation (calling Bob's a week or two in advance is
smart). Note: Your hotel will be eager to call to reserve for you—to
get their commission—but if you let them do it, you won't get the
discount I've negotiated.

Minibus Option: Most of **Bob's Special Tours** use an eight-
seat minibus (and occasionally a 20-seat bus) and therefore have
good access to old-town sights, promote a more casual feel, and
spend less time waiting to load and unload. Calling well in advance
increases your chances of getting a seat (€40 for adults, discount
with this book if you pay cash and book direct, €35 for kids and
students with ID, €30 for kids in car seats, daily at 9:00 and 14:00
year-round, they'll pick you up at your hotel for the morning tour,
afternoon tours leave from Bob's office along the river just east of
Mozartplatz at Rudolfskai 38, tel. 0662/849-511, mobile 0664-
541-7492, www.bobstours.com). Nearly all of Bob's tours stop for a

fun luge ride when the weather is dry (mountain bobsled-€4 extra, generally April-Oct, confirm beforehand). Some travelers looking for Bob's tours at Mozartplatz have been hijacked by other companies...have Bob's pick you up at your hotel (morning only), or meet the bus at their office. If you're unable to book with Bob's, and still want a minibus tour, try **Kultur Tourismus** (€45, tel. 0664/340-1757, www.kultur-tourismus.com, info@kultur-tourismus.com).

Big-Bus Option: Salzburg Panorama Tours depart from their smart kiosk at Mirabellplatz daily at 9:30 and 14:00 year-round (€37, discount with this book if you book direct and pay cash, book by calling 0662/874-029 or online at www.panorama tours.com). Many travelers appreciate their more businesslike feel, roomier buses, and slightly higher vantage point.

Bike Option: For some exercise with your tour, you can meet **Fräulein Maria** at the Mirabell Gardens (at Mirabellplatz 4, 50 yards to the left of palace entry) for a *S.O.M.* bike tour. The main attractions that you'll pass during the seven-mile pedal include the Mirabell Gardens, the horse pond, St. Peter's Cemetery, Nonnberg Abbey, Leopoldskron Palace, and, of course, the gazebo (€24 includes bike, discount with this book, €15 for kids 6-15, €10 for kids under 6, daily May-Sept at 9:30, June-Aug also at 16:30, allow 3.5 hours, family-friendly, reservations requ____ for afternoon tours, tel. 0650/342-6297, www.mariasbicyc____.com). For €8 extra, you're welcome to keep the bike all day.

Beyond Salzburg

Both Bob's and Panorama Tours also offer an extensive array of other day trips from Salzburg (e.g., Berchtesgaden/Eagle's Nest, salt mines, and Salzkammergut lakes and mountains).

Bob's Special Tours offers two particularly well-designed day tours (both depart daily at 9:00; either one costs €80 with a discount if you show this book and book direct, does not include entrance fees). Their *Sound of Music*/**Hallstatt Tour** first covers everything in the standard four-hour *Sound of Music* tour, then continues for a four-hour look at the scenic, lake-speckled Salzkammergut (with free time to explore charming Hallstatt). Bob's **Bavarian Mountain Tour** covers the main things you'd want to do in and around Berchtesgaden (Königsee cruise, Hitler's mountaintop Eagle's Nest, salt mine tour).

Self-Guided Walk

▲▲▲Salzburg's Old Town

I've linked the best sights in the old town into this handy self-guided orientation walk.

• *Begin in the heart of town, just up from the river, near the TI on...*

❶ Mozartplatz

All the happy tourists around you probably wouldn't be here if not for the man honored by this statue—Wolfgang Amadeus Mozart (erected in 1842; locals consider the statue a terrible likeness). Mozart spent much of his first 25 years (1756-1777) in Salzburg, the greatest Baroque city north of the Alps. But the city itself is much older: The Mozart statue sits on bits of Roman Salzburg, and the pink Church of St. Michael that overlooks the square dates from A.D. 800. The first Salzburgers settled right around here. Near you is the TI (with a concert box office), and just around the downhill corner is a pedestrian bridge leading over the Salzach River to the quiet and most medieval street in town, Steingasse (described on page 135).

• *Walk toward the cathedral and into the big square with the huge fountain.*

❷ Residenzplatz

Important buildings have long ringed this square. Salzburg's energetic Prince-Archbishop Wolf Dietrich von Raitenau (who ruled 1587-1612) was raised in Rome, was a cousin of the influential Florentine Medici family, and had grandiose Italian ambitions for Salzburg. After a convenient fire destroyed the town's cathedral, Wolf Dietrich set about building the "Rome of the North." This square, with his new cathedral and palace, was the centerpiece of his Baroque dream city. A series of interconnecting squares—like you'll see nowhere else—make a grand processional way, leading from here through the old town. As we enjoy this heart and soul of historic Salzburg, notice how easily we slip from noisy commercial streets to peaceful, reflective courtyards. Also notice the two dominant kinds of stone around town: a creamy red marble and a chunky conglomerate, both quarried nearby.

For centuries, Salzburg's leaders were both important church officials *and* princes of the Holy Roman Empire, hence the title "prince-archbishop"—mixing sacred and secular authority. But Wolf Dietrich misplayed his hand, losing power and spending his last five years imprisoned in the Hohensalzburg Fortress. (It's a complicated story—basically, the pope counted on Salzburg to hold the line against the Protestants for several generations following the Reformation. Wolf Dietrich was a good Catholic, as were most Salzburgers. But the town's important businessmen and the region's salt miners were Protestant, and for Salzburg's financial good, Wolf Dietrich dealt with them in a tolerant and pragmatic way. So the pope—who couldn't allow any tolerance for Protestants in those heady Counter-Reformation days—had Wolf Dietrich locked up and replaced.)

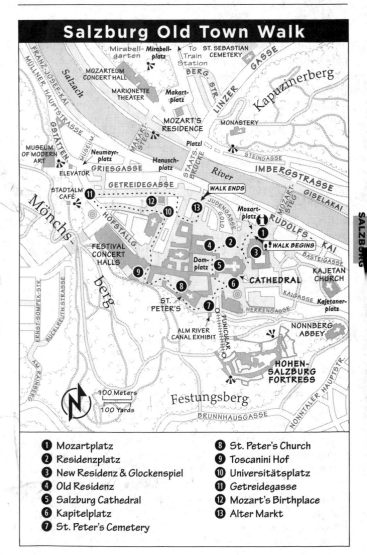

Salzburg Old Town Walk

1. Mozartplatz
2. Residenzplatz
3. New Residenz & Glockenspiel
4. Old Residenz
5. Salzburg Cathedral
6. Kapitelplatz
7. St. Peter's Cemetery
8. St. Peter's Church
9. Toscanini Hof
10. Universitätsplatz
11. Getreidegasse
12. Mozart's Birthplace
13. Alter Markt

The fountain is as Italian as can be, with a Triton matching Bernini's famous Triton Fountain in Rome. Situated on a busy trade route to the south, Salzburg was well aware of the exciting things going on in Italy. Things Italian were respected (as in colonial America, when a bumpkin would "stick a feather in his cap and call it macaroni"). Local artists even Italianized their names in order to raise their rates.

• *Along the left side of Residenzplatz (as you face the cathedral) is the...*

❸ Neue (New) Residenz and Glockenspiel

This former palace, long a government administration building, now houses the central post office, the **Heimatwerk** (a fine shop showing off all the best local handicrafts, Mon-Fri 9:00-18:00, Sat 9:00-17:00, closed Sun), and two worthwhile sights: the fascinating **Salzburg Panorama 1829** exhibit (definitely worth the €2); and the **Salzburg Museum,** which offers the best peek at the history of this one-of-a-kind city (described on page 129).

The famous **glockenspiel** rings atop the Neue Residenz. This bell tower has a carillon of 35 17th-century bells (cast in Antwerp) that chimes throughout the day and plays tunes (appropriate to the month) at 7:00, 11:00, and 18:00. A big barrel with adjustable tabs turns like a giant music-box mechanism, pulling the right bells in the appropriate rhythm. Notice the ornamental top: an upside-down heart in flames surrounding the solar system (symbolizing that God loves all of creation). Seasonal twice-weekly tours let you get up close to watch the glockenspiel action (€2, April-Oct Thu at 17:30 and Fri at 10:30, no tours Nov-March, meet in Salzburg Panorama 1829, just show up).

Look back, past Mozart's statue, to the 4,220-foot-high **Gaisberg**—the forested hill with the television tower. A road leads to the top for a commanding view. Its summit is a favorite destination for local nature-lovers and strong bikers.

• *Head to the opposite end of the square. This building is the...*

❹ Alte (Old) Residenz

Across from the Neue Residenz is Wolf Dietrich's palace, the Alte Residenz, rated ▲, which is connected to the cathedral by a skyway. Its series of ornately decorated rooms is well-described in an included audioguide, which gives you a good feel for the wealth and power of the prince-archbishop. Walking through 15 fancy state rooms (all on one floor), you'll see Renaissance, Baroque, and Classicist styles—200 years of let-them-eat-cake splendor (€8.50, daily 10:00-17:00, tel. 0662/840-4510).

• *Walk under the prince-archbishop's skyway and step into Domplatz (Cathedral Square), where you'll find the...*

❺ Salzburg Cathedral (Salzburger Dom)

This cathedral, rated ▲▲, was one of the first Baroque buildings north of the Alps. It was consecrated in 1628, during the Thirty Years' War. (Pitting Roman Catholics against Protestants, this war devastated much of Europe and brought most grand construction projects to a halt.) Experts differ on what motivated the builders: to emphasize Salzburg's commitment to the Roman Catholic cause and the power of the Church here, or to show that there could be a peaceful alternative to the religious strife that was racking Europe at the time. Salzburg's archbishop was technically the top papal official north of the Alps, but the city managed to steer clear of the war. With its rich salt production, it had enough money to stay out of the conflict and carefully maintain its independence from the warring sides, earning it the nickname "Fortified Island of Peace."

The dates on the iron gates refer to milestones in the church's history: In 774, the previous church (long since destroyed) was founded by St. Virgil, to be replaced in 1628 by the church you see today. In 1959, a partial reconstruction was completed, made necessary by a WWII bomb that had blown through the dome.

Domplatz is surrounded by the prince-archbishop's secular administration buildings. The **statue of Mary** (1771) is looking away from the church, welcoming visitors. If you stand in the rear of the square, immediately under the middle arch, you'll see that she's positioned to be crowned by the two angels on the church facade.

Step inside the cathedral. Enter the cathedral as if part of a festival procession—drawn toward the resurrected Christ by the brightly lit area under the dome, and cheered on by ceiling paintings of the Passion.

The **paintings** lining the nave, showing events leading up to Christ's death, are relatively dark. But the Old Testament themes that foreshadow Jesus' resurrection, and the Resurrection scene painted at the altar, are well-lit. The church has never had stained glass—just clear windows to let light power the message.

The stucco, by a Milanese artist, is exceptional. Sit under the **dome**—surrounded by the tombs of 10 archbishops from the 17th century—and imagine all four organs playing, each balcony filled with musicians...glorious surround-sound. Mozart, who was the organist here for two years, would advise you that the acoustics are best in pews immediately under the dome. Study the symbolism of the decor all around you—intellectual, complex, and cohesive. Think of the altar in Baroque terms, as the center of a stage, with sunrays as spotlights in this dramatic and sacred theater.

In the left transept, stairs lead down into the **crypt** *(Krypta)*, where you can see foundations of the earlier church, more tombs, and a tourist-free chapel (reserved for prayer) directly under the dome.

Built in just 14 years (1614-1628), the church boasts harmonious architecture. When Pope John Paul II visited in 1998, some 5,000 people filled the cathedral (330 feet long and 230 feet tall). The baptismal font (dark bronze, left of the entry) is from the previous cathedral (basin from about 1320, although the lid is modern). Mozart was baptized here (Amadeus means "beloved by God"). Concert and Mass schedules are posted at the entrance; the Sunday Mass at 10:00 is famous for its music.

Cost and Hours: Free, but donation requested; Easter-Oct Mon-Sat 9:00-18:00, Sun 13:00-18:00; Nov-Easter Mon-Sat 10:00-17:00, Sun 13:00-17:00.

Other Cathedral Sights: The **Cathedral Excavations Museum** (outside the church on Residenzplatz and down the stairs) offers a chance to see the foundations of the medieval church, some Roman engineering, and a few Roman mosaics from Roman street level. It has the charm of an old basement garage; unless you've never seen anything Roman, I'd skip it (€2.50, July-Aug daily 9:00-17:00, closed Sept-June).

The **Cathedral Museum** (Dom Museum) has a rich collection of church art (entry at portico, €5, mid-May-Oct Mon-Sat 10:00-17:00, Sun 11:00-18:00, closed Nov-mid-May except during Advent, tel. 0662/8047-1870).

• *From the cathedral, exit left and walk toward the fortress into the next square.*

❻ Kapitelplatz

Head past the underground public WCs (€0.50) to the giant **chessboard.** It's just under the **golden orb** topped by a man gazing up at the castle, trying to decide whether to walk up or shell out €10.50 for the funicular. Every year since 2002, a foundation has commissioned a different artist to create a new work of public art somewhere in the city; this is the piece from 2007. A small road leads uphill to the fortress (and fortress funicular; see arrow pointing to the *Stieglkeller*).

Keep going across the square to the pond. This was a **horse bath,** the 18th-century equivalent of a car wash. Notice the puzzle above it—the artist wove the date of the structure into a phrase. It says, "Leopold the Prince Built Me," using the letters LLDVICMXVXI, which total 1732 (add it up...it works)—the year it was built. With your back to the cathedral, leave the square through a gate in the right corner that reads *zum Peterskeller*. It leads to a waterfall and St. Peter's Cemetery (described later).

The **waterwheel** is part of a clever canal system that has brought water into Salzburg from Berchtesgaden, 15 miles away, since the 13th century. Climb uphill a few steps to feel the medieval water power. The stream was divided into smaller canals and channeled through town to provide fire protection, to flush out the streets (Thursday morning was flood-the-streets day), and to power factories (there were more than 100 watermill-powered firms as late as the 19th century). Because of its water-powered hygiene (relatively good for the standards of the time), Salzburg never suffered from a plague—it's probably the only Austrian town you'll see with no plague monument. For more on the canal system, check out the **Alm River Canal exhibit** (at the exit of the funicular, described on page 133).

Before leaving, drop into the fragrant and traditional **bakery** at the waterfall, which sells various fresh rolls—both sweet and not, explained on the wall, for less than €1 (Thu-Tue 7:00-17:30, Sat until 13:00, closed Wed). There's a good view of the funicular climbing up to the castle from here.

• *Now find the Katakomben sign and step into...*

❼ St. Peter's Cemetery

This collection of lovingly tended mini-gardens abuts the Mönchberg's rock wall (free, silence is requested, daily April-Sept 6:30-19:00, Oct-March 6:30-18:00). Walk in about 50 yards to the intersection of lanes at the base of the cliff marked by a stone ball. You're surrounded by three churches, each founded in the early Middle Ages atop a pagan Celtic holy site. St. Peter's Church is closest to the stone ball. Notice the fine Romanesque stonework on the apse of the chapel nearest you, and the rich guys' fancy Renaissance-style tombs decorating its walls.

Wealthy as those guys were, they ran out of caring relatives. The graves surrounding you are tended by descendants of the deceased. In Austria, gravesites are rented, not owned. Rent bills are sent out every 10 years. If no one cares enough to make the payment, your tombstone is removed.

While the cemetery where the von Trapp family hid out in *The Sound of Music* was a Hollywood set, it was inspired by this one.

Look up the cliff. Legendary medieval hermit monks are said to have lived in the hillside—but "catacombs" they're not. For €1, you can climb lots of steps to see a few old caves, a chapel, and some fine views (May-Sept Tue-Sun 10:30-17:00, closed Mon; Oct-April Wed-Thu 10:30-15:30, Fri-Sun 10:30-16:00, closed Mon-Tue).

To enjoy a peaceful side-trip, stroll past the stark Gothic funeral chapel (1491) to the uphill corner of the cemetery, and return along the high lane to see the finer tombs in the arcade. Tomb #31 belongs to the cathedral's architect—forever facing his creation. Tomb #54, at the catacomb entry, is a chapel carved into the hillside, holding the tombs of Mozart's sister and Joseph Haydn's younger brother Michael, also a composer of great note.

• *Continue downhill through the cemetery and out the opposite end. Just outside, hook right and drop into...*

❽ St. Peter's Church

Just inside, enjoy a carved Romanesque welcome. Over the inner doorway, a fine tympanum shows Jesus on a rainbow flanked by Peter and Paul over a stylized Tree of Life and under a Latin inscription reading, "I am the door to life, and only through me can you find eternal life." Enter the nave and notice how the once purely Romanesque vaulting has since been iced with a sugary Rococo finish. Salzburg's only Rococo interior feels Bavarian (because it is—the fancy stucco work was done by Bavarian artists). Up the right side aisle is the tomb of St. Rupert, with a painting showing Salzburg in 1750 (one bridge, salt ships sailing the river, and angels hoisting barrels of salt to heaven as St. Rupert prays for his city). If you're here during the town's Ruperti-Kirtag festival in late September, you'll see candles and fresh flowers, honoring the city's not-forgotten saint. On pillars farther up the aisle are faded bits of 13th-century Romanesque frescoes. Similar frescoes hide under Rococo whitewash throughout the church.

Leaving the church, notice on the left the recommended Stiftskeller St. Peter restaurant—known for its Mozart Dinner Concert (described on page 140). Charlemagne ate here in A.D. 803, allowing locals to claim that it's the oldest restaurant in Europe. Opposite where you entered the square (look through the arch), you'll see St. Rupert waving you into the next square. Once there, you're surrounded by early 20th-century Bauhaus-style dorms for student monks. Notice the modern crucifix (1926) painted on the far wall. Here's a good place to see the two locally quarried stones (marble and conglomerate) so prevalent in all the town's buildings.
• *Walk through the archway under the crucifix into...*

❾ Toscanini Hof

This square faces the 1925 **Festival Hall.** The hall's three theaters seat 5,000. This is where Captain von Trapp nervously waited before walking onstage (in the movie, he sang "Edelweiss"), just before he escaped with his family. On the left is the city's 1,500-space, inside-the-mountain parking lot; ahead, behind the *Felsenkeller* sign, is a tunnel (generally closed) leading to the actual concert hall; and to the right is the backstage of a smaller hall where carpenters are often building stage sets (door open on hot days). The stairway leads a few flights up to a picnic perch with a fine view, and then up to the top of the cliff and the recommended Stadtalm Café and hostel.

Walk downhill to **Max-Reinhardt-Platz.** Pause here to survey the line of Salzburg Festival concert halls. As the festival was started in the austere 1920s, the city remodeled existing buildings (e.g., the prince-archbishop's stables and riding school) for venues.
• *Continue straight—passing the big church on your left, along with lots of popular wurst stands and a public WC—into...*

❿ Universitätsplatz

This square hosts an **open-air produce market**—Salzburg's liveliest (mornings Mon-Sat, best on Sat). Salzburgers are happy to pay more here for the reliably fresh and top-quality produce.

(These days, half of Austria's produce is grown organically.) The market really bustles on Saturday mornings, when the farmers are in town. Public marketplaces have fountains for washing fruit and vegetables. The fountain here—a part of the medieval water system—plummets down a hole and to the river. The sundial (over the water hole) is accurate (except for the daylight savings hour) and two-dimensional, showing both the time (obvious) and the date (less obvious). The fanciest facade overlooking the square (the yellow one) is the backside of Mozart's Birthplace (we'll see the front soon).

• *Continue past the fountain to the end of the square, passing several characteristic and nicely arcaded medieval tunnels (on right) that connect the square to Getreidegasse (described next). Just for fun, weave between this street and Getreidegasse several times, following these "through houses" as you work your way toward the cliff face. For a look at the giant horse troughs, adjacent to the prince's stables, cross the big road (looking left at the string of Salzburg Festival halls again). Paintings show the various breeds and temperaments of horses in his stable. Like Vienna, Salzburg had a passion for the equestrian arts.*

Turn right (passing a courtyard on your left that once housed a hospital for the poor, and now houses a toy museum and a museum of historic musical instruments), and then right again, which brings you to the start of a long and colorful pedestrian street.

⓫ Getreidegasse

This street, rated ▲▲, was old Salzburg's busy, colorful main drag. It's been a center of trade since Roman times (third century). It's lined with *Schmuck* (jewelry) shops and other businesses. This is the burgher's (businessman's) Salzburg. The buildings, most of which date from the 15th century, are tall for that age, and narrow, and densely packed. Space was tight here because such little land was available between the natural fortifications provided by the mountain and the river, and much of what was available was used up by the Church. Famous for its old wrought-iron signs (best viewed from this end), the architecture on the street still looks much as it did in Mozart's day—though its former elegance is now mostly gone, replaced by chain outlets.

As you walk away from the cliffs, look up and enjoy the traditional signs indicating what each shop made or sold: Watch for spirits, bookmakers, a horn (indicating a place for the postal coach), brewery (the star for the name of the beer, Sternbräu—"Star Brew"), glazier (window-maker), locksmith, hamburgers, pastries, tailor, baker (the pretzel), pharmacy, and a hatter.

On the right at #39, **Sporer** serves up homemade spirits (€1.40 per shot, open 9:30-19:00). This has been a family-run show for a century—fun-loving, proud, and English-speaking. *Nuss* is nut,

Marille is apricot (typical of this region), the *Kletzen* cocktail is like a super-thick Baileys with pear, and *Edle Brande* are the stronger schnapps. The many homemade firewaters are in jugs at the end of the bar.

Continue down Getreidegasse, noticing the old doorbells—one per floor. At #40, **Eisgrotte** serves good ice cream. Across from Eisgrotte, a tunnel leads to the recommended **Balkan Grill** (signed as *Bosna Grill*), the local choice for the very best wurst in town. At #28, Herr Wieber, the iron- and locksmith, welcomes the curious. Farther along, you'll pass McDonald's (required to keep its arches Baroque and low-key).

The knot of excited tourists and salesmen hawking goofy gimmicks marks the home of Salzburg's most famous resident. **Mozart's Birthplace** (*Geburtshaus*, ⑫ on map)—the house where Mozart was born, and where he composed many of his early works—is worth a visit for his true fans (described on page 130). But for most, his Residence, across the river, is more interesting (described on page 135).

At #3, dip into the passage and walk under a whalebone, likely once used to advertise the wares of an exotic import shop. Look up at the arcaded interior. On the right, at the venerable **Schatz Konditorei,** you can enjoy coffee under the vaults with your choice of top-end cakes and pastries (Mon-Fri 8:30-18:30, Sat 8:30-17:00, closed Sun).

Leaving the pastry shop, go straight ahead through the passage to Sigmund-Haffner-Gasse. Before heading right, look left to see the tower of the old City Hall at the end. The blue-and-white ball halfway up is an 18th-century moon clock. It still tells the phase of the moon.

• *Go right, then take your first left to....*

⑬ Alter Markt

Here in Salzburg's old marketplace, you'll find a sausage stand, the recommended **Café Tomaselli,** a fun **candy shop** at #7, and, next door, the beautifully old-fashioned **Alte F. E. Hofapotheke** pharmacy—duck in discreetly to peek at the Baroque shelves and containers (be polite—the people in line are here for medicine, no photography).

• *Our walk is finished. From here, you can circle back to some of the old-town sights (such as those in the Neue Residenz, described next); head up to the Hohensalzburg Fortress on the cliffs over the old town (see page 130); or continue to some of the sights across the river. To reach those sights, head for the river, jog left (past the fast-food fish restaurant and free WCs), climb to the top of the Makartsteg pedestrian bridge, and turn to page 133.*

Sights in Salzburg

In the Old Town

In the Neue (New) Residenz

▲▲**Salzburg Museum**—In 2007, Salzburg finally got the classy history museum it deserves. This two-floor exhibit is the best in town for history—the included audioguide wonderfully describes the great artifacts in the lavish prince-archbishop's residence.

The Salzburg Personalities exhibit fills the first floor with a charming look at Salzburg's greatest historic characters—mostly artists, scientists, musicians, and writers who would otherwise be forgotten. And upstairs is the real reason to come: lavish ceremonial rooms filled with an exhibit called The Salzburg Myth, which traces the city's proud history, art, and culture since early modern times. The focus is on its quirky absolutist prince-archbishop and its long-standing reputation as a fairy-tale "Alpine Arcadia." The *Kunsthalle* in the basement shows off special exhibits.

From the Salzburg Museum, the Panorama Passage (clearly marked from the entry) leads underground to the Salzburg Panorama (described next). This passage is lined with archaeological finds (Roman and early medieval), helping you trace the development of Salzburg from its Roman roots until today.

Cost and Hours: €7, €8 combo-ticket with Salzburg Panorama, both tickets about €2 cheaper on Sun, includes audioguide, Tue-Sun 9:00-17:00, Thu until 20:00, closed Mon except July-Aug and Dec (when it's open Mon 9:00-17:00), tel. 0662/620-808-700, www.smca.at.

▲**Salzburg Panorama 1829**—In the early 19th century, before the advent of photography, 360-degree "panorama" paintings of great cities or events were popular. These creations were even taken on extended road trips. When this one was created, the 1815 Treaty of Vienna had just divvied up post-Napoleonic Europe, and Salzburg had become part of the Habsburg realm. This photo-realistic painting served as a town portrait done at the emperor's request. The circular view, painted by Johann Michael Sattler, shows the city as seen from the top of its castle. When complete, it spent 10 years touring the great cities of Europe, showing off Salzburg's breathtaking setting.

Today, the exquisitely restored painting offers a fascinating look at the city in 1829. The river was slower and had beaches. The old town looks essentially as it does today, and Moosstrasse still leads into idyllic farm country. Paintings from that era of other great cities around the world are hung around the outside wall with numbers but without labels, as a kind of quiz game. A flier gives the cities' names on one side, and keys them to the numbers. See how many 19th-century cities you can identify.

Cost and Hours: €2, €8 combo-ticket with Salzburg Museum, combo-ticket is about €2 cheaper on Sun, open daily 9:00-17:00, Thu until 20:00, Residenzplatz 9.

▲Mozart's Birthplace (Geburtshaus)

Mozart was born here in 1756. It was in this building that he composed most of his boy-genius works. Today it's the most popular Mozart sight in town—for fans, it's almost a pilgrimage. American artist Robert Wilson was hired to spiff up the exhibit, to make it feel more conceptual and less like a museum. Even so, I was unimpressed. If you're tackling just one Mozart sight, skip this one. Instead, walk 10 minutes from here to Mozart's Residence (described on page 135), which provides a more informative visit. But if you want to max out on Mozart, a visit here is worthwhile.

Shuffling through with all the crowds, you'll peruse three floors of rooms with old-school exhibits displaying paintings, letters, personal items, and lots of facsimiles, all attempting to bring life to the Mozart story (and all explained in English). A period living room shows what Wolfgang's world likely looked like, and portraits introduce you to the family. A particular highlight is an old clavichord he supposedly composed on. (A predecessor of the more complicated piano, the clavichord's keys hit the strings with a simple teeter-totter motion that allowed you to play very softly—ideal for composers living in tight apartment quarters.) At the end, there's a room of dioramas dedicated to Mozart's operas.

Cost and Hours: €7, or €12 for combo-ticket that includes Mozart's Residence, daily 9:00-17:30, July-Aug until 20:00, last entry 30 minutes before closing, only the shop has air-con, Getreidegasse 9, tel. 0662/844-313.

Atop the Cliffs Above the Old Town

The main "sight" above town is the Hohensalzburg Fortress. But if you just want to enjoy the sweeping views over Salzburg, you have a couple of cheaper options: Head up to the castle grounds on foot, or take the elevator up the cliffs of Mönchsberg (explained in "Getting Around Salzburg" on page 117).

▲▲Hohensalzburg Fortress (Festung)

Built on a rock (called Festungsberg) 400 feet above the Salzach River, this fortress was never really used. That's the idea. It was a good investment—so foreboding, nobody attacked the town for 1,000 years. The city was never taken by force, but when Napoleon stopped by, Salzburg wisely surrendered. After a stint as a military barracks, the fortress was opened to the public in the 1860s by Habsburg Emperor Franz Josef. Today, it remains one of Europe's mightiest castles, dominating Salzburg's skyline and offering incredible views.

Cost: Your daytime funicular ticket includes admission to the fortress grounds and all the museums inside—whether you want to see them or not (€10.50, €24.50 family ticket). Save €3 by walking up—the climb is much easier than it looks, and the views are fantastic.

Hours: The complex is open daily year-round (May-Sept 9:00-19:00, Oct-April 9:30-17:00, last entry 30 minutes before closing, tel. 0662/8424-3011). On nights when there's a concert, and nightly in July and August, the castle grounds are free and open after the museum closes until 22:00.

Concerts: The fortress also serves as a venue for evening concerts (Festungskonzerte). For details, see "Music in Salzburg," later.

Café: The café between the funicular station and the castle entry is a great place to nibble on apple strudel while taking in the jaw-dropping view.

Orientation: The fortress visit has three parts: a relatively dull courtyard with some fine views from its various ramparts; the fortress itself (with a required and escorted 45-minute audio tour); and the palace museum (by far the best exhibit of the lot). At the bottom of the funicular, you'll pass through an interesting little exhibit on the town's canal system (free, described on page 133).

❍ Self-Guided Tour: From the top of the funicular, head to your right and down the stairs to bask in the view, either from the café or the view terrace a little farther along. Once you're done snapping photos, walk through to the castle grounds and go left, following the path up and around to reach the inner courtyard (labeled *Inneres Schloß*). Immediately inside, circling to the right (clockwise), you'll encounter cannons (still poised to defend Salzburg against an Ottoman invasion), a marionette exhibit, the palace museum, the Kuenburg Bastion, scant ruins of a Romanesque church, the courtyard (with path down for those walking), toilets, shops, a restaurant, and the fortress tour.

• *Begin at the...*

Marionette Exhibit: Several fun rooms show off this local tradition, with three videos playing continuously: two with peeks at Salzburg's ever-enchanting Marionette Theater performances of Mozart classics (described under "Music in Salzburg," later), and one with a behind-the-scenes look at the action. Give the hands-on marionette a whirl.

• *Hiking through the former palace, you'll find the sight's best exhibits at the...*

Palace Museum (Festungsmuseum Carolino Augusteum): The second floor has exhibits on castle life, from music to torture. The top floor shows off fancy royal apartments, a sneak preview of the room used for the nightly fortress concerts, and the Rainer Regiments Museum, dedicated to the Salzburg regiments that fought in both World Wars.

Castle Courtyard: The courtyard was the main square of the castle's medieval residents, a community of 1,000—which could be self-sufficient when necessary. The square was ringed by the shops of craftsmen, blacksmiths, bakers, and so on. The well dipped into a rain-fed cistern. The church is dedicated to St. George, the protector of horses (logical for an army church) and decorated by fine red marble reliefs (c. 1502). Behind the church is the top of the old lift that helped supply the fortress. (From near here, steps lead back into the city, or to the mountaintop "Mönchsberg Walk," described later.) You'll also see the remains of a Romanesque chapel, which are well-described.

• *Near the chapel, turn left into the Kuenburg Bastion (once a garden) for fine city and castle views.*

Kuenburg Bastion: Notice how the castle has three parts: the original castle inside the courtyard, the vast whitewashed walls (built when the castle was a residence), and the lower, beefed-up fortifications (added for extra defense against the expected Ottoman invasion). Survey Salzburg from here and think about fortifying an important city by using nature. Mönchsberg (the cliffs to the left) and Festungsberg (the little mountain you're on) naturally cradle the old town, with just a small gate between the ridge and the river needed to bottle up the place. The new town across the river needed a bit of a wall arcing from the river to its hill. Back then, only one bridge crossed the Salzach into town, and it had a fortified gate.

• *Back inside the castle courtyard, continue your circle. The Round Tower (1497) helps you visualize the inner original castle.*

Fortress Interior: Tourists are allowed in this part of the fortified palace only with an escort. (They say that's for security, though while touring it, you wonder what they're protecting.) A crowd assembles at the turnstile, and every quarter-hour 40 people are issued their audioguides and let in for the escorted walk. You'll go one room at a time, listening to a 45-minute commentary. While the interior furnishings are mostly gone—taken by Napoleon—the rooms survived as well as they did because no one wanted to live here after 1500, so the building was never modernized. Your tour includes a room dedicated to the art of "excruciating questioning" ("softening up" prisoners, in American military jargon)—filled with tools of that gruesome trade. The highlight is the commanding city view from the top of a tower.

• *After seeing the fortress, consider hiking down to the old town, or along the top of Mönchsberg (see "Mönchsberg Walk," below). If you take the funicular down, don't miss (at the bottom of the lift) the...*

Alm River Canal Exhibit: At the base of the funicular, below the castle, is this fine little exhibit on how the river was broken into five smaller streams—powering the city until steam took up the energy-supply baton. Pretend it's the year 1200 and follow (by video) the flow of the water from the river through the canals, into the mills, and as it's finally dumped into the Salzach River. (The exhibit technically requires a funicular ticket—but you can see it by slipping through the exit at the back of the amber shop, just uphill from the funicular terminal.)

Mönchsberg Sights

▲**Mönchsberg Walk**—For a great 30-minute hike, exit the fortress by taking the steep lane down from the castle courtyard. At the first intersection, right leads into the old town, and left leads across the Mönchsberg. The lane leads 20 minutes through the woods high above the city (stick to the high lanes, or you'll end up back in town), taking you to the recommended Gasthaus Stadtalm café (light meals, cheap beds). From the Stadtalm, pass under the medieval wall and walk left along the wall to a tableau showing how it once looked. Take the switchback to the right and follow the lane downhill to the Museum of Modern Art (described next), where the elevator zips you back into town (€2 one-way, €3 round-trip, daily 8:30-19:00, Wed until 21:00, July-Aug daily until 1:00 in the morning, May-Sept starts running at 8:00). If you stay on the lane past the elevator, you eventually pass the Augustine church that marks the rollicking, recommended Augustiner Bräustübl.

In 1669, a huge Mönchsberg landslide killed more than 200 townspeople. Since then the cliffs have been carefully checked each spring and fall. Even today, you might see crews on the cliff, monitoring its stability.

Museum of Modern Art on Mönchsberg—The modern-art museum on top of Mönchsberg, built in 2004, houses Salzburg's Rupertinum Gallery, plus special exhibitions. While the collection is not worth climbing a mountain for, the M32 restaurant has some of the best views in town (€8, €9.70 including elevator ticket, Tue-Sun 10:00-18:00, Wed until 20:00, closed Mon except during festival; restaurant open Tue-Sat 9:00-24:00, Sun 9:00-18:00, closed Mon except during festival; both at top of Mönchsberg elevator, tel. 0662/842-220, www.museumdermoderne.at).

In the New Town, North of the River

The following sights are across the river from the old town. I've connected them with walking instructions.

• *Begin at the Makartsteg pedestrian bridge, where you can survey the...*

Salzach River

Salzburg's river is called "salt river" not because it's salty, but because of the precious cargo it once carried—the salt mines of Hallein are just nine miles upstream. Salt could be transported from here all the way to the Danube, and on to the Mediterranean via the Black Sea. The riverbanks and roads were built when the river was regulated in the 1850s. Before that, the Salzach was much wider and slower-moving. Houses opposite the old town fronted the river with docks and "garages" for boats. The grand buildings just past the bridge (with their elegant promenades and cafés) were built on reclaimed land in the late 19th century, in the Historicist style of Vienna's Ringstrasse.

Scan the cityscape. Notice all the churches. Salzburg, nick-named the "Rome of the North," has 38 Catholic churches (plus two Protestant churches and a synagogue). Find the five streams gushing into the river. These date from the 13th century, when the river was split into five canals running through the town to power its mills. The Stein Hotel (upstream, just left of next bridge) has a popular roof-terrace café (see page 136). Downstream, notice the Museum of Modern Art atop Mönchsberg, with a view restaurant and a faux castle (actually a water reservoir). The Romanesque bell tower with the green copper dome in the distance is the Augustine church, site of the best beer hall in town (the recommended Augustiner Bräustübl).

• *Cross the bridge, pass the recommended Café Bazar (a fine place for a drink), walk two blocks inland, and take a left past the heroic statues into...*

▲Mirabell Gardens and Palace (Schloss)

The bubbly gardens laid out in 1730 for the prince-archbishop have been open to the public since 1850 (thanks to Emperor Franz Josef, who was rattled by the popular revolutions of 1848). The gardens are free and open until dusk. The palace is open only as a concert venue (explained later). The statues and the arbor (far left) were featured in *The Sound of Music*. Walk through the gardens to the palace. Look back, enjoy the garden/cathedral/castle view, and imagine how the prince-archbishop must have reveled in a vista that reminded him of all his secular and religious power. Then go around to the river side of the palace and find the horse.

The rearing **Pegasus statue** (rare and very well-balanced) is the site of a famous *Sound of Music* scene where the kids all danced before lining up on the stairs (with Maria 30 yards farther along). The steps lead to a small mound in the park (made of rubble from a former theater, and today a rendezvous point for Salzburg's gay community).

Nearest the horse, stairs lead between two lions to a pair of tough dwarfs (early volleyball players with spiked mittens) welcoming you to Salzburg's **Dwarf Park.** Cross the elevated walk (noticing the city's fortified walls) to meet statues of a dozen dwarfs who served the prince-archbishop—modeled after real people with real fashions in about 1600. This was Mannerist art, from the hyper-realistic age that followed the Renaissance.

There's plenty of **music** here, both in the park and in the palace. A brass band plays free park concerts (May-Aug Sun at 10:30 and Wed with lighted fountains at 20:30, unless it's raining). To properly enjoy the lavish Mirabell Palace—once the prince-archbishop's summer palace, and now the seat of the mayor—get a ticket to a Schlosskonzerte (my favorite venue for a classical concert—see page 139).

• *To visit Salzburg's best Mozart sight, go a long block southeast to Makartplatz, where, opposite the big and bright Hotel Bristol, you'll find...*

▲▲Mozart's Residence (Wohnhaus)

This reconstruction of Mozart's second home (his family moved here when he was 17) is the most informative Mozart sight in town. The English-language audioguide (included with admission, 1.5 hours) provides fascinating insight into Mozart's life and music, with the usual scores, old pianos, and an interesting 30-minute film (#17 on your audioguide for soundtrack) that runs continuously.

In the main hall—used by the Mozarts to entertain Salzburg's high society—you can hear original instruments from Mozart's time. Mozart was proud to be the first in his family to compose a duet. Notice the family portrait (circa 1780) on the wall, showing Mozart with his sister Nannerl, their father, and their mother—who'd died two years earlier in Paris. Mozart also had silly crude bull's-eyes made for the pop-gun game popular at the time (licking an "arse," Wolfgang showed his disdain for the rigors of high society). Later rooms feature real artifacts that explore his loves, his intellectual pursuits, his travels, and more.

Cost and Hours: €7, or €12 combo-ticket that includes Mozart's Birthplace in the old town, daily 9:00-17:30, July-Aug until 20:00, last entry 30 minutes before closing, allow at least one hour for visit, Makartplatz 8, tel. 0662/8742-2740.

• *From here, you can walk a few blocks back to the main bridge (Staatsbrücke), where you'll find the Platzl, a square once used as a hay market. Pause to enjoy the kid-pleasing little fountain. Near the fountain (with your back to the river), Steingasse leads darkly to the right.*

▲Steingasse Stroll

This street, a block in from the river, was part of the only road in the Middle Ages going south over the Alps to Venice (this was the

SALZBURG

first stop north of the Alps). Today, it's wonderfully tranquil and free of Salzburg's touristy crush. Inviting cocktail bars along here come alive at night (see "Steingasse Pub Crawl" on page 155).

At #9, a plaque (of questionable veracity) shows where Joseph Mohr, who wrote the words to "Silent Night," was born—poor and illegitimate—in 1792. There is no doubt, however, that the popular Christmas carol was composed and first sung in the village of Oberndorf, just outside of Salzburg, in 1818. Stairs lead from near here up to a 17th-century Capuchin monastery.

On the next corner, the wall is gouged out. This scar was left even after the building was restored, to serve as a reminder of the American GI who tried to get a tank down this road during a visit to the town brothel—two blocks farther up Steingasse.

At #19, find the carvings on the old door. Some say these are notices from beggars to the begging community (more numerous after post-Reformation religious wars, which forced many people out of their homes and towns)—a kind of "hobo code" indicating whether the residents would give or not. Trace the wires of the old-fashioned doorbells to the highest floors.

Farther on, you'll find a commanding Salzburg view across the river. Notice the red dome marking the oldest nunnery in the German-speaking world (established in 712) under the fortress and to the left. The real Maria, who inspired *The Sound of Music*, taught in this nunnery's school. In 1927, she and Captain von Trapp were married in the church you see here (not the church filmed in the movie). He was 47. She was 22. Hmmmm.

From here look back, above the arch you just passed through, at part of the town's medieval fortification. The coat of arms on the arch is of the prince-archbishop who paid Bavaria a huge ransom to stay out of the Thirty Years' War (smart move). He then built this fortification (in 1634) in anticipation of rampaging armies from both sides.

Today, this street is for making love, not war. The Maison de Plaisir (a few doors down, at #24) has for centuries been a Salzburg brothel. But the climax of this walk is more touristic.

• *For a grand view, head back to the Platzl and the bridge, enter the Stein Hotel (left corner, overlooking the river), and ride the elevator to...*

Stein Terrasse

This café offers perhaps the best views in town (aside from the castle). Hidden from the tourist crush, it's a trendy, professional, local scene. You can discreetly peek at the view, or enjoy a drink or light meal (small snacks, indoor/outdoor seating, Sun-Thu 9:00-24:00, Fri-Sat 9:00-1:00 in the morning).

• *Back at the Platzl and the bridge, you can head straight up Linzergasse (away from the river) into a neighborhood packed with recommended accommodations, as well as our final new-town sight, the...*

▲St. Sebastian Cemetery

Wander through this quiet oasis (free, daily April-Oct 9:00-18:30, Nov-March 9:00-16:00, entry at Linzergasse 43 in summer; in winter go around the corner to the right, through the arch at #37, and around the building to the doorway under the blue seal). Mozart is buried in Vienna, his mom's in Paris, and his sister is in Salzburg's old town (St. Peter's)—but Wolfgang's wife Constanze ("Constantia") and his father Leopold are buried here (from the black iron gate entrance on Linzergasse, walk 17 paces and look left). When Prince-Archbishop Wolf Dietrich had the cemetery moved from around the cathedral and put here, across the river, people didn't like it. To help popularize it, he had his own mausoleum built as its centerpiece. Continue straight past the Mozart tomb to this circular building (English description at door).

Near Salzburg

▲Hellbrunn Castle—About the year 1610, Prince-Archbishop Sittikus (after meditating on stewardship and Christ-like values) decided he needed a lavish palace with a vast and ornate garden purely for pleasure. He built this and just loved inviting his VIP guests out for fun with his trick fountains. Today, the visit is worthwhile for the Baroque garden, one of the oldest in Europe. More notably, it's full of clever fountains...and tour guides getting sadistic joy from soaking tourists. (Hint: When you see a wet place, cover your camera.) After buying your ticket, you must wait for the English tour and laugh and scramble through the entertaining 40-minute trick-water-toy tour, and are then free to tour the forgettable palace with an included audioguide.

While it can be fun—especially on a hot day or with kids—for many, it's a lot of trouble for a few water tricks. *Sound of Music* fans not taking an *S.O.M.* tour, however, may want to visit just to see the "Sixteen Going on Seventeen" gazebo, now located in the gardens.

Cost and Hours: €9.50, daily May-Sept 9:00-17:30, July-Aug until 21:00—but tours from 18:00 on don't include the castle, mid-March-April and Oct 9:00-16:30, these are last tour times, closed Nov-mid-March, tel. 0662/820-3720, www.hellbrunn.at.

Getting There: Hellbrunn is nearly four miles south of Salzburg (bus #25 from station or from Staatsbrücke bridge, 2-3/hour, 20 minutes). In good weather, it makes a pleasant 30-minute bike excursion along the riverbank from Salzburg (described next).

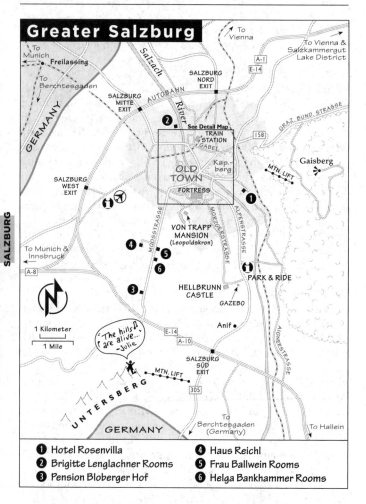

Greater Salzburg

① Hotel Rosenvilla
② Brigitte Lenglachner Rooms
③ Pension Bloberger Hof
④ Haus Reichl
⑤ Frau Ballwein Rooms
⑥ Helga Bankhammer Rooms

▲▲**Riverside or Meadow Bike Ride**—The Salzach River has smooth, flat, and scenic bike lanes along each side (thanks to medieval tow paths—cargo boats would float downstream and be dragged back up by horses). On a sunny day, I can think of no more shout-worthy escape from the city. The nearly four-mile path upstream to Hellbrunn Castle is easy, with a worthy destination (leave Salzburg on castle side). Perhaps the most pristine, meadow-filled farm-country route is the four-mile Hellbrunner Allee from Akademiestrasse. Even a quickie ride across town is a great Salzburg experience. In the evening, the riverbanks are a world of floodlit spires.

Music in Salzburg

▲▲Salzburg Festival (Salzburger Festspiele)

Each summer, from late July to the end of August, Salzburg hosts its famous Salzburg Festival, founded in 1920 to employ Vienna's musicians in the summer. This fun and festive time is crowded, but there are usually plenty of beds (except for a few August weekends). Events take place primarily in three big halls: the Opera and Orchestra venues in the Festival House, and the Landes Theater, where German-language plays are performed. Tickets for the big festival events are generally expensive (€50-600) and sell out well in advance (bookable from January). Most tourists think they're "going to the Salzburg Festival" by seeing smaller non-festival events that go on during the festival weeks. For these lesser events, same-day tickets are normally available (the ticket office on Mozartplatz, in the TI, prints a daily list of concerts and charges a 30 percent fee to book them). For specifics on this year's festival schedule and tickets, visit www.salzburgfestival.at, or contact the Austrian National Tourist Office in the United States (tel. 212/944-6880, fax 212/730-4568, www.austria.info, travel @austria.info).

▲▲Musical Events Year-Round

Salzburg is busy throughout the year, with 2,000 classical performances in its palaces and churches annually. Pick up the events calendar at the TI (free, bimonthly). I've never planned in advance, and I've enjoyed great concerts with every visit. Whenever you visit, you'll have a number of concerts (generally small chamber groups) to choose from. Here are some of the more accessible events:

Concerts at Hohensalzburg Fortress (Festungskonzerte)—Nearly nightly concerts—Mozart's greatest hits for beginners—are held atop Festungsberg, in the "prince's chamber" of the fortress, featuring small chamber groups (open seating after the first six more expensive rows, €31 or €38 plus €3.60 for the funicular; at 19:30, 20:00, or 20:30; doors open 30 minutes early, tel. 0662/825-858 to reserve, pick up tickets at the door). The medieval-feeling chamber has windows overlooking the city, and the concert gives you a chance to enjoy the grand city view and a stroll through the castle courtyard. (The funicular ticket costs €3.60 within an hour of the show—ideal for people who just want to ascend for the view.) For €51, you can combine the concert with a four-course dinner (starts 2 hours before concert).

Concerts at the Mirabell Palace (Schlosskonzerte)—The nearly nightly chamber music concerts at the Mirabell Palace are performed in a lavish Baroque setting. They come with more sophisticated programs and better musicians than the fortress concerts. Baroque music flying around a Baroque hall is a happy bird in the right cage (open seating after the first five pricier rows, €29, usually at 20:00—but check flier for times, doors open one hour ahead, tel. 0662/848-586, www.salzburger-schlosskonzerte.at).

"Five O'Clock Concerts" (5-Uhr-Konzerte)—These concerts—next to St. Peter's in the old town—are cheaper, since they feature young artists (€12, July-Sept Thu-Tue at 17:00, no concerts Wed or Oct-June, 45-60 minutes, tel. 0662/8445-7619, www.5-uhr -konzerte.com). While the series is formally named after the brother of Joseph Haydn, it offers music from various masters.

Mozart Piano Sonatas—St. Peter's Abbey hosts these concerts each weekend (€18, €9 for children, €45 for a family of four, Fri and Sat at 19:00 year-round, in the abbey's Romanesque Hall—a.k.a. Romanischer Saal, tel. 0664/423-5645). This short (45-minute) and inexpensive concert is ideal for families.

Marionette Theater—Salzburg's much-loved marionette theater offers operas with spellbinding marionettes and recorded music. Adults and kids alike are mesmerized by the little people on stage (€18-35, nearly nightly at 17:00 or 19:30 June-Sept except Sun, also 3-4/week in May, some 14:00 matinees, box office open Mon-Sat 9:00-13:00 and 2 hours before shows, near the Mirabell Gardens and Mozart's Residence at Schwarzstrasse 24, tel. 0662/872-406, www.marionetten.at). For a sneak preview, check out the videos playing at the marionette exhibit up in the fortress.

Mozart Dinner Concert—For those who'd like some classical music but would rather not sit through a concert, Stiftskeller St. Peter (see page 152) offers a traditional candlelit meal with Mozart's greatest hits performed by a string quartet and singers in historic costumes gavotting among the tables. In this elegant Baroque setting, tourists clap between movements and get three courses of food (from Mozart-era recipes) mixed with three 20-minute courses of crowd-pleasing music (€51, Mozart-lovers with this guidebook get a discount when booking direct, almost nightly at 20:00, dress is "smart casual," call to reserve at 0662/828-695, www.mozartdinnerconcert.com).

Sound of Salzburg Dinner Show—The show at the recommended Sternbräu Inn is Broadway in a dirndl with tired food. But it's a fun show, and *Sound of Music* fans leave with hands red from clapping. A piano player and a hardworking quartet of singers wearing historical costumes perform an entertaining mix of *S.O.M.* hits and traditional folk songs (€46 for dinner, begins at 19:30). You can also come by at 20:30, pay €32, skip the dinner, and get the show and a drink. Those who book direct (not through a hotel) and pay cash get a discount with this book (nightly mid-

May-mid-Oct, Griesgasse 23, tel. 0662/826-617, www.soundof
salzburgshow.com).

Music at Mass—Each Sunday morning, three great churches offer
a Mass, generally with glorious music. The Salzburg Cathedral
is likely your best bet for fine music to worship by (10:00). The
Franciscan church—the locals' choice—is enthusiastic about its
musical Masses (at 9:00). St. Peter's Church also has music (10:30).
See the Salzburg events guide for details.

Free Brass Band Concert—A traditional brass band plays in the
Mirabell Gardens (May-Aug Sun at 10:30 and Wed at 20:30).

Sleeping in Salzburg

Finding a room in Salzburg, even during its music festival (mid-
July-Aug), is usually easy. Rates rise significantly (20-30 percent)
during the music festival, and sometimes around Easter and
Christmas; these higher prices do not appear in the ranges I've
listed. Many places charge 10 percent extra for a one-night stay.

In the New Town, North of the River

These listings, clustering around Linzergasse, are in a pleasant
neighborhood (with easy parking) a 15-minute walk from the
train station (for directions, see "Arrival in Salzburg," earlier) and
a 10-minute walk to the old town. If you're coming from the old
town, simply cross the main bridge (Staatsbrücke) to the mostly
traffic-free Linzergasse. If driving, exit the highway at Salzburg-
Nord, follow Vogelweiderstrasse straight to its end, and turn right.

Sleep Code

(€1 = about $1.40, country code: 43, area code: 0662)
S = Single, **D** = Double/Twin, **T** = Triple, **Q** = Quad, **b** = bathroom,
s = shower only. Unless otherwise noted, credit cards are
accepted and breakfast is included. All of these places speak
English.

To help you sort easily through these listings, I've divided
the rooms into three categories, based on the price for a
standard double room with bath:

$$$ **Higher Priced**—Most rooms €90 or more.
$$ **Moderately Priced**—Most rooms between €60-90.
$ **Lower Priced**—Most rooms €60 or less.

Prices can change without notice; verify the hotel's
current rates online or by email. For other updates, see www
.ricksteves.com/update.

Salzburg Hotels

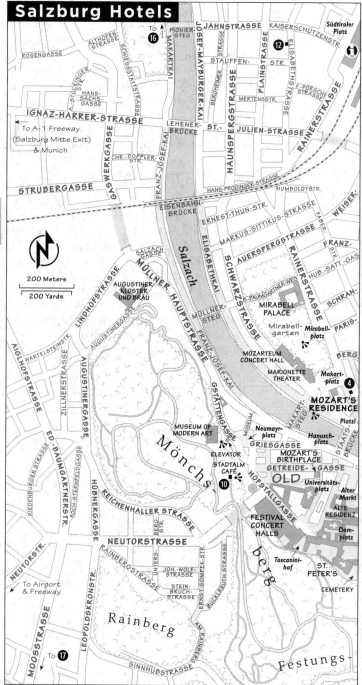

SALZBURG

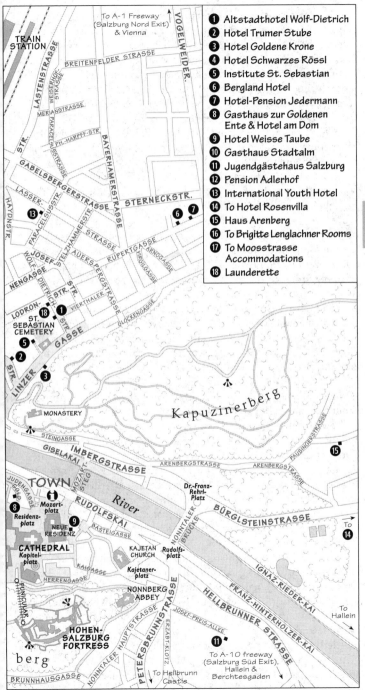

1. Altstadthotel Wolf-Dietrich
2. Hotel Trumer Stube
3. Hotel Goldene Krone
4. Hotel Schwarzes Rössl
5. Institute St. Sebastian
6. Bergland Hotel
7. Hotel-Pension Jedermann
8. Gasthaus zur Goldenen Ente & Hotel am Dom
9. Hotel Weisse Taube
10. Gasthaus Stadtalm
11. Jugendgästehaus Salzburg
12. Pension Adlerhof
13. International Youth Hotel
14. To Hotel Rosenvilla
15. Haus Arenberg
16. To Brigitte Lenglachner Rooms
17. To Moosstrasse Accommodations
18. Launderette

SALZBURG

$$$ Altstadthotel Wolf-Dietrich, around the corner from Linzergasse on pedestrians-only Wolf-Dietrich-Strasse, is well-located (half its rooms overlook St. Sebastian Cemetery). With 27 tastefully plush rooms, it's a good value for a big, stylish hotel (Sb-€80, Db-€120, price depends on size, family deals, €20-40 more during festival, readers of this book get a discount on prevailing price, elevator, Wi-Fi, pool with loaner swimsuits, sauna, free DVD library, Wolf-Dietrich-Strasse 7, tel. 0662/871-275, fax 0662/871-2759, www.salzburg-hotel.at, office@salzburg-hotel.at). Their annex across the street has 14 equally comfortable rooms (but no elevator, and therefore €20 less).

$$$ Hotel Trumer Stube, three blocks from the river just off Linzergasse, has 20 clean, cozy rooms and is warmly run by the Hirschbichler family (official rates: Sb-€65, Db-€105, Tb-€128, Qb-€147—but you can save big by emailing and asking for the best Rick Steves cash-only rate; big made-to-order breakfast, non-smoking, elevator, free Wi-Fi, easy parking, Bergstrasse 6, tel. 0662/874-776, fax 0662/874-326, www.trumer-stube.at, info @trumer-stube.at; the mom and daughter, both named Marianne, may charm you into extending your Salzburg stay).

$$$ Hotel Goldene Krone, about five blocks from the river, is plain and basic, with 20 big, quiet, creaky, and well-kept rooms. Stay a while in their pleasant cliffside garden (Sb-€69, Db-€119, Tb-€159, Qb-€189, ask for discount with this book, dim lights, elevator, Wi-Fi, parking-€12/day, Linzergasse 48, tel. 0662/872-300, fax 0662/8723-0066, www.hotel-goldenekrone.com, office @hotel-goldenekrone.com, Günther Hausknost). Ask Günther about his tours (€10/person, 2 hours, 5 people minimum).

$$ Hotel Schwarzes Rössl is a university dorm that becomes a student-run hotel each July, August, and September. The location couldn't be handier. It looks like a normal hotel from the outside, and its 50 rooms, while a bit spartan, are as comfortable as a hotel on the inside (S-€44, Sb-€54, D-€74, Db-€88, Tb-€120, good breakfast, Internet access and Wi-Fi, no rooms rented Oct-June, just off Linzergasse at Priesterhausgasse 6, tel. 0662/874-426, www.academia-hotels.at/en/salzburg.php, schwarzes.roessl @academiahotels.at).

$$ Institute St. Sebastian is in a somewhat sterile but very clean historic building next to St. Sebastian Cemetery. From October through June, the institute houses female students from various Salzburg colleges, and also rents 40 beds for travelers (men and women). From July through September, the students are gone and they rent all 100 beds (including 20 twin rooms) to travelers. The building has spacious public areas, a roof garden, a piano that guests are welcome to play, and some of the best rooms and dorm beds in town for the money. The immaculate doubles come with modern baths and head-to-toe twin beds (S-€36, Sb-€44, D-€56, Db-€70, Tb-€84, Qb-€98, includes simple breakfast, elevator, self-service laundry-€4/load; reception open daily July-Sept 7:30-12:00 & 13:00-21:30, Oct-June 8:00-12:00 & 16:00-21:00; Linzergasse 41, enter through arch at #37, tel. 0662/871-386, fax 0662/8713-8685, www.st-sebastian-salzburg .at, office@st-sebastian-salzburg.at). Students like the €22 bunks in 4- to 10-bed dorms (€2 less if you have sheets, no lockout time, free lockers, free showers). You'll find self-service kitchens on each floor (fridge space is free; request a key). If you need parking, request it well in advance.

Pensions on Rupertgasse: These two hotels are about five blocks farther from the river on Rupertgasse, a breeze for drivers but with more street noise than the places on Linzergasse. They're both modern and well-run—good values if you don't mind being a bit away from the old town. **$$$ Bergland Hotel** is charming and classy, with comfortable neo-rustic rooms. It's a modern building, and therefore spacious and solid (Sb-€65, Db-€100, Tb-€125, Qb-€155, elevator, Wi-Fi, Internet access, English library, bike rental-€6/day, Rupertgasse 15, tel. 0662/872-318, fax 0662/872-3188, www.berglandhotel.at, office@berglandhotel.at, Kuhn family). The similar, boutique-like **$$$ Hotel-Pension Jedermann,** a few doors down, is tastefully done and comfortable, with an artsy painted-concrete ambience and a backyard garden (Sb-€65, Db-€95, Tb-€120, Qb-€160, much more during festival, elevator, Internet access, Rupertgasse 25, tel. 0662/873-2410, fax 0662/873-2419, www.hotel-jedermann.com, office@hotel-jedermann.com, Herr und Frau Gmachl).

In or Above the Old Town

Most of these hotels are near Residenzplatz. While this area is car-restricted, you're allowed to drive your car in to unload, pick up a map and parking instructions, and head for the €14-per-day garage in the mountain.

$$$ Gasthaus zur Goldenen Ente is in a 600-year-old building with medieval stone arches and narrow stairs. Located above a good restaurant, it's as central as you can be on a pedestrian street in old Salzburg. The 22 rooms are modern and newly renovated, and include classy amenities. While this hotel's advertised rates are too high, travelers with this book get a discount (except in July-Aug), and prices may dip lower according to demand. Ulrike, Franziska, and Anita run a tight ship for the absentee owners (most of the year: Sb-€85, Db-€125; late July-Aug and Dec: Sb-€95, Db-€160; extra person-€30, firm mattresses, elevator, free Internet access, Goldgasse 10, tel. 0662/845-622, fax 0662/845-6229, www.ente.at, hotel@ente.at).

$$$ Hotel Weisse Taube has 30 comfortable rooms in a quiet dark-wood 14th-century building, well-located about a block off Mozartplatz (Sb-€67-85, Db with shower-€98-138, bigger Db with bath-€119-162, discount with this book if you reserve direct and pay cash, elevator, Internet access, tel. 0662/842-404, fax 0662/841-783, Kaigasse 9, www.weissetaube.at, hotel@weisse taube.at).

$$$ Hotel am Dom is perfectly located—on Goldgasse a few steps from the cathedral—and offers 15 chic rooms, some with their original wood-beam ceilings (twin Db-€90-180, standard Db-€140-260, "superior" Db-€150-290, air-con, non-smoking, Wi-Fi, Goldgasse 17, tel. 0662/842-765, fax 0662/8427-6555, www .hotelamdom.at, office@hotelamdom.at).

Hostels

$ Gasthaus Stadtalm (a.k.a. the *Naturfreundehaus*) is a local version of a mountaineer's hut and a great budget alternative. Snuggled in a forest on the remains of a 15th-century castle wall atop the little mountain overlooking Salzburg, it has magnificent town and mountain views. While the 22 beds are designed-for-backpackers basic, the price and view are the best in town—with the right attitude, it's a fine experience (€18.50/person in 4- and 6-bed dorms, same price for room with double bed; includes breakfast, sheets, and shower; lockers, 2 minutes from top of €2 Mönchsberg elevator, Mönchsberg 19C, tel. & fax 0662/841-729, www.diestadtalm .com, info@diestadtalm.com, Peter). Once you've dropped your bags here, it's a five-minute walk down the cliffside stairs into Toscanini Hof, in the middle of the old town (path always lit).

$ Jugendgästehaus Salzburg, just steps from the old town center, is nevertheless removed from the bustle. While its dorm rooms are the standard crammed-with-beds variety—and the hallways will bring back high-school memories—the doubles and family rooms are modern, roomy, and bright, and the public spaces are quite pleasant (bed in 8-person dorm-€23; Db, Tb, and Qb available at much higher prices; includes breakfast and sheets, pay Internet access, free Wi-Fi, *The Sound of Music* plays daily; bike rental-€10/day, €6/half-day; free parking, just around the east side of the castle hill at Josef-Preis-Allee 18; from train station take bus #5 or #25 to the Justizgebäude stop, then head left one block along the bushy wall, cross Petersbrunnstrasse, find shady Josefs-Preis-Allee, and walk a few minutes to the end—the hostel is the big orange/green building on the right; tel. 0662/842-670, fax 0662/841-101, www.jfgh.at/salzburg.php, salzburg@jfgh.at). The hotel at the back of the hostel isn't as cheap, but does offer more standard hotel amenities, such as TVs (Db-€110 depending on season, includes breakfast).

For another hostel (on the other side of the river), consider the International Youth Hostel, listed below.

Near the Train Station

$$ Pension Adlerhof, a plain and decent old pension, is two blocks in front of the train station (left off Kaiserschutzenstrasse), but a 15-minute walk from the sightseeing action. It has a quirky staff, a boring location, and 30 stodgy-but-spacious rooms (Sb-€56, Db-€80, Tb-€115, Qb-€130, price varies a bit with the season and size of room, cash only, elevator, free Wi-Fi, limited free parking, Elisabethstrasse 25, tel. 0662/875-236, fax 0662/873-663, www .gosalzburg.com, adlerhof@pension-adlerhof.at).

$ International Youth Hostel, a.k.a. the "Yo-Ho," is the most lively, handy, and American of Salzburg's hostels. This backpacker haven is a youthful and easygoing place that speaks English first; has cheap meals, 200 beds, lockers, tour discounts, and no curfew; plays *The Sound of Music* free daily at 10:30; runs a lively bar; and welcomes anyone of any age. The noisy atmosphere and lack of a curfew can make it hard to sleep (€18-19 in 4- to 8-bed dorms, €21-22 in dorms with bathrooms, D-€48, Ds-€58, Q-€78, Qs-€90, includes sheets, cheap breakfast, pay Internet access and Wi-Fi, laundry-€4 wash and dry, 6 blocks from station toward Linzergasse and 6 blocks from river at Paracelsusstrasse 9, tel. 0662/879-649, fax 0662/878-810, www.yoho.at, office@yoho.at).

Four-Star Hotels in Residential Neighborhoods away from the Center

If you want plush furnishings, spacious public spaces, generous balconies, gardens, and free parking, consider the following places. These two modern hotels in nondescript residential neighborhoods are a fine value if you don't mind the 15-minute walk from the old town. While not ideal for train travelers, drivers in need of no-stress comfort for a home base should consider these (see map on pages 142-143).

$$$ Hotel Rosenvilla, close to the river, offers 16 rooms with bright furnishings, surrounded by a leafy garden (Sb-€79, Db-€128, bigger Db-€142, Db suite-€188, at least €30 more during festival, free Wi-Fi, Höfelgasse 4, tel. 0662/621-765, fax 0662/625-2308, www.rosenvilla.com, hotel@rosenvilla.com).

$$$ Haus Arenberg, higher up opposite the old town, rents 17 big, breezy rooms—most with generous balconies—in a quiet garden setting (Sb-€79, Db-€125, Tb-€148, Qb-€158, €25 more during music festival, Blumensteinstrasse 8, tel. 0662/640-097, fax 0662/640-0973, www.arenberg-salzburg.at, info@arenberg -salzburg.at, family Leobacher).

Private Rooms

These are generally roomy and comfortable, and come with a good breakfast, easy parking, and tourist information. Off-season, competition softens prices. While they are a bus ride from town, with a €4.20 transit day pass *(Tageskarte)* and the frequent service, this shouldn't keep you away (see map pages 142-143). In fact, most homeowners will happily pick you up at the train station if you simply telephone them and ask. Most will also do laundry for a small fee for those staying at least two nights. I've listed prices for two nights or more—if staying only one night, expect a 10 percent surcharge. Most push tours and concerts to make money on the side. As they are earning a commission, if you go through them, you'll probably lose the discount I've negotiated for my readers who go direct.

Beyond the Train Station

$ Brigitte Lenglachner rents eight basic, well-cared-for rooms in her home in a quiet suburban-feeling neighborhood that's a 25-minute walk, 10-minute bike ride, or easy bus ride away from the center. Frau Lenglachner serves breakfast in the garden (in good weather) and happily provides plenty of local information and advice (S-€25, D-€40, Db-€49, Tb-€68, Qb-€96, 5b-€113; apartment with kitchen-€56 for Db, €95 for Tb, €110 for Qb; apartment requires minimum 3-night stay, easy and free parking, Scheibenweg 8, tel. & fax 0662/438-044, www.bei-brigitte.at, bedandbreakfast4u@yahoo.de). It's a 10-minute walk from the station: Head for the river, cross the pedestrian Pioneer Bridge (Pioniersteg), turn right, and walk along the river to the third street (Scheibenweg). Turn left, and it's halfway down on the right.

On Moosstrasse

The busy street called Moosstrasse, which runs southwest of Mönchsberg (behind the mountain and away from the old town center), is lined with farmhouses offering rooms. To locate these places, see the map on pages 142-143. Handy bus #21 connects Moosstrasse to the center frequently (Mon-Fri 4/hour until 19:00, Sat 4/hour until 17:00, evenings and Sun 2/hour, 20 minutes). To get to these pensions from the train station, take bus #1, #5, #6, or #25 to Makartplatz, where you'll change to #21. If you're coming from the old town, catch bus #21 from Hanuschplatz, just downstream of the Staatsbrücke bridge near the *Tabak* kiosk. Buy a €1.90 *Einzelkarte-Kernzone* ticket (for one trip) or a €4.20 *Tageskarte* (day pass, good for 24 hours) from the streetside machine, and punch it when you board the bus. The bus stop you use for each place is included in the following listings. If you're driving from the center, go through the tunnel, continue straight on Neutorstrasse, and take the fourth left onto Moosstrasse. Drivers exit the autobahn at *Süd* and then head in the direction of *Grodig*. Each place can recommend a favorite Moosstrasse eatery (Reiterhof, at #151, is particularly popular).

$$ Pension Bloberger Hof, while more a hotel than a pension, is comfortable and friendly, with a peaceful, rural location and 20 farmer-plush, good-value rooms. It's the farthest out, but reached by the same bus #21 from the center. Inge and her daughter Sylvia offer a discount to those who have this book, reserve direct, and pay cash (Sb-€50-60, Db-€70, big new Db with balcony-€90, Db suite-€120, extra bed-€20, 10 percent extra for one-night stays, family apartment with kitchen, non-smoking, free Internet access and Wi-Fi, restaurant for guests, free loaner bikes, free station pickup if staying 3 nights, Hammerauer Strasse 4, bus stop: Hammerauer Strasse, tel. 0662/830-227, fax 0662/827-061, www.blobergerhof.at, office@blobergerhof.at).

$$ Haus Reichl, with three good rooms at the end of a long lane, feels the most remote. Franziska offers free loaner bikes for guests (20-minute pedal to the center) and bakes fresh cakes most days (Db-€60-62, Tb-€75-84, Qb-€92-104, cash preferred, doubles and triples have balcony and view, all have tea/coffee in room, non-smoking, between Ballwein and Bankhammer B&Bs, 200 yards down Reiterweg to #52, bus stop: Gsengerweg, tel. & fax 0662/826-248, www.privatzimmer.at/haus-reichl, haus.reichl @telering.at).

$ Frau Ballwein offers four cozy, charming, and fresh rooms in two buildings, some with intoxicating-view balconies (Sb-€35-40, Db-€55-63, Tb-€78, Qb-€80-85, prices depend on season, family deals, cash only, farm-fresh breakfasts amid her hanging teapot collection, non-smoking, small pool, 2 free loaner bikes, free parking, Moosstrasse 69-A, bus stop: Gsengerweg, tel. & fax 0662/824-029, www.haus-ballwein.at, haus.ballwein@gmx.net).

$ Helga Bankhammer rents four nondescript rooms in a farmhouse, with a real dairy farm out back (D-€46, Db-€52, no surcharge for one-night stays, family deals, non-smoking, laundry about €6/load, Moosstrasse 77, bus stop: Marienbad, tel. & fax 0662/830-067, www.privatzimmer.at/helga.bankhammer, bank hammer@aon.at).

Eating in Salzburg

In the Old Town

Salzburg boasts many inexpensive, fun, and atmospheric eateries. Most of these restaurants are centrally located in the old town, famous with visitors but also enjoyed by locals.

Gasthaus zum Wilden Mann is *the* place if the weather's bad

SALZBURG

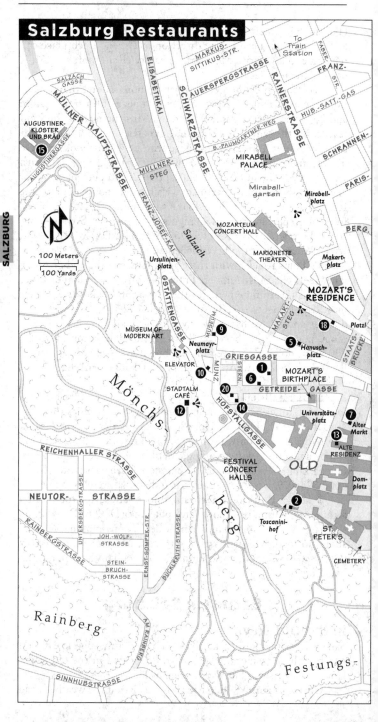

Salzburg Restaurants

SALZBURG

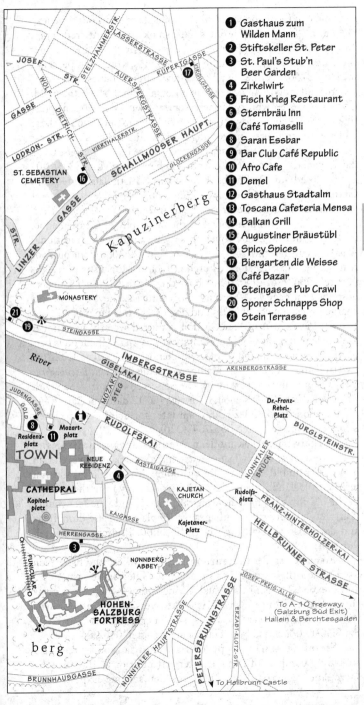

1. Gasthaus zum Wilden Mann
2. Stiftskeller St. Peter
3. St. Paul's Stub'n Beer Garden
4. Zirkelwirt
5. Fisch Krieg Restaurant
6. Sternbräu Inn
7. Café Tomaselli
8. Saran Essbar
9. Bar Club Café Republic
10. Afro Cafe
11. Demel
12. Gasthaus Stadtalm
13. Toscana Cafeteria Mensa
14. Balkan Grill
15. Augustiner Bräustübl
16. Spicy Spices
17. Biergarten die Weisse
18. Café Bazar
19. Steingasse Pub Crawl
20. Sporer Schnapps Shop
21. Stein Terrasse

and you're in the mood for *Hofbräu* atmosphere and a hearty, cheap meal at a shared table in one small, smoky, well-antlered room. Notice the 1899 flood photo on the wall. For a quick lunch, get the *Bauernschmaus*, a mountain of dumplings, kraut, and peasant's meats (€10.50). While they have a few outdoor tables, the atmosphere is all indoors, and the menu is not great for hot-weather food. Owner Robert—who runs the restaurant with Schwarzenegger-like energy—enjoys fostering a convivial ambience (you'll share tables with strangers) and serving fresh traditional cuisine at great prices. I simply love this place (€8 two-course lunch specials, €7-12 daily specials posted on the wall, kitchen open Mon-Sat 11:00-21:00, closed Sun, 2 minutes from Mozart's Birthplace, enter from Getreidegasse 22 or Griesgasse 17, tel. 0662/841-787).

Stiftskeller St. Peter has been in business for more than 1,000 years—it was mentioned in the biography of Charlemagne. It's classy and high-end touristy, serving uninspired traditional Austrian cuisine (€10-25 meals, daily 11:30-22:30, indoor/outdoor seating, next to St. Peter's Church at foot of Mönchsberg, restaurant tel. 0662/841-268). They host the Mozart Dinner Concert described on page 140. Through the centuries, they've learned to charge for each piece of bread and don't serve free tap water.

St. Paul's Stub'n Beer Garden is tucked secretly away under the castle with a decidedly untouristy atmosphere. The food is better than a beer hall, and a young, Bohemian-chic clientele fills its two troll-like rooms and its idyllic tree-shaded garden. *Kasnock'n* is a tasty mountaineers' pasta with cheese served in an iron pan with a side salad for €9—it's enough for two (€6-12 daily specials, €7-15 plates, Mon-Sat 17:00-22:30, open later for drinks only, closed Sun, Herrengasse 16, tel. 0662/843-220).

Zirkelwirt serves modern Mediterranean, Italian, and Austrian dishes, a daily fish special, and always a good vegetarian option. It's an old *Gasthaus* dining room with a medieval tiki-hut terrace a block off Mozartplatz, yet a world away from the tourism of the old town. While the waitstaff, music, and vibe feel young, it attracts Salzburgers of all ages (€9-15 plates, cheese dumplings and daily fish special, nightly 17:00-24:00, Pfeifergasse 14, tel. 0662/843-472).

Fisch Krieg Restaurant, on the river where the fishermen used to sell their catch, is a great value. They serve fast, fresh, and inexpensive fish in a casual dining room—where trees grow through the ceiling—as well as great riverside seating (€2 fishwiches to go, self-serve €7 meals, salad bar, Mon-Fri 8:30-18:30, Sat 8:30-13:00, closed Sun, Hanuschplatz 4, tel. 0662/843-732).

Sternbräu Inn, a sloppy, touristy Austrian food circus, is a sprawling complex of popular eateries (traditional, Italian, self-serve, and vegetarian) in a cheery garden setting. Explore both courtyards before choosing a seat (Bürgerstube is classic, most restaurants open daily 9:00-24:00, enter from Getreidegasse 34, tel. 0662/842-140). One fancy, air-conditioned room hosts the Sound of Salzburg dinner show (described on page 140).

Café Tomaselli (with its Kiosk annex and terrace seating across the way) has long been Salzburg's top place to see and be seen. While pricey, it is good for lingering and people-watching. Tomaselli serves light meals and lots of drinks, keeps long hours daily, and has fine seating on the square, a view terrace upstairs, and indoor tables. Despite its fancy inlaid wood paneling, 19th-century portraits, and chandeliers, it's surprisingly low-key (€3-7 entrées, daily 7:00-21:00, until 24:00 during music festival, Alter Markt 9, tel. 0662/844-488).

Saran Essbar is the product of hardworking Mr. Saran (from the Punjab), who cooks and serves with his heart. This delightful little eatery casts a rich orange glow under medieval vaults. Its fun menu is small (Mr. Saran is committed to both freshness and value), mixing Austrian (great schnitzel and strudel), Italian, and Asian vegetarian, and always offering salads (€9-12 meals, daily 11:00-22:00, often open later, a block off Mozartplatz at Judengasse 10, tel. 0662/846-628).

Bar Club Café Republic, a hip hangout for local young people near the end of Getreidegasse, feels like a theater lobby during intermission. It serves good food with smoky indoor and outdoor seating. It's ideal if you want something mod, untouristy, and un-wursty (trendy breakfasts 8:00-18:00, Asian and international menu, €7-12 plates, lots of hard drinks, daily until late, music with a DJ Fri and Sat from 23:00, Salsa Dance Club Tue night from 21:00, Tango Dance Club Sun from 21:00, no cover, Anton Neumayr Platz 2, tel. 0662/841-613).

Afro Cafe, between Getreidegasse and the Mönchsberg lift, is a hit with local students. Its agenda: to put a fun spin on African cuisine (adapted to European tastes). It serves tea, coffee, cocktails, and tasty food with a dose of '70s funk and a healthy sense of humor. The menu includes pan-African specialties—try the spicy chicken couscous—as well as standard soups and salads (€9-13 entrées, Mon-Fri 10:00-24:00, Sat 9:00-24:00, closed Sun, between Getreidegasse and cliff face at Bürgerspitalplatz 5, tel. 0662/844-888).

Demel, an outpost of Vienna's famed chocolatier (see page 40), is a wonderland of desserts that are as beautiful as they are delectable. Sink into the pink couches upstairs, or have them box up a treat for later (daily 9:00-20:00, near TI and cathedral at Mozartplatz 2, tel. 0662/840-358).

On the Cliffs Above the Old Town: **Gasthaus Stadtalm,** Salzburg's mountaineers' hut, sits high above the old town on the edge of the cliff with cheap prices, good food, and great views. If hiking across Mönchsberg, make this your goal (traditional food, salads, cliffside garden seating or cozy-mountain-hut indoor seating—one indoor view table is booked for a decade of New Year's celebrations, daily 10:00-19:00, July-Aug until 24:00, 2 minutes from top of €3 round-trip Mönchsberg elevator, also reachable by stairs from Toscanini Hof, Mönchsberg 19C, tel. 0662/841-729, Peter). For the location, see map on pages 150-151.

Eating Cheaply in the Old Town

Toscana Cafeteria Mensa is the students' lunch canteen, fast and cheap—with indoor seating and a great courtyard for sitting outside with students and teachers instead of tourists. They serve a daily soup-and-main course special for €5 (Mon-Fri 9:00-15:00, hot meals served 11:00-13:30 only, closed Sat-Sun, behind the Alte Residenz, in the courtyard opposite Sigmund-Haffner-Gasse 16).

Sausage stands *(Würstelstände)* serve the town's favorite "fast food." The best stands (like those on Universitätsplatz) use the same boiling water all day, which gives the weenies more flavor. For a list of helpful terms, see page 102. The Salzburgers' favorite spicy sausage is sold at the 60-year-old **Balkan Grill,** run by chatty Frau Ebner (€2.80; survey the five spicy options—described in English—and choose a number; takeout only, steady and sturdy local crowd, daily 11:00-19:00, hours vary with demand, hiding down the tunnel at Getreidegasse 33 across from Eisgrotte).

Picnickers will appreciate the bustling morning **produce market** (daily except Sun) on Universitätsplatz, behind Mozart's Birthplace.

Away from the Center

Augustiner Bräustübl, a huge 1,000-seat beer garden within a monk-run brewery in the Kloster Mülln, is rustic and raw. On busy nights, it's like a Munich beer hall with no music but the volume turned up. When it's cool outside, you'll enjoy a historic setting inside beer-sloshed and smoke-stained halls. On balmy evenings, it's like a Renoir painting—but with beer breath—under chestnut trees. Local students mix with tourists eating hearty slabs of schnitzel with their fingers or cold meals from the self-serve picnic counter, while children frolic on the playground kegs. For your beer: Pick up a half-liter or full-liter mug, pay the lady (*schank* means self-serve price, *bedienung* is the price with waiter service), wash your mug, give Mr. Keg your receipt and empty mug, and you will be made happy. Waiters only bring beer; they don't bring food—instead, go up the stairs, survey the hallway of deli counters, and assemble your own meal (or, as long as you buy a drink, you can bring in a picnic). Classic pretzels from the bakery and spiraled, salty radishes make great beer even better. For dessert—after a visit to the strudel kiosk—enjoy the incomparable floodlit view of old Salzburg from the nearby Müllnersteg pedestrian bridge and a riverside stroll home (open daily 15:00-23:00, Augustinergasse 4, tel. 0662/431-246). It's about a 15-minute walk along the river (with the river on your right) from the Staatsbrücke bridge. After passing the pedestrian Müllnersteg bridge, just after Café am Kai, follow the stairs up to a busy street, and cross it. From here, either continue up more stairs into the trees and around the small church (for a scenic approach to the monastery), or stick to the sidewalk as it curves around to Augustinergasse. Either way, your goal is the huge yellow building. Don't be fooled by second-rate gardens serving the same beer nearby.

North of the River, near Recommended Linzergasse Hotels

Spicy Spices is a trippy vegetarian-Indian restaurant where Suresh Syal (a.k.a. "Mr. Spicy") serves tasty curry and rice, samosas, organic salads, vegan soups, and fresh juices. It's a *namaste* kind of place, where everything's proudly organic (€6.50 specials, Mon-Fri 10:30-21:30, Sat-Sun 12:00-21:30, takeout available, Wolf-Dietrich-Strasse 1, tel. 0662/870-712).

Biergarten die Weisse, close to the hotels on Rupertgasse and away from the tourists, is a longtime hit with the natives. If a beer hall can be happening, this one—modern, yet with antlers—is it. Their famously good beer is made right there; favorites include their fizzy wheat beer *(Weisse)* and their seasonal beers (on request). Enjoy the beer with their good, cheap traditional food in the great garden seating, or in the wide variety of indoor rooms—sports bar, young and noisy, or older and more elegant (daily specials, Mon-Sat 10:00-24:00, closed Sun, Rupertgasse 10, east of Bayerhamerstrasse, tel. 0662/872-246).

Café Bazar, overlooking the river between Mirabell Gardens and the Staatsbrücke bridge, is as close as you'll get to a Vienna coffeehouse in Salzburg. It's *the* venerable spot for a classy drink with an old-town-and-castle view (light meals, Mon-Sat 7:30-23:00, Sun 9:00-18:00, Schwarzstrasse 3, tel. 0662/874-278).

Steingasse Pub Crawl

For a fun post-concert activity, crawl through medieval Steingasse's trendy pubs (all open until the wee hours). This is a local and hip scene, but accessible to older tourists: dark bars filled with well-dressed Salzburgers lazily smoking cigarettes and talking philosophy as avant-garde Euro-pop throbs on the soundtrack. Most of the pubs are in cellar-like caves...extremely atmospheric. (For more on Steingasse, see page 135.) These four pubs are all within about

100 yards of each other. Start at the Linzergasse end of Steingasse. As they are quite different, survey all before choosing your spot.

Pepe Cocktail Bar, with Mexican decor and Latin music, serves Mexican snacks *con* cocktails (nightly 19:00-3:00 in the morning, live DJs Fri-Sat from 19:00, Steingasse 3, tel. 0662/873-662).

Shrimps Bar-Restaurant, next door and less claustrophobic, is more a restaurant than a bar, serving creative international dishes (spicy shrimp sandwiches and salads, Tue-Sun 18:00-24:00, closed Mon, Steingasse 5, tel. 0662/874-484).

Saiten Sprung wins the "Best Atmosphere" award. The door is kept closed to keep out the crude and rowdy. Ring the bell and enter its hellish interior—lots of stone and red decor, with mountains of melted wax beneath age-old candlesticks and a classic soul music ambience. Stelios, who speaks English with Greek charm, serves cocktails, fine wine, and wine-friendly Italian antipasti (nightly 21:00-4:00 in the morning, Steingasse 11, tel. 0662/881-377).

Fridrich, just next door, is an intimate little place under an 11th-century vault, with lots of mirrors and a silver ceiling fan. Bernd Fridrich is famous for his martinis and passionate about Austrian wines, and has a tattered collection of vinyl that seems to keep the 1970s alive. He serves little dishes to complement the focus, which is socializing and drinking (€5-12 small entrées, nightly from 18:00 in summer or 17:00 in winter, Steingasse 15, tel. 0662/876-218).

Salzburg Connections

By Train

Salzburg's train station, located so close to the German border, is covered not just by Austrian railpasses, but German ones as well.

From Salzburg by Train to: Hallstatt (hourly, 50 minutes to Attnang Puchheim, 20-minute wait, then 1.5 hours to Hallstatt; also consider bus—see below), **Innsbruck** (direct every 2 hours, 2 hours), **Vienna** (2/hour, 2.5-3 hours), **Reutte** (hourly, 5 hours, change either in Munich and Kempten, or in Innsbruck and Garmisch), **Füssen** (roughly hourly, 4 hours, 1-2 changes), **Munich** (2/hour, 1.5-2 hours), **Nürnberg,** Germany (hourly with change in Munich, 3 hours), **Prague** (7/day, 6.5-7.5 hours, via Linz and Český Budějovice, no decent overnight connection), **Interlaken** (7/day, 7.5-8 hours, 2-3 changes), **Florence** (4/day, 8-8.5 hours, 2 changes, 1 overnight connection via Villach), **Ljubljana** (every 2 hours, 4.25-5 hours, some with change in Villach). Train info: tel. 051-717 (to get an operator, dial 2, then 2), www.oebb.at.

By Bus

The bus trip to **Hallstatt** via Bad Ischl is cheaper, more scenic (with views of the Wolfgangsee), and no slower than the train. Bus #150 leaves from the Salzburg train station for Bad Ischl (€8.80, Mon-Fri nearly hourly at :15 past the hour, fewer buses Sat-Sun, 1.5 hours, tel. 0810-222-333, www.postbus.at). It also picks up passengers at Mirabellplatz and Hofwirt (convenient to Linzergasse hotels). At the Bad Ischl station, you have two options: a 25-minute train ride to Hallstatt station (€3.60), and then the boat across the lake to the old town center; or another bus ride, ending at the bus stop in the Lahn section of Hallstatt (€4.20, requires a further change in Gosaumühle).

Route Tips for Drivers

From Salzburg to Hallstatt: Get on the Munich-Vienna autobahn (follow blue *A-1* signs), head for Vienna, exit at Thalgau (#274), and follow signs to *Hof, Fuschl,* and *St. Gilgen.* The Salzburg-Hallstatt road passes two luge rides (see Hallstatt chapter), St. Gilgen (pleasant but touristy), and Bad Ischl (the center of the Salzkammergut, with a spa, the emperor's villa if you need a Habsburg history fix, and a good **TI**, tel. 06132/277-570).

HALLSTATT
and the SALZKAMMERGUT

Commune with nature in the Salzkammergut, Austria's Lake District. "The hills are alive," and you're surrounded by the loveliness that has turned on everyone from Emperor Franz Josef to Julie Andrews. This is *Sound of Music* country. Idyllic and majestic, but not rugged, it's a gentle land of lakes, forested mountains, and storybook villages, rich in hiking opportunities and inexpensive lodging. Settle down in the postcard-pretty, lake-cuddling town of Hallstatt.

Planning Your Time

While there are plenty of lakes and charming villages in the Salzkammergut, Hallstatt is really the only one that matters. One night and a few hours to browse are all you'll need to fall in love. To relax or take a hike in the surroundings, give it two nights and a day. It's a relaxing break between Vienna and Salzburg.

Orientation to Hallstatt

(area code: 06134)

Lovable Hallstatt (HAHL-shtaht) is a tiny town bullied onto a ledge between a selfish mountain and a swan-ruled lake, with a waterfall ripping furiously through its middle. It can be toured on foot in about 15 minutes. Salt veins in the mountain rock drew people here centuries before Christ. The symbol of Hallstatt, which you'll see all over town, consists of two adjacent spirals—a design based on jewelry found in Bronze Age Celtic graves high in the nearby mountains.

Hallstatt has two parts: the tightly packed medieval town center (which locals call the Markt) and the newer, more car-friendly Lahn, a few minutes' walk to the south. A lakeside promenade connects the old center to the Lahn. The tiny "main" boat dock (a.k.a. Market Dock), where boats from the train station arrive, is in the old center of town. Another boat dock is in the Lahn, next to Hallstatt's bus stop and grocery store.

The charms of Hallstatt are the village and its lakeside setting. Come here to relax, nibble, wander, and paddle. While tourist crowds can trample much of Hallstatt's charm in August, the place is almost dead in the off-season. The lake is famous for its good fishing and pure water.

Tourist Information

At the helpful TI, Claudia and her staff can explain hikes and excursions, and find you a room (July-Aug Mon-Fri 9:00-17:00, Sat 10:00-14:00, closed Sun; Sept-June Mon-Fri 9:00-12:00 & 14:00-17:00, closed Sat-Sun; one block from Market Square, across from museum at Seestrasse 169, tel. 06134/8208, www.dachstein -salzkammergut.at).

In the summer, the TI offers 1.5-hour **walking tours** of the town in English and German (€4, mid-May-Sept Sat at 10:00). They can arrange private tours for €75.

Arrival in Hallstatt

By Train: If you're coming on the main train line that runs between Salzburg and Vienna, you'll change trains at Attnang-Puchheim to get to Hallstatt (you won't see Hallstatt on the schedules, but any train to Ebensee and Bad Ischl will stop at Hallstatt). Day-trippers can check their bags at the Attnang-Puchheim station (follow signs for *Schliessfächer*, coin-op lockers are at the street, curbside near track 1, €2.50/24 hours, a ticket serves as your key). Note: Connections can be fast—check the TV monitor.

Hallstatt's train station is a wide spot on the tracks across the lake from town. *Stefanie* (a boat) meets you at the station and glides scenically across the lake to the old town center (€2.20, meets each train until 18:48—don't arrive after that, www.hallstattschifffahrt .at). The last departing boat-train connection leaves Hallstatt at 18:15, and the first boat goes in the morning at 6:50 (8:50 Sat-Sun).

Once in Hallstatt, walk left from the boat dock for the TI; you're steps away from the hotels in the old center, and a 15-minute walk from accommodations in the Lahn.

By Bus: Hallstatt's bus stop is by the boat dock in the Lahn. It takes 15 minutes to walk from the bus stop into the old center along the lakeside path.

By Car: The main road skirts Hallstatt via a long tunnel above the town. Gates close off traffic to the old center, but if you have

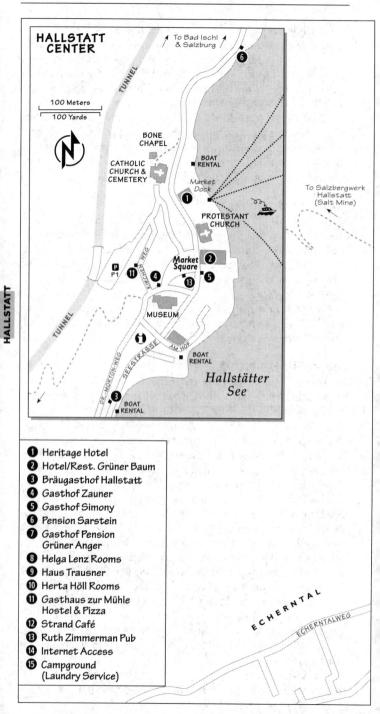

HALLSTATT CENTER

To Bad Ischl & Salzburg

TUNNEL

100 Meters
100 Yards

N

BONE CHAPEL

CATHOLIC CHURCH & CEMETERY

BOAT RENTAL

Market Dock

To Salzbergwerk Hallstatt (Salt Mine)

PROTESTANT CHURCH

P P1

Market Square

MUSEUM

KIRCHEN WEG

DR. MORTON WEG

SEESTRASSE

AM HOF

BOAT RENTAL

TUNNEL

Hallstätter See

BOAT RENTAL

HALLSTATT

1 Heritage Hotel
2 Hotel/Rest. Grüner Baum
3 Bräugasthof Hallstatt
4 Gasthof Zauner
5 Gasthof Simony
6 Pension Sarstein
7 Gasthof Pension Grüner Anger
8 Helga Lenz Rooms
9 Haus Trausner
10 Herta Höll Rooms
11 Gasthaus zur Mühle Hostel & Pizza
12 Strand Café
13 Ruth Zimmerman Pub
14 Internet Access
15 Campground (Laundry Service)

ECHERNTAL

ECHERNTALWEG

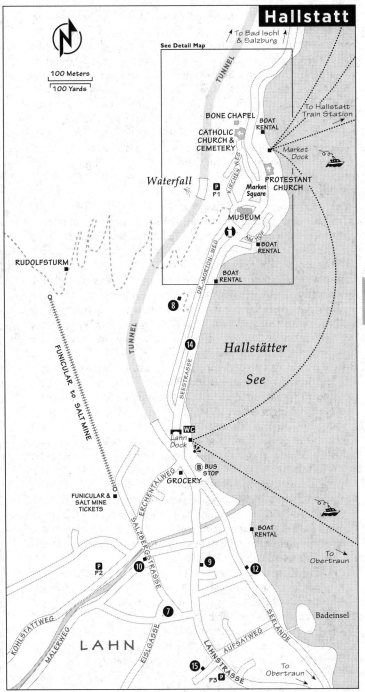

a hotel reservation, the guard will let you drive into town to drop your bags. Ask your hotel for parking suggestions. There are numbered parking areas outside the center (P1 through P5). Parking there is free with a guest card (available from your hotel), and it's a laid-back system—just show your card later. The problem is that the lots are often full, especially P1 (in the tunnel above town); try P2 or P3, in the Lahn, a lovely 15- to 20-minute lakeside walk from the old center. Without a guest card, per-day parking is still quite reasonable (lot P1: €4.20/day, lot P2: €6/day; less after 14:00). Off-season (Nov-April), parking is free and easy. All of the accommodations I recommend in the Lahn have free parking.

Helpful Hints

Internet Access: Try **Hallstatt Umbrella Bar** (€4/hour, summers only, weather permitting—since it's literally under a big umbrella, halfway between the old center and the Lahn along the lake at Seestrasse 145). For free Wi-Fi, drop by the café at the recommended **Heritage Hotel.**

Laundry: The staff of the **campground** in the Lahn will wash and dry (but not fold) your clothes for €8/load (drop off mid-April-mid-Oct daily 8:00-10:00 & 16:00-18:00, pick up in afternoon or next morning, closed off-season, tel. 06134/83224). In the center, the recommended **Hotel Grüner Baum** does laundry for non-guests (€13/load, on Market Square).

Boat Rental: Two places rent electric boats; both rent from two locations in high season. **Riedler** is next to the main boat dock, and 75 yards past Bräugasthof (€13/hour, tel. 06134/20619). **Hemetsberger** is near Gasthof Simony, and by the Lahn boat dock (€12/hour, tel. 06134/8228). Both are open daily until 19:00 in peak season and in good weather. Boats have two speeds: slow and stop. Spending an extra €3/hour gets you a faster, 500-watt boat. Both places also rent rowboats and paddleboats (slightly cheaper).

Parks and Swimming: Green and peaceful lakeside parks line the south end of Lake Hallstatt. If you walk 15 minutes south of the old center to the Lahn, you'll find a grassy public park, playground, mini-golf, and swimming area *(Badestrand)* with the fun Badeinsel play-island.

Views: For a great view over Hallstatt, hike above the recommended Helga Lenz B&B as far as you like, or climb any path leading up the hill. The 40-minute steep hike down from the salt-mine tour gives the best views (see "Sights in Hallstatt," later). While most visitors stroll the lakeside drag between the old and new parts of town, make a point to do the trip once by taking the more higgledy-piggledy high lane called Dr.-Morton-Weg.

Self-Guided Walk

Welcome to Hallstatt

• *This short walk starts at the dock.*

Boat Landing: There was a Hallstatt before there was a Rome. In fact, because of the importance of salt mining here, an entire epoch—the Hallstatt Era, from 800 to 400 B.C.—is named for this important spot. Through the centuries, salt was traded and people came and went by boat. You'll still see the traditional *Fuhr* boats, designed to carry heavy loads in shallow water.

Towering above the town is the **Catholic church.** Its faded St. Christopher—patron saint of travelers, with his cane and baby Jesus on his shoulder—watched over those sailing in and out. Until 1875, the town was extremely remote...then came a real road and the train. The good ship *Stefanie* shuttles travelers back and forth from here to the Hallstatt train station, immediately across the lake. The *Bootverleih* sign advertises boat rentals. By the way, *Schmuck* is not an insult...it means "jewelry."

Notice the one-lane road out of town (below the church). Until 1966, when a bigger tunnel was built above Hallstatt, all the traffic crept single-file right through the town.

Look down the shore at the huge homes. Several families lived in each of these houses, back when Hallstatt's population was about double its present 1,000. Today, the population continues to shrink, and many of these generally underused houses rent rooms to visitors.

Parking is tight here in the tourist season. Locals and hotels have cards getting them into the prime town-center lot. From November through April, the barricade is lifted and anyone can park here. Hallstatt gets about three months of snow each winter, but the lake hasn't frozen over since 1981.

See any swans? They've patrolled the lake like they own it since the 1860s, when Emperor Franz Josef and Empress Sisi—the Princess Diana of her day—made this region their annual holiday retreat. Sisi loved swans, so locals made sure she'd see them here. During this period, the Romantics discovered Hallstatt, many top painters worked here, and the town got its first hotel (now the Heritage Hotel).

Tiny Hallstatt has two big churches: Protestant (bordering the square on the left, with a grassy lakeside playground) and Catholic (up above, with its fascinating bone chapel).

• *Walk over the town's stream, and pop into the...*

Protestant Church: The Catholic Counter-Reformation was very strong in Austria, but pockets of Protestantism survived, especially in mining towns like Hallstatt. In 1860, Emperor Franz Josef finally allowed non-Catholic Christians to build churches. Before that, they were allowed to worship only in low-key "houses of prayer." In 1863, Hallstatt's miners pooled their humble resources and built this fine church. Step inside (free and often open). It's very plain, emphasizing the pulpit and organ rather than fancy art and saints. Check out the portraits: Martin Luther (left of altar), the town in about 1865 with its new church (left wall), and a century of pastors.

• Continue past the church to the...

Market Square (Marktplatz): In 1750, a fire leveled this part of town. The buildings you see now are all late 18th-century structures built of stone rather than flammable wood. The three big buildings on the left are government-subsidized housing (mostly for seniors and people with health problems). Take a close look at the two-dimensional, up-against-the-wall pear tree (it likes the sun-warmed wall). The statue features the Holy Trinity.

• Continue a block past Gasthof Simony. At the first corner, just before the Gemeindeamt (City Hall), jog left across the little square and then right down the tiny lane marked Am Hof, which leads through an intimate bit of domestic town architecture, boat houses, lots of firewood, and maybe a couple of swans hanging out. The lane circles back to the main drag and the...

Museum Square: Because 20th-century Hallstatt was of no industrial importance, it was untouched by World War II. But once upon a time, its salt was worth defending. High above, peeking out of the trees, is Rudolfsturm (Rudolf's Tower). Originally a 13th-century watchtower protecting the salt mines, and later the mansion of a salt-mine boss, it's now a restaurant with a great view. A zigzag trail connects the town with Rudolfsturm and the salt mines just beyond. The big, white houses by the waterfall were water-powered mills that once ground Hallstatt's grain. (If you hike up a few blocks, you'll see the river raging through town.)

Around you are the town's TI, post office, museum, City Hall, and Dachstein Sport Shop (described later). A statue recalls the mine manager who excavated prehistoric graves in about 1850. Much of the Schmuck sold locally is inspired by the jewelry found in the area's Bronze Age tombs.

The memorial wooden stairs in front of the museum are a copy of those found in Hallstatt's prehistoric mine—the original stairs are more than 2,500 years old. For thousands of years, people have been leaching salt out of this mountain. A brine spring sprung here, attracting Bronze Age people in about 1600 B.C. Later, they dug tunnels to mine the rock (which was 70 percent salt), dissolved it into a brine, and distilled out the salt—precious for preserving meat. For a look at early salt-mining implements and the town's story, visit the museum (described later).

Across from the TI, Pension Hallberg has a quirky hallway

full of Nazi paraphernalia and other stuff found on the lake bed (€1). Only recently did local divers realize that, for centuries, the lake had been Hallstatt's garbage can. If something was *kaputt*, locals would just toss it into the lake. In 1945, Nazi medals decorating German and Austrian war heroes suddenly became dangerous to own. Throughout the former Third Reich, hard-earned medals floated down to lonely lake beds, including Hallstatt's.

Under the TI is the "Post Partner"—a government-funded attempt to turn inefficient post offices into something more viable (selling souvenirs, renting bikes, and employing people with disabilities who otherwise wouldn't work). The *Fischerei* provides the town with its cherished fresh lake fish. The county allows two commercial fishermen on the lake. They spread their nets each morning and sell their catch here to town restaurants, or to any locals cooking up a special dinner (Mon-Fri 9:00-12:00, closed Sat-Sun).

• *Nearby, still on Museum Square, find the...*

Dachstein Sport Shop: During a renovation project, the builders dug down and hit a Celtic and ancient Roman settlement. Peek through the glass pavement on the covered porch to see where the Roman street level was. If the shop is open, pop in and go downstairs (free). You'll walk on Roman flagstones and see the small gutter that channeled water to power an ancient hammer mill (used to pound iron into usable shapes). In prehistoric times, people lived near the mines. Romans were the first Hallstatt lakeside settlers. The store's owners are committed to sharing Hallstatt's fascinating history, and often display old town paintings and folk art.

• *From this square, the first right (after the bank) leads up a few stairs to...*

Dr.-Morton-Weg: House #26A dates from 1597. Follow the lane uphill to the left past more old houses. Until 1890, this was the town's main drag, and the lake lapped at the lower doors of these houses. Therefore, many main entrances were via the attic, from this level. Enjoy this back-street view of town. Just after the arch, near #133, check out the old tools hanging outside the workshop, and the piece of wooden piping. It's a section taken from the 25-mile wooden pipeline that carried salt brine from Hallstatt to Ebensee. This was in place from 1595 until the last generation, when the last stretch of wood was replaced by plastic piping. At the pipe, enjoy the lake view and climb down the stairs. From lake level, look back up at the striking traditional architecture (the fine woodwork on the left was recently rebuilt after a fire; parts of the old house on the right date to medieval times).

• *Your tour is finished. From here, you have boat rentals, the salt-mine tour, the town museum, and the Catholic church (with its bone chapel) all within a few minutes' walk.*

Sights in Hallstatt

▲▲**Catholic Church and Bone Chapel**—Hallstatt's Catholic church overlooks the town from above. From near the main boat dock, hike up the covered wooden stairway and follow the *Kath. Kirche* signs. The lovely church has twin altars. The one on the left was made by town artists in 1897. The one on the right is more historic—dedicated in 1515 to Mary, who's flanked by St. Barbara (on right, patron of miners) and St. Catherine (on left, patron of foresters—a lot of wood was needed to fortify the many miles of tunnels, and to boil the brine to distill the salt).

Behind the church, in the well-tended graveyard, is the 12th-century Chapel of St. Michael (even older than the church). Its bone chapel—or charnel house *(Beinhaus)*—contains more than 600 painted skulls. Each skull has been lovingly named, dated, and decorated (skulls with dark, thick garlands are oldest—18th century; those with flowers are more recent—19th century). Space was so limited in this cemetery that bones had only 12 peaceful, buried years here before making way for the freshly dead. Many of the dug-up bones and skulls ended up in this chapel. They stopped this practice in the 1960s, about the same time the Catholic Church began permitting cremation. But one woman (who died in 1983) managed to sneak her skull in later (dated 1995, under the cross, with the gold tooth). The skulls on the books are those of priests.

Cost and Hours: €1.50, free English flier, daily May-Sept 10:00-18:00, Oct 10:00-16:00, closed Nov-April, tel. 06134/8279.

▲**Hallstatt Museum**—This pricey but high-quality museum tells the story of Hallstatt. It focuses on the Hallstatt Era (800-400 B.C.), when this village was the salt-mining hub of a culture that spread from France to the Balkans. Back then, Celtic tribes dug for precious salt, and Hallstatt was, as its name means, the "place of salt." While its treasures are the countless artifacts excavated from prehistoric gravesites around the mine, you'll get the whole gamut—with 26 displays on everything from the region's flora and fauna to local artists and the surge in Hallstatt tourism during the Romantic Age. Everything is labeled in English, and the ring binders have translations of the longer texts.

Cost and Hours: €7.50, May-Sept daily 10:00-18:00, shorter hours off-season, closed Mon-Tue Nov-March, adjacent to TI at Seestrasse 56, tel. 06134/828-015, www.museum-hallstatt.at. On Thursdays in summer, when candlelit boats run, the museum stays open until 20:00 (see "Nightlife in Hallstatt," later).

▲**Lake Trip**—For a quick boat trip, you can ride the *Stefanie* across the lake and back for €4.40. It stops at the tiny Hallstatt train station for 30 minutes (note return time in the boat's window), giving you time to walk to a hanging bridge (ask the captain to point you to the *Hängebrücke*—HENG-eh-brick-eh—a 10-minute lakeside stroll to the left). Longer lake tours are also available (€8/50 minutes, €9.50/75 minutes, sporadic schedules—especially off-season—so check chalkboards by boat docks for today's times). Those into relaxation can rent a sleepy electric motorboat to enjoy town views from the water.

▲**Salt-Mine Tour**—If you have yet to tour a salt mine, consider visiting Hallstatt's, which claims to be the oldest in the world. To get to the mine, take the funicular railway, which starts in the Lahn, close to the bus stop and Lahn boat dock.

After riding the funicular above town, you'll hike 10 minutes to the mine (past excavation sites of many prehistoric tombs and a glass case with 2,500-year-old bones—but there's little to actually see). Report back 10 minutes before the tour time on your ticket, check your bag, and put on old miners' clothes. Then hike 200 yards higher in your funny outfit to meet your guide, who escorts your group down a tunnel dug in 1719. Inside the mountain, you'll watch a slide show, follow your guide through several caverns as you learn about mining techniques over the last 7,000 years, see a silly laser show on a glassy subterranean lake, peek at a few waxy cavemen with pickaxes, and ride the train out. The highlight for most is sliding down two banisters (the second one is longer and ends with a flash for an automatic souvenir photo that clocks your speed—see how you did compared to the rest of your group after the tour).

The presentation is very low-tech, as the mining company owns all three mine tours in the area and sees little reason to invest in the experience when they can simply mine the tourists. While the tour is mostly in German, the guide is required to speak English if you ask...so ask. Be sure to dress for the constant 47-degree temperature.

Cost and Hours: €24 combo-ticket includes mine and funicular round-trip, €16 for mine tour only, buy all tickets at funicular station—note the time and tour number on your ticket, daily May–mid-Sept 9:00-16:00, mid-Sept-Oct 9:00-14:30, later funicular departures miss the last tour of the day, closed Nov-April, no children under age 4, arrive early or late to avoid summer crowds, tel. 06132/200-2400, www.salzwelten.at.

Funicular: You can also just take the funicular without going on the mine tour (€7 one-way, €12 round-trip, 4/hour, daily May-mid-Sept 9:00-18:00, mid-Sept-Oct 9:00-16:30, closed Nov-April).

Returning to Hallstatt: If you skip the funicular down, the scenic 40-minute hike back into town is (with strong knees) a joy. At the base of the funicular, notice the train tracks leading to the Erbstollen tunnel entrance. This lowest of the salt tunnels goes

Salzkammergut

HALLSTATT

many miles into the mountain, where a shaft connects it to the tunnels you just explored. Today, the salty brine from these tunnels flows 25 miles through the world's oldest pipeline—made of wood until quite recently—to the huge modern salt works (next to the highway) at Ebensee.

▲**Local Hikes**—Mountain-lovers, hikers, and spelunkers who use Hallstatt as their home base keep busy for days (ask the TI

for ideas). A good, short, and easy walk is the two-hour round-trip up the Echern Valley to the Waldbachstrub waterfall and back: From the parking lot, follow signs to the salt mines, then follow the little wooden signs marked *Echerntalweg*. With a car, consider hiking around nearby Altaussee (flat, 3-hour hike) or along Grundlsee to Toplitzsee. Regular buses connect Hallstatt with Gosausee for a pleasant hour-long walk around that lake. Or consider walking nine miles halfway around Lake Hallstatt via the town of Steeg (boat to train station, walk left along lake and past idyllic farmsteads, returning to Hallstatt along the old salt trail, *Soleleitungsweg*); for a shorter hike, walk to Steeg along either side of the lake, and catch the train from Steeg back to Hallstatt's station. The TI can also recommend a great two-day hike with an overnight in a nearby mountain hut.

Biking—The best two bike rides take nearly the same routes as the hikes listed previously: up the Echern Valley, and around the lake (bikers do better going via Obertraun along the new lakeside bike path—start with a ride on the *Stefanie*). There's no public bike rental in Hallstatt, but some hotels have loaner bikes for guests.

Near Hallstatt

▲▲Dachstein Mountain Cable Car and Caves

From Obertraun, three miles beyond Hallstatt on the main road (or directly across the lake as the crow flies), a cable car glides up to the Dachstein Plateau. Along the way, you can hop off to tour two different caves: the refreshingly chilly Giant Ice Caves and the less-impressive Mammoth Caves.

Getting to Obertraun: The cable car to Dachstein leaves from the outskirts of Obertraun. To reach the cable car from Hallstatt, the handiest and cheapest option is the bus (€1.70, 5-6/day, leaves from Lahn boat dock, drops you directly at cable-car station). Romantics can take the boat from Hallstatt's main boat dock to Obertraun (€5, 5/day July-Aug, 3/day in June and Sept, 30 minutes, www.hallstattschifffahrt.at)—but it's a 40-minute hike from there to the lift station. The impatient can consider hitching a ride—virtually all cars leaving Hallstatt to the south will pass through Obertraun in a few minutes.

Returning to Hallstatt: Plan to leave by midafternoon. The last bus from the cable-car station back to Hallstatt (at 17:05 in summer) inconveniently leaves before the last cable car down—if you miss the bus, try getting a ride from a fellow cable-car passenger. Otherwise, you can either call a taxi (€13, ask cable-car staff for help), or simply walk back along the lakefront (about one hour).

Dachstein Cable Car—From Obertraun, this mighty gondola goes in three stages high up the Dachstein Plateau—crowned by Dachstein, the highest mountain in the Salzkammergut (9,800 ft). The first segment stops at **Schönbergalm** (4,500 ft, runs May-late Oct), which has a mountain restaurant and two huge caves (described next). The second segment goes to the summit of **Krippenstein** (6,600 ft, runs mid-May-late Oct). The third segment descends to **Gjaidalm** (5,800 ft, runs mid-June-late Oct), where several hikes begin. For a quick high-country experience,

Krippenstein is better than Gjaidalm.

From **Krippenstein,** you'll survey a scrubby, limestone, karstic landscape (which absorbs, through its many cracks, the rainfall that ultimately carves all those caves), with 360-degree views of the surrounding mountains.

Cost and Hours: Round-trip cable-car ride to Schönbergalm and the caves-€15, to Krippenstein-€23, to Gjaidalm-€25; cheaper family rates available, last cable car back down usually at about 17:00, tel. 06131/51310, www.dachsteinwelterbe.at.

Combo-Ticket Tips: The several combo-tickets available for the cable car and caves generally won't save you any money over buying individual tickets. But if you're gung-ho enough to want to visit one or both caves, and plan to ride the cable car farther up the mountain, the €33 same-day combo-ticket makes sense (covers the cable car all the way to Gjaidalm and back, as well as entry to both caves; it's slightly cheaper to buy separate tickets if you're riding only to Krippenstein and skipping one of the caves).

Giant Ice Caves (Riesen-Eishöhle)—Located near the Schönbergalm cable-car stop (4,500 ft), these caves were discovered in 1910. Today, guides lead tours in German and English on an hourlong, half-mile hike through an eerie, icy, subterranean world, passing limestone canyons the size of subway stations.

At the Schönbergalm lift station, report to the ticket window to get your cave appointment. Drop by the little free museum near the lift station—in a local-style wood cabin designed to support 200 tons of snow—to see the cave-system model, exhibits about its exploration, and info about life in the caves. Then hike 10 minutes from the station up to the cave entry. The temperature is just above freezing, and although the 700 steps help keep you warm, you'll want to bring a sweater. The limestone caverns, carved by rushing water, are named for scenes from Wagner's operas—the favorite of the mountaineers who first came here. If you're nervous, note that the iron oxide covering the ceiling takes 5,000 years to form. Things are very stable. Allow 1.5 hours total from the station.

Cost and Hours: €10, €15 combo-ticket with Mammoth Caves, €33 combo-ticket covers the cable car up to Gjaidalm and entry to both caves, open May-late Oct, hour-long tours start at 9:20, last tour at 15:30, stay in front and assert yourself to get English information, tel. 06131/51310.

Mammoth Caves (Mammuthöhle)—While huge and well-promoted, these are much less interesting than the ice caves and—for most—not worth the time. Of the 30-mile limestone labyrinth excavated so far, you'll walk a half-mile with a German-speaking guide.

Cost and Hours: €10, €15 combo-ticket with ice caves, €33 combo-ticket covers the cable car up to Gjaidalm and entry to both caves, open May-late Oct, hour-long tours in English and German 10:15-14:30, entrance a 10-minute hike from lift station.

Luge Rides (Sommerrodelbahnen) on the Hallstatt-Salzburg Road

If you're driving between Salzburg and Hallstatt, you'll pass two luge rides operated by the same company (www.rodelbahnen.at). Each is a ski lift that drags you backward up the hill as you sit on your go-cart. At the top, you ride the cart down the winding metal course. It's easy: Push to go, pull to stop, take your hands off your stick and you get hurt.

Each course is just off the road with easy parking. The ride up and down takes about 15 minutes. The one in **Fuschl am See** (closest to Salzburg, look for *Sommerrodelbahn* sign) is half as long and cheaper (€4.30/ride, 1,970 ft, tel. 06226/8452). The one in **Strobl** near Wolfgangsee (look for *Riesenschutzbahn* sign) is a double course, more scenic with grand lake views (€6.40/ride, €43/10 rides, 4,265 ft, each track is the same speed, tel. 06137/7085). Courses are open May through October from 10:00 to 18:00—but generally closed in bad weather.

Nightlife in Hallstatt

Locals would laugh at the thought. But if you want some action after dinner, you do have a few options: **Gasthaus zur Mühle** is a youth hostel with a rustic sports-bar ambience in its restaurant when drinks replace the food (open late, closed Tue Sept-mid-May, run by Ferdinand). Or, for your late-night drink, savor the Market Square from the trendy little pub called **Ruth Zimmermann,** where locals congregate with soft music, a good selection of drinks, two small rooms, and tables on the square (daily May-Sept 10:00-2:00 in the morning, Oct-April 11:00-2:00, mobile 0664/501-5631). From late July to late August, **candlelit boat rides** leave at 20:30 on Thursday evenings (€13.50, €16 combo-ticket with Hallstatt Museum).

Sleeping in Hallstatt

Hallstatt's TI can almost always find you a room (either in town or at B&Bs and small hotels outside of town—which are more likely to have rooms available and come with easy parking). Drivers, remember to ask if your hotel has in-town parking when you book your room.

Mid-July and August can be tight. Early August is worst. Hallstatt is not the place to splurge—some of the best rooms are *Gästezimmer,* just as nice and modern as rooms in bigger hotels,

Sleep Code

(€1 = about $1.40, country code: 43, area code: 06134)
S = Single, **D** = Double/Twin, **T** = Triple, **Q** = Quad, **b** = bathroom, **s** = shower only. Unless otherwise noted, credit cards are accepted, English is spoken, and breakfast is included.

To help you sort easily through these listings, I've divided the rooms into three categories, based on the price for a standard double room with bath:

$$$ Higher Priced—Most rooms €90 or more.
  $$ Moderately Priced—Most rooms between €60-90.
    $ Lower Priced—Most rooms €60 or less.

Prices can change without notice; verify the hotel's current rates online or by email. For other updates, see www .ricksteves.com/update.

at half the cost. In summer, a double bed in a private home costs about €50 with breakfast. It's hard to get a one-night advance reservation (try calling the TI for help). But if you drop in and they have a spot, one-nighters are welcome. Prices include breakfast, lots of stairs, and a silent night. *"Zimmer mit Aussicht?"* (TSIM-mer mit OWS-zeekt) means "Room with view?"—worth asking for. Unlike many businesses in town, the cheaper places don't take credit cards.

As most rooms here are in old buildings with well-cared-for wooden interiors, dripping laundry is a no-no at Hallstatt pensions. Be especially considerate when hanging laundry over anything but tile—if you must wash larger clothing items here, ask your host about using their clothesline.

$$$ Heritage Hotel, next to the main boat dock, is the town's fanciest place to stay. It has 34 rooms with modern furnishings in a lakeside main building with an elevator; uphill are another 20 rooms in two separate buildings for those willing to climb stairs for better views (Sb-€90, Db-€150, show this book and ask for best Rick Steves price, free sauna, free cable Internet in rooms and Wi-Fi in lobby, laundry service-€13, parking-€10/day, Landungsplatz 120, tel. 06134/20036, fax 06134/20042, www .heritagehotel.at, info@heritagehotel.at).

$$$ Hotel Grüner Baum, on the other side of the church from the main boat dock, has a great location, fronting Market Square and overlooking the lake in back. The owner, Monika, moved here from Vienna and renovated this stately—but still a bit creaky—old hotel with urban taste. Its 22 rooms are huge, each with a separate living area and ancient hardwood floors, but you may not need so much space and the high price that comes with it (suite-like Db-€140-210, price depends on view, discount with this book, family rooms, Internet access in restaurant, laundry service-€13, closed in Nov, 20 yards from boat dock, tel. 06134/82630, fax 06134/826-344, www.gruenerbaum.cc, contact @gruenerbaum.cc).

$$$ Bräugasthof Hallstatt is like a museum filled with antique furniture and ancient family portraits. This former brewery, now a good restaurant, rents eight clean, cozy upstairs rooms. It's run by Virena and her daughter, Virena. Six of the rooms have gorgeous little lakeview balconies (Sb-€55, Db-€98, Tb-€140, free parking, just past TI along lake at Seestrasse 120, tel. 06134/8221, fax 06134/82214, www.brauhaus-lobisser.com, info@brauhaus-lobisser.com, Lobisser family).

$$$ Gasthof Zauner is run by a friendly mountaineer, Herr Zauner, whose family has owned it since 1893. The 13 pricey, pine-flavored rooms near the inland end of Market Square are decorated with sturdy alpine-inspired furniture (sealed not with lacquer but with beeswax, to let the wood breathe out its calming scent). Lederhosen-clad Herr Zauner recounts tales of local mountaineering lore, including his own impressive ascents (Sb-€60, Db-€107, lakeview Db-€112, cheaper mid-Oct-April, Internet access in office, closed Nov-early Dec, Marktplatz 51, tel. 06134/8246, fax 06134/82468, www.zauner.hallstatt.net, zauner@hallstatt.at).

$$$ Gasthof Simony is a well-worn, grandmotherly, 12-room place on the square, with a lake view, balconies, ancient beds, creaky wood floors, slippery rag rugs, antique furniture, and a lakefront garden for swimming. Reserve in advance, and call if arriving late (S-€35, D-€55, Ds-€65, Db-€95, third person-€30-35 extra, cash only, kayaks for guests, Marktplatz 105, tel. & fax 06134/8231, www.gasthof-simony.at, info@gasthof-simony.at, Susanna Scheutz and family).

$$ Pension Sarstein is a big, flower-bedecked house right on the water on the edge of the old center. Its seven renovated rooms are bright, and all have lakeview balconies. You can swim from its plush and inviting lakeside garden (D-€50, Db-€65, Tb-€85; apartments with kitchen: Db-€65, Tb-€75, Qb-€85, apartment prices don't include breakfast; €3 extra per person for 1-night stay, cash only, pay Internet access, 200 yards to the right of the main boat dock at Gosaumühlstrasse 83, tel. 06134/8217, www.pension-sarstein.at.tf, pension.sarstein@aon.at, helpful Isabelle and Klaus Fischer).

$$ Gasthof Pension Grüner Anger, in the Lahn near the bus station and base of the funicular, is practical and modern. It's big and quiet, with 11 rooms and no creaks or squeaks. There are mountain views, but none of the lake (Sb-€43-48, Db-€76-

86, third person-€15, price depends on season, non-smoking, free Internet access and Wi-Fi, free loaner bikes, free parking, Lahn 10, tel. 06134/8397, fax 06134/83974, www.anger.hallstatt.net, anger @aon.at, Sulzbacher family). If arriving by train, have the boat captain call Herr Sulzbacher, who will pick you up at the dock. They run a good-value restaurant, too, with discounts for guests.

$ Helga Lenz rents two fine *Gästezimmer* a steep five-minute climb above Dr.-Morton-Weg (look for the green *Zimmer* sign). This large, sprawling, woodsy house has a nifty garden perch, wins the "Best View" award, and is ideal for those who sleep well in tree houses and don't mind the steps up from town (Db-€50, Tb-€75, €2 more per person for one-night stay, cash only, family room, closed Nov-March, Hallberg 17, tel. 06134/8508, www.hallstatt .net/lenz, haus-lenz@aon.at).

$ Two *Gästezimmer* are a few minutes' stroll south of the center, just past the bus stop/parking lot and over the bridge. **Haus Trausner** has three clean, bright, new-feeling rooms adjacent to the Trausner family home (Ds/Db-€50, 2-night minimum for reservations, cash only, breakfast comes to your room, free parking, Lahnstrasse 27, tel. 06134/8710, trausner1@aon.at, charming Maria Trausner makes you want to settle right in). **Herta Höll** rents out three spacious, modern rooms on the ground floor of her riverside house crawling with kids (Db-€50, apartment for up to five-€60-90, €2 more per person for one-night stay, cash only, free parking, free cable Internet, Salzbergstrasse 45, tel. 06134/8531, fax 06134/825-533, frank.hoell@aon.at).

$ *Hostel:* **Gasthaus zur Mühle Jugendherberge,** below the waterfall and along the gushing town stream, has 46 of the cheapest good beds in town (bed in 3- to 8-bed coed dorms-€14, twin D-€28, family quads, sheets-€4 extra, breakfast-€5, big lockers with a €15 deposit, closed Nov, reception closed Tue Sept-mid-May—so arrange in advance if arriving on Tue, below P1 tunnel parking lot, Kirchenweg 36, tel. & fax 06134/8318, toeroe-f @hallstatturlaub.at, Ferdinand Törö). It's also popular for its great, inexpensive pizza (described below).

Eating in Hallstatt

In this town, when someone is happy to see you, they'll often say, "Can I cook you a fish?" While everyone cooks the typical Austrian fare, fish is your best bet here. *Reinanke* (whitefish) is caught wild out of Lake Hallstatt and served the same day. *Saibling* (lake trout) is also tasty and costs less. You can enjoy good food inexpensively, with delightful lakeside settings. Restaurants in Hallstatt tend to have unreliable hours and close early on slow nights, so don't wait too long to get dinner. Most of the eateries listed here are run by recommended hotels.

Restaurant Bräugasthof, on the edge of the old center, is a good value. The indoor dining room is cozy in cool weather. On a balmy evening, its great lakeside tables offer the best ambience in town—you can feed the swans while your trout is being cooked (€10-14 three-course daily specials, daily May-Oct 11:30-late, closed Nov-April, Seestrasse 120, tel. 06134/8221).

Hotel Grüner Baum is a more upscale option, with elegant service at tables overlooking the lake inside and out (€15-21 main dishes, daily Dec-Oct 8:00-22:00, closed Nov, at bottom of Market Square, tel. 06134/8263).

Gasthof Simony's Restaurant am See serves Austrian cuisine on yet another gorgeous lakeside terrace, as well as indoors (€12-16 main courses, Thu-Tue 11:30-20:00, until 21:00 June-Sept and on winter weekends, closed Wed, tel. 06134/20646).

Gasthaus zur Mühle serves the best pizza in town. Chow down cheap and hearty here with fun-loving locals and the youth-hostel crowd (€7 pizza, lots of Italian, some Austrian, Wed-Mon in summer 16:00-21:00, closed Tue, Kirchenweg 36, tel. 06134/8318, Ferdinand).

Strand Café, a local favorite, is in the Lahn, near Badeinsel, the town beach (€8-15 main courses, plenty of alcohol, Tue-Sun April-mid-Sept 10:00-21:00, mid-Sept-Oct 11:30-20:00, closed Mon and Nov-March, great garden setting on the lake, Seelände 102, tel. 06134/8234).

Picnics and Cheap Eats: The **Zauner** bakery/butcher/grocer, great for picnickers, makes fresh sandwiches to go (Tue-Fri 7:00-12:00 & 15:00-18:00, Sat and Mon 7:00-12:00, closed Sun, uphill to the left from Market Square). The only **supermarket** is Konsum, in the Lahn at the bus stop (Mon-Fri 7:30-12:00 & 15:00-18:00, Sat 7:30-12:00, closed Sun, July-Aug no midday break and until 17:00 on Sat, Sept-April closed Wed). **Snack stands** near the main boat dock and the Lahn boat dock sell *Döner Kebab* and so on for €3 (tables and fine lakeside picnic options nearby).

Hallstatt Connections

By Public Transportation

From Hallstatt by Train: Most travelers leaving Hallstatt are going to Salzburg or Vienna. In either case, you need to catch the shuttle boat (€2.20, departs 15 minutes before every train) to the little Hallstatt train station across the lake, and then ride 1.5 hours to **Attnang-Puchheim** (hourly from about 7:00 to 18:00). Trains are synchronized, so after a short wait in Attnang-Puchheim, you'll catch your onward connection to **Salzburg** (50 minutes) or **Vienna** (2.5 hours). The Hallstatt station has no staff or ticket machines, but you can buy tickets from the conductor without a penalty. In town, your hotel or the TI can help you find schedule information, or check www.oebb.at. Train info: tel. 051-717 (to get an operator, dial 2, then 2).

By Bus: The bus ride from Hallstatt to **Salzburg** is cheaper and more scenic than the train, and only slightly slower. You can still start off from Hallstatt by rail, taking the boat across the lake to the station and then the train toward Attnang-Puchheim—but get off after about 20 minutes in **Bad Ischl,** where you catch bus #150 to Salzburg (€8.80, Mon-Fri almost hourly, less Sat-Sun).

Alternatively, you can reach Bad Ischl by bus from the Hallstatt bus stop (€4.20, change in Gosaumühle), and then catch bus #150 to Salzburg. The Hallstatt TI has a schedule. In Salzburg, bus #150 stops at Hofwirt and Mirabellplatz (convenient to Linzergasse hotels) before ending at the Salzburg train station.

HALLSTATT

BELGIUM

BRUGES

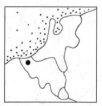

With pointy gilded architecture, stay-a-while cafés, vivid time-tunnel art, and dreamy canals dotted with swans, Bruges is a heavyweight sightseeing destination, as well as a joy. Where else can you ride a bike along a canal, munch mussels and wash them down with the world's best beer, savor heavenly chocolate, and see Flemish Primitives and a Michelangelo, all within 300 yards of a bell tower that jingles every 15 minutes? And do it all without worrying about a language barrier?

The town is Brugge (BROO-ghah) in Flemish, and Bruges (broozh) in French and English. Its name comes from the Viking word for wharf. Right from the start, Bruges was a trading center. In the 11th century, the city grew wealthy on the cloth trade.

By the 14th century, Bruges' population was 35,000, as large as London's. As the middleman in the sea trade between northern and southern Europe, it was one of the biggest cities in the world and an economic powerhouse. In addition, Bruges had become the most important cloth market in northern Europe.

In the 15th century, while England and France were slugging it out in the Hundred Years' War, Bruges was the favored residence of the powerful Dukes of Burgundy—and at peace. Commerce and the arts boomed. The artists Jan van Eyck and Hans Memling had studios here.

But by the 16th century, the harbor had silted up and the economy had collapsed. The Burgundian court left, Belgium became a minor Habsburg possession, and Bruges' Golden Age abruptly ended. For generations, Bruges was known as a mysterious and dead city. In the 19th century, a new port, Zeebrugge, brought renewed vitality to the area. And in the 20th century, tourists discovered the town.

Today, Bruges prospers because of tourism: It's a uniquely well-preserved Gothic city and a handy gateway to Europe. It's no secret, but even with the crowds, it's the kind of place where you don't mind being a tourist.

Bruges' ultimate sight is the town itself, and the best way to enjoy it is to get lost on the back streets, away from the lace shops and ice-cream stands.

Planning Your Time

Bruges needs at least two nights and a full, well-organized day. Even non-shoppers enjoy browsing here, and the Belgian love of life makes a hectic itinerary seem a little senseless. With one day—other than a Monday, when the three museums are closed—the speedy visitor could do the Bruges blitz described below:

9:30 Climb the bell tower on the Markt (Market Square).

10:00 Tour the sights on Burg Square.

11:30 Tour the Groeninge Museum.

13:00 Eat lunch and buy chocolates.

14:00 Take a short canal cruise.

14:30 Visit the Church of Our Lady and see Michelangelo's *Madonna and Child*.

15:00 Tour the Memling Museum.

16:00 Catch the De Halve Maan Brewery tour (note that their last tour runs at 15:00 in winter on weekdays).

17:00 Relax in the Begijnhof courtyard.

18:00 Ride a bike around the quiet back streets of town or take a horse-and-buggy tour.

20:00 Lose the tourists and find dinner.

If this schedule seems insane, skip the bell tower and the brewery—or stay another day.

Orientation to Bruges

The tourist's Bruges—and you'll be sharing it—is less than one square mile, contained within a canal (the former moat). Nearly everything of interest and importance is within a convenient cobbled swath between the train station and the Markt (Market Square; a 20-minute walk). Many of my quiet, charming, recommended accommodations lie just beyond the Markt.

Tourist Information

The main tourist office, called **In&Uit** ("In and Out"), is in the big, red concert hall on the square called 't Zand (daily 10:00-18:00, take a number from the touch-screen machines and wait, 't Zand 34, tel. 050-444-646, www.brugge.be). The other TI is at the train station (Mon-Fri 10:00-17:00, Sat-Sun 10:00-14:00).

The TIs sell the €2.50 *Love Bruges Visitors' Guide,* which comes with a map (costs €0.50 if bought separately), a few well-described self-guided walking tours, and listings of all the sights and services (free with Brugge City Card). You can also pick up a free monthly English-language program called *events@brugge* and a free, fun map/guide "made by locals for young travelers." The TIs have information on train schedules and tours (see "Tours in Bruges," later). Many hotels give out free maps with more detail than the map the TIs sell.

Arrival in Bruges

By Train: Coming in by train, you'll see the bell tower that marks the main square (Markt, the center of town). Upon arrival, stop by the train station TI to pick up the *Love Bruges Visitors' Guide* (with map). The station has ATMs and lockers (€3-4).

The best way to get to the town center is by **bus.** Buses #1-9, #11-17, and #25 go to the Markt (all marked *Centrum*). Simply hop on, pay €1.60 (€1.20 if you buy in advance at Lijnwinkel shop just outside the train station), and in four minutes, you're there (get off at third stop—either Markt or Wollestraat). Buses #4 and #14 continue to the northeast part of town (to the windmills and recommended accommodations on and near Carmersstraat, stop: Gouden Handstraat). If you arrive after 20:30, when the daytime bus routes end, you can still take the bus, but the "evening line" buses run much less frequently (buses marked *Avondlijn Centrum, Avondlijn Noord*—#91, *Avondlijn Oost*—#92, and *Avondlijn Zuid*—#93 all go to the Markt).

The **taxi** fare from the train station to most hotels is about €8.

It's a 20-minute **walk** from the station to the center—no fun with your luggage. If you want to walk to the Markt, cross the busy street and canal in front of the station, head up Oostmeers, and turn right on Zwidzandstraat. You can rent a **bike** at the station for the duration of your stay, but other bike rental shops are closer to the center (see "Helpful Hints," below).

By Car: Park in front of the train station in the handy two-story garage for just €2.50 for 24 hours. The parking fee includes a round-trip bus ticket into town and back for everyone in your car. There are pricier underground parking garages at the square called 't Zand and around town (€9/day, all of them well-marked). Paid parking on the street in Bruges is limited to four hours. Driving in town is very complicated because of the one-way system. The best plan for drivers: Park at the train station, visit the TI at the station, and rent a bike or catch a bus into town.

Helpful Hints

Blue Monday: In Bruges, nearly all museums are open Tuesday through Sunday year-round from 9:30 to 17:00 and are closed on Monday. If you're in Bruges on a Monday, you can still enjoy a bell-tower climb on the Markt, Begijnhof, the De Halve Maan Brewery Tour, Basilica of the Holy Blood, City Hall's Gothic Room, and chocolate shops and museum. You can also join a boat, bus, or walking tour, or rent a bike and pedal into the countryside.

Museum Passes: The 't Zand TI and city museums sell a **museum combo-ticket** (any five museums for €15, valid for 3 days). Because the Groeninge and Memling museums cost €8 each, art lovers will save money with this pass.

The **Brugge City Card** is a more extensive pass covering entry to 22 museums, including all the major sights (€34/48 hours, €39/72 hours, sold at TIs and many hotels). If you'll be doing some serious sightseeing, this card can save you money. Its long list of bonuses and discounts includes a free canal boat ride (March-Nov), a visitors' guide, and discounts on bike rental, parking, and some performances.

Market Days: Bruges hosts markets on Wednesday morning (on the Markt) and Saturday morning ('t Zand). On good-weather Saturdays, Sundays, and public holidays, a flea market hops along Dijver in front of the Groeninge Museum. The Fish Market sells souvenirs and seafood Tuesday through Saturday mornings until 13:00.

Shopping: Shops are generally open from 10:00 to 18:00. Grocery stores are usually closed on Sunday. The main shopping street, Steenstraat, stretches from the Markt to 't Zand Square. The **Hema** department store is at Steenstraat 73 (Mon-Sat 9:00-18:00, closed Sun).

Internet Access: Punjeb Internet Shop, just a block off the Markt, is the most central of the city's many "telephone shops" offering Internet access (€1.50/30 minutes, €2.50/hour, daily 9:00-20:00, Philipstockstraat 4). **Bean Around the World** is a cozy coffeehouse with imported Yankee snacks and free Wi-Fi for customers (€1/15 minutes on their computers, Thu-Mon 10:00-19:00, Wed 11:30-19:00, closed Tue, Genthof 5, tel. 050-703-572, run by American expat Olene).

Post Office: It's on the Markt near the bell tower (Mon-Fri 9:00-18:00, Sat 9:30-15:00, closed Sun, tel. 050-331-411).

Laundry: Bruges has three self-service launderettes, each a five-minute walk from the center; ask your hotelier for the nearest one.

Bike Rental: Bruges Bike Rental is central and cheap, with friendly service and long hours (€3.50/hour, €5/2 hours, €7/4

BRUGES

Bruges

SEE HOTEL & RESTAURANT
DETAIL MAPS

Sights & Services
1. In&Uit Tourist Info (in Concert Hall)
2. De Halve Maan Brewery Tour
3. Dumon Chocolate
4. The Chocolate Line
5. Confiserie De Clerck
6. Choco-Story: The Chocolate Museum
7. Friet Museum
8. Internet Café
9. Bike Rentals (5)
10. City Minibus Tours

Accommodations & Restaurants
11. Hotel Egmond
12. Hotel 't Keizershof
13. To Waterside B&B
14. To B&B AM/PM
15. Snuffel Backpacker Hostel
16. Bistro de Bekoring

P PARKING
B BOAT TOURS
Ⓑ BUS
≈ VIEW

¼ MILE
400 METERS

TO OSTENDE
TO OSTENDE
'T ZAND
TO 14
CONCERT HALL
TO OSTENDE
TO OSTENDE VIA FREEWAY
R-30
STATIONS-PLEIN
TRAIN STATION
TO BRUSSELS

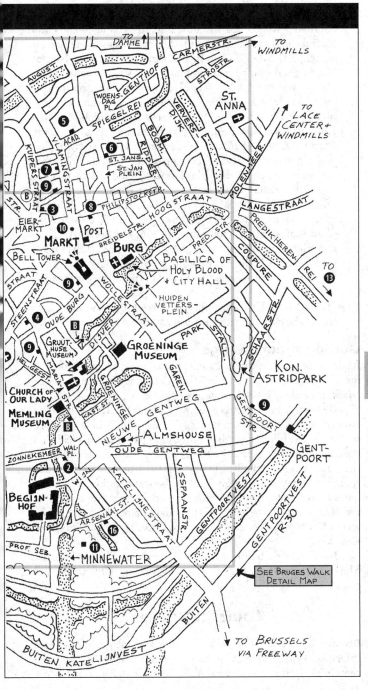

hours, €10/day, show this book to get student rate, no deposit required—just ID, daily 10:00-22:00, free city maps and child seats, behind the far-out iron facade at Niklaas Desparsstraat 17, tel. 050-616-108, Bilal). **Fietsen Popelier Bike Rental** is also good (€4/hour, €8/4 hours, €12/day, 24-hour day is OK if your hotel has a safe place to store bike, no deposit required, daily 10:00-19:00, sometimes open later in summer, free Damme map, Mariastraat 26, tel. 050-343-262). **Koffieboontje Bike Rental** is just under the bell tower on the Markt (€4/hour, €9/day, €20/day for tandem, confirm that you're getting the Rick Steves price, daily 9:00-22:00, free city maps and child seats, Hallestraat 4, tel. 050-338-027).

Other rental places include the less-central **De Ketting** (cheap at €6/day, Mon-Fri 9:00-12:15 & 13:30-18:30 except Mon opens at 10:00, Sat 9:30-12:15, closed Sun, Gentpoortstraat 23, tel. 050-344-196, www.deketting.be) and **Fietspunt Brugge** at the train station (€9.50/day, €6.50/half-day after 14:00, €13 deposit, Mon-Fri 7:00-19:30, closed Sat-Sun, just outside the station and to the left as you exit, tel. 050-302-329).

Best Town View: The bell tower overlooking the Markt rewards those who climb it with the ultimate town view.

Getting Around Bruges

Most of the city is easily walkable, but you may want to take the bus or taxi between the train station and the city center at the Markt (especially if you have heavy luggage).

By Bus: A bus ticket is good for an hour (€1.20 if you buy in advance at Lijnwinkel shop just outside the train station, or €1.60 on the bus). While you can buy various day passes, there's really no need to buy one for your visit. Nearly all city buses go directly from the train station to the Markt and fan out from there; they then return to the Markt and go back to the train station. Note that buses returning to the train station from the Markt also leave from the library bus stop, a block off the square on nearby Kuiperstraat (every 5 minutes). Your key: Use buses that say either *Station* or *Centrum*.

By Taxi: You'll find taxi stands at the station and on the Markt (€8/first 2 km; to get a cab in the center, call 050-334-444 or 050-333-881).

Tours in Bruges

Bruges by Boat—The most relaxing and scenic (though not informative) way to see this city of canals is by boat, with the captain narrating. The city carefully controls this standard tourist activity, so the many companies all offer essentially the same thing: a 30-minute route (roughly 4/hour, daily 10:00-17:00), a price of €7 (cash only), and narration in three or four languages. Qualitative differences are because of individual guides, not companies. Always let them know you speak English to ensure you'll understand the spiel. Two companies give the group-rate discount to individuals with this book: Boten Stael (just over the canal from Memling Museum at Katelijnestraat 4, tel. 050-332-771) and Gruuthuse (Nieuwstraat 11, opposite Groeninge Museum, tel. 050-333-393).

Bruges by Bike—**QuasiMundo Bike Tours** leads daily five-mile English-language bike tours around the city (€25, discount with this book, 2.5 hours, departs March-Oct at 10:00, in Nov only with good weather, no tours Dec-Feb). For more details and contact info, see their listing under "Near Bruges," later.

City Minibus Tour—City Tour Bruges gives a rolling overview of the town in an 18-seat, two-skylight minibus with dial-a-language headsets and video support (€14.50, 50 minutes, pay driver). The tour leaves hourly from the Markt (10:00-20:00 in summer, until 19:00 in spring, until 18:00 in fall, less in winter, tel. 050-355-024, www.citytour.be). The narration, while clear, is slow-moving and a bit boring. But the tour is a lazy way to cruise past virtually every sight in Bruges.

Walking Tour—Local guides walk small groups through the core of town (€9, 2 hours, daily July-Aug, Sat-Sun only mid-April-June and Sept-Oct, depart from TI on 't Zand Square at 14:30—just drop in a few minutes early and buy tickets at the TI desk). Though earnest, the tours are heavy on history and given in two languages, so they may be less than peppy. Still, to propel you beyond the pretty gables and canal swans of Bruges, they're good medicine. In the off-season, "winter walks" leave from the same TI four evenings a week (€9, Nov-Feb Sat-Mon and Wed at 17:00).

Local Guide—A private two-hour guided tour costs €50 (reserve at least one week in advance through TI, tel. 050-448-686). Or contact Christian Scharlé and Daniëlle Janssens, who give two-hour walks for €70, three-hour guided drives for €150, and full-day tours of Bruges and Brussels for €200 (Christian's mobile 0475-659-507, Daniëlle's mobile 0476-493-203, www.tourmanagement belgium.be, tmb@skynet.be).

Horse-and-Buggy Tour—The buggies around town can take you on a clip-clop tour (€36, 35 minutes; price is per carriage, not per person; buggies gather in Minnewater, near entrance to Begijnhof). When divided among four or five people, this can be a good value.

Near Bruges

Popular tour destinations from Bruges are Flanders Fields (famous WWI sites about 40 miles to the southwest) and the picturesque town of Damme (4 easy-to-bike miles to the northeast).

Quasimodo Countryside Tours—This company offers those with extra time two entertaining, all-day, English-only bus tours through the rarely visited Flemish countryside. The "Flanders Fields" tour concentrates on WWI battlefields, trenches, memorials, and poppy-splattered fields (Tue-Sun at 9:15, no tours Mon or in Jan, 8 hours, visit to In Flanders Fields Museum not included). The other tour, "Triple Treat," focuses on Flanders' medieval past and rich culture, with tastes of chocolate, waffles, and beer (departs Mon, Wed, and Fri at 9:15, 8 hours). Be ready for lots of walking.

Tours cost €60, or €50 if you're under 26 (cash preferred, €10 discount on second tour if you've taken the other, includes sandwich lunch, 9- or 30-seat bus depending on demand, non-smoking, reservations required—call 050-370-470, www.quasimodo.be). After making a few big-hotel pickups, the buses leave town from the Park Hotel on 't Zand Square (arrange for pickup when you reserve).

Flanders Fields Battlefield Daytours by Nathan—Nathan (or his right-hand man Karl) leads small groups on minibus day trips to the WWI sights between here and Ypres (Ieper). While pricier than Quasimodo's tour (listed above), Nathan's are more intimate: eight travelers on a minibus rather than a big busload (allowing your guide to tailor the tours to passengers' interests and nationalities); pickup from any hotel or B&B (because the small bus is allowed in the town center); and an included restaurant lunch instead of a picnic. Nathan's tours also include free time at the excellent museums in Ypres and Passchendaele (€65, discount when booked direct using this book, price includes admissions, cash only, departs Tue-Sun around 8:45 from your hotel or B&B, 8.5 hours, call 050-346-060 or toll-free 0800-99133 to reserve, www.visitbruges.org, info@visitbruges.org). In the evening, Nathan offers a shorter **Last Post Evening Tour,** with a stop at Tyne Cot Cemetery en route to the moving 20:00 bugle call at the Menin Gate in Ypres (€40, no discounts, departs Tue-Sun around 18:15 from your B&B/hotel, returns to Bruges around 21:15).

Bike Tours—**QuasiMundo Bike Tours,** which runs bike tours around Bruges (listed earlier) also offers a daily "Border by Bike" tour through the nearby countryside to Damme (€25, discount with this book, March-Oct, departs at 13:00, 15 miles, 4 hours, tel. 050-330-775, www.quasimundo.com). Both their city and border tours include bike rental, a light raincoat (if necessary), water, and a drink in a local café. Meet at the metal "car wash" fountain on Burg Square 10 minutes before departure. If you already have a bike, you're welcome to join either tour for €15. Jos, who leads most departures, is a high-energy and entertaining guide.

Charming Mieke of **Pink Bear Bike Tours** takes small groups on an easy and delightful 3.5-hour guided pedal along a canal to the historic town of Damme and back, finishing with a brief tour of Bruges. English tours go daily through peak season and nearly daily the rest of the year (€22, discount with this book, €15 if you already have a bike, meet at 10:25 under bell tower on the Markt, tel. 050-616-686, mobile 0476-744-525, www.pinkbear.freeservers .com).

For bike rental shops in Bruges, see page 183.

Sights in Bruges

These sights are listed in walking order, from the Markt, to Burg Square, to the cluster of museums around the Church of Our Lady, to the Begijnhof (10-minute walk from beginning to end, without stops).

▲**Markt (Market Square)**—Ringed by a bank, the post office, lots of restaurant terraces, great old gabled buildings, and the iconic bell tower, this square is the modern heart of the city (most city buses run from near here to the train station—it's a block down Kuiperstraat at the library bus stop). Under the bell tower are two great Belgian-style french-fry stands, a quadrilingual Braille description of the old town, and a metal model of the tower. In Bruges' heyday as a trading center, a canal came right up to this square. Geldmuntstraat, just off the square, is a delightful street with many fun and practical shops and eateries.

▲▲**Bell Tower (Belfort)**—Most of this bell tower has presided over the Markt since 1300, serenading passersby with carillon music. The octagonal lantern was added in 1486, making it 290 feet high—that's 366 steps. The view is worth the climb and probably even the €8 (daily 9:30-17:00, 16:15 last-entry time strictly enforced—best to show up before 16:00, €0.30 WC in courtyard).

▲▲**Burg Square**—This opulent square is Bruges' civic center, the historic birthplace of Bruges, and the site of the ninth-century castle of the first count of Flanders. Today, it's an atmospheric place to take in an outdoor concert while surrounded by six centuries of architecture.

▲**Basilica of the Holy Blood**—Originally the Chapel of Saint Basil, this church is famous for its relic of the blood of Christ, which, according to tradition, was brought to Bruges in 1150 after the Second Crusade. The lower chapel is dark and solid—a fine example of Romanesque style. The upper chapel (separate entrance, climb the stairs) is decorated Gothic. An interesting treasury museum is next to the upper chapel (treasury-€1.50;

BRUGES

April-mid-Oct daily 9:30-12:00 & 14:00-18:00; mid-Oct-March Thu-Tue 10:00-12:00 & 14:00-16:00, Wed 10:00-11:45 only; Burg Square, tel. 050-336-792, www.holyblood.com).

▲**City Hall**—This complex houses several interesting sights. Your €2 ticket includes an audioguide; access to a room full of old town maps and paintings; the grand, beautifully restored **Gothic Room** from 1400, starring a painted and carved wooden ceiling adorned with hanging arches (daily 9:30-17:00, last entry 30 minutes before closing, Burg 12); and the less impressive **Renaissance Hall** (Brugse Vrije), basically just one ornate room with a Renaissance chimney (same hours, separate entrance—in corner of square at Burg 11a).

▲▲▲**Groeninge Museum**—This recently renovated museum has one of the world's best collections of the art produced in the city and surrounding area, from Memling to Magritte. In the 1400s, Bruges was northern Europe's richest, most cosmopolitan, and most cultured city. Beautiful paintings were an affordable luxury, like fancy clothes or furniture. Internationally known artists set up studios in Bruges, producing portraits and altarpieces for wealthy merchants from all over Europe.

While there's plenty of worthwhile modern art, the Groeninge's highlights are the vivid and pristine Flemish Primitives. ("Primitive" here means "before the Renaissance.") This early Flemish style, though less appreciated and understood today than the Italian Renaissance art produced a century later, is subtle, technically advanced, and beautiful. Flemish art is shaped by its love of detail, its merchant patrons' egos, and the power of the Church. Lose yourself in the halls of Groeninge: Gaze across 15th-century canals, into the eyes of reassuring Marys, and through town squares littered with leotards, lace, and lopped-off heads.

Cost and Hours: €8, more for special exhibits, Tue-Sun 9:30-17:00, closed Mon, Dijver 12, tel. 050-448-743, www.brugge.be.

Gruuthuse Museum—Once a wealthy brewer's home, this 15th-century mansion is a sprawling smattering of everything from medieval bedpans to a guillotine. An extensive restoration, however, means it's closed from October 2011 until the end of 2012 (when open: €6, includes entry to apse in Church of Our Lady, Tue-Sun 9:30-17:00, closed Mon, Dijver 17, Bruges museums tel. 050-448-711, www.brugge.be).

▲▲**Church of Our Lady (Onze-Lieve-Vrouwekerk)**—The church stands as a memorial to the power and wealth of Bruges in its heyday. A delicate *Madonna and Child* by Michelangelo is near the apse (to the right if you're facing the altar). It's said to be the only Michelangelo statue to leave Italy in his lifetime (thanks to the wealth generated by Bruges' cloth trade). If you like tombs and church art, pay to wander through the apse (Michelangelo viewing is free, art-filled apse-€2, covered by Gruuthuse admission; church open Mon-Fri 9:30-17:00, Sat 9:30-16:45, Sun 13:30-17:00; museum and apse closed Mon, last entry 30 minutes before closing, Mariastraat, www.brugge.be).

▲▲**Memling Museum/St. John's Hospital (Sint Jans-hospitaal)**—The former monastery/hospital complex has a fine museum in what was once the monks' church. The museum offers a glimpse into medieval medicine, displaying surgical instruments, documents, and visual aids as you work your way to the museum's climax: several of Hans Memling's glowing masterpieces. Memling's art was the culmination of Bruges' Flemish Primitive style. His serene, soft-focus, motionless scenes capture a medieval piety that was quickly fading. The popular style made Memling (c. 1430-1494) one of Bruges' wealthiest citizens, and his work was gobbled up by visiting Italian merchants, who took it home with them, cross-pollinating European art. His *Mystical Wedding of St. Catherine* triptych is a highlight, as is the miniature, gilded-oak shrine to St. Ursula.

Cost and Hours: €8, includes fine audioguide, Tue-Sun 9:30-17:00, closed Mon, last entry 30 minutes before closing, across the street from the Church of Our Lady, Mariastraat 38, Bruges museums tel. 050-448-713, www.brugge.be.

▲▲**Begijnhof**—Inhabited by Benedictine nuns, the Begijnhof courtyard (free and always open) almost makes you want to don a habit and fold your hands as you walk under its wispy trees and whisper past its frugal little homes. For a good slice of Begijnhof life, walk through the simple museum, the Beguine's House museum (€2, Mon-Sat 10:00-17:00, Sun 14:30-17:00, shorter hours off-season, English explanations, museum is left of entry gate).

Minnewater—Just south of the Begijnhof is Minnewater, an idyllic world of flower boxes, canals, and swans.

Almshouses—As you walk from the Begijnhof back to the town center, you might detour along Nieuwe Gentweg to visit one of about 20 almshouses in the city. At #8, go through the door marked *Godshuis de Meulenaere 1613* into the peaceful courtyard (free). This was a medieval form of housing for the poor. The rich would pay for someone's tiny room here in return for lots of prayers.

Bruges Experiences: Beer, Chocolate, Windmills, and Biking

▲▲**De Halve Maan Brewery Tour**—Belgians are Europe's beer connoisseurs, and this handy tour is a great way to pay your respects. The brewery makes the only beers brewed in Bruges: Brugse Zot ("Fool from Bruges") and Straffe Hendrik ("Strong Henry"). The happy gang at this working-family brewery gives entertaining and informative, 45-minute tours in three languages.

Avoid crowds by visiting at 11:00 (€6 includes a beer, lots of very steep steps, great rooftop panorama; tours run April-Oct daily on the hour 11:00-16:00, Sat until 17:00; Nov-March Mon-Fri 11:00 and 15:00 only, Sat-Sun on the hour 11:00-16:00; Walplein 26, tel. 050-444-223, www.halvemaan.be).

▲**Chocolate Shops**—Bruggians are connoisseurs of fine chocolate. You'll be tempted by chocolate-filled display windows all over town. While Godiva is the best big-factory/high-price/high-quality brand, there are plenty of smaller, family-run places in Bruges that offer exquisite handmade chocolates. All three of the following chocolatiers are proud of their creative varieties, generous with their samples, and welcome you to assemble a 100-gram assortment of five or six chocolates.

Dumon: Perhaps Bruges' smoothest and creamiest chocolates are at Dumon (€2.20/100 grams). Madame Dumon and her children (Stefaan, Natale, and Christophe) make their top-notch chocolate daily and sell it fresh just off the Markt (Thu-Tue 10:00-18:00 except closes Sun at 17:00, occasionally open Wed, old chocolate molds on display in basement, Eiermarkt 6, tel. 050-346-282; two other Dumon shops around town offer the same chocolate, but not the same experience). The Dumons don't provide English labels because they believe it's best to describe their chocolates in person—and they do it with an evangelical fervor. Try a small mix-and-match box to sample a few out-of-this-world flavors, and come back for more of your favorites.

The Chocolate Line: Locals and tourists alike flock to The Chocolate Line (pricey at €5/100 grams) to taste the *gastronomique* varieties concocted by Dominique Person—the mad scientist of chocolate. His unique creations mix chocolate with various, mostly savory flavors. Even those that sound gross can be surprisingly good (be adventurous). Options include Havana cigar (marinated in rum, cognac, and Cuban tobacco leaves—so therefore technically illegal in the US), lemongrass, lavender, ginger (shaped like a Buddha), saffron curry, spicy chili, Moroccan mint, Pop Rocks/cola chocolate, wine vinegar, fried onions, bay leaf, sake, lime/vodka/passionfruit, wasabi, and tomatoes/olives/basil. The kitchen—busy whipping up 80 varieties—is on display in the back. Enjoy the window display, renewed monthly (daily 9:30-18:00 except Sun-Mon opens at 10:30, between Church of Our Lady and the Markt at Simon Stevinplein 19, tel. 050-341-090).

Confiserie De Clerck: Third-generation chocolate maker Jan sells his handmade chocolates for just €1.20/100 grams, making this one of the best deals in town. Some locals claim his chocolate's just as good as at pricier places—taste it and decide for yourself. The time-warp candy shop itself is so delightfully old-school, you'll want to visit no matter what (Mon-Wed and Fri-Sat 10:00-19:00, closed Sun and Thu, Academiestraat 19, tel. 050-345-338).

Choco-Story: The Chocolate Museum—This museum is rated ▲ for chocoholics. The Chocolate Fairy leads you through 2,600 years of chocolate history—explaining why, in the ancient Mexican world of the Mayas and the Aztecs, chocolate was considered the drink of the gods, and cocoa beans were used as a means of payment. With lots of artifacts well-described in English, the museum fills you in on the production of truffles, bonbons, hollow figures, and solid bars of chocolate. Then you'll view a delicious little video (8 minutes long, repeating continuously, alternating Flemish, French, and then English; peek into the theater to check the schedule. If you have time before the next English showing, visit the exhibits in the top room). Your finale is in the "demonstration room," where—after a 10-minute cooking demo—you get a taste (€7, €11 combo-ticket includes nearby Friet Museum, daily 10:00-17:00; where Wijnzakstraat meets Sint Jansstraat at Sint Jansplein, 3-minute walk from the Markt; tel. 050-612-237, www.choco-story.be). The Chocolate Museum is adjacent to (and offers a combo-ticket with) a lamp museum that's very skippable, unless you're a hard-core lamp enthusiast (in that case, boy, are you in luck).

Friet Museum—It's the only place in the world that enthusiastically tells the story of french fries, which, of course, aren't even French—they're Belgian (not worth €6, €11 combo-ticket includes Chocolate Museum, daily 10:00-17:00, Vlamingstraat 33, tel. 050-340-150, www.frietmuseum.be).

Windmills and Lace by the Moat—A 15-minute walk from the center to the northeast end of town (faster by bike) brings you to four windmills strung along a pleasant grassy setting on the "big moat" canal. The St. Janshuys **windmill** is open to visitors (€2; May-Aug Tue-Sun 9:30-12:30 & 13:30-17:00, closed Mon, last entry at 16:30; Sept same hours but open Sat-Sun only; closed Oct-April; go to the end of Carmersstraat and hang a right).

The **Folklore Museum,** in the same neighborhood, is cute but forgettable (€2, Tue-Sun 9:30-17:00, last entry at 16:30, closed Mon, Balstraat 43, tel. 050-448-764). To find it, ask for the Jerusalem Church. On the same street is a lace shop with a good reputation, **'t Apostelientje** (Tue 13:00-17:00, Wed-Sat 9:30-12:15 & 13:15-17:00, Sun 10:00-13:00, closed Mon, Balstraat 11, tel. 050-337-860, mobile 0495-562-420).

▲▲**Biking**—The Flemish word for bike is *fiets* (pronounced "feets"). While Bruges' sights are close enough for easy walking, the town is a treat for bikers, and a bike quickly gets you into dreamy back lanes without a hint of tourism. Take a peaceful evening ride through the town's nooks and crannies and around the outer canal. Consider keeping a bike for the duration of your stay—it's the way the locals get around in Bruges. Along the canal that circles the town is a park with a delightful bike lane. Rental shops have maps and ideas (see "Bike Rental" on page 183 for more info).

Nightlife in Bruges

Herberg Vlissinghe and **De Garre,** listed under "Eating in Bruges," later, are great places to just nurse a beer and enjoy new friends.

Charlie Rockets is an American-style bar—lively and central—with foosball games, darts, and five pool tables (€9/hour) in the inviting back room. It also runs a youth hostel upstairs and therefore is filled with a young, international crowd (a block off the Markt at Hoogstraat 19). It's open nightly until 3:00 in the morning with non-stop rock 'n' roll.

Nighttime Bike Ride: Great as these pubs are, my favorite way to spend a late-summer evening in Bruges is in the twilight on a rental bike, savoring the cobbled wonders of its back streets, far from the touristic commotion.

Evening Carillon Concerts: The tiny courtyard behind the bell tower has a few benches where people can enjoy the free carillon concerts (generally Mon, Wed, and Sat at 21:00 in the summer; schedule posted on courtyard wall).

Sleeping in Bruges

Bruges is a great place to sleep, with Gothic spires out your window, no traffic noise, and the cheerily out-of-tune carillon heralding each new day at 8:00 sharp. (Thankfully, the bell tower is silent from 22:00 to 8:00.) Most Bruges accommodations are located between the train station and the old center, with the most distant (and best) being a few blocks to the north and east of the Markt (Market Square).

B&Bs offer the best value (listed on page 198). All are on quiet streets and (with a few exceptions) keep the same prices throughout the year.

Bruges is most crowded Friday and Saturday evenings from Easter through October, with July and August weekends being the worst. Many hotels charge a bit more on Friday and Saturday, and won't let you stay just one night if it's a Saturday.

Hotels

$$$ Hotel Heritage offers 24 rooms, with chandeliers that seem hung especially for you, in a solid and completely modernized old building with luxurious public spaces. Tastefully decorated and offering all the amenities, it's one of those places that does everything just right yet still feels warm and inviting—if you can afford

Sleep Code

(€1 = about $1.40, country code: 32)
S = Single, **D** = Double/Twin, **T** = Triple, **Q** = Quad, **b** = bathroom, **s** = shower only. Everyone speaks English. Unless otherwise noted, breakfast is included and credit cards are accepted.

To help you easily sort through these listings, I've divided the rooms into three categories, based on the price for a standard double room with bath:

$$$ Higher Priced—Most rooms €125 or more.
$$ Moderately Priced—Most rooms between €80-125.
$ Lower Priced—Most rooms €80 or less.

Prices can change without notice; verify the hotel's current rates online or by email. For other updates, see www.ricksteves.com/update.

it (Db-€170, superior Db-€218, deluxe Db-€270, extra bed-€60, wonderful buffet breakfast-€21/person, continental breakfast-€11/person, air-con, elevator, free Internet access and Wi-Fi, sauna, tanning bed, fitness room, bike rental, free 2-hour guided city tour, parking-€22/day, Niklaas Desparsstraat 11, a block north of the Markt, tel. 050-444-444, fax 050-444-440, www.hotel-heritage .com, info@hotel-heritage.com). It's run by cheery and hardworking Johan and Isabelle Creytens.

$$$ Hotel Adornes is small and classy—a great value situated in the most charming part of town. This 17th-century canalside house has 20 rooms with full modern bathrooms, free parking (reserve in advance), free loaner bikes, and a cellar lounge with games and videos (small Db-€120, larger Db-€140-150, Tb-€175, Qb-€180, elevator, free Wi-Fi in lobby, some street noise, near Carmersstraat at St. Annarei 26, tel. 050-341-336, fax 050-342-085, www.adornes.be, info@adornes.be). Nathalie runs the family business.

$$ Hotel Patritius, family-run and centrally located, is a grand, circa-1830, Neoclassical mansion with hardwood oak floors in its 16 stately, high-ceilinged rooms. It features a plush lounge, a chandeliered breakfast room, and a courtyard garden. This is the best value in its price range (Db-€100-130, Tb-€140-155, Qb-€165-180, cheaper in off-season, rates depend on room size and demand—check site for best price, extra bed-€25, air-con, elevator, pay Internet access, free Wi-Fi on ground floor, coin-op laundry, parking-€8, garage parking-€14, Riddersstraat 11, tel. 050-338-454, fax 050-339-634, www.hotelpatritius.be, info@hotelpatritius .be, Garrett and Elvi Spaey).

BRUGES

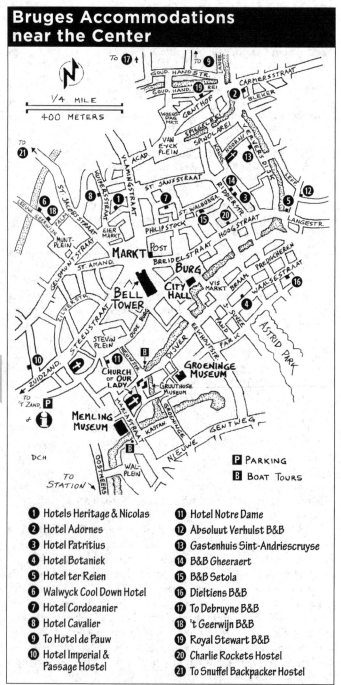

Bruges Accommodations near the Center

1/4 MILE
400 METERS

1 Hotels Heritage & Nicolas
2 Hotel Adornes
3 Hotel Patritius
4 Hotel Botaniek
5 Hotel ter Reien
6 Walwyck Cool Down Hotel
7 Hotel Cordoeanier
8 Hotel Cavalier
9 To Hotel de Pauw
10 Hotel Imperial & Passage Hostel

11 Hotel Notre Dame
12 Absoluut Verhulst B&B
13 Gastenhuis Sint-Andriescruyse
14 B&B Gheeraert
15 B&B Setola
16 Dieltiens B&B
17 To Debruyne B&B
18 't Geerwijn B&B
19 Royal Stewart B&B
20 Charlie Rockets Hostel
21 To Snuffel Backpacker Hostel

P PARKING
B BOAT TOURS

$$ Hotel Egmond is a creaky mansion located in the middle of the quietly idyllic Minnewater. Its eight 18th-century rooms are plain, with small modern baths shoehorned in, and the guests-only garden is just waiting for a tea party. This hotel is ideal for romantics who want a countryside setting—where you sleep surrounded by a park, not a city (Sb-€95, small twin Db-€105, larger Db-€115, Tb-€150, cheaper in winter, free Wi-Fi, parking-€10, Minnewater 15, for location see map on page 199, tel. 050-341-445, fax 050-342-940, www.egmond.be, info@egmond.be, Steven).

$$ Hotel Botaniek, quietly located a block from Astrid Park, is a fine, pint-sized hotel with a comfy lounge, renting nine rooms—some of them quite big (Db-€95 weekday special for my readers, €99 Fri-Sat; Tb-€130 on weekdays, €140 Fri-Sat; Qb-€145, €149 Fri-Sat; less for longer and off-season stays, free museum-discount card, elevator, Waalsestraat 23, tel. 050-341-424, fax 050-345-939, www.botaniek.be, info@botaniek.be, Yasmine).

$$ Hotel ter Reien is big and basic, with 26 rooms overlooking a canal in the town center (Db-€80-110, Tb-€110-130, Qb-€140-160, rates vary widely with demand—check their website for best prices; cheapest rates for weekdays, stays of at least 3 nights, rooms without canal views; extra bed-€24-29, 5 percent Rick Steves discount if you book directly and show this book at check-in, pay Internet access and Wi-Fi, Langestraat 1, tel. 050-349-100, fax 050-340-048, www.hotelterreien.be, info@hotelterreien.be, owned by Diederik and Stephanie Pille-Maes).

$$ Walwyck Cool Down Hotel—a bit of modern comfort, chic design, and English verbiage in a medieval shell—is a nicely located hotel with 18 spacious rooms (small Db-€90, standard Db-€100, "superior" Db-€120, Tb-€135, family room-€155, "superior" family room-€180, Internet access, free Wi-Fi, Leeuwstraat 8, tel. 050-616-360, fax 050-616-560, www.walwyck.com, rooms @walwyck.com).

$$ Hotel Cordoeanier, a charming family-run hotel, rents 22 simple, fresh, hardwood-floor rooms on a quiet street two blocks off the Markt. It's one of the best deals in town (Sb-€70-95, Db-€75-100, twin Db-€85-100, Tb-€95-110, Qb-€125, Quint/b-€145, cheaper with cash if you show this book, breakfast buffet served in their pleasant Café Rose Red, no elevator, pay Internet access, free Wi-Fi, patio, Cordoeanierstraat 16-18, tel. 050-339-051, fax 050-346-111, www.cordoeanier.be, info@cordoeanier.be, Kris).

$ Hotel Cavalier, with more stairs than character, rents eight decent rooms and serves a hearty buffet breakfast in a once-royal setting (Sb-€55, Db-€70, Tb-€85, Qb-€100, two lofty en-suite "back-packers' doubles" on fourth floor-€45-50, book direct and mention this book for special Rick Steves price, pay Wi-Fi,

Kuipersstraat 25, tel. 050-330-207, fax 050-347-199, www.hotel cavalier.be, info@hotelcavalier.be, run by friendly Viviane De Clerck).

$ Hotel de Pauw is tall, skinny, flower-bedecked, and family-run, with eight straightforward rooms on a quiet street next to a church (Sb-€65-75, Db-€70-85, no elevator, free and easy street parking, Sint Gilliskerkhof 8, tel. 050-337-118, fax 050-345-140, www.hoteldepauw.be, info@hoteldepauw.be, Philippe and Hilde).

$ Hotel 't Keizershof is a dollhouse of a hotel that lives by its motto, "Spend a night...not a fortune." (Its other motto: "When you're asleep, we look just like those big fancy hotels.") It's simple and tidy, with seven small, cheery, old-time rooms split between two floors, with a shower and toilet on each (S-€25, D-€44, T-€66, Q-€80, cash only, free and easy parking, laundry service-€7.50, Oostmeers 126, a block in front of station, for location see map on facing page, tel. 050-338-728, www.hotelkeizershof.be, info @hotelkeizershof.be). The hotel is run by Stefaan and Hilde, with decor by their children, Lorie and Fien; it's situated in a pleasant area near the train station and Minnewater, a 15 minute-walk from the Markt.

$ Hotel Nicolas feels like an old-time boarding house that missed Bruges' affluence bandwagon. Its 14 big, plain rooms are a good value, and the location is ideal—on a quiet street a block off the Markt (Sb-€55, Db-€63, Tb-€75, elevator, pay Wi-Fi, TV on request, closed in Jan, Niklaas Desparsstraat 9, tel. 050-335-502, fax 050-343-544, www.hotelnicolas.be, hotel.nicolas@telenet.be, Yi-Ling and Thomas).

$ Hotel Imperial is an old-school hotel with seven old-school rooms. It's simple and well-run in a charming building on a handy, quiet street (Db-€70-90, cash only, no elevator, pay Wi-Fi, Dweersstraat 24, tel. 050-339-014, www.hotelimperial.be, info @hotelimperial.be, Paul Bernolet and Hilde).

$ Hotel Notre Dame is a humble and blocky little budget option, renting 12 worn rooms in the busy thick of things (Db-€70-75, free Internet access and Wi-Fi, Mariastraat 3, tel. 050-333-193, fax 050-337-608, www.hotelnotredame.be, info@hotelnotre dame.be).

Bed-and-Breakfasts

These B&Bs, run by people who enjoy their work, offer a better value than hotels. Most families rent out their entire top floor—generally three rooms and a small sitting area. And most are mod and stylish—they're just in medieval shells. Each is central, with lots of stairs and €70 doubles you'd pay €100 for in a hotel. Most places charge €10 extra for one-night stays. It's possible to find parking on the street in the evening (pay 9:00-19:00, 2-hour

Bruges Accommodations away from the Center

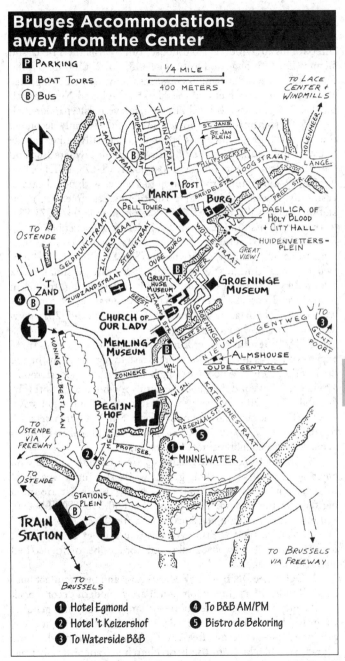

P Parking
B Boat Tours
B Bus

1/4 MILE
400 METERS

TO LACE CENTER + WINDMILLS

TO OSTENDE

MARKT
POST
BURG
BELL TOWER
BASILICA OF HOLY BLOOD + CITY HALL
HUIDENVETTERS-PLEIN
GREAT VIEW!

GRUUT-HUSE MUSEUM
GROENINGE MUSEUM

'T ZAND

CHURCH OF OUR LADY
MEMLING MUSEUM

ALMSHOUSE
OUDE GENTWEG

TO GENT-POORT

ZONNEKE

BEGIJN-HOF

MINNEWATER

TO OSTENDE VIA FREEWAY

TO OSTENDE

STATIONS-PLEIN

TRAIN STATION

TO BRUSSELS VIA FREEWAY

TO BRUSSELS

BRUGES

❶ Hotel Egmond
❷ Hotel 't Keizershof
❸ To Waterside B&B
❹ To B&B AM/PM
❺ Bistro de Bekoring

maximum for metered parking during the day, free overnight).

$$ Absoluut Verhulst is a great, modern-feeling B&B with three rooms in a 400-year-old house, run by friendly Frieda and Benno (Db-€95; huge and lofty suite-€130 for 2, €160 for 3, €180 for 4; €10 more for one-night stays, cash only, non-smoking, free Wi-Fi, 5-minute walk east of the Markt at Verbrand Nieuwland 1, tel. 050-334-515, www.b-bverhulst.com, b-b.verhulst@pandora.be).

$$ Gastenhuis Sint-Andriescruyse offers warmly decorated rooms with high ceilings in a spacious, cheerfully red canalside house a short walk from the Old Town action. Owners Luc and Christiane treat guests like long-lost family (S-€75, D/Db-€100, T-€125, Q-€150, family room for up to 5 comes with board games, cash only, free soft drinks, free Internet access, free pick-up at station, Verversdijk 15A, tel. 050-789-168, mobile 0477-973-933, www.gastenhuisst-andriescruyse.be, luc.cluoet@telenet.be).

$$ B&B Gheeraert is a Neoclassical mansion where Inne rents three huge, bright, comfy rooms (Sb-€85, Db-€95, Tb-€115, two-night minimum stay required, cash only, personal check required for first-night's deposit, strictly non-smoking, fridges in rooms, free Internet access and Wi-Fi, Riddersstraat 9, 5-minute walk east of the Markt, tel. 050-335-627, fax 050-345-201, www.bb-bruges.be, bb-bruges@skynet.be).

$ B&B Setola, run by Lut and Bruno Setola, offers three expansive rooms and a spacious breakfast/living room on the top floor of their house. Wooden ceiling beams give the modern rooms a touch of Old World flair, and the family room has a fun loft (Sb-€60, Db-€70, €20 per extra person, €10 more for one-night stays, free Wi-Fi, 5-minute walk from the Markt, Sint Walburgastraat 12, tel. 050-334-977, fax 050-332-551, www.bedandbreakfast-bruges.com, setola@bedandbreakfast-bruges.com).

$ Koen and Annemie Dieltiens are a friendly couple who enjoy getting to know their guests while sharing a wealth of information on Bruges. You'll eat a hearty breakfast around a big table in their comfortable house (Sb-€60, Db-€70, Tb-€90, €10 more for one-night stays, cash only, free Internet access and Wi-Fi, Waalsestraat 40, three blocks southeast of Burg Square, tel. 050-334-294, www.bedandbreakfastbruges.be, dieltiens@bedandbreakfastbruges.be).

$ Debruyne B&B, run by Marie-Rose and her architect husband, Ronny, offers three rooms with artsy, modern decor (check out the elephant-size white doors—Ronny's design) and genuine warmth (Sb-€60, Db-€65, Tb-€85, €10 more for one-night stays, cash only, Internet access, free Wi-Fi, 7-minute walk north of the Markt, two blocks from the little church at Lange Raamstraat 18, tel. 050-347-606, www.bedandbreakfastbruges.com, mietje debruyne@yahoo.co.uk).

$ 't Geerwijn B&B, run by Chris de Loof, offers homey rooms in the old center. Check out the fun, lofty A-frame room upstairs (Ds/Db-€70-80 depending on season, Tb-€85, cash only, pleasant breakfast room and royal lounge, free Wi-Fi, Geerwijnstraat 14, tel. 050-340-544, fax 050-343-721, www.geerwijn.be, info @geerwijn.be). Chris also rents an apartment that sleeps five.

$ Royal Stewart B&B, run by Scottish Maggie and her husband, Gilbert, has three thoughtfully decorated rooms in a quiet, almost cloistered 17th-century house that was inhabited by nuns until 1953 (S-€48, D/Db-€65, Tb-€85, cash only, pleasant breakfast room, Genthof 25-27, 5-minute walk from the Markt, tel. 050-337-918, fax 050-337-918, www.royalstewart.be, r.stewart @pandora.be).

$ Waterside B&B has two fresh, Zen-like rooms, one floor above a peaceful canal south of the town center (D-€75, €5 more on Sat, continental breakfast, free Wi-Fi, 15-minute walk from Burg Square at Kazernevest 88, for location see map on page 199, tel. & fax 050-616-686, mobile 0476-744-525, www.waterside.be, waterside@telenet.be, run by Mieke of recommended Pink Bear Bike Tours).

$ B&B AM/PM sports three ultramodern rooms in a residential neighborhood just west of the Old Town (Db-€70, Tb-€90, €10 more for one-night stay, cash only, free Internet access—mornings only, free Wi-Fi, 5-minute walk from 't Zand at Singel 10, for location see map on page 199, mobile 0485-071-003, www .bruges-bedandbreakfast.com, info@bruges-bedandbreakfast.com, artsy young couple Tiny and Kevin). From the train station, head left down busy Buiten Begijnevest to the roundabout. Stay to the left, take the pedestrian underpass, then follow the busy road (now on your left). Just before the next bridge, turn right onto the footpath called Buiten Boeverievest, then turn left onto Singel; the B&B is at #10.

BRUGES

Hostels

Bruges has several good hostels offering beds for around €15 in two- to eight-bed rooms. Breakfast is about €3 extra. The American-style **$ Charlie Rockets** hostel (and bar), a backpacker dive, is the liveliest and most central. The ground floor feels like a 19th-century sports bar, with a foosball-and-movie-posters party ambience. Upstairs is an industrial-strength pile of hostel dorms (90 beds, €18/bed with sheets, €20/bed with sheets and breakfast, 4-6 beds/room, D-€50 includes breakfast, lockers, pay Internet access, Hoogstraat 19, tel. 050-330-660, www.charlierockets.com). Other small and loose places are the minimal, funky, and central **$ Passage** (€15/bed with sheets, 4-7 beds/room, D-€50, Db-€65, Dweerstraat 26, tel. 050-340-232, www.passagebruges.com, info@passagebruges.com) and **$ Snuffel Backpacker Hostel,** which is less central and pretty grungy, but friendly and laid-back (60 beds, €15-19/bed includes sheets and breakfast, 4-14 beds/ room, Ezelstraat 47, tel. 050-333-133, www.snuffel.be).

Eating in Bruges

Bruges' specialties include mussels cooked a variety of ways (one order can feed two), fish dishes, grilled meats, and french fries. The town's two indigenous beers are the prizewinning Brugse Zot (Bruges Fool), a golden ale, and Straffe Hendrik, a potent, bitter triple ale.

You'll find plenty of affordable, touristy restaurants on floodlit squares and along dreamy canals. Bruges feeds 3.5 million tourists a year, and most are seduced by a high-profile location. These can be fine experiences for the magical setting and views, but the quality of food and service will likely be low. I wouldn't blame you for eating at one of these places, but I won't recommend any. I prefer the candle-cool bistros that flicker on back streets.

Restaurants

Rock Fort is a chic spot with a modern, fresh coziness and a high-powered respect for good food. Two young chefs, Peter Laloo and Hermes Vanliefde, give their French cuisine a creative and gourmet twist. At the bar, they serve a separate tapas menu. Reservations are required for dinner and recommended for lunch. This place is a winner (€6-12 tapas, great pastas and salads, €15 Mon-Fri lunch special, beautifully presented €19-34 dinner plates, €40 five-tapas special, fancy €50 fixed-price four-course meal, open Mon-Fri 12:00-14:30 & 18:30-23:00, closed Sat-Sun, Langestraat 15, tel. 050-334-113).

Bistro de Bekoring, cute, candlelit, and Gothic, fills two almshouses and a delightful terrace with people thankful for good food. Rotund and friendly Chef Roland and his wife, Gerda, love to tempt the hungry—as the name of their bistro implies. They serve traditional Flemish food (especially eel and beer-soaked stew) from a small menu to people who like holding hands as they dine. Reservations are smart (€15 weekday lunch, €30 fixed-price dinners, €42 with wine, Wed-Sat 11:45-13:45 & 18:30-21:00, closed Sun evening and Mon-Tue; out past the Begijnhof at Arsenaalstraat 53, for location see map on page 199, tel. 050-344-157).

Bistro in den Wittenkop, very Flemish, is a stylishly small, laid-back, old-time place specializing in the local favorites. It's a classy spot to enjoy hand-cut fries, which go particularly well with Straffe Hendrik beer (€37-40 three-course meal, €20-25 plates, Tue-Sat 18:00-21:30, closed Sun-Mon, reserve ahead, terrace in

Bruges Restaurants

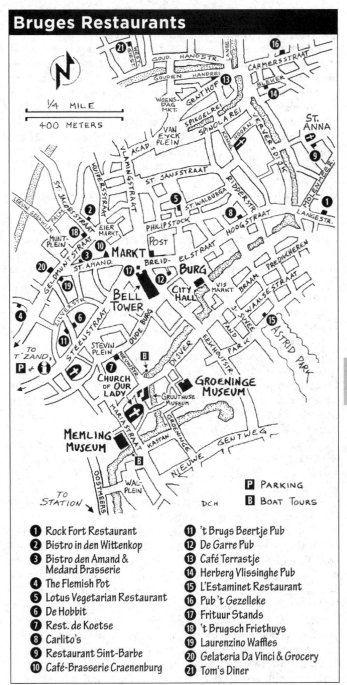

N

1/4 MILE
400 METERS

P PARKING
B BOAT TOURS

DCH

BRUGES

1 Rock Fort Restaurant
2 Bistro in den Wittenkop
3 Bistro den Amand & Medard Brasserie
4 The Flemish Pot
5 Lotus Vegetarian Restaurant
6 De Hobbit
7 Rest. de Koetse
8 Carlito's
9 Restaurant Sint-Barbe
10 Café-Brasserie Craenenburg

11 't Brugs Beertje Pub
12 De Garre Pub
13 Café Terrastje
14 Herberg Vlissinghe Pub
15 L'Estaminet Restaurant
16 Pub 't Gezelleke
17 Frituur Stands
18 't Brugsch Friethuys
19 Laurenzino Waffles
20 Gelateria Da Vinci & Grocery
21 Tom's Diner

back in summer, Sint Jakobsstraat 14, tel. 050-332-059).

Bistro den Amand, with a plain interior and a few outdoor tables, exudes unpretentious quality the moment you step in. In this mussels-free zone, Chef An is enthusiastic about vegetables, as her busy wok and fun salads prove. The creative dishes—some with a hint of Asian influence—are a welcome departure from Bruges' mostly predictable traditional restaurants. It's on a bustling pedestrian lane a half-block off the Markt (€33-35 three-course meal, €20 plates; Mon-Tue and Thu-Sat 12:00-14:00 & 18:00-21:00, closed Wed and Sun; Sint-Amandstraat 4, tel. 050-340-122, An Vissers and Arnout Beyaert). Reservations are smart for dinner.

The Flemish Pot (a.k.a. The Little Pancake House) is a hard-working eatery serving up traditional peasant-style meals. They crank out pancakes (savory and sweet) and homemade *wafels* for lunch. Then, at 18:00, enthusiastic chefs Mario and Rik stow their waffle irons and pull out a traditional menu of vintage Flemish specialties served in little iron pots and skillets. Seating is tight and cluttered. You'll enjoy huge portions, refills from the hovering "fries angel," and a good selection of local beers (€26-30 three-course meals, €16-24 plates, Wed-Sun 12:00-22:00, closed Mon-Tue, reservations smart, family-friendly, just off Geldmuntstraat at Helmstraat 3, tel. 050-340-086).

Lotus Vegetarian Restaurant serves serious lunch plates (€10 *plat du jour* offered daily), salads, and homemade chocolate cake in a pleasantly small, bustling, and upscale setting without a trace of tie-dye. To keep carnivorous companions happy, they also serve several very good, organic meat dishes (Mon-Fri from 11:45, last orders at 14:00, closed Sat-Sun, cash only, just north of Burg Square at Wapenmakersstraat 5, tel. 050-331-078).

De Hobbit, featuring an entertaining menu, is always busy with happy eaters. For a swinging deal, try the all-you-can-eat spareribs with bread and salad for €18.50. It's nothing fancy, just good, basic food served in a fun, crowded, traditional grill house (daily 18:00-23:00, Fri-Sat until 23:30, family-friendly, Kemelstraat 8-10, reservations smart, tel. 050-335-520).

Tom's Diner is a trendy, cozy little candlelit bistro in a quiet, cobbled residential area a 10-minute walk from the center. Young chef Tom gives traditional dishes a delightful modern twist. If you want to flee the tourists and experience a popular neighborhood joint, this is it—the locals love it (€15-20 plates, Wed-Mon 18:00-24:00, closed Tue, north of the Markt near Sint-Gilliskerk at West-Gistelhof 23, tel. 050-333-382).

Restaurant de Koetse is a fine bet for central, good-quality, local-style food. The feeling is traditional, a bit formal (stuffy even), and dressy, yet accessible. The cuisine is Belgian and French, with an emphasis on grilled meat, seafood, and mussels (€30 three-course meals, €20-30 plates include vegetables and a salad, Fri-Wed 12:00-14:30 & 18:00-22:00, closed Thu, non-smoking section, Oude Burg 31, tel. 050-337-680, Piet).

Carlito's is a good choice for basic Italian fare. Their informal space, with whitewashed walls and tea-light candles, is two blocks from Burg Square (€8-13 pizzas and pastas, daily 12:00-14:00 & 18:00-22:30, patio seating in back, Hoogstraat 21, tel. 050-490-075).

Restaurant Sint-Barbe, on the eastern edge of town, serves classy Flemish dishes made from local ingredients in a fresh, modern space on two floors. Their €12 soup-and-main lunch is a great deal (€14-25 main courses, Thu-Mon 11:30-14:30 & 18:00-22:00, closed Tue-Wed, food served until 21:00, St. Annaplein 29, tel. 050-330-999, Evi).

Restaurants on the Markt: Most tourists seem to be eating on the Markt with the bell tower high overhead and horse carriages clip-clopping by. The square is ringed by tourist traps with aggressive waiters expert at getting you to consume more than you intended. Still, if you order smartly, you can have a memorable meal or drink here on one of the finest squares in Europe at a reasonable price. Consider **Café-Brasserie Craenenburg,** with a straightforward menu, where you can get pasta and beer for €15 and spend all the time you want ogling the magic of Bruges (daily 7:30-23:00, Markt 16, tel. 050-333-402).

Cheap Eats: **Medard Brasserie,** just a block off the Markt, serves the cheapest hot meal in town—hearty meat spaghetti (big plate-€3, huge plate-€5.50, sit inside or out, Fri-Wed 11:00-20:30 except opens on Sun at 12:30, closed Thu, Sint Amandstraat 18, tel. 050-348-684).

Bars Offering Light Meals, Beer, and Ambience

My best budget-eating tip for Bruges: Stop into one of the city's atmospheric bars for a simple meal and a couple of world-class beers with great Bruges ambience. The last three pubs listed are in the wonderfully *gezellig* (cozy) quarter, northeast of the Markt.

The **'t Brugs Beertje** is young and convivial. While any pub or restaurant carries the basic beers, you'll find a selection here of more than 300 types, including brews to suit any season. They serve light meals, including pâté, spaghetti, toasted sandwiches, and a traditional cheese plate. You're welcome to sit at the bar and talk with the staff (five cheeses, bread, and salad for €11; Thu-Tue 16:00-24:00, closed Wed, Kemelstraat 5, tel. 050-339-616, run by fun-loving manager Daisy).

De Garre is another good place to gain an appreciation of the Belgian beer culture. Rather than a noisy pub scene, it has a dressy, sit-down-and-focus-on-your-friend-and-the-fine-beer vibe. It's mature and cozy with tables, light meals (cold cuts, pâtés, and toasted sandwiches), and a selection of 150 beers (daily 12:00-24:00, additional seating up tiny staircase, off Breidelstraat between Burg and Markt, on tiny Garre alley, tel. 050-341-029).

Café Terrastje is a cozy pub serving light meals. Experience the grown-up ambience inside, or relax on the front terrace overlooking the canal and heart of the *gezellig* district (€6-8 sandwiches, €10-18 dishes; food served Fri-Mon 12:00-21:00, open until 23:30; Tue 12:00-18:00; closed Wed-Thu; corner of Genthof and Langerei, tel. 050-330-919, Ian and Patricia).

Herberg Vlissinghe is the oldest pub in town (1515). Bruno keeps things simple and laid-back, serving simple plates (lasagna, grilled cheese sandwiches, and famous €8 angel-hair spaghetti) and great beer in the best old-time tavern atmosphere in town. This must have been the Dutch Masters' rec room. The garden outside comes with a *boules* court—free for guests to watch or play (Wed-Sat 11:00-24:00, Sun 11:00-19:00, closed Mon-Tue, Blekersstraat 2, tel. 050-343-737).

L'Estaminet is a youthful, jazz-filled eatery, similar to one of Amsterdam's brown cafés. Don't be intimidated by its lack of tourists. Local students flock here for the Tolkien-chic ambience, hearty €9 spaghetti, and big dinner salads. Since this is Belgium, it serves more beer than wine. For outdoor dining under an all-weather canopy, enjoy the relaxed patio facing peaceful Astrid Park (Fri-Wed 11:30-24:00, Thu 16:00-24:00, Park 5, tel. 050-330-916).

Pub 't Gezelleke lacks the mystique of the Vlissinghe, but it's a true neighborhood pub offering quality fare and a fine chance to drink with locals. Its name is an appropriate play on the word for cozy and the name of a great local poet (Mon-Fri 11:00-24:00, closed Sat-Sun, Carmersstraat 15, tel. 050-338-381, Zena).

Fries, Fast Food, and Picnics

Local french fries *(frites)* are a treat. Proud and traditional *frituur*s serve tubs of fries and various local-style shish kebabs. Belgians dip their *frites* in mayonnaise, but ketchup is there for the Yankees (along with spicier sauces). For a quick, cheap, hot, and scenic snack, hit a *frituur* and sit on the steps or benches overlooking the Markt (convenience benches are about 50 yards past the post office).

Markt *Frituur*s: Twin, take-away fry carts are on the Markt at the base of the bell tower (daily 10:00-24:00). Skip the ketchup and have a sauce adventure. I find the cart on the left more user-friendly.

't Brugsch Friethuys, a block off the Markt, is handy for sit-down fries. Its forte is greasy, fast, deep-fried Flemish fast food. The €11 "menu 1" comes with three traditional gut bombs: shrimp, *frikandel* minced-meat sausage, and "gypsy stick" sausage (daily 11:00-late, at the corner of Geldmuntstraat and Sint Jakobstraat).

Delhaize-Proxy Supermarket is ideal for picnics. Its push-button produce pricer lets you buy as few as one mushroom (Mon-Sat 9:00-19:00, closed Sun, 3 blocks off the Markt on Geldmuntstraat). For midnight snacks, you'll find Indian-run corner grocery stores scattered around town.

Belgian Waffles and Ice Cream

You'll see waffles sold at restaurants and take-away stands. **Laurenzino** is particularly good, and a favorite with Bruges' teens when they get the waffle munchies. Their classic waffle with chocolate costs €2.50 (daily in summer 10:00-22:00, until 23:00 Fri-Sat; winter 10:00-20:00, until 22:00 Fri-Sat; across from Gelateria Da Vinci at Noordzandstraat 1, tel. 050-333-213).

Gelateria Da Vinci, the local favorite for homemade ice cream, has creative flavors and a lively atmosphere. As you approach, you'll see a line of happy lickers. Before ordering, ask to sample the Ferrero Rocher (chocolate, nuts, and crunchy cookie) and plain yogurt (daily 10:00-22:00, until 24:00 April-Sept and in good-weather off-season, Geldmuntstraat 34, run by Sylvia from Austria).

Bruges Connections

From Bruges by Train to: Brussels (2/hour, usually at :31 and :58, 1 hour, €12.90), **Brussels Airport** (2/hour, 1.5 hours, transfer at Brussels Nord), **Delft** (hourly, 3 hours, change in Ghent, Antwerp, and Rotterdam), **Paris** (roughly hourly via Brussels, 2.5 hours on fast Thalys trains—it's best to book by 20:00 the day before), **Amsterdam** (hourly, 3.25-3.75 hours, transfer at Ghent and Antwerp Central or Brussels Midi; transfer can be tight—be alert and check with conductor; some trips via Thalys train, which requires supplement), **Amsterdam's Schiphol Airport** (hourly, 3.5 hours, change in Ghent and/or Antwerp; less frequent connections via Brussels with Thalys save 30 minutes), **Haarlem** (hourly, 3.5 hours, 2-3 changes—avoid Thalys if traveling with a railpass). Train info: tel. 050/302-424.

Trains from London: Bruges is an ideal "Welcome to Europe" stop after London. Take the Eurostar train from London to Brussels (10/day, 2.5 hours), then transfer, backtracking to Bruges (2/hour, 1 hour, entire trip just a few dollars more with Eurostar ticket; see Eurostar details on page 819).

Trains to London: Eurostar trains to London leave from tracks 1 and 2 at Brussels' Midi/Zuid/South Station. Arrive 30 minutes early to get your ticket validated and your luggage and passport checked by British authorities (similar to airport check-in for an international flight).

By Bus to: London (cost can vary, but generally €35 one-way, €70 round-trip, about 9 hours, Eurolines tel. 02-203-0707 in Brussels, www.eurolines.com).

CZECH REPUBLIC

PRAGUE

For many travelers, Prague is their first stop in Eastern Europe. And for good reason. Few places can match Prague's over-the-top romance, evocative Old World charm...and tourist crowds. Whether you use it as a tentative first foray into the East, or a springboard for a lengthy Slavic adventure, Prague (whose name means "threshold" in Czech) has always been a natural entry point to Eastern Europe.

With its privileged position on a major river in the very center of bowl-shaped Bohemia, Prague has long been the beating heart and soul of the Czech people. From the Czechs' humble beginnings under a duke named Wenceslas, to the flourishing of culture under Holy Roman Emperor Charles IV, to the devastating Catholics-versus-Protestants warfare of the 17th century, Prague has seen more than its share of history rumble through its cobbled streets. In the 19th century—back when most of its residents were elite German-speakers proud to be subjects of the Habsburg monarchs—Prague was a low-rent mini-Vienna (and played host to the likes of Mozart). But by century's end, the city had become a hotbed for the Czech national revival, as people across Eastern Europe looked to Prague as the region's cultural capital and standard bearer for shunning imposed Germanic ways and embracing their own deep Slavic roots.

While the 20th century (and its four decades of communism) was hard on Prague, at least the city escaped the bombs of the world wars—making it uniquely well-preserved among Central European capitals. Now that the shroud of communism has lifted, and the facades have been dutifully scrubbed, visitors can fully enjoy the streets and lanes of today's Prague—a veritable textbook of architectural styles. I love bringing first-time visitors to Prague's Old Town Square at twilight. After gaping their way around the square, invariably they nudge me and whisper, "This is better than Disneyland!"

In addition to its glorious buildings, Prague intoxicates visitors with its almost mystically beautiful cityscape, entertains us with an endless array of cheap classical concerts, tickles our inner artist with slinky Art Nouveau works by Alfons Mucha, educates us with its historic sites and sobering Jewish Quarter, bends our minds with the uniquely Czech phenomenon of Black Light Theater, and keeps us lubricated with Europe's best beer. Hike up to the world's biggest castle for a lesson in Czech history and sweeping views across the city's spires and domes. Cross the famous Charles Bridge, communing with vendors, artists, tourists, and a stoic lineup of Czech saints in stone. Escape the crowds into the back lanes and pretend you're strolling through the 18th century. Join the local gang over a *pivo* at a rollicking beer hall and learn some Czech soccer songs. Delve into one of Europe's top stops.

Planning Your Time

Prague demands a minimum of two full days (with three nights, or two nights and a night train). From Munich, Berlin, and Vienna, Prague is a four- to six-hour train ride by day (you also have the option of a longer night train from Vienna).

With two days in Prague, I'd spend one morning seeing the castle and another morning in the Jewish Quarter. Use your afternoons for loitering around the Old Town, Charles Bridge, and the Little Quarter, and split your nights between beer halls and live music. Keep in mind that Jewish Quarter sights close on Saturday. Some museums, mainly in the Old Town, are closed on Monday.

Orientation to Prague

Residents call their town "Praha" (PRAH-hah). It's big, with 1.2 million people, but during a quick visit, you'll focus on its relatively compact old center. As you wander, take advantage of brown street signs directing you to tourist landmarks. Self-deprecating Czechs note that while the signs are designed to help tourists (locals never use them), they're only printed in Czech. Still, thanks to the little icons, the signs can help smart visitors who are sightseeing on foot.

The Vltava River divides the west side (Castle Quarter and Little Quarter) from the east side (New Town, Old Town, Jewish Quarter, Main Train Station, and most of the recommended hotels).

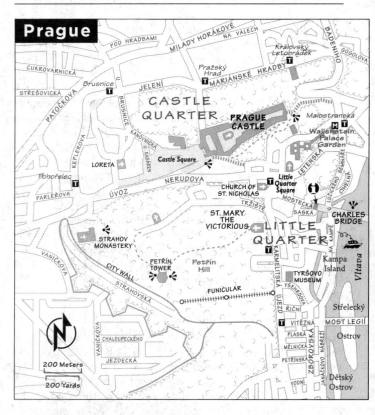

Prague addresses come with references to a general zone: Praha 1 is in the old center on either side of the river; Praha 2 is in the New Town, southeast of Wenceslas Square; Praha 3 (and higher) indicates a location farther from the center. Virtually everything I list is in Praha 1.

Tourist Information

TIs are at several key locations, including: **Old Town Square** (in the Old Town Hall, just to the left of the Astronomical Clock; Easter-Oct Mon-Fri 9:00-19:00, Sat-Sun 9:00-18:00; Nov-Easter Mon-Fri 9:00-18:00, Sat-Sun 9:00-17:00; tel. 224-482-018) and the castle side of **Charles Bridge** (Easter-Oct daily 10:00-18:00, closed Nov-Easter). For general tourist information in English, dial 12444 (Mon-Fri 8:00-19:00) or check the TIs' useful website: www.praguewelcome.cz.

The TIs offer maps, phone cards, a useful transit guide, information on guided walks and bus tours, and bookings for local guides, concerts, hotel rooms, and rooms in private homes.

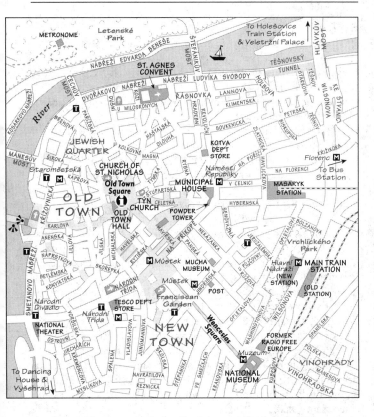

Monthly event guides—all of them packed with ads—include the *Prague Guide* (29 Kč), *Prague This Month* (free), and *Heart of Europe* (free, summer only). The English-language weekly *Prague Post* newspaper is handy for entertainment listings and current events (60 Kč at newsstands).

Arrival in Prague

No matter how you arrive, your first priority is buying a city map, with trams and Metro lines marked and tiny sketches of the sights drawn in for ease in navigating (30-70 Kč, many different brands; sold at kiosks, exchange windows, and tobacco stands). It's a mistake to try doing Prague without a good map—you'll refer to it constantly. The *Kartografie Praha* city map, which shows all the tram lines and major landmarks, includes a castle diagram and a street index. It comes in two versions: 1:15,000 covers the city center, and 1:25,000 includes the whole city. The city center map is easier to navigate, and is sufficient unless you're sleeping in the suburbs.

By Train

In the midst of a multiyear renovation, Prague's **Main Station** (Hlavní Nádraží) serves all international trains; most trains within the Czech Republic, including the high-speed SC Pendolino trains; and the DB-ČD bus to and from Nürnberg. Trains serving Berlin also stop at the secondary **Holešovice Station** (Nádraží Holešovice, located north of the river).

Upon arrival, get money. Both stations have ATMs (best rates) and an exchange bureau (rates are generally bad; consider waiting until you can get to a bank in town to exchange money). Then buy a good map and confirm your departure plans.

Main Train Station (Hlavní Nádraží)

The station's creepy two-floor hall is the work of communist architects who expanded a classy building to make it big, then painted it the compulsory dreary gray with reddish trim. Originally named for Emperor Franz Josef, the station was later renamed for President Woodrow Wilson (see the commemorative plaque in the main exit hall leading away from the tracks), because his promotion of self-determination led to the creation of the free state of Czechoslovakia in 1918. Under the communists (who weren't big fans of Wilson), it was bluntly renamed Hlavní Nádraží—"Main Station." The station is currently undergoing a major renovation: Drunks and homeless people are being pushed out, and an Italian firm is currently refitting the station to Western European standards, filling every empty space with shiny clothing boutiques and convenience stores.

Three parallel tunnels connect the tracks to the arrival hall. The first area you reach (with low ceilings) has an exchange office and signs pointing to the "official" taxi stand to the right (avoid these rip-off cabbies—explained later). If you turn around and go up another floor, you'll find the **Fantova Kavárna,** a decrepit Art Nouveau cupola café. Outside is the stop for the **AE bus** to the airport (buy 50-Kč ticket from driver, runs every half-hour daily 5:35-22:05, 40 minutes) and the **DB-ČD bus** to Nürnberg (6/day, 4 hours).

Straight down from the low-ceilinged area is the main hall, where you'll find four Metro entrances in the center (two for each direction). A Raiffeisen Bank **ATM** is along the right wall (with your back to the tracks, look for a black-and-yellow sign). The **Market Pont Center** (just inside the big glass doors at the front) stocks food perfect for a picnic. You can get Czech mobile-phone SIM cards at the **Vodaphone** store in the main hall.

At the **Student Agency Regiojet** (in the main hall—with your back to tracks, it's to the right under the stairs), Jaromír and Jaroslav offer friendly assistance. Drop by here upon arrival to get a transit ticket without using the ATM (they take euro coins), and to confirm and buy your outbound train tickets. They can help you figure out international train connections, and they sell train tickets to anywhere in Europe—with domestic stopovers if you like—along with tickets for fast local trains (no commission; Mon-Fri 9:00-17:00 or later, Sat 9:00-12:00 & 13:00-16:00, closed Sun, tel. 224-231-949, www.wasteels.cz). You can even leave your bags here for a short time. For a quiet, air-conditioned place to spend your last coins before leaving Prague, the coffee at **Leonidas** (across from Student Agency Regiojet) is good.

The **Czech Railways ticket office** is in the middle of the main hall under the stairs. Its tiny ČD Travel center, on the left as you enter the main office, sells both domestic and international tickets, and is your best bet for information in English (Mon-Fri 9:00-17:00, closed Sat-Sun, tel. 972-241-861, www.cdtravel.cz). The regular ticket desks are faster if you already know your schedule and destination, but attendants are unlikely to speak English.

Touristpoint (with your back to the tracks, it's on your right under the stairs) arranges last-minute rooms in hotels and pensions, as well as car rentals, sightseeing tours, and adrenaline experiences. They accept any currency and credit cards, and also sell maps and international phone cards. A phone is available for calling a cab—the driver will come to the desk to get you (daily 8:00-22:00, tel. 224-946-010, www.touristpoint.cz, info@touristpoint.cz).

Getting from the Main Station to Your Hotel: Even though the Main Station is basically downtown, it can be a little tricky to get to your hotel. The biggest challenge is that the **taxi** drivers at the train station's run-down "official" stand are a gang of no-neck mafia thugs who wait around to charge an arriving tourist five times the regular rate. (This is likely to change as station reconstruction progresses.) To get an honest cabbie, exit the station's main hall through the big glass doors, then cross 50 yards through a park to Opletalova street (a few taxis are usually waiting in front of the Hotel Chopin, on the corner of Jeruzalémská street). You can also call a taxi from the Touristpoint office, described earlier (AAA Taxi—tel. 14-014; City Taxi—tel. 257-257-257). Before getting into a taxi, always confirm the maximum price to your destination, and make sure the driver turns on the meter—it should cost no more than 300 Kč to get to your hotel.

Better yet, take the **Metro.** It's dirt cheap and easy, with frequent departures. Once you're on the Metro, you'll wonder why you would ever bother with a taxi (inside the station's main hall, look for the red *M* with two directions: Háje or Letňany). To purchase tickets from the automated machine by the Metro entrance, you'll need Czech coins (get change at the change machine in the corner near the luggage lockers, or break a bill at a newsstand or

Rip-Offs in Prague

There's no particular risk of violent crime in Prague, but green, rich tourists do get taken by con artists. Simply be on guard, particularly when traveling on trains (thieves thrive on overnight trains), changing money (tellers with bad arithmetic and inexplicable pauses while counting back your change), dealing with taxis (see "Getting Around Prague—By Taxi," later), paying in restaurants (see tips on page 285), and wandering through seedy neighborhoods.

Anytime you pay for something, make a careful mental note of how much it costs, how much you're handing over, and how much you expect back. Count your change. Someone selling you a phone card marked 190 Kč might first tell you it's 790 Kč, hoping to pocket the difference. If you call his bluff, he'll pretend that it never happened.

Plainclothes policemen "looking for counterfeit money" are con artists. Don't show them any cash or your wallet. If you're threatened with an inexplicable fine by a "policeman," conductor, or other official, you can walk away, scare him away by saying you'll need a receipt (which real officials are legally required to provide), or ask a passerby if the fine is legit. On the other hand, do not ignore the plainclothes inspectors on the Metro and trams who show you their badges.

Pickpockets target Western tourists, and can be little children, or adults dressed as professionals—sometimes even as tourists. Many thieves drape jackets over their arms to disguise busy fingers. Thieves work the crowded and touristy places in teams. They use mobile phones to coordinate their bumps and grinds. Be careful if anyone creates a commotion at the door of a Metro or tram car (especially around the Národní Třída and Vodičkova tram stops, or on the made-for-tourists tram #22)—it's a smokescreen for theft.

Car theft is also a big problem in Prague (many Western European car-rental companies don't allow their rentals to cross the Czech border). Never leave anything valuable in your car—not even in broad daylight on a busy street.

The sex clubs on Skořepka and Melantrichova streets, just south and north of Havelská Market, routinely rip off naive tourists and can be dangerous. They're filled mostly with young Russian women and German and Asian men. Lately this district has become the rage for British "stag" parties, for guys who are happy to take a cheap flight to Prague to get to the city's cheap beer and cheap thrills.

This all sounds intimidating. But Prague is safe. It has its share of petty thieves and con artists, but very little violent crime. Don't be scared—just be alert.

PRAGUE

grocery). Validate your ticket in the yellow machines *before* you go down the stairs to the tracks. To get to hotels in the Old Town, catch a Háje-bound train to the Muzeum stop, then transfer to the green line (direction: Dejvická) and get off at either Můstek or Staroměstská; these stops straddle the Old Town.

Most hotels I list in the Old Town are within a 20-minute **walk** of the train station. Exit the station into a small park, walk through the park, and then cross the street on the other side. Head down Jeruzalémská street to the Jindřišská Tower and tram stop, walk under a small arch, then continue slightly to the right down Senovážná street. At the end of the street, you'll see the Powder Gate—the grand entry into the Old Town—to the left. Alternatively, Wenceslas Square in the New Town is a 10-minute walk—exit the station, cross the park, and walk to the left along Opletalova street.

The nearest **tram** stop is to the right as you exit the station (about 200 yards). Tram #9 takes you to the neighborhood near the National Theater and the Little Quarter, but is not useful for most hotels in the Old Town.

For more information on Prague's taxis and public transportation, see "Getting Around Prague," later.

Holešovice Train Station (Nádraží Holešovice)

This station, slightly farther from the center, is suburban mellow. The main hall has all the services of the Main Station in a more compact area. On the left are international and local ticket windows (open 24 hours), an information office, and an AVE (AEX) office with last-minute accommodations (daily 12:00-20:00, tel. 972-224-660). On the right is an uncrowded café with Internet access (1 Kč/minute, daily 8:00-19:30). Two ATMs are just outside the first glass doors, and the Metro is 50 yards to the right (follow signs toward *Vstup,* which means "entrance"; it's three stops to Hlavní Nádraží—the Main Station—or four stops to the city-center Muzeum stop). Taxis and trams are outside to the right (allow 300 Kč for a cab to the center).

By Bus

Prague's main bus station is at Florenc, east of the Old Town (Metro: Florenc). But some connections use other stations, including Roztyly (Metro: Roztyly), Na Knížecí (Metro: Anděl), the Nádraží Holešovice train station (Metro: Nádraží Holešovice), or the main train station (Metro: Hlavní Nádraží). As with trains, be sure to confirm which station your bus uses.

By Plane

Prague's modern, tidy, low-key **Ruzyně Airport,** located 12 miles (about 30 minutes) west of the city center, is as user-friendly as any airport in Western Europe or the US. The new Terminal 2 serves destinations within the EU except for Great Britain (no passport controls); Terminal 1 serves Great Britain and everywhere else. The airport has ATMs (avoid the change desks), desks promoting their transportation services (such as city transit and shuttle buses), kiosks selling city maps and phone cards, and a tourist service with few printed materials. Airport info: tel. 220-113-314, operator tel. 220-111-111.

Getting between the airport and downtown is easy. Leaving either airport terminal, you have five options, listed below from cheapest to priciest:

Dirt Cheap: Take bus #119 to the Dejvická Metro station, or #100 to the Zličín Metro station (20 minutes), then take the Metro into the center (26 Kč, info desk in airport arrival hall).

Budget: Take the airport express (AE) bus to the main train station (50 Kč, runs every half-hour daily 5:35-22:05, 40 minutes, look for the *AE* sign in front of the terminal and pay the driver, www.czech-transport.com). From the main train station, you can take the Metro, hire a taxi, or walk to your hotel. However, note that the Náměstí Republiky station—served by the minibus shuttle described next—is a much handier place to arrive than the main train station, and well worth the negligible extra cost.

Moderate: Take the Čedaz minibus shuttle to the Náměstí Republiky station, at the entrance to the Old Town. The shuttle stop is on V Celnici street, across the street from Hotel Marriott and near the recommended Brasserie La Gare (pay 120 Kč directly to driver, daily 7:30-19:00, 2/hour, info desk in arrival hall).

Expensive: Take a Čedaz minibus directly to your hotel, likely with a couple of stops en route (480 Kč for a group of up to four, tel. 221-111-111). Look for a dispatcher on the curb in front of the arrival hall.

Splurge: Catch a taxi. Cabbies wait at the curb directly in front of the arrival hall. Airport taxi cabbies are honest but more expensive. Carefully confirm the total price before getting in. It should be a fixed rate of 600-700 Kč, with no meter.

Helpful Hints

Medical Help: A 24-hour **pharmacy** is at Palackého 5 (a block from Wenceslas Square, tel. 224-946-982). For standard assistance, there are two state hospitals in the center: the **General Hospital** (open daily 24 hours, moderate wait time, right above Karlovo Náměstí at U Nemocnice 2, Praha 2, use entry G, tel. 224-962-564) and the **Na Františku Hospital** (on the embankment next to Hotel InterContinental, Na Františku 1, go to the main entrance, for English assistance call Mr. Hacker between 8:00-14:00, tel. 222-801-278 or tel. 222-801-371—serious problems only). The reception staff may not speak English, but the doctors do.

For above-standard assistance in English (including dental service), consider the top-quality **Hospital Na Homolce** (less than 1,000 Kč for an appointment, from 8:00 to 16:00 call 252-922-146, for after-hours emergencies call 257-211-111; bus #167 from Anděl Metro station, Roentgenova 2, Praha 5). The **Canadian Medical Care Center** is a small, private clinic with an English-speaking Czech staff at Veleslavínská 1 in Praha 6 (3,000 Kč for an appointment, 4,500 Kč for a house call, halfway between the city and the airport, tel. 235-360-133, after-hours emergency tel. 724-300-301).

Internet Access: Internet cafés are well-advertised and scattered through the Old and New Towns. Consider **Bohemia Bagel** near the Jewish Quarter at Masná 2. **Káva Káva Káva Coffee,** on the boundary between the Old and New Towns, is in the Platýz courtyard off Národní 37.

Laundry: A **full-service laundry** near most of the recommended hotels is at Karolíny Světlé 11 (200 Kč/8-pound load, wash and dry in 3 hours, Mon-Fri 7:30-19:00, closed Sat-Sun, 200 yards from Charles Bridge on Old Town side, mobile 721-030-446); another is at Rybná 27 (290 Kč/8-pound load, same-day pick-up, Mon-Fri 8:00-18:00, Mon and Wed from 7:00, closed Sat-Sun, tel. 224-812-641). Or surf the Internet while your undies tumble-dry at the **self-service launderette** at Korunní 14 (160 Kč/load wash and dry, Internet access-2 Kč/minute, daily 8:00-20:00, near Náměstí Míru Metro stop, Praha 2).

Bike Rental: Prague recently improved its network of bike paths, making bicycles a feasible option for exploring the center of the town and beyond (see http://doprava.praha-mesto.cz for a map). Two bike-rental shops located near the Old Town Square are **Praha Bike** (daily 9:00-22:00, Dlouhá 24, mobile 732-388-880, www.prahabike.cz) and **City Bike** (daily 9:00-19:00, Králodvorská 5, mobile 776-180-284, www.citybike-prague.com). They rent bikes for about 400 Kč for four hours or 500 Kč per day (with a 1,500-Kč deposit), and also organize guided bike tours.

Best Views: Enjoy the "Golden City of a Hundred Spires" during the early evening, when the light is warm and the colors are rich. Good viewpoints—from highest to lowest—include the Strahov Monastery's garden terrace (above the castle), the many balconies and spires at Prague Castle, the Villa Richter restaurants overlooking the city (just below the castle past the Golden Lane), the top of either tower on Charles Bridge, the Old Town Square clock tower (has an elevator), the Restaurant

PRAGUE

u Prince Terrace overlooking the Old Town Square (also with an elevator), and the steps of the National Museum overlooking Wenceslas Square.

Getting Around Prague

You can walk nearly everywhere. But after you figure out the public transportation system, the Metro is slick, the trams fun, and the taxis quick and easy. Prague's tram system is especially wonderful—trams rumble by every 5-10 minutes, and take you just about anywhere. Be bold and you'll swing through Prague like Tarzan with a transit pass. For details, pick up the handy transit guide at the TI. City maps show the Metro, tram, and bus lines.

By Metro, Tram, and Bus

Excellent, affordable public transit is perhaps the best legacy of the communist era (locals ride all month for 550 Kč). The three-line Metro system is handy and simple, but doesn't always get you right to the tourist sights (landmarks such as the Old Town Square and Prague Castle are several blocks from the nearest Metro stops).

Tickets: The Metro, trams, and buses all use the same tickets:

- 20-minute basic ticket with limited transfer options *(základní s omezenou přestupností)*—18 Kč. With this ticket, no transfers are allowed on trams and buses, but on the Metro you can go up to five stops with one transfer (not valid for night trams or night buses).
- 1.25-hour transfer ticket with unlimited transfers *(základní přestupní)*—26 Kč.
- 24-hour pass *(jízdenka na 24 hodin)*—100 Kč.
- 3-day pass *(jízdenka na 3 dny)*—330 Kč.
- 5-day pass *(jízdenka na 5 dní)*—500 Kč.

Buy tickets from your hotel, at newsstand kiosks, or from automated machines (select ticket price, then insert coins). For convenience, buy all the tickets that you think you'll need—but estimate conservatively. Remember, Prague is a great walking town, so unless you're commuting from a hotel far outside the center, you'll likely find that individual tickets work best. Be sure to validate your ticket as you board the tram or bus, or in the Metro station, by sticking it in the machine (which stamps a time on it; watch locals and imitate). Inspectors routinely ambush ticketless riders (including tourists) and fine them 700 Kč on the spot.

Tips: Navigate by signs that list the end stations. When you come to your stop, push the yellow button (if the doors don't automatically open). Although it seems that all Metro doors lead to the neighborhood of Výstup, that's simply the Czech word for "exit." When a tram pulls up to a stop, two different names are

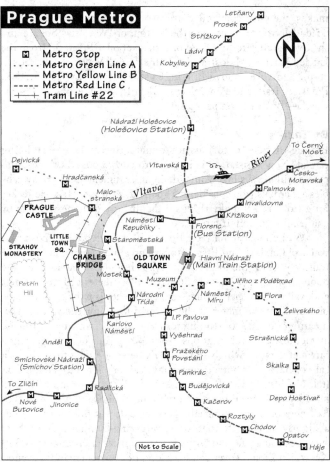

Prague Metro

- Ⓜ Metro Stop
- ···· Metro Green Line A
- —— Metro Yellow Line B
- ---- Metro Red Line C
- ┼┼ Tram Line #22

Letňany Ⓜ
Prosek Ⓜ
Střížkov Ⓜ
Ládví Ⓜ
Kobylisy Ⓜ

Nádraží Holešovice
(Holešovice Station) Ⓜ

To Černý
Most

River

Dejvická Ⓜ
Hradčanská Ⓜ
Malo-
stranská
PRAGUE
CASTLE
STRAHOV
MONASTERY
LITTLE
TOWN
SQ.
CHARLES
BRIDGE
Petřín
Hill
Vltavská Ⓜ
Vltava
Náměstí Ⓜ
Republiky
Staroměstská Ⓜ
OLD TOWN
SQUARE
Můstek Ⓜ
Muzeum
Národní
Třída
I.P. Pavlova
Karlovo
Náměstí
Anděl Ⓜ
Smíchovské Nádraží
(Smíchov Station)
To Zličín
Nové
Butovice
Jinonice
Radlická Ⓜ
Vyšehrad Ⓜ
Pražského
Povstání Ⓜ
Pankrác Ⓜ
Budějovická Ⓜ
Kačerov Ⓜ
Roztyly Ⓜ
Chodov Ⓜ
Opatov Ⓜ
Háje Ⓜ
Náměstí
Míru
Jiřího z Poděbrad Ⓜ
Flora Ⓜ
Želivského Ⓜ
Strašnická Ⓜ
Skalka Ⓜ
Depo Hostivař Ⓜ
Česko-
Moravská Ⓜ
Palmovka Ⓜ
Invalidovna Ⓜ
Křižíkova Ⓜ
Florenc
(Bus Station)
Hlavní Nádraží
(Main Train Station) Ⓜ

Not to Scale

PRAGUE

announced: the name of the stop you're currently at, followed by the name of the stop that's coming up next. Confused tourists, thinking they've heard their stop, are notorious for rushing off the tram one stop too soon.

Schedules and Frequency: Trams run every 5-10 minutes in the daytime (a schedule is posted at each stop). The Metro closes at midnight, and the nighttime tram routes (identified with white numbers on blue backgrounds at tram stops) run all night at 30-minute intervals. You can find more information and a complete route planner in English at www.dpp.cz/en.

Handy Tram: Tram #22 is practically made for sightseeing, connecting the New Town with the Castle Quarter. The tram uses some of the same stops as the Metro (making it easy to get to—or travel on from—the tram route). Of the many stops this tram makes, the most convenient are two in the New Town (Národní Třída Metro stop, between the bottom of Wenceslas Square and the river; and Národní Divadlo, at the National Theater), two in the Little Quarter (Malostranské Náměstí and Malostranská Metro stop), and three above Prague Castle (Královský Letohrádek, Pražský Hrad, and Pohořelec; for details, see "Getting to Prague Castle—By Tram" on page 259).

By Taxi

Prague's taxis—notorious for hyperactive meters—are being tamed. New legislation is in place to curb crooked cabbies, and police will always take your side in an argument. Still, many cabbies are crooks who consider it a good day's work to take one sucker for a ride. You'll make things difficult for a dishonest cabbie by challenging an unfair fare.

While most hotel receptionists and guidebooks advise that you avoid taxis, I find Prague to be a great taxi town and use them routinely. With the local rate, they're cheap (read the rates on the door: drop charge starts at 36 Kč; per-kilometer charge—29 Kč; and waiting time per minute—5 Kč). The key is to be sure the cabbie turns on the meter at the #1 tariff (look for the word *sazba*, meaning "tariff," on the meter). Avoid cabs waiting at tourist attractions and train stations. To improve your odds of getting a fair meter rate—which starts only when you take off—call for a cab (or have your hotel or restaurant call one for you). **AAA Taxi** (tel. 14-014) and **City Taxi** (tel. 257-257-257) are the most likely to have English-speaking staff and honest cabbies. I also find that hailing a passing taxi usually gets me a decent price, although at a slightly higher rate than when reserving by phone. If a cabbie surprises you at the end with an astronomical fare, simply pay 300 Kč, which should cover you for a long ride anywhere in the center. Then go into your hotel. On the miniscule chance that he follows you, the receptionist will back you up.

Tours in Prague

Walking Tours—Many small companies offer walking tours of the Old Town, the castle, and more (for the latest, pick up the walking tour fliers at the TI). Since guiding is a routine side-job for university students, you'll generally get hardworking young guides at good prices. While I'd rather go with my own local guide (described next), public walking tours are cheaper (about 450 Kč for a 4-hour tour), cover themes you might not otherwise consider, connect you with other English-speaking travelers, and allow for spontaneity. The quality depends on the guide rather than the company. Your best bet is to show up at the Astronomical Clock a couple of minutes before 8:00, 10:00, or 11:00, then chat with a few of the umbrella-holding guides there. Choose the one you click with. Guides also have fliers advertising additional walks.

▲▲**Local Guides**—In Prague, hiring a guide is particularly smart—they're twice as helpful for half the price compared with guides in Western Europe. Because prices are usually per hour (not per person), small groups can hire an inexpensive guide for several days. Guides meet you wherever you like and tailor the tour to your interests. Visit their websites in advance for details on various walks, airport transfers, countryside excursions, and other services offered, and then make arrangements by email.

Small Companies: PragueWalker is run by Katka Svobodová, a hardworking historian-guide who knows her stuff and manages a team of enthusiastic and friendly guides (600 Kč/hour for individuals, families, and small groups; mobile 603-181-300, www.praguewalker.com, katerina@praguewalker.com). **Personal Prague Guide Service**'s Šárka Kačabová uses her teaching background to help you understand Czech culture, and has picked a team of personable and knowledgeable guides for her company (600 Kč/hour for 2-3 people, 800 Kč/hour for 4-8 people, fifth hour free, mobile 777-225-205, www.prague-guide.info, saraguide@volny.cz).

Individual Guides: Jana Hronková has a natural style—a welcome change from the more strict professionalism of some of the busier guides—and a penchant for the Jewish Quarter (mobile 732-185-180, www.experience-prague.info, janahronkova@hotmail.com). **Zuzana Tlášková** speaks English as well as Hebrew (mobile 774-131-335, tlaskova@seznam.cz). **Martin Bělohradský,** who guides on the side when not doing his organic chemistry work, is particularly enthusiastic about fine arts and architecture (mobile 723-414-565, martinb@uochb.cas.cz). My readers also recommend **Renata Blažková,** who has a special interest in the history of Prague's Jewish Quarter (tel. 222-716-870, mobile 602-353-186, blazer@volny.cz), and **Václav Štorek,** who specializes in history (mobile 603-743-523, www.storek.guide-prague.cz, vaclavstorek@post.cz). These guides typically charge about 2,000-2,500 Kč for a half-day tour. For a list of more guides, see www.guide-prague.cz.

Jewish-Themed Tours: Jewish guides (of varying quality) meet small groups twice daily in season for three-hour tours of the Jewish Quarter in English. One company is **Wittman Tours,** which charges a 880-Kč fee that includes entry to the Old-New Synagogue and the six other major Jewish Quarter sights (which cost 480 Kč total), so the tour actually costs only 400 Kč (May-Oct Sun-Fri at 10:30 and 14:00, Nov-Dec and mid-March-April Sun-Fri at 10:30 only, no tours Sat and Jan-mid-March, minimum 3 people). Tours meet in the little park (just beyond the café), directly in front of Hotel InterContinental at the end of Pařížská street (tel. 603-168-427 or 603-426-564, www.wittmann-tours .com).

Bus Tours—Although I generally recommend cheap big-bus orientation tours for an efficient, once-over-lightly look at great cities, Prague's sightseeing core (Castle Quarter, Charles Bridge, and the Old Town) is not accessible by bus. In fact, most bus tours of the city are basically walking tours that use buses for pick-ups and transfers. So if you insist on a bus, you're playing basketball with a catcher's mitt.

Bus tours make more sense for day trips out of Prague. Several companies have kiosks on Na Příkopě, where you can comparison-shop. **Premiant City Tours** offers 20 different tours, including one to Terezín Concentration Camp, Karlštejn Castle, and Český Krumlov (1,750 Kč, 10 hours), and a river cruise. The tours feature live guides and depart from near the bottom of Wenceslas Square at Na Příkopě 23. Get tickets at an AVE travel agency, your hotel, on the bus, or at Na Příkopě 23 (tel. 224-946-922, mobile 606-600-123, www.premiant.cz). **Wittman Tours,** listed earlier, offers an all-day minibus tour to Terezín Concentration Camp (www .wittmann-tours.com).

Tour salespeople are notorious for telling you anything to sell a ticket. Some tours, especially those heading into the country-side, can be in as many as four different languages. Hiring a guide, many of whom can drive you around in their car, can be a much better value (described earlier, under "Local Guides").

Cruises—Prague isn't ideal for a boat tour because you might spend half the time waiting to go through the locks. Still, the hour-long Vltava River cruises, which leave from near the castle end of Charles Bridge about hourly, are scenic and relaxing, though not informative (150-200 Kč).

▲Rowboat or Paddleboat Cruises—Renting a rowboat or paddleboat on the island by the National Theater is a better way to enjoy the river. You'll float at your own pace among the swans and watch local lovers cruise by in their own boats (40 Kč/hour for rowboats, 60 Kč/hour for paddleboats, bring photo ID for deposit).

Sights in Prague

I've arranged these sights according to neighborhood: Old Town, New Town, Little Quarter, or Castle Quarter.

The Old Town (Staré Město)

From Prague's dramatic centerpiece, the Old Town Square, sight-seeing options fan out in all directions. Get oriented on the square

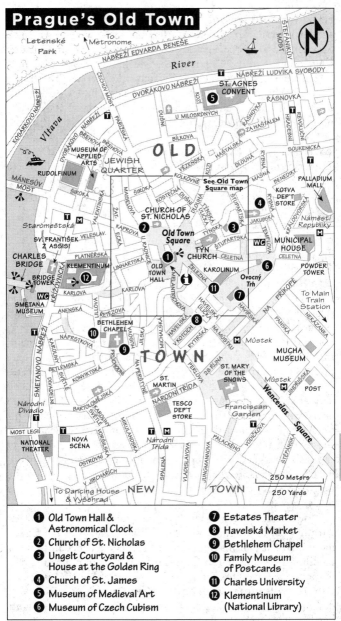

Prague's Old Town

Letenské Park

To Metronome

NÁBŘEŽÍ EDVARDA BENEŠE

STEFÁNIKŮV MOST

N

River

NÁBŘEŽÍ LUDVÍKA SVOBODY

DVOŘÁKOVO NÁBŘEŽÍ

ST. AGNES CONVENT ❺

ŘÁSNOVKA

KOZÍ

Vltava

U MILOSRDNÝCH

ZA HAŠTALEM

HRADEBNÍ

REVOLUČNÍ

SOUKENICKÁ

DUŠNÍ

BÍLKOVA

HAŠTALSKA

RÁSNOVKA

RUDOLFINUM

MUSEUM OF APPLIED ARTS

JEWISH QUARTER

O L D

YÉZENSKÁ

DLOUHÁ

KOZÍ

RYBNÁ

MÁSNÁ

BENEDIKT.

PALLADIUM MALL

MÁNESŮV MOST

See Old Town Square map

KOLKOVNE

ŠIROKÁ

KOSTEČNÁ

MASELNÁ

DUŠNÍ

TÝNSKÁ

ŠTUPARTSKÁ

JAKUBSKÁ

KOTVA DEP'T STORE

Náměstí Republiky

Staroměstská

M

CHURCH OF ST. NICHOLAS ❷

KAPROVA

U RADNICE

Old Town Square

TÝNSKÁ

TÝN CHURCH

❸

ŠTUPARTSKÁ

TEMPLOVÁ

WC

MUNICIPAL HOUSE

M

SV. FRANTIŠEK Z ASSISI

VELESLAV.

EČKA.

ELIŠKY

❶

CELETNÁ

❻

POWDER TOWER

CHARLES BRIDGE

PLATNÉŘSKÁ

LINHARTSKÁ

OLD TOWN HALL

ŽELEZNÁ

KAROLINUM

CELETNÁ

NA PŘÍKOPĚ

To Main Train Station

BRIDGE TOWER

KLEMENTINUM ⓬

KARLOVA

MELANTRICHOVA

❶

❶❶

Ovocný Trh

❼

NEKÁZANKA

SMETANA MUSEUM

WC

KARLOVA

ŘETĚZOVA

HAVELSKÁ ULICKA

PANSKÁ

ANENSKÁ

BETHLEHEM CHAPEL

JILSKÁ

MICHALSKÁ

HAVELSKÁ

❽

M Můstek

NÁPRSTKOVA

⓾

JALOVCOVÁ

V KOTCÍCH

RYTÍŘSKÁ

MUCHA MUSEUM

❾

T O W N

NA MŮSTKU

28. ŘÍJNA

Můstek M

POST

Národní Divadlo

BETLÉMSKÁ

KONVIKTSKÁ

NA PERŠTÝNĚ

PERLOVÁ

ST. MARY OF THE SNOWS

JUNGMANNOVA

Wenceslas Square

MOST LEGII

NATIONAL THEATER

BARTOLOMĚJSKÁ

SVĚTELNÁ

MIKULANDSKÁ

NÁRODNÍ TŘÍDA

ST. MARTIN

TESCO DEP'T STORE

Franciscan Garden

PALACKÉHO

VODIČKOVA

ŠTEPÁNSKÁ

JINDŘIŠSKÁ

DIVADELNÍ

OSTROVNÍ

NOVÁ SCÉNA

VORŠILSKÁ

Národní Třída

SPÁLENÁ

VLADISLAVOVA

250 Meters

250 Yards

JIRCHÁŘÍCH

NEW

TOWN

To Dancing House & Vyšehrad

PRAGUE

❶ Old Town Hall & Astronomical Clock
❷ Church of St. Nicholas
❸ Ungelt Courtyard & House at the Golden Ring
❹ Church of St. James
❺ Museum of Medieval Art
❻ Museum of Czech Cubism
❼ Estates Theater
❽ Havelská Market
❾ Bethlehem Chapel
❿ Family Museum of Postcards
⓫ Charles University
⓬ Klementinum (National Library)

before venturing onward. You can learn about Jewish heritage in the Jewish Quarter (Josefov), a few blocks from the Old Town Square. Closer to the square, you'll find the quaint and historic Ungelt courtyard and Celetná street, which leads to the Museum of Czech Cubism and the landmark Estates Theater. Nearby, Karlova street funnels all the tourists to the famous Charles Bridge. All of the sights described here are within a five-minute walk of the magnificent Old Town Square.

▲▲▲Old Town Square (Staroměstské Náměstí)

The focal point for most visits, Prague's Old Town Square is one of the city's top sights. This has been a market square since the 11th century. It became the nucleus of the Old Town (Staré Město) in the 13th century, when its Town Hall was built. Today, the old-time market stalls have been replaced by outdoor cafés and touristy horse buggies. But under this shallow surface, the square hides a magic power to evoke the history that has passed through here. The square's centerpiece is a memorial to Jan Hus.

Jan Hus Memorial—This monument, erected in 1915 (500 years after the Czech reformer's martyrdom by fire), symbolizes the long struggle for Czech freedom. Walk around the memorial. Jan Hus stands tall between two groups of people: victorious Hussite patriots, and Protestants defeated by the Habsburgs in 1620. One of the patriots holds a chalice (cup)—in the medieval Church, only priests could drink the wine at Communion. Since the Hussites fought for their right to take both the wine and the bread, the cup is their symbol. Hus looks proudly at the Týn Church (described later), which became the headquarters and leading church of his followers. A golden chalice once filled the now-empty niche under the gold bas-relief of the Virgin Mary on the church's facade. After the Habsburg (and, therefore, Catholic) victory over the Czechs in 1620, the Hussite chalice was melted down and made into the image of Mary that shines from that spot high over the square today.

Behind the statue of Jan Hus, the bronze statue of a mother with her children represents the ultimate rebirth of the Czech nation. Because of his bold stance for independence in the way common people worship God, Hus was excommunicated and burned in Germany, a century before the age of Martin Luther.

Old Town Square Orientation Spin-Tour—As this tour is designed to give you your bearings, most of the important sights are described in greater detail later.

Whirl clockwise to get a look at Prague's diverse architectural styles: Gothic, Renaissance, Baroque, Rococo, and Art Nouveau. Start with the green domes of the Baroque **Church of St. Nicholas.** Originally Catholic, now Hussite, this church is a popular venue for concerts. (There's another green-domed Church of St. Nicholas—also popular for concerts—by the same architect, across the Charles Bridge in the Little Quarter.) The Jewish Quarter (Josefov) is a few blocks behind the church, down the uniquely tree-lined Pařížská—"Paris street."

Pařížská, an eclectic cancan of mostly Art Nouveau facades, leads to a bluff that once sported a 100-foot-tall stone statue of Stalin. Demolished in 1962 after Khrushchev exposed Stalin's crimes, it was replaced in 1991 by a giant ticking **metronome**— partly to commemorate Prague's centennial exhibition (the 1891 exhibition is remembered by the Little Quarter's Eiffel-esque Petřín Tower), and partly to send the message that for every power, there's a time to go.

Spin to the right, past the Hus Memorial and the fine yellow Art Nouveau building. The large Rococo palace on the right (with a public WC in the courtyard) is part of the **National Gallery** and houses an exhibit of Asian art (Tue-Sun 10:00-18:00, closed Mon, may close sporadically due to budget cuts—ask at TI).

To the right, you can't miss the towering Gothic **Týn Church** (pronounced "teen"), with its fanciful spires flanking the gold bas-relief of Mary. For 200 years after Hus' death, this was Prague's leading Hussite church. A narrow lane leading to the church's entrance passes the **Via Musica,** the most convenient ticket office in town. Behind the Týn Church is a gorgeously restored medieval courtyard called **Ungelt.** The row of pastel houses in front of Týn Church has a mixture of Gothic, Renaissance, and Baroque facades. To the right of these buildings, shop-lined **Celetná street** leads to a square called Ovocný Trh (with the Estates Theater and Museum of Czech Cubism) and, beyond that, to the Municipal House and Powder Tower in the New Town.

Continue spinning right, taking in more gloriously colorful architecture, until you reach the pointed 250-foot-tall spire marking the 14th-century **Old Town Hall** (with the famous Astronomical Clock and the only elevator-accessible tower in town). The chunk of pink building attached to the tower of the Neo-Gothic City Hall is the town's "memorial" to sore losers. The building once stretched all the way to the Church of St. Nicholas. Then, in the last days of World War II (May 1945), German tanks knocked off this landmark—to the joy of many Prague citizens who considered it an ugly, oversized 19th-century stain on the medieval square. Across the square from the Old Town Hall (opposite the Astronomical Clock), touristy **Melantrichova street** leads directly to the New Town's Wenceslas Square, passing the craft-packed Havelská Market along the way.

Twenty-Seven Crosses—Embedded in the pavement at the base of the Old Town Hall tower (near the snack stand), you'll see white inlaid crosses marking the spot where 27 Protestant nobles, merchants, and intellectuals were beheaded in 1621 after rebelling against the Catholic Habsburgs. The execution ended Czech independence for 300 years and is still one of the grimmest chapters in the country's history.

▲▲**Astronomical Clock**—Join the gang for the striking of the hour on the Town Hall clock (daily 8:00-21:00, until 20:00 in winter). As you wait, see if you can figure out how the clock works.

With revolving discs, celestial symbols, and sweeping hands, this clock keeps several versions of time. Two outer rings show the hour: Bohemian time (gold Gothic numbers on black background, counts from sunset—find the zero, between 23 and 1...supposedly the time of tonight's sunset) and modern time (24 Roman numerals, XII at the top being noon, XII at the bottom being midnight). Five hundred years ago, everything revolved around the earth (the fixed middle background—with Prague marking the center, of course).

To indicate the times of sunrise and sunset, arcing lines and moving spheres combine with the big hand (a sweeping golden sun) and the little hand (a moon that spins to show various stages). Look for the orbits of the sun and moon as they rise through day (the blue zone) and night (the black zone).

If this seems complex to us, it must have been a marvel 500 years ago. Because the clock was heavily damaged during World War II, much of what you see today is a reconstruction. The circle below (added in the 19th century) shows the signs of the zodiac, scenes from the seasons of a rural peasant's life, and a ring of saints' names—one for each day of the year, with a marker showing today's special saint (at top).

Four statues flanking the clock represent the 15th-century outlook on time and prejudices. A Turk with a mandolin symbolizes hedonism, a Jewish moneylender is greed, and the figure staring into a mirror stands for vanity. All these worldly goals are vain in the face of Death, whose hourglass reminds us that our time is unavoidably running out.

At the top of the hour (don't blink—the show is pretty quick): First, Death tips his hourglass and pulls the cord, ringing the bell; then the windows open and the 12 apostles parade by, acknowledging the gang of onlookers; then the rooster crows; and then the hour is rung. The hour is often off because of Daylight Saving Time (completely senseless to 15th-century clockmakers). At the top of the next hour, stand under the tower—protected by a line of banner-wielding concert salespeople in powdered wigs—and watch the tourists.

Clock Tour and Tower Climb: The main TI, to the left of the Astronomical Clock, contains an information desk and sells tickets for these two options: zipping up the Old Town Hall tower by elevator (60 Kč, Tue-Sun 9:00-17:30, Mon 11:00-17:30, good views); or taking a 45-minute tour of the Old Town Hall, which includes a Gothic chapel and a close-up look at the inner guts of the Astronomical Clock (plus its statues of the 12 apostles; 50 Kč, 2/hour).

▲**Týn Church**—Though this church has a long history, it's most notable for its 200-year stint as the leading church of the Hussite movement (generally open to sightseers Tue-Sat 10:00-13:00 & 15:00-17:00). It was Catholic before the Hussites, and was returned to Catholicism after the Hussites were defeated. As if to insult Hus and his doctrine of simplicity, the church's once elegant and pure Gothic columns are now encrusted with noisy Baroque altars. While Gothic, the church interior is uncharacteristically bright because of its clear Baroque windowpanes and whitewash. Read the church's story (posted in English, rear-left side) for a Catholic spin on the church's events—told with barely a mention of Hus. The fine 16th-century, carved John the Baptist altar (right aisle) is worth a look. As you enjoy this church, try to ignore its unwelcoming signs—other than the Catholic-slanted history, the only English words you'll see here are commands that tell you what not to do.

Outside, on the side of the church facing Celetná street, find a statue of the Virgin Mary resting on a temporary column in an ignored niche. The Catholics are still waiting for a chance to re-install Mary in the middle of the Old Town Square, where she stood for about 250 years until being torn down in 1918 by a mob of anti-Habsburg (and therefore anti-Catholic) demonstrators.

Behind Týn Church
▲**Ungelt Courtyard (Týnský Dvůr)**—This fortified courtyard was the commercial nucleus of medieval Prague. Step through its stout gate (immediately behind the Týn Church). The Ungelt courtyard once served as a hostel for foreign merchants, much like a Turkish caravanserai. Here the merchants (usually German) would store their goods and pay taxes before setting up stalls on the Old Town Square (where two old trade routes crossed). Notice that, for the purpose of guaranteeing the safety of goods and merchants, there are only two entrances into the complex. After decades of disuse, the courtyard had fallen into such disrepair by the 1980s that authorities considered demolishing it. Marvelously restored a few years ago, the Ungelt courtyard is now the most pleasant area in the Old Town for dining outdoors (such as at the recommended Indian Jewel). It's a fine place for elegant shopping, too: Sort through wooden crafts, and page through English-language books. Although Prague has undoubtedly lost some of its dreamy

character to the booming tourist industry, places such as Ungelt stand as testimony to the miracles that money can work. Had the communists stayed in power for a few more years, Ungelt would have been a black hole by now. Ungelt also reminds us that Prague, for most of its history, has been a cosmopolitan center quite alien to the rest of the country.

Church of St. James (Kostel Sv. Jakuba)—Perhaps the most beautiful church in the Old Town, the Church of St. James is just behind the Ungelt courtyard. The Minorite Order has occupied this church and the adjacent monastery almost as long as merchants have occupied Ungelt. A medieval city was a complex phenomenon: Commerce, prostitution, and a life of contemplation existed side-by-side. (I guess it's not that much different from today.) Artistically, St. James (along with the Church of the Ascension of St. Mary at Strahov Monastery) is a stunning example of how simple Gothic spaces could be transformed into sumptuous feasts of Baroque decoration. The blue light in the altar highlights one of Prague's most venerated treasures—the bejeweled Madonna Pietatis. Above the *pietà*, as if held aloft by hummingbird-like angels, is a painting of the martyrdom of St. James (free, daily 9:30-12:00 & 14:00-16:00).

As you leave, find the black shriveled-up arm with clenched fingers (15 feet above and to the left of the door). According to legend, a thief attempted to rob the Madonna Pietatis from the altar, but his hand was frozen the moment he touched the statue. The monks had to cut off his arm to get the hand to let go. The desiccated arm now hangs here as a warning—and the entire delightful story is posted nearby in English.

North of the Old Town Square, near the River

▲▲Museum of Medieval Art—The St. Agnes Convent houses the Museum of Medieval Art in Bohemia and Central Europe (1200-1550). The 14th century was Prague's Golden Age, and the religious art displayed in this Gothic space is a testament to the rich cultural life of the period. Each exquisite piece is well-lit and thoughtfully described in English. Follow the arrows on a chronological sweep through Gothic art history. The various Madonnas and saints were gathered here from churches all over Central Europe (100 Kč, Tue-Sun 10:00-18:00, closed Mon, may close sporadically due to budget cuts—ask at TI, two blocks northeast of the Spanish Synagogue, along the river at Anežská 12).

On Celetná Street, Toward the New Town

Celetná, a pedestrian-only street, is a convenient and relatively untouristy way to get from the Old Town Square to the New Town (specifically the Municipal House and Powder Tower, described later). Along the way, at the square called Ovocný Trh, you'll find these sights.

Museum of Czech Cubism—Cubism was a potent force in Prague in the early 20th century. The fascinating Museum of Czech Cubism in the Black Madonna House (Dům u Černé Matky Boží) offers the complete Cubist experience: Cubist architecture (stand back and see how masterfully it makes its statement while mixing with its neighbors...then get up close and study the details), a great café (one flight up), a ground-floor shop, and, of course, a museum. Take the elevator to the top floor and work your way down. On three floors you'll see paintings, furniture, graphics, and architectural drafts by Czech Cubists. Cubists recognized that preservation without growth was stagnation. A city needs growth—but in harmony with its environment. This building is an example of what has long been considered the greatest virtue of Prague's architects: the ability to adapt grandiose plans to the existing cityscape (100 Kč, Tue-Sun 10:00-18:00, closed Mon, corner of Celetná and Ovocný Trh at Ovocný Trh 19, tel. 224-301-003, www.ngprague.cz). Even if you're not interested in touring the museum, consider a drink upstairs in the similarly decorated Grand Café Orient (described on page 293).

Estates Theater (Stavovské Divadlo)—Built by a nobleman in the 1770s, this Classicist building—gently opening its greenish walls onto Ovocný Trh—was the prime opera venue in Prague at a time when an Austrian prodigy was changing the course of music. Wolfgang Amadeus Mozart premiered *Don Giovanni* in this building—he directed many of his works here. Prague's theatergoers would whistle arias from Mozart's works on the streets the morning after they premiered. Today, the Estates Theater (part of the National Theater group) continues to produce *The Marriage of Figaro, Don Giovanni,* and *The Magic Flute.* For a more intimate encounter with Mozart, go to Villa Bertramka (see "Entertainment in Prague," later).

On Melantrichova Street

Skinny, tourist-clogged Melantrichova street leads directly from the Old Town Square's Astronomical Clock to the bottom of Wenceslas Square. But even along this most crowded of streets, a genuine bit of Prague remains...

▲**Havelská Market**—This open-air market, offering crafts and produce, was first set up in the 13th century for the German trading community. Though heavy on souvenirs these days, the market still feeds hungry locals and vagabonds cheaply. It's ideal for a healthy snack—merchants are happy to sell a single vegetable or piece of fruit—and you'll find a washing fountain and plenty of inviting benches midway down the street. The market is also a

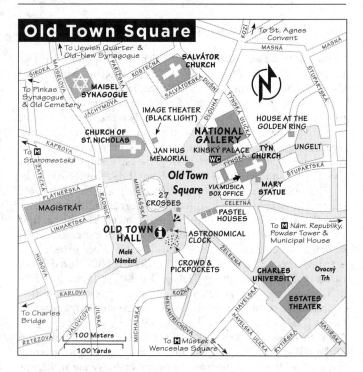

Old Town Square

To St. Agnes Convent

To Jewish Quarter & Old-New Synagogue

SALVÁTOR CHURCH

To Pinkas Synagogue & Old Cemetery

MAISEL SYNAGOGUE

IMAGE THEATER (BLACK LIGHT)

HOUSE AT THE GOLDEN RING

CHURCH OF ST. NICHOLAS

NATIONAL GALLERY

To [M] Staroměstská

JAN HUS MEMORIAL

KINSKÝ PALACE
WC

TÝN CHURCH

UNGELT

Old Town Square

MARY STATUE

27 CROSSES

VIA MUSICA BOX OFFICE

MAGISTRÁT

PASTEL HOUSES

To [M] Nám. Republiky, Powder Tower & Municipal House

OLD TOWN HALL

ASTRONOMICAL CLOCK

Malé Náměstí

CROWD & PICKPOCKETS

CHARLES UNIVERSITY

Ovocný Trh

To Charles Bridge

ESTATES THEATER

100 Meters

100 Yards

To [M] Můstek & Wenceslas Square

fun place to browse for crafts. It's a homegrown, homemade kind of place; you'll often be dealing with the actual artist or farmer (market open daily 9:00-18:00, produce best on weekdays; more souvenirs, puppets, and toys on weekends). The many cafés and little eateries circling the market offer a relaxing vantage point from which to view the action.

From Old Town Square to the Charles Bridge

Karlova Street—Karlova street winds through medieval Prague from the Old Town Square to the Charles Bridge (it zigzags...just follow the crowds). This is a commercial gauntlet, and it's here that the touristy feeding frenzy of Prague is at its ugliest. Street signs keep you on track, and *Karlův most* signs point to the bridge. Obviously, you'll find few good values on this drag. Two favorite places providing a quick break from the crowds are just a few steps off Karlova on Husova street: **Cream and Dream Ice Cream** (Husova 12) and the recommended **U Zlatého Tygra,** a colorful pub that serves great, cheap beer in a classic and untouristy setting (Husova 17).

▲**Klementinum**—The Czech Republic's massive National Library borders touristy Karlova street. The contrast could not be starker: Step out of the most souvenir-packed stretch of Eastern Europe, and enter into the meditative silence of Eastern Europe's biggest library. Jesuits built the Klementinum in the 1600s to house a new college; they had been invited to Prague by the Catholic Habsburgs to offset the influence of the predominantly Protestant Charles University nearby. The building was transformed into a library in the early 1700s, when the Jesuits took firm control of the university. Their books, together with the collections of several noble families (written in all possible languages...except Czech), form the nucleus of the National and University Library, which is now six million volumes strong. (Note that the Klementinum's Chapel of Mirrors is a popular venue for evening concerts.)

▲▲▲Charles Bridge (Karlův Most)

Among Prague's defining landmarks, this much-loved bridge offers one of the most pleasant and entertaining 500-yard strolls in Europe. Enjoy the bridge at different times of day; it's most memorable early—before the crowds—and late, during that photographers' "magic hour" when the sun is low in the sky.

At the Old Town end of the bridge, in a little square, is a statue of the bridge's namesake, **Charles IV** (Karlo Quatro—the guy on the 100-Kč bill), the Holy Roman Emperor who ruled his vast empire from Prague in the 14th century. This statue was erected in 1848 to celebrate the 500th anniversary of Prague's university. Charles is holding a contract establishing the university, the first in Northern Europe. The women around the pedestal symbolize the school's four subjects: the arts, medicine, law, and theology. (From the corner by the busy street, many think the emperor's silhouette makes it appear as if he's peeing on the tourists. Which reminds me—public WCs are in the passageway opposite the statue.)

The magically aligned spot on the Old Town side is occupied by the **bridge tower,** considered one of the finest Gothic gates anywhere. Contemplate the fine sculpture on the Old Town side of the tower, showing the 14th-century hierarchy of kings, bishops, and angels. Climbing the tower rewards you with wonderful views over the bridge (40 Kč, daily 10:00-19:00, as late as 22:00 in summer).

In the 17th century, there were no statues on the bridge—only a **cross,** which you can still see as part of the third sculpture on the right. The gilded Hebrew inscription from the Book of Isaiah celebrates Christ ("Holy, holy, holy is the Lord of hosts"). The inscription was paid for by a fine imposed on a Prague Jew—the result of a rivalry within the Jewish community (fellow Jews turned him in for mocking the cross).

In the space between the third and fourth statues after the cross, look for a small **brass relief** depicting a floating figure with a semicircle of stars above him. This marks the spot where St. John of Nepomuk, the national saint of the Czech people, was tossed off the bridge into the river (I'll tell you that story a bit later). The relief is a replica of a Baroque original that was badly damaged by a flood in 1890, marred by protesters in the 1920s, and finally removed by the communists. In May of 2009, this replacement was installed by Prague's archbishop to help revive traditional celebrations of the saint. Devout pilgrims believe that touching the relief of St. John will make a wish come true. But you get only one chance in life to make this wish, so think carefully before you touch the saint.

The relief is the ideal location from which to survey your surroundings. Looking **downstream** from right to left, you'll see the modern Four Seasons Hotel (doing a pretty good job of fitting in). Farther down, the large Neo-Renaissance facade hides the concert hall of the Czech Philharmonic. Across the river and up the hill, the red needle of a metronome ticks at the spot where a 50-foot-tall granite Joseph Stalin—flanked by eight equally tall deputies—stood from 1955 to 1962. To the right of Stalin's former perch (hiding under the trees and worth the climb on a hot summer day) is Prague's most popular beer garden. Visible between the trees to the left of the metronome is the small but attractive Art Nouveau Havana pavilion, now a fancy restaurant. To the left of it is a red-brick villa, the residence of the Czech prime minister. Finally, the green roof in the shape of an upturned ship along the tree-lined horizon belongs to the Belvedere (also known as the Summer Palace of Queen Anne), an exquisite Renaissance structure.

Looking **upstream,** notice the icebreakers protecting the abutments upon which the bridge sits (ice flow has historically threatened the very survival of the bridge). Look farther upstream for the tiny locks on either side of the weir. While today's river traffic is limited to tourist boats, in the last century timber was floated down the river lashed like rafts. The building with the gilded awning on the left by the next upstream bridge is the National Theater. On the other side of the river, a large sculpture of a chair stands in front of the white Kampa Museum, a private art collection situated in a pleasant public park on Kampa Island.

Pause for a moment to enjoy the musicians, artisans, and parade of people on the bridge itself—my favorite strolling bridge in all of Europe.

Continuing across the bridge, you'll reach the bronze Baroque statue depicting **St. John of Nepomuk** (look for the guy with the five golden stars around his head, near the Little Quarter end of the bridge on the right). This statue always draws a crowd. John was a 14th-century priest to whom the queen confessed all her sins. According to a 17th-century legend, the king wanted to know his wife's secrets, but Father John dutifully refused to tell. He was tortured and eventually killed by being thrown off the bridge. When he hit the water, five stars appeared. The shiny plaque at the base of the statue depicts the heave-ho. Notice the date on the inscription: This oldest statue on the bridge was unveiled in 1683, on the supposed 300th anniversary of the martyr's death.

Most of the other Charles Bridge statues date from the late 1600s and early 1700s. Today, half of them are replicas—the originals are in city museums, out of the polluted air. At the far end of the Charles Bridge, you reach the **Little Quarter,** described later.

▲▲▲Jewish Quarter (Josefov)

Prague's Jewish Quarter neighborhood and its well-presented, profoundly moving museum tell the story of this region's Jews. For me, this is the most interesting collection of Jewish sights in Europe, and well worth seeing. The Jewish Quarter is an easy walk from Old Town Square, up delightful Pařížská street (next to the green-domed Church of St. Nicholas).

As the Nazis decimated Jewish communities in the region, Prague's Jews were allowed to collect and archive their treasures here. While the archivists were ultimately killed in concentration camps, their work survives. Seven sights scattered over a three-block area make up the tourists' Jewish Quarter. Six of the sights—all except the Old-New Synagogue—are called "The Museum" and are covered by one admission ticket. Your ticket comes with a map that locates the sights and lists admission appointments—the times you'll be let in if it's very busy. (Ignore the times unless it's really crowded.) You'll notice plenty of security.

Going from sight to sight in the Jewish Quarter, you'll walk through perhaps Europe's finest Art Nouveau neighborhood. Make a point to enjoy the circa-1900 buildings with their marvelous trimmings and oh-wow entryways. While today's modern grid plan has replaced the higgledy-piggledy medieval streets of old, Široká ("Wide Street") was and remains the main street of the ghetto.

Cost and Hours: A discount ticket covering all seven Jewish Quarter sights is 480 Kč (separately, you'll pay 300 Kč for the six sights that make up the Museum, and 200 Kč for the Old-New Synagogue). The **Museum** sights are open April-Oct Sun-Fri 9:00-18:00; Nov-March Sun-Fri 9:00-16:30; closed year-round on Sat—the Jewish Sabbath—and on Jewish holidays (tel. 222-317-191, www.jewishmuseum.cz). The **Old-New Synagogue** is open Sun-Thu 9:30-18:00, Fri 9:30-17:00 or until sunset, closed Sat and on Jewish holidays (tel. 222-317-191, www.synagogue.cz).

Free View of Cemetery: The Old Jewish Cemetery—with its tightly packed, topsy-turvy tombstones—is, for many, the most evocative part of the experience. Unfortunately, there's no ticket just to see the cemetery, and most of the free viewpoints have been

PRAGUE

Prague's Jewish Quarter

closed off. If the Museum ticket is too steep and you just want a free glimpse of the famous cemetery, climb the steps to the covered porch of the Ceremonial Hall (but don't rest your chin on the treacherous railing).

Photos: While *No Photo* signs are posted everywhere, photos without flash (except during actual prayer times at the Old-New Synagogue) seem to be allowed.

Tours: Because the Museum is scattered throughout the neighborhood, many tourists think they need a guide, but for most, a private guided tour is unnecessary. There's just not a lot to say beyond what's covered in this guidebook and what's thoughtfully posted in English throughout the Museum (unless you're really into Jewish traditions, rituals, and legends that don't necessarily pertain specifically to what you're seeing here in Prague). Group tours flow like chain gangs through the congested and emotional Museum. The 250-Kč audioguide is slow-moving and not worth the time or expense (rent and return at Pinkas Synagogue, ID required).

Touring on Your Own: A do-it-yourself visit is really quite simple: Buy your ticket at Pinkas Synagogue, and tour the synagogue and the adjacent Old Jewish Cemetery, which leads you to the Ceremonial Hall and Klaus Synagogue (at the far side of the cemetery). After visiting those buildings, walk a block to the Old-New Synagogue. Take a coffee break (the recommended

Franz Kafka Café is nearby) before finishing up at the museum-like Maisel Synagogue and the Spanish Synagogue. (Note that Prague's fine Museum of Medieval Art, described earlier, is only a few blocks from the Spanish Synagogue.)

Pinkas Synagogue (Pinkasova Synagóga)—A site of Jewish worship for 400 years, this synagogue (built in 1535) is a poignant memorial to the victims of the Nazis. The walls are covered with the handwritten names of 77,297 Czech Jews who were sent from here to the gas chambers at Auschwitz and other camps. (As you ponder this sad sight, you'll hear the somber reading of the names alternating with a cantor singing the Psalms.) The names are carefully organized by hometown (in gold, listed alphabetically). Family names are in red, followed in black by the individual's first name, birthday, and last date known to be alive. Notice that families generally perished together. Extermination camps are listed on the east wall. Climb eight steps into the women's gallery. When the communists moved in, they closed the synagogue and erased virtually everything. With freedom, in 1989, the Pinkas Synagogue was reopened and the names were rewritten. (The names in poor condition near the ceiling are original.) Note that large tour groups may disturb this small memorial's compelling atmosphere between 10:00 and 12:00.

Upstairs is the **Terezín Children's Art Exhibit** (very well-described in English), displaying art drawn by Jewish children who were imprisoned at Terezín Concentration Camp and later perished. Terezín makes an emotionally moving day trip from Prague (the TI has details on tours and public transportation).

Old Jewish Cemetery (Starý Židovský Hřbitov)—From the Pinkas Synagogue, you enter one of the most wistful scenes in Europe—Prague's Old Jewish Cemetery. As you wander among 12,000 evocative tombstones, remember that from 1439 until 1787, this was the only burial ground allowed for the Jews of Prague. Guides claim the tombs are layered seven or eight deep, and say there are close to 100,000 tombs here. The tombs were piled atop each other because of limited space, the sheer number of graves, and the Jewish belief that the body should not be moved once buried. With its many layers, the cemetery became a small plateau. And as things settled over time, the tombstones got crooked. The Hebrew word for cemetery means "House of Life." Many Jews believe that death is the gateway into the next world. Pebbles on the tombstones are "flowers of the desert," reminiscent of the old days when rocks were placed upon a sandy gravesite to keep the body covered. Wedged under some of the pebbles are scraps of paper that contain prayers.

Ceremonial Hall (Obřadní Síň)—Leaving the cemetery, you'll find a Neo-Romanesque mortuary house (on the left) built in 1911 for the purification of the dead. It's filled with a worthwhile exhibition, described in English, on Jewish medicine, death, and burial traditions. A series of crude but instructive paintings (hanging on walls throughout the house) show how the "burial brotherhood" took care of the ill and buried the dead. As all are equal before God, the rich and poor alike were buried in embroidered linen shrouds similar to the one you'll see on display.

Klaus Synagogue (Klauzová Synagóga)—This 17th-century synagogue (also near the cemetery exit) is the final wing of a museum devoted to Jewish religious practices. Exhibits on the ground floor explain the Jewish calendar of festivals. The central case displays a Torah (the first five books of the Bible) and solid silver pointers used when reading—necessary since the Torah is not to be touched. Upstairs is an exhibit on the rituals of Jewish life (circumcisions, bar and bat mitzvahs, weddings, kosher eating, and so on).

Old-New Synagogue (Staronová Synagóga)—For more than 700 years, this has been the most important synagogue and the central building in Josefov. Standing like a bomb-hardened bunker, it feels as though it has survived plenty of hard times. Stairs take you down to the street level of the 13th century and into the Gothic interior. Built in 1270, it's the oldest synagogue in Eastern Europe. Snare an attendant, who is likely to love showing visitors around. The separate, steep, 200-Kč admission keeps many away, but even if you decide not to pay, you can see the exterior and a bit of the interior. (Go ahead...pop in and crane your cheapskate neck.)

The lobby (down the stairs, where you show your ticket) has two fortified old lockers—in which the most heavily taxed community in medieval Prague stored its money in anticipation of the taxman's arrival. As 13th-century Jews were not allowed to build, the synagogue was erected by Christians (who also built the St. Agnes Convent nearby). The builders were good at four-ribbed vaulting, but since that resulted in a cross, it wouldn't work for a synagogue. Instead, they made the ceiling using clumsy five-ribbed vaulting.

The interior is pure 1300s. The Shrine of the Ark in front is the focus of worship. The holiest place in the synagogue, it holds the sacred scrolls of the Torah. The old rabbi's chair to the right remains empty (notice the thin black chain) out of respect. The red banner is a copy of the one that the Jewish community carried through town during medieval parades. On the banner, you'll see a yellow-pointed hat within the Star of David, which the pope ordered all Jewish men to wear in 1215. Twelve is a popular number (e.g., windows), because it symbolizes the 12 tribes of Israel. The horizontal slit-like windows are an 18th-century addition, allowing women to view the male-only services. While Nazis routinely destroyed synagogues, this most historic synagogue in the country survived because the Nazis intended it to be part of their "Museum of the Extinct Jewish Race."

Maisel Synagogue (Maiselova Synagóga)—This synagogue was built as a private place of worship for the Maisel family during the 16th-century Golden Age of Prague's Jews. Maisel, the wealthy financier of the Habsburg king, lavished his riches on the synagogue's Neo-Gothic interior. In World War II, it served as a warehouse for the accumulated treasures of decimated Jewish communities, a collection that Hitler planned to use for his Jewish museum (explained earlier). Before entering, notice the facade featuring—as is standard in synagogues—the Ten Commandments top and center. Below that is the symbol for Prague's Jewish community: the Star of David, with the pointed hat local Jews wore here through medieval times. The one-room exhibit shows a thousand years of Jewish history in Bohemia and Moravia. Well-explained in English, topics include the origin of the Star of David, Jewish mysticism, the history of discrimination, and the creation of Prague's ghetto. Notice the eastern wall, with the Holy Ark containing the scroll of the Torah. The central case shows the silver ornamental Torah crowns that capped the scroll.

Spanish Synagogue (Španělská Synagóga)—Displays of Jewish history through the 18th, 19th, and tumultuous 20th centuries continue in this ornate, Moorish-style synagogue built in the 1800s. The upstairs is particularly intriguing, with circa-1900 photos of Josefov, an exhibit on the fascinating story of this museum and its relationship with the Nazi regime, and life in Terezín. The Winter Synagogue (also upstairs) shows a trove of silver worshipping aids gathered from countryside Jewish neighborhoods that were depopulated in the early 1940s, giving you a glimpse of the treasures the Nazis stockpiled.

The New Town (Nové Město)

Enough of pretty, medieval Prague—let's leap into the modern era. The New Town, with Wenceslas Square as its focal point, is today's urban Prague. This part of the city offers bustling boulevards and interesting neighborhoods. The New Town is one of the best places to view Prague's remarkable Art Nouveau art and architecture, and to learn more about its recent communist past.

▲▲Wenceslas Square (Václavské Náměstí)

More a broad boulevard than a square (until recently, trams rattled up and down its park-like median strip), this city landmark is named for King Wenceslas—featured both on the 20-Kč coin and the equestrian statue that stands at the top of the boulevard. Wenceslas Square functions as a stage for modern Czech history:

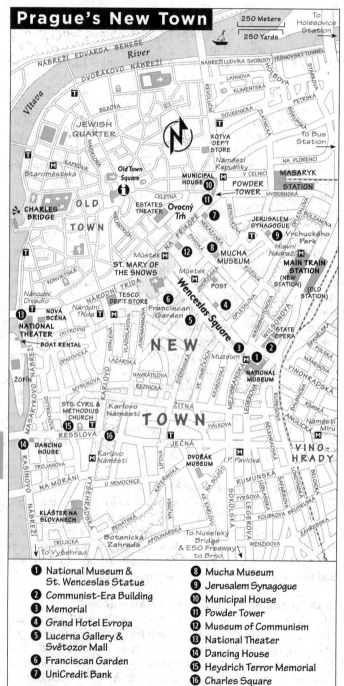

Prague's New Town

250 Meters
250 Yards

❶ National Museum & St. Wenceslas Statue
❷ Communist-Era Building
❸ Memorial
❹ Grand Hotel Evropa
❺ Lucerna Gallery & Světozor Mall
❻ Franciscan Garden
❼ UniCredit Bank
❽ Mucha Museum
❾ Jerusalem Synagogue
❿ Municipal House
⓫ Powder Tower
⓬ Museum of Communism
⓭ National Theater
⓮ Dancing House
⓯ Heydrich Terror Memorial
⓰ Charles Square

The creation of the Czechoslovak state was celebrated here in 1918; in 1968, the Soviets suppressed huge popular demonstrations at the square; and, in 1989, more than 300,000 Czechs and Slovaks converged here to claim their freedom.

◉ Self-Guided Walk: Let's take a stroll down Prague's urban centerpiece.

• *Starting near the Wenceslas statue at the top (Metro: Muzeum), look to the building crowning the top of the square.*

National Museum (Národní Muzeum): This museum—closed for renovation through 2014—stands grandly at the top. While its collection is dull (a skippable assemblage of Czech fossils and animals), the interior is richly decorated in the Czech Revival Neo-Renaissance style that heralded the 19th-century rebirth of the Czech nation. A grand purpose-built national museum made perfect sense in 19th-century Europe. As different political powers wrangled over territory, some groups would end up with countries and others would become "nations without states." During this tumultuous time, people did their best to prove their distinctive identities and affirm their right to exist. The light-colored patches in the museum's columns fill holes where Soviet bullets hit during the crackdown against the 1968 Prague Spring uprising. Masons—defying their communist bosses, who wanted the damage to be forgotten—showed their Czech spirit by intentionally mismatching their patches.

The nearby Metro stop (Muzeum) is the crossing point of two Metro lines built with Russian know-how in the 1970s.

• *To the left of the National Museum (as you face it) is a...*

Communist-Era Building: This structure housed the rubber-stamp Czechoslovak Parliament back when it voted with Moscow. A Socialist Realist statue showing triumphant workers still stands at its base. Between 1994 and 2008, this building was home to Radio Free Europe. After communism fell, RFE lost some of its funding and could no longer afford its Munich headquarters. In gratitude for its broadcasts—which had kept the people of Eastern Europe in touch with real news—the Czech government offered this building to RFE for 1 Kč a year. But as RFE energetically beamed its American message deep into the Muslim world from here, it drew attention—and threats—from Al-Qaeda. So in 2009, RFE moved to a new fortress-like headquarters at an easier-to-defend locale farther from the center.

Today, this building is run by the National Museum and hosts special exhibits. However, the real draw here is to see and get the feel of a typical fancy government building from the days of Brezhnev—visitors are welcome just to stroll its halls. It costs 80 Kč to enter, but you're welcome to pop in and enjoy the Prager café for free—sitting in the same big leather chairs that communist big shots did a generation ago.

• *In front of the National Museum is the equestrian...*

St. Wenceslas Statue: Wenceslas (Václav) is the "good king" of Christmas-carol fame. He was the wise and benevolent 10th-century Duke of Bohemia. A rare example of a well-educated and literate ruler, King Wenceslas I was credited by his people for Christianizing his nation and lifting the culture. He astutely allied the Czechs with Saxony, rather than Bavaria, giving the Czechs a vote when the Holy Roman Emperor was selected (and therefore more political clout).

After his murder in 929, Wenceslas was canonized as a saint. He became a symbol of Czech nationalism and statehood, and remains an icon of Czech unity whenever the nation has to rally. Legend has it that when the Czechs face their darkest hour, Wenceslas will come riding out of Blaník Mountain (east of Prague) with an army of knights to rescue the nation. In 1620, when Austria stripped the Czechs of their independence, many people went to Blaník Mountain to see whether it had opened up. They did the same at other critical points in their history (in 1938, 1948, and 1968), but Wenceslas never emerged. Although the Czech Republic is now safely part of NATO and the EU, Czechs remain realistic: If Wenceslas hasn't come out yet, the worst times must still lie ahead...

Study the statue. Wenceslas, on the horse, is surrounded by the four other Czech patron saints. Notice the focus on books. A small nation without great military power, the Czech Republic chose national heroes who enriched the culture by thinking, rather than fighting. This statue is a popular meeting point. Locals say, "I'll see you under the tail."

Take a moment at this spot to survey the square. You'll see businesspeople, families, dumpster divers, security guards, the Pepsi generation, and students. The vision for the square is a matter of controversy for locals. The city plans to turn it into a long, tree-lined pedestrian mall, with trams running up and down the middle (as they once did), and hide the busy freeway underground (currently it separates the museum from the square).

This freeway originated as part of a 1970s plan by communists to connect the city with inner and outer freeway rings, while running the busiest thoroughfare into the heart of the city. However, due to a lack of funds, they were only able to complete a small portion of their grandiose plan at the time. After 1989, the project moved forward, thanks to the aid of EU funds and a boost in local car production, as manufacturers hoped to realize the dream of a car for every person. (This project is a good illustration of how the last two decades have represented a continuation of trends and policies started under the communists—rather than a break from them.)

Prague's tunnel-to-tunnel inner circle (the city's "Big Dig") was scheduled to be completed by 2012, at an astronomical price. But in elections in the fall of 2010, voters ousted the party that had ruled Prague without interruption since 1989. It remains to be seen whether the current administration has both the will and the means to continue the tunnel project. Until then, automobiles continue to spit their fumes on the museum's facade (the most polluted spot in the city), and few Czechs enjoy strolling in this part of Prague. Notice that locals here are decisively on the run.

• *Begin walking down the square. Thirty yards below the big horse is a small garden with a low-key...*

Memorial: This commemorates victims of communism, such as Jan Palach. In 1969, a group of patriots decided that an act of self-immolation would stoke the fires of independence. Palach, a philosophy student who loved life—but wanted to live in freedom—set himself on fire on the steps of the National Museum for the cause of Czech independence. He died a few days later in a hospital ward. Czechs are keen on anniversaries, and huge demonstrations swept the city on the 20th anniversary of Palach's death. These protests led, 10 months later, to the overthrow of the Czech communist government in 1989.

This grand square is a gallery of modern architectural styles. As you wander downhill, notice the fun mix, all post-1850: Romantic Neo-Gothic, Neo-Renaissance, and Neo-Baroque from the 19th century; Art Nouveau from about 1900; ugly Functionalism from the mid-20th century (the "form follows function" and "ornamentation is a crime" answer to Art Nouveau); Stalin Gothic from the 1950s "communist epoch" (a good example is the Hotel Jalta building, halfway downhill on the right); and the glass-and-steel buildings of the 1970s.

• *Walk a couple of blocks downhill through the real people of Prague (not tourists) to Grand Hotel Evropa, with its dazzling yellow Art Nouveau exterior and plush café interior full of tourists. Stop for a moment to consider the events of...*

November of 1989: This huge square was filled every evening with more than 300,000 ecstatic Czechs and Slovaks who believed freedom was at hand. Assembled on the balcony of the building opposite Grand Hotel Evropa (look for the *Marks & Spencer* sign) were a priest, a rock star (famous for his unconventional style, which constantly unnerved the regime), Alexander Dubček (hero of the 1968 revolt), and Václav Havel (the charismatic playwright, newly released from prison, who was every freedom-loving Czech's Nelson Mandela). Through a sound system provided by the rock star, Havel's voice boomed over the gathered masses, announcing the resignation of the Politburo and saying that the Republic of Czechoslovakia's freedom was imminent. Picture

PRAGUE

that cold November evening, with thousands of Czechs jingling their key chains in solidarity, chanting at the government, "It's time to go now!" (To quell this revolt, government tanks could have given it the Tiananmen Square treatment, which had spilled patriotic blood in China just six months earlier. Locals believe that the Soviet head of state, Mikhail Gorbachev, must have made a phone call recommending a nonviolent response.) This wave of peaceful demonstrations, known as the "Velvet Revolution," ended later that year with the election of Havel as the president of a free Czechoslovakia.

• *Immediately opposite Grand Hotel Evropa is the Lucerna Gallery (use entry marked Pasáž Rokoko and walk straight in).*

Lucerna Gallery: This grand mall retains some of its Art Deco glamour from the 1930s, with shops, theaters, a ballroom in the basement, and the fine Lucerna Café upstairs. You'll see a sculpture—called *Wenceslas Riding an Upside-Down Horse*—hanging like a swing from a glass dome. David Černý, who created the statue in 1999, is one of the Czech Republic's most original contemporary artists. Always aspiring to provoke controversy, Černý has painted a menacing Russian tank pink, attached crawling babies to the rocket-like Žižkov TV tower, defecated inside the National Gallery to protest the policies of its director, and sunk a shark-like Saddam Hussein inside an aquarium. His art hoax *Entropa* was created to commemorate the Czech presidency of the European Union in 2009. But when it was unveiled in Brussels, it insulted many EU nations with its satirical symbolism (Bulgaria was represented by squat toilets, Germany consisted of twisted autobahns hinting at a swastika, and so on).

Inside the gallery, you'll also find a **Ticketpro box office** (with a line on concerts and events, daily 9:30-18:00, 30 Kč fee), a lavish 1930s Prague cinema (under the upside-down horse, shows films in original language with Czech subtitles, 115 Kč), and the popular **Lucerna Music Bar** in the basement ('80s and '90s video parties, 100 Kč, from 21:00 on Fri and Sat, concerts on other nights).

Leave the mall out of the side of the gallery, then cross busy Vodičkova street (with a handy tram stop) and enter **Světozor mall.** The 1930s glass window advertising Tesla, a defunct Czech radio manufacturer, lends a retro brightness to the place. Find the **World of Fruit Bar Světozor,** every local's favorite ice-cream joint. They also sell cakes, milkshakes, and "little breads"—delightful Czech-style open-face sandwiches. Ask at the counter for an English menu.

• *Walk under the* Tesla *sign to exit the mall, and head left into the peaceful...*

Franciscan Garden (Františkánská Zahrada): Its white benches and spreading rosebushes are a universe away from the fast beat of the city, which throbs behind the buildings that surround the garden. Its peacefulness reflects the purpose of its Franciscan origin. (If you need a WC, there's one just out the far side of the garden, and another in the tiny wine bar coming up on this walk.)

Back on Wenceslas Square, if you're in the mood for a mellow hippie teahouse, consider a break at the recommended **Dobrá Čajovna** ("Good Teahouse") near the bottom of the square (#14). Or, if you'd like an old-time wine bar, pop in to the plain **Šenk Vrbovec** (nearby at #10); it comes with a whiff of the communist days, embracing the faintest bits of genteel culture from an age when refinement was sacrificed for the good of the working class. They serve traditional drinks, Czech keg wine, *becherovka* (the 13-herb liqueur), and—only in autumn—*burčák* (this young wine tastes like grape juice turned halfway into wine). Belly up to the bar and choose from four kegs, each serving a different Moravian wine (1 dl for 17 Kč).

The bottom of Wenceslas Square is called **Můstek,** which means "Bridge"; a bridge used to cross a moat here, allowing entrance into the Old Town (you can still see the original Old Town entrance down in the Metro station).

• *From the bottom of Wenceslas Square, you can either head right, to Prague's top Art Nouveau sights (described next) or left, toward the river and the National Theater (described later).*

Na Příkopě: Art Nouveau Prague

At the bottom of Wenceslas Square, the street running to the right is called Na Příkopě. Meaning "On the Moat," this busy boulevard follows the line of the Old Town wall, leading to one of the wall's former gates, the Powder Tower (the black tower spire in the distance). Along the way, it passes the Museum of Communism and two of Prague's best Art Nouveau sights: the Mucha Museum (featuring the work of my favorite Art Nouveau artist) and the Municipal House (with my favorite Art Nouveau interior anywhere). Seeing the interior of the UniCredit Bank building, also on Na Příkopě, will help you understand how the Art Nouveau movement came about.

City tour buses (see "Tours in Prague—Bus Tours," earlier) leave from along this street, which offers plenty of shopping temptations (such as these malls: Slovanský Dům at Na Příkopě 22 and Černá Růže at Na Příkopě 12, next door to Mosers, which has a crystal showroom upstairs).

• *Start strolling up Na Příkopě. Turn right at Panská to reach the...*

▲▲**Mucha Museum**—This is one of Europe's most enjoyable little museums. I find the art of Alfons Mucha (MOO-kah, 1860-1939) insistently likeable. See the crucifixion scene he painted as an eight-year-old boy. Read how this popular Czech artist's posters,

PRAGUE

Mucha's *Slav Epic*

Alfons Mucha (1860-1939), born in the small Moravian town of Ivančice, made a hugely successful commercial career for himself in Paris and in the US as *the* Art Nouveau poster artist and illustrator. In Paris, Mucha conceived the idea of dedicating the second half of his life to a work that would edify his nation. Throughout history, bards in every culture have composed poems eulogizing the best moments of their tradition. Mucha would do the same for the Czechs and the Slavs, on a grand, epic scale...and on canvas.

Mucha convinced the Chicago industrialist Charles Crane to sponsor his project. Both men believed that the purpose of a truly patriotic work was to inspire human beings to understand one another better, and thereby bring humanity closer together. Mucha returned home, and by 1912 finished the first of three paintings (each 25 by 20 feet). It was another 16 years before Mucha completed the cycle of 20 enormous canvases known as the *Slav Epic*. The response of his fellow artists was lukewarm—in the experimental age of Picasso, Mucha's slinky style and overt nationalism were out of fashion.

During World War II, the patriotic work was hidden from the Nazis and damaged. After years of restoration, the paintings were unveiled in 1963 and put on display in a castle in the town of Moravský Krumlov, near Mucha's birthplace. Although Mucha had originally dedicated the *Slav Epic* to Prague, the gift came with strings: Prague was to build a suitable structure in which to display the paintings. But rather than finding a good location and raising the necessary funds, Prague officials simply waited until the end of 2009—60 years after Mucha's death—when the copyright on his work expired. Then they cited the dilapidated condition of the Krumlov castle as legal grounds to "temporarily relocate" the canvases to Prague's National Gallery—over the objections of Mucha's family and the people of Moravský Krumlov. Following a series of highly publicized standoffs and court battles, in October of 2010, several canvases of the *Slav Epic* were stripped from the walls of Moravský Krumlov's castle, rolled up, and taken to Prague.

Where to See It: Depending on the timing of your visit, you may see some, all, or none of the *Slav Epic* in Prague (in the National Gallery's Veletržní Palace). For a while, some panels stayed in Moravský Krumlov, but by the time of your visit the entire work should be reunited in Prague. The *Slav Epic* will be on display in Prague for about two years, until the château in Moravský Krumlov has been refurbished. Check with the TI or call before you visit to confirm the *Epic's* location and hours.

Cost and Hours: 250 Kč, Tue-Sun 10:00-18:00, closed Mon, tel. 224-301-122, www.ngprague.cz.

Getting There: Veletržní Palace is located near Holešovice Station at Dukelských Hrdinů 47. Take tram #17 from the Staroměstská Metro stop for five stops to Veletržní (direction: Výstaviště or Vozovna Kobylisy).

Viewing the Paintings: The entire work is described below; depending on which canvases are currently on display in Prague, you may not see all of this.

Although Mucha's magnum opus continues to be scorned by many Czech intellectuals because of its overtly nationalistic theme, the *Slav Epic* rises above the typically shallow products of the politicized 19th century. A brilliant craftsman and designer, Mucha captures the viewer's attention with his strong composition and sense of color. Like any true artistic masterpiece, Mucha's work goes beyond the style of the time, beyond Art Nouveau, beyond Slavic.

Consider contemplating Mucha's canvases on three levels. First, use the captions (or handouts, if available) to understand what the paintings are depicting. The great feast is the celebration of the Slavic pagan god; the zealous preacher is Jan Hus (the revolutionary Czech priest); and the subdued old man contemplating the dark horizon is the first Czech exile and great educator, John Amos Comenius. Red is the color of war, white is the color of peace, blue is the past, and orange is the future.

When you get tired of being told what's what, step back and figure out Mucha's intention. His technique will help you. The grand-scale background, which shows the historic events, is executed in egg-based tempera. Against that low-resolution foggy base, the figures painted in oil come sharply into focus: the terrified couple, the mother and child, the bearded sage with the young man, the face of the lady-in-waiting. The lucid detail tells the experience of these single, often-anonymous individuals, suggesting that the *Slav Epic* is not about the monumental depiction of a particular event, but about the fate of the individual against the backdrop of history. The entire weight of events is condensed into the expressions on their faces. In the scene of a print shop, the young man in the foreground is Mucha's self-portrait.

Finally, step even farther back and contemplate the painting as a work of an Impressionist or an abstract artist. The fusion of colors stands far beyond any particular meaning. Like the tones of a 19th-century symphony, Mucha's visual concert has the power to stir the deepest emotions.

filled with Czech symbols and expressing his people's ideals and aspirations, were patriotic banners that aroused the national spirit. And check out the photographs of his models. With the help of an abundant supply of slinky models, Mucha was a founding father of the Art Nouveau movement. Partly overseen by Mucha's grandson, the museum is two blocks off Wenceslas Square and wonderfully displayed on one comfortable floor.

The included 30-minute video is definitely worthwhile (in English, generally at :15 and :45 past the hour—check the starting time); it describes the main project of Mucha's life, the *Slav Epic* (see sidebar).

Cost and Hours: 160 Kč, daily 10:00-18:00, good English descriptions, Panská 7. Tel. 224-233-355, www.mucha.cz.

• *Backtrack to Na Příkopě and turn right. At the corner of Na Příkopě and Nekázanka is the...*

▲UniCredit Bank (Pre-Art Nouveau)—Pop into this bank building to understand the origins of Art Nouveau. Climb up the stairs and sit in the main hall. The Neo-Renaissance UniCredit Bank building (formerly Živnostenská Banka, Prague's oldest banking institution) was, until the early 1990s, the only place in town to get hard currency or traveler's checks. Any Czech who traveled would sit here dreaming of upcoming adventures.

But let's go back not 20 years, but 100 years—to when cool air (created by ice that filled the vaults below) flowed out of the circa-1880s air-conditioning vents that flank the top of the staircase. You're surrounded by textbook Historicism. In the 19th century, Prague existed in the Viennese cultural realm, and this was it: a Neo-Renaissance celebration of the professions (identify the statues), with the coats of arms of cities in the Czech realm. Imagine a young Alfons Mucha or Gustav Klimt sitting in a lobby similar to this one—talented young artists surrounded by all this, with their deep-seated need to escape this conformity on steroids...to secede. In simple terms, that was what the Secessionist movement (born in Vienna, circa 1897, and kicking off the Art Nouveau era) was all about.

• *Continue one more block up Na Příkopě to the...*

▲▲Municipal House (Obecní Dům)—The Municipal House, which celebrated its centennial birthday in 2011, is the "pearl of Czech Art Nouveau." Stand in front and study the Homage to Prague mosaic on the building's striking facade. Featuring a goddess-like Praha presiding over a land of peace and high culture, the image stoked cultural pride and nationalist sentiment.

The building (1905-1911) is Neo-Baroque with a dusting of Art Nouveau. It was financed by cultural and artistic leaders, who wanted a ceremonial palace to reinforce the self-awareness of the Czech nation. Built under Catholic Habsburg rule, it was drenched

PRAGUE

in patriotic Czech themes to emphasize how the Protestant Czechs were a distinct culture. In 1918, Czechoslovakia's independence was declared from the building's balcony.

While the exterior is impressive, the highlight is inside—arguably Europe's finest Art Nouveau interior. The Municipal House features Prague's largest concert hall, a recommended Art Nouveau café (Kavárna Obecní Dům), and two other restaurants. While you can poke around its entrance halls (daily 10:00-18:00) or wander around the lobby of the concert hall, there are two ways to really appreciate the building: Attend a concert or take a tour.

Tours: Daily one-hour tours give you a guided look at all the sumptuous halls and banquet rooms (English-only, 180 Kč, usually 3/day, generally at 12:00, 14:00 and 17:00). Buy your ticket (and pay 55 Kč extra to take photos) from the ground-floor shop where tours depart. Tel. 222-002-101, www.obecnidum.cz.

Concerts: Performances are held regularly in the lavish Smetana Hall. Note that many concerts brag they are held in the Municipal House, but are performed in a smaller, less impressive hall in the same building.

Powder Tower—Next to the Municipal House, the big, black Powder Tower (not worth touring inside) was the Gothic gate of the town wall, built to house the city's gunpowder. The decoration on the tower is the best 15th-century sculpture in town. This is the only surviving bit of wall that was built to defend the city in the 1400s. Look at your city map and conceptualize medieval Prague's smart design. The city was encircled by the river and its wall (now a main street), which arced from a bend in the river. The only river crossing back then was the fortified Charles Bridge. The road from Vienna arrived at the foot of the Powder Tower—it was the city's formal front door. When Empress Maria Theresa was crowned the Queen of Bohemia here, she came down that road and through this gate. Go back 500 years and look up at the impressive welcoming committee, reminding all of the hierarchy of our mortal existence: from artisans flanking Prague's coat of arms, up to a pair of Czech kings with seals of alliance of neighboring regions, and finally to angels heralding the heavenly zone with Saints Peter and Paul flanking Jesus.

• OK, got it...let's go in. Pass through the tower to reach commercial and touristy Celetná Street, which leads directly to the Old Town Square (see page 226).

Národní Třída: Communist Prague

From Můstek at the bottom of Wenceslas Square, you can head west on Národní Třída (in the opposite direction from Na Příkopě and the Art Nouveau sights) for an interesting stroll through urban Prague to the National Theater and the Vltava River. But first, consider dropping into the Museum of Communism, a few steps down Na Příkopě (on the right).

▲▲**Museum of Communism**—This museum traces the story of communism in Prague: the origin, dream, reality, and nightmare; the cult of personality; and, finally, the Velvet Revolution—all thoughtfully described in English. Along the way, it gives a fascinating review of the Czech Republic's 40-year stint with Soviet economics, "in all its dreariness and puffed-up glory." You'll find propaganda posters, busts of communist All-Stars (Marx, Lenin, Stalin), and a photograph of the massive stone Stalin that overlooked Prague until 1962.

Slices of communist life are re-created here, from a bland store counter to a typical classroom (with textbooks using Russia's Cyrillic alphabet—no longer studied—and a poem on the chalkboard that extols the virtues of the tractor). Don't miss the Jan Palach exhibit and the 20-minute video (plays continuously, English subtitles) that shows how the Czech people chafed under the big Red yoke from 1969 through 1989.

Cost and Hours: 180 Kč, daily 9:00-21:00, Na Příkopě 10, above a McDonald's and next to a casino—Lenin is turning over in his Red Square mausoleum. Tel. 224-212-966, www.muzeum komunismu.cz.

Národní Třída and the Velvet Revolution—Národní Třída (National Street) is where you feel the pulse of the modern city. The street, which connects Wenceslas Square with the National Theater and the river, is a busy thoroughfare running through the heart of urban Prague. In 1989, this unassuming boulevard played host to the first salvo of a Velvet Revolution that would topple the communist regime.

Make your way down Národní Třída until you hit the tram tracks (just beyond the Tesco department store). On the left, look for the photo of Bill Clinton playing saxophone, with Václav Havel on the side (this is the entrance to **Reduta,** Prague's best jazz club; next door are two recommended eateries, **Café Louvre** and **Le Patio**). Just beyond that, you'll come to a short corridor with white arches. Inside this arcade is a simple **memorial** to the hundreds of students injured here by the police in the Velvet Revolution, which took place on November 17, 1989.

Along the Vltava River

I've listed these sights from north to south, beginning at the grand, Neo-Renaissance National Theater, which is five blocks south of Charles Bridge and stands along the riverbank at the end of Národní Třída.

National Theater (Národní Divadlo)—Opened in 1883 with Smetana's opera *Libuše,* this theater was the first truly Czech venue in Prague. From the very start, it was nicknamed the "Cradle of Czech Culture." The building is a key symbol of the Czech national revival that began in the late 18th century. In 1800, "Prag" was predominantly German. The Industrial Revolution brought Czechs from the countryside into the city, their new urban identity defined by patriotic teachers and priests. By 1883, most of the city spoke Czech, and the opening of this theater represented the birth of the modern Czech nation. It remains an important national icon: The state annually pours more subsidies into this theater than into all of Czech film production. It's the most beautiful venue in town for opera and ballet, often with world-class singers (for more details on performances, see "Entertainment in Prague," later).

Next door (just inland, on Národní Třída) is the boxy, glassy facade of the **Nová Scéna.** This "New National Theater" building, dating from 1983 (the 100th anniversary of the original National Theater building), reflects the bold and stark communist aesthetic.

Across the street from the National Theater is the former haunt of Prague's intelligentsia, the recommended **Grand Café Slavia,** a Viennese-style coffeehouse that is fine for a meal or drink with a view of the river.

• *Just south of the National Theater in the Vltava, you'll find...*

Prague's Islands—From the National Theater, the Legions' Bridge (Most Legií) leads across the island called **Střelecký Ostrov.** Covered with chestnut trees, this island boasts Prague's best beach (on the sandy tip that points north to Charles Bridge). You might see a fisherman pulling out trout from a river that's now much cleaner than it used to be. Bring a swimsuit and take a dip just a stone's throw from Europe's most beloved bridge. In summer, the island hosts open-air movies (most in English or with English subtitles, nightly mid-July-early Sept at about 21:00, www.strelak.cz).

In the mood for boating instead of swimming? On the next island up, **Slovanský Ostrov,** you can rent a boat (40 Kč/hour for rowboats, 60 Kč/hour for paddleboats, bring a picture ID as deposit). A lazy hour paddling around Střelecký Ostrov—or just floating sleepily in the middle of the river surrounded by this great city's architectural splendor—is a delightful experience on a sunny day. It's cheap, easy fun (and it's good for you).

• *A 10-minute walk (or one stop on tram #17) south from the National Theater, beyond the islands, is Jirásek Bridge (Jiráskův Most), where you'll find the...*

Dancing House (Tančící Dům)—If ever a building could get your toes tapping, it would be this one, nicknamed "Fred and Ginger" by American architecture buffs. This metallic samba is the work of Frank Gehry (who designed the equally striking Guggenheim Museum in Bilbao, Spain, and Seattle's Experience

Music Project). Eight-legged Ginger's wispy dress and Fred's metal mesh head are easy to spot. Some Czechs prefer to think that the two "figures" represent the nation's greatest 20th-century heroes, Jozef Gabčík and Jan Kubiš (see the next listing).

The building's top-floor restaurant, **Céleste,** is a fine place for a fancy French meal. Whether you go up for lunch (reasonable, 12:00-14:30), a drink (16:00-18:00), or an expensive dinner, you'll be a louse in the Gehry haircut (tel. 221-984-160).

• *Two blocks up Resslova street is the Sts. Cyril and Methodius Church, which contains in its crypt the...*

▲**National Memorial to the Heroes of the Heydrich Terror**—In 1942, WWII paratroopers Jozef Gabčík and Jan Kubiš assassinated the SS second-in-command Reinhard Heydrich, who controlled the Nazi-occupied Czech lands and was one of the main architects of the Holocaust. In the weeks following his assassination, the two paratroopers hid, along with other freedom fighters, in the crypt of the Greek Orthodox Sts. Cyril and Methodius Church on Resslova street. Today, a modest exhibition in the church's crypt retells their story, along with the history of the Czech resistance movement. Outside, notice the small memorial, including bullet holes, plaque, and flowers on the street. Around the corner is the entry into the museum and the crypt (75 Kč, Tue-Sun 9:00-17:00, closed Mon, 2 blocks up from the Dancing House at Resslova 9A, tel. 224-916-100, full history explained in small 25-Kč booklet).

• *Farther up Resslova street is...*

Charles Square (Karlovo Náměstí)—Prague's largest square is covered by lawns, trees, and statues of Czech writers. It's a quiet antidote to the bustling Wenceslas and Old Town squares. The Gothic New Town Hall at the top-left corner of the square has excellent views and labeled panoramic photographs that help you orient yourself. The little parlor across the street has some of the best gelato in town.

The Little Quarter (Malá Strana)

This charming neighborhood, huddled under the castle on the west bank of the river, is low on blockbuster sights but high on ambience. The most enjoyable approach from the Old Town is across Charles Bridge. From the end of the bridge (TI in tower), Mostecká street leads two blocks up to the Little Quarter Square (Malostranské Náměstí) and the huge Church of St. Nicholas. But before you head up there, consider a detour to Kampa Island.

Between Charles Bridge and Little Quarter Square

Kampa Island—One hundred yards from the castle end of the Charles Bridge, stairs on the left lead down to the main square of Kampa Island (mostly created from the rubble of the Little Quarter, which was destroyed in a 1540 fire). The island features relaxing pubs, a breezy park, hippies, lovers, a fine contemporary art gallery, and river access. From the main square, Hroznová lane (on the right) leads to a bridge. The high-water mark at the end of the bridge dates from 1890. The **old water wheel** is the last survivor of many mills that once lined the canal here. Each mill had its own protective water spirit *(vodník)*. Notice the padlocks. These are the scourge of romantic spots throughout Europe these days, popular with not-very-creative Romeos who think that clinching a lock onto something (mill, bridge, whatever) proves their enduring love.

• *Fifty yards beyond the bridge (on the right, under the trees) is the...*

Lennon Wall (Lennonova Zeď)—While Lenin's ideas hung like a water-soaked trench coat upon the Czech people, rock singer John Lennon's ideas gave many locals hope and a vision. When Lennon was killed in 1980, a large wall was spontaneously covered with memorial graffiti. Night after night, the police would paint over the "All You Need Is Love" and "Imagine" graffiti. And day after day, it would reappear. Until independence came in 1989, travelers, freedom-lovers, and local hippies gathered here. Silly as it might seem, this wall is remembered as a place that gave hope to locals craving freedom. Even today, while the tension and danger associated with this wall are gone, people come here to imagine. *"John žije"* is Czech for "John lives."

• *From here, continue up to the Little Quarter Square.*

On or near Little Quarter Square

The focal point of this neighborhood, the Little Quarter Square (Malostranské Náměstí) is dominated by the huge Church of St. Nicholas. Note that there's a handy Via Musica ticket office across from the church.

Church of St. Nicholas (Kostel Sv. Mikuláše)—When the Jesuits came to Prague, they found the perfect piece of real estate for their church and its associated school—right on Little Quarter Square. The church (built 1703-1760) is the best example of High Baroque in town. It's giddy with curves and illusions. The altar features a lavish gold-plated Nicholas, flanked by the two top Jesuits: the founder, St. Ignatius Loyola, and his missionary follower, St. Francis Xavier.

Climb up the **gallery** through the staircase in the left transept for a close-up look at a collection of large canvases and illusionary frescoes by Karel Škréta, who is considered the greatest Czech Baroque painter. Notice that at first glance the canvases are utterly dark, but as sunbeams shine through the window, various parts of the painting brighten up. Like a looking-glass, the image reflects the light, creating a play of light and dark. This painting technique

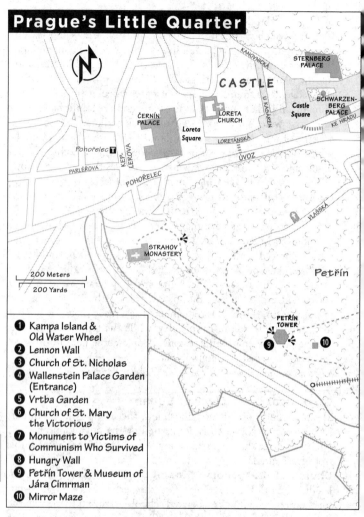

Prague's Little Quarter

1 Kampa Island & Old Water Wheel
2 Lennon Wall
3 Church of St. Nicholas
4 Wallenstein Palace Garden (Entrance)
5 Vrtba Garden
6 Church of St. Mary the Victorious
7 Monument to Victims of Communism Who Survived
8 Hungry Wall
9 Petřín Tower & Museum of Jára Cimrman
10 Mirror Maze

represents a central Baroque belief: The world is full of darkness, and the only hope that makes it come alive comes from God. The church walls seem to nearly fuse with the sky, suggesting that happenings on earth are closely connected to heaven. In the center of the ceiling, find St. Nick with his bishop's miter, on his way to heaven.

Cost and Hours: 60 Kč, church open daily 9:00-17:00, opens at 8:30 for prayer.

Tower Climb: For a good look at the city and the church's 250-foot dome, climb 215 steps up the bell tower (50 Kč, April-Oct daily 10:00-18:00, closed Nov-March, tower entrance is outside the right transept).

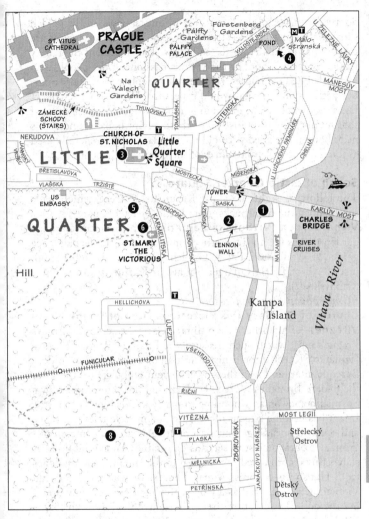

Concerts: The church is also an evening concert venue; tickets are usually on sale at the door (450 Kč, generally nightly except Tue, at 18:00, www.psalterium.cz).

• *From here, you can hike 10 minutes uphill to the castle (and five more minutes to the Strahov Monastery). For information on these sights, see "The Castle Quarter," later. If you're walking up to the castle, consider going via...*

Nerudova Street—This steep, cobbled street, leading from Little Quarter Square to the castle, is named for Jan Neruda, a gifted 19th-century journalist (and somewhat less-talented fiction writer). It's lined with old buildings still sporting the characteristic doorway signs (e.g., the lion, three violinists, house of the golden suns) that once served as street addresses. The surviving signs are carefully restored and protected by law. They represent the family name, the occupation, or the various passions of the people who once inhabited the houses. (If you were to replace your house number with a symbol, what would it be?) In 1777, in order to collect taxes more effectively, Habsburg empress Maria Theresa decreed that numbers be used instead of these quaint house names. This neighborhood is filled with old noble palaces, now generally used as foreign embassies and offices of the Czech Parliament.

South of Little Quarter Square

The following sights lie along Karmelitská street, which leads south (along the tram tracks) from Little Quarter Square.

Vrtba Garden (Vrtbovská Zahrada)—This terraced Baroque garden makes for an interesting comparison to the Renaissance garden at Wallenstein Palace Garden (100 Kč, daily 10:00-18:00, just south of Little Quarter Square at Karmelitská 25, www .vrtbovska.cz).

• *Continue past the gardens to the...*

Church of St. Mary the Victorious (Kostel Panny Marie Vítězné)—This otherwise ordinary Carmelite church displays Prague's most worshipped treasure, the Infant of Prague (Pražské Jezulátko). Kneel at the banister in front of the tiny lost-in-gilded-Baroque altar, and find the prayer in your language (of the 13 in the folder). Brought to Czech lands during the Habsburg era by a Spanish noblewoman who came to marry a Czech nobleman, the Infant has become a focus of worship and miracle tales in Prague and Spanish-speaking countries. South Americans come on pilgrimage to Prague just to see this one statue. An exhibit upstairs shows tiny embroidered robes given to the Infant, including ones from Habsburg Empress Maria Theresa of Austria (1754) and Vietnam (1958), as well as a video showing a nun lovingly dressing the doll-like sculpture (free, Mon-Sat 9:30-17:30, Sun 13:00-17:00, English-language Mass Sun at 12:00, Karmelitská 9, www .pragjesu.info).

• *Continue a few more blocks down Karmelitská to the south end of the Little Quarter (where the street is called Újezd, roughly across the Legions' Bridge from the National Theater). Here you find yourself at the base of...*

Petřín Hill

This hill, topped by a replica of the Eiffel Tower, features several unusual sights.

Monument to Victims of Communism Who Survived—The figures walking down the steps in the hillside are gradually atrophied by the totalitarian regime. They do not die but slowly disappear, one limb at a time. The statistics say it all: In Czechoslovakia alone, 205,486 people were imprisoned, 248 were executed, 4,500 died in prison, 327 were shot attempting to cross the border, and 170,938 left the country.

• *To the left of the monument is the...*

Hungry Wall—This medieval defense wall was Charles IV's 14th-century equivalent of FDR's work-for-food projects.

• *On the right (50 yards away) is the base of a handy **funicular**—hop on to reach Petřín Tower (uses tram/Metro ticket, runs daily, every 10-15 minutes from 8:00-22:00).*

Summit and Tower—The summit of Petřín Hill is considered the best place in Prague to take your date for a romantic city view. Built for an exhibition in 1891, the 200-foot-tall **Petřín Tower** is one-fifth the height of its Parisian big brother, which was built two years earlier. But, thanks to this hill, the top of the tower sits at the same elevation as the real Eiffel Tower. Climbing the 400 steps rewards you with amazing views of the city. Czech wives drag their men to Petřín Hill each May Day to reaffirm their love with a kiss under a blooming sour-cherry tree.

• *In the tower's basement is the...*

Museum of Jára Cimrman, Genius Who Did Not Become Famous—The museum, the funniest sight in Prague, traces the fictional life of the greatest Czech who never lived, including pictures and English descriptions of the thinker's overlooked inventions.

Cost and Hours: 100 Kč includes tower and Cimrman museum, daily 10:00-22:00; the mirror maze next door is nothing special, but fun to wander through quickly since you're already here—50 Kč, daily 10:00-22:00).

The Castle Quarter (Hradčany)

Looming above Prague, dominating its skyline, is the Castle Quarter. Prague Castle and its surrounding sights are packed with Czech history, as well as with tourists. In addition to the castle, I enjoy visiting the nearby Strahov Monastery—which has a fascinating old library and beautiful views over all of Prague.

Castle Square (Hradčanské Náměstí)—right in front of the castle gates—is at the center of this neighborhood. Stretching along the promontory away from the castle is a regal neighborhood that ends at the Strahov Monastery. Above the castle are the Royal Gardens, and below the castle are more gardens and lanes leading down to the Little Quarter.

Getting to Prague Castle

If you're not up for a hike, the tram offers a sweat-free ride up to

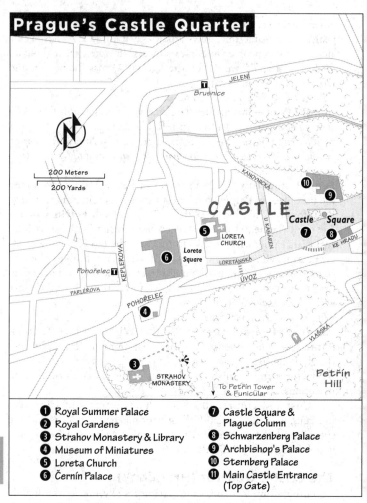

Prague's Castle Quarter

200 Meters
200 Yards

JELENÍ
Brusnice

CASTLE

Castle Square

LORETA
CHURCH

Loreta
Square

KANOVNICKÁ

U KASÁREN

KE HRADU

Pohořelec

KEPLEROVA

LORETÁNSKÁ

ÚVOZ

PARLEROVA

POHOŘELEC

VLAŠSKÁ

STRAHOV
MONASTERY

To Petřín Tower
& Funicular

Petřín
Hill

① Royal Summer Palace
② Royal Gardens
③ Strahov Monastery & Library
④ Museum of Miniatures
⑤ Loreta Church
⑥ Černín Palace
⑦ Castle Square & Plague Column
⑧ Schwarzenberg Palace
⑨ Archbishop's Palace
⑩ Sternberg Palace
⑪ Main Castle Entrance (Top Gate)

PRAGUE

the castle. Taxis are expensive, as they have to go the long way around (200 Kč).

By Foot: Begin in the Little Quarter, just across Charles Bridge from the Old Town. Hikers can follow the main cobbled road (Mostecká) from Charles Bridge to Little Quarter Square, marked by the huge, green-domed Church of St. Nicholas. (The nearest Metro stop is Malostranská, from which Valdštejnská street leads down to Little Quarter Square.) From Little Quarter Square, hike uphill along Nerudova street (described earlier). After about 10 minutes, a steep lane on the right leads to the castle. (If you continue straight, Nerudova becomes Úvoz and climbs to the Strahov Monastery.)

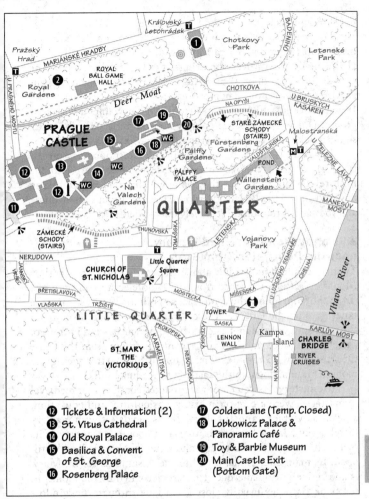

12 Tickets & Information (2)
13 St. Vitus Cathedral
14 Old Royal Palace
15 Basilica & Convent
   of St. George
16 Rosenberg Palace
17 Golden Lane (Temp. Closed)
18 Lobkowicz Palace &
   Panoramic Café
19 Toy & Barbie Museum
20 Main Castle Exit
   (Bottom Gate)

By Tram: Tram #22 takes you up to the castle. While you can catch the tram in various places, these three stops are particularly convenient: at the Národní Třída Metro stop (between Wenceslas Square and the National Theater in the New Town); in front of the National Theater (Národní Divadlo, on the riverbank in the New Town); and at Malostranská (the Metro stop in the Little Quarter).

Which Tram Stop for the Castle? After rattling up the hill, the tram makes three stops near the castle. To choose the best stop for your visit, consider the time of day, as the castle is plagued with crowds.

The first castle stop, **Královský Letohrádek,** allows a scenic but slow approach through the Royal Gardens.

For the quickest commute to the castle, stay on the tram one more stop to get off at **Pražský Hrad,** then simply walk along U Prašného Mostu over the bridge into the castle. To beat the crowds, be at the door of St. Vitus Cathedral right when it opens at 9:00 (except on Sunday mornings, when it's closed for Mass). If you arrive just 10-15 minutes later, it'll be swamped with tour groups. (I'd avoid the castle entirely mid-morning.) See the castle sights quickly, then hike up to the Strahov Monastery.

If you'd rather visit the castle in the afternoon, stay on the tram for two more stops—passing the Brusnice stop—to the **Pohořelec** stop, then tour the Strahov Monastery before hiking down to the castle. By late afternoon, the tour groups are napping and the castle grounds are relatively uncrowded.

▲Strahov Monastery and Library, near the Pohořelec Tram Stop

Twin Baroque domes high above the castle mark the Strahov Monastery. It's best reached from the Pohořelec stop on tram #22 (from the stop, follow the tram tracks uphill for 50 yards, enter the fancy gate on the left near the tall red-brick wall, and you'll see the twin spires of the monastery; the library entrance is in front of the church on the right). If you're coming on foot from the Little Quarter, allow 15 minutes for the uphill hike. After seeing the monastery, hike down to the castle (a five-minute walk).

Monastery: As you enter the grounds, consider that medieval monasteries were a mix of industry, agriculture, and education, as well as worship and theology. In its heyday, the monastery (Strahovský Klášter Premonstrátů) had a booming economy of its own, with vineyards, a brewery, and a sizeable beer hall—all still open. Its main church, dedicated to the Assumption of St. Mary, is an originally Romanesque structure decorated by the monks in textbook Baroque (usually closed, but look through the window inside the front door to see its interior).

Library: The adjacent library (Strahovská Knihovna) offers a peek at how enlightened thinkers in the 18th century influenced learning (80 Kč, daily 9:00-11:45 & 13:00-17:00, www.strahov skyklaster.cz). Cases in the library gift shop show off illuminated manuscripts, described in English. Some are in old Czech, but because the Enlightenment promoted the universality of knowledge (and Latin was the universal language of Europe's educated elite), there was little place for regional dialects—therefore, few books here are in the Czech language.

Two rooms (seen only from the door) are filled with 10th- to 17th-century books, shelved under elaborately painted ceilings. The theme of the first and bigger hall is philosophy, with the history of man's pursuit of knowledge painted on the ceiling. The other hall focuses on theology. As the Age of Enlightenment began to take hold in Europe at the end of the 18th century, monasteries still controlled the books. Notice the gilded, locked case containing the *libri prohibiti* (prohibited books) at the end of the room. Only the abbot had the key, and you had to have his blessing to read these books—by writers such as Nicolas Copernicus and Jan Hus, and even including the French encyclopedia. The hallway connecting these two library rooms was filled with cases illustrating the new practical approach to natural sciences. Find the dried-up elephant trunks, baby dodo bird (which became extinct in the 17th century), and one of the earliest models of an electricity generator.

Nearby Views: Just downhill from the monastery, past the venerable linden trees (a symbol of the Czech people) and through the gate, the views from the **monastery garden** are among the finest in Prague. The Bellavista Restaurant, with perhaps the city's best view tables, serves basic food at high prices. From the public perch beneath the tables, you can see St. Vitus Cathedral (the heart of the castle complex), the green dome of the Church of St. Nicholas (marking the center of the Little Quarter), the two dark towers fortifying both ends of Charles Bridge, and the fanciful black spires of the Týn Church (marking the Old Town Square). On the horizon is the modern **Žižkov TV and radio tower** (conveniently marking the liveliest nightlife zone in town). Begun in the 1980s, the tower was partly meant to jam Radio Free Europe's broadcast from Munich. By the time it was finished, communism was dead, and Radio Free Europe's headquarters had moved to Prague.

Getting to the Castle: To reach the castle from Strahov Monastery, take Loretánská (the upper road, passing Loreta Square, with Loreta Church—described later); this is a more interesting route than the lower road, Úvoz, which takes you down a steep hill, below Castle Square.

• *Or, for one more little sight, consider visiting the Museum of Miniatures. From the monastery garden viewpoint, backtrack through the gate to the big linden trees and leave through a passage on your right. At the door is the miniscule...*

Museum of Miniatures: You'll see 40 teeny exhibits, each under a microscope, crafted by an artist from St. Petersburg. Yes, you could fit the entire museum in a carry-on-size suitcase, but good things sometimes come in very, very small packages—it's fascinating to see minutiae such as a padlock on the leg of an ant. An English loaner flier explains it all. Notice how the Russian staff has a certain gentility (70 Kč, kids-50 Kč, daily 9:00-17:00, tel. 233-352-371, www.muzeumminiatur.com).

On Loreta Square, Between Strahov Monastery and Castle Square

From the monastery, take Loretánská street to Loreta Square (Loretánské Náměstí).

Loreta Church—This church has been a hit with pilgrims for centuries, thanks to its dazzling bell tower, peaceful yet plush cloister, sparkling treasury, and much-venerated Holy House.

Once inside, follow the one-way clockwise route. While you stroll along the cloister, notice that the ceiling is painted with the many places Mary has miraculously appeared to the faithful in Europe.

In the garden-like center of the cloister stands the ornate **Santa Casa (Holy House),** considered by some pilgrims to be part of Mary's home in Nazareth. Because many pilgrims returning from the Holy Land docked at the Italian port of Loreto, it's called the Loreta Shrine. The Santa Casa is the "little Bethlehem" of Prague. It is the traditional departure point for Czech pilgrims setting out on the long, arduous journey to Europe's most important pilgrimage site, Santiago de Compostela, in northwest Spain. Inside, on the left wall, hangs what some consider to be an original beam from the house of Mary. It's overseen by a much-venerated statue of the Black Virgin. The Santa Casa itself might seem like a bit of a letdown, but consider that you're entering the holiest spot in the country for generations of believers.

The small **Baroque church** behind the Santa Casa is one of the most beautiful in Prague. The decor looks rich—but the marble and gold are all fake (tap the columns). From the window in the back, you can see a stucco relief on the Santa Casa that shows angels rescuing the house from a pagan attack in Nazareth and making a special delivery to Loreto in Italy.

Continue around the cloister. In the last corner is **"St. Bearded Woman"** (Svatá Starosta). This patron saint of unhappy marriages is a woman whose family arranged for her to marry a pagan man. She prayed for an escape, sprouted a beard...and the guy said, "No way." While she managed to avoid the marriage, it angered her father, who crucified her. The many candles here are from people suffering through unhappy marriages.

Take a left just before the exit and head upstairs, following signs to the **treasury**—a room full of jeweled worship aids (well-described in English). The highlight here is a monstrance (Communion wafer holder) from 1699, with more than 6,000 diamonds.

Enjoy the short **carillon concert** at the top of the hour; from the lawn in front of the main entrance, you can see the racks of bells being clanged. (At the exit, you'll see a schedule of English-language Masses and upcoming *pout*—pilgrimages—departing from here.)

Cost and Hours: 110 Kč, Tue-Sun 9:00-12:15 & 13:00-16:30, closed Mon, tel. 220-516-740, www.loreta.cz.

Castle Square (Hradčanské Náměstí)

This is the central square of the Castle Quarter. Enjoy the awesome city view and the two entertaining bands that play regularly at the gate. (If the Prague Castle Orchestra is playing, say hello to friendly, mustachioed Josef, and consider getting the group's terrific CD.) The recommended **Espresso Kajetánka** café, with dramatic city views, hides a few steps down (immediately to the right as you face the castle). From the café, stairs lead down to the Little Quarter.

Castle Square was a kind of medieval Pennsylvania Avenue—the king, the most powerful noblemen, and the archbishop lived here. Look uphill from the gate. The Renaissance **Schwarzenberg Palace** (on the left, with the big, envelope-like rectangles scratched on the wall) was where the Rožmberks "humbly" stayed when they were in town visiting from their Český Krumlov estates. The Schwarzenberg family inherited the Krumlov estates and aristocratic prominence in Bohemia, and stayed in the palace until the 20th century. The palace now houses the National Gallery's collection of Czech Baroque paintings, displayed in recently restored rooms that have great views of the city (150 Kč, Tue-Sun 10:00-18:00, cheaper after 16:00, closed Mon; may close sporadically due to budget cuts—ask at TI).

The archbishop still lives in the yellow Rococo **palace** across the square (with the three white goose necks in the red field—the coat of arms of Prague's archbishops).

Through the portal on the left-hand side of the palace, a lane leads to the **Sternberg Palace** (Šternberský Palác), filled with the National Gallery's collection of European paintings—including minor works by Albrecht Dürer, Peter Paul Rubens, Rembrandt, and El Greco (150 Kč, Tue-Sun 10:00-18:00, closed Mon; may close sporadically due to budget cuts—ask at TI).

The black Baroque sculpture in the middle of the square is a **plague column.** Erected as a token of gratitude to the saints who saved the population from the epidemic, these columns are an integral part of the main square of many Habsburg towns.

The statue marked *TGM* honors **Tomáš Garrigue Masaryk** (1850-1937), a university prof and a pal of Woodrow Wilson. At the end of World War I, Masaryk united the Czechs and the Slovaks into one nation and became its first president.

▲▲Prague Castle (Pražský Hrad)

For more than a thousand years, Czech leaders have ruled from Prague Castle. Today, Prague's Castle is, by some measures, the biggest on earth. Several stops stand out, and are explained here: St. Vitus Cathedral, Old Royal Palace, Basilica of St. George, and Lobkowicz Palace. (The Golden Lane, another highlight, is closed for renovation.)

Cost: Get the short-tour ticket (250 Kč), which covers the cathedral, Old Royal Palace, Basilica of St. George, and Rosenberg Palace (buy in the palace or at the ticket offices on the two castle courtyards—look for the green *i*). The comprehensive long-tour ticket (350 Kč) includes a few additional sights that aren't worth visiting.

Hours: Castle sights are open daily April-Oct 9:00-18:00, Nov-March 9:00-16:00, last entry 15 minutes before closing; grounds are open daily 5:00-24:00. St. Vitus Cathedral is closed Sunday mornings for Mass. Be warned that the cathedral can be closed unexpectedly due to special services—consider calling ahead to confirm (tel. 224-373-368 or 224-372-434). If you're not interested in entering the museums, you could try a nighttime visit—the castle grounds are safe, peaceful, floodlit, and open late.

Tours: Hour-long tours in English depart from the main ticket office near the cathedral entrance about three times a day, but they cover only the cathedral and Old Royal Palace (100 Kč plus entry ticket, tel. 224-373-368). You can rent an **audioguide** for 200 Kč (good all day)—pick it up at the main desk, show this book, and ask for a special Rick Steves price. It's perfectly shareable if you have a cheek-to-cheek partner and not much money. The audioguide also entitles you to priority entrance at the cathedral—when the line in front of the entrance is long, walk to the exit door on the right and show the audioguide to the guard to be let in.

Crowd-Beating Tips: Huge throngs of tourists turn the castle grounds into a sea of people during peak times (9:30-12:30). St. Vitus Cathedral is the most crowded part of the castle complex. If you're visiting in the morning, be at the cathedral entrance promptly at 9:00, when the doors open. For 10 minutes you'll have the sacred space to yourself (after about 9:15, tour guides jockey unwieldy groups from tomb to tomb, forming a noisy human traffic jam). Late afternoon is least crowded. The grounds are free, romantically lit, and all yours after dark.

Eateries: The castle complex has several forgettable cafés scattered throughout; a good bet is the scenic and creative Panoramic Café at Lobkowicz Palace (at the end of this tour). Otherwise, seek out recommended eateries located nearby in the Castle Quarter (see map on pages 258-259) or Little Quarter (see map on pages 254-255).

Sightseeing Plan: Begin at Castle Square, then tour St. Vitus

Cathedral, the Old Royal Palace, and the Basilica of St. George, ending with Lobkowicz Palace.

Castle Gate and Courtyards—Standing in the square, survey the castle—the tip of a 1,500-foot-long series of courtyards, churches, and palaces. The guard changes on the hour from 5:00-23:00 at every gate: top, bottom, and side. The most ceremony and music occurs at noon at the top gate.

Walk under the fighting giants, under an arch, through the passageway, and into the courtyard. The modern green awning with the golden-winged cat (just to the right of the fountain) marks the offices of the Czech president, who is elected by the parliament rather than by popular vote and serves as more of a figurehead than a power broker. The current president is Václav Klaus. His consistent politics have brought him popularity from like-minded Czechs, but bitter resentment from those who see him as incapable of considering points of view other than his own. Outside the Czech Republic, Klaus is known for his unconstructive criticism of the European Union and denunciation of the campaign against global warming (the reality of which he denies).

• *As you walk through another passageway, you'll find yourself facing...*

▲▲▲**St. Vitus Cathedral (Katedrála Sv. Víta)**—The Roman Catholic cathedral symbolizes the Czech spirit—it contains the tombs and relics of the most important local saints and kings, including the first three Habsburg kings.

Cathedral Facade: Before entering, check out the facade. What's up with the guys in suits carved into the facade beneath the big, round window? They're the architects and builders who finished the church. Started in 1344, construction was stalled by wars and plagues. But, fueled by the 19th-century rise of Czech nationalism, Prague's top church was finished in 1929 for the 1,000th anniversary of the death of St. Wenceslas. While it looks all Gothic, it's actually two distinct halves: the original 14th-century Gothic area around the high altar and the modern Neo-Gothic nave. For 400 years, a temporary wall sealed off the functional, yet unfinished, cathedral.

Mucha Stained-Glass Window: Enter through the gate on the left with the fenced-off queuing area and find the third window on the left. This masterful 1931 Art Nouveau window was designed by Czech artist Alfons Mucha, though the work was actually done by a craftsman (if you like this, you'll love the Mucha Museum in the New Town and Mucha's masterpiece, *Slav Epic*—described on pages 245 and 246 respectively).

Notice Mucha's stirring nationalism: Methodius and Cyril, widely considered the fathers of Slavic-style Christianity, are top and center. Cyril—the monk in black holding the Bible—brought the word of God to the Slavs. They had no written language in the

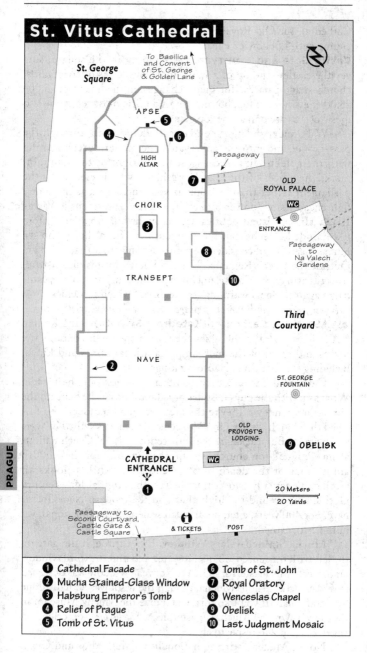

St. Vitus Cathedral

St. George Square

To Basilica
and Convent
of St. George
& Golden Lane

APSE

❹

❺

❻

HIGH
ALTAR

Passageway

❼

OLD
ROYAL PALACE

WC

CHOIR

ENTRANCE

❸

Passageway
to
Na Valech
Gardens

❽

TRANSEPT

❿

Third
Courtyard

NAVE

ST. GEORGE
FOUNTAIN

❷

OLD
PROVOST'S
LODGING

❾ OBELISK

WC

CATHEDRAL
ENTRANCE

❶

Passageway to
Second Courtyard,
Castle Gate &
Castle Square

& TICKETS

POST

20 Meters
20 Yards

PRAGUE

❶ Cathedral Facade
❷ Mucha Stained-Glass Window
❸ Habsburg Emperor's Tomb
❹ Relief of Prague
❺ Tomb of St. Vitus

❻ Tomb of St. John
❼ Royal Oratory
❽ Wenceslas Chapel
❾ Obelisk
❿ Last Judgment Mosaic

ninth century, so he designed the necessary alphabet (Glagolitic, which later developed into Cyrillic). Methodius, the bishop, is shown baptizing a mythic, lanky, long-haired Czech man—a reminder of how he brought Christianity to the Czech people. Scenes from the life of Cyril on the left, and scenes from the life of Methodius on the right, bookend the stirring and epic Slavic scene. In the center are a kneeling boy and a prophesying elder—that's young St. Wenceslas and his grandmother, St. Ludmila. In addition to being specific historical figures, these characters are also symbolic: The old woman, with closed eyes, stands for the past and memory; the young boy, with a penetrating stare, represents the hope and future of a nation. Notice how master designer Mucha draws your attention to these two figures through the use of colors—the dark blue on the outside gradually turns into green, then yellow, and finally the gold of the woman and the crimson of the boy in the center. In Mucha's color language, blue stands for the past, gold for the mythic, and red for the future. Besides all the meaning, Mucha's art is simply a joy to behold. (And on the bottom, the tasteful little ad for *Banka Slavie*, which paid for the work, is hardly noticeable.)

Habsburg Emperor's Tomb: Continue circulating around the church. A slight incline near the middle takes you into the older, 14th-century section (you will need to show your ticket here). The big royal tomb (within the black iron fence) is that of Ferdinand I, the first Habsburg emperor. It dates from 1590, when Prague was a major Habsburg city.

Relief of Prague: As you walk around the high altar (Neo-Gothic, circa 1900), study the fascinating carved-wood relief of Prague. It depicts the action after the Battle of White Mountain, while the Protestant King Frederic escapes over the Charles Bridge (before it had any statues). Carved in 1630, 10 years after the famous event occurred, the relief also gives you a peek at Prague in 1620, stretching from the Týn Church to the cathedral (half-built at that time, up to where you are now). Notice that back then, the Týn Church was Hussite, so the centerpiece of its facade is not the Virgin Mary, but a chalice, a symbol of Jan Hus' ideals. The old city walls—now replaced by the main streets of the city—stand strong. The Jewish Quarter (the slummy, muddy zone along the riverside below the bridge on the left) fills land no one else wanted.

Apse: Circling around the high altar, you pass graves of bishops, including the tomb of St. Vitus (with a rooster at his feet). The stone sarcophagi contain kings from the Přemysl dynasty (12th-14th centuries). Locals claim the gigantic, shiny tomb of St. John of Nepomuk has more than a ton of silver (for more on St. John of Nepomuk, see page 234). About three yards after the tomb (above on the right) is a finely carved wood relief, circa 1630. It gives a

Counter-Reformation spin on the Wars of Religion, showing the "barbaric" Protestant nobles destroying the Catholic icons in the cathedral after their short-lived victory.

Ahead on the left, look up at the royal oratory, a box supported by busy late-Gothic vine-like ribs. This is where the king would go to attend Mass in his jammies (an elevated corridor connected his private apartment with his own altar-side box pew).

• *From here, walk 25 paces and look left through the crowds and door to see the richly decorated chapel containing the tomb of St. Wenceslas. The best views are around the corner, ahead and to the left.*

Wenceslas Chapel: A fancy roped-off chapel (right transept) houses the tomb of St. Wenceslas, surrounded by walls encrusted with precious and semi-precious stones. (Lead us not into temptation.) The scene evokes heavenly Jerusalem to anyone entering with a 14th-century mindset. Above are circa-1590 frescoes showing scenes of the saint's life and a locked door leading to the crown jewels. Get as close as you can. Notice the Tupperware-toned stained-glass windows from the 1950s. The Czech kings used to be crowned right here in front of the coffin, draped in red. You can view the chapel from either door (if the door facing the nave is crowded, duck around to the left to find a door that is most likely open).

Back Outside the Cathedral: Leaving the cathedral, turn left (past the clean and free public WC). The **obelisk** was erected in 1928—a single piece of granite celebrating the 10th anniversary of the establishment of Czechoslovakia and commemorating the soldiers who fought for its independence. It was originally much taller, but broke in transit—an inauspicious start for a nation destined to last only 70 years. Up in the fat, green tower of the cathedral is the Czech Republic's biggest bell, nicknamed "Zikmund." In June 2002, it cracked, and two months later, the worst flood in recorded history hit the city—the locals saw this as a sign. As a nation sandwiched between great powers, Czechs are deeply superstitious when it comes to the tides of history. Often feeling unable to influence the course of their own destiny, they helplessly look at events as we might look at the weather and other natural phenomena—trying to figure out what fate has in store for them next.

Find the 14th-century **mosaic** of the Last Judgment outside on the right transept (above the church's "golden gate"). It was commissioned in the Italian style by King Charles IV, who, in 1370 was modern, cosmopolitan, and ahead of his time. Jesus oversees the action, as some go to heaven and some go to hell. The Czech king and queen kneel directly beneath Jesus and the six patron saints. On coronation day, they would walk under this arch, which would remind them (and their subjects) that even those holding great power are not above God's judgment. The royal crown and national jewels are kept in a chamber (see the grilled windows) above this entryway, which was the cathedral's main entry for centuries while the church remained uncompleted.

• *Across the square and 20 yards to the right, a door leads into the Old Royal Palace (in the lobby, there's a WC with a window shared by the men's and women's sections—meet your partner to enjoy the view).*

Old Royal Palace (Starý Královský Palác)—Starting in the 12th century, this was the seat of the Bohemian princes. While extensively rebuilt, the **large hall** is late Gothic, designed as a multipurpose hall for the old nobility. It was big enough for jousts—even the staircase (which you'll use as you exit) was designed to let a mounted soldier gallop in. It was filled with market stalls, giving nobles a chance to shop without actually going into town. In the 1400s, the nobility met here to elect their king. The tradition survived until modern times, as the parliament crowded into this room until the late 1990s to elect the president of Czechoslovakia, and later, the Czech Republic (though the last three elections happened in another, far more lavish hall in the castle). Look up at the flower-shaped, vaulted ceiling.

On your immediate right, enter the two small Renaissance rooms known as the **"Czech Office."** From these rooms (empty today except for their 17th-century porcelain heaters), two governors used to oversee the Czech lands for the Habsburgs in Vienna. In 1618, angry Czech Protestant nobles poured into these rooms and threw the two Catholic governors out of the window. An old law actually permits this act—called defenestration—which usually targets bad politicians. Old prints on the wall show the second of Prague's many defenestrations. The two governors landed—fittingly—in a pile of horse manure. Even though they suffered only broken arms and bruised egos, this event kicked off the huge and lengthy Thirty Years' War.

Look down on the chapel from the end, and go out on the balcony for a sweeping view of Prague. Is that Paris' Eiffel Tower in the distance? No, it's Petřín Tower (described earlier), a fine place for a relaxing day at the park, offering sweeping views over Prague.

As you reenter the main hall, find the display case (just to the left of the exit gate) with replicas of the Czech crown jewels. The originals are locked up inside the cathedral.

As you leave through the side door, pause at the door to consider the subtle yet racy little Renaissance knocker. Go ahead—play with it for a little sex in the palace (be gentle).

• *Across from the palace exit is the...*

Basilica and Convent of St. George (Bazilika Sv. Jiří)—Step into the beautiful-in-its-simplicity Basilica of St. George to see

Prague's best-preserved Romanesque church and the burial place of Czech royalty. Notice the characteristic double windows on the gallery, as well as the walls made of limestone (the bedrock underlying Prague). In those early years, the building techniques were not yet advanced, and the ceiling is made of wood, rather than arched with stone. St. Wenceslas' grandmother, St. Ludmila, who established this first Bohemian convent, was reburied here in 973. Her stone tomb is in the space just to the right of the altar. Look for the restored Gothic fresco (from the 12th century) depicting this cultured woman (under the arch, to the right of the altar space). The St. John of Nepomuk chapel (through which you exit the church) comes with scary-looking bones under the altar. (These are replicas—neither St. John's nor real.)

• *Continue walking downhill through the castle grounds. You'll pass* **Rosenberg Palace,** *now open to visitors and included in the basic castle ticket while the Golden Lane is closed. Gutted in communist times, the palace is barely worth wandering through, featuring a string of rooms that shows the life of an 18th-century noblewoman. The next street on the left leads to the curiously popular* **Golden Lane,** *which is closed for several years for a thorough renovation.*

At the bottom of the castle complex is...

▲▲Lobkowicz Palace (Lobkowiczký Palác)

This palace displays the private collection of a prominent Czech noble family, including paintings, ceramics, and musical scores. The Lobkowiczes' property was confiscated twice in the 20th century: first by the Nazis at the beginning of World War II, and then by the communists in 1948. In 1990, William Lobkowicz, then a Boston investment banker, returned to Czechoslovakia to fight a legal battle to reclaim his family's property and, eventually, to restore the castles and palaces to their former state.

A conscientious host, William himself narrates the delightful, included audioguide. As you pass by the portraits of his ancestors, listen to their stories, including that of Polyxena, whose determination saved the two Catholic governors defenestrated next door (according to family legend, she hid the bruised officials under the folds of her skirt). The museum's highlights are Peter Brueghel the Elder's magnificently preserved *Haymaking,* from 1565, one of the earliest entirely secular landscape paintings in Europe (showing an idyllic and almost heroic connection between peasants and nature), along with the manuscript of Beethoven's *Heroica* (dedicated to his sponsor, Prince Lobkowicz), displayed near Mozart's reorchestration of Handel's *Messiah.* While the National Gallery may seem a more logical choice for the art enthusiast, the obvious care that went into creating this museum, the collection's variety, and the personal insight that it opens into the past and present of Czech nobility make the Lobkowicz worth an hour of your time.

Cost and Hours: 275 Kč, includes audioguide, not included in any castle tickets, daily 10:00-18:00, last entry one hour before closing, tel. 233-312-925, www.lobkowiczevents.cz.

Eating: The Panoramic Café by the exit has a creative cosmopolitan menu and stunning views of the city (daily 10:00-18:00). If a charming young man is selling ice cream out front, it may be William's son, Will.

Toy and Barbie Museum (Muzeum Hraček)

Across the street from Lobkowicz Palace, a courtyard and a long wooden staircase lead to two entertaining floors of old toys and dolls, thoughtfully described in English. You'll see a century of teddy bears, some 19th-century model train sets, old Christmas decor, and an incredible Barbie collection (the entire top floor). Find the buxom 1959 first edition, and you'll understand why these capitalistic sirens of material discontent weren't allowed here until 1989 (70 Kč, 120 Kč family ticket, not included in any castle tickets, daily 9:30-17:30, WC next to entrance).

Leaving the Castle Quarter

Tourists squirt slowly through a fortified door at the bottom end of the castle. From there, you can head to the nearest Metro station or walk to the Little Quarter.

To Malostranská Metro: You can follow the steep lane directly back to the riverbank...or turn right about halfway down the steps to visit the Fürstenberg Gardens, with 3,500 flowering plants and 2,200 rose bushes (80 Kč, April-Oct daily from 10:00 until one hour before sunset). For a gentler descent, start heading down the steep lane. About 40 yards below the castle exit, a gate on the left leads you through a scenic vineyard and past the Villa Richter restaurants (described under "Eating in Prague," later) to the station.

To the Little Quarter: You have several options. As you leave the castle gate, take a hard right and stroll through the long, delightful park. Along the way, notice the Modernist layout of the Na Valech Gardens, designed by the 1920s court architect, Jože Plečnik of Slovenia. Halfway through the long park is a viewpoint overlooking the terraced Pálffy Gardens (80 Kč, April-Oct daily 10:00-18:00, closed Nov-March). You can zigzag down through these gardens into the Little Quarter. Or, if you want to go to Castle Square, continue uphill along the castle wall and through the garden. From the square, you can get to Little Quarter either by taking the staircase, or the cobbled street leading to historic Nerudova street (see page 255).

Congratulations. You've conquered the castle.

Entertainment in Prague

Prague booms with live and inexpensive theater, classical music, jazz, and pop entertainment. Everything is listed in several monthly cultural events programs (free at TIs) and in the *Prague Post* newspaper (60 Kč at newsstands).

You'll be tempted to gather fliers as you wander through the town. Don't bother. To really understand all your options (the street Mozarts are pushing only their concerts), drop by a **Via Musica** box office. There are two: One is next to Týn Church on the Old Town Square (daily 10:30-19:30, tel. 224-826-969), and the other is in the Little Quarter across from the Church of St. Nicholas (daily 10:30-18:00, tel. 257-535-568). The event schedule posted on the wall clearly shows everything that's playing today and tomorrow, including tourist concerts, Black Light Theater, and marionette shows, with photos of each venue and a map locating everything (www.viamusica.cz).

Ticketpro sells tickets for the serious concert venues and most music clubs (daily 8:00-12:00 & 12:30-16:30, Rytířská 31, between Havelská Market and Estates Theater; also has a booth in Tourist Center at Rytířská 12, daily 9:00-20:00; English-language reservations tel. 296-329-999, www.ticketpro.cz). As with most ticket box offices, you'll pay about 30 Kč extra per ticket.

Locals dress up for the more "serious" concerts, opera, and ballet, but many tourists wear casual clothes—as long as you don't show up in shorts, sneakers, or flip-flops, you'll be fine.

Black Light Theater

A kind of mime/modern dance variety show, Black Light Theater has no language barrier and is, for many, more entertaining than a classical concert. Unique to Prague, Black Light Theater originated in the 1960s as a playful and mystifying theater of the absurd. These days, aficionados and critical visitors lament that it's becoming a cheesy variety show, while others are uncomfortable with the sexual flavor of some acts. Still, it's an unusual theater experience that most enjoy. Shows last about an hour and a half. Avoid the first four rows, which get you so close that it ruins the illusion. Each theater has its own spin on what Black Light is supposed to be:

Ta Fantastika is traditional and poetic, with puppets and a little artistic nudity (*Aspects of Alice* nightly at 21:30, 650 Kč, reserved seating, near east end of Charles Bridge at Karlova 8, tel. 222-221-366, www.tafantastika.cz).

Image Theater has more mime and elements of the absurd, with shows including *Black Box, Cabinet,* and *The Best of Image:*

"It's precisely the fact that we are all so different that unites us" (shows nightly at 18:00 and 20:00, 480 Kč, open seating—arrive early to grab a good spot, just off Old Town Square at Pařížská 4, tel. 222-314-448, www.imagetheatre.cz).

Laterna Magica, in the big, glassy building next to the National Theater, mixes Black Light techniques with film projection into a multimedia performance that draws Czech audiences (*Wonderful Circus, Rendezvous, Graffiti,* shows Mon-Sat at 20:00, no shows on Sun, 680 Kč, tel. 224-931-482, www.laterna.cz).

The other Black Light theaters advertised around town aren't as good.

Classical Concerts

Touristy Concerts: Each day, six to eight classical concerts designed for tourists fill delightful Old World halls and churches with music of the crowd-pleasing sort: Vivaldi, Best of Mozart, Most Famous Arias, and works by the famous Czech composer Antonín Dvořák. Concerts typically cost 400-1,000 Kč, start anywhere from 13:00 to 21:00, and last about an hour. Typical venues include two buildings on the Little Quarter Square (the Church of St. Nicholas and the Prague Academy of Music in Liechtenstein Palace), the Klementinum's Chapel of Mirrors, the Old Town Square (in a different Church of St. Nicholas), and the stunning Smetana Hall in the Municipal House (see page 248). Musicians vary from excellent to amateurish.

Serious Concerts: To ensure a memorable venue and top-notch musicians, choose a concert in one of three places (Municipal House's Smetana Hall, Rudolfinum, or National Theater) featuring Prague's finest ensembles (such as the Prague Symphony Orchestra or Czech Philharmonic). The **Prague Symphony Orchestra** plays in the gorgeous Art Nouveau Municipal House. Their ticket office is on the right side of the building, on U Obecního Domu street opposite Hotel Paris (Mon-Fri 10:00-18:00, tel. 222-002-336, www.fok.cz, pokladna@fok.cz). A smaller selection of tickets is sold in the information office inside the Municipal House. The **Czech Philharmonic** performs in the classical Neo-Renaissance Rudolfinum in the Jewish Quarter. Their ticket office is on the right side of the Rudolfinum, under the stairs (250-1,000 Kč, open Mon-Fri 10:00-18:00, and until just before the show starts on concert days, on Palachovo Náměstí on the Old Town side of Mánes Bridge, tel. 227-059-352, www.ceskafilharmonie.cz, info @cfmail.cz). Both orchestras perform in their home venues about five nights a month from September through June. Most other nights these spaces are rented to agencies that organize tourist concerts of varying quality for double the price (as described

PRAGUE

earlier). Check first whether your visit coincides with either ensemble's performance.

Mozart's Villa: During his frequent visits to Prague, Austrian Wolfgang Amadeus Mozart (1756-1791) stayed with his friends in the beautiful, small, Neoclassical **Villa Bertramka,** now the Mozart Museum. Surrounded by a peaceful garden, the villa preserves the time when the Salzburg prodigy felt more appreciated in Prague than in Austria. Intimate concerts are held some afternoons and evenings, either in the garden or in the small concert hall (110 Kč, daily April-Oct 9:30-18:00, Nov-March 9:30-17:00, Mozartova 169, Praha 5; from Metro: Anděl, it's a 10-minute walk—head to Hotel Mövenpick and then go up alley behind hotel; tel. 257-317-465, www.bertramka.cz).

Jam Session: A good bet is the jam session held every Monday at 17:00 at **St. Martin in the Wall,** where some of Prague's best musicians gather to tune in and chat with one another (400 Kč, Martinská street, just north of the Tesco department store in the Old Town).

Buskers: The **Prague Castle Orchestra,** one of Prague's most entertaining acts, performs regularly on Castle Square. This trio—Josef on flute, Radek on accordion, and Zdeněk on bass—plays a lively Czech mélange of Smetana, swing, old folk tunes, and 1920s cabaret songs. Look for them if you're visiting the castle, and consider picking up their fun CD. They're also available for private functions (mobile 603-552-448, josekocurek@volny.cz).

Opera and Ballet

The **National Theater** (Národní Divadlo, on the New Town side of Legií Bridge)—with a must-see Neo-Renaissance interior (see page 250)—is best for opera and ballet (shows from 19:00, 300-1,000 Kč, tel. 224-912-673, www.nationaltheatre.cz). The **Estates Theater** (Stavovské Divadlo) is where Mozart premiered and personally directed many of his most beloved works (see page 231). *Don Giovanni, The Marriage of Figaro,* and *The Magic Flute* are on the program a couple of times each month (shows from 20:00, 800-1,400 Kč, between the Old Town Square and the New Town on a square called Ovocný Trh, tel. 224-214-339, www.estates theatre.cz). A handy ticket office for both of these theaters is in the little square (Ovocný Trh) behind the Estates Theater, next to a pizzeria.

The **State Opera** (Státní Opera) operates on a smaller budget and is also not as architecturally rewarding as the National Theater (shows at 19:00 or 20:00, 400-1,200 Kč, buy tickets at the theater, 101 Wilsonova, on the busy street between the main train station and Wenceslas Square—see map on page 240, tel. 224-227-693, www.opera.cz).

Festivals

World-class musicians are in town during these musical festivals: **Prague Spring** (mid-May-early June, www.festival.cz), **Prague Proms** (late June-late July, www.pragueproms.cz), and the newer **Dvořák's Prague** (Aug-Sept, www.dvorakovapraha.cz).

Shopping in Prague

Prague's entire Old Town seems designed to bring out the shopper in visitors. Puppets, glass, and ceramics are traditional. Shop your way from the Old Town Square up Celetná street to the Powder Tower, then along Na Příkopě to the bottom of Wenceslas Square. The city center is tourist-oriented—most locals do their serious shopping in the suburbs.

Celetná is lined with big stores selling all the traditional Czech goodies. Tourists wander endlessly here, mesmerized by the window displays. Celetná Crystal, about midway down the street, offers the largest selection of affordable crystal. You can have the glass safely shipped home directly from the shop.

Náměstí Republiky (Republic Square) boasts Prague's newest and biggest mall, Palladium (Sun-Wed 9:00-21:00, Thu-Sat 9:00-22:00). It's hidden behind a pink Neo-Romanesque facade and the brown steel-and-glass 1980s department store Kotva (Anchor), an obsolete beast on the verge of extinction (Mon-Fri 9:00-20:00, Sat-Sun 10:00-18:00).

Na Příkopě has a couple of good modern malls. The best is Slovanský Dům (daily 10:00-20:00, Na Příkopě 22), where you'll wander deep past a 10-screen multiplex into a world of classy restaurants and designer shops surrounding a peaceful, park-like inner courtyard. Another modern mall is Černá Růže (daily 10:00-20:00, Na Příkopě 12), with a great Japanese restaurant around a small garden. Next door is Moser, which has a museum-like crystal showroom upstairs. The Galerie Myslbek, directly across the street, has fancy stores in a space built to Prague's scale.

Národní Třída (National Street) is less touristy and lined with some inviting stores. The big Tesco department store in the middle sells anything you might need, from a pin for a broken watchband to a swimsuit (generally daily 9:00-21:00, Národní Třída 26).

Crystal: Along with shops on Celetná and Na Příkopě, a small square just off the Old Town Square, Malé Náměstí, is ringed by three major crystal retailers (generally open daily 10:00-20:00): Moser, Rott Crystal, and Crystalex (which claims to have "factory-direct" prices, at #6 on the square).

"Bohemian Garnets": These fiery red gemstone-quality garnets, with unique refractive—some claim even curative—properties, were mined from a mountainous area of Bohemia. This region was the major source of garnet gems from the Renaissance through the Victorian Age, and is now largely mined-out. The traditional hand-crafted designs pack many small garnets together, and much of the authentic jewelry you'll see today is Victorian-era. Of the many garnet shops in Prague's shopping districts, Turnov Granát Co-op has the largest selection (with shops at Dlouhá 28 and Panská 1, www.granat.eu). If you buy garnet jewelry, shop around, use a reputable dealer, and ask for a certificate of authenticity to avoid buying a glass imitation.

Sleeping in Prague

Peak months for hotels in Prague are May, June, and September. Easter and New Year's are the most crowded times, when prices are jacked up a bit. I've listed peak-time prices—if you're traveling in July or August, you'll find rates generally 15 percent lower, and from November through March, about 30 percent lower. It's often possible to negotiate a discount off the published rack rate.

Room-Booking Services

Prague is awash with fancy rooms on the push list; private, small-time operators with rooms to rent in their apartments; and roving agents eager to book you a bed and earn a commission. You can save about 30 percent by showing up without a reservation and finding accommodations upon arrival. However, it can be a hassle, and you won't necessarily get your ideal choice. If you're coming in by train or car, you'll encounter booking agencies. They can almost always find you a reasonable room, and, if it's in a private guest house, your host can even come and lead you to the place.

Athos Travel has a line on 200 properties (ranging from hostels to five-star hotels), 90 percent of which are in the Old Town. To book a room, call them or use their handy website, which allows you to search for a room, based on various criteria (best to arrange in advance during peak season, can also help with last-minute booking off-season, tel. 241-440-571, fax 241-441-697, www.a -prague.com, info@a-prague.com). Readers report that Athos is aggressive with its business policies—although there's no fee to cancel well in advance, they strictly enforce penalties on cancellations within 48 hours.

Touristpoint, at the main train station (Hlavní Nádraží), is another booking service (daily 8:00-22:00). They have a slew of hotels and small pensions available (2,000-Kč pension doubles in the Old Town, 1,500-Kč doubles a Metro ride away). You can reserve by email, using your credit card as a deposit (tel. 224-946-010, www.touristpoint.cz, info@touristpoint.cz), or just show up at

Sleep Code

(20 Kč = about $1, country code: 420)
S = Single, **D** = Double/Twin, **T** = Triple, **Q** = Quad, **b** = bathroom, **s** = shower only. Unless otherwise noted, credit cards are accepted, and breakfast and tax are included. Everyone listed here speaks English.

To help you sort easily through these listings, I've divided the rooms into three categories based on the price for a standard double room with bath:

$$$ Higher Priced—Most rooms 3,500 Kč or more.
$$ Moderately Priced—Most rooms between 2,500-3,500 Kč.
$ Lower Priced—Most rooms 2,500 Kč or less.

Prices can change without notice; verify the hotel's current rates online or by email. For other updates, see www.ricksteves.com/update.

the office and request a room. Be clear on the location before you make your choice.

Lída Jánská's **Magic Praha** can help with accommodations (mobile 604-207-225, www.magicpraha.cz, magicpraha@magic praha.cz. Lída rents a well-located apartment with a river view near the Jewish Quarter.

Web-booking services, such as Priceline.com and Bidding fortravel.com, enable budget travelers to snare fancy rooms on the push list for half the rack rate. It's not unusual to find a room in a four-star hotel for 1,300 Kč—but keep in mind that many of these international business-class hotels are far from the city center.

Old Town Hotels and Pensions

You'll pay higher prices to stay in the Old Town, but for many travelers, the convenience is worth the expense. These places are all within a 10-minute walk of the Old Town Square.

$$$ Hotel Metamorphis is a splurge, with solidly renovated rooms in Prague's former caravanserai (hostel for foreign merchants). Its breakfast room is in a spacious medieval cellar with modern artwork. Some of the street-facing rooms, located above two popular bars, are noisy at night (Db-4,800 Kč, check website for discounts, Malá Štupartská 5, tel. 221-771-011, fax 221-771-099, www.metamorphis.cz, hotel@metamorphis.cz).

$$$ Hotel Maximilian is a sleek, mod, 70-room place with Art Deco black design; big, plush living rooms; and all the business services and comforts you'd expect in a four-star hotel. It faces a church on a perfect little square just a short walk from the

PRAGUE

Hotels in Prague's Old Town

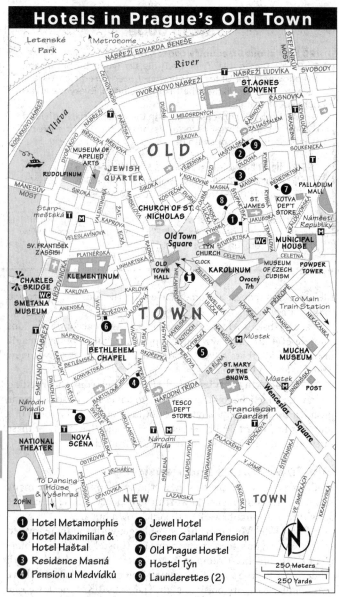

1 Hotel Metamorphis
2 Hotel Maximilian &
  Hotel Haštal
3 Residence Masná
4 Pension u Medvídků
5 Jewel Hotel
6 Green Garland Pension
7 Old Prague Hostel
8 Hostel Týn
9 Launderettes (2)

250 Meters
250 Yards

PRAGUE

action (Db-4,000 Kč, extra bed-1,500 Kč, 20 percent discount on weekends, 15 percent discount if you stay three nights or more, check website for discounts, Internet access, Haštalská 14, tel. 225-303-111, fax 225-303-110, www.maximilianhotel.com, reservation @maximilianhotel.com).

$$ Residence Masná rents 12 apartments in an elegant 1930s building with a marble staircase. Apartments vary somewhat in size, but all have hardwood floors, a kitchen, basic furniture, and a few plants (Db-3,125 Kč, extra person-125 Kč, ask about discount when you book direct and mention this book, breakfast in room or in ultramodern café next door, Masná 9, tel. 222-311-244, mobile 724-744-395, www.heartofprague.cz, info@heartofprague.cz).

$$ Pension u Medvídků has 31 comfortably renovated rooms in a big, rustic, medieval shell with dark wood furniture. Upstairs, you'll find lots of beams—or, if you're not careful, they'll find you (Sb-2,000 Kč, Db-3,000 Kč, Tb-4,000 Kč, extra bed-500 Kč, "historical" rooms-10 percent more, apartment-20 percent more, ask about discount with cash and this book if you book direct, Internet access, Na Perštýně 7, tel. 224-211-916, fax 224-220-930, www .umedvidku.cz, info@umedvidku.cz). The pension runs a popular beer-hall restaurant with live music most Fridays and Saturdays until 23:00—request an inside room for maximum peace.

$$ Jewel Hotel (U Klenotníka), with 11 modern, comfortable rooms in a plain building, is three blocks off the Old Town Square (Sb-2,000 Kč, small double-bed Db-2,750 Kč, bigger twin-bed Db-3,300 Kč, Tb-3,750 Kč, ask about discount when you book direct and mention this book, Wi-Fi, Rytířská 3, tel. 224-211-699, fax 224-221-025, www.uklenotnika.cz, info@uklenotnika.cz, Helena and Katka).

$ Green Garland Pension (U Zeleného Věnce), on a central but delightfully quiet cobbled lane, has a warm and personal feel rare for the Old Town. Located in a thick 14th-century building with open beams, it has a blond-hardwood charm decorated with a woman's touch. Its nine rooms are clean and simply furnished (big Sb-1,700 Kč, Db-2,200 Kč, bigger Db-2,500 Kč, Tb-2,800 Kč, family suite, Wi-Fi, Řetězová 10, tel. 222-220-178, fax 224-248-791, www.uzv.cz, pension@uzv.cz).

$ Hotel Haštal is next to Hotel Maximilian (listed earlier) on the same quiet, hidden square in the Old Town. A popular hotel back in the 1920s, it has been renovated to complement the neighborhood's vibrant circa-1900 architecture. Its 24 rooms are comfortable, but the walls are a bit thin (Sb-1,500 Kč, Db-2,000 Kč, extra bed-550 Kč, book via email to avoid their online booking fee, air-con, Wi-Fi, Haštalská 16, tel. 222-314-335, www.hastal.com, info@hastal.com). The hotel's small restaurant is understandably popular for its reasonably priced lunch specials and draft beer.

Under the Castle, in the Little Quarter

The first and third listings below are buried on quiet lanes deep in the Little Quarter, among cobbles, quaint restaurants, rummaging tourists, and embassy flags. Hotel Julián is a 10-minute walk up the river on a quiet and stately street, with none of the intense medieval cityscape of the others.

$$$ Vintage Design Hotel Sax's 22 rooms are decorated in a retro, meet-the-Jetsons fashion. With a fruity atrium and a distinctly modern, stark feel, this is a stylish, no-nonsense place (Sb-3,800-4,300 Kč, Db-3,800-4,500 Kč, Db suite-5,000 Kč, extra bed-750 Kč, ask about discount with this book, elevator, Internet access, Jánský Vršek 3, tel. 257-531-268, fax 257-534-101, www.sax.cz, hotel@sax.cz).

$$$ Hotel Julián is an oasis of professional, predictable decency in an untouristy neighborhood. Its 32 spacious, fresh, well-furnished rooms and big, homey public spaces hide behind a noble Neoclassical facade. The staff is friendly and helpful. Their official "rack rates" are ridiculous, but with the Rick Steves discount, you can generally get a double here for around 1,875 Kč (Sb-3,725 Kč, Db-3,975 Kč, suites and bigger rooms available, check website for discounts, ask about discount when you book direct and mention this book, air-con, Wi-Fi, elevator, plush and inviting lobby, summer roof terrace, parking lot; Metro: Anděl, then an 8-minute walk, or take tram #6, #9, #12, or #20 for two stops; Elišky Peškové 11, Praha 5, reservation tel. 257-311-150, reception tel. 257-311-145, fax 257-311-149, www.julian.cz, info@julian.cz). Free lockers and a shower are available for those needing a place to stay after checkout (for example, while waiting for an overnight train).

$$ Dům u Velké Boty ("House at the Big Boot"), on a quiet square in front of the German Embassy, is the rare quintessential family hotel in Prague: homey, comfy, and extremely friendly. Charlotta, Jan, and their two sons treat every guest as a (thirsty) friend, and the wellspring of their stories never runs dry. Each of their 12 rooms is uniquely decorated, most in a tasteful, 19th-century Biedermeier style (tiny Sb-2,100 Kč, two D rooms that share a bathroom-2,250 Kč each, Db-2,900-3,600 Kč, extra bed-725 Kč, ask about discount with advance reservation and this book, prices can be soft when slow, cash only, children up to age 10 sleep free—toys provided, free Internet access and Wi-Fi, Vlašská 30, tel. 257-532-088, www.bigboot.cz, info@bigboot.cz). There's no hotel sign on the house—look for the splendid geraniums that Jan nurtures in the windows.

Away from the Center

Moving just outside central Prague saves you money—and gets you away from the tourists and into some more workaday residential neighborhoods. The following listings are great values compared with the downtown hotels listed previously, and are all within a 5- to 15-minute tram or Metro ride from the center. For locations, see the map on the next page.

Beyond Wenceslas Square

These hotels are in urban neighborhoods on the outer fringe of the New Town, beyond Wenceslas Square. But they're still within several minutes' walk of the sightseeing zone, and are well-served by trams.

$$$ Sieber Hotel, with 20 rooms, is a quality four-star, business-class hotel in an upscale, circa-1900 residential neighborhood (Vinohrady) that has recently become popular with Prague's expat community. They do a good job of being homey and welcoming (Sb-4,480 Kč, Db-4,780 Kč, extra bed-990 Kč, fourth night free, ask about discount when you book direct and mention this book, discount for last-minute reservations, air-con, elevator, Internet access, 3-minute walk to Metro: Jiřího z Poděbrad, or tram #11, Slezská 55, Praha 3, tel. 224-250-025, fax 224-250-027, www .sieber.cz, reservations@sieber.cz).

$$ Hotel 16 is a sleek and modern business-class place with an intriguing Art Nouveau facade, polished cherry-wood elegance, high ceilings, and 14 fine rooms (Sb-2,800 Kč, Db-3,500 Kč, bigger Db-3,700 Kč, Tb-4,400 Kč, ask about discount when you book direct and mention this book, check website for last-minute discounts, triple-paned windows, back rooms facing the garden are quieter, air-con, elevator, Internet access, 10-minute walk south of Wenceslas Square, Metro: I.P. Pavlova, Kateřinská 16, Praha 2, tel. 224-920-636, fax 224-920-626, www.hotel16.cz, hotel16@hotel16.cz).

$ Hotel Anna offers 24 bright, simple, pastel rooms and basic service. It's a bit closer to the action—just 10 minutes by foot east of Wenceslas Square (Sb-1,600 Kč, Db-1,900 Kč, Tb-2,100 Kč, check website for discounts, elevator, Budečská 17, Praha 2, Metro: Náměstí Míru, tel. 222-513-111, fax 222-515-158, www.hotelanna .cz, sales@hotelanna.cz). They run a similar hotel (same standards and prices) nearby.

The Best Values, Farther from the Center

These accommodations are a 10- to 20-minute tram ride from the center, but once you make the trip, you'll see it's no problem— and you'll feel pretty smug saving $50-100 a night per double by not sleeping in the Old Town. Hotel u Šemíka and Guest House Lída are within a stone's throw of peaceful Vyšehrad Park, with a legendary castle on a cliff overlooking the Vltava River. Hotel Adalbert is on the grounds of an ancient monastery, and Pension Větrník is adjacent, with two of Prague's best-preserved natural areas (Star Park and Šárka) just a short walk away.

PRAGUE

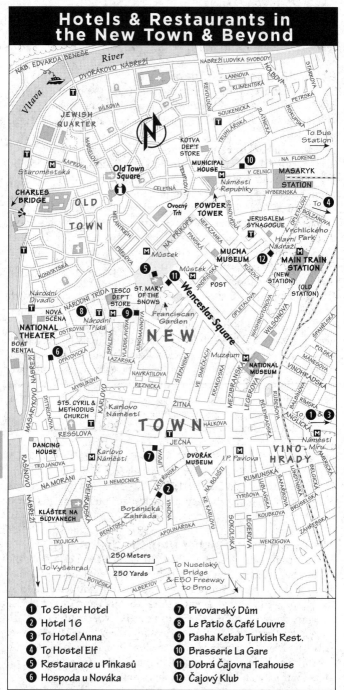

Hotels & Restaurants in the New Town & Beyond

1. To Sieber Hotel
2. Hotel 16
3. To Hotel Anna
4. To Hostel Elf
5. Restaurace u Pinkasů
6. Hospoda u Nováka
7. Pivovarský Dům
8. Le Patio & Café Louvre
9. Pasha Kebab Turkish Rest.
10. Brasserie La Gare
11. Dobrá Čajovna Teahouse
12. Čajový Klub

PRAGUE

$$ Hotel Adalbert occupies an 18th-century building in the Břevnov Monastery (one of the Czech Republic's oldest monastic institutions, founded in 993). Meticulously restored after the return of the Benedictine monks in the 1990s, the monastery complex is the ultimate retreat for those who come to Prague for soul-searching or just wanting a quiet place away from the bustle. Join the monks for morning (7:00) and evening (18:00) Mass in the St. Margaret Basilica, a large and elegant Baroque church decorated with unusual simplicity. You can help yourself in the monastery fruit orchard and eat in the atmospheric monastery pub (Klášterní Šenk). The hotel itself caters primarily to business clientele and takes ecology seriously: recycling, water conservation, and free tram tickets for guests. I prefer the first-floor rooms, as some of the attic rooms—room numbers in the 200s—feel a bit cramped (Sb-2,300 Kč, Db-3,200 Kč, extra bed-1,050 Kč, less on weekends, ask about Rick Steves discount when you reserve, Wi-Fi, free parking, halfway between city and airport at Markétská 1, Praha 6, tram #22 to Břevnovský Klášter; 5 minutes by tram beyond the castle, 20 minutes from Old and New Towns; tel. 220-406-170, fax 220-406-190, www.hoteladalbert.cz, info@hoteladalbert.cz).

$$ Hotel u Šemíka, named for a heroic mythical horse, offers 25 rooms in a quiet residential neighborhood just below Vyšehrad Castle and the Slavín cemetery where Dvořák, Mucha, and Čapek are buried. It's a 10-minute tram ride south of the Old Town (Sb-2,000 Kč, Db-2,650 Kč, apartment-3,350-3,700 Kč for 2-4 people, extra bed-600 Kč, ask about the "direct booking" Rick Steves discount when you reserve, Internet access; from the center, take tram #3, #17, or #21 to Výtoň, go under rail bridge, and walk 3 blocks uphill to Vratislavova 36; Praha 2, tel. 224-920-736, fax 224-911-602, www.usemika.cz, usemika@usemika.cz).

$ Pension Větrník fills an attractive white-and-orange former 18th-century windmill in one of Prague's most popular residential areas, right next to the Břevnov Monastery and midway between the airport and the city. The talkative owner, Miloš Opatrný, is a retired prizewinning Czech chef whose culinary work took him as far as Japan. On request, he will gladly prepare a meal you won't forget. The six rooms here are the pride of the Opatrný family, who live on the upper floors. The garden has a red-clay tennis court—rackets and balls are provided (Db-2,200 Kč, suite-3,300 Kč, extra bed-550 Kč, Internet access, U Větrníku 1, Praha 6; airport bus #179 stops near the house, tram #18 goes straight to Charles Bridge, both take 20 minutes; tel. 220-612-404, fax 220-513-390, www.vetrnik1722.cz, pension@vetrnik1722.cz).

$ Guest House Lída, with 12 homey and spacious rooms, fills a big house in a quiet residential area farther inland, a 15-minute tram ride from the center. Jan, Jitka, Jiří, and Jana Prouzas—who

PRAGUE

run the place—are a wealth of information and know how to make people feel at home (Sb-1,380 Kč, small Db-1,440 Kč, Db-1,760 Kč, Tb-2,110 Kč, Qb-2,530 Kč, cash only, family rooms, top-floor family suite with kitchenette, Internet access, parking garage-200 Kč/day, Metro: Pražského Povstání; exit Metro and turn left on Lomnického between the Metro station and big blue-glass ČSOB building, follow Lomnického for 500 yards, then turn left on Lopatecká, go uphill and ring bell at Lopatecká #26; Praha 4, tel. & fax 261-214-766, www.lidabb.eu, lidabb@seznam.cz). The Prouzas brothers also rent two **apartments** across the river, an equal distance from the center (Db-1,400 Kč, Tb-1,700 Kč, Qb-2,000 Kč).

Hostels in the Center

It's tough to find a double for less than 2,500 Kč in the old center. But Prague has an abundance of fine hostels—each with a distinct personality, and each excellent in its own way for anyone wanting a 300-500-Kč dorm bed or an extremely simple twin-bedded room for about 1,300 Kč. With travelers seeking cheaper options these days, it's good to keep in mind that hostels are no longer the exclusive domain of backpackers. The first two hostels are centrally located, but lack in care and character; the last two are found in workaday neighborhoods and have atmospheric interiors.

$ **Old Prague Hostel** is a small place with 70 beds on the second and third floors of an apartment building on a back alley near the Powder Tower. The spacious rooms were once apartment bedrooms, so it feels less institutional than most hostels. You can hang out in the comfy TV lounge/breakfast room (D-1,400 Kč, bunk in 4- to 8-person room-400-500 Kč; includes breakfast, sheets, towels, lockers, and free Internet access; in summer reserve 2 weeks ahead for doubles, a few days ahead for bunks; Benediktská 2, see map on page 278 for location, tel. 224-829-058, fax 224-829-060, www.oldpraguehostel.com, oldpraguehostel@seznam.cz).

$ **Hostel Týn** is a quiet, mature, and sterile place hidden in a silent courtyard two blocks from the Old Town Square. The management is very aware of its valuable location, so they don't have to bother being friendly (D-1,240 Kč, T-1,410 Kč, bunk in 4- to 5-bed co-ed room-420 Kč, lockers, Internet access, kitchen, no breakfast, reserve one week ahead, Týnská 19, see map on page 278 for location, tel. 224-828-519, mobile 776-122-057, www.hosteltyn.com, roomservice@seznam.cz).

$ **Sir Toby's** is in a 1930s working-class neighborhood—a newly popular residential and dining-out area that's a 12-minute tram ride from the center. The owners have taken great pains to stamp the place with character: restored hardwood floors, a back garden with tables made out of sewing machines, and rooms filled with vintage 1930s furniture and photographs. Amenities include self- and full-service laundry, an on-site pub, and a friendly staff (120 beds, S-1,200 Kč, Db-1,640 Kč, Tb-1,840 Kč, bunk in 4- to 6-bed co-ed room-480 Kč, bunk in 8- to 10-bed co-ed room-340 Kč, take tram #5 from the main train station or tram #3 from the middle of Wenceslas Square to Dělnická, at Dělnická 24, Praha 7, tel. 246-032-610, www.sirtobys.com). They also run two contemporary-design hostels in Vinohrady.

$ Hostel Elf, a 10-minute walk from the main train station or one bus stop from the Florenc Metro station, is fun-loving; ramshackle; covered with noisy, self-inflicted graffiti; and the wildest of these hostels. They offer cheap, basic beds, a helpful staff, and lots of creative services—kitchen, free luggage room, free Internet access, laundry, no lockout, free tea, cheap beer, a terrace, and lockers (120 beds, D-1,100 Kč, bunk in 6- to 11-person room-320 Kč, includes sheets and breakfast, cash only, reserve four days ahead, Husitská 11, Praha 3, take bus #133 or #207 from Florenc Metro station for one stop to U Památníku, tel. 222-540-963, www.hostel elf.com, info@hostelelf.com).

Eating in Prague

A big part of Prague's charm is found in wandering aimlessly through the city's winding old quarters, marveling at the architecture, watching the people, and sniffing out fun restaurants. You can eat well here for very little money. What you'd pay for a basic meal in Vienna or Munich will get you a feast in Prague. In addition to meat-and-potatoes Czech cuisine , you'll find trendy, student-oriented bars and lots of fine ethnic eateries. For ambience, the options include traditional, dark Czech beer halls; elegant Art Nouveau dining rooms; and hip, modern cafés.

Watch out for scams. Many restaurants put more care into ripping off green tourists (and even locals) than into their cooking. Tourists are routinely served cheaper meals than what they ordered, given a menu with a "personalized" price list, charged extra for things they didn't get, or shortchanged. Speak Czech. Even saying "Hello" in Czech (*dobrý den,* DOH-bree dehn) will get you better service. Avoid any menu without clear and explicit prices. Be careful of waiters padding the tab. Closely examine your itemized bill and understand each line (a 10 percent service charge is sometimes added—in that case, there's no need to tip extra). Tax is always included in the price, so it shouldn't be tacked on later.

Make it a habit to pay for your meals with cash that you've withdrawn from an ATM. Part with very large bills only if necessary, and deliberately count your change. If you pay with a credit card, never let it out of your sight.

Remember, there are two parallel worlds in Prague: the tourist town and the real city. Generally, if you walk two minutes away from the tourist flow, you'll find better value, atmosphere, and service. (For more on scams, see "Rip-Offs in Prague" on page 216.)

I've listed these eating and drinking establishments by neighborhood. The most options—and highest prices—are in the Old Town. For a light meal, consider one of Prague's many cafés (see "Cafés in the Old and New Towns" section). Many of the places listed here are handy for an efficient lunch, but may not offer fine evening dining. Others make less sense for lunch, but are great for a slow, drawn-out dinner. Read the descriptions to judge which is which.

Fun, Touristy Neighborhoods: Several areas are pretty and well-situated for sightseeing, but lined only with touristy restaurants. While these places are not necessarily bad values, I've listed only a few of your many options—just survey the scene in these spots and choose whatever looks best. Kampa Square, just off the Charles Bridge, feels like a small-town square. Havelská Market is surrounded by colorful little eateries, any of which offer a nice perch for viewing the market scene while you munch. The massive Old Town Square is the place to nurse a drink or enjoy a meal while watching the tide of people, both tourists and locals, sweep back and forth. There's often some event on this main square, and its many restaurants provide tasty and relaxing vantage points.

Dining with a View: For great views, consider these options: **Restaurant u Prince Terrace** (rooftop dining above a fancy hotel, completely touristy but with awesome views, described on page 292); **Villa Richter** (next to Prague Castle, above Malostranská Metro stop, described on page 298); the **Bellavista Restaurant** at Strahov Monastery; **Petřínské Terasy** and **Nebozízek** next to the funicular stop halfway up Petřín Hill; and the many overpriced but elegant places serving scenic meals along the riverbanks. For the best cheap riverside dinner, have a picnic on a paddleboat (see page 224). There's nothing like drifting down the middle of the Vltava River as the sun sets, while munching on a picnic meal and sipping a beer with your favorite travel partner.

Cheap-and-Cheery Sandwich Shops: All around town you'll find modern little sandwich shops (like the Panería chain) offering inexpensive fresh-made sandwiches (grilled if you like), pastries, salads, and drinks. You can get the food to go, or eat inside at simple tables.

In the Old and New Towns
Characteristically Czech Places

With the inevitable closing of cheap student pubs (replaced by shops and hotels that make more money), it's getting difficult to

Restaurants in the Old Town

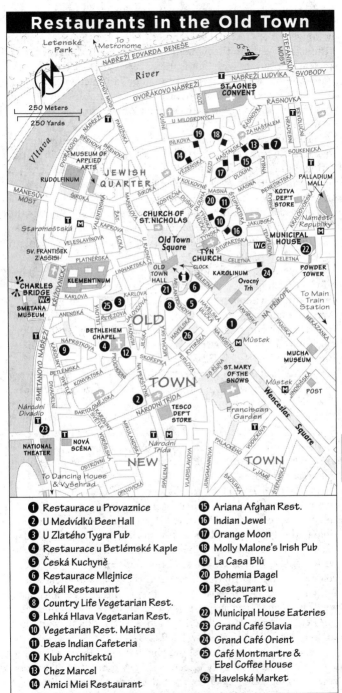

1. Restaurace u Provaznice
2. U Medvídků Beer Hall
3. U Zlatého Tygra Pub
4. Restaurace u Betlémské Kaple
5. Česká Kuchyně
6. Restaurace Mlejnice
7. Lokál Restaurant
8. Country Life Vegetarian Rest.
9. Lehká Hlava Vegetarian Rest.
10. Vegetarian Rest. Maitrea
11. Beas Indian Cafeteria
12. Klub Architektů
13. Chez Marcel
14. Amici Miei Restaurant
15. Ariana Afghan Rest.
16. Indian Jewel
17. Orange Moon
18. Molly Malone's Irish Pub
19. La Casa Blů
20. Bohemia Bagel
21. Restaurant u Prince Terrace
22. Municipal House Eateries
23. Grand Café Slavia
24. Grand Café Orient
25. Café Montmartre & Ebel Coffee House
26. Havelská Market

find a truly Czech pub in the historic city center. Most Czechs no longer go to "traditional" eateries, preferring the cosmopolitan taste of the world to the mundane taste of sauerkraut. As a result, ancient institutions with "authentic" Czech ambience have become touristy—but they're still great fun, a good value, and respected by locals. Expect wonderfully rustic spaces, smoke, surly service, and reasonably good, inexpensive food. Understand every line on your bill.

Restaurace u Pinkasů, founded in 1843, is known among locals as the first place to serve Pilsner beer. You can sit in its traditional interior, in front to watch the street action, or out back in a garden shaded by the Gothic buttresses of the St. Mary of the Snows Church. While the prices are straightforward, some of the waiters could win the rudest-service award (daily 9:00-24:00, 90-Kč lunch menu, near the bottom of Wenceslas Square, between Old and New towns—see map on page 282, Jungmannovo Náměstí 16, tel. 221-111-150).

Restaurace u Provaznice ("By the Ropemaker's Wife") has all the Czech classics, peppered with the story of a once-upon-a-time-faithful wife. (Check the menu for details of the gory story.) Natives congregate under bawdy frescoes for the famously good "pig leg" with horseradish and Czech mustard (daily 11:00-24:00, a block into the Old Town from the bottom of Wenceslas Square at Provaznická 3, tel. 224-232-528).

U Medvídků ("By the Bear Cubs") started out as a brewery in 1466 and is now a flagship beer hall of the Czech Budweiser. The one large room is bright, noisy, touristy, and a bit smoky (daily 11:30-23:00, a block toward Wenceslas Square from Bethlehem Square at Na Perštýnì 7, tel. 224-211-916). The small beer bar next to the restaurant (daily 16:00-3:00 in the morning) is used by university students during emergencies—such as after most other pubs have closed.

U Zlatého Tygra ("By the Golden Tiger") has long embodied the proverbial Czech pub, where beer turns strangers into kindred spirits, who cross the fuzzy line between memory and imagination as they tell their hilarious life stories to each other. Today, "The Tiger" is a buzzing shrine to one of its longtime regulars, the writer Bohumil Hrabal, whose fictions immortalize many of the colorful characters that once warmed the wooden benches here. Only regulars have reserved tables. If you find a rare empty spot, you'll be treated as a surprise guest rather than a customer. Feel privileged if you actually do land a beer (daily 15:00-23:00, just south of Karlova at Husova 17, tel. 222-221-111).

Hospoda u Nováka, behind the National Theater (i.e., not so central), is emphatically Czech, with few tourists. It takes good care of its regulars (you'll see the old monthly beer tabs in a rack just inside the door). Nostalgic communist-era signs are everywhere. During that time, pubs like this were close-knit communities where regulars escaped from the depression of daily life. Today, the U Nováka is a bright and smoky hangout where you can still happily curse whatever regime you happen to live under. While the English menu lists the well-executed Czech classics, it doesn't list the cheap daily specials (daily 10:00-23:00, V Jirchářích 2—see map on page 282, tel. 224-930-639).

Pivovarský Dům ("The Brewhouse"), on the corner of Ječná and Lípová in the New Town, is popular with locals for its rare variety of fresh beers (yeast, wheat, and fruit-flavored), fine classic Czech dishes, and an inviting interior that mixes traditional and modern (daily 11:00-23:00, reservations recommended in the evenings; walk up Štěpánská street from Wenceslas Square for 10 minutes, or take tram #22 for two stops from Národní to Štěpánská; Lípová 15—see map on page 282, tel. 296-216-666, variety of beer mugs sold).

Restaurace u Betlémské Kaple, behind Bethlehem Chapel, is not "ye olde" Czech. It has light wooden decor, cheap lunch deals, and fish specialties that attract natives and visitors in search of a good Czech bite for good Czech prices (daily 11:00-23:00, Betlémské Náměstí 2, tel. 222-221-639).

Česká Kuchyně ("Czech Kitchen") is a blue-collar cafeteria serving steamy old Czech cuisine. It's fast, practical, cheap, and traditional as can be. There's no English inside, so if you want apple charlotte, but not tripe soup, be sure to review the small English menu in the window outside before entering. Note the numbers of your preferred dishes (they correspond to the Czech menu inside), pick up your tally sheet as you enter, grab a tray, point to whatever you'd like, and keep the paper to pay as you exit. It's extremely cheap...unless you lose your paper. As you enter, you'll come across serving stations in this order: salads, fruit dumplings and sweets, soups, main dishes, and finally, drinks (daily 9:00-20:00, very central, across from Havelská Market at Havelská 23, tel. 224-235-574).

Restaurace Mlejnice ("The Mill") is a fun little pub strewn with farm implements and happy eaters, located just out of the tourist crush two blocks from the Old Town Square. They serve hardy traditional and modern Czech plates for 150-180 Kč. Reservations are smart in the evening (daily 11:00-24:00, between Melantrichova and Železná at Kožná 14, tel. 224-228-635).

Lokál ("The Dump") is a new hit with residents for its good-quality Czech classics at low prices. Filling a long, gray, tube-like space, the restaurant plays on customers' nostalgia: the uninviting interior is a deliberate 1980's retro design, and the waiters have been instructed to be curt (but not impolite)—just as if they were serving in one of Prague's notorious train station "dumps" (daily 11:00-1:00 in morning, ask for English menu at the front by the tap, Dlouhá 33, tel. 222-316-265).

Hip Restaurants

Country Life Vegetarian Restaurant is a bright, easy, non-smoking cafeteria with a well-displayed buffet of salads and hot veggie dishes. It's midway between the Old Town Square and the bottom of Wenceslas Square. They're serious about their vegetarianism, serving only plant-based, unprocessed, and unrefined food. Its quiet dining area is elegant for a cafeteria, with a few tables outside in the courtyard (Sun-Thu 9:00-20:30, Fri 9:00-17:00, closed Sat, through courtyard at Melantrichova 15/Michalská 18, tel. 224-213-366).

Lehká Hlava Vegetarian Restaurant ("Clear Head"), tucked away on a cul-de-sac, has a mission to provide a "clear atmosphere for enjoying food." Sitting in an enchanted-forest setting, diners enjoy dishes from around the world. Reserve in advance for evenings (100-150-Kč plates, two-course 90-Kč daily special, no eggs, no smoke, lots of vegan dishes, daily 11:30-23:30, between Bethlehem Chapel and the river at Boršov 2, tel. 222-220-665).

Vegetarian Restaurant Maitrea, just off the Old Town Square alongside the Týn Church, serves imaginative dishes in a swoopy modern interior where every inch is curved to ensure the "unobstructed flow of energy." Its organic woody basement is even more seductive than the ground floor. The 105-Kč lunch special is a great value (Mon-Fri 11:30-23:30, Sat-Sun 12:00-23:30, Týnská ulička 6, tel. 221-711-631).

Beas Indian Cafeteria is a spartan little vegetarian restaurant ruled by a Punjabi chef. Diners grab a steel tray and point to whatever looks good. The food is sold by weight—you'll likely spend 140 Kč for lunch. Tucked away in a courtyard behind the Týn Church, this place is popular with university students (Mon-Sat 11:00-20:00, Sun 12:00-18:00, Týnská 19, mobile 608-035-727).

Klub Architektů, next to Bethlehem Chapel, is a modern hangout in a medieval cellar with a fun menu offering excellent original dishes, hearty salads, Moravian wines, and Slovak beer (daily 11:30-24:00, Betlémské Náměstí 169, tel. 224-401-214).

Le Patio, on the big and busy Národní Třída, has a hip, continental feel. But for a place that also sells furniture (head straight back and down the stairs), it definitely needs comfier dining chairs. Hanging lanterns and live music (Fri-Sat) contribute to the pleasant atmosphere. Dishes are from India, France, and points in between, and there's always a serious vegetarian option (200-350-Kč plates, daily 8:00-23:00, Národní 22—see map on page 282, tel. 224-934-375).

Pasha Kebab Turkish Restaurant, near the bottom of Wenceslas Square, has American fast-food chain ambience, good ingredients, and wonderful, authentic ready-to-eat Turkish dishes (120-Kč meals, daily 10:00-22:00, a block from Můstek Metro stop, just beyond Franciscan garden at Jungmannova 27, see map on page 282, tel. 224-948-481).

Brasserie La Gare, just off Náměstí Republiky, opened with the mission to prove to Czechs that French food can be simple and inexpensive. The menu includes such classics as d'escargots de Bourgogne and coq au vin. The red-hued, modern interior also contains a French bakery and a deli (250-Kč entreés, 89-Kč lunch specials, daily 11:00-24:00, V Celnici 3, tel. 222-313-712).

Ethnic Eateries and Bars near Dlouhá Street

Dlouhá, the wide street leading away from the Old Town Square behind the Jan Hus Memorial, is lined with ethnic restaurants catering mostly to cosmopolitan locals. Within a couple of blocks, you can eat your way around the world. From Dlouhá, wander the Rámová/Haštalská/Vězeňská area to survey a United Nations of eateries: You'll find French (Chez Marcel at Haštalská 12); Italian (the expensive Amici Miei at Vězeňská 5 that prides itself on fresh *pesci* and *frutti di mare*); and Afghan (Ariana at Rámová 6). These five deserve special consideration:

Indian: Indian Jewel, in the Ungelt courtyard behind the Týn Church, is the best place in Prague to find a full Indian menu that actually tastes Indian. Located in a pleasant, artfully restored courtyard, this is my choice for outdoor dining, with seriously executed sub-continental classics and good-value lunch specials (daily 11:00-23:00, Týn 6, tel. 222-310-156).

Thai: Orange Moon specializes in Thai curries, but you'll also find dishes from Myanmar (Burma) and India, served in a space delightfully decorated with artwork from Southeast Asia. This restaurant attracts a mixture of locals, expats, and tourists (daily 11:30-23:30, reservations recommended, Rámová 5, tel. 222-325-119).

Irish: Molly Malone's Irish Pub may seem like a strange recommendation in Prague—home of some of the world's best beer—but it has the kind of ambience that locals (and few tourists) seek out. Expats have favored Molly's for Guinness ever since the Velvet Revolution enabled the Celts to return to one of their homelands. Worn wooden floors, dingy walls, and the Irish manager transport you right into the heart of blue-collar Dublin—which is, after all, a popular place for young Czechs to seek jobs in the high-tech industry (daily 11:00-24:00, U Obecního Dvora 4, tel. 224-818-851).

Latin American: La Casa Blů, with cheap lunch specials,

Mexican plates, Staropramen beer, and greenish mojitos, is your own little pueblo in Prague. It's one of the last student bastions in the Old Town. Painted in warm oranges and reds, energized by upbeat music, and guarded by creatures from Mayan mythology, La Casa Blů attracts a fiesta of happy eaters and drinkers (Mon-Sat 11:00-23:00, Sun 14:00-23:00, non-smoking, on the corner of Kozí and Bílkova, tel. 224-818-270).

North American: **Bohemia Bagel** is hardly authentic—exasperated Czechs insist that bagels have nothing to do with Bohemia. Owned by an American, this practical café caters mostly to youthful tourists, with good sandwiches (100-125 Kč), a little garden out back, and Internet access. If homesick, you'll love the menu, with everything from Philly cheesesteaks to bacon and eggs (daily 7:00-24:00, Masná 2, tel. 224-812-560). Outside of meal times, it's a quiet and comfy hangout.

In the Jewish Quarter

These three eateries are well-located to break up a demanding tour of the Jewish Quarter—all within two blocks of each other on or near Široká (see map on page 236). Also consider the nearby ethnic eateries listed above.

Kolkovna, the flagship restaurant of a chain owned by Pilsner Urquell, is big and woody, yet modern, serving a fun mix of Czech and international cuisine—ribs, salads, cheese plates, and beer. It feels a tad formulaic...but in a good way (a bit overpriced but good energy, daily 11:00-24:00, across from Spanish Synagogue at V Kolkovně 8, tel. 224-819-701).

Franz Kafka Café, with a cool, dark interior strewn with historic photos of the ghetto and a few good sidewalk tables, is great for a relaxing salad, sandwich, snack, or drink (150-Kč salads, daily 10:00-21:00, one block from the cemetery at Široká 12).

Restaurace U Knihovny ("By the Library"), situated steps away from the City and National Libraries as well as the Pinkas Synagogue, is a favorite lunch spot for locals who work nearby. Their cheap daily lunch specials consist of seven imaginative variations on traditional Czech themes. The service is friendly and the stylish red-brick interior is warm (daily 11:00-23:00, smoke-free at lunch, on the corner of Veleslavínova and Valentinská, mobile 732-835-876).

Dining with an Old Town Square View

Restaurant u Prince Terrace, in the five-star U Prince Hotel facing the Astronomical Clock, is designed for foreign tourists. A sleek elevator takes you to its rooftop, where every possible inch is used to serve good food (international with plenty of fish) from their open-air grill. The view is arguably the best in town—

especially at sunset. The menu is a fun but overpriced mix, with photos that make ordering easy. Being in such a touristy spot, waiters are experts at nicking you with confusing menu charges; don't be afraid to confirm exact prices before ordering. This place is also great for a drink at sunset or late at night (fine salads, 240-300-Kč plates, daily until 24:00, brusque staff, outdoor heaters when necessary, Staroměstské Náměstí 29, tel. 224-213-807, no reservations possible).

Art Nouveau Splendor in the Municipal House

The **Municipal House** (Obecní Dům), the sumptuous Art Nouveau concert hall, has three restaurants: a café, a French restaurant, and a beer cellar (all at Náměstí Republiky 5). The dressy café, **Kavárna Obecní Dům,** is drenched in chandeliered, Art Nouveau elegance and offers the best value and experience here. Light, pricey meals and drinks come with great atmosphere and bad service (280-Kč three-course special daily for lunch or dinner, open daily 7:30-23:00, live piano or jazz trio 16:00-20:00, tel. 222-002-763). The fine and formal French restaurant in the next wing oozes Mucha elegance (700-1,000-Kč meals, daily 12:00-16:00 & 18:00-23:00, tel. 222-002-777). The beer cellar is overpriced and touristy (daily 11:30-23:00).

Cafés in the Old and New Towns

Dripping with history, these places are as much about the ambience as they are about the coffee. Most cafés also serve sweets and light meals.

Grand Café Slavia, across from the National Theater (facing the Legií Bridge on Národní street), is a fixture in Prague, famous as a hangout for its literary elite. Today, it's tired and clearly past its prime, with an Art Deco interior, lousy piano entertainment, and celebrity photos on the wall. But its iconic status makes it a fun stop for a coffee—skip the food (daily 8:00-23:00, sit as near the river as possible, tel. 224-218-493). Notice the *Drinker of Absinthe* painting on the wall (and on the menu for 55 Kč)—with the iconic Czech writer struggling with reality.

Café Louvre is a longtime elegant favorite (opened in 1902) that still draws an energetic young crowd. From the big and busy Národní street, you walk upstairs into a venerable world of newspapers on sticks (including English) and waiters in vests and aprons. The back room has long been the place for billiard tables (100 Kč/hour). An English flier tells its history (200-Kč plates, 120-Kč two-course lunch offered 11:00-15:00, open daily 8:00-23:30, Národní 22—see map on page 282, tel. 224-930-949).

Grand Café Orient is just one flight up off busy Celetná street, yet a world away from the crush of tourism below. Located in the Black Madonna House, the café is upstairs, above the entrance to the Museum of Czech Cubism and fittingly decorated with a Cubist flair. With its stylish, circa-1910 decor toned to dark green, this space is full of air and light—and a good value as well. The café takes its Cubism seriously: Traditionally round desserts are served square (salads, sandwiches, great balcony seating, Mon-Fri 9:00-22:00, Sat-Sun 10:00-22:00, Ovocný Trh 19, at the corner of Celetná near the Powder Tower, tel. 224-224-240).

Café Montmartre, on a small street parallel to Karlova, combines Parisian ambience with unbeatable Czech prices for coffee (no food served). Dreamy Czech minds found their quiet asylum here after Grand Café Slavia (listed earlier) and other longtime favorites either closed down or became stuck in their past. The main room is perfect for discussing art and politics; the intimate room behind the courtyard is where you recite poetry to your partner (Mon-Fri 9:00-23:00, Sat-Sun 12:00-23:00, Řetězová 7, tel. 222-221-244).

Ebel Coffee House, next door to Café Montmartre, prides itself on its wide assortment of fresh brews from every coffee-bean-growing country in the world, inviting cakes, and a colorful setting that delights the mind as much as the caffeine (daily 9:00-22:00, Řetězová 3, tel. 224-895-788).

Teahouses

Many Czech people are bohemian philosophers at heart and prefer the mellow, smoke-free environs of a teahouse to the smoky, traditional beer hall. Young Czechs are much more interested in traveling to exotic destinations like Southeast Asia, Africa, or Peru than to Western Europe, so the Oriental teahouses set their minds in vacation mode.

While there are teahouses all over town, a fine example in a handy locale is Prague's original one, established in 1991—a year after freedom. **Dobrá Čajovna** ("Good Teahouse"), just a few steps off the bustle of Wenceslas Square, takes you into a very peaceful world that elevates tea to an almost religious ritual. You'll be given an English menu—which lovingly describes each tea—and a bell. The menu lists a world of tea (very fresh, prices by the small pot), "accompaniments" (such as Exotic Miscellany), and light meals "for hungry tea drinkers." When you're ready to order, ring your bell to beckon a tea monk—likely a member of the Lovers of Tea Society (Mon-Sat 10:00-21:30, Sun 14:00-21:30, near the base of Wenceslas Square, opposite McDonald's at Václavské Náměstí 14, see map on page 282, tel. 224-231-480).

For an actual taste of tea from Prague's newly emerging Chinese middle class (rather than from some Czech's dreams of the Orient), head to **Čajový Klub** ("Tea Club"), just opposite the Jerusalem Synagogue. Creatively run by a cultured man from Beijing, here you'll find red cherry-wood decor, expertly served tea, and the freshest green leaves in town (Mon-Sat 10:00-21:00, closed Sun, Jeruzalémská 10, see map on page 282, tel. 222-721-072).

In the Little Quarter

These characteristic eateries are handy for a bite before or after your Prague Castle visit. For locations, see the map on pages 296-297.

Malostranská Beseda, in the impeccably restored former Town Hall, weaves together an imaginative menu of traditional Czech dishes (both classic and little known), vegetarian fare, and fresh fish. You can eat either in the non-smoking ground-floor restaurant or in the packed beer hall downstairs (daily 11:00-23:00, Malostranské Náměstí 21, tel. 257-409-112). It's also home to a recommended nightclub.

U Sedmi Švábů ("By the Seven Roaches") is an ever-more-touristy den where even the cuisine is medieval. Since America had not yet been discovered in the Middle Ages, you won't find any corn, potatoes, or tomatoes on the menu. The salty yellow things that come with the Krušovice beer are chickpeas. Carnivores thrive here: Try the skewered meats *(špíz u Sedmi Švábů)*, flaming beef *(flambák)*, or pork knuckle (daily 11:00-23:00, Janský Vršek 14, tel. 257-531-455).

U Osla v Kolébce ("By the Donkey in the Cradle") fills a peaceful courtyard just a minute off the touristy hubbub of Nerudova. The laid-back scene consists of two restaurants with nearly identical simple menus, dominated by tasty sausages and salads (daily 10:00-22:00, Jánský Vršek 8, below Nerudova, next door to U Sedmi Švábů, mobile 731-407-036).

U Hrocha ("By the Hippo"), a very authentic little pub packed with beer-drinkers and smoke, serves simple, traditional meals—basically meat starters with bread. Just below the castle near Little Quarter Square (Malostranské Náměstí), it's actually the haunt of many members of Parliament, which is located around the corner (daily 12:00-23:00, chalkboard lists daily meals in English, Thunovská 10, tel. 257-533-389).

Campanulla Café, in the courtyard on the other side of the Lennon Wall, is a secluded spot serving fresh sandwiches, raspberry drinks, and Italian coffee next to a flower garden, an English lawn, and one of the oldest trees in Prague (daily 11:00-22:00, Velkopřevorské Náměstí 4, look for small gate at left end of Lennon Wall, entrance to indoor seating area is another 20 yards to the left, tel. 257-217-736).

Restaurace Rybářský Klub, on Kampa Island overlooking the river, is run by the Society of Czech Fishermen and serves one of the widest selections of freshwater fish in Prague. Dine on

Restaurants & Hotels in the Little Quarter & Castle Quarter

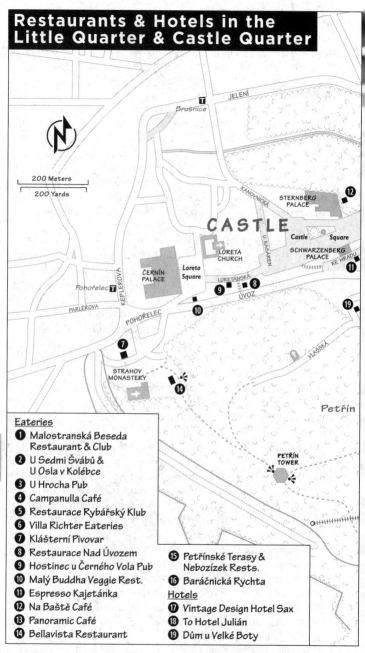

Eateries

1. Malostranská Beseda Restaurant & Club
2. U Sedmi Švábů & U Osla v Kolébce
3. U Hrocha Pub
4. Campanulla Café
5. Restaurace Rybářský Klub
6. Villa Richter Eateries
7. Klášterní Pivovar
8. Restaurace Nad Úvozem
9. Hostinec u Černého Vola Pub
10. Malý Buddha Veggie Rest.
11. Espresso Kajetánka
12. Na Baště Café
13. Panoramic Café
14. Bellavista Restaurant
15. Petřínské Terasy & Nebozízek Rests.
16. Baráčnická Rychta

Hotels

17. Vintage Design Hotel Sax
18. To Hotel Julián
19. Dům u Velké Boty

PRAGUE

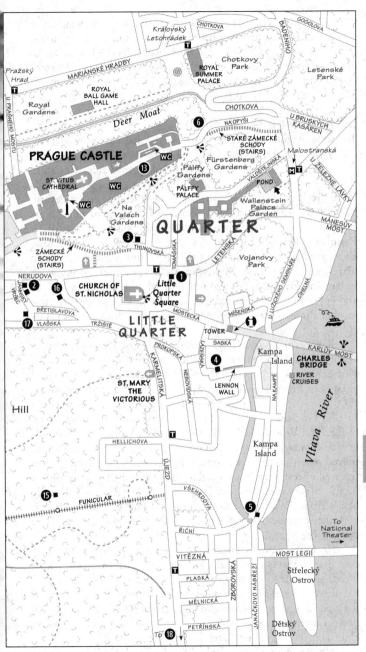

fish-cream soup, pike, trout, carp, or catfish under the imaginative artwork of Little Quarter painter Mr. Kuba. On warm evenings, late May through October, the Society fills its dock with tables (three-course meal for around 500 Kč, riverside menu not as extensive as indoor restaurant menu, daily 12:00-23:00, U Sovových Mlýnů 1, tel. 257-534-200).

In the Castle Quarter

To locate the following restaurants, see the map on pages 296-297.

Villa Richter, at the end of the castle promontory (closest to the river) and surrounded by newly replanted vineyards, consists of three classy restaurants, each with killer Prague views. Forty yards below the lower castle gate, you'll see a gate leading to a vineyard. Stroll downhill through the vineyard and you'll come upon three distinct restaurants (all open daily 10:00-23:00, tel. 257-219-079). **Panorama Pergola** consists of a string of outdoor tables lining a vineyard terrace overlooking the city (wine, sandwiches, cold plates, and hot views). **Piano Nobile** is more pretentious, with Italian and French dishes and romantic white-linen tables indoors and out—it's the perfect place to propose (1,000-Kč three-course meals). **Piano Terra** serves more affordable Czech dishes (200-300-Kč entrées).

Klášterní Pivovar ("Monastery Brewery"), founded by an abbot in 1628 and reopened in 2004, has two large rooms and a pleasant courtyard. This is the place to taste rare unpasteurized yeast beer, brewed on the premises. The wooden decor and circa-1900 newspaper clippings (including Habsburg Emperor Franz Josef's "Proclamation to My Nations," announcing the beginning of the First World War) evoke the era when Vienna was Europe's artistic capital, Prague was building its faux Eiffel Tower, and life moved much slower. To accompany the beer, try the strong beer-flavored cheese served on toasted black-yeast bread (daily 10:00-22:00, Strahovské Nádvoří 301, tel. 233-353-155). It's directly across from the entrance to the Strahov Library (don't confuse it with the enormous, tour group–oriented Klášterní Restaurace next door, to the right).

Restaurace Nad Úvozem is hidden in the middle of a staircase that connects Loretánská and Úvoz streets. This spot, which boasts super views of the Little Quarter and Petřín Hill, is good for unexceptional food in a quiet, secluded space. Check your bill for "special charges" before you pay (daily 12:00-21:00; as you go down Loretánská watch for pans, scoops, and spoons hanging on chains on your right at #15; tel. 220-511-532).

Hostinec u Černého Vola ("By the Black Ox") is a smoky, dingy old-time pub—its survival in the midst of all the castle splendor and tourism is a marvel. It feels like a kegger on the banks of the river Styx, with classic bartenders serving up Kozel beer (traditional "Goat" brand with excellent darks) and beer-friendly gut-bomb snacks (fried cheese, local hot dogs). The pub is located on Loretánská (50 yards from Loreta Church, no sign outside, sniff for cigarette smoke and look for the only house on the block without an arcade, daily 10:00-22:00, English menu on request, tel. 220-513-481).

Malý Buddha ("Little Buddha") serves delightful food—especially vegetarian—and takes its theme seriously. You'll step into a mellow, low-lit escape of bamboo and peace, where you'll be served by people with perfect complexions and almost no pulse to the no-rhythm of meditative music. Eating in their little back room is like being in a temple (100-200-Kč meals, Tue-Sun 12:00-22:30, closed Mon, non-smoking, between the castle and Strahov Monastery at Úvoz 46, tel. 220-513-894).

Espresso Kajetánka, just off Castle Square, has magnificent city views. It's a handy, though overpriced, place for a coffee in a plastic cup or a snack as you start or end your castle visit (daily 10:00-20:00, Ke Hradu, tel. 257-533-735).

Na Baště, serene but not as scenic, is in a garden through the gate to the left of the main castle entry. The outdoor seating, among Jože Plečnik's ramparts and obelisks, is the castle at its most sublime (100-Kč sandwiches, 250-Kč salads, daily 10:00-18:00, tel. 281-933-010).

Prague Connections

Centrally located Prague is a logical gateway between Eastern and Western Europe. From here, there are convenient, direct night trains to Amsterdam, Frankfurt, and Zurich; several trains leave daily to Munich, Berlin, and Vienna. From the east, Prague is connected by night trains with Budapest, Kraków, and Warsaw. You'll find handy Czech train and bus schedules at www.idos.cz; for trains, you can also check out Germany's all-Europe timetable at http://bahn.hafas.de/bin/query.exe/en. Remember that for all train connections, it's important to confirm which of Prague's stations to use.

From Prague by Train to: Terezín (train to Bohušovice station, nearly hourly, 1-1.5 hours; then 5-minute taxi or bus ride), **Český Krumlov** (8/day, 1/day direct, 4 hours—bus is faster, cheaper, and easier), **Budapest** (3/day, 7 hours; more with 2-3 changes, 8.5 hours; 1 night train, 7.5 hours), **Kraków** (1/day direct, 7.5 hours; 4/day with 1-2 changes, 8.25 hours; 1 night train, 9.5 hours), **Warsaw** (1/day direct, 8.75 hours; 3/day with 1-2 changes, 8.5-10 hours; 1 night train, 10 hours), **Vienna**—*Vídeň* in Czech (5/day direct, 4.75 hours, more with 1 change, 5-6 hours; 1 night train,

8 hours), **Berlin** (6/day, 4.5-5 hours), **Salzburg** (5/day, 6.5 hours, change in Český Budějovice and Linz, no decent overnight connection), **Munich** (2/day direct, 6.25 hours; 6/day via ExpressBus to Nürnberg then train to Munich, 5.25 hours total; no night train), **Frankfurt** (almost hourly, 7-8.25 hours), **Dresden** (about hourly, 2-2.5 hours), **Paris** (5/day, 12.5-13.5 hours, night train possible via Mannheim or Berlin).

From Prague by Bus to: **Terezín** (hourly, 50 minutes, departs from Nádraží Holešovice train station), **Český Krumlov** (7/day, 3.5 hours, some leave from Florenc station, others leave from Na Knížecí station or Roztyly station).

By Car with a Driver: Mike's Chauffeur Service is a reliable, family-run company with fair and fixed rates around town and beyond. Friendly Mike's motto is, "We go the extra mile for you" (round-trip fares, with waiting time included: Český Krumlov-3,800 Kč, Terezín-1,900 Kč, Karlštejn-1,700 Kč, 4 percent surcharge for credit-card payment; these prices for up to 4 people, minibus for up to 7 also available; tel. 241-768-231, mobile 602-224-893, www.mike-chauffeur.cz, mike.chauffeur@cmail.cz). On the way to Český Krumlov, Mike will stop at no extra charge at Hluboká Castle or České Budějovice, where the original Bud beer is made.

Mike also offers "Panoramic Transfers" to **Vienna** (7,000 Kč, depart Prague at 8:00, arrive Český Krumlov at 10:00, stay up to 6 hours, 1-hour scenic Czech riverside-and-village drive, then a 2-hour autobahn ride to your Vienna hotel, maximum 4 people); **Budapest** (8,900 Kč, 6 hours, Bratislava or Český Krumlov options); and **Kraków** (8,900 Kč, Auschwitz stop). Check Mike's website for special deals on last-minute transfers (see the "Hot News" column at right), including super-cheap "deadhead" rides when you travel in the opposite direction of a full-fare client.

By Plane: For information on Prague's airport, see page 217.

FRANCE

PARIS

Paris—the City of Light—has been a beacon of culture for centuries. As a world capital of art, fashion, food, literature, and ideas, it stands as a symbol of all the fine things human civilization can offer. Come prepared to celebrate, rather than judge the cultural differences, and you'll capture the romance and joie de vivre that Paris exudes.

Paris offers sweeping boulevards, chatty crêpe stands, chic boutiques, and world-class art galleries. Sip decaf with deconstructionists at a sidewalk café, then step into an Impressionist painting in a tree-lined park. Climb Notre-Dame and rub shoulders with the gargoyles. Cruise the Seine, zip up the Eiffel Tower, and saunter down avenue des Champs-Elysées. Master the Louvre and Orsay museums. Save some after-dark energy for one of the world's most romantic cities.

Planning Your Time

For up to five very busy but doable days in Paris, I've listed sights in descending order of importance in the planning sections that follow. Therefore, if you have only one day, just do Day 1; for two days, add Day 2; and so on. When planning where to plug in Versailles, keep in mind that the Château is closed on Mondays and especially crowded on Sundays and Tuesdays—try to avoid these days.

Day 1
Morning: Follow this chapter's Historic Paris Walk, featuring the Ile de la Cité, Notre-Dame, the Latin Quarter, and Sainte-Chapelle.

Afternoon: Tour the Louvre.

Evening: Enjoy the Trocadéro scene and a twilight ride up the Eiffel Tower.

Day 2

Morning: Wander the Champs-Elysées from the Arc de Triomphe down the grand avenue des Champs-Elysées to the Tuileries Garden.

Afternoon: Cross the pedestrian bridge from the Tuileries Garden, then tour the Orsay Museum.

Evening: Take one of the nighttime tours by taxi, bus, or retro-chic Deux Chevaux car. (If you're staying more than two days, save this for your last-night finale.)

Day 3

Morning: Catch the RER suburban train by 8:00 to arrive early at Versailles (before it opens at 9:00). Tour the palace's interior.

Midday: Have lunch in the gardens at Versailles.

Afternoon: Spend the afternoon touring the gardens, the Trianon Palaces, and Domaine de Marie-Antoinette.

Evening: Have dinner in Versailles town or return to Paris. For dessert, cruise the Seine River.

Day 4

Morning: Visit Montmartre and the Sacré-Cœur Basilica. Have lunch on Montmartre.

Afternoon: Continue your Impressionist theme by touring the Orangerie and the Rodin Museum, or change themes entirely and tour the Army Museum and Napoleon's Tomb.

Evening: Enjoy dinner on Ile St. Louis, then a floodlit walk by Notre-Dame.

Day 5

Morning: Ride scenic bus #69 to the Marais and tour this neighborhood, including the Pompidou Center.

Afternoon: Tour the Opéra Garnier (English tours available), and end your day enjoying the glorious rooftop views at the Galeries Lafayette and Printemps department stores.

Evening: Stroll the Champs-Elysées at night.

Orientation to Paris

Paris (population of city center: 2,170,000) is split in half by the Seine River, divided into 20 arrondissements (proud and independent governmental jurisdictions), circled by a ring-road freeway (the *périphérique*), and speckled with Métro stations. You'll find

---

Rick Steves' Free Audio Tours

I've produced free, self-guided audio versions of my tours of the major sights in Paris (download them via www.ricksteves .com/audioeurope, iTunes, or the Rick Steves Audio Europe smartphone app). These user-friendly, easy-to-follow, fun, and enlightening audio tours are available for the Louvre, the Orsay, the palace at Versailles, and my Historic Paris Walk. If you don't mind me in your ear, these audio tours are hard to beat: Nobody will stand you up, the quality is reliable, you can take the tour exactly when you like, and they're free.

Paris easier to navigate if you know which side of the river you're on, which arrondissement you're in, and which Métro stop you're closest to. If you're north of the river (the top half of any city map), you're on the Right Bank (Rive Droite). If you're south of it, you're on the Left Bank (Rive Gauche). The bull's-eye of your Paris map is Notre-Dame, which sits on an island in the middle of the Seine. Most of your sightseeing will take place within five blocks of the river.

Arrondissements are numbered, starting at the Louvre and moving in a clockwise spiral out to the ring road. The last two digits in a Parisian zip code indicate the arrondissement number. The abbreviation for "Métro stop" is "Mo." In Parisian jargon, the Eiffel Tower is on *la Rive Gauche* (the Left Bank) in the *7ème* (7th arrondissement), zip code 75007, Mo: Trocadéro.

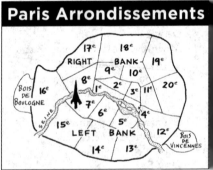

Paris Métro stops are used as a standard aid in giving directions, even for those not taking the Métro. As you're tracking down addresses, these words and pronunciations will help: Métro (may-troh), *place* (plahs—square), *rue* (roo—road), *avenue* (ah-vuh-noo), *boulevard* (boo-luh-var), and *pont* (pohn—bridge).

Tourist Information

Paris' TIs have long lines, offer little information, and may charge for maps. All you really need are this book and one of the freebie maps available at any hotel (or in the front of this book). On the plus side, TIs sell individual tickets to sights (see "Avoiding Lines

Paris Neighborhoods

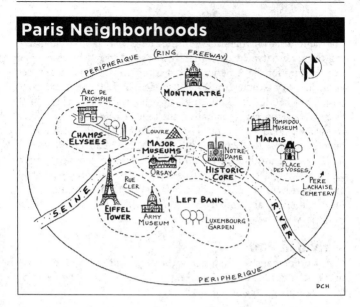

with Advance Tickets" in "Helpful Hints," later) as well as Paris Museum Passes, but if you plan to get a Museum Pass, it's quicker to buy these at participating sights. Paris' TIs share a single phone number: 08 92 68 30 00 (from the US, dial 011 33 8 92 68 30 00).

If you must visit a TI, you can do so at several locations, including **Pyramides** (daily 9:00-19:00, at Pyramides Métro stop between the Louvre and Opéra), **Gare de Lyon** (Mon-Sat 8:00-18:00, closed Sun), **Gare du Nord** (daily 8:00-18:00), and **Montmartre** (two branches: one on place du Tertre, daily 10:00-19:00, and the other above the Anvers Métro stop, daily 10:00-18:00). The official website for Paris' TIs is www.parisinfo.com. Both **airports** have handy information offices (called ADP) with long hours and short lines. *Pariscope:* The weekly €0.40 *Pariscope* magazine (or one of its clones, available at any newsstand) lists museum hours, art exhibits, concerts, festivals, plays, movies, and nightclubs. Smart sightseers rely on this for the latest listings.

Other Publications: Look for the *Paris Times,* which provides helpful English information and fresh insights into living in Paris (available at English-language bookstores, French-American establishments, and the American Church). *L'Officiel des Spectacles* (€0.35), which is similar to *Pariscope,* also lists goings-on around town (in French). The *Paris Voice,* with snappy reviews of concerts, plays, and current events, is available only online at www.paris voice.com. For a schedule of museum hours and English museum tours, get the free *Musées, Monuments Historiques, et Expositions* booklet at any museum.

American Church and Franco-American Center: This interdenominational church—in the rue Cler neighborhood, facing the river between the Eiffel Tower and Orsay Museum—is a nerve center for the American expat community. Worship services are held every Sunday (traditional services at 9:00 and 11:00, contemporary service at 13:30); the coffee hour after church and the free Sunday concerts (generally Sept-June at 17:00—but not every week) are a good way to get a taste of émigré life in Paris (reception open Mon-Sat 9:00-12:00 & 13:00-22:00, Sun 14:30-19:00, 65 quai d'Orsay, Mo: Invalides, tel. 01 40 62 05 00, www.acparis.org). It's also a handy place to pick up free copies of *Paris Times* (described earlier) and *France-USA Contacts* (an advertisement paper with info on housing and employment for the 50,000 Americans living in Paris, www.fusac.fr).

Arrival in Paris

For a comprehensive rundown of the city's train stations and airports, see "Paris Connections," near the end of this chapter. For information on parking a car, see page 308.

Helpful Hints

Theft Alert: Troublesome thieves thrive near famous monuments and on Métro and RER lines that serve high-profile tourist sights. Beware of pickpockets working busy lines (e.g., at train station ticket windows). Pay attention when it's your turn and your back is to the crowd—keep your bag firmly gripped in front of you.

In general, it's smart to wear a money belt, put your wallet in your front pocket, loop your day bag over your shoulders, and keep a tight grip on your purse or shopping bag. Muggings are rare, but they do occur. If you're out late, avoid the dark riverfront embankments and any place where the lighting is dim and pedestrian activity is minimal.

Paris is taking action to combat crime by stationing an abundance of police at monuments, on streets, and on the Métro, as well as security cameras at key sights. You'll go through quick and reassuring airport-like security checks at many major attractions.

Tourist Scams: Be aware of the latest scams, including these current favorites. The "found ring" scam involves an innocent-looking person who picks up a ring off the ground, and asks if you dropped it. When you say no, the person examines the ring more closely, then shows you a mark "proving" that it's pure gold. He offers to sell it to you for a good price—several times more than he paid for it before dropping it on the sidewalk.

In the "friendship bracelet" scam, a vendor approaches

you and asks if you'll help him with a demonstration. He proceeds to make a friendship bracelet right on your arm. When finished, he asks you to pay for the bracelet he created just for you. And because you can't easily take it off on the spot, he counts on your feeling obliged to pay up.

Distractions by a stranger—often a "salesman," or someone asking you to sign a petition, or posing as a deaf person to show you a small note to read—can all be tricks that function as a smokescreen for theft. As you try to wriggle away from the pushy stranger, an accomplice picks your pocket.

In popular tourist spots (such as in front of Notre-Dame) young ladies politely ask if you speak English, then pretend to beg for money while actually angling to get your wallet.

To all these scammers, simply say "no" firmly. Don't apologize, don't smile, and step away purposefully.

Street Safety: Parisian drivers are notorious for ignoring pedestrians. Look both ways (many streets are one-way) and be careful of seemingly quiet bus/taxi lanes. Don't assume you have the right of way, even in a crosswalk. When crossing a street, keep your pace constant and don't stop suddenly. By law, drivers are allowed to miss pedestrians by up to just one meter—a little more than three feet (1.5 meters in the countryside). Drivers carefully calculate your speed so they won't hit you, provided you don't alter your route or pace.

Watch out for bicyclists when you're crossing streets. This popular—and silent—transportation may come at you from unexpected places and directions—cyclists have a right to use lanes reserved for buses and taxis. Also, bikes commonly go against traffic, as many bike paths are on one-way streets. Again, always look both ways.

Museum Strategies: The worthwhile Paris Museum Pass, covering most sights in Paris, is sold at TIs, museums, FNAC stores, and monuments. For detailed information, see "Paris Museum Pass" on page 331.

Avoiding Lines with Advance Tickets: Throughout Paris, TIs and FNAC department stores sell individual *"coupe-file"* tickets, which allow you to use the Museum Pass entrance at sights and thereby skip ticket lines. TIs sell these tickets for no extra fee, but FNAC stores add a surcharge of 10-20 percent (possibly worth it, given the convenience of FNAC's many locations). For sights that can otherwise have long waits (such as the Arc de Triomphe, Opéra Garnier, and Versailles), these tickets are a good idea. (Note that Versailles and the Arc de Triomphe are covered by the Paris Museum Pass—also sold, without surcharge, at TIs and FNAC stores.)

You can go online to buy Paris Museum Passes and tickets

for several major sights at no surcharge (no more than three weeks in advance, http://en.parisinfo.com/express-booking). You'll print out vouchers, which you'll need to redeem at a Paris TI for the actual passes or tickets (or you can opt to have the passes or tickets mailed to you in the US, allow 5-7 days, postage fee added).

Bookstores: Paris has many English-language bookstores, where you can pick up guidebooks (at nearly double their American prices). Most stores carry Rick Steves titles.

My favorite is the friendly **Red Wheelbarrow Bookstore** in the Marais neighborhood, run by mellow Penelope (Mon 10:00-18:00, Tue-Sat 10:00-19:00, Sun 14:00-18:00, 22 rue St. Paul, Mo: St. Paul, tel. 01 48 04 75 08).

Other options include the following:

Shakespeare and Company (some used travel books, Mon-Fri 10:00-23:00, Sat-Sun 11:00-23:00, 37 rue de la Bûcherie, across the river from Notre-Dame, Mo: St. Michel, tel. 01 43 25 40 93).

W. H. Smith (Mon-Sat 9:00-19:00, Sun 12:30-19:00, 248 rue de Rivoli, Mo: Concorde, tel. 01 44 77 88 99).

Village Voice (Mon 14:00-19:30, Tue-Sat 10:00-19:30, Sun 12:00-18:00, near St. Sulpice Church at 6 rue Princesse, tel. 01 46 33 36 47).

San Francisco Book Company (Mon-Sat 11:00-21:00, Sun 14:00-19:30, 17 rue Monsieur le Prince, tel. 01 43 29 15 70).

Public WCs: Public toilets are free (though it's polite to leave a small tip if there's an attendant). Modern, sanitary street-booth toilets provide both relief and a memory (don't leave small children inside unattended). The restrooms in museums are free and the best you'll find. Or walk into any sidewalk café like you own the place, and find the toilet in the back. Keep toilet paper or tissues with you, as some WCs are poorly supplied.

Parking: Street parking is generally free at night (19:00 to 9:00), all day Sunday, and anytime in August, when many Parisians are on vacation. To pay for streetside parking, you must go to a *tabac* and buy a parking card *(une carte parking)*, sold in €10, €20, and €30 denominations. Insert the card into the meter and punch the desired amount of time (generally €1-2/ hour), then take the receipt and put it inside your windshield. Meters limit street parking to a maximum of two hours. For a longer stay, park for less at an airport (about €10/day) and take public transport or a taxi into the city. Underground lots are numerous in Paris—you'll find them under Ecole Militaire, St. Sulpice Church, Les Invalides, the Bastille, and the

Panthéon; all charge about €27-36/day (€58/3 days, €10/day more after that, for locations see www.vincipark.com). Some hotels offer parking for less—ask your hotelier.

Tobacco Stands *(Tabacs):* These little kiosks—usually just a counter inside a café—sell cards for parking meters, some public-transit tickets, postage stamps (though not all sell international postage—to mail something home, use two domestic stamps, or go to a post office), prepaid phone cards, and...oh yeah, cigarettes. To find one anywhere in Paris, just look for a *Tabac* sign and the red cylinder-shaped symbol above certain cafés.

Winter Activities: The City of Light sparkles year-round. For background on what to do and see here in winter months, see www.ricksteves.com/pariswinter.

Getting Around Paris

Paris is easy to navigate. Your basic choices are Métro (in-city subway), RER (suburban rail tied into the Métro system), public bus, and taxi. (Also consider the hop-on, hop-off bus and boat tours, described under "Tours in Paris," later.) You can buy tickets and passes at Métro stations and at many *tabac* shops. Keep change on hand, as some smaller Métro stations don't have staffed ticket windows, only ticket-vending machines, for which you'll need coins (some take bills; none takes American credit cards).

Public-Transit Tickets: The Métro, RER, and buses all work on the same tickets. You can make as many transfers as you need on a single ticket, except when transferring between the Métro/RER system and the bus system, which requires using an additional ticket. A **single ticket** costs €1.70. To save money, buy a ***carnet*** (kar-nay) of 10 tickets for €12 (cheaper for ages 4-10). *Carnets* can be shared among travelers.

Passes: The transit system has a chip-embedded card, called the **Passe Navigo** (though for most tourists, *carnets* are still the better deal). You pay a one-time €5 fee for the Navigo card itself (which also requires a postage stamp-size photo of yourself—bring your own, or use the €4 photo booths in major Métro stations). For a weekly *(hebdomadaire)* version, you'll pay €22.50, which gives you free run of the bus, Métro, and non-suburban RER system from Monday to Sunday (expiring on Sunday, even if you buy it on Friday). A monthly version for €60 is good for one calendar month.

To use the Passe Navigo, whether at a Métro turnstile or on the bus, touch the card to the purple pad, wait for the green validation light and the "ding," and you're on your way. The basic pass covers only central Paris, not regional destinations such as Versailles.

Navigo or *Carnet?* It's hard to beat the *carnet.* Two 10-packs of *carnets*—enough for most travelers staying a week—cost €23.40, are shareable, and don't expire until they're used. The Passe Navigo only becomes worthwhile for visitors who stay a full week or more and use the system a lot.

Other Passes: A handy one-day bus/Métro pass (called **Mobilis**) is available for €5.90. The overpriced **Paris Visite** passes are poorly designed for tourists, and offer minor reductions at minor sights (1 day/€9, 2 days/€15, 3 days/€20, 5 days/€29).

By Métro

In Paris, you're never more than a 10-minute walk from a Métro station. Europe's best subway allows you to hop from sight to sight quickly and cheaply (runs daily 5:30-24:30 in the morning). Learn to use it. Color Métro maps are free at Métro stations and included on freebie Paris maps at your hotel.

How the Métro Works: To get to your destination, determine the closest "Mo" stop and which line or lines will get you there. The lines are color-coded and numbered, and are known by their end-of-the-line stops. For example, the La Défense/Château de Vincennes line, also known as line 1 (yellow), runs between La Défense, on its west end, and Vincennes on its east end. Once in the Métro station, you'll see the color-coded line numbers and/ or blue-and-white signs directing you to the train going in your direction (e.g., *direction: La Défense*). Insert your ticket in the automatic turnstile, reclaim your ticket, pass through, and keep it until you exit the system (some stations require you to pass your ticket through a turnstile to exit).

Be warned that fare inspectors regularly check for cheaters and accept absolutely no excuses—keep that ticket or pay a minimum fine of €25.

Transfers are free and can be made wherever lines cross, provided you do so within 1.5 hours. When you transfer, follow the appropriately colored line number for your next train, or find orange *correspondance* (connection) signs leading you to the part of the station where you'll find your next line.

Be prepared to walk significant distances within Métro stations to reach your platform (especially when you transfer). Escalators are common, but they're often out of order. To limit excessive walking, avoid transferring at these sprawling stations: Montparnasse-Bienvenüe, Châtelet-Les Halles, Charles de Gaulle-Etoile, Gare du Nord, and Bastille. (Taking buses require less walking than the Métro—for more, see "By City Bus," later.)

When you reach your destination, look for the blue-and-white *sortie* signs pointing you to the exit. Before leaving the station, check the helpful *plan du quartier* (map of the neighborhood) to get your bearings. At stops with several *sorties,* you can save lots of walking by choosing the best exit.

After you exit the system, toss or tear your used ticket so you don't confuse it with unused tickets—they look almost identical.

Beware of Pickpockets: Thieves dig the Métro and RER. Be on guard. For example, if your pocket is picked as you pass through a turnstile, you end up stuck on the wrong side (after the turnstile bar has closed behind you) while the thief gets away. Stand away from Métro doors to avoid being a target for a theft-and-run just before the doors close. Any jostling or commotion—especially when boarding or leaving trains—is likely the sign of a thief or a team of thieves in action. Make any fare inspector show proof of identity (ask locals for help if you're not certain). Never show anyone your wallet.

By RER

The RER (Réseau Express Régionale; air-ay-air) is the suburban arm of the Métro, serving outlying destinations such as Versailles, Disneyland Paris, and the airports. These routes are indicated by thick lines on your subway map and identified by the letters A, B, C, and so on.

Within the city center, the RER works like the Métro and can be speedier if it serves your destination directly, because it makes fewer stops. Métro tickets and the Passe Navigo card are good on the RER when traveling in the city center. You can transfer between the Métro and RER systems with the same ticket. But to travel outside the city (to Versailles or the airport, for example), you'll need to buy a separate, more expensive ticket. Unlike the Métro, not every train stops at every station along the way; check the sign over the platform to see if your destination is listed as a stop ("*toutes les gares*" means it makes all stops along the way), or confirm with a local before you board. For RER trains, you may need to insert your ticket in a turnstile to exit the system.

By City Bus

Paris' excellent bus system is worth figuring out. Buses don't seem as romantic as the famous Métro and are subject to traffic jams, but savvy travelers know that buses can have you swinging through the city like Tarzan in an urban jungle. Buses require less walking and fewer stairways than the Métro, and you can see Paris unfold as you travel.

Bus stops are everywhere, and every stop comes complete with all the information you need: a good city bus map, route maps showing exactly where each bus that uses this stop goes, a frequency chart and schedule, a *plan du quartier* map of the immediate neighborhood, and a *soirées* map explaining night service, if available.

Just like with the Métro, every bus stop has a name, and every bus is headed to one end-of-the-line stop or the other. First, find your stop on the chart, then find your destination stop. Now, find out exactly where to catch the bus going in that direction. (On the maps showing the bus route, notice the triangle-shaped arrows pointing in the direction the bus is headed. With so many one-way streets in Paris, it's easy to get on the bus in the wrong direction.) When the bus pulls up, double-check that the sign on the front of the bus has the end-of-the-line stop going in your direction.

Buses use the same tickets and passes as the Métro and RER. One Zone 1 ticket buys you a bus ride anywhere in central Paris within the freeway ring road *(le périphérique)*. Use your Métro ticket or buy one on board for €0.10 more. (The ticket system has a few quirks—see "More Bus Tips," below.)

Board your bus through the front door (or on long buses, you can push the green button by the other doors to open them). If you already have a ticket, validate it in the yellow machine. If you have a Passe Navigo, scan it on the purple touch pad. Otherwise, buy a ticket from the driver. Keep track of what stop is coming up next by following the on-board diagram or listening to recorded announcements. When you're ready to get off, push the red button to signal you want a stop, then exit through the rear door. Even if you're not certain you've figured out the system, do some joyriding.

More Bus Tips: Avoid rush hour (Mon-Fri 8:00-9:30 & 17:30-19:30), when buses are jammed and traffic doesn't move. Not all city buses are air-conditioned, so they can become rolling greenhouses on summer days. You can transfer from one bus to another on the same ticket (within 1.5 hours, re-validate your ticket in the next bus's yellow machine), but you can't do a round-trip or hop on and off on the same line. Neither can you transfer between the bus and the Métro/RER systems on a single ticket. Also, you can't transfer between buses with a ticket bought on board—go figure.

Handy bus-system maps *(plans des autobus)* are available in any Métro station (and in the €6 *Paris Pratique* map book sold at newsstands). For longer stays, consider buying the €6 *Le Bus* book of bus routes. While the Métro shuts down at about 24:30 in the morning, some buses continue much later (called Noctilien lines, www.noctilien.fr).

I've listed the handiest bus routes for each recommended hotel neighborhood in the "Sleeping in Paris" section, later.

By Taxi

Parisian taxis are reasonable, especially for couples and families. The meters are tamper-proof. Fares and supplements (described in English on the rear windows) are straightforward and tightly regulated.

A taxi can fit three people comfortably, and a fourth for €3 extra. (Cabbies are legally required to accept four passengers, though they don't always like it.) Groups of up to five can use a larger vehicle, which must be booked in advance—ask your hotelier to call. For a sample taxi tour of the city at night, see page 376.

Rates: All Parisian taxis start with €2.20 on the meter, and have a minimum charge of €6.10. A 20-minute ride (e.g., Bastille to Eiffel Tower) costs about €20 (versus €1.20/person to get anywhere in town using a *carnet* ticket on the Métro or bus). Drivers charge higher rates at rush hour and at night, all day Sunday, and to any of the airports. Each piece of luggage you put in the trunk is €1 extra (though it won't appear on the meter, it is a legitimate charge). To tip, round up to the next euro (at least €0.50).

How to Catch *un Taxi:* You can try waving down a taxi, but it's often easier to ask someone for the nearest taxi stand (*"Où est une station de taxi?"*; oo ay ewn stah-see-ohn duh "taxi"). Taxi stands are indicated by a circled "T" on good city maps, and on many maps in this chapter. To order a taxi, call 3607, or ask your hotelier for help. When you summon a taxi by phone, the meter starts running as soon as the call is received, often adding €6 or more to the bill.

Taxis are tough to find during rush hour, when it's raining, and on Friday and Saturday nights, especially after the Métro closes (around 24:30 in the morning). If you need to catch a train or flight early in the morning, book a taxi at least the day before (especially for weekday departures). Some taxi companies require a €5 reservation fee by credit card for weekday morning rush-hour departures (7:00-10:00) and only have a limited number of reservation spots.

By Bike

Paris is surprisingly easy by bicycle. The city is flat, and riders have access to more than 370 miles of bike lanes and the many priority lanes for buses and taxis. I biked along the river from Notre-Dame to the Eiffel Tower in 15 wonderfully scenic minutes.

Urban cyclists will find Paris a breeze. First-timers will get the hang of it quickly enough by following some simple rules. Always stay to the right in your lane, bike single-file, stay off sidewalks, watch out for opening doors on parked cars, signal with your arm before making turns, and use bike paths when available. Obey the traffic laws as if you were driving a car.

Parisians use the same road rules as Americans, with two exceptions: When passing vehicles or other bikes, always pass on the left (it's illegal to pass on the right); and where there is no stoplight, always yield to incoming traffic on your right. You'll find a bell on your bike; use it like a horn to warn pedestrians who don't see you.

The TIs have a helpful "Paris à Vélo" map, which shows all the dedicated bike paths. Many other versions are available for sale at newsstand kiosks, some bookstores, and department stores.

Both bike companies listed below rent bikes at good rates, sell maps, and also offer organized tours by bike (listed under "Tours in Paris," next).

Bike About Tours is your best bet for bike rental. Their bikes are also foldable, which allows you to collapse your bike and jump on the Métro if the weather turns bad or you tire too early (€15/day during office hours, €20/24 hours; includes locks, helmets, and comfy gel seats; daily 9:00-11:30 & 14:30-16:30, closed mid-Dec-mid-Feb, shop located near Hôtel de Ville at 4 rue de Lobau in Vinci parking garage—see map on page 322, Mo: Hôtel de Ville, www.bikeabouttours.com, info@bikeabouttours.com). They sell detailed maps for €6 (free for Rick Steves readers with bike rental) and are full of advice for routes and things to see.

Fat Tire Bike Tours has some bikes for rent—call ahead to check availability (€4/hour, €25/24 hours, includes helmets and locks, credit-card imprint required for deposit, discount with this book for daily rental, office open daily 9:00-18:30, May-Aug bike rental only after 11:30 as priority is given to those taking a tour, request map of suggested routes, 24 rue Edgar Faure—see map on page 346, Mo: Dupleix, tel. 01 56 58 10 54, www.fattirebiketours paris.com).

Bike Freedom for Parisians: You're sure to see Vélib' rental bikes and racks around town—the bikes are geared mainly for residents to rent (the machines take chip-embedded European credit cards, and American Express cards—but otherwise no other American cards). For tourists, the plus side of the popular, highly touted Vélib' program is that it has prompted the city to add more bike paths, and has helped Parisian drivers learn to share the road with bicycles.

By Scooter

Left Bank Scooters will deliver and pick-up rental scooters to daring travelers over 20 years old with a valid driver's license (€70-90/day, price depends on size of the scooter and how long you keep it, tel. 06 82 70 13 82, www.leftbankscooters.com).

Tours in Paris

By Bus

Bus Tours—**Paris Vision** offers bus tours of Paris, day and night (advertised in hotel lobbies). I'd consider a Paris Vision tour only for their nighttime tour (see page 375). During the day, the hop-on, hop-off bus tours and the Batobus (both described in this section) are a better value, providing both transportation between sights as well as commentary.

Hop-on, Hop-off Bus Tours—Double-decker buses connect Paris' main sights, allowing you to hop on and off along the way. You get a disposable set of ear plugs to listen to a basic running commentary (dial English for the so-so narration). You can get off at any stop, tour a sight, then catch a later bus. These are best in good weather, when you can sit up top. There are two companies: L'Open Tours and Les Cars Rouges (pick up their brochures showing routes and stops from any TI or on their buses). You can start either tour at just about any of the major sights, such as the Eiffel Tower (both companies stop on avenue Joseph Bouvard).

L'Open Tours uses bright-yellow buses and provides more extensive coverage (and slightly better commentary) on four different routes, rolling by most of the important sights in Paris. Their Paris Grand Tour (the green route) offers the best introduction. The same ticket gets you on any of their routes within the validity period. Buy your tickets from the driver (1 day-€29, 2 days-€32, kids 4-11 pay €15 for 1 or 2 days, allow 2 hours per tour). Two to four buses depart hourly from about 10:00 to 18:00; expect to wait 10-15 minutes at each stop (stops can be tricky to find—look for yellow signs; tel. 01 42 66 56 56, www.paris-opentour.com). A combo-ticket covers both the Batobus boats (described later) and L'Open Tours buses (€44, kids under 12 pay €20, valid 3 days).

Les Cars Rouges' bright red buses offer largely the same service, with only one route and just nine stops, for less (recorded narration, adult-€24, kids 4-12 pay €12, good for 2 days, 10 percent cheaper when booked online, tel. 01 53 95 39 53, www.carsrouges .com).

By Boat

Seine Cruises—Several companies run one-hour boat cruises on the Seine. For the best experience, cruise at twilight or after dark. (To dine while you cruise, see "Dinner Cruises" on page 430.) Two of the companies—Bateaux-Mouches and Bateaux Parisiens—are convenient to the rue Cler hotels, and both run daily year-round (April-Oct 10:00-22:30, 2-3/hour; Nov-March shorter hours, runs hourly). Some offer discounts for early online bookings.

Bateaux-Mouches, the oldest boat company in Paris, departs from pont de l'Alma's right bank, and has the biggest open-top, double-decker boats (higher up means better views). But this company often has too many tour groups, causing these boats to get packed (€10, kids 4-12 pay €5, tel. 01 40 76 99 99, www.bateaux -mouches.com).

Bateaux Parisiens has smaller covered boats with handheld audioguides, fewer crowds, and only one deck. It leaves from right

Affording Paris' Sights

Paris is an expensive city for tourists, with lots of pricey sights, but—fortunately—lots of freebies, too. Smart, budget-minded travelers begin by buying and getting the most out of a **Paris Museum Pass** (see page 331), then considering these frugal sightseeing options.

Free Museums: Museums that are always free (with the possible exception of special exhibits) include the Carnavalet, Petit Palais, Victor Hugo's House, and Fragonard Perfume Museum. Many of Paris' most famous museums offer free entry on the first Sunday of the month, including the Louvre, Orsay, Rodin, Cluny, Pompidou Center, and Delacroix museums (expect big crowds on these days). You can also visit the Orsay Museum for free at 17:00 (or Thu at 21:00), an hour before the museum closes. One of the best everyday values is the Rodin Museum's garden, where it costs just €1 to experience many of Rodin's finest works in a lovely outdoor setting.

Other Freebies: Many worthwhile sights don't charge entry, including the Notre-Dame Cathedral, Père Lachaise Cemetery, Deportation Memorial, Holocaust Memorial, Paris Plage (summers only), Sacré-Cœur Basilica, St. Sulpice Church (with organ recital), and La Défense (though there is a charge to enter La Grande Arche).

Paris' glorious, entertaining parks are free, of course. These include Luxembourg Garden, Champ de Mars (under the Eiffel Tower), Tuileries Garden (between the Louvre and place de la Concorde), Palais Royal Courtyards, Jardin des Plantes, the Promenade Plantée walk, and Versailles' gardens (except on Fountain Spectacle weekends).

Reduced Price: Several museums offer a discount if you enter later in the day, including the Louvre (after 18:00 on Wed and Fri), Orsay (Fri-Wed after 16:15 and Thu after 18:00), Army Museum and Napoleon's Tomb (one hour before closing), and Versailles' Château (after 15:00) and Trianon Palaces and Domaine de Marie-Antoinette (after 16:00).

in front of the Eiffel Tower (€11, kids 3-12 pay €5, half-price if you have a valid France or France-Switzerland railpass—does not use up a day of a flexipass, tel. 01 76 64 14 45 or toll 08 25 01 01 01, www.bateauxparisiens.com).

Vedettes du Pont Neuf offers essentially the same one-hour tour as Bateaux Parisiens, but starts and ends at pont Neuf, closer to recommended hotels in the Marais and Luxembourg Garden neighborhoods. The boats feature a live guide whose delivery (in English and French) is as stiff as a recorded narration—and as hard to understand, given the quality of their sound system (€12, kids 4-12 pay €6, tip requested, check for online advance-purchase discounts, nearly 2/hour, daily 10:30-22:30, tel. 01 46 33 98 38,

Free Concerts: Venues offering free or cheap (€6-8) concerts include the American Church, Hôtel des Invalides, St. Sulpice Church, La Madeleine Church, and Notre-Dame Cathedral. For a listing of free concerts, check *Pariscope* magazine (under the "Musique" section) and look for events marked *entrée libre*.

Self-Guided Bus Tour: Instead of paying €25 for a tour company to give you an overview of Paris, ride city bus #69 for the cost of a Métro ticket. This scenic route crosses the city east-west, running between the Eiffel Tower and Père Lachaise Cemetery, and passing these great monuments and neighborhoods: Eiffel Tower, Ecole Militaire, rue Cler, Les Invalides (Army Museum and Napoleon's Tomb), Louvre Museum, Ile de la Cité, Ile St. Louis, Hôtel de Ville, Pompidou Center, Marais, Bastille, and Père Lachaise. You don't have to do the whole enchilada; get on and off wherever you like (though you'll have to buy a new ticket each time you board).

You can hop on daily until 22:30 (last departure from Eiffel Tour stop). It's best to avoid weekday rush hours (8:00-9:30 & 17:30-19:30) and hot days (no air-con). Sundays are quietest, and it's easy to get a window seat. Evening bus rides are magical from fall through spring (roughly Sept-April), when it gets dark early enough to see the floodlit monuments before the bus stops running. In the rue Cler area, catch bus #69 eastbound at the Eiffel Tower on avenue Joseph Bouvard (the first stop is at the southwestern end of the avenue, across from the Eiffel Tower; the second stop is at the eastern end).

Good-Value Tours: At €12-15, Paris Walks' tours are a good value. The €10-12 Seine River cruises, best after dark, are also worthwhile.

Pricey... but worth it? Certain big-ticket items—primarily the Eiffel Tower, Louvre, and Versailles—are expensive and crowded, but offer once-in-a-lifetime experiences. Think of it as you would a spree in Vegas—budget in a little "gambling" money you expect to lose, then just relax...and enjoy.

www.vedettesdupontneuf.com).

Hop-on, Hop-Off Boat Tour—Batobus allows you to get on and off as often as you like at any of eight popular stops along the Seine: Eiffel Tower, pont Alexandre III (closest to Champs-Elysées), Orsay/place de la Concorde, the Louvre, Notre-Dame, the Institut de France (closest to St. Germain-des-Prés), Hôtel de Ville, and Jardin des Plantes. Safe glass enclosures turn the boats into virtual ovens on hot days (1 day-€12, 2 days-€16, 5 days-€20, boats run June-Aug 10:00-21:30, mid-March-May and Sept-Oct 10:00-19:00, Nov-early Jan and Feb-mid-March 10:30-16:30, no service last three weeks in Jan, every 15-20 minutes, 45 minutes one-way, 1.5-hour round-trip, worthless narration, www.batobus.com). If you use this for getting around—sort of a scenic, floating alternative to the Métro—it can be worthwhile, especially with a 5-day pass. But if you just want a guided boat tour, Batobus is not as good a value as the regular tour boats described above.

Low-Key Cruise on a Tranquil Canal—**Canauxrama** runs a lazy 2.5-hour cruise on a peaceful canal out of sight of the Seine. Tours start from place de la Bastille and end at Bassin de la Villette (near Mo: Stalingrad). During the first segment of your trip, you'll pass through a long tunnel (built at the order of Napoleon in the early 19th century, when canal boats were vital for industrial transport). Once outside, you glide—not much faster than you can walk—through sleepy Parisian neighborhoods and slowly climb through four double locks as a guide narrates the trip in French and English (€16, check online for discounts for advance booking, departs at 9:45 and 14:30 across from Opéra Bastille, just below boulevard de la Bastille, opposite #50—where the canal meets place de la Bastille, tel. 01 42 39 15 00, www.canauxrama.com). The same tour also goes in the opposite direction, from Bassin de la Villette to place de la Bastille (departs at 9:45 and 14:45). It's OK to bring a picnic on board.

On Foot

Paris Walks—This company offers a variety of two-hour walks, led by British and American guides. Tours are thoughtfully prepared and entertaining. Don't hesitate to stand close to the guide to hear (€12-15, generally 2/day—morning and afternoon, private tours available, family guides and Louvre tours a specialty, call 01 48 09 21 40 for schedule in English, or check printable online schedule at www.paris-walks.com). Tours focus on the Marais (4/week), Montmartre (3/week), medieval Latin Quarter (Mon), Ile de la Cité/Notre-Dame (Mon), the "Two Islands" (Ile de la Cité and Ile St. Louis, Wed), the Revolution (Wed), and Hemingway's Paris (Fri). Call a day or two ahead to hear the current schedule and starting point. Most tours don't require reservations, but specialty tours (such as the Louvre or Chocolate tour) require advance reservations and prepayment with credit card (not refundable if you cancel less than two days in advance).

Context Paris—These "intellectual by design" walking tours are geared for serious learners and led by docents (historians, architects, and academics). They cover both museums and specific neighborhoods (see website for details). It's best to book in advance—groups are limited to six participants and can fill up (€55-90/person plus admissions, generally 3 hours long, tel. 01 72 81 36 35, US tel. 800-691-6036, www.contextparis.com). They also

PARIS

offer private tours and excursions outside Paris.

Classic Walks—The antithesis of Context Paris' walks, these lowbrow, low-information, but high-fun walking tours are run by Fat Tire Bike Tours. Their 3.5-hour "Classic Walk" covers most major sights (€20, March-Oct, daily at 10:00, meet at their office—see their listing under "By Bike," below). They also do two-hour walks on various themes and neighborhoods: Montmartre, French Revolution, World War II, and Latin Quarter (€12-20, ask about discount with this book, leaves several times a week—see website for details, 24 rue Edgar Faure, Mo: Dupleix, tel. 01 56 58 10 54, www.classicwalksparis.com).

Local Guides—For many, Paris merits hiring a Parisian as a personal guide. **Arnaud Servignat** is an excellent licensed guide (€160/half-day, €270/day, also does car tours of the countryside around Paris for a little more, tel. 06 68 80 29 05, www.french -guide.com, arnotour@me.com). **Thierry Gauduchon** is a terrific guide well worth his fee (€180/half-day, €350/day, tel. 01 56 98 10 82, mobile 06 19 07 30 77, tgauduchon@aol.com). **Elizabeth Van Hest** is another likeable and capable guide (€160/half-day, €270/ day, tel. 01 43 41 47 31, elisa.guide@gmail.com).

By Bike

Paris is terrific by bike (see "Getting Around Paris—By Bike," earlier) and made easier by bike tour. Both companies below sell bottled water and bike maps of Paris, and can give advice on biking routes of the city. Their tour routes cover different parts of the city, so you could do both tours without much repetition.

Bike About Tours—Run by Christian (American) and Paul (New Zealander), this company offers easygoing tours with a focus on the eastern half of the city.

The four-hour tours run daily year-round at 10:00 (also at 15:00 June-Aug). You'll meet at the statue of Charlemagne in front of Notre-Dame, then walk to the nearby rental office to get bikes (in Vinci parking garage at corner of rue de Lobau and rue de Rivoli). The tour includes a good back-street visit of the Marais, the Rive Gauche outdoor sculpture park, the Ile de la Cité, the heart of the Latin Quarter (with a lunch break), the Louvre, Les Halles, and the Pompidou Center. Group tours have a 12-person maximum—reserve online to guarantee a spot, or show up and take your chances (€30, discount with this book, maximum 2 discounts per book, 15 percent discount for families, includes helmets upon request, private tours available, see listing on page 314 for contact info).

Fat Tire Bike Tours—A hardworking gang of young American expats runs an extensive program of bike, Segway, and walking tours.

PARIS

Their high-energy guides run four-hour bike tours of Paris, by day and by night. Reservations aren't necessary—just show up. On the day tour, you'll pedal with a pack of 10-20 riders, mostly in parks and along bike lanes, with a lunch stop in the Tuileries Garden (€28, show this book for a discount, maximum 2 discounts per book, English only, tours leave daily rain or shine at 11:00, April-Oct at 15:00 as well). Night tours are more lively, and include a boat cruise on the Seine (€28, discount with this book, April-Oct daily at 19:00, March daily at 18:00, end of Feb and all of Nov Tue, Thu, and Sat-Sun at 18:00, no night tours Dec-mid-Feb). Both tours meet at the south pillar of the Eiffel Tower, where you'll get a short history lesson, then walk six minutes to the Fat Tire office to pick up bikes (helmets available upon request at no extra charge, for contact info see listing on page 314). They also run bike tours to Versailles and Giverny (reservations required, see website for details). Their office has Internet access with English keyboards.

Fat Tire's pricey four-hour **City Segway Tours**—on stand-up motorized scooters—are novel in that you learn to ride a Segway while exploring Paris (you'll get the hang of it after about half an hour). These tours take no more than eight people at a time, so reservations are required (€75, daily at 9:30, April-Oct also at 14:00 and 18:30, March and Nov also at 14:00, www.citysegwaytours .com).

Excursions from Paris

Most of the **local guides** listed earlier will do excursion tours from Paris using your rental car. Or consider these companies, which provide transportation:

Paris Webservices, a reliable outfit, offers many services, including day trips with English-speaking chauffeur-guides in cushy minivans for private groups (figure €90-120/person for groups of 4 or more, ask for Rick Steves discount—use promo code "RSteves 07," see contact info in listing on page 436).

Many companies offer bus tours to regional sights. **Paris Vision** runs minivan and bus tours to several popular regional destinations, including the Loire Valley, Champagne region, D-Day beaches, and Mont St. Michel. Minivan tours are pricier, but more personal and given in English, and most offer convenient pickup at your hotel (€90-190/person). Their full-size bus tours are multilingual, mass-marketed, and nothing special, but cheaper than the minivan tours—worthwhile for some travelers simply for the ease of transportation to the sights (about €70, destinations include Versailles and Giverny). Paris Vision's full-size buses depart from 214 rue de Rivoli (Mo: Tuileries, tel. 01 42 60 30 01, www.paris vision.com).

Self-Guided Walk

Historic Paris Walk

(This information is distilled from the Historic Paris Walk chapter in *Rick Steves' Paris*, by Rick Steves, Steve Smith, and Gene Openshaw. You can download a free audio version of this walk for your mobile device via www.ricksteves.com/audioeurope, iTunes, or the Rick Steves Audio Europe smartphone app.

Allow four hours to do justice to this three-mile walk. Start where the city did—on the Ile de la Cité. Face Notre-Dame and follow the gray line on the "Historic Paris Walk" map.

• *Start at Notre-Dame Cathedral on the island in the Seine River, the physical and historic bull's-eye of your Paris map. The closest Métro stops are Cité, Hôtel de Ville, and St. Michel, each a short walk away.*

On the square in front of the cathedral, stand far enough back to take in the whole facade. View it from the bronze plaque on the ground marked "Point Zero" (30 yards from the central doorway). You're standing at the center of France, the point from which all distances in France are measured. Find the circular window in the center of the cathedral's facade.

▲▲▲Notre-Dame Cathedral

This 700-year-old cathedral is packed with history and tourists. Study its sculpture and windows, take in a Mass, eavesdrop on guides, and walk all around the outside.

Cost and Hours: Free, cathedral open daily 8:00-18:45, Sat-Sun until 19:15; Treasury-€3, not covered by Museum Pass, daily 9:30-18:00, Sat-Sun until 18:30; audioguide-€5, ask about free English tours—normally Wed and Thu at 14:00, Sat at 14:30; Mo: Cité, Hôtel de Ville, or St. Michel. Tel. 01 42 34 56 10, www.cathedraledeparis.com. The international Mass is held Sun at 11:30, with an organ concert at 16:30. Call or check the website for a full schedule. On Good Friday and the first Friday of the month at 15:00, the (physically underwhelming) relic known as Jesus' Crown of Thorns goes on display.

➋ Self-Guided Tour: The **cathedral facade** is worth a close look. The church is dedicated to "Our Lady" *(Notre Dame)*. Mary is center stage—cradling God, right in the heart of the facade, surrounded by the halo of the rose window. Adam is on the left and Eve is on the right.

Below Mary and above the arches is a row of 28 statues known as the Kings of Judah. During the French Revolution, these biblical kings were mistaken for the hated French kings, and Notre-Dame represented the oppressive Catholic hierarchy. The citizens stormed the church, crying, "Off with their heads!" All were decapitated, but have since been recapitated.

PARIS

Historic Paris Walk

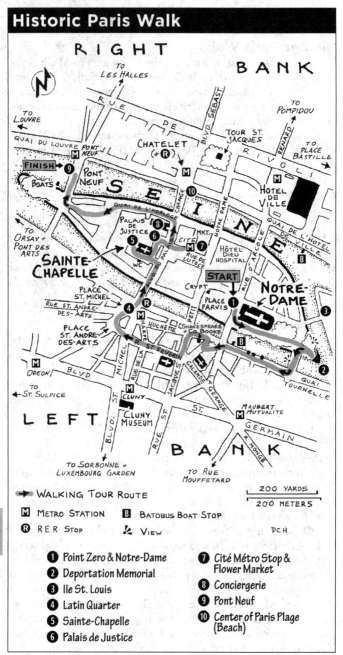

TO LES HALLES

RIGHT BANK

TO LOUVRE

QUAI DU LOUVRE

RUE DE

BLVD. SEBAST.

TOUR ST. JACQUES

RENARD

TO POMPIDOU

CHATELET (+ⓇR)

RIVOLI

TO PLACE BASTILLE

FINISH ⑨

PONT NEUF

PONT NEUF

Ⓜ

S E I N E

QUAI DE L'HORLOGE

CHANGE

HOTEL DE VILLE

QUAI DE L'HOTEL DE VILLE

BOATS

TO ORSAY & PONT DES ARTS

PALAIS DE JUSTICE ⑧ CONCIERGERIE

⑥ CITÉ MKT.

⑤ ⑦ RUE DE LUTECE

QUAI D'ARGENT

SAINTE-CHAPELLE

WC

HÔTEL DIEU HOSPITAL

CRYPT

START

NOTRE-DAME

PLACE ST. MICHEL

Ⓡ

PLACE PARVIS

①

③

RUE ST. ANDRE-DES-ARTS

④ Ⓜ

HUCHETTE

SHAKESPEARE CO. BOOKS

B

PLACE ST. ANDRE-DES-ARTS

RUE DE LA

RUE ST. SEVERIN

GALANDE

②

QUAI TOURNELLE

Ⓜ ODEON

BLVD.

MICHEL

RUE

ST. JACQUES

CLUNY

CLUNY MUSEUM

GRANGE

MAUBERT MUTUALITE Ⓜ

TO ST. SULPICE

GERMAIN

R MONGE

L E F T   B A N K

TO SORBONNE & LUXEMBOURG GARDEN

TO RUE MOUFFETARD

200 YARDS

200 METERS

➤ WALKING TOUR ROUTE

Ⓜ METRO STATION

Ⓡ RER STOP

B BATOBUS BOAT STOP

View

DCH

① Point Zero & Notre-Dame

② Deportation Memorial

③ Ile St. Louis

④ Latin Quarter

⑤ Sainte-Chapelle

⑥ Palais de Justice

⑦ Cité Métro Stop & Flower Market

⑧ Conciergerie

⑨ Pont Neuf

⑩ Center of Paris Plage (Beach)

PARIS

Speaking of decapitation, look at the carving to the left of the doorway on the left. The man with his head in his hands is St. Denis. Back when there was a Roman temple on this spot, Christianity began making converts. The fourth-century bishop of Roman Paris, Denis was beheaded as a warning to those forsaking the Roman gods. But those early Christians were hard to keep down. The man who would become St. Denis got up, tucked his head under his arm, headed north, paused at a fountain to wash it off, and continued until he found just the right place to meet his maker: Montmartre. (Although the name "Montmartre" comes from the Roman "Mount of Mars," later generations—thinking of their beheaded patron, St. Denis—preferred a less pagan version, "Mount of Martyrs.") The Parisians were convinced by this miracle, Christianity gained ground, and a church soon replaced the pagan temple.

Medieval art was OK if it embellished the house of God and told biblical stories. For a good example, move to the base of the central column (at the foot of Mary, about where the head of St. Denis could spit if he were really good). Working around from the left, find God telling a barely created Eve, "Have fun, but no apples." Next, the sexiest serpent I've ever seen makes apples à la mode. Finally, Adam and Eve, now ashamed of their nakedness, are expelled by an angel. This is a tiny example in a church covered with meaning.

Step inside. You'll be routed around the ambulatory, in much the same way medieval pilgrims were. Notre-Dame has the typical basilica floor plan shared by so many Catholic churches: a long central nave lined with columns and flanked by side aisles. It's designed in the shape of a cross, with the altar placed where the crossbeam intersects. The church can hold up to 10,000 faithful, and it's probably buzzing with visitors now, just as it was 600 years ago. The quiet, deserted churches we see elsewhere are in stark contrast to the busy, center-of-life places they were in the Middle Ages. Don't miss the **rose windows** that fill each of the transepts. Just past the altar is the **"choir,"** enclosed with carved-wood walls, where more intimate services can be held in this spacious building. Circle the choir—the back side of the choir walls features **scenes of the resurrected Jesus** (c. 1350). Just ahead on the right is the **Treasury.** It contains lavish robes, golden reliquaries, and the humble tunic of King (and St.) Louis IX, but it probably isn't worth the €3 entry fee.

Back outside, walk around the church through the park on the riverside for a close look at the **flying buttresses.** The Neo-Gothic 300-foot **spire** is a product of the 1860 reconstruction of the dilapidated old church. Around its base (visible as you approach the back end of the church) are apostles and evangelists (the green men) as well as Eugène-Emmanuel Viollet-le-Duc, the architect in charge of the work. The apostles look outward, blessing the city, while the architect (at top) looks up the spire, marveling at his fine work.

Nearby: The **archaeological crypt** is a worthwhile 15-minute stop if you have a Paris Museum Pass (€4 without Museum Pass, Tue-Sun 10:00-18:00, last entry 30 minutes before closing, closed Mon, enter 100 yards in front of cathedral). You'll see remains of the many structures that have stood on this spot in the center of Paris: Roman buildings that surrounded a temple of Jupiter; a wall that didn't keep the Franks out; the main medieval road that once led grandly up the square to Notre-Dame; and even (wow) a 19th-century sewer.

Tower: You can climb to the top of the facade between the towers, and then to the top of the south tower, 400 steps total, for a grand view (€8, covered by Museum Pass but no bypass line for passholders, daily April-Sept 10:00-18:30, June-Aug Sat-Sun until 23:00, Oct-March 10:00-17:30, last entry 45 minutes before closing, arrive before 10:00 or after 17:00 to avoid long lines).

• *Behind Notre-Dame, cross the street and enter through the iron gate into the park at the tip of the island. Look for the stairs and head down to reach the...*

▲Deportation Memorial (Mémorial de la Déportation)

This memorial to the 200,000 French victims of the Nazi concentration camps (1940-1945) draws you into their experience. France was quickly overrun by Nazi Germany, and Paris spent the war years under Nazi occupation. Jews and dissidents were rounded up and deported—many never returned.

As you descend the steps, the city around you disappears. Surrounded by walls, you have become a prisoner. Your only freedom is your view of the sky and the tiny glimpse of the river below.

Enter the dark, single-file chamber up ahead. Inside, the circular plaque in the floor reads, "They went to the end of the earth and did not return." The hallway stretching in front of you is lined with 200,000 lighted crystals, one for each French citizen who died. Flickering at the far end is the eternal flame of hope. The tomb of the unknown deportee lies at your feet. Above, the inscription reads, "Dedicated to the living memory of the 200,000 French deportees sleeping in the night and the fog, exterminated in the Nazi concentration camps." The side rooms are filled with triangles—reminiscent of the identification patches inmates were forced to wear—each bearing the name of a concentration camp. Above the exit as you leave is the message you'll find at many other Holocaust sites: "Forgive, but never forget."

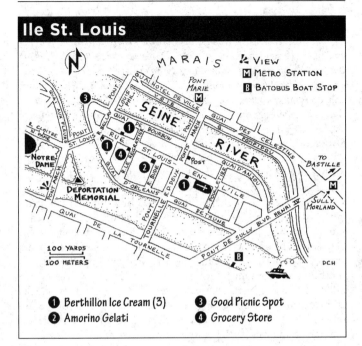

Ile St. Louis

▲ VIEW
M METRO STATION
B BATOBUS BOAT STOP

1 Berthillon Ice Cream (3) **3** Good Picnic Spot
2 Amorino Gelati **4** Grocery Store

Cost and Hours: Free, Tue-Sun April-Sept 10:00-19:00, Oct-March 10:00-18:00, closed Mon year-round, Mo: Cité.

• *Back on street level, look across the river (north) to the island called...*

Ile St. Louis

If the Ile de la Cité is a tug laden with the history of Paris, it's towing this classy little residential dinghy, laden only with high-rent apartments, boutiques, characteristic restaurants (see page 421), and famous ice-cream shops.

This island wasn't developed until much later than the Ile de la Cité (17th century). What was a swampy mess is now harmonious Parisian architecture and one of Paris' most exclusive neighborhoods.

If you won't have time to return here for an evening stroll (see page 374), consider taking a brief detour across the pedestrian bridge. Pont St. Louis connects the two islands, leading right to rue St. Louis-en-l'Ile. This spine of the island is lined with interesting shops and reasonably priced restaurants. A short stroll takes you to the famous Berthillon ice cream parlor at #31 (there are two more—one across the street, and yet another around the corner on rue Bellay). Gelato-lovers head instead to Amorino Gelati at #47. Loop back to the pedestrian bridge along the parklike quays (walk north to the river and turn left). This walk is about as peaceful and

PARIS

romantic as Paris gets.

• *From the Deportation Memorial, cross the bridge onto the Left Bank and enjoy the riverside view of Notre-Dame; window-shopping among the green book stalls; and browsing through used books, vintage posters, and souvenirs. Page through books at the atmospheric* **Shakespeare and Company,** *a reincarnation of the original 1920s shop (37 rue de la Bûcherie), then venture inland a few blocks, basically arcing through the Latin Quarter. Before returning to the island, walk a block behind Shakespeare and Co. and take a spin through the...*

▲Latin Quarter

This area's touristy fame relates to its intriguing, artsy, bohemian character. This was perhaps Europe's leading university district in the Middle Ages, when Latin was the language of higher education. The neighborhood's main boulevards (St. Michel and St. Germain) are lined with cafés—once the haunts of great poets and philosophers, now the hangouts of tired tourists. Though still youthful and artsy, much of this area has become a tourist ghetto filled with cheap North African eateries. Exploring a few blocks up or downriver from here gives you a better chance of feeling the pulse of what survives of Paris' classic Left Bank. For colorful wandering and café-sitting, afternoons and evenings are best.

Walking along rue St. Séverin, you can still see the shadow of the medieval sewer system. The street slopes into a central channel of bricks. In the days before plumbing and toilets, when people still went to the river or neighborhood wells for their water, flushing meant throwing it out the window. At certain times of day, maids on the fourth floor would holler, *"Garde de l'eau!"* ("Watch out for the water!") and heave it into the streets, where it would eventually wash down into the Seine.

Consider a visit to the Cluny Museum for its medieval art and unicorn tapestries (see page 352). The Sorbonne—the University of Paris' humanities department—is also nearby; visitors can ogle the famous dome, but they are not allowed to enter the building (two blocks south of the river on boulevard St. Michel).

This square, place St. Michel (facing the pont St. Michel), is the traditional core of the Left Bank's artsy, liberal, hippie, bohemian district of poets, philosophers, and winos. In less commercial times, place St. Michel was a gathering point for the city's malcontents and misfits. In 1830, 1848, and again in 1871, the citizens took the streets from the government troops, set up barricades *Les Miz*-style, and fought against royalist oppression. During World War II, the locals rose up against their Nazi oppressors (read the plaques under the dragons at the foot of the St. Michel fountain).

In the spring of 1968, a time of social upheaval all over the world, young students battled riot batons and tear gas, took over the square, and declared it an independent state. Factory workers followed their call to arms and went on strike, challenging the de Gaulle government and forcing change. Eventually, the students were pacified, the university was reformed, and the Latin Quarter's original cobblestones were replaced with pavement, so future scholars could never again use the streets as weapons. Even today, whenever there's a student demonstration, it starts here.

• *From place St. Michel, look across the river and find the prickly steeple of the Sainte-Chapelle church. Head toward it. Cross the river on pont St. Michel and continue north along the boulevard du Palais. On your left, you'll see the doorway to Sainte-Chapelle.*

You'll need to pass through a strict security checkpoint to get into the Sainte-Chapelle complex. (This is more than a tourist attraction—France's Supreme Court meets to the right of Sainte-Chapelle.) Bags are screened, and sharp objects (e.g., Swiss Army knives) will be confiscated. Past security, you'll enter the courtyard outside Sainte-Chapelle, where you'll find WCs and information about upcoming church concerts (for concert details, see page 372). The ticket-buying line into the church may be long.

If you have a Museum Pass or a Conciergerie combo-ticket, you may be able to skip some of the security line (look for signs), and can certainly bypass the ticket-buying line. You can also bypass it by buying your ticket or Museum Pass from the tabac *shop across the street from the security entrance.*

Enter the humble ground floor.

▲▲▲Sainte-Chapelle

This triumph of Gothic church architecture is a cathedral of glass like no other. It was speedily built between 1242 and 1248 for King Louis IX—the only French king who is now a saint—to house the supposed Crown of Thorns. Its architectural harmony is due to the fact that it was completed under the direction of one architect and in only five years—unheard of in Gothic times. Recall that Notre-Dame took over 200 years.

Inside, the layout clearly shows an *ancien régime* approach to worship. The low-ceilinged basement was for staff and other common folks—worshipping under a sky filled with painted fleurs-de-lis, a symbol of the king. Royal Christians worshipped upstairs. The paint job, a 19th-century restoration, helps you imagine how grand this small, painted, jeweled chapel was. (Imagine Notre-Dame painted like this...) Each capital is carved with a different plant's leaves.

Climb the spiral staircase to the Chapelle Haute. Fill the place with choral music, crank up the sunshine, face the top of the altar, and really believe that the Crown of Thorns is there, and this becomes one awesome space.

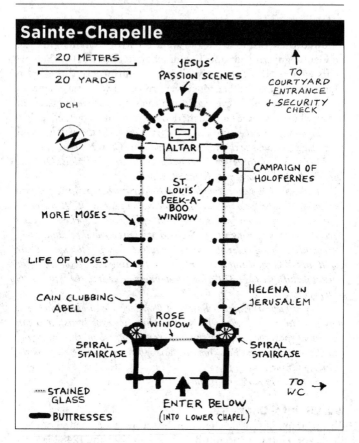

Sainte-Chapelle

20 METERS

20 YARDS

DCH

JESUS' PASSION SCENES

TO COURTYARD ENTRANCE & SECURITY CHECK

ALTAR

CAMPAIGN OF HOLOFERNES

ST. LOUIS' PEEK-A-BOO WINDOW

MORE MOSES

LIFE OF MOSES

CAIN CLUBBING ABEL

HELENA IN JERUSALEM

ROSE WINDOW

SPIRAL STAIRCASE

SPIRAL STAIRCASE

TO WC →

···· STAINED GLASS

━━ BUTTRESSES

ENTER BELOW (INTO LOWER CHAPEL)

Fiat lux. "Let there be light." From the first page of the Bible, it's clear: Light is divine. Light shines through stained glass like God's grace shining down to earth. Gothic architects used their new technology to turn dark stone buildings into lanterns of light. The glory of Gothic shines brighter here than in any other church.

There are 15 separate panels of stained glass (6,500 square feet—two thirds of it 13th-century original), with more than 1,100 different scenes, mostly from the Bible. These cover the entire Christian history of the world, from the Creation in Genesis (first window on the left, as you face the altar), to the coming of Christ (over the altar), to the end of the world (the round "rose"-shaped window at the rear of the church). Each individual scene is interesting, and the whole effect is overwhelming.

The altar was raised up high to better display the Crown of Thorns, the relic around which this chapel was built. The supposed crown cost King Louis three times as much as this church. Today, it is kept by the Notre-Dame Treasury (though it's occasionally brought out for display).

Cost and Hours: €8, €11 combo-ticket with Conciergerie, kids under 18 free, covered by Museum Pass, March-Oct daily 9:00-18:00, possibly Wed in summer until 21:30, Nov-Feb daily 9:00-17:00, last entry 30 minutes before closing, English tours most days at 10:45 and 14:45 and possibly also Wed at 18:30 and 20:00, 4 boulevard du Palais, Mo: Cité.

• *Exit Sainte-Chapelle. Back outside, as you walk around the church exterior, look down to see the foundation and take note of how much Paris has risen in the 750 years since Sainte-Chapelle was built.*

Next door to Sainte-Chapelle is the...

Palais de Justice

Sainte-Chapelle sits within a huge complex of buildings that has housed the local government since ancient Roman times. It was the site of the original Gothic palace of the early kings of France. The only surviving medieval parts are Sainte-Chapelle and the Conciergerie prison.

Most of the site is now covered by the giant Palais de Justice, built in 1776, home of the French Supreme Court. The motto *Liberté, Egalité, Fraternité* over the doors is a reminder that this was also the headquarters of the Revolutionary government. Here they doled out justice, condemning many to imprisonment in the Conciergerie downstairs or to the guillotine.

• *Now pass through the big iron gate to the noisy boulevard du Palais. Cross the street to the wide, pedestrian-only rue de Lutèce and walk about halfway down.*

Cité "Metropolitain" Métro Stop

Of the 141 original early-20th-century subway entrances, this is one of only a few survivors—now preserved as a national art treasure. (New York's Museum of Modern Art even exhibits one.) It marks Paris at its peak in 1900—on the cutting edge of Modernism, but with an eye for beauty. The curvy, plantlike ironwork is a textbook example of Art Nouveau, the style that rebelled against the erector-set squareness of the Industrial Age. Other similar Métro stations in Paris are Abbesses and Porte Dauphine.

The flower and plant market on place Louis Lépine is a pleasant detour. On Sundays this square flutters with a busy bird market. And across the way is the Préfecture de Police, where Inspector Clouseau of *Pink Panther* fame used to work, and where the local resistance fighters took the first building from the Nazis in August of 1944, leading to the Allied liberation of Paris a week later.

• *Pause here to admire the view. Sainte-Chapelle is a pearl in an ugly architectural oyster. Double back to the Palais de Justice, turn right onto boulevard du Palais, and enter the...*

▲Conciergerie

Though pretty barren inside, this former prison echoes with history (and is free with the Museum Pass—remember that pass-holders can skip any ticket-buying lines). Positioned next to the courthouse, the Conciergerie was the gloomy prison famous as the last stop for 2,780 victims of the guillotine, including France's last *ancien régime* queen, Marie-Antoinette. Before then, kings had used the building to torture and execute failed assassins. (One of its towers along the river was called "The Babbler," named for the pain-induced sounds that leaked from it.) When the Revolution (1789) toppled the king, the building kept its same function, but without the torture. The progressive Revolutionaries proudly unveiled a modern and more humane way to execute people—the guillotine.

Inside, pick up a free map and breeze through. See the spacious, low-ceilinged Hall of Men-at-Arms (Room 1), used as the guards' dining room, with four large fireplaces (look up the chimneys). This big room gives a feel for the grandeur of the Great Hall (upstairs, not open to visitors), where the Revolutionary tribunals grilled scared prisoners on their political correctness. You'll also see a re-creation of Marie-Antoinette's cell, which houses a collection of her mementos. In another room, a list of those made "a foot shorter at the top" by the "national razor" includes ex-King Louis XVI, Charlotte Corday (who murdered the Revolutionary writer Jean-Paul Marat in his bathtub), and—oh, the irony—Maximilien de Robespierre, the head of the Revolution, the man who sent so many to the guillotine.

Cost and Hours: €7, €11 combo-ticket with Sainte-Chapelle, covered by Museum Pass, daily March-Oct 9:30-18:00, Nov-Feb 9:00-17:00, last entry 30 minutes before closing, 4 boulevard du Palais, Mo: Cité, tel. 01 53 40 60 97, www.monum.fr.

• *Back outside, turn left on boulevard du Palais and head north. On the corner is the city's oldest public clock. The mechanism of the present clock is from 1334, and even though the case is Baroque, it keeps on ticking.*

Turn left onto quai de l'Horloge and walk west along the river, past the "Babbler" tower. The bridge up ahead is the pont Neuf, where we'll end this walk. At the first corner, veer left into a sleepy triangular square called place Dauphine. Marvel at how such coziness could be lodged in the midst of such greatness. At the equestrian statue of Henry IV, turn right onto the old bridge and take refuge in one of the nooks on the Eiffel Tower side; or continue through the park to the end of the island (the departure point for Seine river cruises offered by Vedettes du Pont Neuf, described under "By Boat" on page 316).

Pont Neuf

This "New Bridge" is now Paris' oldest. Built during Henry IV's reign (about 1600), its arches span the widest part of the river. Unlike other bridges, this one never had houses or buildings growing on it. The turrets were originally for vendors and street entertainers. In the days of Henry IV, who promised his peasants "a chicken in every pot every Sunday," this would have been a lively scene. From the bridge, look downstream (west) to see the next bridge, the pedestrian-only pont des Arts. Ahead on the Right Bank is the long Louvre Museum. Beyond that, on the Left Bank, is the Orsay. And what's that tall black tower in the distance?

• *As for now, you can tour the Seine by boat, continue to the Louvre, or (if it's summer) head to the...*

Paris Plage (Beach)

The Riviera it's not, but this fanciful faux beach—assembled in summer along a two-mile stretch of the Seine on the Right Bank—is a fun place to stroll, play, and people-watch on a sunny day. Each summer since 2002, the Paris city government has closed the embankment's highway and trucked in potted palm trees, hammocks, lounge chairs, and 2,000 tons of sand to create a colorful urban beach. You'll also find "beach cafés," climbing walls, prefab pools, trampolines, *boules,* a library, beach volleyball, badminton, and Frisbee.

Cost and Hours: Free, mid-July-mid-Aug daily 7:00-24:00, no beach off-season; on Right Bank of Seine, just north of Ile de la Cité, between pont des Arts and pont de Sully.

Sights in Paris

Paris Museum Pass

In Paris there are two classes of sightseers—those with a Paris Museum Pass, and those who stand in line. The pass admits you to many of Paris' most popular sights, allowing you to skip ticket-buying lines. Serious sightseers save time and money by getting this pass.

Buying the Pass

The pass pays for itself with four key admissions in two days (for example, the Louvre, Orsay, Sainte-Chapelle, and Versailles), and lets you skip the ticket line at most sights (2 days/€32, 4 days/€48, 6 days/€64, no youth or senior discount). It's sold at participating museums, monuments, FNAC department stores, and TIs (even at airports; see "Paris Connections," near the end of this chapter). Try to avoid buying the pass at a major museum (such as the Louvre), where the supply can be spotty and lines long. For more info, visit

Paris Sights

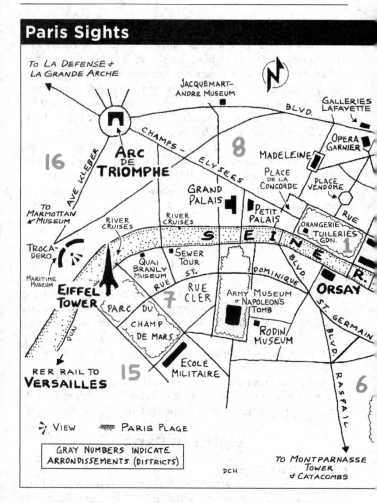

To La Défense & La Grande Arche

JACQUEMART-ANDRE MUSEUM

BLVD.

GALLERIES LAFAYETTE

OPERA GARNIER

MADELEINE

CHAMPS - ELYSEES

8

16

AVE KLEBER

ARC DE TRIOMPHE

To MARMOTTAN MUSEUM

GRAND PALAIS

PLACE DE LA CONCORDE

PLACE VENDOME

RUE

ORANGERIE TUILERIES GDN.

PETIT PALAIS

SEINE

1

RIVER CRUISES

RIVER CRUISES

TROCA-DERO

MARITIME MUSEUM

SEWER TOUR

QUAI BRANLY MUSEUM

ST.

RUE

RUE CLER

ARMY MUSEUM & NAPOLEON'S TOMB

DOMINIQUE

BLVD.

ST. GERMAIN

ORSAY

R

EIFFEL TOWER

PARC DU CHAMP DE MARS

7

RODIN MUSEUM

QUAI

RER RAIL TO VERSAILLES

15

ECOLE MILITAIRE

BLVD. RASPAIL

6

VIEW

PARIS PLAGE

GRAY NUMBERS INDICATE ARRONDISSEMENTS (DISTRICTS)

DCH

To MONTPARNASSE TOWER & CATACOMBS

www.parismuseumpass.com or call 01 44 61 96 60.

Tally up what you want to see from the list on page 334—and remember, an advantage of the pass is that you skip to the front of most lines, which can save you hours of waiting, especially in summer. At a few sights (including the Louvre, Sainte-Chapelle, Notre-Dame's tower, and the Château de Versailles), everyone has to shuffle through the slow-moving baggage-check lines for security—but you still save time by avoiding the ticket line.

Families: The pass isn't worth buying for children and teens, as most museums are free or discounted for those under 18 (teen-agers may need to show ID as proof of age). Kids can usually skip ticket lines if you have a Museum Pass, although a few places (such as the Arc de Triomphe and Army Museum) require you to stand

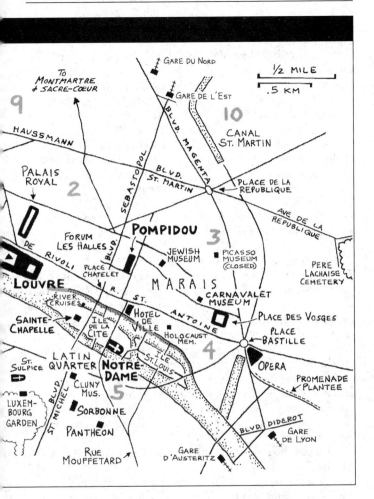

in line to collect your child's free ticket. Of the few museums that charge for children, some allow kids in for free if their parents have a Museum Pass, whereas others charge admission, depending on age (the cutoff age varies from 5 to 18). The free directory that comes with your pass lists the current hours of sights, phone numbers, and the price that kids pay.

What the Paris Museum Pass Covers

Most of the sights listed in this chapter are covered by the pass. Notable exceptions are the Eiffel Tower, Montparnasse Tower, Marmottan Museum, Opéra Garnier, Notre-Dame Treasury, Jacquemart-André Museum, Grand Palais, La Grande Arche at La Défense, Catacombs, Montmartre Museum, Sacré-Cœur's

dome, Dalí Museum, Museum of Erotic Art, and the ladies of
Pigalle.

Here's a list of some of the included sights and their admission
prices without the pass:

Louvre (€10)	Notre-Dame Tower (€8)
Orsay Museum (€8)	Paris Archaeological Crypt (€4)
Orangerie Museum (€7.50)	Paris Sewer Tour (€4.30)
Sainte-Chapelle (€8)	Cluny Museum (€8)
Arc de Triomphe (€9.50)	Pompidou Center (€10-12)
Rodin Museum (€6)	Jewish Art and History Museum (€7)
Army Museum (€9)	National Maritime Museum (€7)
Conciergerie (€7)	Delacroix Museum (€5)
Panthéon (€8)	Quai Branly Museum (€8.50)

Versailles (€25 total—€15 for Château, €10 for Trianon Palaces
and Domaine de Marie-Antoinette)

Activating and Using the Pass

Think ahead to make the most of your pass. Validate it only when
you're ready to tackle the covered sights on consecutive days. Make
sure the sights you want to visit will be open (many museums are
closed Mondays or Tuesdays). The Paris Museum Pass even covers most of Versailles (your other option for Versailles is the Le
Passeport pass; described on page 439). Keep in mind that sights
such as the Arc de Triomphe and Pompidou Center are open later
in the evening, and that the Louvre and Orsay have late hours on
selected evenings, allowing you to stretch the day for your Paris
Museum Pass. On days that you don't have pass coverage, visit free
sights as well as those not covered by the pass (see page 316 for a
list of free sights).

The pass isn't activated until the first time you use it (write the
starting date on the pass).

To use your pass at sights, boldly walk to the front of the ticket
line (after passing security, if necessary), hold up your pass, and
ask the ticket-taker: *"Entrez, pass?"* (ahn-tray pahs). You'll either
be allowed to enter at that point or you'll be directed to a special
entrance. For major sights, such as the Louvre and Orsay museums,
I've identified passholder entrances on the maps in this chapter.

With the pass you can pop into sights as you're walking by
(even for a few minutes) that otherwise might not be worth the
expense (e.g., the Conciergerie or Paris Archaeological Crypt).

Major Museums Neighborhood

Paris' grandest park, the Tuileries Garden, was once the private
property of kings and queens. Today it links the Louvre, Orangerie,
Jeu de Paume, and Orsay museums. And across from the Louvre
are the tranquil, historic courtyards of the Palais Royal.

Major Museums Neighborhood

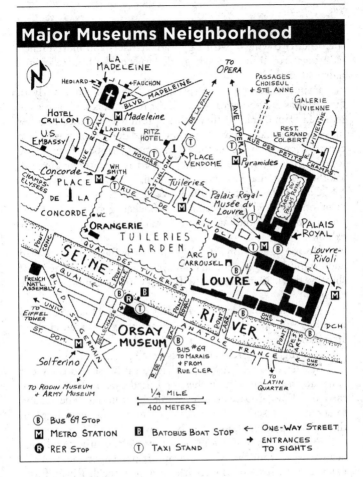

B Bus #69 Stop
M Metro Station
R RER Stop
B Batobus Boat Stop
T Taxi Stand
← One-Way Street
→ Entrances to Sights

▲▲▲Louvre (Musée du Louvre)

This is Europe's oldest, biggest, greatest, and second-most-crowded museum (after the Vatican). Housed in a U-shaped, 16th-century palace (accentuated by a 20th-century glass pyramid), the Louvre is Paris' top museum and one of its key landmarks. It's home to *Mona Lisa, Venus de Milo,* and hall after hall of Greek and Roman masterpieces, medieval jewels, Michelangelo statues, and paintings by the greatest artists from the Renaissance to the Romantics (mid-1800s).

Touring the Louvre can be overwhelming, so be selective. Focus on the Denon wing (south, along the river), with Greek sculptures, Italian paintings (by Raphael and da Vinci), and—of course—French paintings (Neoclassical and Romantic). For extra credit, tackle the Richelieu wing (north, away from the river), displaying works from ancient Mesopotamia (today's Iraq), as well as

PARIS

French, Dutch, and Northern art; or the Sully wing (connecting the other two wings), with Egyptian artifacts and more French paintings. You'll find my self-guided tour of the Louvre's highlights on page 338.

Expect Changes: The sprawling Louvre is constantly in flux. Rooms are periodically closed for renovation, and pieces are removed from display if they're being restored or loaned to other museums. Several collections may be closed during your visit while construction continues on the exciting new Islamic art wing, due to open sometime in 2012. To find the artwork you're looking for, ask the nearest guard for its new location.

Cost: €10, €6 after 18:00 on Wed and Fri, free on first Sun of month, covered by Museum Pass. Tickets good all day; reentry allowed. Optional additional charges apply for temporary exhibits.

Hours: Wed-Mon 9:00-18:00, most wings stay open Wed and Fri until 21:45 (except on holidays), closed Tue. Galleries start shutting down 30 minutes early. The last entry is 45 minutes before closing.

When to Go: Crowds are worst on Sun, Mon, Wed, and mornings. Evening visits are peaceful, and the glass pyramid glows after dark.

Getting There: You have a variety of options:

By Métro: The Métro stop Palais Royal-Musée du Louvre is closer to the entrance than the stop called Louvre-Rivoli. From the Palais Royal-Musée du Louvre stop, you can stay underground to enter the museum, or exit above ground if you want to go in through the pyramid (more details below).

By Bus: Handy bus #69 runs every 10-20 minutes. Buses headed west from the Marais drop off passengers next to the Palais Royal-Musée du Louvre Métro stop on rue de Rivoli. Buses headed east from rue Cler drop off along the Seine River (at quai François Mitterand).

By Taxi: You'll find a taxi stand on rue de Rivoli, next to the Palais Royal-Musée du Louvre Métro station.

Getting In: Enter through the pyramid, or opt for shorter lines elsewhere.

Main Pyramid Entrance: There is no grander entry than through the main entrance at the pyramid in the central courtyard, but metal detectors (not ticket-buyers) can create a long line.

Museum Pass/Group Entrance: Museum Pass-holders can use the group entrance in the pedestrian passageway (labeled *Pavilion Richelieu*) between the pyramid and rue de Rivoli. It's under the arches, a few steps north of the pyramid; find the uniformed guard at the security checkpoint entrance, at the down escalator.

Underground Mall Entrance: You can enter the Louvre from

The Louvre

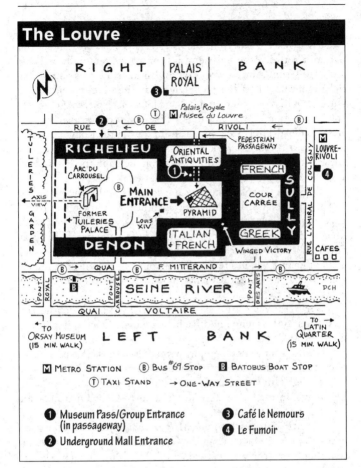

RIGHT BANK

PALAIS ROYAL
❸

Palais Royale
Ⓜ Musée du Louvre
Ⓣ
❷ Ⓑ
RUE DE RIVOLI Ⓑ
←
Ⓜ LOUVRE-RIVOLI

PEDESTRIAN PASSAGEWAY

RICHELIEU
ORIENTAL ANTIQUITIES ❶
FRENCH

ARC DU CARROUSEL
Ⓑ MAIN ENTRANCE →
COUR CARREE
S U L L Y
❹

TUILERIES GARDEN
AXIS VIEW
PYRAMID

FORMER TUILERIES PALACE
Louis XIV
ITALIAN & FRENCH
GREEK
RUE L'AMIRAL DE COLIGNY

DENON
WINGED VICTORY
CAFES

QUAI
Ⓑ → F. MITTERAND Ⓑ Ⓑ
PONT ROYAL
Ⓑ
PONT CARROUSEL
SEINE RIVER
PONT DES ARTS
PCH

QUAI VOLTAIRE

TO ORSAY MUSEUM (15 MIN. WALK)
LEFT BANK
TO LATIN QUARTER (15 MIN. WALK)

Ⓜ METRO STATION   Ⓑ BUS #69 STOP   Ⓑ BATOBUS BOAT STOP
Ⓣ TAXI STAND   → ONE-WAY STREET

❶ Museum Pass/Group Entrance (in passageway)
❷ Underground Mall Entrance
❸ Café le Nemours
❹ Le Fumoir

its less crowded underground entrance, accessed through the Carrousel du Louvre shopping mall. Enter the mall at 99 rue de Rivoli (the door with the red awning) or directly from the Métro stop Palais Royal-Musée du Louvre (stepping off the train, exit at the end of the platform, following signs to *Musée du Louvre-Le Carrousel du Louvre*). Museum Pass-holders can skip to the head of the underground-mall security line.

Information: Pick up the free *Plan/Information* in English at the information desk under the pyramid as you enter. Tel. 01 40 20 53 17, recorded info tel. 01 40 20 51 51, www.louvre.fr.

Buying Tickets: Located under the pyramid, the self-serve ticket machines are faster to use than the ticket windows (machines accept euro notes, coins, and Visa cards). The *tabac* in the underground mall at the Louvre sells tickets to the Louvre, Orsay, and Versailles, plus Museum Passes, for no extra charge.

Tours: Ninety-minute English-language **guided tours** leave twice daily except Sun from the *Accueil des Groupes* area, under the pyramid between the Sully and Denon wings (normally at 11:00 and 14:00, sometimes more often in summer; €5 plus your entry ticket, tour tel. 01 40 20 52 63). Digital **audioguides** provide eager students with commentary on about 130 masterpieces (€6, available at entries to the three wings, at the top of the escalators). You can download a free Rick Steves **audio tour** of the Louvre for your mobile device via www.ricksteves.com/audioeurope, iTunes, or the Rick Steves Audio Europe smartphone app. You'll also find English explanations throughout the museum.

Baggage Check: The free *Bagagerie* is under the pyramid, to the right of the Denon wing entrance. Large bags must be checked, and you can also check small bags to lighten your load. They will not take coats unless they're stuffed into bags. (The coat check, or *Vestiaire*, is near the Richelieu wing.) The baggage-claim clerk might ask you in French, "Does your bag contain anything of value?" You can't check cameras, money, passports, or other valuables.

Services: WCs are located under the pyramid, behind the escalators to the Denon and Richelieu wings. Once you're in the galleries, WCs are scarce.

Photography: Photography without a flash is allowed. (Flash photography damages paintings and distracts viewers.)

➲ Self-Guided Tour: Start in the Denon Wing and visit the highlights, in the following order (thanks to Gene Openshaw for his help writing this tour).

Find the famous *Venus de Milo (Aphrodite)* statue. This goddess of love (c. 100 B.C., from the Greek island of Melos) created a sensation when she was discovered in 1820. Most "Greek" statues are actually later Roman copies, but *Venus* is a rare Greek original. She, like Golden Age Greeks, epitomizes stability, beauty, and balance. After viewing *Venus,* wander through the **ancient Greek and Roman works** to see the Parthenon frieze (stone fragments that once decorated the exterior of the greatest Athenian temple), mosaics from Pompeii, Etruscan sarcophagi, and Roman portrait busts.

Later Greek art was Hellenistic, adding motion and drama. For a good example, see the exciting *Winged Victory of Samothrace* (*Victoire de Samothrace,* on the landing). This statue of a woman with wings, poised on the prow of a ship, once stood on a hilltop to commemorate a naval victory. This is the *Venus de Milo* gone Hellenistic.

The **Italian collection** is on the other side of the *Winged Victory* in the Grand Gallery. In painting, the Renaissance meant realism, and for the Italians, realism was spelled "3-D." Painters

PARIS

were inspired by the realism and balanced beauty of Greek sculpture. Painting a 3-D world on a 2-D surface is tough, and after a millennium of Dark Ages, artists were rusty. Living in a religious age, they painted mostly altarpieces full of saints, angels, Madonnas-and-bambinos, and crucifixes floating in an ethereal gold-leaf heaven. Gradually, though, they brought these otherworldly scenes down to earth. (The Italian collection—including the *Mona Lisa*—is scattered throughout the rooms of the long Grand Gallery—look for **two Botticelli frescoes** as you enter.)

Two masters of the Italian High Renaissance (1500-1600) were Raphael (see his *La Belle Jardinière*, showing the Madonna, Child, and John the Baptist) and Leonardo da Vinci. The Louvre has the greatest collection of Leonardos in the world—five of them, including the exquisite *Virgin, Child, and St. Anne*; the neighboring *Virgin of the Rocks*; and the androgynous *John the Baptist*. His most famous, of course, is the *Mona Lisa*.

The ***Mona Lisa*** (*La Joconde* in French) is in the Salle des Etats, midway down the Grand Gallery, on the right. After several years and a €5 million renovation, Mona is alone behind glass on her own false wall.

Leonardo was already an old man when François I invited him to France. Determined to pack light, he took only a few paintings with him. One was a portrait of a Lisa del Giocondo, the wife of a wealthy Florentine merchant. When Leonardo arrived, François immediately fell in love with the painting, making it the centerpiece of the small collection of Italian masterpieces that would, in three centuries, become the Louvre museum. He called it *La Gioconda (La Joconde* in French)—both her last name and a play on the Italian word for "happy woman." We know it as a contraction of the Italian for "my lady Lisa"—*Mona Lisa*. Warning: François was impressed, but *Mona* may disappoint you. She's smaller than you'd expect, darker, engulfed in a huge room, and hidden behind a glaring pane of glass.

The overall mood is one of balance and serenity, but there's also an element of mystery. *Mona's* smile and long-distance beauty are subtle and elusive, tempting but always just out of reach, like strands of a street singer's melody drifting through the Métro tunnel. *Mona* doesn't knock your socks off, but she winks at the patient viewer.

The huge canvas opposite *Mona* is Paolo Veronese's ***The Marriage at Cana***, showing the Renaissance love of beautiful things gone hog-wild. Venetian artists like Veronese painted the good life of rich, happy-go-lucky Venetian merchants.

Now for something **Neoclassical.** Exit behind *Mona Lisa* and turn right into the Salle Daru to find *The Coronation of Napoleon* by Jacques-Louis David. Neoclassicism, once the rage in France

(1780-1850), usually features Greek subjects, patriotic sentiment, and a clean, simple style. After Napoleon quickly conquered most of Europe, he insisted on being made emperor (not merely king) of this "New Rome." He staged an elaborate coronation ceremony in Paris, and rather than let the pope crown him, he crowned himself. The setting was Notre-Dame Cathedral, with Greek columns and Roman arches thrown in for effect. Napoleon's mom was also added, because she couldn't make it to the ceremony. A key on the frame describes who's who in the picture.

The **Romantic** collection, in an adjacent room (Salle Mollien), has works by Théodore Géricault (*The Raft of the Medusa*—one of my favorites) and Eugène Delacroix *(Liberty Leading the People).* Romanticism, with an emphasis on motion and emotion, is the flip side of cool, balanced Neoclassicism, though they both flourished in the early 1800s. Delacroix's *Liberty,* commemorating the stirrings of democracy in France, is also a fitting tribute to the Louvre, the first museum ever opened to the common rabble of humanity. The good things in life don't belong only to a small, wealthy part of society, but to everyone. The motto of France is *Liberté, Egalité, Fraternité*—liberty, equality, and the brotherhood of all.

Exit the room at the far end (past the Café Mollien) and go downstairs, where you'll bump into the bum of a large, twisting male nude looking like he's just waking up after a thousand-year nap. The two *Slaves* (1513-1515) by Michelangelo are a fitting end to this museum—works that bridge the ancient and modern worlds. Michelangelo, like his fellow Renaissance artists, learned from the Greeks. The perfect anatomy, twisting poses, and idealized faces appear as if they could have been created 2,000 years earlier. Michelangelo said that his purpose was to carve away the marble to reveal the figures God put inside. The *Rebellious Slave,* fighting against his bondage, shows the agony of that process and the ecstasy of the result.

Although this makes for a good first tour, there's so much more. After a break (or on a second visit), consider a stroll through a few rooms of the Richelieu wing, which contain some of the Louvre's oldest and biggest pieces. Bible students, amateur archaeologists, and Iraq War vets may find the collection especially interesting.

Palais Royal Courtyards

Across from the Louvre are the lovely courtyards of the stately Palais Royal. Although the palace is closed to the public, the courtyards are open. Enter through a whimsical (locals say tacky) courtyard filled with stubby, striped columns and playful fountains (with fun, reflective metal balls). Next, you'll pass into another, perfectly Parisian garden. This is where in-the-know Parisians come to take a quiet break, walk their poodles and kids, or enjoy a rendezvous—amid flowers and surrounded by a serene arcade and a handful of historic restaurants. Bring a picnic and create your own quiet break, or have a drink at one of the outdoor cafés at the courtyard's northern end. This is Paris.

Exiting the courtyard at the side facing away from the Seine brings you to the Galeries Colbert and Vivienne, good examples of shopping arcades from the early 1900s and worth a look.

Cost and Hours: Courtyards are free and always open. The Palais Royal is directly north of the Louvre on rue de Rivoli (Mo: Palais Royal-Musée du Louvre).

▲▲Orangerie Museum (Musée de l'Orangerie)

Step out of the tree-lined, sun-dappled Impressionist painting that is the Tuileries Garden, and into the Orangerie (oh-rahn-zheh-ree), a little bijou of select works by Claude Monet and his contemporaries. You'll start with the museum's claim to fame: Monet's water lilies. These eight mammoth-scale paintings are displayed exactly as Monet intended them—surrounding you in oval-shaped rooms—so you feel as though you're immersed in his garden at Giverny. Working from his home there, Monet built a special studio with skylights and wheeled easels to accommodate the canvases—1,950 square feet in all. Each canvas features a different part of the pond, painted from varying angles at distinct times of day—but the true subject of these works is the play of reflected light off the surface of the pond. Downstairs you'll find a tight selection of works by Utrillo, Cézanne, Renoir, Matisse, and Picasso. Together they provide a snapshot of what was hot in the world of art, circa 1920.

Cost and Hours: €7.50, mandatory temporary exhibitions may raise price, €13 combo-ticket with Orsay Museum valid four days (one visit per sight), under 18 free, covered by Museum Pass, audioguide-€5, Wed-Mon 9:00-18:00, closed Tue, located in Tuileries Garden near place de la Concorde, Mo: Concorde. Tel. 01 44 77 80 07, www.musee-orangerie.fr.

▲▲▲Orsay Museum (Musée d'Orsay)

The Musée d'Orsay (mew-zay dor-say) houses French art of the 1800s and early 1900s (specifically, 1848-1914), picking up where the Louvre's art collection leaves off. For us, that means Impressionism, the art of sun-dappled fields, bright colors, and crowded Parisian cafés. The Orsay houses the best general collection anywhere of Manet, Monet, Renoir, Degas, Van Gogh, Cézanne, and Gauguin.

The museum shows art that is also both old and new, conservative and revolutionary. The most important part of the

Orsay Museum—Ground Floor

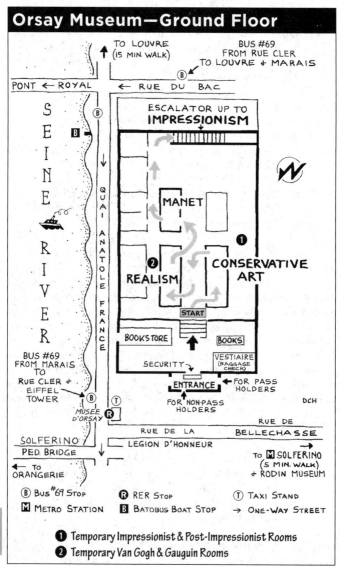

TO LOUVRE (15 MIN. WALK)

BUS #69 FROM RUE CLER TO LOUVRE & MARAIS

Ⓑ

PONT ← ROYAL   ← RUE DU BAC

SEINE RIVER

QUAI ANATOLE FRANCE

Ⓑ
Ⓑ

ESCALATOR UP TO **IMPRESSIONISM**

MANET

❶ CONSERVATIVE ART

❷ REALISM

START

BOOKSTORE   BOOKS

SECURITY   VESTIAIRE (BAGGAGE CHECK)

ENTRANCE ← FOR PASS HOLDERS

FOR NON-PASS HOLDERS

BUS #69 FROM MARAIS TO RUE CLER & EIFFEL TOWER

Ⓑ Ⓣ
Ⓡ
MUSÉE D'ORSAY

DCH

RUE DE LA   RUE DE BELLECHASSE

SOLFERINO PED. BRIDGE

LEGION D'HONNEUR

← TO ORANGERIE

TO Ⓜ SOLFERINO (5 MIN. WALK) & RODIN MUSEUM

Ⓑ Bus #69 Stop   Ⓡ RER Stop   Ⓣ Taxi Stand
Ⓜ Metro Station   Ⓑ Batobus Boat Stop   → One-Way Street

❶ Temporary Impressionist & Post-Impressionist Rooms
❷ Temporary Van Gogh & Gauguin Rooms

museum—the Impressionist collection on the top floor—may be closed for renovation when you visit. During the construction, some Impressionist works are on display on other levels (pick up a free English floor plan upon entering).

In general, the ground floor holds the Conservatives and the early rebels (like Manet and Gustave Courbet) who paved the way for the Impressionists. Here, sappy soft-focus Venuses (popular with the 18th-century bourgeoisie) are displayed alongside the grittier work of the Realists. The museum's Impressionist collection, whether you find it on the top floor or scattered throughout the museum, has many pictures you've probably seen in books, such as Renoir's *Dance at the Moulin de la Galette,* Monet's *Cathedral of Rouen,* Degas' *The Dance Class,* James Abbott McNeill Whistler's *Portrait of the Artist's Mother,* Van Gogh's *The Church at Auvers-sur-Oise,* Cézanne's *The Card Players,* and Henri de Toulouse-Lautrec's *Jane Avril Dancing.* You'll also see Primitive works by Gauguin and Henri Rousseau. As you approach these beautiful, easy-to-enjoy paintings, remember that there is more to this art than meets the eye.

Background: Here's a primer on Impressionism: After the camera was invented, it threatened to make pictoral artists obsolete. A painter's original function was to record reality faithfully, like a journalist. Now a machine could capture a better likeness faster than you could say "Etch-a-Sketch."

But true art is more than just painting reality. It gives us reality from the artist's point of view, with the artist's personal impressions of the scene. Impressions are often fleeting, so you have to work quickly.

The Impressionist painters rejected camera-like detail for a quick style more suited to capturing the passing moment. Feeling stifled by the rigid rules and stuffy atmosphere of the Academy, the Impressionists took as their motto, "Out of the studio, into the open air." They grabbed their berets and scarves and went on excursions to the country, where they set up their easels (and newly invented tubes of premixed paint) on riverbanks and hillsides, or they sketched in cafés and dance halls. Gods, goddesses, nymphs, and fantasy scenes were out; common people and rural landscapes were in.

The quick style and everyday subjects were ridiculed and called childish by the "experts." Rejected by the Salon (where works were displayed to the buying public), the Impressionists staged their own exhibition in 1874. They brashly took their name from an insult thrown at them by a critic who laughed at one of Monet's "impressions" of a sunrise. During the next decade, they exhibited their own work independently. The public, opposed at first, was slowly won over by the simplicity, the color, and the vibrancy of Impressionist art.

Cost: €8, €5.50 Fri-Wed after 16:15 and Thu after 18:00, free first Sun of month, covered by Museum Pass. Tickets are good all day. Combo-tickets are available with the Orangerie Museum (€13, valid four days) or Rodin Museum (€12, valid same day).

Hours: Tue-Sun 9:30-18:00, Thu until 21:45, closed Mon, last entry one hour before closing (45 minutes before on Thu). When open, the top-floor Impressionist galleries begin closing 45 minutes early, frustrating unwary visitors. Tuesdays are particularly crowded, because the Louvre is closed.

Free Entry near Closing Time: Right when the ticket booth stops selling tickets, you're welcome to scoot in free of charge (Tue-Wed and Fri-Sun at 17:00, Thu at 21:00; they won't let you in much after that, however). Make a beeline for the Impressionist galleries (if they're open), which start shutting down first.

Renovation: The Orsay's top-floor Impressionist and Post-Impressionist rooms may be closed for renovation during your visit. Until at least late 2011, some paintings are in storage or on loan. Fortunately, most are temporarily displayed on the ground floor. After the reopening, the Impressionist art will likely return to the top floor, but some Post-Impressionist art may be moved downstairs to the second level. Regardless of when you visit, you'll see most of the Orsay's masterpieces.

Getting There: The museum sits above the RER-C stop called Musée d'Orsay. The nearest Métro stop is Solférino, three blocks southeast of the Orsay. Bus #69 from the Marais neighborhood stops at the museum on the river side (quai Anatole France); from the rue Cler area, it stops behind the museum on the rue du Bac. From the Louvre, catch bus #69 along rue de Rivoli; otherwise, it's a lovely 15-minute walk through the Tuileries Garden and across the river on the pedestrian bridge. The museum is at 1 rue de la Légion d'Honneur. A taxi stand is in front of the entrance on quai Anatole France. The Batobus boat also makes a stop here (see page 317).

Getting In: The ticket-buying line can be long, but if you have a Museum Pass or advance ticket, you can waltz right in (tickets can be purchased in person at FNAC department stores and TIs, or online for pick-up in Paris; for options and fees, see the Orsay website, www.musee-orsay.fr). As you face the front of the museum from rue de la Légion d'Honneur (with the river on your left), passholders and ticket-holders enter on the right side of the museum (Entrance C). Ticket-purchasers enter closer to the river (Entrance A).

Information: The booth inside the entrance provides free floor plans in English that can help you navigate the museum while it's under renovation. Tel. 01 40 49 48 14, www.musee-orsay.fr.

Tours: Audioguides cost €6. English guided tours usually run daily (except Sun) at 11:30 (€7.50/1.5 hours). Occasionally, some tours are offered at other times (inquire when you arrive). You can download a free Rick Steves audio tour of the Orsay for your mobile device via www.ricksteves.com/audioeurope, iTunes, or the Rick Steves Audio Europe smartphone app.

Cloakroom *(Vestiaire):* Checking bags or coats is free. Day bags (but nothing big) are allowed in the museum. No valuables can be stored in checked bags. The cloakroom clerk might ask you in French not to check cameras, passports, or anything particularly precious.

Photography: Photography is forbidden.

Cuisine Art: A pricey but *très* elegant restaurant is on the second floor, with affordable tea and coffee served 14:45-17:30 (daily except Thu). A fifth-floor café is sandwiched between the Impressionists.

Eiffel Tower and Nearby

▲▲▲**Eiffel Tower (La Tour Eiffel)**—It's crowded, expensive, and there are probably better views in Paris, but this 1,000-foot-tall ornament is worth the trouble. Visitors to Paris may find *Mona Lisa* to be less than expected, but the Eiffel Tower rarely disappoints, even in an era of skyscrapers.

Built a hundred years after the French Revolution (and in the midst of an industrial one), the tower served no function but to impress. In 1889, the first visitor to Paris' Universal Exposition walked beneath the "arch" formed by the newly built Eiffel Tower and entered the fair grounds. The World's Fair celebrated both the centennial of the French Revolution and France's position as a global superpower. Bridge-builder Gustave Eiffel (1832-1923) won the contest to build the fair's centerpiece by beating out such rival proposals as a giant guillotine.

To a generation hooked on technology, the tower was the marvel of the age, a symbol of progress and human ingenuity. Not all were so impressed, however; many found it a monstrosity. Writer Guy de Maupassant (1850-1893) routinely ate lunch in the tower just so he wouldn't have to look at it.

Delicate and graceful when seen from afar, the Eiffel Tower is massive—even a bit scary—close up. You don't appreciate its size until you walk toward it; like a mountain, it seems so close but takes forever to reach. But despite the tower's 7,300 tons of metal and 60 tons of paint, it is so well-engineered that it weighs no more per square inch at its base than a linebacker on tiptoes.

There are three observation platforms, at 200, 400, and 900 feet. (The higher you go, the more you pay.) To get to the top, you need to take two different elevators. The first takes you to the second level. (You must bypass the first level on the way up and see it on the way back down.) A separate elevator—with another line—shuttles between the second and third levels. Although being on the windy top of the Eiffel Tower is a thrill you'll never forget, the view is better from the second level, where you can actually see Paris' monuments. Budget three hours to wait in line, get to the top, and sightsee your way back down. With online reservations

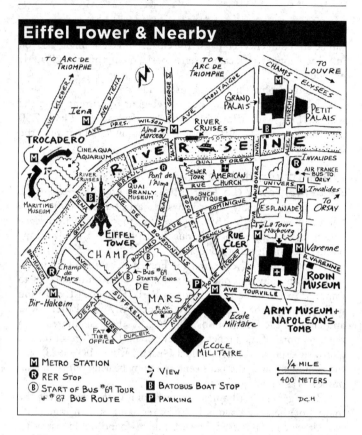

Eiffel Tower & Nearby

and/or no crowds, figure 1.5 hours to the top and back (with time for sightseeing).

The stairs—yes, you can walk up to the first and second levels—are next to the entrance to the pricey Jules Verne restaurant. As you ascend through the metal beams, imagine being a worker, perched high above nothing, riveting this thing together.

The **top level,** called *le sommet*, is tiny. (It can close temporarily without warning when it reaches capacity.) All you'll find here are wind and grand, sweeping views. The city lies before you, with a panorama guide. On a good day, you can see for 40 miles.

The **second level** (400 feet) has the best views because you're closer to the sights, and the monuments are more recognizable. (The best views are up the short stairway, on the platform without the wire-cage barriers.) This level has souvenir shops, public telephones to call home, and a small stand-up café. Although you won't save money, consider taking the elevator up and the stairs down (five minutes from second level to first, five minutes more to ground) for good exercise and views.

The **first level** (200 feet) has more great views, all well-described by the tower's panorama displays. There are a number of photo exhibits on the tower's history, WCs, a conference hall (closed to tourists), an ATM, and souvenirs. A small café sells pizza and sandwiches (outdoor tables in summer). The 58 Tour Eiffel restaurant (listed on page 411) has more *accessible* prices than the Jules Verne Restaurant, and also is run by Alain Ducasse (for Jules Verne, allow €200/person for dinner or weekend lunch at the restaurant, €85 for weekday lunch, reserve three months in advance). In winter, part of the first level is set up for winter activities (most recently as an ice-skating rink).

Videos shown in the small theater (some permanent, some rotating) document the tower's construction, paint job, place in pop culture, and a century of fireworks, capped by the entire millennium blast.

Seeing It All: If you don't want to miss a single level, here's a plan for getting the most out of your visit. Ride the elevator to the second level, then immediately line up for the other elevator to the top. Enjoy the views on top, then ride back down to the second level. Frolic there for a while and take in some more views. When you're ready, head to the first level by taking the stairs (no line) or lining up for the elevator. Explore the shops and exhibits on the first level and have a snack. Once you're ready to leave, you can line up for the elevator, but it's quickest and most memorable to take the stairs back to earth.

Cost: €13.10 all the way to the top, €8.10 if you're only going up to the two lower levels, not covered by Museum Pass. You can skip the elevator line and climb the stairs to the first and second level for €4.50, or for €3.50 if you're under 25. (Elevators and stairs are both free going down.) Once inside the tower, you can buy your way to the top with no penalty—ticket booths and machines on the first and second levels sell supplements for €5 (€3.50 if you're under 25; walkers need to climb to second level to ride elevator up).

Hours: Daily mid-June-Aug 9:00-24:45 in the morning, last ascent to top at 23:00 and to lower levels at 24:00; Sept-mid-June 9:30-23:45, last ascent to top at 22:30 and to lower levels at 23:00 (elevator) or 18:00 (stairs). During windy weather, the top level may close to tourists.

Reservations: At www.toureiffel.fr, you can book an entry time (e.g., June 12 at 16:30) and skip the line—at no extra cost. You just pay online with a credit card and print your own ticket (or have confirmation sent to your mobile phone). At the tower, go to the entrance for *visitors with reservation,* where attendants scan your ticket and put you on the first available elevator. Note that even if you have a reservation, when you want to get from the second level to the summit, you'll still have to wait in line like everybody else (and show your ticket again).

The website is easy, but here are a few tips: First, when you "Choose a ticket," make sure you select "Lift entrance ticket with access to the summit" in order to go all the way to the top. For "Type of ticket," it doesn't really matter whether you pick "Group" or "Individual"; a "Group" ticket just gives you one piece of paper covering everyone in your party. You must enter a "Mobile phone number" for identification purposes, so if you don't have one, make one up—and jot it down so you won't forget it. To print the ticket, follow their specifications carefully (white paper, blank on both sides, etc.). If you're on the road without a printer, try forwarding your email confirmation notice to your hotel reception. They can click on a link to the website, where you can enter your information and print out your ticket.

When to Go: For the best of both worlds, arrive with enough light to see the views, then stay as it gets dark to see the lights. The views are grand whether you ascend or not. At the top of the hour, a five-minute lighting display features thousands of sparkling lights (best viewed from place du Trocadéro or the grassy park below).

Avoiding Lines: Crowds overwhelm this place much of the year, with one- to two-hour waits to get in. Weekends and holidays are worst, but prepare for ridiculous crowds almost any time. The best solution is to make an online reservation (see above). If you don't have a reservation, go early; get in line 30 minutes before it opens. Going later is the next-best bet (after 19:00 May-Aug, after 17:00 off-season; see "Hours," earlier, for last ascent times). If you're in line to buy tickets, estimate about 20 minutes for every 100 yards, plus 30 minutes more after you reach the security check near the ticket booths. You can bypass some (but not all) elevator lines if you have a reservation at either of the tower's view restaurants. There's less of a line for the stairs.

Getting There: The Bir-Hakeim and Trocadéro Métro stops, and the Champ de Mars-Tour Eiffel RER stop, are each about a 10-minute walk away. The Ecole Militaire Métro stop in the rue Cler area is 20 minutes away. Buses #69 and #87 stop nearby on avenue Joseph Bouvard in the Champ de Mars park.

Nearby: Before or after your tower visit, you can catch the Bateaux Parisiens boat for a Seine cruise (near the base of Eiffel Tower, see page 430).

Information: An Eiffel Tower information office is between the north and east pillars. Each level on the tower has displays pointing out the landmarks and monuments visible below. Tel. 01 44 11 23 23, www.toureiffel.fr.

Pickpockets: Tourists in crowded elevators are like fish in a barrel for predatory thieves. *En garde.*

Security Check: Bags larger than 19" × 8" × 12" are not allowed and there is no baggage check. All bags are subject to a security search. No knives, glass bottles, or cans are allowed.

Services: There are free WCs at the base of the tower, behind the east pillar. Inside the tower itself, WCs are on all levels, but they're small, with long lines.

Photography: All photos and videos are allowed.

Best Views: The best place to view the tower is from place du Trocadéro to the north. It's a 10-minute walk across the river, a happening scene at night, and especially fun for kids. Consider arriving at the Trocadéro Métro stop for the view, then walking toward the tower. Another delightful viewpoint is the Champ de Mars park to the south. However impressive it may be by day, the tower is an awesome thing to see at twilight, when it becomes engorged with light, and virile Paris lies back and lets night be on top. When darkness fully envelops the city, the tower seems to climax with a spectacular light show at the top of each hour...for five minutes.

Quai Branly Museum (Museé du Quai Branly)—This is the best collection I've seen anywhere of so-called Primitive Art from Africa, Polynesia, Asia, and America. It's presented in a wild, organic, and strikingly modern building that caused a stir in Paris when it opened in 2006. Masks, statuettes, musical instruments, clothes, voodoo dolls, and a variety of temporary exhibits and activities are artfully presented and exquisitely lit. It's not, however, accompanied by much printed English information—to really appreciate the exhibit, use the €5 audioguide. It's a 10-minute walk east (upriver) of the Eiffel Tower, along the river. Even if you skip the museum, drop by its garden café for its fair prices and fine Eiffel Tower views (closes 30 minutes before museum).

Cost and Hours: €8.50, more for temporary exhibits, covered by Museum Pass, Tue-Sun 11:00-19:00, Thu-Sat until 21:00, closed Mon, 37 quai Branly, RER: Champ de Mars-Tour Eiffel or Pont de l'Alma. Tel. 01 56 61 70 00, www.quaibranly.fr.

National Maritime Museum (Musée National de la Marine)—This extensive museum houses an amazing collection of ship models, submarines, torpedoes, cannonballs, *beaucoup* bowsprits, and naval you-name-it, including a small boat made for Napoleon. Don't miss the model and story of how the obelisk on place de la Concorde was delivered from Egypt to Paris entirely by waterways; look for the model and story (behind stairs leading down to special exhibits space). Your ticket (or Museum Pass) includes a good audioguide that explains key exhibits and adds important context to your visit. Kids love it, too.

Cost and Hours: Adults-€7, 18 and under free but pay €2

for audioguide, more during special exhibits, covered by Museum Pass, Wed-Mon 10:00-18:00, closed Tue, on left side of place du Trocadéro with your back to Eiffel Tower. Tel. 01 53 65 69 69, www.musee-marine.fr.

▲**Paris Sewer Tour (Les Egouts de Paris)**—Discover what happens after you flush. This quick, interesting, and slightly stinky visit (a perfumed hanky helps) takes you along a few hundred yards of water tunnels in the world's first underground sewer system. Pick up the helpful English self-guided tour, then drop down into Jean Valjean's world of tunnels, rats, and manhole covers. (Victor Hugo was friends with the sewer inspector when he wrote *Les Misérables*.) You'll pass well-organized displays with helpful English information explaining the history of water distribution in Paris, from Roman times to the present. The evolution of this amazing network of sewers is surprisingly interesting. More than 1,500 miles of tunnels carry 317 million gallons of water daily through this underworld. It's the world's longest sewer system—so long, they say, that if it was laid out straight, it would stretch from Paris all the way to Istanbul.

Ask about the slideshow in the gift shop and occasional tours in English. The WCs are just beyond the gift shop.

Cost and Hours: €4.30, covered by Museum Pass; Sat-Wed May-Sept 11:00-17:00, Oct-April 11:00-16:00; closed Thu-Fri; located where pont de l'Alma greets the Left Bank—on the right side of the bridge as you face the river, Mo: Alma-Marceau, RER: Pont de l'Alma. Tel. 01 53 68 27 81.

▲▲**Army Museum and Napoleon's Tomb (Musée de l'Armée)**—The Hôtel des Invalides—a former veterans' hospital built by Louis XIV—houses Napoleon's over-the-top-ornate tomb, as well as Europe's greatest military museum. Visiting the Army Museum's different sections, you can watch the art of war unfold from stone axes to Axis powers.

At the center of the complex, Napoleon lies majestically dead inside several coffins under a grand dome—a goose-bumping pilgrimage for historians. The dome overhead glitters with 26 pounds of thinly pounded gold leaf, and tombs of other French war heroes surround the emperor. Follow signs to the crypt to find Roman Empire–style reliefs that list the accomplishments of Napoleon's administration.

Your visit continues through an impressive range of military museums that surround a central courtyard, complete with good English explanations. See medieval armor, Napoleon's stuffed and mounted horse, Louis XIV-era uniforms and weapons, and much more. The best part is the section dedicated to the two World Wars, especially World War II.

Cost: €9, ticket includes Napoleon's Tomb, all museums

within Les Invalides complex, and audioguide for tomb. All covered by the Museum Pass except for €1 audioguide. Price drops to €7 an hour before closing time; always free for all military personnel in uniform.

Hours: Daily April-Sept 10:00-18:00, Sun until 18:30 and Tue until 21:00, July-Aug tomb stays open until 19:00; daily Oct-March 10:00-17:00, Sun until 17:30; last tickets sold 30 minutes before closing; Oct-June closed first Mon of every month, Charles de Gaulle Museum (within the complex) closed Mon year-round.

Location: The Hôtel des Invalides is at 129 rue de Grenelle; Mo: La Tour Maubourg, Varenne, or Invalides. Tel. 01 44 42 38 77 or toll 08 10 11 33 99, www.invalides.org.

▲▲**Rodin Museum (Musée Rodin)**—This user-friendly museum is filled with passionate works by the greatest sculptor since Michelangelo.

Auguste Rodin (1840-1917) sculpted human figures on an epic scale, revealing through the body their deepest thoughts and feelings. Like many of Michelangelo's unfinished works, Rodin's statues rise from the raw stone around them, driven by the life force. With missing limbs and scarred skin, these are prefab classics, making ugliness noble. Rodin's people are always moving restlessly. Even the famous *Thinker* is moving—though he's plopped down solidly, his mind is a million miles away.

Rodin worked with many materials—he chiseled marble (though not often), modeled clay, cast bronze, worked plaster, painted, and sketched. He often created different versions of the same subject in different media.

Rodin lived and worked in this mansion, renting rooms alongside Henri Matisse, poet Rainer Maria Rilke (Rodin's secretary), and dancer Isadora Duncan. The well-displayed exhibits trace Rodin's artistic development, explain how his bronze statues were cast, and show some of the studies he created to work up to his masterpiece (the unfinished *Gates of Hell*). Learn about Rodin's tumultuous relationship with his apprentice and lover, Camille Claudel. Mull over what makes his sculptures some of the most evocative since the Renaissance. And stroll the gardens, packed with many of his greatest works (including *The Thinker, Balzac,* the *Burghers of Calais,* and the *Gates of Hell*). The beautiful gardens are ideal for artistic reflection.

Cost and Hours: €6, under 18 free, free on first Sun of the month, €12 same-day combo-ticket with Orsay Museum, covered by Museum Pass. It costs €1 to get into the gardens only—which may be Paris' best deal, as many works are on display there (also covered by Museum Pass). Audioguides are €4, and baggage check is mandatory. Open Tue-Sun 10:00-17:45, closed Mon, gardens close at 18:45, last entry 30 minutes before closing. It's near the

PARIS

Army Museum and Napoleon's Tomb, 79 rue de Varenne, Mo: Varenne. Tel. 01 44 18 61 10, www.musee-rodin.fr.

▲▲Marmottan Museum (Musée Marmottan Monet)—The Marmottan has the best collection of works by master Impressionist Claude Monet. In this mansion on the fringe of urban Paris, you can walk through Monet's life, from black-and-white sketches to colorful open-air paintings to the canvas that gave Impressionism its name. The museum's highlights are scenes of his garden at Giverny, including larger-than-life water lilies. In addition, the Marmottan features a world-class collection of works by Berthe Morisot.

The ground floor usually displays Paul Marmottan's eclectic collection of non-Monet objects—period furnishings, a beautifully displayed series of illuminated manuscript drawings, and non-Monet paintings created in the seamless-brushstroke style that Monet rebelled against. The permanent collection (mainly Monet) is generally in the basement and on the first floor. The basement displays Monet's large-scale works from his gardens at Giverny, whereas the first floor hosts special exhibits and paintings by Impressionist colleagues Pierre-Auguste Renoir, Camille Pissarro, Berthe Morisot, and more.

Cost and Hours: €9, not covered by Museum Pass, Tue 11:00-21:00, Wed-Sun 11:00-18:00, closed Mon, last entry 30 minutes before closing, 2 rue Louis-Boilly, Mo: La Muette. Tel. 01 44 96 50 33, www.marmottan.com.

Left Bank

Opposite Notre-Dame, on the left bank of the Seine, is the Latin Quarter.

▲▲Cluny Museum (Musée National du Moyen Age)—This treasure trove of Middle Ages *(Moyen Age)* art fills old Roman baths, offering close-up looks at stained glass, Notre-Dame carvings, fine goldsmithing and jewelry, and rooms of tapestries. The highlights are several original stained-glass windows from Sainte-Chapelle, and the exquisite *Lady and the Unicorn* series of six tapestries: A delicate, as-medieval-as-can-be noble lady introduces a delighted unicorn to the senses of taste, hearing, sight, smell, and touch. This museum helps put the Middle Ages in perspective, reflecting a time when Europe was awakening from a thousand-year slumber and Paris was emerging on the world stage. Trade was booming, people actually owned chairs, and the Renaissance was moving in like a warm front from Italy.

Cost and Hours: €8, more for temporary exhibits, free on first Sun of month, covered by Museum Pass, Wed-Mon 9:15-17:45, closed Tue, last entry at 17:15, near corner of boulevards St. Michel and St. Germain at 6 place Paul Painlevé; Mo: Cluny-La

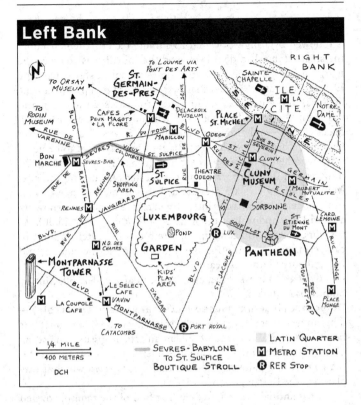

Left Bank

RIGHT BANK

To Louvre via Pont des Arts

ST. GERMAIN-DES-PRES

SAINTE-CHAPELLE

ILE DE LA CITE

To Orsay Museum

SEINE

To Rodin Museum

NOTRE DAME

CAFES DEUX MAGOTS & LA FLORE

Delacroix Museum

PLACE ST. MICHEL

BLVD

RUE DE VARENNE

BLVD

RUE DU FOUR MABILLON

BLVD

ODEON

RUE ST. SEVERIN

CLUNY

BON MARCHE

Sevres-Bab.

VIEUX COLOMBIER

ST. SULPICE

RUE DE RENNES

RUE DE SEVRES

RASTAIL

SHOPPING AREA

THEATRE ODEON

RUE DES

CLUNY MUSEUM

GERMAIN

MAUBERT MUTUALITE

RENNES

VAUGIRARD

RUE DE RENNES

ST. SULPICE

ECOLES

SORBONNE

CARD. LEMOINE

BLVD.

RUE DE

LUXEMBOURG GARDEN

POND

R LUX.

SOUFFLOT

ST. ETIENNE DU MONT

PANTHEON

N.D. DES CHAMPS

MONTPARNASSE TOWER

KIDS' PLAY AREA

ST. JACQUES

BLVD

RUE MONGE

RUE MOUFFETARD

PLACE MONGE

BLVD.

LE SELECT CAFE

VAVIN

DASSAS

La COUPOLE CAFE

MONTPARNASSE

To CATACOMBS

R PORT ROYAL

1/4 MILE
400 METERS

DCH

SEVRES-BABYLONE TO ST. SULPICE BOUTIQUE STROLL

LATIN QUARTER

M METRO STATION

R RER STOP

Sorbonne, St. Michel, or Odéon. Tel. 01 53 73 78 16, www.musee
-moyenage.fr.

St. Germain-des-Prés—A church was first built on this site in
A.D. 452. The church you see today was constructed in 1163 and is
all that's left of a once sprawling and influential monastery. The
colorful interior reminds us that medieval churches were originally
painted in bright colors. The surrounding area hops at night with
venerable cafés, fire-eaters, mimes, and scads of artists (free, daily
8:00-20:00, Mo: St. Germain-des-Prés).

▲**St. Sulpice Church and Organ Concert**—This grand church
was featured in *The Da Vinci Code,* and has since become a trendy
stop for the book's many fans. But the real reason to visit is to see
and hear its intimately accessible organ. For pipe-organ enthusiasts, this is one of Europe's great musical treats. The Grand
Orgue at St. Sulpice Church has a rich history, with a succession
of 12 world-class organists—including Charles-Marie Widor
and Marcel Dupré—that goes back 300 years. Widor started the
tradition of opening the loft to visitors after the 10:30 service on
Sundays. Daniel Roth (or his understudy) continues to welcome
guests in three languages while playing five keyboards.

The 10:30-11:30 Sunday Mass (come appropriately dressed) is followed by a high-powered 25-minute recital. Then, at noon, the small, unmarked door is opened (left of entry as you face the rear). Visitors scamper like 16th notes up spiral stairs, past the 19th-century StairMasters that five men once pumped to fill the bellows, into a world of 7,000 pipes. You can see the organ and visit with Daniel (or his substitute, who might not speak English). Space is tight—only 15 people are allowed in at a time, and only a few can gather around the organist at once—you need to be quick to allow others a chance to meet him. You'll likely have about 20 minutes to kill before watching the master play during the next Mass (church views are great and there's a small lounge to wait in); you can leave at any time. If you're late or rushed, show up around 12:30 and wait at the little door (last entry is at 13:00). As someone leaves, you can slip in, climb up, and catch the rest of the performance. Tempting boutiques surround the church, and Luxembourg Garden is nearby.

Cost and Hours: Free, church open daily 7:30-19:30, Mo: St. Sulpice or Mabillon.

Delacroix Museum (Musée National Eugène Delacroix)—

This museum for Eugène Delacroix (1798-1863) was once his home and studio. A friend of bohemian artistic greats—including George Sand and Frédéric Chopin—Delacroix is most famous for the flag-waving painting *Liberty Leading the People*, which is displayed at the Louvre, not here.

Cost and Hours: €5, free on first Sun of the month, covered by Museum Pass, Wed-Mon 9:30-17:00, Sat-Sun until 17:30 in summer, closed Tue, last entry 30 minutes before closing, 6 rue de Furstenberg, Mo: St. Germain-des-Prés. Tel. 01 44 41 86 50, www.musee-delacroix.fr.

▲Luxembourg Garden (Jardin du Luxembourg)—Paris'

most beautiful, interesting, and enjoyable garden/park/recreational area, le Jardin du Luxembourg, is a great place to watch Parisians at rest and play. These 60-acre gardens, dotted with fountains and statues, are the property of the French Senate, which meets here in the Luxembourg Palace. Luxembourg Garden has special rules governing its use (for example, where cards can be played, where dogs can be walked, where joggers can run, and when and where music can be played). The brilliant flower beds are completely changed three times a year, and the boxed trees are brought out of the *orangerie* in May. Children enjoy rentable toy sailboats, pony rides, and marionette shows (Les Guignols, or Punch and Judy). Challenge the card and chess players to a game (near the tennis courts), or find a free chair near the main pond and take a well-deserved break (park open daily dawn until dusk, Mo: Odéon, RER: Luxembourg).

The grand Neoclassical-domed Panthéon (next listing), now a mausoleum housing the tombs of great French notables, is three blocks away.

If you enjoy Luxembourg Garden and want to see more green spaces, you could visit the more elegant **Parc Monceau** (Mo: Monceau), the colorful **Jardin des Plantes** (Mo: Jussieu or Gare d'Austerlitz, RER: Gare d'Austerlitz), or the hilly and bigger **Parc des Buttes-Chaumont** (Mo: Buttes-Chaumont).

▲**Panthéon**—This state-capitol-style Neoclassical monument celebrates France's illustrious history and people, balances Foucault's pendulum, and is the final home of many French VIPs. Inside the vast building (360' × 280' × 270') are monuments tracing the celebrated struggles of the French people: a beheaded St. Denis (painting on left wall of nave), St. Geneviève saving the fledgling city from Attila the Hun, and scenes of Joan of Arc (left transept).

Foucault's pendulum swings gracefully at the end of a 220-foot cable suspended from the towering dome. It was here in 1851 that scientist Léon Foucault first demonstrated the rotation of the Earth. Stand a few minutes and watch the pendulum's arc (appear to) shift as you and the earth rotate beneath it.

Stairs in the back lead down to the crypt, where a pantheon of greats is buried. Rousseau is along the right wall as you enter, Voltaire faces him across the hall. Also buried here are scientist Marie Curie, Victor Hugo *(Les Misérables, The Hunchback of Notre-Dame)*, Alexandre Dumas *(The Three Musketeers, The Count of Monte Cristo)*, and Louis Braille, who invented the script for the blind.

From the main floor you can climb 206 steps to the dome gallery for great views of the interior as well as the city (accessible only with an escort). Visits leave every hour until 17:30 from the bookshop near the entry—see schedule as you go in.

Cost and Hours: €8, covered by Museum Pass, daily 10:00-18:30 in summer, until 18:00 in winter, last entry 45 minutes before closing, Mo: Cardinal Lemoine. Ask about occasional English tours or call ahead for schedule. Tel. 01 44 32 18 00, www.monum.fr.

Montparnasse Tower (La Tour Montparnasse)—This sadly out-of-place 59-story superscraper has one virtue: its sensational views are cheaper and far easier to access than the Eiffel Tower's. Come early in the day for clearest skies and be treated to views from a comfortable interior and from up on the rooftop. (Some say it's the very best view in Paris, as you can see the Eiffel Tower clearly...and you can't see the Montparnasse Tower at all.) Exit the elevator at the 56th floor, passing the eager photographer (they'll superimpose your group's image with the view) to views of *tout Paris*. Have a drink or a light lunch (OK prices) with a view, peruse the gift shop, and find good WCs. There may be plenty of dioramas identifying highlights of the star-studded vista, but the €3 "M-56" photo-guide makes a fun souvenir. Explore every corner of the floor for best views—from here it's easy to admire Haussmann's grand-boulevard scheme.

Enjoy fascinating historic black-and-white photos, and a plush little theater playing a worthwhile video that celebrates the big views of this grand city (free, 12 minutes, shows continuously). Climb to the open terrace on the 59th floor to enjoy the surreal scene of a lonely man in a box, and a helipad surrounded by the window-cleaner track. Here, 690 feet above Paris, you can scan the city with the wind in your hair, noticing the lush courtyards hiding behind grand street fronts.

Cost and Hours: €11, not covered by Museum Pass, daily April-Sept 9:30-23:30; Oct-March 9:30-22:30, Fri-Sat until 23:00; last entry 30 minutes before closing, sunset is great but views are disappointing after dark, entrance on rue de l'Arrivée, Mo: Montparnasse-Bienvenüe—from the Métro stay inside the station and follow the signs for *La Tour*. Tel. 01 45 38 52 56, www.tourmontparnasse56.com.

▲**Catacombs**—These underground tunnels contain the anonymous bones of six million permanent Parisians. In 1786, the citizens of Paris decided to relieve congestion and improve sanitary conditions by emptying the city cemeteries (which traditionally surrounded churches) into an official ossuary. They found the perfect locale in the many miles of underground tunnels from limestone quarries, which were, at that time, just outside the city. For decades, priests led ceremonial processions of black-veiled, bone-laden carts into the quarries, where the bones were stacked into piles five feet high and as much as 80 feet deep behind neat walls of skull-studded tibiae. Each transfer was completed by placing a plaque, indicating the church and district where the bones came from and the date that they arrived. Note to wannabe Hamlets: An attendant checks your bag at the exit for stolen souvenirs. A flashlight is handy. Being under 6'2" is helpful.

Cost and Hours: €8, not covered by Museum Pass, Tue-Sun 10:00-17:00, ticket booth closes at 16:00, closed Mon. Be warned that lines are long (figure an hour wait) and hard to avoid. Arrive no later than 14:30 or risk not getting in. Take the Métro to Denfert-Rochereau, then find the lion in the big traffic circle; if he looked left rather than right, he'd stare right at the green entrance to the Catacombs at 1 place Denfert-Rochereau. Tel. 01 43 22 47 63.

Champs-Elysées and Nearby

▲▲**Champs-Elysées**—This famous boulevard is Paris' backbone, with its greatest concentration of traffic. From the Arc de Triomphe down avenue des Champs-Elysées, all of France seems

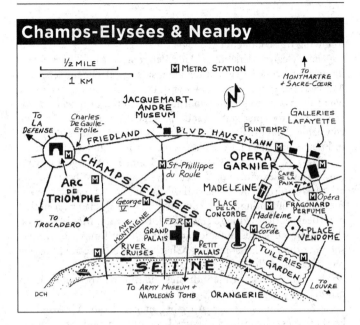

Champs-Elysées & Nearby

to converge on place de la Concorde, the city's largest square. And though the Champs-Elysées has become as international as it is Parisian, a walk here is still a must.

In 1667, Louis XIV opened the first section of the street as a short extension of the Tuileries Garden. This year is considered the birth of Paris as a grand city. The Champs-Elysées soon became *the* place to cruise in your carriage. (It still is today; traffic can be gridlocked even at midnight.) One hundred years later, the café scene arrived.

From the 1920s until the 1960s, this boulevard was pure elegance. Parisians actually dressed up to come here. It was mainly residences, rich hotels, and cafés. Then, in 1963, the government pumped up the neighborhood's commercial metabolism by bringing in the RER (commuter train). Suburbanites had easy access, and *pfft*—there went the neighborhood.

The *nouveau* Champs-Elysées, revitalized in 1994, has new benches and lamps, broader sidewalks, all-underground parking, and a fleet of green-suited workers who drive motorized street cleaners. Blink away the modern elements, and it's not hard to imagine the boulevard pre-1963, with only the finest structures lining both sides all the way to the palace gardens.

⊘ Self-Guided Walk: To reach the top of the Champs-Elysées, take the Métro to the Arc de Triomphe (Mo: Charles de Gaulle-Etoile), then saunter down the grand boulevard (Métro stops every few blocks, including Charles de Gaulle-Etoile, George

V, and Franklin D. Roosevelt). Start here, then head downhill, following this commentary.

Fancy car dealerships include **Peugeot,** at #136 (showing off its futuristic concept cars, often alongside the classic models), and **Mercedes-Benz,** a block down at #118, where you can pick up a Mercedes watch to go with your new car. In the 19th century this was an area for horse stables; today, it's the district of garages, limo companies, and car dealerships. If you're serious about selling cars in France, you must have a showroom on the Champs-Elysées.

Next to Mercedes is the famous **Lido,** Paris' largest cabaret (and a multiplex cinema). You can walk all the way inside, if you ask nicely, until 18:00. Paris still offers the kind of burlesque-type spectacles combining music, comedy, and scantily clad women that have been performed here since the 19th century. Moviegoing on the Champs-Elysées provides another kind of fun, with theaters showing the very latest releases. Check to see if there are films you recognize, then look for the showings *(séances)*. A "v.o." *(version originale)* next to the time indicates the film will be shown in its original language.

The flagship store of leather-bag makers **Louis Vuitton** may be the largest single-brand luxury store in the world. Step inside. The store insists on providing enough salespeople to treat each customer royally—if there's a line, it means shoppers have overwhelmed the place.

Fouquet's café-restaurant (#99), under the red awning, is a popular spot among French celebrities, serving the most expensive shot of espresso I've found in downtown Paris (€8). Opened in 1899 as a coachman's bistro, Fouquet's gained fame as the hangout of France's WWI biplane fighter pilots—those who weren't shot down by Germany's infamous "Red Baron." It also served as James Joyce's dining room.

Since the early 1900s, Fouquet's has been a favorite of French actors and actresses. The golden plaques at the entrance honor winners of France's Oscar-like film awards, the Césars (one is cut into the ground at the end of the red carpet). Look for the plaques for Gérard Depardieu, Catherine Deneuve, Roman Polanski, Juliette Binoche, and many famous Americans (but not Jerry Lewis). Recent winners are shown on the floor just inside.

The hushed interior is at once classy and intimidating—and also a grand experience...if you dare (to say "I'm just looking" in French, say *"Je regarde"*—zhuh ruh-gard). The outdoor setting is more relaxed. Fouquet's was recently saved from foreign purchase and eventual destruction when the government declared it a historic monument. For his election-night victory party in 2007, the flamboyant President Sarkozy celebrated at Fouquet's, along with France's glitterati—including the "French Elvis," Johnny Hallyday.

France's first lady, Carla Bruni-Sarkozy, is often seen dining here.

Ladurée (two blocks downhill at #75, with green-and-purple awning) is a classic 19th-century tea salon/restaurant/*pâtisserie*. Its interior is right out of the 1860s. Nonpatrons can discreetly wander in through the door farthest downhill and peek into the cozy rooms upstairs (no photos). A coffee here is *très élégant* (only €3.50). The bakery sells traditional *macarons*, cute little cakes, and gift-wrapped finger sandwiches to go (your choice of four mini-*macarons* for €7.50).

▲▲▲**Arc de Triomphe**—Napoleon had the magnificent Arc de Triomphe commissioned to commemorate his victory at the battle of Austerlitz. There's no triumphal arch bigger (165 feet high, 130 feet wide). And, with 12 converging boulevards, there's no traffic circle more thrilling to experience—either from behind the wheel or on foot (take the underpass).

The foot of the arch is a stage on which the last two centuries of Parisian history have played out—from the funeral of Napoleon to the goose-stepping arrival of the Nazis to the triumphant return of Charles de Gaulle after the Allied liberation. Examine the carvings on the pillars, featuring a mighty Napoleon and excitable Lady Liberty. Pay your respects at the Tomb of the Unknown Soldier. Then climb the 284 steps to the observation deck up top, with sweeping skyline panoramas and a mesmerizing view down onto the traffic that swirls around the arch.

Cost and Hours: Outside—free, always viewable. Interior—€9.50, under 18 free, free on first Sun of month Oct-March, covered by Museum Pass, daily April-Sept 10:00-23:00, Oct-March 10:00-22:30, last entry 30 minutes before closing, place Charles de Gaulle, use underpass to reach arch, Mo: Charles de Gaulle-Etoile. Tel. 01 55 37 73 77, www.arc-de-triomphe .monuments-nationaux.fr.

▲**Opéra Garnier**—This gleaming grand theater of the belle époque was built for Napoleon III and finished in 1875. The building is huge—though the auditorium itself seats only 2,000. The real show was before and after the performance, when the elite of Paris—out to see and be seen—strutted their elegant stuff in the extravagant lobbies. Think of the grand marble stairway as a theater. As you wander the halls and gawk at the decor, imagine the place filled with the beautiful people of its day. The massive foundations straddle an underground lake (inspiring the mysterious world of the *Phantom of the Opera*). Visitors can peek from two boxes into the actual red-velvet performance hall to view Marc Chagall's colorful ceiling (1964) playfully dancing around the eight-ton chandelier (guided tours take you into the performance hall; you can't enter when they're changing out the stage). Note the box seats next to the stage—the most expensive in the house, with an obstructed view of the stage...but just right if you're here only to be seen.

The elitism of this place prompted President François Mitterrand to have a people's opera house built in the 1980s, symbolically on place de la Bastille, where the French Revolution started in 1789. This left the Opéra Garnier home only to ballet and occasional concerts. The library/museum will interest opera buffs, but anyone will enjoy the second-floor grand foyer and Salon du Glacier, iced with decor typical of 1900.

For a novel souvenir, pick up a jar of honey cultivated from beehives on the Opéra's roof. The hives are tended by staff and can be seen from the seventh floor of Galleries Lafayette (behind the Opéra).

Cost and Hours: €9, not covered by Museum Pass, generally daily 10:00-16:30, July-Aug until 17:30, closed during rehearsals (schedule on website), 8 rue Scribe, Mo: Opéra, RER: Auber, www.operadeparis.fr.

Tours: English tours of the building run during summer and off-season on weekends and Wed, usually at 11:30 and 14:30—call to confirm schedule (€12.50, includes entry, 1.5 hours, tel. 08 25 05 44 05, press 2 for tours).

Nearby: The Fragonard Perfume Museum (next) is on the left side of the Opéra, and the venerable Galeries Lafayette department store (marvelous views from roof terrace) is just behind. Across the street, the illustrious Café de la Paix has been a meeting spot for the local glitterati for generations. If you can afford the coffee, this spot offers a delightful break.

Fragonard Perfume Museum—Near Opéra Garnier, this perfume shop masquerades as a museum. Housed in a beautiful 19th-century mansion, it's the best-smelling museum in Paris—and you'll learn a little about how perfume is made, too (ask for the English handout).

Cost and Hours: Free, daily 9:00-17:30, 9 rue Scribe, tel. 01 47 42 04 56, www.fragonard.com.

▲▲Jacquemart-André Museum (Musée Jacquemart-André)—This thoroughly enjoyable museum (with an elegant café) showcases the lavish home of a wealthy, art-loving, 19th-century Parisian couple. After wandering the grand boulevards, get inside for an intimate look at the lifestyles of the Parisian rich and fabulous. Edouard André and his wife Nélie Jacquemart—who had no children—spent their lives and fortunes designing, building, and then decorating this sumptuous mansion. What makes the visit so rewarding is the excellent audioguide tour (in English, free with admission, plan on spending an hour with the audioguide). The place is strewn with paintings by Rembrandt, Botticelli, Uccello,

Mantegna, Bellini, Boucher, and Fragonard—enough to make a painting gallery famous.

Cost and Hours: €10, not covered by Museum Pass, daily 10:00-18:00, 158 boulevard Haussmann, Mo: Miromesnil or St. Philippe-de-Roule, bus #80 makes a convenient connection to Ecole Militaire. Tel. 01 45 62 11 59, www.musee-jacquemart-andre .com.

After Your Visit: Consider a break in the sumptuous museum tearoom, with delicious cakes and tea (daily 11:45-17:30). From here walk north on rue de Courcelles to see Paris' most beautiful park, Parc Monceau.

▲Petit Palais (and its Musée des Beaux-Arts)—This free museum displays a broad collection of paintings and sculpture from the 1600s to the 1900s. It's a museum of second-choice art, but the building itself is impressive, and there are a few 19th-century diamonds in the rough, including pieces by Courbet, Monet, the American painter Mary Cassatt, and other Impressionists. The Palais also has a pleasant garden courtyard and café.

Cost and Hours: Free, Tue-Sun 10:00-18:00, Thu until 20:00 for temporary exhibits, closed Mon, across from Grand Palais on avenue Winston Churchill, a l-o-o-ong block west of place de la Concorde. Tel. 01 53 43 40 00, www.petitpalais.paris.fr.

Grand Palais—This grand exhibition hall, built for the 1900 World's Fair, is used for temporary exhibits. The building's Industrial Age, erector-set, iron-and-glass exterior is grand, but the steep entry price is only worthwhile if you're interested in any of the several different exhibitions (each with different hours and costs, located in various parts of the building). Many areas are undergoing renovations, which may still be underway during your visit. Get details on the current schedule from the TIs, in *Pariscope*, or from the website.

Cost and Hours: Admission prices and hours vary with each exhibition. It's open daily, though some parts of the building are closed Mon, and others are closed Tue. Major exhibitions are usually €11 and not covered by the Museum Pass. Generally open 10:00-20:00, Wed 10:00-22:00, closed between exhibitions, avenue Winston Churchill, Mo: Rond Point or Champs-Elysées. Tel. 01 44 13 17 17, www.grandpalais.fr.

▲La Défense and La Grande Arche—Though Paris keeps its historic center classic and skyscraper-free, this district, nicknamed "le petit Manhattan," offers an impressive excursion into a side of Paris few tourists see: that of a modern-day economic superpower. La Défense was first conceived more than 60 years ago as a US-style forest of skyscrapers that would accommodate the business needs of the modern world. Today La Défense is a thriving business and shopping center, home to 150,000 employees and 55,000 residents.

For an interesting visit, take the Métro to the La Défense, Grande Arche stop and ride the elevator to the top of La Grande Arche for great city views. Then stroll among the glass buildings to the Esplanade de la Défense Métro station, and return home from there.

La Grande Arche de la Fraternité is the centerpiece of this ambitious complex. Inaugurated in 1989 on the 200th anniversary of the French Revolution, it was, like the Revolution, dedicated to human rights and brotherhood. The place is big—Notre-Dame Cathedral could fit under its arch. The "cloud"—a huge canvas canopy under the arch—is an attempt to cut down on the wind-tunnel effect this gigantic building creates.

Glass capsule elevators whisk you scenically up to a grand open-air view, a thrilling 20-minute movie (with English subtitles) on the mammoth construction project, and models of the arch. You can also visit an exhibit on computer history, and take advantage of its free Internet access. Kids like the small video-game museum, and everyone seems fascinated by the set of digital portraits by French artist Dimitri, illustrating *remanence*—"after imagery." After staring at one of these colorful portraits for 30 seconds, close your eyes and see a clear image of the face...behind your eyelids.

Cost and Hours: La Grande Arche elevator and exhibits–€10, kids–€8.50, family deals, not covered by Museum Pass, check online for discounts, daily 10:00-19:00, RER or Mo: La Défense, Grande Arche, follow signs to *La Grande Arche*. Tel. 01 49 07 27 55, www.grandearche.com.

After Your Visit: If you're hungry, head over to glassy Le Dome, which serves good sandwiches and salads to go. Have lunch with a view on the steps of La Grande Arche (cafés also available nearby).

The Esplanade: La Défense is much more than its eye-catching arch. Wander from the arch back toward the city center (and to the next Métro stop) along the Esplanade (a.k.a. "le Parvis")—a virtual open-air modern art gallery, sporting pieces by Joan Miró (blue), Alexander Calder (red), and Yaacov Agam (the fountain with colorful stripes and rhythmically dancing spouts), among others. *La Défense de Paris,* the statue that gave the area its name, recalls the 1871 Franco-Prussian war—it's a rare bit of old Paris out here in the 'burbs. Notice how the Wallace Fountain and *boules* courts are designed to integrate tradition into this celebration of modern commerce. Walking toward the Nexity Tower, you'll come to the Esplanade de la Défense Métro station, which zips you out of all this modernity and directly back into town.

Marais Neighborhood & Nearby

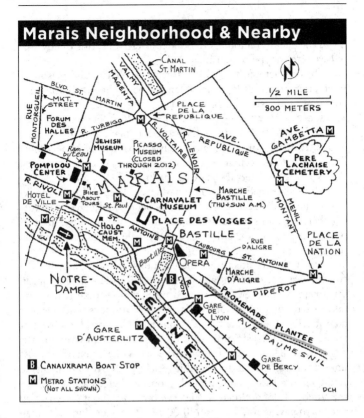

Marais Neighborhood and Nearby

The Marais neighborhood extends along the Right Bank of the Seine, from the Pompidou Center to the Bastille. With more pre-Revolutionary lanes and buildings than anywhere else in town, the Marais is more atmospheric than touristy. It's medieval Paris, and the haunt of the old nobility. During the reign of Henry IV, this area—originally a swamp *(marais)*—became the hometown of the French aristocracy. In the 17th century, big shots built their private mansions *(hôtels)* close to Henry's stylish place des Vosges. With the Revolution, the aristocratic splendor of this quarter passed, and the Marais became a working-class quarter, filled with gritty shops, artisans, immigrants, and a Jewish community. Today this thriving, trendy, real community is a joy to explore.

It looks the way much of the city did until the mid-1800s, when Napoleon III had Baron Georges-Eugène Haussmann blast out the narrow streets to construct broad boulevards (wide enough for the guns and ranks of the army, too wide for revolutionary barricades), thus creating modern Paris. When strolling the Marais, stick to the west-east axis formed by rue Ste. Croix de la Bretonnerie, rue des Rosiers (heart of Paris' Jewish community), and rue St. Antoine. On Sunday afternoons, this trendy area pulses with shoppers and café crowds.

Don't waste time looking for the **Bastille,** the prison of Revolution fame. It's Paris' most famous nonsight—the building is long gone and just the square remains.

▲**Place des Vosges**—Henry IV (r. 1589-1610) built this centerpiece of the Marais in 1605 and called it "place Royal." As he'd hoped, it turned the Marais into Paris' most exclusive neighborhood. Walk to the center, where Louis XIII on horseback gestures, "Look at this wonderful square my dad built." He's surrounded by locals enjoying their community park. You'll see children frolicking in the sandbox, lovers warming benches, and pigeons guarding their fountains while trees shade this escape from the glare of the big city (you can refill your water bottle in the center of the square).

Study the architecture: nine pavilions (houses) per side. The two highest—at the front and back—were for the king and queen (but were never used). Warm red brickwork—some real, some fake—is topped with sloped slate roofs, chimneys, and another quaint relic of a bygone era: TV antennas. Victor Hugo lived at #6—at the southeast corner of the square, marked by the French flag—from 1832 to 1848. This was when he wrote much of his most important work, including his biggest hit, *Les Misérables*. Inside you'll wander through eight plush rooms and enjoy a fine view of the square (free, optional special exhibits cost about €7—usually not worth paying for, Tue-Sun 10:00-18:00, closed Mon, last entry at 17:40, 6 place des Vosges, tel. 01 42 72 10 16, www.musee-hugo .paris.fr).

Leave the place des Vosges through the doorway at the southwest corner of the square and pass through the elegant **Hôtel de Sully** (great example of a Marais mansion, grand courtyard open daily 10:00-19:00, fine bookstore inside) to rue St. Antoine.

▲▲**Pompidou Center (Centre Pompidou)**—One of Europe's greatest collections of far-out modern art is housed in the Musée National d'Art Moderne, on the fourth and fifth floors of this colorful exhibition hall. The building itself is "exoskeletal" (like Notre-Dame or a crab), with its functional parts—the pipes, heating ducts, and escalator—on the outside, and the meaty art inside. It's the epitome of Modern architecture, where "form follows function." Created ahead of its time, the 20th-century art in this collection is still waiting for the world to catch up.

Buy your ticket on the ground floor, then ride up the escalator (or run up the down escalator to get in the proper mood). When you see the view, your opinion of the Pompidou's exterior should improve a good 15 percent. Find the permanent collection—the entrance is either on the fourth or fifth floor (it varies). Enter, show your ticket, and get the current floor plan *(plan du musée)*.

The 20th century—accelerated by technology and fragmented by war—was exciting and chaotic, and the art reflects the turbulence of that century of change. In this free-flowing and airy museum (with great views over Paris), you'll come face to face with works by Henri Matisse, Pablo Picasso, Marc Chagall, Salvador Dalí, Andy Warhol, Wassily Kandinsky, Max Ernst, Jackson Pollock, and many more. After so many Madonnas-and-children, a piano smashed to bits and glued to the wall is refreshing.

Cost and Hours: €10-12 depending on current exhibits, free on first Sun of month, Museum Pass covers permanent collection and view escalators (but not special exhibitions), Wed-Mon 11:00-21:00, open Thu until 23:00 when special exhibits are on, closed Tue, ticket counters close at 20:00, Mo: Rambuteau or farther-away Hôtel de Ville. Tel. 01 44 78 12 33, www.centrepompidou.fr.

View from the Pompidou: Even if you don't go inside, you can ride the escalator for a great city view from the top (€3 Panorama ticket covers ride but not exhibit, also covered by museum ticket or Museum Pass).

Nearby: The Pompidou Center and the square that fronts it are lively, with lots of people, street theater, and activity inside and out—a perpetual street fair. Kids of any age enjoy the fun, colorful fountain (called *Homage to Stravinsky*) next to the Pompidou Center. Consider either eating at the good mezzanine-level café, or for a light meal or snack, try the places lining the Stravinsky fountain: Dame Tartine and Crêperie Beaubourg, both with reasonable prices (to the right as you face the museum entrance).

▲**Jewish Art and History Museum (Musée d'Art et Histoire du Judaïsme)**—This fine museum, located in a beautifully restored Marais mansion, tells the story of Judaism in France and throughout Europe, from the Roman destruction of Jerusalem to the theft of famous artworks during World War II. Displays illustrate the cultural unity maintained by this continually dispersed population. You'll learn about the history of Jewish traditions, from bar mitzvahs to menorahs, and see the exquisite traditional costumes and objects central to daily life. The museum also displays paintings by famous Jewish artists, including Marc Chagall, Amedeo Modigliani, and Chaim Soutine. The English explanations posted in many rooms provide sufficient explanation for most; free audioguides provide greater detail.

Cost and Hours: €7, more during special exhibits, includes audioguide, covered by Museum Pass, Mon-Fri 11:00-18:00, Sun 10:00-18:00, closed Sat, last entry 45 minutes before closing, 71 rue du Temple, Mo: Rambuteau or Hôtel de Ville a few blocks farther away. Tel. 01 53 01 86 60, www.mahj.org.

PARIS

Rue des Rosiers—Jewish Quarter—Located along rue des Rosiers, the tiny yet colorful Jewish district of the Marais was once considered the largest in Western Europe. Today, rue des Rosiers is lined with Jewish shops and kosher eateries—and the district is being squeezed by the trendy boutiques of modern Paris (visit any day but Saturday, when most businesses are closed—best on Sunday). The intersection of rue des Rosiers and rue des Ecouffes marks the heart of the small neighborhood that Jews call the Pletzl ("little place"). Lively rue des Ecouffes, named for a bird of prey, is a derogatory nod to the moneychangers' shops that once lined this lane.

If you're visiting at lunchtime, you'll be tempted by kosher pizza and plenty of cheap fast-food joints selling falafel "to go" *(emporter)*. The falafel at L'As du Falafel, with its bustling New York-deli atmosphere, is terrific (at #34, sit-down or to go). The Sacha Finkelsztajn Yiddish bakery at #27 is also good (Polish and Russian cuisine, pop in for a tempting treat, sit for the same price as take-away). Nearby, recommended Chez Marianne cooks up traditional Jewish meals and serves excellent falafel to go (at corner of rue des Rosiers and rue des Hospitalières-St.-Gervais; long hours daily). The Jewish Quarter is also home to the Holocaust Memorial (described later).

▲▲**Picasso Museum (Musée Picasso)**—This museum, which has been closed for a major renovation, should re-open sometime in 2012. Tucked into a corner of the Marais and worth ▲▲▲ if you're a Picasso fan, it contains the world's largest collection of Picasso's paintings, sculptures, sketches, and ceramics, along with his small collection of Impressionist art. The art is well-displayed in a fine old mansion with a peaceful garden café. Room-by-room English introductions help make sense of Picasso's work—from the Toulouse-Lautrec–like portraits at the beginning of his career to his gray-brown Cubist period to his return-to-childhood, Salvador Dalí-like finish. The well-done English guidebook helps Picassophiles appreciate the context of his art and learn more about his interesting life. Most will be happy reading the posted English explanations while moving at a steady pace through the museum—the ground and first floors satisfied my curiosity.

Cost and Hours: Reopens in 2012, entry about €7, likely covered by Museum Pass, additional fees for temporary exhibits, hours likely Wed-Mon 9:30-18:00, may be closed Tue, 5 rue de Thorigny, Mo: St. Paul or Chemin Vert, tel. 01 42 71 25 21, www .musee-picasso.fr.

▲▲**Carnavalet Museum (Musée Carnavalet)**—The tumultuous history of Paris—starring the Revolutionary years—is well-portrayed in paintings, models, and a few original artifacts. You'll get a good overview of everything from Louis XIV period rooms to Napoleon to the belle époque. The sprawling Carnavalet is housed in two Marais mansions connected by a corridor; it can be hard to navigate but is great for browsing. The first half of the museum (pre-Revolution) dates from a period when people generally accepted the notion that some were born to rule, and most were born to be ruled. Lovers of Louis XIV-, XV-, and XVI-period furniture will enjoy this section. Others can see it quickly, then concentrate on the Revolution and beyond.

The Revolution is the museum's highlight. A dozen rooms of fascinating exhibits cover this bloody period of French history, when atrocious acts were committed in the name of government "by, for, and of the people." The exhibits take you from events that led up to the Revolution to the storming of the 100-foot-high walls of the Bastille to the royal beheadings, and through the reigns of terror that followed. The rest of the museum traces the rise and fall of Napoleon, France's struggle between monarchy and democracy, the Paris Commune, and the elegance of Paris during the belle époque. Though explanations are in French only, many displays are fairly self-explanatory.

Cost and Hours: Free, occasional fees for optional temporary exhibits, Tue-Sun 10:00-18:00, closed Mon; avoid lunchtime (12:00-14:00), when many rooms close; 23 rue de Sévigné, Mo: St. Paul. Tel. 01 44 59 58 58, www.carnavalet.paris.fr.

Holocaust Memorial (Mémorial de la Shoah)—Commemorating the lives of the more than 76,000 Jews deported from France in World War II, this memorial's focal point is underground, where victims' ashes are buried. Displaying original deportation records, the museum takes you through the history of Jews in Europe and France, from medieval pogroms to the Nazi era.

Cost and Hours: Free, Sun-Fri 10:00-18:00, Thu until 22:00, closed Sat and certain Jewish holidays, 17 rue Geoffroy l'Asnier. Tel. 01 42 77 44 72, www.memorialdelashoah.org.

Promenade Plantée Park (Viaduc des Arts)—This two-mile-long, narrow garden walk on an elevated viaduct was once used for train tracks and is now a good place for a refreshing stroll. Botanists appreciate the well-maintained and varying vegetation, and runners adore the separated pathway. At a few spots, gaps in the planted path have you walking along the street for a bit until you pick up the next segment. The shops at street level below the viaduct's arches take creative advantage of once-wasted urban space, and make for entertaining window shopping (mostly modern furnishings).

Cost and Hours: Free, opens Mon-Fri at 8:00, Sat-Sun at 9:00, closes at sunset (17:30 in winter, 20:30 in summer). It runs from place de la Bastille (Mo: Bastille) along avenue Daumesnil to St. Mandé (Mo: Michel Bizot), passing within a block of Gare de Lyon. From place de la Bastille (exit the Métro following *Sortie rue de Lyon*), walk a l-o-o-ong block down rue de Lyon hugging the Opéra on your left. Find the steps up the red-brick wall a block after the Opéra.

▲**Père Lachaise Cemetery (Cimetière du Père Lachaise)**—Littered with the tombstones of many of the city's most illustrious dead, this is your best one-stop look at Paris' fascinating, romantic past residents. Enclosed by a massive wall and lined with 5,000 trees, the peaceful, car-free lanes and dirt paths of Père Lachaise cemetery encourage parklike meandering. Named for Father *(Père)* La Chaise, whose job was listening to Louis XIV's sins, the cemetery is relatively new, having opened in 1804 to accommodate Paris' expansion. Today, this city of the dead (pop. 70,000) still accepts new residents, but real estate prices are sky high (a 21-square-foot plot costs more than €11,000).

The 100-acre cemetery is big and confusing, with thousands of graves and tombs crammed every which way, and only a few pedestrian pathways to help you navigate. The maps available from any of the nearby florists will direct you to the graves of Frédéric Chopin, Molière, Edith Piaf, Oscar Wilde, Gertrude Stein, Jim Morrison, Héloïse and Abélard, and many more.

Cost and Hours: Free, Mon-Sat 8:30-17:30, Sun 9:00-18:00. It's two blocks from Mo: Gambetta (not Mo: Père Lachaise) and two blocks from bus #69's last stop. Tel. 01 55 25 82 10, www.pere-lachaise.com.

Montmartre

Stroll along Paris' highest hilltop (420 feet) for a different perspective on the City of Light. Walk in the footsteps of the people who've lived here—monks stomping grapes (1200s), farmers grinding grain in windmills (1600s), dust-coated gypsum miners (1700s), Parisian liberals (1800s), Modernist painters (1900s), and all the struggling artists, poets, dreamers, and drunkards who came here for cheap rent, untaxed booze, rustic landscapes, and cabaret nightlife. With vineyards, wheat fields, windmills, animals, and a village tempo of life, it was the perfect escape from grimy Paris.

Getting There: To reach Montmartre, you have several options: You can take the Métro to the Anvers stop (to avoid the stairs up to Sacré-Cœur Basilica, buy one more Métro ticket and ride the funicular, though it's sometimes closed for maintenance). The Abbesses stop is closer but less scenic. Or you can go to place Pigalle, then take the tiny electric Montmartrobus, which drops you right by place du Tertre, near Sacré-Cœur. A taxi to the top of the hill saves time and avoids sweat (about €13, €20 at night). For restaurant recommendations, see page 428.

▲▲**Sacré-Cœur**—The Sacré-Cœur (Sacred Heart) Basilica's exterior, with its onion domes and bleached-bone pallor, looks ancient, but was finished only a century ago by Parisians humiliated by German invaders. Otto von Bismarck's Prussian army laid siege to Paris for more than four months in 1870. Things got so bad for residents that urban hunting for dinner (to cook up dogs, cats, and finally rats) became accepted behavior. Convinced they were being punished for the country's liberal sins, France's Catholics raised money to build the church as a "praise the Lord anyway" gesture. The five-domed, Roman-Byzantine–looking basilica took 44 years to build (1875-1919). It stands on a foundation of 83 pillars sunk 130 feet deep, necessary because the ground beneath was honeycombed with gypsum mines. The exterior is laced with gypsum, which whitens with age.

Take a clockwise spin around the crowded interior to see impressive mosaics, and to give St. Peter's bronze foot a rub. For an unobstructed panoramic view of Paris, climb 260 feet (300 steps) up the tight and claustrophobic spiral stairs to the top of the dome (especially worthwhile if you have kids with excess energy).

Cost and Hours: Church interior free, open daily 6:00-23:00, last entry at 22:15; €5 to climb dome, not covered by Museum Pass, daily June-Sept 9:00-19:00, Oct-May 10:00-18:00.

The Heart of Montmartre—One block from the church, the **place du Tertre** was the haunt of Henri de Toulouse-Lautrec and the original bohemians. Today, it's mobbed with tourists and unoriginal bohemians, but it's still fun (to beat the crowds, go early in the morning). From here follow rue des Saules (a block west, passing near the Dalí Museum—described next) and find Paris' lone vineyard and the **Montmartre Museum** (described later). Return uphill, then follow rue Lépic down to the old windmill, **Moulin de la Galette,** which once pressed monks' grapes and farmers' grain, and crushed gypsum rocks into powdery plaster of Paris (there were once 30 windmills on Montmartre). When the gypsum mines closed (c. 1850) and the vineyards sprouted apartments, this windmill turned into the ceremonial centerpiece of a popular outdoor dance hall. Farther down rue Lépic, you'll pass near the former homes of **Toulouse-Lautrec** (at rue Tourlaque—look for the brick-framed art-studio windows under the heavy mansard roof) and **Vincent van Gogh** (54 rue Lépic).

Dalí Museum (L'Espace Dalí)—This beautifully lit black gallery (well-described in English) offers a walk through statues, etchings, and paintings by the master of Surrealism. The Spaniard found fame in Paris in the 1920s and '30s. He lived in Montmartre for a while, hung with the Surrealist crowd in Montparnasse, and shocked the world with his dreamscape paintings and experimental films. Don't miss the printed interview on the exit stairs.

Cost and Hours: €10, not covered by Museum Pass, daily 10:00-18:00, July-Aug until 20:00, 11 rue Poulbot. Tel. 01 42 64 40 10, www.daliparis.com.

Montmartre Museum (Musée de Montmartre)—This 17th-century home re-creates the traditional cancan and cabaret Montmartre scene, with paintings, posters, photos, music, and memorabilia.

Cost and Hours: €8, includes good audioguide, not covered by Museum Pass, Tue-Sun 11:00-18:00, closed Mon, 12 rue Cortot. Tel. 01 49 25 89 39, www.museedemontmartre.fr.

Pigalle—Paris' red light district, the infamous "Pig Alley," is at the foot of Butte Montmartre. *Ooh la la.* It's more racy than dangerous. Walk from place Pigalle to place Blanche, teasing desperate barkers and fast-talking temptresses. In bars, a €150 bottle of (what would otherwise be) cheap champagne comes with a friend. Stick to the bigger streets, hang on to your wallet, and exercise good judgment. Cancan can cost a fortune, as can con artists in topless bars. After dark, countless tour buses line the streets, reminding us that tour guides make big bucks by bringing their groups to touristy nightclubs like the famous Moulin Rouge (Mo: Pigalle or Abbesses).

Museum of Erotic Art (Musée de l'Erotisme)—Paris' sexy museum has five floors of risqué displays—mostly paintings and drawings—ranging from artistic to erotic to disgusting, with a few circa-1920 porn videos and a fascinating history of local brothels tossed in. It's in the center of the Pigalle red light district.

Cost and Hours: €8, €6/person for small groups of four or more, no...it's not covered by Museum Pass, daily 10:00-2:00 in the morning, 72 boulevard de Clichy, Mo: Blanche. Tel. 01 42 58 28 73, www.musee-erotisme.com.

Entertainment in Paris

Paris is brilliant after dark. Save energy from your day's sightseeing and experience the City of Light lit. Whether it's a concert at Sainte-Chapelle, a boat ride on the Seine, a walk in Montmartre, a hike up the Arc de Triomphe, or a late-night café, you'll see Paris at its best. Night walks in Paris are wonderful.

The *Pariscope* magazine (€0.40 at any newsstand, in French) offers a complete weekly listing of music, cinema, theater, opera, and other special events. The *Paris Voice* website, in English, has a helpful monthly review of Paris entertainment (www.parisvoice.com).

Music

Jazz and Blues Clubs—With a lively mix of American, French, and international musicians, Paris has been an internationally acclaimed jazz capital since World War II. You'll pay €12-25 to enter a jazz club (may include one drink; if not, expect to pay €5-10 per drink; beer is cheapest). See *Pariscope* magazine under "Musique" for listings, or, even better, the American Church's *Paris Voice* website for a good monthly review. You can also check each club's website (all have English versions), or drop by the clubs to check out the calendars posted on their front doors. Music starts after 21:00 in most clubs. Some offer dinner concerts from about 20:30 on. Here are several good bets:

Caveau de la Huchette, a characteristic, old jazz/dance club, fills an ancient Latin Quarter cellar with live jazz and frenzied dancing every night (admission about €12 on weekdays, €14 on weekends, €6-8 drinks, daily 21:30-2:30 in the morning or later, 5 rue de la Huchette, Mo: St. Michel, recorded info tel. 01 43 26 65 05, www.caveaudelahuchette.fr).

For a spot teeming with late-night activity and jazz, go to the two-block-long rue des Lombards, at boulevard Sébastopol, midway between the river and the Pompidou Center (Mo: Châtelet). **Au Duc des Lombards** is one of the most popular and respected jazz clubs in Paris, with concerts nightly in a great, plush, 110-seat theater-like setting (admission €20-30, buy online and arrive early for best seats, cheap drinks, shows at 20:00 and 22:00, 42 rue des Lombards, tel. 01 42 33 22 88, www.ducdeslombards.fr). **Le Sunside,** run for 16 years by Stephane Portet, is just a block away. The club offers two little stages (ground floor and downstairs): "le Sunset" stage tends toward contemporary world jazz; "le Sunside" stage features more traditional and acoustic jazz—Dixieland and big band (concerts range from free to €20, check their website; generally at 20:00, 21:00, and 22:00; 60 rue des Lombards, tel. 01 40 26 21 25, www.sunset-sunside.com).

For a less pricey—and less central—concert club, try **Utopia.** From the outside it's a hole in the wall, but inside it's filled with devoted fans of rock and folk blues. Though Utopia is officially a private club (and one that permits smoking), you can pay €3 to join for an evening, then pay a reasonable charge for the concert (usually €10 or under, concerts start about 22:00). It's located in the Montparnasse area (79 rue de l'Ouest, Mo: Pernety, tel. 01 43 22 79 66, www.utopia-cafeconcert.fr).

Old-Time Parisian Cabaret on Montmartre: Au Lapin Agile—This historic cabaret maintains the atmosphere of the heady days when bohemians would gather here to enjoy wine, song, and sexy jokes. For €24 (€17 for students) you gather with about 25 French people in a dark room for a drink and as many as 10 different performers—mostly singers with a piano. Performers range from sweet and innocent Amélie types to naughty Maurice Chevalier types. And though tourists are welcome, it's exclusively

French, with no accommodation for English speakers (except on their website), so non-French-speakers will be lost. You sit at carved wooden tables in a dimly lit room, taste the traditional drink (brandy with cherries), and are immersed in a true Parisian ambience. The soirée covers traditional French standards, love ballads, sea chanteys, and more. The crowd sings along, as it has here for a century (€7 drinks, Tue-Sun 21:00-2:00 in the morning, closed Mon, best to reserve ahead, 22 rue des Saules, tel. 01 46 06 85 87, www.au-lapin-agile.com).

A Modern Cabaret near Canal St. Martin: Chez Raymonde—This club proves that the art of dinner cabaret is still alive in Paris. Your evening begins with a good three-course dinner (including apéritif, wine, a half-bottle of champagne, and coffee) in an intimate dining room, where you get to know your neighbors. Around 22:00 the maître d'hôtel and the chef himself kick off the performance with a waltz together. Then it's feather boas, song, and dance—audience participation is encouraged (€55-100/person based on how elaborate a *menu* you choose, Fri-Sat evenings only, dinner starts at 20:00 when *le chef* greets you in person, performance usually finishes about 23:00, reservations necessary, 119 avenue Parmentier, Mo: Goncourt, Parmentier, or République, tel. 01 43 55 26 27, www.chez-raymonde.com). On Sunday afternoons, you can also attend a performance over lunch (same prices, starts at 12:30).

Classical Concerts—For classical music on any night, consult *Pariscope* magazine (check "Concerts Classiques" under "Musique" for listings) and look for posters at tourist-oriented churches.

From March through November, these churches regularly host concerts: St. Sulpice, St. Germain-des-Prés, La Madeleine, St. Eustache, St. Julien-le-Pauvre, and Sainte-Chapelle.

At **Sainte-Chapelle**, it's well worth the money for the pleasure of hearing Mozart, Bach, or Vivaldi, surrounded by the stained glass of the tiny church (unheated—bring a sweater). The acoustical quality is surprisingly good. There are usually two concerts per evening, at 19:00 and 20:30; specify which one you want when you buy or reserve your ticket. "Prestige" tickets get you a seat in the first seven rows; "normal" tickets are everything else. Seats are unassigned, so arrive at least 30 minutes early to snare a good view and to get through the security line. Two companies put on concerts—pick up schedules and tickets during the day at the small ticket booth to the left of the chapel entrance gate (€30 prestige, €25 normal; 4 boulevard du Palais, Mo: Cité; call 01 42 77 65 65 or 06 67 30 65 65 for schedules and reservations, you can leave your message in English—just speak clearly and spell your name; www.archetspf.asso.fr). Flavien from Euromusic offers discounts with this book (limit 2 tickets per book, prestige tickets discounted to €25, normal discounted to €16, offer applies to

Euromusic concerts and must be purchased with cash only at the Sainte-Chapelle ticket booth). The evening entrance is at 4 boulevard du Palais, between the gilded gate of the Palais de Justice and the Conciergerie. You'll enter through the law courts hall, directly into the royal upper chapel, just as St. Louis once did.

The **Salle Pleyel** hosts world-class artists, from string quartets and visiting orchestras to international opera stars. Tickets are usually expensive and hard to come by, so it's best to order online in advance (252 rue du Faubourg St. Honoré, Mo: Ternes, tel. 01 42 56 13 13, www.sallepleyel.fr).

Look also for daytime concerts in parks, such as the Luxembourg Garden. Even the Galeries Lafayette department store offers concerts. Many concerts are free *(entrée libre),* such as the Sunday atelier concert sponsored by the American Church (generally Sept-June at 17:00 but not every week, 65 quai d'Orsay, Mo: Invalides, RER: Pont de l'Alma, tel. 01 40 62 05 00, www.acparis.org).

Opera—Paris is home to two well-respected opera venues. The **Opéra Bastille** is the massive modern opera house that dominates place de la Bastille. Come here for state-of-the-art special effects and modern interpretations of classic ballets and operas. In the spirit of this everyman's opera, unsold seats are available at a big discount to seniors and students 15 minutes before the show. Standing-room-only tickets for €15 are also sold for some performances (Mo: Bastille). The **Opéra Garnier,** Paris' first opera house, hosts opera and ballet performances. Come here for less expensive tickets and grand belle époque decor (Mo: Opéra). To get tickets for either opera house, it's easiest to reserve online at www.operadeparis.fr, or call 01 71 25 24 23 outside France or toll tel. 08 92 89 90 90 inside France. You can also go direct to the Opéra Bastille's ticket office (open daily 11:00-18:00).

Art in the Evening

Various museums are open late on different evenings, offering the opportunity for more relaxed, less crowded visits.

In summer, sound-and-light displays at the Notre-Dame Cathedral illuminate its history. They generally run twice a week (free, in French with English subtitles, usually Thu and Sat at 21:00 but schedule varies—check www.cathedraledeparis.com). There is also an elaborate sound-and-light show at the Château in Versailles on Saturdays (€21, June-Aug at 21:00, www.chateauversailles.fr).

Night Walks

Go for an evening walk to best appreciate the City of Light. Break for ice cream, pause at a café, and enjoy the sidewalk entertainers

PARIS

as you join the post-dinner Parisian parade. Remember to avoid poorly lit areas and stick to main thoroughfares. Consider the following suggestions:

▲▲▲**Trocadéro and Eiffel Tower**—This is one of Paris' most spectacular views at night. Take the Métro to the Trocadéro stop and join the party on place du Trocadéro for a magnificent view of the glowing Eiffel Tower (see "Best Views" on page 349). It's a festival of hawkers, gawkers, drummers, and entertainers. To enjoy the same view from a comfortable seat with a drink in your hand, find **Café de l'Homme** on the west side of the terrace (daily 12:00 until "the heart of the night," but closed on occasion for private events, 17 place du Trocadéro, enter through Musée de la Marine, tel. 01 44 05 30 15).

Walk down the stairs, passing the fountains and rollerbladers, then cross the river to the base of the tower, worth the effort even if you don't go up (tower open daily mid-June-Aug until 24:45, Sept-mid-June until 23:45; see listing on page 345).

From the Eiffel Tower you can stroll through the Champ de Mars park past tourists and romantic couples, and take the Métro home (Ecole Militaire stop, across avenue de la Motte-Picquet from far southeast corner of park). Or there's a handy RER stop (Champ de Mars-Tour Eiffel) two blocks west of the Eiffel Tower.

▲▲**Champs-Elysées and the Arc de Triomphe**—The avenue des Champs-Elysées glows after dark. Start at the Arc de Triomphe (observation deck open daily, April-Sept until 23:00, Oct-March until 22:30), then stroll down Paris' lively grand promenade. A right turn on avenue George V leads to the Bateaux-Mouches river cruises. A movie on the Champs-Elysées is a fun experience (weekly listings in *Pariscope* under "Cinéma"), and a drink or snack at Renault's futuristic car café is a kick (at #53, toll tel. 08 11 88 28 11).

▲**Ile St. Louis and Notre-Dame**—This stroll features floodlit views of Notre-Dame and a taste of the Latin Quarter. Take the Métro (line 7) to the Pont Marie stop, then cross pont Marie to Ile St. Louis. Turn right up rue St. Louis-en-l'Ile, stopping for dinner—or at least a Berthillon ice cream (several locations) or Amorino Gelati at #47. At the end of Ile St. Louis, cross pont St. Louis to Ile de la Cité, with a great view of Notre-Dame. Wander to the Left Bank on quai de l'Archevêché, and drop down to the river to the right for the best floodlit views. From May through September you'll find several permanently moored barges *(péniches)* that operate as bars. Although I wouldn't eat dinner on one of these barges, the atmosphere is great for a drink, often including live music on weekends (daily until 2:00 in the morning, closed Oct-April, live music often Thu-Sun from 21:00). End your walk on place du Parvis Notre-Dame in front of Notre-Dame (on Sat-

Sun June-Aug, tower open until 23:00), or go back across the river to the Latin Quarter.

After-Dark Tours

Several companies offer evening tours of Paris. You can take a traditional, mass-produced bus tour for €28 per person, or for about the same price (€90 for 3 people) take a vintage car tour with a student guide. Do-it-yourselfers can save money by hiring a cab for a private tour (€50 for one hour). All options are described here.

▲▲▲**Deux Chevaux Car Tours**—If rumbling around Paris, sticking your head out of the rolled-back top of a funky old 2CV car *à la* Inspector Clouseau sounds like your kind of fun, do this. Paris Authentic has assembled a veritable fleet of these "tin-can" cars (not made since 1985) for giving tourists tours of Paris day and night. Night is best.

The student-guides are informal, speak English, and are passionate about showing you their city. The tours are flexible—you tell them where you'd like to go (use the taxi tour route described later). Trust your guide's detour suggestions and ask to get out as often as you like. Appreciate the simplicity of the vehicle you're in (France's version of the VW "bug"). Notice the bare-bones dashboard. Ask your guide to honk the horn, to run the silly little wipers, and to open and close the air vent—*c'est magnifique!* They'll pick you up and drop you at your hotel or wherever you choose (€80/hour for 1-2 person tour, €90/hour for 3 people, their 2-hour tour includes Montmartre and a bottle of champagne, 10 percent tip is appropriate, 23 rue Jean Jacques Rousseau, mobile 06 64 50 44 19, www.parisauthentic.com, paris@parisauthentic.com).

Nighttime Bus Tours—I list two different tours run by Paris Vision. Tickets are sold through your hotel (no booking fee, brochures in lobby) or directly at the Paris Vision office at 214 rue de Rivoli, across the street from the Tuileries Métro stop.

The nightly **Paris Vision** tour connects all the great illuminated sights of Paris with a 100-minute bus tour in 12 languages. The double-decker buses have huge windows, but the most desirable front seats are sometimes reserved for customers who've bought tickets for the overrated Moulin Rouge. Left-side seats are better. Visibility is fine in the rain.

These tours are not for everyone. You'll stampede on with a United Nations of tourists, get a set of headphones, dial up your language, and listen to a recorded spiel (which is interesting, but includes an annoyingly bright TV screen and a pitch for the other, more expensive excursions). Uninspired as it is, the ride provides an entertaining overview of the city at its floodlit and scenic best. Bring your city map to stay oriented as you go. You're always on the bus, but the driver slows for photos at viewpoints (€28/person, kids under 12 ride free, 1.5 hours, departs from 214 rue de Rivoli at 19:00 Nov-March, at 22:00 April-Oct, reserve one day in advance, arrive 30 minutes early to wait in line for best seats, tel. 01 42 60 30 01, www.parisvision.com). Skip the pricier minivan night tours.

L'Open Tour uses open-top, double-decker buses, and the guides don't hawk other packages (€25-30, departs from 2 rue des Pyramides at 22:00, 1.5 hours, June Fri-Sat only, daily July-Sept, closed Oct-May, must book in advance, tel. 01 42 66 56 56, www.parislopentour.com). If it's warm out, this is a great option.

▲▲▲**Do-It-Yourself Floodlit Paris Taxi Tour**—Seeing the City of Light floodlit is one of Europe's great travel experiences and a great finale to any day in Paris. For less than the cost of two seats on a big bus tour, you can hire your own cab (maximum four passengers) and have a glorious hour of illuminated Paris on your terms and schedule. The downside: You don't have the high vantage point and big windows, and taxi drivers can be moody. The upside: It's cheaper, you go when and where you like, and you can jump out anywhere to get the best views and pictures. I recommend a loop trip that takes about an hour and connects these sights: the Louvre Museum, Hôtel de Ville, Notre-Dame, Ile St. Louis, the Orsay Museum, esplanade des Invalides, Champ de Mars park at place Jacques Rueff (five-minute stop), Eiffel Tower from place du Trocadéro (five-minute stop), Arc de Triomphe, Champs-Elysées, and place de la Concorde. The trip should cost you about €45 (taxis have a strict meter of €33/hour plus about €1/km).

Sleeping in Paris

I've focused most of my recommendations in four safe, handy, and colorful neighborhoods: the village-like rue Cler (near the Eiffel Tower), the artsy and trendy Marais (near place de la Bastille), the historic core (on the two islands in the Seine, Ile St. Louis and Ile de la Cité), and the lively and Latin yet classy Luxembourg (on the Left Bank). Before choosing a hotel, read the descriptions of the neighborhoods closely. Each offers different pros and cons, and your neighborhood is as important as your hotel for the success of your trip.

Reserve ahead for Paris—the sooner, the better. In August and at other times when business is slower, some hotels offer lower rates to fill their rooms. Check their websites for the best deals.

If you're arriving on an overnight flight or train, your room probably won't be ready first thing in the morning. You should be able to safely check your bag at the hotel and dive right into Paris.

Old, characteristic, budget Parisian hotels have always been cramped. Retrofitted with toilets, private showers, and elevators (as most are today), they are even more cramped. French hotels must

Sleep Code

(€1 = about $1.40, country code: 33)

S = Single, **D** = Double/Twin, **T** = Triple, **Q** = Quad, **b** = bathroom, **s** = shower only, * = French hotel rating system (0-4 stars). Unless otherwise noted, hotel staff speak basic English, credit cards are accepted, and breakfast is not included (but is usually optional). All hotels in these listings have elevators, air-conditioning, Internet access (a public terminal in the lobby for guests to use), and Wi-Fi for travelers with laptops or other wireless devices, unless otherwise noted. "Wi-Fi only" means there's no public computer available.

To help you easily sort through these listings, I've divided the rooms into three categories based on the price for a standard double room with bath during high season:

$$$ Higher Priced—Most rooms €150 or more.

$$ Moderately Priced—Most rooms between €100-150.

$ Lower Priced—Most rooms €100 or less.

Prices can change without notice; verify the hotel's current rates online or by email. For other updates, see www.ricksteves.com/update.

charge a daily room tax *(taxe du séjour)* of about €1-2 per person per day. Some hotels include it in the price list, but most add it to your bill. Get advice from your hotel for safe parking (for parking basics, see page 308).

In the Rue Cler Neighborhood
(7th arrondissement, Mo: Ecole Militaire, La Tour Maubourg, or Invalides)

Rue Cler, lined with open-air produce stands six days a week, is a safe, tidy, village-like pedestrian street. It's so French that when I step out of my hotel in the morning, I feel like I must have been a poodle in a previous life. How such coziness lodged itself between the high-powered government district and the wealthy Eiffel Tower and Les Invalides areas, I'll never know. This is a neighborhood of wide, tree-lined boulevards, stately apartment buildings, and lots of Americans. The American Church and Franco-American Center (see page 306), American Library, American University, and many of my readers call this area home. Hotels here are a relatively good value, considering the elegance of the neighborhood and the higher prices of the more cramped hotels in other central areas. And for sightseeing, you're within walking distance of the Eiffel Tower, Army Museum, Quai Branly Museum, Seine River, Champs-Elysées, and Orsay and Rodin museums.

PARIS

Become a local at a rue Cler café for breakfast, or join the afternoon crowd for *une bière pression* (a draft beer). On rue Cler you can eat and browse your way through a street full of cafés, pastry shops, delis, cheese shops, and colorful outdoor produce stalls. Afternoon *boules* (outdoor bowling) on the esplanade des Invalides is a relaxing spectator sport (look for the dirt area to the upper right as you face the front of Les Invalides. The manicured gardens behind the golden dome of the Army Museum are free, peaceful, and filled with flowers (at southwest corner of grounds, closes at about 19:00).

Though hardly a happening nightlife spot, rue Cler offers many low-impact after-dark activities. Take an evening stroll above the river through the parkway between pont de l'Alma and pont des Invalides. For an after-dinner cruise on the Seine, it's a 15-minute walk to the river and the Bateaux-Mouches (see page 430). For a post-dinner cruise on foot, saunter into the Champ de Mars park to admire the glowing Eiffel Tower. For more ideas on Paris after hours, see "Entertainment in Paris," earlier.

Services: There's a large **post office** at the end of rue Cler on avenue de la Motte-Picquet, and a handy **SNCF Boutique** at 80 rue St. Dominique (Mon-Sat 8:30-19:30, closed Sun, get there when it opens to avoid a long wait). At both of these offices, take a number and wait your turn. A smaller post office is closer to the Eiffel Tower on avenue Rapp, one block past rue St. Dominique toward the river.

Markets: Cross the Champ de Mars park to mix it up with bargain-hunters at the twice-weekly open-air market, **Marché Boulevard de Grenelle,** under the Métro, a few blocks southwest of the Champ de Mars park (Wed and Sun until 12:30, between Mo: Dupleix and Mo: La Motte-Picquet-Grenelle). Two grocery stores, both on rue de Grenelle, are open until midnight: **Epicerie de la Tour** (at #197) and **Alimentation** (at corner with rue Cler). **Rue St. Dominique** is the area's boutique-browsing street and well worth a visit if shopping for clothes.

Internet Access: Two Internet cafés compete in this neighborhood: **Com Avenue** is best (about €5/hour, shareable and multiuse accounts, Mon-Sat 10:00-20:00, closed Sun, 24 rue du Champ de Mars, tel. 01 45 55 00 07); **Cyber World Café** is more expensive (and may close in 2012), but stays open later (about €7/hour, Mon-Sat 12:00-22:00, Sun 12:00-20:00, 20 rue de l'Exposition, tel. 01 53 59 96 54).

Laundry: Launderettes are omnipresent; ask your hotel for the nearest. Here are three handy locations: on rue Augereau (between rue St. Dominique and rue de Grenelle), on rue Amélie (between rue St. Dominique and rue de Grenelle), and at the southeast corner of rue Valadon and rue de Grenelle.

Métro Connections: Key Métro stops are Ecole Militaire, La Tour Maubourg, and Invalides. The useful RER-C line runs from the pont de l'Alma and Invalides stations, serving Versailles to the southwest; the Marmottan Museum to the northwest; and the Orsay Museum, Latin Quarter (St. Michel stop), and Austerlitz train station to the east.

Bus Routes: Smart travelers take advantage of these helpful bus routes (see "Rue Cler Hotels" map for stop locations):

Line #69 runs east-west along rue St. Dominique and serves Les Invalides, Orsay, Louvre, Marais, and Père Lachaise Cemetery.

Line #63 runs along the river (the quai d'Orsay), serving the Latin Quarter along boulevard St. Germain to the east (ending at Gare de Lyon), and Trocadéro and the Marmottan Museum to the west.

Line #92 runs along avenue Bosquet, north to the Champs-Elysées and Arc de Triomphe (far better than the Métro) and south to the Montparnasse Tower and Gare Montparnasse.

Line #87 runs from avenue Joseph Bouvard in the Champ de Mars park up avenue de la Bourdonnais and serves St. Sulpice, Luxembourg Garden, the Sèvres-Babylone shopping area, the Bastille, and Gare de Lyon (also more convenient than Métro for these destinations).

Line #80 runs on avenue Bosquet, crosses the Champs-Elysées, and serves Gare St. Lazare.

Line #28 runs on boulevard de la Tour Maubourg and serves Gare St. Lazare.

Line #42 runs from avenue Joseph Bouvard in the Champs de Mars park (same stop as #87) to Gare du Nord—a long ride but less tiring than the subway if you're carrying suitcases.

In the Heart of Rue Cler

Many of my readers stay in the rue Cler neighborhood. If you want to disappear into Paris, choose a hotel elsewhere. The first six hotels listed in this section are within Camembert-smelling distance of rue Cler; the others are within a five- to ten-minute stroll.

$$$ Hôtel Relais Bosquet*** is an excellent value with generous public spaces and comfortable rooms that are large by local standards and feature effective darkness blinds. The staff are politely formal (standard Db-€185-205, bigger Db-€225-245, book direct and ask about discount with this book, good €15 breakfast buffet with eggs and sausage, extra bed-€30, 19 rue du Champ de Mars, tel. 01 47 05 25 45, fax 01 45 55 08 24, www.relaisbosquet .com, hotel@relaisbosquet.com).

$$$ Hôtel du Cadran***, perfectly located a *boule* toss from rue Cler, is daringly modern—with a chocolate shop/bar in the

Rue Cler Hotels

1 Hôtel Relais Bosquet
2 Hôtel du Cadran
3 Hôtel de la Motte Picquet
4 Hôtel Valadon
5 Hôtel Beaugency
6 Grand Hôtel Lévêque
7 Hôtel du Champ de Mars
8 Hôtel Duquesne Eiffel
9 Hôtel La Bourdonnais
10 Hôtel de France
11 Hôtel de Turenne
12 Hôtel de Londres Eiffel
13 Hôtel de la Tulipe
14 Hôtel St. Dominique
15 Hôtel de la Tour Eiffel
16 Hôtel Kensington
17 Hôtel Les Jardins d'Eiffel
18 Hôtel Tour Eiffel Invalides
19 Hôtel Muguet
20 Hôtel de l'Empereur
21 Best Western Eiffel Park
22 Hôtel Eber Mars
23 Hôtel Prince
24 Hôtel la Serre
25 Hôtel Royal Phare
26 Paris Home Studios
27 SNCF Boutique
28 Internet Cafés (2)
29 Launderettes (3)

M METRO STATION
B BUS STOP w/ ROUTE #
P PARKING
T TAXI STAND
   PEDESTRIAN ZONE

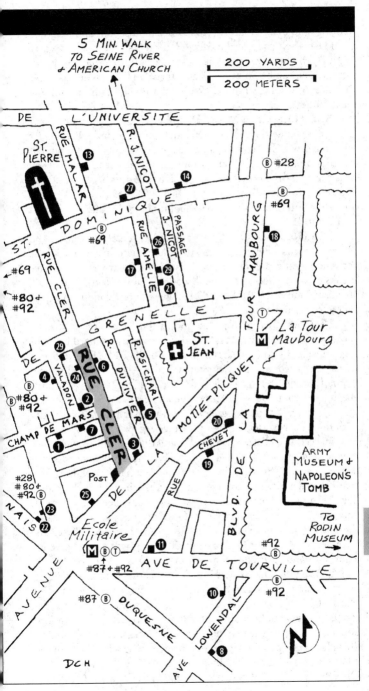

5 MIN. WALK
TO SEINE RIVER
& AMERICAN CHURCH

200 YARDS

200 METERS

DE L'UNIVERSITE

ST. PIERRE

RUE MALAR

R. J. NICOT

DE DOMINIQUE

ST.

RUE CLER

B #69

RUE AMELIE

J. NICOT

PASSAGE

B #28

B #69

18

B #69

GRENELLE

ST. JEAN

RUE CLER

VALADON

R. DUVIVIER

R. PSICHARI

La Tour Maubourg

TOUR MAUBOURG

MOTTE-PICQUET

BLVD. DE LA

ARMY MUSEUM & NAPOLEON'S TOMB

CHEVET

CHAMP DE MARS

DE

#80 & #92

#28 #80 & #92 B

NAIS

Post

Ecole Militaire

#87 & #92

AVE DE TOURVILLE

#92

B #92

AVENUE

#87 B

DUQUESNE

AVE

DCH

LOWENDAL

TO RODIN MUSEUM

PARIS

lobby, efficient staff, and stylish rooms featuring cool colors, mood lighting, and every comfort (Db-€210-240, discount and free (big) breakfast when you use the code "RickSteves" and book by email or through their website, discount not valid on website promo rates, which can be far better deals; 10 rue du Champ de Mars, tel. 01 40 62 67 00, fax 01 40 62 67 13, www.hotelducadran.com, info @cadranhotel.com).

$$$ Hôtel de la Motte Picquet*,** at the corner of rue Cler and avenue de la Motte-Picquet, is an intimate little place with narrow halls, comfortable but pricey rooms, and a terrific staff (Moe and Tina). Get a room off the street to avoid street noise (standard Db-€200, bigger Db-€250, Tb/Qb-€300, 30 avenue de la Motte-Picquet, tel. 01 47 05 09 57, fax 01 47 05 74 36, www.hotelmottepicquetparis.com, book@hotelmottepicquet paris.com).

$$$ Hôtel Valadon,** cute and quiet, rents 12 spacious and pleasing rooms a block from the rue Cler action. It's owned by the recommended Hôtel du Cadran (listed above), where you'll have breakfast, and offers the same discounts (Db-€155-165, Tb-€190, 16 rue Valadon, tel. 01 47 53 89 85, www.hotelvaladon.com, info @hotelvaladon.com).

$$ Hôtel Beaugency*,** a good value on a quieter street a short block off rue Cler, has 30 small rooms with standard furnishings and a lobby you can stretch out in (Sb-€112-125, Db-€125-165, occasional discounts for Rick Steves readers—ask when you book, 21 rue Duvivier, tel. 01 47 05 01 63, fax 01 45 51 04 96, www.hotel -beaugency.com, infos@hotel-beaugency.com).

Warning: The next two hotels are super values, but very busy with my readers (reserve long in advance).

$$ Grand Hôtel Lévêque,** ideally located on rue Cler, greets travelers with red and gray tones, and a sliver-sized slow-dance elevator. This busy, less personal hotel has a sleek breakfast room that doubles as a lounge, but no real lobby. Half the rooms have been nicely renovated and cost more, some need new carpets, and those on rue Cler come with fun views but morning noise as the market sets up (S-€75-95, Db-€95-145, Tb-€140-175, 29 rue Cler, tel. 01 47 05 49 15, fax 01 45 50 49 36, www.hotel-leveque .com, info@hotel-leveque.com, helpful staff).

$ Hôtel du Champ de Mars,** with adorable rooms and serious owners Françoise and Stephane, is a cozy rue Cler option. This plush little hotel has a small-town feel from top to bottom. The rooms are snug but lovingly kept, and single rooms can work as tiny doubles. It's an excellent value despite the lack of air-conditioning. This place gets mixed reviews from readers, who wish the management was more professionally good-natured at all times (Sb-€95, Db-€98, Tb-€129, 30 yards off rue Cler at 7 rue du Champ de

Mars, tel. 01 45 51 52 30, fax 01 45 51 64 36, www.hotelduchamp
demars.com, reservation@hotelduchampdemars.com).

Near Rue Cler, Close to Ecole Militaire Métro Stop

The following listings are a five-minute walk from rue Cler, near
Métro stop Ecole Militaire or RER: Pont de l'Alma.

$$$ Hôtel Duquesne Eiffel***, a few blocks farther from the
action, is calm, hospitable, and expertly run. It features handsome
rooms (some with terrific Eiffel Tower views for only €20 more), a
welcoming lobby, and a big, hot breakfast for €13 (Db-€180-230,
price grows with room size, Tb-€250, ask for discount with this
book, check website for better deals, 23 avenue Duquesne, tel. 01
44 42 09 09, fax 01 44 42 09 08, www.hde.fr, hotel@hde.fr).

$$$ Hôtel La Bourdonnais*** is *très* Parisian, mixing an
Old World feel with creaky, comfortable rooms and generous
public spaces. Its mostly spacious rooms are traditionally decorated, and its bathrooms are due for an upgrade (Db-€180-210,
Tb-€210, Qb-€235, ask about discount with this book, check website for better deals, 111 avenue de la Bourdonnais, tel. 01 47 05 45
42, fax 01 45 55 75 54, www.hotellabourdonnais.fr, hlb@hotella
bourdonnais.fr).

$$ Hôtel de France** is a good mid-range option away
from most other hotels I list. It's well-run by a brother-sister team
(Alain and Marie-Hélène) with a small bar/lounge and 60 fairly
priced and well-maintained rooms, some with knockout views of
Invalides' golden dome. Rooms on the courtyard are very quiet
(Sb-€95, standard Db-€115, bigger Db-€155, Tb-€165, connecting
rooms possible for families, no air-con, 102 boulevard de la Tour
Maubourg, tel. 01 47 05 40 49, fax 01 45 56 96 78, www.hotelde
france.com, hoteldefrance@wanadoo.fr).

$ Hôtel de Turenne** is modest, with the cheapest air-
conditioned rooms I've found and a lobby with windows on the
world. Rooms are simple but comfortable, and the price is right.
There are five true singles and several connecting rooms good for
families (Sb-€70, Db-€84-104, Tb-€130, Wi-Fi only, 20 avenue
de Tourville, tel. 01 47 05 99 92, fax 01 45 56 06 04, www.hotel
-turenne-paris.com, hotel.turenne.paris7@wanadoo.fr).

Near Rue Cler, Closer to Rue St. Dominique (and the Seine)

$$$ Hôtel de Londres Eiffel*** is my closest listing to the Eiffel
Tower and the Champ de Mars park. Here you get immaculate,
warmly decorated rooms (several are connecting for families), cozy
public spaces, and a service-oriented staff. Some rooms are tight—
request a bigger room. It's less convenient to the Métro (10-minute
walk), but handy to buses #69, #80, #87, and #92, and to RER-C:

Pont de l'Alma (Sb-€165, small Db-€190, bigger Db-€205, Db with Eiffel Tower view-€230, Tb-€260, 1 rue Augereau, tel. 01 45 51 63 02, fax 01 47 05 28 96, www.londres-eiffel.com, info@londres-eiffel.com). The owners also run a good two-star hotel with similar comfort in the cheaper Montparnasse area, **$$ Hôtel Apollon Montparnasse** (Db-€115-145, look for web deals, 91 rue de l'Ouest, Mo: Pernety, tel. & fax 01 43 95 62 00, www.paris-hotel-paris.net, apollonm@wanadoo.fr).

$$$ Hôtel de la Tulipe*,** three blocks from rue Cler toward the river, feels pricey but unique. The 20 small but artistically decorated rooms—each one different—come with stylish little bathrooms and surround a seductive, wood-beamed lounge and a peaceful, leafy courtyard (Db-€160, Tb-€180, two-room suite for up to five people-€295, no air-con, no elevator, pay Wi-Fi, 33 rue Malar, tel. 01 45 51 67 21, fax 01 47 53 96 37, www.paris-hotel-tulipe.com, hoteldelatulipe@wanadoo.fr).

$$ Hôtel St. Dominique,** well-located in the thick of rue St. Dominique, has fair rates, formal service, an inviting lobby, a small courtyard, a lovely breakfast room and traditionally decorated rooms—most with minibars (standard Db-€140, big Db-€160, extra bed-€20, no air-con, no elevator, Wi-Fi only, 62 rue St. Dominique, tel. 01 47 05 51 44, fax 01 47 05 81 28, www.hotelstdominique.com, saint-dominique.reservations@wanadoo.fr).

$ Hôtel de la Tour Eiffel** is a fair two-star value on a quiet street near several of my favorite restaurants. The rooms are well-designed but have thin walls, and some are desperately in need of new carpets (snug Db-€89-105, bigger Db-€105-129, no air-con, no breakfast offered, Wi-Fi only, 17 rue de l'Exposition, tel. 01 47 05 14 75, fax 01 47 53 99 46, www.hotel-toureiffel.com, hte7@wanadoo.fr).

$ Hôtel Kensington** is a good budget value close to the Eiffel Tower and run by elegant, though formal, Daniele. It's an unpretentious place with mostly small, simple, but well-kept rooms (Sb-€63, Db-€80, big Db on back side-€96, Eiffel Tower views for those who ask, no air-con, pay Internet access, 79 avenue de la Bourdonnais, tel. 01 47 05 74 00, fax 01 47 05 25 81, www.hotel-kensington.com, hk@hotel-kensington.com).

Near La Tour Maubourg Métro Stop

The next four listings are within three blocks of the intersection of avenue de la Motte-Picquet and boulevard de la Tour Maubourg.

$$$ Hôtel Les Jardins d'Eiffel*,** on a quiet street, feels like the modern motel it is, with professional service, its own parking garage (€24/day), and a spacious lobby. Rooms are spacious and peaceful (for Paris) and come in modern or traditional decor (Db-€215-240; ask about Rick Steves discount when you book direct, or check website for special discounts; 8 rue Amélie, tel. 01 47 05 46 21, fax 01 45 55 28 08, www.hoteljardinseiffel.com, paris@hoteljardins eiffel.com).

$$$ Hôtel Tour Eiffel Invalides* advertises its Best Western status proudly and offers a generous-size lobby with a small courtyard and good, traditionally decorated rooms with big beds but no firm prices (the Internet decides). Allow about €210 for a double, but look for better rates on their website (35 boulevard de la Tour Maubourg, tel. 01 45 56 10 78, fax 01 47 05 65 08, www .timhotel.fr, invalides@timhotel.fr).

$$$ Hôtel Muguet*,** a peaceful, stylish, immaculate refuge, gives you three-star comfort for a two-star price. This delightful spot offers 43 tasteful rooms, a greenhouse lounge, and a small garden courtyard. The hands-on owner, Catherine, gives her guests a restful and secure home in Paris (Sb-€115, Db-€150-200, Db with view-€175-205, Tb-€205, 11 rue Chevert, tel. 01 47 05 05 93, fax 01 45 50 25 37, www.hotelmuguet.com, muguet@wanadoo .fr, gentle Jacqueline runs reception).

$$$ Hôtel de l'Empereur** is well-run and offers good service. It delivers smashing views of Invalides from most of its very comfortable and tastefully designed rooms. Fifth-floor rooms have small balconies, and all rooms have queen-size beds (Sb-€130, Db-€160-180, Tb-€195, two-room Qb-€340, 2 rue Chevert, tel. 01 45 55 88 02, fax 01 45 51 88 54, www.hotelempereurparis.com, contact@hotelempereur.com).

Lesser Values in the Rue Cler Area
Given how nice this area is, these are acceptable last choices.

$$$ Best Western Eiffel Park* is a dead-quiet concrete business hotel with all the comforts, 36 pleasant if sterile rooms, and a rooftop terrace (Db-€270, bigger "premium" Db-€340, check online for promotional rates, 17 bis rue Amélie, tel. 01 45 55 10 01, fax 01 47 05 28 68, www.eiffelpark.com, reservation@eiffel park.com).

$$ Hôtel Eber Mars has larger-than-most rooms with weathered furnishings, oak-paneled public spaces, and a beam-me-up-Jacques coffin-sized elevator. Half the rooms are newly renovated, air-conditioned, and pricey; the higher rates listed are for those rooms (Db-€130-190, 20 percent cheaper Nov-March and July-Aug, 117 avenue de la Bourdonnais, tel. 01 47 05 42 30, fax 01 47 05 45 91, www.hotelebermars.com, reservation@hoteleber mars.com).

$$ Hôtel Prince,** across from the Ecole Militaire Métro stop, has a spartan lobby, drab halls, and plain-but-acceptable rooms for the price (Sb-€90, Db with shower-€115, Db with tub-€130, Tb-€150, Wi-Fi only, 66 avenue Bosquet, tel. 01 47 05 40 90, fax 01 47 53 06 62, www.hotelparisprince.com, paris@hotel-prince .com).

$$ Hôtel la Serre****, a modest place with basic comfort, some rough edges, and acceptable rates, is right on rue Cler (D–€80-140, 24 rue Cler, tel. 01 47 05 52 33, fax 01 40 62 95 66, www.hotella serreparis.com, hotellaserre@wanadoo.fr).

$ Hôtel Royal Phare****, facing the busy Ecole Militaire Métro stop, is a humble place. The 34 basic, pastel rooms are unimaginative but sleepable. Rooms on the courtyard are quietest, with peek-a-boo views of the Eiffel Tower from the fifth floor up (Sb–€84, Db with shower–€98, Db with tub–€108, Tb–€120, fridges in rooms, no air-con but fans, no Wi-Fi, 40 avenue de la Motte-Picquet, tel. 01 47 05 57 30, fax 01 45 51 64 41, www.hotel-royalphare-paris .com, hotel-royalphare@wanadoo.fr, friendly manager Hocin).

In the Marais Neighborhood

(4th arrondissement, Mo: Bastille, St. Paul, and Hôtel de Ville)
Those interested in a more SoHo/Greenwich Village–type locale should make the Marais their Parisian home. Once a forgotten Parisian backwater, the Marais—which runs from the Pompidou Center to the Bastille (a 15-minute walk)—is now one of Paris' most popular residential, tourist, and shopping areas. This is jumbled, medieval Paris at its finest, where classy stone mansions sit alongside trendy bars, antiques shops, and fashion-conscious boutiques. The streets are a fascinating parade of artists, students, tourists, immigrants, and baguette-munching babies in strollers. The Marais is also known as a hub of the Parisian gay and lesbian scene. This area is *sans doute* livelier (and louder) than the rue Cler area.

In the Marais you have these major sights close at hand: the Carnavalet Museum, Victor Hugo's House, the Jewish Art and History Museum, the Pompidou Center, and the Picasso Museum (closed for a multiyear renovation). You're also a manageable walk from Paris' two islands (Ile St. Louis and Ile de la Cité), home to Notre-Dame and Sainte-Chapelle. The Opéra Bastille, Promenade Plantée park, place des Vosges (Paris' oldest square), Jewish Quarter (rue des Rosiers), the Latin Quarter, and nightlife-packed rue de Lappe are also walkable. Strolling home (day or night) from Notre-Dame along the Ile St. Louis is marvelous. (For Marais sight descriptions, see page 363; for the Opéra, see page 373.)

Most of my recommended hotels are located a few blocks north of the Marais' main east-west drag, rue St. Antoine/rue de Rivoli.

Tourist Information: The nearest TI is in Gare de Lyon (Mon-Sat 8:00-18:00, closed Sun, all-Paris TI toll tel. 08 92 68 30 00).

Services: Most banks and other services are on the main street, rue de Rivoli, which becomes rue St. Antoine. Marais **post offices** are on rue Castex and at the corner of rue Pavée and rue des Francs Bourgeois. There's a busy **SNCF Boutique** where you can take care of all train needs on rue St. Antoine at rue de Turenne (Mon-Sat 8:30-20:30, closed Sun). A quieter SNCF Boutique is nearer Gare de Lyon at 5 rue de Lyon (Mon-Sat 8:30-18:00, closed Sun).

Markets: The Marais has two good open-air markets: the sprawling **Marché de la Bastille,** along boulevard Richard Lenoir, on the north side of place de la Bastille (Thu and Sun until 14:30, arts market Sat 10:00-19:00); and the more intimate, untouristy **Marché de la place d'Aligre** (Tue-Sun 9:00-14:00, closed Mon, cross place de la Bastille and walk about 10 blocks down rue du Faubourg St. Antoine, turn right at rue de Cotte to place d'Aligre; or, take Métro line 8 from Bastille in the direction of Créteil-Préfecture, get off at the Ledru-Rollin stop, and walk a few blocks southeast). A small **grocery** is open until 23:00 on rue St. Antoine (near intersection with rue Castex). To shop at a Parisian Sears, find the **BHV** next to Hôtel de Ville. Paris' oldest covered market, **Marché des Enfants Rouges,** lies a 10-minute walk north of rue de Rivoli.

Bookstore: The Marais is home to the friendliest English-language bookstore in Paris, **Red Wheelbarrow.** Penelope sells most of my guidebooks at good prices, and carries a great collection of other books about Paris and France for both adults and children (Mon 10:00-18:00, Tue-Sat 10:00-19:00, Sun 14:00-18:00, 22 rue St. Paul, Mo: St. Paul, tel. 01 48 04 75 08).

Internet Access: Try **Paris CY** (Mon-Sat 10:00-20:00, Sun 13:00-20:00, 8 rue de Jouy, Mo: St. Paul, tel. 01 42 71 37 37).

Laundry: There are many launderettes; ask your hotelier for the nearest. Here are three you can count on: on impasse Guéménée (north of rue St. Antoine), on rue Ste. Croix de la Bretonnerie (just east of rue du Temple), and on rue du Petit Musc (south of rue St. Antoine).

Métro Connections: Key Métro stops in the Marais are, from east to west: Bastille, St. Paul, and Hôtel de Ville (Sully-Morland, Pont Marie, and Rambuteau stops are also handy). Métro connections are excellent, with direct service to the Louvre, Champs-Elysées, Arc de Triomphe, and La Défense (all on line 1); the rue Cler area and Opéra Garnier (line 8 from Bastille stop); and four major train stations: Gare de Lyon, Gare du Nord, Gare de l'Est, and Gare d'Austerlitz (all accessible from Bastille stop).

Bus Routes: For stop locations, see the "Marais Hotels" map.

Line #69 on rue St. Antoine takes you eastbound to Père Lachaise Cemetery and westbound to the Louvre, Orsay, and

Marais Hotels

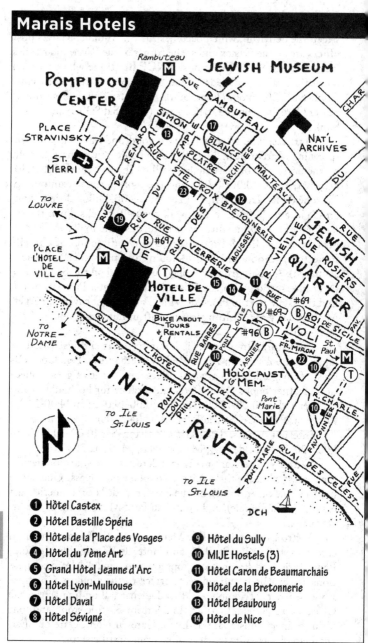

1 Hôtel Castex
2 Hôtel Bastille Spéria
3 Hôtel de la Place des Vosges
4 Hôtel du 7ème Art
5 Grand Hôtel Jeanne d'Arc
6 Hôtel Lyon-Mulhouse
7 Hôtel Daval
8 Hôtel Sévigné
9 Hôtel du Sully
10 MIJE Hostels (3)
11 Hôtel Caron de Beaumarchais
12 Hôtel de la Bretonnerie
13 Hôtel Beaubourg
14 Hôtel de Nice

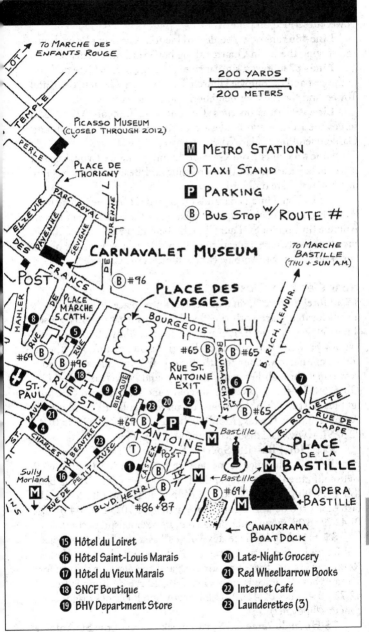

To MARCHE DES ENFANTS ROUGE

200 YARDS
200 METERS

PICASSO MUSEUM
(CLOSED THROUGH 2012)

Ⓜ METRO STATION
Ⓣ TAXI STAND
Ⓟ PARKING
Ⓑ BUS STOP w/ ROUTE #

PLACE DE THORIGNY

CARNAVALET MUSEUM

To MARCHE BASTILLE
(THU + SUN A.M.)

POST

Ⓑ #96   PLACE DES VOSGES

BOURGEOIS

PLACE MARCHE S. CATH.

❽

❺

#69 Ⓑ   Ⓑ #96

❶❽

#65 Ⓑ   Ⓑ #65

RUE ST. ANTOINE EXIT

❻

Ⓣ

❼

ST. PAUL

RUE ST.

❾   ❸

❷❸   ❷⓪   ❷

#69 Ⓑ   Ⓟ

Ⓑ #65

❷❶

❹

ANTOINE   Bastille   Ⓜ

❷❸

Ⓣ   POST

RUE DE LAPPE
ROQUETTE

Sully Morland

❶❻

Ⓜ

Ⓑ

IV

Ⓑ

BLVD. HENRI

#86 + #87

Ⓜ —Bastille

Ⓑ #69

PLACE DE LA BASTILLE

Ⓜ

OPERA BASTILLE

Ⓜ

CANAUXRAMA BOAT DOCK

⓯ Hôtel du Loiret
⓰ Hôtel Saint-Louis Marais
⓱ Hôtel du Vieux Marais
⓲ SNCF Boutique
⓳ BHV Department Store

⓴ Late-Night Grocery
㉑ Red Wheelbarrow Books
㉒ Internet Café
㉓ Launderettes (3)

Rodin museums, plus the Army Museum, ending at the Eiffel Tower (described on page 317).

Line #86 runs down boulevard Henri IV, crossing Ile St. Louis and serving the Latin Quarter along boulevard St. Germain.

Line #87 follows a similar route, but also serves Gare de Lyon to the east and St. Sulpice Church/Luxembourg Garden, the Eiffel Tower, and the rue Cler neighborhood to the west.

Line #96 runs on rues Turenne and François Miron and serves the Louvre and boulevard St. Germain (near Luxembourg Garden), ending at Gare Montparnasse.

Line #65 runs from Gare de Lyon up rue de Lyon, around place de la Bastille, and then up boulevard Beaumarchais to Gare de l'Est and Gare du Nord.

Taxis: You'll find taxi stands on place de la Bastille (where boulevard Richard Lenoir meets the square), on the south side of rue St. Antoine (in front of St. Paul Church), behind the Hôtel de Ville on rue du Lobau (where it meets rue de Rivoli), and a quieter one on the north side of rue St. Antoine (where it meets rue Castex).

Near Place des Vosges

$$$ Hôtel Castex***, on a quiet street near place de la Bastille, is a well-located place with tile-floored rooms (that amplify noise). Their clever system of connecting rooms allows families total privacy between two rooms, each with its own bathroom. The 30 rooms are narrow. Your fourth night is free in August and from November through February, except around New Year's (Sb-€130, Db-€160, Tb-€230, ask about discount and free but mediocre buffet breakfast with this book, just off place de la Bastille and rue St. Antoine at 5 rue Castex, Mo: Bastille, tel. 01 42 72 31 52, fax 01 42 72 57 91, www.castexhotel.com, info@castexhotel.com).

$$$ Hôtel Bastille Spéria***, a short block off place de la Bastille, offers business-type service in a great location. The 42 well-configured rooms are modern and comfortable, with big beds (Sb-€115-140, Db-€135-180, child's bed-€20, good buffet breakfast-€13, 1 rue de la Bastille, Mo: Bastille, tel. 01 42 72 04 01, fax 01 42 72 56 38, www.hotelsperia.com, info@hotelsperia.com).

$$ Hôtel de la Place des Vosges** is a shy, low–brow place brilliantly located between rue St. Antoine and place des Vosges. Rooms are spare, there's no air-con, and the elevator skips floors 5 and 6, but the price is right (Db-€107, 12 rue de Biraque, tel. 01 42 72 60 46, fax 01 42 72 02 64, www.hotelplacedesvosges.com, contact@hpdv.net).

$$ Hôtel du 7ème Art**, two blocks south of rue St. Antoine toward the river, is a young, carefree, Hollywood-nostalgia place with a full-service café-bar and Charlie Chaplin murals. Its 23 good-value rooms have brown 1970s decor, but are comfortable enough. Sadly, smoking is allowed in all rooms, so you might detect an odor. The large rooms are American-spacious (small Db-€95, standard Db-€110, large Db-€125-150, Tb-€145-170, extra bed-€20, no elevator, 20 rue St. Paul, Mo: St. Paul, tel. 01 44 54 85 00, fax 01 42 77 69 10, www.paris-hotel-7art.com, hotel7art @wanadoo.fr).

$ Grand Hôtel Jeanne d'Arc**, a lovely little hotel with thoughtfully appointed rooms, is ideally located for (and very popular with) connoisseurs of the Marais. It's a good value and worth booking way ahead (three months in advance, if possible). Sixth-floor rooms have views, and corner rooms are wonderfully bright in the City of Light. Rooms on the street can be noisy until the bars close (Sb-€63-91, Db-€91, larger twin Db-€118, Tb-€148, good Qb-€162, no air-con, Wi-Fi only, 3 rue de Jarente, Mo: St. Paul, tel. 01 48 87 62 11, fax 01 48 87 37 31, www.hoteljeannedarc .com, information@hoteljeannedarc.com).

$ Hôtel Lyon-Mulhouse**, well-managed by gregarious Nathalia, is located on a busy street barely off place de la Bastille. Though less intimate than some, it is a solid deal, with pleasant, relatively large rooms—five are true singles with partial Eiffel Tower views (Sb-€74, Db-€100, Tb-€130, Qb-€150, 8 boulevard Beaumarchais, Mo: Bastille, tel. 01 47 00 91 50, fax 01 47 00 06 31, www.1-hotel-paris.com, hotelyonmulhouse@wanadoo.fr).

$ Hôtel Daval**, an unassuming place on the *wild side* of place de la Bastille, is ideal for night owls. The rooms are tiny and the halls are narrow, but the rates are good for an air-conditioned place. Ask for a quieter room on the courtyard side if sleep matters (Sb-€81, Db-€89-98, Tb-115, Qb-€130, Wi-Fi only, 21 rue Daval, Mo: Bastille, tel. 01 47 00 51 23, fax 01 40 21 80 26, www.hotel daval.com, hoteldaval@wanadoo.fr, Didier).

$ Hôtel Sévigné**, run by straight-faced owner Monsieur Mercier, is a simple little hotel with lavender halls and 30 tidy, comfortable rooms at good prices (Sb-€72, Db-€86-97, Tb-€100-117; one-night, no-refund policy for any cancellation; Wi-Fi only, air-con turned off overnight, 2 rue Malher, Mo: St. Paul, tel. 01 42 72 76 17, fax 01 42 78 68 26, www.le-sevigne.com, contact@le -sevigne.com).

$ Hôtel du Sully, sitting right on rue St. Antoine, is basic, cheap, central, and run by friendly Monsieur Zeroual. The rooms are frumpy, dimly lit, and can smell of smoke, and the entry is narrow, but the hotel offers a fair deal (Db-€70, Tb-€84, Qb-€94, no elevator, no air-con, Wi-Fi only, 48 rue St. Antoine, Mo: St. Paul, tel. 01 42 78 49 32, fax 01 44 61 76 50, www.sullyhotelparis.com, sullyhotel@orange.fr).

$ MIJE Youth Hostels: The Maison Internationale de la Jeunesse et des Etudiants (MIJE) runs three classy old residences, ideal for budget travelers. Each is well-maintained, with simple, clean, single-sex (unless your group takes a whole room), one- to four-bed rooms for travelers of any age. The hostels are **MIJE Fourcy** (biggest and loudest, €11 dinners available with a membership card, 6 rue de Fourcy, just south of rue de Rivoli), **MIJE Fauconnier** (no elevator, 11 rue du Fauconnier), and **MIJE Maubisson** (smallest and quietest, no outdoor terrace, 12 rue des Barres). None has double beds or air-conditioning; all have private showers in every room (all prices per person: Sb-€50, Db-€37, Tb-€33, Qb-€31, credit cards accepted, includes breakfast but not towels, required membership card-€2.50 extra/person, 7-day maximum stay, rooms locked 12:00-15:00, curfew at 1:00 in the morning). They all share the same contact information (tel. 01 42 74 23 45, fax 01 40 27 81 64, www.mije.com, info@mije.com) and Métro stop (St. Paul). Reservations are accepted (six weeks ahead online, 10 days ahead by phone), though you must show up by noon, or call the morning of arrival to confirm a later arrival time.

Near the Pompidou Center

These hotels are farther west, closer to the Pompidou Center than to place de la Bastille. The Hôtel de Ville Métro stop works well for all of these hotels, unless a closer stop is noted.

$$$ Hôtel Caron de Beaumarchais*,** on a busy corner, feels like a fluffy folk museum, with 20 pricey but cared-for and character-filled rooms. Its small lobby is cluttered with bits from an elegant 18th-century Marais house (small Db in back-€160, larger Db facing the front-€185, Wi-Fi only, 12 rue Vieille du Temple, tel. 01 42 72 34 12, fax 01 42 72 34 63, www.carondebeaumarchais .com, hotel@carondebeaumarchais.com).

$$ Hôtel de la Bretonnerie*,** three blocks from the Hôtel de Ville, makes a good Marais home. It has a warm, welcoming lobby and 29 well-appointed, good-value rooms with an antique, open-beam warmth (standard "classic" Db-€135, bigger "charming" Db-€165, Db suite-€195, Tb/Qb-€200, Tb/Qb suite-€220, no air-con, between rue Vieille du Temple and rue des Archives at 22 rue Ste. Croix de la Bretonnerie, tel. 01 48 87 77 63, fax 01 42 77 26 78, www.bretonnerie.com, hotel@bretonnerie.com).

$$ Hôtel Beaubourg*** is a solid three-star value on a small street in the shadow of the Pompidou Center. The lounge is inviting, and the 28 rooms are comfy, well-appointed, and quiet (standard Db-€140, bigger twin or king-size Db-€160 and worth the extra cost, rates vary wildly by season, 11 rue Simon Le Franc, Mo: Rambuteau, tel. 01 42 74 34 24, fax 01 42 78 68 11, www.hotel beaubourg.com, reservation@hotelbeaubourg.com).

$$ Hôtel de Nice,** on the Marais' busy main drag, features a turquoise-and-fuchsia "Marie-Antoinette-does-tie-dye" decor. Its narrow halls are littered with paintings and layered with carpets, and its 23 Old World rooms have thoughtful touches and tight bathrooms. Twin rooms, which cost the same as doubles, are larger and on the street side—but have effective double-paned windows (Sb-€95, Db-€120, Tb-€145, extra bed-€25, Wi-Fi only, reception on second floor, 42 bis rue de Rivoli, tel. 01 42 78 55 29, fax 01 42 78 36 07, www.hoteldenice.com, contact@hoteldenice.com, laissez-faire management).

$ Hôtel du Loiret* is a centrally located and rare Marais budget hotel. It's basic, but the rooms are surprisingly sharp, considering the price and location (Db-€70-90, Tb-€100, no air-con, pay Internet access, no Wi-Fi, expect some noise, 8 rue des Mauvais Garçons, tel. 01 48 87 77 00, fax 01 48 04 96 56, www.hotel-du -loiret.fr, hotelduloiret@hotmail.com).

Lesser Values in the Marais

These hotels are located on the map on pages 388-389.

$$ Hôtel Saint-Louis Marais,** small and tranquil, is tucked away on a residential street between the river and rue St. Antoine. The lobby and 19 rooms have character, but need attention (small Db-€115, standard Db-€140, Tb-€160, no air-con, no elevator, pay Wi-Fi only, parking-€20, 1 rue Charles V, Mo: Sully Morland, tel. 01 48 87 87 04, fax 01 48 87 33 26, www.saintlouismarais.com, marais@saintlouishotels.com).

$$ Hôtel du Vieux Marais,** with a quirky owner and modern rooms but a lobby perpetually under construction, lies on a quiet street two blocks east of the Pompidou Center. Say *bonjour* to friendly bulldog Leelou, who runs the little lobby (Sb-€110-125, Db-€130-165, Wi-Fi only, just off rue des Archives at 8 rue du Plâtre, Mo: Rambuteau or Hôtel de Ville, tel. 01 42 78 47 22, fax 01 42 78 34 32, www.vieuxmarais.com, hotel@vieuxmarais.com).

In the Historic Core of Paris
(4th arrondissement; Mo: Pont Marie, Sully-Morland, and Cité; RER: St. Michel)

This area is smack-dab in the middle of the city, in the peaceful kernel of this busy metropolis. You won't find any budget values here, but the islands' village ambience and proximity to the Marais, Notre-Dame, and the Latin Quarter help compensate for higher rates. For background on these two islands, see page 325 of the "Historic Paris Walk."

On Ile St. Louis

The peaceful, residential character of this river-wrapped island, its brilliant location, and its homemade ice cream have drawn Americans for decades, allowing hotels to charge dearly. All of the

PARIS

Hotels & Restaurants on Ile St. Louis

1 Hôtel du Jeu de Paume
2 Hôtel de Lutèce & Grocery
3 Hôtel des Deux-Iles
4 Hôtel Saint-Louis
5 Le Tastevin Rest.
6 Rests. La Taverne du Sergeant Recruteur & Nos Ancêtres les Gaulois
7 La Brasserie de l'Ile St. Louis
8 L'Orangerie & Auberge de la Reine Blanche
9 Café Med
10 Berthillon Ice Cream (3)
11 Amorino Gelati
12 Good Picnic Spot

following hotels are on the island's main drag, rue St. Louis-en-l'Ile, where I list several restaurants (see page 421). Use Mo: Pont Marie or Sully-Morland.

$$$ Hôtel du Jeu de Paume****, occupying a 17th-century tennis center, is the most expensive hotel I list in Paris. When you enter its magnificent lobby, you'll understand why. Greet Scoop, *le chien*, then take a spin in the glass elevator for a half-timbered-tree-house experience. The 30 quite comfortable rooms are carefully designed and *très* tasteful, though small for the price (you're paying for the location and sensational public spaces—check for deals on their website). Most rooms face a small garden; all are pin-drop peaceful (standard Db-€335, larger Db-€420, deluxe Db-€480, check for Web deals, €18 breakfast, 54 rue St. Louis-en-l'Ile, tel. 01 43 26 14 18, fax 01 40 46 02 76, www.jeudepaumehotel.com, info@jeudepaumehotel.com).

$$$ Hôtel de Lutèce*** charges top euro for its island address but comes with a sit-awhile wood-paneled lobby, a real fireplace, and warmly designed rooms. Twin rooms are larger and the same

PARIS

price as double rooms (Db-€200, Tb-€235, 65 rue St. Louis-en-l'Ile, tel. 01 43 26 23 52, fax 01 43 29 60 25, www.hoteldelutece.com, info@hoteldelutece.com).

$$$ Hôtel des Deux-Iles* is bright and colorful, with marginally smaller rooms than other hotels on this street (Db-€200, Wi-Fi only, 59 rue St. Louis-en-l'Ile, tel. 01 43 26 13 35, fax 01 43 29 60 25, www.hoteldesdeuxiles.com, info@hoteldesdeuxiles.com).

$$$ Hôtel Saint-Louis* has less personality but good enough rooms with parquet floors and comparatively good rates. The hotel was entirely renovated in 2011, so expect some change in rates (Db-€150-165, superior Db-€240, extra bed-€50, Wi-Fi only, 75 rue St. Louis-en-l'Ile, tel. 01 46 34 04 80, fax 01 46 34 02 13, www.hotelsaintlouis.com, slouis@noos.fr).

On Ile de la Cité

$$ Hôtel Dieu Hospitel Paris is the only Paris hotel with an Ile de la Cité address. It's located in the oldest city hospital of Paris, on the square in front of Notre-Dame (find the hospital on the map on page 322). The present building dates from 1877. Originally intended to receive families of patients, it now offers rooms for tourists as well. With just 14 rooms, you must book well in advance. You'll be surprised by the modern, comfortable decor and may even forget you're in a hospital (Sb-€125, Db-€135, some rooms have peek-a-boo views of Notre-Dame, 1 place du Parvis, tel. 01 44 32 01 00, www.hotel-hospitel.com, hospitelhoteldieu@wanadoo.fr). Enter the hotel's main entrance, turn right, follow signs to wing B2, and take the elevator to the sixth floor.

Luxembourg Garden Area
(St. Sulpice to Panthéon)
(5th and 6th arrondissements, Mo: St. Sulpice, Mabillon, Odéon, and Cluny-La Sorbonne; RER: Luxembourg)

This neighborhood revolves around Paris' loveliest park and offers quick access to the city's best shopping streets and grandest café-hopping. Hotels in this central area are expensive; sleeping in the Luxembourg area offers visitors a true Left Bank experience without a hint of the low-end commotion of the nearby Latin Quarter tourist ghetto. The Luxembourg Garden, boulevard St. Germain, Cluny Museum, and Latin Quarter are all at your doorstep. Here you get the best of both worlds: youthful Left Bank energy and the classic trappings that surround the monumental Panthéon and St. Sulpice Church.

Having the Luxembourg Garden as your backyard allows strolls through meticulously cared-for flowers, a great kids' play area, and a purifying escape from city traffic. Place St. Sulpice

PARIS

Hotels near Luxembourg Garden

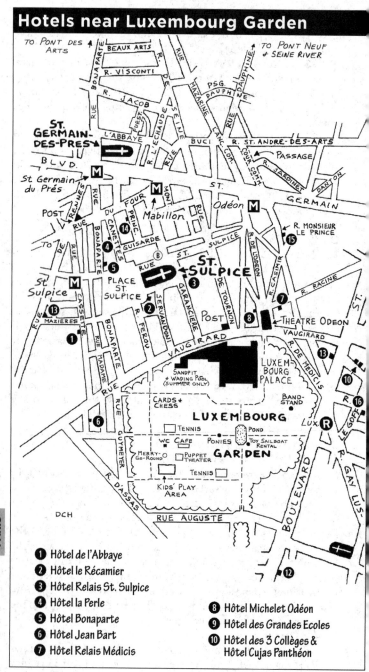

❶ Hôtel de l'Abbaye
❷ Hôtel le Récamier
❸ Hôtel Relais St. Sulpice
❹ Hôtel la Perle
❺ Hôtel Bonaparte
❻ Hôtel Jean Bart
❼ Hôtel Relais Médicis

❽ Hôtel Michelet Odéon
❾ Hôtel des Grandes Ecoles
❿ Hôtel des 3 Collèges &
   Hôtel Cujas Panthéon

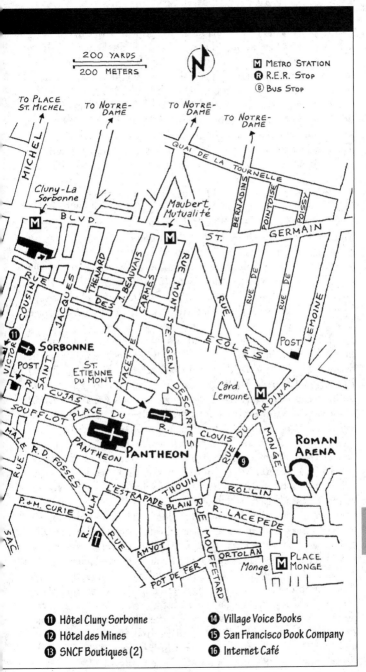

11 Hôtel Cluny Sorbonne
12 Hôtel des Mines
13 SNCF Boutiques (2)
14 Village Voice Books
15 San Francisco Book Company
16 Internet Café

presents an elegant, pedestrian-friendly square and quick access to some of Paris' best boutiques. Sleeping in the Luxembourg area also puts several movie theaters at your fingertips (at Métro stop: Odéon), as well as lively cafés on boulevard St. Germain, rue de Buci, rue des Canettes, place de la Sorbonne, and place de la Contrescarpe, all of which buzz with action until late.

Although it takes only 15 minutes to walk from one end of this neighborhood to the other, I've located the hotels by the key monument they are close to (St. Sulpice Church, the Odéon Theater, and the Panthéon). Most hotels are within a five-minute walk of the Luxembourg Garden (and none is more than 15 minutes away).

Services: The nearest **TI** is across the river in Gare de Lyon (Mon-Sat 8:00-18:00, closed Sun, all-Paris TI toll tel. 08 92 68 30 00). There are two useful **SNCF Boutiques** for easy train reservations and ticket purchase: at 79 rue de Rennes and at 54 boulevard St. Michel (Mon-Sat 8:30-18:00, closed Sun).

Markets: The colorful street market at the south end of rue Mouffetard is a worthwhile 10- to 15-minute walk from these hotels (Tue-Sat 8:00-12:00 & 15:30-19:00, Sun 8:00-12:00, closed Mon, five blocks south of place de la Contrescarpe, Mo: Place Monge).

Bookstores: The **Village Voice** bookstore carries a full selection of English-language books (including mine), and is near St. Sulpice. Say hello to Michael but don't ask his opinion of *The Da Vinci Code* (Mon 14:00-19:30, Tue-Sat 10:00-19:30, Sun 12:00-18:00, 6 rue Princesse, tel. 01 46 33 36 47). **San Francisco Book Company** is a welcoming bookstore (Mon-Sat 11:00-21:00, Sun 14:00-19:30, 17 rue Monsieur le Prince, tel. 01 43 29 15 70).

Internet Access: You'll find it at **Le Milk** (always open, between the Luxembourg Garden and Panthéon at 17 rue Soufflot).

Métro Connections: Métro lines 10 and 4 serve this area (10 connects to the Austerlitz train station, and 4 runs to the Montparnasse, Est, and Nord train stations). Neighborhood stops are Cluny-La Sorbonne, Mabillon, Odéon, and St. Sulpice. RER-B (Luxembourg station is handiest) provides direct service to Charles de Gaulle airport and Gare du Nord trains, and access to Orly airport on the Orlybus (transfer at Denfert-Rochereau).

Bus Routes: Buses #63, #86, and #87 run eastbound through this area on or near boulevard St. Germain, and westbound along rue des Ecoles, stopping on place St. Sulpice. Lines #63 and #87 provide direct connections west to the rue Cler area. Line #63 also serves the Orsay, Army, Rodin, and Marmottan museums to the west and Gare de Lyon to the east. Lines #86 and #87 run east to the Marais, and #87 continues to Gare de Lyon. Line #96 stops at place St. Sulpice southbound en route to Gare Montparnasse and runs north along rue de Rennes and boulevard St. Germain into the Marais.

Hotels near St. Sulpice Church

These hotels are all within a block of St. Sulpice Church and two blocks from famous boulevard St. Germain. This is nirvana for boutique-minded shoppers—and you'll pay extra for the location. Métro stops St. Sulpice and Mabillon are equally close.

$$$ Hôtel de l'Abbaye**** is a lovely refuge just west of Luxembourg Garden, and is a find for well-heeled connoisseurs of this area. The hotel's four-star luxury includes refined lounges inside and out, with 44 sumptuous rooms and every amenity at surprisingly reasonable rates (standard Db-€240-260, bigger Db-€352-380, suites and apartments available for €550, includes breakfast, 10 rue Cassette, tel. 01 45 44 38 11, fax 01 45 48 07 86, www.hotel-abbaye.com, hotel.abbaye@wanadoo.fr).

$$$ Hôtel le Récamier** romantically tucked in the corner of place St. Sulpice, is high-end defined, with designer public spaces, elaborately appointed rooms, and professional service (classic Db-€260, deluxe Db-€290, traditional Db-€330, deluxe rooms offer best value, fitness room, 3 bis place St. Sulpice, tel. 01 43 26 04 89, fax 01 43 26 35 76, www.hotelrecamier.com, contact@hotel recamier.com).

$$$ Hôtel Relais St. Sulpice***, burrowed on the small street just behind St. Sulpice Church, is a little boutique hotel with a cozy lounge and 26 pricey and stylish rooms, most surrounding a leafy glass atrium. Top-floor rooms get more light and are worth requesting (Db-€213-260 depending on size, much less off-season, includes breakfast, sauna free for guests, Wi-Fi only, 3 rue Garancière, tel. 01 46 33 99 00, fax 01 46 33 00 10, www.relais-saint-sulpice.com, relaisstsulpice@wanadoo.fr).

$$$ Hôtel la Perle***, is a spendy pearl in the thick of the lively rue des Canettes, a block off place St. Sulpice. At this snappy, modern, business-class hotel, sliding glass doors open onto the traffic-free street, and you're greeted by a fun lobby built around a central bar and atrium (standard Db-€210, bigger Db-€225, luxury Db-€250, check website or call for last-minute deals within five days of your stay, includes breakfast, 14 rue des Canettes, tel. 01 43 29 10 10, fax 01 46 34 51 04, www.hotellaperle.com, booking@hotel laperle.com).

$$ Hôtel Bonaparte**, an unpretentious place wedged between boutiques, is a few steps from place St. Sulpice. Although the 29 Old World rooms don't live up to the handsome entry, they're plenty comfortable and spacious by Paris standards, with big bathrooms, traditional decor, and molded ceilings (Sb-€107-132, Db-€140-163, big Db-€175, Tb-€182, includes basic breakfast,

61 rue Bonaparte, tel. 01 43 26 97 37, fax 01 46 33 57 67, www
.hotelbonaparte.fr, reservation@hotelbonaparte.fr; helpful Fréd-
eric, Sabine, and Eric at reception).

West of Luxembourg Garden

$ Hôtel Jean Bart** feels like it's from another era—prices
included. Run by smiling Madame Lechopier, it's a rare budget
hotel find in this otherwise swanky neighborhood, one block from
Luxembourg Garden. Beyond the dark, retirement home–like
lobby, you'll find 33 simple, spotless rooms with creaking floors
and tight bathrooms. The cheapest rooms share one shower on the
first floor (S-€53, Sb-€71, D-€54, Db-€72, cash only, no air-con,
9 rue Jean-Bart, tel. 01 45 48 29 13, fax 01 45 48 10 79, hotel.jean
.bart@gmail.com).

Near the Odéon Theater

These two hotels are between the Odéon Métro stop and
Luxembourg Garden (five blocks east of St. Sulpice), and may have
rooms when others don't. In addition to the Odéon Métro stop,
the RER-B Luxembourg stop is a short walk away.

$$$ Hôtel Relais Médicis*** is perfect in every way—if
you've always wanted to live in a Monet painting and can afford
it. A glassy entry hides 16 rooms surrounding a fragrant little
garden courtyard and fountain, giving you a countryside break fit
for a Medici in the heart of Paris. This delightful refuge is taste-
fully decorated with floral Old World charm, and is permeated
with thoughtfulness (Sb-€172, Db-€208-228, deluxe Db-€258,
Tb-€298, Qb-€388, €30 cheaper mid-July-Aug and Nov-March,
includes extravagant continental breakfast, faces the Odéon
Theater at 23 rue Racine, tel. 01 43 26 00 60, fax 01 40 46 83 39,
www.relaismedicis.com, reservation@relaismedicis.com).

$$ Hôtel Michelet Odéon** sits in a corner of place de
l'Odéon with big windows on the square. Though it lacks person-
ality, it's a fair value in this pricey area, with 24 simple rooms with
modern decor and views of the square (Db-€115-135, Tb-€170,
Qb-€190, no air-con, pay Wi-Fi, 6 place de l'Odéon, tel. 01 53
10 05 60, fax 01 46 34 55 35, www.hotelmicheletodeon.com, hotel
@micheletodeon.com).

Near the Panthéon and Rue Mouffetard

$$ Hôtel des Grandes Ecoles*** is idyllic. A private cobbled lane
leads to three buildings that protect a flower-filled garden court-
yard, preserving a sense of tranquility rare in this city. Its 51 rooms
are French-countryside–pretty, spotless, and reasonably spacious,
but have no air-conditioning. This romantic spot is deservedly
popular, so book ahead, though reservations are not accepted more

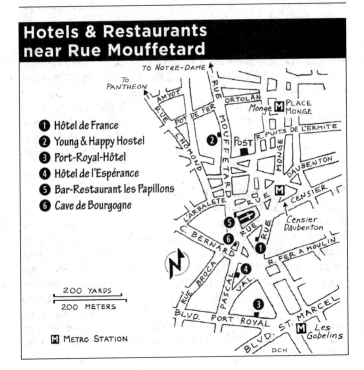

Hotels & Restaurants near Rue Mouffetard

1 Hôtel de France
2 Young & Happy Hostel
3 Port-Royal-Hôtel
4 Hôtel de l'Espérance
5 Bar-Restaurant les Papillons
6 Cave de Bourgogne

200 YARDS
200 METERS

M METRO STATION

than four months in advance (Db-€118-143 depending on size, extra bed-€20, pricey breakfast, parking garage-€30, pay Wi-Fi, 75 rue du Cardinal Lemoine, Mo: Cardinal Lemoine, tel. 01 43 26 79 23, fax 01 43 25 28 15, www.hotel-grandes-ecoles.com, hotel .grandes.ecoles@wanadoo.fr, mellow Marie speaks English, Mama does not).

$$ Hôtel des 3 Collèges** greets clients with a bright lobby, narrow hallways, and unimaginative rooms...but fair rates (Sb-€83-108, Db-€108-150, Tb-€150-170, pay Wi-Fi only, 16 rue Cujas, tel. 01 43 54 67 30, fax 01 46 34 02 99, www.3colleges.com, hotel@3colleges.com).

$$ Hôtel Cujas Panthéon** gives traditional two-star comfort *sans* air-conditioning at fair prices (Db-€99-110, Tb-€149, Wi-Fi only, 18 rue Cujas, tel. 01 43 54 58 10, fax 01 43 25 88 02, www .hotelcujaspantheon.com, hotel-cujas-pantheon@wanadoo.fr).

$ Hôtel Cluny Sorbonne** is a modest place warmly run by Monsieur and Madame Berber. It's located in the thick of things across from the famous university and below the Panthéon. Rooms are well-worn with thin walls, but are clean and comfortable (small Db-€95, really big Db/Tb/Qb-€160, check website for deals, no air-con, Wi-Fi only, 8 rue Victor Cousin, tel. 01 43 54 66 66, fax 01 43 29 68 07, www.hotel-cluny.fr, cluny@club-internet.fr).

South of Luxembourg Garden

$$$ Hôtel des Mines** is less central but worth the walk. Its 50 well-maintained rooms are a fair value, and come with updated bathrooms and an inviting lobby (Db-€165, Tb-€195, Qb-€225, less for last-minute bookings and for 3 nights or more, frequent Web deals, between Luxembourg and Port-Royal stations on the RER-B line, a 10-minute walk from Panthéon, one block past Luxembourg Garden at 125 boulevard St. Michel, tel. 01 43 54 32 78, fax 01 46 33 72 52, www.hoteldesminesparis.com, hotel @hoteldesminesparis.com).

Budget Accommodations away from the Center

Acceptable budget accommodations in central neighborhoods are few and far between in Paris. I've listed the best I could find in the neighborhoods above, most at about €100 for a double room. These are great (moderate) budget options, but if you want lower rates or greater selection, you need to look farther away from the river (prices drop proportionally with distance from the Seine). Below you'll find more budget listings in less-central, but still-appealing neighborhoods. You'll spend more time on the Métro or bus getting to sights, but find fewer tourists and save money by sleeping in these areas.

Bottom of Rue Mouffetard

These hotels, away from the Seine and other tourists in an appealing workaday area, offer more room for your euro. Rue Mouffetard is the bohemian soul of this area. Two thousand years ago, it was the principal Roman road south to Italy. Today, this small, meandering street has a split personality. The lower half thrives in the daytime as a pedestrian shopping street. The upper half sleeps during the day, but comes alive after dark. Use Métro stop Censier Daubenton or Les Gobelins. A terrific Saturday market sprawls along boulevard Port Royal, just east of the Port Royal Métro stop.

$$ Hôtel de France**, on a busy street, offers modern rooms with little character. The best and quietest are *sur la cour* (on the courtyard). Stay here only if you score a great promo deal when room prices drop by over 50 percent, which is not unusual (Db-€135-155, Tb-€150-175, 108 rue Monge, Mo: Censier Daubenton, tel. 01 47 07 19 04, fax 01 43 36 62 34, www.hotelfrancequartier latin.com, hotel.de.fce@wanadoo.fr).

$ Young & Happy Hostel is easygoing, well-run, and English-speaking, with Internet access, kitchen facilities, and acceptable hostel conditions. It sits dead-center in the rue Mouffetard action... which can be good or bad (all rates per person: bunk in 4- to 10-bed dorm-€26, in 3- to 5-bed dorm-€28, in double room-€30, includes breakfast, sheets-€2.50, credit cards accepted, no air-con, no lockers but safety box at reception, 11:00-16:00 lockout but reception stays open, no curfew, 80 rue Mouffetard, Mo: Place Monge, tel. 01 47 07 47 07, fax 01 47 07 22 24, www.youngandhappy.fr, smile @youngandhappy.fr).

$ Port-Royal-Hôtel* has only one star, but don't let that fool you. Its 46 rooms are polished top to bottom and have been well-run by the same proud family for 68 years. You could eat off the floors of its spotless, comfy rooms...but you won't find air-conditioning, Internet access, or Wi-Fi. Ask for a room away from the street (S-€42-56, D-€56, Db-€80-90 depending on size, big shower down the hall-€3, cash only, nonrefundable cash deposit required, on busy boulevard de Port-Royal at #8, Mo: Les Gobelins, tel. 01 43 31 70 06, fax 01 43 31 33 67, www.hotelportroyal.fr, portroyal hotel@wanadoo.fr).

$ Hôtel de L'Espérance** is a terrific two-star value. It's quiet and cushy, with soft rooms, canopy beds, and nice public spaces (Sb-€75-80, Db-€80-90, Tb-€107, 15 rue Pascal, Mo: Censier Daubenton, tel. 01 47 07 10 99, fax 01 43 37 56 19, www.hotelde lesperance.fr, hotel.esperance@wanadoo.fr).

Montmartre

Montmartre is surprisingly quiet once you get away from the touristy top of the hill. The neighborhood is young, trendy, and popular with the *bobo* crowd (*bourgeois bohemian*, French for "hipster"). Young and budget-minded travelers will find good deals on hotel rooms and a lively atmosphere.

Most of the action is centered around rue des Abbesses, starting at place des Abbesses, and stretching several blocks to rue Lépic. Rue Lépic is also lively, but the lower you go the seedier it gets—scammers and shady characters swarm the base of the hill after hours (along boulevard Clichy and boulevard Rouchechouart where you'll find what's left of Paris' red light district). Métro line 12 is the handiest (use the Abbesses stop). Line 2 is also close, using the Blanche, Pigalle, or Anvers stops, but requires a four-block uphill walk to reach my recommended hotels. There's only one bus line here—the Montmartobus electric bus—which connects Pigalle, Abbesses, and Place du Tertre in 10 minutes (4/hour). For restaurant suggestions, see page 428.

$$ Hôtel Regyn's Montmartre** is located directly on the lively Abbesses square, with 22 small but comfortable rooms, no air-conditioning, and mediocre bathrooms. Rooms in the front come with pleasant views and noise from the square. Guests in fourth- and fifth-floor rooms can see all the way to the Eiffel Tower (Sb-€79-99, Db-€91-120, check website for specials, pay

PARIS

Hotels & Restaurants in Montmartre

200 YARDS
200 METERS

1 Hôtel Regyn's Montmartre
2 My Hôtel in France Montmartre
3 Plug-Inn Boutique Hostel
4 Hôtel Bonséjour Montmartre
5 Restaurant Chez Plumeau
6 Moulin de la Galette
7 L'Eté en Pente Douce
8 Au Relais Café
9 Le Grenier à Pain
10 Le Chinon Brasserie
11 Le Relais Gascon

M METRO STATION
B BUS STOP
IIII STAIRS
i INFO KIOSK
↗ VIEW

MOULIN ROUGE

BLVD Blanche M

PARIS

Wi-Fi, 18 place des Abbesses, tel. 01 42 54 45 21, fax 01 42 23 76 69, www.hotel-regyns-paris.com, hrm18@club-internet.fr).

$ My Hôtel in France Montmartre, a chain hotel, has 41 basic but well-maintained rooms on six floors, with no elevator or air-conditioning. Twin rooms are larger than doubles for the same price. Continental breakfast and a sandwich lunch-box are included (Sb-€80-89, Db-€90-99, prices vary greatly depending

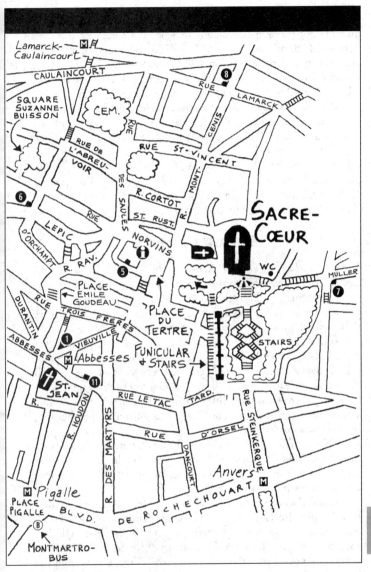

on occupancy, 57 rue des Abbesses, tel. 01 42 51 50 00, fax 01 42 51 08 68, www.book-your-hotel.com, montmartre@my-hotel-in -france.com).

$ Plug-Inn Boutique Hostel is part hotel and part hostel, but with a hotel vibe. Half a block off of rue des Abbesses, it has a young clientele, bathrooms in all 30 rooms, free Wi-Fi, and several public computer terminals. Early arrivals can leave their luggage and take a shower. Not all rooms are available online, so book direct (all prices per person: bunk in 4-bed dorm-€23-29, in 6-bed dorm-€22-28, private Db room-€33-43, female-only rooms available, sheets and towels-€2, includes breakfast, kitchen facilities, elevator, 24-hour front desk staff, no curfew, 7 rue Aristide Bruant, tel. 01 42 58 42 58, www.plug-inn.fr, bonjour@plug-inn.fr).

$ Hôtel Bonséjour Montmartre, run by eager Michel and his family, is an old, worn, hostelesque place with dirt-cheap prices. All rooms have sinks but share hallway toilets. Some rooms share one public shower on main floor, and others have oddly placed shower cabins right next to the bed (S-€35-50, D-€56-69, Tb-€78, higher price for private shower, no elevator, no air-con, 11 rue Burq, tel. 01 42 54 22 53, fax 01 42 54 25 92, www.hotel-bonsejour-montmartre .fr, hotel-bonsejour-montmartre@wanadoo.fr).

Eating in Paris

The Parisian eating scene is kept at a rolling boil. Entire books (and lives) are dedicated to the subject. Paris is France's wine-and-cuisine melting pot. Though it lacks a style of its own (only French onion soup is truly Parisian), it draws from the best of France. Paris could hold a gourmet Olympics and import nothing.

Cafés and brasseries are happy to serve a *plat du jour* (garnished plate of the day, about €12-18) or a chef-like salad (about €10-12) day or night, whereas restaurants expect you to enjoy a full dinner. Restaurants open for dinner at about 19:00, and small local favorites get crowded after 21:00. Most of the following restaurants accept credit cards. Before choosing a seat outside, remember that smokers love outdoor tables.

To save money, go to bakeries for quick take-out lunches, or stop at a café for a lunch salad or *plat du jour,* but linger longer over dinner. To save even more, consider picnics (tasty take-out dishes available at charcuteries).

Good Picnic Spots: The Palais Royal (across place du Palais Royal from the Louvre) and place des Vosges in the Marais make exquisite spots for peaceful, royal picnics. The little triangular Henry IV park on the west tip of Ile de la Cité and the bench-equipped pedestrian pont des Arts bridge, across from the Louvre, offer great river views. Parks, such as the Tuileries and Luxembourg Garden, make for ideal picnics—as do the gardens behind Les Invalides, and the Champ de Mars park below the Eiffel Tower (eat at the sides of the park; the central area is off-limits). Parks, including the grassy area on the place des Vosges, close at dusk. For an urban setting and terrific people-watching, try the Pompidou Center (by the *Homage to Stravinsky* fountains) or the courtyard around the pyramid of the Louvre.

PARIS

Restaurant Price Code

To help you choose among these listings, I've divided the restaurants into three categories, based on the price for a typical main course.

$$$ **Higher Priced**—Most main courses €25 or more
$$ **Moderately Priced**—Most main courses between €15-25.
$ **Lower Priced**—Most main courses €15 or less.

Restaurants

My recommendations are centered on the same great neighborhoods listed in "Sleeping in Paris"; you can come home exhausted after a busy day of sightseeing and find a good selection of restaurants right around the corner. And evening is a great time to explore any of these delightful neighborhoods, even if you're sleeping elsewhere. Most restaurants I've listed in these areas have set-price meals *(menus)* between €15 and €30. In most cases, the few extra euros you pay are well-spent, and open up a variety of better choices. You decide. Remember that service is always included (so little or no tipping is expected), and consider dinner picnics (great take-out dishes available at charcuteries).

If you plan to travel outside of Paris, save your splurges for the countryside, where you'll enjoy regional cooking for less money. Many Parisian department stores have supermarkets in the basement, along with top-floor cafeterias offering not-really-cheap but low-risk, low-stress, what-you-see-is-what-you-get meals.

In the Rue Cler Neighborhood

The rue Cler neighborhood caters to its residents. Its eateries, while not destination places, have an intimate charm. I've provided a full range of choices from cozy ma-and-pa diners to small and trendy boutique restaurants to classic big, boisterous bistros. For all restaurants listed in this area, use the Ecole Militaire Métro stop (unless another station is listed).

On Rue Cler

$ **Café du Marché** boasts the best seats, coffee, and prices on rue Cler. The owner's philosophy: Brasserie on speed—crank out good food at great prices to chic locals and savvy tourists. It's high-energy, with young waiters who barely have time to smile...*très* Parisian. This place is ideal if you don't mind a limited section and want to eat an inexpensive one-course meal among a commotion of people. The chalkboard lists your choices: good, hearty €10 salads or more filling €10-12 *plats du jour*. If coming for dinner, arrive

Rue Cler Restaurants

1. Café du Marché & Tribeca Italian Rest.
2. Le Petit Cler
3. Crêperie Ulysée en Gaule
4. Petite Brasserie PTT
5. Le Florimond
6. Restaurant Pasco
7. Café le Bosquet
8. La Terrasse du 7ème
9. Le Petit Niçois
10. Chez Pierrot
11. To 58 Tour Eiffel & Jules Verne
12. Le P'tit Troquet
13. Billebaude Bistro
14. La Casa Campana
15. "The Constant Line-Up"
16. To Pâtisserie de la Tour Eiffel
17. La Varangue
18. La Gourmandise Pizzeria
19. Late-Night Groceries (2)
20. Café la Roussillon
21. O'Brien's Pub
22. La Fontaine de Mars
23. L'Ami Jean

PARIS

M METRO STATION
B BUS STOP w/ ROUTE #
P PARKING
T TAXI STAND
   PEDESTRIAN ZONE

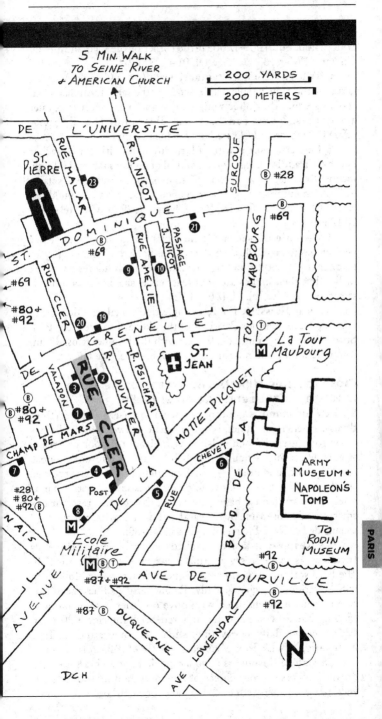

5 MIN. WALK TO SEINE RIVER & AMERICAN CHURCH

200 YARDS
200 METERS

DE L'UNIVERSITE

RUE MALAR
R. J. NICOT
SURCOUF

ST. PIERRE

23

B #28

B #69

ST. DOMINIQUE

RUE AMELIE
J. NICOT
PASSAGE

21

B #69

#69

9 10

RUE CLER

#80 & #92

20 19

GRENELLE

DE

VALADON

RUE CLER

R. DUVIVIER
R. PSICHARI

ST. JEAN

T La Tour
M Maubourg

MOTTE-PICQUET

2

B #80 & #92

3

1

CHAMP DE MARS

BLVD. DE LA TOUR MAUBOURG

ARMY MUSEUM & NAPOLEON'S TOMB

7

CHEVET

6

#28 #80 & #92 B

4

Post

5

RUE DE LA

8

M

Ecole Militaire

M B T
#87 & #92

AVE DE TOURVILLE

TO RODIN MUSEUM

#92

B #92

NAIS

AVENUE

#87 B

DUQUESNE

LOWENDAL

AVE

DCH

N

PARIS

before 19:30; it's packed at 21:00, and service can be slow (Mon-Sat 11:00-23:00, Sun 11:00-17:00, at the corner of rue Cler and rue du Champ de Mars, 38 rue Cler, tel. 01 47 05 51 27).

$ Tribeca Italian Restaurant, next door to Café du Marché, is run by the same people with essentially the same formula and an Italian accent. They offer similar value and more space, a calmer ambience, and more patient service. This family-friendly eatery offers €12 pizzas and €13 Italian *plats* (open daily).

$ Le Petit Cler is a popular, tiny café with long leather booths, a traditional interior, a handful of outdoor tables, and fine, inexpensive dishes (€9 omelets, €7 soup of the moment, €12 salads, €14 *plats,* mouthwatering *petit-pots* of chocolate or vanilla pudding, closed Mon, next to Grand Hôtel Lévêque at 29 rue Cler, tel. 01 45 50 17 50).

$ Crêperie Ulysée en Gaule offers cheap seats on rue Cler with crêpes to go (€3-10). Readers of this book don't have to pay an extra charge to sit if they buy a drink. The family adores its Greek dishes, but their crêpes are your least expensive hot meal on this street (28 rue Cler, tel. 01 47 05 61 82).

$ Petite Brasserie PTT, a simple traditional café delivering fair-value fare, reminds Parisians of the old days on rue Cler. Rick Steves diners are promised a free *kir* with their dinner (closed Sun, 2-minute walk from most area hotels, opposite 53 rue Cler).

Close to Ecole Militaire, Between Rue de la Motte-Picquet and Rue de Grenelle

$$ Le Florimond is good for a special occasion. The setting, though spacious and quiet, is also intimate and welcoming. Locals come for classic French cuisine with elegant indoor or breezy streetside seating. Friendly English-speaking Laurent—whose playful ties change daily—and Bénédicte gracefully serve one small room of tables and love to give suggestions. Try the explosively tasty stuffed cabbage (€36 *menu,* closed Sun, reservations smart, good house wine by the carafe, affordable wine selection, 19 avenue de la Motte-Picquet, tel. 01 45 55 40 38).

$$ Restaurant Pasco, perched elegantly overlooking Les Invalides, is semi-dressy and has a special enthusiasm for fish. The hardworking owner, Pasco Vignes, attracts a loyal following with selections that change daily. The modern Mediterranean cuisine is generously endowed with olive oil. There's some outdoor seating, but I'd come for the cozy red-brick interior (€20 *plats,* €22-36 *menus,* daily, reservations smart, 74 boulevard de la Tour Maubourg, Mo: La Tour Maubourg, tel. 01 44 18 33 26).

$$ Café le Bosquet is a modern, chic Parisian brasserie with dressy waiters and your choice of a mod-elegant interior or sidewalk tables on a busy street. Come here for a bowl of French onion soup; a good-value deal featuring roast chicken with fries and a dessert (€14); or a full meal with inexpensive fish and meat choices. There's always one *plat du jour* for about €11. Say *bonjour* to lanky owner Jean-François (a.k.a. Jeff). The escargots are tasty, and the house red wine is plenty good (€15-20 *plats*, continental breakfast for €5-6, free Wi-Fi, closed Sun, reservations smart Fri-Sat, corner of rue du Champ de Mars and avenue Bosquet, 46 avenue Bosquet, tel. 01 45 51 38 13).

$$ La Terrasse du 7ème is a sprawling, happening café with grand outdoor seating and a living room–like interior with comfy love seats. Located on a corner, it overlooks a busy intersection with a constant parade of people. Chairs are set up facing the street, as a meal here is like dinner theater—and the show is slice-of-life Paris (€16 daily *plats*, no fixed-price *menu*, good €12 *salade niçoise* and €14-18 *plats*, daily until at least 24:00 and sometimes until 2:00 in the morning, at École Militaire Métro stop, tel. 01 45 55 00 02).

Between Rue de Grenelle and the River, East of Avenue Bosquet

$$ Le Petit Niçois is all about fish. Come here for everything from *bouillabaisse* to bass to paella to mussels and enjoy the area's top seafood at fair prices. The *marmite du pêcheur*—my favorite—is a delicious version of *bouillabaisse;* the puréed potatoes are sinful; and the *café gourmand* dessert just about did me in. The atmosphere is warm though formal, the welcome is genuine, and the cuisine is excellent—though some find the portions small (€29 two-course *menu*, €32 three-course *menu*, daily, 10 rue Amélie, Mo: La Tour Maubourg, tel. 01 45 51 83 65).

$$ Chez Pierrot, across from Le Petit Niçois, is an inviting 14-table bistro, drawing mostly tourists who appreciate the low-key setting and large portions of traditional fare. Dishes from Lyon are a specialty—try the *salade lyonnaise* and the quenelles (fish dumplings in white cream sauce). The *pot-au-feu*—beef stew—is tasty, as is the *canard à l'orange*—duck in orange sauce (€18 *plats,* good wine list, 9 rue Amélie, Mo: La Tour Maubourg, tel. 01 45 51 50 08).

Between Rue de Grenelle and the River, West of Avenue Bosquet

$$$ 58 Tour Eiffel is in the Eiffel Tower's first level (about 300 feet up). It's the latest creation of famed French chef Alain Ducasse. Reserve at least a month in advance for a view table on a weekend, or a few days ahead for a viewless spot on weekdays. Lunch is first-come, first-served (€20 lunches, €65 dinners, daily 11:30-23:00, dinner seatings at 18:30 and 21:00; Mo: Bir-Hakeim or Trocadéro, RER: Champ de Mars-Tour Eiffel; within France dial toll tel. 08 25 56 66 62; if calling outside France, use tel. 01 76 64 14 64;

www.restaurants-toureiffel.com). Drop by the kiosk between the north/*nord* and east/*est* pillars to buy your Eiffel Tower ticket. You can skip the line for the elevator to the first level (lunchtime rate-€4.50, dinnertime rate-€13).

$$$ La Fontaine de Mars is a longtime favorite, charmingly situated on a tiny, jumbled square with tables jammed together for the serious business of eating. Reserve in advance for a table on the ground floor or on the square. Skip the upstairs room (€20-30 plats du jour, superb foie gras, superb-er desserts, 129 rue St. Dominque, tel. 01 47 05 46 44).

$$ Le P'tit Troquet, a petite eatery taking you back to the Paris of the 1920s, is gracefully and earnestly run by Dominique. The fragile elegance makes you want to hug a flapper. Dominique is particularly proud of her foie gras and lamb, and of her daughter's breads and pastries. The delicious three-course €31 *menu* comes with traditional choices. Delicate charm and gourmet flair make this restaurant a favorite of connoisseurs (opens at 18:00, closed Sun, reservations smart, 28 rue de l'Exposition, tel. 01 47 05 80 39).

$$ Billebaude, run by patient Pascal, is an authentic Parisian bistro popular with locals. The focus is on what's fresh, including catch-of-the-day fish and meats from the hunt (available in the fall and winter). Chef Sylvain, an avid hunter, is determined to deliver quality at a fair price (€31 *menu,* closed Sun-Mon, 29 rue de l'Exposition, tel. 01 45 55 20 96).

$$ La Casa Campana is worth a visit if you're sleeping in the rue Cler area and crave Italian food. The gentle owners moved to Paris from southern Italy, bringing their delicious and unspoiled cuisine with them. The handmade ravioli are bellisimo (*menus* from €20, daily, 20 rue de l'Exposition, tel. 01 45 51 37 71).

$$-$$$ The Constant Lineup: Ever since leaving the venerable Hôtel Crillon, famed chef Christian Constant has made a career of taking the "snoot" out of French cuisine—and making it accessible to people like us. Today you'll find four of his restaurants strung along one block of rue St. Dominique between rue Augereau and rue de l'Exposition, each offering a different experience and price range. The restaurants go from the lively **$$ Café Constant** (my favorite, described below), to the refined **$$$ Le Violon d'Ingres** (where Christian won his first Michelin star and reservations are essential), to **$$ Les Cocottes** (a trendy, bar-stool-only place serving simple dishes in small iron pots to yuppie Parisians), to **$$$ Les Fables de la Fontaine** (a tiny, classy place serving fish only, reservations necessary). For more details, check out www.leviolondingres.com.

$$ Café Constant is a cool, two-level place that feels more like a small bistro-wine bar than a café. Delicious and affordably priced dishes are served in a fun setting to a well-established clientele. Arrive early to get a table (downstairs seating is better); the friendly staff speaks English (€11 entrées, €16 *plats*, €7 desserts, closed Sun-Mon, no reservations, corner of rue Augereau and rue St. Dominique, next to recommended Hôtel Londres Eiffel, tel. 01 47 53 73 34).

$$ L'Ami Jean offers top Basque specialties at fair prices with tight but fun seating. The chef has made his reputation on the quality of his cuisine. Arrive by 19:30 or call ahead (€38 menu, closed Sun-Mon, 27 rue Malar, Mo: La Tour Maubourg, tel. 01 47 05 86 89).

$ Pâtisserie de la Tour Eiffel offers inexpensive salads, quiches, and sandwiches. Enjoy the views of the Eiffel Tower (daily, outdoor and indoor seating, one block southeast of the tower at 21 avenue de la Bourdonnais, tel. 01 47 05 59 81).

$ La Varangue is an entertaining one-man show featuring English-speaking Philippe, who lives upstairs, and has found his niche serving a mostly American clientele, who are all on a first-name basis. The food is cheap and basic, the tables are few, and he opens at 17:30. Norman Rockwell would dig his miniscule dining room—with the traditional kitchen sizzling just over the counter. Philippe is so fun and accessible that you are welcome to join him in the kitchen and help cook your meal. Try his snails and chocolate cake...but not together (€12 *plats*, €18 *menu*, always a vegetarian option, closed Sun, 27 rue Augereau, tel. 01 47 05 51 22).

$ La Gourmandise is a kid-friendly cheap pizzeria across from La Varangue (closed Sun, eat in or take out, 28 rue Augereau, tel. 01 45 55 45 16).

Picnicking near Rue Cler

Rue Cler is a moveable feast that gives "fast food" a good name. The entire street is clogged with connoisseurs of good eating. Only the health-food store goes unnoticed. A festival of food, the street is lined with people whose lives seem to be devoted to their specialty: polished produce, rotisserie chicken, crêpes, or cheese.

For a magical picnic dinner at the Eiffel Tower, assemble it in no fewer than five shops on rue Cler. Then lounge on the best grass in Paris, with the dogs, Frisbees, a floodlit tower, and a cool breeze in the Champ de Mars park (picnics are allowed off to the sides of the central area, which is off-limits).

Asian delis (generically called *traiteurs asiatique*) provide tasty, low-stress, low-price take-out treats (€8 dinner plates, the one on rue Cler near rue du Champ de Mars has tables). **Crêperie Ulysée en Gaule,** the Greek restaurant on rue Cler across from Grand Hôtel Lévêque, sells take-away crêpes (described earlier). There's a small **late-night grocery** at 197 rue de Grenelle (open daily until midnight), and another where rues Cler and Grenelle cross.

Breakfast on Rue Cler

Hotel breakfasts, though convenient, are generally not a good value. For a rue Cler start to your day, drop by the **Petite Brasserie PTT,** where Alexi promises Rick Steves readers a *deux pour douze* breakfast special (2 "American" breakfasts—juice, a big coffee, croissant, bread, ham, and eggs—for €12; closed Sun, 53 rue Cler). For a continental breakfast for about €6, try nearby **Café le Bosquet** (closed Sun, 46 avenue Bosquet).

Nightlife in Rue Cler

This sleepy neighborhood was not made for night owls, but there are a few notable exceptions. **La Terrasse du 7ème** and **Café du Marché** (both listed earlier) attract a Franco-American crowd until at least midnight, as does the younger **Café la Roussillon** (good French pub atmosphere, corner of rue de Grenelle and rue Cler). **O'Brien's Pub** is a relaxed Parisian rendition of an Irish pub, full of Anglophones (77 avenue St. Dominique, Mo: La Tour Maubourg).

In the Marais Neighborhood

The trendy Marais is filled with diners enjoying good food in colorful and atmospheric eateries. The scene is competitive and changes all the time. I've listed an assortment of eateries—all handy to recommended hotels—that offer good food at decent prices, plus a memorable experience.

On Romantic Place des Vosges

This square offers Old World Marais elegance, a handful of eateries, and an ideal picnic site until 20:30, when the park closes (use Bastille or St. Paul Métro stops). Strolling around the arcade after dark is more important than dining here—fanciful art galleries alternate with restaurants and cafés. Choose a restaurant that best fits your mood and budget; most have arcade seating and provide big space heaters to make outdoor dining during colder months an option. Also consider a drink or dessert on the square at Café Hugo or Carette after eating elsewhere.

$$$ Ma Bourgogne is a vintage eatery where you'll sit under warm arcades in a whirlpool of Frenchness, as bow-tied and black-aproned waiters serve you traditional French specialties: blood-red steak (try the *brochette de bœuf*), piles of fries, escargot, and good red wine. Monsieur Cougoureux (koo-goo-ruh) has commanded this ship because de Gaulle was sniveling at Americans. He offers anyone with this book a free *amuse-bouche* ("amusement for your mouth") of his homemade *steak tartare.* This is your chance to try this "raw spiced hamburger" delicacy without dedicating an entire meal to it (€37 *menu,* daily, cash only, at northwest corner at #19, tel. 01 42 78 44 64).

$$ Carette is a welcoming, modern café specializing in desserts, fine teas, big salads, and bistro fare served with smiles under the arcades (€16 dinner salads, €20 *plats*, daily from 12:00, 28 place des Vosges, tel. 01 48 87 94 07).

$$ Royal Turenne is smothered in Auvergnant (south-central France) culture and serves up mostly meat-based dishes at good prices. Try the *marquise de bœuf* or the beefy salad topped with foie gras. Clients take their cue from the gregarious owner Philippe—don't come here for a romantic soirée. There's live music on weekends and lively crowds most evenings (daily, where rue de Turenne meets the place des Vosges at 24 rue de Turenne, tel. 01 42 72 04 53).

$$ Les Bonnes Soeurs, barely off the square, blends modern and traditional fare with light-hearted and contemporary ambience. Portions are big and inventive. The delicious and filling *pressé de chèvre* starter (a hunk of goat cheese topped with tapenade and tomatoes) begs to be shared. The French hamburger would feed a soccer team and comes with a salad, and easygoing owner Cécile serves the best fries I've tasted in Paris (*plats* from €16, no *menu*, daily, 8 rue du pas de la Mule, tel. 01 42 74 55 80).

$ Nectarine is small and demure—with a wicker, pastel, and feminine atmosphere. This peaceful teahouse serves €11 salads, quiches, and €13 *plats du jour* day and night. Its *menu* lets you mix and match omelets and crêpes, and the huge desserts are splittable (daily, at #16, tel. 01 42 77 23 78).

$ Café Hugo, named for the square's most famous resident, is best for drinks only, as the cuisine does not live up to its setting (daily, at #22, tel. 01 42 72 64 04).

Near the Bastille
To reach these restaurants, use the Bastille Métro stop.

$$ Brasserie Bofinger, an institution for over a century, is famous for fish and traditional cuisine with Alsatian flair. You're surrounded by brisk, black-and-white-attired waiters. The sprawling interior features elaborately decorated rooms reminiscent of the Roaring Twenties. Eating under the grand 1919 *coupole* is a memorable treat (as is using the "historic" 1919 WC downstairs). Check out the boys shucking and stacking seafood platters out front before you enter. Their €25 two-course and €32 three-course *menus*, while not top cuisine, are a good value. If you've always wanted one of those picturesque seafood platters, this is a good place—you can take the standard platter or create one à la carte (open daily for lunch and for dinner, fun kids' menu, reasonably priced wines, 5 rue de la Bastille, don't be confused by the lesser "Petite" Bofinger across the street, tel. 01 42 72 87 82).

PARIS

Marais Restaurants

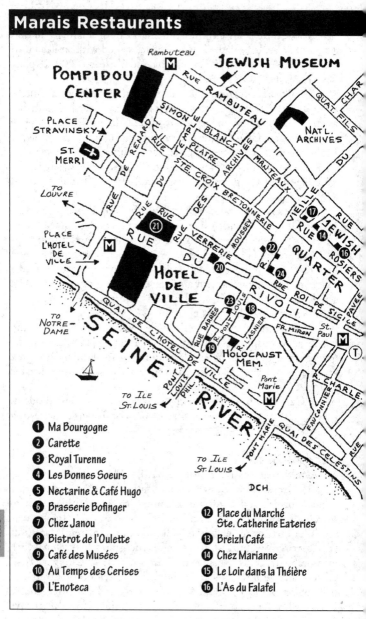

1 Ma Bourgogne

2 Carette

3 Royal Turenne

4 Les Bonnes Soeurs

5 Nectarine & Café Hugo

6 Brasserie Bofinger

7 Chez Janou

8 Bistrot de l'Oulette

9 Café des Musées

10 Au Temps des Cerises

11 L'Enoteca

12 Place du Marché
Ste. Catherine Eateries

13 Breizh Café

14 Chez Marianne

15 Le Loir dans la Théière

16 L'As du Falafel

PARIS

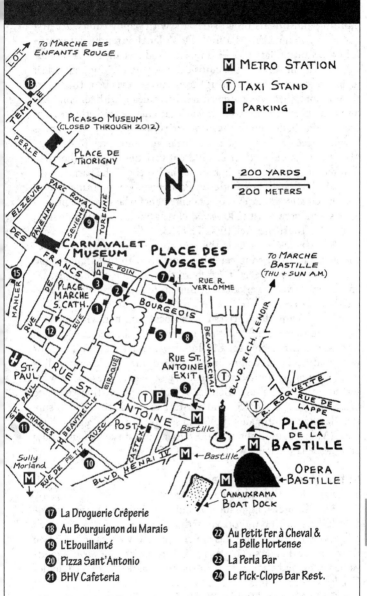

M METRO STATION
T TAXI STAND
P PARKING

200 YARDS
200 METERS

To MARCHE DES ENFANTS ROUGE

Picasso Museum (CLOSED THROUGH 2012)

PLACE DE THORIGNY

CARNAVALET MUSEUM

PLACE DES VOSGES

To MARCHE BASTILLE (THU + SUN A.M.)

RUE R. VERLOMME

PLACE MARCHE S. CATH.

BOURGEOIS

RUE ST. ANTOINE EXIT

ST. PAUL

RUE ST. ANTOINE

Post

Bastille

PLACE DE LA BASTILLE

OPERA BASTILLE

Sully Morland

BLVD. HENRI IV

Bastille

CANAUXRAMA BOAT DOCK

17 La Droguerie Crêperie
18 Au Bourguignon du Marais
19 L'Ebouillanté
20 Pizza Sant'Antonio
21 BHV Cafeteria

22 Au Petit Fer à Cheval & La Belle Hortense
23 La Perla Bar
24 Le Pick-Clops Bar Rest.

$$ Chez Janou, a Provençal bistro, tumbles out of its corner building and fills its broad sidewalk with happy eaters. At first glance, you know this is a find. Don't let the trendy and youthful crowd intimidate you—it's relaxed and charming, with helpful and patient service. The curbside tables are inviting, but I'd sit inside (with very tight seating) to immerse myself in the happy commotion. The style is French Mediterranean, with an emphasis on vegetables (€16-19 *plats du jour* that change with the season, daily from 19:45—book ahead or arrive when it opens, 2 blocks beyond place des Vosges at 2 rue Roger Verlomme, tel. 01 42 72 28 41). They're proud of their 81 different varieties of *pastis* (licorice-flavored liqueur, €3.50 each, browse the list above the bar).

$$ At **Bistrot de l'Oulette,** Parisians pile into a tiny spot to test the creative inventions of a talented chef who gives traditional dishes a modern twist (€30 *menu,* closed Sun, reservations smart, 38 rue des Tournelles, tel. 01 42 71 43 33).

$ Café des Musées is the real thing—an unspoiled, zinc-countered bistro serving traditional dishes with little fanfare and a €19 daily *menu* special that's hard to beat. The place is just far enough away to be overlooked by tourists (daily, 49 rue de Turenne, tel. 01 42 72 96 17).

$ Au Temps des Cerises is a *très* local wine bar, with a woody 1950s atmosphere, tight seating, and wads of character. Although they serve three-course, €16 lunch *menus,* I'd come here for wine and heavy munchies pre- or post-dinner—or even for dinner. "Dinner" is limited to bread, dry sausage, cheese, and wine served by goateed Yves, Michele, or Sara. Their small mixed plate of cheese (€5), meat (€5), and a carafe of good wine (€4-8) surrounded by the intimate Old World setting can make a good light meal (Mon-Sat until about 22:00, closed Sun, at rue du Petit-Musc and rue de la Cerisaie, tel. 01 42 72 08 63).

In the Heart of the Marais

These are closest to the St. Paul Métro stop.

$$ L'Enoteca, high-spirited and half-timbered, serves affordable Italian cuisine (no pizza) with a tempting *antipasti* bar. It's a fun, open setting with busy, blue-aproned waiters serving two floors of local eaters (€17 pastas, €30 three-course *menu,* good-value wines, daily, at rue St. Paul and rue Charles V, 25 rue Charles V, tel. 01 42 78 91 44).

$ *On place du Marché Ste. Catherine:* This small, romantic square, just off rue St. Antoine, is an international food festival cloaked in extremely Parisian, leafy-square ambience. On a balmy evening, this is clearly a neighborhood favorite, with a handful of restaurants offering €20-30 three-course meals. Study the square, and you'll find two popular French bistros (**Le Marché** and **Au**

Bistrot de la Place, each open daily with €23 three-course *menus* and tight seating on flimsy chairs indoors and out) and other inviting eateries serving a variety of international food—Russian, Korean, Italian, and so on. You'll eat under the trees, surrounded by a futuristic-in-1800 planned residential quarter.

$ Breizh (Brittany) Café is a find for lovers of things pure and unaffected. This simple Breton place serves organic crêpes and small rolls made for dipping in rich sauces and salted butter. Try a sparkling cider, a Breton cola, or my favorite—*lait ribot*, a butter-milk-like drink (€7-11 dinner crêpes and *plats*, serves nonstop from 12:00 to late, closed Mon-Tue, 109 rue du Vielle du Temple, tel. 01 42 72 13 77).

$ Several hardworking **Asian fast-food eateries,** great for a €8 meal, line rue St. Antoine.

On Rue des Rosiers in the Jewish Quarter

To reach the Jewish Quarter, use the St. Paul Métro stop.

$ Chez Marianne is a neighborhood fixture that blends deli-cious Jewish cuisine with Parisian *élan*. Choose from several indoor zones with a cluttered wineshop/deli feeling, or sit outside. You'll select from two dozen *Zakouski* elements to assemble your €15 *plat*. Vegetarians will find great options (€8 falafel sandwich—only €6 if you order it to go, long hours daily, corner of rue des Rosiers and rue des Hospitalières-St.-Gervais, tel. 01 42 72 18 86). For take-out, pay inside first and get a ticket before you order outside.

$ Le Loir dans la Théière is a cozy, mellow teahouse offering a welcoming ambience for tired travelers. It's ideal for weekend brunch, baked goods, and hot drinks (Mon-Fri 12:00-19:00, Sat-Sun 10:00-19:00, 3 rue des Rosiers, tel. 01 42 72 90 61).

$ L'As du Falafel rules the falafel scene in the Jewish quarter. Monsieur Isaac, the "Ace of Falafel" here since 1979, brags, "I've got the biggest pita on the street...and I fill it up." (Apparently it's Lenny Kravitz's favorite, too.) Your inexpensive meal comes on plastic plates, in a bustling setting that seems to prove he's earned his success. The €7 "special falafel" is the big hit, but many Americans enjoy his lighter chicken version *(poulet grillé)* or the tasty and filling *assiette de falafel*. Their take-out service draws a constant crowd (day and night until late, closed Sat, air-con, 34 rue des Rosiers, tel. 01 48 87 63 60).

$ La Droguerie, a full-service outdoor crêpe stand a few blocks farther down rue des Rosiers, is an option if falafels don't work for you, but cheap does (€5 dinner crêpes, closed Sun-Mon, rue des Rosiers).

Closer to Hôtel de Ville

These eateries appear on the map on pages 416-417. To reach them,

PARIS

use the Hôtel de Ville Métro stop.

$$ Au Bourguignon du Marais is a handsome wine-bar/bistro for Burgundy-lovers, where excellent wines (Burgundian only, available by the glass) blend with a good selection of well-designed dishes and efficient service. The *œufs en meurette* were the best I've ever had, and the *bœuf bourguignon* could feed two (€10-14 starters, €18-22 *plats*, closed Sun-Mon, pleasing indoor and outdoor seating, 52 rue Francois Miron, tel. 01 48 87 15 40).

$ L'Ebouillanté is a breezy crêperie-café, romantically situated near the river on a broad, cobbled lane behind a church. With great outdoor seating and an artsy, cozy interior, it's perfect for an inexpensive and relaxing tea, snack, or lunch—or for dinner on a warm evening. Have a *Brick,* a Tunisian-inspired dish that looks like a stuffed omelet (several filling options) and comes with a small salad; it left me stuffed (€13 *plats* and big salads, Tue-Sun 12:00-21:30, closed Mon in winter, 6 rue des Barres, tel. 01 42 71 09 69).

$ Pizza Sant'Antonio is bustling and cheap, serving up €11 pizzas and salads on a fun Marais square (daily, barely off rue de Rivoli on place du Bourg Tibourg, 1 rue de la Verrerie).

$ BHV Department Store's fifth-floor cafeteria provides nice views, good prices, and no-brainer, point-and-shoot cafeteria cuisine (Mon-Sat 11:30-18:00, closed Sun, at intersection of rue du Temple and rue de la Verrerie, one block from Hôtel de Ville).

Picnicking in the Marais
Picnic at peaceful place des Vosges (closes at dusk) or on the Ile St. Louis *quais* (described later). Stretch your euros at the basement supermarket of the **Monoprix** department store (closed Sun, near place des Vosges on rue St. Antoine). You'll find small **groceries** open until 23:00 at 48 rue St. Antoine and on the Ile St. Louis.

Nightlife in the Marais
Trendy cafés and bars—popular with gay men—cluster on rue des Archives and rue Ste. Croix de la Bretonnerie (closing at about 2:00 in the morning). There's also a line of bars and cafés providing front-row seats for the buff parade on rue Vieille du Temple, a block north of rue de Rivoli (the horseshoe-shaped **Au Petit Fer à Cheval** bar-restaurant and the atmospheric **La Belle Hortense** bookstore/wine bar are the focal points of the action). Nearby, rue des Rosiers bustles with youthful energy, but there are no cafés to observe from. **La Perla** is full of Parisian yuppies in search of the perfect margarita (26 rue François Miron).

$ Le Pick-Clops bar-restaurant is a happy peanuts-and-lots-of-cocktails diner with bright neon, loud colors, and a garish local crowd. It's perfect for immersing yourself in today's Marais world—a little boisterous, a little edgy, a little gay, fun-loving, easygoing...and no tourists. Sit inside on old-fashioned diner stools, or streetside to watch the constant Marais parade. The name means "Steal the Cigarettes"—but you'll pay €11 for your big salad (daily 7:00-24:00, 16 rue Vieille du Temple, tel. 01 40 29 02 18).

The best scene for hardcore clubbers is the dizzying array of wacky eateries, bars, and dance halls on **rue de Lappe.** Just east of the stately place de la Bastille, it's one of the wildest nightspots in Paris and not for everyone.

The most enjoyable peaceful evening may be simply mentally donning your floppy "three musketeers" hat and slowly strolling place des Vosges, window-shopping the art galleries.

In the Historic Core, on Ile St. Louis

This romantic and peaceful neighborhood is filled with promising and surprisingly inexpensive possibilities—it merits a trip for dinner even if your hotel is elsewhere. Cruise the island's main street for a variety of options, from cozy *crêperies* to Italian eateries to traditional brasseries and romantic bistros. After dinner, sample Paris' best ice cream and stroll across to the Ile de la Cité to see a floodlit Notre-Dame. These recommended spots line the island's main drag, rue St. Louis-en-l'Ile (see map on page 394; to get here use the Pont Marie Métro stop).

$$$ Le Tastevin is an intimate mother-and-son-run restaurant serving top-notch traditional French cuisine with white-tablecloth, candlelit, gourmet elegance under heavy wooden beams. The romantic setting (and the elegantly romantic local couples enjoying the place) naturally makes you whisper. The three-course *menus* start at about €39-52 and offer a handful of classic choices that change with the season to ensure freshness (daily, reserve for late-evening dining, good wine list, 46 rue St. Louis-en-l'Ile, tel. 01 43 54 17 31, owner Madame Puisieux and her gentle son speak just enough English).

$$$ *Medieval Theme Restaurants:* La Taverne du Sergeant Recruteur, famous for its rowdy, medieval-cellar atmosphere, is ideal for hungry warriors and their wenches who like to swill hearty wine. For as long as anyone can remember, they've served up a rustic all-you-can-eat buffet with straw baskets of raw veggies and bundles of sausage (cut whatever you like with your dagger), massive plates of pâté, a meat course, and all the wine you can stomach for €41. The food is just food; burping is encouraged. If you want to eat a lot, drink a lot of wine, be surrounded with tourists (mostly French), and holler at your friends while receiving smart-aleck buccaneer service, this food fest can be fun. And it comes with a historic twist: The "Sergeant Recruiter" used to get young Parisians drunk and stuffed here, then sign them into the army (daily from 19:00, #37 rue St. Louis-en-l'Ile, tel. 01 43 54 75 42). Next door, **Nos Ancêtres les Gaulois** is a bit goofier and grittier, and serves the same basic formula. As the name implies ("Our Ancestors the Gauls"), this place makes barbarians feel right at home (tel. 01 46 33 66 07). You might swing by both and choose the..."ambience" is not quite the right word...that fits your mood.

$$ La Brasserie de l'Ile St. Louis is situated at the prow of the island's ship as it faces Ile de la Cité, offering purely Alsatian cuisine (try the *choucroute garnie* for €18), served in a vigorous, Teutonic setting with no-nonsense, slap-it-down service and wine-stained paper tablecloths. This is a good balmy-evening perch for watching the Ile St. Louis promenade. If it's chilly, the interior is plenty characteristic for a memorable night out (closed Wed, no reservations, 55 quai de Bourbon, tel. 01 43 54 02 59).

$$ L'Orangerie is an inviting place with soft lighting and comfortable seating where diners speak in hushed voices so that everyone can appreciate the delicious cuisine and tasteful setting (€35 three-course *menu*, €27 two-course *menu*, closed Mon, open at 19:00, 28 rue St. Louis-en-l'Ile, tel. 01 46 33 93 98).

$ Auberge de la Reine Blanche's friendly owner Michel welcomes diners willing to rub elbows with their neighbors in a cozy setting while enjoying delicious cuisine at unbeatable prices (€20 two-course *menu*, €25 three-course *menu*, daily from 18:00, 30 rue St. Louis-en-l'Ile, tel. 01 46 33 07 87).

$ Café Med, near the pedestrian bridge to Notre-Dame at #77, has inexpensive salads, crêpes, *plats* and a €14-20 *menu* served in a tight but cheery setting (open daily, limited wine list, tel. 01 43 29 73 17). Two similar *crêperies* are just across the street.

Riverside Picnic for Impoverished Romantics

On sunny lunchtimes and balmy evenings, the *quai* on the Left Bank side of Ile St. Louis is lined with locals who have more class than money, spreading out tablecloths and even lighting candles for elegant picnics. And tourists can enjoy the same budget meal. A handy grocery store at #67 on the main drag (Wed-Mon until 22:00, closed Tue) has tabouli and other simple, cheap take-away dishes for your picnicking pleasure.

Ice-Cream Dessert

Half the people strolling Ile St. Louis are licking ice-cream cones, because this is the home of *les glaces Berthillon*. The original **Berthillon** shop, at 31 rue St. Louis-en-l'Ile, is marked by the line of salivating customers (closed Mon-Tue). Another Berthillon shop is across the street, and there's one more around the corner on rue Bellay (all are located on map on page 394). The three shops are so popular that the wealthy people who can afford to live on this fancy island complain about the congestion they cause. For a less famous but at least as satisfying treat, the homemade Italian gelato a block away at **Amorino Gelati** is giving Berthillon competition (no line, bigger portions, easier to see what you want, and they offer little tastes—Berthillon doesn't need to, 47 rue St. Louis-en-l'Ile, tel. 01 44 07 48 08). Having some of each is not a bad thing.

In the Luxembourg Garden Area

Sleeping in the Luxembourg neighborhood puts you near many appealing dining and after-hours options. Because my hotels in this area cluster near St. Sulpice Church and the Panthéon (see page 395), I've organized restaurant listings the same way. Restaurants around St. Sulpice tend to be boisterous; those near the Panthéon are calmer; it's a short walk from one area to the other. Anyone sleeping in this area is close to the inexpensive eateries that line the always-bustling rue Mouffetard. You're also within a 15-minute walk of the *grands cafés* of St. Germain and Montparnasse (with Paris' first café and famous artist haunts).

Near St. Sulpice Church:
Rue des Canettes and Rue Guisarde

For locations, see the map on the next page. These eateries are served by the St. Sulpice, Mabillon, and St. Germain-des-Prés Métro stops.

Roam the streets between the St. Sulpice Church and boulevard St. Germain, abounding with restaurants, *créperies*, wine bars, and jazz haunts (use Mo: St. Sulpice). Find rue des Canettes and rue Guisarde, and window-shop the many French and Italian eateries—most with similar prices, but each with a slightly different feel. For yummy crêpes, try **$ La Crêpe Rit du Clown** (Mon-Sat 12:00-23:00, closed Sun, 6 rue des Canettes, tel. 01 46 34 01 02). For comfortable atmosphere and above-average bistro fare in a zone where every restaurant looks the same, consider **$$ Lou Pescadou-Chez Julien** (daily, some outdoor seating, 16 rue Mabillon, tel. 01 43 54 56 08). Another option is **$$ Boucherie Rouliere,** crammed with locals in search of a good steak or other meat dish (€7 *entrées,* €16 *plats,* €7 desserts, closed Mon, 24 rue des Canettes). **$ Santa Lucia** draws rave reviews with wood-fired pizza, good pasta, and killer tiramisu (€12-14 pizza and pastas, closed Mon-Tue, 22 rue des Canettes, tel. 01 43 26 42 68).

And for a bohemian pub lined with black-and-white photos of the artsy and revolutionary French '60s, have a drink at **Chez Georges.** Sit in a cool little streetside table nook, or venture downstairs to find a hazy, drippy-candle, traditionally French world in the Edith Piaf–style dance cellar (cheap drinks from old-fashioned

PARIS

Restaurants near Luxembourg Garden

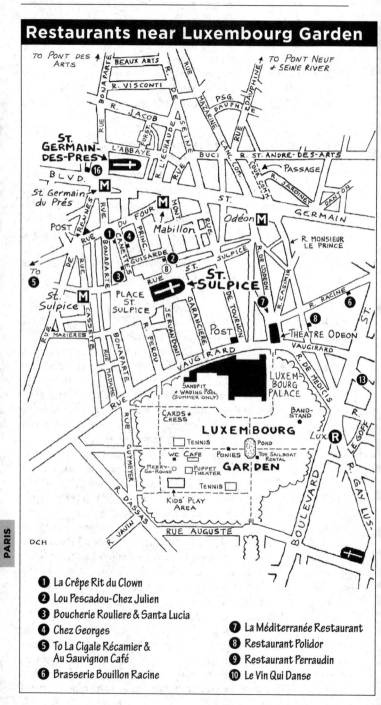

1. La Crêpe Rit du Clown
2. Lou Pescadou-Chez Julien
3. Boucherie Rouliere & Santa Lucia
4. Chez Georges
5. To La Cigale Récamier & Au Sauvignon Café
6. Brasserie Bouillon Racine

7. La Méditerranée Restaurant
8. Restaurant Polidor
9. Restaurant Perraudin
10. Le Vin Qui Danse

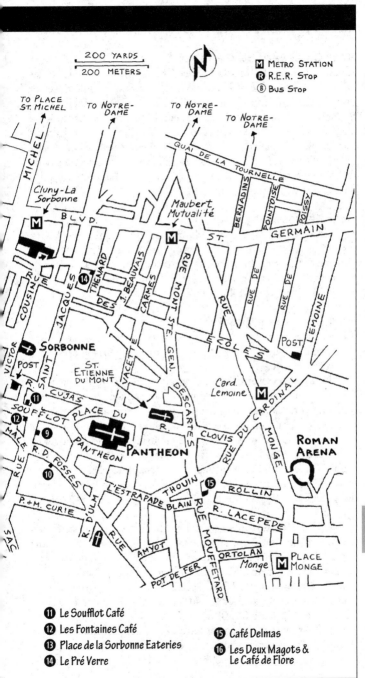

200 YARDS
200 METERS

Ⓜ METRO STATION
Ⓡ R.E.R. STOP
Ⓑ BUS STOP

TO PLACE ST. MICHEL
TO NOTRE-DAME
TO NOTRE-DAME
TO NOTRE-DAME
TO NOTRE-DAME

QUAI DE LA TOURNELLE

Cluny-La Sorbonne

Maubert Mutualité

BLVD.

ST. GERMAIN

RUE COUSINE
RUE SAINT JACQUES
THENARD
J. BEAUVAIS
DES
CARMES
RUE MONT STE.
RUE DES ÉCOLES
RUE BERNADINS
POINTOISE
POSSI
RUE DE
RUE DE LEMOINE

⑭

Sorbonne
POST
VICTOR
ST. ETIENNE DU MONT
VACETTE
RUE GEN. DESCARTES
Card. Lemoine
Ⓜ

R. SAINT
⑪ CUJAS
SOUFFLOT
⑫
MALE
RUE R.D. FOSSES
⑨
PLACE DU PANTHEON
PANTHEON
R.
CLOVIS
RUE DU CARDINAL
MONGE

ROMAN ARENA

P. & M. CURIE
RUE D'ULM
L'ESTRAPADE
THOUIN
BLAIN
⑮
ROLLIN
R. LACEPEDE

SAC.
AMYOT
RUE MOUFFETARD
ORTOLAN
Monge Ⓜ
PLACE MONGE

POT DE FER

PLACE MONGE

PARIS

⑪ Le Soufflot Café
⑫ Les Fontaines Café
⑬ Place de la Sorbonne Eateries
⑭ Le Pré Verre
⑮ Café Delmas
⑯ Les Deux Magots &
Le Café de Flore

menu, Tue-Sat 14:00-2:00 in the morning, closed Sun-Mon and in Aug, 11 rue des Canettes, tel. 01 43 26 79 15).

Near Boulevard St. Germain

A five-minute walk from St. Sulpice Church, this venerable boulevard is home to some of Paris' most famous cafés and best pre- or post-dinner strolling. Consider a light dinner with a table facing the action at Hemingway's **Les Deux Magots** or at Sartre's **Le Café de Flore** (figure about €10 for an omelet and €16-25 for a salad or *plat*). A block north (toward the river), **rue de Buci** offers a lineup of bars, cafés, and bistros targeted to a young clientele who are more interested in how they look than how the food tastes. It's terrific theater for passersby.

Near Sèvres-Babylone

$$ La Cigale Récamier is a classy place for a quiet meal with appealing indoor and outdoor seating. It's about 10 minutes west of place St. Sulpice, on a short pedestrian alley a block off rue de Sèvres (€20 *plats*, à la carte only, closed Sun, 4 rue Récamier, Mo: Sèvres-Babylone, tel. 01 46 48 86 58).

Near the Odéon Theater

To reach these, use the Odéon Métro stop. In this same neighborhood, you'll find the historic Café le Procope, Paris' more-than-300-year-old café.

$$ Brasserie Bouillon Racine takes you back to 1906 with an Art Nouveau carnival of carved wood, stained glass, and old-time lights reflected in beveled mirrors. The over-the-top decor, energetic waiters, and affordable prices combine to give it an inviting conviviality. Check upstairs before choosing a table. Their roast suckling pig (€18) is a house favorite, but I'd skip their bouillon soups. There's good beer on tap and a fascinating history on the menu (€18-23 *plats*, €31 *menu*, a few fish options and lots of meat, daily 12:00-14:00 & 19:00-23:00, 3 rue Racine, tel. 01 44 32 15 60, Phillipe).

$$ La Méditerranée is all about having fish in a pastel and dressy setting...with similar clientele. The scene and the cuisine are sophisticated yet accessible, and the view of the Odéon is *formidable*. The sky-blue tablecloths and the lovingly presented dishes add to the romance (€27 two-course *menus*, €32 three-course *menus*, daily, smart to book ahead, facing the Odéon at 2 place de l'Odéon, tel. 01 43 26 02 30).

$ Restaurant Polidor, a bare-bones neighborhood fixture since the 19th century, is much loved for its unpretentious quality cooking, fun old-Paris atmosphere, and fair value. Stepping inside,

PARIS

you know this is a winner—noisy, happy diners squeeze in at shared tables as waiters chop and serve fresh bread. The selection features classic bourgeois *plats* from every corner of France; their *menu fraîcheur* is designed for lighter summer eating (€12-15 *plats*, €20-30 three-course *menus*, daily 12:00-14:30 & 19:00-23:00, cash only, no reservations, 41 rue Monsieur-le-Prince, tel. 01 43 26 95 34).

Near the Panthéon

For locations, see the map on pages 424-425. These eateries are served by the Cluny-La Sorbonne Métro stop and the RER-B Luxembourg station.

$$ Restaurant Perraudin is a family-run, red-checkered-tablecloth eatery understandably popular with tourists. Monsieur Correy serves classic *cuisine bourgeoise* with an emphasis on Burgundian dishes in air-conditioned comfort (€20 lunch *menus*, €30 dinner *menus*, daily, *bœuf bourguignon* is a specialty here, between the Panthéon and Luxembourg Garden at 157 rue St. Jacques, tel. 01 46 33 15 75).

$$ Le Vin Qui Danse is a warm little place serving a good selection of tasty dishes and well-matched wines to appreciative clients (€27 two-course *menu*, add €15 for three wines selected to complement your meal, daily, 4 rue des Fossés St. Jacques, tel. 01 43 54 80 81).

$ Le Soufflot Café, between the Panthéon and Luxembourg Garden, is well-positioned for afternoon sun and soft light in the evening. It has a nifty library-like interior, lots of outdoor tables, point-blank views of the Panthéon, and happy waiters (Frédéric and Serge are owners). The cuisine is café-classic, day or night: good €10 salads and omelets, and €12-15 *plats du jour* (daily, a block below the Panthéon on the right side of rue Soufflot as you walk toward Luxembourg Garden, tel. 01 43 26 57 56).

$ Les Fontaines Café offers similar café fare and ambience on the other side of rue Soufflot, but has a more elaborate wine list and features glass-enclosed sidewalk tables with protected views of the Pantheon (daily, 9 rue Soufflot, tel. 01 43 26 42 80).

$ *Place de la Sorbonne:* This cobbled and green square, with a small fountain facing the Sorbonne University just a block from the Cluny Museum, offers several opportunities for a quick outdoor lunch or light dinner. At amiable Carole's tiny **Baker's Dozen,** you'll pay take-away prices for light fare you can sit down to eat (€5 salads and sandwiches, Mon-Fri until 15:30, closed Sun). **Café de l'Ecritoire** is a typical, lively brasserie with happy diners enjoying €11 salads, €13 *plats,* and fine square seating (daily, tel. 01 43 54 60 02). **Patios,** with appealing decor inside and out, serves inexpensive Italian fare, including pizza (daily until late, tel. 01 45 38 71 19).

PARIS

$ Le Pré Verre, a block from the Cluny Museum, is a chic wine bistro—a refreshing alternative in a part of the Latin Quarter mostly known for low-quality, tourist-trapping eateries. Offering imaginative, modern cuisine at fair prices, the place is always packed. The bargain lunch *menu* includes a starter, main course, glass of wine, and coffee for €14. At €29, the three-course dinner *menu* is worth every penny. They pride themselves equally on their small-producers' wine list, so follow your server's advice (closed Sun-Mon, 8 rue Thénard, reservations necessary, tel. 01 43 54 59 47).

On Rue Mouffetard

Lying several blocks behind the Panthéon, rue Mouffetard is a conveyer belt of comparison-shopping eaters with wall-to-wall budget options (fondue, crêpes, Italian, falafel, and Greek). Come here to sift through the crowds and eat cheaply (you get what you pay for). This street stays up late and likes to party (particularly around place de la Contrescarpe). The gauntlet begins on top, at thriving place de la Contrescarpe, and ends below where rue Mouffetard stops at St. Médard Church. Both ends offer fun cafés where you can watch the action. The upper stretch is pedestrian and touristy; the bottom stretch is purely Parisian. Anywhere between is no-man's land for consistent quality. Still, strolling with so many fun-seekers is enjoyable, whether you eat or not. To get here, use the Censier Daubenton Métro stop.

$$ Café Delmas, at the top of rue Mouffetard on picturesque place de la Contrescarpe, is *the* place to see and be seen. Come here for a before- or after-dinner drink on the broad outdoor terrace, or for typical but pricey café cuisine (€15 salads, €22 *plats,* great chocolate ice cream, daily).

$ Bar-restaurant Les Papillons is a down-and-dirty local diner where a few outdoor tables tangle with pedestrians, and no one seems to care. Join the fun. As smiling owner Eric says, "Everyone sings after zee wine" (€12 *plats,* closed Sun-Mon, 129 rue Mouffetard, tel. 01 43 31 66 50).

$ Cave de Bourgogne, a young and local hangout, has reasonably priced café fare at the bottom of rue Mouffetard. The outside has picture-perfect tables on a raised terrace; the interior is warm and lively (€13-16 *plats,* specials listed on chalkboards, daily, 144 rue Mouffetard).

In Montmartre

Much of Montmartre is extremely touristy, with mindless mobs following guides to cancan shows. But the ambience is undeniably fun, and an evening overlooking Paris is a quintessential experience in the City of Light.

Near Sacré-Cœur

The steps in front of Sacré-Cœur are perfect for a picnic with a view, though the spot comes with lots of company. Along the touristy main drag (near place du Tertre and just off it), several fun piano bars serve crêpes along with great people-watching. To reach this area, use the Anvers Métro stop. For locations, see the map on pages 404-405.

$$ Restaurant Chez Plumeau, just off jam-packed place du Tertre, is touristy yet moderately priced, with formal service but great seating on a tiny, charming square (elaborate €17 salads, €18-22 *plats,* closed Wed, place du Calvaire, tel. 01 46 06 26 29).

$$ Moulin de la Galette lets you dine with Renoir under the historic windmill in a comfortable setting with good prices. Find the old photos scattered about the place (€17 two-course *menu,* €25 three-course *menu,* daily, 83 rue Lépic, Mo: Abbesses, tel. 01 46 06 84 77).

$ L'Eté en Pente Douce is a good Montmartre choice, hiding under the generous branches of street trees. Just downhill from the crowds on a classic neighborhood corner, it features cheery indoor and outdoor seating, €10 *plats du jour* and salads, vegetarian options, and good wines (daily, many steps below Sacré-Cœur to the left as you leave, down the stairs below the WC, 23 rue Muller, tel. 01 42 64 02 67).

$ Au Relais, on the backside of Montmartre with no hint of tourists, is a neighborhood café, offering a two-course lunch *menu du jour* with a coffee for €11 and good-value dinners (daily, 48 rue Lamarck, at the intersection with rue Mont Cenis, outdoor seating, tel. 01 46 06 68 32). From place du Tertre, walk north on rue Mont Cenis, down two long staircases to rue Lamarck. If you don't want to brave the steps back up after you've finished your meal, head for the closest Métro stop, Lamarck-Caulaincourt (turn right out of the café).

Near Rue des Abbesses

At the bottom of Montmartre, residents pile into a long lineup of brasseries and cafés along rue des Abbesses (Mo. Abbesses). The food is average; the atmosphere is anything but. Come here for a lively, tourist-free scene. The street is perfect for a picnic-gathering stroll with cheese shops, delis, wine stores, and bakeries. In fact, the baker at **Le Grenier à Pain** won the award for the Best Baguette in Paris in 2010 (Thu-Mon 7:30-20:00, closed Tue-Wed, 38 rue des Abbesses, tel. 01 42 23 85 36). For locations, see the map on pages 404-405.

$ Le Chinon Brasserie offers good seating inside and out and is the best bet for café/wine bar ambience and fare (daily, 49 rue des Abbesses, tel. 01 42 62 07 17).

PARIS

$ Le Relais Gascon serves giant salads (€12) topped with their signature garlic *frites* and a selection of grilled meats (€12-15) in a narrow dining room on two floors (nonstop service daily 10:30-24:00, 6 rue des Abbesses, just after the post office as you leave place des Abbesses, tel. 01 42 58 58 22).

Elsewhere in Paris
Next to the Galerie Vivienne, Behind the Palais Royal

$$$ Le Grand Colbert, appropriately located in the elegant Galerie Colbert, gives its clients the feel of a luxury restaurant at relatively moderate prices. It's a stylish, grand brasserie with hurried waiters, leather booths, and brass lamps, serving all the classic dishes from steak *frites* to escargots (*menus* from €42, daily, 4 rue Vivienne, Mo: Palais Royal/Musée du Louvre or Pyramides, tel. 01 42 86 82 38).

Along Canal St. Martin, North of République

Escape the crowded tourist areas and enjoy a breezy canalside experience. Take the Métro to place de la République and walk down rue Beaurepaire to Canal St. Martin. There you'll find a few worthwhile cafés with similarly reasonable prices. **$ La Marine** is a good choice (daily, 55 bis quai de Valmy, tel. 01 42 39 69 81). In summertime most bars and cafés offer beer and wine to go *(à emporter)*, so you can take it to the canal's edge and picnic there with the younger crowd.

Dinner Cruises

The following companies offer dinner cruises (reservations required). Bateaux-Mouches and Bateaux Parisiens have the best reputations and the highest prices. They offer multicourse meals and music in aircraft carrier-size dining rooms with glass tops and good views. For both, proper dress is required—no denim, shorts, or sport shoes; Bateaux-Mouches requires a jacket and tie for men. The main difference between these companies is the music: Bateaux-Mouches offers violin and piano to entertain your romantic evening, whereas Bateaux Parisiens boasts a lively atmosphere with a singer, band, and dance floor.

Bateaux-Mouches, started in 1949, is hands-down the most famous. You can't miss its sparkling port on the north side of the river at Pont de l'Alma. The boats usually board 19:30-20:15, depart at 20:30, and return at 22:45 (€95-130/person, RER: Pont de l'Alma, tel. 01 42 25 96 10, www.bateauxmouches.com).

Bateaux Parisiens leaves from Port de la Bourdonnais, just east of the bridge under the Eiffel Tower. Begin boarding at 19:45, leave at 20:30, and return at 23:00 (€65/person for 18:30 departure with dinner, €100-145/person for 20:30 departure, price depends on view seating and *menu* option, tel. 01 76 64 14 45, www.bateaux parisiens.com). The middle level is best. Pay the few extra euros to get seats next to the windows—it's more romantic and private, with sensational views.

Le Capitaine Fracasse offers the budget option (€50/person, €70 with wine and coffee; tables are first-come, first-serve, so get there early; boarding times vary by season and day of week, closed Mon, walk down stairs in the middle of Bir Hakeim bridge near the Eiffel Tower to Iles aux Cygne, Mo: Bir-Hakeim or RER: Champ de Mars-Tour Eiffel, tel. 01 46 21 48 15, www.croisiere -paris.com).

Paris Connections

When leaving Paris, get to your departure point early to allow time for waiting in lines. Figure on 2-3 hours for an overseas flight; 1-2 hours for flights within Europe (particularly if flying with one of the budget airlines, which tend to have long check-in lines); and 40 minutes for a train trip or long-distance bus ride, if you're doing anything beyond simply boarding (Eurostar trains require you to check in at least 30 minutes early). Whether arriving or departing, always keep your luggage safely near you. Pickpockets prey on jet-lagged tourists on shuttle trains and buses.

Don't take an unauthorized taxi from cabbies greeting you on arrival. Official taxi stands are well-signed.

Trains

Paris is Europe's rail hub, with six major stations and one minor one, each serving different regions:

- Gare du Nord (northern France and Europe)
- Gare Montparnasse (northwestern France and TGV service to France's southwest)
- Gare de Lyon (southeastern France and Italy)
- Gare de l'Est (northeastern France and eastbound international trains)
- Gare St. Lazare (northwestern France)
- Gare d'Austerlitz (southwestern France and Europe)
- Gare de Bercy (smaller station, departure point for most night trains to Italy)

All six main train stations have banks or currency exchanges, ATMs, train information desks, telephones, cafés, newsstands, and clever pickpockets (pay attention in ticket lines—keep your bag firmly gripped in front of you). Because of security concerns, not all have baggage checks. Any train station has schedule information, can make reservations, and can sell tickets for any

PARIS

destination. Buying tickets is handier from an SNCF neighborhood office.

Each station offers two types of rail service: long distance to other cities, called Grandes Lignes (major lines); and suburban service to nearby areas, called Banlieue, Transilien, or RER. You also may see ticket windows identified as *Ile de France*. These are for Transilien trains serving destinations outside Paris in the Ile de France region (usually no more than an hour from Paris).

Paris train stations can be intimidating, but if you slow down, take a deep breath, and ask for help, you'll find them manageable and efficient. Bring a pad of paper for clear communication at ticket/info windows. All stations have helpful information booths *(accueil);* the bigger stations have roving helpers, usually wearing red or blue vests. They're capable of answering rail questions more quickly than the staff at the information desks or ticket windows. I make a habit of confirming my track number and departure time with these helpers.

Paris' Train Stations

Métro and RER trains, as well as buses and taxis, are well-marked at every station. When arriving by Métro, follow signs for *Grandes Lignes–SNCF* to find the main tracks.

Gare du Nord
Key Destinations Served by Gare du Nord Grandes Lignes:
Bruges (at least hourly, 2.5 hours, change in Brussels), **Amsterdam** (8-10/day, 3.5 hours direct), **Berlin** (6/day, 9 hours, 1-2 changes, via Belgium, better connections from Gare de l'Est), **Copenhagen** (7/day, 14-18 hours, two night trains), and **London** by Eurostar Chunnel train (15/day, 2.5 hours, toll tel. 08 36 35 35 39; for details, see "To Paris or Brussels via Eurostar Train" on page 819). Routes via **Brussels** (e.g., to Amsterdam and Bruges) require taking the pricey Thalys train; for details and tips, see "Amsterdam Connections" on page 1240.

By Banlieue/RER Lines: Charles de Gaulle Airport (4/hour, 30 minutes, runs 5:00-24:00, track 4).

Gare Montparnasse
Key Destinations Served by Gare Montparnasse: Chartres (10/day, 65 minutes), **Madrid** (3/day, 13 hours, expensive direct overnight trains require reservations more than 2 weeks in advance), and **Lisbon** (1/day, 21.5 hours via Irun).

Gare de Lyon
Key Destinations Served by Gare de Lyon: Avignon (9/day in 2.5 hours to Avignon TGV station, 4/day in 3.5 hours to Avig-

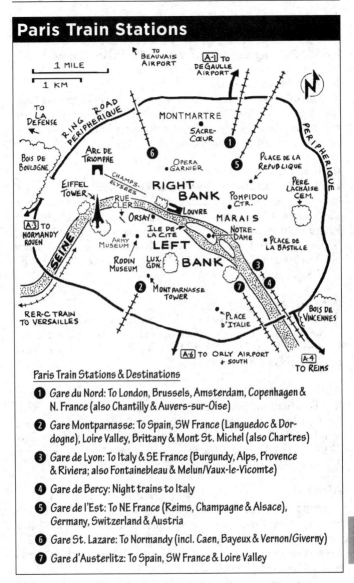

Paris Train Stations

Paris Train Stations & Destinations

1 Gare du Nord: To London, Brussels, Amsterdam, Copenhagen & N. France (also Chantilly & Auvers-sur-Oise)

2 Gare Montparnasse: To Spain, SW France (Languedoc & Dordogne), Loire Valley, Brittany & Mont St. Michel (also Chartres)

3 Gare de Lyon: To Italy & SE France (Burgundy, Alps, Provence & Riviera; also Fontainebleau & Melun/Vaux-le-Vicomte)

4 Gare de Bercy: Night trains to Italy

5 Gare de l'Est: To NE France (Reims, Champagne & Alsace), Germany, Switzerland & Austria

6 Gare St. Lazare: To Normandy (incl. Caen, Bayeux & Vernon/Giverny)

7 Gare d'Austerlitz: To Spain, SW France & Loire Valley

non Centre-Ville station, more connections with change—3-4 hours), **Arles** (11/day, 2 direct TGVs—4 hours, 9 with change in Avignon—5 hours), **Nice** (10/day, 6 hours, may require change, 11-hour night train possible out of Gare d'Austerlitz), **Venice** (3/ day, 10-12 hours with change in Milan; 1 direct overnight, 13 hours, important to reserve ahead, 2 more night trains with changes), **Rome** (4/day, 11-13 hours, plus several overnight options, important to reserve ahead), **Interlaken** (5/day, 6-6.5 hours, 2-3 changes, 7 more from Gare de l'Est), and **Barcelona** (3/day, 9 hours, 1-2 changes; night train possible from Gare d'Austerlitz).

Gare de Bercy

This smaller station handles some night train service to Italy (Mo: Bercy, one stop east of Gare de Lyon on line 14, exit the Métro station and it's across the street). Facilities are limited—just a WC and a sandwich-fare takeout café.

Gare de l'Est

Key Destinations Served by Gare de l'Est: Interlaken (7/day, 6-7 hours, 1-2 changes, 5 more from Gare de Lyon), **Vienna** (7/day, 12-17 hours, 1-3 changes, night train via Munich or Frankfurt), **Prague** (5/day, 12.5-13.5 hours, night train via Mannheim or Berlin), **Munich** (4/day, 6-7 hours, most with 1 change, 1 direct night train), and **Berlin** (6/day, 8-9 hours, 1-2 changes; 1 direct night train, 11.25 hours).

Gare St. Lazare

Key Destinations Served by Gare St. Lazare: Bayeux (9/day, 2.5 hours, some change in Caen), **Caen** (14/day, 2 hours), and **Pontorson/Mont St. Michel** (2/day, 4-5.5 hours, via Caen; more trains from Gare Montparnasse).

Gare d'Austerlitz

Key Destinations Served by Gare d'Austerlitz: Versailles (RER line C, 4/hour, 30-40 minutes), **Barcelona** (1/night, 12 hours, make mandatory reservation at least 2 weeks ahead; day trains from Gare de Lyon), and **Madrid** (2/night, 13 hours direct, 16 hours via Irun; day trains from Gare Montparnasse).

Airports

Charles de Gaulle Airport

Paris' primary airport has three terminals: T-1, T-2, and T-3 (see map). Most flights from the US use T-1 or T-2. To find out which terminal serves your airline, check your ticket or contact the airport (toll tel. 3950, www.adp.fr).

Transportation Between Charles de Gaulle Airport and Paris: Three public-transportation routes, airport vans, and taxis link the airport's terminals with central Paris. If you're traveling with one or two companions, carrying lots of baggage, or are just plain tired, taxis are worth the extra cost (for reasons explained later in this section, avoid airport vans going in the airport-to-Paris direction).

Roissy-Buses run to the Opéra Métro stop (€9.40, 4/hour,

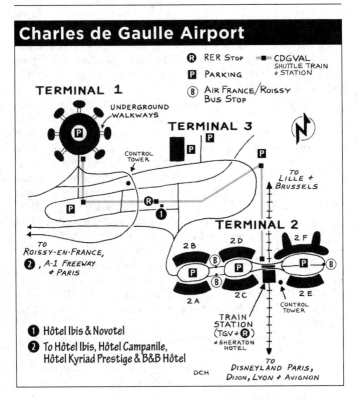

Charles de Gaulle Airport

R RER Stop
P Parking
B Air France/Roissy Bus Stop
■ CDGVAL Shuttle Train + Station

TERMINAL 1

UNDERGROUND WALKWAYS

P

CONTROL TOWER

TERMINAL 3

P
P
P

N

TO LILLE + BRUSSELS

P
R
❶

TO ROISSY-EN-FRANCE, **❷**, A-1 FREEWAY + PARIS

TERMINAL 2

2 B   2 D   2 F

B   **B**

P   **P**   **P**   **B**

B

2 A   2 C   2 E

CONTROL TOWER

TRAIN STATION (TGV + **R**) + SHERATON HOTEL

TO DISNEYLAND PARIS, DIJON, LYON + AVIGNON

❶ Hôtel Ibis & Novotel
❷ To Hôtel Ibis, Hôtel Campanile, Hôtel Kyriad Prestige & B&B Hôtel

DCH

runs 6:30-21:00, 50 minutes, buy ticket on bus). You'll arrive at a bus stop on rue Scribe on the left side of the Opéra building. To get to the Métro entrance, turn left out of the bus and walk counterclockwise around the lavish Opéra building. The Métro station entrance faces the Opéra's front. You can also take a taxi (about €12) to any of my listed hotels from behind the Opéra (the stand is in front of Galeries Lafayette department store).

"Les Cars" Air France buses serve central Paris on two routes (€16, at least 2/hour, runs 5:45-23:00, toll tel. 08 92 35 08 20, www.cars-airfrance.com). Bus #2 runs between the airport and the Arc de Triomphe and Porte Maillot (45 minutes). Bus #4 runs to Gare de Lyon (45 minutes) and continues to the Montparnasse Tower/train station (1 hour). A third line runs to Orly Airport (see page 436).

Taxis cost about €60 for up to three people with bags (more if traffic is bad). Your hotel can call for a taxi to the airport. Specify that you want a real taxi *(un taxi normal),* and not a limo service that costs €20 more (and gives your hotel a kickback).

Airport vans work like those at home, packing several passengers from different hotels into a van and taking them to or from the airport. They work best for trips from your hotel to the airport. They don't work as well for trips from the airport because you must book a set pick-up time in advance, even though you don't know exactly when you'll arrive, get your baggage, and so on (the exception is Paris Webservices, which meets you inside the terminal). The hotel-to-airport service takes longer than a taxi because you make several hotel stops on the way, but is a particularly good deal for single travelers or families of four or more (which is too many people for a taxi). If your hotel doesn't work with a van service, reserve directly (book at least a day in advance—most hoteliers will make the call for you). Airport vans cost about €30 for one person, €43 for two, and €55 for three. Here are a couple of companies to consider: **Paris Shuttles Network** (tel. 01 45 26 01 58, www. shuttlesnetwork.com), **Airport Connection** (tel. 01 43 65 55 55, www.airport-connection.com), and **Paris Webservices** (meets you inside the terminal, €160-180/up to 4 people round-trip, about €30 more for 6 people, use promo code "RSteves 07" for 10 percent discount, excursions available—see page 320, sells Museum Passes with no extra fee—order ahead, tel. 01 53 62 02 29, fax 01 53 01 35 84, www.pariswebservices.com, contactpws @pariswebservices.com).

A **Disneyland shuttle van** is at each terminal (€17, runs every 20 minutes daily 8:30-20:00ish, 30 minutes). TGV trains also run to Disneyland from the airport in 10 minutes, but leave less frequently (hourly) and require shuttle buses at each end—take the shuttle van instead.

Sleeping at or near Charles de Gaulle Airport
$$ Hôtel Ibis**, outside the T-3 RER stop, is huge and offers standard airport accommodations (Db-€95-130, tel. 01 49 19 19 19, fax 01 49 19 19 21, www.ibishotel.com, h1404@accor.com).

$$ Novotel*** is nearby and the next step up (Db-€130-180, can rise to €280 for last-minute rooms, tel. 01 49 19 27 27, fax 01 49 19 27 99, www.novotel.com, h1014@accor.com). Both places have restaurants, and are cheapest when booked well in advance.

Orly Airport
This airport feels small. It's good for rental-car pickup and drop-off, as it's closer to Paris and far easier to navigate than Charles de Gaulle Airport.

Transportation Between Orly Airport and Paris: Choose between shuttle buses *(navettes)*, the RER, taxis, and airport vans. They all connect Paris with either terminal.

"Les Cars" Air France buses run to Gare Montparnasse, Invalides, and Etoile Métro stops, all of which have connections to several Métro lines. Bus #1 goes only to Gare Montparnasse.

Bus #1* (with an asterisk) hits Gare Montparnasse, Invalides, and Etoile. For the rue Cler neighborhood, take the #1* bus to Invalides, then the Métro to La Tour Maubourg or Ecole Militaire. Both buses depart from Ouest exit D or Sud exit L: Look for signs to *navettes* (€11.50, buy ticket from driver, 4/hour, 40 minutes to Invalides).

The **Orlybus** goes directly to the Denfert-Rochereau Métro stop. From there you can catch the Métro or RER-B to central Paris, including the Luxembourg area, Notre-Dame Cathedral, and Gare du Nord. The Orlybus departs from Ouest exit D and Sud exit H (€6.60, 2/hour, 30 minutes).

A different bus called **"Paris par le train"** takes you to the Pont d'Orly RER station, where you can catch the RER-C to Gare d'Austerlitz, St. Michel/Notre-Dame, Musée d'Orsay, Invalides (change here for rue Cler hotels), and Pont de l'Alma. Catch this bus at Ouest exit G or Sud exit F (€6.50 total, 4/hour, 40 minutes).

Taxis are to the far right as you leave the terminal, at Gate M. Allow €38 with bags for a taxi into central Paris.

Airport vans are good for single travelers or families of four or more (too many for a taxi) if going from Paris to the airport (see page 435; from Orly, figure about €23/1 person, €30/2 people, less per person for larger groups and kids).

Beauvais Airport

Budget airlines such as Ryanair use this small airport, offering dirt-cheap airfares but leaving you 50 miles north of Paris. Still, this airport has direct buses to Paris (see below), and is handy for travelers heading to Normandy or Belgium (car rental available; airport toll tel. 08 92 68 20 66, www.aeroportbeauvais.com; Ryanair toll tel. 08 92 68 20 73, www.ryanair.com).

Transportation Between Beauvais Airport and Paris: Buses depart from the airport when they're full (about 20 minutes after flights arrive) and take 1.5 hours to reach Paris. Buy your ticket (€14 one-way) at the little kiosk to the right as you exit the airport. Buses arrive at Porte Maillot on the west edge of Paris (on Métro line 1 and RER-C). The closest taxi stand is at Hôtel Concorde-Lafayette. Buses heading to Beauvais Airport leave from Porte Maillot about 3.25 hours before scheduled flight departures. Catch the bus in the parking lot on boulevard Pershing next to Hôtel Concorde-Lafayette. Arrive with enough time to purchase your bus ticket before boarding (bus toll tel. 08 92 68 20 64).

Trains connect Beauvais' city center and Paris' Gare du Nord (20/day, 80 minutes).

Taxis run from Beauvais Airport to Beauvais' train station or city center (€14) or central Paris (allow €125).

Versailles

If you've ever wondered why your American passport has French writing in it, you'll find the answer at Versailles (vehr-"sigh")—every king's dream palace. The powerful court of Louis XIV at Versailles set the standard of culture for all of Europe, right up to modern times. Today, if you're planning to visit just one palace in all of Europe, make it Versailles.

Visiting Versailles can seem daunting because of its size and hordes of visitors. But it's manageable. Arm yourself with a pass to skip ticket-buying lines; arrive early or late to avoid the crowds; and use this self-guided tour to focus on the highlights. I've provided all the details in "Orientation," below.

Orientation to Versailles

Cost: I recommend buying either a Paris Museum Pass or Versailles' "Le Passeport" Pass, both of which give you access to the most important parts of the complex (see "Passes," below). As costs, hours, entries, and special events at Versailles can change from season to season, get the latest information at the helpful Versailles website—www.chateauversailles.fr.

If you don't get a pass, you can buy individual tickets for each of the three different sections:

The Château, the main palace, costs €15 (€13 after 15:00, under 18 always free, includes audioguide). Your Château ticket includes the famous Hall of Mirrors, the king and queen's living quarters, many lesser rooms, and any temporary exhibitions. On the first Sunday of off-season months (Nov-March), entry is free.

The Trianon Palaces and Domaine de Marie-Antoinette costs €10 (€6 after 16:00 and Nov-March, under 18 always free). This ticket gives you access to the far corner of the Gardens, the small palaces called the Grand Trianon and Petit Trianon, the queen's Hamlet, and a smattering of nearby buildings.

The Gardens are free, except on certain days (generally weekends April-Oct) when the fountains blast, and then the price is €8 (described later, under "Fountain Spectacles in the Gardens").

Passes: The following passes can save money and allow you to skip the long ticket-buyer lines (though everyone must endure security checks before entering the palaces).

The **Paris Museum Pass** (see page 331) covers the Château and the Trianon/Domaine area (a €25 value) and is the best solution for most, but doesn't include the Gardens on Fountain Spectacle days (you'll have to buy an extra ticket for that).

The **Le Passeport** one-day pass covers your entrance to the Château, the Trianon/Domaine area, and the Gardens, including the weekend Fountain Spectacles. Le Passeport costs €18 except when the fountains play, when it costs €25.

Buying Passes and Tickets: The Château box office (to the left as you face the palace) usually has long lines. It's best to buy tickets or Le Passeport in advance. In the city of Versailles, you can get them at the TI (but only Le Passeport, not tickets) or at Café Bleu Roi (on the right side of the parking lot as you approach the Château, 7 rue Colbert—see map on the next page). They're also available at any Paris FNAC department store, or online at www.chateauversailles.fr (print out your pass/ticket or pick it up near the entrance).

Hours: The **Château** is open April-Oct Tue-Sun 9:00-18:30, Nov-March Tue-Sun 9:00-17:30, closed Mon.

The **Trianon Palaces and Domaine de Marie-Antoinette** are open April-Oct Tue-Sun 12:00-18:30, closed Mon; Nov-March Tue-Sun 12:00-17:30, closed Mon (off-season only the two Trianon Palaces are open, not the Hamlet or other outlying buildings).

The **Gardens** are open April-Oct daily 9:00-20:30, but may close earlier for special events; Nov-March Tue-Sun 8:00-18:00, closed Mon.

Last entry to all of these areas is 30 minutes before closing.

Crowd-Beating Strategies: Versailles is a zoo May-Sept 10:00-13:00, especially Tue and Sun. Lines to buy tickets and go through security are long, and the Château is a slow shuffle of shoulder-to-shoulder tourists.

You can skip the ticket-buying line by using a Paris Museum Pass or Le Passeport, by buying tickets in advance, or by booking a guided tour (discussed later). Everyone—including advanced ticket and passholders—must wait in line to go through security (longest lines 10:00-12:00). Before queuing up at the security entrance, check for signs that they might have opened up a special, shorter line for passholders (but don't count on it).

For fewer crowds, go early or late. If you go early, arrive by 9:00 (when the palace opens), and tour the Château first, then the Gardens. If you arrive later, tour the Gardens first (remembering that the Trianon/Domaine area opens at noon), then visit the Château after 13:00, when crowds dissipate. Avoid Tue and Sun, when the place is packed from open to close.

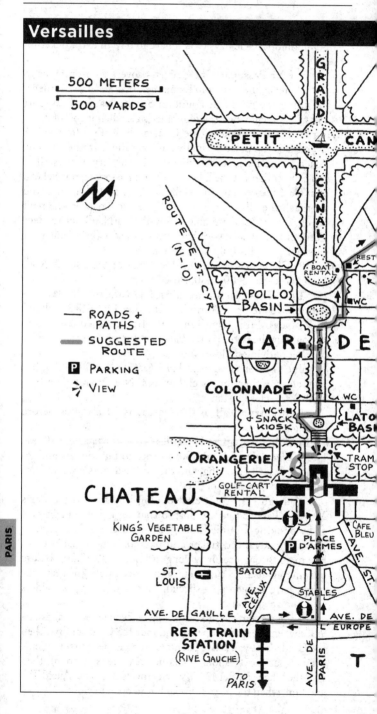

Versailles

500 METERS
500 YARDS

GRAND CANAL

PETIT CAN...

ROUTE DE ST. CYR (N-10)

BOAT RENTAL

REST...

APOLLO BASIN

WC

ROADS & PATHS

SUGGESTED ROUTE

P PARKING

VIEW

G A R ... D E

COLONNADE

WC

LATO... BASI...

WC & SNACK KIOSK

TRAM STOP

ORANGERIE

GOLF-CART RENTAL

CHATEAU

KING'S VEGETABLE GARDEN

CAFE BLEU

PLACE D'ARMES

P

AVE. ST.

ST. LOUIS

SATORY

STABLES

AVE. DE GAULLE

AVE. SCEAUX

AVE. DE L'EUROPE

RER TRAIN STATION
(RIVE GAUCHE)

AVE. DE PARIS

TO PARIS

T

PARIS

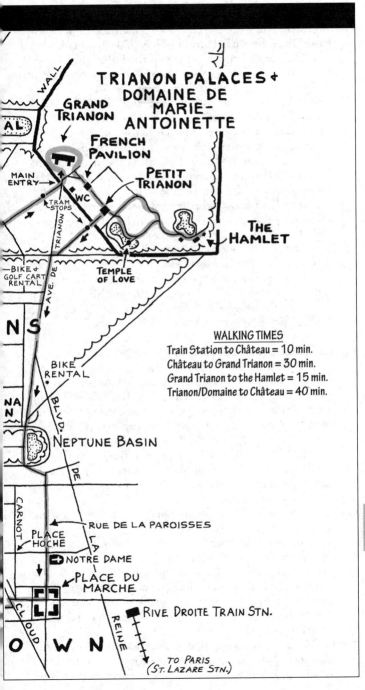

TRIANON PALACES &
DOMAINE DE MARIE-
ANTOINETTE

GRAND TRIANON

WALL

AL

FRENCH PAVILION

MAIN ENTRY

PETIT TRIANON

TRAM STOPS

WC

AVE. DE TRIANON

THE HAMLET

BIKE & GOLF CART RENTAL

TEMPLE OF LOVE

NS

WALKING TIMES
Train Station to Château = 10 min.
Château to Grand Trianon = 30 min.
Grand Trianon to the Hamlet = 15 min.
Trianon/Domaine to Château = 40 min.

BIKE RENTAL

BLVD.

NA N

NEPTUNE BASIN

DE

RUE DE LA PAROISSES

CARNOT

PLACE HOCHE

NOTRE DAME

LA

PLACE DU MARCHE

RIVE DROITE TRAIN STN.

C LOUD

O W N

REINE

TO PARIS
(St. LAZARE STN.)

Pickpockets: Assume pickpockets are working the tourist crowds.

Getting There: The town of Versailles is 30 minutes southwest of Paris. Take the **RER-C train** (4/hour, 30-40 minutes one-way, €6.20 round-trip) from any of these Paris RER stops: Gare d'Austerlitz, St. Michel, Musée d'Orsay, Invalides, Pont de l'Alma, and Champ de Mars. Scan the list of departing trains. Any train whose name starts with a V (e.g., "Vick") goes to Versailles; don't board other trains. Get off at the last stop (Versailles R.G., or "Rive Gauche"). Exit through the turnstiles by inserting your ticket. To reach the palace, turn right out of the train station, then left at the first boulevard, and walk 10 minutes. To return to Paris, all trains serve all downtown Paris RER stops on the C line.

Versailles has two other train stations—Rive Droite and Chantiers—that are not as useful to travelers. Trains run from Paris' Gare St. Lazare to both of these stations.

Taxis for the 30-minute ride (without traffic) between Versailles and Paris cost about €55.

By **car**, get on the *périphérique* freeway that circles Paris, and take the toll-free A13 autoroute toward Rouen. Exit at Versailles, follow signs to "Versailles Château," and park in the huge pay lot at place d'Armes (€5.50/2 hours, €10/4 hours, €14.80/8 hours).

Information: Before you go, check their excellent website—www.chateauversailles.fr. The palace's general contact number is tel. 01 30 83 78 00. Versailles has two information offices, and both sell Paris Museum Passes and Le Passeport. You'll pass the (uncrowded, helpful) town TI on your walk from the main RER station to the palace—it's just past the Pullman Hôtel (daily April-Sept 9:00-19:00, Oct-March 9:00-18:00, tel. 01 39 24 88 88). The information office at the Château (long waits) is on the left side of the courtyard as you face the Château (toll tel. 08 10 81 16 14). Pick up the free, useful map as you enter the sight.

Guided Tours: The 1.5-hour English guided tour gives you access to a few extra rooms (the line-up varies) and lets you skip ticket-buying lines. Ignore the tours hawked as you leave the train station. Book at the information office in the Château courtyard; bypass the ticket-buying line and find the guided tour desk just to the right of the ticket office. Reserve immediately upon arrival, because tours can sell out by 13:00 (€14.50, or €7.50 if you already have Château admission or pass, runs about every 45 minutes 9:00-15:00).

Audio Tours: A free audioguide to the Château is included in admission. You can download a free Rick Steves audio tour for your mobile device via www.ricksteves.com/audioeurope, iTunes, or the Rick Steves Audio Europe smartphone app. Other podcasts and digital tours are available in the "multimedia" section at www.chateauversailles.fr.

Length of This Day Trip: With the usual lines, allow 1.5 hours each for the Château, the Gardens, and the Trianon/Domaine. Add another two hours for round-trip transit, plus another hour for lunch...and, at around eight hours, Versailles is a full day trip from Paris.

Baggage Check: To enter the Château and the two Trianons, you must use the free baggage check if you have large bags or baby strollers (your best bet is to use a baby backpack or hire a babysitter for the day).

WCs: Reminiscent of the days when dukes urinated behind the potted palm trees, WCs at the Château are few and far between, and some come with long lines. There are WCs immediately upon entering the Château (Entrance H); near the Grand Café d'Orléans; in the Gardens near the Latona Basin; at the Grand Canal; in the Grand Trianon and Petit Trianon; and at several other places scattered around the grounds. Any café generally has a WC.

Cuisine Art: To the left of the Château's Royal Gate entrance, the Grand Café d'Orléans has a restaurant (€13 salads, €20 *plats*) and a take-out bar (€5 sandwiches, great for picnicking in the Gardens). In the Gardens, you'll find several restaurants, cafés, and snack stands. Most are clustered near the Latona Fountain (less crowded) and the Grand Canal (more crowds and more choices, including two restaurants).

In the **town,** restaurants are on the street to the right of the parking lot (as you face the Château). A handy McDonald's (with WC) is immediately across from the train station (Internet café next door). The best choices are on rue de Satory between the station and the palace, and on the lively place du Marché Notre-Dame in the town center.

Photography: Allowed, but no flash indoors.

Fountain Spectacles in the Gardens: On spring and summer weekends, the Gardens charge a mandatory admission fee for these spectacles. Loud classical music fills the king's backyard, and the Garden's fountains are in full squirt. Louis XIV had his engineers literally reroute a river to fuel these gushers. Even by today's standards, they are impressive.

The fountains run April-Oct Sat-Sun 11:00-12:00 & 15:30-17:00, with the finale 17:20-17:30. On these "spray days," the Gardens cost €8. (Pay at the Gardens entrance; covered by Le Passeport but not Paris Museum Pass.) The calendar of spectacles also includes a few music-only days (on the rare Tue, €7) and elaborate sound-and-light displays on Sat

PARIS

June-Aug at 21:00 (€21). Check the Versailles website for what's happening during your particular visit.

Starring: Luxurious palaces, endless gardens, Louis XIV, Marie-Antoinette, and the *ancien régime*.

Overview

The main sights to see at Versailles are the Château, the landscaped Gardens in the "backyard," and the Trianon Palaces and Domaine de Marie-Antoinette, located at the far end of the Gardens. If your time is limited, skip the Trianon/Domaine, which is a full 40-minute walk from the Château.

In the Château, the highlights are the State Apartments of the King and Queen and the Hall of Mirrors.

Self-Guided Tour

Welcome to Versailles

This commentary, which leads you through the various attractions at Versailles, covers just the basics. For a detailed room-by-room rundown, consider *Rick Steves' Paris* (buy in the US or at any of the English-language bookstores in Paris listed earlier in this chapter) or the guidebook called *The Châteaux, the Gardens, and Trianon* (sold at Versailles).

Stand in the huge courtyard and face the palace, or Château. The original golden Royal Gate in the center of the courtyard, nearly 260 feet long and decorated with 100,000 gold leaves, is a recent replica of the original. The ticket-buying and guided-tour offices are to the left. The entrance to the Château (once you have your ticket or pass) is through the modern concrete-and-glass security checkpoint, marked Entrance A.

After passing through security at Entrance A, you spill out into the open-air courtyard inside the golden Royal Gate. Enter the Château from the courtyard at Entrance H—the State Apartments. Once inside, you'll find an info desk (get a free map), WCs, and free audioguides.

The Château: The one-way walk through the palace leads you past the dazzling 700-seat **Royal Opera House;** by the intimate, two-tiered **Royal Chapel;** and through the glamorous **State Apartments.** In the **King's Wing** you'll see a billiard room, a royal make-out room, the Swiss bodyguard room, Louis' official bedroom, and his grand throne room (the **Apollo Room**)—with a 10-foot-tall canopied throne—and war rooms.

Next you'll visit the magnificent **Hall of Mirrors**—250 feet long, with 17 arched mirrors matching 17 windows looking out upon royal garden views. The mirrors—a luxury at the time—reflect an age when beautiful people loved to look at themselves. In

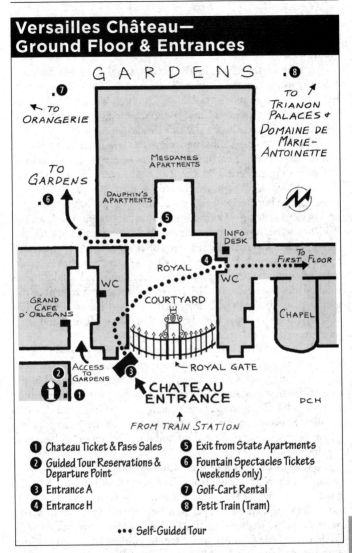

Versailles Château—
Ground Floor & Entrances

GARDENS

TO ORANGERIE

TO TRIANON PALACES & DOMAINE DE MARIE-ANTOINETTE

TO GARDENS

MESDAMES APARTMENTS

DAUPHIN'S APARTMENTS

INFO DESK

To FIRST FLOOR

ROYAL

WC

WC

GRAND CAFE D'ORLEANS

COURTYARD

CHAPEL

ACCESS TO GARDENS

ROYAL GATE

CHATEAU ENTRANCE

FROM TRAIN STATION

DCH

- ❶ Chateau Ticket & Pass Sales
- ❷ Guided Tour Reservations & Departure Point
- ❸ Entrance A
- ❹ Entrance H
- ❺ Exit from State Apartments
- ❻ Fountain Spectacles Tickets (weekends only)
- ❼ Golf-Cart Rental
- ❽ Petit Train (Tram)

••• Self-Guided Tour

another age altogether, this was the room in which the Treaty of Versailles was signed, ending World War I.

You'll finish in the **Queen's Wing,** where you'll see the Queen's bedchamber, the guard room where Louis XVI and Marie-Antoinette surrendered to the Revolution, and Napoleon's coronation room.

Getting Around the Gardens: It's a 40-minute walk from the palace, down to the Grand Canal, past the two Trianon palaces, to the Hamlet at the far end of Domaine de Marie-Antoinette.

Allow more time if you stop along the way. After enduring the slow Château shuffle, stretching your legs out here feels pretty good.

A **bike** rental station by the Grand Canal gives you the most freedom to explore the Gardens economically (€6.50/hour or €15/half-day, kid-size bikes available). Although you can't take your bike inside the grounds of the Trianon/Domaine, you can park it near an entrance while you sightsee inside.

The fast-looking, slow-moving *petit train* (tram) leaves from behind the Château (north side). It stops at the Grand Canal and at the Grand and Petit Trianons (two of the entrance points to the Trianon/Domaine). You can hop on and off as you like (€7 day pass, €3.50 single trip, free for kids under 11, 4/hour). Another option is to rent a **golf cart** for a fun drive through the Gardens (€30/hour, rent down by the canal or at Orangerie side of palace).

Palace Gardens: The Gardens offer a world of royal amusements. The warmth from the Sun King was so great that he could even grow orange trees in chilly France. Louis XIV had a thousand of these to amaze his visitors. In winter they were kept in the greenhouses (beneath your feet) that surround the courtyard. On sunny days they were wheeled out in their silver planters and scattered around the grounds.

With the palace behind you, it seems as if the grounds stretch out forever. Versailles was laid out along an eight-mile axis that included the grounds, the palace, and the town of Versailles itself, one of the first instances of urban planning since Roman times and a model for future capitals, such as Washington, DC, and Brasilia. A promenade leads from the palace to the Grand Canal, where France's royalty floated up and down in imported Venetian gondolas.

Trianon Palaces and Domaine de Marie-Antoinette: Versailles began as an escape from the pressures of kingship. But in a short time the Château had become as busy as Paris ever was. Louis XIV needed an escape from his escape and built a smaller palace out in the boonies. Later, his successors retreated still farther from the Château and French political life, ignoring the real world that was crumbling all around them. They expanded the Trianon area, building a fantasy world of palaces and pleasure gardens—the enclosure called Marie-Antoinette's Domaine.

The beautifully restored **Grand Trianon Palace** is as sumptuous as the main palace, but much smaller. With its pastel-pink colonnade and more human scale, this is a place you'd like to call home. Nearby are the **French Pavilion,** Marie-Antoinette's **Theater,** and the octagonal **Belvedere** palace.

You can almost see princesses bobbing gaily in the branches as you walk through the enchanting forest, past the white marble

Temple of Love to the queen's fake-peasant **Hamlet** *(le Hameau)*. Marie-Antoinette's happiest days were spent at the Hamlet, under a bonnet, tending her perfumed sheep and manicured gardens in a thatch-happy wonderland.

The **Petit Trianon** is a masterpiece of Neoclassical architecture. Despite her bad reputation with the public, Marie-Antoinette was a sweet girl from Vienna who never quite fit in with the fast, sophisticated crowd at Versailles. Here at the Petit Trianon, she could get away and re-create the simple home life she remembered from her childhood. Here she played, while in the cafés of faraway Paris, revolutionaries plotted the end of the *ancien régime*.

If you have more time to spend at Versailles, consider one of the following, lesser sights near the palace:

The Equestrian Performance Academy (Académie du Spectacle Equestre): On most weekends from May through mid-December, you can watch the basic training sessions (no choreography), or enjoy choreographed performances—including "equestrian fencing"—performed to classical music (€12 training sessions, Sat-Sun and some Thu at 11:15; €25 musical shows, Sun and some Thu at 15:00 plus Sat at 20:00 May-July and at 18:00 Sept-Dec, but schedule is sporadic—check website for closure dates and extra performances; information tel. 01 39 02 07 14, reservations toll tel. 08 92 68 18 91, www.acadequestre.fr). The stables (Grandes Ecuries) are across the parking square from the Château, next to the post office.

The King's Vegetable Garden (Le Potager du Roi): When Louis XIV demanded fresh asparagus in the middle of winter, he got it, thanks to his vegetable garden. The 22-acre garden—still productive—is open to visitors. Stroll through symmetrically laid-out plots planted with vegetables both ordinary and exotic, among thousands of fruit trees. The garden is surrounded by walls and sunk below street level to create its own microclimate. Overseeing the central fountain is a statue of the agronomist Jean de la Quintinie, who wowed Louis XIV's court with Versailles-sized produce (€4.50 weekdays, €6.50 weekends, April-Oct Tue-Sun 10:00-18:00, closed Mon; limited hours in winter; 10 rue du Maréchal Joffre, tel. 01 39 24 62 62, www.potager-du-roi.fr).

PARIS

PROVENCE

This magnificent region is shaped like a giant wedge of quiche. From its sunburned crust, fanning out along the Mediterranean coast from the Camargue to Marseille, it stretches north along the Rhône Valley to Orange. The Romans were here in force and left many ruins—some of the best anywhere. Seven popes, artists such as Vincent van Gogh and Paul Cézanne, and author Peter Mayle all enjoyed their years in Provence. This destination features a splendid recipe of arid climate, oceans of vineyards, dramatic scenery, captivating cities, and adorable hill-capping villages.

Explore France's greatest Roman ruin, the Pont du Gard. Spend a few starry, starry nights with Van Gogh in Arles. Youthful but classy Avignon bustles in the shadow of its brooding Palace of the Popes.

Planning Your Time

Make Arles or Avignon your sightseeing base—particularly if you have no car. Italophiles prefer smaller Arles, while poodles pick urban Avignon. Arles has a blue-collar quality; the entire city feels like Van Gogh's bedroom. Avignon—double the size of Arles—feels sophisticated, with more nightlife and shopping, and makes a good base for non-drivers thanks to its convenient public-transit options.

When budgeting your time, you'll want a full day for sightseeing in Arles (best on Wed or Sat, when it's market day); a half-day for Avignon; and a day or two for the villages and sights in the countryside. Pont du Gard is a short hop west of Avignon.

Provence

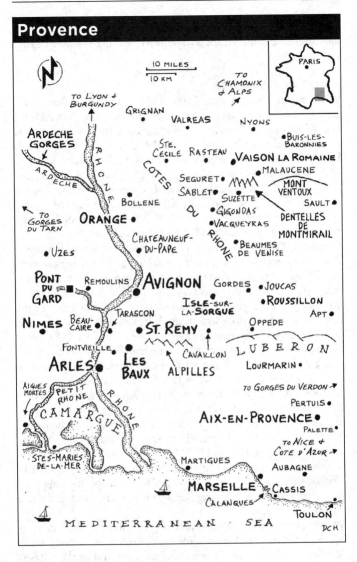

Getting Around Provence

By Bus or Train: Public transit is good between cities and decent to some towns, but marginal at best to the villages. Frequent trains link Avignon and Arles (about 30 minutes between each). From Avignon you can bus to Pont du Gard.

By Car: The region is made to order for a car. The yellow Michelin Local maps #332 and #340 are worth considering; the larger-scale orange Michelin map #527 also includes the Riviera. Avignon (pop. 100,000) is a headache for drivers. Arles (pop. 52,000) is easier, but still urban. Be wary of thieves: Park only in well-monitored spaces and leave nothing valuable in your car.

Tours of Provence

Wine Safari—Dutchman Mike Rijken runs a one-man show, taking travelers through the region he adopted more than 20 years ago. Mike came to France to train as a chef, later became a wine steward, and has now found his calling as a driver/guide. His English is fluent, and though his focus is wine and wine villages, Mike knows the region thoroughly and is a good teacher of its history (€55/half-day, €100/day, priced per person, group size varies from 2 to 6; pickups possible in Arles, Avignon, Lyon, Marseille, or Aix-en-Provence; tel. 04 90 35 59 21, mobile 06 19 29 50 81, www.winesafari.net, mikeswinesafari@wanadoo.fr).

Avignon Wine Tour—For a playful, informative, and distinctly French perspective on wines of the Côtes du Rhône region, contact François Marcou, who runs his tours with passion and energy, offering different itineraries every day. Based in Avignon, François can pick you up at your Avignon hotel, the TI, or at either of the city's train stations (€75/person for all-day wine tours that include 4-5 tastings, €350 for private groups, mobile 06 28 05 33 84, www.avignon-wine-tour.com, avignon.wine.tour@modulonet.fr).

Imagine Tours—Unlike most tour operators, this organization runs on a not-for-profit basis, with a focus on cultural excursions. It offers low-key, personalized tours that allow visitors to discover the "true heart of Provence." The itineraries adapt to your interests, and the volunteer guides will meet you at your hotel or the departure point of your choice (€150/half-day, €275/day, prices are for up to 4 people, mobile 06 89 22 19 87, fax 04 90 24 84 26, www.imagine-tours.net, imagine.tours@gmail.com). They also offer free assistance to travelers, should you want advice planning your itinerary, need help booking hotel rooms, or run into problems during your trip.

Wine Uncovered—Passionate Englishman (is that an oxymoron?) Olivier Hickman takes small groups on focused tours of selected wineries in Châteauneuf-du-Pape and in the villages near Vaison la Romaine. Olivier is serious about French wine, and knows his subject matter inside and out. His in-depth tastings include three wineries for €55 per person (his minimum half-day fee is €155; full-day is €195). If you need transportation, he can help arrange it (mobile 06 75 10 10 01, www.wine-uncovered.com, olivier.hickman@wine-uncovered.com).

Visit Provence—This company runs trips from Avignon (and a few from Arles), and provides introductory commentary to what you'll see (but no guiding at the actual sights). They have

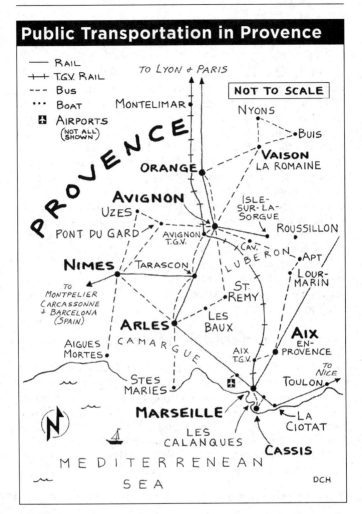

Public Transportation in Provence

eight-seat minivans (about €60/half-day, €100/day; they'll pick you up at your hotel in Avignon). Ask about their cheaper big-bus excursions, or consider hiring a van and driver for your own private use (plan on €210/half-day, €400/day, tel. 04 90 14 70 00, check website for current destinations, www.provence-reservation .com).

Madeleine's Culinary and Active Adventures—Madeleine Vedel, an effervescent American expat, plans small group tours from Avignon and Arles to visit food artisans and wineries. Madeleine also leads kid-friendly hikes in the countryside (€300/day, flat rate for 1-5 people, mobile 06 82 15 51 74, www.cuisine provencale.com).

Arles

By helping Julius Caesar defeat Marseille, Arles (pronounced "arl") earned the imperial nod and was made an important port city. With the first bridge over the Rhône River, Arles was a key stop on the Roman road from Italy to Spain, the Via Domitia. After reigning as the seat of an important archbishop and a trading center for centuries, the city became a sleepy backwater of little importance in the 1700s. Vincent van Gogh settled here in the late 1800s, but left only a chunk of his ear (now long gone). American bombers destroyed much of Arles in World War II as the townsfolk hid out in its underground Roman galleries. But today Arles thrives again, with its evocative Roman ruins, an eclectic assortment of museums, made-for-ice-cream pedestrian zones, and squares that play hide-and-seek with visitors.

The city's unpolished streets and squares are not to everyone's taste. This workaday city has not sold out to tourism, so you won't see dolled-up lanes and perfectly preserved buildings. But to me, that's part of its charm.

Orientation to Arles

Arles faces the Mediterranean, turning its back on Paris. And though the town is built along the Rhône, it largely ignores the river. Landmarks hide in Arles' medieval tangle of narrow, winding streets. Virtually everything is close—but first-timers can walk forever to get there. Hotels have good, free city maps, and Arles provides helpful street-corner signs that point you toward sights and hotels. Racing cars enjoy Arles' medieval lanes, turning sidewalks into tightropes and pedestrians into leaping targets.

Tourist Information

The **main TI** is on the ring road boulevard des Lices, at esplanade Charles de Gaulle (April-Sept daily 9:00-18:45; Oct-March Mon-Sat 9:00-16:45, Sun 10:00-13:00; tel. 04 90 18 41 20, www.arlestourisme.com). There's also a **train station TI** (Mon-Fri 9:00-13:30 & 14:30-16:45, closed Sat-Sun).

At either TI, pick up the city map, note the bus schedules (displayed in binders), and get English information on nearby destinations such as the Camargue wildlife area. Ask about "bullgames" (Provence's more humane version of bullfights—described later, under "Events in Arles") and walking tours of Arles. Skip the useless €1 brochure describing several walks in Arles, including one that locates Van Gogh's "easels." Both TIs can help you reserve hotel rooms (credit card required for deposit).

PROVENCE

Arrival in Arles

By Train: The train station is on the river, a 10-minute walk from the town center. Before heading into town, get what you need at the train station TI. There's no baggage storage at the station, but you can walk 10 minutes to stow it at Hôtel Régence (see "Helpful Hints," later).

To reach the town center, turn left out of the train station and walk 15 minutes; or wait for the free Starlette bus at the shelter across the street (3/hour, Mon-Sat only). Taxis usually wait in front of the station, but if you don't see any, call the posted telephone numbers, or dial 04 89 73 36 00. If the train station TI is open, you can ask them to call. Taxi rates are fixed—allow about €10 to any of my recommended hotels.

By Bus: The Centre-Ville bus station is a few blocks below the main TI, located on the ring road at 16-24 boulevard Georges Clemenceau.

By Car: Most hotels have parking nearby—ask for detailed directions (€1.50/hour at most meters, free 12:00-14:00 & 19:00-9:00). For most hotels, first follow signs to *Centre-Ville,* then *Gare SNCF* (train station). You'll come to a big roundabout (place Lamartine) with a Monoprix department store to the right. You can park along the city wall and find your hotel on foot; the hotels I list are no more than a 10-minute walk away (best not to park here overnight due to theft concerns and markets on Wed and Sat). Fearless drivers can plunge into the narrow streets between the two stumpy towers via rue de la Calade, and follow signs to their hotel. Again, theft is a problem; leave nothing in your car, and trust your hotelier's advice on where to park.

If you can't find parking near your hotel, Parking des Lices (Arles' only parking garage), near the TI on boulevard des Lices, is a good fallback (€3/hour, €8/24 hours).

Helpful Hints

Market Days: The big markets are on Wednesdays and Saturdays.

Meetings and Festivals: An international photo event jams hotels in early July. The let-'er-rip, twice-a-year Féria draws crowds over Easter and in mid-September (see www.arlestourisme .com for dates).

Internet Access: Internet cafés in Arles change with the wind. Ask your hotelier or at the TI.

Baggage Storage and Bike Rental: The recommended **Hôtel Régence** (see page 465) will store your bags for €3 (daily 7:30-22:00 mid-March-mid-Nov, closed in winter). They also rent bikes (€6/hour, €14/day, one-way rentals within Provence possible, same hours as baggage storage). Ask about their electric bikes—handy on windy days, but with limited power.

Arles

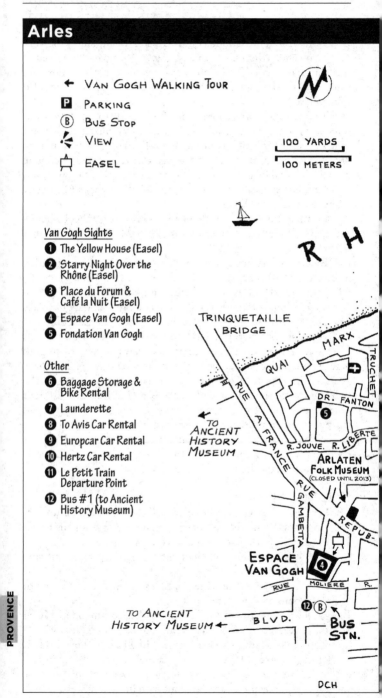

← VAN GOGH WALKING TOUR
P PARKING
(B) BUS STOP
View
EASEL

100 YARDS
100 METERS

Van Gogh Sights
1 The Yellow House (Easel)
2 Starry Night Over the Rhône (Easel)
3 Place du Forum & Café la Nuit (Easel)
4 Espace Van Gogh (Easel)
5 Fondation Van Gogh

Other
6 Baggage Storage & Bike Rental
7 Launderette
8 To Avis Car Rental
9 Europcar Car Rental
10 Hertz Car Rental
11 Le Petit Train Departure Point
12 Bus #1 (to Ancient History Museum)

R H

TRINQUETAILLE BRIDGE

MARX

TRUCHET

QUAI

RUE A. FRANCE

DR. FANTON

TO ANCIENT HISTORY MUSEUM

R. JOUVE. R. LIBERTE

ARLATEN FOLK MUSEUM (CLOSED UNTIL 2013)

RUE GAMBETTA

REPUB-

ESPACE VAN GOGH

RUE

MOLIERE

R.

TO ANCIENT HISTORY MUSEUM ←

BLVD.

BUS STN.

DCH

PROVENCE

TO TRAIN STATION

TO LES BAUX, FONTVIEILLE & AVIGNON

AVE. STALIN.

MONOPRIX

❷

PLACE LAMARTINE

PETANQUE

GATE

BLVD.

R H O N E

QUAI LAMARTINE

RUE JOUVEAU

RUE CAVALERIE

JULES FERRY

❻

BALZAC

R.L. BLUM

PLACE VOLTAIRE

R. CONDORCET

EMILE COMBES

REATTU MUSEUM

DORMOY

RUE DU GRAND PRIEURE

GRILLE

𝆑

RUE DU QUATRE SEPT.

R. AMPH.

R. BARBES

R. VOLTAIRE

RUE PORTAGNEL

❼

R. TARDIEU

DU FOUR

❿

RUE

R. REFUGE

RASPAIL

ENTER

ROMAN ARENA

NOTRE DAME

SUISSES

RUE DE HOTEL DE VILLE

SAUVAGE

BALE

FAURE

BAST.

PLACE DU ❸ FORUM

RUE DES ARENES

R. NIC.

R. DIDEROT

R. BALZE

RUE CALADE

DE LAURE

ANCIENT CITY WALLS

EMILE COMBES

ST. TROPHIME

WC

PLACE REPUBLIQUE

RUE DE CLOITRE

PORTE DE

CLASSICAL THEATER

LIQUE

ROTONDE

RUE JAURES

CLOISTERS

JARDIN D'ETE

MONTEE VAUBAN

BLVD. V. HUGO

❾

DES

LICES

❶❶

POST & TAXIS

P

PLAYGROUND

R. E. FASSIN

TO ❽

TO LES AYLSCAMPS CEMETERY

Laundry: There's a launderette at 12 rue Portagnel (daily 7:00-21:30, you can stay later to finish if you're already inside, English instructions).

Car Rental: Avis is at the train station (tel. 04 90 96 82 42), and **Europcar** and **Hertz** are downtown (Europcar is at 2 bis avenue Victor Hugo, tel. 04 90 93 23 24; Hertz is closer to place Lamartine at 10 boulevard Emile Combes, tel. 04 90 96 75 23).

Local Guide: Charming **Jacqueline Neujean,** an excellent guide, knows Arles and nearby sights intimately and loves her work (€90/2 hours, tel. & fax 04 90 98 47 51).

English Book Exchange: A small exchange is available at the recommended **Soleileis** ice-cream shop (see page 470).

Cooking Courses: Food-lovers enjoy cooking classes and market tours offered by gentle Erick Vedel (tel. 04 90 49 69 20).

Public Pools: Arles has three public pools (indoor and outdoor). Ask at the TI or your hotel.

Boules: The local "*boul*ing alley" is by the river on place Lamartine. After their afternoon naps, the old boys congregate here for a game of *pétanque.*

Getting Around Arles

In this flat city, everything's within **walking** distance. Only the Ancient History Museum requires a healthy walk (or you can take a taxi or bus). The elevated riverside promenade provides Rhône views and a direct route to the Ancient History Museum (to the southwest) and the train station (to the northeast). Keep your head up for *Starry Night* memories, but eyes down for decorations by dogs with poorly trained owners.

Arles' **taxis** charge a set fee of about €10, but nothing except the Ancient History Museum is worth a taxi ride. To call a cab, dial 04 89 73 36 00 or 04 90 96 90 03.

The free **Starlette bus** circles the town (3/hour, Mon-Sat only), but is only useful for access to the train station.

Le Petit Train d'Arles provides a helpful orientation to the lay of the land—if you prefer sitting to walking (€6.50, 35 minutes, stops in front of the main TI and at the Arena).

Sights in Arles

Most sights cost €3.50-7, and while any sight warrants a few minutes, many aren't worth their individual admission price. The TI sells three different monument passes (called Passeports). **Le Passeport Avantage** covers almost all of Arles' sights (€13.50, under 18 for €12; Fondation Van Gogh discounted); the €9 **Le Passeport Arelate** covers Arles' four Roman sights and the Ancient

History Museum; and the €9 **Le Passeport Liberté** lets you choose any five monuments (one must be a museum). Depending on your interests, one of the €9 Passeports is probably best.

Start at the Ancient History Museum for a helpful overview (drivers should try to do this museum on their way into Arles), then dive into the city-center sights. Remember, many sights stop selling tickets 30-60 minutes before closing (both before lunch and at the end of the day).

▲▲Ancient History Museum (Musée de l'Arles et de la Provence Antiques)

Begin your town visit here, for Roman Arles 101. Located on the site of the Roman chariot racecourse (the arc of which is built into the parking lot), this air-conditioned, all-on-one-floor museum is just west of central Arles along the river. Models and original sculptures (with almost no posted English translations but a decent handout) re-create the Roman city, making workaday life and culture easier to imagine.

Cost and Hours: €6, Wed-Mon April-Oct 9:00-19:00, Nov-March 10:00-18:00, closed Tue year-round, presqu'île du Cirque Romain.

Information: Ask for the English booklet, which provides a helpful if not in-depth background on the collection, and inquire whether there are any free English tours (usually daily July-Sept at 17:00, 1.5 hours). Tel. 04 90 18 88 88, www.arles-antique.cg13.fr.

Getting There: To reach the museum on foot from the city center (a 20-minute **walk**), turn left at the river and take the riverside path to the big, blue, modern building. As you approach the museum, you'll pass the verdant Hortus Garden—designed to recall the Roman circus and chariot racecourse that were located here, and to give residents a place to gather and celebrate civic events. A **taxi** ride costs €10 (museum can call a taxi for your return). **Bus #1** gets you within a few minutes' walk (€0.80, 3/hour Mon-Sat, none Sun). Catch the bus in Arles (clockwise direction on boulevard des Lices), then get off at the Musée de l'Arles Antique stop (before the stop, you'll see the bright-blue museum ahead on the right). Turn left as you step off the bus, and follow the sidewalk. (To return to the center, the bus stop is across the street from where you got off.)

◐ Self-Guided Tour: A huge map of the Roman Arles region greets visitors and shows the key Roman routes accessible to Arles. Find the impressive row of pagan and early-Christian **sarcophagi** (from the second to fifth centuries). These would have lined the Via Aurelia outside the town wall. In the early days of the Church, Jesus was often portrayed beardless and as the good shepherd, with a lamb over his shoulder.

Next you'll see **models** of every Roman structure in (and near) Arles. These are the highlight for me, as they breathe life into the buildings as they looked 2,000 years ago. Start with the model of Roman Arles, and imagine the city's splendor. Find the Forum—still the center of town today, though only two columns survive. Look at the space Romans devoted to their Arena and huge racecourse—a reminder that an emphasis on sports is not unique to modern civilizations. The model also illustrates how little Arles seems to have changed over two millennia, with its houses still clustered around the city center, and warehouses still located on the opposite side of the river.

Look for individual models of the major buildings shown in the city model: the elaborately elegant forum; the floating bridge that gave Arles a strategic advantage (over the widest, and therefore slowest, part of the river); the theater (with its magnificent stage wall); the Arena (with its movable stadium cover to shelter spectators from sun or rain); and the circus, or chariot racecourse. Part of the original racecourse was just outside the windows, and while long gone, it must have resembled Rome's Circus Maximus in its day—its obelisk is now the centerpiece of Arles' place de la République.

Finally, check out the **3-D model** of the hydraulic mill of Barbegal, with its 16 waterwheels and 8 grain mills cascading down a nearby hillside.

Other rooms in the museum display pottery, jewelry, fine metal and glass artifacts, and well-crafted mosaic floors that make it clear that Roman Arles was a city of art and culture. The many **statues** that you see are all original, except for the greatest—the *Venus of Arles,* which Louis XIV took a liking to and had moved to Versailles. It's now in the Louvre—and, as locals say, "When it's in Paris...bye-bye."

In Central Arles

Ideally, visit these sights in the order listed here. I've included some walking directions to connect the dots.

▲▲**Forum Square (Place du Forum)**—Named for the Roman forum that once stood here, place du Forum was the political and religious center of Roman Arles. Still lively, this café-crammed square is a local watering hole and popular for a *pastis* (anise-based apéritif). And though the bistros on the square are no place for a fine dinner, they can put together a decent salad or *plat du jour*—and when you sprinkle on the ambience, that's €10 well spent.

At the corner of Grand Hôtel Nord-Pinus (a favorite of Pablo Picasso), a plaque shows how the Romans built a foundation of galleries to make the main square level in order to compensate for Arles' slope down to the river. The two columns are all that survive from the upper story of the entry to the Forum. Steps leading to the entrance are buried—the Roman street level was about 20 feet below you (you can get a glimpse of it by peeking through the street-level openings under the Hôtel d'Arlatan, two blocks below place du Forum on rue Sauvage).

The statue on the square is of **Frédéric Mistral** (1830-1914). This popular poet, who wrote in the local dialect rather than in French, was a champion of Provençal culture. After receiving the Nobel Prize in Literature in 1904, Mistral used his prize money to preserve and display the folk identity of Provence. He founded the regional folk museum (the Arlaten Folk Museum, closed for renovation until 2013) at a time when France was rapidly centralizing. (The local mistral wind—literally "master"—has nothing to do with his name.)

The **bright-yellow café**—called Café la Nuit—was the subject of one of Vincent van Gogh's most famous works in Arles. While his painting showed the café in a brilliant yellow from the glow of gas lamps, the facade was bare limestone, just like the other cafés on this square. The café's current owners have painted it to match Van Gogh's version...and to cash in on the Vincent-crazed hordes who pay too much to eat or drink here.

• *Walk a block uphill (past Grand Hôtel Nord Pinus) and turn left. Walk through the Hôtel de Ville's vaulted entry (or take the next right if it's closed), and pop out onto the big...*

Republic Square (Place de la République)—This square used to be called "place Royale"...until the French Revolution. The obelisk was the former centerpiece of Arles' Roman Circus. The lions at its base are the symbol of the city, whose slogan is (roughly) "the gentle lion." Find a seat and watch the peasants—pilgrims, locals, and street musicians. There's nothing new about this scene.

• *Near the corner of the square where you entered, look for...*

▲▲St. Trophime Church—Named after a third-century bishop of Arles, this church sports the finest Romanesque main entrance (west portal) I've seen anywhere.

Like a Roman triumphal arch, the church facade trumpets the promise of Judgment Day. The tympanum (the semicircular area above the door) is filled with Christian symbolism. Christ sits in majesty, surrounded by symbols of the four evangelists: Matthew (the winged man), Mark (the winged lion), Luke (the ox), and John (the eagle). The 12 apostles are lined up below Jesus. It's Judgment Day...some are saved and others aren't. Notice the condemned (on the right)—a chain gang doing a sad bunny-hop over the fires of hell. For them, the tune trumpeted by the three angels above Christ is not a happy one. Below the chain gang, St. Stephen is being stoned to death, with his soul leaving through his mouth and instantly being welcomed by angels. Ride the exquisite detail back to a simpler age. In an illiterate medieval world, long before the vivid images of our Technicolor time, this was a neon billboard over the town square.

Enter the church (free, daily April-Sept 9:00-12:00 & 14:00-18:30, Oct-March 9:00-12:00 & 14:00-17:00). Just inside the door on the right, a chart locates the interior highlights and helps explain the carvings you just saw on the tympanum.

Tour the church counterclockwise. The tall 12th-century Romanesque nave is decorated by a set of tapestries showing scenes from the life of Mary (17th century, from the French town of Aubusson). Amble around the Gothic apse. Just to the left of the high altar, check out the relic chapel—with its fine golden boxes that hold long-venerated bones of obscure saints. Farther down is a chapel built on an early-Christian sarcophagus from Roman Arles (dated about A.D. 300). The heads were lopped off during the French Revolution.

This church is a stop on the ancient pilgrimage route to Santiago de Compostela in northwest Spain. For 800 years pilgrims on their way to Santiago have paused here...and they still do today. As you leave, notice the modern-day pilgrimages advertised on the far right near the church's entry.

• *Leaving the church, turn left, then left again through a courtyard to enter the cloisters.*

The adjacent **cloisters** are worth a look only if you have a pass (big cleaning underway, enter at the far end of the courtyard). The many small columns were scavenged from the ancient Roman theater. Enjoy the sculpted capitals, the rounded 12th-century Romanesque arches, and the pointed 14th-century Gothic ones. The pretty vaulted hall exhibits 17th-century tapestries showing scenes from the First Crusade to the Holy Land. On the second floor, you'll walk along an angled rooftop designed to catch rainwater—notice the slanted gutter that channeled the water into a cistern and the heavy roof slabs covering the tapestry hall below (€3.50, daily March-Oct 9:00-18:00, Nov-Feb 10:00-17:00).

• *Turn right out of the cloisters, then take the first right on rue de la Calade to reach the...*

Classical Theater (Théâtre Antique)—This first-century B.C. Roman theater once seated 10,000. This theater was an elegant, three-level structure with 27 arches radiating out to the street level. From the outside, it looked much like a halved version of Arles' Roman Arena.

Start with the video outside, which provides helpful background information and images that make it easier to put the scattered stones back in place (crouch in front to make out the small English subtitles). Next, walk to a center aisle and pull up a stone seat. To appreciate the theater's original size, look to the upper-left side of the tower and find the protrusion that supported the highest seating level. The structure required 33 rows of seats covering three levels to accommodate demand. During the Middle Ages, the old theater became a convenient town quarry—St. Trophime Church was built from theater rubble. Precious little of the original theater survives—though it still is used for events, with seating for 3,000 spectators.

Two lonely Corinthian columns are all that remain of a three-story stage wall that once featured more than 100 columns and statues painted in vibrant colors. The orchestra section is defined by a semicircular pattern in the stone in front of you. Stepping up onto the left side of the stage, look down to the slender channel that allowed the brilliant-red curtain to disappear below, like magic. The stage, which was built of wood, was about 160 feet across and 20 feet deep. Go backstage and browse through the actors' changing rooms, then loop back to the entry behind the grass (€3, daily May-Sept 9:00-19:00, March-April and Oct 9:00-12:00 & 14:00-18:00, Nov-Feb 10:00-12:00 & 14:00-17:00). Budget travelers can peek over the fence from rue du Cloître, and see just about everything for free.

• *A block uphill is the...*

▲▲▲**Roman Arena (Amphithéâtre)**—Nearly 2,000 years ago, gladiators fought wild animals here to the delight of 20,000 screaming fans. Today, local daredevils still fight wild animals here—"bullgame" posters around the Arena advertise upcoming spectacles (described later, under "Events in Arles"). A lengthy restoration process is well underway, giving the amphitheater an almost bleached-teeth whiteness.

In Roman times, games were free (sponsored by city bigwigs), and fans were seated according to social class. The many exits allowed for rapid dispersal after the games—fights would break out among frenzied fans if they couldn't leave quickly. Through medieval times and until the early 1800s, the arches were bricked up and the stadium became a fortified town—with 200 humble homes crammed within its circular defenses. Three of the medieval towers survive (the one above the ticket booth is open and rewards those who climb it with terrific views). To see two still-sealed arches—complete with cute medieval window frames—turn right as you leave, walk to the Andaluz restaurant, and look back to the second floor (€6, daily May-Sept 9:00-19:00, March-April and Oct 9:00-18:00, Nov-Feb 10:00-17:00).

• *The next three attractions are back across town. The Fondation Van Gogh is near the Trinquetaille Bridge (in spring 2012 it moves here from its temporary digs on rue des Suisses). The Arlaten Folk Museum (closed until 2013) is close to place du Forum, and the Réattu Museum is near the river.*

▲**Fondation Van Gogh**—A refreshing stop for modern-art–lovers and Van Gogh fans, this two-level gallery displays works by contemporary artists (including Roy Lichtenstein and Robert Rauschenberg) who pay homage to Vincent through thought-provoking interpretations of his works. The black-and-white photographs (both art and shots of places that Vincent painted) complement the paintings. (But be warned that the collection contains no Van Gogh originals.) Unfortunately, this collection is often on the road July through September, when non-Van Gogh material is displayed (€6, €4 with Le Passeport Avantage; good collection of Van Gogh souvenirs, prints, and postcards for sale in gift shop; Tue-Sat 10:00-12:30 & 14:00-17:00, closed Sun-Mon; 17 rue des Suisses until Spring 2012, then moves to 35 rue du Dr. Fanton; tel. 04 90 49 94 04, www.fondationvangogh-arles.org).

▲**Arlaten Folk Museum (Musée Arlaten/Museon Arlaten)**—This museum, which normally explains the ins and outs of daily Provençal life, is closed for renovation until 2013 (www.museon arlaten.fr).

Réattu Museum (Musée Réattu)—Housed in the former Grand Priory of the Knights of Malta, this mildly interesting, mostly modern art collection includes 57 Picasso drawings (some two-sided and all done in a flurry of creativity—I like the bullfights best), a room of Henri Rousseau's Camargue watercolors, and an unfinished painting by the Neoclassical artist Jacques Réattu...but none with English explanations. Occasional special exhibits show off the museum's impressive permanent collection, which is mostly in storage (€7, Tue-Sun July-Sept 10:00-19:00, Oct-June 10:00-12:30 & 14:00-18:30, closed Mon year-round, last entry 30 minutes before closing for lunch or at end of day, 10 rue du Grand Prieuré, tel. 04 90 96 37 68, www.museereattu.arles.fr).

Events in Arles

▲▲**Markets**—On Wednesday and Saturday mornings, Arles' ring road erupts into an open-air festival of fish, flowers, produce, and you-name-it. The main event is on Saturday, with vendors jamming the ring road from boulevard Emile Combes to the east, along boulevard des Lices near the TI (the heart of the market), and continuing down boulevard Georges Clemenceau to the west. Wednesday's market runs only along boulevard Emile Combes, between place Lamartine and bis avenue Victor Hugo; the segment nearest place Lamartine is all about food, and the upper half features clothing, tablecloths, purses, and so on. On the first Wednesday of the month, a flea market doubles the size of the usual Wednesday market along boulevard des Lices near the main TI. Join in: Buy some flowers for your hotelier, try the olives, sample some wine, and swat a pickpocket. Both markets are open until 12:30.

▲▲**Bullgames (Courses Camarguaises)**—Occupy the same seats that fans have used for nearly 2,000 years, and take in Arles' most memorable experience—the *courses camarguaises* in the ancient Arena. The nonviolent "bullgames" are more sporting than bloody bullfights (though traditional Spanish-style bullfights still take place on occasion). The bulls of Arles (who, locals stress, "die of old age") are promoted in posters even more boldly than their human foes. In the bullgame, a ribbon *(cocarde)* is laced between the bull's horns. The *razeteur*, with a special hook, has 15 minutes to snare the ribbon. Local businessmen encourage a *razeteur* (dressed in white with a red cummerbund) by shouting out how much money they'll pay for the *cocarde*. If the bull pulls a good stunt, the band plays the famous "Toreador" song from *Carmen*. The following day, newspapers report on the games, including how many *Carmens* the bull earned.

Three classes of bullgames—determined by the experience of the *razeteurs*—are advertised in posters: The *course de protection* is for rookies. The *trophée de l'Avenir* comes with more experience— and the *trophée des As* features top professionals. During Easter and the fall rice-harvest festival *(Féria du Riz)*, the Arena hosts traditional Spanish bullfights (look for *corrida*) with outfits, swords, spikes, and the whole gory shebang. Bullgame tickets run €5-15, while bullfights are pricier (€14-80). Schedules change every year—ask at the TI or check online at www.arenes-arles.com.

Don't pass on a chance to see *Toro Piscine,* a silly spectacle for warm summer evenings where the bull ends up in a swimming pool (uh-huh...get more details at TI). Nearby villages stage *courses camarguaises* in small wooden bullrings nearly every weekend; TIs have the latest schedule.

Sleeping in Arles

Hotels are a great value here; many are air-conditioned, though few have elevators. The Calendal, Musée, and Régence hotels offer exceptional value.

$$$ Hôtel le Calendal*** is a seductive place located between the Arena and Classical Theater. Enter an expertly run hotel with airy lounges and a lovely palm-shaded courtyard. Enjoy the elaborate €12 buffet breakfast, have lunch in the courtyard or at the inexpensive sandwich bar (daily 12:00-15:00), and take advantage of their four free laptops for guests. You'll also find a Jacuzzi and a "spa" with a Turkish bath, a hot pool, and massages at good rates. The comfortable rooms sport Provençal decor and come in all shapes and sizes (standard Db-€100-115, Db with

Sleep Code

(€1 = about $1.40, country code: 33)
S = Single, **D** = Double/Twin, **T** = Triple, **Q** = Quad, **b** = bathroom,
s = shower only, ***** = French hotel rating system (0-4 stars).
Unless otherwise noted, credit cards are accepted and English is spoken.

To help you sort easily through these listings, I've divided the rooms into three categories based on the price for a standard double room with bath:

$$$ Higher Priced—Most rooms €85 or more.
  $$ Moderately Priced—Most rooms between €65-85.
    $ Lower Priced—Most rooms €65 or less.

Prices can change without notice; verify the hotel's current rates online or by email. For other updates, see www.ricksteves.com/update.

balcony-€135-165, Tb-€120-170, Qb-€140-180, price depends on room size, air-con, Wi-Fi, reserve ahead for parking-€10, just above Arena at 5 rue Porte de Laure, tel. 04 90 96 11 89, fax 04 90 96 05 84, www.lecalendal.com, contact@lecalendal.com).

$$$ Hôtel d'Arlatan***, built on the site of a Roman basilica, is classy in every sense of the word. It has sumptuous public spaces, a tranquil terrace, a designer pool, a turtle pond, and antique-filled rooms, most with high, wood-beamed ceilings and stone walls. In the lobby of this 15th-century building, a glass floor looks down into Roman ruins (standard Db-€137, bigger Db-€157, Db/Qb suites-€180, apartments-€200-250, excellent buffet breakfast-€15, air-con, bathrobes, ice machines, elevator, Wi-Fi, parking garage-€14, 1 block below place du Forum at 26 rue Sauvage—tricky by car, tel. 04 90 93 56 66, fax 04 90 49 68 45, www.hotel-arlatan.fr, hotel-arlatan@wanadoo.fr).

$$ Hôtel du Musée** is a quiet and affordable manor-home hideaway tucked deep in Arles (tough to find by car). This delightful refuge comes with 28 air-conditioned and wood-floored rooms, a flowery two-tiered courtyard, and comfortable lounges. Lighthearted Claude and English-speaking Laurence, the gracious owners, are eager to help (Sb-€50, Db-€60-70, Tb-€75-90, Qb-€95, Wi-Fi, laptop available for guests, garage-€10, follow signs to *Réattu Museum* to 11 rue du Grand Prieuré, tel. 04 90 93 88 88, fax 04 90 49 98 15, www.hoteldumusee.com, contact @hoteldumusee.com).

$$ Hôtel de la Muette**, with reserved owners Brigitte and Alain, is another good choice. Located in a quiet corner of Arles, this low-key hotel is well-kept, with stone walls, brown tones, and a small terrace in front. You'll pay a bit more for the upgraded rooms, but it's money well-spent (most Db-€66, bigger Db-€75, Tb-€77, Qb-€92, buffet breakfast-€8, air-con, Internet access and Wi-Fi, private garage-€8, 15 rue des Suisses, tel. 04 90 96 15 39, fax 04 90 49 73 16, www.hotel-muette.com, hotel.muette @wanadoo.fr).

$ Hôtel Régence**, a top budget deal, has a riverfront location, immaculate and comfortable Provençal rooms, safe parking, and easy access to the train station (Db-€50-60, Tb-€65-70, Qb-€75-80, good buffet breakfast-€6, choose river view or quieter courtyard rooms, most rooms have showers, air-con, no elevator but only two floors, Internet access and Wi-Fi; from place Lamartine, turn right immediately after passing between towers to reach 5 rue Marius Jouveau; tel. 04 90 96 39 85, fax 04 90 96 67 64, www.hotel-regence.com, contact@hotel-regence.com). The gentle Nouvions speak some English.

$ Hôtel Acacias**, just off place Lamartine and inside the old city walls, is a modern hotel with less personality. The pretty pastel rooms are on the small side, but they're reasonably priced (standard Sb or Db-€53, larger Db-€64-78, extra bed-€15, breakfast-€6, air-con, elevator, Wi-Fi, 2 rue de la Cavalerie, tel. 04 90 96 37 88, fax 04 90 96 32 51, www.hotel-acacias.com, contact@hotel-acacias .com).

$ Hôtel Voltaire* rents 12 small and questionably clean rooms with ceiling fans and nifty balconies overlooking a fun square. A block below the Arena, it's good for starving artists. Smiling owner "Mr." Ferran (fur-ran) loves the States (his dream is to travel there), and hopes you'll add to his postcard collection (D-€30, Ds-€35, Db-€40, 1 place Voltaire, tel. 04 90 96 49 18, fax 04 90 96 45 49, levoltaire13@aol.com). They also serve a good-value lunch and dinner in their recommended restaurant.

Eating in Arles

You can dine well in Arles on a modest budget—in fact, it's hard to blow a lot on dinner here (most of my listings have *menus* for €22 or less). The bad news is that restaurants here change regularly, so double-check my suggestions. Before dinner, go local on place du Forum and enjoy a *pastis*. This anise-based apéritif is served straight in a glass with ice, plus a carafe of water—dilute to taste. Sunday is a dead night for restaurants, though most eateries on place du Forum are open.

For **picnics,** a big, handy Monoprix supermarket/department store is on place Lamartine (Mon-Sat 8:30-19:25, closed Sun).

Arles Hotels & Restaurants

← Van Gogh Walking Tour

P Parking

B Bus Stop

↙ View

⌂

100 YARDS
100 METERS

❶ Hôtel/Rest. le Calendal

❷ Hôtel d'Arlatan

❸ Hôtel du Musée

❹ Hôtel de la Muette

❺ Hôtel Acacias

❻ Hôtel Régence

❼ Hôtel/Rest. Voltaire

❽ To La Peiriero & Domaine de Laforest Hôtels

❾ To Mas du Petit Grava Hôtel

❿ Le 16, Le Gaboulet & Au Bryn du Thym Restaurants

⓫ Bistrot à Vins Restaurant

⓬ La Guele de Loup Restaurant

⓭ La Cuisine de Comptoir Rest.

⓮ Café de la Major (Coffee/Tea)

⓯ Le Grillon Restaurant

⓰ Le Criquet Restaurant

⓱ Media Luna Restaurant

⓲ L'Atelier & A Côté Restaurants

⓳ Soleileis Ice Cream

RH

TRINQUETAILLE BRIDGE

QUAI MARX

TRUCHET

RUE A. FRANCE

DR. FANTON

TO ANCIENT HISTORY MUSEUM

R. JOUVE. R. LIBERTE

⓭

ARLATEN FOLK MUSEUM
(CLOSED UNTIL 2013)

RUE GAMBETTA

REPUB-

ESPACE VAN GOGH

RUE MOLIERE R.

TO ANCIENT HISTORY MUSEUM ←

BLVD.

B

BUS STN.

DCH

PROVENCE

TO
TRAIN
STATION

TO LES BAUX,
FONTVIEILLE
& AVIGNON

8

AVE. STALIN.

MONOPRIX

PLACE
LAMARTINE

R H O N E

PETANQUE

GATE

BLVD.

RUE JOUVEAU

RUE

JULES FERRY

CAVALERIE

6 5

QUAI LAMARTINE

R. L. BLUM

7

BALZAC

EMILE COMBES

REATTU
MUSEUM

17

PLACE
VOLTAIRE

R. CONDORCET

DORMOY

RUE DE LA GRILLE

QUATRE SEPT.

R. AMPH.

VOLTAIRE

RUE PORTAGNEL

RUE DU

GRAND PRIEURE

f

R. BARBES

RUE TARDIEU

DU FOURAGNEL

3

RUE DU

RASPAIL

R. REFUGE

RUE
DU SAUVAGE

2

14

SUISSES

FAURE

ENTER

10

BALE

4

BAST.

ROMAN
ARENA

11

HOTEL DE VILLE

RUE DES   ARENES

19

12

PLACE
DU
FORUM

RUE DE

R. NIC.   R. DIDEROT

NOTRE
DAME

R. BALZE

RUE CALADE

FOND.
V.G.

ANCIENT
CITY
WALLS

WC

ST.
TROPHIME

1 15

RUE DE CLOITRE

PORTE DE LAURE

16

PLACE
REPUB-
LIQUE

LIQUE

CLASSICAL
THEATER

18

RUE

JAURES

JARDIN
D. ETE

MONTEE VAUBAN

BLVD. EMILE COMBES

ROTONDE

CLOISTERS

DES

LICES

POST
& TAXIS

P

TO 9

V. HUGO

i

PLAYGROUND

R. E. FASSIN

TO LES AYLSCAMPS
CEMETERY

On or near Place du Forum

Great atmosphere and mediocre food at fair prices await on place du Forum. By all accounts, the garish yellow Café la Nuit is worth avoiding. Most other cafés on the square deliver acceptable quality and terrific ambience. A half-block below the Forum, on rue du Dr. Fanton, you'll find a lineup of more tempting restaurants. The first three are popular, and all have good indoor and outdoor seating.

Le 16 is a warm and affordable place to enjoy a fresh salad (€10)—though it's almost too popular for its own good (€13 *plats*, €21 three-course *menu*, closed Sat-Sun, 16 rue du Dr. Fanton, tel. 04 90 93 77 36).

Le Gaboulet has created a buzz in Arles by blending a cozy interior, classic French cuisine, and service with a smile (thanks to owner Frank). It's the most expensive of the places I list on this street, but it's still jammed every night—book ahead or come early (€27 *menu*, great fries, closed Sun-Mon, 18 rue du Dr. Fanton, tel. 04 90 93 18 11).

Au Brin de Thym, next door, has long been reliable and specializes in traditional Provençal cuisine at fair prices—the bull steak is delicious. Arrive early for an outdoor table or call ahead, and let hardworking and sincere Monsieur and Madame Colombaud take care of you. Monsieur does *le cooking* while Madame does *le serving* (€19 three-course *menu*, closed Tue, 22 rue du Dr. Fanton, tel. 04 90 49 95 96).

Bistrot à Vins suits wine-lovers who enjoy pairing food and drink, and those in search of a good glass of *vin*. Sit at a convivial counter or at one of five tables while listening to light jazz (book ahead for a table). Affable Ariane speaks enough English and offers a limited selection of simple, tasty dishes. Her savory *tartes* and fresh green salad make a great meal (€10-16), and the wines— many available by the glass—are well-priced (indoor dining only from 18:30 to 22:00, closed Mon-Tue, 2 rue du Dr. Fanton, tel. 04 90 52 00 65).

La Gueule du Loup is a small, traditional place with a loyal following (reserve ahead). Its good blend of Provençal and classic French cuisine is served in an intimate setting under wood beams in an upstairs room (€31 three-course *menu*, closed Wed, 39 rue des Arènes, tel. 04 90 96 96 69).

At **La Cuisine de Comptoir,** a cool little bistro, locals of all ages abandon Provençal decor. Welcoming owners Alexandre and Vincent offer light *tartine* dinners—a delicious cross between pizza and bruschetta, served with soup or salad for just €10 (a swinging deal). Sit at the counter and watch *le chef* at work (closed Sun, indoor dining only, just off place du Forum's lower end at 10 rue de la Liberté, tel. 04 90 96 86 28).

Café de la Major is the place to go to recharge with some serious coffee or tea (closed Sun, 7 bis rue Réattu, tel. 04 90 96 14 15).

Near the Roman Arena

For about the same price as on place du Forum, you can enjoy regional cuisine with a point-blank view of the Arena. Because they change regularly, the handful of (mostly) outdoor eateries that overlook the Arena are pretty indistinguishable.

Le Grillon owns the best view above the Arena and serves good-enough salads, crêpes, and *plats du jour* for €9-12 (closed all day Wed and Sun nights, at the top of the Arena on rond-point des Arènes, tel. 04 90 96 70 97).

Le Criquet is a sweet little place serving Provençal classics at good prices two blocks above the Arena (€18 three-course *menu*, closed Mon, indoor dining only, 21 rue Porte de Laure, tel. 04 90 96 80 51).

Hôtel le Calendal serves lunch in its lovely courtyard (€12-18, daily 12:00-15:00) or delicious little sandwiches for €2 each (three make a good meal) at its small café (also listed under "Sleeping in Arles," earlier).

Hôtel Voltaire, well-situated on a pleasing square, serves simple three-course lunches and dinners at honest prices to a loyal clientele (€13 *menus;* hearty *plats* and filling salads for €10—try the *salade fermière, salade Latine,* or the filling *assiette Provençale;* closed Sun evening, a few blocks below the Arena at 1 place Voltaire, tel. 04 90 96 49 18; also listed under "Sleeping in Arles," earlier).

Media Luna, a good choice for vegetarians, uses fresh, organic ingredients in its flavorful dishes. It's open on Sundays (rare in Arles) and welcomes guests with easygoing service (€14-16 *plats,* filling €15 vegetarian dish, organic wines, closed Tue, between the river and place Voltaire at 65 rue Amédée Pichot, tel. 04 90 97 81 89).

A Gastronomic Dining Experience

One of France's most recognized chefs, Jean-Luc Rabanel, has created a sensation with two different-as-night-and-day dining options 50 yards from place de la République (at 7 rue des Carmes). They sit side by side, both offering indoor and terrace seating.

L'Atelier is so intriguing that people travel great distances just for the experience. Diners fork over €90 (at lunch, you'll spoon out €50) and trust the chef to create a memorable meal...which he does. There is no menu, just an onslaught of delicious taste sensations served on artsy dishes. Don't plan on a quick dinner, and don't come for the setting—it's a contemporary, shoebox-shaped dining room, but several outdoor tables are also available. The get-to-know-your-neighbor atmosphere means you can't help but join the party. You'll probably spot the famous chef (hint: he has long brown hair), as he is very hands-on with his waitstaff (closed Mon-Tue, best to book ahead, friendly servers will hold your hand through this palate-widening experience, tel. 04 90 91 07 69, www .rabanel.com).

A Côté saddles up next door, offering a smart wine bar/bistro ambience and top-quality cuisine for far less. Here you can sample the famous chef's talents for as little as €16 (daily *plat*) or as much as €32 (three-course *menu*, smallish servings, reasonably priced wines, open daily, tel. 04 90 47 61 13).

And for Dessert...

Soleileis has Arles' best ice cream, with all-natural ingredients and unusual flavors such as *fadoli*—olive oil mixed with nougatine. There's also a shelf of English books for exchange (open daily 14:00-18:30, across from recommended Le 16 restaurant at 9 rue du Dr. Fanton).

Arles Connections

Some trains in and out of Arles require a reservation. These include connections with Nice to the east and Bordeaux to the west (including intermediary stops). Ask at the station.

From Arles by Train to: Paris (11/day, 2 direct TGVs—4 hours, 9 with transfer in Avignon—5 hours), **Avignon Centre-Ville** (11/day, 20 minutes, less frequent in the afternoon), **Nîmes** (9/day, 30 minutes), **Nice** (11/day, 3.75-4.5 hours, most require transfer in Marseille or Avignon), **Barcelona** (2/day, 6 hours, transfer in Montpellier), **Italy** (3/day, transfer in Marseille and Nice; from Arles it's 4.5 hours to Ventimiglia on the border, 8 hours to Milan, 9.5 hours to Cinque Terre, 11 hours to Florence, and 13 hours to Venice or Rome).

From Arles Train Station to Avignon TGV Station: If you're connecting from Arles to the TGV in Avignon, it's easiest to take the SNCF bus directly from Arles' train station to Avignon's TGV station (10/day, 1 hour). Another option—which takes the same amount of time, but adds more walking—is to take the regular train from Arles to Avignon's Centre-Ville Station, then catch the *navette* (shuttle bus) to the TGV station from there.

From Arles by Bus to: Nîmes (6/day, 1 hour). The bus station is at 16-24 boulevard Georges Clemenceau (2 blocks below main TI, next to Café le Wilson). Bus info: tel. 04 90 49 38 01 (unlikely to speak English).

Avignon

Famous for its nursery rhyme, medieval bridge, and brooding Palace of the Popes, contemporary Avignon (ah-veen-yohn) bustles and prospers behind its mighty walls. During the 68 years (1309-1377) that Avignon starred as the *Franco Vaticano,* it grew from a quiet village into a thriving city. With its large student population and fashionable shops, today's Avignon is an intriguing blend of medieval history, youthful energy, and urban sophistication. Street performers entertain the international throngs who fill Avignon's ubiquitous cafés and trendy boutiques. If you're here in July, be prepared for big crowds and higher prices, thanks to the rollicking theater festival. (Reserve your hotel far in advance.) Clean, sharp, and popular with tourists, Avignon is more impressive for its outdoor ambience than for its museums and monuments.

Orientation to Avignon

The cours Jean Jaurès, which turns into rue de la République, runs straight from the Centre-Ville train station to place de l'Horloge and the Palace of the Popes, splitting Avignon in two. The larger eastern half is where the action is. Climb to Le Jardin du Rochers des Doms for the town's best view, consider touring the pope's immense palace, lose yourself in Avignon's back streets (you can follow my "Discovering Avignon's Back Streets" self-guided walk on page 481), and find a shady square to call home. Avignon's shopping district fills the traffic-free streets near where rue de la République meets place de l'Horloge.

Tourist Information

The main TI is between the Centre-Ville train station and the old town, at 41 cours Jean Jaurès (April-Oct Mon-Sat 9:00-18:00—until 19:00 in July, Sun 9:45-17:00; Nov-March Mon-Fri 9:00-18:00, Sat 9:00-17:00, Sun 10:00-12:00; tel. 04 32 74 32 74, www.avignon-tourisme.com). From April through mid-October, branch TI offices are open inside the St. Bénezet Bridge entrance (daily 10:00-13:00 & 14:00-18:00) and inside Les Halles market (Fri-Sun 10:00-13:00, closed Mon-Thu). At any TI, get the helpful map. If you're staying awhile, pick up the free *Guide Pratique* (info on bike rentals, hotels, apartment rentals, events, and museums).

Everyone should pick up the free **Avignon Passion Pass** (valid 15 days, for up to five family members). Get the pass stamped when you pay full price at your first sight, and then receive reductions at the others (for example, €2 less at the Palace of the Popes and €3 less at the Petit Palais). The discounts add up—always show your Passion Pass when buying a ticket. The pass comes with the Avignon "Passion" map and guide, which includes several good (but tricky-to-follow) walking tours.

Arrival in Avignon

By Train

Avignon has two train stations: TGV (linked to downtown by frequent shuttle buses) and Centre-Ville. While most TGV trains serve only the TGV train station, some serve Centre-Ville—verify your station in advance.

TGV Station (Gare TGV): This shiny new station, on the outskirts of town, has no baggage storage (bags can be stored only at Centre-Ville Station).

To get to the city center, take the *navette*/**shuttle bus** (marked *Navette/Avignon Centre;* €1.20, buy ticket from driver, 3/hour, 15 minutes). To find the bus stop, leave the station by the north exit *(sortie nord)*, walk down the stairs, and find the long bus shelter to the left. In downtown Avignon, you'll arrive at a stop just inside the city walls, in front of the post office on cours Président Kennedy (see the map on pages 474-475). From here you're three blocks from the city's main TI, and two blocks from Centre-Ville Station. A **taxi** ride between the TGV station and downtown Avignon costs about €16-20 (to find taxis, exit the TGV station via *sortie nord*).

To pick up a **rental car** at the TGV train station, walk out the south exit *(sortie sud)* to find the *location de voitures* in the parking lot. If you're driving directly to Arles, leave the station following signs to *Avignon Sud*, then *La Rocade*. You'll soon see exits to Arles.

If you're heading from the Avignon TGV train station to the **Arles train station,** catch the direct SNCF bus from the TGV station's bus stop (10/day, 1 hour, schedule available at any information booth inside the TGV station).

Centre-Ville Station (Gare Avignon Centre-Ville): All non-TGV trains (and a few TGV trains) serve the central station. You can stash your bags here—exit the station to the left and look for the *consignes* sign (confirm closing time when you leave your bag). To reach the town center, cross the busy street in front of the station and walk through the city walls onto cours Jean Jaurès. The TI is three blocks down, at #41.

By Bus

The dingy bus station *(gare routière)* is 100 yards to the right as you leave the Centre-Ville train station (beyond and below Ibis Hôtel).

By Car

Drivers entering Avignon follow *Centre-Ville* and *Gare SNCF* (train station) signs. You'll find central pay lots (about €10/half-day, €14/day) in the garage next to Centre-Ville Station, at the Parking Jean Jaurès under the ramparts across from the train station; or at the Parking Palais des Papes (follow signs on the riverside road, boulevard St. Lazare, just past St. Bénezet Bridge). There are two free lots nearby with free shuttle buses to the center (follow *P Gratuit* signs): One is just across Daladier Bridge (pont Daladier), and the other is along the river past the Palace of the Popes, just northeast of the walls. Leave nothing in your car. Hotels have advice for smart overnight parking and can get you big discounts at pay lots.

Helpful Hints

Book Ahead for July: During the July theater festival, rooms are sparse—reserve very early, or stay in Arles.

Local Help: David at **Imagine Tours** (a nonprofit group whose goal is to promote this region) can help you with hotel emergencies or tickets to special events (mobile 06 89 22 19 87, www.imagine-tours.net, imagine.tours@gmail.com).

Internet Access: The TI has a current list of Internet cafés, or ask your hotelier.

English Bookstore: Try **Shakespeare Bookshop** (Tue-Sat 9:30-12:00 & 14:00-18:30, closed Sun-Mon, 155 rue Carreterie, in Avignon's northeast corner, tel. 04 90 27 38 50).

Baggage Storage: You can leave your bags at Centre-Ville train station (see "Arrival in Avignon," earlier).

Laundry: The launderette at 66 place des Corps-Saints, where rue Agricol Perdiguier ends, has English instructions and is handy to most hotels (daily 7:00-20:00).

Grocery Store: **Carrefour City** is central and has long hours (Mon-Sat 7:00-21:00, Sun 9:00-12:00, next to McDonald's, 2 blocks from the TI, toward place de l'Horloge on rue de la République).

Bike Rental: You'll see many **Vélopop** city bikes stationed at key points in Avignon, making one-way and short-term rental a breeze. But note that the machines only accept American Express and chip-and-PIN credit cards (see page 11). You can also rent bikes and scooters at **Provence Bike** (52 boulevard St. Roch, tel. 04 90 27 92 61, www.provence-bike.com). You'll enjoy riding on the Ile de la Barthélasse.

Car Rental: The TGV train station has the car-rental agencies (open long hours daily).

Shuttle Boat: A free shuttle boat, the *Navette Fluviale*, plies back and forth across the river (as it did in the days when the town had no functioning bridge) from near St. Bénezet Bridge (daily July-Aug 11:00-21:00, Sept-June roughly 10:00-12:30

Avignon

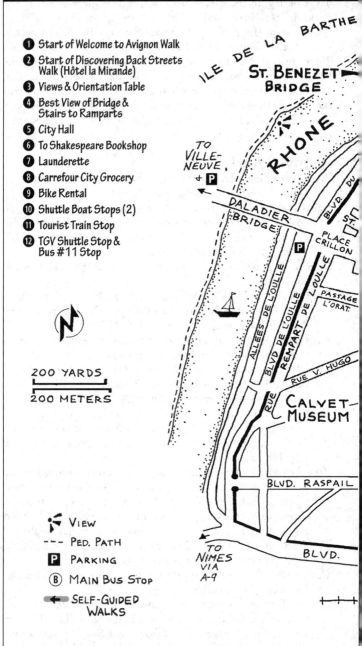

1. Start of Welcome to Avignon Walk
2. Start of Discovering Back Streets Walk (Hôtel la Mirande)
3. Views & Orientation Table
4. Best View of Bridge & Stairs to Ramparts
5. City Hall
6. To Shakespeare Bookshop
7. Launderette
8. Carrefour City Grocery
9. Bike Rental
10. Shuttle Boat Stops (2)
11. Tourist Train Stop
12. TGV Shuttle Stop & Bus #11 Stop

200 YARDS
200 METERS

ILE DE LA BARTHE

ST. BENEZET BRIDGE

RHONE

TO VILLE-NEUVE & P

DALADIER BRIDGE

BLVD. DU ST.

PLACE CRILLON

P

PASSAGE L'ORAT.

ALLEES DE L'OULLE

BLVD DE L'OULLE

REMPART DE L'OULLE

RUE V. HUGO

RUE

CALVET MUSEUM

BLVD. RASPAIL

TO NIMES VIA A-9

BLVD.

View
--- Ped. Path
P   Parking
B   Main Bus Stop
⬅   Self-Guided Walks

PROVENCE

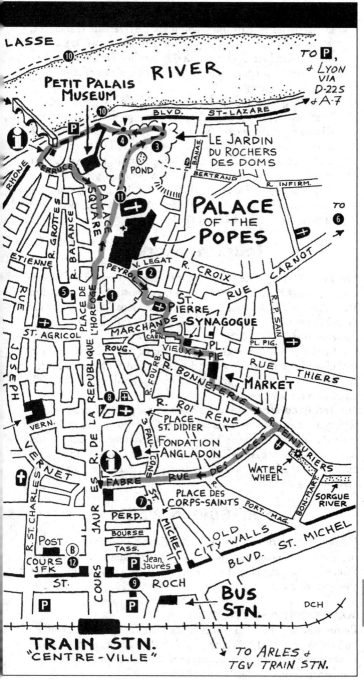

LASSE

RIVER

Petit Palais Museum

TO P, & LYON VIA D-225 & A-7

BLVD. ST-LAZARE

Le Jardin Du Rochers Des Doms

POND

BERTRAND

R. INFIRM.

PALACE OF THE POPES

TO 6

R. GROTES

R. BALANCE

PLACE DE L'HORLOGE

PALACE SQUARE

RHONE

TERRUCE

ETIENNE

RUE

V. LEGAT

PEYRO

R. CROIX

RUE

CARNOT

St. PIERRE

SYNAGOGUE

MARCHANDS

PL. CARN.

VIEUX PIE

PL. PIE

PL. PIG.

RUE THIERS

ROUG.

R. FOURB.

R. BONNETERIE

MARKET

ST. AGRICOL

JOSEPH

RUE

R. ROI RENE

PLACE ST. DIDIER

FONDATION ANGLADON

R. TEINTURIERS

VERNET

VERN.

R. DE LA REPUBLIQUE

FAC. CONS.

FABRE

RUE DES LICES

WATER-WHEEL

SORGUE RIVER

BON-MART.

PLACE DES CORPS-SAINTS

PORT. MAG.

R. ST. CHARLES

PERP.

BOURSE

TASS.

MICHEL

OLD CITY WALLS

ST. MICHEL

Post

B

COURS JFK

JAURES

COURS

BLVD.

Jean Jaures

ST.

ROCH

BUS STN.

DCH

P

P

P

TRAIN STN. "CENTRE-VILLE"

TO ARLES & TGV TRAIN STN.

PROVENCE

& 14:00-18:00, 3/hour). It drops you on the peaceful Ile de la Barthélasse, with its recommended riverside restaurant, grassy walks, and bike rides with terrific city views. If you stay on the island for dinner, check the schedule for the last return boat—or be prepared for a taxi ride or a pleasant 25-minute walk back to town.

Commanding City Views: For great views of Avignon and the river, walk or drive across Daladier Bridge, or ferry across the Rhône on the *Navette Fluviale* (described above). I'd take the boat across the river, walk the view path to Daladier Bridge, and then cross back over the bridge (45-minute walk over mostly level ground). You can enjoy other impressive vistas from the top of Le Jardin du Rochers des Doms, from the tower in the Palace of the Popes, and from the end of the famous, broken St. Bénezet Bridge.

Tours in Avignon

Walking Tours—The TI offers informative two-hour English walking tours of Avignon (€11, discounted with Avignon Passion Pass, April-Oct Wed and Fri-Sat at 10:00, depart from main TI; Nov-March on Sat only, depart from Palace of the Popes).

Tourist Trains—The little train leaves regularly from in front of the Palace of the Popes and gives a decent overview of the city, including Le Jardin du Rochers des Doms and St. Bénezet Bridge (€7, 2/hour, 40 minutes, mid-March-mid-Oct daily 10:00-19:00, English commentary).

Guided Excursions—Several minivan tour companies based in Avignon offer tours to destinations around Provence, including Pont du Gard (about €65-75/person for all-day tours). See "Tours of Provence" on page 450 (note that guides Madeleine Vedel and François Marcou, as well as Imagine Tours, are all based in Avignon).

Self-Guided Walks

Combine these two walks—one ("Welcome to Avignon") covering the major sights, and the other ("Discovering Avignon's Back Streets") along the lanes less taken—to get beyond the surface of this historic city.

▲▲Welcome to Avignon

Before starting this walk—which connects the city's top sights—be sure to pick up the Avignon Passion Pass at the TI, then show it when entering each attraction to receive discounted admission (explained earlier, under "Tourist Information").

• *Start your tour where the Romans did, on place de l'Horloge, in front of City Hall (Hôtel de Ville).*

Place de l'Horloge

This café square was the town forum during Roman times and the market square through the Middle Ages. (Restaurants here offer good people-watching, but they also have less ambience and low-quality meals—you'll find better squares elsewhere to hang your beret in.) Named for a medieval clock tower that the City Hall now hides (find plaque in English), this square's present popularity arrived with the trains in 1854. Walk a few steps to the center of the square, and look down the main drag, rue de la République. When the trains came to Avignon, proud city fathers wanted a direct, impressive way to link the new station to the heart of the city (just like in Paris)—so they plowed over homes to create rue de la République and widened place de l'Horloge. This main drag's Parisian feel is intentional—it was built not in the Provençal manner, but in the Haussmann style that is so dominant in Paris (characterized by broad, straight boulevards lined with stately buildings).

• *Walk uphill past the carousel (public WCs behind). You'll see a golden statue of Mary, floating high above the buildings. Veer right at the street's end, and continue into...*

Palace Square (Place du Palais)

This grand square is lined with the Palace of the Popes, the Petit Palais, and the cathedral. In the 1300s, the entire headquarters of the Catholic Church was moved to Avignon. The Church bought Avignon and gave it a complete makeover. Along with clearing out vast spaces like this square and building this three-acre palace, the Church erected more than three miles of protective wall (with 39 towers), "appropriate" housing for cardinals (read: mansions), and residences for its entire bureaucracy. The city was Europe's largest construction zone. Avignon's population grew from 6,000 to 25,000 in short order. (Today, 13,000 people live within the walls.) The limits of pre-papal Avignon are outlined on city maps: Rues Joseph Vernet, Henri Fabre, des Lices, and Philonarde all follow the route of the city's earlier defensive wall.

The Petit Palais (Little Palace) seals the uphill end of the square and was built for a cardinal; today, it houses medieval paintings (museum described later). The church just to the left of the Palace of the Popes is Avignon's cathedral. It predates the Church's purchase of Avignon by 200 years. Its small size reflects Avignon's modest, pre-papal population. The gilded Mary was added in 1854, when the Vatican established the doctrine of her Immaculate Conception. Mary is taller than the Palace of the

Popes by design: The Vatican never accepted what it called the "Babylonian Captivity" and had a bad attitude about Avignon long after the pope was definitively back in Rome. There hasn't been a French pope since the Holy See returned to Rome—over 600 years. That's what I call a grudge.

Directly across the square from the palace's main entry stands a cardinal's residence built in 1619 (now the Conservatoire National de Musique). Its fancy Baroque facade was a visual counterpoint to the stripped-down Huguenot aesthetic of the age. During this time, Provence was a hotbed of Protestantism—but, buried within this region, Avignon was a Catholic stronghold. Notice the stumps in front and nearby. Nicknamed *bites* (slang for the male anatomy), they effectively keep cars from double-parking in areas designed for people. Many of the metal ones slide up and down by remote control to let privileged cars come and go.

• *You can visit the massive Palace of the Popes (described on page 480) now, but it works better to visit that palace at the end of this walk, then continue directly to the "Back Streets" walk, described later.*

Now is a good time to take in the...

Petit Palace Museum (Musée du Petit Palais)

This former cardinal's palace now displays the Church's collection of mostly medieval Italian painting (including one delightful Botticelli) and sculpture. All 350 paintings deal with Christian themes. A visit here before going to the Palace of the Popes helps furnish and populate that otherwise barren building, and a quick peek into its courtyard shows the importance of cardinal housing (€6, €2 English brochure, some English explanations posted; June-Sept Wed-Mon 10:00-13:00 & 14:00-18:00, closed Tue; Oct-May Wed-Mon 9:30-13:00 & 14:00-17:30, closed Tue; at north end of Palace Square, tel. 04 90 86 44 58).

From Palace Square, we'll head up to the rocky hilltop where Avignon was first settled, then drop down to the river (park gates open daily April-Sept 7:30-20:00, Oct-March 7:30-18:00). With this short loop, you can enjoy a park, hike to a grand river view, and visit Avignon's beloved broken bridge—an experience worth ▲▲.

• *Start by climbing to the church level, then take the switchback ramps up to...*

▲▲Le Jardin du Rochers des Doms

While the park itself is a delight—with a sweet little café (good prices for food and drinks) and public WCs—don't miss the climax: a panoramic view of the Rhône River Valley and the broken bridge. For the best views (and the favorite make-out spot for local teenagers later in the evening), find the terrace behind the odd zodiac display (across the grass from the pond-side park café, facing the statue of Jean Althen). On a clear day, the tallest peak you see, with its white limestone cap, is Mont Ventoux ("Windy Mountain"). Below and just to the right, you'll spot free passenger ferries shuttling across the river (great views from path on other side of the river), and—tucked amidst the trees on the far side of the river—a highly recommended restaurant, Le Bercail. The island in the river is the Ile de la Barthélasse, a nature preserve where Avignon can breathe.

St. André Fortress (across the river on the hill; see the info plaque to the left) was built by the French in 1360, shortly after the pope moved to Avignon, to counter the papal incursion into this part of Europe. The castle was across the border, in the kingdom of France. Avignon's famous bridge was a key border crossing, with towers on either end—one was French, and the other was the pope's. The French one, across the river, is the Tower of Philip the Fair (described on page 484).

• *From this viewpoint, take the stairs to the left (closed at night) down to the tower. As the stairs spiral down, just before St. Bénezet Bridge, catch a glimpse of the...*

Ramparts

The only bit of the rampart you can walk on is accessed from St. Bénezet Bridge (pay to enter—see next listing). When the pope came in the 1360s, small Avignon had no town wall...so he built one. What you see today was restored in the 19th century.

• *When you come out of the tower on street level, take the right-side exit and walk left along the river. Pass under the old bridge to find its entrance shortly after.*

▲▲St. Bénezet Bridge (Pont St. Bénezet)

This bridge, whose construction and location were inspired by a shepherd's religious vision, is the "pont d'Avignon" of nursery-rhyme fame. The ditty (which you've probably been humming all day) dates back to the 15th century: *Sur le pont d'Avignon, on y danse, on y danse, sur le pont d'Avignon, on y danse tous en rond* ("On the bridge of Avignon, we will dance, we will dance, on the bridge of Avignon, we will dance all in a circle").

But the bridge was a big deal even outside of its kiddie-tune fame. Built between 1171 and 1185, it was the only bridge crossing the mighty Rhône in the Middle Ages. It was damaged several times by floods and subsequently rebuilt, until 1668, when most of it was knocked down by a disastrous icy flood. Lacking a government stimulus package, the townsfolk decided not to rebuild this time, and for more than a century, Avignon had no bridge across the Rhône. And though only four arches survive today, the original bridge was huge: Imagine a 22-arch, 3,000-foot-long bridge extending from Vatican territory to the lonely Tower of Philip the Fair, which marked the beginning of France (see displays of the bridge's original length). A Romanesque chapel on the bridge is dedicated to St. Bénezet. While there's not much to see on the bridge, the audioguide included with your ticket tells a good enough story. It's also fun to be in the breezy middle of the river with a city view.

Cost and Hours: €4.50, €13 combo-ticket includes Palace of the Popes, same hours as the Palace of the Popes (see next listing), tel. 04 90 27 51 16. The ticket booth is housed in what was a medieval hospital for the poor (funded by bridge tolls). Admission includes a small room dedicated to the song of Avignon's bridge and your only chance to walk a bit of the ramparts (enter both from the tower).

• *To get to the Palace of the Popes from here, exit left, then turn left again back into the walls. Walk to the end of the short street, then turn right following signs to* Palais des Papes. *Look for the brown signs leading left under the passageway. After a block of uphill walking, find the stairs to the palace.*

▲Palace of the Popes (Palais des Papes)

In 1309, a French pope was elected (Pope Clément V). At the urging of the French king, His Holiness decided that dangerous Italy was no place for a pope, so he moved the whole operation to Avignon for a secure rule under a supportive king. The Catholic Church literally bought Avignon (then a two-bit town), and popes resided here until 1403. Meanwhile, Italians demanded a Roman pope, so from 1378 on, there were twin popes—one in Rome and one in Avignon—causing a schism in the Catholic Church that wasn't fully resolved until 1417.

A visit to the mighty yet barren papal palace comes with an audioguide that leads you along a one-way route and does a credible job of overcoming the complete lack of furnishings. It teaches the basic history while allowing you to tour at your own pace.

As you wander, ponder that this palace—the largest surviving Gothic palace in Europe—was built to accommodate 500 people as the administrative center of the Holy See and home of the pope. This was the most fortified palace of the age (remember, the pope left Rome to be more secure). Nine popes ruled from here, making this the center of Christianity for 100 years. You'll walk through the pope's personal quarters (frescoed with happy hunting scenes), see many models of how the various popes added to the building, and learn about its state-of-the-art plumbing. The rooms are huge. The "pope's chapel" is twice the size of the adjacent Avignon cathedral.

Although the last pope checked out in 1403 (escaping a siege),

PROVENCE

the Church owned Avignon until the French Revolution in 1789. During this interim period, the pope's "legate" (official representative, normally a nephew) ruled Avignon from this palace. Avignon residents, many of whom had come from Rome, spoke Italian for a century after the pope left, making it a linguistic ghetto within France. In the Napoleonic age, the palace was a barracks, housing 1,800 soldiers. You can see cuts in the wall where high ceilings gave way to floor beams. Climb the tower (Tour de la Gâche) for grand views and a rooftop café with surprisingly good food at very fair prices.

A room at the end of the tour (called *la boutellerie*) is dedicated to the region's wines, of which they claim the pope was a fan. Sniff "Le Nez du Vin"—a black box with 54 tiny bottles designed to develop your "nose." (Blind-test your travel partner.) The nearby village of Châteauneuf-du-Pape is where the pope summered in the 1320s. Its famous wine is a direct descendant of his wine. You're welcome to taste here (€6 for three to five fine wines and souvenir tasting cup).

Cost and Hours: €10.50 (more during special exhibits), €13 combo-ticket includes St. Bénezet Bridge, daily mid-March-Oct 9:00-19:00, until 20:00 July and Sept, until 21:00 in Aug, Nov-mid-March 9:30-17:45, last entry one hour before closing, tel. 04 90 27 50 74, www.palais-des-papes.com.

• *You'll exit at the rear of the palace, where my "Back Streets" walking tour begins (described next). Or, to return to Palace Square, make two rights after exiting the palace.*

▲▲Discovering Avignon's Back Streets

Use the map on pages 474-475 or the TI map to navigate this easy, level, 30-minute walk. This self-guided tour begins in the small square (place de la Mirande) behind the Palace of the Popes. If you've toured the palace, this is where you exit. Otherwise, from the front of the palace, follow the narrow, cobbled rue Peyrollerie—carved out of the rock—around the palace on the right side as you face it.

• *Our walk begins at the...*

Hôtel la Mirande: Located on the square, Avignon's finest hotel welcomes visitors. Find the atrium lounge and consider a coffee break amid the understated luxury (€12 afternoon tea served daily 15:00-18:00, includes a generous selection of pastries). Inspect the royal lounge and dining room (recommended on page 491); cooking demos are offered in the basement below. Rooms start at about €400 in high season.

• *Turn left out of the hotel and left again on rue Peyrollerie ("Copper-smiths Street"), then take your first right on rue des Ciseaux d'Or. On the small square ahead you'll find the...*

Church of St. Pierre: The original chestnut doors were carved in 1551, when tales of New World discoveries raced across Europe. (Notice the Indian headdress, top center of left-side door.) The fine Annunciation (eye level on right-side door) shows Gabriel giving Mary the exciting news in impressive Renaissance 3-D. Now take 10 steps back from the door and look way up. The tiny statue breaking the skyline of the church is the pagan god Bacchus, with oodles of grapes. What's he doing sitting atop a Christian church? No one knows. The church's interior holds a beautiful Baroque altar. For recommended restaurants near the Church of St. Pierre, see "Eating in Avignon," later.

• *With your back to the church, follow the alley to the right, which was covered and turned into a tunnel during the town's population boom. It leads into...*

Place des Châtaignes: The cloister of St. Pierre is named for the chestnut *(châtaigne)* trees that once stood here (now replaced by plane trees). The practical atheists of the French Revolution destroyed the cloister, leaving only faint traces of the arches along the church side of the square.

• *Continue around the church and cross busy place Carnot to the Banque Chaix. Across the small lane to the right of the bank, find the classy...*

15th-Century Building: With its original beamed eaves showing, this is a rare vestige from the Middle Ages. Notice how this building widens the higher it gets. A medieval loophole based taxes on ground-floor square footage—everything above was tax-free. Walking down the pedestrian street, rue des Fourbisseurs ("Street of the Animal Furriers"), notice how the top floors almost meet. Fire was a constant danger in the Middle Ages, as flames leapt easily from one home to the next. In fact, the lookout guard's primary responsibility was watching for fires, not the enemy. Virtually all of Avignon's medieval homes have been replaced by safer structures.

• *Turn left from rue des Fourbisseurs onto the traffic-free rue du Vieux Sextier ("Street of the Balance," for weighing items); another left under the first arch leads 10 yards to Avignon's...*

Synagogue: Jews first arrived in Avignon with the Diaspora (exile) of the first century. Avignon's Jews were nicknamed "the Pope's Jews" because of the protection that the Vatican offered to Jews expelled from France. This synagogue dates from the 1220s; in the mid-19th century it was completely rebuilt in a Neoclassical Greek-temple style by a non-Jewish architect. This is the only synagogue under a rotunda that you'll see anywhere. It's an intimate, classy place dressed with white colonnades and walnut furnishings. To visit the synagogue, press the buzzer (free, Mon-Fri 10:00-12:00 & 15:00-17:00, closed Sat-Sun, 2 place Jerusalem, tel. 04 90 55 21 24).

• *Retrace your steps to rue du Vieux Sextier and turn left, then continue to the big square and find the big, boxy...*

Market (Les Halles): In 1970, the town's open-air market was replaced by this modern one. The market's jungle-like green wall reflects the changes of seasons and helps mitigate its otherwise stark exterior (open Tue-Sun until 13:00, closed Mon, small TI inside open Fri-Sun). Step inside for a sensual experience of organic breads, olives, and festival-of-mold cheeses. The rue des Temptations cuts down the center. Cafés and cheese shops are on the right—as far as possible from the stinky fish stalls on the left. Follow your nose away from the fish and have a coffee with the locals.

• *Exit out the back door of Les Halles, turn left on rue de la Bonneterie ("Street of Hosiery"), and track the street for five minutes to the plane trees, where it becomes...*

Rue des Teinturiers: This "Street of the Dyers" is a tie-dyed, tree- and stream-lined lane, home to earthy cafés and galleries. This was the cloth industry's dyeing and textile center in the 1800s (a *teinturier* is a dyer). The stream is a branch of the Sorgue River. Those stylish Provençal fabrics and patterns you see for sale everywhere were first made here, modeled after a pattern imported from India.

About three small bridges down, you'll pass the Grey Penitents chapel on the right. The upper facade shows the GPs, who dressed up in robes and pointy hoods to do their anonymous good deeds back in the 13th century (long before the KKK dressed this way). As you stroll on, you'll see the work of amateur sculptors, who have carved whimsical car barriers out of limestone.

Trendy restaurants on this atmospheric street are recommended later, under "Eating in Avignon."

• *Farther down rue des Teinturiers, you'll come to the...*

Waterwheel: Standing here, imagine the Sorgue River—which hits the mighty Rhône in Avignon—being broken into several canals in order to turn 23 such wheels. In about 1800, waterwheels powered the town's industries. The little cogwheel above the big one could be shoved into place, kicking another machine into gear behind the wall.

• *To return to the real world, double back on rue des Teinturiers and turn left on rue des Lices, which traces the first medieval wall. (Lice is the no-man's-land along a wall.) After a long block, you'll pass a striking four-story building that was a home for the poor in the 1600s, an army barracks in the 1800s, a fine-arts school in the 1900s, and is a deluxe condominium today (much of this neighborhood is going high-class residential). Eventually you'll return to rue de la République, Avignon's main drag.*

More Sights in Avignon

Most of Avignon's top sights are covered by the walking tours, described earlier. With more time, consider these options.

Fondation Angladon-Dubrujeaud—Visiting this museum is like being invited into the elegant home of a rich and passionate art collector. It mixes a small but enjoyable collection of art from Post-Impressionists to Cubists (including Paul Cézanne, Vincent van Gogh, Honoré Daumier, Edgar Degas, and Pablo Picasso) with re-created art studios and furnishings from many periods. It's a quiet place with a few superb paintings (€6, Tue-Sun 13:00-18:00, closed Mon, 5 rue Laboureur, tel. 04 90 82 29 03, www .angladon.com).

Calvet Museum (Musée Calvet)—This fine-arts museum impressively displays its collection, highlighting French Baroque works. While the museum goes ignored by most, you'll find a few diamonds in the rough upstairs: Géricault, Soutine, and one painting each from Manet, Sisley, Bonnard, Dufy, and Vlamnick (€6, includes audioguide, Wed-Mon 10:00-13:00 & 14:00-18:00, closed Tue, in the quieter western half of town at 65 rue Joseph Vernet, antiquities collection a few blocks away at 27 rue de la République—same hours and ticket, tel. 04 90 86 33 84, www .musee-calvet.org).

Near Avignon

Villeneuve-lès-Avignon—For a refreshing village escape from Avignon, cross the Rhône River and explore Avignon's little sister city of Villeneuve-lès-Avignon (take bus #11 from in front of Avignon's post office on cours Président Kennedy, 2/hour Mon-Sat, none Sun—see map on pages 486-487; or drive 5 minutes across Daladier Bridge and follow signs).

As you approach Villeneuve, bus #11 stops near the **Tower of Philip the Fair** (Tour Philippe-le-Bel). Built in 1307 to protect access to St. Bénezet Bridge, this massive tower offers a terrific view over Avignon and the Rhône basin. It's best late in the day (€2.10; April-Sept daily 10:00-12:30 & 14:00-18:30; Oct-Nov Tue-Sat 10:00-12:30 & 14:00-17:00, closed Sun-Mon; closed Dec-March).

Once in Villeneuve, you'll find fewer tourists and a smattering of good restaurants and local cafés among its peaceful lanes and small squares. You'll also uncover a handful of worthwhile sights (the Avignon Passion Pass offers discounts for most). Climb to the monumental **Fort St. André** for film gobbling views from its ramparts and towers and roam the lovely **Abbey Gardens** inside the fort's walls with more views (fort-€5, daily Oct-March 10:00-17:00, April-Sept 9:30-18:00; abbey-€5, Tue-Sun 10:00-12:30 & 14:00-18:00, closed Mon). Or rattle around a romantic abbey at the

Chartreuse du Val de Bénédiction (€7, same hours as fort, 58 rue de la République).

Sleeping in Avignon

(€1 = about $1.40, country code: 33)

Hotel values are better in Arles, though I've found some good values in Avignon and have listed them here. Avignon is particularly popular during its July festival, when you must book ahead (expect inflated prices). Drivers should ask about parking deals.

Near Avignon's Centre-Ville Station

The first five listings are a five- to ten-minute walk from the Centre-Ville train station. (For hotels Colbert, Parc, and Splendid, turn right off cours Jean Jaurès on rue Agricol Perdiguier.)

$$$ Hôtel Bristol*** is a big, professionally run place on the main drag, offering predictable "American" comforts, including spacious public spaces, large rooms decorated in neutral tones, duvets on the beds, a big elevator, air-conditioning, and a generous buffet breakfast (standard Db-€88-103, bigger Db-€126, Tb/Qb-€153, breakfast-€12, parking-€12, 44 cours Jean Jaurès, tel. 04 90 16 48 48, fax 04 90 66 22 72, www.bristol-hotel-avignon.com, contact@bristol-avignon.com).

$$$ Hôtel Colbert** is a solid two-star hotel and a good mid-range bet, with richly colored, comfortable rooms in many sizes. Your efficient hosts—Patrice, Annie, and *le chien* Brittany—care for this restored manor house, with its warm public spaces and sweet little patio. It's a popular place, so it's best to book well in advance (Sb-€65, small Db-€78, bigger Db-€84-100, some tight bathrooms, no triples available, creative homemade breakfast-€10, air-con, Wi-Fi, 7 rue Agricol Perdiguier, tel. 04 90 86 20 20, fax 04 90 85 97 00, www.lecolbert-hotel.com, contact@avignon-hotel-colbert.com).

$$ Hôtel du Parc* is a spotless value with white walls, some tiny bathrooms, and stone accents. Since it's likely to be under new ownership, these prices are *très* tentative (S-€32, Sb-€45, Ds-€65, Db-€70, Ts-€75; no TVs, phones, or air-con; tel. 04 90 82 71 55, fax 04 90 85 64 86, http://perso.modulonet.fr/hoduparc, hotel.parc@modulonet.fr). This place is homier than Hôtel le Splendid, across the street.

$$ At Hôtel Boquier**, engaging Madame Sendra offers 12 quiet, good-value, and homey rooms under wood beams in a central location (small Db-€58, bigger Db-€72, Tb-€80, Qb-€94, air-con, Internet access and Wi-Fi, steep and narrow stairways to some rooms, no elevator, parking-€7, near the TI at 6 rue du portail Boquier, tel. 04 90 82 34 43, fax 04 90 86 14 07,

Avignon Hotels & Restaurants

1. Hôtel Bristol
2. Hôtel Colbert
3. Hôtel du Parc
4. Hôtel le Splendid
5. Hôtel Boquier
6. Hôtel d'Europe
7. Hôtel Mercure Cité des Papes
8. Hôtel Pont d'Avignon
9. Hôtel Médiéval
10. To Le Clos du Rempart & Lumani B&Bs
11. To Auberge Bagatelle (Hostel) & Jardin de Bacchus Rooms
12. Church of St. Pierre Eateries
13. Place Crillon Eateries
14. Place des Corps-Saints Eateries
15. Restaurant Françoise
16. La Cave des Passages Wine Bar
17. L'Empreinte Restaurant
18. To Restaurant Numéro 75
19. L'Isle Sonnante Restaurant
20. La Cantina Restaurant
21. Le Caveau du Théâtre Rest.
22. Hôtel la Mirande Restaurant
23. La Vache à Carreaux Rest.
24. L'Epice and Love Rest.
25. Le Bercail Rest.
26. Carrefour City Grocery

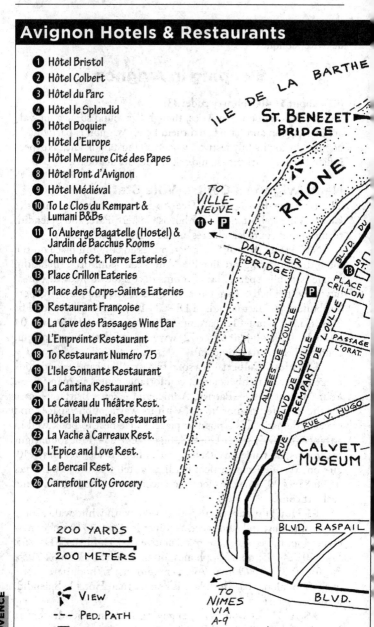

PROVENCE

www.hotel-boquier.com, contact@hotel-boquier.com).

$ Hôtel le Splendid* rents 17 acceptable rooms with faux-wood floors, most of which could use a little attention (Sb-€48, Db-€62, bigger Db with air-con-€72, Tb with air-con-€82, three Db apartments-€92, Internet access and Wi-Fi, 17 rue Agricol Perdiguier, tel. 04 90 86 14 46, fax 04 90 85 38 55, www.avignon-splendid-hotel.com, splendidavignon@gmail.com).

In the Center, near Place de l'Horloge

$$$ Hôtel d'Europe****, with Avignon's most prestigious address, lets peasants sleep royally without losing their shirts—but only if you land one of the 10 surprisingly reasonable "standard" rooms. Enter a shady courtyard, linger in the lounges, and savor every comfort. The hotel is located on the handsome place Crillon, near the river (standard Db-€200, superior Db-€360, prestige Db-€495, breakfast-€17, elevator, Internet access, garage-€17, near Daladier Bridge at 12 place Crillon, tel. 04 90 14 76 76, fax 04 90 14 76 71, www.heurope.com, reservations@heurope.com). The hotel's restaurant is Michelin-rated (one star) and serves an upscale €48 *menu* in its formal dining room or front courtyard.

$$$ Hôtel Mercure Cité des Papes*** is a modern chain hotel within spitting distance of the Palace of the Popes. It has 89 smartly designed, small rooms (Sb-€135, Db-€145-180, promotional deals best if booked 15 days ahead, many rooms have views over place de l'Horloge, air-con, elevator, 1 rue Jean Vilar, tel. 04 90 80 93 00, fax 04 90 80 93 01, www.mercure.com, h1952@accor.com).

$$$ Hôtel Pont d'Avignon***, just inside the walls near St. Bénezet Bridge, is part of the same chain as the Hôtel Mercure Cité des Papes, with the same prices for its 87 rooms (direct access to a garage makes parking easier than at the other Mercure hotel, elevator, on rue Ferruce, tel. 04 90 80 93 93, fax 04 90 80 93 94, www.mercure.com, h0549@accor.com).

$$ Hôtel Médiéval** is burrowed deep a few blocks from the Church of St. Pierre. Built as a cardinal's home, this massive stone mansion has a small garden and friendly-as-they-get Mike at the helm. It has 35 wood-paneled, air-conditioned, unimaginative rooms (Sb-€49, Db-€62-77, bigger Db or Tb-€85-92, kitchenettes available but require 3-night minimum stay, Wi-Fi, 5 blocks east of place de l'Horloge, behind Church of St. Pierre at 15 rue Petite Saunerie, tel. 04 90 86 11 06, fax 04 90 82 08 64, www.hotelmedieval.com, hotel.medieval@wanadoo.fr).

Chambres d'Hôte

$$$ At Le Clos du Rempart, a 10-minute walk from the center, Madame Assad rents two comfortable rooms and one apartment on a peaceful courtyard with Middle Eastern decor (Db-€120-150 depending on season and room size, 2-bedroom apartment for 4 with kitchen-€800-1,100/week, includes breakfast, cash only, air-con, Wi-Fi, one parking spot in garage, inside the walls east of the Palace of the Popes at 35-37 rue Crémade—call or check website for directions, tel. & fax 04 90 86 39 14, www.closdurempart.com, aida@closdurempart.com).

$$$ Lumani provides the ultimate urban refuge just inside the city walls, a 15-minute walk from the Palace of the Popes. In this graceful old manor house, gentle Elisabeth and Jean welcome guests to their art-gallery-cum-bed-and-breakfast that surrounds a fountain-filled courtyard with elbow room. She paints, he designs buildings, and both care about your experience in Avignon. The five rooms are decorated with flair—no two are alike, and all overlook the shady garden (small Db-€100, big Db-€140, Db suites-€170, extra person-€30, includes breakfast, credit cards OK except American Express, Internet access and Wi-Fi, music studio, parking-€10 or easy on street, 37 rue de Rempart St Lazare, tel. 04 90 82 94 11, www.avignon-lumani.com, lux@avignon-lumani .com).

On the Outskirts of Town

$ Auberge Bagatelle's hostel offers dirt-cheap beds, a lively atmosphere, a café, a grocery store, a launderette, great views of Avignon, and campers for neighbors (D-€44, Ds-€48, T-€60, Ts-€67, Tb-€82, Q-€73, Qb-€100, dorm bed-€18, includes breakfast, across Daladier Bridge on Ile de la Barthélasse, bus #10 from main post office, tel. 04 90 86 71 31, fax 04 90 27 16 23, www .aubergebagatelle.fr, auberge.bagatelle@wanadoo.fr).

Near Avignon

$$$ At Jardin de Bacchus, just 15 minutes northwest of Avignon and convenient to Pont du Gard, enthusiastic and English-speaking Christine and Erik offer three rooms in their rural farmhouse overlooking little Tavel's famous vineyards (Db-€85-105, €30 extra for one-night stays, breakfast-€10, fine dinner possible, Wi-Fi, tel. 04 66 90 28 62, www.jardindebacchus.fr, jardindebacchus@free .fr). To learn about their small-group food and wine tours, check their website.

Eating in Avignon

Skip the overpriced places on place de l'Horloge and find a more intimate location for your dinner. Avignon has many delightful squares filled with tables ready to seat you.

Near the Church of St. Pierre

The church divides two enchanting squares. One is quiet and intimate, the other is lively.

L'Epicerie, sitting alone on an intimate square, serves the highest-quality—and highest-priced—cuisine around the Church of St. Pierre, with a focus on products from the south of France. Expect lots of color and a dash of spice (€18-24 *plats,* closed Sun off-season, cozy interior good in bad weather, 10 place St. Pierre, tel. 04 90 82 74 22).

On Place des Châtaignes: Pass under the arch by L'Epicerie restaurant and enter enchanting place des Châtaignes, with a fun commotion of tables. Peruse your options. The **Crêperie du Cloître** makes mediocre dinner crêpes and salads (daily, cash only). **Restaurant Nem,** tucked in the corner, is Vietnamese and family-run (*menus* from €12, cash only). **Pause Gourmande** is a small, lunch-only eatery with €9 *plats du jour* and always a veggie option (closed Sun).

Place Crillon

This more refined square just off the river attracts a stylish crowd and houses a variety of dining choices. Traditional French **Restaurant les Artistes** and *italiano* **La Piazza** are both popular and owned by the same folks (good €11 lunch deals, €17 dinner *menus* with interesting choices, daily, tel. 04 90 82 23 54). **La Comédie** serves €9 crêpes and salads with mod seating (closed Sun).

Place des Corps-Saints

You'll find several youthful and reasonable eateries with tables sprawling under big plane trees on this locally popular square. **Bistrot à Tartines** specializes in—you guessed it—*tartines* (big slices of toast smothered with toppings), and has the coziest interior and best desserts on the square (€8 *tartines* and salads, daily, tel. 04 90 85 58 70). I also enjoy the €10 pizzas and friendly service at **Le Pili** (daily, tel. 04 90 27 39 53). **Zeste** is a friendly, modern deli offering fresh soups, pasta salads, wraps, smoothies, and more. Get it to go, or eat inside or on the scenic square—all at unbeatable prices (closed Sun, tel. 09 51 49 05 62).

By the Market (Les Halles)

Here you'll find a good selection of eateries with good prices. **Restaurant Françoise** is a pleasant café and tea salon, where fresh-baked tarts—savory and sweet—and a variety of salads and soups make a healthful meal, and vegetarian options are plentiful (€7-12 dishes, Mon-Sat 8:00-19:00, closed Sun, free Wi-Fi, 6 rue Général Leclerc, tel. 04 32 76 24 77).

Rue des Teinturiers

This "tie-dye" street has a wonderful concentration of eateries popular with the natives, and justifies the long walk. It's a youthful, trendy area, recently spiffed up with a canalside ambience and little hint of tourism. Survey the eateries listed here before choosing (all line up near the waterwheel).

La Cave des Passages makes a colorful pause before dinner. The owners enjoy serving you a fragrant €2.50 glass of regional wine. Choose from the blackboard by the bar that lists all the bottles open today, then join the gang outside by the canal. In the evening, this place is a hit with the young local crowd for its wine and weekend concerts (Mon-Sat 10:00-15:00 & 18:00-1:00 in the morning, closed Sun, no food in evening, across from waterwheel at 41 rue des Teinturiers).

L'Empreinte is good for North African cuisine. Choose a table in its tent-like interior, or sit canalside on the cobbles (copious couscous or *tajine* for €13-16, take-out and veggie options available, daily, 33 rue des Teinturiers, tel. 04 32 76 31 84).

Restaurant Numéro 75 is worth the walk (just past where the cobbles end on rue des Teinturiers). It fills the Pernod mansion (of *pastis* liquor fame) and a large, romantic courtyard with outdoor tables. The menu is limited to Mediterranean cuisine, but everything's *très* tasty. It's best to go with the options offered by your young black-shirted server (€20 two-course lunch *menu* with wine and coffee, dinner *menus:* €27/appetizer and main course or main course and dessert, €33/3 courses; Mon-Sat 12:00-14:00 & 20:00-22:00, closed Sun, 75 rue Guillaume Puy, tel. 04 90 27 16 00).

Elsewhere in Avignon

At **L'Isle Sonnante,** join chef Boris and his wife, Anne, to dine intimately in their formal and charming one-room *bistrot.* You'll choose from a small menu offering only fresh products and be served by owners who care (*menus* from €30, closed Sun-Mon, 100 yards from the carousel on place de l'Horloge at 7 rue Racine, tel. 04 90 82 56 01, best to book ahead).

La Cantina delivers fine Italian cuisine in a beautiful courtyard (€15 pizzas, €20-30 *plats,* closed Sun evening, 83 rue Joseph Vernet, tel. 04 90 85 99 04).

Le Caveau du Théâtre is a welcoming place where Richard invites diners to have a glass of wine or dinner at a sidewalk table, or inside in one of two carefree rooms (€13 *plats,* €18 *menus,* fun ambience for free, closed for lunch Sat and all day Sun, 16 rue des Trois Faucons, tel. 04 90 82 60 91).

Hôtel la Mirande is the ultimate Avignon splurge. Reserve ahead here for understated elegance and Avignon's top cuisine (€35 lunch *menu,* €105 dinner tasting *menu;* closed Tue-Wed—but for a price break, dine in the kitchen with the chef on these "closed" days for €85-140 including wine; behind Palace of the Popes, 4 place de la Mirande, tel. 04 90 86 93 93, www.la-mirande.fr).

La Vache à Carreaux is a unique place with a passion for cheese in all its forms (non-cheese dishes are also available). The decor is as warm as the welcome, the wine list is extensive and reasonable, and it's a hit with the locals—so reserve ahead (€12-20 *plats*, daily, just behind Palace of the Popes at 14 rue Peyrollerie, tel. 04 90 80 09 05).

At **L'Epice and Love** (the name is a fun French-English play on words, pronounced "lay peace and love"), English-speaking owner Marie creates a playful atmosphere in her cozy, friendly restaurant. A few colorfully decorated tables and tasty meat, fish, and vegetarian dishes at good prices greet the hungry traveler (*menus* from €16, daily, 30 rue des Lices, tel. 04 90 82 45 96).

Across the River

Le Bercail offers a fun opportunity to get out of town (barely) and take in *le fresh air* with a terrific riverfront view of Avignon, all while enjoying inexpensive Provençal cooking served in big portions. Book ahead, as this restaurant is popular (*menus* from €17, serves late, daily April-Oct, tel. 04 90 82 20 22). To get there, take the free shuttle boat (located near St. Bénezet Bridge) to the Ile de la Barthélasse, turn right, and walk five minutes. As the boat usually stops running at about 18:00 (except in July-Aug, when it runs until 21:00), you can either taxi home or walk 25 minutes along the pleasant riverside path and over Daladier Bridge.

Avignon Connections

Trains

Remember, there are two train stations in Avignon: the suburban TGV Station, and the Centre-Ville Station in the city center (€1.20 shuttle buses connect to both stations, buy ticket from driver, 3/hour, 15 minutes). TGV trains usually serve the TGV train station only, though a few depart from Centre-Ville train station (check your station). Only Centre-Ville Station has baggage storage (see "Arrival in Avignon" on page 472). Car rental is available only at the TGV Station. Some cities are served by slower local trains from Centre-Ville Station as well as by faster TGV trains from the TGV Station; I've listed the most convenient stations for each trip.

From Avignon's Centre-Ville Station by Train to: Arles (11/day, 20 minutes, less frequent in the afternoon), **Lyon** (10/day, 2 hours, also from TGV Station—see below), **Paris** (4/day direct, 3.5 hours; more with change, 3-4 hours, also from TGV Station—see below), **Barcelona** (2/day, 6-9 hours, transfer in Montpellier).

From Avignon's TGV Station to: **Arles** (by SNCF bus, 10/day, 1 hour), **Nice** (20/day, most via TGV, 4 hours, most require transfer in Marseille), **Lyon** (12/day, 1.5 hours, also from Centre-Ville Station—see above), **Paris**' Gare de Lyon (9/day direct, 2.5 hours; also from Centre-Ville Station—see above), **Paris**' Charles de Gaulle airport (7/day, 3 hours).

Buses

The bus station *(gare routière)* is just past and below Ibis Hôtel, to the right as you exit the train station (info desk open Mon-Sat 8:00-19:30, closed Sun, tel. 04 90 82 07 35, staff speaks English). Nearly all buses leave from this station (buy tickets on bus, small bills only). The biggest exception is the SNCF bus service from the Avignon TGV train station to Arles (explained earlier). The Avignon TI has schedules. Service is reduced or nonexistent on Sundays and holidays. Check your departure time beforehand and make sure to verify your destination with the driver.

From Avignon to Pont du Gard: Buses go to this famous old aqueduct (3-5/day, 40-50 minutes, departs from bus station, usually from stall #11), but the schedule doesn't work well for day-trippers from Avignon; instead, consider a taxi one way and bus back.

Pont du Gard

Throughout the ancient world, aqueducts were like flags of stone that heralded the greatness of Rome. A visit to this sight still works to proclaim the wonders of that age. This perfectly preserved Roman aqueduct was built in about 19 B.C. as the critical link of a 30-mile canal that, by dropping one inch for every 350 feet, supplied nine million gallons of water per day (about 100 gallons per second) to Nîmes—one of ancient Europe's largest cities. Though most of the aqueduct is on or below the ground, at Pont du Gard it spans a canyon on a massive bridge—one of the most remarkable surviving Roman ruins anywhere. Wear sturdy shoes if you plan to climb around the aqueduct (footing is tricky), and bring swimwear and flip-flops if you plan to backstroke beneath the monument.

Getting to Pont du Gard

The famous aqueduct is between Remoulins and Vers-Pont du Gard on D-981, 13 miles from Avignon.

By Car: Pont du Gard is a 25-minute drive due west of Avignon (follow N-100 from Avignon, tracking signs to *Nîmes* and *Remoulins,* then *Pont du Gard* and *Rive Gauche*), and 45 minutes northwest of Arles (via Tarascon on D-15). Parking is available

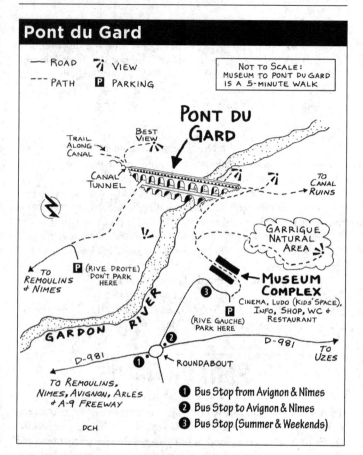

Pont du Gard

— ROAD 🕅 VIEW
--- PATH P PARKING

NOT TO SCALE:
MUSEUM TO PONT DU GARD
IS A 5-MINUTE WALK

PONT DU GARD

TRAIL ALONG CANAL

BEST VIEW

CANAL TUNNEL

TO CANAL RUINS

GARRIGUE NATURAL AREA

TO REMOULINS & NÎMES

P (RIVE DROITE) DON'T PARK HERE

MUSEUM COMPLEX
CINEMA, LUDO (KIDS' SPACE), INFO, SHOP, WC & RESTAURANT

3

P (RIVE GAUCHE) PARK HERE

GARDON RIVER

D-981 TO UZÈS

D-981

2

1 ROUNDABOUT

TO REMOULINS, NÎMES, AVIGNON, ARLES & A-9 FREEWAY

DCH

1 Bus Stop from Avignon & Nîmes
2 Bus Stop to Avignon & Nîmes
3 Bus Stop (Summer & Weekends)

on the Rive Droite (Right Bank), but it's farther away from the museum than parking on the Rive Gauche (Left Bank). If going to Arles from Pont du Gard, follow signs to *Nîmes* (not Avignon), then follow D-986 and then D-15 to Arles.

By Bus: Buses run to Pont du Gard (on the Rive Gauche side) from Avignon (3/day, 50 minutes), Nîmes, and Uzès (confirm times locally). Consider this plan: Take the midday bus from Avignon to Pont du Gard (12:05 in 2011), then take the afternoon bus (16:55 in 2011) on to Nîmes (55 minutes), where trains run almost hourly back to Avignon. Or take a taxi back (see next page).

Buses stop at the traffic roundabout 300 yards from the aqueduct. In summer and on weekends, however, buses usually drive into the Pont du Gard site and stop at the parking lot's ticket booth. Confirm where the bus stops at the parking booth inside the Pont du Gard site.

At the roundabout, the stop for buses coming from Avignon

PROVENCE

and Nîmes (and going to Uzès) is on the side opposite Pont du Gard; the stop for buses to Nîmes and to Avignon is on the same side as Pont du Gard (a block to your left as you exit Pont du Gard onto the main road). Make sure you're waiting for the bus on the correct side of the traffic circle (stops have schedules posted), and wave your hand to signal the bus to stop for you (otherwise, it'll chug on by). Buy your ticket when you get on and verify your destination with the driver.

By Taxi: From Avignon it's about €42 for a taxi ride to Pont du Gard. If you're staying in Avignon and only want to see Pont du Gard, consider splurging on a taxi to the aqueduct in the morning, then take the early-afternoon bus back.

Orientation to Pont du Gard

There are two riversides to Pont du Gard: the Left Bank (Rive Gauche) and Right Bank (Rive Droite). Park on the Rive Gauche, where you'll find museums, ticket booth, ATM, cafeteria, WCs, and shops—all built into a modern plaza. You'll see the aqueduct in two parts: first the fine museum complex, then the actual river gorge spanned by the ancient bridge.

Cost and Hours: The aqueduct, museum, film, outdoor *garrigue* nature area, and related attractions are covered by the €15 parking fee (those arriving by bus or bike pay nothing). The museum is open daily May-Sept 9:00-19:00, Oct-April 9:00-17:00, closed two weeks in Jan. The aqueduct itself is open until 1:00 in the morning, as is the parking lot. Toll tel. 08 20 90 33 30, www.pontdugard.fr. The *garrigue* is always open.

Tours and Information: For an extra €6, you can rent an **audioguide** with detailed explanations of the aqueduct in English. Call ahead or visit the website for information on **guided walks** on top of the aqueduct. Consider the helpful €4 English **booklet** about the *garrigue*—the extensive nature area featuring historic crops and landscapes of the Mediterranean.

Canoe Rental: Floating under Pont du Gard by canoe is an experience you won't soon forget. Collias Canoes will pick you up at Pont du Gard (or elsewhere, if pre-arranged) and shuttle you to the town of Collias. You'll float down the river to the nearby town of Remoulins, where they'll pick you up and take you back to Pont du Gard (€18/person, €9/child under 12, usually 2 hours, though you can take as long as you like, good idea to reserve the day before in July-Aug, tel. 04 66 22 85 54).

Plan Ahead for Swimming: Pont du Gard is perhaps best enjoyed on your back and in the water—bring along a swimsuit, and flip-flops for the rocks.

Sights at Pont du Gard

▲**Museum**—In this state-of-the-art museum (well-presented in English), you'll enter to the sound of water and understand the critical role fresh water played in the Roman "art of living." You'll see examples of lead pipes, faucets, and siphons; walk through a mock rock quarry; and learn how they moved those huge rocks into place and how those massive arches were made. While actual artifacts from the aqueduct are few, the exhibit shows the immensity of the undertaking as well as the payoff. Imagine the excitement as this extravagant supply of water finally tumbled into Nîmes. A relaxing highlight is the scenic video of a helicopter ride along the entire 30-mile course of the structure, from its start at Uzès all the way to the Castellum in Nîmes.

Other Activities—Several additional attractions are designed to give the sight more meaning—and they do (but for most visitors, the museum is sufficient). A corny, romancing-the-aqueduct 25-minute **film** plays in the same building as the museum and offers good information in a flirtatious French-Mediterranean style...and a cool, entertaining, and cushy break. The nearby **kids' museum,** called Ludo, offers a scratch-and-sniff teaching experience (in English) of various aspects of Roman life and the importance of water. The extensive outdoor *garrigue* **natural area,** closer to the aqueduct, features historic crops and landscapes of the Mediterranean.

▲▲▲**Viewing the Aqueduct**—A park-like path leads to the aqueduct. Until a few years ago, this was an actual road—adjacent to the aqueduct—that had spanned the river since 1743. Before you cross the bridge, pass under it and hike about 300 feet along the riverbank for a grand viewpoint from which to study the world's second-highest standing Roman structure. (Rome's Colosseum is only 6 feet taller.)

This was the biggest bridge in the whole 30-mile-long aqueduct. It seems exceptional because it is: The arches are twice the width of standard aqueducts, and the main arch is the largest the Romans ever built—80 feet (so it wouldn't get its feet wet). The bridge is about 160 feet high and was originally about 1,100 feet long. Today, 12 arches are missing, reducing the length to 790 feet.

Although the distance from the source (in Uzès) to Nîmes was only 12 miles as the eagle flew, engineers chose the most economical route, winding and zigzagging 30 miles. The water made the trip in 24 hours with a drop of only 40 feet. Ninety percent of the aqueduct is on or under the ground, but a few river canyons like this required bridges. A stone lid hides a four-foot-wide, six-foot-

PROVENCE

tall chamber lined with waterproof mortar that carried the stream for more than 400 years. For 150 years, this system provided Nîmes with good drinking water. Expert as the Romans were, they miscalculated the backup caused by a downstream corner, and had to add the thin extra layer you can see just under the lid to make the channel deeper.

The bridge and the river below provide great fun for holidaygoers. While parents suntan on rocks, kids splash into the gorge from under the aqueduct. Some daredevils actually jump from the aqueduct's lower bridge—not knowing that crazy winds scrambled by the structure cause painful belly flops (and sometimes even accidental deaths). For the most refreshing view, float flat on your back underneath the structure.

The appearance of the entire gorge changed in 2002, when a huge flood flushed lots of greenery downstream. Those floodwaters put Roman provisions to the test. Notice the triangular-shaped buttresses at the lower level—designed to split and divert the force of any flood *around* the feet of the arches rather than *into* them. The 2002 floodwaters reached the top of those buttresses. Anxious park rangers winced at the sounds of trees crashing onto the ancient stones...but the arches stood strong.

The stones that jut out—giving the aqueduct a rough, unfinished appearance—supported the original scaffolding. The protuberances were left, rather than cut off, in anticipation of future repair needs. The lips under the arches supported wooden templates that allowed the stones in the round arches to rest on something until the all-important keystone was dropped into place. Each stone weighs four to six tons. The structure stands with no mortar—taking full advantage of the innovative Roman arch, made strong by gravity.

Hike over the bridge for a closer look and the best views. Steps lead up a high trail (marked *panorama*) to a superb viewpoint (go right at the top; best views are soon after the trail starts descending). You'll also see where the aqueduct meets a rock tunnel. Walk through the tunnel and continue for a bit, following a trail that meanders along the canal's path.

Back on the museum side, steps lead up to the Rive Gauche (parking lot) end of the aqueduct, where you can follow the canal path along a trail (marked with red-and-white horizontal lines) to find some remains of the Roman canal. You'll soon reach another *panorama* with great views of the aqueduct. Hikers can continue along the path, following the red-and-white markings that lead through a forest, after which you'll come across more remains of the canal (much of which are covered by vegetation). There's not much left to see because of medieval cannibalization—frugal

NICE ON THE FRENCH RIVIERA

La Côte d'Azur

A hundred years ago, celebrities from London to Moscow flocked to the French Riviera to socialize, gamble, and escape the dreary weather at home. Today, budget vacationers and heat-seeking Europeans fill belle époque resorts at France's most sought-after fun-in-the-sun destination.

Some of the Continent's most stunning scenery and intriguing museums lie along this strip of land—as do millions of sun-worshipping tourists. Evenings on the Riviera, a.k.a. La Côte d'Azur, were made for a promenade and outdoor dining.

My favorite (and the most convenient) home base is Nice, the region's capital and France's fifth-largest city. With easy train and bus connections to most regional sights, it's practical for train travelers. Urban Nice has a full palette of world-class museums, a splendid beachfront promenade, a seductive old town, and all the drawbacks of a major city (traffic, crime, pollution, and so on). Nice also has the best selection of hotels in all price ranges, and good nightlife options. A car is a headache in Nice, though it's easily stored at one of the many pricey parking garages or for free at an outer tram station.

Getting Around the Riviera

Nice is perfectly situated for exploring the Riviera by public transport. Monaco, Villefranche-sur-Mer, Antibes, and Cannes are all within about a one-hour bus or train ride. Boats go from Nice to Monaco and St-Tropez.

By Train and Bus: All trains serving Nice arrive at and depart from the Nice-Ville station. Many key Riviera destinations are connected by direct bus or train service from Nice, and some

NICE

The French Riviera

are served by both. Since bus fare is only €1 (except on express airport buses), the pricier train is only a better choice when it saves you time (which it generally does—there is no faster way to move about the Riviera than by train).

You make the call—both modes of transportation work well. Unless otherwise noted, the following bus frequencies are for Monday-Saturday (Sunday often has limited or no service). All prices are one-way.

Destination	Bus from Nice	Train from Nice
Villefranche-sur-Mer	4/hr daily, 15 min	2/hr, 10 min, €1.90
Monaco	4/hr Mon-Sat, 3/hr Sun, 45 min	2/hr, 20 min, €3.60
Antibes	2-4/hr, 1-1.5 hrs	2/hr, 15-30 min, €4
Cannes	2-4/hr, 1.5-1.75 hrs	2/hr, 30-40 min, €6.20

Public Transportation on the French Riviera

NICE

FRANCE

NOT TO SCALE

TO GRENOBLE

ITALY

VENTIMIGLIA

TO GENOA & CINQUE TERRE

EZE-LE-VILLAGE

LA TURBIE

ST. AUBAN

DIGNE

TO AIX-EN-PROVENCE

EZE-BORD-DE-MER

MONACO

MENTON

VENCE

NICE

CAP D'AIL

TOURETTES

BEAULIEU

BAR

ST. PAUL

CAP FERRAT

VILLEFRANCHE

BIOT

VALL.

ANTIBES

JUAN-LES-PINS

GRASSE

CAP D'ANTIBES

ST. RAPHAEL

CANNES

RIVIERA

TO MARSEILLE AVIGNON & PARIS

ST. TROPEZ

RAIL

T.G.V. RAIL

BUS

BOAT

AIRPORTS (NOT ALL SHOWN)

MEDITERRENEAN SEA

DCH

By Minivan Excursion: Sylvie Di Cristo offers terrific full-day tours throughout the French Riviera in a car or minivan. She adores educating people about this area's culture and history, and loves adapting her tour to your interests, from overlooked hill towns to wine, cuisine, art, or perfume (€170/person for 2-3 people, €120/person for 4-6 people, €100/person for 7-8 people, 2-person minimum, mobile 06 09 88 83 83, www.frenchrivieraguides.net, sylvie.di.cristo@wanadoo.fr).

The TI and most hotels have information on other minivan excursions from Nice (roughly €50-60/half-day, €80-110/day). **Med-Tour** is one of many (tel. 04 93 82 92 58, mobile 06 73 82 04 10, www.med-tour.com); **Tour Azur** is another (tel. 04 93 44 88

77, www.tourazur.com). **Revelation Tours** specializes in English-language excursions (tel. 04 93 53 69 85, www.revelation-tours .com). All also offer private tours by the day or half-day (check with them for their outrageous prices, about €90/hour).

By Boat: From June to mid-September, **Trans Côte d'Azur** offers scenic trips from Nice to Monaco and Nice to St-Tropez. Boats leave in the morning and return in the evening, giving you all day to explore your destination. Drinks and WCs are available on board. Boats to **Monaco** depart at 9:30 and 16:00, and return at 11:00 and 18:00 (€32 round-trip, €27 if you don't get off in Monaco, 45 minutes each way, June-Sept Tue, Thu, and Sat only). Boats to **St-Tropez** depart at 9:00 and return at 19:00 (€55 round-trip, 2.5 hours each way; July-Aug Tue-Sun, no boats Mon; late June and early Sept Tue, Thu, and Sun only). Reservations are required for both boats, and tickets for St-Tropez often sell out, so book a few days ahead (tel. 04 92 98 71 30 or 04 92 00 42 30, www.trans-cote -azur.com, croisieres@trans-cote-azur.com). The boats leave from Nice's port, bassin des Amiraux, just below Castle Hill—look for the blue ticket booth *(billeterie)* on quai de Lunel (see map on pages 504-505). The same company also runs one-hour round-trip cruises along the coast to Cap Ferrat (see "Tours in Nice," later).

Nice

Nice (sounds like "niece"), with its spectacular Alps-to-Mediterranean surroundings, is an enjoyable big-city highlight of the Riviera. Its traffic-free old city mixes Italian and French flavors to create a spicy Mediterranean dressing, while its broad seaside walkways invite lounging and people-watching. Nice may be nice, but it's hot and jammed in July and August—reserve ahead and get a room with air-conditioning *(une chambre avec climatisation)*. Everything you'll want to see in Nice is either within walking distance, or a short bus or tram ride away.

Orientation to Nice

Everything of interest lies between the beach and the train tracks (about 15 blocks apart). The city revolves around its grand place Masséna, where pedestrian-friendly avenue Jean Médecin meets Old Nice and the Albert 1er parkway (with quick access to the beaches). It's a 20-minute walk (or a €10 taxi ride) from the train station to the beach, and a 20-minute walk along the promenade from the fancy Hôtel Negresco to the heart of Old Nice.

A 10-minute ride on the smooth-as-silk tramway takes you

through the center of the city, connecting the train station, place Masséna, Old Nice, the bus station, and the port (from nearby place Garibaldi). The tram and all city and regional buses cost only €1 per trip, making this one of the cheapest and easiest cities in France to get around in (see "Getting Around Nice," later).

Tourist Information

Nice's helpful TI has three locations: at the **airport** (in Terminal 1, daily 8:00-21:00, closed Sun off-season), next to the **train station** (usually busy; summer Mon-Sat 8:00-20:00, Sun 9:00-18:00; rest of year Mon-Sat 9:00-19:00, Sun 10:00-17:00), and facing the **beach** at 5 promenade des Anglais (usually quiet, daily 9:00-18:00, until 20:00 July-Aug, closed Sun off-season, toll tel. 08 92 70 74 07—€0.34/minute, www.nicetourisme.com). Pick up the thorough *Practical Guide to Nice* and a free Nice map (or find a better one at your hotel). You can also get information here on day trips.

Arrival in Nice

By Train: All trains stop at Nice's main station, Nice-Ville (baggage storage at the far right with your back to the tracks, lockers open daily 8:00-21:00). The station area is gritty and busy: Never leave your bags unattended and don't linger here longer than necessary.

Turn left out of the station to find a **TI** next door. Continue a few more blocks down for the Gare Thiers **tram stop** (this will take you to place Masséna, the old city, bus station, and port). Board the tram heading toward the right, direction Pont Michel (see "Getting Around Nice," later). You'll find many recommended hotels a 10- to 20-minute walk down the same street (those listed under "Between Nice Etoile and the Sea," on page 524), though it's easier taking the tram to place Masséna and walking from there.

To walk to other recommended hotels (those listed under "Between the Train Station and Nice Etoile" on page 521 and "Between Boulevard Victor Hugo and the Sea" on page 528), cross avenue Thiers in front of the station, go down the steps by Hôtel Interlaken, and continue walking down avenue Durante. Follow this same route for the fastest path from the station to the beach— avenue Durante turns into rue des Congrés. You'll soon reach the heart of Nice's beachfront promenade.

Taxis and **buses to the airport** (#23 and #99) wait in front of the train station. **Car rental** offices are to the right as you exit the station.

By Bus: Nice's bus station *(gare routière)* is sandwiched between boulevard Jean Jaurès and avenue Félix Faure, next to the old city. Cross boulevard Jean Jaurès to enter Old Nice, or cross avenue Félix Faure to get to my recommended hotels near Nice

NICE

Nice

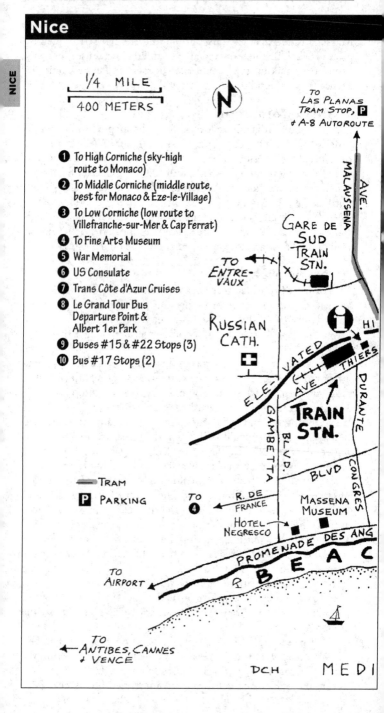

1/4 MILE
400 METERS

N

① To High Corniche (sky-high route to Monaco)
② To Middle Corniche (middle route, best for Monaco & Eze-le-Village)
③ To Low Corniche (low route to Villefranche-sur-Mer & Cap Ferrat)
④ To Fine Arts Museum
⑤ War Memorial
⑥ US Consulate
⑦ Trans Côte d'Azur Cruises
⑧ Le Grand Tour Bus Departure Point & Albert 1er Park
⑨ Buses #15 & #22 Stops (3)
⑩ Bus #17 Stops (2)

— TRAM
P PARKING

TO LAS PLANAS TRAM STOP, P & A-8 AUTOROUTE

AVE. MALAUSSENA

GARE DE SUD TRAIN STN.

TO ENTRE-VAUX

RUSSIAN CATH.

ELEVATED AVE

GAMBETTA BLVD.

BLVD

THIERS

DURANTE

TRAIN STN.

CONGRES

BLVD

TO 4

R. DE FRANCE

MASSENA MUSEUM

HOTEL NEGRESCO

PROMENADE DES ANG

TO AIRPORT

BEAC

TO ANTIBES, CANNES & VENCE

DCH

MEDI

NICE

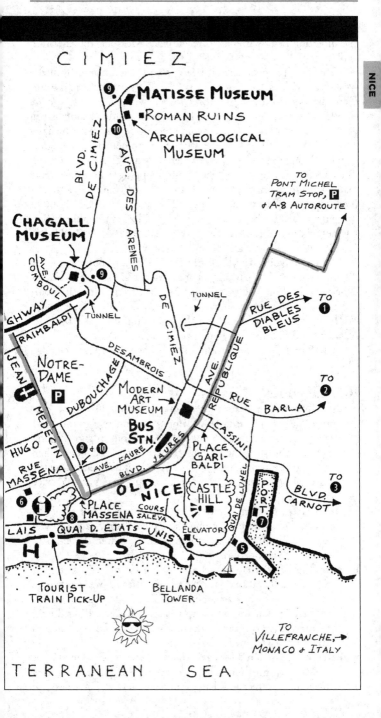

CIMIEZ

MATISSE MUSEUM
■ ROMAN RUINS
ARCHAEOLOGICAL
MUSEUM

TO
PONT MICHEL
TRAM STOP, P
& A-8 AUTOROUTE

**CHAGALL
MUSEUM**

AVE. BOUL COMBOUL

BLVD. DE CIMIEZ

AVE. DES ARENES

DE CIMIEZ

TUNNEL

GHWAY

RAIMBALDI

TUNNEL

JEAN MEDECIN

NOTRE-DAME
P

DUBOUCHAGE

DESAMBROIS

TUNNEL

RUE DES DIABLES BLEUS

TO
❶

AVE. REPUBLIQUE

RUE BARLA

TO
❷

HUGO

RUE MASSENA

Modern Art Museum

BUS STN.

9 & 10

AVE. FAURE

BLVD. JAURES

CASSINI

PLACE GARI-BALDI

OLD NICE

CASTLE HILL

QUAI DE LUNEL

PORT
❼

TO
❸

BLVD. CARNOT

6
i
8

PLACE MASSENA

Cours SALEYA

ELEVATOR

LAIS
QUAI D. ETATS-UNIS

H E S

TOURIST TRAIN PICK-UP

BELLANDA TOWER

❺

TO
VILLEFRANCHE,→
MONACO & ITALY

TERRANEAN   SEA

NICE

Etoile. Trams run along boulevard Jean Jaurès; take the tram in the direction of Las Planas to reach place Masséna and the train station.

By Car: To reach the city center on the autoroute from the west, take the first Nice exit (for the airport—called Côte d'Azur, Central) and follow signs for *Nice Centre* and *Promenade des Anglais*. (Be ready to cross three left lanes of traffic as soon as you get off the autoroute.) Try to avoid arriving at rush hour (usually Mon-Fri 8:00-9:30 & 17:00-19:30), when promenade des Anglais grinds to a halt. Hoteliers know where to park (allow €15-26/day). The parking garage at the Nice Etoile shopping center on avenue Jean Médecin is pricey but near many of my recommended hotels (ticket booth on third floor, about €20/day, €11 from 20:00-8:00). The garage next to the recommended Hôtel Ibis at the train station has better rates. All on-street parking is metered (9:00-18:00 or 19:00), but usually free all day on Sunday.

You can avoid driving in the center—and park for free—by ditching your car at a parking lot at a remote tram stop (Las Planas is best) and taking the tram into town (€1, 15 minutes, 10/hour, don't leave anything in your car, tramway described later under "Getting Around Nice"). From the A-8 autoroute, take the *Nice Nord* exit and find the Las Planas tram station.

By Plane: For information on Nice's handy airport, see page 536.

Helpful Hints

Theft Alert: Nice has its share of pickpockets. Thieves target fanny packs: Have nothing important on or around your waist, unless it's in a money belt tucked out of sight. Don't leave anything visible in your car; be wary of scooters when standing at intersections; don't leave things unattended on the beach while swimming; and stick to main streets in Old Nice after dark.

Medical Help: Riviera Medical Services has a list of English-speaking physicians all along the Riviera. They can help you make an appointment or call an ambulance (tel. 04 93 26 12 70, www.rivieramedical.com).

Events: The Riviera is famous for staging major events. Unless you're actually taking part in the festivities, these events give you only room shortages and traffic jams. The three biggies are the **Nice Carnival** (www.nicecarnaval.com), **Grand Prix of Monaco** (www.grand-prix-monaco.com), and the **Cannes Film Festival** (www.festival-cannes.com).

Sightseeing Tips: On Mondays, the following sights are closed: the Modern and Contemporary Art Museum, Fine Arts Museum, and the cours Saleya produce market. On Tuesdays, the Chagall, Matisse, and Archaeological museums are closed. Nice's city museums are free of charge (except the Chagall Museum and the Russian Cathedral).

Internet Access: There's no shortage of places to get online in Nice—they're everywhere. Ask at your hotel, or just look up as you walk (keep your eye out for the @ symbol).

English Bookstore: The Cat's Whiskers has an eclectic selection of novels and regional travel books, including mine (Tue-Sat 10:00-12:00 & 14:00-19:00, closed Sun-Mon, 26-30 rue Lamartine—see map on pages 522-523, tel. 04 93 80 02 66).

Laundry: You'll find launderettes everywhere in Nice—ask your hotelier for the nearest one. The self-service **Point Laverie** is centrally located (daily 8:00-20:00, at the corner of rue Alberti and rue Pastorelli, next to Hôtel Vendôme—see map on pages 522-523).

Grocery Store: The big **Monoprix** on avenue Jean Médecin and rue Biscarra has it all, including a deli counter, a bakery, and cold drinks (Mon-Sat 8:30-21:00, closed Sun, see map on pages 532-533). You'll also find many small grocery stores (some open Sun and/or until late hours) near my recommended hotels.

Renting a Bike (and Other Wheels): Roller Station rents bikes (*vélos*, €5/hour, €10/half-day, €15/day), rollerblades (*rollers*, €6/day), Razor-type scooters (*trotinettes*, €6/half-day, €9/day), and skateboards (€6/half-day, €9/day). You'll need to leave your ID as a deposit (daily 9:30-19:00, July-Aug until 20:00, next to yellow awnings of Pailin's Asian restaurant at 49 quai des Etats-Unis—see map on pages 522-523, another location at 10 rue Cassini near place Garibaldi, tel. 04 93 62 99 05, owner Eric). If you need more power, try the electric-assisted bikes or scooters at **Energy Scoot** (2 rue St. Philippe, near the promenade des Anglais and avenue Gambetta, tel. 04 97 07 12 64).

Car Rental: Renting a car is easiest at Nice's airport, which has offices for all the major companies. You'll also find most companies represented at Nice's train station and near Albert 1er Park.

English Radio: Tune in to Riviera-Radio at FM 106.5.

Views: For panoramic views, climb Castle Hill (see page 514), or take a one-hour boat trip (described later, under "Tours in Nice").

Beach Gear: To make life tolerable on the rocks, swimmers should buy a pair of the cheap plastic beach shoes sold at many shops (flip-flops fall off in the water). **Go Sport** at #13 on place Masséna sells beach shoes, flip-flops, and cheap sunglasses (daily 10:00-19:00—see map on pages 526-527).

Getting Around Nice

Although you can walk to most attractions in Nice, smart travelers make good use of the buses and tram. Both are covered by the same single-ride €1 ticket (good for 74 minutes in one direction, including transfers between bus and tram; can't be used for a round-trip). An all-day pass is €4 (valid on local buses and trams, as well as buses to nearby destinations—see "Getting Around the Riviera" on page 499).

The **bus** is handy to reach the Chagall and Matisse museums and the Russian Cathedral. Make sure to validate your ticket in the machine just behind the driver—watch locals do it and imitate.

Nice's **tramway** makes an "L" along avenue Jean Médecin and boulevard Jean Jaurès, and connects the main train station (Gare Thiers stop), place Masséna (Masséna stop, a few blocks' walk from the sea), Old Nice (Opéra-Vieille Ville), the bus station (Cathédrale-Vieille Ville), and the Modern and Contemporary Art Museum and port (Place Garibaldi).

Taking the tram in the direction of Pont Michel takes you from the train station toward the beach and bus station (direction Las Planas goes the other way). Buy tickets at the machines on the platforms (coins only, no credit cards). Choose the English flag to change the display language, turn the round knob and push the green button to select your ticket, press it twice at the end to get your ticket, or press the red button to cancel. Once you're on the tram, validate your ticket by inserting it into the top of the white box, then reclaiming it.

Taxis are useful for getting to Nice's outlying sights, and worth it if you're nowhere near a bus or tram stop (figure €15 from promenade des Anglais). They normally only pick up at taxi stands (*tête de station)*, or you can call 04 93 13 78 78.

The hokey **tourist train** gets you up Castle Hill (see "Tours in Nice," below).

Tours in Nice

Bus Tour—Le Grand Tour Bus provides a 12-stop, hop-on, hop-off service on an open-deck bus with headphone commentary (2/hour, 1.5-hour loop) that includes the promenade des Anglais, old port, Cap de Nice, and the Chagall and Matisse museums on Cimiez Hill (€20/1-day pass, €23/2-day pass, cheaper for seniors and students, €10 for last tour of the day at about 18:00, some hotels offer €3 discounts, buy tickets on bus, main stop is near where promenade des Anglais and quai des Etats-Unis meet, across from plage Beau Rivage, tel. 04 92 29 17 00). This tour is a pricey way to get to the Chagall and Matisse museums, but it's an acceptable option if you also want a city overview. Check the schedule if you plan to use this bus to visit the Russian Cathedral, as it may be faster to walk there.

Tourist Train—For €7 (or €3 for children under 9), you can spend 40 embarrassing minutes on the tourist train tooting along the promenade, through the old city, and up to Castle Hill. This is a sweat-free way to get to Castle Hill...but so is the elevator, which is much cheaper (every 30 minutes, daily 10:00-18:00, June-Aug until 19:00, recorded English commentary, meet train near Le Grand Tour Bus stop on quai des Etats-Unis, tel. 04 93 62 85 48).

▲**Boat Cruise**—Here's your chance to join the boat parade and see Nice from the water. On this one-hour, star-studded tour, you'll cruise in a comfortable yacht-size vessel to Cap Ferrat and past Villefranche-sur-Mer, then return to Nice with a final lap along promenade des Anglais. It's a scenic and worthwhile trip (the best views are from the seats on top).

French (and sometimes English-speaking) guides play Robin Leach, pointing out mansions owned by some pretty famous people, including Elton John (just as you leave Nice, it's the soft-yellow square-shaped place right on the water), Sean Connery (on the hill above Elton, with rounded arches and tower), and Microsoft co-founder Paul Allen (in saddle of Cap Ferrat hill, above yellow-umbrella beach with sloping red-tile roof). Guides also like to point out the mansion where the Rolling Stones recorded *Exile on Main Street* (between Villefranche-sur-Mer and Cap Ferrat). I wonder if this gang ever hangs out together (€15; May-Oct Tue-Sun 2/day, usually at 11:00 and 15:00, no boats Mon; March-April Tue-Wed, Fri, and Sun at 15:00; no boats Nov-Feb; call ahead to verify schedule, arrive 30 minutes early to get best seats, drinks and WCs available). For directions to the dock and contact information, see "Getting Around the Riviera—By Boat" on page 502.

Walking Tours—The TI on promenade des Anglais organizes weekly walking tours of Old Nice in French and English (€12, May-Oct only, usually Sat morning at 9:30, 2.5 hours, reservations necessary, depart from TI, tel. 08 92 70 74 07). They also have evening art walks on Fridays at 19:00.

Nice's cultural association (Centre du Patrimoine) offers incredibly cheap €5 walks on varying themes (in English, minimum 5 people). Call 04 92 00 41 90 a few days ahead to make a reservation. Most tours start at their office near the beach at 75 quai des Etats-Unis; look for the red plaque next to Musée des Ponchettes.

Local Guides—**Sylvie Di Cristo** gives expert tours of Nice (for contact info, see page 501). **Sofia Villavicencio** can guide you expertly in Nice and around the Riviera. Her English is flawless, and her passion is art (€135/half-day, €200/full-day, tel. 04 93 32 45

92, mobile 06 68 51 55 52, sofia.villavicencio@laposte.net). Lovely **Pascale Rucker** tailors her tours in Nice to your interests. Book in advance, though it's also worth a try on short notice (€179/half-day, €274/day, tel. & fax 04 93 87 77 89, mobile 06 16 24 29 52).

Les Petits Farcis Cooking Tour and Classes—Charming Canadian Francophile Rosa Jackson, a food journalist and Cordon Bleu–trained cook, offers popular cooking classes in Old Nice. Her single-day classes include a morning trip to the open-air market on cours Saleya to pick up ingredients, and an afternoon session spent creating an authentic Niçois meal from your purchases (€195/person, mobile 06 81 67 41 22, www.petitsfarcis.com).

Self-Guided Walk

▲▲A Scratch-and-Sniff Walk Through Old Nice

• *See the map on pages 526–527, and start at Nice's main market square...*

Cours Saleya (koor sah-lay-yuh): Named for its broad exposure to the sun *(soleil)*, this commotion of color, sights, smells, and people has been Nice's main market square since the Middle Ages (produce market held Tue-Sun until 13:00—on Mon, an antiques market takes center stage). Amazingly, part of this square was a parking lot until 1980, when the mayor of Nice had an underground garage built.

The first section is devoted to the Riviera's largest flower market (all day Tue-Sun and in operation since the 19th century). Here you'll find the ubiquitous plants and flowers that grow effortlessly in this climate, including the local favorites: carnations, roses, and jasmine. Fresh flowers are perhaps the best value in this otherwise pricey city.

The boisterous produce section trumpets the season with mushrooms, strawberries, white asparagus, zucchini flowers, and more—whatever's fresh gets top billing.

Place Pierre Gautier (also called Plassa dou Gouvernou—bilingual street signs include the old Niçoise language, an Italian dialect) is where farmers set up stalls to sell their produce and herbs directly.

Continue down the center of cours Saleya, stopping when you see the La Cambuse restaurant on your left. In front, hovering over the black-barrel fire with the paella-like pan on top, is the self-proclaimed **Queen of the Market,** Thérèse (tehr-ehz). When she's not looking for a husband, Thérèse is cooking *socca,* Nice's chickpea crêpe specialty (until about 13:00). Spend €3 for a wad of *socca* (careful—it's hot, but good). If she doesn't have a pan out, that means it's on its way (watch for the frequent scooter deliveries). Wait in line...or else it'll be gone when you return.

• *Continue down cours Saleya. The golden building that seals the end of the square is where Henri Matisse spent 17 years with a brilliant view onto Nice's world. Turn left a block before the end of the square and head down...*

Rue de la Poissonnerie: Look up at the first floor of the first building on your right. **Adam and Eve** are squaring off, each holding a zucchini-like gourd. This scene (post-apple) represents the annual rapprochement in Nice to make up for the sins of a too-much-fun Carnival (Mardi Gras). Residents of Nice have partied hard during Carnival for more than 700 years.

A few steps away, check out the small **Baroque church** (Notre-Dame-de-l'Annonciation) dedicated to St. Rita, the patron saint of desperate causes. She holds a special place in locals' hearts, making this the most popular church in Nice.

• *Turn right on the next street, where you'll pass Old Nice's most happening café/bar (Distilleries Ideales), with a lively happy hour (18:00-20:00) and a Pirates-of-the-Caribbean–style interior. Now turn left on "Right" Street (rue Droite), and enter an area that feels like a Little Naples.*

Rue Droite: In the Middle Ages, this straight, skinny street provided the most direct route from wall to wall, or river to sea. Stop at **Espuno's bakery** (at place du Jésus, closed Mon-Tue) and say *bonjour* to the friendly folks. Thirty years ago, this baker was voted the best in France—the trophies you see were earned for bread-making, not bowling. His son now runs the place. Notice the firewood stacked by the oven. Try the house specialty, *tourte aux blettes* (pastry stuffed with pine nuts, raisins, and white beets).

Farther along, at #28, Thérèse (whom you met earlier) cooks her *socca* in the wood-fired oven here before she carts it to her barrel on cours Saleya. The balconies of the mansion in the next block mark the **Palais Lascaris** (1647, gorgeous at night), a rare souvenir from one of Nice's most prestigious families. It's worth popping inside for its Baroque Italian architecture, antique musical instruments, tapestries, and furniture (free, Wed-Mon 10:00-18:00, closed Tue). Look up and make faces back at the guys under the balconies.

• *Turn left on rue de la Loge, then left again on rue Centrale, to reach...*

Place Rossetti: The most Italian of Nice's piazzas, place Rossetti feels more like Roma than Nice. This square comes alive after dark. **Fenocchio** is popular for its many gelato flavors, ranging from classic to innovative (daily March-Nov 9:00-24:00; mouthwatering preview at www.fenocchio.fr). Walk to the fountain and stare back at the church. This is the **Cathedral of St. Réparate**—an unassuming building for a major city's cathedral. It was relocated here in the 1500s, when Castle Hill was temporarily converted to military-only. The name comes from Nice's patron saint, a teenage virgin named Réparate whose martyred body floated to Nice in the fourth century accompanied by angels. The interior of the cathedral gushes Baroque, a response to the Protestant Reformation. With the Catholic Church's Counter-Reformation, the theatrical energy of churches was cranked up—with re-energized, high-powered saints and eye-popping decor.

• *Our walk is over. Castle Hill is straight up the stepped lane opposite the cathedral.*

Sights in Nice

Walks and Beach Time

▲▲▲**Promenade des Anglais**—Welcome to the Riviera. There's something for everyone along this four-mile-long seafront circus. Watch the Europeans at play, admire the azure Mediterranean, anchor yourself on a blue seat, and prop your feet up on the made-to-order guardrail. Later in the day, come back to join the evening parade of tans along the promenade.

The broad sidewalks of the promenade des Anglais ("walkway of the English") were financed by upper-crust English tourists who wanted a safe place to stroll and admire the view. The walk was done in marble in 1822 for aristocrats who didn't want to dirty their shoes or smell the fishy gravel. Strolling like a belle époque English aristocrat, visit the following sights along the promenade to Castle Hill (starting at the pink-domed Hôtel Negresco). This walk is ideally done at sunset, as a pre-dinner stroll.

Hôtel Negresco—Nice's finest hotel is also a historic monument, offering up the city's most expensive beds (see "Sleeping in Nice," later) and a free "museum" interior (always open—provided you're dressed decently, absolutely no beach attire). The hotel underwent a massive renovation in 2010, so expect some changes to the following description.

March straight through the lobby (as if you're staying here) into the exquisite **Salon Royal,** a cozy place for a drink and a frequent host to art exhibits (opens at 11:00). The chandelier hanging from the Eiffel-built dome is made of 16,000 pieces of crystal. It was built in France for the Russian czar's Moscow palace...but because of the Bolshevik Revolution in 1917, he couldn't take delivery. Read the explanation of the bucolic dome scene, painted in 1913 for the hotel, then saunter around the perimeter counterclockwise. If the bar door is open (after about 15:00), wander up the marble steps for a look. Farther along, nip into the toilets for either an early 20th-century powder room or a Battle of Waterloo experience. The chairs nearby were typical of the age (cones of silence for an afternoon nap sitting up).

Bay of Angels (Baie des Anges)—Grab a blue chair and face the sea. The body of Nice's patron saint, Réparate, was supposedly escorted into this bay by angels in the fourth century. To your right is where you might have been escorted into France—Nice's airport, built on a massive landfill. On that tip of land way beyond the runway is Cap d'Antibes. Until 1860, Antibes and Nice were in different countries—Antibes was French, but Nice was a protectorate of the Italian kingdom of Savoy-Piedmont, a.k.a. the Kingdom of Sardinia. (During that period, the Var River—just west of Nice—was the geographic border between these two peoples.) In 1850, the people here spoke Italian and ate pasta. As Italy was uniting, the region was given a choice: Join the new country of Italy or join good old France (which was enjoying good times under the rule of Napoleon III). The vast majority voted in 1860 to go French...and voilà!

The first green hill to your left (Castle Hill) marks the end of this walk. Farther left lies Villefranche-sur-Mer (marked by the tower at land's end, and home to lots of millionaires), then Monaco (which you can't see, with more millionaires), then Italy (with lots of, uh, Italians). Behind you are the foothills of the Alps (Alpes Maritimes), which trap threatening clouds, ensuring that the Côte d'Azur enjoys sunshine more than 300 days each year. Though half a million people live here, pollution is carefully treated—the water is routinely tested and very clean.

Stroll the promenade with the sea starboard, and contemplate beach time on your way to the Albert 1er Park.

Beaches—Dig your feet into the smooth pebbles and consider your options: you can play beach volleyball, table tennis, or *boules;* rent paddleboats, personal watercraft, or windsurfing equipment; explore ways to use your zoom lens and pretend you're a paparazzo; or snooze on a comfy beach bed.

To rent a spot on the beach, compare rates, as prices vary—beaches on the east end of the bay are usually cheaper (chair and mattress—*chaise longue* and *transat*-€12-18, umbrella-€3-5, towel-€4). Some hotels have special deals with certain beaches for discounted rentals (check with your hotel for details). Consider having lunch in your bathing suit (€12 salads and pizzas in bars and restaurants all along the beach). Or, for a peaceful café au lait on the Mediterranean, stop here first thing in the morning before the crowds hit. *Plage Publique* signs explain the 15 beach no-nos (translated into English).

Albert 1er Park—The park is named for the Belgian king who enjoyed wintering here. While the English came first, the Belgians and Russians were also big fans of 19th-century Nice. That tall statue at the edge of the park commemorates the 100-year anniversary of Nice's union with France.

If you detour from the promenade into the park and continue down the center of the grassy strip, you'll be walking over Nice's river, the Paillon (covered since the 1800s). For centuries this river was Nice's natural defense to the north and west (the sea protected the south, and Castle Hill defended the east). Imagine the fortified wall that ran along its length from the hills to the sea. With the arrival of tourism in the 1800s, Nice expanded over and beyond the river (toward the train station).

▲**Castle Hill (Colline du Château)**—This hill—in an otherwise flat city center—offers sensational views over Nice, the port (to the east), the foothills of the Alps, and the Mediterranean. The views are best early or at sunset, or whenever the weather's really clear (park closes at 20:00 in summer, earlier off-season). The city of Nice was first settled here by Greeks circa 400 B.C. In the Middle Ages, a massive castle stood there, with turrets, high walls, and soldiers at the ready. Nice's medieval seawall ran between cours Saleya and quai des Etats-Unis. With the river guarding one side and the sea the other, this mountain fortress seemed strong— until Louis XIV leveled it in 1706. Today, you'll find a waterfall, a playground, two cafés (with fair prices), and a cemetery—but no castle—on Castle Hill. You can get to the top by foot, by elevator (€0.70 one-way, €1.10 round-trip, runs daily 10:00-19:00, until 20:00 in summer, next to beachfront Hôtel Suisse), or by pricey tourist train (described under "Tours in Nice," earlier).

Nice's port, where you'll find Trans Côte d'Azur's boat cruises (also described in "Tours in Nice"), is just below on the east edge of Castle Hill.

Bike Routes—Meandering along Nice's seafront on foot or by bike is a must. To rev up the pace of your saunter, rent a bike and glide along the coast in both directions (about 30 minutes each way; for rental info see "Helpful Hints," earlier). Both of the following paths start along promenade des Anglais.

The path to the **west** stops just before the airport, at perhaps the most scenic *boules* courts in France. Pause here to watch the old-timers while away their afternoon tossing shiny metal balls. If you take the path heading **east,** you'll curve below Castle Hill—passing a scenic cape and the town's memorial to both world wars—to the harbor of Nice, with a chance to survey some fancy yachts. Pedal around the harbor and follow the coast past the Corsica ferry terminal (you'll need to carry your bike up a flight of steps). From there the path leads you to an appealing tree-lined residential district.

Museums and Monuments

To bring culture to the masses, the city of Nice has nixed the entry fee to all municipal museums—so it's free to enter all of the following sights except the Chagall Museum and the Russian Cathedral. Cool.

The first two museums (Chagall and Matisse) are a long walk northeast of Nice's city center. Because they're in the same direction and served by the same bus line (buses #15 and #22 stop at both museums), it makes sense to visit them on the same trip. From place Masséna, the Chagall Museum is a 10-minute bus ride or 30-minute walk, and the Matisse Museum is a 20-minute bus ride or one-hour walk.

▲▲▲Chagall Museum (Musée National Marc Chagall)— Even if you're suspicious of modern art, this museum—with the world's largest collection of Marc Chagall's work in captivity—is a delight. After World War II, Chagall returned from the United States to settle in Vence, not far from Nice. Between 1954 and 1967, he painted a cycle of 17 large murals designed for, and donated to, this museum. These paintings, inspired by the biblical books of Genesis, Exodus, and the Song of Songs, make up the "nave," or core, of what Chagall called the "House of Brotherhood."

Each painting is a lighter-than-air collage of images that draw from Chagall's Russian folk-village youth, his Jewish heritage, biblical themes, and his feeling that he existed somewhere between heaven and earth. He believed that the Bible was a synonym for nature, and that color and biblical themes were key ingredients for understanding God's love for his creation. Chagall's brilliant blues and reds celebrate nature, as do his spiritual and folk themes. Notice the focus on couples. To Chagall, humans loving one another mirrored God's love of creation.

Cost and Hours: €7.50, free first Sun of the month (but crowded), open Wed-Mon 10:00-17:00, May-Oct until 18:00, closed Tue year-round, avenue Docteur Ménard, tel. 04 93 53 87 20, www.musee-chagall.fr.

Getting to the Chagall Museum: You can reach the museum, located on avenue Docteur Ménard, by bus or on foot.

Buses #15 and #22 serve the Chagall Museum from the Masséna Guitry stop, near place Masséna (5/hour Mon-Sat, 3/hour Sun, €1; stop faces eastbound on rue Sacha Guitry, a block east of Galeries Lafayette department store—see map on pages 532-533). The museum's bus stop (called Musée Chagall, shown on the bus shelter) is on boulevard de Cimiez (walk uphill from the stop to find the museum).

To **walk** from central Nice to the Chagall Museum (30 minutes), go to the train-station end of avenue Jean Médecin and turn right onto boulevard Raimbaldi. Walk four long blocks along the elevated road, then turn left onto avenue Raymond Comboul, and follow *Musée Chagall* signs.

Leaving the Museum: To take **buses** #15 or #22 back to downtown Nice, turn right out of the museum, then make another right down boulevard de Cimiez, and catch the bus heading

NICE

downhill. To continue on to the Matisse Museum, catch buses #15 or #22 using the uphill stop located across the street. **Taxis** usually wait in front of the museum. It's about €12 for a ride to the city center.

To **walk** to the train station area from the museum (20 minutes), turn left out of the museum grounds, then left again on the street behind it (avenue Docteur Ménard). As the street bends right, take the ramps and staircases down on your left, turn left at the bottom, cross under the freeway and the train tracks, then turn right onto boulevard Raimbaldi to reach the station.

Cuisine Art and WCs: An idyllic café (€10 salads and *plats*) awaits in the corner of the garden. A spick-and-span WC is next to the ticket desk (there's one inside, too).

▲**Matisse Museum (Musée Matisse)**—This small museum contains the world's largest collection of Henri Matisse paintings. It offers a painless introduction to the artist, whose style was shaped by Mediterranean light and by fellow Côte d'Azur artists Pablo Picasso and Pierre-Auguste Renoir. The collection—which includes several early paintings, models of his famous Rosary Chapel, papier mâché cut-outs, and personal objects—lacks a certain je ne sais quoi when compared to the Chagall Museum.

Matisse, the master of leaving things out, could suggest a woman's body with a single curvy line—letting the viewer's mind fill in the rest. Ignoring traditional 3-D perspective, he used simple dark outlines saturated with bright blocks of color to create recognizable but simplified scenes composed into a decorative pattern to express nature's serene beauty. You don't look "through" a Matisse canvas, like a window; you look "at" it, like wallpaper.

Matisse understood how colors and shapes affect us emotionally. He could create either shocking, clashing works (Fauvism) or geometrical, balanced, harmonious ones (later pieces). While other modern artists reveled in purely abstract design, Matisse (almost) always kept the subject matter at least vaguely recognizable. He used unreal colors and distorted lines not just to portray what an object looks like, but to express its inner nature (even inanimate objects). Meditating on his paintings helps you connect with nature—or so Matisse hoped.

Cost and Hours: Free, Wed-Mon 10:00-18:00, closed Tue, 164 avenue des Arènes de Cimiez, tel. 04 93 81 08 08, www.musee-matisse-nice.org. The museum is housed in a beautiful Mediterranean mansion set in an olive grove amid the ruins of the Roman city of Cemenelum.

Getting to the Matisse Museum: It's a long uphill walk from the city center. Take the bus (details follow) or a cab (about €15 from promenade des Anglais). Once here, walk into the park to find the pink villa. **Buses #15, #17, and #22** offer regular service to the Matisse Museum from just off place Masséna on rue Sacha Guitry (Masséna Guitry stop, a block east of the Galeries Lafayette department store—see map on pages 532-533; 20 minutes; note that bus #17 does not stop at the Chagall Museum). **Bus #20** connects the port to the museum. On any bus, get off at the Arènes-Matisse bus stop.

Leaving the Museum: When leaving the museum, find the stop for buses #15 and #22 (frequent service downtown and stops en route at the Chagall Museum): Turn left out of the Matisse Museum into the park and keep straight, exiting the park at the Archeological Museum, then turn right. Pass the bus stop across the street (#17 goes to the city center but not the Chagall Museum, and #20 goes to the port), and walk to the small roundabout. Cross the roundabout to find the shelter (facing downhill) for buses #15 and #22 by the apartment building with the oval portico (see map on pages 504-505).

▲**Modern and Contemporary Art Museum (Musée d'Art Moderne et d'Art Contemporain)**—This ultramodern museum features an explosively colorful, far-out, yet manageable collection focused on American and European-American artists from the 1960s and 1970s (Pop Art and New Realism styles are highlighted). The exhibits cover three floors and include a few works by Andy Warhol, Roy Lichtenstein, and Jean Tinguely, and small models of Christo's famous wrappings. You'll find rooms dedicated to Robert Indiana, Yves Klein, and Niki de Saint Phalle (my favorite). The temporary exhibits can be as appealing to modern-art-lovers as the permanent collection: Check the museum website for what's playing. And don't leave without exploring the rooftop terrace.

Cost and Hours: Free, Tue-Sun 10:00-18:00, closed Mon, about a 15-minute walk from place Masséna, near bus station on promenade des Arts, tel. 04 93 62 61 62, www.mamac-nice.org.

Fine Arts Museum (Musée des Beaux-Arts)—Housed in a sumptuous Riviera villa with lovely gardens, this museum holds 6,000 works from the 17th to 20th centuries. Start on the first floor and work your way up to experience an appealing array of paintings by Monet, Sisley, Bonnard, and Raoul Dufy, as well as a few sculptures by Rodin and Carpeaux (free, Tue-Sun 10:00-18:00, closed Mon, 3 avenue des Baumettes, inconveniently located at the western end of Nice, take buses #12 or #23 from the train station or bus #38 from the bus station to the Rosa Bonheur stop, tel. 04 92 15 28 28, www.musee-beaux-arts-nice.org).

Molinard Perfume Museum—The Molinard family has been making perfume in Grasse (about an hour's drive from Nice) since 1849. Their Nice store has a small museum in the rear that illustrates the story of their industry. Back when people believed water spread the plague (Louis XIV supposedly bathed less than once a year), doctors advised people to rub fragrances into their skin and then powder their body. At that time, perfume was a necessity of everyday life.

Tiny Room 1 shows photos of the local flowers, roots, and other parts of plants used in perfume production. Room 2 explains the earliest (18th-century) production method. Petals would be laid out in the sun on a bed of animal fat, which would absorb the essence of the flowers as they baked. Petals were replaced daily for two months until the fat was saturated. Models and old photos show the later distillation process (660 pounds of lavender produced only a quarter-gallon of essence). Perfume is "distilled like cognac and then aged like wine." The small bottles on the table in the corner demonstrate the role of the "blender" and the perfume mastermind called the "nose" (who knows best). Notice the photos of these lab-coat–wearing perfectionists. Of the 150 real "noses" in the world, more than 100 are French. You are welcome to enjoy the testing bottles.

Cost and Hours: Free, daily July-Aug 10:00-19:00, Sept-June 10:00-13:00 & 14:00-18:30, sometimes closed Mon off-season, just between beach and place Masséna at 20 rue St. François de Paule, see map on pages 526-527, tel. 04 93 62 90 50, www.molinard.com.

Other Nice Museums—Both of these museums are acceptable rainy-day options, and free of charge.

The **Archaeological Museum** (Musée Archéologique) displays various objects from the Romans' occupation of this region. It's convenient—just below the Matisse Museum—but has little of interest to anyone but ancient Rome aficionados. You also get access to the Roman bath ruins...which are, sadly, overgrown with weeds (free, very limited information in English, Wed-Mon 10:00-18:00, closed Tue, near Matisse Museum at 160 avenue des Arènes de Cimiez, tel. 04 93 81 59 57, www.musee-archeologique-nice .org).

The **Masséna Museum** (Musée Masséna), like Nice's main square, is named in honor of Jean-André Masséna, a commander during France's Revolutionary and Napoleonic Wars. This beachfront mansion is worth a gander for its lavish decor and lovely gardens alone (pick up your free ticket at the boutique just outside).

The ground floor shows rotating exhibits, and the upstairs floors offer a folk-museum–like look at Nice through the years, with antique posters, models of the old casino destroyed in World War II, many 18th- and 19th-century paintings (mostly by artists from Nice), and other collections relevant to the city's tumultuous history. Find the images of Nice before they covered the river that runs under place Masséna. You'll also come across some Napoleon paraphernalia; Josephine's cape and tiara are impressive, and I'd look good in Napoleon's vest. Check out the paintings of the Italian

NICE

patriot and Nice favorite Giuseppe Garibaldi, as well as his burial sheet (free, daily 10:00-18:00, 35 promenade des Anglais, tel. 04 93 91 19 10).

▲**Russian Cathedral (Cathédrale Russe)**—Nice's Russian Orthodox church—claimed to be the finest outside Russia—is worth a visit. Five hundred rich Russian families wintered in Nice in the late 19th century. Since they couldn't pray in a Catholic church, the community needed a worthy Orthodox house of worship. Czar Nicholas I's widow provided the land (which required tearing down her house), and Czar Nicholas II gave this church to the Russian community in 1912. (A few years later, Russian comrades who *didn't* winter on the Riviera assassinated him.) Here in the land of olives and anchovies, these proud onion domes seem odd. But, I imagine, so did those old Russians.

Step inside (pick up English info sheet). The one-room interior is filled with icons and candles, and the old Russian music adds to the ambience. The wall of icons (iconostasis) divides things between the spiritual world and the temporal world of the worshippers. Only the priest can walk between the two worlds, by using the "Royal Door." Take a close look at items lining the front (starting in the left corner). The angel with red boots and wings—the protector of the Romanov family—stands over a symbolic tomb of Christ. The tall black hammered-copper cross commemorates the massacre of Nicholas II and his family in 1918. Notice the Jesus icon to the right of the Royal Door. According to a priest here, as worshippers meditate, staring deep into the eyes of Jesus, they enter a lake where they find their soul. Surrounded by incense, chanting, and your entire community...it could happen. Farther to the right, the icon of the unhappy-looking Virgin and Child is decorated with semiprecious stones from the Ural Mountains. Artists worked a triangle into each iconic face—symbolic of the Trinity.

Cost and Hours: €3, Mon-Sat 9:00-12:00 & 14:30-18:00, Sun 14:30-18:00, until 17:00 off-season, chanted services Sat at 17:30 or 18:00, Sun at 10:00, no tourist visits during services, no short shorts, 17 boulevard du Tzarewitch, tel. 04 93 96 88 02, www .acor-nice.com. The park around the church stays open at lunch and makes a nice setting for picnics.

Getting to the Russian Cathedral: It's a 10-minute walk from the train station. Exit the station to the right onto avenue Thiers, turn right on avenue Gambetta, go under the freeway, and turn left following *Eglise Russe* signs. Or, from the station, take any bus heading west on avenue Thiers and get off at avenue Gambetta (then follow the previous directions).

Nightlife in Nice

Promenade des Anglais, cours Saleya, and rue Masséna are all worth an evening walk. Nice's bars play host to a happening late-night scene, filled with jazz, rock, and trolling singles. Most activity focuses on Old Nice. Rue de la Préfecture is ground zero for bar life, though place Rossetti and rue Droite are also good targets. **Distilleries Ideales** is a good place to start or end your evening, with a lively international crowd and a fun interior (where rues de la Poissonnerie and Barillerie meet, happy hour 18:00-20:00). **Wayne's Bar** is a happening spot for the younger, English-speaking backpacker crowd (15 rue Préfecture). Along the promenade des Anglais, the plush bar at **Hôtel Negresco** is fancy-cigar old English.

Plan on a cover charge or expensive drinks where music is involved. If you're out very late, avoid walking alone. Nice is well-known for its lively after-dark action.

Sleeping in Nice

Don't look for charm in Nice. Go for modern and clean, with a central location and, in summer, air-conditioning. The rates listed here are for April through October. Prices generally drop €15-30 from November through March but go sky-high during the Nice Carnival, the Cannes Film Festival, and the Grand Prix of Monaco. Between the film festival and the Grand Prix, the second half of May is very tight every year. Nice is also one of Europe's

---

Sleep Code

(€1 = about $1.40, country code: 33)
S = Single, **D** = Double/Twin, **T** = Triple, **Q** = Quad, **b** = bathroom, **s** = shower only, ***** = French hotel rating (0-4 stars). Hoteliers speak English, and hotels have elevators and accept credit cards unless otherwise noted.

To help you sort easily through these listings, I've divided the rooms into three categories based on the price for a standard double room with bath:

$$$ Higher Priced—Most rooms €110 or more.
  $$ Moderately Priced—Most rooms between €75-110.
    $ Lower Priced—Most rooms €75 or less.

Prices can change without notice; verify the hotel's current rates online or by email. For other updates, see www.ricksteves.com/update.

top convention cities, and June is convention month here. Reserve early if visiting May through August, especially during these times. For parking, ask your hotelier (several hotels have limited private parking), or see "Arrival in Nice—By Car" on page 506.

I've divided my sleeping recommendations into three areas: between the train station and Nice Etoile shopping center (easy access to the train station and Old Nice on the sleek new tramway, 20-minute walk to promenade des Anglais); between Nice Etoile and the sea (east of avenue Jean Médecin, good access to Old Nice and the sea at quai des Etats-Unis); and between boulevard Victor Hugo and the sea (a somewhat classier area, offering better access to the promenade des Anglais but longer walks to the train station and Old Nice). I've also listed a hotel near the airport and a hostel on the outskirts.

Check hotel websites for deals (which are more common at larger hotels).

Between the Train Station and Nice Etoile

This area offers Nice's cheapest sleeps, though most hotels near the station ghetto are overrun, overpriced, and loud. The following hotels are the pleasant exceptions (most are near avenue Jean Médecin), and are listed in order of proximity to the train station, going toward the beach.

$$ Hôtel Ibis Nice Centre Gare**, 100 yards to the right as you leave the station, gives those in need of train station access a secure refuge in this seedy area. It's modern, with two-star business comfort (Db-€90-105, air-con, Wi-Fi, bar, café, 14 avenue Thiers, tel. 04 93 88 85 85, fax 04 93 88 58 00, www.ibishotel.com, h1396@accor.com).

$$ At Hôtel Durante**, you know you're on the Mediterranean as soon as you enter this cheery, way-orange building with its rooms wrapped around a flowery courtyard. Every one of its quiet rooms overlooks a spacious and well-maintained patio/garden with an American-style Jacuzzi. The rooms are good enough (mostly big beds) and the price is right enough (Ds-€72-80, bigger Db-€100-150, Tb-€130-170, air-con, Wi-Fi, 16 avenue Durante, tel. 04 93 88 84 40, fax 04 93 87 77 76, www.hotel-durante.com, info@hotel-durante.com).

$$ Hôtel St. Georges**, five blocks from the station toward the sea, has a backyard garden, reasonably clean and comfortable high-ceilinged rooms, orange tones, blue halls, fair rates, and friendly Houssein at the reception (Sb-€85, Db-€85-100, Tb with 3 beds-€120, extra bed-€20, air-con, Wi-Fi, 7 avenue Georges Clemenceau, tel. 04 93 88 79 21, fax 04 93 16 22 85, www.hotel saintgeorges.fr, contact@hotelsaintgeorges.fr).

Nice Hotels

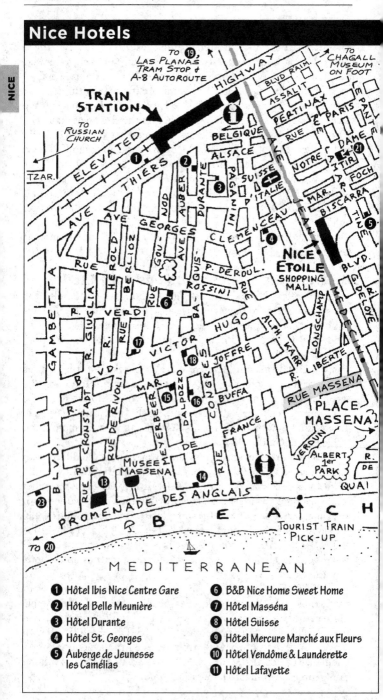

1. Hôtel Ibis Nice Centre Gare
2. Hôtel Belle Meunière
3. Hôtel Durante
4. Hôtel St. Georges
5. Auberge de Jeunesse les Camélias
6. B&B Nice Home Sweet Home
7. Hôtel Masséna
8. Hôtel Suisse
9. Hôtel Mercure Marché aux Fleurs
10. Hôtel Vendôme & Launderette
11. Hôtel Lafayette

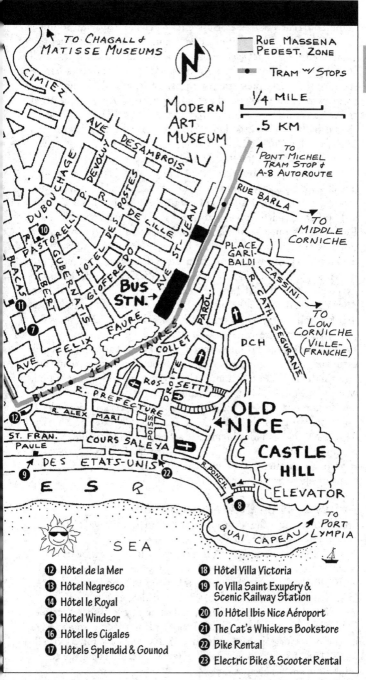

TO CHAGALL &
MATISSE MUSEUMS

RUE MASSENA
PEDEST. ZONE

TRAM W/ STOPS

¼ MILE
.5 KM

MODERN ART MUSEUM

TO PONT MICHEL TRAM STOP & A-8 AUTOROUTE

RUE BARLA

TO MIDDLE CORNICHE

PLACE GARIBALDI

CASSINI

BUS STN.

TO LOW CORNICHE (VILLEFRANCHE)

DCH

OLD NICE

CASTLE HILL

ELEVATOR

TO PORT LYMPIA

QUAI CAPEAU

SEA

⑫ Hôtel de la Mer
⑬ Hôtel Negresco
⑭ Hôtel le Royal
⑮ Hôtel Windsor
⑯ Hôtel les Cigales
⑰ Hôtels Splendid & Gounod

⑱ Hôtel Villa Victoria
⑲ To Villa Saint Exupéry & Scenic Railway Station
⑳ To Hôtel Ibis Nice Aéroport
㉑ The Cat's Whiskers Bookstore
㉒ Bike Rental
㉓ Electric Bike & Scooter Rental

$ Hôtel Belle Meunière*, in a fine old mansion built for Napoleon III's mistress, offers cheap beds and private rooms a block below the train station. Lively and youth hostel-esque, this simple but well-kept place attracts budget-minded travelers of all ages with basic-but-adequate rooms and charismatic Mademoiselle Marie-Pierre presiding (with perfect English). Tables in the front yard greet guests and provide opportunities to meet other travelers (bunk in 4-bed dorm-€23 with private bath, €18 with shared bath, Db-€60, includes breakfast, Wi-Fi, laundry service, 21 avenue Durante, tel. 04 93 88 66 15, fax 04 93 82 51 76, www.bellemeuniere.com, hotel.belle.meuniere@cegetel.net).

$ Auberge de Jeunesse les Camélias is a laid-back youth hostel with a great location and modern facilities. Rooms accommodate between four and eight people in bunk beds (136 beds in all) and come with showers and sinks—WCs are down the hall. Reservations must be made on the website in advance or on the same day by phone. If you don't have a reservation, call by 10:00 or, better, try to snag a bunk in person. The place is popular but worth a try for last-minute availability (€23/bed, one-time €15 extra charge without hostel membership, includes breakfast, rooms closed 11:00-15:00 but can leave bags, Internet access, laundry, kitchen, safes, bar, 3 rue Spitalieri, tel. 04 93 62 15 54, www.hihostels.com, nice-camelias@fuaj.org).

$ B&B Nice Home Sweet Home is a great value. Gentle Genevieve (a.k.a. Jennifer) Levert rents out three large rooms and one small single in her home. Her rooms are simply decorated, with high ceilings, big windows, lots of light, and space to spread out. One room comes with private bath; otherwise, it's just like at home...down the hall (S-€31-38, D-€61-70, Db-€65-75, Tb-€74-84, Q-€80-90, includes breakfast, air-con units available in summer, no elevator, two floors up, washer/dryer-€5, kitchen access, 35 rue Rossini at intersection with rue Auber, mobile 06 19 66 03 63, www.nicehomesweethome.com, glevert@free.fr).

Between Nice Etoile and the Sea

These hotels are either on the sea or within an easy walk of it, and are the closest to Old Nice.

$$$ Hôtel Masséna****, in a classy building a few blocks from place Masséna, is a "professional" hotel (popular with tour groups) with 100 rooms at almost-reasonable rates and mod public spaces (5 small Db-€160, larger Db-€200, still larger Db-€295, extra bed-€30, skip the €20 breakfast, call same day for special rates—prices drop big time when hotel is not full, sixth-floor rooms have balconies, reserve parking ahead-€25/day, 58 rue Giofreddo, tel. 04 92 47 88 88, fax 04 92 47 88 89, www.hotel-massena-nice.com, info@hotel-massena-nice.com).

$$$ Hôtel Suisse***, below Castle Hill, has Nice's best ocean and city views for the money, and is surprisingly quiet given the busy street below. Rooms are quite comfortable, the decor is classy, and the staff is professional. There's no reason to sleep here if you don't land a view, so I've listed prices only for view rooms—many of which have balconies (Db-€170-205, extra bed-€36, breakfast-€15, 15 quai Rauba Capeu, tel. 04 92 17 39 00, fax 04 93 85 30 70, www.hotels-ocre-azur.com, hotel.suisse@hotels-ocre-azur.com).

$$$ Hôtel Mercure Marché aux Fleurs*** is ideally situated across from the sea and behind cours Saleya. Rooms are tastefully designed and well-maintained (some with beds in a loft). Prices are reasonable, though rates vary dramatically depending on demand: Be sure to check their website for deals (standard Db-€135, superior Db-€165 and worth the extra euros, sea view-€50 extra, air-con, 91 quai des Etats-Unis, tel. 04 93 85 74 19, fax 04 93 13 90 94, www.hotelmercure.com, h0962@accor.com). Don't confuse this Mercure with the four others in Nice.

$$$ Hôtel Vendôme*** gives you a whiff of the belle époque, with pink pastels, high ceilings, and grand staircases in a mansion set off the street. Its public spaces are delightful. The rooms are modern and come in all sizes; the best have balconies (on floors 4 and 5)—request *une chambre avec balcon* (Sb-€115, Db-€150, Tb-€165, air-con, Internet access and Wi-Fi, book ahead for limited parking-€12/day, 26 rue Pastorelli, tel. 04 93 62 00 77, fax 04 93 13 40 78, www.vendome-hotel-nice.com, contact@vendome-hotel-nice.com).

$$$ Hôtel Lafayette***, in a handy location a block behind the Galeries Lafayette department store, is a great value. The hotel may look average from the outside, but inside it's comfortable and homey, with 18 well-designed, mostly spacious rooms, all one floor up from the street. It's family-run by Kirill, Tina, and little Victor. Rooms not overlooking rue de l'Hôtel des Postes are quieter and worth requesting (standard Db-€105-120, spacious Db-€115-130, extra bed-€24, coffee service in rooms, air-con, no elevator, 32 rue de l'Hôtel des Postes, tel. 04 93 85 17 84, fax 04 93 80 47 56, www.hotellafayettenice.com, info@hotellafayettenice.com).

$$ Hôtel de la Mer** is a humble place with an enviable position overlooking place Masséna, just steps from Old Nice (of my listings, it's among the closest to the old town). Although this small hotel has a few rough edges, new (and very helpful) owner Pierre seems to be on top of things, the beds are firm, and it's quiet (small Db-€100, bigger Db facing place Masséna-€130, Tb-€145, air-con, Wi-Fi, 4 place Masséna, tel. 04 93 92 09 10, fax 04 93 85 00 64, www.hoteldelamernice.com, hotel.mer@wanadoo.fr).

NICE

NICE

Old Nice Hotels & Restaurants

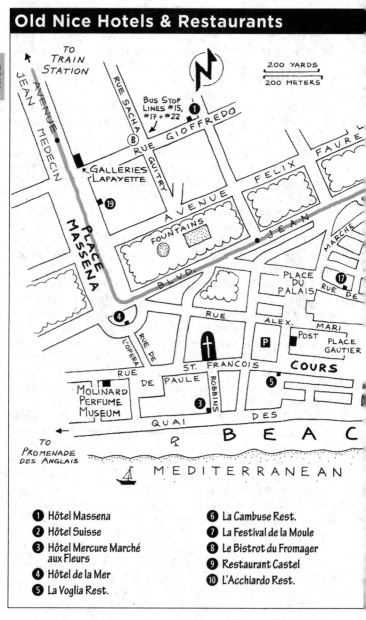

TO TRAIN STATION

200 YARDS
200 METERS

BUS STOP LINES #15, #17 + #22

RUE GIOFFREDO

RUE SACHA GUITRY

JEAN MEDECIN AVENUE

GALLERIES LAFAYETTE

PLACE MASSENA

AVENUE JEAN

FELIX FAURE

FOUNTAINS

BLVD

MARCHE

PLACE DU PALAIS

RUE DE

RUE

ALEX.

MARI

POST

PLACE GAUTIER

RUE DE L'OPERA

ST. FRANCOIS

COURS

RUE DE PAULE

ROBBINS

MOLINARD PERFUME MUSEUM

QUAI

DES

R

BEAC

TO PROMENADE DES ANGLAIS

MEDITERRANEAN

1 Hôtel Massena
2 Hôtel Suisse
3 Hôtel Mercure Marché aux Fleurs
4 Hôtel de la Mer
5 La Voglia Rest.

6 La Cambuse Rest.
7 La Festival de la Moule
8 Le Bistrot du Fromager
9 Restaurant Castel
10 L'Acchiardo Rest.

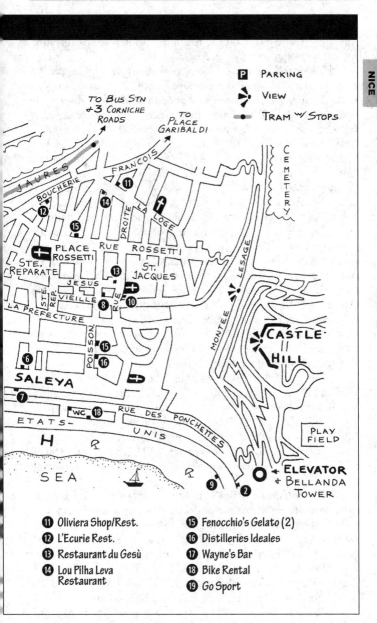

P — PARKING

View

Tram w/ Stops

⑪ Oliviera Shop/Rest.
⑫ L'Ecurie Rest.
⑬ Restaurant du Gesù
⑭ Lou Pilha Leva Restaurant

⑮ Fenocchio's Gelato (2)
⑯ Distilleries Ideales
⑰ Wayne's Bar
⑱ Bike Rental
⑲ Go Sport

Between Boulevard Victor Hugo and the Sea

These hotels are either on the beach or within walking distance, and closest to promenade des Anglais.

$$$ Hôtel Negresco**** owns Nice's most prestigious address on promenade des Anglais and knows it. Still, it's the kind of place that, if you were to splurge just once in your life... Rooms are opulent (see page 512 for more description), and tips are expected (viewless Db-€360, Db with sea view-€460-580, view suite-€770-1,900, breakfast-€30, Old World bar, 37 promenade des Anglais, tel. 04 93 16 64 00, fax 04 93 88 35 68, www.hotel-negresco-nice .com, reservations@hotel-negresco.com).

$$$ Hôtel le Royal*** stands shoulder-to-shoulder on promenade des Anglais with the big boys (the Negresco, Palais, and Westminster hotels). With 140 rooms, big lounges, and hallways that stretch forever, it feels a bit institutional. But the prices are reasonable considering the solid air-conditioned comfort and terrific location—and sometimes they have rooms when others don't (viewless Db-€125, Db with sea view-€155-175, bigger view room-€175-195 and worth it, extra person-€25, 23 promenade des Anglais, tel. 04 93 16 43 00, fax 04 93 16 43 02, www.hotel-royal -nice.cote.azur.fr, royal@vacancesbleues.com).

$$$ Hôtel Windsor*** is a snazzy garden retreat that feels like a cross between a modern-art museum and a health spa. Some of the contemporary rooms, designed by modern artists, defy explanation. It has a full-service bar, a small outdoor swimming pool and gym (both free for guests), an €11 sauna, €55 massages, and full meal service in the cool, shaded garden area (standard Db-€125, bigger Db-€155, big Db with balcony-€180, extra bed-€20, rooms over garden worth the higher price, air-con, Internet access and Wi-Fi, 11 rue Dalpozzo, tel. 04 93 88 59 35, fax 04 93 88 94 57, www.hotelwindsornice.com, reservation@hotelwindsornice .com).

$$$ Hôtel les Cigales*** is one of my favorites. It's a smart little pastel place with tasteful decor, 19 plush rooms (most with tub-showers), air-conditioning, and a nifty upstairs terrace, all well-managed by friendly Mr. Valentino, with Veronique and Elaine. Book directly through the hotel and show this book for a surprise treat on arrival (standard Db-€135-160, Tb-€160-180, free Wi-Fi, 16 rue Dalpozzo, tel. 04 97 03 10 70, fax 04 97 03 10 71, www.hotel-lescigales.com, info@hotel-lescigales.com).

$$$ Hôtel Splendid**** is a worthwhile splurge if you miss your Marriott. The panoramic rooftop pool, Jacuzzi, bar, restaurant, and breakfast room almost justify the cost...but throw in solid rooms (four of the six floors are non-smoking), a free gym, spa services, and air-conditioning, and you're as good as home

(Db-€235, deluxe Db with terrace-€280, suites-€360-410, breakfast-€16, check website for special deals, parking-€24/day, 50 boulevard Victor Hugo, tel. 04 93 16 41 00, fax 04 93 16 42 70, www.splendid-nice.com, info@splendid-nice.com).

$$$ Hôtel Gounod*** is behind Hôtel Splendid, and because the two share the same owners, Gounod's guests are allowed free access to Splendid's pool, Jacuzzi, and other amenities. Don't let the lackluster lobby fool you—most rooms are richly decorated, with high ceilings and air-conditioning (Db-€170, palatial 4-person suites-€270, parking-€15/day, 3 rue Gounod, tel. 04 93 16 42 00, fax 04 93 88 23 84, www.gounod-nice.com, info@gounod-nice.com).

$$$ Hôtel Villa Victoria*** is managed by cheery Marlena, who welcomes travelers into this spotless, classy old building with a green awning and an open, attractive lobby overlooking a generous garden. Rooms are traditional and well-kept, with space to stretch out (streetside Db-€150, garden-side Db-€180, Tb-€160-185, suites-€210-235, breakfast-€15, air-con, minibar, Wi-Fi, parking-€18, 33 boulevard Victor Hugo, tel. 04 93 88 39 60, fax 04 93 88 07 98, www.villa-victoria.com, contact@villa-victoria.com).

Barely Beyond Nice

$ Villa Saint Exupéry, a service-oriented hostel, is a haven two miles north of the city center. Its amenities and 60 comfortable, spick-and-span rooms create a friendly climate for budget-minded travelers of any age. Often filled with energetic youth, the place can be noisy. There are units for one, two, and up to six people. Many have private bathrooms and views of the Mediterranean—some come with balconies. You'll also find a laundry room, complete kitchen facilities, and a lively bar. There's easy Internet access with a wall of computers in the lobby and Wi-Fi in all the rooms (bed in dorm-€30/person, S-€50-70, Db-€60-90, Tb-€115, includes big breakfast, no curfew; take bus #23 from the airport or train station, or take the tram—direction: Las Planas—to the Compte de Falicon stop and walk 10 minutes; ask about free pickup at train station, 22 avenue Gravier, toll-free tel. 08 00 30 74 09, fax 04 92 09 82 94, www.vsaint.com, reservations@vsaint.com).

Closer to the Airport

$$ Hôtel Ibis Nice Aéroport** offers a handy port in the storm for those with early flights or just stopping in for a single night (Db-€78-98 when no special events in town, parking-€7, 359 promenade des Anglais, tel. 04 93 83 30 30, fax 04 93 21 19 43, www.ibisnice.com, reception@ibisnice.com). Hotel chains Etap, Campanile, and Novotel also have hotels at the airport.

Eating in Nice

Remember, you're in a resort. Seek ambience and fun, and lower your palate's standards. Italian is a low-risk and regional cuisine. The listed restaurants are concentrated in neighborhoods close to my recommended hotels. Several offer fixed-price, multicourse meals *(menus)*. Promenade des Anglais is ideal for picnic dinners on warm, languid evenings. Old Nice has the best and busiest dining atmosphere (and best range of choices), while the Nice Etoile area is more local, convenient, and also offers a good range of choices. To feast cheaply, eat on rue Droite in Old Nice, or explore the area around the train station. Allow yourself one dinner at a beachfront restaurant in Nice, and for terribly touristy trolling, wander the wall-to-wall eateries lining rue Masséna. Yuck.

In Old Nice

Nice's dinner scene converges on cours Saleya, which is entertaining enough in itself to make the generally mediocre food a good deal. It's a fun, festive spot to compare tans and mussels. Even if you're eating elsewhere, wander through here in the evening. For locations, see the map on pages 526-527.

La Voglia is all about good Italian food at fair prices. It's popular with locals, lively, and offers fun inside and outside seating (€14 pizza and pasta, open daily, at the western edge of cours Saleya at 2 rue St Francois de Paule, tel. 04 93 80 99 16).

La Cambuse is a classy place by cours Saleya standards, and may be the only restaurant along here that doesn't try to reel in passersby. The cuisine is Franco-Italian with an emphasis on Italy. There's attentive service and good seating indoors and out (€14 starters, €18-24 *plats*, 5 cours Saleya, tel. 04 93 80 82 40).

La Festival de la Moule is a simple, touristy place for lovers of mussels (or for just plain hungry folks). For €14 you get all-you-can-eat mussels (11 sauces possible) and fries in a youthful outdoor setting. Let twins Alex and Marc tempt you with their spicy and cream sauces—be daring and try several (other bistro fare available, across the square from la Cambuse, 20 cours Saleya, tel. 04 93 62 02 12).

Le Bistrot du Fromager's owner is crazy about cheese and wine. Come here to escape the heat and dine in cool vaulted cellars surrounded by shelves of wine. All dishes use cheese as their base ingredient, although you'll also find pasta, ham, and salmon (with cheese, of course). This is a good choice for vegetarians (€10 entrees, €12-14 *plats*, €6 desserts, closed Sun, just off place de Gésu at 29 rue Benoit Bunico, tel. 04 93 13 07 83).

Restaurant Castel is a fun eat-on-the-beach option, thanks to its location at the very east end of Nice looking over the bay.

Dining here, you almost expect Don Ho to step up and grab a mic. Lose the city hustle and bustle by dropping down the steps below Castle Hill. The views are unforgettable even if the cuisine is not; you can even have lunch at your beach chair if you've rented one here (€10/half-day, €14/day). Dinner here is best: Arrive before sunset and find a waterfront table perfectly positioned to watch evening swimmers get in their last laps as the sky turns pink and city lights flicker on. Linger long enough to merit the few extra euros the place charges (€16 salads and pastas, €20-26 main courses, 8 quai des Etats-Unis, tel. 04 93 85 22 66).

Dining Cheap *à la Niçoise*

Try at least one of these five places—not just because they're terrific budget options, but primarily because they offer authentic *niçoise* cuisine.

L'Acchiardo, hidden away in the heart of Old Nice, is a dark and homey eatery that does a good job mixing a loyal clientele with hungry tourists. Its simple, hearty *niçoise* cuisine is served for fair prices by gentle Monsieur Acchiardo. The small plaque under the menu outside says it's been run by father and son since 1927 (€7 starters, €14 *plats*, €5 desserts, cash only, closed Sat-Sun, indoor seating only, 38 rue Droite, tel. 04 93 85 51 16).

Oliviera venerates the French olive. This shop/restaurant sells a variety of oils, offers free tastings, and serves a menu of dishes paired with specific oils (think of a wine pairing). Welcoming owner Nadim, who speaks excellent English, knows all of his producers personally and provides "Olive Oil 101" explanations with his tastings (best if you buy something afterward or have a meal). You'll learn how passionate he is about his products, and once you come to taste, you'll want to stay and eat (€14-22 main dishes, Tue-Sat 10:00-22:00, closed Sun-Mon, indoor seating only, 8 bis rue du Collet, tel. 04 93 13 06 45).

L'Ecurie, a favorite for Nice residents, is off the beaten path in Old Nice. The cuisine is a mix of traditional *niçoise* and Italian specialties, and the ambience is warm inside and out (€23 three-course *menu*, €11 wood-fired pizza, open daily, 4 rue du Marché, tel. 04 93 62 32 62).

Restaurant du Gesù, a happy-go-lucky greasy spoon, squeezes plastic tables into a slanting square deep in the old city (sailors accustomed to dining off-balance will feel right at home). Arrive early or join the mobs waiting for an outside table; better yet, have fun in the soccer-banner-draped interior. The *raviolis sauce daube* is popular (€10 pizzas and pastas, closed Sun, 1 place du Jésus, tel. 04 93 62 26 46).

Lou Pilha Leva delivers fun, cheap lunch or dinner options with *niçoise* specialties and outdoor-only benches that are

NICE

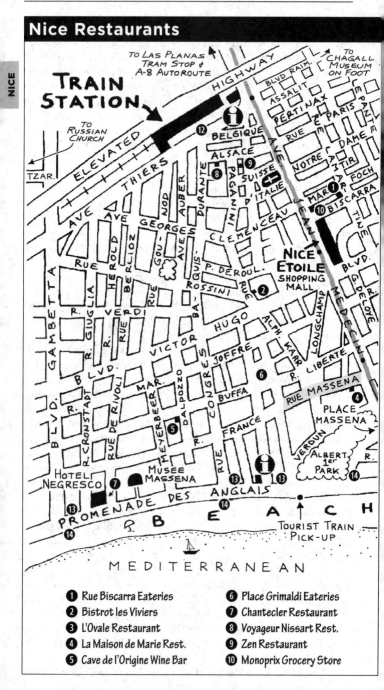

Nice Restaurants

TO LAS PLANAS
TRAM STOP &
A-8 AUTOROUTE

HIGHWAY

TO CHAGALL MUSEUM ON FOOT

TRAIN STATION

TO RUSSIAN CHURCH

TZAR.

ELEVATED

THIERS

AVE.

AVE.

BELGIQUE

ALSACE

BLVD RAIM. ASSALIT

PERTINAX

RUE

PARIS

NOTRE DAME

ITIR

FOCH

PAGANINI

SUISSE

D'ITALIE

MAR.

BISCARRA

BLVD.

DE LOYE

GEORGES

GOU-NOD

AUBER

DURANTE

BERLION

CLEMENCEAU

P. DEROUL.

RUE

NICE ETOILE SHOPPING MALL

GAMBETTA

RUE

HEROLD

R. GIUGLIA

VERDI

RUE

ROSSINI

HUGO

ALPH. KARR

LONGCHAMP

LIBERTE

BLVD.

R. CRONSTADT

RUE DE RIVOLI

VICTOR

MEYERBEER

MAR.

DALPOZZO

CONGRES

JOFFRE

BUFFA

R. MASSENA

RUE MASSENA

PLACE MASSENA

FRANCE

RUE

VERDUN

ALBERT 1er PARK

R.

HOTEL NEGRESCO

MUSEE MASSENA

PROMENADE DES ANGLAIS

BEACH

TOURIST TRAIN PICK-UP

MEDITERRANEAN

❶ Rue Biscarra Eateries		❻ Place Grimaldi Eateries	
❷ Bistrot les Viviers		❼ Chantecler Restaurant	
❸ L'Ovale Restaurant		❽ Voyageur Nissart Rest.	
❹ La Maison de Marie Rest.		❾ Zen Restaurant	
❺ Cave de l'Origine Wine Bar		❿ Monoprix Grocery Store	

NICE

① Buses #15 & #22 to Chagall & Matisse Museums; Bus #17 to Matisse Museum

⑫ Buses #99 & #23 to Airport

⑬ Bus #98 to Airport

⑭ Bus #98 from Airport

swimming in pedestrians (open daily, located where rues de la Loge and Centrale meet in Old Nice).

And for Dessert...

Gelato-lovers should save room for the tempting ice-cream stands in Old Nice. **Fenocchio** is the city's favorite, with mouthwatering displays of 86 flavors ranging from tomato to lavender to avocado— all of which are surprisingly good (daily March-Nov until 24:00, two locations: 2 place Rossetti and 6 rue de la Poissonnerie).

Near Nice Etoile

If you're not up for eating in Old Nice, try one of these spots around the Nice Etoile shopping mall.

On rue Biscarra: An appealing lineup of bistros overflowing with outdoor tables stretches along the broad sidewalk on traffic-free rue Biscarra (just east of avenue Jean Médecin behind Nice Etoile, all closed Sun). Come here to dine with area residents away from the tourists. These three places are all good choices, with good interior and exterior seating: **Le Cenac** seems most popular and features cuisine from southwest France (such as duck, foie gras, and omelets with *cèpe* mushrooms, €14-23 *plats*). **L'Authentic** has the most creative cuisine and comes with two memorable owners: burly Philippe and sleek Laurent (€22 two-course *menus,* €25 three-course *menus,* reasonable pasta dishes, tel. 04 93 62 48 88). **Le 20 sur Vin** is a neighborhood favorite with a cozy, wine-bar-meets-café ambience. It offers *(bien sûr)* good wines at fair prices, and basic bistro fare (tel. 04 93 92 93 20).

Bistrot les Viviers attracts those who require attentive service and authentic *niçoise* cuisine with a big emphasis on fish. This classy splurge offers two intimate settings as different as night and day: a soft, formal restaurant (€50 *menu,* €28-35 *plats*), and a relaxed *bistrot* next door (€35 weekday *menu,* €25-32 *plats,* bouillabaisse-€41, bourride-€25). I'd reserve a table in the atmospheric *bistrot,* where some outdoor seating is available (restaurant closed Sun, *bistrot* open daily, 5-minute walk west of avenue Jean Médecin at 22 rue Alphonse Karr, tel. 04 93 16 00 48).

L'Ovale is a find. Named for the shape of a rugby ball, how this ever-so-local and rugby-loving café survives in a tourist mecca, I'll never know. It's a well-run, welcoming bistro with quality food at respectable prices. Dine inside on big *plats* for €13; consider their specialty, *cassoulet* (€35 for two people, though it's enough for three); or enjoy *la planche de charcuterie* as a meaty, filling first course. The *salade de manchons* with duck and walnuts is incredible (excellent €17 three-course *menu,* €12 monster salads, closed Sun, air-con, 29 rue Pastorelli, tel. 04 93 80 31 65). Effervescent Johanna ensures good service.

La Maison de Marie is a surprisingly good-quality refuge off touristy rue Masséna, where most other restaurants serve mediocre food to tired travelers. Enter through a deep-red arch to a bougainvillea-draped courtyard, and enjoy the fair prices and good food that draw neighborhood regulars and out-of-towners alike. The interior tables are as appealing as those in the courtyard (*menus* from €22, open daily, look for the square red sign at 5 rue Masséna, tel. 04 93 82 15 93).

Near Promenade des Anglais

Cave de l'Origine is a warm, local spot run by kind Isabelle and Carlo, where you'll find a quality food shop *(épicerie)* and wine bar/*bistrot* serving a small selection. Carlo loves talking about his all-natural wines and other products. Stop by for a glass of wine, to peruse the shop, or, better, to reserve a table for a meal (€10 starters, €19 *plats,* open Tue-Sat for lunch, Thu-Sat for dinner, reservations smart, indoor seating only; shop open Tue-Sat 10:00-20:00, closed Sun-Mon; 3 rue Dalpozzo, tel. 04 83 50 09 60).

Place Grimaldi nurtures several appealing restaurants with good indoor and outdoor seating along a broad sidewalk and under tall sycamore trees. **Crêperie Bretonne** is the only crêperie I list in Nice (€8 dinner crêpes, closed Sun, 3 place Grimaldi, tel. 04 93 82 28 47). **Le Grimaldi** is popular for its café fare (€12 pasta and pizza, €15-19 *plats,* closed Sun, 1 place Grimaldi, tel. 04 93 87 98 13).

Chantecler has Nice's most prestigious address—inside the Hôtel Negresco. This is everything a luxury restaurant should be: elegant, soft, and top-quality. If your trip is ending in Nice, call or email for reservations—you've earned this splurge (*menus* from €90, closed Mon-Tue, 37 promenade des Anglais, tel. 04 93 16 64 00, chantecler@hotel-negresco.com).

Near the Train Station

Both of the following restaurants provide good indoor and outdoor seating.

Voyageur Nissart has blended good-value cuisine with cool Mediterranean ambience and friendly service since 1908. Alexis and Max could not be kinder hosts, making this a top option for those on a budget (€16 three-course *menus,* €7 fine *salade niçoise,* €10 *plats,* closed Mon, 19 rue d'Alsace-Lorraine, tel. 04 93 82 19 60).

Zen provides a Japanese break from French cuisine. Its friendly staff, pleasing contemplative decor, and tasty specialties draw a strong following (€16 three-course *menu,* €8-13 sushi, open daily, 27 rue d'Angleterre, tel. 04 93 82 41 20).

Nice Connections

For rough train, bus, and boat schedules from Nice to nearby towns, see "Getting Around the Riviera" on page 499. Note that most long-distance train connections to other French cities require a change in Marseille. The Grande Ligne train to Bordeaux (serving Antibes, Cannes, Toulon, Arles, Carcassonne, and other stops en route) requires a reservation.

From Nice by Train to: Marseille (18/day, 2.5 hours), **Arles** (11/day, 3.75-4.5 hours, most require transfer in Marseille or Avignon), **Avignon** (20/day, most of which are via TGV, 4 hours, most require transfer in Marseille), **Paris**' Gare de Lyon (10/day, 6 hours, may require change; 11-hour night train goes to Paris' Gare d'Austerlitz), **Munich** (4/day, 12-13 hours with 2-4 transfers, night trains possible via Italy), **Interlaken** (6/day, 9-11 hours, 2-5 transfers), **Florence** (6/day, 7-9 hours, 1-3 transfers), **Venice** (5/day, 8-9 hours, all require transfers), **Barcelona** (1/day via Montpelier, 10.5 hours, more with multiple changes).

Nice's Airport

Nice's easy-to-navigate airport (Aéroport de Nice Côte d'Azur) is on the Mediterranean, a 20- to 30-minute drive west of the city center. Planes leave about hourly to Paris (one-hour flight, about the same price as a train ticket, check www.easyjet.com for the cheapest flights to Paris' Orly airport). The two terminals (Terminal 1 and Terminal 2) are connected by frequent shuttle buses *(navettes)*. Both terminals have banks, ATMs, taxis, baggage storage (open daily 6:00-23:00), and buses to Nice. The TIs for Nice and Monaco are in Terminal 1 (tel. 08 20 42 33 33 or 04 89 88 98 28, www.nice.aeroport.fr).

Taxis into the center are expensive considering the short distance (figure €35 to recommended hotels, 10 percent more from 19:00-7:00 and all day Sun). Taxis stop outside door *(Porte)* A-1 at Terminal 1 and outside *Porte* A-3 at Terminal 2. Notorious for overcharging, Nice taxis are not always so nice. If your fare for a ride into town is much higher than €35 (or €40 at night or on Sun), refuse to pay the overage. If this doesn't work, tell the cabbie to call a *gendarme* (police officer). It's always a good idea to ask for a receipt *(reçu)*.

Airport shuttle vans work with some of my recommended hotels, but they only make sense when going *to* the airport, not when arriving on an international flight. Unlike taxis, shuttle vans offer a fixed price that doesn't rise on Sundays, early mornings, or evenings. Prices are best for groups (figure €25 for one person, and only a little more for additional people). **Nice Airport Shuttle** is one option (€25/one person, €32/two people, mobile 06 60 33 20

54, www.nice-airport-shuttle.com), or ask your hotelier for recommendations.

Three bus lines connect the airport with the city center, offering good alternatives to high-priced taxis. **Bus #99** (airport express) runs from both terminals to Nice's main train station (€4, 2/hour, 8:00-21:00, 30 minutes, drops you within a 10-minute walk of many recommended hotels). To take this bus *to* the airport, catch it right in front of the train station (departs on the half-hour). If your hotel is within walking distance of the station, #99 is a breeze.

Bus #98 serves both terminals, and runs along promenade des Anglais to Nice's main bus station *(gare routière),* which is near Old Nice (€4, 3/hour, from the airport 6:00-23:00, to the airport until 21:00, 30 minutes, see map on pages 532-533 for stops). The slower, cheaper local **bus #23** serves only Terminal 1, and makes every stop between the airport and train station (€1, 5/hour, 6:00-20:00, 40 minutes, direction: St. Maurice).

For all buses, buy tickets in the information office just outside either terminal, or from the driver. To reach the bus information office and stops at Terminal 1, turn left after passing customs and exit the doors at the far end. Buses serving Terminal 2 stop across the street from the airport exit (information kiosk and ticket sales to the right as you exit).

If you take bus #98 or #99, hang on to your €4 ticket—it's good all day on any public bus and the tramway in Nice, and for buses between Nice and nearby towns (see page 499 for details). Note that if you take your big bag onto any non-airport bus, you may be charged an extra €5.

GERMANY

BAVARIA AND TIROL

Füssen • King's Castles • Reutte, Austria

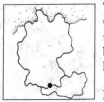

Two hours south of Munich, between Germany's Bavaria and Austria's Tirol, is a timeless land of fairy-tale castles, painted buildings shared by cows and farmers, and locals who still yodel when they're happy.

In Germany's Bavaria, tour "Mad" King Ludwig II's ornate Neuschwanstein Castle, Europe's most spectacular. Just over the border in Austria's Tirol, explore the ruined Ehrenberg Castle.

My favorite home base for exploring Bavaria's castles is actually in Austria, in the Tirolean town of Reutte. Reutte's hotels offer better value to those with a car. Füssen, in Germany, is more touristy, but a handier home base for train travelers.

Planning Your Time and Getting Around Bavaria

While Germans and Austrians vacation here for a week or two at a time, the typical speedy American traveler will find two days' worth of sightseeing. With a car and more time, you could enjoy three or four days.

By Public Transportation

Where you stay determines which sights you can see most easily. Train travelers use **Füssen** as a base, and bus or bike the three miles to Neuschwanstein and the Tegelberg luge or gondola. Although **Reutte** is the least convenient base if you're carless, travelers staying there can easily bike or hike to the Ehrenberg ruins, and can reach Neuschwanstein by bus (via Füssen), bike (1.5 hours), or taxi (€35 one-way); if you stay at the recommended Gutshof zum Schluxen hotel (between Reutte and Füssen, in Pinswang, Austria)

it's a one-hour hike through the woods to Neuschwanstein. Those staying in **Füssen** can day-trip by bus to Reutte and the Ehrenberg ruins.

By Bike

This is great biking country. Many hotels loan bikes to guests, and shops in Reutte and at the Füssen train station rent bikes for €8-15 per day. The ride from Reutte to Neuschwanstein and the Tegelberg luge (1.5 hours) is a natural.

Füssen

Dramatically situated under a renovated castle on the lively Lech River, Füssen (FEW-sehn) is a handy home base for exploring the region. This town has been a strategic stop since ancient times. Its main street sits on the Via Claudia Augusta, which crossed the Alps (over the Brenner Pass) in Roman times. Going north, early traders could follow the Lech River downstream to the Danube, and then cross over to the Main and Rhine valleys—a route now known to modern travelers as the "Romantic Road." Today, while Füssen is overrun by tourists in the summer, few venture to the back streets...which is where you'll find the real charm. Apart from my self-guided walk and the Füssen Heritage Museum, there's little to do here. It's just a pleasant small town with a big history and lots of hardworking people in the tourist business.

Halfway between Füssen and the border (as you drive, or a woodsy walk from the town) is the **Lechfall,** a thunderous water-fall (with a handy WC).

Orientation to Füssen

(area code: 08362)
Füssen's train station is a few blocks from the TI, the town center (a cobbled shopping mall), and all my hotel listings.

Tourist Information
The TI is in the center of town (June-mid-Sept Mon-Fri 9:00-18:00, until 17:00 off-season, Sat 10:00-14:00, Sun 10:00-12:00, one free Internet terminal, 3 blocks down Bahnhofstrasse from station at Kaiser-Maximilian-Platz 1, tel. 08362/93850, www.fuessen.de). If necessary, the TI can help you find a room. After hours, the little self-service info pavilion near the front of the TI features an automated room-finding service with a phone to call hotels.

Arrival in Füssen
From the train station (lockers available, €2-3), exit to the left and walk a few blocks to reach the center of town and the TI. Buses to Neuschwanstein, Reutte, and elsewhere leave from a parking lot next to the station.

Helpful Hints
Internet Access: Beans & Bytes is the best place to get online, with fast terminals and good drink service (€2/2 hours, Wi-Fi, Skype, disc-burning, daily 10:00-22:00, down the pedestrian

alley off the main drag at Reichenstrasse 33, tel. 08362/926-8960).

Bike Rental: Bike Station, sitting right where the train tracks end, outfits sightseers with good bikes and tips on two-wheeled fun in the area (€8-10/24 hours, March-Oct Mon-Fri 9:00-18:00, Sat 9:00-13:00, Sun in good weather 10:00-12:00, closed Nov-Feb, tel. 08362/505-9155, mobile 0176-2205-3080, www.ski-sport-luggi.de).

Car Rental: Peter Schlichtling, in the town center, rents cars for reasonable prices (€62/day, includes insurance, Mon-Fri 8:00-18:00, Sat 9:00-12:00, closed Sun, Kemptener Strasse 26, tel. 08362/922-122, www.schlichtling.de).

Auto Osterried/Europcar rents at similar prices, but is an €8 taxi ride away from the train station. Their cheapest car goes for about €59 per day (daily 8:00-19:00, past waterfall on road to Austria, Tiroler Strasse 65, tel. 08362/6381).

Local Guide: Silvia Beyer speaks English, knows the region very well, and can even drive you to sights that are hard to reach by train (€30/hour, silliby@web.de, mobile 0160-901-13431).

Self-Guided Walk

Welcome to Füssen

For most, Füssen is just a touristy home base for visiting Ludwig's famous castles. But the town has a rich history and hides some evocative corners, as you'll see when you follow this short orientation walk. Throughout the town, "City Tour" information plaques explain points of interest in English. Use them to supplement the information I've provided.

• *Begin at the square in front of the TI, three blocks from the train station.*

❶ **Kaiser-Maximilian-Platz:** The entertaining "Seven Stones" fountain on this square (in front of the TI) was built in 1995 to celebrate Füssen's 700th birthday. The stones symbolize community, groups of people gathering, conviviality...each is different, with "heads" nodding and talking. It's granite on granite. The moving heads are not connected, and nod only with water-power. While frozen in winter, it's a popular and splashy play zone for kids on hot summer days.

• *Just half a block down the busy street stands...*

❷ **Hotel Hirsch and the Medieval Wall:** Hotel Hirsch, one of the first hotels in town, dates from the 19th century, when aristocratic tourists started coming to appreciate the castles and natural wonders of the Alps. Across the busy street stands one of two surviving towers from Füssen's medieval town wall (c. 1515). Farther down the street (50 yards, just before the second tower), a

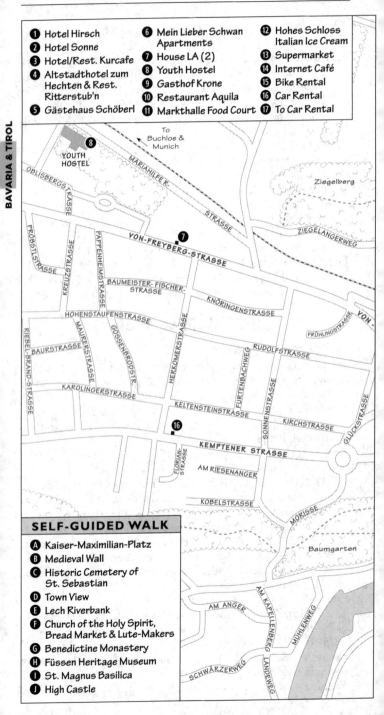

1 Hotel Hirsch
2 Hotel Sonne
3 Hotel/Rest. Kurcafe
4 Altstadthotel zum Hechten & Rest. Ritterstub'n
5 Gästehaus Schöberl
6 Mein Lieber Schwan Apartments
7 House LA (2)
8 Youth Hostel
9 Gasthof Krone
10 Restaurant Aquila
11 Markthalle Food Court
12 Hohes Schloss Italian Ice Cream
13 Supermarket
14 Internet Café
15 Bike Rental
16 Car Rental
17 To Car Rental

BAVARIA & TIROL

YOUTH HOSTEL
Ziegelberg
To Buchloe & Munich
MARIAHILFER R.
OBLISBERGSTRASSE
STRASSE
ZIEGELANGERWEG
PRÖBSTLSTRASSE
KREUZSKYLPLATZ
PAPPENHEIMSTRASSE
VON-FREYBERG-STRASSE
BAUMEISTER-FISCHER-STRASSE
KNÖRINGENSTRASSE
VON-
HOHENSTAUFENSTRASSE
HERKOMERSTRASSE
FRÜHLINGSTRASSE
RIEBEL-BRAND-STRASSE
BAURSTRASSE
MAURERSTRASSE
GOSSENBRODSTR.
RUDOLFSTRASSE
KAROLINGERSTRASSE
KELTENSTEINSTRASSE
FURTENBACHWEG
SONNENSTRASSE
KIRCHSTRASSE
GLÜCKSTRASSE
KEMPTENER STRASSE
FLORIAN-STRASSE
AM RIESENANGER
KOBELSTRASSE
MORISSE
Baumgarten
AM ANGER
AM KAPELLENBERG
MÜHLENWEG
SCHWÄRZERWEG
LANDEWEG

SELF-GUIDED WALK

A Kaiser-Maximilian-Platz
B Medieval Wall
C Historic Cemetery of St. Sebastian
D Town View
E Lech Riverbank
F Church of the Holy Spirit, Bread Market & Lute-Makers
G Benedictine Monastery
H Füssen Heritage Museum
I St. Magnus Basilica
J High Castle

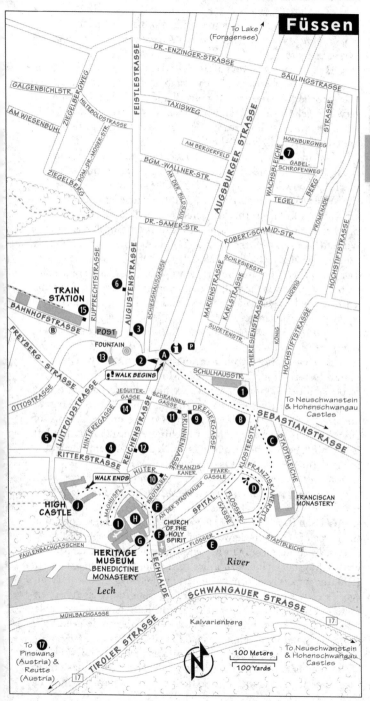

Füssen

To Lake (Forggensee)

DR.-ENZINGER-STRASSE

SÄULINGSTRASSE

GALGENBICHLSTR.

AM WIESENBÜHL

ZIEGELBERGWEG

HILTEBOLDSTRASSE

BGM.-DR.-MOSER-STR.

ZIEGELBERG

FEISTLESTRASSE

TAXISWEG

AM BERGERFELD

BGM.-WALLNER-STR.

AN DER BLEICHE

DR.-SAMER-STR.

AUGSBURGER STRASSE

HORNBURGWEG

GABEL-SCHROFENWEG

WACHSBLEICHE

TEGEL

BERG

PROMENADE

STRASSE

ROBERT-SCHMID-STR.

MARIENSTRASSE

SCHLESIERSTR.

KARLSTRASSE

THERESIENSTRASSE

SUDETENSTR.

KÖNIG

LUDWIG

HOCHSTIFTSTRASSE

HOCHSTIFTSTRASSE

TRAIN STATION

BAHNHOFSTRASSE

FREYBERG-STRASSE

RUPPRECHTSTRASSE

AUGUSTENSTRASSE

SCHIESSHAUSGASSE

POST

FOUNTAIN

SCHULHAUSSTR.

OTTOSTRASSE

LUITPOLDSTRASSE

JESUITER-GASSE

HINTEREGASSE

REICHENSTRASSE

SCHRANNEN-GASSE

BRUNNENGASSE

DREHERGASSE

KLOSTERSTR.

SEBASTIANSTRASSE

STADTBLEICHE

To Neuschwanstein & Hohenschwangau Castles

RITTERSTRASSE

HUTER-GASSE

FRANZIS-KANER.

FRANZISKANERPL.

FRANZISKANER MONASTERY

BROTMARKT

MAGNUSPL.

AN DER STADTMAUER

SPITAL

PFARR-GASSE

FLÖSSER-GASSE

WALK ENDS

HIGH CASTLE

FAULENBACHGÄSSCHEN

HERITAGE MUSEUM

BENEDICTINE MONASTERY

CHURCH OF THE HOLY SPIRIT

LECHHALDE

FLÖSSER-

STADTBLEICHE

River

Lech

MÜHLBACHGASSE

SCHWANGAUER STRASSE

Kalvarienberg

17

To Pinswang (Austria) & Reutte (Austria)

17

TIROLER STRASSE

To Neuschwanstein & Hohenschwangau Castles

100 Meters

100 Yards

BAVARIA & TIROL

WALK BEGINS

gate leads into the old town (read the information plaque).

• *Step through the gate (onto today's Klosterstrasse), and immediately turn left into the...*

❸ Historic Cemetery of St. Sebastian (Alter Friedhof): This peaceful oasis of Füssen history, established in the 16th century, fills a corner between the town wall and the Franciscan monastery. It's technically full, and only members of great and venerable Füssen families (who already own plots here) can join those who are buried (free, daily 7:30-19:00).

Just inside the gate (on the right) is the tomb of Dominic Quaglio, who painted the Romantic scenes decorating the walls of Hohenschwangau Castle in 1835. Over on the old city wall is the World War I memorial, listing all the names of men from this small town killed in that devastating conflict (along with each one's rank and place of death). A bit to the right, also along the old wall, is a statue of the hand of God holding a fetus—a place to remember babies who died before being born. And in the corner, farther to the right, are the simple wooden crosses of Franciscans who lived just over the wall in the monastery. Note the fine tomb art from many ages collected here, and the loving care this community gives its cemetery.

• *Exit on the far side, just past the dead Franciscans, and continue toward the big church.*

❹ Town View from Franciscan Monastery (Franziskanerkloster): From the Franciscan Monastery (which still has big responsibilities, but only a handful of monks in residence), there's a fine view over the medieval town. The Church of St. Magnus and the High Castle (the summer residence of the Bishops of Augsburg) break the horizon. The chimney (c. 1886) on the left is a reminder that when Ludwig built Neuschwanstein, the textile industry (linen and flax) was very big here.

• *Go down the steps into the flood zone, and stay left, following the roar of the charging river, through the medieval "Bleachers' Gate," to the riverbank.*

❺ Lech Riverbank: This low end of town, the flood zone, was the home of those whose work depended on the river—bleachers, rafters, and fishermen. In its heyday, the Lech River was an expressway to Augsburg (about 70 miles to the north). Around the year 1500, the rafters established the first professional guild in Füssen. As Füssen was on the Via Claudia, cargo from Italy passed here en route to big German cities farther north. Rafters would assemble rafts, and pile them high with goods—or with people needing a lift. If the water was high, they could float all the way to Augsburg in as little as one day. There they'd disassemble their raft and sell off the lumber along with the goods they'd carried, then make their way home to raft again. Today you'll see no modern-day rafters here, as there's a hydroelectric plant just downstream.

• *Walk upstream a bit, and head inland immediately after crossing under the bridge.*

❻ **Church of the Holy Spirit, Bread Market, and Lute-Makers:** Climbing uphill, you pass the colorful Church of the Holy Spirit (Heilig-Geist-Spitalkirche) on the left. As this was the church of the rafters, their patron, St. Christopher, is prominent on the facade. Today it's the church of Füssen's old folks' home (it's adjacent—notice the easy-access skyway).

Farther up the lane (opposite the entry to the big monastery) is Bread Market Square (Brotmarkt), with its fountain honoring the famous 16th-century lute-making family, the Tieffenbruckers. In its day, Füssen was a huge center of violin- and lute-making, with about 200 workshops. Today only two survive.

• *Backtrack and enter the courtyard in the huge monastery just across the street.*

❼ **Benedictine Monastery (Kloster St. Mang):** From 1717 until secularization in 1802, this was the powerful center of town. Today the courtyard is popular for concerts, and the building houses the City Hall and Füssen Heritage Museum (and a public WC).

❽ **Füssen Heritage Museum:** This is Füssen's one must-see sight (€2.50, €3 combo-ticket includes painting gallery and castle tower; April-Oct Tue-Sun 11:00-17:00, closed Mon; Nov-March Fri-Sun 13:00-16:00, closed Mon-Thu; tel. 08362/903-146, www .fuessen.de). Pick up the loaner English translations and follow the one-way route. In the St. Anna Chapel, you'll see the famous *Dance of Death.* This was painted shortly after a plague devastated the community in 1590. It shows 20 social classes, each dancing with the Grim Reaper—starting with the pope and the emperor. The words above say, essentially, "You can say yes or you can say no, but you must ultimately dance with death."

Leaving the chapel, you walk over the metal lid of the crypt. Upstairs, exhibits illustrate the rafting trade and violin- and lute-making (with a complete workshop). The museum also includes an exquisite *Festsaal* (main festival hall), an old library, an exhibition on textile production, and a King Ludwig–style "castle dream room."

• *Leaving the courtyard, hook left around the monastery and uphill. The square tower marks...*

❾ **St. Magnus Basilica (Basilika St. Mang):** St. Mang (or Magnus) is Füssen's favorite saint. In the eighth century, he worked miracles all over the area with his holy rod. For centuries, pilgrims came from far and wide to enjoy art depicting the great works of St. Magnus. Above the altar dangles a glass cross containing his relics (including that holy stick). Just inside the door is a chapel remembering a much more modern saint—Franz Seelos

(1819-1867), the local boy who went to America (Pittsburgh and New Orleans) and lived such a saintly life that in 2000 he was made a saint. If you're in need of a miracle, fill out a request card next to the candles.

• *From the church, a lane leads high above, into the courtyard of the...*

❶ **High Castle (Hohes Schloss):** This castle, long the summer residence of the Bishop of Augsburg, houses a painting gallery (the upper floor is labeled in English) and a tower with a view over the town and lake (included in the €3 Füssen Heritage Museum combo-ticket, otherwise €2.50, same hours as museum). Its courtyard is interesting for the striking perspective tricks painted onto its flat walls. From below the castle, the city's main drag (once the Roman Via Claudia, and now Reichenstrasse) leads from a grand statue of St. Magnus past lots of shops, cafés, and strolling people to Kaiser-Maximilian-Platz and the TI...where you began.

BAVARIA & TIROL

Sleeping in Füssen

(country code: 49, area code: 08362)

Though I prefer sleeping in Reutte, convenient Füssen is just three miles from Ludwig's castles and offers a cobbled, riverside retreat. It's very touristy, but it has plenty of rooms, and is the region's best base for those traveling by train. All recommended accommodations are within a few handy blocks of the train station and the town center. Parking is easy at the station. Prices listed are for one-night stays; most hotels give about 5-10 percent off for two-night stays—always request this discount. Competition is fierce, and off-season prices are soft. High season is mid-June–September. Rooms are generally 10-15 percent less in shoulder season and much cheaper in off-season. Ask if the city hotel tax (€1.60 per person, per night) is included; some places add it on.

Big, Fancy Hotels in the Center of Town

$$$ Hotel Hirsch is a romantic, well-maintained, old-style tour-class hotel with 53 rooms on the main street two blocks from the station. Their standard rooms are fine, and their rooms with historical and landscape themes are a fun splurge (Sb-€65-85, standard Db-€105-140, theme Db-€145-180, lower prices are for Nov-March and during slow times, family rooms, elevator, expensive Internet access, free Wi-Fi, free parking, Kaiser-Maximilian-Platz 7, tel. 08362/93980, fax 08362/939-877, www.hotelhirsch.de, info@hotelhirsch.de).

$$$ Hotel Sonne, in the heart of town, has a modern lobby and takes pride in decorating (some would say over-decorating) its 50 stylish rooms (Sb-€89-111, Db-€111-165, Tb-€139-193, Qb-€179-205, higher prices are for huge rooms in the new wing,

Sleep Code

(€1 = about $1.40, Germany country code: 49, Austria country code: 43)

S = Single, **D** = Double/Twin, **T** = Triple, **Q** = Quad, **b** = bathroom, **s** = shower only. Unless otherwise noted, credit cards are accepted, English is spoken, and breakfast is included.

To help you sort easily through these listings, I've divided the rooms into three categories, based on the price for a standard double room with bath:

$$$ **Higher Priced**—Most rooms €100 or more.

$$ **Moderately Priced**—Most rooms between €60-100.

$ **Lower Priced**—Most rooms €60 or less.

Prices can change without notice; verify the hotel's current rates online or by email. For other updates, see www.ricksteves.com/update.

lower prices are for Nov-March, 5 percent discount if you book on their website, elevator, free Internet access and Wi-Fi, free sauna, parking-€5-7/day, kitty-corner from TI at Prinzregentenplatz 1, tel. 08362/8000, fax 08362/908-100, www.hotel-sonne.de, info @hotel-sonne.de).

$$$ Hotel Kurcafe, a block from the station, has all of the amenities. The standard rooms are comfortable, and the newer, bigger rooms have elegant touches and fun decor—such as canopy drapes and cherubic frescoes over the bed (Sb-€89-99, standard Db-€109-129, bigger Db-€135-169 depending on size, Tb-€135-155, Qb-€149-169, 4-person suite-€205-229, high prices are for May-Sept, €10 more for weekends and holidays, you'll likely save money by booking via their website, elevator, free Wi-Fi, parking-€5/day, a block from station at Bahnhofstrasse 4, tel. 08362/930-180, fax 08362/930-1850, www.kurcafe.com, info@kurcafe.com, Norbert and the Schöll family).

Smaller, Mid-Priced Hotels and Pensions

$$ Altstadthotel zum Hechten, offers 35 modern rooms in a friendly, traditional building right under Füssen Castle in the old-town pedestrian zone (Sb-€59, Db-€90-98, Tb-€120, Qb-€140, ask for best Rick Steves price, also mention if you're very tall as most beds can be short, non-smoking rooms, lots of stairs, free Internet access in lounge, free Wi-Fi and parking with this book, laundry-€10/load, fun miniature bowling alley in basement, electrobike rental-€20/day; from TI, walk down pedestrian street and take second right to Ritterstrasse 6; tel. 08362/91600, fax

08362/916-099, www.hotel-hechten.com, info@hotel-hechten
.com, Pfeiffer and Tramp families).

$$ Gästehaus Schöberl, run by the head cook at Altstadthotel
zum Hechten, rents six attentively furnished, modern rooms a
five-minute walk from the train station. One room is in the own-
ers' house, and the rest are in the building next door (Sb-€40-50,
Db-€65-75, Tb-€85-95, Qb-€100-120, lower prices are for Jan-Feb
and Nov or for longer stays, cash only, free parking, Luitpold-
strasse 14-16, tel. 08362/922-411, www.schoeberl-fuessen.de,
info@schoeberl-fuessen.de, Pia and Georg Schöberl).

$$ Mein Lieber Schwan, a block from the train station, is
a former private house with four superbly outfitted apartments,
each with a double bed, sofa bed, and kitchen. The catch is the
three-night minimum stay (Sb-€66-77, Db-€75-86, Tb-€84-95,
Qb-€93-104, price depends on apartment size, slightly cheaper
off-season, cash or PayPal only, no breakfast, free Wi-Fi, free
parking, laundry facilities, garden, from station turn left at traffic
circle to Augustenstrasse 3, tel. 08362/509-980, fax 08362/509-
914, www.meinlieberschwan.de, fewo@meinlieberschwan.de,
Herr Bletschacher).

Füssen's Budget Beds

$ House LA, run by energetic mason Lahdo Algül, has two
branches. The backpacker house has 11 basic, clean four-bed dorm
rooms at rock-bottom prices about a 10-minute walk from the
station (€18/bed, D-€42, breakfast-€2, free Wi-Fi, free parking,
Wachsbleiche 2). A second building has five family apartments with
kitchen and bath, each sleeping 4-6 people (apartment-€60-90,
breakfast-€2, free Wi-Fi, free parking, 6-minute walk back along
tracks from station to von Freybergstrasse 26; contact info for both:
tel. 08362/607-366, mobile 0170-624-8610, fax 08362/505-9181,
www.housela.de, info@housela.de). Lahdo plans to open a third
branch in the near future.

$ Füssen Youth Hostel occupies a pleasant modern build-
ing in a grassy setting an easy walk from the center (bed in 2- to
6-bed dorm rooms-€21, D-€50, €3 more for nonmembers, includes
breakfast and sheets, guests over age 26 pay €4 penalty for being
so old, laundry-€3.20/load, dinner-€4.20, office open 7:00-12:00
& 17:00-23:00, until 22:00 off-season, Internet access, free parking, from station backtrack 10 minutes along tracks, Mariahilfer
Strasse 5, tel. 08362/7754, fax 08362/2770, www.fuessen.jugend
herberge.de, jhfuessen@djh-bayern.de).

$ Gasthof Krone, a rare bit of pre-glitz Füssen in the pedes-
trian zone, has dumpy halls and stairs and 12 big, worn, time-warp
rooms—left unrenovated by the owner. Still, the location makes
it worth considering as an alternative to the youth hostel (S-€26,

D-€46, T-€69, €3 less per person for 2-night stays, no breakfast but bakeries across the street, closed Nov-early June; from TI, head down pedestrian street and take first left to Schrannengasse 17; tel. 08362/7824, fax 08362/37505, www.krone-fuessen.de, info @krone-fuessen.de).

Eating in Füssen

Restaurant Aquila serves modern international dishes in a simple, traditional *Gasthaus* setting with great seating outside on the delightful little Brotmarkt Square (€10-16 entrées, serious €8-9 salads, Wed-Mon 11:30-14:30 & 17:30-22:00, closed Tue, Brotmarkt 9, tel. 08362/6253).

Restaurant Ritterstub'n offers delicious, reasonably priced fish, salads, veggie plates, and a fun kids' menu. They have three eating zones: modern decor in front, traditional Bavarian in back, and a courtyard. Demure Gabi serves while her husband cooks standard Bavarian fare (€7-14 entrées, €5 lunch specials, €15-18 three-course fixed-price dinners, Tue-Sun 11:30-14:30 & 17:30-23:00, closed Mon, Ritterstrasse 4, tel. 08362/7759).

Schenke & Wirtshaus (inside the recommended Altstadthotel zum Hechten) dishes up hearty, traditional Bavarian fare. They specialize in pike *(Hecht)* pulled from the Lech River, served with a tasty fresh-herb sauce (€8-14 entrées, salad bar, cafeteria ambience, daily 10:00-22:00, Ritterstrasse 6, tel. 0836/91600).

Hotel Kurcafe's fine restaurant, right on Füssen's main traffic circle, has good weekly specials and live Bavarian zither music most Fridays and Saturdays during dinner. Choose between a traditional dining room and a pastel winter garden (open daily 11:30-14:30 & 18:00-22:00, Bahnhofstrasse 4, tel. 08362/930-180).

Markthalle, just across the street from Gasthof Krone, is a fun food court offering a wide selection of reasonably priced, wurst-free food. Located in an old warehouse from 1483, it's now home to a fishmonger; Chinese, Turkish, and Italian delis; a fruit stand; a bakery; and a wine bar. Buy your food from one of the vendors, park yourself at any one of the tables, then look up and admire the Renaissance ceiling (Mon-Fri 8:00-18:30, Sat 8:00-14:00, closed Sun, corner of Schrannengasse and Brunnengasse).

Gelato: **Hohes Schloss Italian Ice Cream** is a good *gelateria* on the main drag, with cheap ice cream to go and an inviting perch for a coffee or dessert while people-watching (Reichenstrasse 14).

Picnic Supplies: Bakeries and *Metzger*s (butcher shops) abound and frequently have ready-made sandwiches. For groceries, try the underground **Netto** supermarket at the roundabout on your way into town from the train station (Mon-Sat 7:00-20:00, closed Sun).

Füssen Connections

From Füssen to: Neuschwanstein (bus #73 or #78, departs from train station, most continue to Tegelberg lift station after castles, 1-2/hour, 10 minutes, €1.90 one-way, €3.80 round-trip; taxis cost €10 one-way), **Reutte** (bus #74, Mon-Fri almost hourly, last bus 19:00, Sat-Sun every 2 hours, last bus 18:00, 45 minutes, €3.90 one-way; taxis cost €30 one-way), **Munich** (hourly trains, 2 hours, some change in Buchloe), **Innsbruck** (take bus #74 to Reutte, then train from Reutte to Innsbruck, 5/day, 3.5 hours), **Salzburg** (hourly, 4 hours, 1-2 changes), **Rothenburg ob der Tauber** (every 1-2 hours, 5 hours, often with changes in Augsburg, Treuchtlingen, and Steinach), **Frankfurt** (hourly, 5-6 hours, 1-2 changes). Train info: toll tel. 0180-599-6633 (€0.14/minute), www.bahn.de.

BAVARIA & TIROL

The King's Castles

The most popular tourist destinations in Bavaria are the "King's Castles" (Königsschlösser). The older Hohenschwangau, King Ludwig's boyhood home, is less touristy but more historic. The more dramatic Neuschwanstein, which inspired Walt Disney, is the one everyone visits. I'd recommend visiting both, and planning some time to hike above Neuschwanstein to Mary's Bridge—and if you enjoy romantic hikes, down through the gorge below. Reservations are a magic wand to smooth out your visit. With fairy-tale turrets in a fairy-tale alpine setting built by a fairy-tale king, these castles are understandably a huge hit.

Getting There

If arriving by **car**, note that road signs in the region refer to the sight as *Königsschlösser*, not Neuschwanstein. There's plenty of parking (all lots-€4.50). The first lots require more walking. Drive right through Touristville and past the ticket center, and park in lot #4 by the lake for the same price.

From **Füssen**, those without cars can catch **bus** #73 or #78 (1-2/hour, €1.90 one-way, €3.80 round-trip, 10 minutes, catch bus at train station, extra buses often run when crowded), take a **taxi** (€10 one-way), or ride a rental **bike** (two level miles). The bus drops you at the tourist office; it's a one-minute walk from there to the ticket office.

From **Reutte**, take bus #74 to the Füssen train station, then hop on bus #73 or #78 to the castles. Or pay €35 for a taxi right to the castles.

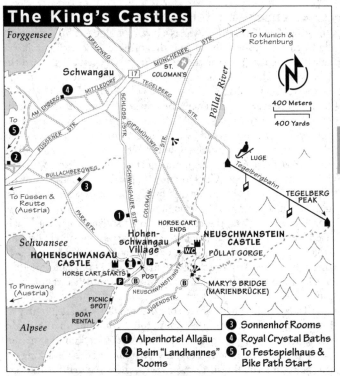

The King's Castles

Forggensee

To Munich & Rothenburg

Schwangau

ST. COLOMAN'S

KREUZWEG

MÜNCHENER STR.

MITTLEDORF

TEGELBERG STR.

Pöllat River

AM EHBERG

FÜSSENER STR.

SCHLOSS STR.

GIPSMÜHLWEG

STR.

400 Meters

400 Yards

BULLACHBERGWEG

COLOMAT STR.

To Füssen & Reutte (Austria)

PARK STR.

SCHWANGAUER STR.

LUGE

Tegelbergbahn

TEGELBERG PEAK

Schwansee

HOHENSCHWANGAU CASTLE

Hohen-schwangau Village

HORSE CART ENDS

NEUSCHWANSTEIN CASTLE

WC

PÖLLAT GORGE

HORSE CART STARTS

POST

NEUSCHWANSTEINSTR.

P

To Pinswang (Austria)

PICNIC SPOT

JUGENDSTR.

MARY'S BRIDGE (MARIENBRÜCKE)

BOAT RENTAL

Alpsee

❶ Alpenhotel Allgäu
❷ Beim "Landhannes" Rooms
❸ Sonnenhof Rooms
❹ Royal Crystal Baths
❺ To Festspielhaus & Bike Path Start

BAVARIA & TIROL

▲▲▲Hohenschwangau Castle

Standing quietly below Neuschwanstein, the big, yellow Hohenschwangau Castle was Ludwig's boyhood home. Originally built in the 12th century, it was ruined by Napoleon. Ludwig's father, King Maximilian II, rebuilt it in 1830. Hohenschwangau (hoh-en-SHVAHN-gow, loosely translated as "High Swanland") was used by the royal family as a summer hunting lodge until 1912.

The interior decor is harmonious, cohesive, and original—all done in 1835, with paintings inspired by Romantic themes. The Wittelsbach family (which ruled Bavaria for nearly seven centuries) still owns the place (and lived in the annex—today's shop—until the 1970s). As you tour the castle, imagine how the paintings must have inspired young Ludwig. For 17 years, he lived here at his dad's place and followed the construction of his dream castle across the way—you'll see the telescope still set up and directed at Neuschwanstein.

The excellent 30-minute tours give a better glimpse of Ludwig's life than the more-visited and famous Neuschwanstein Castle tour. Tours here are smaller (35 people rather than 60) and more relaxed.

▲▲▲Neuschwanstein Castle

Imagine "Mad" King Ludwig as a boy, climbing the hills above his dad's castle, Hohenschwangau, dreaming up the ultimate fairy-tale castle. Inheriting the throne at the young age of 18, he had the power to make his dream concrete and stucco. Neuschwanstein (noy-SHVAHN-shtine, roughly "New Swanstone") was designed first by a theater-set designer...then by an architect. It looks medieval, but it's modern iron-and-brick construction with a sandstone veneer—only about as old as the Eiffel Tower. It feels like something you'd see at a home show for 19th-century royalty. Built from 1869 to 1886, it's the epitome of the Romanticism popular in 19th-century Europe. Construction stopped with Ludwig's death (only a third of the interior was finished), and within six weeks, tourists were paying to go through it.

During WWII, the castle took on a sinister role. The Nazis used Neuschwanstein as one of their primary secret storehouses for stolen art. After the war, it took Allied authorities a year to sort through and redistribute the art, which filled 49 rail cars from this one location alone. It was the only time the unfinished rooms were put to use.

Today, guides herd groups of 60 through the castle, giving an interesting—if rushed—30-minute tour. You'll go up and down more than 300 steps, through lavish rooms based on Wagnerian opera themes, the king's gilded-lily bedroom, and his extravagant throne room. You'll visit 15 rooms with their original furnishings and fanciful wall paintings. After the tour, before you descend to the king's kitchen, see the 20-minute video about the king's life and passions accompanied by Wagner's music (next to the café, alternates between English and German, schedule board at the entry says what's playing and what's on deck). After the kitchen (state of the art for this high-tech king in its day), you'll see a room lined with fascinating drawings (described in English) of the castle plans, construction, and drawings from 1883 of Falkenstein—a whimsical, over-the-top, never-built castle that makes Neuschwanstein look stubby. Falkenstein occupied Ludwig's fantasies the year he died.

Visiting the Castles

Cost: Each castle costs €9, a *Königsticket* for both castles costs €17, and children under 18 (accompanied by an adult) are admitted free.

Hours: Both castles are open April-Sept daily from 9:00 with last tour departing at 18:00, Oct-March daily from 10:00 with last tour at 16:00.

Getting Tickets for the Castles: Every tour bus in Bavaria converges on Neuschwanstein, and tourists flush in each morning from Munich. A handy reservation system sorts out the chaos for smart travelers. Tickets come with admission times. If you miss your appointed tour time, you can't get in. To tour both castles, you must do Hohenschwangau first (logical, since this gives a better introduction to Ludwig's short life). You'll get two tour times: Hohenschwangau and then, two hours later, Neuschwanstein.

A **ticket center** for both castles is located at street level between the two (daily April-Sept 8:00-17:00, Oct-March 9:00-15:00, last tickets sold for Neuschwanstein one hour before closing, for Hohenschwangau 30 minutes before closing). If you have a reservation, there's a short line for picking up tickets. If you don't have a reservation...welcome to the very long line. Arrive by 8:00 in summer, and you'll likely be touring by 9:00. During August, the busiest month, tickets for English tours usually run out between 16:00 and 17:00.

Reservations: It's smart to reserve in peak season (July-Sept, especially Aug). Reservations cost €1.80 per person per castle, and must be made no later than 17:00 on the previous day by phone (tel. 08362/930-830), email (info@ticket-center-hohenschwangau.de), or online (www.ticket-center-hohenschwangau.de). You must pick up reserved tickets well before the appointed entry time (30 minutes before your Hohenschwangau tour, one hour before your Neuschwanstein tour). Why the long wait? Sure, it takes a while to walk to the castles. But many of the businesses serving tourists are owned by the old royal family...so they require more waiting time than necessary in the hope that you'll spend more money.

Getting up to the Castles: From the ticket booth, Hohenschwangau is an easy 10-minute climb, and Neuschwanstein is a steep 30-minute hike. To minimize hiking to Neuschwanstein, you can take a shuttle bus (leaves every few minutes from in front of Hotel Lisl, just above ticket office and to the left) or a horse-drawn carriage (in front of Hotel Müller, just above ticket office and to the right), but neither gets you to the castle doorstep. The shuttle bus drops you off near Mary's Bridge (Marienbrücke), leaving you a steep, 10-minute downhill walk to the castle—so be sure to see the view from Mary's Bridge *before* hiking down (€1.80 one-way, the €2.60 round-trip is not worth it since you have to hike uphill to the bus stop for your return trip). Carriages (€6 up, €3 down) are slower than walking and stop below Neuschwanstein, leaving you a five-minute uphill hike. Here's the most economic and least strenuous plan: Ride the bus to Mary's Bridge for the view, hike down to Neuschwanstein, and then catch the horse carriage from the castle back down to the parking lot.

Entry Procedure: For each castle, tourists jumble at the entry, waiting for their ticket number to light up on the board. When it does, power through the mob (most waiting there are holding higher numbers) and go to the turnstile. Warning: You must use your ticket while your number is still on the board. If you space out while waiting for a polite welcome, you'll miss your entry window and never get in.

Services: The helpful TI, bus stop, ATM, WC (€0.50), and telephones cluster around the main intersection (TI open daily June-Sept 11:00-19:00, Oct-March 11:00-17:00, April-May 11:00-18:00, tel. 08362/819-765, www.schwangau.de).

Eating: The "village" at the foot of Europe's Disney castle feeds off the droves of hungry, shop-happy tourists. The **Bräustüberl cafeteria** serves the cheapest grub (€6-7 gut-bomb grill meals, often with live folk music, from 11:00, close to end of road and lake). The Alpsee lake is ideal for a picnic, but there are no grocery shops nearby. Your best bets are to bring along a picnic, get food to go from one of the many bratwurst stands (between the ticket center and TI), or buy a sandwich at the shop adjacent to the ticket booth. Enjoy a lazy lunch at the lakeside park or in one of the old-fashioned rowboats (rented by the hour in summer).

Near the Castles

Mary's Bridge (Marienbrücke)—Before or after the Neuschwanstein tour, climb up to Mary's Bridge to marvel at Ludwig's castle, just as Ludwig did. This bridge was quite an engineering accomplishment 100 years ago. From the bridge, the frisky can hike even higher to the *Beware—Danger of Death* signs and an even more glorious castle view. (Access to the bridge is closed in bad winter weather, but many travelers walk around the barriers to get there—at their own risk, of course.) For the most interesting hike from Neuschwanstein (15 minutes longer but worth it, steel walkways and railings that make the slippery area safer), follow signs to the Pöllat Gorge *(Pöllatschlucht).*

▲**Tegelberg Gondola**—Just north of Neuschwanstein is a fun play zone around the mighty Tegelberg Gondola. For €17 round-trip (€10 one-way), you can ride the lift to the 5,500-foot summit (daily 9:00-17:00, closed Nov, 4/hour, last ride at 16:30, in bad weather call first to confirm, tel. 08362/98360, www.tegelberg bahn.de; most buses #73 and #78 from Füssen continue from the castles to Tegelberg).

On a clear day, you get great views of the Alps and Bavaria and the vicarious thrill of watching hang gliders and paragliders leap into airborne ecstasy. Weather permitting, scores of adventurous Germans line up and leap from the launch ramp at the top of the lift. With someone leaving every two or three minutes, it's great for spectators. Thrill-seekers with exceptional social skills may talk themselves into a tandem ride with a paraglider. From the top of Tegelberg, it's a steep and demanding 2.5-hour hike down to Ludwig's castle. (Avoid the treacherous trail directly below the gondola.) At the base of the gondola, you'll find a playground, a cheery eatery, the stubby remains of an ancient Roman villa, and a luge ride.

▲**Tegelberg Luge**—Next to the Tegelberg Gondola is a luge *(Sommerrodelbahn)* course. A luge is like a bobsled on wheels. This stainless-steel track is heated, so it's often dry and open even when drizzly weather shuts down the concrete luges. A funky cable system pulls riders (in their sleds) to the top without a ski lift. Push the stick forward to go faster, pull back to apply brakes, keeping both hands on your stick. To avoid getting into a bumper-to-bumper traffic jam, let the person in front of you get way ahead before you start. You'll emerge from the course with a windblown hairdo and a smile-creased face (€2.60/ride, 6-ride sharable card-€10.50, July-Sept daily 10:00-18:00, otherwise same hours as gondola, in winter sometimes opens late due to wet track, in bad weather call first to confirm, waits can be long in good weather, no children under 6, tel. 08362/98360, www.tegelbergbahn.de).

Sleeping near the King's Castles

(€1 = about $1.40, country code: 49, area code: 08362)
Inexpensive farmhouse B&Bs abound in the Bavarian countryside around Neuschwanstein, offering drivers a decent value. Look for *Zimmer Frei* signs ("room free," i.e., vacancy). The going rate is about €50-65 for a double, including breakfast. Though a bit inconvenient for those without a car, my three listings here are a quick taxi ride from the Füssen train station.

$$ Alpenhotel Allgäu is a small, family-run hotel with 18 rooms in a bucolic setting. It's a 15-minute walk from the castle ticket office, not far beyond the humongous parking lot (small Sb without balcony-€48, Sb-€58, perfectly fine older Db-€80, newer Db-€88, Tb-€115, these are book-direct prices, ask about discount with cash and this book, all rooms except one single have porches or balconies—some with castle views, family rooms, free Wi-Fi, elevator, free parking, just before tennis courts at Schwangauer Strasse 37, tel. 08362/81152, fax 08362/987-028, www.alpenhotel -allgaeu.de, info@alpenhotel-allgaeu.de, Frau Reiss).

$ Beim "Landhannes," a 200-year-old working dairy farm run by Conny Schön, rents three creaky but sunny rooms, and keeps flowers on the balconies, big bells and antlers in the halls, and cows in the yard (Sb-€30, Db-€60, €5 less per person for 3 or more nights, also rents apartments with kitchen with a 5-night minimum, cash only, poorly signed in the village of Horn on the Füssen side of Schwangau, look for the farm down a tiny lane through the grass 100 yards in front of Hotel Kleiner König, Am Lechrain 22, tel. 08362/8349, www.landhannes.de, mayr@landhannes.de).

$ Sonnenhof is a big woody old house with four spacious, traditionally decorated rooms (all with balconies) and a cheery garden. It's a 15-minute walk through the fields to the castles (S-€35, D-€50, Db-€60, cash only, all rooms non-smoking; at Pension Schwansee on the Füssen-Neuschwanstein road, follow the small lane 100 yards to Sonnenweg 11; they'll pick you up from the Füssen train station if you request ahead, tel. 08362/8420, Frau Görlich, English spoken).

Reutte, Austria

Reutte (ROY-teh, with a rolled *r*), a relaxed Austrian town of 5,700, is located 20 minutes across the border from Füssen. While overlooked by the international tourist crowd, it's popular with Germans and Austrians for its climate. Doctors recommend its "grade 1" air. I like Reutte for the opportunity to simply be in a real community. As an example of how the town is committed to its character, real estate can be sold only to those using it as a primary residence. (Many formerly vibrant alpine towns made a pile of money but lost their sense of community by becoming resorts. They allowed wealthy foreigners—who just drop in for a week or two a year—to buy up all the land, and are now shuttered up and dead most of the time.)

Reutte's one claim to fame with Americans: As Nazi Germany was falling in 1945, Hitler's top rocket scientist, Werner von Braun, joined the Americans (rather than the Russians) in Reutte. You could say that the American space program began here.

Reutte isn't featured in any other American guidebook. While its generous sidewalks are filled with smart boutiques and lazy coffeehouses, its charms are subtle. It was never rich or important. Its castle is ruined, its buildings have painted-on "carvings," its churches are full, its men yodel for each other on birthdays, and its energy is spent soaking its Austrian and German guests in *Gemütlichkeit*. Most guests stay for a week, so the town's attractions are more time-consuming than thrilling.

Orientation to Reutte

(country code: 43, area code: 05672)
Tourist Information
Reutte's TI is a block in front of the train station (Mon-Fri 8:00-12:00 & 14:00-17:00, no midday break July-Aug, Sat 8:30-12:00, closed Sun, Untermarkt 34, tel. 05672/62336, www.reutte.com).

Go over your sightseeing plans, ask about a folk evening, pick up city and biking maps and the *Sommerprogramm* events schedule (in German only), and ask about discounts with the hotel guest cards. Their free informational booklet has a good self-guided town walk.

Arrival in Reutte

If you're coming by car from Germany, skip the north *(Nord)* exit and take the south *(Süd)* exit into town. For parking in town, blue lines denote pay-and-display spots. There is a free lot (P-1) near the train station on Muhlerstrasse.

While Austria requires a **toll sticker** *(Vignette)* for driving on its highways (€8/10 days, buy at the border, gas stations, car-rental agencies, or *Tabak* shops), those just dipping into Tirol from Bavaria do not need one.

Ask your hotel to give you an **Aktiv-Card,** which gives free travel on local buses (including the Reutte-Füssen route) as well as small discounts on sights and activities.

Helpful Hints

Internet Access: Get online at **Café Alte Post** (daily 7:00-19:00, Untermarkt 15).

Laundry: There isn't an actual launderette in town, but the recommended Hotel Maximilian lets non-guests use its laundry service (€8/load).

Bike Rental: Try **Intersport** (€15/day, Mon-Fri 9:00-18:00, Sat 9:00-17:00, closed Sun, Lindenstrasse 25, tel. 05672/62352), or check at the recommended Hotel Maximilian.

Taxi: **STM Shuttle Service** promises 24-hour service (mobile tel. 0664/113-3277).

Car Rental: **Autoreisen Köck** rents cars at Mühlerstrasse 12 (tel. 05672/62233, www.koeck-tours.com, winfried@koeck-tours .com).

"Nightlife": Reutte is pretty quiet. For any action at all, there's a strip of bars, dance clubs, and Italian restaurants on Lindenstrasse.

Sights in and near Reutte

▲▲Ehrenberg Castle Ensemble (Festungsensemble Ehrenberg)

If Neuschwanstein was the medieval castle dream, Ehrenburg is the medieval castle reality. About two miles outside of Reutte are the brooding ruins of four castles that once made up the largest fort in Tirol. This impressive "castle ensemble" was built to defend against the Bavarians and to bottle up the strategic Via Claudia

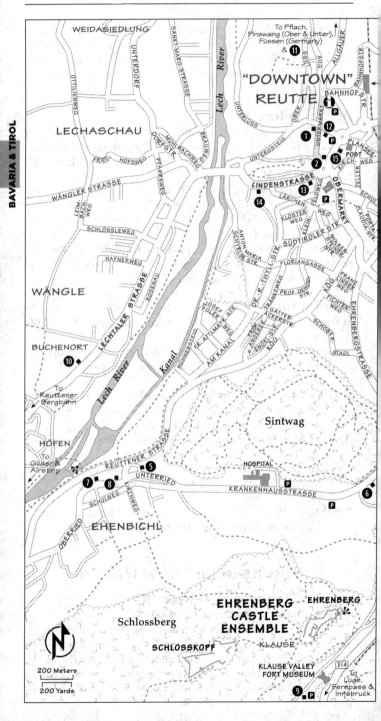

BAVARIA & TIROL

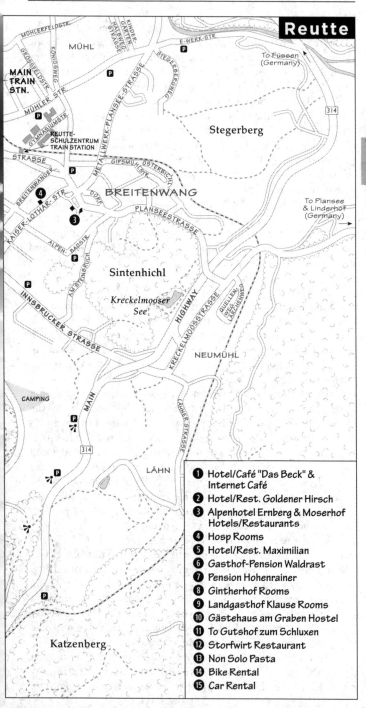

Reutte

1. Hotel/Café "Das Beck" & Internet Café
2. Hotel/Rest. Goldener Hirsch
3. Alpenhotel Ernberg & Moserhof Hotels/Restaurants
4. Hosp Rooms
5. Hotel/Rest. Maximilian
6. Gasthof-Pension Waldrast
7. Pension Hohenrainer
8. Gintherhof Rooms
9. Landgasthof Klause Rooms
10. Gästehaus am Graben Hostel
11. To Gutshof zum Schluxen
12. Storfwirt Restaurant
13. Non Solo Pasta
14. Bike Rental
15. Car Rental

trade route, which cut through the Alps as it connected Italy and Germany. Today, these castles have become a European "castle museum," showing off 500 years of military architecture in one swoop. The European Union is helping fund the project (paying a third of its €9 million cost) because it promotes the heritage of a multinational region—Tirol—rather than a country.

The complex has four parts: the fortified Klause toll booth on the valley floor, the oldest castle on the first hill above (Ehrenberg), a mighty and more modern castle high above (Schlosskopf, built in the age when cannons positioned there made the original castle vulnerable), and a smaller fourth castle across the valley (Fort Claudia, an hour's hike away). All four were a fortified complex once connected by walls. Signs posted throughout the castle complex help visitors find their way and explain some background on the region's history, geology, geography, culture, flora, and fauna. (While the castles are free and open all the time, the museum and multimedia show at the fort's parking lot charge admission.)

Getting to the Castle Ensemble: The Klause, Ehrenberg, and Schlosskopf castles are on the road to Lermoos and Innsbruck. These are a pleasant 30- to 45-minute walk or a short bike ride from Reutte; bikers can use the *Radwanderweg* along the Lech River (the TI has a good map). Local buses run from Reutte to Ehrenberg several times a day (see www.vvt.at for schedules—the stop name is "Ehrenberger Klause").

▲**Klause Valley Fort Museum**—Historians estimate that about 10,000 tons of precious salt passed through this valley (along the route of Rome's Via Claudia) each year in medieval times, so it's no wonder the locals built this complex of fortresses and castles. Beginning in the 14th century, the fort controlled traffic and levied tolls on all who passed. Today, these scant remains hold a museum and a theater with a multimedia show (€7.50 for museum, €10.50 combo-ticket also includes multimedia show, €17.80 family pass for 2 adults and any number of kids, daily 10:00–17:00, closed Nov-mid-Dec, tel. 05672/62007, www.ehrenberg.at).

While there are no real artifacts here (other than the sword used in A.D. 2008 to make me the honorary First Knight of Ehrenberg), the clever, kid-friendly **museum** takes one 14th-century decade (1360-1370) and attempts to bring it to life. It's a hands-on experience, well-described in English. You can try on a set of armor (and then weigh yourself), see the limited vision knights had to put up with when wearing their helmet, empathize with victims of the plague, and join a Crusade.

The **multimedia show** takes you on a 30-minute spin through the 2,000-year history of this valley's fortresses, with images projected on the old stone walls and modern screens (50-minute

English version at 13:00 or sometimes by request).

Eating: Next to the museum, the **Landgasthof Klause** is a self-service café serving light meals (€7-11 entrées, Tue-Sun 10:00-18:00, closed Mon, closed Nov and Jan-Feb, tel. 05672/62213). They also rent a few rooms if you'd like to stay right at Ehrenberg (see page 567).

▲▲**Ehrenberg Ruins**—Ehrenberg, a 13th-century rock pile, provides a super opportunity to let your imagination off its leash. Hike up 30 minutes from the parking lot of the Klause Valley Fort Museum for a great view from your own private ruins. Ehrenberg (which means "Mountain of Honor") was the first castle here, built in 1296. Thirteenth-century castles were designed to stand boastfully tall. With the advent of gunpowder, castles dug in. (Notice the 18th-century **ramparts** around you.)

Approaching Ehrenberg Castle, look for the small **door** to the left. It's the night entrance (tight and awkward, and therefore safer against a surprise attack). Entering this castle, you go through two doors. Castles allowed step-by-step retreat, giving defenders time to regroup and fight back against invading forces.

Before climbing to the top of the castle, follow the path around to the right to a big, grassy courtyard with commanding views and a fat, newly restored **turret.** This stored gunpowder and held a big cannon that enjoyed a clear view of the valley below. In medieval times, all the trees approaching the castle were cleared to keep an unobstructed view.

Look out over the valley. The pointy spire marks **Breitenwang,** which was a stop on the ancient Via Claudia. In A.D. 46, there was a Roman camp there. In 1489, after the Reutte bridge crossed the Lech River, Reutte (marked by the onion-domed church) was made a market town and eclipsed Breitenwang in importance. Any gliders circling? They launch from just over the river in Höfen.

For centuries, this castle was the seat of government—ruling an area called the "judgment of Ehrenberg" (roughly the same as today's "district of Reutte"). When the emperor came by, he stayed here. In 1604, the ruler moved downtown into more comfortable quarters, and the castle was no longer a palace.

Now climb to the top of Ehrenberg Castle. Take the high ground. There was no water supply here—just kegs of wine, beer, and a cistern to collect rain.

Ehrenberg repelled 16,000 Swedish soldiers in the defense of Catholicism in 1632. Ehrenberg saw three or four other battles, but its end was not glorious. In the 1780s, a local businessman bought the castle in order to sell off its parts. Later, in the late 19th century, when vagabonds moved in, the roof was removed to make squatting miserable. With the roof gone, deterioration quickened, leaving only this evocative shell and a whiff of history.

▲**Schlosskopf**—From Ehrenberg, you can hike up another 30 minutes to the mighty Schlosskopf ("Castle Head"). When the Bavarians captured Ehrenberg in 1703, the Tiroleans climbed up to the bluff above it to rain cannonballs down on their former fortress. In 1740, a mighty new castle—designed to defend against modern artillery—was built on this sky-high strategic location. By the end of the 20th century, the castle was completely overgrown with trees—you literally couldn't see it from Reutte. But today the trees are shaved away, and the castle has been excavated. In 2008, the Castle Ensemble project, led by local architect Armin Walch, opened the site with English descriptions and view platforms. One spot gives spectacular views of the strategic valley. The other looks down on the older Ehrenberg Castle ruins, illustrating the strategic problems presented with the advent of cannon.

In the Town

Reutte Museum (Museum Grünes Haus)—Reutte's cute city museum offers a quick look at the local folk culture and the story of the castles. There are exhibits on Ehrenberg and the Via Claudia, local painters, and more—ask to borrow the English translations (€3; May-Oct Tue-Sat 13:00-17:00, Thu until 19:00, closed Sun-Mon; early Dec-Easter Wed-Sat 14:00-17:00, Thu until 19:00, closed Sun-Tue; closed Easter-April and Nov-early Dec; in the bright-green building at Untermarkt 25, around corner from Hotel Goldener Hirsch, tel. 05672/72304, www.museum-reutte.at).

▲▲**Tirolean Folk Evening**—Ask the TI or your hotel if there's a Tirolean folk evening scheduled. During the summer (July-Aug), nearby towns (such as Höfen on Tuesdays) occasionally put on an evening of yodeling, slap dancing, and Tirolean frolic. These are generally free and worth the short drive. Off-season, you'll have to do your own yodeling. There are also weekly folk concerts featuring the local choir or brass band in Reutte's Zeiller Platz (free, July-Aug only, ask at TI). For listings of these and other local events, pick up a copy of the German-only *Sommerprogramm* schedule at the TI.

Sleeping in and near Reutte

(€1 = about $1.40, country code: 43, area code: 05672)

Reutte is a mellow Füssen with fewer crowds and easygoing locals with a contagious love of life. Come here for a good dose of Austrian ambience and lower prices. While it's not impossible by public transport, staying here makes most sense for those with a car. Reutte is popular with Austrians and Germans, who come here year after year for one- or two-week vacations. The hotels are big, elegant, and full of comfy carved furnishings and creative ways to spend lots of time in one spot. They take great pride in their restaurants, and the owners send their children away to hotel-management schools. All include a great breakfast, but few accept credit cards. Most hotels give a small discount for stays of two nights or longer.

The Reutte TI has a list of 50 private homes that rent out generally good rooms *(Zimmer)* with facilities down the hall, pleasant communal living rooms, and breakfast. Most charge €20 per person per night, and the owners speak little or no English. As these are family-run places, it is especially important to cancel in advance if your plans change. I've listed a few favorites below, but the TI can always find you a room when you arrive.

Reutte is surrounded by several distinct "villages" that basically feel like suburbs—many of them, such as Breitenwang, within easy walking distance of the Reutte town center. If you want to hike through the woods to Neuschwanstein Castle, stay at Gutshof zum Schluxen. To locate these accommodations, see the Reutte map.

In Central Reutte

These two hotels are the most practical if you're traveling by train or bus.

$$ Hotel "Das Beck" offers 16 clean, sunny rooms (many with balconies) filling a modern building in the heart of town close to the train station. It's a great value, and guests are personally taken care of by Hans, Inge, Tamara, and Pipi. Their small café offers tasty snacks and specializes in Austrian and Italian wines. Expect good conversation overseen by Hans (Sb-€46, Db-€70, Tb suite-€95, Qb suite-€112, ask for best Rick Steves price, all rooms non-smoking, Internet access and Wi-Fi free for Rick Steves readers, free parking, Untermarkt 11, tel. 05672/62522, fax 05672/625-2235, www.hotel-das-beck.at, info@hotel-das-beck.at).

$$ Hotel Goldener Hirsch, also in the center of Reutte just two blocks from the station, is a grand old hotel with 56 rooms and one lonely set of antlers (Sb-€58-62, Db-€85-92, Db suite-€90-98, Tb-€125-135, Qb-€140-145, less for 2 nights, elevator, free Wi-Fi, restaurant, Mühlerstrasse 1, tel. 05672/62508, fax 05672/625-087, www.goldener-hirsch.at, info@goldener-hirsch.at; Monika, Helmut, and daughters Vanessa and Nina).

In Breitenwang

Now basically a part of Reutte, the older and quieter village of Breitenwang has good *Zimmer* and a fine bakery. It's a 20-minute walk from the Reutte train station: From the post office, follow Planseestrasse past the onion-dome church to the pointy straight-dome church near the two hotels. The Hosps—as well as other

B&Bs—are along Kaiser-Lothar-Strasse, the first right past this church. If your train stops at the tiny Reutte-Schulzentrum station, hop out here—you're just a five-minute walk from Breitenwang.

$$ Alpenhotel Ernberg's 26 fresh rooms are run with great care by friendly Hermann, who combines Old World elegance with modern touches. Nestle in for some serious coziness among the carved-wood eating nooks, tiled stoves, and family-friendly backyard (Sb-€55, Db-€90, less for 2 nights, free Wi-Fi, popular restaurant, Planseestrasse 50, tel. 05672/71912, fax 05672/719-1240, www.ernberg.at, info@ernberg.at).

$$ Moserhof Hotel has 35 new-feeling rooms plus an elegant dining room (Sb-€53, Db-€92, confirm you're getting Rick Steves rates, extra bed-€35, most rooms have balconies, elevator, free Wi-Fi, restaurant, sauna and whirlpool, free parking, Planseestrasse 44, tel. 05672/62020, fax 05672/620-2040, www.hotel-moserhof.at, info@hotel-moserhof.at, Hosp family).

$ Walter and Emilie Hosp rent three rooms in a comfortable, quiet, and modern house two blocks from the Breitenwang church steeple. You'll feel like you're staying at Grandma's (D-€40, T-€60, Q-€80, cash only, Kaiser-Lothar-Strasse 29, tel. 05672/65377).

In Ehenbichl, near the Ehrenberg Ruins

The next listings are a bit farther from central Reutte, a couple of miles upriver in the village of Ehenbichl (under the Ehrenberg ruins). From central Reutte, go south on Obermarkt and turn right on Kög, which becomes Reuttener Strasse, following signs to Ehenbichl. These listings are best for car travelers—you'll need to take a taxi if you arrive by train.

$$ Hotel Maximilian offers 30 rooms at a great value. It includes table tennis, play areas for children (indoors and out), a pool table, and the friendly service of Gabi, Monika, and the rest of the Koch family. They host many special events, and their hotel has lots of wonderful extras such as a sauna and a piano (Sb-€48-55, Db-€76-90, confirm you're getting Rick Steves rate, family deals, elevator, free Internet access and Wi-Fi, laundry service-€6/load, good restaurant, Reuttenerstrasse 1, tel. 05672/62585, fax 05672/625-8554, www.maxihotel.com, info@hotelmaximilian.at). They rent cars to guests only (€0.72/km, book in advance) and bikes to anyone (€5/half-day, €8/day, more if you're not a guest, those staying at the hotel have free use of older bikes).

$$ Gasthof-Pension Waldrast, separating a forest and a meadow, is run by the farming Huter family and their dog, Picasso. The place feels hauntingly quiet and has no restaurant, but it's inexpensive and offers 10 nice rooms with generous sitting areas and castle-view balconies (Sb-€38, Db-€64, Tb-€77, Qb-€95, ask about discount with this book, cash only, all rooms non-smoking,

Internet access, free parking; about a mile from Reutte, just off main drag toward Innsbruck, past campground and under castle ruins on Ehrenbergstrasse; tel. & fax 05672/62443, www.waldrast tirol.com, info@waldrasttirol.com, Gerd).

$$ Pension Hohenrainer, a big, quiet, no-frills place, is a good value with 12 modern rooms and some castle-view balconies (Sb-€31-36, Db-€61-67, €3/person less for 2 nights, cheaper in April-June and Sept-Oct, cash only, family rooms, non-smoking rooms, free Internet access and Wi-Fi, restaurant and reception in Gasthof Schlosswirt across the street, follow signs up the road behind Hotel Maximilian into village of Ehenbichl, Unterried 3, tel. 05672/62544 or 05672/63262, fax 05672/62052, www.hohen rainer.at, hohenrainer@aon.at).

$ Gintherhof is a working farm that provides its guests with fresh milk, butter, and bacon. Annelies Paulweber offers geranium-covered balconies, six nice rooms with carved-wood ceilings, and a Madonna in every corner (Db-€56, Db suite-€60, €3/person less for second night, cash only, Internet access, Unterried 7, just up the road behind Hotel Maximilian, tel. 05672/67697, www.gintherhof .com, gintherhof@aon.at).

At the Ehrenberg Ruins

$$ Landgasthof Klause café, just below the Ehrenberg ruins and next to the castle museum, rents six non-smoking rooms with balconies on its upper floor. The downside is you'll have to go out for dinner (the café closes at 18:00), and you'll need a car to get anywhere besides Ehrenberg (Sb-€33, Db-€66, Tb-€99, closed Nov and Jan-Feb, tel. 05672/62007, fax 05672/62077, www.ehrenberg .at, info@ehrenberg.at).

A Hostel Across the River

The homey **$ Gästehaus am Graben hostel** has 4-6 beds per room and includes breakfast and sheets. It's lovingly run by the Reyman family—Frau Reyman, Rudi, and Gabi keep the 50-bed place traditional, clean, and friendly. This is a super value less than two miles from Reutte, and the castle views are fantastic. If you've never hosteled and are curious (and have a car or don't mind a bus ride), try it. If traveling with kids, this is a great choice. The double rooms are hotel-grade, and they accept nonmembers of any age (dorm bed-€23, hotel-style Db-€60, cash only, non-smoking, expensive Internet access, laundry service-€9, no curfew, closed April and Nov-mid-Dec; from downtown Reutte, cross bridge and follow main road left along river, or take the bus—hourly until 19:30, ask for Graben stop; Graben 1, tel. 05672/626-440, fax 05672/626-444, www.hoefen.at, info@hoefen.at).

In Pinswang

The village of Pinswang is closer to Füssen (and Ludwig's castles), but still in Austria.

$$ Gutshof zum Schluxen gets the "Remote Old Hotel in an Idyllic Setting" award. This family-friendly farm offers rustic elegance draped in goose down and pastels. Its picturesque meadow setting will turn you into a dandelion-picker, and its proximity to Neuschwanstein will turn you into a hiker—the castle is just an hour's hike away (Sb-€45-50, Db-€80-92, extra person-€28, confirm you're getting Rick Steves rate, lower prices are for off-season, 5 percent discount for stays of three or more nights, free Wi-Fi in common areas, self-service laundry-€7, mountain-bike rental-€10/day or €5/half-day, restaurant, fun bar, between Reutte and Füssen in village of Pinswang, free pick-up from Reutte or Füssen but call 24 hours ahead if you'll arrive after 18:00, tel. 05677/8903, fax 05677/890-323, www.schluxen.com, welcome@schluxen.com).

For a romantic twist, hike or mountain-bike from the trailhead nearby. When the dirt road forks at the top of the hill, go right (downhill), cross the Austria-Germany border (marked by a sign and deserted hut), and follow the narrow paved road to the castles. It's a 1- to 1.5-hour hike or a great circular bike trip (allow 30 minutes; cyclists can return to Schluxen from the castles on a different 30-minute bike route via Füssen).

Eating in Reutte

The hotels here take great pride in serving local cuisine at reasonable prices to their guests and the public. Rather than go to a cheap restaurant, eat at a hotel. Most offer €8-14 dinners from 18:00 to 21:00 and are closed one night a week. Reutte itself has plenty of inviting eateries, including traditional, ethnic, fast food, grocery stores, and delis.

Since hospitality is such a big part of the local scene, **hotel restaurants** are generally your best bet for a good meal. Many of the Reutte hotels recommended earlier—including Hotel Goldener Hirsch, Alpenhotel Ernberg, Moserhof Hotel, and Hotel Maximilian—offer fine restaurants.

Storfwirt is *the* place for a quick and cheap weekday lunch. You can get the usual sausages here, as well as baked potatoes and salads (€5.50-9 daily specials, salad bar, always something for vegetarians, Mon-Fri 9:00-14:30, closed Sat-Sun, Schrettergasse 15, tel. 05672/62640).

Non Solo Pasta, just off the traffic circle, is a local favorite for Italian food (€7-8 pizzas, €8-12 entrées, Mon-Fri 11:30-14:00 & 18:00-23:00, Sat 18:00-23:00, closed Sun, Lindenstrasse 1, tel. 05672/72714).

Picnic Supplies: **Billa** supermarket has everything you'll need (across from TI, Mon-Fri 7:15-19:30, Sat 7:15-18:00, closed Sun).

Reutte Connections

From Reutte by Train to: Garmisch (almost hourly, 1 hour), **Munich** (every 2 hours, 2.5 hours, change in Garmisch), **Salzburg** (hourly, 5 hours, change either in Munich and Kempten, or in Innsbruck and Garmisch). Train info: toll tel. 0180-599-6633 (€0.14/minute), www.bahn.de.

By Bus to: Füssen (Mon-Fri almost hourly, Sat-Sun every 2 hours, 45 minutes, €3.90 one-way, buses depart from train station, pay driver).

Taxis cost €30 one-way to Füssen, or €35 to the King's Castles.

ROTHENBURG

In the Middle Ages, when Frankfurt and Munich were just wide spots on the road, Rothenburg ob der Tauber was a "free imperial city" beholden only to the Holy Roman Emperor. With a whopping population of 6,000, it was one of Germany's largest. Today, it's the country's best-preserved medieval walled town, enjoying tremendous tourist popularity without losing its charm.

During Rothenburg's heyday, from 1150 to 1400, it was a strategic stop on the trade routes between northern and southern Europe. Now that route is known as the "Romantic Road," linking Frankfurt and Munich through a medieval heartland strewn with picturesque villages, farmhouses, onion-domed churches, and walled cities.

Today, Rothenburg's great trade is tourism: Two-thirds of the townspeople are employed to serve you. While 2.5 million people visit each year, a mere 500,000 spend the night. Rothenburg is yours after dark, when the groups vacate and the town's floodlit cobbles wring some romance out of any travel partner.

Too often, Rothenburg brings out the shopper in visitors before they've had a chance to see the historic town. True, this is a fine place to do your German shopping, but appreciate Rothenburg's great history and sights, too.

Planning Your Time

If time is short, you can make just a two- to three-hour midday stop in Rothenburg, but the town is really best appreciated after the day-trippers have gone home. Spend at least one night in Rothenburg (hotels are cheap and good). With two nights and a day, you'll be able to see more than the essentials and actually relax a little.

Rothenburg in one day is easy, with four essential experiences: the Medieval Crime and Punishment Museum, Tilman Riemenschneider's wood carving in St. Jakob's Church, a walk along the city wall, and the entertaining Night Watchman's Tour. With more time, there are several mediocre but entertaining museums, scenic hikes and bike rides in the nearby countryside, and lots of cafés and shops.

Rothenburg is very busy through the summer and in the Christmas Market month of December. Spring and fall are a joy, but it's pretty bleak from January through March—when most locals are hibernating or on vacation. Many shops stay open on Sundays during the tourist season, but close on Sundays in November and from Christmas to Easter.

There are several Rothenburgs in Germany, so make sure you are going to **Rothenburg ob der Tauber** (not "ob der" any other river); people really do sometimes drive or ride the train to other, nondescript Rothenburgs by accident.

Orientation to Rothenburg

(area code: 09861)

To orient yourself in Rothenburg, think of the town map as a human head. Its nose—the castle garden—sticks out to the left, and the skinny lower part forms a wide-open mouth, with the youth hostel and a recommended hotel in the chin. The town is a delight on foot. No sights or hotels are more than a 15-minute walk from the train station or each other.

Most of the buildings you'll see were in place by 1400. The city was born around its long-gone castle—built in 1142, destroyed in 1356—which was located where the castle garden is now. You can see the shadow of the first town wall, which defines the oldest part of Rothenburg, in its contemporary street plan. A few gates (called *Tor*—such as the Rödertor or the Spitaltor) from this wall still survive. The richest and biggest houses were in this central part. The commoners built higgledy-piggledy (read: picturesque) houses farther from the center, but still inside the present walls. Rothenburg's classic street scene is the Plönlein ("Little Square"), a picture-perfect tableau of a yellow house wedged between two towers at a diverging road (3 blocks due south of Market Square).

Tourist Information

The TI is on Market Square (May-Oct and Dec Mon-Fri 9:00-19:00, Sat-Sun 10:00-17:00; Nov and Jan-April Mon-Fri 9:00-17:00, Sat 10:00-13:00, closed Sun; Marktplatz 2, tel.

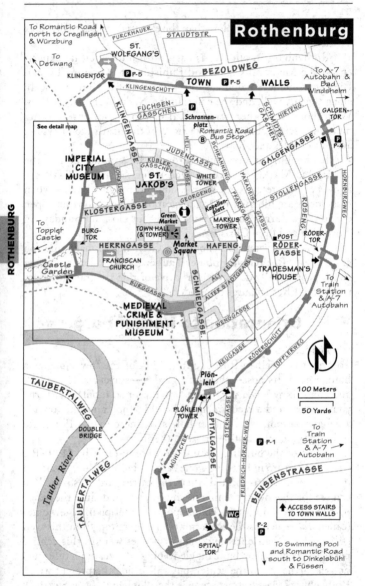

09861/404800, www.rothenburg.de). If there's a long line, just raid the rack where they keep all the free pamphlets. The free *Map & Guide* comes with a walking guide to the town. The free *RoTour* monthly magazine lists all the events and entertainment (mostly in German); look for current concert listing posters here and at your hotel. Ask about the daily English walking tour at 14:00 (€6, April-Oct and Dec; see "Tours in Rothenburg," later). The TI has one free Internet terminal (15-minute maximum). Visitors who arrive after closing can check the handy map highlighting which hotels have rooms available, with a free direct phone connection to them; it's just outside the door. A pictorial town map is available for free with this book at the Friese shop, two doors west from the TI (toward St. Jakob's Church; see "Shopping in Rothenburg," later).

Arrival in Rothenburg

By Train: It's a 10-minute walk from the station to Rothenburg's Market Square (following the brown *Altstadt* signs, exit left from station, turn right on Ansbacher Strasse, and head straight into the Middle Ages). Day-trippers can leave luggage in station lockers (€1-2, on platform) or at a local shop (try the Friese shop on Market Square, or Passage 12—both listed on page 586). Free WCs are behind the snack bar next door to the station. Taxis wait at the station (€5-6 to any hotel).

By Car: While much of the town is closed to traffic, anyone with a hotel reservation can drive in and through pedestrian zones to get to their hotel. The easiest way to enter and leave Rothenburg is generally via Spitalgasse and the Spitaltor (south end). But driving in town can be a nightmare, with many narrow, one-way streets. If you're packing light, just park outside the walls and walk five minutes to the center. Parking lots line the town walls: P1 costs €5 per day; P5 and the south half of P4 are free. Only those with a hotel reservation can park within the walls after hours (but not during festivals). It's smart to ask your hotel for advice, especially as plans are afoot to tighten parking restrictions and increase prices.

Helpful Hints

Festivals: Each spring, *Biergartens* spill out into the street and Rothenburgers dress up in medieval costumes to celebrate Mayor Nusch's Meistertrunk victory; the story of the draught that saved the town is described under "Meistertrunk Show" on page 576, more info at www.meistertrunk.de). The Reichsstadt festival every September celebrates Rothenburg's history.

Christmas Market: Rothenburg is dead in November, January, and February, but December is its busiest month—the entire town cranks up the medieval cuteness with concerts and costumes, shops with schnapps, stalls filling squares, hot spiced wine, giddy nutcrackers, and mobs of earmuffed Germans. Christmas markets are big all over Germany, and Rothenburg's is considered one of the best. The market takes place each year during Advent. Virtually all sights listed in this chapter are open longer hours during these four weeks. Try to avoid Saturdays and Sundays, when big-city day-trippers really clog the grog.

Internet Access: Most hotels have Internet access. If yours doesn't, the **Nuschhaus Café,** just below Market Square, has terminals (€3/hour) and Wi-Fi (€2/hour, Mon-Thu 10:00-19:00, Fri-Sun 10:00-20:30, Obere Schmiedgasse 23, tel. 09861/976-838). The **TI** has one free terminal for brief use (maximum 15 minutes), and the **Passage 12** souvenir shop at Obere Schmiedgasse 12 offers limited free use of the computer at their desk upstairs (see page 586).

Laundry: A handy launderette is near the station, off Ansbacher Strasse (€5.50/load, includes soap, English instructions, owner isn't always around to make change so it's smart to bring coins, opens at 8:00, last load Mon-Fri at 18:00, Sat at 14:00, closed Sun, Johannitergasse 9, tel. 09861/2775).

Bike Rental: You can rent a bike and follow the suggested route on page 585. **Fahrradhaus Krauss** is a big, cheap, reliable bike shop a 10- to 15-minute walk from the old town that rents eight-gear bikes. From the old town, head toward the train station, then continue along Ansbacher Strasse, bearing right over the train tracks (€5/6 hours, €10/24 hours, €15/weekend, Mon-Fri 9:00-18:00, Sat 9:00-13:00, closed Sun but ask about arranging return, no helmets, Ansbacher Strasse 85, tel. 09861/3495, www.fahrradhaus-krauss.de). Another rental shop—more expensive but closer to town—is **Rad & Tat** (€9/6 hours, €12/24 hours, Bensenstrasse 17, tel. 09861/87984, www.mietraeder.de).

Taxi: For a taxi, call 09861/2000 or 09861/7227.

Haircuts: At **Salon Wack** (pronounced vack, not wack), Horst and his team speak English and welcome both men and women (wash and cut: €18.50 for men, €28.50-33.50 for women; Tue-Fri 8:00-12:00 & 13:30-18:00, Sat 8:30-14:00, closed Sun-Mon, in the old center just off Wenggasse at Goldene Ringgasse 8, tel. 09861/7834).

Swimming: Rothenburg has a fine swimming complex, with a heated outdoor pool *(Freibad)* from mid-May to mid-September, and an indoor pool and sauna the rest of the year. It's about a 15-minute walk south of the Spitaltor along the main road toward Dinkelsbühl (adults-€4, kids-€2, swimsuit rental-€2, towel rental-€2.50; outdoor pool Fri-Tue 9:00-20:00, Wed 6:30-20:00, Thu 10:00-20:00; indoor pool Mon 14:00-21:00, Tue-Thu 9:00-21:00, Fri-Sun 9:00-18:00; Nördlinger Strasse 20, tel. 09861/4565).

Tours in Rothenburg

▲▲**Night Watchman's Tour**—This tour is flat-out the most entertaining hour of medieval wonder anywhere in Germany. The Night Watchman (a.k.a. Hans-Georg Baumgartner) jokes like a medieval Jerry Seinfeld as he lights his lamp and takes tourists on his rounds, telling slice-of-gritty-life tales of medieval Rothenburg (€6, Easter-Dec nightly at 20:00, in English, meet at Market Square, www.nightwatchman.de). This is the best evening activity in town. Night Watchman fans can also visit his store (see page 587).

Old Town Historic Walk—The TI offers 1.5-hour guided walking tours in English (€6, April-Oct and Dec daily at 14:00, Jan-March Sat only at 11:00, no tours in Nov, departs from Market Square). While the Night Watchman's Tour is fun, take this tour for the serious side of Rothenburg's history, and to make sense of the town's architecture. The tours are completely different, and it would be a shame not to take advantage of this informative tour just because you took the other.

Local Guides—A local historian can really bring the ramparts alive. Prices are standardized (€62/1.5 hours, €80/2 hours). Reserve a guide by emailing the TI (info@rothenburg.de; more info under "Guided Tours" at www.rothenburg.de). I've had good experiences with **Martin Kamphans,** who also works as a potter (tel. 09861/7941, www.stadtfuehrungen-rothenburg.de, post @stadtfuehrungen-rothenburg.de).

Self-Guided Walk

Welcome to Rothenburg

This one-hour circular walk weaves Rothenburg's top sights together.

• *Start the walk on Market Square.*

Market Square Spin-Tour

Stand at the bottom of Market Square (10 feet below the wooden post on the corner) and spin 360 degrees clockwise, starting with the Town Hall tower. Now do it again, this time more slowly, following these notes:

Town Hall and Tower: Rothenburg's tallest spire is the Town Hall tower (Rathausturm). At 200 feet, it stands atop the old Town Hall, a white Gothic 13th-century building. Notice the tourists enjoying the best view in town from the black top of the tower (€2 and a rigorous but interesting climb, 214 steps, narrow and steep near the top—watch your head, April-Oct daily 9:30-12:30 & 13:00-17:00, closed Nov-March, enter on Market Square through

Rothenburg Self-Guided Walk

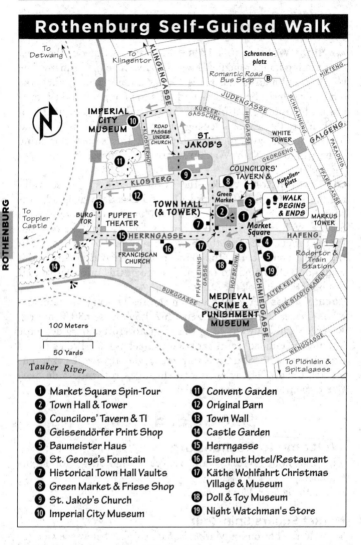

To Detwang
To Klingentor
KLINGENGASSE
Schrannen-platz
Romantic Road Bus Stop (B)
JUDENGASSE
HIRTENG.
SCHRANNEN
GALGENG.
PFARGASSE
PARADEIS

KÜBLER-GASSCHEN
HEUGASSE
WHITE TOWER
GEORGENG.

IMPERIAL CITY MUSEUM ⑩
ROAD PASSES UNDER CHURCH
ST. JAKOB'S
KLOSTERHOF
KLOSTERG.
⑪
⑨
COUNCILORS' TAVERN & ⑧
Kapellen-platz
③ WALK BEGINS & ENDS ①
MARKUS TOWER

⑫
TOWN HALL (& TOWER)
Green Market ②
Market Square

⑬
BURG-TOR
PUPPET THEATER
⑦
④

To Toppler Castle
HERRNGASSE ⑮
⑯ ⑰
HAFENG.
⑤
⑲
To Rödertor & Train Station

FRANCISCAN CHURCH
⑱
⑥
HOFBRONN
PFAFFLEINS-GASSE

⑭
CASTLE GARDEN
BURGGASSE
MEDIEVAL CRIME & PUNISHMENT MUSEUM
SCHMIEDGASSE
ALTER KELLER
ALTER STADTGRABEN

100 Meters
50 Yards
Tauber River
WENGGASSE
To Plönlein & Spitalgasse

① Market Square Spin-Tour
② Town Hall & Tower
③ Councilors' Tavern & TI
④ Geissendörfer Print Shop
⑤ Baumeister Haus
⑥ St. George's Fountain
⑦ Historical Town Hall Vaults
⑧ Green Market & Friese Shop
⑨ St. Jakob's Church
⑩ Imperial City Museum
⑪ Convent Garden
⑫ Original Barn
⑬ Town Wall
⑭ Castle Garden
⑮ Herrngasse
⑯ Eisenhut Hotel/Restaurant
⑰ Käthe Wohlfahrt Christmas Village & Museum
⑱ Doll & Toy Museum
⑲ Night Watchman's Store

middle arch of new Town Hall). After a fire in 1501 burned down part of the original building, a new Town Hall was built alongside what survived of the old one (fronting the square). This half of the rebuilt complex is in the Renaissance style from 1570.

Meistertrunk Show: At the top of Market Square stands the proud Councilors' Tavern (clock tower from 1466). In its day, the city council—the rich guys who ran the town government—drank here. Today, it's the TI and the focus of most tourists' attention when the little doors on either side of the clock flip open and the wooden figures (from 1910) do their thing. Be on Market Square at 11:00, 12:00, 13:00, 14:00, 15:00, 20:00, 21:00, or 22:00 for the ritual gathering of the tourists to see the less-than-breathtaking reenactment of the Meistertrunk ("Master Draught") story:

In 1631, in the middle of the Thirty Years' War, the Catholic army took the Protestant town and was about to do its rape, pillage, and plunder thing. As was the etiquette, the mayor had to give the conquering general a welcoming drink. The general enjoyed a huge tankard of local wine. Feeling really good, he told the mayor, "Hey, if you can drink this entire three-liter tankard of wine in one gulp, I'll spare your town." The mayor amazed everyone by drinking the entire thing, and Rothenburg was saved.

While this is a nice story, it was dreamed up in the late 1800s for a theatrical play designed (effectively) to promote a romantic image of the town. In actuality, if Rothenburg was spared, it happened because it bribed its way out of a jam. It was occupied and ransacked several times in the Thirty Years' War, and it never recovered—which is why it's such a well-preserved time capsule today.

For the best show, don't watch the clock; watch the open-mouthed tourists gasp as the old windows flip open. At the late shows, the square flickers with camera flashes.

Bottom of Market Square: At the bottom end of the square, the cream-colored building on the corner has a fine **print shop** around back (described under "Shopping in Rothenburg," later). Adjoining that is the **Baumeister Haus,** featuring a famous Renaissance facade with statues of the seven virtues and the seven vices—the former supporting the latter. The statues are copies; the originals are in the Imperial City Museum (described later on this walk). The green house below that is the former home of the 15th-century Mayor Toppler (it's now the recommended Gasthof Goldener Greifen).

Keep circling to the big 17th-century **St. George's fountain.** The long metal gutters slid, routing the water into the villagers' buckets. Rothenburg had an ingenious water system. Built on a rock, it had one real source above the town, which was plumbed to serve a series of fountains; water flowed from high to low through Rothenburg. Its many fountains had practical functions beyond providing drinking water (some were stocked with fish on market days and during times of siege). Water was used for fighting fires, and because of its plentiful water supply—and its policy of requiring relatively wide lanes as fire breaks—the town never burned entirely, as so many neighboring villages did.

Two fine buildings behind the fountain show the old-time lofts with warehouse doors and pulleys on top for hoisting. All over town, lofts were filled with grain and corn. A year's supply was required by the city so they could survive any siege. The building behind the fountain is an art gallery showing off work by members of the local artists' association (free, Tue-Sun 14:00-18:00, closed Mon). To the right is Marien Apotheke, an old-time pharmacy mixing old and new in typical Rothenburg style.

The broad street running under the Town Hall tower is **Herrngasse**. The town originated with its castle (built in 1142 but now long gone; only the castle garden remains). Herrngasse connected the castle to Market Square. The last leg of this circular walking tour will take you from the castle garden up Herrngasse back to where you are standing. For now, walk a few steps down Herrngasse and stop by the arch under the Town Hall tower (between the new and old town halls). On the left wall are the town's measuring rods—a reminder that medieval Germany was made of 300 independent little countries, each with its own weights and measures. Merchants and shoppers knew that these were the local standards: the rod (4.3 yards), the *Schuh* (or shoe, roughly a foot), and the *Ell* (from elbow to fingertip—four inches longer than mine...try it). Notice the protruding cornerstone. These are all over town—originally to protect buildings from reckless horse carts (and vice versa).

• *Under the arch, you'll find the...*

▲Historical Town Hall Vaults (Historiengewölbe)

This grade-schoolish little museum gives a waxy but interesting look at Rothenburg during the Catholics-vs.-Protestants Thirty Years' War. With helpful English descriptions, it offers a look at "the fateful year 1631," a replica of the mythical Meistertrunk tankard, and a dungeon complete with three dank cells and some torture lore (€2.50, daily May-Oct 9:30-17:30, shorter hours April and Dec, closed Nov and Jan-March, tel. 09861/86751).

• *Leaving the museum, turn left (past a much-sketched and photographed venerable door), and walk through the courtyard to a square called...*

Green Market (Grüner Markt)

Once a produce market, this parking lot fills with Christmas shops during December. Notice the clay-tile roofs. These "beaver tail" tiles became standard after thatched roofs were outlawed to prevent fires. Today, all of the town's roofs are made of these. The little fences keep the snow from falling, and catch tiles that blow off during storms. The free public WC is on your left, the recommended Friese shop is on your right, and straight ahead is St. Jakob's Church.

Outside the church, you'll see 14th-century statues (mostly original) showing Jesus praying at Gethsemane, a common feature of Gothic churches. The artist is anonymous, because in the Gothic age (pre-Albrecht Dürer) artists were just nameless craftspeople working only for the glory of God. Five yards to the left (on the wall), notice the nub of a sandstone statue—a rare original, looking pretty bad after 500 years of weather and, more recently, pollution. Most original statues are now in the city museum. The better-preserved statues you see on the church are copies.

• *If it's your wedding day, take the first entrance. Otherwise, use the second (downhill) door to enter...*

▲▲St. Jakob's Church (St. Jakobskirche)

Built in the 14th century, this church has been Lutheran since 1544. The interior was "purified" by Romantics in the 19th century—cleaned of everything Baroque or not original, and refitted in the Neo-Gothic style. (For example, the baptismal font and the pulpit above the second pew *look* Gothic, but are actually Neo-Gothic.) The stained-glass windows behind the altar, which are most colorful in the morning light, are originals from the 1330s (€2, daily April-Oct 9:00-17:15, Dec 10:00-16:45, Nov and Christmas-March 10:00-12:00 & 14:00-16:00, on Sun wait to enter until services end at 10:45, free helpful English info sheet, concerts and tour schedule posted on the door). There are guided tours in English for no extra charge on Saturdays at 15:00.

At the back of the church, take the stairs that lead up behind the pipe organ. In the loft, you'll find the artistic highlight of Rothenburg and perhaps the most wonderful wood carving in all of Germany: the glorious 500-year-old, 35-foot-high *Altar of the Holy Blood.* Tilman Riemenschneider, the Michelangelo of German woodcarvers, carved this from 1499 to 1504 to hold a precious rock-crystal capsule, set in a cross that contains a scrap of tablecloth miraculously stained in the shape of a cross by a drop of communion wine. It's a realistic commotion, showing that Riemenschneider—while a High Gothic artist—was ahead of his time. Below, in the scene of the Last Supper, Jesus gives Judas a piece of bread, marking him as the traitor, while John lays his head on Christ's lap. Everything is portrayed exactly as described in the Bible. On the left: Jesus enters Jericho, with the shy tax collector Zacchaeus looking on from his tree. Notice the fun attention to detail—down to the nails on the horseshoe. On the right: Jesus prays in the Garden of Gethsemane. Judas, with his big bag of cash, could be removed from the scene—illustrated by photos on the wall nearby—as was the tradition for the four days leading up to Easter.

Head back down the stairs to the church's main hall. Go up front to take a close look at the **main altar** (from 1466, by Friedrich Herlin). Below Christ are statues of six saints. St. James (Jakob in German) is the one with the shell. He's the saint of pilgrims,

ROTHENBURG

and this church was a stop on the medieval pilgrimage route to Santiago ("St. James" in Spanish) de Compostela in Spain. Study the painted panels—ever see Peter with spectacles? Around the back of the altarpiece (upper left) is a painting of Rothenburg's Market Square in the 15th century—looking much like it does today, with the exception of the full-Gothic Town Hall (as it was before the big fire of 1501). Notice Christ's face on the veil of Veronica (center of back side). It follows you as you walk from side to side—it must have given the faithful the religious heebie-jeebies four centuries ago.

The **small altar** to the left is also worth a look. It's a century older than the main altar. Notice the unusual Trinity: the Father and Son are literally bridged by a dove, which represents the Holy Spirit. Stepping back, you can see that Jesus is standing on a skull—clearly "overcoming death."

Before leaving the front of the church, notice the old **medallions** above the carved choir stalls. They feature the coats of arms of Rothenburg's leading families and portraits of city and church leaders.

• *Leave the church and, from its outside steps, walk around the corner to the right and under the chapel (built over the road). Go two blocks down Klingengasse and stop at the corner of Klosterhof Street. Looking down Klingengasse, you see the...*

Klingentor

This cliff tower was Rothenburg's water reservoir. From 1595 until 1910, a copper tank high in the tower provided clean spring water (pumped up by river power) to the privileged. To the right of the Klingentor is a good stretch of wall rampart to walk. To the left, the wall is low and simple, lacking a rampart because it guards only a cliff. Now find the shell decorating a building on the street corner next to you. That's the symbol of St. James (pilgrims commemorated their visit to Santiago de Compostela with a shell), indicating that this building is associated with the church.

• *Turn left down Klosterhof, passing the shell and, on your right, the colorful, recommended Altfränkische Weinstube am Klosterhof pub, to reach the...*

▲▲Imperial City Museum (Reichsstadt-Museum)

You'll get a scholarly sweep through Rothenburg's history at this museum, housed in a former Dominican convent. Cloistered nuns used the lazy Susan embedded in the wall (to the right of the museum door) to give food to the poor without being seen.

Highlights include the *Rothenburg Passion*, a 12-panel series of paintings from 1492 showing scenes leading up to Christ's crucifixion (in the *Konventsaal*); an exhibit of Jewish culture in Rothenburg through the ages *(Judaika);* a 14th-century convent kitchen *(Klosterküche)* with a working model of the lazy Susan and a massive chimney; romantic paintings of the town *(Gemäldegalerie);* the fine Baumann collection of weapons and armor; and sandstone statues from the church and Baumeister Haus (the seven vices and seven virtues). Follow the *Rundgang/Tour* signs (€4, daily April-Oct 9:30-17:30, Nov-March 13:00-16:00, English info sheet and descriptions, Klosterhof 5, tel. 09861/939-043, www.reichsstadt museum.rothenburg.de).

• *Leaving the museum, go around to the right and into the Convent Garden (when locked at night, continue straight to the T-intersection and see the barn three doors to the right).*

Convent Garden

This spot is a peaceful place to work on your tan...or mix a poisoned potion (free, same hours as museum). Enjoy the herb garden. Monks and nuns, who were responsible for concocting herbal cures in the olden days, often tended herb gardens. Smell (but don't pick) the *Pfefferminze, Juniper* (gin), *Chamomilla* (disinfectant), and *Origanum.* Don't smell the plants in the poison corner (potency indicated by the number of crosses, like spiciness stars in a Chinese restaurant).

• *Exit opposite from where you entered, angling left through the nuns' garden (site of the now-gone Dominican church), eventually leaving via an arch at the far end. Looking to your left, you'll see the back end of an...*

Original Barn

This is the back side of a complex that fronts Herrngasse. Medieval Germans often lived in large structures like this that were like small villages in themselves, with a grouping of buildings and open spaces. The typical design included a house, a courtyard, a stable, a garden, and, finally, a barn. Notice how the bulging wall is corseted by a brace with iron washers. Crank on its nuts and the building will stand up straight.

• *Now go downhill to the...*

Town Wall

This part of the wall (view through bars, look to far right) takes advantage of the natural fortification provided by the cliff, and is therefore much smaller than the ramparts. Angle left along the wall to the big street (Herrngasse), then right under the Burgtor tower. Notice the tiny "eye of the needle" door cut into the big door. If trying to get into town after curfew, you could bribe the guard to let you through this door (which was small enough to keep out any fully armed attackers).

• *Step through the gate and outside the wall. Look around and imagine being locked out in the year 1400. This was a wooden drawbridge (see the chain slits above). Notice the "pitch nose" mask—designed to pour boiling Nutella on anyone attacking. High above is the town coat of arms: a red castle* (roten Burg).

Castle Garden (Burggarten)

The garden before you was once that red castle (destroyed in the 14th century). Today, it's a picnic-friendly park. The chapel (50 yards into the park on the left) is the only bit of the original castle to survive. It's now a memorial to local Jews killed in a 1298 slaughter. A few steps beyond that is a grapevine trellis that provides a fine picnic spot. If you walk all the way out to the garden's far end, you'll find a great viewpoint (well past the tourists, and considered the best place to kiss by romantic local teenagers). But the views of the lush Tauber River Valley below are just as good from the top end of the park. Facing the town, on the left, a path leads down to the village of Detwang (you can see the church spire below)—a town even older than Rothenburg (for a walk to Detwang, see "A Walk in the Countryside," page 584). To the right is a fine view of the fortified Rothenburg and the "Tauber Riviera" below.

• *Return to the tower, cross carefully under the pitch nose, and hike back up Herrngasse to your starting point.*

Herrngasse

Many towns have a Herrngasse, where the richest patricians and merchants (the *Herren*) lived. Predictably, it's your best chance to see the town's finest old mansions. Strolling back to Market Square, you'll pass the old-time puppet theater (German only, on left), and the Franciscan church (from 1285, oldest in town, on right). The house at #18 is the biggest patrician house on the street. The family, which has lived here for three centuries, disconnected the four old-time doorbells. Their door—big enough to allow a carriage in (with a human-sized door cut into it)—is typical of the age. To see the traditional house-courtyard-stables-garden-barn layout, pop into either #14 (now an apartment block) or—if that's closed—the shop across the street, at #11. The Hotel Eisenhut, with its recommended restaurant, is Rothenburg's fanciest hotel and worth a peek inside. The Käthe Wohlfahrt Christmas shops (at Herrngasse 1 and 2; described later, under "Shopping in Rothenburg") are your last, and perhaps greatest, temptations before reaching your starting and ending point: Market Square.

Sights in Rothenburg

Museums Within a Block of Market Square

▲▲Medieval Crime and Punishment Museum (Mittel-alterliches Kriminalmuseum)—This museum is the best of its kind, specializing in everything connected to medieval criminal justice. Learn about medieval police, medieval criminal law, and above all, instruments of punishment and torture—even a special cage complete with a metal gag for nags. The museum is more eclectic than its name, and includes exhibits on general history, superstition, biblical art, and temporary displays in a second building. Follow the yellow arrows—the one-way traffic system makes it hard to double back. Exhibits are tenderly described in English (€4, daily May-Oct 10:00-18:00, Nov and Jan-Feb 14:00-16:00, Dec and March 13:00-16:00, April 11:00-17:00, last entry 45 minutes before closing, fun cards and posters, Burggasse 3-5, tel. 09861/5359, www.kriminalmuseum.rothenburg.de). If you insist on trying a *Schneeball,* the museum café (located in the next building down Burggasse) sells mini-*Schneeballen* for €0.40 (open May-Oct, closed Nov-April, no museum admission required for café after 13:00).

▲Doll and Toy Museum (Puppen- und Spielzeugmuseum)—These two floors of historic *Kinder* cuteness are a hit with many little kids. Pick up the free English binder (just past the entry curtain) for an extensive description of the exhibits (€4, family ticket-€10, daily March-Dec 9:30-18:00, Jan-Feb 11:00-17:00, just off Market Square, downhill from the fountain at Hofbronnengasse 11-13, tel. 09861/7330, www.spielzeugmuseum.rothenburg.de).

▲German Christmas Museum (Deutsches Weihnachts-museum)—This excellent museum, upstairs in the giant Käthe Wohlfahrt Christmas Village shop, tells the history of Christmas decorations. There's a unique and thoughtfully described collection of Christmas-tree stands, mini-trees sent in boxes to WWI soldiers at the front, early Advent calendars, old-time Christmas cards, and a look at tree decorations through the ages—including the Nazi era and when you were a kid. The museum is not just a ploy to get shoppers to spend more money, but a serious collection managed by professional curator Felicitas Höptner (€4, April-Dec daily 10:00-18:00, Jan-March Sat-Sun 10:00-18:00 and irregularly on weekdays, last entry at 17:00, Herrngasse 1, tel. 09861/409-365, www.germanchristmasmuseum.com).

More Sights in Rothenburg

▲▲Walk the Wall—Just longer than a mile and a half around, providing great views and a good orientation, this walk can be done by those under six feet tall in less than an hour (unless your camera can't stop snapping). The hike requires no special sense of balance. This walk is covered and is a great option in the rain. Photographers will stay very busy, especially before breakfast or at sunset, when the lighting is best and the crowds dissipate . You can enter or exit the ramparts at nearly every tower. The best fortifications are in the Spitaltor (south end). Climb the Rödertor en route (described next). The names you see along the way belong to people who donated money to rebuild the wall after World War II, and those who've more recently donated €1,000 per meter for the maintenance of Rothenburg's heritage.

▲**Rödertor**—The wall tower nearest the train station is the only one you can climb. It's worth the 135 steps for the view and a short but fascinating rundown on the bombing of Rothenburg in the last weeks of World War II, when the east part of the city was destroyed (€1.50, pay at top, unreliable hours, usually open daily April-Oct 10:00-16:00, closed Nov-March, WWII photos have English translations). If you climb this, you can skip the more claustrophobic Town Hall tower climb.

▲▲**The Allergic-to-Tourists Wall and Moat Walk**—For a quiet and scenic break from the tourist crowds and a chance to appreciate the marvelous fortifications of Rothenburg, consider this hike: From the Castle Garden, go right and walk outside the wall to the Klingentor. At the Klingentor, climb up to the ramparts and walk on the wall past the Galgentor to the Rödertor. Then descend, leave the old town, and hike through the park (once the moat) down to the Spitaltor. Explore the fortifications here before hiking a block up Spitalgasse, turning left to pass the youth hostel, popping back outside the wall, and heading along the upper scenic reaches of the "Tauber Riviera" and above the vineyards back to the Castle Garden.

▲**Tradesman's House (Alt-Rothenburger Handwerkerhaus)**—See the everyday life of a Rothenburger in the town's heyday in this restored 700-year-old home (€2.50; Easter-Oct Mon-Fri 11:00-17:00, Sat-Sun 10:00-17:00; Dec daily 14:00-16:00; closed Nov and Jan-Easter; Alter Stadtgraben 26, near Markus Tower, tel. 09861/5810).

St. Wolfgang's Church—This fortified Gothic church is built into the medieval wall at the Klingentor. Its dungeon-like passages and shepherd's-dance exhibit are pretty lame (€1.50, Wed-Mon April-Sept 10:00-13:00 & 14:30-17:00, Oct 10:00-16:00, closed Tue and Nov-March).

Near Rothenburg
▲**A Walk in the Countryside**—From the *Burggarten* (castle garden), head into the Tauber Valley. With your back to town,

go down the hill, exiting the castle garden on your left. Once outside of the wall, walk around, keeping the castle and town on your right. The trail becomes really steep, taking you down to the wooden covered bridge on the valley floor. Across the bridge, the road goes left to Toppler Castle and right (downstream, with a pleasant parallel footpath) to Detwang.

Toppler Castle (Topplerschlösschen) is cute, skinny, sky-blue, and 600 years old. It was the castle/summer home of the medieval Mayor Toppler. The tower's top looks like a house—a sort of tree fort for grownups. It's in a farmer's garden, and it's open whenever he's around and willing to let you in (€1.50, normally Fri-Sun 13:00-16:00, closed Mon-Thu and Nov, one mile from town center at Taubertalweg 100, tel. 09861/7358). People say the mayor had this valley-floor escape built to get people to relax about leaving the fortified town...or to hide a mistress.

To extend your stroll, walk back to the bridge and follow the river downstream (passing the Unter den Linden beer garden—described on page 596) to the peaceful village of **Detwang.** One of the oldest villages in Franconia (a medieval German dukedom), Detwang dates from 968. Like Rothenburg, it has a Riemenschneider altarpiece in its church.

Franconian Bike Ride—To get a fun, breezy look at the countryside around Rothenburg, rent a bike from Fahrradhaus Krauss (see "Helpful Hints" on page 574). For a pleasant half-day pedal, escape the old town through the Rödertor, bike along Topplerweg to the Spitaltor, and follow the curvy road down into the Tauber Riviera. Turn right at the yellow *Leutzenbronn* sign to cross the double-arcaded bridge. From here a peaceful road follows the river downstream to **Detwang,** passing the cute Toppler Castle (described above). From Detwang, follow the main road to the old mill, and turn left to follow the *Liebliches Taubertal* bike path signs as far up the Tauber River (direction: Bettwar) as you like. After 2.5 miles, you'll arrive in the sleepy farming town of **Bettwar;** claim a spot among the chickens and the apple trees for a picnic or have a drink at one of the two restaurants in town.

Franconian Open-Air Museum (Fränkisches Freiland- museum)—A 20-minute drive from Rothenburg—in the undiscovered "Rothenburgy" town of Bad Windsheim—is an open-air folk museum that, compared with others in Europe, is a bit humble. But it tries very hard and gives you the best look around at traditional rural Franconia (€5, daily mid-March-Sept 9:00-18:00, Oct-mid-Dec 10:00-16:00, closed mid-Dec-mid-March, last entry one hour before closing, tel. 09841/66800, www.freiland museum.de).

Shopping in Rothenburg

Be warned...Rothenburg is one of Germany's best shopping towns. Do it here and be done with it. Lovely prints, carvings, wine glasses, Christmas-tree ornaments, and beer steins are popular. Rödergasse is the old town's everyday shopping street. There is also a modern shopping center across the street from the train station.

Christmas Souvenirs

Rothenburg is the headquarters of the **Käthe Wohlfahrt** Christmas trinkets empire, which is spreading across the half-timbered reaches of Europe. In Rothenburg, tourists flock to two Käthe Wohlfahrt stores (at Herrngasse 1 and 2, just off Market Square). Start with the **Christmas Village** (Weihnachtsdorf) at Herrngasse 1. This Christmas wonderland is filled with enough twinkling lights (196,000—mostly LEDs) to require a special electrical hookup. You're greeted by instant Christmas mood music (best appreciated on a hot day in July), and American and Japanese tourists hungrily filling little woven shopping baskets with €5-8 goodies to hang on their trees. (OK, I admit it, my Christmas tree sports a few KW ornaments.) Let the spinning flocked tree whisk you in, but pause at the wall of Steiffs, jerking uncontrollably and mesmerizing little kids. The **Christmas Museum** upstairs is described earlier, under "Sights in Rothenburg."

The smaller **Christmas Market** (Weihnachtsmarkt), across the street at Herrngasse 2, specializes in finely crafted wooden ornaments. A third, much smaller store is at Untere Schmiedgasse 19 (all stores open Mon-Sat 9:00-18:00, May-Dec also most Sun 10:00-18:00, Jan-April closed Sun but museum and museum shop open, ask about discount on official KW products with this book, tel. 09861/4090, www.wohlfahrt.com). Käthe started the business in Stuttgart in 1964, and it's now run by her son Harald Wohlfahrt, who lives in Rothenburg.

Traditional German Souvenirs

Cuckoo with friendliness, trinkets, and souvenirs, the **Friese shop** has been welcoming readers of this book for more than 20 years (on the smaller square just off Market Square, west of TI, on corner across from free public WC). Ask about a discount and a free pictorial map (normally €1.50) with this book. Anneliese Friese, who runs the place with her son Bernie, charges only her cost for shipping and lets tired travelers leave their bags in her back room for free. (Mon-Sat 9:00-17:00, Sun 10:00-16:00, Grüner Markt 8, tel. 09861/7166, fax 09861/936-619, friese-kabalo@gmx.de).

Passage 12, a huge, more commercial souvenir shop with a vast selection of steins, knives, and noisy clocks, is locked in tooth-gnashing competition with the Friese shop. It's just a block below Market Square at Obere Schmiedgasse 12. Ask about a discount with this book. Customers can check their email for free upstairs, use the WC, and stash their bags in lockers in the storage room (April-Dec Mon-Sat 9:00-19:00, Sun 10:00-18:00; Jan-March Mon-Sat 10:00-18:00, usually closed Sun; tel. 09861/8196).

Werkstattladen Lebenshilfe sells tasteful, original, unconventional toys and souvenirs made in sheltered workshops by Germans with disabilities. It's a tiny shop down the side street behind Herrngasse 10 (May-Dec daily 10:30-18:00; April Mon-Sat 10:30-18:00, closed Sun; closed Jan-March; Kirchgasse 1, tel. 09861/938-401).

The **Night Watchman's Store** (Nachtwächterladen), run by the watchman's wife, gives Night Watchman fans a chance to try on the Night Watchman's hat, blow through a drinking horn, or browse medieval clothing (March-Dec daily 10:00-19:00; Jan-Feb Sat-Sun 10:00-19:00, closed Mon-Fri; just below Market Square at Untere Schmiedgasse 7, tel. 09861/938633). See page 575 for details on the Night Watchman's entertaining tour.

Romantic Prints: The Ernst Geissendörfer print shop has sold fine prints, etchings, and paintings on the corner of Market Square since 1908. To find the shop, walk a few steps down Hafengasse (it's on your right, just before the Bosporus Café). If you're interested in more expensive prints and etchings than those on display, ask Frau Geissendörfer to take you upstairs—she'll offer you a free shot of German brandy while you browse. Show this book and ask about a discount (May-Dec daily 11:00-18:00; March-April Mon-Sat 11:00-18:00, closed Sun; closed Jan-Feb; Obere Schmiedgasse 1 at corner of Hafengasse, tel. 09861/2005, www.geissendoerfer.de).

Wine Stuff: For characteristic wine glasses, winemaking gear, and the real thing from the town's oldest winemakers, drop by the **Weinladen am Plönlein** (daily 10:00-18:00, Untere Schmiedgasse 27—see page 597 for info on wine-tasting). Although Rothenburg is technically in Bavaria, the region around the town is often called by its medieval name, *Franken* (Franconia). You'll recognize Franconian wines by the shape of the bottle—short, stubby, and round.

Books: A good bookstore is **Rothenburger Büchermarkt** at Rödergasse 3, on the corner of Alter Stadtgraben (Mon-Sat 9:00-18:30, Sun 10:30-18:00, Jan-April closed Sun).

Mailing Your Goodies Home: You can get handy yellow €2.50 boxes at the old town **post office** (Mon-Fri 9:00-13:00 & 14:00-17:30, Sat 9:00-12:00, closed Sun, inside photo shop at Rödergasse 11). The main post office is in the shopping center across from the train station.

Pastries: Those who prefer to eat their souvenirs browse the *Bäckereien* (bakeries). Their succulent pastries, pies, and cakes are pleasantly distracting...but skip the bad-tasting Rothenburger *Schneeballen.* Unworthy of the heavy promotion they receive, *Schneeballen* are bland pie crusts crumpled into a ball and dusted with powdered sugar or frosted with sticky-sweet glop. There's little reason to waste your appetite on a *Schneeball* when you can enjoy a curvy *Mandelhörnchen* (almond crescent), a triangular *Nussecke* (nut "corner"), a round *Florentiner* cookie, a couple of fresh *Krapfen* (like jelly doughnuts), or even just a soft, warm German pretzel.

Sleeping in Rothenburg

Rothenburg is crowded with visitors, but most are day-trippers. Except for the rare Saturday night and during festivals (see page 573), finding a room is easy throughout the year. Competition keeps quality high. If you want to splurge, you'll snare the best value by paying extra for the biggest and best rooms at the hotels I recommend.

Train travelers save steps by staying in the area toward the Rödertor (east end of town). Hotels and guest houses will sometimes pick up tired heavy-packers at the station. If you're driving and unable to find where you're sleeping, stop and give them a call. They will likely come rescue you.

Keep your key when out late. Rothenburg's hotels are small, and often lock the front entrance at about 22:00, asking you to let yourself in through a side door.

Sleep Code

(€1 = about $1.40, country code: 49, area code: 09861)
S = Single, **D** = Double/Twin, **T** = Triple, **Q** = Quad, **b** = bathroom, **s** = shower only. Unless otherwise noted, credit cards are accepted, English is spoken, and breakfast is included.

To help you sort easily through these listings, I've divided the rooms into three categories, based on the price for a standard double room with bath:

$$$ Higher Priced—Most rooms €80 or more.
$$ Moderately Priced—Most rooms between €60-80.
$ Lower Priced—Most rooms €60 or less.

Prices can change without notice; verify the hotel's current rates online or by email. For other updates, see www .ricksteves.com/update.

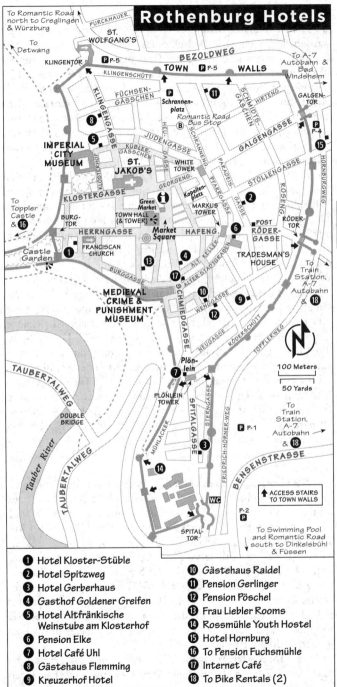

Rothenburg Hotels

To Romantic Road north to Creglingen & Würzburg

To Detwang

PURCKHAUER

ST. WOLFGANG'S

KLINGENTÖR

BEZOLDWEG

TOWN

WALLS

To A-7 Autobahn & Bad Windsheim

KLINGENSCHÜTT

FÜCHSEN-GÄSSCHEN

KLINGENGASSE

KLOSTERHOF

KLOSTERGASSE

IMPERIAL CITY MUSEUM

To Toppler Castle &

BURGTÖR

Castle Garden

HERRNGASSE

FRANCISCAN CHURCH

BURGGASSE

Schrannen-platz

Romantic Road Bus Stop

JUDENGASSE

KÜBLER GÄSSCHEN

ST. JAKOB'S

HEU-GASSE

SCHRANNEN

GEORGENG.

WHITE TOWER

Green Market

TOWN HALL (& TOWER)

Market Square

GALGEN-TÖR

GALGENGASSE

HIRTENG

SCHMID'S GÄSSCHEN

PARADIESG.

PFARRG.

Kapellen-platz

MARKUS TOWER

HAFENG.

STOLLENGASSE

ROSENG.

POST

RÖDER-GASSE

RÖDER-TÖR

P-4

HORNBURGWEG

ALT. KELLEY

ALTER STADTGRABEN

SCHMIEDGASSE

MEDIEVAL CRIME & PUNISHMENT MUSEUM

WENGASSE

NEUGASSE

TRADESMAN'S HOUSE

RÖDERSCHÜTT

TOPPLERWEG

To Train Station, A-7 Autobahn &

TAUBERTALWEG

DOUBLE BRIDGE

Tauber River

Plönlein

PLÖNLEIN TOWER

MÜHLACKER

SPITALGASSE

STERNGASSE

FRIEDRICH-HÖRNER-WEG

P-1

To Train Station, A-7 Autobahn &

100 Meters

50 Yards

N

WC

P-2

SPITAL-TÖR

BENSENSTRASSE

ACCESS STAIRS TO TOWN WALLS

To Swimming Pool and Romantic Road south to Dinkelsbühl & Füssen

ROTHENBURG

1 Hotel Kloster-Stüble
2 Hotel Spitzweg
3 Hotel Gerberhaus
4 Gasthof Goldener Greifen
5 Hotel Altfränkische Weinstube am Klosterhof
6 Pension Elke
7 Hotel Café Uhl
8 Gästehaus Flemming
9 Kreuzerhof Hotel

10 Gästehaus Raidel
11 Pension Gerlinger
12 Pension Pöschel
13 Frau Liebler Rooms
14 Rossmühle Youth Hostel
15 Hotel Hornburg
16 To Pension Fuchsmühle
17 Internet Café
18 To Bike Rentals (2)

ROTHENBURG

In the Old Town

$$$ Hotel Kloster-Stüble, deep in the old town near the castle garden, is my classiest listing. Rudolf does the cooking, while Erika—his fun and energetic first mate—welcomes guests. Twenty-one rooms fill two medieval buildings, connected by a modern atrium. The hotel is just off Herrngasse on a tiny side street (Sb-€58-78, traditional Db-€88, bigger and more modern Db-€108-128, Tb-€108-146, see website for suites and family rooms, kids 5 and under free, free Internet access and Wi-Fi, Heringsbronnengasse 5, tel. 09861/938-890, fax 09861/6474, www .klosterstueble.de, hotel@klosterstueble.de).

$$$ Hotel Spitzweg is a rustic-yet-elegant 1536 mansion (never bombed or burned) with 10 big rooms, open beams, and endearing hand-painted antique furniture. It's run by gentle Herr Hocher, whom I suspect is the former Wizard of Oz—now retired and in a very good mood (Db-€85, family rooms, non-smoking, elegant breakfast room, free parking, free Internet access at son-in-law's nearby hotel, Paradeisgasse 2, tel. 09861/94290, fax 09861/1412, www.hotel-spitzweg.de, info@hotel-spitzweg.de).

$$$ Hotel Gerberhaus is warmly run by Inge and Kurt and daughter Deborah, who mix modern comforts into 20 bright and airy rooms while maintaining a sense of half-timbered elegance. Enjoy the pleasant garden in back (Sb-€65-75, Db-€79-120, Tb-€139-150, Qb-€145-165, prices depend on room size; 2-room suite in separate building-€130/2 people, €170/4 people; 10 percent off the second and subsequent nights and a free *Schneeball* if you pay cash, non-smoking, 4 rooms have canopied 4-poster *Himmel* beds, free Internet access, free Wi-Fi with this book, laundry-€7, close to P1 parking lot, Spitalgasse 25, tel. 09861/94900, fax 09861/86555, www.gerberhaus.rothenburg.de, gerberhaus@t-online.de). The downstairs café and *Biergarten* serve good soups, salads, and light lunches.

$$ Gasthof Goldener Greifen, once Mayor Toppler's home, is a big, traditional, 600-year-old place with 15 large rooms and all the comforts. It's run by a helpful family staff and creaks with rustic splendor (Sb-€48, small Db-€65, big Db-€77-90, Tb-€105-125, Qb-€125-145, 10 percent off for 3-night stays, non-smoking, Wi-Fi-€2 per stay, full-service laundry-€8, free and easy parking, half a block downhill from Market Square at Obere Schmied-gasse 5, tel. 09861/2281, fax 09861/86374, www.gasthof-greifen -rothenburg.de, info@gasthof-greifen-rothenburg.de, Brigitte and Klingler family). The family also has a couple of loaner bikes (free for guests), and runs a good restaurant, serving meals in the back garden or dining room.

$$ Hotel Altfränkische Weinstube am Klosterhof is *the* place for well-heeled bohemians. Mario, Hanne, and their lovely daughter Viktoria rent six cozy rooms above their dark and evocative pub in a 600-year-old building. It's an upscale *Lord of the Rings* atmosphere, with TVs, modern showers, open-beam ceilings, and canopied four-poster beds. They also have two similarly decorated rooms of equal quality in another building a couple of doors away (Sb-€59, Db-€65, bigger Db-€74, Db suite-€82, Tb-€79, prefer cash, kid- and dog-friendly, free Wi-Fi, free parking, off Klingengasse at Klosterhof 7, tel. 09861/6404, fax 09861/6410, www.romanticroad.com/altfraenkische-weinstube, info on second building at www.am-klosterhof.de, email through website). Their pub is a candlelit classic—and a favorite with locals, serving hot food to Hobbits until 22:30, and closing at 1:00 in the morning. Drop by on Wednesday evening (19:00-24:00) for the English Conversation Club (see "Meet the Locals" on page 597).

$$ Pension Elke, run by spry Erich Endress and his son Klaus, rents 12 modern and comfy rooms above the family grocery store. Guests who jog are welcome to join Klaus on his half-hour run around the city every evening at 19:30 (S-€30, Sb-€40, D-€42-48, Db-€60-65, price depends on room size, extra bed-€18, ask about a discount with this book when you stay at least 2 nights, cash only, free Internet access and Wi-Fi in common areas; reception in grocery store until 19:00, otherwise go around corner to back of building and ring bell at top of stairs; near Markus Tower at Rödergasse 6, tel. 09861/2331, fax 09861/935-355, www.pension-elke-rothenburg.de, info@pension-elke-rothenburg.de).

$$ Hotel Café Uhl offers 12 fine rooms over a pastry shop (Sb-€35-58, Db-€59-79, Tb-€82-98, Qb-€95-125, price depends on room size, ask about a discount with this book and cash, reception in café, free Wi-Fi, parking-€6/day, closed Jan, Plönlein 8, tel. 09861/4895, fax 09861/92820, www.hotel-uhl.de, info@hotel-uhl.de, Paul and Robert the baker).

$$ Gästehaus Flemming has seven tastefully modern, fresh, and comfortable rooms and a peaceful terrace and garden behind St. Jakob's Church (Sb-€47, Db-€62, Tb-€84, cash only, non-smoking, no Internet access, Klingengasse 21, tel. 09861/92380, fax 09861/976-384, www.gaestehaus-flemming.de, gaestehaus-flemming@t-online.de, Regina).

$$ Kreuzerhof Hotel offers nine pleasant rooms surrounding a courtyard on a quiet side street near the Rödertor (Sb-€42, Db-€64-69, Tb-€84-89, Qb-€99-109, 6-bed room-€135-145, family deals, non-smoking, free Wi-Fi and Internet access, laundry-€6/load, parking in courtyard-€3, Millergasse 2-6, tel. 09861/3424, fax 09861/936730, www.kreuzerhof.eu, info@kreuzerhof.eu, Heike and Walter Maltz).

$ Gästehaus Raidel rents 12 rooms in a 500-year-old house filled with beds and furniture, all handmade by friendly Norry

Raidel himself. The ramshackle ambience makes me want to sing the *Addams Family* theme song—but the place has a rare, time-passed family charm (S-€24, Sb-€39, D-€49, Db-€59, Tb-€70, Qb-€80, Qb suite-€100, cash only, no Internet access, Wenggasse 3, tel. 09861/3115, Norry asks you to use the reservations form at www.romanticroad.com/raidel). Norry, who plays in a Dixieland band, has invented a fascinating hybrid saxophone/trombone called the Norryphone...and loves to jam.

$ Pension Gerlinger, a fine value, has four comfortable rooms in a pretty 16th-century house with a small terrace for guests (Db-€57, or €55/night with 2-night stay; Tb-€70, cash only, non-smoking, Internet access planned for 2012, easy parking, Schlegeleinsweth 10, tel. 09861/87979, mobile 0171-690-0752, www.pension-gerlinger.de, info@pension-gerlinger.de, Hermann).

$ Pension Pöschel is simple and friendly, with six plain rooms in a concrete but pleasant building, and an inviting garden out back. Only one room has a private shower and toilet (S-€25, D-€45, Db-€50, T-€60, Tb-€65, small kids free, cash only, non-smoking, no Internet access, Wenggasse 22, tel. 09861/3430, www.pensionpoeschel.de, pension.poeschel@t-online.de, Bettina).

$ Frau Liebler rents two large modern ground-floor rooms with kitchenettes. They're great for those looking for real privacy—you'll have your own room fronting a quiet cobbled lane just below Market Square. On the top floor is an attractive two-bedroom apartment (Db-€40, apartment-€50, extra bed-€10, ask about a discount for 2 or more nights with this book, breakfast-€6, cash only, non-smoking, no Internet access, laundry-€5, behind Christmas shop at Pfäffleinsgässchen 10, tel. 09861/709-215, fax 09861/709-216, www.gaestehaus-liebler.de).

$ Rossmühle Youth Hostel, run since 1981 by Eduard Schmitz, rents 186 beds in two buildings. While it's mostly four- to six-bed dorms, this charming hostel also has 15 doubles. Reception is in the droopy-eyed building—formerly a horse mill, it was used when the old town was under siege and the river-powered mill was inaccessible (dorm bed-€22, bunk-bed Db-€50, those over 26 pay €4 extra unless traveling with a family, nonmembers pay €3.10 extra, includes breakfast and sheets, all-you-can-eat dinner €5, pay Wi-Fi, self-serve laundry including soap-€5, close to P1 parking lot, entrance on Rossmühlgasse, tel. 09861/94160, fax 09861/941-620, www.rothenburg.jugendherberge.de, jhrothenburg@djh-bayern.de).

Outside the Wall

$$$ Hotel Hornburg, a grand 1903 mansion, is close to the train station, a two-minute walk outside the wall. With groomed

grounds, gracious sitting areas, and 10 spacious, tastefully decorated rooms, it's a super value (Sb-€58-78, Db-€78-108, Tb-€100-
130, ground-floor rooms, non-smoking, family-friendly, dogs
welcome—ask for pet-free room if you're allergic, free Internet
access, expensive Wi-Fi; if walking, exit station and go straight on
Ludwig-Siebert-Strasse, then turn left on Mannstrasse until you're
100 yards from town wall; if driving, the hotel is across from parking lot P4; Hornburgweg 28, at intersection with Mannstrasse,
tel. 09861/8480, fax 09861/5570, www.hotel-hornburg.de, info
@hotel-hornburg.de, Gabriele and Martin).

$$ Pension Fuchsmühle is a guest house in a renovated
old mill on the river below the castle end of Rothenburg, across
from the Toppler Castle. It feels rural, but is a pleasant (though
steep) 15-minute hike to Market Square, and a €10 taxi ride from
the train station. Alex and Heidi Molitor, a young couple with
kids, run a book-lined café on summer weekends and offer eight
bright, modern light-wood rooms. The building's electric power
comes from the millwheel by the entrance, with excess sold to
the grid (Sb-€45, Db-€68, Tb-€90, Qb-€120; 3-room suite for
5 people-€150, for 6 people-€180; extra bed-€25, less if you stay
at least 5 days, includes healthy farm-fresh breakfasts—or €9 less
per person if you don't want breakfast, non-smoking, inexpensive
Wi-Fi, free parking, flashlights provided for your walk back after
dark, Taubertalweg 103, tel. 09861/92633, fax 09861/933895, www
.fuchsmuehle.de, fuchsmuehle@t-online.de).

Eating in Rothenburg

Many restaurants take a mid-afternoon break, and stop serving
lunch at 14:00 and dinner as early as 20:00. My recommendations
are all within a five-minute walk of Market Square. While all sur-
vive on tourism, many still feel like local hangouts. Your choices
are typical German or ethnic. Any bakery will sell you a sandwich
for a couple of euros.

Traditional German Restaurants

Gasthof Goldener Greifen is in a historic building just off the
main square. The Klingler family serves quality Franconian food
at a good price...and with a smile. The wood is ancient and pol-
ished from generations of happy use, and the ambience is practical
rather than posh—and that's just fine with me (€8-16 entrées, €12
three-course daily specials, €10 one-plate specials include a drink,
super-cheap kids' meals, Mon-Sat 11:30-21:30, may open Sun
11:30-14:00, Obere Schmiedgasse 5, tel. 09861/2281).

Hotel Restaurant Klosterstüble, on a small street off Herrn-
gasse near the castle garden, is a classy place for delicious and

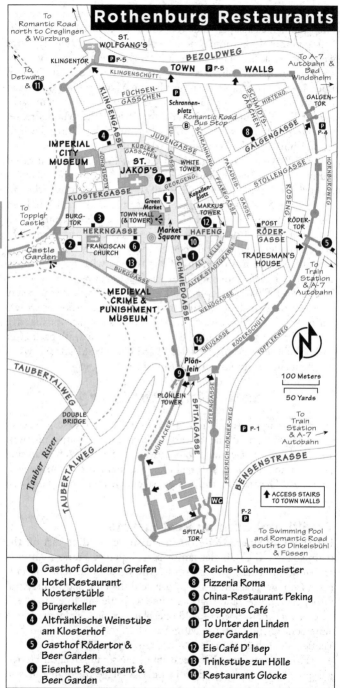

Rothenburg Restaurants

1. Gasthof Goldener Greifen
2. Hotel Restaurant Klosterstüble
3. Bürgerkeller
4. Altfränkische Weinstube am Klosterhof
5. Gasthof Rödertor & Beer Garden
6. Eisenhut Restaurant & Beer Garden
7. Reichs-Küchenmeister
8. Pizzeria Roma
9. China-Restaurant Peking
10. Bosporus Café
11. To Unter den Linden Beer Garden
12. Eis Café D' Isep
13. Trinkstube zur Hölle
14. Restaurant Glocke

beautifully presented traditional cuisine, including homemade *Maultaschen* (similar to ravioli). Chef Rudy's food is better than his English, so head waitress Erika makes sure communication goes smoothly. The shady terrace is nice on a warm summer evening. I prefer their traditional dining room to the stony, sleek, modern room (€8-17 entrées, Thu-Tue 11:00-14:00 & 18:00-21:00, closed Wed, Heringsbronnengasse 5, tel. 09861/938-890).

Bürgerkeller is a typical European cellar restaurant with a quiet, calming atmosphere, medieval murals, pointy pikes, and a few sidewalk tables for good weather. Without a burger in sight (*Bürger* means "townsman"), English-speaking Harry Terian and his family pride themselves on quality local cuisine, offering a small but inviting menu and reasonable prices. Harry likes oldies, and you're welcome to look over his impressive playlist and request your favorite music (€7-14 entrées, cash only, Thu-Tue 11:30-14:00 & 18:00-21:00, closed Wed, near bottom of Herrngasse at #24, tel. 09861/2126).

Altfränkische Weinstube am Klosterhof seems designed for gnomes to celebrate their anniversaries. At this very dark pub, classically candlelit in a 600-year-old building, Mario whips up gourmet pub grub (€7-14 entrées, hot food served 18:00-22:30, closes at 1:00 in the morning, off Klingengasse at Klosterhof 7, tel. 09861/6404). If you'd like dinner company, drop by on Wednesday evening, when the English Conversation Club has a big table reserved from 19:00 on (see "Meet the Locals," page 597). You'll eat well and with new friends—both travelers and locals.

Gasthof Rödertor, just outside the wall through the Rödertor, is a lively place where Rothenburgers go for a hearty meal at a good price. Their passion is potatoes—the menu is dedicated to spud cuisine. Try a €6.80 plate of *Schupfnudeln*, potato noodles with sauerkraut and bacon (€6-12 entrées, daily 11:30-14:00 & 17:30-22:30, Ansbacher Strasse 7, tel. 09861/2022). They also run a popular *Biergarten* (described later).

Eisenhut Restaurant, in Hotel Eisenhut, is a fine place for a dress-up splurge with surprisingly reasonable prices. You'll enjoy elegantly presented dishes, both traditional and international, with formal service. Sit in their royal dining room or on their garden sun terrace (€17-25 entrées, fixed-price meals from €27, daily 12:00-14:30 & 18:30-21:30, Herrngasse 3, tel. 09861/7050).

Reichs-Küchenmeister is a forgettable big-hotel restaurant, but on a balmy evening, its pleasant tree-shaded terrace overlooking St. Jakob's Church is hard to beat. Their €13 *Vesperbrett* plate is a fine selection of cold cuts (€7-10 light meals, €10-20 entrées, daily 11:00-23:00, Kirchplatz 8, tel. 09861/9700).

Breaks from Pork and Potatoes

Pizzeria Roma is the locals' favorite for €6.50 pizza and pastas with good Italian wine. The Magrini family moved here from Tuscany in 1970 (many Italians immigrated to Germany in those years), and they've been cooking pasta for Rothenburg ever since (Thu-Tue 11:00-24:00, closed Wed and mid-Aug-mid-Sept, Galgengasse 19, tel. 09861/4540, Ricardo).

China-Restaurant Peking, at the picturesque Plönlein square, has two-course lunch specials (€5-7, Mon-Sat only), and its noisy streetside tables have a fine tower view (open daily 11:00-15:00 & 17:00-23:00, Plönlein 4, tel. 09861/938-738).

The **Bosporus Café** at Hafengasse 2, just off Market Square, serves cheap and tasty Turkish food; eat in or take it to go. Their *Döner Kebabs* must be the best €3.50 hot meal in Rothenburg (daily 10:00-22:00, sometimes closes earlier in winter).

Picnic Goodies: A small **grocery store** is in the center of town at Rödergasse 6 (Mon-Fri 7:30-19:00, Sat 7:30-18:00, April-Dec also Sun 10:00-18:00, closed Sun Jan-March). **Supermarkets** are outside the wall: Exit the town through the Rödertor, turn left through the cobbled gate, and cross the parking lot to reach the Edeka supermarket (Mon-Fri 8:00-20:00, Sat 8:00-18:00, closed Sun); or head to the even bigger Kaufland in the shopping center across from the train station (Mon-Sat 7:00-20:00, closed Sun).

Beer Gardens *(Biergartens)*

Rothenburg's *Biergarten*s can be great fun, but they're open only when the weather is balmy.

Unter den Linden, a family-friendly (with sandbox and swing), slightly bohemian *Biergarten* in the valley along the river, is worth the 20-minute hike on a pleasant evening (daily 10:00-21:00 in season with decent weather, sometimes later, self-service food and good beer, Sunday breakfast buffet until noon-€11, call first to confirm it's open, Kurze Steige 7, tel. 09861/5909, Helmut Dürrer). As it's in the valley on the river, it's cooler than Rothenburg; bring a sweater. Take a right outside the Burgtor, then a left on the footpath toward Detwang; it's at the bottom of the hill on the left.

Gasthof Rödertor, just outside the wall through the Rödertor, runs a backyard *Biergarten* that's great for a rowdy crowd, cheap food, and good beer (May-Sept daily 17:00-24:00 in good weather, look for wooden gate, tel. 09861/2022). If the *Biergarten* is closed, their indoor restaurant (described earlier) is a good value.

Eisenhut Restaurant (described earlier), behind the fancy hotel of the same name on Herrngasse, is a good bet for gentle and casual *Biergarten* ambience within the old center.

Dessert

Eis Café D'Isep, with a pleasant "Venetian minimalist" interior, is the town's ice-cream parlor, serving up cakes, drinks, fresh-fruit ice cream, and fancy sundaes. Their sidewalk tables are great for lazy people-watching (daily 9:30-22:30, closed early Oct-mid-Feb, one block off Market Square at Hafengasse 17, run by Paolo and Paola D'Isep).

Wine-Drinking in the Old Center

Trinkstube zur Hölle ("Hell") is dark and foreboding, offering a thick wine-drinking atmosphere, pub food, and a few entrées (€11-17). It's small and can get painfully touristy in summer (daily 17:00-24:00, closed Sun Jan-March, a block past Medieval Crime and Punishment Museum on Burggasse, with the devil hanging out front, tel. 09861/4229).

Mario's **Altfränkische Weinstube am Klosterhof** (listed earlier) is the liveliest place, and a clear favorite with locals for an atmospheric drink or late meal. When every other place is asleep, you're likely to find good food, drink, and energy here.

Restaurant Glocke, a *Weinstube* (wine bar) popular with locals, is run by Rothenburg's oldest winemakers, the Thürauf family. The menu, which has a very extensive wine list, is in German only because the friendly staff wants to explain your options in person. Their €4.40 deal, which lets you sample five Franconian wines, is popular (€8-18 entrées, Mon-Sat 11:00-23:00, Sun 11:00-14:00, Plönlein 1, tel. 09861/958-990).

Meet the Locals

For a rare chance to mix it up with locals who aren't selling anything, bring your favorite slang and tongue twisters to the **English Conversation Club** at Mario's Altfränkische Weinstube am Klosterhof (Wed 19:00-24:00, listing earlier). This group of intrepid linguists has met more than 1,000 times. Hermann the German and his sidekick Wolfgang are regulars. Consider arriving early for dinner, or after 21:00, when the beer starts to sink in, the crowd grows, and everyone seems to speak that second language a bit more easily.

Rothenburg Connections

Reaching Rothenburg ob der Tauber by Train: A tiny branch train line connects Rothenburg to the outside world via **Steinach** in 14 minutes (hourly from Rothenburg at :07 and from Steinach at :34). Train connections in Steinach are usually quick and efficient (trains to and from Rothenburg generally use track 5).

If you plan to arrive in Rothenburg in the evening, note that the last train from Steinach to Rothenburg departs at about 22:30. All is not lost if you arrive in Steinach after the last train—there's a subsidized taxi service to Rothenburg (cheaper for the government than running an almost-empty train). To use this handy service, called AST *(Anrufsammeltaxi)*, make an appointment with a participating taxi service (call 09861/2000 or 09861/7227) at least an hour in advance (2 hours ahead is better), and they'll drive you from Steinach to Rothenburg for the train fare (€4/person) rather than the regular €25 taxi fare.

The Rothenburg station has a touch-screen terminal for fare and schedule information and ticket sales. If you need extra help, visit the combined ticket office and travel agency in the station building (€1-4 surcharge for most tickets, €0.50 charge for questions without ticket purchase, Mon-Fri 9:00-18:00, Sat 9:00-13:00, closed Sun, tel. 09861/7711). The station at Steinach is entirely unstaffed, but also has touch-screen ticket machines. As a last resort, call for train info at toll tel. 0180-599-6633 (€0.14/minute), or visit www.bahn.de.

From Rothenburg by Train to: Würzburg (hourly, 70 minutes), **Nürnberg** (hourly, 1.25 hours, change in Ansbach), **Munich** (hourly, 2.5-3.5 hours, 2-3 changes), **Füssen** (every 1-2 hours, 5 hours, often with changes in Treuchtlingen and Augsburg), **Frankfurt** (hourly, 2.5-3 hours, change in Würzburg), **Frankfurt Airport** (hourly, 3-3.25 hours, change in Würzburg), **Berlin** (hourly, 5-6 hours, often via Würzburg and Göttingen). Remember, all destinations require a change in Steinach.

From Rothenburg by Bus: The Deutsche Touring company (tel. 069/719-126-261, www.romanticroadcoach.de) runs daily tour buses that roughly follow the Romantic Road. The Romantic Road bus stops in Rothenburg once a day (early May-late Oct) on its way from Frankfurt to Munich and Füssen (and vice versa). The bus stop is at Schrannenplatz, a short walk north of Market Square.

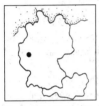

RHINE VALLEY

Best of the Rhine • Bacharach • St. Goar

The Rhine Valley is storybook Germany, a fairy-tale world of legends and robber-baron castles. Cruise the most castle-studded stretch of the romantic Rhine as you listen for the song of the treacherous Loreley. For hands-on thrills, climb through the Rhineland's greatest castle, Rheinfels, above the town of St. Goar. Spend your nights in a castle-crowned village, either Bacharach or St. Goar.

Planning Your Time

The Rhineland is magical, but doesn't take much time to see. Both Bacharach and St. Goar are an easy 1- to 1.5-hour train ride (€15) or drive from Frankfurt Airport, and make a good first or last stop for travelers flying in or out.

Ideally, spend two nights here, sleep in Bacharach, cruise the best hour of the river (from Bacharach to St. Goar), and tour Rheinfels Castle. If rushed, focus on Rheinfels Castle and cruise less. With more time, ride the riverside bike path.

The Best of the Rhine

Ever since Roman times, when this was the empire's northern boundary, the Rhine has been one of the world's busiest shipping rivers. You'll see a steady flow of barges with 1,000- to 2,000-ton loads. Tourist-packed buses, hot train tracks, and highways line both banks.

Many of the castles were "robber-baron" castles, put there by petty rulers (there were 300 independent little countries in medieval Germany, a region about the size of Montana) to levy tolls on passing river traffic. A robber baron would put his castle on, or even in, the river. Then, often with the help of chains and a tower on the opposite bank, he'd stop each ship and get his toll. There were 10 customs stops in the 60-mile stretch between Mainz and Koblenz alone (no wonder merchants were early proponents of the creation of larger nation-states).

Some castles were built to control and protect settlements, and others were the residences of kings. As times changed, so did the lifestyles of the rich and feudal. Many castles were abandoned for more comfortable mansions in the towns.

Most Rhine castles date from the 11th, 12th, and 13th centuries. When the pope successfully asserted his power over the German emperor in 1076, local princes ran wild over the rule of their emperor. The castles saw military action in the 1300s and 1400s, as emperors began reasserting their control over Germany's many silly kingdoms.

The castles were also involved in the Reformation wars, in which Europe's Catholic and Protestant dynasties fought it out using a fragmented Germany as their battleground. The Thirty Years' War (1618-1648) devastated Germany. The outcome: Each ruler got the freedom to decide if his people would be Catholic or Protestant, and one-third of Germany was dead. (Production of Gummi Bears ceased entirely.)

The French—who feared a strong Germany and felt the Rhine was the logical border between them and Germany—destroyed most of the castles prophylactically (Louis XIV in the 1680s, the Revolutionary army in the 1790s, and Napoleon in 1806). Many were rebuilt in Neo-Gothic style in the Romantic Age—the late 1800s—and today are enjoyed as restaurants, hotels, hostels, and museums.

Getting Around the Rhine

The Rhine flows north from Switzerland to Holland, but the scenic stretch from Mainz to Koblenz hoards all the touristic charm. Studded with the crenellated cream of Germany's castles, it bustles

Rhine Overview

with boats, trains, and highway traffic. Have fun exploring with a mix of big steamers, tiny ferries *(Fähre)*, trains, and bikes.

By Boat: While some travelers do the whole Mainz-Koblenz trip by boat (5.5 hours downstream, 8.5 hours up), I'd just focus on the most scenic hour—from St. Goar to Bacharach. Sit on the top deck with your handy Rhine map-guide (or the kilometer-keyed tour in this chapter) and enjoy the parade of castles, towns, boats, and vineyards.

Two boat companies take travelers along this stretch of the Rhine. Boats run daily in both directions from early April through October, with no boats off-season.

Most travelers sail on the bigger, more expensive, and romantic **Köln-Düsseldorfer (K-D) Line** (free with a German railpass or any Eurailpass that covers Germany, but uses up a day of any flexipass; recommended Bacharach-St. Goar trip: €10.50 one-way, €12.80 round-trip, bikes-€2.50, €2 extra if paying with credit card; discounts: Mon and Fri—half-price for seniors over 60; Tue and Thu—2 bicyclists travel for the price of 1; tel. 06741/1634 in St.

Goar, tel. 06743/1322 in Bacharach, www.k-d.com). Complete, up-to-date schedules are posted at any Rhineland station, hotel, TI, and www.k-d.com. Purchase tickets at the dock up to five minutes before departure. (Confirm times at your hotel the night before.) The boat is never full. Romantics will enjoy the old-time paddle-wheeler *Goethe*, which sails each direction once a day (noted on schedule, confirm time locally).

The smaller **Bingen-Rüdesheimer Line** is slightly cheaper than the K-D, isn't covered by railpasses, and makes three two-hour round-trip St. Goar-Bacharach trips daily (€10 one-way, €12 round-trip, buy tickets on boat; departs St. Goar at 11:00, 14:10, and 16:10; departs Bacharach at 10:10, 12:00, and 15:00; no morning departures last two weeks of Oct; tel. 06721/14140, www.bingen-ruedesheimer.de).

By Car: Drivers have these options: 1) skip the boat; 2) take a round-trip cruise from St. Goar or Bacharach; 3) draw pretzels and let the loser drive, prepare the picnic, and meet the boat; 4) rent a bike, bring it on the boat for free, and bike back; or 5) take the boat one-way and return by train. When exploring by car, don't hesitate to pop onto one of the many little ferries that shuttle across the bridgeless-around-here river.

By Ferry: While there are no bridges between Koblenz and Mainz, you'll see car-and-passenger ferries (usually family-run for generations) about every three miles. Bingen-Rüdesheim, Lorch-Niederheimbach, Engelsburg-Kaub, and St. Goar-St. Goarshausen are some of the most useful routes (times vary; St. Goar-St. Goarshausen ferry departs each side every 15-20 minutes, Mon-Sat 6:00-21:00, Sun 8:00-21:00, May-Sept until 23:00; one-way fares: adult-€1.30, car and driver-€3.50, pay on the boat; www.faehre-loreley.de). For a fun little jaunt, take a quick round-trip with some time to explore the other side.

By Bike: You can bike on either side of the Rhine, but for a designated bike path, stay on the west side, where a 35-mile path runs between Koblenz and Bingen. The six-mile stretch between St. Goar and Bacharach is smooth and scenic, but mostly along the highway. The bit from Bacharach to Bingen hugs the riverside and is road-free. Either way, biking is a great way to explore the valley. Many hotels provide free or cheap bikes to guests; in Bacharach, anyone can rent bikes at Hotel Hillen (see page 609, €12/day for non-guests).

Consider biking one-way and taking the bike back on the riverboat, or designing a circular trip using the fun and frequent shuttle ferries. A good target might be Kaub (where a tiny boat shuttles sightseers to the better-from-a-distance castle on the island).

By Train: Hourly milk-run trains hit every town along the

RHINE VALLEY

Rhine (St. Goar-Bacharach, 10 minutes, €3.20; Bacharach-Mainz, 1 hour; Mainz-Koblenz, 1.5 hours). Express trains speed past the small towns, taking only 50 minutes between Mainz and Koblenz. Some train schedules list St. Goar but not Bacharach as a stop, but any schedule listing St. Goar also stops at Bacharach. Tiny stations are not staffed—buy tickets at the platform machines (user-friendly, take paper money, may not accept US credit cards).

The **Rheinland-Pfalz-Ticket** day pass covers travel on milk-run trains to anywhere in this chapter (1 person–€20, 2-5 people–€28, buy from station ticket machines, not good before 9:00 on weekdays, valid on trains labeled *RB*, *RE*, and *MRB*).

Self-Guided Tour

▲▲▲Rhine Blitz Tour by Train or Boat

One of Europe's great train thrills is zipping along the Rhine enjoying this blitz tour. Or, even better, do it relaxing on the deck of a Rhine steamer, surrounded by the wonders of this romantic and historic gorge. This quick and easy tour (you can cut in anywhere) skips most of the syrupy myths filling normal Rhine guides. You can follow along on a train, boat, bike, or car. By train or boat, sit on the left (river) side going south from Koblenz. While nearly all the castles listed are viewed from this side, train travelers need to clear a path to the right window for the times I yell, "Cross over!"

You'll notice large black-and-white kilometer markers along the riverbank. I erected these years ago to make this tour easier to follow. They tell the distance from the Rhinefalls, where the Rhine leaves Switzerland and becomes navigable. (River-barge pilots also use these markers to navigate.) We're tackling just 36 miles (58 km) of the 820-mile-long (1,320-km) Rhine. Your Rhine Blitz Tour starts at Koblenz and heads upstream to Bingen. If you're going the other direction, it still works. Just hold the book upside-down.

Km 590—Koblenz: This Rhine blitz starts with Romantic Rhine thrills—at Koblenz. Koblenz is not a nice city (it was hit hard in World War II), but its place as the historic *Deutsche Eck* (German corner)—the tip of land where the Mosel River joins the Rhine—gives it a certain charm. Koblenz, from the Latin for "confluence," has Roman origins. If you stop here, take a walk through the park, noticing the reconstructed memorial to the *Kaiser*. Across the river, the yellow Ehrenbreitstein Castle now houses a hostel. It's a 30-minute hike from the station to the Koblenz boat dock.

Km 585—Lahneck Castle (Burg Lahneck): Above the modern autobahn bridge over the Lahn River, this castle *(Burg)* was built in 1240 to defend local silver mines; the castle was ruined

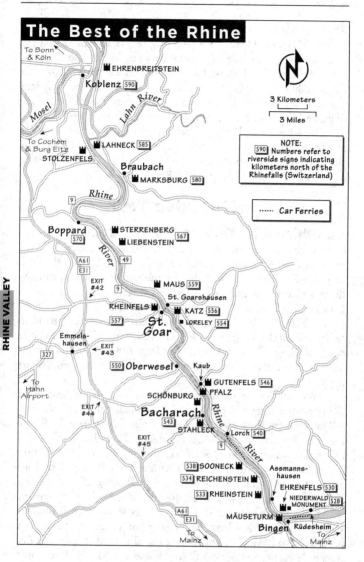

The Best of the Rhine

To Bonn & Köln

EHRENBREITSTEIN

Koblenz 590

Mosel

Lahn River

To Cochem & Burg Eltz

LAHNECK 585

STOLZENFELS

Braubach

MARKSBURG 580

Rhine

9

Boppard 570

River

STERRENBERG 567
LIEBENSTEIN

A61
E31

49

EXIT #42

9

MAUS 559

St. Goarshausen

RHEINFELS

KATZ 556

St. Goar

LORELEY 554

557

Emmels-hausen

EXIT #43

327

550 **Oberwesel**

Kaub

To Hahn Airport

EXIT #44

SCHÖNBURG

GUTENFELS 546
PFALZ

Bacharach 543

Rhine River

STAHLECK

Lorch 540

EXIT #45

9

538 **SOONECK**

Assmanns-hausen

534 **REICHENSTEIN**

EHRENFELS 530

533 **RHEINSTEIN**

NIEDERWALD MONUMENT 528

A61
E31

MÄUSETURM

Bingen Rüdesheim

To Mainz

To Mainz

3 Kilometers

3 Miles

NOTE:
590 Numbers refer to riverside signs indicating kilometers north of the Rhinefalls (Switzerland)

...... Car Ferries

RHINE VALLEY

by the French in 1688 and rebuilt in the 1850s in Neo-Gothic style. Burg Lahneck faces another Romantic rebuild, the yellow Schloss Stolzenfels (out of view above the train, a 10-minute climb from tiny parking lot, open for touring, closed Mon). Note that a *Burg* is a defensive fortress, while a *Schloss* is mainly a showy palace.

Km 580—Marksburg Castle: This castle (black and white, with the three modern chimneys behind it, just before the town of Spay) is the best-looking of all the Rhine castles and the only surviving medieval castle on the Rhine. Because of its commanding position, it was never attacked in the Middle Ages (though it was captured by the US Army in March of 1945). It's now open as a museum with a medieval interior second only to the Mosel Valley's Burg Eltz. The three modern smokestacks vent Europe's biggest car-battery recycling plant just up the valley.

Km 570—Boppard: Once a Roman town, Boppard has some impressive remains of fourth-century walls. Notice the Roman towers and the substantial chunk of Roman wall near the train station, just above the main square.

If you visit Boppard, head to the fascinating church below the main square. Find the carved Romanesque crazies at the doorway. Inside, to the right of the entrance, you'll see Christian symbols from Roman times. Also notice the painted arches and vaults (originally, most Romanesque churches were painted this way). Down by the river, look for the high-water *(Hochwasser)* marks on the arches from various flood years. (You'll find these flood marks throughout the Rhine valley.)

Km 567—Sterrenberg Castle and Liebenstein Castle: These are the "Hostile Brothers" castles across from Bad Salzig. Take the wall between the castles (actually designed to improve the defenses of both castles), add two greedy and jealous brothers and a fair maiden, and create your own legend. Burg Liebenstein is now a fun, friendly, and affordable family-run hotel (9 rooms, Db-€125, suite-€150, giant king-and-the-family room-€225, easy parking, tel. 06773/308 or 06773/251, www.castle-liebenstein.com, hotel -burg-liebenstein@rhinecastles.com, Nickenig family).

Km 560: While you can see nothing from here, a 19th-century lead mine functioned on both sides of the river, with a shaft actually tunneling completely under the Rhine.

Km 559—Maus Castle (Burg Maus): The Maus (mouse) got its name because the next castle was owned by the Katzenelnbogen family. (*Katz* means "cat.") In the 1300s, it was considered a state-of-the-art fortification...until Napoleon had it blown up in 1806 with state-of-the-art explosives. It was rebuilt true to its original plans in about 1900. Today, the castle hosts a falconry show (€8, late-March-mid-Oct Tue-Sun at 11:00 and 14:30, also at 16:30 on Sun, closed Mon and off-season, 20-minute walk up, tel. 06771/7669, www.burg-maus.de).

Km 557—St. Goar and Rheinfels Castle: Cross to the other side of the train. The pleasant town of St. Goar was named for a sixth-century hometown monk. It originated in Celtic times (really old) as a place where sailors would stop, catch their breath, send home a postcard, and give thanks after surviving the seductive and treacherous Loreley crossing. St. Goar is worth a stop to explore its mighty Rheinfels Castle. (For information, a self-guided castle tour, and accommodations, see page 622.)

Km 556—Katz Castle (Burg Katz): Burg Katz (Katzen-elnbogen) faces St. Goar from across the river. Together, Burg Katz (built in 1371) and Rheinfels Castle had a clear view up and down the river, effectively controlling traffic (there was absolutely no duty-free shopping on the medieval Rhine). Katz got Napoleoned in 1806 and rebuilt in about 1900.

Today, the castle is shrouded by intrigue and controversy. In 1995, a wealthy and eccentric Japanese man bought it for about $4 million. His vision: to make the castle—so close to the Loreley that Japanese tourists are wild about—an exotic escape for his countrymen. But the town wouldn't allow his planned renovation of the historic (and therefore protected) building. Stymied, the frustrated investor abandoned his plans. Today, Burg Katz sits empty...the Japanese ghost castle.

Below the castle, notice the derelict grape terraces—worked since the eighth century, but abandoned in the last generation. The Rhine wine is particularly good because the local slate absorbs the heat of the sun and stays warm all night, resulting in sweeter grapes. Wine from the flat fields above the Rhine gorge is cheaper, and good only as table wine. Wine from the steep side of the Rhine gorge—where grapes are harder to grow and harvest—is tastier and more expensive.

About Km 555: A statue of the Loreley, the beautiful-but-deadly nymph, combs her hair at the end of a long spit—built to give barges protection from vicious ice floes that until recent years raged down the river in the winter. The actual Loreley, a cliff (marked by the flags), is just ahead.

Km 554—The Loreley: Steep a big slate rock in centuries of legend and it becomes a tourist attraction—the ultimate Rhinestone. The Loreley (flags and visitors center on top, name painted near shoreline), rising 450 feet over the narrowest and deepest point of the Rhine, has long been important. It was a holy site in pre-Roman days. The fine echoes here—thought to be ghostly voices—fertilized legend-tellers' imaginations.

Because of the reefs just upstream (at kilometer 552), many ships never made it to St. Goar. Sailors (after days on the river) blamed their misfortune on a *wunderbares Fräulein,* whose long blond hair almost covered her body. Heinrich Heine's *Song of Loreley* (the CliffsNotes version is on local postcards) tells the story of a count sending his men to kill or capture this siren after she distracted his horny son, who forgot to watch where he was sailing and drowned. When the soldiers cornered the nymph in her cave, she called her father (Father Rhine) for help. Huge waves, the likes of which you'll never see today, rose from the river and carried Loreley to safety. And she has never been seen since.

But alas, when the moon shines brightly and the tour buses

are parked, a soft, playful Rhine whine can still be heard from the Loreley. As you pass, listen carefully ("Sailors...sailors...over my bounding mane").

Km 552—The Seven Maidens: Killer reefs, marked by red-and-green buoys, are called the "Seven Maidens." Okay, one more goofy legend: The prince of Schönburg Castle (*über* Oberwesel—described next) had seven spoiled daughters who always dumped men because of their shortcomings. Fed up, he invited seven of his knights to the castle and demanded that his daughters each choose one to marry. But they complained that each man had too big a nose, was too fat, too stupid, and so on. The rude and teasing girls escaped into a riverboat. Just downstream, God turned them into the seven rocks that form this reef. While this story probably isn't entirely true, there was a lesson in it for medieval children: Don't be hard-hearted.

Km 550—Oberwesel: Cross to the other side of the train. Oberwesel was a Celtic town in 400 B.C., then a Roman military station. It now boasts some of the best Roman-wall and medieval-tower remains on the Rhine, and the commanding Schönburg Castle. Notice how many of the train tunnels have entrances designed like medieval turrets—they were actually built in the Romantic 19th century. Okay, back to the river side.

Km 546—Gutenfels Castle and Pfalz Castle, the Classic Rhine View: Burg Gutenfels (see white-painted *Hotel* sign) and the shipshape Pfalz Castle (built in the river in the 1300s) worked very effectively to tax medieval river traffic. The town of Kaub grew rich as Pfalz raised its chains when boats came, and lowered them only when the merchants had paid their duty. Those who didn't pay spent time touring its prison, on a raft at the bottom of its well. In 1504, a pope called for the destruction of Pfalz, but the locals withstood a six-week siege, and the castle still stands. Notice the overhanging outhouse (tiny white room—with faded medieval stains—between two wooden ones). Pfalz (also known as Pfalzgrafenstein) is tourable but bare and dull (€3 ferry from Kaub, €3 entry; March-Oct Tue-Sun 10:00-18:00, until 17:00 in March, closed Mon; Nov and Jan-Feb Sat-Sun 10:00-17:00, closed Mon-Fri; closed Dec; last entry one hour before closing, mobile 0172-262-2800).

In Kaub, on the riverfront directly below the castles, a green statue honors the German general Gebhard von Blücher. He was Napoleon's nemesis. In 1813, as Napoleon fought his way back to Paris after his disastrous Russian campaign, he stopped at Mainz—hoping to fend off the Germans and Russians pursuing him by controlling that strategic bridge. Blücher tricked Napoleon. By building the first major pontoon bridge of its kind here at the Pfalz Castle, he crossed the Rhine and outflanked the French. Two years later, Blücher and Wellington teamed up to defeat Napoleon once and for all at Waterloo.

Km 544—"The Raft Busters": Immediately before Bacharach, at the top of the island, buoys mark a gang of rocks notorious for busting up rafts. The Black Forest, upstream from here, was once poor, and wood was its best export. Black Foresters would ride log booms down the Rhine to the Ruhr (where their timber fortified coal-mine shafts) or to Holland (where logs were sold to shipbuilders). If they could navigate the sweeping bend just before Bacharach and then survive these "raft busters," they'd come home reckless and likely horny—the German folkloric equivalent of American cowboys after payday.

Km 543—Bacharach and Stahleck Castle (Burg Stahleck): Cross to the other side of the train. The town of Bacharach is a great stop (see details and accommodations on the next page). Some of the Rhine's best wine is from this town, whose name likely derives from "altar to Bacchus." Local vintners brag that the medieval Pope Pius II ordered Bacharach wine by the cartload. Perched above the town, the 13th-century Burg Stahleck is now a hostel.

Km 540—Lorch: This pathetic stub of a castle is barely visible from the road. Check out the hillside vineyards. These vineyards once blanketed four times as much land as they do today, but modern economics have driven most of them out of business. The vineyards that do survive require government subsidies. Notice the small car ferry (3/hour, 10 minutes), one of several along the bridgeless stretch between Mainz and Koblenz.

Km 538—Sooneck Castle: Cross back to the other side of the train. Built in the 11th century, this castle was twice destroyed by people sick and tired of robber barons.

Km 534—Reichenstein Castle and **Km 533—Rheinstein Castle:** Stay on the other side of the train to see two of the first castles to be rebuilt in the Romantic era. Both are privately owned, tourable, and connected by a pleasant trail.

Km 530—Ehrenfels Castle: Opposite Bingerbrück and the Bingen station, you'll see the ghostly Ehrenfels Castle (clobbered by the Swedes in 1636 and by the French in 1689). Since it had no view of the river traffic to the north, the owner built the cute little *Mäuseturm* (mouse tower) on an island (the yellow tower you'll see near the train station today). Rebuilt in the 1800s in Neo-Gothic style, it's now used as a Rhine navigation signal station.

Km 528—Niederwald Monument: Across from the Bingen station on a hilltop is the 120-foot-high Niederwald monument, a memorial built with 32 tons of bronze in 1877 to commemorate "the re-establishment of the German Empire." A lift takes tourists to this statue from the famous and extremely touristy wine town of Rüdesheim.

From here, the Romantic Rhine becomes the industrial Rhine, and our tour is over.

Bacharach

Once prosperous from the wine and wood trade, charming Bacharach (BAHKH-ah-rahkh, with a guttural *kh* sound) is now just a pleasant half-timbered village of a thousand people working hard to keep its tourists happy.

Orientation to Bacharach

Tourist Information

The TI, on the main street in the Posthof courtyard next to the church, will store bags for day-trippers. Note that the TI might move to the train station, so check there first if you arrive by train (April-Oct Mon-Fri 9:00-17:00, Sat-Sun 10:00-15:00; Nov-March Mon-Fri 9:00-12:00, closed Sat-Sun; Oberstrasse 45, from train station turn right and walk 5 blocks down main street with castle high on your left, tel. 06743/919-303, www.bacharach.de or www .rhein-nahe-touristik.de, Herr Kuhn and his team).

Helpful Hints

Shopping: The **Jost** German gift store, across the main square from the church, carries most everything a souvenir-shopper could want—from beer steins to cuckoo clocks—and can ship purchases to the US. Ask about discounts with this book (March-Oct Mon-Fri 8:30-18:00, Sat 8:30-17:00, possibly Sun 10:00-16:00; Nov-Feb shorter hours and closed Sun; Blücherstrasse 4, tel. 06743/1224, www.phil-jost-germany .com, phil.jost@t-online.de).

Internet Access: The Rhine's cheapest Internet café is in the basement of the Lutheran-church–run kindergarten at Koblenzer Strasse 10, a few doors past the Altes Haus (€1/hour, Mon-Tue and Thu-Fri 16:00-21:00, closed Sat-Sun and Wed). The TI has a coin-op terminal (€0.50/15 minutes).

Post Office: It's inside a news agents' shop, across from the church and Altes Haus, at Oberstrasse 56 (Mon-Fri 7:30-12:30 & 14:00-18:30, Sat 7:30-12:30, closed Sun).

Grocery Store: Pick up picnic supplies at **Nahkauf,** a basic grocery store (Mon-Fri 8:00-12:30 & 14:00-18:30, Sat 8:30-14:00, closed Sun, Koblenzer Strasse 2).

Bike Rental: While many hotels loan bikes to guests, the only real bike-rental business in the town center is run by Erich

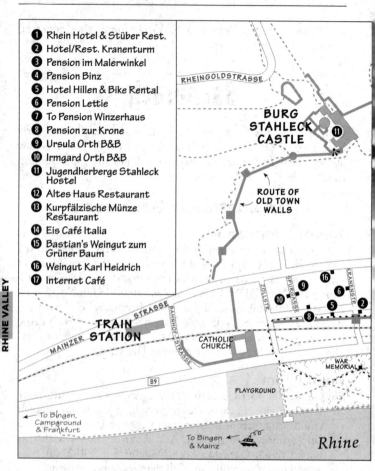

1. Rhein Hotel & Stüber Rest.
2. Hotel/Rest. Kranenturm
3. Pension im Malerwinkel
4. Pension Binz
5. Hotel Hillen & Bike Rental
6. Pension Lettie
7. To Pension Winzerhaus
8. Pension zur Krone
9. Ursula Orth B&B
10. Irmgard Orth B&B
11. Jugendherberge Stahleck Hostel
12. Altes Haus Restaurant
13. Kurpfälzische Münze Restaurant
14. Eis Café Italia
15. Bastian's Weingut zum Grüner Baum
16. Weingut Karl Heidrich
17. Internet Café

at the recommended **Hotel Hillen** (€12/day for non-guests, €7/day for guests, 35 bikes available, daily 9:00 until dark, Langstrasse 18, tel. 06743/1287).

Local Guides: Get acquainted with Bacharach by taking a walking tour with guides who enjoy sharing their town with visitors: **Birgit Wessels** (tel. 06743/937-514, wessels.birgit@t-online .de) or Aussie **Joanne Augustin** (€30/1.5 hours, tel. 06743/919-300, mobile 0179-231-1389, jopetit90@yahoo.com). Or take my self-guided walk below.

Self-Guided Walks

Welcome to Bacharach

· *Start at the Köln-Düsseldorfer ferry dock (next to a fine picnic park).*
   Riverfront: View the town from the parking lot—a modern

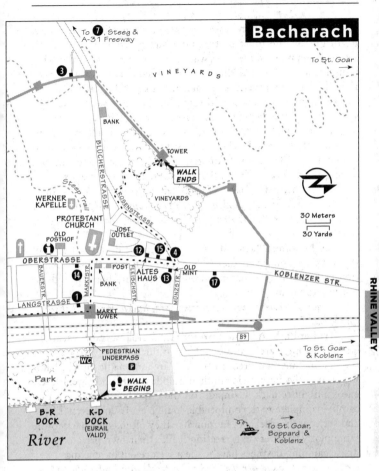

landfill. The Rhine used to lap against Bacharach's town wall, just over the present-day highway. Every few years the river floods, covering the highway with several feet of water. The **castle** on the hill is now a youth hostel. Two of the town's original 16 towers are visible from here (up to five if you look really hard). The huge roadside keg declares that this town was built on the wine trade.

Reefs farther upstream forced boats to unload upriver and reload here. Consequently, in the Middle Ages, Bacharach became the biggest wine-trading town on the Rhine. A riverfront crane hoisted huge kegs of prestigious "Bacharach" wine (which, in practice, was from anywhere in the region). The tour buses next to the dock and the flags of the biggest spenders along the highway remind you that today's economy is basically founded on tourism.

• *Before entering the town, walk upstream through the...*

Riverside Park: This park was laid out in 1910 in the English style: Notice how the trees were planted to frame fine town views, highlighting the most picturesque bits of architecture. Until recently, stepping on the grass was verboten. The dark, sad-looking monument—its "eternal" flame long snuffed out—is a war memorial. The German psyche is permanently scarred by war memories. Today, many Germans would rather avoid monuments like this, which revisit the dark periods before Germany became a nation of pacifists. Take a close look at the monument. Each panel honors sons of Bacharach who died for the Kaiser: in 1864 against Denmark, in 1866 against Austria, in 1870 against France, in 1914 during World War I. The military Maltese cross—flanked by classic German helmets—has a W at its center, for Kaiser Wilhelm.

• *Continue to where the park meets the playground, and then cross the highway to the fortified riverside wall of the Catholic church, decorated with...*

High-Water Marks: These recall various floods. Check out the metal ring on the medieval slate wall. Before the 1910 reclamation project, the river extended out to here, and boats would use the ring to tie up.

• *Upstream from here, there's a trailer park, and beyond that there's a campground.*

Trailer Park and Campground: In Germany, trailer vacationers and campers are two distinct subcultures. Folks who travel in trailers, like many retirees in the US, are a nomadic bunch, hauling around the countryside in their mobile homes and paying a few euros a night to park. Campers, on the other hand, tend to set up camp—complete with comfortable lounge chairs and even TVs—and stay put for weeks, even months. They often come back to the same plot year after year, treating it like their own private estate. These camping devotees have made a science out of relaxing.

• *At the church, go under the 1858 train tracks and hook right past the yellow floodwater yardstick and up the stairs onto the town wall. Atop the wall, turn left and walk under the long arcade. After a few steps, on your left, notice a...*

Well: This is one of 40 such wells that, until 1900, provided water to the townsfolk.

• *Pass the recommended Rhein Hotel (hotel is before the Markt tower, which marks one of the town's 15 original 14th-century gates), descend, pass another well, and follow Marktstrasse toward the town center, the two-tone church, and the town's...*

Main Intersection: From here, Bacharach's main street (Oberstrasse) goes right to the half-timbered red-and-white Altes Haus (from 1368, the oldest house in town) and left 400 yards to the train station.

• *To the left (south) of the church, a golden horn hangs over the old...*

Posthof: The postal horn symbolizes the postal service

throughout Europe. In olden days, when the postman blew this, traffic stopped and the mail sped through. This post station (now home to the TI) dates from 1724, when stagecoaches ran from Köln to Frankfurt and would change horses here, Pony Express–style.

Step past the old oak doors into the courtyard—once a carriage house and inn that accommodated Bacharach's first VIP visitors. Notice the fascist eagle (from 1936, on the left as you enter; a swastika once filled its center) and the fine view of the church and a ruined chapel above. The Posthof is on a charming square. Spin around to enjoy the higgledy-piggledy building style.

Two hundred years ago, Bacharach's main drag was the only road along the Rhine. Napoleon widened it to fit his cannon wagons. The steps alongside the church lead to the castle.

• *Return to the church, passing the recommended Italian ice-cream café (Eis Café Italia), where friendly Mimo serves his special invention: Riesling wine–flavored gelato.*

Protestant Church: Inside the church (daily May-Sept 10:00-18:00, closed Oct-April, English info on table near door), you'll find Grotesque capitals, brightly painted in medieval style, and a mix of round Romanesque and pointed Gothic arches. To the left of the altar, some medieval frescoes survive where an older Romanesque arch was cut by a pointed Gothic one.

• *Continue down Oberstrasse to the recommended...*

Altes Haus: Notice the 14th-century building style—the first floor is made of stone, while upper floors are half-timbered (in the ornate style common in the Rhine Valley). Some of its windows still look medieval, with small, flattened circles as panes (small because that's all that glass-blowing technology of the time would allow), pieced together with molten lead. Frau Weber welcomes visitors to enjoy the fascinating ground floor of the Altes Haus, with its evocative old photos and etchings (consider eating here later).

• *Keep going down Oberstrasse to the...*

Old Mint (Münze): The old mint is marked by a crude coin in its sign. Across from the mint, the recommended **Bastian** family's wine garden is the liveliest place in town after dark. Above you in the vineyards stands a lonely white-and-red tower—your final destination.

• *At the next street, look right and see the mint tower, painted in the medieval style (illustrating that the Dark Ages weren't really that dark), and then turn left. Wander 30 yards up Rosenstrasse to the **well**. Notice the sundial and the wall painting of 1632 Bacharach with its walls intact. (You can walk along the route of the old town walls, described later, by following the Stadtmauer-Rundweg signs in town.) Climb the tiny-stepped lane behind the well up into the vineyard and to the...*

Tall Tower: The slate steps lead to a small path through the vineyard that deposits you at a viewpoint atop the stubby remains of the old town wall. If the tower's open, hike to its top floor for the best view.

Romantic Rhine View: A grand medieval town spreads before you. For 300 years (1300-1600), Bacharach was big (population 4,000), rich, and politically powerful.

From this perch you can see the chapel ruins and six surviving **city towers.** Visually trace the wall to the castle. The castle was actually the capital of Germany for a couple of years in the 1200s. When Holy Roman Emperor Frederick Barbarossa went away to fight the Crusades, he left his brother (who lived here) in charge of his vast realm. Bacharach was home of one of seven electors who voted for the Holy Roman Emperor in 1275. To protect their own power, these elector-princes did their best to choose the weakest guy on the ballot. The elector from Bacharach helped select a two-bit prince named Rudolf von Habsburg (from a no-name castle in Switzerland). However, the underestimated Rudolf brutally silenced the robber barons along the Rhine and established the mightiest dynasty in European history. His family line, the Habsburgs, ruled much of Central and Eastern Europe from Vienna until 1918.

Plagues, fires, and the Thirty Years' War (1618-1648) finally did in Bacharach. The town, with a population of about a thousand, has slumbered for several centuries. Today, the castle houses commoners—40,000 overnights annually by youth hostelers.

In the mid-19th century, painters such as J. M. W. Turner and writers such as Victor Hugo were charmed by the Rhineland's romantic mix of past glory, present poverty, and rich legend. They put this part of the Rhine on the old Grand Tour map as the "Romantic Rhine." Victor Hugo pondered the ruined 15th-century chapel that you see under the castle. In his 1842 travel book, *Excursions Along the Banks of Rhine,* he wrote, "No doors, no roof or windows, a magnificent skeleton puts its silhouette against the sky. Above it, the ivy-covered castle ruins provide a fitting crown. This is Bacharach, land of fairy tales, covered with legends and sagas." If you're enjoying the Romantic Rhine, thank Victor Hugo and company.

• *To get back into town, take the level path away from the river that leads along the once-mighty wall up the valley past the next tower. Then cross the street into the parking lot. Pass Pension Malerwinkel on your right, being careful not to damage the old arch with your head. Follow the creek past a delightful little series of half-timbered homes and cheery gardens known as "Painters' Corner" (Malerwinkel). Resist looking into some pervert's peep show (on the right) and continue downhill back to the village center. Nice work.*

Walk Along the Old Town Walls

A well-maintained and clearly marked walking path follows the remains of Bacharach's old town walls and makes for a good hour's workout. The TI has maps that show the entire route. The path starts near the train station, then climbs up to the youth hostel, descends into the side valley, and then continues up the other side to the tower in the vineyards before returning to town. To start the walk at the train station, find the house at Oberstrasse 2 and climb up the stairway to its left. Then follow the *Stadtmauer-Rundweg* signs. Good bilingual signposts tell the history of each of the towers along the wall—some are intact, one is a private residence, and others are now only stubs.

Sleeping in Bacharach

(area code: 06743)

Parking in Bacharach is simple along the highway next to the tracks (3-hour daytime limit is generally not enforced) or, better, in the big lot by the boat dock. For locations, see the map on pages 610-611.

$$$ Rhein Hotel, with 14 spacious and comfortable rooms, is classy, well-run and decorated with modern flair, and overlooks the river. Since it's right on the train tracks, its river- and train-side rooms come with four-paned windows and air-conditioning. This place has been in the Stüber family for six generations (Sb-€55, Db-€90, confirm you're getting Rick Steves rate with this book and direct reservation, cheaper for longer stays and off-season, half-board €16-20/person, non-smoking, free loaner bikes for guests, pay Wi-Fi, directly inland from the K-D boat dock at Langstrasse 50, tel. 06743/1243, fax 06743/1413, www.rhein-hotel-bacharach .de, info@rhein-hotel-bacharach.de). For a culinary splurge, consider dining here.

$$ Hotel Kranenturm, offering castle ambience without the climb, combines hotel comfort with *Privatzimmer* coziness right downtown. Run by hardworking Kurt Engel and his intense but friendly wife, Fatima, this 17-room hotel is part of the medieval town wall. The rooms in its former *Kran* (crane) tower have the best views. When the riverbank was higher, cranes on this tower loaded barrels of wine onto Rhine boats. While just 15 feet from the train tracks, a combination of medieval sturdiness, triple-paned windows, and included earplugs makes the riverside rooms sleepable (Sb-€40-46, small Db-€57-62, regular Db-€59-65, Db in huge tower rooms with castle and river views-€73-80, Tb-€85-95, Qb great for families with small kids-€100-110, honeymoon special-€85-105, lower prices are for 3-night stay, family deals, cash preferred—€2 extra if paying with credit card, Rhine views come with train noise, back rooms are quiet, non-smoking, showers can

RHINE VALLEY

RHINE VALLEY

Sleep Code

(€1 = about $1.40, country code: 49)

S = Single, **D** = Double/Twin, **T** = Triple, **Q** = Quad, **b** = bathroom, **s** = shower only. Staff at all hotels speak at least some English. Breakfast is included, and credit cards are accepted unless otherwise noted.

To help you sort easily through these listings, I've divided the rooms into three categories, based on the price for a standard double room with bath:

$$$ Higher Priced—Most rooms €80 or more.

$$ Moderately Priced—Most rooms between €55-80.

$ Lower Priced—Most rooms €55 or less.

Prices can change without notice; verify the hotel's current rates online or by email. For other updates, see www.ricksteves.com/update.

The Rhine is an easy place for cheap sleeps. B&Bs and *Gasthäuser* with €25-30 beds abound (and normally discount their prices for longer stays). Rhine-area hostels offer €15-19 beds to travelers of any age. Each town's TI is eager to set you up, and finding a room should be easy any time of year (except for wine-festival weekends in Sept and Oct). Bacharach and St. Goar, the best towns for an overnight stop, are 10 miles apart, connected by milk-run trains, riverboats, and a riverside bike path. Bacharach is a much more interesting town, but St. Goar has the famous castle (for St. Goar recommendations, see page 629).

be temperamental, kid-friendly, good breakfast, free Internet access and Wi-Fi, laundry service-€13, Langstrasse 30, tel. 06743/1308, fax 06743/1021, www.kranenturm.com, hotel-kranenturm@t -online.de). Kurt, a good cook, serves €8-14 dinners.

$$ Pension im Malerwinkel sits like a grand gingerbread house that straddles the town wall in a quiet little neighborhood so charming it's called "Painters' Corner" *(Malerwinkel)*. The Vollmer family's 20-room place is super-quiet and comes with a sunny garden on a brook, views of the vineyards, and easy parking (Sb-€40; Db-€65 for 1 night, €59 for 2 nights, €56 for 3 nights or more; family rooms, cash only, some rooms have balconies, no train noise, non-smoking, free Wi-Fi, bike rental-€6/day; from Oberstrasse, turn left at the church, and stay to the left of the babbling brook until you reach Blücherstrasse 41-45; tel. 06743/1239, fax 06743/93407, www.im-malerwinkel.de, pension@im-maler winkel.de, Armin and Daniela).

$$ Pension Binz offers four large, bright, plainly furnished rooms in a good location with no train noise (Sb-€37, Db-€60,

Tb-€78, slightly cheaper for 3 nights or more, apartment with kitchen but no breakfast and 2-night minimum-€65, Koblenzer Strasse 1, tel. 06743/1604, fax 06743/937-9916, http://pensionbinz .funpic.de, pension.binz@freenet.de, warm Carla speaks a little English).

$ **Hotel Hillen,** a block south of the Hotel Kranenturm, has less charm and similar train noise (with the same ultra-thick windows). It offers spacious rooms, good food, and friendly owners (S-€30, Sb-€35, D-€40, Ds-€45, Db-€50, Tb-€65, Qb-€80, confirm you're getting Rick Steves rate with a 2-night stay and this book, €5 more for 1-night stays, closed mid-Nov-mid-March, family rooms, Langstrasse 18, tel. 06743/1287, fax 06743/1037, hotel-hillen@web.de, kind Iris speaks some English). The hotel also rents bikes (see page 609).

$ At **Pension Lettie,** effervescent and eager-to-please Lettie offers four bright rooms. Lettie speaks English (she worked for the US Army before they withdrew) and does laundry for €12/load (Sb-€38, Db-€55, Tb-€75, Qb-€90, Quint/b-€105, confirm you're getting the Rick Steves rate with this book, reserve direct rather than through TI, €3-5 discount for 2-night stays, 10 percent more if paying with credit card, strictly non-smoking, buffet breakfast with waffles and eggs, no train noise, free Wi-Fi, a few doors inland from Hotel Kranenturm, Kranenstrasse 6, tel. 06743/2115, pension.lettie@t-online.de).

$ **Pension Winzerhaus,** a 10-room place run by friendly Sybille and Stefan, is outside the town walls, 200 yards up the side-valley road from the town gate, directly under the vineyards. Though you can't hear the train, you might hear slight noise from passing cars. The rooms are simple, clean, and modern, and parking is easy (Sb-€33, Db-€49, Tb-€65, Qb-€75, show this book at check-in for best price, cash only, non-smoking, free Wi-Fi, free loaner bikes for guests, Blücherstrasse 60, tel. 06743/1294, www .pension-winzerhaus.de, winzerhaus@gmx.de).

$ **Pension zur Krone** is close to the station but with no train noise. Emilja Banfi and her husband Milan, a computer programmer, sell used books online and rent four simple rooms crowded with furniture (Db-€40, cash only, dog on premises, Langstrasse 7, tel. 06743/947-209, banfi.emilja@web.de).

$ **Orth** *Zimmer:* Delightful sisters-in-law run two fine little B&Bs across the lane from each other (from station, walk down Oberstrasse, turn right on Spurgasse, and look for *Orth* sign). **Ursula Orth** rents five basic rooms, speaks a smidge of English, and is proud of her homemade jam (Sb-€22, Db-€37, Tb-€48, cash only, non-smoking, rooms 4 and 5 on ground floor, Spurgasse 3, tel. 06743/1557). **Irmgard Orth** rents three fresh rooms, two of which share a bathroom on the hall. She speaks even less English but is exuberantly cheery and serves homemade honey with breakfast (S-€22, D-€36, Db-€38, cash only, non-smoking, Spurgasse 2, look for *Honig* signs with picture of a beehive, tel. 06743/1553, speak slowly). Their excellent prices assume you're booking direct, instead of through the TI.

$ Jugendherberge Stahleck hostel is a 12th-century castle on the hilltop—350 steps above Bacharach—with a royal Rhine view. Open to travelers of any age, this is a gem with 168 beds and a private modern shower and WC in most rooms. The steep 20-minute climb on the trail from the town church is worth it for the view, even if you're not sleeping there. The hostel offers hearty €7.50 all-you-can-eat buffet dinners, and its pub serves cheap local wine and snacks until midnight. If you're arriving at the train station with luggage, it's an €8.50 taxi ride to the hostel—call 06743/1653 (€19 dorm beds with breakfast and sheets, non-members-€3.10 extra, couples can share one of five €49 Db, no smoking in rooms, pay Internet access and Wi-Fi, laundry-€6; reception open 7:30-20:00, after that check in at bar until 21:30; curfew at 22:00, tel. 06743/1266, fax 06743/2684, www.diejugendherbergen.de, bacharach@diejugendherbergen.de). If driving, don't go in the driveway; park on the street and walk 200 yards.

Eating in Bacharach

Restaurants

You can easily find reasonably priced, atmospheric restaurants offering indoor and outdoor dining. Two of the recommended hotels—Rhein and Kranenturm—have good restaurants. Non-German options on the main street include a pizzeria and *Döner Kebab* joint (open daily until late) and an Irish pub.

The Rhein Hotel's **Stüber Restaurant** is Bacharach's best top-end choice. Chef Andreas Stüber is of the sixth generation to prepare regional, seasonal plates, served on river- and track-side seating or indoors with a spacious wood-and-white-tablecloth elegance. Consider their €14.50 William Turner pâté sampler plate, named after the British painter who liked Bacharach (€10-19 entrées, €27-35 fixed-price meals, March-mid-Dec Wed-Mon 11:30-14:15 & 17:30-21:15, closed Tue and mid-Dec-Feb, call to reserve on weekends or for an outdoor table, facing the K-D boat dock just below the center of town, Langstrasse 50, tel. 06743/1243).

Altes Haus, the oldest building in town (see page 613), serves reliably good food with Bacharach's most romantic atmosphere. Find the cozy little dining room with photos of the opera singer who sang about Bacharach, adding to its fame (€9-15 entrées, May-Oct Thu-Tue 12:00-15:30 & 18:00-23:00, April and Nov weekends only, closed Dec-Easter and Wed year-round, dead center by the church, tel. 06743/1209).

Kurpfälzische Münze, while more expensive than Altes Haus, is a popular standby for lunch or a drink on its sunny terrace or in its pubby, low-beamed interior (€7-18 entrées, daily 10:00-22:00, in the old mint, a half-block down from Altes Haus; tel. 06743/1375).

Hotel Kranenturm is another good value, with hearty dinners (Kurt prides himself on his *Sauerbraten*—marinated beef with potato dumplings and red cabbage) and good main-course salads. If you're a train-spotter, sit on their track-side terrace and trade travel stories with new friends over dinner, letting screaming trains punctuate your conversation. If you prefer charming old German decor, sit inside (€9-15 entrées, open 6 days a week 17:00-21:00—closed day varies, restaurant closed Dec-Feb). Kurt and Fatima are your hosts.

Eis Café Italia, on the main street and run by friendly Mimo Calabrese, is known for its refreshing, not-too-sweet Riesling-flavored gelato. Notice the big sundae bowls on the shelves. To enjoy your *Eis* German-style, sit down and order ice cream off the menu, or just stop by for a cone before an evening stroll (€0.70/scoop, no tastes offered, April-mid-Oct daily 10:00-22:00, closed off-season, opposite Posthof at Oberstrasse 48).

Wine-Tasting

Bacharach is proud of its wine. Two places in town—Bastian's rowdy and rustic Grüner Baum, and sophisticated Weingut Karl Heidrich—offer visitors an inexpensive chance to join in on the fun. Each creates carousels of local wines that small groups of travelers (who don't mind sharing a glass) can sample and compare.

At **Bastian's Weingut zum Grüner Baum,** groups of 2-6 people pay €19 for a wine carousel of 15 glasses—14 different white wines and one lonely rosé—and a basket of bread. Your mission: Team up with others who have this book to rendezvous here after dinner. Spin the Lazy Susan, share a common cup, and discuss the taste. Doris Bastian insists: "After each wine, you must talk to each other." They offer soup and cold cuts, and good ambience indoors and out (Mon-Wed and Fri from 13:00, Sat-Sun from 12:00, closed Thu and Feb-mid-March, just past Altes Haus, tel. 06743/1208). To make a meal of a carousel, consider the €8 *Käseteller* (seven different cheeses—including *Spundekäse,* the local soft cheese—with bread and butter).

Weingut Karl Heidrich is a fun family-run wine shop and *Stube* in the town center (at Oberstrasse 16-18, near Hotel Kranenturm), where Markus proudly shares his family's wine while passionately explaining its fine points to travelers. They offer a variety of carousels with English descriptions, six wines, and bread (€10), which are ideal for the more sophisticated wine taster (Easter-Oct Thu-Tue 11:00-22:00, closed Wed and Nov-Easter, tel. 06743/93060).

Bacharach Connections

Train Connections from the Rhine

Milk-run trains stop at Rhine towns each hour starting as early as 6:00, connecting at Mainz and Koblenz to trains farther afield. Trains between St. Goar and Bacharach depart at about :20 after the hour in each direction (€3.20, buy tickets from the machine in the unstaffed stations). The ride times listed below are calculated from Bacharach; for St. Goar, the difference is only 10 minutes. Train info: toll tel. 0180-599-6633 (€0.14/minute), www.bahn.de.

From Bacharach by Train to: St. Goar (hourly, 10 minutes), **Frankfurt Airport** (hourly, 1-1.5 hours, change in Mainz or Bingen), **Frankfurt** (hourly, 1.25-1.75 hours, change in Mainz or Bingen), **Rothenburg ob der Tauber** (every 2 hours, 4.25 hours, 3-4 changes), **Munich** (hourly, 5 hours, 2 changes), **Berlin** (hourly, 6.5-7.5 hours, 1-3 changes), **Amsterdam** (hourly, 7 hours, change in Köln, sometimes 1-2 more changes).

St. Goar

St. Goar (sahnkt gwahr) is a classic Rhine town. Its hulk of a castle overlooks a half-timbered shopping street and leafy riverside park, busy with sightseeing ships and contented strollers. Rheinfels Castle, once the mightiest on the Rhine, is the single best Rhineland ruin to explore. From the riverboat docks, the main drag—a dull pedestrian mall without history—cuts through town before ending at the road up to the castle.

While the town of St. Goar itself isn't much more than a few hotels and restaurants—and is less interesting than Bacharach—it still makes a good base for hiking or biking the region. A tiny car ferry will shuttle you back and forth across the busy Rhine from here. (One of my favorite pastimes in St. Goar is chatting with friendly Heike at the K-D boat kiosk.) For train connections, see "Bacharach Connections," earlier.

Orientation to St. Goar

Tourist Information

The helpful St. Goar TI, which books rooms and stores bags for free, is on the pedestrian street, three blocks from the K-D boat dock and train station (May-Sept Mon-Fri 9:00-12:30 & 13:30-18:00,

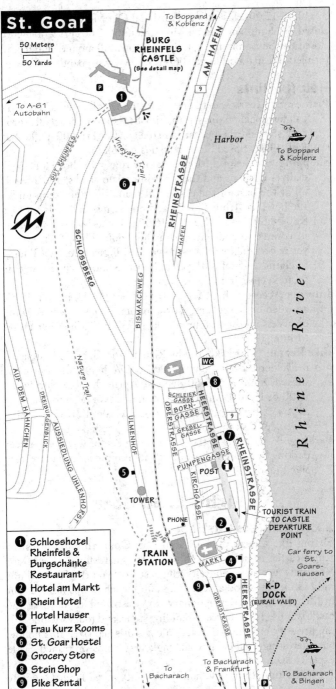

St. Goar

50 Meters
50 Yards

To A-61
Autobahn

BURG
RHEINFELS
CASTLE
(See detail map)

To Boppard
& Koblenz

AM HAFEN

9

Harbor

To Boppard
& Koblenz

GUT RHEINFELS

Vineyard Trail

SCHLOSSBERG

BISMARCKWEG

RHEINSTRASSE

AM HAFEN

P

Nature Trail

ULMENHOF

AUF DEM HAHNCHEN

DREIBURGENBLICK

AUSSIEDLUNG UHLENHOST

SCHLEIER-GASSE
OBERSTRASSE
BORN-GASSE
GREBEL-GASSE
HEERSTRASSE
RHEINSTRASSE

WC

8

9

7

PUMPENGASSE

POST

i

KIRCHGASSE

TOWER

PHONE

5

2

TRAIN
STATION

MARKT

4

3

OBERSTRASSE

9

HEERSTRASSE

TOURIST TRAIN
TO CASTLE
DEPARTURE
POINT

Car ferry to St.
Goars-
hausen

K-D
DOCK
(EURAIL VALID)

Rhine River

To Bacharach

To Bacharach
& Frankfurt

To Bacharach
& Bingen

1 Schlosshotel
   Rheinfels &
   Burgschänke
   Restaurant
2 Hotel am Markt
3 Rhein Hotel
4 Hotel Hauser
5 Frau Kurz Rooms
6 St. Goar Hostel
7 Grocery Store
8 Stein Shop
9 Bike Rental

Sat 10:00-12:00, closed Sun; April and Oct Mon-Fri until 17:00, closed Sat-Sun; Nov-March Mon-Thu until 17:00, Fri 9:00-14:00, closed Sat-Sun; from train station, go downhill around church and turn left, Heerstrasse 86, tel. 06741/383, www.st-goar.de).

Helpful Hints

Picnics: St. Goar's waterfront park is hungry for picnickers. You can buy picnic fixings at the tiny **St. Goarer Stadtladen** grocery store on the pedestrian street (Mon-Fri 8:00-18:00, Sat 8:00-13:00, closed Sun, Heerstrasse 106).

Shopping: The helpful Montag family runs two shops (one specializes in steins and the other in cuckoo clocks) and a hotel, all at the base of the castle hill road. The stein shop under the hotel has Rhine guides and fine steins (daily March-Oct 8:30-18:00, Nov-Feb 10:00-16:00). Ask at both shops about discounts on souvenirs with this book. They'll ship, or if you're carrying purchases home, they'll give you a VAT form to claim your refund at the airport. Another good souvenir shop is across from the K-D boat dock.

Internet Access: The **TI** is your best bet (€3/hour), but if it's crowded or closed, the backup option is the expensive coin-op access (€6/hour, 6 terminals) or Wi-Fi (€5/hour) at **Hotel Montag** (Heerstrasse 128).

Bike Rental: Goar Bike, run by Richard and Gabriele Langhans, is five doors from the train station (€7/6 hours, €10/day, must show ID and leave €50 deposit, April-Oct Tue-Sun 9:00-13:00 & 15:00-19:00, closed Mon and Nov-March, go right as you exit station, Oberstrasse 44, tel. 06741/1735, goarbike @web.de). Ask the TI for maps and suggested routes.

Parking: A free lot is at the downstream end of town. On-street parking by the K-D boat dock and recommended hotels costs about €4/day.

Sights in St. Goar

▲▲▲Rheinfels Castle

Sitting like a dead pit bull above St. Goar, this mightiest of Rhine castles rumbles with ghosts from its hard-fought past. Burg Rheinfels *was* huge—once the biggest castle on the Rhine (built in 1245). It withstood a siege of 28,000 French troops in 1692. But in 1797, the French Revolutionary army destroyed it. For years, the castle was used as a source of building stone, and today—while still mighty—it's only a small fraction of its original size. This hollow but interesting shell offers your single best hands-on ruined-castle experience on the river.

Cost and Hours: €4, family card-€10; mid-March-Oct daily

St. Goar's Rheinfels Castle

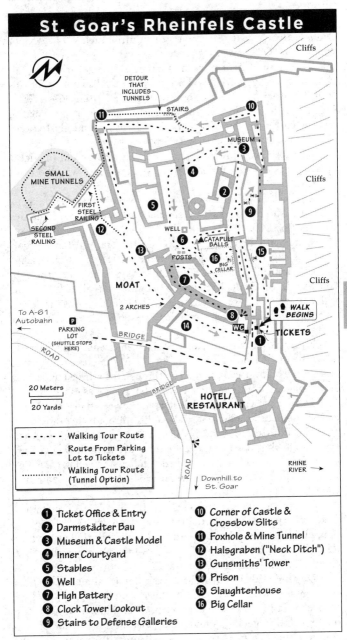

Cliffs

DETOUR THAT INCLUDES TUNNELS

STAIRS

SMALL MINE TUNNELS

MUSEUM

FIRST STEEL RAILING

SECOND STEEL RAILING

WELL

CATAPULT BALLS

POSTS

BIG CELLAR

MOAT

2 ARCHES

To A-61 Autobahn

P PARKING LOT (SHUTTLE STOPS HERE)

BRIDGE

ROAD

WALK BEGINS

WC

TICKETS

Cliffs

Cliffs

RHINE VALLEY

20 Meters
20 Yards

BRIDGE

HOTEL/ RESTAURANT

ROAD

Downhill to St. Goar

RHINE RIVER →

- - - - - Walking Tour Route
— — — Route From Parking Lot to Tickets
· · · · · Walking Tour Route (Tunnel Option)

1 Ticket Office & Entry
2 Darmstädter Bau
3 Museum & Castle Model
4 Inner Courtyard
5 Stables
6 Well
7 High Battery
8 Clock Tower Lookout
9 Stairs to Defense Galleries
10 Corner of Castle & Crossbow Slits
11 Foxhole & Mine Tunnel
12 Halsgraben ("Neck Ditch")
13 Gunsmiths' Tower
14 Prison
15 Slaughterhouse
16 Big Cellar

9:00–18:00, last entry at 17:00; Nov–mid-March Sat–Sun only 11:00–17:00, last entry at 16:00—weather permitting; tel. 06741/7753, in winter 06741/383, www.st-goar.de.

Tours and Information: Call in advance or gather 10 English-speaking tourists and beg to get an English tour—perhaps from Günther, the "last knight of Rheinfels" (tel. 06741/7753). Otherwise, follow my self-guided tour. The castle map is helpful, and the €2 English booklet is good, with history and illustrations. If it's damp, be careful of slippery stones.

Services: A handy WC is immediately across from the ticket booth (check out the guillotine urinals—stand back when you pull to flush).

Let There Be Light: If planning to explore the mine tunnels, bring a flashlight, or do it by candlelight (museum sells candles with matches, €0.50).

Getting to the Castle by Taxi or Mini-Train: A taxi up from town costs €5 (tel. 06741/7011). Or take the kitschy "tschu-tschu" tourist train (€2 one-way, €3 round-trip, 8 minutes to the top, April–Oct daily 10:00–17:30 but sometimes unpredictable, 2/hour, waits at square between station and K-D dock or wave it down, complete with lusty music, mobile 0171-496-3762, www.st-goarer-burgexpress.de).

Hiking Up to the Castle: Two steep but scenic paths take you up to the castle from the town (allow 15–20 minutes up). You can also simply follow the main road up through the railroad underpass at the top end of the pedestrian street, but it's not as much fun.

To take the **vineyard trail,** start at the beer-stein shop at the end of the pedestrian street, walk uphill through the underpass, make an immediate right on Bismarcksweg along the railroad tracks following the *Fussweg Burg Rheinfels* and yellow *Zur Burg* signs, pass the youth hostel, and then follow the yellow *Zur Burg* signs up the hill through the vineyard. The last couple hundred yards are along the road.

To take the **nature trail,** start at the St. Goar train station. Take the underpass under the tracks at the north end of the station, climb the steep stairs uphill, and turn right (following *Burg Rheinfels* signs) along the path just above the old city wall, which takes you to the castle in 10 minutes.

◑ **Self-Guided Tour:** Rather than wander aimlessly, visit the castle by following this tour. The basic route below can be done without a flashlight or any daring acts of chivalry. To go through the tunnels, bring a light or buy candles at the castle entrance, and choose either the full-strength, small-mine-tunnel plan or the medium-strength, big-mine-tunnel option.

Pick up the free map and use its commentary to navigate from red signpost to signpost through the castle. The route I suggest below is very similar to the one marked on the castle map (that official map, the map on page 623 of this book, and this tour all use the same numbering system), but offers you varying levels of spookiness depending on how much of the castle tunnels you want to explore.

• *The ticket office is under the castle's clock tower, labeled* ❶ Uhrturm. *Walk through the entranceway and continue straight. Pass the big cellar (signed* ⓰ Grosser Keller) *on the left—where we'll end this tour— and walk through an internal gate. Pass the part of the castle called* ❷ Darmstädter Bau *on your left and the* ❾ zu den Wehrgängen *("to the defense galleries") sign on the right—we'll go there later. Walk uphill to the* ❸ Treppenturm *signpost to find the...*

Museum and Castle Model: The pleasant museum, located in the only finished room of the castle, has good English descriptions, but it's not as important as seeing the castle itself. Skip the museum if you're short on time (museum open mid-March-Oct daily 10:00-12:30 & 13:00-17:30, closed Nov-mid-March, included in castle entry).

The seven-foot-tall carved stone immediately inside the door (marked *Flammensäule*)—a tombstone from a nearby Celtic grave—is from 400 years before Christ. There were people here long before the Romans...and this castle. Find the old wooden library chair near the tombstone. If you pull the chair's back forward, it becomes stairs for accessing the highest shelves—smile sweetly, and the man behind the desk may demonstrate.

The sweeping castle history exhibit in the center of the room is well-described in English. The massive fortification was the only Rhineland castle to withstand Louis XIV's assault during the 17th century. At the far end of the room is a model reconstruction of the castle (not the one with the toy soldiers) showing how much bigger it was before French Revolutionary troops destroyed it in the 18th century. Study this. Find where you are. (Hint: Look for the tall tower.) This was the living quarters of the original castle, which was only the smallest ring of buildings around the tiny central courtyard (13th century). The ramparts were added in the 14th century. By 1650, the fortress was largely complete. Since its destruction by the French in the late 18th century, it's had no military value. While no WWII bombs were wasted on this ruin, it served St. Goar as a stone quarry for generations. The basement of the museum shows the castle pharmacy and an exhibit of Rhine-region odds and ends, including tools, an 1830 loom, and photos of icebreaking on the Rhine. While once routine, icebreaking hasn't been necessary here since 1963.

• *Exit the museum and walk 30 yards directly out, slightly uphill into the castle courtyard, where you'll see a sign for the inner courtyard (*❹ Innenhof).

Medieval Castle Courtyard: Five hundred years ago, the entire castle encircled this courtyard. The place was self-sufficient and ready for a siege, with a bakery, pharmacy, herb garden, brewery, well (top of yard), and livestock. During peacetime, 300-600 people lived here; during a siege, there would be as many as 4,000. The walls were plastered and painted white. Bits of the original 13th-century plaster survive.

• *Continue through the courtyard under the* Erste Schildmauer *(first shield wall) sign, turn left into the next courtyard, pass the stables (*❺ Marstall*), and walk straight to the two old wooden upright posts. Find the pyramid of stone catapult balls on your left.*

Castle Garden: Catapult balls like these were too expensive not to recycle—they'd be retrieved after any battle. Across from the balls is a well (❻ *Brunnen*)—essential for any castle during the age of sieges. Look in. Spit. The old posts are for the ceremonial baptizing of new members of the local trading league. While this guild goes back centuries, it's now a social club that fills this court with a huge wine party the third weekend of each September.

• *If weary, skip the next paragraph; otherwise, climb the cobbled path up past the high battery (*❼ Hohe Batterie*) to the castle's best viewpoint—up where the German flag waves (signed* ❽ Uhrturm*).*

Highest Castle Tower Lookout: Enjoy a great view of the river, the castle, and the forest. Remember, the fortress once covered five times the land it does today. Notice how the other castles (across the river) don't poke above the top of the Rhine canyon. That would make them easy for invading armies to see.

• *Return to the catapult balls, walk past the well down through the tunnel, veer left through the arch marked* ❾ zu den Wehrgängen *("to the defense galleries"), go down two flights of stairs, and turn left into the dark, covered passageway. From here, we'll begin a rectangular walk taking us completely around (counterclockwise) the perimeter of the castle.*

Covered Defense Galleries with "Minutemen" Holes: Soldiers—the castle's "minutemen"—had a short commute: defensive positions on the outside, home in the holes below on the left. Even though these living quarters were padded with straw, life was unpleasant.

• *Continue straight through the dark gallery and to the corner of the castle, where you'll see a white painted arrow at eye level and a red signpost with the number* ❿. *Stand with your back to the arrow on the wall.*

Corner of Castle: Look up. A three-story, half-timbered building originally rose beyond the highest stone fortification. The two stone tongues near the top just around the corner supported the toilet. (Insert your own joke here.) Turn around and face the wall. The crossbow slits below the white arrow were once steeper. The bigger hole on the riverside was for hot pitch.

• *Follow that white arrow along the outside to the next corner. Midway you'll pass stairs on the right leading down to the foxhole and mine tunnel (⓫, zu den Minengängen sign on upper left). Adventurers with flashlights can detour here (described later, under "Optional Detour—Into the Small Mine Tunnels") and may, if lucky, re-emerge around the next corner. Otherwise, stay with me, walking level to the corner. At the corner, turn left.*

Thoop...You're Dead: Look ahead at the smartly placed crossbow slit. While you're lying there, notice the stonework. The little round holes were for scaffolds used as they built up. They indicate this stonework is original. Notice also the fine stonework on the chutes. More boiling pitch...now you're toast, too.

• *Continue along the castle wall around the corner. At the gray railing, look up the valley and uphill where the sprawling fort stretched. Below, just outside the wall, is land where attackers would gather. The mine tunnels are under there, waiting to blow up any attackers.*

Keep going along the perimeter, jog left, go down five steps and into an open field, and walk toward the wooden bridge. The "old" wooden bridge is actually modern. Angle left (under the zum Verliess sign, before the bridge) through two arches and through the rough entry to the ⓮ Verliess (prison) on the left.

Prison: This is one of six dungeons. You just walked through an entrance prisoners only dreamed of 400 years ago. They came and went through the little square hole in the ceiling. The holes in the walls supported timbers that thoughtfully gave as many as 15 residents something to sit on to keep them out of the filthy slop that gathered on the floor. Twice a day, they were given bread and water. Some prisoners actually survived longer than two years in here. While the town could torture and execute, the castle had permission only to imprison criminals in these dungeons. Consider this: According to town records, the two men who spent the most time down here—2.5 years each—died within three weeks of regaining their freedom. Perhaps after a diet of bread and water, feasting on meat and wine was simply too much.

• *Continue through the next arch, under the white arrow, then turn left and walk 30 yards to the ⓯ Schlachthaus.*

Slaughterhouse: Any proper castle was prepared to survive a six-month siege. With 4,000 people, that's a lot of provisions. The cattle that lived within the walls were slaughtered in this room. The castle's mortar was congealed here (by packing all the organic waste from the kitchen into kegs and sealing it). Notice the drainage gutters. "Running water" came through from drains built into the walls (to keep the mortar dry and therefore strong...and less smelly).

• *Back outside, climb the modern stairs to the left (look for the zum*

RHINE VALLEY

Ausgang *sign). A skinny, dark passage (yes, that's the one) leads you into the...*

Big Cellar: This ⑯ *Grosser Keller* was a big pantry. When the castle was smaller, this was the original moat—you can see the rough lower parts of the wall. The original floor was 13 feet deeper. The drawbridge rested upon the stone nubs on the left. When the castle expanded, the moat became this cellar. Halfway up the walls on the entrance side of the room, square holes mark spots where timbers made a storage loft, perhaps filled with grain. In the back, an arch leads to the wine cellar (sometimes blocked off) where finer wine was kept. Part of a soldier's pay was wine...table wine. This wine was kept in a single 180,000-liter stone barrel (that's 47,550 gallons), which generally lasted about 18 months.

The count owned the surrounding farmland. Farmers got to keep 20 percent of their production. Later, in more liberal feudal times, the nobility let them keep 40 percent. Today, the German government leaves the workers with 60 percent...and provides a few more services.

• *You're free. Climb out, turn right, and leave. For coffee on a terrace with a great view, visit Schlosshotel Rheinfels, opposite the entrance.*

Optional Detour—Into the Small Mine Tunnels: In about 1600, to protect their castle, the Rheinfellers cleverly booby-trapped the land just outside their walls by building tunnels topped with thin slate roofs and packed with explosives. By detonating the explosives when under attack, they could kill hundreds of invaders. In 1626, a handful of underground Protestant Germans blew 300 Catholic Spaniards to—they figured—hell. You're welcome to wander through a set of never-blown-up tunnels. But be warned: It's 600 feet long, assuming you make no wrong turns; it's pitch-dark, muddy, and claustrophobic, with confusing dead-ends; and you'll never get higher than a deep crouch. It cannot be done without a light (candles available at entrance). Be sure to bring the castle map, which shows the tunnels in detail.

To tour the Small Mine Tunnels, start at the red signpost ⑩ at the crossbow slits (described earlier). Follow the stairs on the right leading down to the mine (*zu den Minengängen* sign on upper left). The ⑪ *Fuchsloch* (foxhole) sign welcomes you to a covered passageway. Walk level (take no stairs) past the first steel railing (where you hope to emerge later) around a few bends to the second steel railing. Climb down.

The "highway" in this foxhole is three feet high. The ceiling may be painted with a white line indicating the correct path. Don't venture into the narrower side aisles. These were once filled with the gunpowder. After a small decline, take the second right. At the T-intersection, go right (uphill). After about 10 feet, go left.

Take the next right and look for a light at the end of the tunnel. Head up a rocky incline under the narrowest part of the tunnel and you'll emerge at that first steel railing. The stairs on the right lead to freedom. Cross the field, walk under the bigger archway, and continue uphill toward the old wooden bridge. Angle left through two arches (before the bridge) and through the rough entry to the ⑭ *Verliess* (prison) on the left. Rejoin the tour here.

Compromise Option—The Big Mine Tunnels: The castle also has a larger, less claustrophobic set of tunnels that you can walk through. You can mostly stand up in them, and there's some daylight, but you still need a flashlight and candles, as the floor is uneven and there can be puddles if it rains.

To go through the bigger mine tunnels, you'll need the map that the castle ticket office hands out; the route it shows runs through the big mine tunnels from signposts ⑪ through ⑭. From signpost ⑩, follow the stairs on the right leading down, and look for the *zu den Minengängen* sign on upper left. Go into the passageway at the ⑪ *Fuchsloch* (foxhole) sign, and continue along it, but don't go down the stairway by the steel railings into the small mine tunnels. Instead, follow the route on the castle map through the big mine tunnels, emerging across a courtyard where you'll see the ⑫ *Halsgraben* sign, into the ⑬ *Büchsenmacherturm* (gunsmiths' tower), and then back outside, turning left through an archway to emerge by the ⑭ *Verliess* (prison) sign.

Sleeping in St. Goar

(€1 = about $1.40, country code: 49, area code: 06741)
Parking in St. Goar is tight; ask at your hotel.

$$$ Schlosshotel Rheinfels ("Rheinfels Castle Hotel") is an overpriced 64-room place across from the castle entrance. My advice: Stay at a good-value hotel in town, put on a clean shirt, and hike up here for a luxurious breakfast overlooking the river (non-guest breakfast-€16, served daily 7:00-11:00; airless Db under the roof-€120-130 and up; view Db with train noise-€210-225; elevator doesn't go to top floor, non-smoking rooms, free Internet access, indoor pool and sauna, dressy restaurant, free parking, Schlossberg 47, tel. 06741/8020, fax 06741/802-802, www.schloss -rheinfels.de, info@schloss-rheinfels.de).

$$ Hotel am Markt, recently purchased by the Marx family (no relation to Karl), is rustic and a good deal, with all the modern comforts. It features a hint of antler with a pastel flair, 17 bright rooms, and a good restaurant. It's a good value and a stone's throw from the boat dock and train station (S-€40, Sb-€50, standard Db-€65, bigger riverview Db-€80, cheaper March-mid-April and Oct, closed Nov-Feb, free Internet access and Wi-Fi, parking-€5,

RHINE VALLEY

Markt 1, tel. 06741/1689, fax 06741/1721, www.hotel-am-markt -sankt-goar.de, hotel.am.markt@gmx.de).

$$ Rhein Hotel, two doors down from Hotel am Markt and run with enthusiasm by energetic Gil Velich (a trained chef), has 10 quality rooms in a spacious building and its own restaurant (Sb-€50, Db-€65, river-view Db-€85-95, non-smoking, free Wi-Fi, laundry-€12/load, closed mid-Nov-Feb, Heerstrasse 71, tel. 06741/981-240, fax 06741/981-267, www.rheinhotel-st-goar.de, info@rheinhotel-st-goar.de).

$ Hotel Hauser, across the square from Hotel am Markt, is another good value, warmly run by Marianne Velich (Gil's distant relative). Its 12 simple rooms sit over a fine restaurant (S-€23, D-€46, Db-€54, great Db with Rhine-view balconies-€58, confirm you're getting the Rick Steves rate, show this book and pay cash for best prices, family rooms, cash preferred, flexible à la carte half-pension-€14, free Wi-Fi, Heerstrasse 77, tel. 06741/333, fax 06741/1464, www.hotelhauser.de, hotelhauser@t-online.de).

$ Frau Kurz offers St. Goar's best B&B, renting three delightful rooms (sharing 2.5 bathrooms) with bathrobes, a breakfast terrace, garden, fine view, and homemade marmalade (S-€30, D-€52, 2-night minimum, D-€48 if you stay at least 4 nights, cash only, non-smoking, free and easy parking, honor your reservation or call to cancel, ask about apartment with kitchen if staying at least 5 days, Ulmenhof 11, tel. 06741/459, www.gaestehaus -kurz.de, jeanette.kurz@superkabel.de). It's a memorably steep five-minute hike from the train station: Exit left from the station, take an immediate left at the yellow phone booth, pass under the tracks, go up the stairs, and follow the zigzag path, turning right through an archway onto Ulmenhof; #11 is just past tower.

$ St. Goar Hostel, the big beige building down the hill from the castle, rents 126 beds, mostly in 4- to 10-bed dorms but also in 18 doubles. The facilities hark back to an earlier age of hosteling, with shared baths down the hall (hence the low price), but it has Rhine views, a nice terrace, and hearty €6 dinners (dorm beds-€15, D-€36, includes breakfast, non-members-€3.10 extra, non-smoking, open all day, curfew 22:30—but you can borrow the key, reconfirm reservation by phone the day before, Bismarckweg 17, tel. 06741/388, fax 06741/2869, www.diejugendherbergen.de, st-goar@diejugendherbergen.de). It's a fairly level 10-minute walk from the train station: Veer left and go all the way down narrow red-brick Oberstrasse, then turn left through the underpass and make an immediate right on Bismarcksweg, following the red *Jugendherberge* signs.

Eating in St. Goar

Hotel am Markt serves tasty traditional meals with plenty of game and fish (specialties include marinated roast beef and homemade cheesecake) at fair prices with good atmosphere and service (€9-15 entrées, March-Oct daily 8:00-21:00, closed Nov-Feb, Markt 1, tel. 06741/1689).

Burgschänke, on the ground floor of Schlosshotel Rheinfels across from the castle ticket office (enter through the souvenir shop) offers the only reasonably priced lunches up at Rheinfels Castle. It's family-friendly and has a Rhine view from its outdoor terrace (€9-13 entrées, Sun-Thu 11:00-18:00, Fri-Sat 11:00-21:00, tel. 06741/802-806). Upstairs, the **Schlosshotel Rheinfels** dining room is your Rhine splurge, with an incredible indoor view terrace in an elegant, dressy setting (€16 breakfast for non-guests, €19-24 entrées, €32-36 three-course fixed-price meals, daily 7:00-11:00 & 12:00-14:15 & 18:30-21:15, call to reserve a window table, tel. 06741/8020; see also hotel listing, earlier).

Other Options: St. Goar has a couple of Italian eateries, and the grocery has plenty for a picnic to enjoy on the riverside park or up at the castle. For more restaurants, take the quick train to Bacharach, which leaves and returns hourly (last train at 22:00).

BERLIN

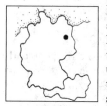

No tour of Germany is complete without a look at its historic and reunited capital. Over the last two decades, Berlin has been a construction zone. Standing over ripped-up tracks and under a canopy of cranes, visitors witnessed the rebirth of a great European capital. Today, as we enjoy the thrill of walking over what was the Wall and through the well-patched Brandenburg Gate, it's clear that history is not contained in some book, but is an exciting story that we are a part of. Historians find Berlin exhilarating.

Berlin had a tumultuous 20th century. After the city was devastated in World War II, it was divided by the Allied powers: The American, British, and French sectors became West Berlin, and the Soviet sector, East Berlin. In 1948 and 1949, the Soviet Union tried to starve the Western half into submission, but the siege was foiled by the Western Allies' Berlin Airlift, which flew in supplies from Frankfurt. The East-West division was set in stone in 1961, when the East German government boxed in West Berlin by building the Berlin Wall. The Wall stood for 28 years. In 1990, less than a year after the Wall fell, the two Germanys—and the two Berlins—officially became one. When the dust settled, Berliners from both sides of the once-divided city faced the monumental challenge of reunification.

While the work is far from over, a new Berlin has emerged. Berliners joke that they don't need to go anywhere because their city's always changing. Spin a postcard rack to see what's new. A 10-year-old guidebook on Berlin covers a different city.

Reunification has had its negative side, and locals are fond of saying, "The Wall survives in the minds of some people." Some "Ossies" (impolite slang for Easterners) miss their security. Some

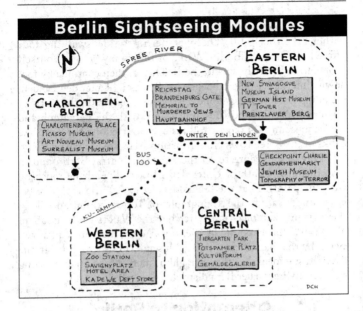

Berlin Sightseeing Modules

SPREE RIVER

N

EASTERN BERLIN

New Synagogue
Museum Island
German Hist Museum
TV Tower
Prenzlauer Berg

CHARLOTTEN-BURG

Charlottenburg Palace
Picasso Museum
Art Nouveau Museum
Surrealist Museum

Reichstag
Brandenburg Gate
Memorial to
Murdered Jews
Hauptbahnhof

UNTER DEN LINDEN

BUS 100

Checkpoint Charlie
Gendarmenmarkt
Jewish Museum
Topography of Terror

KU-DAMM

CENTRAL BERLIN

Tiergarten Park
Potsdamer Platz
Kulturforum
Gemäldegalerie

WESTERN BERLIN

Zoo Station
Savignyplatz
Hotel Area
KaDeWe Dept Store

DCH

"Wessies" miss their easy ride (military deferrals, subsidized rent, and tax breaks offered to West Germans willing to live in an isolated city surrounded by the communist world). For free spirits, walled-in West Berlin was a citadel of freedom within the East.

The city government has been eager to charge forward, with little nostalgia for anything that was associated with the East. Big corporations and the national government have moved in, and the dreary swath of land that was the Wall and its notorious "death strip" has been transformed. City planners have boldly made Berlin's reunification and the return of the national government a good opportunity to make Berlin a great capital once again. When the Wall fell, the East was a decrepit wasteland and the West was a paragon of commerce and materialism. More than 20 years later, the roles are reversed: It is the East that feels the vibrant pulse of the city, while the West seems like yesterday's news.

Today, Berlin feels like the nuclear fuel rod of a great nation. It's so vibrant with youth, energy, and an anything-goes-and-anything's-possible buzz that Munich feels spent in comparison. Berlin is both extremely popular and surprisingly affordable. As tourist attraction, it's booming. But the city is so spread out, you'll often feel like you have the place to yourself.

Planning Your Time

Because of Berlin's inconvenient location, try to enter and/or leave by either night train or plane. I'd give Berlin at least two days and spend them this way:

Day 1: Begin your day getting oriented to this huge city. Either take the 10:00 "Discover Berlin" guided walking tour offered by Original Berlin Walks or follow my "Do-It-Yourself Orientation Tour" by bus to the Reichstag, then continue by foot down Unter den Linden. Focus on sights along Unter den Linden, including the Reichstag dome (reservations required), the German History Museum, and Museum Island (with the Pergamon and Neues museums). Take a stroll (or boat tour) along the park-like banks of the Spree River from Museum Island to the Chancellery.

Day 2: Concentrate on the sights in central Berlin and in eastern Berlin south of Unter den Linden. Spend the morning with the paintings at the Gemäldegalerie. After lunch, hike via Potsdamer Platz to the Topography of Terror exhibit and along the surviving Zimmerstrasse stretch of the Wall to the Museum of The Wall at Checkpoint Charlie. If you're not museum-ed out yet, swing by the magnificent Jewish Museum. Finish your day in the lively East—ideally in the once glum, then edgy, now fun-loving and trendy Prenzlauer Berg district.

Orientation to Berlin

(area code: 030)

Berlin is huge, with 3.4 million people. But the tourist's Berlin can be broken into three digestible chunks:

1. Eastern Berlin has the highest concentration of notable sights and colorful neighborhoods. Near the landmark Brandenburg Gate, you'll find the Reichstag building, Pariser Platz, and the Holocaust Memorial. From Brandenburg Gate, the famous Unter den Linden boulevard runs eastward through former East Berlin, passing the marvelous German History Museum and Museum Island (Pergamon Museum, Neues Museum, and Berlin Cathedral) on the way to Alexanderplatz (TV Tower). The intersection of Unter den Linden and Friedrichstrasse has reclaimed its place as the center of the city. South of Unter den Linden, you'll find the delightful Gendarmenmarkt square, most Nazi sites (including the Topography of Terror), the best Wall-related sights (Museum of The Wall at Checkpoint Charlie and East Side Gallery), the Jewish Museum, and the colorful Turkish neighborhood of Kreuzberg. North of Unter den Linden are these worth-a-wander neighborhoods: around Oranienburger Strasse (Jewish Quarter and New Synagogue), Hackescher Markt, and Prenzlauer Berg (several recommended hotels and a very lively restaurant/nightlife zone). Eastern Berlin's pedestrian-friendly Spree riverbank is also worth a stroll (or a river cruise).

2. Central Berlin is dominated by the giant Tiergarten park. South of the park are Potsdamer Platz and the Kulturforum museum cluster (including the Gemäldegalerie, New National Gallery, Musical Instruments Museum, and Philharmonic Concert Hall). To the north, the huge Hauptbahnhof (main train station) straddles the former Wall in what was central Berlin's no-man's-land.

3. **Western Berlin** centers on the Bahnhof Zoo (Zoo train station, often marked "Zoologischer Garten" on transit maps) and the grand Kurfürstendamm boulevard, nicknamed "Ku'damm" (transportation hub, tours, information, shopping, and recommended hotels). The East is all the rage. But the West, while staid in comparison, is bouncing back—with lots of big-name stores and destination restaurants that keep the area buzzing. During the Cold War, this "Western Sector" was the hub for Western visitors. Capitalists visited the West, with a nervous side-trip beyond the Wall into the grim and foreboding East. (Cubans, Russians, Poles, and Angolans stayed behind the Wall and did their sightseeing in the East.) Remnants of this Iron Curtain–era Western focus have left today's visitors with a stronger focus on the Ku'damm and Bahnhof Zoo than the district really deserves.

Tourist Information

With any luck, you won't have to use Berlin's TIs—they're for-profit agencies working for the city's big hotels, which colors the information they provide. TI branches, appropriately called "infostores," are unlikely to have the information you need (tel. 030/250-025, www.berlin-tourist-information.com). You'll find them at the **Hauptbahnhof** train station (daily 8:00-22:00, by main entrance on Europaplatz), **Ku'damm** (Kurfürstendamm 21, in the glass-and-steel Neues Kranzler Eck building, Mon-Sat 10:00-20:00, Sun 10:00-18:00, shorter hours in winter), and the **Brandenburg Gate** (daily 10:00-18:00).

Skip the TI's €1 map, and instead pick up any of the walking tour companies' brochures—they include better maps for free (most hotels also provide free city maps). While the TI does sell the three-day Museumspass (described next), it's also available at major museums. If you take a walking tour, your guide is likely a better source of nightlife or shopping tips than the TI. The TI offers a €3 room-finding service (but only for hotels that give them kickbacks—many don't).

Museum Passes: The three-day **Museumspass** (a.k.a. SchauLUST MuseenBERLIN) gets you into 70 museums, including the national museums and most of the recommended biggies, on three consecutive days for €19. As you'll routinely spend €5-10 per admission, this pays for itself in a hurry. And you'll enjoy the ease of popping in and out of museums that you might not otherwise want to pay for. Buy it at the TI or any participating

Berlin

······ COURSE OF FORMER WALL
+●+ ELEVATED S-BAHN LINE & STATION

½ MILE
1 KM

CHARLOTTEN-
BURG

SPREE R.

VICTORY
COLUMN

ERNST-
REUTER-
PLATZ

STRASSE

DES

17

BISMARCK- STR.

TIERGAR

SAVIGNY-
PLATZ

BAHNHOF
ZOO

HARD.

ZOO

BAUHAUS
ARCHIVE

KULTUR

K ANTSTR.

EUROPA
CENTER

GERMAN
RESIST.
MUSEUM

KU'DAMM

MEMORIAL
CHURCH

KUFURSTEN-

LIETZEN- STR.

KOLLWITZ
MUSEUM

KaDeWe
STORE

KLEISTSTR.

DCH

BERLIN

museum. Note that if a museum is closed on one of the days of your Museumspass, you have access to that museum on a fourth day to make up for lost time. The pass won't, however, enable you to skip lines: Many museums require passholders to stand in line to get a free ticket that lets you through the turnstile. The €14 **Museum Island Pass** (Bereichskarte Museumsinsel) covers all the museums on the island (otherwise €8-10 each) and is a fine value—but for €5 more, the three-day Museumspass gives you triple the days and many more entries. TIs also sell the **WelcomeCard,** a transportation pass that also includes some museum discounts (described later, under "Getting Around Berlin").

Local Publications: Various magazines can help make your time in Berlin more productive (all available at the TI and most at newsstands). *Berlin Programm* is a comprehensive German-language monthly, especially strong in high culture, that lists upcoming events and museum hours (€2, www.berlin-programm .de). *Berlin To Go* is a sketchier German/English TI-produced bimonthly magazine offering timely features on Berlin and a partial calendar of events (€1). *Exberliner Magazine,* the only real English monthly (published mostly by expat Brits who love to poke fun at expat Americans), is very helpful for curious travelers. It has an

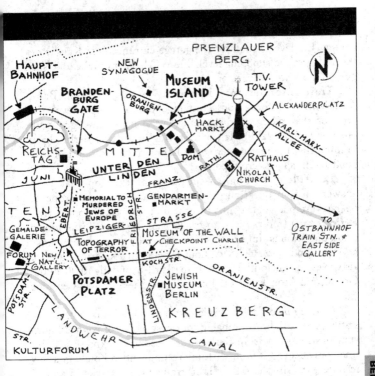

edgy, somewhat pretentious, youthful focus and gives a fascinating insider's look at this fast-changing city (€2 but often given away at theaters or on the street, www.exberliner.com).

Arrival in Berlin

By Train

Berlin's newest and grandest train station is **Berlin Hauptbahnhof** (main train station, a.k.a. simply "der Bahnhof"). All long-distance trains arrive here, at Europe's biggest, mostly underground train station. Tracks 1-8 are in the lowest underground level, while tracks 11-16 (along with the S-Bahn) are a floor above ground level, marked +1.

It's a "transfer station"—unique for its major lines coming in at right angles—where the national train system meets the city's train system (S-Bahn). It's also the home of 80 shops with long hours—some locals call the station a "shopping mall with trains" (daily 8:00-22:00, only stores selling travel provisions are open Sun). The Kaisers supermarket (on the underground shopping level, marked -1) is handy for assembling a picnic for the ride.

Services: The easy way to store your luggage is at the Gepäck Center, an efficient and secure deposit service (€4/day per bag, always open, on the upper level directly under track 14). Luggage lockers (€3-5) are difficult to find since they're in the parking garage (P-3 level). Look for the garage entrance near Kaisers on the underground shopping level. The WC Center (public toilets) is next to the Virgin Megastore.

Train Information: The station has two DeutscheBahn *Reisezentrum* information counters (one on the upper level, the other on the underground shopping level—just follow signs; both open daily 6:00-22:00). If you're staying in western Berlin, keep in mind that the info center at the Bahnhof Zoo station is just as good and much less crowded.

EurAide is an English-speaking information desk with answers to your questions about train travel around Europe. It operates from a single counter in the underground shopping level *Reisezentrum* (follow signs to tracks 5-6). It's American-run, so communication is simple. This is an especially good place to make fast-train and *couchette* reservations for later in your trip. EurAide also gives out a helpful free city map (April-Sept daily 10:00-19:00; Oct-March Mon-Fri 11:00-18:00, closed Sat-Sun; www.euraide .com).

Getting into Town: While taxis and buses await outside the station, the S-Bahn is probably your best means of connecting to your destination within Berlin. The cross-town express S-Bahn line connects the station with my recommended hotels in a few minutes. It's simple: All S-Bahn trains are on tracks 15 and 16 at the top of the station. All trains on track 15 go east (toward the Ostbahnhof and Hackescher Markt, with connections to Prenzlauer Berg), and trains on track 16 go west (toward Bahnhof Zoo and Savignyplatz). Your train ticket or railpass into the station covers you on your connecting S-Bahn ride into town (and your ticket out includes the transfer via S-Bahn to the Hauptbahnhof). U-Bahn rides are not covered by tickets or railpasses.

If you're sleeping at my recommended hotels in eastern Berlin's Prenzlauer Berg neighborhood, take any train on track 15 two stops to Hackescher Markt, then catch tram #M1 north (see map on page 688).

If you're sleeping at my recommended hotels in western Berlin, catch any train on track 16 to Savignyplatz, and you're a five-minute walk from your hotel (see map on pages 694-695). Savignyplatz is one stop after **Bahnhof Zoo** (rhymes with "toe;" a.k.a. Bahnhof Zoologischer Garten), the once-grand train hub now eclipsed by the Hauptbahnhof. Nowadays it's useful mainly for its shops, uncrowded train-information desk, and BVG transit office (outside the entrance, amid the traffic).

The Berlin Hauptbahnhof is not well-connected to the city's U-Bahn (subway) system—yet. The station's sole U-Bahn line—U55—only goes two stops to the Brandenburger Tor station and doesn't really connect to the rest of the system. It's part of a planned extension of the U5 line to Alexanderplatz that's far from completion. But for transit junkies, it is an interesting ride on Europe's newest and shortest subway line.

By Plane

For information on reaching the city center from Berlin's airports, see "Berlin Connections" at the end of this chapter.

Helpful Hints

Medical Help: "Call a Doc" is a non-profit referral service designed for tourists (toll tel. 01805-321-303, phone answered 24 hours a day, www.calladoc.com). Payment is arranged between you and the doctor, and is likely far more affordable than similar care in the US. The US Embassy also has a list of local English-speaking doctors (tel. 030/832-9233, www.usembassy.de).

Museum Tips: Some major Berlin museums are closed on Monday. The €14 Museum Island Pass (Bereichskarte Museumsinsel) covers all of the museums on the island (otherwise €8-10 each), but for €5 more, the three-day Museumspass gives you triple the days and many more entries. If a museum is closed on one of the days of your Museumspass, you can visit that museum on a fourth day.

Monday Activities: Since several museums close on Monday, save the day for Berlin Wall sights, the Reichstag dome (requires reservations—see page 650), my "Do-It-Yourself Orientation Tour" and strolling Unter den Linden, walking/bus tours, the Jewish Museum, churches, the zoo, or shopping (the Kaufhaus des Westens—KaDeWe—department store is a sight in itself). Be aware that when Monday is a holiday—as it is several times a year—museums are open then and closed Tuesday.

Addresses: Many Berlin streets are numbered with odd and even numbers on the same side of the street, often with no connection to the other side (for example, Ku'damm #212 can be across the street from #14). To save steps, check the white street signs on curb corners; many list the street numbers covered on that side of the block.

Internet Access: You'll find Internet access in most hotels and hostels, as well as at small Internet cafés all over the city. Near Savignyplatz, **Internet-Terminal** is at Kantstrasse 38. In eastern Berlin, try **Netlounge** at Auguststrasse 89, or **Surf Inn** at Alexanderplatz 9. The Zoo, Friedrichstrasse, and Hauptbahnhof train stations have coin-operated Internet terminals (though these unmanned machines can come with greater security risks).

Bookstore: Berlin Story, a big, cluttered, fun bookshop, has the best selection anywhere in town of English-language books on Berlin. They also have a fascinating free little museum in the back with a model of Unter den Linden from 1930 and a room showing a good 25-minute Berlin history video (in English). The shop has a knowledgeable staff and stocks an amusing mix of knickknacks and East Berlin nostalgia souvenirs (daily 10:00-20:00, Unter den Linden 26, second location farther to the east, tel. 030/2045-3842, www.berlinstory.de).

Laundry: Schnell und Sauber Waschcenter is a chain of handy launderettes, including a location in eastern Berlin at Torstrasse 115, around the corner from the recommended Circus hostel (€5-9/load wash and dry, daily 6:00-23:00). Also near my recommended hotels in Prenzlauer Berg, try **Eco-Express Waschsalon** (€4-9/load wash and dry, daily 6:00-22:00, self- or full-serve, attached café, Danziger Strasse 7).

Travel Agency: Last Minute Flugbörse can help you find a flight in a hurry (discount flights, no train tickets, in Europa Center near Bahnhof Zoo, Mon-Sat 10:00-20:00, closed Sun, tel. 030/2655-1050, www.lastminuteflugboerse.de). **American Express** is a few blocks off Unter den Linden at Friedrichstrasse 172 (sells train tickets for €4 service fee, Mon-Fri 9:00-19:00, Sat 10:00-14:00, closed Sun, tel. 030/201-7400).

Getting Around Berlin

Berlin's sights spread far and wide. Right from the start, commit yourself to the city's fine public-transit system.

By Public Transit: Subway, Train, Tram, and Bus

Berlin's many modes of transportation are consolidated into one system that uses the same tickets: U-Bahn (*Untergrund-Bahn*, Berlin's subway), S-Bahn (*Stadtschnellbahn*, or "fast urban train," mostly aboveground and with fewer stops), *Strassenbahn* (street-cars, called "trams" by locals), and buses.

Ticket Options: You have several options for tickets:

• A basic ticket *(Einzelfahrschein)* for two hours of travel in one direction on buses or subways—€2.30. It's easy to make this ticket stretch to cover several rides...as long as they're all in the same direction.

• A cheap, short-ride ticket *(Kurzstrecke)* for a single ride of six bus stops or three subway stations (one transfer allowed)—€1.40.

• A four-trip ticket *(4-Fahrten-Karte),* four basic tickets at a small discount—€8.20.

• A day pass *(Tageskarte)* covering zones A and B, the city proper—€6.30 (good until 3:00 the morning after). For longer stays, a 7-day pass—*Sieben-Tage-Karte*—is also available for €27.20. Or consider the WelcomeCard—good for up to 5 days (described next). The *Kleingruppenkarte* lets groups of up to five travel all day for €15.

• If you plan to cover a lot of ground using public transportation during a two- or three-day visit, the **WelcomeCard** (available at TIs) is usually the best deal. For longer stays, there's even a five-day option. It covers all public transportation and gives you up to 50 percent discounts on lots of minor and a few major museums (including Checkpoint Charlie), sightseeing tours (including 25 percent off the recommended Original Berlin Walks), and music and theater events (www.visitberlin.de/welcomecard). The Berlin-only option covers transit zones A and B (€17/48 hours, €23/72 hours). If you're a museum junkie, consider the **WelcomeCard Museumsinsel** (€32/72 hours), which combines travel in zones A and B with unlimited access to the five museums on Museum Island. Families get an extra price break: The A/B versions are valid for one adult and up to three kids younger than 14.

Buying Tickets: You can buy U- and S-Bahn tickets from machines at stations. (They are also sold at BVG pavilions at train stations, airports, and the TI, and aboard trams and buses—drivers give change.) *Erwachsener* means "adult"—anyone 14 or older. Don't be afraid of the automated machines: First select the type of ticket you want, then load in the coins or paper bills. As you board the bus or tram, or enter the subway system, punch your ticket in a red or yellow clock machine to validate it (or risk a €40 fine; for an all-day or multiday pass, stamp it only the first time you ride). Within Berlin, Eurailpasses are good only on S-Bahn connections from the train station when you're arriving and to the station when you're departing.

Transit Tips: The S-Bahn crosstown express is a river of public transit through the heart of the city, in which many lines converge on one basic highway. Get used to this, and you'll leap within a few minutes between key locations: Savignyplatz (hotels), Bahnhof Zoo (Ku'damm, bus #100, Original Berlin Walks tour meeting spot), Hauptbahnhof (all major trains in and out of Berlin), Friedrichstrasse (heart of Unter den Linden), Hackescher Markt (Museum Island, restaurants, nightlife, connection to Prenzlauer Berg hotels and eateries), and Alexanderplatz (eastern end of Unter den Linden).

Sections of the U- or S-Bahn sometimes close temporarily for repairs. In this situation, a bus route often replaces the train (*Ersatzverkehr*, or "replacement transportation").

Berlin's public transit is operated by BVG (except the S-Bahn, run by DeutscheBahn). Bus schedules are available on the helpful BVG website (www.bvg.de).

By Taxi

Taxis are easy to flag down, and taxi stands are common. A typical ride within town costs €8-10, and a cross-town trip (for example, Bahnhof Zoo to Alexanderplatz) will run you about €15.

Money-Saving Taxi Tip: For any ride of less than two kilometers (about a mile), you can save several euros if you take advantage of the *Kurzstrecke* (short-stretch) rate. To get this rate, it's important that you flag the cab down on the street—not at or even near a taxi stand. Also, you must ask for the *Kurzstrecke* rate as soon as you hop in: Confidently say *"Kurzstrecke, bitte"* (KOORTS-shtreh-keh BIT-teh), and your driver will grumble and flip the meter to a fixed €4 rate.

By Bike

Flat Berlin is a very bike-friendly city, but be careful—Berlin's motorists don't brake for bicyclists (and bicyclists don't brake for pedestrians). Fortunately, some roads and sidewalks have special red-painted bike lanes. Just don't ride on the regular sidewalk—it's verboten.

In eastern Berlin, **Take a Bike** near the Friedrichstrasse S-Bahn station is owned by a lovely Dutch couple who know a lot about bikes and have a huge inventory (€12.50/day, €19/2 days, slightly cheaper on weekdays, daily 9:30-19:00, 8 Neustädtische Kirchstrasse, tel. 030/2065-4730, info@takeabike.de). To find it, leave the S-Bahn station via the Friedrichstrasse exit, turn right, go through a triangle-shaped square, and hang a left on Neustädtische Kirchstrasse.

In western Berlin, you can rent good bikes at the **Bahnhof Zoo** left-luggage counter, next to the lockers at the back of the station (€10/day, €23/3 days, €35/7 days; bikes come with lock, air pump, and mounted basket; daily 7:00-21:00, there's a limited supply of bikes and they've been known to run out).

Tours in Berlin

▲▲▲Walking Tours

Berlin is an ideal city to explore on a walking tour. The city is a battle zone of extremely competitive and creative walking-tour companies, all offering employment to American and British expats and students—and cheap, informative tours to visiting travelers. Unlike many other European countries, Germany has no regulations controlling who can give city tours. Berlin is home to a large number of expatriates and academics, and it seems that every year some of them get together and form a new tour company. Some of these upstarts run great tours, but you'll generally get the best quality with one of the more established companies.

All give variations on the same themes: general introductory walk, Hitler and Nazi sites walk, and a communism walk. The youth-oriented outfits also do nightly pub crawls. For details, see the various websites.

Original Berlin Walks—This is the most established operation, with tours aimed at a clientele that's curious about the city's history. I've enjoyed the help of O.B.W.'s high-quality, high-energy guides for many years, and routinely hire them when my tour groups are in town. I'm always impressed with founder Nick Gay's ability to assemble guides of such high caliber. Tours generally cost €12 (€9 with WelcomeCard, €10 if you're under 26). Ask about a discount with this book.

There's no need to reserve ahead—just show up. All tours meet at the taxi stand in front of the Bahnhof Zoo train station and start at 10:00 unless otherwise noted. The Discover Berlin and Jewish Life tours have a second departure point 30 minutes later opposite eastern Berlin's Hackescher Markt S-Bahn station, outside the Weihenstephaner restaurant; if you're staying in eastern Berlin, save time by meeting the group there.

Discover Berlin, O.B.W.'s flagship introductory walk, covers the birthplace of the city, Museum Island, then heads up Unter den Linden, stops at the Reichstag, and goes on to Checkpoint Charlie (no interior visits, 4 hours, English only, daily year-round, meet at 10:00 at Bahnhof Zoo, April-Oct also daily at 13:30). Other tours include: **Infamous Third Reich Sites** (June-Aug Tue, Thu, and Sun at 10:00, Sat at 14:30, less frequently off-season—check their website or pick up a flier for the schedule); **Jewish Life in Berlin** (April-Oct Mon at 10:00 at Bahnhof Zoo); and **Nest of Spies** (April-Oct only, Sat at 10:00). Many of the Third Reich and Jewish history sights are difficult to pin down without these excellent walks.

You can confirm these starting times at EurAide or by phone with Nick or Serena, his wife and business partner (tel. 030/301-9194, www.berlinwalks.de, info@berlinwalks.de).

Vive Berlin—The shining new star on Berlin's tour scene, Vive Berlin was started by some of the city's most experienced guides, who came together to form Berlin's first "guiding collective" (in which everyone at the company has a say). All tours meet at Potsdamer Platz 10, in front of Balzac Coffee (U2/S-Bahn: Potsdamer Platz, use Stresemannstrasse exit). The lineup includes **Essential Berlin** (€12, daily at 10:00, also Thu and Fri at 17:00), **East Berlin** (€12, Mon, Wed, and Sat at 17:00, Sun at 10:00), and **Third Reich** (€16, Wed and Fri at 10:00, Sat at 13:00). Vive Berlin also offers one of the few dedicated tours of **West Berlin** (€12, Tue, Fri, and Sat at 17:00, Mon at 10:00). If you can, try to join one of Ben Spalding's tours (tel. 0157/845-46696, www.viveberlintours.de).

New Berlin Tours—This company offers essentially the same itineraries as O.B.W., but targets a younger crowd and offers "free" introductory tours. (Though these walks are billed as free, tips are expected; the company takes a €3/person cut, so if guides don't get enough in tips, they have to pay the rest out of pocket.) Tours meet at the Old Post Office on the corner of Oranienburger Strasse and Tucholskystrasse (S-Bahn: Oranienburger Strasse). The basic introductory city walks leave daily at 11:00, 13:00, and 16:00 and last 3.5 hours (meet in front of Starbucks at Brandenburg Gate/Pariser Platz, just show up). Paid tours include their wildly popular €12 pub crawls (nightly; for more info, see page 686) and their excellent Alternative Berlin Tour, which explores Berlin's gritty counterculture, squats, and urban life (daily at 14:00; €12, €10 for students; ask about discount with this book, tel. 030/5105-0030, www.newberlintours.com).

Berlin Underground Association (Berliner Unterwelten Verein)—Much of Berlin's history lies beneath the surface, and this group has an exclusive agreement with the city to explore and research what is hidden underground. Their one-of-a-kind tour of a WWII air-raid bunker features a chilling explanation of the air war over Berlin (Thu-Mon at 11:00). They also have access to the inside of the Humboldthain air defense tower (April-Oct Thu, Sat, and Sun at 16:00) and a completely stocked and fully functional nuclear emergency bunker (Fri-Mon at 13:00 year-round, April-Oct also Thu at 13:00). The English tours are usually led by Nick Jackson, one of the best tour guides in the city (all tours cost €9, meet in the hall of the Gesundbrunnen U-Bahn/S-Bahn station, follow signs to Humboldthain/Brunnenstrasse exit and walk up the stairs to their office, tel. 030/4991-0517, www.berlinerunterwelten.de).

Local Guides—Both **Nick Jackson** (from the Berlin Underground Association, mobile 0176-633-64975, nick.jackson@berlin.de) and **Lee Evans** (my longtime helper in Berlin, mobile 0177-423-5307, lee.evans@berlin.de) enjoy sharing the story of their adopted hometown with visitors. If they are busy, try **Jennifer DeShirley** at Berlin and Beyond; this company has a crew of excellent, professional guides with an academic bent (mobile 0176-633-55565, info@berlinandbeyond.de).

Bus Tours

Full-Blown Bus Tours—**Severin & Kühn** offers a long list of bus tours in and around Berlin; their three-hour "Big Berlin Tour" is a good introduction (€19, daily at 10:00, Fri-Sun also at 14:00, two stops: Checkpoint Charlie and Brandenburg Gate, live guides in two languages, interesting historical photos displayed on bus monitors, departs from Ku'damm 216, buy ticket at bus, tel. 030/880-4190, www.berlinerstadtrundfahrten.de).

Hop-on, Hop-off City Circle Tours—Several companies cooperate so that you can make a circuit of the city with unlimited hop-on, hop-off privileges (about 14 stops) on buses with boring recorded commentary (4/hour, daily 10:00-18:00, last bus leaves all stops at 16:00, 2-hour loop). Just hop on where you like and pay the driver. On a sunny day, when some convertible double-decker buses go topless, these are a photographer's delight, cruising slowly by just about every major sight in town. In the winter (Nov-March), the buses come only twice an hour, and the last departure is at 15:00. Basic tickets cost €20 and cover 24 hours. You can also get package deals combining the bus tour with one of the following: a one-hour river cruise (€29), the Panoramapunkt (€25), or Charlottenburg Palace (€29).

Bike Tours

Fat Tire Bike Tours—Choose among three different four-hour, six-mile tours (€20 each): City Tour (daily March-April and Oct-Nov at 11:00, May-Sept also at 16:00, Dec-Feb Wed and Sat at 11:00), Berlin Wall Tour (April-Oct Mon, Thu, and Sat at 10:30), and Third Reich Tour (April-Oct Wed, Fri, and Sun at 10:30). For any tour, meet at the TV Tower at Alexanderplatz—but don't get distracted by the Russians pretending to be Fat Tire (no need to reserve for the Wall or Third Reich tours, tel. 030/2404-7991, www.fattirebiketours.com, berlin@fattirebiketours.com).

Boat Tours

Spree River Cruises—Several boat companies offer one-hour €10 trips up and down the river. They used to be boring, but now a relaxing hour on one of these boats can be time and money well-spent. You'll listen to excellent English audioguides, see lots of wonderful new government-commissioned architecture, and enjoy the lively park action fronting the river. Boats leave from various docks that cluster near the bridge at the Berlin Cathedral (just off Unter den Linden). I enjoyed the Historical Sightseeing Cruise from **Stern und Kreisschiffahrt** (mid-March-Nov daily 10:30-18:30, leaves from Nikolaiviertel Dock—cross bridge from Berlin Cathedral toward Alexanderplatz and look right, tel. 030/536-3600, www.sternundkreis.de). Confirm that the boat you choose comes with English commentary.

Self-Guided Tour

Do-It-Yourself Orientation Tour: Bus #100 from Bahnhof Zoo to the Reichstag

This tour narrates the route of convenient bus #100, which connects my recommended hotel neighborhood in western Berlin

BERLIN

with the sights in eastern Berlin. If you have the €20 and two hours for a hop-on, hop-off bus tour, take that instead. But this short €2.30 bus ride provides a fine city introduction. Bus #100 is a sightseer's dream, stopping at Bahnhof Zoo, the Berlin Zoo, Victory Column (Siegessäule), Reichstag, Brandenburg Gate, Unter den Linden, Pergamon Museum, and Alexanderplatz. While you could ride it to the end, it's more fun to get out at the Reichstag and walk down Unter den Linden at your own pace (using my commentary on page 656). When combined with the self-guided walk down Unter den Linden, this tour merits ▲▲▲. Before you take this bus into eastern Berlin, consider checking out the sights in western Berlin (see page 681).

The Tour Begins: Buses start from Hardenbergplatz in front of Bahnhof Zoo (from elsewhere in the city, just take the S-Bahn to Bahnhof Zoo). Buses come every 10 minutes, and single tickets are good for two hours—so take advantage of hop-on-and-off privileges. Climb aboard, stamp your ticket (giving it a starting time), and grab a seat on top. This is about a 15-minute ride. The upcoming stop will light up on the reader board inside the bus.

● On your left and then straight ahead you'll see the bombed-out hulk of the **Kaiser Wilhelm Memorial Church,** with its postwar sister church (under restoration through 2012, and described on page 682), and the **Europa Center.** This shopping district, once the center of West Berlin, is still a bustling people zone with big department stores nearby. When the Wall came down, East Berliners flocked to this area's department stores (especially KaDeWe, described on page 684). Soon after, the biggest, swankiest new stores were built in the East. Now western Berlin is trying to win those shoppers back by building even bigger and better shopping centers around the Europa Center.

● At the stop in front of Hotel Palace: On the left, the elephant gates mark the entrance to the **Berlin Zoo** and its aquarium (described on page 684).

● Cruising down Kurfürstenstrasse, you'll pass several Asian restaurants—a reminder that the best food in cosmopolitan Berlin is not necessarily German. Turning left, with the huge Tiergarten park in the distance ahead, you'll cross a canal and see the **Bauhaus Archive** behind the trees on the right (hard to see—it's the off-white, blocky building with scoopy roof ducts). The Bauhaus movement ushered in a new age of modern architecture, emphasizing the notion that function is a part of beauty, and art is a functional part of our daily lives. The movement gave rise to all of those blocky steel-and-glass skyscrapers in big cities around the world.

On the left is Berlin's **embassy row.** The first interesting embassy is Mexico's, with columns that seem to move when you're driving past them (how do they do that?). The big turquoise wall marks the communal home of all five Nordic embassies. This building is very "green," run entirely on solar power.

> ● The bus enters the 400-acre **Tiergarten** park, packed with cycling paths, joggers, and—on hot days—nude sunbathers. Straight ahead, the **Victory Column** (Siegessäule, with the gilded angel, described on page 677) towers above this vast city park that was once a royal hunting grounds, now nicknamed the "green lungs of Berlin."

> ● A block after leaving the Victory Column (on the left) is the 18th-century late-Rococo **Bellevue Palace.** Formerly the official residence of the Prussian (and later German) crown prince, and at one time a Nazi VIP guest house, it's now the residence of the federal president (whose power is mostly ceremonial—the chancellor wields the real power). If the flag's out, he's in.

> ● Driving along the Spree River, look left for the next sights: This park area was a residential district before World War II. Now it's filled with the buildings of the **national government.** The huge brick "brown snake" complex was built to house government workers—but it didn't sell, so now its apartments are available to anyone. A metal Henry Moore sculpture titled *Butterfly* floats in front of the slope-roofed House of World Cultures (Berliners have nicknamed this building "the pregnant oyster"). The modern tower (next on left) is a carillon with 68 bells (from 1987).

> ● Leap out at the Platz der Republik stop. (While you could continue on bus #100, it's better on foot from here.) Through the trees on the left you'll see Germany's sprawling **Chancellery.** Started during the more imperial rule of Helmut Kohl, it's now considered overly grand. The big open space is **Platz der Republik,** where the Victory Column stood until Hitler moved it. The Hauptbahnhof (Berlin's vast main train station, marked by its tall tower with the *DB* sign) is across the field between the Chancellery and the Reichstag. Watch your step—excavators found a 250-pound undetonated American bomb here.

> ● Just down the street stands an old building with a new dome...the **Reichstag.**

Sights in Eastern Berlin

I've arranged the following sights in order of a convenient self-guided orientation walk, picking up where the bus #100 part of my "Do-It-Yourself Orientation Tour" leaves off. Allow a comfortable hour for this walk from the Reichstag to Alexanderplatz, including time for lingering (but not museum stops).

▲▲▲Reichstag

The parliament building—the heart of German democracy—has a

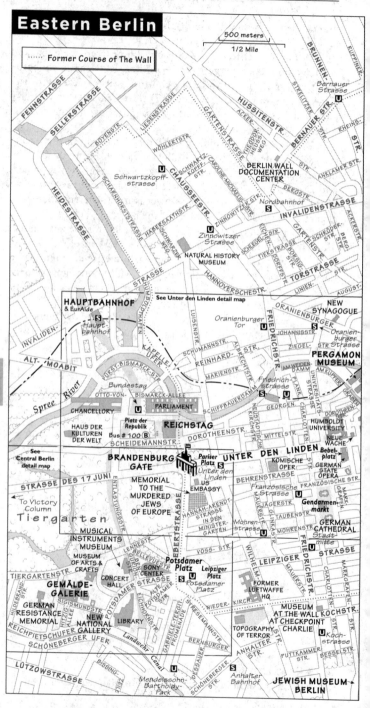

Eastern Berlin

500 meters
1/2 Mile

.... Former Course of The Wall

FENNSTRASSE
SELLERSTRASSE
BÖYENSTR.
LIESENSTRASSE
WÖHLERTSTR.
SCHWARTZ-KOPFF-STR.
SCHWARTZ-KOPFF-STRASSE
CAROLINE-MICHAELIS-STR.
HEIDESTRASSE
SCHARNHORSTSTRASSE
HABERSAATHSTR.
SCHWARZER WEG
Zinnowitzer Strasse
ZINNOWITZER STR.
GARTENSTRASSE
ACKERSTR.
THEODOR-WEG
BERGSTR.
HUSSITENSTR.
Bernauer Strasse
BERNAUER STR. U
STREUTZER STR.
RHEINSBERGER STR.
KÜPPNER STR.
ANKLAMER STR.

BERLIN WALL
DOCUMENTATION
CENTER
Nordbahnhof S
INVALIDENSTRASSE
GARTENSTR.
SCHRÖDER STR.
BERG. STR.
DERGL. STR.
TORSTRASSE

NATURAL HISTORY
MUSEUM
SCHLEGEL-STR.
TIECKSTR.
DORFELTSTR.
BÖRSIG STR.
LINIEN-STR.
AUGUST-

HANNOVERSCHESTR.

See Unter den Linden detail map

HAUPTBAHNHOF
& EurAide
Haupt-bahnhof
INVALIDEN-STRASSE
ALT-MOABIT
KAPELLE UFER
LUISENSTR.
SCHUMANNSTR.
REINHARD-STR.
ALBRECHTSTR.
MARIENSTR.
Oranienburger
Tor
FRIEDRICHSTR.
JOHANNISSTR.
ZIEGEL-STR.
NEW
SYNAGOGUE
ORANIENBURGER
ORANIENBURGER STR.
Oranien-burger
Strasse
PERGAMON
MUSEUM

Bundestag
OTTO-VON- BISMARCK-ALLEE
FÜRST-BISMARCK-STR.
Spree River
CHANCELLORY
HAUS DER
KULTUREN
DER WELT
PARLIAMENT U
Platz der
Republik
Bus # 100 B
SCHEIDEMANNSTR.
REICHSTAG
DOROTHEENSTR.
SCHIFFBAUERDAMM
Friedrich-strasse
S
AM WEIDEN-DAMM
PLANK-STR.
NEUSTÄDTISCHE KIRCHSTR.
GEORGEN-
MITTELSTR.
UNIVERSITÄTS-STRASSE
CHARLOTTEN-STR.
AM KUPFER-GRABEN
DOROTHEE-STR.
HUMBOLDT
UNIVERSITY
NEUE
WACHE

See
Central Berlin
detail map
STRASSE DES 17 JUNI
BRANDENBURG
GATE
MEMORIAL
TO THE
MURDERED
JEWS OF
EUROPE
EBERTSTRASSE
ENTLASTUNGSSTR.
Pariser
Platz S
UNTER DEN LINDEN
Unter den
Linden
US
EMBASSY
BEHRENSTRASSE
Französische
Strasse
JÄGERSTR.
TAUBENSTR.
MOHRENSTR.
KOMISCHE
OPER
Bebel-platz
GERMAN
STATE
OPERA
FRANZÖSISCHE STR. U
Gendarmen-markt
GERMAN
CATHEDRAL
Stadt-mitte

To Victory
Column
Tiergarten
MUSICAL
INSTRUMENTS
MUSEUM
MUSEUM
OF ARTS &
CRAFTS
HANNAH-ARENDT-
STRASSE
IN DEN
MINISTER-
GÄRTEN
Mohren-strasse
VOSS- STR.
WILHELMSTRASSE
FORMER
LUFTWAFFE
HQ
LEIPZIGER
STRASSE
FRIEDRICHSTR.
CHARLOTTEN STR.
MARKGRAFEN-STR.

TIERGARTENSTR.
GEMÄLDE-
GALERIE
GERMAN
RESISTANCE
MEMORIAL
HILDEBRAND-STR.
SIGISMUNDSTR.
HITZIG-
NEW
NATIONAL
GALLERY
REICHPIETSCHUFER
SCHÖNEBERGER UFER
LENNESTR.
BELLEVUE-STR.
GABRIELE-TERGIT-PROMENADE
Potsdamer
Platz
SONY
CENTER
CONCERT
HALL
LIBRARY
POTSDAMER STRASSE
ALTE POTSDAMER STR.
EICHHORNSTR.
Leipziger
Platz
Potsdamer
Platz S U
LINK-STR.
ST. RESEMANNSTR.
NIEDER-
KIRCH-
STR.
TOPOGRAPHY
OF TERROR
FORMER
MUSEUM
AT THE WALL
AT CHECKPOINT
CHARLIE
KOCHSTR.
Koch-strasse U

LÜTZOWSTRASSE
BISSING-STR.
ZEILE
Mendelssohn-Bartholdy-Park U
SCHÖNEBERGER STR.
BERNBURGER STR.
DESSAUER STR.
ANHALTER
STR.
Anhalter
Bahnhof S
PUTTKAMMER-STR.
BESSELSTR.
JEWISH MUSEUM
BERLIN

Landwehr Canal

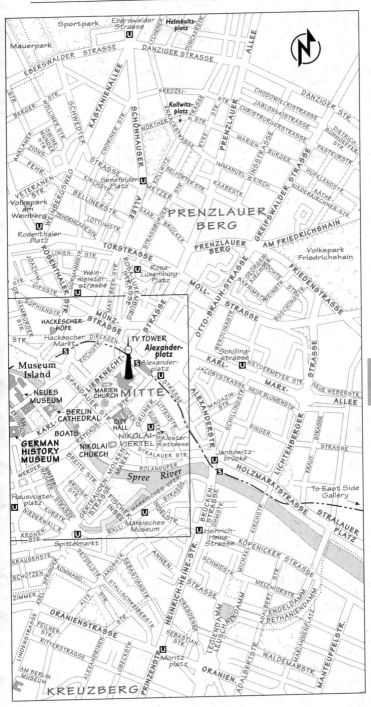

short but complicated and emotional history. When it was inaugurated in the 1890s, the last emperor, Kaiser Wilhelm II, disdainfully called it the "chatting home for monkeys" *(Reichsaffenhaus)*. It was placed outside of the city's old walls—far from the center of real power, the imperial palace. It was from here that the German Republic was proclaimed in 1918.

In 1933, this symbol of democracy nearly burned down. The Nazis—whose influence on the German political scene was on the rise—blamed a communist plot. Dutch Communist Marinus van der Lubbe was eventually convicted and guillotined for the crime. Others believed that Hitler himself planned the fire, using it as a handy excuse to frame the communists and grab power. Even though van der Lubbe was posthumously pardoned by the German government in 2008, most modern historians concede that he most likely was guilty, that he acted alone, and that the Nazis were just incredibly lucky.

The Reichstag was hardly used from 1933 to 1999. Despite the fact that the building had lost any of its symbolic value, Stalin ordered his troops to take the Reichstag from the Nazis by May 1, 1945 (the workers' holiday). More than 1,500 Nazi soldiers (mostly French SS troops) made their last stand here—extending World War II by two days. On April 30, after fierce fighting on this rooftop, the Reichstag fell to the Red Army.

For the building's 101st birthday in 1995, the Bulgarian-American artist Christo wrapped it in silvery-gold cloth. It was then wrapped again—in scaffolding—and rebuilt by British architect Lord Norman Foster into the new parliamentary home of the Bundestag (Germany's lower house, similar to the US House of Representatives). To many Germans, the proud resurrection of the Reichstag symbolizes the end of a terrible chapter in their country's history.

The **glass cupola** rises 155 feet above the ground. Its two sloped ramps spiral 755 feet to the top for a grand view. Inside the dome, a cone of 360 mirrors reflects natural light into the legislative chamber below. Lit from inside at night, this gives Berlin a memorable nightlight. The environmentally friendly cone also helps with air circulation, drawing hot air out of the legislative chamber (no joke) and pulling in cool air from below.

Cost and Hours: Free, daily 8:00-24:00, last entry at 22:00, reservations required—see below, metal detectors, no big luggage allowed, some hour-long English tours when parliament is not sitting. Platz der Republik 1, S- or U-Bahn: Friedrichstrasse or Brandenburger Tor. Tel. 030/2273-2152, www.bundestag.de.

Reservations: Because of security concerns, the procedure for visiting the dome has been in flux. As of summer 2011, visitors were required to make a free advance reservation at www.bundestag

.de/besuche/besucherdienst/index.jsp (in German only). Plan ahead--slots book up several days ahead (up to two weeks in the busiest summer months). Those reserving a table at the Dachgarten rooftop restaurant can also access the dome, but those slots book up even earlier--up to three months ahead during peak season (call 030/2262-9933, lunch from €15, dinner from €20, daily 9:30–16:30 & 18:30–24:00). At times when it's not too crowded, you may be able to get in without a reservation (though it's unlikely).

Audioguide: The free GPS-driven audioguide explains the building and narrates the view as you wind up the spiral ramp to the top of the dome, but may not be available while stringent security measures are in place.

Touring the Reichstag: Security measures may impact the tour route; use the following information as a general guide but be prepared for changes.

As you approach the building, look above the door, surrounded by stone patches from WWII bomb damage, to see the motto and promise: *Dem Deutschen Volke* ("To the German People"). The open, airy lobby towers 100 feet high, with 65-foot-tall colors of the German flag. See-through glass doors show the **central legislative chamber.** The message: There will be no secrets in government. Look inside. The seats are "Reichstag blue," a lilac-blue color designed by the architect to brighten the otherwise gray interior. Spreading his wings behind the podium is the *Bundestagsadler* (a.k.a. "the fat hen"), a stylized German eagle representing the Bundestag (each branch of government has its own symbolic eagle). Notice the doors marked *Ja* (Yes), *Nein* (No), and *Enthalten* (Abstain)...an homage to the Bundestag's traditional "sheep jump" way of counting votes by exiting the chamber through the corresponding door (although for critical issues, all 669 members vote with electronic cards).

An elevator takes you to the base of the glass **dome,** where an excellent exhibit tells the Reichstag story. Study the surrounding architecture: a broken collage of new on old, torn between antiquity and modernity, like Germany's history. Notice the dome's giant and unobtrusive sunscreen that moves as necessary with the sun. Peer down through the skylight to look over the shoulders of the elected representatives at work. For Germans, the best view from here is down—keeping a close eye on their government.

Take a 360-degree survey of the city as you hike up the **double ramp:** First, the big park is the **Tiergarten,** the "green lungs of Berlin." Beyond that is the **Teufelsberg,** or "Devil's Hill" (built of rubble from the destroyed city in the late 1940s, it was famous during the Cold War as a powerful ear of the West—notice the telecommunications tower on top). Knowing the bombed-out and bulldozed story of their city, locals say, "You have to be suspicious when you see the nice, green park." Find the **Victory Column** (Siegessäule). This was moved by Hitler in the 1930s from in front of the Reichstag to its present position in the Tiergarten, as the first step in creating a grandiose axis he envisioned for postwar Berlin. Next, scenes of the new Berlin spiral into your view—**Potsdamer Platz,** marked by the conical glass tower that houses Sony's European headquarters. The yellow building to the right is the Berlin Philharmonic Concert Hall, marking the museums at the Kulturforum. Continue circling left, and find the green chariot atop the **Brandenburg Gate.** The **Memorial to the Murdered Jews of Europe** stretches south of the Brandenburg Gate. Next, you'll see **former East Berlin** and the city's next huge construction zone, with a forest of 300-foot-tall skyscrapers in the works. Notice the TV Tower, the Berlin Cathedral's massive dome, the red tower of the City Hall, the golden dome of the New Synagogue, and the Reichstag's **Dachgarten Restaurant.**

Follow the train tracks in the distance to the left toward Berlin's huge main train station, the **Hauptbahnhof.** Just in front of it, alone in a field, is the Swiss Embassy. It used to be surrounded by buildings, but now it's the only one left. Complete your spintour with the blocky **Chancellery,** nicknamed by Berliners "the washing machine." It may look like a pharaoh's tomb, but it's the office and home of Germany's most powerful person, the chancellor (currently Angela Merkel). To remind the chancellor who he or she works for, the Reichstag, at about 130 feet, is about six feet taller than the Chancellery.

Near the Reichstag

• *As you leave the Reichstag, look for the park across from the main entry. Embedded in the ground is the...*

Memorial to Politicians Who Opposed Hitler—This row of slate slabs (looks like a fancy slate bicycle rack) is a memorial to the 96 members of the Reichstag (the equivalent of our members of Congress) who were murdered and persecuted because their politics didn't agree with Chancellor Hitler's. They were part of the Weimar Republic, the weak and ill-fated attempt at post-WWI democracy in Germany. These were the people who could have stopped Hitler...so they became his first victims. Each slate slab remembers one man—his name, party (mostly KPD—Communists, and SPD—Social Democrats), and date and location of death—generally in concentration camps. (*KZ* stands for "concentration camp.") They are honored here, in front of the building in which they worked.

• *Circle around the Reichstag to enjoy the...*

Spree Riverfront—Admire the wonderful architecture incorporating the Spree River into the people's world. It's a poignant spot because this river was once a symbol of division—the East German regime put nets underwater to stymie those desperate for freedom who might swim to the West. When kings ruled Prussia, government buildings went right up to the river. But today, the city is incorporating the river thoughtfully into a people-friendly cityscape. From the Reichstag, a delightful riverside path leads around the curve, past "beach cafés," to the Chancellery. For a slow, low-impact glide past this zone, consider one of the river cruises described on page 645 (we'll pass the starting point—on Museum Island—later on this walk).

• *Let's continue our walk and cross what was the Berlin Wall. Leaving the Reichstag, return to the busy road and walk around the building. At the rear of the building (across the street, at the edge of the park on the corner of Scheidemannstrasse and Ebertstrasse) is a small memorial of white crosses. This is the...*

Berlin Wall Victims Memorial—This monument commemorates some of the East Berliners who died trying to cross the Wall. This 100-mile-long "Anti-Fascist Protective Rampart," as it was called by the East German government, was erected almost overnight in 1961 to stop the outward flow of people (three million leaked out between 1949 and 1961). Look at the faces of these exceptionally free spirits. Notice that the last person shot while trying to escape was 20-year-old Chris Gueffroy, who was killed nine months before the Wall fell. (He was shot through the heart and died in no-man's-land.) This monument used to stand right on the Berlin Wall behind the Reichstag. The Wall was built on August 13, 1961. Of these people—many of whom perished within months of the wall's construction—most died trying to swim the river to freedom.

In the park just behind this memorial, another memorial is planned. It will remember the Roma (Gypsy) victims of the Holocaust. The Roma, as disdained by the Nazis as the Jews were, lost the same percentage of their population to Hitler. Unfortunately, the project is stalled for lack of a well-funded individual or group to finance it.

• *From here, head to the Brandenburg Gate. Stay on the park side of the street for a better view of the gate ahead. As you cross at the light, notice the double row of* **cobblestones**—*it goes around the city, marking where the Wall used to stand.*

Brandenburg Gate and Nearby

▲▲**Brandenburg Gate (Brandenburger Tor)**—The historic Brandenburg Gate (1791) was the grandest—and is the last survivor—of 14 gates in Berlin's old city wall (this one led to the neighboring city of Brandenburg). The gate was the symbol of Prussian Berlin...and later the symbol of a divided Berlin. It's crowned by a majestic four-horse chariot with the Goddess of Peace at the reins. Napoleon took this statue to the Louvre in Paris in 1806. After the Prussians defeated Napoleon and got it back (1813), she was renamed the Goddess of Victory.

The gate sat unused, part of a sad circle dance called the Wall, for more than 25 years. Now postcards all over town show the ecstatic day—November 9, 1989—when the world enjoyed the sight of happy Berliners jamming the gate like flowers on a parade float. Pause a minute and think about struggles for freedom—past and present. (There's actually a special room built into the gate for this purpose.) Around the gate, look at the information boards with pictures of how much this area changed throughout the 20th century. The latest chapter: The shiny white gate was completely restored in 2002 (but you can still see faint patches marking war damage). The TI within the gate is open daily (10:00-18:00, S-Bahn: Brandenburger Tor).

The Brandenburg Gate, the center of old Berlin, sits on a major boulevard running east to west through Berlin. The western segment, called Strasse des 17 Juni (named for a workers' uprising against the DDR government on June 17, 1953), stretches for four miles from the Brandenburg Gate and Victory Column to the Olympic Stadium. But we'll follow this city axis in the opposite direction, east, walking along what is known as Unter den Linden—into the core of old imperial Berlin and past what was once the palace of the Hohenzollern family who ruled Prussia and then Germany. The palace—the reason for just about all you'll see—is a phantom sight, long gone. Alexanderplatz, which marks the end of this walk, is near the base of the giant TV Tower hovering in the distance.

• *Cross through the gate into...*

▲**Pariser Platz**—"Parisian Square," so named after the Prussians defeated Napoleon in 1813, was once filled with important government buildings—all bombed to smithereens in World War II. For decades, it was an unrecognizable, deserted no-man's-land—cut off from both East and West by the Wall. But now it's rebuilt, and the banks, hotels, and embassies that were here before the bombing have reclaimed their original places...with a few additions: a palace of coffee (Starbucks) and the small Kennedys Museum (described later). The winners of World War II enjoy this prime real estate: The American, French, British, and Soviet (now Russian) embassies are all on or near this square.

Face the gate and look to your left. The **US Embassy** reopened in its historic location in 2008. The building has been controversial: For safety's sake, Uncle Sam wanted more of a security zone around the building, but the Germans wanted to keep Pariser Platz a welcoming people zone. (Throughout the world, American embassies are the most fortified buildings in town.) The compromise: The extra security the US wanted is actually built into the structure. The building is pretty low-key; easy-on-the-eyes barriers keep potential car bombs at a distance, and its front door is on the side farthest from the Brandenburg Gate.

Just to the left, the **DZ Bank building** is by Frank Gehry, the unconventional American architect famous for Bilbao's organic Guggenheim Museum, Prague's Dancing House, Seattle's Experience Music Project, Chicago's Millennium Park, and Los Angeles' Walt Disney Concert Hall. Gehry fans might be surprised at the DZ Bank building's low profile. Structures on Pariser Platz are designed to be bland so as not to draw attention away from the Brandenburg Gate. (The glassy facade of the Academy of Arts, next to Gehry's building, is controversial for drawing attention to itself.) For your fix of the good old Gehry, step into the lobby and check out its undulating interior. It's a fish—and you feel like you're both inside and outside of it. The architect's vision is explained on a nearby plaque. The best view of Gehry's creation is from the Reichstag dome.

• Next door is the **Academy of Arts** (Akademie der Kunst), with its notorious glass facade. Its doors lead to a mall (daily 10:00-22:00), which leads directly to the vast...

▲▲Memorial to the Murdered Jews of Europe (Denkmal für die Ermordeten Juden Europas)—This Holocaust memorial, consisting of 2,711 gravestone-like pillars and completed in 2005, is an essential stop for any visit to Berlin. It is the first formal, German government-sponsored Holocaust memorial. Jewish American architect Peter Eisenman won the competition for the commission (and built it on time and on budget—€27 million). It's controversial for the focus—just Jews—but the government promises to make memorials to the other groups targeted by the Nazis.

The pillars are made of hollow concrete, each chemically coated for easy removal of graffiti. (Ironically, the chemical coating was developed by a subsidiary of the former IG Farben group—the company infamous for supplying the Zyklon B gas used in Nazi death camps.) The number of pillars, symbolic of nothing, is simply how many fit on the provided land.

Once you enter the memorial, notice that people seem to appear and disappear between the columns, and that no matter where you are, the exit always seems to be up. Is it a labyrinth... symbolic cemetery...intentionally disorienting? The meaning is entirely up to the visitor to derive. The idea is for you to spend time pondering this horrible chapter in human history.

The pondering takes place under the sky. For the learning, go under the field of concrete pillars to the state-of-the-art information center (there may be a short line because visitors must go through a security check). This studies the Nazi system of extermination, humanizes the victims, and lists 200 different places of genocide. Exhibits trace the stories of six individuals and their experiences during the Holocaust (all well-explained in English). Remember: Behind these six stories are millions more tales of despair, tragedy, and survival.

The memorial's location—where the Wall once stood—is coincidental. It's just a place where lots of people will experience it. Nazi propagandist Joseph Goebbels' bunker was discovered during the work and left buried under the northeast corner of the memorial. Hitler's bunker is just 200 yards away, under a nondescript parking lot. Such Nazi sites are intentionally left hidden to discourage neo-Nazi elements from creating shrines.

Cost and Hours: Free, memorial always open, information center open Tue-Sun April-Sept 10:00-20:00, Oct-March 10:00-19:00, closed Mon, last entry 45 minutes before closing, S-Bahn: Brandenburger Tor or Potsdamer Platz, tel. 030/2639-4336, www.stiftung-denkmal.de. The €3 audioguide augments the experience.

• *Now backtrack to Pariser Platz (through the yellow building). Across the square, consider dropping into...*

The Kennedys Museum—This crisp private enterprise facing the Brandenburg Gate recalls John F. Kennedy's Germany trip in 1963, with great photos and video clips as well as a photographic shrine to the Kennedy clan in America. It's a small, overpriced, yet delightful experience with interesting mementos—such as JFK's notes with the phonetic "ish bin ein Bear lee ner." Jacqueline Kennedy commented on how strange it was that this was her husband's most quotable quote (€7, reduced to €3.50 for a broad array of visitors—dream up a discount and ask for it, daily 10:00-18:00, Pariser Platz 4a, www.thekennedys.de, tel. 030/2065-3570).

• *Leave Pariser Platz and begin strolling...*

▲▲Unter den Linden

The street called Unter den Linden is the heart of former East Berlin. In Berlin's good old days, Unter den Linden was one of Europe's grand boulevards. In the 15th century, this carriageway led from the palace to the hunting grounds (today's big Tiergarten). In the 17th century, Hohenzollern princes and princesses moved in and built their palaces here so they could be near the Prussian king.

Named centuries ago for its thousand linden trees, this was the most elegant street of Prussian Berlin before Hitler's time, and the main drag of East Berlin after his reign. Hitler replaced the venerable trees—many 250 years old—with Nazi flags. Popular discontent actually drove him to replant linden trees. Today, Unter den Linden is no longer a depressing Cold War cul-de-sac, and its pre-Hitler strolling café ambience has returned. Notice how it is divided, roughly at Friedrichstrasse, into a business section that stretches toward the Brandenburg Gate, and a culture section that spreads out toward Alexanderplatz. Frederick the Great wanted to have culture, mainly the opera and the university, closer to his palace, and to keep business (read: banks) farther away, near the city walls.

◗ Self-Guided Walk: As you walk toward the giant TV Tower, the big building you see jutting out into the street on your right is the **Hotel Adlon.** It hosted such notables as Charlie Chaplin, Albert Einstein, and Greta Garbo. This was the setting for Garbo's most famous line, "I want to be alone," in the film *Grand Hotel.* And, perhaps fresher in your memory, this is where the late Michael Jackson shocked millions by dangling his baby, Blanket, over the railing (second balcony up, on the side of the hotel next to the Academy of Art). Destroyed by Russians just after World War II, the grand Adlon was rebuilt in 1996. See how far you can get inside.

Descend into the Brandenburger Tor S-Bahn station ahead of you. It's one of Berlin's former **ghost subway stations.** During the Cold War, most underground train tunnels were simply blocked at the border. But a few Western lines looped through the East. To make a little hard Western cash, the Eastern government rented the use of these tracks to the West, but the stations (which happened to be in East Berlin) were strictly off-limits. For 28 years, the stations were unused, as Western trains slowly passed through and passengers saw only eerie DDR (East German) guards and lots of cobwebs. Literally within days of the fall of the Wall, these stations were reopened, and today they are a time warp (looking essentially as they did when built in 1931, with dreary old green tiles and original signage). Walk along the track (the walls are lined with historic photos of the Reichstag through the ages) and exit on the other side, following signs to *Russische Botschaft* (the Russian Embassy).

The **Russian Embassy** was the first big postwar building project in East Berlin. It's built in the powerful, simplified Neoclassical style that Stalin liked. While not as important now as it was a few years ago, it's immense as ever. It flies the Russian white, blue, and red. Find the hammer-and-sickle motif decorating the window frames—a reminder of the days when this was the USSR embassy.

Continuing past the Aeroflot airline offices, look across Glinkastrasse to the right to see the back of the **Komische Oper** (Comic Opera; program and view of ornate interior posted in window). While the exterior is ugly, the fine old theater interior—amazingly missed by WWII bombs—survives.

Eastern Berlin's Unter den Linden

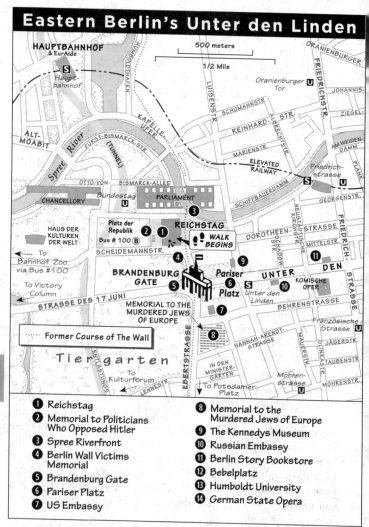

① Reichstag
② Memorial to Politicians Who Opposed Hitler
③ Spree Riverfront
④ Berlin Wall Victims Memorial
⑤ Brandenburg Gate
⑥ Pariser Platz
⑦ US Embassy
⑧ Memorial to the Murdered Jews of Europe
⑨ The Kennedys Museum
⑩ Russian Embassy
⑪ Berlin Story Bookstore
⑫ Bebelplatz
⑬ Humboldt University
⑭ German State Opera

Back on the main drag, at #26, is a great bookstore, **Berlin Story.** In addition to a wide range of English-language books, this shop has a free museum (with a dusty model of 1930s Unter den Linden) and a 25-minute English film about the history of Berlin (daily 10:00-20:00; for more details, see page 640). This is also a good opportunity to pick up some nostalgic knickknacks from the Cold War. The West lost no time in consuming the East; consequently, some are feeling a wave of *Ost*-algia for the old days of East Berlin. In 2006 local elections, nearly half of East Berlin's voters—and 6 percent of West Berliners—voted for the

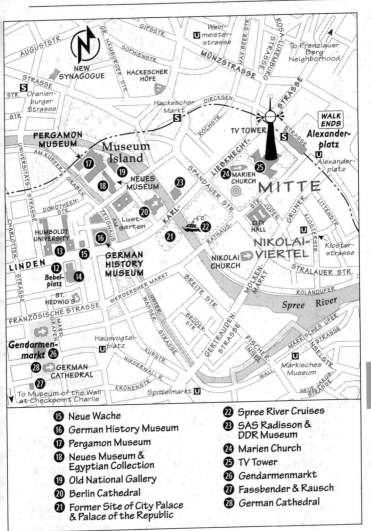

15 Neue Wache
16 German History Museum
17 Pergamon Museum
18 Neues Museum & Egyptian Collection
19 Old National Gallery
20 Berlin Cathedral
21 Former Site of City Palace & Palace of the Republic
22 Spree River Cruises
23 SAS Radisson & DDR Museum
24 Marien Church
25 TV Tower
26 Gendarmenmarkt
27 Fassbender & Rausch
28 German Cathedral

extreme left party, which has ties to the bygone Communist Party. More recently, debate raged about whether to close Tempelhof Airport—which West Berliners remember fondly from the days of the Berlin Airlift, which provided them with desperately needed supplies during the early days of the Wall. For the referendum about whether to keep the old airport running, voter turnout in the former West was 63 percent (an overwhelming number of them in favor of keeping Tempel)—while only 8 percent of Easterners came to the polls. The overall low turnout meant the measure was defeated, and the airport was closed.

One symbol of that era has been given a reprieve. As you continue to Friedrichstrasse, look at the DDR-style pedestrian lights, and you'll realize that someone had a sense of humor back then. The perky red and green men—*Ampelmännchen*—were under threat of replacement by the far less jaunty Western signs. Fortunately, after a 10-year court battle, the DDR signals were kept after all. This communist-era icon has been popping up as far away as Munich—hardly a bastion of sympathy for East German culture.

At **Friedrichstrasse,** look right. Before the war, the Unter den Linden/Friedrichstrasse intersection was the heart of Berlin. In the 1920s, Berlin was famous for its anything-goes love of life. This was the cabaret drag, a springboard to stardom for young and vampy entertainers like Marlene Dietrich. (Born in 1901, Dietrich starred in the first German talkie—*The Blue Angel*—and then headed straight to Hollywood.) Over the last few years, this boulevard—lined with super department stores (such as Galeries Lafayette) and big-time hotels (such as the Hilton and Regent)—is attempting to replace Ku'damm as the grand commerce-and-café boulevard of Berlin. (More recently, western Berlin is retaliating with some new stores of its own. And so far, Friedrichstrasse gets little more than half the pedestrian traffic that Ku'damm gets in the West. Why? Locals complain that this area has no daily life—no supermarkets, not much funky street food, and so on.) Consider detouring to Galeries Lafayette, with its cool marble and glass waste-of-space interior (Mon-Sat 9:30-20:00, closed Sun; belly up to its amazing ground-floor viewpoint, or have lunch in its recommended basement cafeteria).

If you continued down Friedrichstrasse, you'd wind up at the sights listed under "South of Unter den Linden," on page 668—including the Museum of The Wall at Checkpoint Charlie (a 10-minute walk from here). But for now, continue along Unter den Linden. You'll notice big, colorful **water pipes** around here and throughout Berlin. As long as the city remains a gigantic construction zone, it will be laced with these drainage pipes—key to any building project. Berlin's high water table means any new basement comes with lots of pumping out.

The **VW Automobil Forum** shows off the latest models from the many car companies owned by VW (free, corner of Friedrichstrasse and Unter den Linden, VW art gallery in the basement).

Continue down Unter den Linden a few more blocks, past the large equestrian statue of Frederick II ("the Great"), and turn right into the square called **Bebelplatz.** Stand on the glass window in the center.

Frederick the Great—who ruled from 1740 to 1786—established Prussia not just as a military power, but as a cultural and intellectual heavyweight as well. This square was the center of the "new Athens" that Frederick envisioned. His grand palace was just down the street (explained later).

Look down through the glass you're standing on (center of Bebelplatz): The room of empty bookshelves is a memorial to the notorious Nazi **book burning.** It was on this square in 1933 that staff and students from the university threw 20,000 newly forbidden books (like Einstein's) into a huge bonfire on the orders of the Nazi propaganda minister Joseph Goebbels. A memorial plaque nearby reminds us of the prophetic quote by the German poet Heinrich Heine. In 1820, he wrote, "Where they burn books, at the end they also burn people." The Nazis despised Heine because he was Jewish before converting to Christianity. A century later, his books were among those that went up in flames on this spot.

Great buildings front Bebelplatz. Survey the square counter-clockwise:

Humboldt University, across Unter den Linden, is one of Europe's greatest. Marx and Lenin (not the brothers or the sisters) studied here, as did the Grimms (both brothers) and more than two dozen Nobel Prize winners. Einstein, who was Jewish, taught here until taking a spot at Princeton in 1932 (smart guy).

The former **state library** is where Vladimir Lenin studied during much of his exile from Russia. If you climb to the second floor of the library and go through the door opposite the stairs, you'll see a 1968 vintage stained-glass window depicting Lenin's life's work with almost biblical reverence. On the ground floor is Tim's Canadian Deli, a great little café with light food, student prices, and garden seating (€3 plates, Mon-Sat 7:00-20:00, closed Sun, handy WC).

The **German State Opera** was bombed in 1941, rebuilt to bolster morale and to celebrate its centennial in 1943, and bombed again in 1945.

The round, Catholic **St. Hedwig's Church**—nicknamed the "upside-down teacup"—was built by the pragmatic Frederick the Great to encourage the integration of Catholic Silesians after his empire annexed their region in 1742. (St. Hedwig is the patron saint of Silesia, a region now shared by Germany, Poland, and the Czech Republic.) When asked what the church should look like, Frederick literally took a Silesian teacup and slammed it upside-down on a table. Like all Catholic churches in Berlin, St. Hedwig's is not on the street, but stuck in a kind of back lot—indicating inferiority to Protestant churches. You can step inside the church to see the cheesy DDR government renovation.

Continue down Unter den Linden. The next square on your right holds the **Opernpalais,** formerly a Prussian royal residence.

Preening with fancy prewar elegance, it hosts the recommended but pricey Operncafé. With the best desserts and the longest dessert bar in Europe, it's popular with Berliners for *Kaffee und Kuchen*.

Cross Unter den Linden to the university side. The Greek-temple-like building set in the small chestnut-tree-filled park is the **Neue Wache** (the emperor's "New Guardhouse," from 1816). When the Wall fell, this memorial to the victims of fascism was transformed into a national memorial. Look inside, where a replica of the Käthe Kollwitz statue, *Mother with Her Dead Son*, is surrounded by thought-provoking silence. This marks the tombs of Germany's unknown soldier and the unknown concentration camp victim. The inscription in front reads, "To the victims of war and tyranny." Read the entire statement in English (on wall, left of entrance). The memorial, open to the sky, incorporates the elements—sunshine, rain, snow—falling on this modern-day *pietà*.

• *After the Neue Wache, the next building you'll see is Berlin's pink-yet-formidable Zeughaus (arsenal). Dating from 1695, it's considered the oldest building on the boulevard and now houses the...*

▲▲▲German History Museum (Deutsches Historisches Museum)

This fantastic museum is a two-part affair: the pink former Prussian arsenal building and the I. M. Pei–designed annex. The main building (fronting Unter den Linden) houses the permanent collection. Two huge rectangular floors are packed with more than 8,000 artifacts telling the story of Germany—making this the top history museum in town. Historical objects, photographs, and models are intermingled with multimedia stations to help put everything in context. The first floor traces German history from 1 B.C. to 1918, with exhibits on early cultures, the Middle Ages, Reformation, Thirty Years' War, German Empire, and World War I. Exhibits on the ground floor continue with the Weimar Republic, Nazism, World War II, Allied occupation, and a divided Germany, wrapping up with reunification and a quick look at Germany today.

For architecture buffs, the big attraction is the Pei annex behind the history museum, which complements the museum with often-fascinating temporary history exhibits. From the old building (with the Pei glass canopy over its courtyard), take a tunnel to the new wing, emerging under a striking glass spiral staircase that unites four floors with surprising views and lots of light. It's here that you'll experience why Pei—famous for his glass pyramid at Paris' Louvre—is called the "perfector of classical modernism," "master of light," and a magician of uniting historical buildings with new ones. (If the museum is closed, or you don't have a ticket, venture down the street—Hinter dem Giesshaus—to the left of the museum to see the Pei annex from the outside.)

Cost and Hours: €5, daily 10:00-18:00, excellent €3 audioguide has six hours of info for you to choose from, tel. 030/2030-4751, www.dhm.de.

• *Back on Unter den Linden, head toward the Spree River. Just before the bridge, wander left along the canal through a tiny but colorful arts-and-crafts market (weekends only; a larger flea market is just outside the Pergamon Museum). Continue up the riverbank two blocks and cross the footbridge over the Spree. This takes you to...*

Museum Island (Museumsinsel)

This island, home of Berlin's first museum, is undergoing a formidable renovation. The grand vision is to integrate the city's major museums with a grand entry and tunnels that will lace the complex together (intended completion date: 2015, www.museumsinsel-berlin.de). The complex was originally built around 1871, when Germany was newly unified as one nation—and when Berlin was calling itself the "Athens on the Spree River." Today, its imposing Neoclassical buildings host five grand museums: the Pergamon (classical antiquities); the Altes Museum ("Old Museum," archaeological treasures and a huge collection of Celtic goldwork); the recently renovated Neues Museum ("New Museum," housing the Egyptian Collection, with the bust of Queen Nefertiti); the Old National Gallery (19th-century German Romantic painting); and the Bode Museum (European statuary through the ages, coins, and Byzantine art).

Cost: The €14 Museum Island Pass combo-ticket is a far better value than buying individual €8-10 entries. All of the museums are also included in the city's €19 Museumspass (described on page 635). Plus, with a pass, you can visit museums that you might not otherwise go to.

Hours: Neues Museum open daily 10:00-18:00, Thu-Sat until 20:00; Pergamon, Altes, and Bode museums open daily 10:00-18:00, Thu until 22:00; Old National Gallery open same hours except closed Mon. Tel. 030/2090-5577, www.smb.museum.

Required Reservation for Neues/Egyptian Museum: Visiting the Neues Museum requires an additional *Zeitfensterticket* ("time-window ticket") that gives you a 30-minute appointment to enter the museum (included with your admission). Once inside, you can stay as long as you like. Reserve your time online, or in person at the Neues Museum ticket office (but not at any of the other museums).

Getting There: The nearest S-Bahn station is Hackescher Markt. You can also visit any Museum Island attraction before continuing our walk. I've described the top attractions below. Once

BERLIN

you're finished, skip down to "Museum Island to Alexanderplatz," page 666, to resume the self-guided walk.

▲▲**Pergamon Museum**—This world-class museum, part of Berlin's Collection of Classical Antiquities (Antikensammlung), stars the fantastic Pergamon Altar. From a second-century B.C. Greek temple, the altar shows the Greeks under Zeus and Athena beating the giants in a dramatic pig pile of mythological mayhem. Check out the action spilling onto the stairs. The Babylonian Ishtar Gate (glazed blue tiles from the sixth century B.C.) and many ancient Greek and Mesopotamian treasures are also impressive. The superb "Pergamon in 30 Minutes" audioguide (free with admission) covers the museum's highlights and broadens your experience by introducing you to wonders you might not otherwise notice.

▲▲**Neues (New) Museum and Egyptian Collection**—Filling a good chunk of the recently rebuilt Neues Museum is one of the world's top collections of Egyptian art. The curator welcomes you on the included audioguide and encourages a broader approach to the museum than just seeing its claim to fame, the bust of Queen Nefertiti. The fine audioguide celebrates new knowledge about ancient Egyptian civilization and offers fascinating insights into workaday Egyptian life as it describes the vivid papyrus collection, slice-of-life artifacts, and dreamy wax portraits decorating mummy cases.

But let's face it: The main reason to visit is to enjoy one of the great thrills in art appreciation—gazing into the still-young-and-beautiful face of 3,000-year-old **Queen Nefertiti,** the wife of King Akhenaton. This bust of Queen Nefertiti (c. 1340 B.C.) is the most famous piece of Egyptian art in Europe. Discovered in 1912, Nefertiti—with all the right beauty marks: long neck, symmetrical face, and the perfect amount of makeup—is called "Berlin's most beautiful woman." The bust never left its studio, but served as a master model for all other portraits of the queen. (That's probably why the left eye was never inlaid.)

How the queen arrived in Germany is a tale out of *Indiana Jones.* The German archaeologist Ludwig Borchardt uncovered her in the Egyptian desert in 1912. The Egyptian Department of Antiquities had first pick of all the artifacts excavated on their territory. After the first takings, the rest would be divided up 50/50. When Borchardt presented Nefertiti to the Egyptians, they passed her over, never bothering to examine her closely. Unsubstantiated rumors persist that Borchardt misled the Egyptians in order to keep the bust for himself—rumors that have prompted some Egyptians to call for the return of Nefertiti (just as the Greeks are lobbying the British to return the Parthenon marbles currently housed in the British Museum). Although this bust is not particularly representative of Egyptian art in general—and despite increasing claims that her long neck suggests she's a Neoclassical fake—Nefertiti has become a symbol of Egyptian art by popular acclaim.

Old National Gallery (Alte Nationalgalerie)—This gallery, behind the Neues Museum and Altes Museum, is designed to look like a Greek temple. Spanning three floors, it shows mostly paintings, with French and German Impressionists on the second and Romantic German paintings (which I find most interesting) on the top. The included audioguide explains the highlights.

Other Sights on Museum Island

Lustgarten—For 300 years, the island's big central square has flip-flopped between being a military parade ground and a people-friendly park, depending upon the political tenor of the time. During the revolutions of 1848, the Kaiser's troops dispersed the protesting crowd here, sending demonstrators onto footpaths. Karl Marx later commented that "it is impossible to have a revolution in a country where people stay off the grass."

Until the last half-century, it was verboten to relax or walk on the Lustgarten's grass. But in 1999, the Lustgarten was made into a park (read the history posted in corner opposite church). On a sunny day, it's packed with relaxing locals and is one of Berlin's most enjoyable public spaces.

Berlin Cathedral (Berliner Dom)—This century-old church towers over Museum Island (€5 includes access to dome gallery, €8 with audioguide, not covered by Museum Island ticket, Mon-Sat 9:00-20:00, Sun 12:00-20:00, until 19:00 in winter, www .berliner-dom.de; many organ concerts—generally Sat at 20:00, tickets about €10 always available at the door, tel. 030/2026-9136). Inside, the great reformers (Luther, Calvin, and company) stand around the brilliantly restored dome like stern saints guarding their theology. Frederick I rests in an ornate tomb (right transept, near entrance to dome). The 270-step climb to the outdoor dome gallery is tough but offers pleasant, breezy views of the city at the finish line (last entry 45 minutes before closing). The crypt downstairs is not worth a look.

Former Site of the City Palace and the Palace of the Republic—Across Unter den Linden from Berlin Cathedral is a big lawn that once held the decrepit Palace of the Republic—formerly East Berlin's parliament building/futuristic entertainment complex, and a showy symbol of the communist days. Even earlier, this was the site of the City Palace (Stadtschloss), the grand urban residence of the rulers of Brandenburg and Prussia since the 15th century. Much of the palace actually survived World War II but was replaced by the communists with a blocky Soviet-style building. The landmark building fell into disrepair after reunification and was eventually dismantled in 2007.

After much debate, the German parliament decided to construct a building featuring a rebuilt facade of Frederick's original Hohenzollern palace along with a huge public venue filled with museums, shops, galleries, and concert halls. All of this was highly controversial, not in the least due to the €1.2 billion price tag. Many Berliners saw the reconstruction as a complete waste of money that could be better spent elsewhere. So the federal government has decided to cut off all funding for the project until 2015. For now, the site of the kings' palace—and the people's palace during communist times—is just a very plain, wide-open grassy park.

Spree River Cruises—If you want a break from our walk, the recommended Spree River boat tours depart from the riverbank near the bridge by the Berlin Cathedral. For details, see page 645.

Museum Island to Alexanderplatz

Continue walking down Unter den Linden. Before crossing the bridge (and leaving Museum Island), look across the river. The pointy twin spires of the 13th-century Nikolai Church mark the center of medieval Berlin. This **Nikolaiviertel** (*Viertel* means "quarter") was restored by the DDR and was trendy in the last years of communism. Today, it's a lively-at-night riverside restaurant district.

As you cross the bridge, look left in the distance to see the gilded **New Synagogue** dome, rebuilt after WWII bombing (described on page 674).

Across the river to the left of the bridge is the giant **SAS Radisson Hotel** and shopping center, with a huge aquarium in the center. The elevator goes right through the middle of a deep-sea world. (You can see it from the unforgettable Radisson hotel lobby—tuck in your shirt and walk past the guards with the confidence of a guest who's sleeping there.) Here in the center of the old communist capital, it seems that capitalism has settled in with a spirited vengeance.

At the river side of the SAS Radisson Hotel, the little **DDR Museum** offers an interesting peek at a humbler life before capitalism took hold. You'll crawl through a Trabant car, see a DDR kitchen, and be surrounded by former DDR residents reminiscing about the bad old days (steep €5.50 admission, daily 10:00-20:00, Karl-Liebknecht Strasse 1, tel. 030/847-123-731, www.ddr-museum.de).

In the park immediately across the street (a big jaywalk from the Radisson) are grandfatherly statues of **Marx and Engels** (nicknamed "the old pensioners"). Surrounding them are stainless-steel monoliths with evocative photos that show the struggles of the workers of the world. (Rumor has it that these may be moved to make way for the extension of the U5 subway line.)

Walk toward **Marien Church** (from 1270), just left of the base of the TV Tower. An artist's rendering helps you follow the interesting but very faded old "Dance of Death" mural that wraps around the narthex inside the door.

The big red-brick building past the trees on the right is the **City Hall,** built after the revolutions of 1848 and arguably the first democratic building in the city.

The 1,200-foot-tall **TV Tower** (Fernsehturm) has a fine view from halfway up (€9.50, daily March-Oct 9:00-24:00, Nov-Feb 10:00-24:00, www.tv-turm.de). The tower offers a handy city orientation and an interesting view of the flat, red-roofed sprawl of Berlin—including a peek inside the city's many courtyards (*Höfe*). Consider a kitschy trip to the observation deck for the view and lunch in its revolving restaurant (mediocre food, €12 plates, horrible lounge music, reservations smart for dinner, tel. 030/242-3333). It's very retro and somewhat trendy these days, so expect a line for the elevator—but in bad weather, remember: If you can't see the top from the ground, you can't see the ground from the top. Built (with Swedish know-how) in 1969 for the 20th anniversary of the communist government, the tower was meant to show the power of the atheistic state at a time when DDR leaders were having the crosses removed from church domes and spires. But when the sun shined on their tower—the greatest spire in East Berlin—a huge cross was reflected on the mirrored ball. Cynics called it "The Pope's Revenge." East Berliners dubbed the tower the "Tele-Asparagus." They joked that if it fell over, they'd have an elevator to the West.

Farther east, pass under the train tracks into **Alexanderplatz.** This area—especially the Kaufhof department store—was the commercial pride and joy of East Berlin. Today, it's still a landmark, with a major U- and S-Bahn station. The once-futuristic, now-kitschy "World Time Clock" is nostalgic for old-timers and has been left here as a reminder of a popular meeting point back in DDR times.

• *Our orientation stroll or bus ride (this is the last stop for bus #100) is finished. From here, you can hike back a bit to take the riverboat tour or take in the sights south of Unter den Linden, venture into the colorful Prenzlauer Berg neighborhood, or consider extending this foray into eastern Berlin to...*

Karl-Marx-Allee

The buildings along Karl-Marx-Allee in East Berlin (just beyond Alexanderplatz) were completely leveled by the Red Army in 1945. As an expression of their adoration to the "great Socialist

Father" (the "cult of Stalin" was in full gear), the DDR government decided to rebuild the street better than ever (the USSR provided generous subsidies) and made it intentionally one meter wider than the Champs-Elysées. They named it Stalinallee. Today, this street, done in the bold "Stalin Gothic" style so common in Moscow in the 1950s, has been restored, renamed after Karl Marx, and lined with "workers' palaces"—providing a rare look at Berlin's communist days. Distances are a bit long for convenient walking, but you can cruise Karl-Marx-Allee by taxi, or ride the U-Bahn to Strausberger Platz (which was built to resemble an Italian promenade) and walk to Frankfurter Tor, reading the good information posts along the way. Notice the Social Realist reliefs on the buildings and the lampposts, which incorporate the wings of a phoenix (rising from the ashes) in their design. Once a "workers' paradise," the street now hosts a two-mile-long capitalist beer festival the first weekend in August.

The **Café Sibylle,** just beyond the Strausberger Platz U-Bahn station, is a fun spot for a coffee, traditional DDR ice-cream treats, and a look at its free informal museum that tells the story of the most destroyed street in Berlin. While the humble exhibit is nearly all in German, it's fun to see the ear (or buy a €10 plaster replica) and half a moustache from what was the largest statue of Stalin in Germany (the centerpiece of the street until 1961). It also provides a few intimate insights into apartment life in a DDR flat. The café is known for its good coffee and *Schwedeneisbecher mit Eierlikor*—an ice-cream sundae with a shot of egg liqueur, popular among those nostalgic for communism (daily 10:00-20:00, Karl-Marx-Allee 72, at intersection with Koppenstrasse, a block from U-Bahn: Strausberger Platz, tel. 030/2935-2203).

Heading out to Karl-Marx-Allee (just beyond the TV Tower), you're likely to notice a giant colorful **mural** decorating a blocky communist-era skyscraper. This was the Ministry of Education, and the mural is a tile mosaic trumpeting the accomplishments of the DDR's version of "No Child Left Behind."

South of Unter den Linden

The following sights—heavy on Nazi and Wall history—are listed roughly north to south (as you reach them from Unter den Linden).

▲▲Gendarmenmarkt

This delightful, historic square is bounded by twin churches, a tasty chocolate shop, and the Berlin Symphony's concert hall (designed by Karl Friedrich Schinkel, the man who put the Neoclassical stamp on Berlin). In summer, it hosts a few outdoor cafés, *Biergartens*, and sometimes concerts. Wonderfully symmetrical, the square is considered by Berliners to be the finest in town. The name of the square—part French and part German (after the *Gens d'Armes*, Frederick the Great's royal guard who were headquartered here)—reminds us that in the 17th century, a fifth of all Berliners were French émigrés, Protestant Huguenots fleeing Catholic France. Back then, tolerant Prussia was a magnet for the persecuted. These émigrés vitalized Berlin with new ideas and know-how.

The German Cathedral (described later) on the square has an exhibit worthwhile for history buffs. The French Cathedral (Französischer Dom) offers a humble museum on the Huguenots (€2, Tue-Sun 12:00-17:00, closed Mon, U-Bahn: Französische Strasse or Stadtmitte). Fun fact: Neither of these churches are true cathedrals, as they never contained a bishop's throne; their German title of *Dom* (cathedral) is actually a mistranslation from the French word *dôme* (cupola).

Fassbender & Rausch, on the corner near the German Cathedral, claims to be Europe's biggest chocolate store. After 150 years of chocolate-making, this family-owned business proudly displays its sweet delights—250 different kinds—on a 55-foot-long buffet. Truffles are sold for about €0.60 each—it's fun to compose a fancy little eight-piece box of your own for about €5. Upstairs is an elegant hot chocolate café with fine views. If this isn't enough to entice you, I have three words: "Erupting Chocolate Volcano" (daily 10:00-20:00, opens Sun at 11:00, corner of Mohrenstrasse at Charlottenstrasse 60, tel. 030/2045-8440).

Gendarmenmarkt is buried in what has recently emerged as Berlin's "Fifth Avenue" shopping district. For the ultimate in top-end shops, find the corner of Jägerstrasse and Französische Strasse and wander through the **Quartier 206** (Mon-Fri 10:30-19:30, Sat 10:00-18:00, closed Sun, www.quartier206.com).

• *Of the two matching churches on Gendarmenmarkt, the one to the south (bottom end of square) is the...*

▲**German Cathedral (Deutscher Dom)**—This cathedral (not to be confused with the Berlin Cathedral on Unter den Linden) was bombed flat in the war and rebuilt only in the 1980s. It houses the thought-provoking *Milestones, Setbacks, Sidetracks (Wege, Irrwege, Umwege)* exhibit, which traces the history of the German parliamentary system. The parliament-funded exhibit—while light on actual historical artifacts—is well done and more interesting than it sounds. It takes you quickly from the revolutionary days of 1848 to the 1920s, and then more deeply through the tumultuous 20th century. There are no English descriptions, but you can follow the essential, excellent, and free 1.5-hour English audioguide or buy the wonderfully detailed €10 guidebook. If you think this museum is an attempt by the German government to develop a more sophisticated and educated electorate in the interest of stronger democracy, you're exactly right. Germany knows (from its own troubled history) that a dumbed-down electorate, manipulated by clever spin-meisters and sound-bite media blitzes, is a dangerous thing (free, Tue-Sun May-Sept 10:00-19:00, Oct-April 10:00-18:00, closed Mon year-round, tel. 030/2273-0431).

Nazi Sites on Wilhelmstrasse

Surviving stretches of the Wall are virtually nonexistent in downtown Berlin. One of the most convenient places to see a bit is at the intersection of Wilhelmstrasse and Zimmerstrasse/ Niederkirchnerstrasse, a few blocks southwest of Gendarmenmarkt. This is also the site of some significant Nazi history.

▲▲**Topography of Terror (Topographie des Terrors)**—The park behind the chunk of Wall marks what was once the most feared addresses in Berlin: the headquarters of the Reich Main Security Office (Reichssicherheitshauptamt). Located on the street formerly known as Prinz-Albrecht-Strasse, these offices served as the engine room of the Nazi dictatorship as well as the command center of the Gestapo (Secret Police) and SS (Hitler's personal bodyguards). This trio of bodies grew to become a state-within-a-state, with their talons in every corner of German society. It was from these headquarters that the Nazis administered concentration camps, firmed up plans for the "Final Solution" of the "Jewish Question," and organized the domestic surveillance of anyone opposed to the regime. The building was also equipped with dungeons, where the Gestapo imprisoned and tortured thousands of prisoners.

In 2010—after 25 years of building, tearing down, and rebuilding—a permanent exhibition hall opened on this spot (the excavated dungeons are still accessible). It's one of the few memorial sites that focuses on the perpetrators and not on the victims of the Nazis. It's a chilling but fascinating experience to see just how seamlessly and bureaucratically the Nazi institutions and state structures merged to become a well-oiled terror machine. While you could read this story anywhere, to take this in while standing atop the Gestapo headquarters is a powerful experience.

Cost and Hours: Free, daily 10:00-18:00, Niederkirchnerstrasse 8, tel. 030/2548-6703, www.topographie.de.

German Finance Ministry (Bundesministerium der Finanzen)—Across the street (facing the Wall chunk) are the former headquarters of the Nazi Luftwaffe (Air Force), the only major Hitler-era government building that survived the war's bombs. Notice how the whole building gives off a monumental feel, making the average person feel small and powerless. After the war, the communists used the building to house their—no joke—

BERLIN

Ministry of Ministries. Walk up Wilhelmstrasse (to the north) to see an entry gate (on your left) that looks much like it did when Germany occupied nearly all of Europe. On the north side of the building (farther up Wilhelmstrasse, at corner with Leipziger Strasse) is a wonderful example of communist art. The mural, Max Lingner's *Aufbau der Republik* (*Building the Republic*, 1953), is classic Socialist Realism, showing the entire society—industrial laborers, farm workers, women, and children—all happily singing the same patriotic song. This was the communist ideal. For the reality, look at the ground in the courtyard in front of the mural to see an enlarged photograph from a 1953 uprising here against the communists...quite a contrast.

Checkpoint Charlie

▲▲▲**Museum of The Wall at Checkpoint Charlie (Mauermuseum Haus am Checkpoint Charlie)**—While the famous border checkpoint between the American and Soviet sectors is long gone, its memory is preserved by one of Europe's most cluttered museums. During the Cold War, the House at Checkpoint Charlie stood defiantly—spitting distance from the border guards—showing off all the clever escapes over, under, and through the Wall. Today, while the drama is over and hunks of the Wall stand like victory scalps at its door, the museum still tells a gripping history of the Wall, recounts the many ingenious escape attempts (early years—with a cruder wall—saw more escapes), and includes plenty of video coverage of those heady days when people-power tore down the Wall. While dusty, disorganized, and slightly overpriced, with lots of reading involved, all of that just adds to its borderline-kitschy charm. It's the best place in Berlin to get a handle on the Cold old days.

If you're pressed for time, this is a decent after-dinner sight. With extra time, consider the "Hear We Go" audioguide about the Wall that takes you outside the museum (€7, 1.5 hours, leave ID as deposit).

Cost and Hours: €12.50, assemble 20 tourists and get in for €7.50 each, €3 audioguide, discount with WelcomeCard but not covered by Museumspass, cash only, daily 9:00-22:00, U6 to Kochstrasse or—better from Zoo—U2 to Stadtmitte, Friedrichstrasse 43-45, tel. 030/253-7250, www.mauermuseum.de.

▲▲**Checkpoint Charlie Street Scene**—Where Checkpoint Charlie once stood, notice the thought-provoking post with larger-than-life posters of a young American soldier facing east and a young Soviet soldier facing west. The area has become a Cold War freak show. The rebuilt guard station now hosts two actors playing American guards who pose for photos. (Across the street is Snack Point Charlie.) The old checkpoint was not named for a person,

BERLIN

but because it was checkpoint number three—as in Alpha (at the East-West German border, a hundred miles west of here), Bravo (as you enter Berlin proper), and Charlie (the most famous because it was where most foreigners would pass). A fine photo exhibit stretches down the street, with great English descriptions telling the story of the Wall. While you could get this information from a book, it's poignant to stand here in person and ponder the gripping history of this place. A few yards away (on Zimmerstrasse), a glass panel describes the former checkpoint. From there, a double row of cobbles in Zimmerstrasse traces the former path of the Wall. These innocuous cobbles run throughout the city, even through some modern buildings.

Farther down on Zimmerstrasse, before Charlottenstrasse, find the **Memorial to Peter Fechter** (set just off the sidewalk, barely inside the Wall marker). On August 17, 1962, East German soldiers shot Fechter as he was trying to climb over the Wall. For more than an hour, Fechter lay bleeding to death while soldiers and bystanders on both sides of the Wall did nothing. In 1997, a German court sentenced three former border guards to two years in prison for manslaughter.

▲▲▲Jewish Museum Berlin (Jüdisches Museum Berlin)

This museum is one of Europe's best Jewish sights. The highly conceptual building is a sight in itself, and the museum inside— an overview of the rich culture and history of Europe's Jewish community—is excellent. The Holocaust is appropriately remembered, but it doesn't overwhelm this celebration of Jewish life. Even though the museum is in a nondescript residential neighborhood (a 10-minute walk from the Hallesches Tor U-Bahn station or Checkpoint Charlie), it's well worth the trip.

Designed by American architect Daniel Libeskind (who is redeveloping New York City's World Trade Center site), the zinc-walled building's zigzag shape is pierced by voids symbolic of the irreplaceable cultural loss caused by the Holocaust. Enter through the 18th-century Baroque building next door, then go through an underground tunnel to reach the museum interior.

Before you reach the exhibit, your visit starts with three memorial spaces. Underground, follow the Axis of Exile to a disorienting slanted garden with 49 pillars. Then the Axis of Holocaust leads to an eerily empty tower shut off from the outside world. A detour near the bottom of the long stairway leads to the "Memory Void," a thought-provoking space of "fallen leaves": heavy metal faces that you walk on, making un-human noises with each step.

Finally, climb the stairs to the top of the museum, from where you stroll chronologically through the 2,000-year story of Judaism in Germany. The exhibit, on two floors, is engaging. Interactive bits (for example, spell your name in Hebrew) make it lively for kids. English explanations interpret both the exhibits and the design of the very symbolic building.

Cost and Hours: €5, covered by Museumspass, discount with WelcomeCard, daily 10:00-20:00, Mon until 22:00, last entry one hour before closing, closed on Jewish holidays. Tight security includes bag check and metal detectors. If you're here in December, be sure to check out their "Hannumas" holiday market. Tel. 030/2599-3300, www.jmberlin.de.

Getting There: Take the U-Bahn to Hallesches Tor, find the exit marked *Jüdisches Museum*, exit straight ahead, then turn right on Franz-Klühs-Strasse. The museum is a five-minute walk ahead on your left, at Lindenstrasse 9.

Eating: The museum's restaurant, Liebermanns, offers good Jewish-style meals, albeit not kosher (€9 daily specials, lunch served 12:00-16:00, snacks at other times, tel. 030/2593-9760).

More Sights South of Unter den Linden

East Side Gallery—The biggest remaining stretch of the Wall is now "the world's longest outdoor art gallery." It stretches for nearly a mile and is covered with murals painted by artists from around the world. The murals (classified as protected monuments) got a facelift in 2009, when the city invited the original artists back to re-create their work for the 20th anniversary of the fall of the Wall. This segment of the Wall makes another poignant walk. For a quick look, take the S-Bahn to the Ostbahnhof station (follow signs to Stralauerplatz exit; once outside, TV Tower will be to your right; go left and at next corner look to your right—the Wall is across the busy street). The gallery is slowly being consumed by developers. If you walk the entire length of the East Side Gallery, you'll find a small Wall souvenir shop at the end and a bridge crossing the river to a subway station at Schlesisches Tor (in Kreuzberg). The bridge, a fine example of Brandenburg Neo-Gothic brickwork, has a fun neon "rock, paper, scissors" installment poking fun at the futility of the Cold War.

Kreuzberg—This district—once abutting the dreary Wall and inhabited mostly by poor Turkish guest laborers and their families—is still run-down, with graffiti-riddled buildings and plenty of student and Turkish street life. It offers a gritty look at melting-pot Berlin, in a city where original Berliners are as rare as old buildings. Berlin is the largest Turkish city outside of Turkey itself, and Kreuzberg is its "downtown." But to call it a "little Istanbul" insults the big one. You'll see *Döner Kebab* stands, shops decorated with spray paint, and mothers wrapped in colorful scarves looking like they just got off a donkey in Anatolia. But lately, an influx of immigrants from many other countries has diluted the Turkish-ness of Kreuzberg. Berliners come here for fun ethnic eateries. For a dose of Kreuzberg without getting your fingers dirty, joyride on bus #129 (catch it near Jewish Museum). For a colorful stroll, take the U-Bahn to Kottbusser Tor and wander—ideally on Tuesday and Friday between 12:00 and 18:00, when the Turkish Market sprawls along the Maybachufer riverbank.

North of Unter den Linden

While there are few major sights to the north of Unter den Linden, this area has some of Berlin's trendiest, most interesting neighborhoods.

▲**New Synagogue (Neue Synagogue)**—A shiny gilded dome marks the New Synagogue, now a museum and cultural center on Oranienburger Strasse. Only the dome and facade have been restored—a window overlooks the vacant field marking what used to be the synagogue. The largest and finest synagogue in Berlin before World War II, it was desecrated by Nazis on "Crystal Night" (Kristallnacht) in 1938, bombed in 1943, and partially rebuilt in 1990. Inside, past tight security, there's a small but moving exhibit on the Berlin Jewish community through the centuries with some good English descriptions (ground floor and first floor). On its facade, the *Vergesst es nie* message—added by East Berlin Jews in 1966—means "Never forget." East Berlin had only a few hundred Jews, but now that the city is reunited, the Jewish community numbers about 12,000.

Cost and Hours: €3; March-Oct Sun-Mon 10:00-20:00, Tue-Thu 10:00-18:00, Fri 10:00-17:00, closed Sat; Nov-Feb Sun-Thu 10:00-18:00, Fri 10:00-14:00, closed Sat; Oranienburger Strasse 28/30, S-Bahn: Oranienburger Strasse, tel. 030/8802-8300 and press 1, www.cjudaicum.de.

Nearby: Cheer things up 50 yards away with every local kid's favorite traditional candy shop—**Bonbonmacherei**—where you can see candy being made the old-fashioned way (at Oranienburger Strasse 32, in another example of a classic Berlin courtyard).

A block from the synagogue, walk 50 yards down **Grosse Hamburger Strasse** to a little park. This street was known for 200 years as the "street of tolerance" because the Jewish community donated land to Protestants so that they could build a church. Hitler turned it into the "street of death" *(Todes Strasse)*, bulldozing 12,000 graves of the city's oldest Jewish cemetery and turning a Jewish nursing home into a deportation center. Because of the small but growing radical Islamic element in Berlin, and a smattering of persistent neo-Nazis, several police officers and an Israeli secret agent keep watch over this park and the Jewish high school nearby.

▲**Oranienburger Strasse**—Berlin is developing so fast, it's impossible to predict what will be "in" from year to year. The area around Oranienburger Strasse is definitely trendy (but is being challenged by hip Friedrichshain, farther east, and Prenzlauer Berg, described later). While the area immediately around the synagogue is dull, 100 yards away things get colorful. The streets behind Grosse Hamburger Strasse flicker with atmospheric cafés, *Kneipen* (pubs), and art galleries. At night (from about 20:00), techno-prostitutes line Oranienburger Strasse. Prostitution is legal throughout Germany. Prostitutes pay taxes and receive health care insurance like anyone else. On this street, they hire security guards (lingering nearby) for safety.

A good place to watch this part of Berliner life is the pub **Aufsturz,** which serves more than 100 different beers and 40 varieties of whiskey, traditional Berliner pub grub—like nachos—and great potato soup for under €5. The traditional Berlin platter for €14 can easily feed three voracious carnivores. Aufsturz is also a hangout for local tour guides who don't mind if you join them to talk shop (daily from 12:00 until "at least" 2:00 in the morning, across from the old Imperial Post Office at Oranienburger Strasse 67, tel. 030/2804-7407).

Hackescher Markt—This area, in front of the S-Bahn station of the same name, is a great people scene day and night. The brick trestle supporting the train track is another classic example of the city's Brandenburg Neo-Gothic brickwork. Most of the brick archways are now filled with hip shops, which have official—and newly trendy—addresses such as "S-Bahn Arch #9, Hackescher Markt." Within 100 yards of the S-Bahn station, you'll find Hackesche Höfe (described next), recommended Turkish and Bavarian restaurants, walking-tour and pub-crawl departure points, and tram #M1 to Prenzlauer Berg.

Hackesche Höfe (a block in front of the Hackescher Markt S-Bahn station) is a series of eight courtyards bunny-hopping through a wonderfully restored 1907 *Jugendstil* building. Berlin's apartments are organized like this—courtyard after courtyard leading off the main roads. This complex is full of trendy restaurants (including the recommended Turkish eatery, Hasir), theaters, and cinemas (playing movies in their original languages). This is a wonderful example of how to make huge city blocks livable. Two decades after the Cold War, this area has reached the final evolution of East Berlin's urban restoration—this is where Prenzlauer Berg is heading. (These courtyards also serve a useful lesson for visitors: Much of Berlin's charm hides off the street front.)

▲**Prenzlauer Berg**—Young, in-the-know locals agree that "Prenzl'berg" is one of Berlin's most colorful neighborhoods (roughly between Helmholtzplatz and Kollwitzplatz and along Kastanienallee, U2: Senefelderplatz and Eberswalder Strasse; or take the S-Bahn to Hackescher Markt and catch tram #M1 north). This part of the city was largely untouched during World War II, but its buildings slowly rotted away under the communists. After the Wall fell, it was overrun with laid-back hipsters, energetic young families, and clever entrepreneurs who breathed life back into its classic old apartment blocks, deserted factories, and long-forgotten breweries. Ten years of rent control kept things affordable for its bohemian residents. But now landlords are free to charge what the market will bear, and the vibe is changing. Locals complain that these days the cafés and bars cater to yuppies sipping prosecco, while the working class and artistic types have been pushed out. While it has changed plenty, I still find Prenzlauer Berg a celebration of life and a joy to stroll through. Though it's a few blocks farther out than the neighborhoods described previously, it's a fun area to explore and have a meal (see page 698) or spend the night (see page 687).

Natural History Museum (Museum für Naturkunde)—This museum is worth a visit just to see the largest dinosaur skeleton ever assembled. While you're there, meet "Bobby" the stuffed ape. The museum is a magnet for the city's children, who love the interactive displays, the "History of the Universe in 120 Seconds" exhibit, and the cool virtual-reality glasses that put meat and skin on all of the dinosaur skeletons (€6, Tue-Fri 9:30-17:00, Sat-Sun 10:00-18:00, closed Mon, last entry 30 minutes before closing, Invalidenstrasse 43, U6: Zinnowitzer Strasse, tel. 030/2093-8591, www.naturkundemuseum-berlin.de).

Berlin Wall Documentation Center (Dokumentations-zentrum Berliner Mauer)—The last surviving complete "Wall system" (with both sides of its Wall and its no-man's-land, or "death strip," all still intact) is now part of a sober memorial and "Doku-Center." Though it's directed at German speakers and far from other sights, it's handy enough to the S-Bahn that any Wall aficionado will find it worth a quick visit. The Documentation Center has a photo gallery and rooftop viewpoint (accessible by elevator), from which you can view the "Wall system." It's poignantly located where a church was destroyed to make way for the Wall; today, a memorial chapel has been built where the church once stood (free, April-Oct Tue-Sun 10:00-18:00, Nov-March until 17:00, closed Mon year-round, Bernauer Strasse 111, tel. 030/464-1030, www.berliner-mauer-dokumentationszentrum.de). Take the S-Bahn to Nordbahnhof and walk 200 yards along Bernauer Strasse, which is still lined with a long chunk of Wall.

Central Berlin

To Reichstag

BRANDENBURG GATE

Pariser Platz

Unter den Linden

500 meters

1/2 Mile

STRASSE DES 17 JUNI

MEMORIAL TO THE MURDERED JEWS OF EUROPE

US EMBASSY

HANNAH-ARENDT-STRASSE

VICTORY COLUMN

Tiergarten

ENTLASTUNGSSTR.

LENNÉSTRASSE

EBERTSTRASSE

VOSSSTR.

..... Former Course of The Wall

MUSICAL INSTRUMENTS MUSEUM

STÜLERSTR.

BELLEVUESTR.

Potsdamer Platz

Leipziger Platz

SONY CENTER

Potsdamer Platz

TIERGARTENSTRASSE

MUSEUM OF ARTS & CRAFTS

GEMÄLDE-GALERIE

CONCERT HALL

POTSDAMER STRASSE

ALTE POTSDAMER

EICHHORNSTR.

To Zoo & Memorial Church

HILDEBRANDSTR.

HIROSHIMASTR.

BAUHAUS ARCHIVE

GERMAN RESISTANCE MEMORIAL

SIGISMUNDSTR.

HITZIGALLEE

NEW NATIONAL GALLERY

LIBRARY

GABRIELE-TERGIT-PROMENADE

STRESEMANNSTR.

REICHPIETSCHUFER

Landwehr Canal

N

Sights in Central Berlin

Tiergarten Park and Nearby

Berlin's "Central Park" stretches two miles from Bahnhof Zoo to the Brandenburg Gate.

Victory Column (Siegessäule)—The Tiergarten's centerpiece, the Victory Column, was built to commemorate the Prussian defeat of Denmark in 1864...then reinterpreted after the defeat of France in 1870. The pointy-helmeted Germans rubbed it in, decorating the tower with French cannons and paying for it all with francs received as war reparations. The three lower rings commemorate Bismarck's victories. I imagine the statues of Moltke and other German military greats—which lurk in the trees nearby—goose-stepping around the floodlit angel at night.

Originally standing at the Reichstag, in 1938 the tower was moved to this position and given a 25-foot lengthening by Hitler's architect Albert Speer, in anticipation of the planned re-envisioning of Berlin as "Germania"—the capital of a world-wide Nazi empire. Streets leading to the circle are flanked by surviving Nazi guardhouses, built in the stern style that fascists loved. At the memorial's first level, notice how WWII bullets chipped the fine marble columns. From 1989 to 2003, the column was the epicenter of the Love Parade (Berlin's city-wide techno-hedonist street party) and the backdrop for Barack Obama's summer 2008 visit to Germany as a presidential candidate. (He asked to speak in front of the Brandenburg Gate, but German Chancellor Angela Merkel wanted to save that symbol from "politics.")

Climbing its 285 steps earns you a breathtaking Berlin-wide view and a close-up look at the gilded bronze statue of the goddess Victoria (go ahead, call her "the chick on a stick"—everybody here does). You might recognize Victoria from Wim Wenders' 1987

BERLIN

art-house classic *Wings of Desire,* or the *Stay (Faraway, So Close!)* video he directed for U2.

Cost and Hours: €2.20; April-Sept Mon-Thu 9:30-18:30, Fri-Sun 9:30-19:00; Oct-March daily 9:30-17:30; closes in the rain, WCs for paying guests only, no elevator, bus #100, tel. 030/8639-8560. From the tower, the grand Strasse des 17 Juni leads east to the Brandenburg Gate.

Flea Market—A colorful flea market with great antiques, more than 200 stalls, collector-savvy merchants, and fun German fast-food stands thrives weekends on Strasse des 17 Juni (Sat-Sun 6:00-16:00, right next to S-Bahn: Tiergarten).

German Resistance Memorial (Gedenkstätte Deutscher Widerstand)—This memorial and museum, just south of the Tiergarten, tells the story of several organized German resistance movements and the more than 42 separate assassination attempts against Hitler. The Bendlerblock was a military headquarters where an ill-fated attempt to assassinate Hitler was plotted (the actual attempt occurred in Rastenburg, eastern Prussia; the event was dramatized in the 2009 Tom Cruise film *Valkyrie*). Claus Schenk Graf von Stauffenberg and several of his co-conspirators were shot here in the courtyard. While posted explanations are in German only and there are no real artifacts, the spirit that haunts the place is multilingual (free, Mon-Fri 9:00-18:00, Thu until 20:00, Sat-Sun 10:00-18:00, free and good English audioguide with passport, €3 printed English translation, no crowds, near Kulturforum at Stauffenbergstrasse 13, enter in courtyard, door on left, main exhibit is on third floor, bus #M29, tel. 030/2699-5000).

Potsdamer Platz and Nearby

The "Times Square of Berlin," and possibly the busiest square in Europe before World War II, Potsdamer Platz was cut in two by the Wall and left a deserted no-man's-land for 40 years. Today, this immense commercial/residential/entertainment center, sitting on a futuristic transportation hub, is home to the European corporate headquarters of several big-league companies.

▲Potsdamer Platz

The new Potsdamer Platz was a vision begun in 1991, when it was announced that Berlin would resume its position as capital of Germany. Sony, Daimler, and other major corporations have turned the square once again into a center of Berlin. Like great Christian churches built upon pagan holy grounds, Potsdamer Platz—with its corporate logos flying high and shiny above what was the Wall—trumpets the triumph of capitalism.

While Potsdamer Platz tries to give Berlin a common center,

the city has always been—and remains—a collection of towns. Locals recognize 28 distinct neighborhoods that may have grown together but still maintain their historic orientation. While Munich has the single dominant Marienplatz, Berlin will always have Charlottenburg, Savignyplatz, Kreuzberg, Prenzlauer Berg, and so on. In general, Berliners prefer these characteristic neighborhoods to an official city center. They're unimpressed by the grandeur of Potsdamer Platz, simply considering it a good place to go to the movies, with overpriced, touristy restaurants.

While most of the complex just feels big (the arcade is like any huge, modern, American mall), the entrance to the complex and Sony Center are worth a visit, and German-film buffs will enjoy the Deutsche Kinemathek museum (described later).

For an overview of the construction, and a scenic route to the Sony Center, start at the Bahnhof Potsdamer Platz (east end of Potsdamer Strasse, S- and U-Bahn: Potsdamer Platz, exit following *Leipziger Platz* signs to see the best view of skyscrapers as you emerge). Find the green hexagonal **clock tower** with the traffic lights on top. This is a replica of the first automatic traffic light in Europe, which once stood at the six-street intersection of Potsdamer Platz. On either side of Potsdamer Strasse, you'll see enormous cubical entrances to the new underground Potsdamer Platz train station. Near these entrances, notice the slanted **glass cylinders** sticking out of the ground. The mirrors on the tops of the tubes move with the sun to collect light and send it underground (saving piles of euros in energy costs). A line in the pavement indicates where the **Berlin Wall** once stood. Notice also the slabs of the Wall re-erected where the Wall once stood. Imagine when the first piece was cut out (see photo and history on nearby panel). These hang at the gate of Fort Capitalism...look up at the towering corporate headquarters: Market forces have won a clear victory. Now descend into one of the train station entrances and follow signs to *Sony Center*.

You'll come up the escalator into the **Sony Center** under a grand canopy (designed to evoke Mount Fuji). At night, multicolored floodlights play on the underside of this tent. Office workers and tourists eat here by the fountain, enjoying the parade of people. The modern Bavarian Lindenbräu beer hall—the Sony boss wanted a *Bräuhaus*—serves traditional food (€5-16, daily 11:00-24:00, big salads, three-foot-long taster boards of eight different beers, tel. 030/2575-1280). The adjacent Josty Bar is built around a surviving bit of a venerable hotel that was a meeting place for Berlin's rich and famous before the bombs (expensive, daily 10:00-24:00, tel. 030/2575-9702). CineStar is a rare cinema that plays mainstream movies in their original language (www.cinestar.de).

Sights near Potsdamer Platz

▲**Deutsche Kinemathek Film and TV Museum**—This exhibit is the most interesting place to visit in the Sony Center. Your admission ticket gets you into several floors of exhibits (third floor is permanent exhibits, first and fourth floor are temporary exhibits) made meaningful by the included (and essential) English audioguide. The film section takes you from the German film industry's beginnings, with emphasis on the Weimar Republic period in the 1920s, when Berlin rivaled Hollywood (*Metropolis* was a 1927 German production). Three rooms are dedicated to Marlene Dietrich, and another section features Nazi use of film as propaganda. The TV section tells the story of *das Idioten Box* from its infancy (when it was primarily used as a Nazi propaganda tool) to today. The 30-minute kaleidoscopic review—kind of a frantic fast-forward montage of greatest hits in German TV history—is great fun even if you don't understand a word of it (it plays all day long, with 10-minute breaks). Upstairs is a TV archive where you can dial through a wide range of new and classic German TV standards (€6, includes 1.5-hour audioguide, Tue-Sun 10:00-18:00, Thu until 20:00, closed Mon, tel. 030/2474-9888, www.deutsche-kinemathek.de). The Kino Arsenal theater downstairs shows offbeat art-house films in their original language.

Panoramapunkt—Across Potsdamer Strasse from the Film and TV Museum, you can ride what's billed as "the fastest elevator in Europe" to skyscraping rooftop views. You'll travel at nearly 30 feet per second to the top of the 300-foot-tall Kollhoff Tower. Its sheltered but open-air view deck provides a fun opportunity to survey Berlin's ongoing construction from above. While you're up top, check out the "highest section of the Berlin Wall," which is basically just a publicity stunt (€6.50, daily 11:00-20:00, until 22:00 in summer, last elevator at 19:30, in red-brick building at Potsdamer Platz 1, tel. 030/2529-4372, www.panoramapunkt.de).

Kulturforum

Just west of Potsdamer Platz, Kulturforum is the city's cultural heart, with several top museums and Berlin's concert hall—home of the world-famous Berlin Philharmonic orchestra (admission to all Kulturforum sights covered by a single €8 Bereichskarte Kulturforum combo-ticket or the Museumspass; phone number for all museums: tel. 030/266-2951). Of its sprawling museums, only the Gemäldegalerie is a must (S- or U-Bahn to Potsdamer Platz, then walk along Potsdamer Platz; or from Bahnhof Zoo, take bus #200 to Philharmonie).

▲▲▲**Gemäldegalerie**—Germany's top collection of 13th-18th-century European paintings (more than 1,400 canvases) is beautifully displayed in a building that's a work of art in itself. Follow the excellent free audioguide. The North Wing starts with German paintings of the 13th to 16th centuries, including eight by Albrecht Dürer. Then come the Dutch and Flemish—Jan van Eyck, Pieter Brueghel, Peter Paul Rubens, Anthony van Dyck, Frans Hals, and Jan Vermeer. The wing finishes with German, English, and French 18th-century art, such as Thomas Gainsborough and Antoine Watteau. An octagonal hall at the end features an impressive stash of Rembrandts. The South Wing is saved for the Italians—Giotto, Botticelli, Titian, Raphael, and Caravaggio (open Tue-Sun 10:00-18:00, Thu until 22:00, closed Mon, clever little loaner stools, great salad bar in cafeteria upstairs, Matthäikirchplatz 4).

New National Gallery (Neue Nationalgalerie)—This features 20th-century art, with ever-changing special exhibits (Tue-Fri 10:00-18:00, Thu until 22:00, Sat-Sun 11:00-18:00, closed Mon, café downstairs, Potsdamer Strasse 50).

Museum of Decorative Arts (Kunstgewerbemuseum)— Wander through a thousand years of applied arts—porcelain, fine *Jugendstil* furniture, Art Deco, and reliquaries. There are no English descriptions and no crowds (Tue-Fri 10:00-18:00, Sat-Sun 11:00-18:00, closed Mon, Herbert-von-Karajan-Strasse 10).

▲Musical Instruments Museum (Musikinstrumenten Museum)—This impressive hall is filled with 600 exhibits from the 16th century to modern times. Wander among old keyboard instruments and funny-looking tubas. There's no English, aside from a €0.10 info sheet, but it's fascinating if you're into pianos (Tue-Fri 9:00-17:00, Thu until 22:00, Sat-Sun 10:00-17:00, closed Mon, low-profile white building east of the big yellow Philharmonic Concert Hall, tel. 030/254-810).

Philharmonic Concert Hall—Poke into the lobby of Berlin's yellow Philharmonic building and see if there are tickets available during your stay (ticket office open Mon-Fri 15:00-18:00, Sat-Sun 11:00-14:00, must purchase tickets in person, box office tel. 030/2548-8132). You can often get inexpensive and legitimate tickets sold on the street before the performance. The interior is famous for its extraordinary acoustics. Even from the outside, this is a remarkable building, designed by a nautical engineer to look like a ship—notice how different it looks from each angle.

Sights in Western Berlin

Throughout the Cold War, Western travelers—and most West Berliners—got used to thinking of western Berlin's Kurfürstendamm boulevard as the heart of the city. But those days have gone the way of the Wall. With the huge changes the city has undergone since 1989, the real "city center" is now, once again, Berlin's historic center (the Mitte district, around Unter den

Linden and Friedrichstrasse). While western Berlin has long had the best infrastructure to support your visit, and still works well as a home base, it's no longer the obvious place from which to explore Berlin. After the new Hauptbahnhof essentially put the Bahnhof Zoo out of business in 2006, the area was left with an identity crisis. Now, more than 20 years after reunification, the west side is back and has fully embraced its historical role as a chic, classy suburb.

In the Heart of Western Berlin

A few interesting sights sit within walking distance of Bahnhof Zoo and the Savignyplatz hotels. For a detailed map of this area, see pages 694-695.

▲**Kurfürstendamm**—Western Berlin's main drag, Kurfürstendamm boulevard (nicknamed "Ku'damm"), starts at Kaiser Wilhelm Memorial Church and does a commercial cancan for two miles. In the 1850s, when Berlin became a wealthy and important capital, her "new rich" chose Kurfürstendamm as their street. Bismarck made it Berlin's Champs-Elysées. In the 1920s, it became a chic and fashionable drag of cafés and boutiques. During the Third Reich, as home to an international community of diplomats and journalists, it enjoyed more freedom than the rest of Berlin. Throughout the Cold War, economic subsidies from the West made sure that capitalism thrived on Ku'damm. And today, while much of the old charm has been hamburgerized, Ku'damm is still a fine place to enjoy elegant shops (around Fasanenstrasse), department stores, and people-watching.

▲**Kaiser Wilhelm Memorial Church (Gedächtniskirche)**—This church was originally dedicated to the first emperor of Germany. Reliefs and mosaics show great events in the life of Germany's favorite *Kaiser,* from his coronation in 1871 to his death in 1888. The church's bombed-out ruins have been left standing as a poignant memorial to the destruction of Berlin in World War II.

The church is actually an ensemble of buildings: a new church, the matching bell tower, a meeting hall, and the bombed-out ruins of the old church, with its Memorial Hall. The church is likely to be undergoing renovation when you visit (though the interior should still be open to visitors). Slated for completion around fall of 2012, the renovations will strengthen the foundations of all four buildings and make it possible for visitors to get to the top of the church for the first time in 60 years. Until then, the church will be surrounded by an aluminum tent to prevent dust contamination of the area and to make it easier to work in inclement weather. (In fact, in an attempt to revitalize the western part of the city, the entire area around the church and Breitscheid Platz will be under reconstruction.)

Under a Neo-Romanesque mosaic ceiling, the **Memorial Hall** features a small exhibit of interesting photos about the bombing and before-and-after models of the church. After the war, some Berliners wanted to tear down the ruins and build it anew. Instead, it was decided to keep what was left of the old church as a memorial and stage a competition to design a modern, add-on section. The winning entry—the short, modern building (1961) next to the Memorial Hall—offers a world of 11,000 little blue windows. The blue glass was given to the church by the French as a reconciliation gift. For more information on both churches, pick up the English booklet (€2.60).

As you enter the **church,** turn immediately right to find a simple charcoal sketch of the Virgin Mary wrapped in a shawl. During the Battle of Stalingrad, German combat surgeon Kurt Reuber rendered the Virgin on the back of a stolen Soviet map to comfort the men in his care. On the right are the words "Light, Life, Love" from the gospel of John; on the left, "Christmas in the cauldron 1942"; and at the bottom, "Fortress Stalingrad." Though Reuber died in captivity a year later, his sketch had been flown out of Stalingrad on the last medical evacuation flight, and post-war Germany embraced it as a symbol of the wish for peace. Copies of the drawing, now known as the *Stalingrad Madonna,* hang in the Berlin Cathedral, in England's Coventry, and in Russia's Volgograd (formerly Stalingrad), as a sign of peaceful understanding between the nations. As another act of reconciliation, every Friday at 13:00 there is a "Prayers for Peace" service held simultaneously with the cathedral in Coventry.

The lively square between the churches and the Europa Center (a once-impressive, shiny high-rise shopping center built as a showcase of Western capitalism during the Cold War) usually attracts street musicians and performers—especially in the summer. Berliners call the funky fountain "the wet meatball."

Cost and Hours: Church—free, daily 9:00-19:00; Memorial Hall—free, Mon-Sat 10:00-16:00, closed Sun. Located on Breitscheidplatz, U2/U9 and S-Bahn: Zoologischer Garten or U1/U9: Kurfürstendamm, www.gedaechtniskirche.com.

The Story of Berlin—Filling most of what seems like a department store right on Ku'damm (at #207), this sprawling history exhibit is a business venture making money by telling the stormy 800-year story of Berlin in a creative way. While there are almost no real historic artifacts, the exhibit does a good job of cobbling together many dimensions of the life and tumultuous times of this great city (€10, daily 10:00-20:00, last entry two hours before closing, tel. 030/8872-0100, www.story-of-berlin.de). However, for similar information, the German History Museum on Unter den Linden is a far better use of your time and money (see page 662).

BERLIN

▲**Käthe Kollwitz Museum**—This local artist (1867-1945), who experienced much of Berlin's stormiest century, conveys some powerful and mostly sad feelings about motherhood, war, and suffering through the stark faces of her art. This small yet fine collection (the only one in town of Kollwitz's work) consists of three floors of charcoal drawings, topped by an attic with a handful of sculptures (€6, €1 pamphlet has necessary English explanations of a few major works, daily 11:00-18:00, a block off Ku'damm at Fasanenstrasse 24, U-Bahn: Uhlandstrasse, tel. 030/882-5210, www.kaethe-kollwitz.de).

▲**Kaufhaus des Westens (KaDeWe)**—The "Department Store of the West" has been a Berlin tradition for more than a century. With a staff of 2,100 to help you sort through its vast selection of 380,000 items, KaDeWe claims to be the biggest department store on the Continent. You can get everything from a haircut and train ticket (basement) to souvenirs (third floor). The theater and concert box office on the sixth floor charges an 18 percent booking fee, but they know all your options (cash only). The sixth floor is a world of gourmet taste treats. The biggest selection of deli and exotic food in Germany offers plenty of classy opportunities to sit down and eat. Ride the glass elevator to the seventh floor's glass-domed Winter Garden, a self-service cafeteria—fun but pricey (Mon-Thu 10:00-20:00, Fri 10:00-21:00, Sat 9:30-20:00, closed Sun, S-Bahn: Zoologischer Garten or U-Bahn: Wittenbergplatz, tel. 030/21210, www.kadewe.de). The Wittenbergplatz U-Bahn station (in front of KaDeWe) is a unique opportunity to see an old-time station. Enjoy its interior.

Berlin Zoo (Zoologischer Garten Berlin)—More than 1,400 different kinds of animals call Berlin's famous zoo home...or so the zookeepers like to think. Germans enjoy seeing the pandas at play (straight in from the entrance). I enjoy seeing the Germans at play (€12 for zoo, €12 for world-class aquarium, €18 for both, children half-price, daily mid-March-mid-Oct generally 9:00-19:00, mid-Oct-mid-March generally 9:00-17:00, aquarium closes 30 minutes earlier; feeding times—*Fütterungszeiten*—posted on map just inside entrance, the best feeding show is the sea lions—generally at 15:30; enter near Europa Center in front of Hotel Palace or opposite Bahnhof Zoo on Hardenbergplatz, Budapester Strasse 34, tel. 030/254-010, www.zoo-berlin.de).

Erotic Art Museum—This offers two floors of graphic art (especially East Asian), old-time sex-toy knickknacks, and a special exhibit on the queen of German pornography, the late Beate Uhse. This amazing woman, a former test pilot for the Third Reich and groundbreaking purveyor of condoms and sex ed in the 1950s, was the female Hugh Hefner of Germany and CEO of a huge chain of porn shops. She is famously credited with bringing sex out of the bedroom and onto the kitchen table, "where it belonged" (€6, Mon-Sat 9:00-24:00, Sun 13:00-24:00, last entry at 23:00, hard-to-beat gift shop, at corner of Kantstrasse and Joachimstaler-strasse, a block from Bahnhof Zoo, tel. 030/8862-6613). FYI: You'll see much more sex for half the price in a private video booth next door.

Nightlife in Berlin

Berlin is a happening place for nightlife—whether it's clubs, pubs, jazz music, cabaret, hokey-but-fun German variety shows, theater, or concerts.

Sources of Entertainment Info: *Berlin Programm* lists a non-stop parade of concerts, plays, exhibits, and cultural events (€2, in German, www.berlin-programm.de); *Exberliner Magazine* (€2, www.exberliner.com) and the TI-produced *Berlin To Go* (€1) have less information, but are in English (all sold at kiosks and TIs). For the young and determined sophisticate, *Zitty* and *Tip* are the top guides to alternative culture (in German, sold at kiosks). Also pick up the free schedules *Flyer* and *030* in bars and clubs. Visit KaDeWe's ticket office for your music and theater options (sixth floor, 18 percent fee but access to all tickets; see page 684). Ask about "competitive improvisation" and variety shows.

Berlin Jazz—To enjoy live music near my recommended Savignyplatz hotels in western Berlin, consider **A Trane Jazz Club** (all jazz, great stage and intimate seating, €7-18 cover depending on act, opens at 21:00, live music nightly 22:00-2:00 in the morning, Bleibtreustrasse 1—see map on pages 694-695, tel. 030/313-2550, www.a-trane.de). **B-Flat Acoustic Music and Jazz Club,** in the heart of eastern Berlin, also has live music and really starts hopping at 22:00 (Rosenthaler Strasse 13—see map on pages 688-689, tel. 030/283-86835, www.b-flat-berlin.de).

Berliner Rock and Roll—Berlin has a vibrant rock and pop scene, with popular venues at the Spandau Citadel and at the outdoor Waldbühne ("Forest Stage"). Check out what's playing on posters in the U-Bahn, in *Zitty*, or at any ticket agency. Great Berlin bands include Wir Sind Helden, The Beatsteaks, Jennifer Rostock, and the funky ska band Seeed.

Cabaret—**Bar Jeder Vernunft** offers modern-day cabaret a short walk from my recommended hotels in western Berlin. This variety show—under a classic old tent perched atop a modern parking lot—is a hit with German speakers, but can still be worthwhile for those who don't speak the language (as some of the music shows are in a sort of "Denglish"). Even some Americans perform here periodically. Tickets are generally about €20, and shows change regularly (performances start Mon-Sat at 20:30, Sun at 20:00, Wed is non-smoking, seating can be a bit cramped, south of Ku'damm at Schaperstrasse 24, tel. 030/883-1582, www.bar-jeder-vernunft.de).

German Variety Show—To spend an evening enjoying Europe's largest revue theater, consider "YMA—Too Beautiful to be True" at the **FriedrichstadtPalast**. It's a passionate visual spectacle, a weird ballet that pulsates like a visual poem (€21-94, Thu-Sat at 19:30, Sat also at 15:30, Tue and Sun at 18:30, no shows Mon or Wed, U6: Oranienburger Tor, tel. 030/2326-2326, www.show -palace.eu).

The Friedrichstrasse area around the Palast and to the south has been synonymous with entertainment for at least 200 years. The East German government built the current Palast in 1984 on the ruins of an older theater, which itself was a horse barn for the Prussian Army. The current exterior is meant to mimic the interior design of the older theater.

Nightclubs and Pubs—Oranienburger Strasse's trendy scene (page 675) is being eclipsed by the action at Friedrichshain (farther east). To the north, you'll find the hip Prenzlauer Berg neighborhood, packed with everything from smoky pubs to small art bars and dance clubs (best scene is around Helmholtzplatz, U2: Eberswalder Strasse; see page 676).

Dancing—Cut a rug at **Clärchens Ballhaus,** an old ballroom that's been a Berlin institution since 1913. At some point everyone in Berlin comes through here, as the dance hall attracts an eclectic Berlin-in-a-nutshell crowd of grannies, elegant women in evening dresses, yuppies, scenesters, and hippies. The music (swing, waltz, tango, or cha-cha) changes every day, with live music on Friday and Saturday (daily from 10:00 until the last person goes home, in the heart of the Auguststrasse gallery district at Auguststrasse 24, S-Bahn: Oranienburger Strasse, tel. 030/282-9295, www.ball haus.de). Dancing lessons are also available (€8, Mon-Tue and Thu at 19:00, 1.5 hours). The restaurant serves decent food and good pizzas.

Art Galleries—Berlin, a magnet for new artists, is a great city for gallery visits. Galleries—many of which stay open late—welcome visitors who are "just looking." The most famous gallery district is in eastern Berlin's Mitte neighborhood, along **Auguststrasse** (branches off from Oranienburger Strasse at the Tacheles building). Check out the Berlin outpost of the edgy-yet-accessible art of the New Leipzig movement at **Galerie Eigen+Art** (Tue-Sat 11:00-18:00, closed Sun-Mon, Auguststrasse 26, tel. 030/280-6605, www.eigen-art.com). The other gallery area is in western Berlin, along **Fasanenstrasse.**

Pub Crawl—New Berlin Tours offers a popular €12 pub crawl. "The New Berlin Pub Crawl" starts nightly at 20:15 from the Oranienburger Strasse S-Bahn station, with free beer until 21:00.

Sleep Code

(€1 = about $1.40, country code: 49, area code: 030)
S = Single, **D** = Double/Twin, **T** = Triple, **Q** = Quad, **b** = bathroom,
s = shower only. Unless otherwise noted, credit cards are
accepted, English is spoken, and breakfast is included.

To help you sort easily through these listings, I've divided
the rooms into three categories, based on the price for a
standard double room with bath:

$$$ **Higher Priced**—Most rooms €125 or more.
$$ **Moderately Priced**—Most rooms between €85-125.
$ **Lower Priced**—Most rooms €85 or less.

Prices can change without notice; verify the hotel's
current rates online or by email. For other updates, see www
.ricksteves.com/update.

Organizers are fairly adamant about their slogan, "Our mission:
To show you Berlin's great nightlife...not to hospitalize you." The
(unrelated) binge-drinking death of a 16-year-old teenager in
Berlin a few years ago has reinforced the tour's strict 18-year-old
minimum age limit. The pub crawl generally visits four bars and
two clubs, and provides a great way to drink it up with new friends
from around the world while getting a peek at Berlin's bar scene...
or at least how its bars look when invaded by 50 loud tourists.

Sleeping in Berlin

When in Berlin, I used to sleep in the former West, on or near
Savignyplatz. But now the focus of Berlin is moving farther east.
If you're interested in staying in a lively, colorful district in the
heart of the *Kiez* (literally "gravel," meaning a homey, homogenous
neighborhood in Berlin), I've listed some suggestions in eastern
Berlin's youthful and increasingly popular Prenzlauer Berg neighborhood.

Berlin is packed and hotel prices go up on holidays, including
Green Week in mid-January, Easter weekend, the first weekend
in May, Ascension weekend in May, German Unity Day (Oct 3),
Christmas, and New Year's. Keep in mind that many hotels have
limited staff after 20:00, so if you're planning to arrive after that,
let the hotel know in advance.

In Eastern Berlin
Prenzlauer Berg
If you want to sleep in the former East Berlin, set your sights on

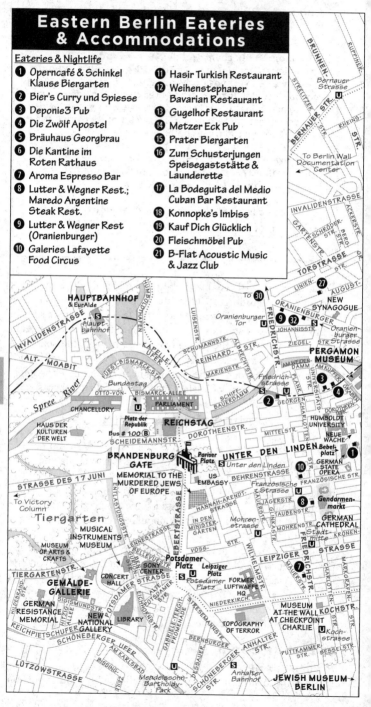

Eastern Berlin Eateries & Accommodations

Eateries & Nightlife

1. Operncafé & Schinkel Klause Biergarten
2. Bier's Curry und Spiesse
3. Deponie3 Pub
4. Die Zwölf Apostel
5. Bräuhaus Georgbrau
6. Die Kantine im Roten Rathaus
7. Aroma Espresso Bar
8. Lutter & Wegner Rest.; Maredo Argentine Steak Rest.
9. Lutter & Wegner Rest (Oranienburger)
10. Galeries Lafayette Food Circus
11. Hasir Turkish Restaurant
12. Weihenstephaner Bavarian Restaurant
13. Gugelhof Restaurant
14. Metzer Eck Pub
15. Prater Biergarten
16. Zum Schusterjungen Speisegaststätte & Launderette
17. La Bodeguita del Medio Cuban Bar Restaurant
18. Konnopke's Imbiss
19. Kauf Dich Glücklich
20. Fleischmöbel Pub
21. B-Flat Acoustic Music & Jazz Club

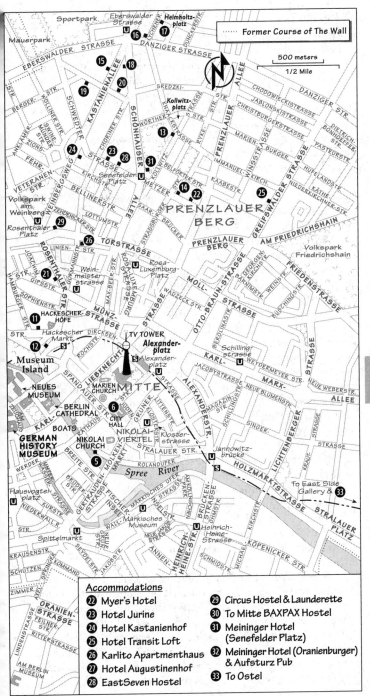

...... Former Course of The Wall

500 meters
1/2 Mile

Sportpark

Mauerpark

Eberswalder Strasse

Helmholtz-platz

EBERSWALDER STRASSE

DANZIGER STRASSE

SREDZKI-

Kollwitz-platz

PRENZLAUER BERG

PRENZLAUER BERG

Volkspark am Weinberg

Rosenthaler Platz

TORSTRASSE

Rosa-Luxemburg-Platz

Wein-meister-strasse

Volkspark Friedrichshain

AM FRIEDRICHSHAIN

MOLL-STRASSE

Hackescher Höfe

Hackescher Markt

TV TOWER
Alexander-platz

Alexanderplatz

Museum Island

NEUES MUSEUM

BERLIN CATHEDRAL

MARIEN CHURCH

MITTE

CITY HALL

NIKOLAI-VIERTEL

KARL-STRASSE

Schilling-strasse

MARX-ALLEE

GERMAN HISTORY MUSEUM

NIKOLAI CHURCH

Kloster-strasse

Jannowitz-brücke

Spree River

HOLZMARKTSTRASSE

To East Side Gallery &

Hausvogtel-platz

Spittelmarkt

Märkisches Museum

Heinrich-Heine-Strasse

STRALAUER PLATZ

ORANIEN-STRASSE

AM BERLIN MUSEUM

Accommodations

22 Myer's Hotel
23 Hotel Jurine
24 Hotel Kastanienhof
25 Hotel Transit Loft
26 Karlito Apartmenthaus
27 Hotel Augustinenhof
28 EastSeven Hostel

29 Circus Hostel & Launderette
30 To Mitte BAXPAX Hostel
31 Meininger Hotel (Senefelder Platz)
32 Meininger Hotel (Oranienburger) & Aufsturz Pub
33 To Ostel

BERLIN

the colorful and fun Prenzlauer Berg district (or "Prenzl'berg" for short). After decades of neglect, this corner of eastern Berlin has quickly come back to life. Gentrification has brought Prenzlauer Berg great hotels, tasty ethnic and German eateries (listed later, under "Eating in Berlin"), and a happening nightlife scene. Think of all the graffiti as just some people's way of saying they care. The huge and impersonal concrete buildings are now enlivened with a street fair of fun little shops and eateries. Prenzlauer Berg is about 1.5 miles north of Alexanderplatz, roughly between Kollwitzplatz and Helmholtzplatz, and to the west, along Kastanienallee (known affectionately as "Casting Alley" for its generous share of beautiful people). The closest U-Bahn stops (U2 line) are Senefelderplatz at the south end of the neighborhood and Eberswalder Strasse at the north end. Or, for less walking, take the S-Bahn to Hackescher Markt, then catch tram #M1 north.

$$ Myer's Hotel is a boutique-hotel renting 52 simple, small, but elegant rooms. The gorgeous public spaces include a patio and garden. Details done right and impeccable service set this place apart. This peaceful hub—off a quiet courtyard and tree-lined street, just a five-minute walk from Kollwitzplatz or the nearest U-Bahn stop (Senefelderplatz)—makes it hard to believe you're in a capital city (Sb-€65-75, Db-€85-125, price depends on size of room, Metzer Strasse 26, tel. 030/440-140, fax 030/4401-4104, www.myershotel.de, info@myershotel.de).

$$ Hotel Jurine (yoo-REEN) is a pleasant 53-room business-style hotel whose friendly staff aims to please. Enjoy the breakfast buffet surrounded by modern art, or relax in the lush backyard (Sb-€85, Db-€110, Tb-€147, extra bed-€37, prices can zoom up during conventions, check website for discounts in July-Aug, parking garage-€13/day, Schwedter Strasse 15, 10-minute walk to U2: Senefelderplatz, tel. 030/443-2990, fax 030/4432-9999, www.hotel-jurine.de, mail@hotel-jurine.de).

$$ Hotel Kastanienhof is a basic, less-classy hotel offering 35 sleepable but slightly overpriced rooms in a great location on Kastanienallee (Sb-€79, Db-€105, reception closed 22:00-6:30, 20 yards from the #M1 tram stop at Kastanienallee 65, tel. 030/443-050, fax 030/4430-5111, www.kastanienhof.biz, info@kastanienhof.biz).

$ Hotel Transit Loft is technically a hostel, but feels more like an upscale budget hotel. Located in a refurbished factory, it offers clean, bright, modern, new-feeling, mostly blue rooms with an industrial touch. The reception—staffed by friendly, hip Berliners—is open 24 hours, with a bar serving drinks all night long (4- to 6-bed dorms-€21/bed, Sb-€62, Db-€72, Tb-€96, includes sheets and breakfast, no age limit, cheap Internet access, fully wheelchair-accessible, Immanuelkirchstrasse 14A; U2/U5/

U8 or S-Bahn: Alexanderplatz, then tram #M4 to Hufelandstrasse and walk 50 yards; tel. 030/4849-3773, fax 030/4405-1074, www .transit-loft.de, loft@hotel-transit.de).

$ Karlito Apartmenthaus offers nine well-located, modern, and comfortable apartments near Hackescher Markt (Sb-€62, Db-€77, Tb-€93, Qb-€108, cash only, up to 2 children under 8 sleep free with 2 paying adults, fully equipped as if you live there, breakfast in Café Lois-€4, bike rental-€8/day, Linienstrasse 60—enter on Gormannstrasse, 350 yards from S-Bahn: Hackescher Markt, even closer to U8: Rosenthaler Platz, mobile 0179-704-9041, www .karlito-apartments.de, info@karlito-apartments.de).

Near Oranienburger Strasse: **$$$ Hotel Augustinenhof** is a clean hotel with spacious rooms and some of the most comfortable beds in Berlin. While not exactly in Prenzlauer Berg, the hotel is on a side street near all of the Oranienburger Strasse action. Rooms in front overlook the courtyard of the Imperial Post Office. If you want quiet, ask for a room in the back (official rates: Sb-€119, Db-€151, but you'll almost always pay closer to Db-€99, Auguststrasse 82, 50 yards from S-Bahn: Oranienburger Strasse, tel. 030/308-860, fax 030/308-86100, www.hotel-augustinenhof.de).

Hostels in Eastern Berlin

Berlin is known among budget travelers for its fun, hip hostels. Here are some good bets. The first three options are in Prenzlauer Berg; Meininger is a chain with several locations; and Ostel is (in every sense) farther East.

$ EastSeven Hostel rents the best cheap beds in Prenzlauer Berg. It's sleek and modern, with all the hostel services and more: 24-hour reception, inviting lounge, fully equipped guests' kitchen, lockers, garden, and bike rental. Children are welcome. While most hostels—especially in Prenzlauer Berg—feel annoyingly young to those over 30, easygoing people of any age are comfortable here (S-€38, D-€52, T-€66, €22/bed in 4-bed dorms, €18/ bed in 8-bed dorms, bathrooms always down the hall, free Internet access and Wi-Fi, laundry-€5, 100 yards from U2: Senefelderplatz at Schwedter Strasse 7, tel. 030/9362-2240, www.eastseven.de, info@eastseven.de).

$ Circus is a brightly colored, well-run place with 230 beds, a Dylanesque ambience, and a bar downstairs (€19/bed in 4- to 8-bed dorms, S-€43, Sb-€53, D-€56, Db-€70, T-€75, Q-€92, 2-person apartment with kitchen-€85, 4-person apartment-€140, breakfast-€5, no curfew, Internet access; Weinbergsweg 1a, U8: Rosenthaler Platz, tel. 030/2839-1433, www.circus-berlin.de, info@circus-berlin.de).

$ Mitte BAXPAX Hostel is another option, at the western edge of Prenzlauer Berg (€19/bed in 9-bed dorms, S-€37-39,

D-€58-32, Db-€66-70, T-€78, Q-€88, sheets-€2.50, no breakfast, could be cleaner, no curfew, Internet access, English newspapers, laundry, bike rental, Chausseestrasse 102, U6: Zinnowitzer Strasse, tel. 030/2839-0965, fax 030/2839-0935, www.backpacker.de, reservation@backpacker.de).

$ **Meininger** is a Europe-wide budget-hotel chain with five locations in Berlin. The most convenient branches are at the Hauptbahnhof (Ella-Traebe-Strasse 9) and Prenzlauer Berg (Schönhauser Allee 19 on Senefelder Platz). Its newest location is at Oranienburger Strasse 67, next to the Aufsturz pub (€14/bed in 8-bed dorms, Sb-€57, Db-€72, Tb-€93, tel. 030/666-36100, www.meininger-hostels.de).

$ **Ostel** is a fun retro-1970s-DDR apartment building that re-creates the lifestyle and interior design of a country relegated to the dustbin of history. All the furniture and room decorations have been meticulously collected and restored to their former socialist glory—only the psychedelic wallpaper is a replica. Guests buy ration vouchers (€6.50/person) for breakfast in the attached restaurant. Kitschy and tacky, sure—but also clean and memorable (€9/bed in a 4- or 6-bed "Pioneer Camp" room, S-€33, Sb-€40, D-€54, Db-€61, 4-person apartments-€120, Wi-Fi, free bike rental, free parking, free collective use of the people's own barbeque, right behind Ostbahnhof station on the corner of Strasse der Pariser Kommune at Wriezener Karree 5, tel. 030/2576-8660, www.ostel.eu, contact@ostel.eu).

In Western Berlin:
Near Savignyplatz and Bahnhof Zoo

While Bahnhof Zoo and Ku'damm are no longer the center of the action, this western Berlin neighborhood is still a comfortable and handy home base (thanks to its easy transit connections to the rest of the city and proximity to the starting point of Original Berlin Walks' guided tours). The streets around the tree-lined Savignyplatz (a 10-minute walk behind the station) have a neighborhood charm, with simple, small, friendly, good-value places abound here. The area has an artsy aura going back to the cabaret days in the 1920s, when it was the center of Berlin's gay scene. The hotels and pensions I list here—which are all a 5- to 15-minute walk from Bahnhof Zoo and Savignyplatz (with S- and U-Bahn stations)—are generally located a couple of flights up in big, run-down buildings. Inside, they're clean and spacious enough so that their well-worn character is actually charming. Asking for a quieter room in back gets you away from any street noise. Of the accommodations listed here, Pension Peters offers the best value for budget travelers.

BERLIN

$$$ Hecker's Hotel is an ultramodern four-star business hotel with 69 rooms and all the sterile Euro-comforts (Sb-€95, Db-€180, all rooms €200 during conferences but generally only €100 July-Aug, breakfast-€16, non-smoking rooms, elevator, parking-€12-18/day, between Savignyplatz and Ku'damm at Grolmanstrasse 35, tel. 030/88900, fax 030/889-0260, www.heckers-hotel.com, info@heckers-hotel.com).

$$ Hotel Askanischerhof is the oldest B&B in Berlin, posh as can be with 16 sprawling, antique-furnished living rooms you can call home. Photos on the walls brag of famous movie-star guests. Frau Glinicke offers Old World service and classic Berlin atmosphere (Sb-€110, Db-€117, Tb-€127, elevator, free parking, Ku'damm 53, tel. 030/881-8033, fax 030/881-7206, www.askanischer-hof.de, info@askanischer-hof.de).

$$ Hotel Astoria is a friendly three-star business-class hotel with 32 comfortably furnished rooms and affordable summer and weekend rates (Db-€108-126, check their website for deals, breakfast-€10 extra, non-smoking floors, elevator, Internet access, parking-€5/day, around corner from Bahnhof Zoo at Fasanenstrasse 2, tel. 030/312-4067, fax 030/312-5027, www.hotelastoria.de, info@hotelastoria.de).

$$ Hotel Carmer 16, with 30 bright and airy (if a bit dated) rooms, is both businesslike and homey, and has an inviting lounge and charming balconies (Db-€87-160, ask about Rick Steves discount, extra person-€20, some rooms have balconies, elevator and a few stairs, Carmerstrasse 16, tel. 030/3110-0500, fax 030/3110-0510, www.hotel-carmer16.de, info@hotel-carmer16.de).

$$ Hotel-Pension Funk, the former home of a 1920s silent-movie star, is delightfully quirky. Kind manager Herr Michael Pfundt offers 14 elegant old rooms with rich Art Nouveau furnishings (S-€42, Ss-€60, Sb-€72, D-€72, Ds-€85, Db-€105, extra person-€23, cash preferred, a long block south of Ku'damm at Fasanenstrasse 69, tel. 030/882-7193, fax 030/883-3329, www.hotel-pensionfunk.de, berlin@hotel-pensionfunk.de).

$$ Hotel Bogota is a once-elegant old slumbermill renting 115 rooms in a sprawling maze of a building that used to house the Nazi Chamber of Culture. Today, pieces of the owner's modern-art collection lurk around every corner (S-€49, Ss-€62, Sb-€98, D-€77, Ds-€84, Db-€89-150, extra bed-€21, children under 12 free, elevator, 10-minute walk from Savignyplatz at Schlüterstrasse 45, tel. 030/881-5001, fax 030/883-5887, www.bogota.de, info@hotel-bogota.de).

$$ Hotel Pension Alexandra is located in an area of art galleries and place-to-be cafés on Pariser Strasse just a five-minute walk south of Ku'damm. Set in a remodeled historical building,

BERLIN

Western Berlin

1. Hecker's Hotel
2. Hotel Askanischerhof
3. Hotel Astoria
4. Hotel Carmer 16
5. Hotel-Pension Funk
6. Hotel Bogota
7. Hotel Pension Alexandra
8. Pension Peters
9. Restaurant Marjellchen
10. Dicke Wirtin Pub
11. Die Zwölf Apostel Rest.
12. Zillemarkt Restaurant
13. To Genazvale Rest.
14. Technical University Mensa
15. Ullrich Supermarkt
16. Schleusenkrug Beer Garden
17. A Trane Jazz Club
18. Bar Jeder Vernunft (Cabaret)
19. Internet Café

the hotel features stylish and contemporary custom-made furniture inspired by Art Deco design, and a bistro with outdoor seating (Sb-€79-109, Db-€99-129, lower prices off-season, extra bed-€35-55, breakfast-€12.50, parking-€7-12, free Wi-Fi, Pariser Strasse 37, tel. 030/887-1650, fax 030/887-16565, www.hotelalexandra.de, info@hotelalexandra.de, Frau Kuhn).

$ Pension Peters, run by a German-Swedish couple, is sunny and central, with a cheery breakfast room and a super-friendly staff that goes out of their way to help their guests. With its sleek Scandinavian decor and 37 renovated rooms, it's a good choice. Some of the ground-floor rooms are a bit dark—and cheaper for the inconvenience (Sb-€58, D-€52, Db-€79, extra bed-€10, family room-€85, up to 2 kids under 13 free with 2 paying adults, cash preferred, Internet access, 10 yards off Savignyplatz at Kantstrasse 146, tel. 030/3150-3944, fax 030/312-3519, www.pension-peters-berlin.de, info@pension-peters-berlin.de, Annika and Christoph).

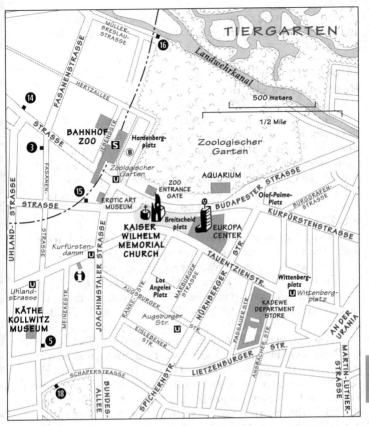

Eating in Berlin

Don't be too determined to eat "Berlin-style." The city is known only for its mildly spicy sausage. Still, there is a world of restaurants to choose from in this ever-changing city. Your best approach may be to select a neighborhood, rather than a particular restaurant.

Colorful pubs—called *Kneipen*—offer light, quick, and easy meals and the fizzy local beer, *Berliner Weiss*. Ask for it *mit Schuss* for a shot of fruity syrup in your suds. Germans—especially Berliners—consider their food old-school; when they go out to eat, they're not usually looking for the "traditional local fare" many travelers are after. Nouveau German is California cuisine with scant memories of wurst, kraut, and pumpernickel.

If the kraut is getting the wurst of you, try one of the many Turkish, Italian, and Balkan restaurants. Eat cheap at *Imbiss* snack stands, bakeries (sandwiches), and falafel/kebab counters. Train stations have grocery stores, as well as bright and modern fruit-and-sandwich bars. And remember: Smoking is banned in Berlin's restaurants.

In Eastern Berlin

Near Unter den Linden

See the map on pages 688-689 for locations.

At the Opera House (Opernpalais): The **Operncafé** is perhaps the classiest coffee stop in Berlin, with a selection of 50—count 'em: 50—different decadent desserts (daily 8:00-24:00, across from university and war memorial at Unter den Linden 5, tel. 030/202-683). The **Schinkel Klause Biergarten** serves good €9-14 meals on its shady terrace with a view of the Unter den Linden scene when sunny, or in its cellar otherwise (daily 11:30-24:00. tel. 030/2026-8450).

Cheap Eats on Friedrichstrasse: **Bier's Curry und Spiesse**, under the tracks at the Friedrichstrasse S-Bahn stop, is a great, greasy, cheap, and generous place for an old-fashioned German hot dog. This is the local favorite near Unter den Linden for *Currywurst*. Experiment with variations (the *Flieschspiess* is excellent) and sauces—and don't hold the *Zwiebeln* (fried onions). You'll likely munch standing at a counter, where the people-watching is great.

Near the Pergamon Museum: Georgenstrasse, a block behind the Pergamon Museum and under the S-Bahn tracks, is lined with fun eateries filling the arcade of the train trestle—close to the sightseeing action but in business mainly for students from nearby Humboldt University. **Deponie3** is a trendy Berlin *Kneipe* usually filled with students. Garden seating in the back is nice if you don't mind the noise of the S-Bahn passing directly above you. The interior is a cozy, wooden wonderland of a bar with several inviting spaces. They serve basic sandwiches, salads, traditional Berlin dishes, and hearty daily specials (€3-7 breakfasts, €5-11 lunches and dinners, great €8 brunch Sun 10:00-15:00, open daily from 9:00, sometimes live music, Georgenstrasse 5, tel. 030/2016-5740). For Italian food, a branch of **Die Zwölf Apostel** is nearby (daily until 24:00; described later, under "Near Savignyplatz").

In the Heart of Old Berlin's Nikolai Quarter: The *Nikolaiviertel* marks the original medieval settlement of Cölln, which would eventually become Berlin. The area was destroyed during the war but was rebuilt for Berlin's 750th birthday in 1987. The whole area has a cute, cobbled, and characteristic old town...Middle Ages meets Socialist Realism. Today, the district is pretty soulless by day but a popular restaurant zone at night. **Bräuhaus Georgbrau** is a thriving beer hall serving homemade suds on a picturesque courtyard overlooking the Spree River. Eat in the lively and woody but mod-feeling interior, or outdoors with fun riverside seating—

thriving with German tourists. It's a good place to try one of the few typical Berlin dishes: *Eisbein* (boiled ham hock) with sauerkraut and mashed peas with bacon (€9.99 with a beer and schnapps). The statue of St. George once stood in the courtyard of Berlin's old castle—until the Nazis deemed it too decadent and not "German" enough, and removed it (€9-13 plates, three-foot-long sampler board with a dozen small glasses of beer, daily 10:00-24:00, 2 blocks south of Berlin Cathedral and across the river at Spreeufer 4, tel. 030/242-4244).

In City Hall: Consider lunching at one of Berlin's many *Kantine*. Located in government offices and larger corporations, *Kantine* offer fast, filling, and cheap lunches, along with a unique opportunity to see Germans at work (though the food can hardly be considered gourmet). There are thousands of *Kantine* in Berlin, but the best is **Die Kantine im Roten Rathaus,** in the basement of City Hall. For less than €4, you can get filling German dishes like *Leberkäse* (German-style baloney) or stuffed cabbage (Mon-Fri 11:00-15:00, closed Sat-Sun, Rathausstrasse 15).

Near Gendarmenmarkt, South of Unter den Linden

The twin churches of Gendarmenmarkt seem to be surrounded by people in love with food. The lunch and dinner scene is thriving with upscale restaurants serving good cuisine at highly competitive prices to local professionals (see map on pages 688-689 for locations). If in need of a quick-yet-classy lunch, stroll around the square and along Charlottenstrasse.

Aroma Espresso Bar offers fresh, made-to-order sandwiches in the shadow of Checkpoint Charlie. Israeli-born Sagi makes his own bread daily and piles on the fixins for under €7. Aroma also makes great coffee, and the mint-infused lemonade can't be beat on a hot afternoon (daily 10:00-19:00, Friedrichstrasse 200, tel. 030/206-16693).

Lutter & Wegner Restaurant is well-known for its Austrian cuisine (*Schnitzel* and *Sauerbraten*) and popular with business-people. It's dressy, with fun sidewalk seating or a dark and elegant interior (€8-17 entrées, €34 fixed-price gourmet dinner, daily 11:00-24:00, Charlottenstrasse 56, tel. 030/202-9540). They have a second location at Oranienburger Strasse 52, near the New Synagogue.

Maredo Argentine Steak Restaurant, a family-friendly chain restaurant, is generally a good value with a fine €6.50 salad bar that can make a healthy and cheap meal (behind French Cathedral at Gendarmenmarkt, at Charlottenstrasse 57, tel. 030/2094-5230).

Galeries Lafayette Food Circus is a French festival of fun eateries in the basement of the landmark department store (Mon-Sat 10:00-20:00, closed Sun, U-Bahn: Französische Strasse, tel. 030/209-480).

At Hackescher Markt

Hasir Turkish Restaurant is your chance to dine with candles, hardwood floors, and happy Berliners savoring meaty Anatolian specialties. As Berlin is the world's largest Turkish city outside of Asia Minor, it's no wonder you can find some good Turkish restaurants here. But while most locals think of Turkish food as fast and cheap, this is a dining experience. The restaurant, in a courtyard next to the Hackesche Höfe shopping complex (see pages 688-689), offers indoor and outdoor tables filled with an enthusiastic local crowd. The service can be a bit questionable, so bring some patience (€14 plates, large and splittable portions, daily from 11:30 until late, a block from the Hackescher Markt S-Bahn station at Oranienburger Strasse 4, tel. 030/2804-1616).

Weihenstephaner Bavarian Restaurant serves upmarket Bavarian traditional food for around €15 a plate, offers an atmospheric cellar and a busy people-watching street-side terrace, and, of course, has excellent beer (daily 11:00-24:00, Neue Promenade 5 at Hackescher Markt, tel. 030/2576-2871).

In Prenzlauer Berg

Prenzlauer Berg is packed with fine restaurants—German, ethnic, and everything in between. (For more on this district, see page 676; for restaurant locations, see the map on pages 688-689.) Before making a choice, I'd spend half an hour strolling and browsing through this bohemian wonderland of creative eateries. **Kollwitzplatz** is an especially good area to prowl for dinner—this square, home of the DDR student resistance in 1980s, is now trendy and upscale. With its leafy playground park in the center, it's a good place for upmarket restaurants. Walk the square and choose. Just about every option offers sidewalk seats in the summer—these are great on a balmy evening. Nearby **Helmholtzplatz** (especially Lychener Strasse) is a somewhat younger, hipper, and edgier place to eat and drink.

Gugelhof, right on Kollwitzplatz, is the Prenzlauer Berg stop for visiting dignitaries. It's an institution famous for its Alsatian German cuisine. You'll enjoy French quality with German proportions. It's highly regarded with a boisterous and enthusiastic local crowd filling its minimalist yet classy interior (€25 three-course meal, daily from 16:00, reservations required during peak times, where Knaackstrasse meets Kollwitzplatz, tel. 030/442-9229).

Metzer Eck is a time-warp *Kneipe* with a family tradition dating to 1913 and a cozy charm. It serves cheap basic typical Berlin food with Czech Budvar beer on tap (€5-7 meals, daily from 18:00, Metzer Strasse 33, on the corner of Metzer Strasse and Strassburger Strasse, tel. 030/442-7656).

Prater Biergarten offers two great eating opportunities: a rustic restaurant indoors and a mellow, shady, super-cheap, and family-friendly beer garden outdoors—each proudly pouring Prater's own microbrew. In the beer garden—Berlin's oldest—you step up to the counter and order (simple €3-5 plates and an intriguing selection of beer munchies). The restaurant serves serious traditional *Biergarten* cuisine and good salads. A playground for the kids invites families to linger (€8-14 plates, Mon-Sat 18:00-24:00, Sun 12:00-24:00, cash only, Kastanienallee 7, tel. 030/448-5688).

Zum Schusterjungen Speisegaststätte ("The Cobbler's Apprentice") is a classic old-school, German-with-attitude eatery that retains its circa-1986 DDR decor. Famous for its schnitzel and its filling €7-8 meals, it's a no-frills place with quality ingredients and a strong local following. It serves the eating needs of those Berliners lamenting the disappearance of solid traditional German cooking amid the flood of ethnic eateries (small 40-seat dining hall, daily 11:00-24:00, corner of Lychener Strasse and Danziger Strasse 9, tel. 030/442-7654).

La Bodeguita del Medio Cuban Bar Restaurant is purely fun-loving Cuba—Christmas lights, graffiti-caked walls, Che Guevara posters, animated staff, and an ambience that makes you want to dance. Come early to eat or late to drink. This restaurant has been here for more than a decade—and in fast-changing Prenzlauer Berg, that's an eternity. Cuban ribs and salad for €7 is a hit. Main dishes are big enough to split. There's live Cuban music on Wednesdays, and you can puff a Cuban cigar any day (€5-10 tapas, struggle with a menu in German and Spanish, daily 17:00-24:00, 1 block from U2: Eberswalder Strasse at Lychener Strasse 6, tel. 030/4171-4276).

Konnopke's Imbiss, a super-cheap German-style sausage stand, has been a Berlin institution for more than 70 years—it was family-owned even during DDR times. Berliners say Konnopke's cooks up the city's best *Currywurst* (grilled bratwurst with curry-infused ketchup, €2). Located beneath the U2 viaduct, the stand was demolished in summer 2010 during roadwork. Berliners rioted, and Konnopke's was rebuilt in a slick glass-and-steel hut (Mon-Fri 10:00-20:00, Sat 12:00-20:00; Kastanienallee dead-ends at the elevated train tracks, and under them you'll find Konnopke's at Schönhauser Allee 44A). Don't confuse this with the nearby Currystation—look for the real Konnopke's.

For After-Dinner Dessert and Drinks: **Kauf Dich Glücklich** makes a great capper to a Prenzlauer Berg dinner. It serves an enticing array of sweet Belgian waffles and ice cream (best pistachio ice cream in Berlin) in a candy-sprinkled, bohemian, retro setting under WWII bullet holes on a great Prenzlauer Berg street (daily until late, indoor and outdoor seating, Oderberger Strasse 44—it's the only un-renovated building on the street, tel. 030/4435-2182). Also on Oderberger Strasse, **Fleischmöbel** ("Meat Furniture") is a fun place to drink with locals, despite the lack of beer on tap. Its two smallish rooms unashamedly offer a bit of 1960s retro in an increasingly trendy part of Prenzlauer Berg (daily 12:00 until "whenever," Oderberger Strasse 2).

In Western Berlin
Near Savignyplatz

Many good restaurants are on or within 100 yards of Savignyplatz, near my recommended western Berlin hotels (see map on pages 694-695 for locations). Take a walk and survey these; continue your stroll along Bleibtreustrasse to discover many trendier, more creative little eateries.

Restaurant Marjellchen is a trip to East Prussia. Dine in soft, jazzy elegance in one of two six-table rooms. While it doesn't have to be expensive (€27 for two courses), plan to go the whole nine yards here, as this can be a great Prussian experience with caring service. The menu is inviting, and all the recipes were brought to Berlin by the owner's mother after being expelled from East Prussia. The Königsberg meatballs are the specialty. Reservations are smart (daily 17:00-23:30, family-run, Mommsenstrasse 9, tel. 030/883-2676).

Dicke Wirtin is a pub with traditional old-Berlin *Kneipe* atmosphere, six good beers on tap, and solid home cooking at reasonable prices—such as their famously cheap *Gulaschsuppe* (€3.50). Their interior is fun and pubby; their streetside tables are also inviting (€5 daily specials, open daily from 12:00 with dinner served from 18:00, just off Savignyplatz at Carmerstrasse 9, tel. 030/312-4952).

Die Zwölf Apostel ("The Twelve Apostles") is trendy for good Italian food. Choose between indoors with candlelit ambience, outdoors on a sun-dappled patio, or overlooking the people-parade on its pedestrian street. A dressy local crowd packs this restaurant for excellent €10 pizzas and €15-30 meals (daily 7:00-1:00 in the morning, cash only, immediately across from Savignyplatz S-Bahn entrance, Bleibtreustrasse 49, tel. 030/312-1433).

Zillemarkt Restaurant, which feels like an old-time Berlin *Biergarten,* serves traditional Berlin specialties in the garden or in the rustic candlelit interior. Their *Berliner Allerlei* is a fun way to sample a bit of nearly everything (cabbage, pork, sausage, potatoes and more for a minimum of two people...but it can feed up to five). They have their own microbrew (€10 meals, daily 12:00-24:00, near the S-Bahn tracks at Bleibtreustrasse 48A, tel. 030/881-7040).

Genazvale ("Best Friends") serves traditional fare from the

Republic of Georgia, and is popular with Berlin's immigrant Russian community. Sample some Georgian wines—virtually impossible to find in North America—and try their warm *catchapuri* (cheese bread) or a delicious plate of *chinkali* (cheese dumplings). The best way to enjoy Georgian food is to order several appetizers and split an entrée, which is usually grilled meat or stew (€7-16 entrées, daily 15:00-23:00, live music and dancing on Georgian holidays, on the corner of Kantstrasse at Windscheidstrasse 14, tel. 030/4508-6026).

Technical University Mensa, a student cafeteria with impossibly cheap prices, puts you in a modern university scene with fine food and good indoor or streetside seating (€3-5 meals, Mon-Fri 11:00-15:30, closed Sat-Sun, general public entirely welcome but pays the highest of the three prices, cheap coffee bar downstairs with Internet access, just north of Uhlandstrasse at Hardenbergstrasse 34).

Supermarket: The neighborhood grocery store is **Ullrich** (Mon-Sat 9:00-22:00, Sun 11:00-22:00, Kantstrasse 7, under the tracks near Bahnhof Zoo). There's plenty of fast food near Bahnhof Zoo and on Ku'damm.

Near Bahnhof Zoo

Schleusenkrug beer garden is hidden in the park between the Bahnhof Zoo and Tiergarten stations. Choose from an ever-changing self-service menu of huge salads, pasta, and some German dishes. English breakfast is served until 15:00 (€7-12 plates, €3-5 grill snacks, daily 10:00-24:00, Müller-Breslau-Strasse; standing in front of Bahnhof Zoo, turn left and follow the path into the park between the zoo and train tracks; tel. 030/313-9909).

Self-Service Cafeterias: The top floor of the famous department store, **KaDeWe,** holds the Winter Garden Buffet view cafeteria, and its sixth-floor deli/food department is a picnicker's nirvana. Its arterials are clogged with more than 1,000 kinds of sausage and 1,500 types of cheese (Mon-Thu 10:00-20:00, Fri 10:00-21:00, Sat 9:30-20:00, closed Sun, U-Bahn: Wittenbergplatz). **Wertheim** department store, a half-block from Kaiser Wilhelm Memorial Church, has cheap food counters in the basement and a city view from its self-service cafeteria, Le Buffet, located up six banks of escalators (Mon-Sat 9:30-20:00, closed Sun, U-Bahn: Kurfürstendamm). **Marche,** a chain that's popped up in big cities all over Germany, is another inexpensive self-service cafeteria within a half-block of Kaiser Wilhelm Memorial Church (Mon-Thu 8:00-22:00, Fri-Sat 8:00-24:00, Sun 10:00-22:00, plenty of salads, fruit, made-to-order omelets, Ku'damm 14, tel. 030/882-7578).

Berlin Connections

Trains

Berlin used to have several major train stations. But now that the Hauptbahnhof has emerged as the single, massive central station, all the others have wilted into glorified subway stations. Virtually all long-distance trains pass through the Hauptbahnhof—ignore the other stations.

EurAide is an agent of the German Railway that sells reservations for high-speed and overnight trains, with staff that can answer your travel questions in English (located in the Hauptbahnhof; see "Arrival in Berlin," on page 637).

From Berlin by Train to: Frankfurt (hourly, 4 hours), **Bacharach** (hourly, 6.5-7.5 hours, 1-3 changes), **Rothenburg** (hourly, 5-6 hours, often via Göttingen and Würzburg), **Nürnberg** (hourly, 4.5 hours), **Munich** (1-2/hour, 6-6.75 hours, every 2 hours direct, otherwise change in Göttingen), **Amsterdam** (6/day direct to Amsterdam Zuid, 6.5 hours), **London** (5/day, 10-11.5 hours, 2 changes—but you're better off flying cheap on easyJet or Air Berlin, even if you have a railpass), **Paris** (5/day, 8-9 hours, 1 change in Köln—via Belgium—or in Mannheim, 1 direct 12-hour night train), **Prague** (6/day, 4.5-5 hours, no overnight trains), **Vienna** (8/day, most with 1 change, 9.5 hours, some via Czech Republic; the Berlin-Vienna via Passau train avoids Czech Republic—nightly at 20:55—as do connections with a change in Nürnberg or Munich). It's wise but not required to reserve in advance for trains to or from Amsterdam or Prague. Train info: toll tel. 0180-599-6633 (€0.14/minute), www.bahn.de. Before buying a ticket for any long train ride from Berlin (over 7 hours), consider taking a cheap flight instead (buy it well in advance to get a super fare).

There are **night trains** from Berlin to these cities: Munich, Frankfurt, Köln, Paris, Vienna, Warsaw, Malmö (Sweden, near Copenhagen), Basel, and Zürich. There are no night trains from Berlin to anywhere in Italy or Spain. A *Liegeplatz,* or *couchette* berth (€13-36), is a great deal; inquire at EurAide at the Hauptbahnhof for details. Beds generally cost the same whether you have a first- or second-class ticket or railpass. Trains are often full, so reserve your *couchette* a few days in advance from any travel agency or major train station in Europe.

Berlin's Airports

Berlin is in the process of whittling down to a single airport. A new airport, called Willy Brandt Berlin-Brandenburg International, is slated to open in 2012 and will handle all air traffic for the area.

Until then, **Tegel Airport** handles most flights from the United States and Western Europe (4 miles from center, no subway trains, catch the faster bus #X9 to Bahnhof Zoo, or bus #109 to Ku'damm and Bahnhof Zoo for €2.10; bus #TXL goes between Tegel Airport, the Hauptbahnhof, and Alexanderplatz in eastern Berlin; taxi from Tegel Airport costs €15 to Bahnhof Zoo, €25 to Alexanderplatz; taxis from Tegel levy a €0.50 surcharge).

Flights from the east and discount airlines usually arrive at **Schönefeld Airport** (12.5 miles from center). It's just a three-minute walk to the train station, where you catch a regional express train into the city (ignore the S-Bahn, as there are no direct S-Bahn trains to the city center). The Airport Express RE and RB trains go direct to Ostbahnhof, Alexanderplatz, Friedrichstrasse, Hauptbahnhof, and Bahnhof Zoo (€2.60, every 30 minutes, take trains in the direction of Nauen or Dessau, railpass valid). A taxi to the city center costs about €35.

The central toll telephone number for both airports is 01805-000-186. For British Air, toll tel. 01805-266-522; Delta, toll tel. 01803-337-880; SAS, toll tel. 01805-117-002; Lufthansa, toll tel. 01803-803-803.

Berlin, the Discount Airline Hub: Berlin's Schönefeld Airport is now the continental European hub for discount airlines such as easyJet (with lots of flights to Spain, Italy, Eastern Europe, the Baltics, and more—book long in advance to get the incredible €30-and-less fares, www.easyjet.com). Ryanair (www.ryanair.com) and German Wings (www.germanwings.com) are also making the London-Berlin trip (and other routes) dirt-cheap, so consider this option before booking an overnight train. Consequently, British visitors to the city are now outnumbered only by Americans. But not every budget line uses Schönefeld; Air Berlin flies out of Tegel (www.airberlin.com).

BERLIN

GREAT BRITAIN

LONDON

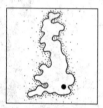

London is more than 600 square miles of urban jungle. With eight million people, it's a world in itself and a barrage on all the senses. On my first visit, I felt extremely small.

London is more than its museums and landmarks. It's a living, breathing, thriving organism...a coral reef of humanity. The city has changed dramatically in recent years, and many visitors are surprised to find how "un-English" it is. ESL (English as a second language) seems like the city's first language, as white people are now a minority in major parts of the city that once symbolized white imperialism. Arabs have nearly bought out the area north of Hyde Park. Chinese takeouts outnumber fish-and-chips shops. Eastern Europeans pull pints in British pubs. Many hotels are run by people with foreign accents (who hire English chambermaids), while outlying suburbs are home to huge communities of Indians and Pakistanis. London is a city of eight million separate dreams, inhabiting a place that tolerates and encourages them. With the English Channel Tunnel and discount airlines making travel between Britain and the Continent easier than ever, London is learning—sometimes fitfully—to live as a microcosm of its formerly vast empire. The city, which has long attracted tourists, seems perpetually at your service, with an impressive slate of sights, entertainment, and eateries, linked by a great transit system. In anticipation of the 2012 Olympic Games and a greater onslaught of tourists than usual, London is busy spiffing up the place, especially its rapidly developing Olympic Park in East London.

With just a few days here, you'll get no more than a quick splash in this teeming human tidal pool. But with a good orientation, you'll find London manageable and fun. You'll get a sampling of the city's top sights, history, and cultural entertainment, and a good look at its ever-changing human face.

Blow through the city on the open deck of a double-decker orientation tour bus, and take a pinch-me-I'm-in-London walk through the West End. Ogle the crown jewels at the Tower of London, hear the chimes of Big Ben, and see the Houses of Parliament in action. Cruise the Thames River, and take a spin on the London Eye. Hobnob with the tombstones in Westminster Abbey, and visit with Leonardo, Botticelli, and Rembrandt in the National Gallery. Enjoy Shakespeare in a replica of the Globe Theatre and marvel at a glitzy, fun musical at a modern-day theater. Whisper across the dome of St. Paul's Cathedral, then rummage through our civilization's attic at the British Museum. And sip your tea with pinky raised and clotted cream dribbling down your scone.

Planning Your Time

The sights of London alone could easily fill a trip to Britain. It's worth at least three busy days. You won't be able to see everything, so don't try. You'll keep coming back to London. After dozens of visits myself, I still enjoy a healthy list of excuses to return. Especially if you hope to enjoy a play or concert, a night or two of jet lag is bad news.

Here's a suggested three-day schedule:

Day 1

9:00 Tower of London (crown jewels first, then Beefeater tour, then White Tower).

13:00 Grab a picnic, catch a boat at Tower Pier, and relax with lunch on the Thames while cruising to Westminster Pier.

14:30 Tour Westminster Abbey, and consider their evensong service (at 15:00 Sat-Sun, at 17:00 Mon-Fri).

17:00 (or after evensong) Follow my self-guided Westminster Walk. When you're finished, if it's a Monday or Tuesday, you could return to the Houses of Parliament and pop in to see the House of Commons in action (until 22:30).

Day 2

8:30 Take a double-decker hop-on, hop-off London sightseeing bus tour (from Green Park or Victoria) and hop off for the Changing of the Guard.

11:00 Buckingham Palace (guards change most days May-July at 11:30, alternate days Aug-April—confirm).

12:00 Walk through St. James's Park to enjoy London's

Rick Steves' Free Audio Tours

I've produced free, self-guided audio versions of my tours of the major sights in London (download them via www.rick steves.com/audioeurope, iTunes, or the Rick Steves Audio Europe smartphone app). These user-friendly, easy-to-follow, fun, and enlightening audio tours are available for the British Museum, the British Library, St. Paul's Cathedral, the Westminster neighborhood, and The City. If you don't mind me in your ear, these audio tours are hard to beat: Nobody will stand you up, the quality is reliable, you can take the tour exactly when you like, and they're free.

	delightful park scene.
13:00	Covent Garden for lunch, shopping, and people-watching.
14:30	Tour the British Museum.
Evening	Have a pub dinner before a play, concert, or evening walking tour.

Day 3

Choose among these remaining London highlights: National Gallery, British Library, Cabinet War Rooms and Churchill Museum, Imperial War Museum, the two Tates (Tate Modern on the south bank for modern art, Tate Britain on the north bank for British art), St. Paul's Cathedral, or the Museum of London; take a spin on the London Eye or a cruise to Kew or Greenwich; enjoy a Shakespearean play at Shakespeare's Globe; do some serious shopping at one of London's elegant department stores or open-air markets; or take another historic walking tour.

Orientation to London

(area code: 020)

To grasp London more comfortably, see it as the old town in the city center without the modern, congested sprawl. (Even at that, it's still huge.)

The Thames River (pronounced "tems") runs roughly west to east through the city, with most of the visitor's sights on the north bank. Mentally, maybe even physically, with scissors, trim down your map to include only the area between the Tower of London (to the east), Hyde Park (west), Regent's Park (north), and the South Bank (south). This is roughly the area bordered by the Tube's Circle Line. This four-mile stretch between the Tower and Hyde Park (about a 1.5-hour walk) looks like a milk bottle on its

London's Neighborhoods

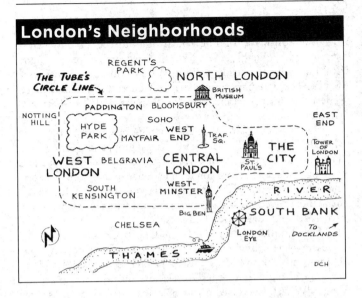

side (see map above), and holds 80 percent of the sights mentioned in this chapter.

Sprawling London becomes much more manageable if you think of it as a collection of neighborhoods:

Central London: This area contains Westminster and what Londoners call the West End. The **Westminster** district includes Big Ben, Parliament, Westminster Abbey, and Buckingham Palace—the grand government buildings from which Britain is ruled. Trafalgar Square, London's gathering place, has many major museums. The **West End** is the center of London's cultural life, with bustling squares: Piccadilly Circus and Leicester Square (pronounced "LESS-ter") host cinemas, tourist traps, and nighttime glitz. Soho and Covent Garden are thriving people-zones with theaters, restaurants, pubs, and boutiques. And Regent and Oxford streets are the city's main shopping zones.

North London: Neighborhoods in this part of town—including Bloomsbury, Fitzrovia, and Marylebone—contain such major sights as the British Museum and the overhyped Madame Tussauds Waxworks. Nearby, along busy Euston Road, is the British Library plus a trio of train stations (one of them, St. Pancras International Station, is linked to Paris and Brussels by the Eurostar "Chunnel" train).

The City: Today's modern financial district, called simply "The City," was a walled town in Roman times. Gleaming skyscrapers are interspersed with historical landmarks such as St. Paul's Cathedral, legal sights (Old Bailey), and the Museum of London. The Tower of London and Tower Bridge lie at The City's eastern border.

The South Bank: The South Bank of the Thames River offers major sights (Tate Modern, Shakespeare's Globe, London Eye) linked by a riverside walkway. Within this area, **Southwark** (SUTH-uck) stretches from the Tate Modern to London Bridge. Pedestrian bridges connect the South Bank with The City and Trafalgar Square.

West London: This huge area contains neighborhoods such as Mayfair, Belgravia, Chelsea, South Kensington, and Notting Hill. It's home to London's wealthy, and has many trendy shops and enticing restaurants. Here you'll find a range of museums (Victoria and Albert Museum, Tate Britain, and more), my top hotel recommendations, lively Victoria Station, and the vast green expanses of Hyde Park and Kensington Gardens.

East London: Just east of The City is the **East End**—the increasingly gentrified former stomping ground of Cockney ragamuffins and Jack the Ripper. Even farther to the east, London's version of Manhattan—the **Docklands**—has sprung up around Canary Wharf. Energized by big businesses, the Docklands show you London at its most modern. Historic **Greenwich** lies just south of the Docklands/Canary Wharf area, across the Thames. And the **2012 Olympic Park** is being built in the once-dreary Stratford district, a short train ride to the north.

Tourist Information

The **Britain and London Visitors Centre,** just a block off Piccadilly Circus, is the best tourist information service in town (June-Sept Mon-Fri 9:30-18:30, Sat 9:00-17:00, Sun 10:00-16:00; Oct-May Mon-Fri 9:30-18:00, Sat-Sun 10:00-16:00; 1 Lower Regent Street—but may move in 2012, tel. 020/8846-9000, toll tel. 0870-156-6366, www.visitbritain.com, www.visitlondon.com). If you visit only one TI, make it this one. Unfortunately, London's many "Tourist Information Centres" (which represent themselves as TIs at major train and bus stations and airports) are now simply businesses, selling advertising space to companies with fliers to distribute.

The Britain and London Visitors Centre has many different departments. It's a great one-stop shopping place to get tourist information, buy advance tickets to big sights, buy sightseeing passes, arrange coach tours, buy theater tickets, plan travel beyond London, and even book trains to the Continent. Bring your itinerary and a checklist of questions.

Entering the lobby, check out the various departments and get in the right line for what you need. At the Tourist Information desk handling both London and Britain inquiries, pick up various free publications: the *London Planner* (a free monthly that lists all

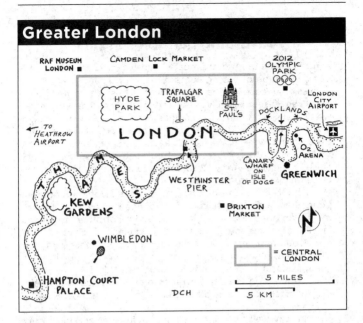

Greater London

RAF MUSEUM
LONDON ■

CAMDEN LOCK MARKET ■

2012 OLYMPIC PARK

HYDE PARK

TRAFALGAR SQUARE

ST. PAUL'S

DOCKLANDS

LONDON CITY AIRPORT

← TO HEATHROW AIRPORT

L O N D O N

O₂ ARENA

CANARY WHARF ON ISLE OF DOGS

GREENWICH

WESTMINSTER PIER

T H A M E S

KEW GARDENS

● WIMBLEDON

■ BRIXTON MARKET

N

■ HAMPTON COURT PALACE

DCH

= CENTRAL LONDON

5 MILES

5 KM

the sights, events, and hours), walking tours info, a theater guide,
London bus map, and the *Guide to River Thames Boat Services*. The
staff sells a good £1 map and all the various sightseeing passes,
including the London Pass (described below).

The Entertainment and Tickets desk sells tickets to plays
(steep 20 percent booking fee). The Hotels and Travel desk sells
long-distance bus tickets and passes, train tickets (convenient for
reservations), and Fast Track tickets to some of London's attractions. These tickets, which allow you to skip the queue at the sights
at no extra cost, are worthwhile for places that can have long ticket
lines, such as the Tower of London, the London Eye, and Madame
Tussauds Waxworks. (If you're going to the Waxworks, buy tickets
here, since—at £22.50—they're cheaper than at the sight itself.)

The Visitors Centre reserves hotel rooms, but you can avoid
their £5 booking fee by contacting hotels on your own. A Rail
Europe section books the Eurostar and train travel or train passes
on the Continent.

Upstairs, you'll find more brochures, Internet access (£1/20
minutes), and comfy chairs where you can read or get organized.

The **London Pass** is pricey, and only worth considering for
the most rabid sightseer (£40/1 day, £55/2 days, £63/3 days, £90/6
days; days are calendar days rather than 24-hour periods; includes
160-page guidebook, toll tel. 0870-242-9988, www.londonpass
.com). It lets you skip the lines and covers plenty of sights that
cost £11-17, including the Tower of London, St. Paul's Cathedral,

Affording London's Sights

London is one of Europe's most expensive cities, with the dubious distinction of having some of the world's most expensive admission prices. Fortunately, many of its best sights are free.

Free Museums: Many of the city's biggest and best museums won't cost you a dime. Free sights include the British Museum, British Library, National Gallery, National Portrait Gallery, Tate Britain, Tate Modern, Wallace Collection, Imperial War Museum, Victoria and Albert Museum, Natural History Museum, Science Museum, National Army Museum, Sir John Soane's Museum, the Museum of London, and the Geffrye.

About half of these museums request a donation of a few pounds, but whether you contribute or not is up to you. If I spend money for an audioguide, I feel fine about not otherwise donating. If that makes you uncomfortable, donate.

Free Churches: Smaller churches let worshippers (and tourists) in free, although they may ask for a donation. The big sightseeing churches—Westminster Abbey and St. Paul's—charge steep admission fees, but offer free evensong services daily. Westminster Abbey also offers free organ recitals most Sundays at 17:45.

Other Freebies: There are plenty of free performances, such as lunch concerts at St. Martin-in-the-Fields (see page 741) and summertime movies at The Scoop amphitheater near City Hall (Tube: London Bridge, schedule at www.morelondon.com—click on "The Scoop"). For other freebies, check out www.freelondon listings.co.uk. There's no charge to enjoy the pageantry of the Changing of the Guard, rants at Speaker's Corner in Hyde Park, displays at Harrods, the people-watching scene at Covent Garden, and the colorful streets of the East End. It's free to view the legal action at the Old Bailey and the legislature at work in the Houses of Parliament. And you can get into a bit of the Tower of London by attending Sunday services in the Tower's chapel (chapel access only).

Sightseeing Deals: If you buy a paper One-Day Travelcard or rail ticket at a National Rail station (such as Paddington or Victoria), you may be eligible for two-for-one discounts at many popular sights, such as the London Eye, Tower of London, Tate Modern, and Madame Tussauds Waxworks. Get details and print vouchers at www.daysoutguide.co.uk, or look for brochures with coupons at major train stations.

Good-Value Tours: The £5-8 city walking tours with professional guides are one of the best deals going. (Note that the guides for the "free" walking tours are unpaid and expect tips—

I'd pay for a professionally-guided tour instead.) Hop-on, hop-off big-bus tours (£22-26), while expensive, provide a great overview, and include free boat tours as well as city walks. A one-hour Thames ride to Greenwich costs £9.50 one-way, but most boats come with an entertaining commentary. A three-hour bicycle tour is about £16-19.

Pricey...But Worth It? Big-ticket sights worth their hefty admission fees are Kew Gardens (£13.50), Shakespeare's Globe (£10.50), and the Cabinet War Rooms, with its fine Churchill Museum (£14.95).

The London Eye has become a London must-see—though if you're on a tight budget, it's difficult to justify its very high cost (£18). The Queen charges big time to open her palace to the public: Buckingham Palace (£16.50, Aug-Sept only) and her art gallery and carriage museum (adjacent to the palace, £8.75 and £7.75, £15 for both) are expensive but interesting. Madame Tussauds Waxworks is pricey but still fun and popular (£28, £22.50 if purchased at TI, drops to £14 after 17:00 if booked online). The Vinopolis wine museum provides a way to get a buzz and call it museum-going (from £20, entry includes tastes of wine).

Many smaller museums cost only around £5. My favorites include the Courtauld Gallery (free on Mon until 14:00) and the Wellington Museum at Apsley House (£6, www.english-heritage .org.uk).

Not Worth It: The London Dungeon, at £22.50, is gimmicky, overpriced, and a terrible value...despite the long line at the door.

Theater: Compared with Broadway's prices, London theater is a bargain. Seek out the freestanding "tkts" booth at Leicester Square to get discounts from 25 to 50 percent on good seats (though not necessarily for the hottest shows; see page 776). If you're willing to settle for the cheapest seats (possibly with obstructed views), ask the theater's box office for their best deal (even the hottest shows generally have some £10-20 tickets). A £5 "groundling" ticket for a play at Shakespeare's Globe is the best theater deal in town (see page 776). Tickets to the Open Air Theatre at north London's Regent's Park start at £12 (see page 777).

London doesn't come cheap. But with its many free museums and affordable plays, this cosmopolitan, cultured city offers days of sightseeing thrills without requiring you to pinch your pennies (or your pounds).

Shakespeare's Globe, Cabinet War Rooms, Windsor Castle, and Kew Gardens. If you saw just these sights without the pass, you'd pay about £90, the cost of a six-day London Pass. Busy sightseers can make a short pass work for a longer trip by seeing only covered sights during the validity of the pass, and touring London's many free sights (listed on page 712) before or after the pass' validity period. Note that the pass doesn't include Westminster Abbey, the London Eye, or Madame Tussauds Waxworks. Think through your sightseeing plans carefully, and do the math before you buy.

Arrival in London

By Train: London has nine major train stations, all connected by the Tube (subway). All have ATMs, and many of the larger stations also have shops, fast food, exchange offices, and luggage storage. From any station, you can ride the Tube or taxi to your hotel. For more info on train travel, see www.nationalrail.co.uk.

By Bus: The main intercity bus station is Victoria Coach Station, one block southwest of Victoria train station (and the Victoria Tube station). For more on bus travel, see www.national express.com.

By Plane: London has five airports. Most tourists arrive at Heathrow or Gatwick airports, although flights from elsewhere in Europe may land at Stansted, Luton, or London City airports. For specifics on getting from London's airports to downtown London, see "London Connections" near the end of this chapter; for hotels near Heathrow and Gatwick, see page 798.

Helpful Hints

Theft Alert: Wear your money belt. The Artful Dodger is alive and well in London. Be on guard, particularly on public transportation and in places crowded with tourists, who, considered naive and rich, are targeted. The Changing of the Guard scene is a favorite for thieves. And more than 7,500 purses are stolen annually at Covent Garden alone.

Pedestrian Safety: Cars drive on the left side of the road—which can be as confusing for foreign pedestrians as for foreign drivers. Before crossing a street, I always look right, look left, then look right again just to be sure. Most crosswalks are even painted with instructions, reminding foreign guests to "Look right" or "Look left."

Medical Problems: Local hospitals have good-quality 24-hour-a-day emergency care centers where any tourist who needs help can drop in and, after a wait, be seen by a doctor. Your hotel has details. St. Thomas' Hospital, immediately across the river from Big Ben, has a fine reputation.

Getting Your Bearings: London is well-signed for visitors. A new initiative called Legible London is erecting thoughtfully designed, pedestrian-focused maps around town. In this sprawling city—where predictable grid-planned streets are relatively rare—it's also smart to buy and use a good map. The *Benson's London Street Map* (£2.75), sold at many newsstands and bookstores, is my favorite for efficient sightseeing.

Festivals: For one week in February and another in September, fashionistas descend on the city for **London Fashion Week** (www.londonfashionweek.co.uk). The famous **Chelsea Flower Show** blossoms in late May (book ahead for this popular event at www.rhs.org.uk/chelsea). During the annual **Trooping the Colour** in June, there are military bands and pageantry, and the Queen's birthday parade (www.trooping-the-colour .co.uk). Tennis fans pack the stands at the **Wimbledon Tennis Championship** on June 25-July 8 in 2012 (www.wimbledon .org), and partygoers head for the **Notting Hill Carnival** in late August.

Winter: London dazzles year-round, so consider visiting in winter, when airfares and hotel rates are generally cheaper and there are fewer tourists. For ideas on what to do, see the "Winter Activities in London" article at www.ricksteves.com/winteracts.

Internet Access: As nearly all hotels offer Internet access and cafés all over town have free Wi-Fi, there are fewer actual Internet cafés. If you need to get online, you'll find Internet cafés near Trafalgar Square (456 Strand), on Oxford Street (at #358, opposite Bond Street Tube station), and near Victoria Station (at 164 Victoria Street).

Travel Bookstores: Located between Covent Garden and Leicester Square, the very good **Stanfords Travel Bookstore** stocks current editions of many of my books (Mon-Fri 9:00-19:30, Thu 9:00-20:00, Sat 10:00-20:00, Sun 12:00-18:00, 12-14 Long Acre, Tube: Leicester Square, tel. 020/7836-1321, www.stanfords.co.uk).

Two impressive **Waterstone's** bookstores have the biggest collection of travel guides in town: on Piccadilly (Mon-Sat 9:00-22:00, Sun 12:00-18:00, Costa Café, 203 Piccadilly, tel. 020/7851-2400) and on Trafalgar Square (Mon-Sat 9:30-21:00, Sun 12:00-18:00, Costa Café on second floor, tel. 020/7839-4411).

Baggage Storage: Train stations have replaced their lockers with more secure baggage storage counters, known locally as "left luggage." Each bag must go through a scanner (just like at the airport), so lines can be slow. Expect long waits in the morning to check in (up to 45 minutes) and in the afternoon to pick up (each item-£8/24 hours, most stations daily 7:00-23:00). You can also store bags at the airports (similar rates and hours, www.excess-baggage.com). If leaving London and returning later, you may be able to leave a box or bag at your hotel for free—assuming you'll be staying there again.

Bike Rental: Barclays Cycle Hire rents bikes from self-service docking stations (most likely won't work with US credit or debit cards, www.tfl.gov.uk).

Getting Around London

To travel smart in a city this size, you must get comfortable with public transportation. London's excellent taxis, buses, and subway (Tube) system make a private car unnecessary.

If you do have a car, stow it—you don't want to drive in London. If you need convincing, here's one more reason: A £10 **congestion charge** is levied on any private car entering the city center during peak hours (Mon-Fri 7:00-18:00, no charge Sat-Sun and holidays, fee payable at gas stations, convenience stores, and self-service machines at public parking lots, or online at www.cclondon.com). Traffic cameras photograph and identify every vehicle that enters the fee zone; if you get spotted and don't pay up by midnight that day (or pay £12 until midnight of the following day), you'll get socked with at least a £60 penalty. The system has been effective in cutting down traffic jam delays and bolstering London's public transit. The revenue that's raised subsidizes the buses, which are now cheaper, more frequent, and even more user-friendly than before. Today, the vast majority of vehicles in the city center are buses, taxis, and service trucks. (Drivers—or American city planners—can find more information on the congestion charge at www.cclondon.com.)

Public-Transit Passes

London has the most expensive public transit in the world—save money on your Tube and bus rides using a multi-ride pass. You have three options: pay double by buying individual tickets as you go; buy a £5 Oyster card and top it up as needed to travel like a local for about £1-2 per ride; or get a Travelcard for unlimited travel on one or seven days.

The transit system has six zones. Since almost all of my recommended accommodations, restaurants, and sights are within Zones 1 and 2, those are the prices I've listed here—but you'll pay more to go farther afield. Specific fares and other details change constantly; for a complete and updated list of prices, check www.tfl.gov.uk.

Individual Transit Tickets

These days in London, individual paper tickets are dinosaurs; there's no point buying one unless you're literally taking just one ride your entire time in the city. Because individual fares (£4 per Tube ride, £2 per bus ride) are about double the cost of using a pay-as-you-go Oyster card (explained below), in just two or three rides you'll recoup the £5 added deposit for the Oyster. If you do buy a single ticket, avoid ticket-window lines in Tube stations by using the coin-op machines; practice on the punchboard to see how the system works (hit "Adult Single" and your destination). These tickets are valid only on the day of purchase.

Oyster Cards

A pay-as-you-go Oyster card (a plastic card embedded with a computer chip) is the standard, smart way to economically ride the Tube, buses, Docklands Light Railway (DLR), and Overground. On each type of transport, you simply lay the card flat against the yellow card reader at the turnstile or entrance, it flashes green, and the fare is automatically deducted. (You'll also touch your card again to exit the Tube and DLR turnstiles, but not to exit buses.)

With an Oyster card, rides cost about half the price of individual paper tickets (£1.90 or £2.50 per Tube ride—depending on time of day, £1.20 per bus ride). You buy the card itself at any Tube station ticket window for a £5 deposit, then load it up with as much credit as you want. (For extra peace of mind, ask about registering your card against theft or loss.) When your balance gets low, you simply add credit—or "top up"—at a ticket window or machine. A price cap on the pay-as-you-go Oyster card guarantees you'll never pay more than the One-Day Travelcard price within a 24-hour period.

You can see how much credit remains on your card or review the trips you've taken so far by swiping it at any automatic ticket machine. Oyster card balances never expire (though they need reactivating at a ticket window every two years), so you can use the card whenever you're in London, or lend it to someone else. If you're done with the card (and don't mind a short wait), you can turn it in to reclaim your £5 deposit at any ticket window.

Travelcards

Like the Oyster card, Travelcards are valid on the Tube, buses, Docklands Light Railway (DLR), and Overground. The difference is that Travelcards let you ride as many times as you want within a one- or seven-day period for one fixed price.

Before you buy a card, estimate where you'll be going; there's a card for Zones 1 and 2, and another for Zones 1-6 (which includes Heathrow Airport). If Heathrow is the only ride you're taking outside Zones 1-2 (which is likely), you can pay a small supplement to make the Zones 1-2 Travelcard stretch to cover that one ride.

The **One-Day Travelcard** gives you unlimited travel for a day

(Zones 1-2: £8, off-peak version £6.60; Zones 1-6: £15, off-peak version £8; cheaper off-peak versions are good for travel after 9:30 on weekdays and anytime on weekends). This Travelcard works like a traditional paper ticket: You buy it at any Tube station ticket window or machine, then feed it into a turnstile (and retrieve it) to enter and exit the Tube. On a bus, just show it to the driver when you get on.

The **Seven-Day Travelcard** is a great option if you're staying four or more days and plan to use the buses and Tube a lot. It's actually issued on a plastic Oyster card, but gives you unlimited travel anytime, anywhere in Zones 1 and 2 for a week (£27.60 plus the refundable £5 deposit for the Oyster card). As with an Oyster card, you'll touch it to the yellow pad when entering or exiting a Tube turnstile, or when boarding a bus.

Discounts

Groups: A gang of 10 or more adults can travel all day on the Tube for £4 each (but not on buses). Kids ages 11-17 pay £1.50 when part of a group of 10.

Families: A paying adult can take up to four kids (aged 10 and under) for free on the Tube, Docklands Light Railway (DLR), and Overground all day, every day (kids 10 and under are always free on buses). At the Tube station, use the manual gate, rather than the turnstiles, to be waved in. Other child and student discounts are explained at www.tfl.gov.uk/tickets.

River Cruises: A Travelcard gives you a 33 percent discount on most Thames cruises (see "Cruises" on page 728). If you pay for Thames Clippers (including the Tate-to-Tate museum boat) with your pay-as-you go Oyster card, you'll get a 10 percent discount.

Sightseeing Deal: Buy a paper One-Day Travelcard or rail ticket at a National Rail station, and you may qualify for two-for-one discounts at many popular sights (look for brochures with coupons at major train stations, or print vouchers at www.daysout guide.co.uk).

Passes: The Bottom Line

Struggling to choose which pass works best for your trip? First of all, skip the individual tickets. On a short visit (three days or fewer), if you think you'll be zipping around a lot, consider a One-Day Travelcard for each day you're here (or at least for your busiest days); if you'll be taking fewer, more focused rides, get an Oyster card and pay as you go. If you're in London four days or longer, the Seven-Day Travelcard will likely pay for itself.

By Tube

London's subway system (called the Tube or Underground—but

never "subway," which refers to a pedestrian underpass) is one of this planet's great people-movers and often the fastest long-distance transport in town (runs Mon-Sat about 5:00-24:00, Sun about 7:00-23:00). While technically not part of the Tube, two other commuter rail lines are tied into the network: The Docklands Light Railway (called DLR, runs to the Docklands, 2012 Olympics site, and Greenwich) and the Overground.

Get your bearings by studying a map of the system (free at any station). Each line has a name (such as Circle, Northern, or Bakerloo) and two directions (indicated by the end-of-the-line stops). Find the line that will take you to your destination, and figure out roughly what direction (north, south, east, or west) you'll need to go to get there.

You can use an Oyster card, Travelcard, or individual tickets (all explained earlier) to pay for your journey. At the Tube station, touch your Oyster card flat against the turnstile's yellow card reader, both when you enter and exit the station. If you have a regular paper ticket or a One-Day Travelcard, feed it into the turnstile, reclaim it, and hang on to it—you'll need it later.

Find your train by following signs to your line and the (general) direction it's headed (such as Central Line: east). Since some tracks are shared by several lines, double-check before boarding a train: First, make sure your destination is one of the stops listed on the sign at the platform. Also, check the electronic signboards that announce which train is next, and make sure the destination (the end-of-the-line stop) is the direction you want. Some trains, particularly on the Circle and District lines, split off for other directions, but each train has its final destination marked above its windshield.

Trains run roughly every 3-10 minutes. If one train is absolutely packed and you notice another to the same destination is coming in three minutes, wait to avoid the sardine routine. Rush hours (8:00-10:00 and 16:00-19:00) can be packed and sweaty. Bring something to do to make your waiting time productive. If you get confused, ask for advice from a local, a blue-vested staff person, or at the information window located before the turnstile entry.

You can't leave the system without touching your Oyster card to an electronic reader, or feeding your ticket or One-Day Travelcard into the turnstile. (If you have a single-trip paper ticket, the turnstile will eat your now-expired ticket; if it's a One-Day Travelcard, it will spit out your still-valid card.) Save walking time by choosing the best street exit—check the maps on the walls or ask any station personnel.

The system can be fraught with construction delays and breakdowns (the Circle Line is notorious for problems). This will

Handy Bus Routes

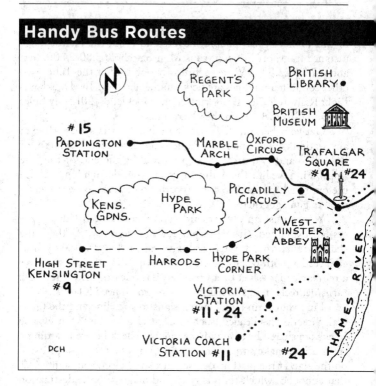

be especially noticeable as London gears up for the 2012 Olympics. Most construction is scheduled for weekends. Closures are known and publicized in advance (online at www.tfl.gov.uk and with posters in the Tube). Pay attention to signs and announcements explaining necessary detours. Closed Tube lines are often replaced by temporary bus service, but it can be faster to figure out alternate routes on the Tube; since the lines cross each other constantly, there are several ways to make any journey. For help, check out the "Journey Planner" at www.tfl.gov.uk.

Tube Etiquette

- When your train arrives, stand off to the side and let riders exit the train before you try to board.
- Avoid using the hinged seats near the doors of some trains when the car is jammed; they take up valuable standing space.
- If you're blocking the door when the train stops, step out of the car and off to the side, let others off, then get back on.
- Talk softly in the cars. Listen to how quietly Londoners communicate and follow their lead.
- On escalators, stand on the right and pass on the left. But note

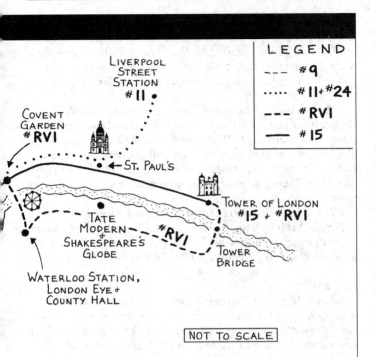

that in some passageways or stairways, you might be directed to walk on the left (the direction Brits go behind the wheel).

- When leaving a station, it's polite to hold the door for the person behind you.
- Discreet eating and drinking are fine (nothing smelly); drinking alcohol and smoking are not.

By Bus

If you figure out the bus system, you'll easily conquer sprawling London. Pick up a free bus map at a TI, transport office, or some major museums; it will list the bus routes best for sightseeing.

Buses are covered by Travelcards and Oyster cards (see page 717). Or you can buy individual tickets from a machine at bus stops (no change given). Any bus ride in downtown London costs £2 for those paying cash, or £1.20 if using an Oyster card (with a cap of £3.90 maximum per day). If you're staying longer, consider the £16.60 Seven-Day bus pass.

The first step in mastering London's bus system is learning how to decipher the bus stop signs. In the first column, find your destination on the list—e.g., Paddington. In the next column, find a bus that goes there—the #23. The final column has a letter within a circle (e.g., "M") that tells you exactly which bus stop you need to stand at to catch your bus. (You'll find the same letter marked on a neighborhood map nearby.) Make your way to that stop—you'll know it's yours because it will have the same letter on its pole—and wait for the bus with your number on it to arrive. Hop on, and you're good to go.

As you board, touch your Oyster card to the electronic card reader, or, if you have a paper ticket or a One-Day Travelcard, show it to the driver. On "Heritage Routes" #9 and #15 (which use older double-decker buses), you may still pay a conductor; take a seat, and he or she will come around to collect your fare or verify your pass. There's no need to tap your card or show your ticket when you hop off.

If you have an Oyster card or Travelcard, save your feet and get in the habit of hopping buses for quick little straight shots, even just to get to a Tube stop. During bump-and-grind rush hours (8:00-10:00 and 16:00-19:00), you'll usually go faster by Tube.

By Taxi

London is the best taxi town in Europe. Big, black, carefully regulated cabs are everywhere. (While historically known as "black cabs," some of London's official taxis are now covered with wildly colored ads.) Some cabs are switching to biofuels—a good use for frying oil used for all those fish-and-chips.

I've never met a crabby cabbie in London. They love to talk, and they know every nook and cranny in town. I ride in a taxi each day just to get my London questions answered (drivers must pass a rigorous test on "The Knowledge" of London geography to earn their license).

If a cab's top light is on, just wave it down. Drivers flash lights when they see you wave. They have a tight turning radius (on new cabs, the back tires actually pivot), so you can hail cabs going in either direction. If waving doesn't work, ask someone where you can find a taxi stand. Telephoning a cab will get you one in a few minutes, but costs a little more (toll tel. 0871-871-8710; £2 surcharge, plus extra fee to book ahead by credit card).

Rides start at £2.20. The regular tariff #1 covers most of the day (Mon-Fri 6:00-20:00), tariff #2 is during "unsociable hours" (Mon-Fri 20:00-22:00 and Sat-Sun 6:00-22:00), and tariff #3 is at night (nightly 22:00-6:00) and on holidays. Rates go up about 15-20 percent with each higher tariff. All extra charges are explained in writing on the cab wall. Tip a cabbie by rounding up (maximum 10 percent).

Connecting downtown sights is quick and easy, and will cost you about £6-8 (for example, St. Paul's to the Tower of London). For a short ride, three adults in a cab generally travel at close to

Tube prices—and groups of four or five adults should taxi everywhere. All cabs can carry five passengers, and some take six, for the same cost as a single traveler.

Don't worry about meter cheating. Licensed British cab meters come with a sealed computer chip and clock that ensures you'll get the correct tariff. The only way a cabbie can cheat you is by taking a needlessly long route. Another pitfall is taking a cab when traffic is bad to a destination efficiently served by the Tube. On one trip to London, I hopped in a taxi at South Kensington for Waterloo Station and hit bad traffic. Rather than spending 20 minutes and £2 on the Tube, I spent 40 minutes and £16 in a taxi.

If you overdrink and ride in a taxi, be warned: Taxis charge £40 for "soiling" (a.k.a., pub puke). If you forget this book in a taxi, call the Lost Property office and hope for the best (toll tel. 0845-330-9882).

Tours in London

▲▲▲Hop-on, Hop-off Double-Decker Bus Tours

Two competitive companies (Original and Big Bus) offer essentially the same two tours of the city's sightseeing highlights, with nearly 30 stops on each route. Big Bus tours are a little more expensive (£26), while Original tours are cheaper (£22 with this book) and nearly as good.

These 2-3-hour, once-over-lightly bus tours drive by all the famous sights, providing a stress-free way to get your bearings and see the biggies. They stop at a core group of sights regardless of which overview tour you're on: Piccadilly Circus, Trafalgar Square, Big Ben, St. Paul's, the Tower of London, Marble Arch, Victoria Station, and elsewhere. With a good guide and nice weather, I'd sit back and enjoy the entire tour. (If you don't like your guide, you can hop off and try your luck with the next departure.)

Each company offers at least one route with live (English-only) guides, and a second (sometimes slightly different route) comes with recorded, dial-a-language narration. In addition to the overview tours, both Original and Big Bus include the Thames River boat trip by City Cruises (similar to the £13 "River Red Rover" ticket explained on page 729) and three 1.5-hour walking tours.

Pick up a map from any flier rack or from one of the countless salespeople, and study the complex system. Sunday morning—when the traffic is light and many museums are closed—is a fine time for a tour. Unless you're using the bus tour mainly for hop-on, hop-off transportation, consider saving time and money by taking a night tour (described later).

Buses run about every 10-15 minutes in summer, every 20 minutes in winter, and operate daily. They start at about 8:30 and run until early evening in summer, or until late afternoon in winter. The last full loop usually leaves Victoria Station about 17:00 (confirm by checking the schedule or asking the driver).

You can buy tickets from drivers or from staff at street kiosks (credit cards accepted at kiosks at major stops such as Victoria, ticket good for 24 hours).

Original London Sightseeing Bus Tour—There are two versions of their basic highlights loop: **The Original Tour** (live guide, marked with a yellow triangle on the front of the bus) and the **City Sightseeing Tour** (essentially the same route but with recorded narration, a kids' soundtrack option, and a stop at Madame Tussauds; bus marked with a red triangle). Other routes include the blue-triangle **Museum Tour** (connecting far-flung museums and major shopping stops), and green, black, and purple triangle routes (linking major train stations to the central route). All routes are covered by the same ticket. Keep it simple and just take one of the city highlights tours (£25, discount with this book, limit two discounts per book, they'll rip off the corner of this page; also online deals, info center at 17 Cockspur Street, tel. 020/8877-1722, www.theoriginaltour.com).

Big Bus London Tours—For £26 (up to 30 percent discount if you book low-use times online—requires printer), you get the same basic overview tours: Red buses come with a live guide, while the blue route has a recorded narration and a longer path (one hour longer) around Hyde Park. These pricier Big Bus tours tend to have better, more dynamic guides than the Original tours, and more departures as well—meaning shorter waits for those hopping on and off (daily 8:30-18:00, winter until 16:30, info center at 48 Buckingham Palace Road, tel. 020/7233-9533, www.bigbustours .com).

London by Night Sightseeing Tour—This tour offers a two-hour circuit, but after hours, with no extras (e.g., walks, river cruises), and at a lower price. While the narration can be pretty lame, the views at twilight are grand—though note that it stays light until late on summer nights, and London just doesn't do floodlighting as well as Paris (£16, £11 online, drivers take cash only). From May through late September, there are nightly departures at 19:30 (open top), 20:00 (open top), 20:30 (closed top), and 21:30 (open top) from Victoria Station (Jan-April and late Sept-late Dec departs at 19:30 only with closed-top bus, no tours between Christmas and New Year's). Buses leave from the curb immediately in front of Victoria Station (closest to building at muster point C; or you can board at any stop, such as Paddington Station, Marble Arch, Trafalgar Square, London Eye, or Tower of London; tel.

020/8545-6109, www.london-by-night.net). For a memorable and economical evening, munch a scenic picnic dinner on the top deck. (There are plenty of take-away options within the train stations and near the various stops.)

▲▲Walking Tours

Several times a day, top-notch local guides lead (sometimes big) groups through specific slices of London's past. Look for brochures at TIs or ask at hotels, although the latter usually push higher-priced bus tours. *Time Out,* the weekly entertainment guide (£3 at newsstands), lists some, but not all, scheduled walks. Check with the various tour companies by phone or online to get their full picture.

To take a walking tour, you simply show up at the announced location and pay the guide. Then enjoy two chatty hours of Dickens, Harry Potter, the Plague, Shakespeare, Legal London, the Beatles, Jack the Ripper, or whatever is on the agenda.

The Essential London Walk—Blue Badge Tourist Guides offer a basic two-hour walk for £5, 365 days a year at 10:00 (from the Eros statue on Piccadilly Circus—look for the guide with the Blue Badge umbrella, www.touristguides.org.uk). Tours go rain or shine, and there's no need to pre-book—just show up. This is the best deal going, as you know you'll get a well-trained guide leading you through the historic core of London (from Piccadilly, you walk to Trafalgar Square, Whitehall, Westminster Abbey, the Houses of Parliament, and the Thames, and end at Buckingham Palace—just in time for the last part of the Changing of the Guard).

London Walks—This leading company lists its extensive and creative daily schedule in a beefy, plain *London Walks* brochure. Pick it up at TIs, hotels, or St. Martin-in-the-Fields' Café in the Crypt on Trafalgar Square, or access it on their website. Just perusing their fascinating lineup of tours inspires me to stay longer in London. Their two-hour walks, led by professional guides and actors, cost £8 (cash only, walks offered year-round, private tours for groups-£120, tel. 020/7624-3978 for a live person, tel. 020/7624-9255 for a recording of today's or tomorrow's walks and the Tube station they depart from, www.walks.com).

London Walks also offers "Explorer Days" tours into the countryside, a good option for those with limited time and transportation (£14 plus £10-46 for transportation and any admission costs, cash only: Stonehenge/Salisbury, Oxford/Cotswolds, Cambridge, Bath, and so on). These are economical in part because everyone gets group discounts for transportation and admissions.

Sandemans New London "Free Royal London Tour"—This company employs English-speaking students (rather than licensed guides) who recite three-hour spiels covering the basic London sights. While the fast-moving, youthful tours are light and irreverent, and can be both entertaining and fun, it's misleading to call the tours "free," as tips are expected (the guides are unpaid). With the Essential London Walk (listed earlier) offered daily at a reasonable price by professional Blue Badge guides, taking this "free" tour makes no sense to me (daily at 11:00 and 13:00, meet at Wellington Arch, Tube: Hyde Park Corner, Exit 2). Sandemans also has other guided tours for a charge, including a Pub Crawl (£12, Tue-Sat at 19:30, meet at Belushi's at 9 Russell Street, Tube: Covent Garden, www.newlondon-tours.com).

Beatles Walks—Fans of the still-Fab Four can take one of three Beatles walks (London Walks, listed earlier, has two that run 5 days/week; Big Bus, also listed earlier, includes a daily walk with their bus tour).

Jack the Ripper Walks—Each walking tour company seems to make most of its money with "haunted" and Jack the Ripper tours. Many guides are historians and would rather not lead these lightweight tours—but, in tourism as in journalism, "if it bleeds, it leads" (which is why the juvenile London Dungeon is one of London's busiest sights).

Two reliably good two-hour tours start every night at the Tower Hill Tube station exit. **Ripping Yarns** is guided by off-duty Yeoman Warders—the Tower of London "Beefeaters" (£7, pay at end, nightly at 18:45, no tours between Christmas and New Year's, mobile 07813-559-301, www.jack-the-ripper-tours.com). **London Walks'** guides leave from the same spot later each night (£7, pay at the start, nightly at 19:30, tel. 020/7624-3978, recorded info tel. 020/7624-9255, www.jacktheripperwalk.com). After taking both, I found the London Walks more entertaining, informative, and with a better route (along quieter, once-hooker-friendly lanes, with less traffic), starting at Tower Hill and ending at Liverpool Street Station rather than returning to Tower Hill. Groups can be huge for both, but there's always room—just show up.

Private Walks with Local Guides—Standard rates for London's registered Blue Badge guides are about £125 for four hours, and £200 or more for nine hours (tel. 020/7780-4060, www.tourist guides.org.uk or www.blue-badge.org.uk). I know and like four fine local guides: **Sean Kelleher** (tel. 020/8673-1624, mobile 07764-612-770, seankelleher@btinternet.com), **Britt Lonsdale** (£150/half-day, £250/day, great with families, tel. 020/7386-9907, mobile 07813-278-077, brittl@btinternet.com), and two others who work in London when they're not on the road leading my Britain tours, **Tom Hooper** (mobile 07986-048-047, tomh@ricksteves.net) and **Gillian Chadwick** (mobile 07889-976-598, gillianc@ricksteves .net).

Driver-Guides—These two guides have cars or a minibus (particularly helpful for travelers with limited mobility) and charge around £290/half-day and £420/day for London tours (see websites and contact them for details): **Robina Brown** (tel. 020/7228-2238, www.driverguidetours.com, robina@driverguidetours.com) and **Janine Barton** (tel. 020/7402-4600, http://seeitinstyle.synthasite .com, jbsiis@aol.com).

London Duck Tours

A bright-yellow amphibious WWII-vintage vehicle (the model that landed troops on Normandy's beaches on D-Day) takes a gang of 30 tourists past some famous sights on land—Big Ben, Trafalgar Square, Piccadilly Circus—then splashes into the Thames for a cruise. All in all, it's good fun at a rather steep price. The live guide works hard, and it's kid-friendly to the point of goofiness (£20, April-Sept daily 10:30-18:00, shorter hours Oct-March, 1-4/hr, 1.25 hours—45 minutes on land and 30 minutes in the river, £3 booking fee online, these book up in advance, departs from Chicheley Street—you'll see the big, ugly vehicle parked 100 yards behind the London Eye, Tube: Waterloo or Westminster, tel. 020/7928-3132, www.londonducktours.co.uk).

Bike Tours

London, like Paris, is committed to creating more bike paths, and many of its best sights can be laced together with a pleasant pedal through its parks. A bike tour is a fun way to see the sights and enjoy the city on two wheels.

London Bicycle Tour Company—Three tours covering London are offered daily from their base at Gabriel's Wharf on the south bank of the Thames. Sunday is the best, as there is less car traffic (**Central Tour**—£15.95, April-Oct daily at 10:30, Nov-March only on Mon-Fri, 6 miles, 2.5 hours, includes Westminster, Covent Garden, and St. Paul's; **Royal West Tour**—£18.95, April-Oct Sat-Sun at 12:00, Nov-March only on Sun, 9 miles, 3.5 hours, includes Westminster, Hyde Park, Buckingham Palace, and Covent Garden; **East Tour**—£18.95, April-Oct Sat-Sun at 14:00, Nov-March only on Sat at 12:00, 9 miles, 3.5 hours, includes south side of the river to Tower Bridge, then The City to the East End; book ahead for off-season tours). They also rent bikes (£3.50/hour, £20/day; office open daily 10:00-18:00, west of Blackfriars Bridge on the South Bank, 1a Gabriel's Wharf, tel. 020/7928-6838, www .londonbicycle.com).

Fat Tire Bike Tours—Daily bike tours cover the highlights of downtown London on two different itineraries (£2 discount with this book): Royal London (£20, daily March-Nov at 11:00,

June-Aug also at 15:30, 7 miles, 4 hours, meet at Queensway Tube station; includes Parliament, Buckingham Palace, Hyde Park, and Trafalgar Square) and River Thames (£30, mid-March-Nov Thu-Sat at 10:30, 5 hours, meet at Waterloo Tube station—exit 2; includes London Eye, St. Paul's, Tower of London, Trafalgar Square, Covent Garden, and boat trip on the Thames). The spiel is light and irreverent rather than scholarly, but the price is right. Reservations are easy online and required for River Thames tours and kids' bikes (off-season tours by arrangement, mobile 078-8233-8779, www.fattirebiketourslondon.com). The schedule changes often—confirm online or by phone.

▲▲Cruises

Boat tours with entertaining commentaries sail regularly from many points along the Thames. The options are confusing, since several companies offer essentially the same trip. Your basic options are to use the boats either for a scenic joyride cruise within central London, or for transportation to an outlying sight (such as Greenwich or Kew Gardens).

Boats come and go from several docks in central London. The most popular places to embark are Westminster Pier (at the base of Westminster Bridge across the street from Big Ben) and Waterloo Pier (at the London Eye, across the river).

Buy boat tickets at the kiosks on the docks. While individual Tube and bus tickets don't work on the boats, a Travelcard can snare you a 33 percent discount on most cruises (just show the card when you pay for the cruise; no discount with the pay-as-you-go Oyster card except on Thames Clippers). Because different companies vary in the discounts they offer, always ask. Children and seniors generally get discounts. You can purchase drinks and scant, pricey snacks on board. Clever budget travelers pack a picnic and munch while they cruise.

Round-trip fares are only a bit more than one-way. Still, for pleasure and efficiency, consider combining a one-way cruise (to Kew, Greenwich, or wherever) with a Tube or train ride back.

Tourist-Oriented Cruises in Central London

London offers many made-for-tourist cruises on slow-moving, open-top boats accompanied by commentary about passing sights.

City Cruises runs boats from Westminster Pier across the river to Waterloo Pier, then downriver to Tower Pier and on to Greenwich (tel. 020/7740-0400, www.citycruises.com). If you want just a sample, hop on their 30-minute cruise only as far as Tower Pier (£8 one-way, £10.50 round-trip, daily April-Oct roughly 10:00-19:00, until 18:00 in winter, 2/hr). City Cruises also offers a £13 "River Red Rover" ticket good for all-day hop-on, hop-off travel (also included with the bus tours described on page 723)—though the line's limited stops in central London make this a lesser deal than it might seem.

Thames River Services runs a similar service with even fewer stops: Westminster to St. Katharine's Pier to Greenwich (tel. 020/7930-4097, www.thamesriverservices.co.uk). They have classic boats and feel a little friendlier and more old-fashioned. For more details, see "Cruising Downstream, to Greenwich and the Docklands," later.

The **Circular Cruise** offered by Crown River Services is a handy hop-on, hop-off route with stops at the Westminster, Festival, Embankment, Bankside, London Bridge, and St. Katharine's piers (£3 to go one stop, £8 one-way for a longer trip, £10.50 for an all-day ticket, daily 11:00-18:30, every 30 minutes late May-early Sept, fewer stops and less frequent off-season, tel. 020/7936-2033, www.crownriver.com).

The **London Eye** operates its own river cruise, offering a 40-minute live-guided circular tour from Waterloo Pier. As it's much pricier than the alternatives for just a short loop, it's a poor value (£12, reservations recommended, 10 percent discount if you pre-book online, no Travelcard discounts, departures daily generally at :45 past the hour, April-Oct 10:45-18:45, Nov-March 11:45-16:45, closed mid-Jan-mid-Feb, toll tel. 0870-500-0600, www.londoneye.com).

Careening at Top Speed Along the Thames: Two competing companies invite you aboard a small, 12-person, high-speed rigid inflatable boat (RIB—similar to a Zodiac) for an adrenaline-fueled tour of the city (London RIB Voyages: stand-up comedian guides, £32.50/50 minutes, £45/1.25 hours, tel. 020/7928-8933, www.londonribvoyages.com; Thames RIB Experience: £29/50 minutes, £45/1.5 hours, toll tel. 0870-224-4200, www.thamesribexperience.com).

Away from the Thames, on Regent's Canal: Consider exploring London's canals by taking a cruise on historic Regent's Canal in north London. The good ship *Jenny Wren* offers 1.5-hour guided canal boat cruises from Walker's Quay in Camden Town through scenic Regent's Park to Little Venice (£9; Aug daily at 10:30, 12:30, 14:30, and 16:30; April-July and Sept-Oct daily at 12:30 and 14:30, Sat-Sun also at 16:30; Walker's Quay, 250 Camden High Street, 3-minute walk from Tube: Camden Town; tel. 020/7485-4433, www.walkersquay.com). While in Camden Town, stop by the popular, punky Camden Lock Market to browse through trendy arts and crafts (daily 10:00-18:00, busiest on weekends, a block from Walker's Quay, www.camdenlockmarket.com).

London

Commuting by Clipper

Thames Clippers, with their fast, sleek, 220-seat catamarans, are designed for commuters rather than sightseers. Think of the clippers as express buses in the river—they zip no-nonsense through London every 20 minutes, stopping at most of the major docks en route: Embankment, Waterloo, Blackfriars or Bankside, London Bridge, Tower, Canary Wharf (Docklands), and Greenwich (roughly 20 minutes from Embankment to Tower, 10 more minutes to Docklands, 10 more minutes to Greenwich). However, the clippers are less pleasant for joyriding than the cruises described earlier. There's no commentary, and no open deck up top (the only outside access is on a crowded deck at the exhaust-choked back of the boat, where you're jostling for photos). Any one-way ride costs £5.30, and a River Roamer all-day ticket costs £12 (33 percent discount with Travelcard, 10 percent off with a pay-as-you-go Oyster card, tel. 020/7001-2222, www.thamesclippers.com).

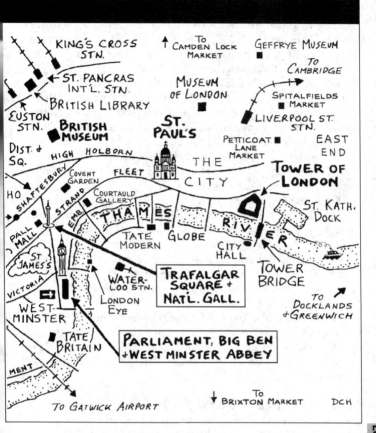

The company also offers two express trips. The **"Tate to Tate"** boat service, which directly connects Tate Britain (Millbank Pier) and the Tate Modern (Bankside Pier), is made for art-lovers (£5 one-way, covered by £12 River Roamer day ticket; buy ticket at gallery desk, at kiosk by the dock, or onboard; daily 10:00-17:00, runs every 40 minutes, 18-minute trip, www.tate.org.uk/tatetotate). The **O2 Express** runs only on nights when there are events going on at the O_2 Arena (formerly the Millennium Dome; from Waterloo Pier, £6 one-way, £12 round-trip, 30 minutes).

Cruising Downstream, to Greenwich and the Docklands

Greenwich: Both of the big tour companies (City Cruises and Thames River Services, described earlier) head to Greenwich from Westminster Pier. The cruises are usually narrated by the captain, with most commentary given on the way to Greenwich.

The companies' prices are the same (£9.50 one-way, £12.50 round-trip), though their itineraries are slightly different: **City Cruises** stops at Waterloo/London Eye Pier and Tower Pier on the way to Greenwich (if you buy their £13 River Red Rover ticket, you can hop on and off all day long; daily April-Oct generally 10:00-17:00, less off-season, 2/hour, 1.25 hours from Westminster to Greenwich; cheaper to go from Tower Pier to Greenwich—£8 one-way, £10.50 round-trip, only 30 minutes to Greenwich—but you miss all the scenery in central London). **Thames River Services** stops only at St. Katharine's Pier on the way to Greenwich, making the trip a little faster (April-Oct 10:00-16:00, July-Aug until 17:00, daily 2/hour; Nov-March shorter hours and runs every 40 minutes; 1 hour from Westminster to Greenwich).

The **Thames Clippers**, described earlier, are cheaper, faster, and make more stops downtown, but have no commentary and no seating up top (£5.30 one-way, £12 for an all-day pass, 3/hour, about 45 minutes from Westminster to Greenwich).

To maximize both efficiency and sightseeing, I'd take a boat to Greenwich one way, and go the other way on the DLR (Docklands Light Railway), with a stop in the Docklands (Canary Wharf station).

The Docklands: Thames Clippers connect the Docklands' Canary Wharf Pier to both central London and Greenwich (£5.30 one-way, £12 for an all-day pass, no commentary, 3/hour, roughly 10 minutes to Tower, 30 minutes to Waterloo, 15 minutes to Greenwich).

Cruising Upstream to Kew Gardens

Boats operated by the Westminster Passenger Services Association leave for Kew Gardens from Westminster Pier (£12 one-way, £18 round-trip, cash only; 4/day, April-Oct daily at 10:30, 11:15, 12:00, and 14:00; 1.5 hours, about half the trip is narrated, tel. 020/7930-2062, www.wpsa.co.uk). Romantic as these rides sound, it can be a long trip...especially upstream.

Self-Guided Walk

Westminster Walk

Just about every visitor to London strolls along historic Whitehall from Big Ben to Trafalgar Square. This quick, nine-stop walk gives meaning to that touristy ramble. Under London's modern traffic and big-city bustle lie 2,000 fascinating years of history. You'll get a whirlwind tour as well as a practical orientation to London. (You can download a free Rick Steves audio tour of this walk for your mobile device via www.ricksteves.com/audioeurope, iTunes, or the Rick Steves Audio Europe smartphone app.).

Westminster Walk

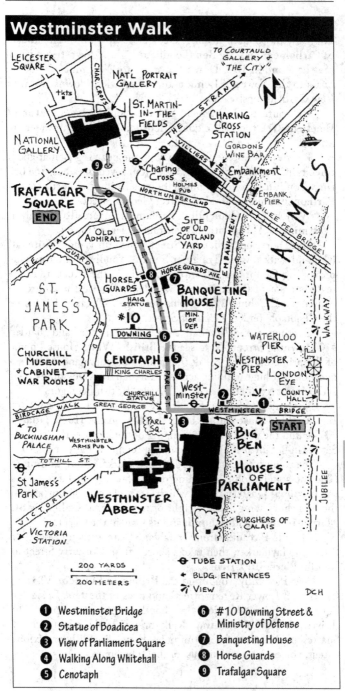

TO COURTAULD GALLERY & "THE CITY"

LEICESTER SQUARE

NAT'L PORTRAIT GALLERY

ST. MARTIN-IN-THE-FIELDS

THE STRAND

CHARING CROSS STATION

GORDON'S WINE BAR

tkts

CHAR CROSS

VILLIERS ST.

NATIONAL GALLERY

TRAFALGAR SQUARE

END

Charing Cross

S. HOLMES PUB

NORTHUMBERLAND

Embankment

EMBANK. PIER

JUBILEE PED BRIDGE

THE MALL

OLD ADMIRALTY

Site OF OLD SCOTLAND YARD

EMBANKMENT

THAMES

GUARDS ROAD

ST. JAMES'S PARK

HORSE GUARDS

HAIG STATUE

HORSE GUARDS AVE.

BANQUETING HOUSE

MIN. OF DEF.

VICTORIA

WALKWAY

#10 DOWNING

WATERLOO PIER

CHURCHILL MUSEUM & CABINET WAR ROOMS

CENOTAPH

KING CHARLES

WESTMINSTER PIER

LONDON EYE

COUNTY HALL

PARL ST.

West-minster

BIRDCAGE WALK

GREAT GEORGE

CHURCHILL STATUE

WESTMINSTER BRIDGE

TO BUCKINGHAM PALACE

WESTMINSTER ARMS PUB

PARL. SQ.

START

TOTHILL ST.

BIG BEN

St James's Park

VICTORIA ST.

WESTMINSTER ABBEY

HOUSES OF PARLIAMENT

JUBILEE

TO VICTORIA STATION

BURGHERS OF CALAIS

LONDON

200 YARDS
200 METERS

⊖ TUBE STATION
← BLDG. ENTRANCES
⌐ VIEW

DCH

1 Westminster Bridge
2 Statue of Boadicea
3 View of Parliament Square
4 Walking Along Whitehall
5 Cenotaph

6 #10 Downing Street & Ministry of Defense
7 Banqueting House
8 Horse Guards
9 Trafalgar Square

Start halfway across **Westminster Bridge** (❶) for that "Wow, I'm really in London!" feeling. Get a close-up view of the **Houses of Parliament** and **Big Ben** (floodlit at night). Downstream you'll see the **London Eye.** Down the stairs to Westminster Pier are boats to the Tower of London and Greenwich (downstream) or Kew Gardens (upstream).

En route to Parliament Square, you'll pass a **statue of Boadicea** (❷), the Celtic queen defeated by Roman invaders in A.D. 60.

For fun, call home from a pay phone near Big Ben at about three minutes before the hour, to let your loved ones hear the bell ring. You'll find four red phone booths lining the north side of **Parliament Square** (❸) along Great George Street.

Wave hello to Churchill in Parliament Square. To his right is **Westminster Abbey** with its two stubby, elegant towers.

Head north up Parliament Street, which turns into **Whitehall** (❹), and walk toward Trafalgar Square. You'll see the thought-provoking **Cenotaph** (❺) in the middle of the street, reminding passersby of Britain's many war dead. To visit the Churchill Museum and Cabinet War Rooms (see page 737), take a left before the Cenotaph, on King Charles Street.

Continuing on Whitehall, stop at the barricaded and guarded **#10 Downing Street** (❻) to see the British "White House," home of the prime minister. Break the bobby's boredom and ask him a question. The huge building across Whitehall from Downing Street is the **Ministry of Defense** (MOD), the "British Pentagon."

Nearing Trafalgar Square, look for the 17th-century **Banqueting House** across the street (❼) and the **Horse Guards** (❽) behind the gated fence (Changing of the Horse Guards Mon-Sat at 11:00, Sun at 10:00, dismounting ceremony daily at 16:00).

The column topped by Lord Nelson marks **Trafalgar Square** (❾). The stately domed building on the far side of the square is the **National Gallery** (free), which has a classy café upstairs in the Sainsbury wing. To the right of the National Gallery is **St. Martin-in-the-Fields Church** and its Café in the Crypt.

To get to Piccadilly from Trafalgar Square, walk up Cockspur Street to Haymarket, then take a short left on Coventry Street to colorful **Piccadilly Circus.**

Near Piccadilly, you'll find the **Britain and London Visitors Centre** (on Lower Regent Street) and piles of theaters. **Leicester Square** (with its half-price "tkts" booth for plays—see page 776) thrives just a few blocks away. Walk through seedy **Soho** (north of Shaftesbury Avenue) for its fun pubs. From Piccadilly or Oxford Circus, you can take a taxi, bus, or the Tube home.

Sights in London

Central London

Westminster

▲▲▲Westminster Abbey—The greatest church in the English-speaking world, Westminster Abbey is the place where England's kings and queens have been crowned and buried since 1066. Like a stony refugee camp huddled outside St. Peter's Pearly Gates, Westminster Abbey has many stories to tell. The steep admission includes an excellent audioguide—worthwhile if you have the time and interest. To experience the church more vividly, take a live tour, or attend evensong or an organ concert (see below).

Two tiny **museums** ring the cloisters. The Chapter House, where the monks had daily meetings, features fine architecture and stained glass with faded but well-described medieval art. The Abbey Museum has exhibits on royal coronations, funerals, Abbey history, a close-up look at medieval stained glass, and replicas of the crown jewels used for coronation practice. Look into the impressively realistic eyes of Elizabeth I, Charles II, Admiral Nelson, and a dozen others, part of a compelling series of wax-and-wood statues that, for three centuries, graced coffins during funeral processions.

Cost: £15, £30 family ticket (covers 2 adults and 1 child), cash only, includes cloisters, audioguide, and Abbey Museum.

Hours: Abbey open Mon-Fri 9:30-16:30, Wed until 19:00 (main church only), Sat 9:30-14:30, last entry one hour before closing, closed Sun to sightseers but open for services; Abbey Museum open daily 10:30-16:00; cloisters open daily 8:00-18:00; 1.5-hour guided tour-£3, up to 5/day in summer; Tube: Westminster or St. James's Park. Info desk tel. 020/7222-5152 or 020/7654-4834, www.westminster-abbey.org.

Crowd-Beating Tips: The main entrance, on the Parliament Square side, often has a sizable line; visit early, during lunch, or late to avoid tourist hordes. Sat and Mon are worst. Midmornings are also crowded, while weekdays after 14:30 are less congested; come then and stay for the 17:00 evensong.

Music: The church hosts evensong performances daily, sung every night but Wednesday, when it may be spoken (Mon-Fri at 17:00; Sat-Sun at 15:00). A free 30-minute organ recital is often held on Sunday at 17:45.

▲▲Houses of Parliament (Palace of Westminster)—This Neo-Gothic icon of London, the royal residence from 1042 to 1547, is now the meeting place of the legislative branch of government. The Houses of Parliament are located in what was once the Palace of Westminster—long the palace of England's medieval kings—until it was largely destroyed by fire in 1834. The palace was rebuilt in the Victorian Gothic style (a move away from Neoclassicism back to England's Christian and medieval heritage, true to the Romantic Age) and completed in 1860.

Tourists are welcome to view debates in either the bickering House of Commons or the genteel House of Lords. You're only allowed inside when Parliament is in session, indicated by a flag flying atop the Victoria Tower at the south end of the building (generally Mondays through Thursdays). During the summer recess, when Parliament is not in session, visitors can still take a guided tour. While the actual debates are generally quite dull, it is a thrill to be inside and see the British government in action.

Cost and Hours: Free, both Houses usually open Mon-Tue 14:30-22:30, Wed-Thu 11:30-17:50, closed Fri-Sun and most of Aug-Sept, generally less action and no lines after 18:00, Tube: Westminster. Tel. 020/7219-4272, see www.parliament.uk for schedule. The House of Lords has more pageantry, shorter lines, and less interesting debates (tel. 020/7219-3107 for schedule, visit www.parliamentlive.tv for a preview).

Visiting the Houses of Parliament (HOP): Enter the venerable HOP midway along the west side of the building (across the street from Westminster Abbey) through the Visitor Entrance (with the tourist ramp, next to the St. Stephen's Entrance—if lost, ask a guard). As you enter, you'll be asked if you want to visit the House of Commons or the House of Lords. Inquire about the wait—an hour or two is not unusual. If there's a long line for the House of Commons and you just want a quick look inside the grand halls of this majestic building, start with the House of Lords. Once inside, you can switch if you like.

Just past security (where you'll be photographed and given a badge to wear around your neck), you enter the vast and historic **Westminster Hall,** which survived the 1834 fire. The cavernous hall was built in the 11th century, and its famous self-supporting hammer-beam roof was added in 1397. Racks of brochures here explain how the British government works, and plaques describe the hall. The Jubilee Café, open to the public, has live video feeds showing exactly what's going on in each house. Just seeing the café video is a fun experience (and can help you decide which house—if either—you'd like to see). Walking through the hall and up the stairs, you'll enter the busy world of government with all its high-powered goings-on.

Houses of Parliament Tours: Though Parliament is in recess during much of August and September, you can get a behind-the-scenes peek at the royal chambers of both houses during these months with a tour (£14, 1.25 hours, generally Mon-Fri, times vary, so confirm in advance; book ahead through www.ticket master.co.uk). The same tours are offered Saturdays year-round.

Jewel Tower: Across the street from the Parliament building's St. Stephen's Gate, the Jewel Tower is a rare remnant of the old Palace of Westminster used by kings until Henry VIII. The crude stone tower (1365-1366) was a guard tower in the palace wall, overlooking a moat. It contains a fine little exhibit on Parliament and the tower (£3, daily March-Oct 10:00-17:00, Nov-Feb 10:00-16:00, tel. 020/7222-2219). Next to the tower (and free) is a quiet courtyard with picnic-friendly benches.

Big Ben: The clock tower (315 feet high) is named for its 13-ton bell, Ben. The light above the clock is lit when the House of Commons is sitting. The face of the clock is huge—you can actually see the minute hand moving. For a good view of it, walk halfway over Westminster Bridge.

▲▲▲**Churchill Museum and Cabinet War Rooms**—This is a fascinating walk through the underground headquarters of the British government's fight against the Nazis in the darkest days of the Battle for Britain. The attraction includes two parts: the war rooms themselves, and a top-notch museum dedicated to the man who steered the war from here, Winston Churchill. For details on all the blood, sweat, toil, and tears, pick up the excellent, essential, and included audioguide at the entry, and dive in.

Cabinet War Rooms: The 27-room, heavily fortified nerve center of the British war effort was used from 1939 to 1945. Churchill's room, the map room, and other rooms are just as they were in 1945. As you follow the one-way route, be sure to take advantage of the audioguide, which explains each room and offers first-person accounts of wartime happenings here (it takes about 45 minutes, not counting the Churchill Museum). Be patient—it's well worth it. While the rooms are spartan, you'll see how British gentility survived even as the city was bombarded—posted signs informed those working underground what the weather was like outside, and a cheery notice reminds you to turn off the light switch to conserve electricity.

Churchill Museum: Don't bypass this museum, which occupies a large hall about a half-dozen rooms into the war rooms. It dissects every aspect of the man behind the famous cigar, bowler hat, and V-for-victory sign. It's extremely well-presented and engaging, using artifacts, quotes, political cartoons, clear explanations, and high-tech interactive exhibits to bring the colorful statesman to life; this museum alone deserves an hour. You'll get a taste of Winston's wit, irascibility, work ethic, passion for painting, American ties, writing talents, and drinking habits. The exhibit shows Winston's warts as well: It questions whether his party-switching was just political opportunism, examines the basis for his opposition to Indian self-rule, and reveals him to be an intense taskmaster who worked 18-hour days and was brutal to his staffers (who deeply respected him nevertheless).

A long touch-the-screen timeline lets you zero in on events in his life from birth (November 30, 1874) to his first appointment as prime minister in 1940. Many of the items on display—such as a European map divvied up in permanent marker, which Churchill brought home from the postwar Potsdam Conference—drive home the remarkable span of history this man lived through. Imagine: Churchill began his military career riding horses in the cavalry, and ended it speaking out against the proliferation of nuclear armaments. It's all the more amazing considering that, in the 1930s, the man who would become my vote for greatest statesman of the 20th century was once considered a washed-up loony ranting about the growing threat of fascism.

Cost and Hours: £14.95, daily 9:30-18:00, last entry one hour before closing; on King Charles Street, 200 yards off Whitehall, follow the signs, Tube: Westminster. Tel. 020/7930-6961, www .iwm.org.uk. The museum's gift shop is great for anyone nostalgic for the 1940s. Note that this wonderful museum is far superior to the Winston Churchill's Britain at War Experience (next to the London Dungeon on the South Bank); give that one—and the London Dungeon—a miss.

Eating: If you're hungry, get your rations at the Switch Room café (in the museum) or, for a nearby pub lunch, try the Westminster Arms (food served downstairs, on Storey's Gate, a couple of blocks south of Cabinet War Rooms).

Horse Guards—The Horse Guards change daily at 11:00 (10:00 on Sun), and there's a colorful dismounting ceremony daily at 16:00. The rest of the day, they just stand there—terrible for video cameras (on Whitehall, between Trafalgar Square and #10 Downing Street, Tube: Westminster, www.changing-the-guard .com). Buckingham Palace pageantry is canceled when it rains, but the horse guards change regardless of the weather.

▲Banqueting House—England's first Renaissance building (1619-1622) was designed by Inigo Jones. Built by King James I and decorated by his son Charles I, the Banqueting House came to symbolize the Stuart kings' "divine right" management style—the belief that God himself had anointed them to rule. The house is one of the few London landmarks spared by the 1698 fire, and the only surviving part of the original Palace of Whitehall. Today it opens its doors to visitors, who enjoy a restful 20-minute audio-visual history, a 30-minute audio tour, and a look at the exquisite banqueting hall itself. As a tourist attraction, it's basically one big room—but what a grand room it is, with sumptuous ceiling paintings by Peter Paul Rubens. At Charles I's request, these paintings drove home the doctrine of the legitimacy of the divine right of kings. Ironically, in 1649—divine right ignored—King Charles I

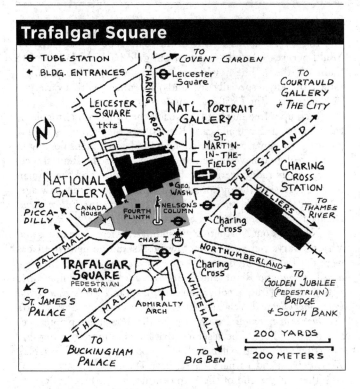

Trafalgar Square

- TUBE STATION
- BLDG. ENTRANCES

TO COVENT GARDEN

Leicester Square

LEICESTER SQUARE tkts

CHARING CROSS

NAT'L. PORTRAIT GALLERY

ST. MARTIN-IN-THE-FIELDS

TO COURTAULD GALLERY & THE CITY

THE STRAND

CHARING CROSS STATION

VILLIERS

NATIONAL GALLERY

TO PICCA-DILLY

CANADA House

GEO. WASH.

FOURTH PLINTH

NELSON'S COLUMN

Charing Cross

TO THAMES RIVER

CHAS. I

Charing Cross

NORTHUMBERLAND

PALL MALL

TRAFALGAR SQUARE PEDESTRIAN AREA

TO ST. JAMES'S PALACE

THE MALL

ADMIRALTY ARCH

WHITEHALL

TO GOLDEN JUBILEE (PEDESTRIAN) BRIDGE & SOUTH BANK

TO BUCKINGHAM PALACE

TO BIG BEN

200 YARDS

200 METERS

was famously executed right here.

Cost and Hours: £4.80, includes audioguide, Mon-Sat 10:00-17:00, closed Sun, last entry at 16:30, subject to closure for government functions, aristocratic WC, immediately across Whitehall from the Horse Guards, Tube: Westminster. Tel. 020/3166-6154 or 020/3166-6155, www.hrp.org.uk.

On Trafalgar Square

▲▲**Trafalgar Square**—London's recently renovated central square, the climax of most marches and demonstrations, is a thrilling place to simply hang out. Lord Nelson stands atop his 185-foot-tall fluted granite column, gazing out toward Trafalgar, where he lost his life but defeated the French fleet. Part of this 1842 memorial is made from his victims' melted-down cannons. He's surrounded by spraying fountains, giant lions, hordes of people, and—until recently—even more pigeons. A former London mayor decided that London's "flying rats" were a public nuisance and evicted Trafalgar Square's venerable seed salesmen (Tube: Charing Cross).

▲▲▲**National Gallery**—Displaying Britain's top collection of European paintings from 1250 to 1900—including works by

Leonardo, Botticelli, Velázquez, Rembrandt, Turner, Van Gogh, and the Impressionists—this is one of Europe's great galleries. You'll peruse 700 years of art—from gold-backed Madonnas to Cubist bathers. The newly remodeled museum is surprisingly family-friendly (especially on Sunday mornings), with a variety of kids' activities. The £3.50 audioguide tour is excellent.

Pick up a free map and approach the collection chronologically. In the medieval and early Renaissance rooms you'll see shiny paintings of saints, angels, Madonnas, and crucifixions floating in an ethereal gold never-never land. Then comes the Renaissance, where artists rediscovered the beauty of nature and the human body, expressing the optimism and confidence of this new age. Look for Botticelli's *Venus and Mars,* Michelangelo's *Entombment,* Raphael's *Pope Julius II,* and Leonardo's *The Virgin of the Rocks.*

Next seek out Northern Protestant art, where Greek gods and Virgin Marys were out, hometown folks and hometown places were in. Two highlights are Vermeer's *A Young Woman Standing at a Virginal* and Rembrandt's *Belshazzar's Feast.* The museum's outstanding Baroque collection includes Van Dyck's *Equestrian Portrait of Charles I,* Velázquez's *The Rokeby Venus,* and Caravaggio's *The Supper at Emmaus.* It's no surprise that hometown painters get lots of space here. The reserved British were more comfortable cavorting with nature than with lofty gods, as seen in Constable's *The Hay Wain* and Turner's *The Fighting Téméraire.*

Then, at the end of the 19th century, a new breed of artists broke out of the stuffy confines of the studio. They donned scarves and berets and set up their canvases in farmers' fields or carried their notebooks into crowded cafés, dashing off quick sketches in order to catch a momentary...impression. There's a mother lode of Impressionist and Post-Impressionist masterpieces here, such as Monet's *Gare St. Lazare,* Renoir's *Boating on the Seine,* Seurat's *Bathers at Asnières,* Van Gogh's *Sunflowers,* and Cézanne's *Bathers.*

Cost and Hours: Free, but suggested donation of £2-3; daily 10:00-18:00, Fri until 21:00; last entry to special exhibits 45 minutes before closing, free one-hour overview tours daily at 11:30 and 14:30, plus Fri at 19:00; no photography, on Trafalgar Square, Tube: Charing Cross or Leicester Square. Recorded info tel. 020/7747-2885, switchboard tel. 020/7839-3321, www.national gallery.org.uk.

Eating: The excellent-but-pricey museum restaurant called the National Dining Rooms is a good spot to split afternoon tea. Two cheaper eateries, also in the museum, are located near the Getty Entrance: the National Café (with both a table-service restaurant and an easier-on-the-budget sandwich/soup/salad/pastry buffet) and the Espresso Bar (sandwiches, soft couches, and ArtStart computers).

▲▲National Portrait Gallery—Put off by halls of 19th-century characters who meant nothing to me, I used to call this "as interesting as someone else's yearbook." But a selective walk through this 500-year-long *Who's Who* of British history is quick and free, and puts faces on the story of England. The collection is well-described, not huge, and in historical sequence, from the 16th century on the second floor to today's royal family on the ground floor.

Some highlights: Henry VIII and wives; portraits of the "Virgin Queen" Elizabeth I, Sir Francis Drake, and Sir Walter Raleigh; the only real-life portrait of William Shakespeare; Oliver Cromwell and Charles I with his head on; portraits by Gainsborough and Reynolds; the Romantics (William Blake, Lord Byron, William Wordsworth, and company); Queen Victoria and her era; and the present royal family, including the late Princess Diana.

Cost and Hours: Free, but suggested donation of £5, temporary exhibits extra; daily 10:00-18:00, Thu-Fri until 21:00, first and second floors open Mon at 11:00, last entry to special exhibits 45 minutes before closing, excellent themed audioguides-£3; entry 100 yards off Trafalgar Square, around corner from National Gallery, opposite Church of St. Martin-in-the-Fields; Tube: Charing Cross or Leicester Square. Tel. 020/7306-0055, recorded info tel. 020/7312-2463, www.npg.org.uk.

Eating: The elegant Portrait Restaurant on the top floor is pricey but has a fine view of Trafalgar Square (£15-20 entrées, reservations smart, tel. 020/7312-2490). The Portrait Café in the basement (take the lift down) is cheaper and offers sandwiches, salads, and pastries.

▲St. Martin-in-the-Fields—The church, built in the 1720s with a Gothic spire atop a Greek-type temple, is an oasis of peace on the wild and noisy Trafalgar Square. St. Martin cared for the poor. "In the fields" was where the first church stood on this spot (in the 13th century), between Westminster and The City. Stepping inside, you still feel a compassion for the needs of the people in this neighborhood—the church serves the homeless and houses a Chinese community center. The modern east window—with grill-work bent into the shape of a warped cross—was installed in 2008 to replace one damaged in World War II.

A new freestanding glass pavilion to the left of the church serves as the entrance to the church's underground areas. There you'll find the concert ticket office, a gift shop, brass-rubbing center, and the recommended support-the-church Café in the Crypt.

Cost and Hours: Church entry free, donations welcome, £3.50 audioguide at shop downstairs; hours vary but generally Mon-Fri 8:30-13:00 & 14:00-18:00, Sat 9:30-13:00 & 14:00-18:00,

LONDON

West End & Nearby

⊖ TUBE STATION
← BLDG. ENTRANCES
↗ VIEW

Sun 15:30-17:00; Tube: Charing Cross. Tel. 020/7766-1100, www2 .stmartin-in-the-fields.org.

Music: The church is famous for its concerts. Consider a free lunchtime concert (Mon, Tue, and Fri at 13:00), an evening concert (£6-25, several nights a week at 19:30), or Wednesday night jazz in the church's café (£5-10, at 20:00). See the website for the concert schedule.

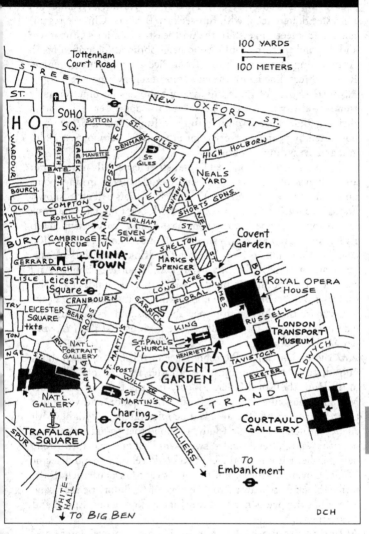

The West End and Nearby

▲**Piccadilly Circus**—Although this square is slathered with neon billboards and tacky attractions, the surrounding streets are packed with great shopping opportunities and swimming with youth on the rampage. For overstimulation in a grimy mall that smells like teen spirit, drop by the extremely trashy Trocadero Center for its Funland arcade games, multiplex cinema, and 10-lane bowling alley (admission to Trocadero is free; individual attractions have separate admissions; located between Piccadilly and Leicester squares on Coventry Street). Nearby Shaftesbury Avenue and Leicester Square teem with fun-seekers, theaters, Chinese restaurants, and street singers. To the northeast is London's Chinatown and, beyond that, the funky Soho neighborhood (described next). And curling to the northwest from Piccadilly Circus is genteel Regent Street, lined with the city's most exclusive shops.

▲**Soho**—North of Piccadilly, seedy Soho has become seriously trendy and is well worth a gawk. It's the epicenter of London's thriving and colorful youth, a fun and funky *Sesame Street* scene populated by people of every color of the racial rainbow...straight, gay, and everything in between.

Soho is also London's red light district (especially near Brewer and Berwick Streets), where "friendly models" wait in tiny rooms up dreary stairways, and voluptuous con artists sell strip shows. Though venturing up a stairway to check out a model is interesting, anyone who goes into any one of the shows will be ripped off. Every time. Even a £5 show in a "licensed bar" comes with a £100 cover or minimum (as it's printed on the drink menu) and a "security man." You may accidentally buy a £200 bottle of bubbly. And suddenly, the door has no handle. While this all sounds creepy, it's easy to avoid trouble if you're not looking for it. In fact, the sleazy joints share the block with respectable pubs and restaurants, and elderly couples out for a stroll pass neon signs that flash *Licensed Sex Shop in Basement.*

▲▲**Covent Garden**—The centerpiece of this boutique-ish shopping district is an iron-and-glass arcade. The "Actors' Church" of St. Paul, the Royal Opera House, and the London Transport Museum (described next) all border the square, and venerable theaters are nearby. The area is a people-watcher's delight, with cigarette eaters, Punch-and-Judy acts, food that's good for you (but not your wallet), trendy crafts, sweet whiffs of marijuana, two-tone hair (neither natural), and faces that could set off a metal detector (Tube: Covent Garden). For better Covent Garden lunch deals, walk a block or two away from the eye of this touristic hurricane (check out the places north of the Tube station, along Endell and Neal Streets).

▲**London Transport Museum**—This modern, well-presented museum, located right at Covent Garden, is fun for kids and thought-provoking for adults (if a bit overpriced). Whether you're cursing or marveling at the buses and Tube, the growth of Europe's third-biggest city (after Moscow and Istanbul) has been made possible by its public transit system.

Cost and Hours: £10, includes optional £2 donation, Sat-Thu 10:00-18:00, Fri 11:00-18:00, open some Fri until 22:00 for special events, last entry 45 minutes before closing, pleasant upstairs café with Covent Garden view, in southeast corner of Covent Garden courtyard, Tube: Covent Garden. Switchboard tel. 020/7379-6344 or recorded info tel. 020/7565-7298, www.ltmuseum.co.uk.

▲**Courtauld Gallery**—While less impressive than the National Gallery, this wonderful collection of paintings is still a joy. The gallery is part of the Courtauld Institute of Art, and the thoughtful description of each piece of art reminds visitors that the gallery is still used for teaching. You'll see medieval European paintings and works by Rubens, the Impressionists (Manet, Monet, and Degas), Post-Impressionists (such as Cézanne), and more. Besides the permanent collection, a quality selection of loaners and temporary exhibits are often included in the entry fee.

Cost and Hours: £5, free Mon until 14:00; open daily 10:00-18:00, last entry at 17:30; downstairs cafeteria, lockers, and WC; bus #6, #9, #11, #13, #15, or #23 from Trafalgar Square; Tube: Temple or Covent Garden. Shop tel. 020/7848-2579, recorded info tel. 020/7848-2526, www.courtauld.ac.uk.

Somerset House: The Courtauld Gallery is located at Somerset House, a grand 18th-century civic palace that offers a marvelous public space (housing temporary exhibits) and a riverside terrace with several eateries (between the Strand and the Thames). The palace once held the national registry that recorded Britain's births, marriages, and deaths: "...where they hatch 'em, match 'em, and dispatch 'em." Step into the courtyard to enjoy the fountain. Go ahead...walk through it. The 55 jets get playful twice an hour. In the winter, this becomes a popular ice-skating rink with a toasty café for viewing the scene (www.somerset-house.org.uk).

Buckingham Palace

There are three palace sights that require admission: the State Rooms (Aug-Sept only), Queen's Gallery, and Royal Mews. You can pay for each separately, or buy a combo-ticket. The combo-ticket for £30.50 admits you to all three sights; a cheaper version for £15 covers the Queen's Gallery and Royal Mews. Many tourists are more interested in the Changing of the Guard, which costs nothing at all to view.

▲**State Rooms at Buckingham Palace**—This lavish home has been Britain's royal residence since 1837. When the Queen's at home, the royal standard flies (a red, yellow, and blue flag); otherwise, the Union Jack flaps in the wind. The Queen opens her palace to the public—but only in August and September, when she's out of town.

Cost and Hours: £17 for lavish State Rooms and throne room, includes audioguide; Aug-Sept only, daily 9:45-18:00, last admission 15:45; only 8,000 visitors a day by timed entry; come early to the palace's Visitor Entrance (opens 9:15) or book ahead in person

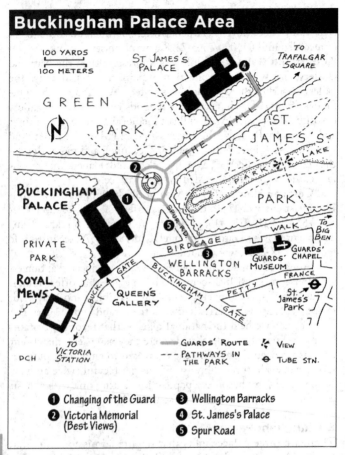

Buckingham Palace Area

100 YARDS
100 METERS

ST JAMES'S PALACE

TO TRAFALGAR SQUARE

GREEN PARK

N

THE MALL

ST. JAMES'S

ST. JAMES'S PARK

LAKE

PARK

BUCKINGHAM PALACE

PRIVATE PARK

ROYAL MEWS

SPUR RD.

BIRDCAGE

WALK

TO BIG BEN

GUARDS' CHAPEL

GUARDS' MUSEUM

WELLINGTON BARRACKS

BUCK. GATE

QUEEN'S GALLERY

BUCKINGHAM GATE

PETTY FRANCE

St James's Park

TO VICTORIA STATION

DCH

GUARDS' ROUTE — VIEW
PATHWAYS IN THE PARK · · · TUBE STN.

1. Changing of the Guard
2. Victoria Memorial (Best Views)
3. Wellington Barracks
4. St. James's Palace
5. Spur Road

LONDON

or by phone or online (£1.25 extra); Tube: Victoria. Tel. 020/7766-7300, www.royalcollection.org.uk.

▲**Queen's Gallery at Buckingham Palace**—Queen Elizabeth's personal collection of art is on display in a wing adjoining the palace. Her 7,000 paintings make up the finest private art collection in the world, rivaling Europe's biggest national art galleries. It's actually a collection of collections, built on by each successive monarch since the 16th century. She rotates her paintings, enjoying some privately in her many palatial residences while sharing others with her subjects in public galleries in Edinburgh and London. Small, thoughtfully presented, and always exquisite displays fill the five rooms open to the public. As you're in "the most important building in London," security is tight.

In addition to the permanent collection, you'll see temporary exhibits and a small room glittering with the Queen's personal jewelry. Compared to the crown jewels at the Tower, it may be Her Majesty's bottom drawer—but it's still a dazzling pile of diamonds. Temporary exhibits change about twice a year, and are lovingly described by the included audioguide. While admission tickets come with an entry time, this is only enforced during rare days when crowds are a problem.

Cost and Hours: £8.75, daily 10:00-17:30, last entry one hour before closing, Tube: Victoria. Tel. 020/7766-7301, but Her Majesty rarely answers. Men shouldn't miss the mahogany-trimmed urinals.

Royal Mews—Located to the left of Buckingham Palace, the Queen's working stables, or "mews," are open to visitors. The visit is likely to be disappointing unless you follow the included audioguide or the hourly guided tour, in which case it's thoroughly entertaining—especially if you're interested in horses and/or royalty. The 40-minute tours show off a few of the Queen's 30 horses, a fancy car, and a bunch of old carriages, finishing with the Gold State Coach (c. 1760, 4 tons, 4 mph). Queen Victoria said absolutely no cars. When she died, in 1901, the mews got its first Daimler. Today, along with the hay-eating transport, the stable is home to five Bentleys and Rolls-Royce Phantoms, with one on display.

Cost and Hours: £7.75, April-July and Oct Sat-Thu 11:00-16:00, Aug-Sept 10:00-17:00, last entry 45 minutes before closing, closed Fri and Nov-March, guided tours on the hour, Buckingham Palace Road, Tube: Victoria. Tel. 020/7766-7302.

▲▲Changing of the Guard at Buckingham Palace—This is the spectacle every visitor to London has to see at least once: stone-faced, red-coated, bearskin-hatted guards changing posts with much fanfare, in an hour-long ceremony accompanied by a brass band.

It's 11:00 at Buckingham Palace, and the on-duty guards are ready to finish their shift. Nearby at St. James's Palace (a half-mile northwest), a second set of guards is also ready for a break. At a third location, fresh replacement guards gather for a review and inspection at Wellington Barracks, 500 yards east of the palace (on Birdcage Walk).

At 11:15, the tired St. James's guards head out to the Mall, and then take a right turn for Buckingham Palace. At 11:30, the replacement troops, led by the band, also head for Buckingham Palace. Meanwhile, a fourth group—the Horse Guard—passes by along the Mall on their way back to Hyde Park Corner from their own changing-of-the-guard ceremony on Whitehall (which just took place at Horse Guards Parade at 11:00, or 10:00 on Sun).

At 11:45, the tired and fresh guards converge on Buckingham Palace in a perfect storm of Red Coat pageantry. Everyone parades around, the guard changes (passing the regimental flag, or "color") with much shouting, the band plays a happy little concert, and then they march out. At noon, two bands escort two detachments of guards away: the tired guards to Wellington Barracks and the fresh guards to St. James's Palace. As the fresh guards set up at St. James's Palace and the tired ones dress down at the barracks, the tourists disperse.

Cost and Hours: Free, daily May-July at 11:30, every other day Aug-April, no ceremony in very wet weather; exact schedule subject to change—call 020/7766-7300 for the day's plan, or check www.changing-the-guard.com or www.royalcollection.org.uk (click "Visit," then "Changing the Guard"); Buckingham Palace, Tube: Victoria, St. James's Park, or Green Park. Or hop into a big black taxi and say, "Buck House, please" (a.k.a. Buckingham Palace).

Sightseeing Strategies: Most tourists just show up and get lost in the crowds, but those who know the drill will enjoy the event more. The action takes place in stages over the course of an hour, at several different locations. The main event is in the forecourt right in front of Buckingham Palace (between Buckingham Palace and the fence) from 11:30 to 12:00. To see it close up, you'll need to get here no later than 10:30 to get a place right next to the fence.

But there's plenty of pageantry elsewhere. Get out your map and strategize. You could see the guards mobilizing at Wellington Barracks or St. James's Palace (11:00-11:15). Or watch them parade with bands down The Mall and Spur Road (11:15-11:30). After the ceremony at Buckingham Palace is over (and many tourists have gotten bored and gone home), the parades march back along those same streets (12:10).

Pick one event and find a good, unobstructed place from which to view it. The key is to either get right up front along the road or fence, or find some raised elevation to stand or sit on—a balustrade or a curb—so you can see over people's heads.

For the best overall view, stake out the high ground on the circular Victoria Memorial (come before 11:00 to get a place). From the Memorial, you have good views of the palace as well as the arriving and departing parades along The Mall and Spur Road. The actual changing of the guard in front of the palace is a nonevent. It is interesting, however, to see nearly every tourist in London gathered in one place at the same time. Afterward, stroll through nearby St. James's Park.

North London

▲▲▲**British Museum**—Simply put, this is the greatest chronicle of civilization...anywhere. A visit here is like taking a long hike through *Encyclopedia Britannica* National Park. While the vast British Museum wraps around its Great Court (the huge entrance hall), the most popular sections of the museum fill the ground

North London

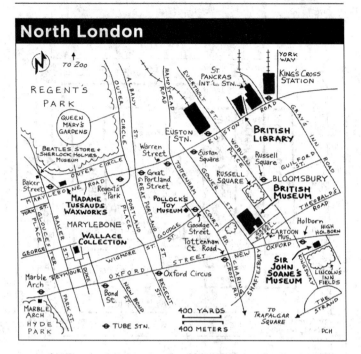

floor: Egyptian, Assyrian, and ancient Greek, with the famous Elgin Marbles from the Athenian Parthenon. The museum's stately Reading Room—famous as the place where Karl Marx hung out while formulating his ideas on communism and writing *Das Kapital*—sometimes hosts special exhibits.

From the Great Court, doorways lead to all wings. Huge winged lions (which guarded an Assyrian palace 800 years before Christ) guard these great galleries. For a brief tour, connect these ancient dots:

Start with the **Egyptian** section. Wander from the Rosetta Stone past the many statues. At the end of the hall, climb the stairs to mummy land.

Back at the winged lions, explore the dark, violent, and mysterious **Assyrian** rooms. The Nimrud Gallery is lined with royal propaganda reliefs and wounded lions (from the ninth century B.C.).

The most modern of the ancient art fills the **Greek** section. Find Room 11, behind the winged lions, and start your walk through Greek art history with the simple and primitive Cycladic fertility figures. Later, painted vases show a culture really into partying. The finale is the Elgin Marbles. The much-wrangled-over bits of the Athenian Parthenon (from about 450 B.C.) are even more impressive than they look. To best appreciate these ancient carvings, take the audioguide tour (described later).

British Museum Overview

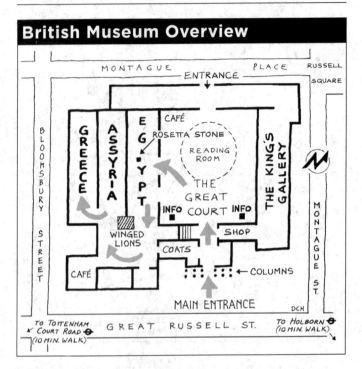

Be sure to venture upstairs to see artifacts from **Roman Britain** (Room 50) that surpass anything you'll see at Hadrian's Wall or elsewhere in Britain. Nearby, the Dark Age Britain exhibits offer a worthwhile peek at that bleak era; look for the Sutton Hoo Burial Ship artifacts from a seventh-century royal burial on the east coast of England (Room 41). A rare Michelangelo cartoon (preliminary sketch) is in Room 90.

Cost and Hours: Free but a £4, $6, or €5 donation requested; temporary exhibits extra, daily 10:00-17:30, Thu-Fri until 20:30—but not all galleries open after 17:30, least crowded weekday late afternoons, Great Russell Street, Tube: Tottenham Court Road. Switchboard tel. 020/7323-8000, general info tel. 020/7323-8299, collection questions tel. 020/7323-8838, www.britishmuseum.org.

Tours: The 1.5-hour Highlights tours, led by licensed guides, are expensive but meaty, giving an introduction to the museum's masterpieces (£8, daily at 10:30, 13:00, and 15:00). The free 30- to 40-minute eyeOpener tours are led by volunteers, who focus on select rooms (daily 11:00-15:30, generally every half-hour, plus Thu at 18:15 and 19:15).

The £4.50 **audioguide** (called a "Multimedia Guide") offers dial-up audio commentary and video on 200 objects, as well as several theme tours (for example, 1.5-hour Highlights tour or

Parthenon Sculptures tour). They're substantial and cerebral (must leave photo ID). There's also a fun children's audioguide (£3).

You can download a free Rick Steves **audio tour** of the British Museum for your mobile device via www.ricksteves.com/audio europe, iTunes, or the Rick Steves Audio Europe smartphone app.

▲▲▲**British Library**—Here, in just two rooms, called "The Treasures of the British Library," are the literary treasures of Western civilization, from early Bibles to the Magna Carta to Shakespeare's *Hamlet* to Lewis Carroll's *Alice's Adventures in Wonderland*. You'll see the Lindisfarne Gospels transcribed on an illuminated manuscript, as well as Beatles lyrics scrawled on the back of a greeting card. The British Empire built its greatest monuments out of paper, and it's with literature that England made her lasting contribution to civilization and the arts.

Cost and Hours: Free but £2 suggested donation, temporary exhibits extra, Mon-Fri 9:30-18:00, Tue until 20:00, Sat 9:30-17:00, Sun 11:00-17:00, helpful free computers give you extra info, ground-floor café, self-service cafeteria upstairs, Tube: King's Cross St. Pancras—walk a block west to 96 Euston Road, Euston Tube station is also nearby; bus #10, #30, #73, #91, #205, or #390. Tel. 019/3754-6060 or 020/7412-7676, www.bl.uk.

Audio Tour: You can download a free Rick Steves audio tour of the British Library for your mobile device via www.ricksteves .com/audioeurope, iTunes, or the Rick Steves Audio Europe smartphone app.

▲**Wallace Collection**—Sir Richard Wallace's fine collection of 17th-century Dutch Masters, 18th-century French Rococo, medieval armor, and assorted aristocratic fancies fills the sumptuously furnished Hertford House on Manchester Square. From the rough and intimate Dutch lifescapes of Jan Steen to the pink-cheeked Rococo fantasies of François Boucher, a wander through this little-visited mansion makes you nostalgic for the days of the empire. While this collection would be a big deal in a mid-sized city, it's small potatoes here in London...but enjoyable nevertheless.

Cost and Hours: Free, daily 10:00-17:00, £4 audioguide, free guided tours or lectures almost daily—call to confirm times, just north of Oxford Street on Manchester Square, Tube: Bond Street. Tel. 020/7563-9500, www.wallacecollection.org.

▲**Madame Tussauds Waxworks**—This is gimmicky and expensive, but dang good...a hit with the kind of travelers who skip the British Museum. The original Madame Tussaud did wax casts of heads lopped off during the French Revolution (such as Marie-Antoinette's). She took her show on the road and ended up in London in 1835. Now it's all about squeezing Tom Cruise's bum, gambling with George Clooney, and partying with Beyoncé, Britney, and Brangelina. In addition to posing with all the eerily realistic wax dummies—from Johnny Depp to Barack Obama to the Beatles—you'll have the chance to tour a hokey haunted-house exhibit; learn how they create this waxy army; hop on a people-mover and cruise through a kid-pleasing "Spirit of London" time trip; and meet your favorite Marvel super heroes before heading into an auditorium for a nine-minute "4-D" show—a 3-D movie heightened by wind, "back ticklers," and other special effects.

Cost and Hours: £28, no waiting in line if you buy ticket on their website (10 percent discount), or TI (£22.50), £41 combo-ticket with London Eye, cheaper for kids. From 17:00 to closing, it's £14 if you buy in advance online. Children under 5 are always free. Open Mon-Fri 9:30-19:30, Sat-Sun 9:00-20:00, mid-July-Aug and school holidays daily 9:00-21:00, last entry two hours before closing; Marylebone Road, Tube: Baker Street. Toll tel. 0871-894-3000, www.madametussauds.com. Check the website for discounts on this pricey waxtravaganza.

Crowd-Beating Tips: This popular attraction can be swamped by crowds. To avoid the hassle, buy your tickets and reserve an entry time in advance, either online (10 percent discount) or by phone (same price as box office). If you wait to buy tickets at the attraction, you'll discover that the ticket-buying line twists endlessly once inside the door (believe the posted signs warning you how long the wait will be—an hour or more is not unusual at busy times). If you buy your tickets at the door, try to arrive after 15:00.

▲**Sir John Soane's Museum**—Architects love this quirky place, as do fans of interior decor, eclectic knickknacks, and Back Door sights. Tour this furnished home on a bird-chirping square and see 19th-century chairs, lamps, and carpets, wood-paneled nooks and crannies, and stained-glass skylights. The townhouse is cluttered with Soane's (and his wife's) collection of ancient relics, curios, and famous paintings, including Hogarth's series on *The Rake's Progress* (read the fun plot) and several excellent Canalettos. In 1833, just before his death, Soane established his house as a museum, stipulating that it be kept as nearly as possible in the state he left it. If he visited today, he'd be entirely satisfied. You'll leave wishing you'd known the man.

Cost and Hours: Free but donations much appreciated, Tue-Sat 10:00-17:00, first Tue of the month also 18:00-21:00, closed Sun-Mon, last entry 30 minutes before closing, long entry lines on Sat and first Tue, good £1 brochure, £5 guided tour Sat at 11:00, 13 Lincoln's Inn Fields, quarter-mile southeast of British Museum, Tube: Holborn. Tel. 020/7405-2107, www.soane.org.

Cartoon Museum—This humble but interesting museum is located in the shadow of the British Museum. While its three rooms are filled with British cartoons unknown to most Americans, the satire of famous bigwigs and politicians—from Napoleon to Margaret Thatcher, the Queen, and Tony Blair—shows the power of parody to deliver social commentary. Upstairs, you'll see pages spanning from *Tarzan* to *Tank Girl*, and *Andy Capp* to the British *Dennis the Menace*—interesting only to comic-book die-hards.

Cost and Hours: £5.50, Tue-Sat 10:30-17:30, Sun 12:00-17:30, closed Mon, 35 Little Russell Street—go one block south of the British Museum on Museum Street and turn right, Tube: Tottenham Court Road. Tel. 020/7580-8155, www.cartoonmuseum.org.

Pollock's Toy Museum—This rickety old house, with glass cases filled with toys and games lining its walls and halls, is a time-warp experience that brings back childhood memories to people who grew up without batteries or computer chips. Though the museum is small, you could spend a lot of time here, squinting at the fascinating toys and dolls that entertained the children of 19th- and early 20th-century England. The included information is great. The story of Theodore Roosevelt refusing to shoot a bear cub while on a hunting trip was celebrated in 1902 cartoons, resulting in a new, huggable toy: the Teddy Bear. It was popular for good reason: it could be manufactured during World War I without rationed products; it coincided with the new belief that soft toys were good for a child's development; it was an acceptable "doll for boys"; and it's *the* toy children keep long after they've grown up.

Cost and Hours: £5, kids-£2, generally Mon-Sat 10:00-17:00, closed Sun, last entry 30 minutes before closing, 1 Scala Street, Tube: Goodge Street. Tel. 020/7636-3452, www.pollockstoy museum.com.

The City

When Londoners say "The City," they mean the one-square-mile business center in East London that 2,000 years ago was Roman Londinium. The outline of the Roman city walls can still be seen in the arc of roads from Blackfriars Bridge to Tower Bridge. Within The City are 23 churches designed by Sir Christopher Wren, mostly just ornamentation around St. Paul's Cathedral. Today, while home to only 5,000 residents, The City thrives with nearly 500,000 office workers coming and going daily. It's a fascinating district to wander on weekdays, but since almost nobody actually lives there, it's dull in the evenings and on Saturday and Sunday. You can download a free Rick Steves audio tour of The City for your mobile device via www.ricksteves.com/audioeurope, iTunes, or the Rick Steves Audio Europe smartphone app.

St. Paul's Cathedral and Nearby

▲▲▲**St. Paul's Cathedral**—Wren's most famous church is the great St. Paul's, its elaborate interior capped by a 365-foot dome.

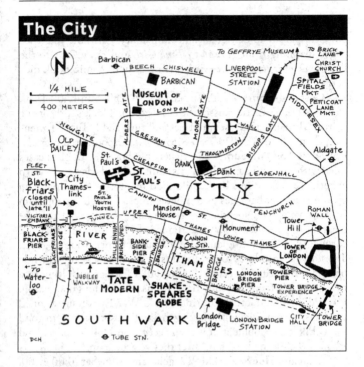

The City

Since World War II, St. Paul's has been Britain's symbol of resistance. Despite 57 nights of bombing, the Nazis failed to destroy the cathedral, thanks to the St. Paul's volunteer fire watchmen, who stayed on the dome.

St. Paul's is England's national church. There's been a church on this spot since 604. After the Great Fire of 1666 destroyed the old cathedral, Wren created a Baroque masterpiece. Even now, as skyscrapers encroach, the dome of St. Paul's rises majestically above the rooftops of the neighborhood.

Inside, this big church *feels* big. At 515 feet long and 250 feet wide, it's Europe's fourth-largest, after Rome (St. Peter's), Sevilla, and Milan. The spaciousness is accentuated by the relative lack of decoration. The simple, cream-colored ceiling and the clear glass in the windows light everything evenly.

There are many legends buried here: Horatio Nelson, who wore down Napoleon; the Duke of Wellington, who finished Napoleon off; and even Charles Cornwallis, who was finished off by George Washington at Yorktown. Often the site of historic funerals (Queen Victoria and Winston Churchill), St. Paul's most famous ceremony was a wedding—when Prince Charles married Lady Diana Spencer in 1981.

During your visit, you can climb the dome for a great city view and have some fun in the Whispering Gallery. Whisper sweet nothings into the wall, and your partner (and anyone else) standing far away can hear you. For best effects, try whispering (not talking) with your mouth close to the wall, while your partner stands a few dozen yards away with his or her ear to the wall. The crypt (included with admission) is a world of historic bones and interesting cathedral models.

Cost and Hours: £12.50, includes church entry and dome climb; Mon-Sat 8:30-16:30, last church entry for sightseeing 16:00, last dome entry 16:15, closed Sun except for worship, £3 tours and £4 audioguides; download free Rick Steves audio tour for your mobile device via www.ricksteves.com/audioeurope, iTunes, or the Rick Steves Audio Europe smartphone app; no photography allowed, cheery café and pricier restaurant in crypt, Tube: St. Paul's; bus #4, #11, #15, #23, or #26. Recorded info tel. 020/7236-4128, reception tel. 020/7246-8350, www.stpauls.co.uk.

Music: The evensong services are free, but nonpaying visitors are not allowed to linger afterward (Mon-Sat at 17:00, Sun at 15:15, 40 minutes).

▲**Old Bailey**—To view the British legal system in action—lawyers in little blond wigs speaking legalese with a British accent—spend a few minutes in the visitors' gallery at the Old Bailey, called the "Central Criminal Court." Don't enter under the dome; signs point you to the two visitors' entrances.

Cost and Hours: Free, generally Mon-Fri 10:00-13:00 & 14:00-16:30 depending on caseload, closed Sat-Sun, reduced hours in Aug; no kids under 14; no bags, mobile phones, cameras, iPods, or food, but small purses OK; Eddie at Bailey's Café across the street at #27 stores bags for £2; 2 blocks northwest of St. Paul's on Old Bailey Street, follow signs to public entrance, Tube: St. Paul's. Tel. 020/7248-3277.

▲**Museum of London**—This museum tells the fascinating story of London, taking you on a walk from its pre-Roman beginnings to the present. It features London's distinguished citizens through history—from Neanderthals to Romans to Elizabethans to Victorians to Mods to today. The museum's displays are chronological, spacious, and informative without being overwhelming. Scale models and costumes help you visualize everyday life in the city at different periods. There are enough whiz-bang multimedia displays (including the Plague and the Great Fire) to spice up otherwise humdrum artifacts. This regular stop for the local school kids gives the best overview of London history in town.

Cost and Hours: Free, daily 10:00-18:00, last entry 30 minutes before closing, see the day's events board for special talks and tours, Tube: Barbican or St. Paul's plus a five-minute walk. Tel. 020/7814-5530, recorded info tel. 020/7001-9844, www.museum oflondon.org.uk.

The Monument—Wren's 202-foot-tall tribute to London's Great Fire was recently restored. Climb the 331 steps inside the column for a view of The City that is still monumental (£3, daily 9:30-17:30, last entry at 17:00, junction of Monument Street and Fish Street Hill, Tube: Monument, tel. 020/7626-2717, www.the monument.info).

Tower of London and Nearby

▲▲▲**Tower of London**—The Tower has served as a castle in wartime, a king's residence in times of peace, and, most notoriously, as the prison and execution site of rebels. You can see the crown jewels, take a witty Beefeater tour, and ponder the executioner's block that dispensed with Anne Boleyn, Sir Thomas More, and troublesome heirs to the throne.

William I, still getting used to his new title of "the Conqueror," built the stone "White Tower" (1077-1097) to keep the Londoners in line. The Tower also served as an effective lookout for seeing invaders coming up the Thames. His successors enlarged it to its present 18-acre size. Because of the security it provided, it has served over the centuries as the Royal Mint, the Royal Jewel House, and as a prison and execution site.

The Tower's hard stone and glittering jewels represent the ultimate power of the monarch. The crown jewels include the world's largest cut diamond—the 530-carat Star of Africa—placed in the royal scepter. When Queen Elizabeth II opens Parliament, she checks out the Imperial State Crown with its 3,733 jewels, including Elizabeth I's pearl earrings.

You'll find more bloody history per square inch in this original tower of power than anywhere else in Britain, though the actual execution site (in the courtyard) looks just like a lawn. Not all prisoners died at the block—Richard III supposedly ordered two teenage princes strangled in their prison cells because they were a threat to his throne.

Today, while the Tower's military purpose is history, it's still home to the Beefeaters (the 25 Yeoman Warders and their families), who host three million visitors a year. Although these men (and one woman) are no longer expected to protect the monarch, the Beefeaters have evolved into great entertainers, leading groups of tourists through the Tower.

For a refreshingly different Tower experience, come on Sunday mornings, when visitors are welcome on the grounds for free to worship in the Royal Chapel. You get in without the lines, but you can only see the chapel—no sightseeing (9:15 Communion or 11:00

service with fine choral music, meet at west gate 30 minutes early, dress for church).

Cost and Hours: £17, family-£47; audioguide-£4; March-Oct Tue-Sat 9:00-17:30, Sun-Mon 10:00-17:30; Nov-Feb Tue-Sat 9:00-16:30, Sun-Mon 10:00-16:30; last entry 30 minutes before closing; no photography allowed of jewels or in chapels; Tube: Tower Hill. Switchboard toll tel. 0844-482-7777.

Getting Tickets: The long but fast-moving ticket lines are worst on Sundays. Avoid lines anytime by buying your ticket online (www.hrp.org.uk), at the Trader's Gate gift shop down the steps from the Tower Hill Tube stop, at the Tower Welcome Centre to the left of the normal ticket line (credit card only), in advance at any London TI (no extra charge), or by phone (£2 extra fee, tel. 0844-482-7799 within UK, tel. 011-44-20-3166-6000 from the US). After your visit, consider taking the boat to Greenwich from here (see "Cruises" on page 728).

More Sights near the Tower—The best remaining bit of London's **Roman Wall** is just north of the Tower (at the Tower Hill Tube station).

The iconic **Tower Bridge** (often mistakenly called London Bridge) has been freshly painted and is undergoing restoration. The hydraulically powered drawbridge was built in 1894 to accommodate the growing East End. While fully modern, its design was a retro Neo-Gothic look.

You can tour the bridge at the **Tower Bridge Experience,** with a history exhibit and a peek at the Victorian engine room that lifts the span (£7, daily 10:00-18:00 in summer, 9:30-17:30 in winter, last entry 30 minutes before closing, good view, poor value, enter at the northwest tower, tel. 020/7403-3761, Tube: Tower Hill, www.towerbridge.org.uk). The visit is most interesting when the drawbridge lifts to let ships pass, as it does a thousand times a year; for the bridge-lifting schedule, see the website or call 020/7940-3984.

The chic **St. Katharine Dock,** just east of Tower Bridge, has private yachts, mod shops, and the classic Dickens Inn, fun for a drink or pub lunch. Across the bridge is the South Bank, with the upscale Butlers Wharf area, City Hall, museums, and the Jubilee Walkway.

Northeast of The City

▲Geffrye Museum—This low-key but well-organized museum—housed in an 18th-century almshouse—is located north of Liverpool Street Station in the trendy Shoreditch area. Walk past 11 English living rooms, furnished and decorated in styles from 1600 to 2000, then descend the circular stairs to see changing exhibits on home decor. In summer, explore the fragrant herb garden.

The South Bank

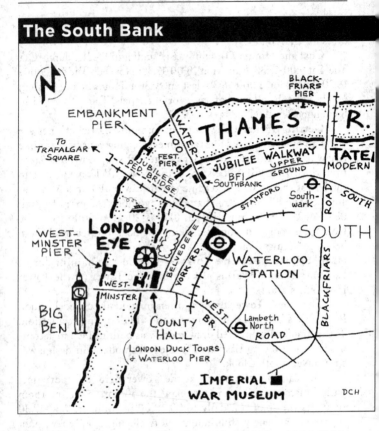

Cost and Hours: Free, Tue-Sat 10:00-17:00, Sun 12:00-17:00, closed Mon, garden open April-Oct, 136 Kingsland Road. Tel. 020/7739-9893, www.geffrye-museum.org.uk. To get here, take the Tube to Liverpool Street, then it's a 10-minute ride north on bus #149 or #242. Or take the East London line on the Overground to the Hoxton stop, which is right next to the museum.

South Bank

▲**Jubilee Walkway**—The South Bank is a thriving arts and cultural center tied together by this riverside path, a popular, pub-crawling pedestrian promenade called the Jubilee Walkway. Stretching from Tower Bridge past Westminster Bridge, it offers grand views of the Houses of Parliament and St. Paul's. On a sunny day, this is the place to see London out strolling. The Walkway hugs the river except just east of London Bridge, where it cuts inland for a couple of blocks. Plans are underway to expand the path into a 60-mile "Greenway" encircling the city, scheduled to open in 2012 for the Olympic Games and Elizabeth's 60th year

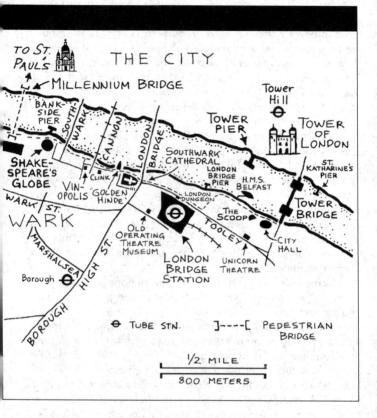

as queen (www.jubileewalkway.org.uk).

▲▲**London Eye**—This giant Ferris wheel, towering above London opposite Big Ben, is the world's highest observational wheel and London's answer to the Eiffel Tower. While the experience is memorable, London doesn't have much of a skyline, and the price is borderline outrageous. But whether you ride or not, the wheel is a sight to behold.

Designed like a giant bicycle wheel, it's a pan-European undertaking: British steel and Dutch engineering, with Czech, German, French, and Italian mechanical parts. It's also very "green," running extremely efficiently and virtually silently. Twenty-five people ride in each of its 32 air-conditioned capsules for the 30-minute rotation (you go around only once). Each capsule has a bench, but most people stand. From the top of this 443-foot-high wheel—the highest public viewpoint in the city—even Big Ben looks small. Built to celebrate the new millennium, the Eye's original five-year lease has been extended, and it's becoming a permanent fixture on the London skyline.

After buying your ticket inside, you'll be aggressively ushered into *The London Eye 4-D Experience,* a brief (four-minute) and engaging show combining a 3-D movie with wind and water effects. It basically feels like a bombastic ad for the attraction you already bought a ticket for, and in some ways is more exciting than riding the Eye itself. You can politely skip the show if you want to just get on the wheel, and have the option of coming back later to see the movie.

Cost and Hours: £18, or £41 combo-ticket with Madame Tussauds Waxworks—see page 751, other packages available. Buy tickets at the box office (in the corner of the County Hall building nearest the Eye), in advance by calling 0870-500-0600, or save 10 percent by booking online at www.londoneye.com. Open daily July-Aug 10:00-21:30, June and Sept 10:00-21:00, Oct-May 10:00-20:00, these are last-ascent times, closed Dec 25 and a few days in Jan for annual maintenance, Tube: Waterloo or Westminster. Thames boats come and go from here using the Waterloo Pier at the foot of the wheel.

Crowd-Beating Tips: While not as popular as when it opened, the London Eye can still be crowded at certain times (busiest between 11:00 and 17:00, especially on weekends year-round and every day July-Aug). At the busiest times, you might have to wait up to 30 minutes to buy your ticket, then another 30-45 minutes to board your capsule. If you plan to visit during one of those times, call ahead or go online to pre-book your ticket, then punch your confirmation code into the automated machine in the ticket office (no wait to get the ticket, but you'll still wait to board the wheel). You can pay an extra £10 for a Fast Track ticket that lets you jump the queue, but the time savings are probably not worth the expense.

By the Eye: The area next to the London Eye has developed a cotton-candy ambience of kitschy, kid-friendly attractions. There's an aquarium, game arcade, and "Movieum" dedicated to movies filmed in London, from *Harry Potter* to *Star Wars.*

▲▲**Imperial War Museum**—This impressive museum covers the wars of the last century—from World War I biplanes to the rise of fascism to Montgomery's Africa campaign tank to the Cold War, the Cuban Missile Crisis, the Troubles in Northern Ireland, the wars in Iraq, and terrorism.

Allow plenty of time, as this powerful museum—with lots of artifacts and video clips—can be engrossing. The core of the permanent collection, located downstairs, takes you step by step through World Wars I and II. A special exhibit called "Monty: Master of the Battlefield" celebrates Field Marshal Bernard Montgomery. Then you move on to conflicts since 1945. Most of the displays are low-tech—glass cases hold dummies in uniforms, weapons, newspaper clippings, ordinary objects from daily life—but have excellent explanations and video clips. The Trench Experience lets you walk through a dark, chaotic, smelly WWI trench. The Blitz Experience film assaults the senses with the noise and intensity of a WWII air raid on London. Also, the cinema shows a rotating selection of films.

In the entry hall are the large exhibits—including Monty's tank, several field guns, and, dangling overhead, vintage planes. Imagine the awesome power of the 50-foot V-2 rocket, the kind the Nazis rained down on London, which could arrive silently and destroy a city block. Its direct descendant was the Polaris missile, capable of traveling nearly 3,000 miles in 20 minutes and obliterating an entire city.

Two other sections are not to be missed: The "Secret War" peeks into the intrigues of espionage in World Wars I and II and in conflicts since. The section on the Holocaust, one of the best on the subject anywhere, tells the story with powerful videos, artifacts, and fine explanations.

War wonks will love the place, as will general history buffs who enjoy patiently reading displays. For the rest, there are enough multimedia exhibits and submarines for the kids to climb in to keep it interesting.

Rather than glorify war, the museum does its best to shine a light on the 100 million deaths of the 20th century. It shows everyday life for people back home and never neglects the powerful human side of one of humankind's most persistent traits.

The museum (which sits in an inviting park equipped with an equally inviting café) is housed in what was the Royal Bethlam Hospital. Also known as "the Bedlam asylum," the place was so wild that it gave the world a new word for chaos. Back in Victorian times, locals—without reality shows and YouTube—paid admission to visit the asylum on weekends for entertainment.

Cost and Hours: Free, daily 10:00-18:00, temporary exhibits extra, often guided tours on weekends—ask at info desk, £4 audioguide, Tube: Lambeth North or bus #12 or bus #159. Tel. 020/7416-5000, www.iwm.org.uk.

▲▲**Tate Modern**—Dedicated in the spring of 2000, the striking museum across the river from St. Paul's opened the new century with art from the previous one. Its powerhouse collection of Monet, Matisse, Dalí, Picasso, Warhol, and much more is displayed in a converted powerhouse. Of equal interest are the many temporary exhibits featuring cutting-edge art. Each year, the main hall features a different monumental installation by a prominent artist.

Cost and Hours: Free but £3 donations appreciated, fee for special exhibitions, daily 10:00-18:00, Fri-Sat until 22:00—good times to visit, last entry to temporary exhibitions 45 minutes before closing, audioguide-£3.50; free 45-minute guided tours at 11:00, 12:00, 14:00, and 15:00—confirm at info desk; view restaurant on top floor, cross the Millennium Bridge from St. Paul's; Tube: Southwark, London Bridge or Mansion House plus a 10-15-minute walk; or connect by "Tate to Tate" boat from Tate Britain for £5 one-way or £12 for day ticket, 33 percent discount with Travelcard or Oyster card, buy ticket on board. Tel. 020/7887-8888, www .tate.org.uk.

▲**Millennium Bridge**—The pedestrian bridge links St. Paul's Cathedral and the Tate Modern across the Thames. This is London's first new bridge in a century. When it first opened, the $25 million bridge wiggled when people walked on it, so it promptly closed for an $8 million, 20-month stabilization; now it's stable and open again. Nicknamed the "blade of light" for its sleek minimalist design (370 yards long, four yards wide, stainless steel with teak planks), its clever aerodynamic handrails deflect wind over the heads of pedestrians.

▲▲**Shakespeare's Globe**—This replica of the original Globe Theatre was built, half-timbered and thatched, as it was in Shakespeare's time. (This is the first thatched roof constructed in London since they were outlawed after the Great Fire of 1666.) The Globe originally accommodated 2,200 seated and another 1,000 standing. Today, slightly smaller and leaving space for reasonable aisles, the theater holds 800 seated and 600 groundlings. Its promoters brag that the theater melds "the three A's"—actors, audience, and architecture—with each contributing to the play. The working theater hosts authentic performances of Shakespeare's plays with actors in period costumes, modern interpretations of his works, and some works by other playwrights (generally all summer at 14:00 and 19:30—but confirm). For details on seeing a play, see page 776.

The complex has three parts: the theater itself, the box office, and a museum. The Globe Exhibition ticket (£10.50) includes both a tour of the theater and the museum. First, you browse on your own through the **museum's** displays of Elizabethan-era costumes, music, script-printing, and special effects. There are early folios and objects that were dug up on site. A video and scale models help put Shakespearean theater within the context of the times. (The Globe opened one year after England mastered the seas by defeating the Spanish Armada. The debut play was Shakespeare's *Julius Caesar*.)

Next comes the tour of the **theater**—you must take the tour at the time stamped on your ticket, but you can come back to the museum afterward; tickets are good all day. The guide (usually an actor) leads you into the theater to see the stage and the different seating areas for the different classes of people. You take a seat and learn how the new Globe is similar to the old Globe (open-air performances, standing-room by the stage, no curtain) and how it's different (female actors today, lights for night performances, concrete floor). It's not a backstage tour—you don't see dressing rooms or costume shops or sit in on rehearsals, though you may see workers building sets for a new production. You mostly sit and listen. The guides are energetic, theatrical, and knowledgeable, bringing the Elizabethan period to life.

When matinee performances are going on, you can't tour the theater. But you can see the museum, then tour the nearby (and less interesting) Rose Theatre instead.

Cost and Hours: £10.50 includes museum and 40-minute tour, £7.50 when only the Rose Theatre is available for touring, tickets good all day; complex open daily 9:00-17:00; exhibition and tours: May-Sept—Globe tours offered mornings only with Rose Theatre tours in afternoon; Oct-April—Globe tours run all day, tours start every 15-30 minutes; on the South Bank directly across Thames over Southwark Bridge from St. Paul's, Tube: Mansion House or London Bridge plus a 10-minute walk. Tel. 020/7902-1400 or 020/7902-1500, www.shakespeares-globe.org.

Eating: The Swan at the Globe café offers a sit-down restaurant (for lunch and dinner, reservations recommended, tel. 020/7928-9444), a drinks-and-plates bar, and a sandwich-and-coffee cart (daily 9:00-closing, depending on performance times).

Vinopolis: City of Wine—While it seems illogical to have a huge wine museum in beer-loving London, Vinopolis makes a good case. Built over a Roman wine store and filling the massive vaults of an old wine warehouse, the museum offers an excellent audioguide with a light yet earnest history of wine to accompany your sips of various mediocre reds and whites, ports, and champagnes. Allow some time, as the audioguide takes 1.5 hours—and the sipping can slow things down pleasantly. This place is popular. Booking ahead for Friday and Saturday nights is a must.

Cost and Hours: Self-guided tour options range from £20 to £65—each includes about five wine tastes and an audioguide. Other options are available for guided tours. Some packages also include whiskey (the new wine), other spirits, or a meal. Thu-Sat 12:00-22:00, Sun 12:00-18:00, closed Mon-Wed, last entry 2.5 hours before closing, between the Globe and Southwark Cathedral at 1 Bank End, Tube: London Bridge. Tel. 020/7940-8300, www.vinopolis.co.uk.

Southwark

These sights are in Southwark, on the South Bank. The area stretching from the Tate Modern to London Bridge, known as

Southwark (SUTH-uck), was for centuries the place Londoners would go to escape the rules and decency of the city and let their hair down. Bearbaiting, brothels, rollicking pubs, and theater—you name the dream, and it could be fulfilled just across the Thames. A run-down warehouse district through the 20th century, it's been gentrified with classy restaurants, office parks, pedestrian promenades, major sights (such as the Tate Modern and Shakespeare's Globe), and this colorful collection of lesser sights. The area is easy on foot and a scenic—though circuitous—way to connect the Tower of London with St. Paul's.

The Clink Prison Museum—Proudly the "original clink," this was, until 1780, where law-abiding citizens threw Southwark troublemakers. Today, it's a low-tech torture museum filling grotty old rooms with papier-mâché gore. Unfortunately, there's little that seriously deals with the fascinating problem of law and order in Southwark, where 18th-century Londoners went for a good time.

Cost and Hours: Overpriced at £5; July-Sept daily 10:00-21:00; Oct-June Mon-Fri 10:00-18:00, Sat-Sun until 19:30; 1 Clink Street, Tube: London Bridge. Tel. 020/7403-0900, www.clink .co.uk.

Golden Hinde Replica—This is a full-size replica of the 16th-century warship in which Sir Francis Drake circumnavigated the globe from 1577 to 1580. Commanding this ship, Drake earned the reputation as history's most successful pirate. The original is long gone, but this boat has logged more than 100,000 miles, including a voyage around the world. While the ship is fun to see, its interior is not worth touring.

Cost and Hours: £6, daily 10:00-17:00; may be closed if rented out for pirate birthday parties, school groups, or weddings; Tube: London Bridge. Tel. 020/7403-0123, www.goldenhinde.com.

Southwark Cathedral—While made a cathedral only in 1905, it's been the neighborhood church since the 13th century, and comes with some interesting history. The enthusiastic docents give impromptu tours if you ask.

Cost and Hours: Free but £4 suggested donation, daily 8:00-18:00, last entry 30 minutes before closing, £2.50 guidebook, no photos without permission, Tube: London Bridge. Tel. 020/7367-6700, http://cathedral.southwark.anglican.org.

Music: The cathedral hosts evensong services (weekdays at 17:30, Sat at 16:00, Sun at 15:00, no service on Wed or alternate Mon).

▲**Old Operating Theatre Museum and Herb Garret**—Climb a tight and creaky wooden spiral staircase to a church attic where you'll find a garret used to dry medicinal herbs, a fascinating exhibit on Victorian surgery, cases of well-described 19th-century medical paraphernalia, and a special look at "anesthesia, the defeat of pain." Then you stumble upon Britain's oldest operating theater, where limbs were sawed off way back in 1821.

Cost and Hours: £5.80, cash only, daily 10:30-16:45, 9a St. Thomas Street, Tube: London Bridge. Tel. 020/7188-2679, www.thegarret.org.uk.

HMS *Belfast*—"The last big-gun armored warship of World War II" clogs the Thames just upstream from the Tower Bridge. This huge vessel—now manned with wax sailors—thrills kids who always dreamed of sitting in a turret shooting off their imaginary guns. If you're into WWII warships, this is the ultimate. Otherwise, it's just lots of exercise with a nice view of the Tower Bridge.

Cost and Hours: £12.95, includes audioguide, daily March-Oct 10:00-18:00, Nov-Feb 10:00-17:00, last entry one hour before closing, Tube: London Bridge. Tel. 020/7940-6300, www.hms belfast.iwm.org.uk.

City Hall—The glassy, egg-shaped building near the south end of Tower Bridge is London's City Hall, designed by Sir Norman Foster, the architect who worked on London's Millennium Bridge and Berlin's Reichstag. City Hall houses the office of London's mayor—the blond, flamboyant, conservative former journalist and author Boris Johnson. He consults here with the Assembly representatives of the city's 25 districts. An interior spiral ramp allows visitors to watch and hear the action below in the Assembly Chamber—ride the lift to the second floor (the highest visitors can go) and spiral down. On the lower ground floor is a large aerial photograph of London, an information desk, and a handy cafeteria. Next to City Hall is the outdoor amphitheater called The Scoop.

Cost and Hours: City Hall is free and open to visitors Mon-Thu 8:00-18:00, Fri 8:00-17:30, closed Sat-Sun; Tube: London Bridge station plus 10-minute walk, or Tower Hill station plus 15-minute walk. Tel. 020/7983-4000.

West London

▲▲Tate Britain—One of Europe's great art houses, Tate Britain specializes in British painting from the 16th century through modern times. The museum has a good representation of William Blake's religious sketches, the Pre-Raphaelites' realistic art, and J. M. W. Turner's swirling works. This is people's art, with realistic paintings rooted in the people, landscape, and stories of the British Isles. You'll see Hogarth's stage sets, Gainsborough's ladies, Blake's angels, Constable's clouds, Turner's tempests, the swooning realism of the Pre-Raphaelites, and the camera-eye portraits of Hockney and Freud. What you won't see here are the fleshy goddesses, naked baby angels, and Madonna-and-child altarpieces so popular elsewhere in Europe. The largely Protestant English

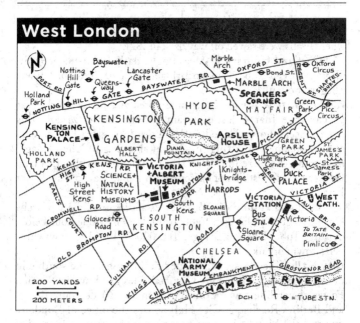

West London

abhorred the "graven images" of the wealthy Catholic world.

The collection is constantly in motion but the basic layout stays the same: a roughly chronological walk through British paintings from 1500 to 1901 in the west half of the building, the 20th century in the east, and the works of J. M. W. Turner in the adjoining Clore Gallery.

Cost and Hours: Free, £2 donation requested, temporary exhibits extra; daily 10:00-18:00, last entry to special exhibitions at 17:15, first Fri of the month until 22:00, last entry to special exhibitions at 20:30; no photography allowed without advance permission, café and restaurant; Tube: Pimlico, then 7-minute walk; take the "Tate to Tate" boat directly to the museum from Tate Modern; or take bus #87 from National Gallery or bus #88 from Oxford Circus. Switchboard tel. 020/7887-8888, recorded info tel. 020/7887-8008, www.tate.org.uk.

Tours: Free tours are offered Mon-Fri at 11:00 (art from 1500 to 1800), 12:00 (art from 1800 to 1900), 14:00 (Turner), and 15:00 (art from the 20th century). Weekend tours cover the collection's highlights (Sat-Sun 12:00 and 15:00); call to confirm schedule. The £3.50 audioguide (with photos and video clips) is useful.

▲**Apsley House (Wellington Museum)**—Having beaten Napoleon at Waterloo, Arthur Wellesley, the First Duke of Wellington, was once the most famous man in Europe. He was given a huge fortune with which he purchased London's ultimate address, #1 London. His refurbished mansion offers a nice interior, a handful of world-class paintings, and a glimpse at the life of the great soldier and two-time prime minister. Those who know something about Wellington ahead of time will appreciate the place much more than those who don't, as there's scarce biographical background. The place is well-described by the included audioguide, which has sound bites from the current Duke of Wellington (who still lives at Apsley).

Cost and Hours: £6, free on June 18—Waterloo Day, April-Oct Wed-Sun 11:00-17:00, Nov-March until 16:00, closed Mon-Tue, 20 yards from Hyde Park Corner Tube station. Tel. 020/7499-5676, www.english-heritage.org.uk. Hyde Park's pleasant and picnic-friendly rose garden is nearby.

Note that the **Wellington Arch,** which stands just across the street, is open to the public but not worth the £4 charge (elevator up, lousy views and boring exhibits).

▲**Hyde Park and Speakers' Corner**—London's "Central Park," originally Henry VIII's hunting grounds, has more than 600 acres of lush greenery, the huge man-made Serpentine Lake, the royal Kensington Palace and Orangery (described later), and the ornate Neo-Gothic Albert Memorial across from the Royal Albert Hall. The western half of the park is known as Kensington Gardens.

On Sundays, from just after noon until early evening, **Speakers' Corner** offers soapbox oratory at its best (northeast corner of the park, Tube: Marble Arch). Characters climb their stepladders, wave their flags, pound emphatically on their sandwich boards, and share what they are convinced is their wisdom. Regulars have resident hecklers who know their lines and are always ready with a verbal jab or barb. "The grass roots of democracy" is actually a holdover from when the gallows stood here and the criminal was allowed to say just about anything he wanted to before he swung. I dare you to raise your voice and gather a crowd—it's easy to do.

The **Princess Diana Memorial Fountain** honors the "People's Princess," who once lived in nearby Kensington Palace. The low-key circular stream, great for cooling off your feet on a hot day, is in the south central part of the park, near the Albert Memorial and Serpentine Gallery. (Don't be confused by signs to the Diana, Princess of Wales Memorial Playground, in the northwest corner of the park.)

▲▲▲**Victoria and Albert Museum**—The world's top collection of decorative arts (vases, stained glass, fine furniture, clothing, jewelry, carpets, and more) is a surprisingly interesting assortment of crafts from the West, as well as Asian and Islamic cultures. The British Galleries are grand, but there's much more to see, including Raphael's tapestry cartoons and a cast of Trajan's Column that depicts the emperor's conquests.

The V&A grew out of the Great Exhibition of 1851, that ultimate celebration of the Industrial Revolution. Now "art" could be brought to the masses through modern technology and mass production. The museum was founded on the idealistic Victorian notion that anyone can be continually improved by education and example. After much support from Queen Victoria and Prince Albert, the museum was renamed for the royal couple, and its present building was opened in 1909.

The V&A is in the midst of a 10-year update and expansion. Changes so far include a new café, sculpture gallery, Islamic room, and refurbished Medieval and Renaissance galleries. During this chaotic time, exhibits may be rearranged, so check with the information desk for current room closures, carry a copy of the museum's detailed map, and ask a nearby guard if you can't find one of the objects I mention below.

You could spend days in this place. The museum is large and gangly, with 150 rooms and more than 12 miles of corridors. Pick up the much-needed museum map (£1 suggested donation). While just wandering works well here, consider catching one of the free one-hour orientation tours or buying the fine £5 *V&A Guide Book*.

Here are a few highlights:

The **British Galleries** sweeps chronologically through 400 years of British high-class living (1500-1900)—all laid out over two floors, and beautifully described.

In Room 46A are the plaster casts of **Trajan's Column**—a copy of Rome's 140-foot spiral relief telling the story of the conquest of Dacia (modern-day Romania).

Room 46B has plaster casts of **Renaissance sculptures** by Michelangelo and others, which allowed 19th-century art students who couldn't afford a railpass to go study the classics. Compare Michelangelo's monumental *David* with Donatello's girlish *David* (at the other end of the room), and see Ghiberti's bronze Baptistery doors that inspired the Florentine Renaissance.

In Room 48A are **Raphael's "cartoons,"** seven of the full-size designs by Raphael that were used to produce tapestries for the Sistine Chapel (approximately 13 feet by 17 feet, done in tempera on paper, now mounted on canvas). The cartoons were sent to factories in Brussels, cut into strips (see the lines), and placed on the looms. The scenes are the reverse of the final product—lots of left-handed saints.

Cost and Hours: Free, £3 donation requested, possible pricey fee for special exhibits, daily 10:00-17:45, Fri until 22:00, free one-hour tours daily on the half-hour 10:30-15:30, Tube: South Kensington, from the Tube station a long tunnel leads directly to museum. Tel. 020/7942-2000, www.vam.ac.uk.

▲▲**Natural History Museum**—Across the street from Victoria and Albert, this mammoth museum is housed in a giant and wonderful Victorian, Neo-Romanesque building. In the main hall, above a big dinosaur skeleton and under a massive slice of sequoia tree, Charles Darwin sits as if upon a throne overseeing it all. Built in the 1870s specifically for the huge collection (50 million specimens), the building has two halves: the Life Galleries (creepy-crawlies, human biology, "our place in evolution," and awe-inspiring dinosaurs) and the Earth Galleries (meteors, volcanoes, earthquakes, and so on).

Exhibits are wonderfully explained, with lots of creative, interactive displays. Pop in, if only for the wild collection of dinosaurs and to hear English children exclaim, "Oh my goodness!" Get oriented by talking with one of the many "visit planners" (helpful guides scattered throughout the museum), review the "What's on Today" board for special events and tours, and note which sections are closed (rather than "renovating," they say "we are evolving"). While the dinosaur hall often has a long line, everything else is wide open. Don't miss the vault in the mineralogy section (top floor of the green zone), with rare and precious stones (including a meteorite from Mars and the Aurora Pyramid of Hope, displaying 296 diamonds showing their full range of natural colors).

Cost and Hours: Free, fees for special exhibits, daily 10:00-17:50, last entry at 17:30, occasional tours, long tunnel leads directly from South Kensington Tube station to museum. Tel. 020/7942-5000, exhibit info and reservations tel. 020/7942-5011, www.nhm.ac.uk.

▲**Science Museum**—Next door to the Natural History Museum, this sprawling wonderland for curious minds is kid-perfect, with themes such as measuring time, exploring space, and the evolution of modern medicine. It offers hands-on fun, from moonwalks to deep-sea exploration, with trendy technology exhibits, an IMAX theater (£8, kids-£6.25), and cool rotating themed exhibits.

Cost and Hours: Free, daily 10:00-18:00, Exhibition Road, Tube: South Kensington. Toll tel. 0870-870-4868, www.sciencemuseum.org.uk.

Kensington Palace—In 1689, King William and Queen Mary moved from Whitehall in central London to the more pristine and peaceful village of Kensington (now engulfed by London). Sir Christopher Wren renovated an existing house into Kensington Palace, which became the center of English court life until 1760, when the royal family moved into Buckingham Palace. Since then, lesser royals have bedded down in Kensington Palace. Princess Diana lived here from her 1981 marriage to Prince Charles until her death in 1997. Today it's home to three of Charles' cousins. The palace, while still functioning as a royal residence, also welcomes visitors with an impressive string of royal apartments and a few rooms of royal dresses.

While generally a ▲▲ attraction, the palace is currently being renovated, and until June 2012 it's not worth your time or money. Rather than close it during restoration, they've created a silly "Enchanted Palace" theatrical show replacing the historic artifacts of the palace (such as the wonderful royal dress collection, splendid 17th-century furniture of the William and Mary apartments, and the bed where Queen Victoria was born—fully clothed, it is said) with cheesy modern props. The only good thing about the Enchanted Palace is that it enables unwitting tourists to help pay for the £12 million renovation.

Cost and Hours: £12.50, daily 10:00-18:00, until 17:00 in winter, last entry one hour before closing, a 10-minute hike through Kensington Gardens from either Queensway or High Street Kensington Tube station. Toll tel. 0870-751-5170 or 0844-482-7777, www.hrp.org.uk.

Eating: Garden enthusiasts enjoy popping into the secluded Sunken Garden, 50 yards from the exit. Consider afternoon tea at the nearby Orangery, built as a greenhouse for Queen Anne in 1704 (tea served 12:00-18:00, £15 "Orangery tea," £35 "Tregothnan tea," à la carte treats, no reservations taken, tel. 020/3166-6113).

Victoria Station—From underneath this station's iron-and-glass canopy, trains depart for the south of England and Gatwick Airport. While Victoria Station is famous and a major Tube stop, few tourists actually take trains from here—most just come to take in the exciting bustle. It's a fun place to just be a "rock in a river" teeming with commuters and services. The station is surrounded by big red buses, taxis, travel agencies, and lousy eateries. It's next to the main intercity bus station (Victoria Coach Station) and the best inexpensive lodgings in town.

Westminster Cathedral—This cathedral, the largest Catholic church in England and just a block from Victoria Station, is striking, but not very historic or important to visit. Opened in 1903, it has a brick Neo-Byzantine flavor (surrounded by glassy office blocks). While it's definitely not Westminster Abbey, half the tourists wandering around inside seem to think it is. The highlight is the lift to the viewing gallery atop its 273-foot bell tower (£5 for the lift, tower open daily 9:30-12:30 & 13:00-17:00).

Cost and Hours: Free entry, daily 7:00-19:00; 5-minute walk from Victoria Station or take bus #11, #24, #148, #211, or #507 to museum's door; just off Victoria Street, Tube: Victoria; www.westminstercathedral.org.uk.

National Army Museum—This museum is not as awe-inspiring as the Imperial War Museum, but it's still fun, especially for kids into soldiers, armor, and guns. And while the Imperial War Museum is limited to wars of the 20th century, the National Army Museum tells the story of the British army from 1415 through the Bosnian conflict and Iraq, with lots of Redcoat lore and a good look at Waterloo. Kids enjoy trying on a Cromwellian helmet, seeing the skeleton of Napoleon's horse, and peering out from a World War I trench through a working periscope.

Cost and Hours: Free, daily 10:00-17:30, Royal Hospital Road, Chelsea, Tube: Sloane Square. Tel. 020/7730-0717 or 020/7881-2455, www.national-army-museum.ac.uk.

Greater London
West of Central London

▲▲**Kew Gardens**—For a fine riverside park and a palatial greenhouse jungle to swing through, take the Tube or the boat to every botanist's favorite escape, Kew Gardens. While to most visitors the Royal Botanic Gardens of Kew are simply a delightful opportunity to wander among 33,000 different types of plants, to the hardworking organization that runs the gardens, it's a way to promote understanding and preservation of the botanical diversity of our planet. The Kew Tube station drops you in an herbal little business community, a two-block walk from Victoria Gate (the main garden entrance). Pick up a map brochure and check at the gate for a monthly listing of best blooms.

Garden-lovers could spend days exploring Kew's 300 acres. For a quick visit, spend a fragrant hour wandering through three buildings: the **Palm House,** a humid Victorian world of iron, glass, and tropical plants built in 1844; a **Waterlily House** that Monet would swim for; and the **Princess of Wales Conservatory,** a modern greenhouse with many different climate zones growing countless cacti, bug-munching carnivorous plants, and more. The latest addition to the gardens is the **Rhizotron and Xstrata Treetop Walkway,** a 200-yard-long scenic steel walkway that puts you high in the canopy 60 feet above the ground.

Cost and Hours: £13.50, discounted to £11.50 45 minutes before closing, kids under 17 free, £5 for Kew Palace only; April-Aug Mon-Fri 9:30-18:30, Sat-Sun 9:30-19:30; closes earlier Sept-March, last entry to gardens 30 minutes before closing, galleries and conservatories close at 17:30 in high season—earlier off-season; free one-hour walking tours daily at 11:00 and 14:00; £4 narrated 40-minute hop-on, hop-off joyride on Kew Explorer tram departs on the hour from 11:00 from near Victoria Gate; Tube: Kew Gardens, boats run April-Oct between Kew Gardens and Westminster Pier—see page 732. Switchboard tel. 020/8332-5000, recorded info tel. 020/8332-5655, www.kew.org.

Eating: For a sun-dappled lunch or afternoon tea, walk 10 minutes from the Palm House to the Orangery (£8-12 lunches, £15-18 afternoon tea, daily 10:00-18:00, until 17:00 in winter, closes early for events, tel. 0844-482-7777 www.hrp.org.uk).

Northeast of Central London
2012 London Olympic Park—From July 27 to August 12, 2012, all eyes will be on London as it hosts athletes from 205 nations in the 30th Olympiad. Though events will take place throughout the city, festivities will center around Olympic Park, filling the Lea Valley in Stratford, about seven miles northeast of central London. Work is scheduled to be complete in the summer of 2011, when a rigorous 12-month testing process will begin. Locals whine about the cost—as locals have whined about big public building projects, I imagine, since the days when great cities built great Gothic churches. But the $14 billion project is a stimulus plan, with 90 percent local investment and employment.

A viewpoint on a nearby greenway (called "The View Tube") comes with information boards, a lookout tower, a café (already well-known for its coffee and brownies), and a WC. It's free and a short walk from the Pudding Mill Lane DLR station. Along the way, you'll see some of the legion of Nepali Gurkhas employed here for security. To get here, ride the Tube (Jubilee Line) from central London to Stratford, where you can change to the DLR to Pudding Mill Lane. To go direct on the DLR, take a Stratford-bound train from Bank (in central London, also accessible from the Monument Tube station) or from Canary Wharf (in the Docklands), and get off at Pudding Mill Lane.

Tours: Blue Badge guides lead 1.5-hour guided walks of the area, weaving background about its Industrial Age heritage into the excitement of today's building project and impressive vision (£8, pay guide directly in cash, online reservations recommended but not required, daily at 11:00, www.toursof2012sites.com). Meet at Bromley-by-Bow Tube station (District or Hammersmith Line).

Note that the Stratford, Pudding Mill Lane, and Bromley-by-Bow stations are (barely) inside Zone 2, which means the trip is covered by any Tube ticket or pass covering Zones 1-2.

Entertainment in London

Theater (a.k.a. "Theatre")
London's theater rivals Broadway's in quality and usually beats it in price. Choose from 200 offerings—Shakespeare, musicals, comedies, thrillers, sex farces, cutting-edge fringe, revivals starring movie celebs, and more. London does it all well. I prefer big, glitzy—even bombastic—musicals over serious chamber dramas,

simply because London can deliver the lights, sound, dancers, and multimedia spectacle I rarely get back home. (If you're a regular visitor to Broadway or Las Vegas—where you have access to similar spectacles—you might prefer some of London's more low-key offerings.)

There are also plenty of enticing plays to choose from, ranging from revivals of classics to cutting-edge works by the hottest young playwrights. Many star huge-name celebrities (you'll see the latest offerings advertised all over the Tube and elsewhere). London is a magnet for movie stars who want to stretch their acting chops. For example, since 2003, Kevin Spacey has been the artistic director of the Old Vic theatre. He has directed and appeared in several productions, and has enlisted many big-name film directors and actors for others (www.oldvictheatre.com).

Most theaters, marked on tourist maps, are found in the West End between Piccadilly and Covent Garden. Box offices, hotels, and TIs offer a handy free *London Theatre Guide* and *Entertainment Guide*. From home, it's easy to check www.officiallondontheatre .co.uk for the latest on what's currently playing in London.

Performances are nightly except Sunday, usually with one or two matinees a week (Shakespeare's Globe is the rare theater that does offer performances on Sun, May-Sept). Tickets range from about £15 to £60. Matinees are generally cheaper and rarely sell out.

To book a seat, simply call the theater box office (which may ring through to a central ticketing office), ask about seats and available dates, and buy a ticket with your credit card. You can call from the US as easily as from England. Arrive about 30 minutes before the show starts to pick up your ticket and avoid lines.

For a booking fee, you can reserve online. Most theater websites link you to a preferred ticket vendor, usually www.ticket master.co.uk or www.seetickets.com. In the US, Keith Prowse Ticketing is also handy by phone or online (US tel. 212/398-4175, www.keithprowse.com).

Although booking through an agency is quick and easy, prices are inflated by a standard 25 percent fee. Ticket agencies (whether in the US, at London's TIs, or scattered throughout the city) are scalpers with an address. If you're buying from an agency, look at the ticket carefully (your price should be no more than 30 percent over the printed face value; the 20 percent VAT is already included in the face value), and understand where you're sitting according to the floor plan (if your view is restricted, it will state this on the ticket; for floor plans of the various theaters, see www.theatre monkey.com).

Agencies are worthwhile only if a show you've just got to see is sold out at the box office. They scarf up hot tickets, planning

London's Major Theaters

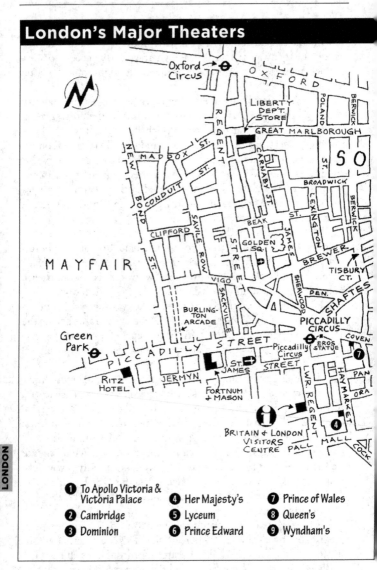

1 To Apollo Victoria & Victoria Palace
2 Cambridge
3 Dominion
4 Her Majesty's
5 Lyceum
6 Prince Edward
7 Prince of Wales
8 Queen's
9 Wyndham's

to make a killing after the show is sold out. US booking agencies get their tickets from another agency, adding even more to your expense by involving yet another middleman. Many tickets sold on the street are forgeries. Although some theaters use booking agencies to handle their advance sales, you'll stand a good chance of saving money by avoiding the middleman and simply calling the box office directly to purchase your tickets (international phone calls are cheap, and credit cards make booking a snap).

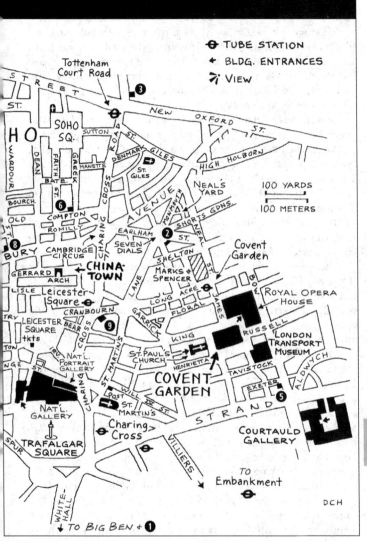

Theater Lingo: stalls (ground floor), dress circle (first balcony), upper circle (second balcony), balcony (sky-high third balcony), slips (cheap seats on the fringes). Many cheap seats have a restricted view (behind a pillar).

Cheap Theater Tricks: Most theaters offer cheap returned tickets, standing-room, matinee, and senior or student standby deals. These "concessions" (discounted tickets) are indicated with a "conc" or "s" in the listings. Picking up a late return can get you a great seat at a cheap-seat price. Even if a show is "sold out," there's usually a way to get a seat. Call the theater box office and ask how.

If you don't care where you sit, you can often buy the absolutely cheapest seats—those with an obstructed view or in the nosebleed section—at the box office; these tickets generally cost less than £20. Many theaters are so small that there's hardly a bad seat. After the lights go down, scooting up is less than a capital offense. Shakespeare did it.

Half-Price "tkts" Booth: This famous ticket booth at Leicester Square sells discounted tickets for top-price seats to shows on the push list—but only on the day of the performance (generally £3 service charge per ticket, Mon-Sat 10:00-19:00, Sun 11:00-16:00, lines often form early, list of shows available online at www.tkts.co.uk). Most tickets are half-price; other shows are discounted 25 percent. Note that the real half-price booth (with its "tkts" name) is a freestanding kiosk at the edge of the garden in Leicester Square. Several dishonest outfits nearby advertise "official half-price tickets"—avoid these.

Here are sample prices: A top-notch seat to *Chicago* costs £59 if you buy directly from the theater; the same seat costs £32.50 at Leicester Square. The cheapest balcony seat is £25 through the theater. Half-price tickets can be a good deal, unless you want the cheapest seats or the hottest shows. But check the board; occasionally they sell cheap tickets to good shows.

West End Theaters: The commercial (nonsubsidized) theaters cluster around Soho (especially along Shaftesbury Avenue) and Covent Garden. With a centuries-old tradition of pleasing the masses, these present London theater at its glitziest.

Royal Shakespeare Company: If you'll ever enjoy Shakespeare, it'll be in Britain. The RSC performs at various theaters around London and in Stratford-upon-Avon year-round. To get a schedule, contact the RSC (Royal Shakespeare Theatre, Stratford-upon-Avon, toll tel. 0844-800-1110, www.rsc.org.uk).

Shakespeare's Globe: To see Shakespeare in a replica of the theater for which he wrote his plays, attend a play at the Globe. In this round, thatch-roofed, open-air theater the plays are performed much as Shakespeare intended—under the sky with no amplification.

The play's the thing from late April through early October (usually Mon 19:30, Tue-Sat 14:00 and 19:30, Sun either 13:00 and/or 18:30, tickets can be sold out months in advance). You'll pay £5 to stand and £15-35 to sit, usually on a backless bench. Because only a few rows and the pricier Gentlemen's Rooms have seats with backs, £1 cushions and £3 add-on back rests are considered a good investment by many. Dress for the weather. The £5 "groundling" tickets—which are open to rain—are most fun. Scurry in early to stake out a spot on the stage's edge, where the most interaction with the actors occurs. You're a crude peasant. You can lean your elbows on the stage, munch a picnic dinner (yes, you can bring in food), or walk around. I've never enjoyed Shakespeare as much as here, performed as it was meant to be in the "wooden O." If you can't get a ticket, consider waiting around. Plays can be long, and many groundlings leave before the end. Hang around outside and beg or buy a ticket from someone leaving early (groundlings are allowed to come and go). A few non-Shakespeare plays are also presented each year.

To reserve tickets for plays, call or drop by the theater box office (Mon-Sat 10:00-18:00, Sun 10:00-17:00, open one hour later on performance days, New Globe Walk entrance, no extra charge to book by phone, tel. 020/7401-9919). You can also reserve online (www.shakespeares-globe.org, £2 booking fee). If the tickets are sold out, don't despair; a few often free up at the last minute. Try calling around noon the day of the performance to see if the box office expects any returned tickets. If so, they'll advise you to show up a little more than an hour before the show, when these tickets are sold (first-come, first-served).

The theater is on the South Bank, directly across the Thames over the Millennium Bridge from St. Paul's Cathedral (Tube: Mansion House or London Bridge). The Globe is inconvenient for public transport, but the courtesy phone in the lobby lets you get a minicab in minutes. (These minicabs have set fees—e.g., £8 to South Kensington—but generally cost less than a metered cab and provide fine and honest service.) During theater season, there's a regular supply of black cabs outside the main foyer on New Globe Walk.

Outdoor Theater in Summer: Enjoy Shakespearean drama and other plays under the stars at the Open Air Theatre, in leafy Regent's Park in north London. Food is allowed: You can bring your own picnic; order à la carte from the theater menu; or pre-order a £22.50 picnic supper from the theater at least 36 hours in advance (tickets £12-50; season runs late May-mid-Sept, box office open April-late May Mon-Sat 10:00-18:00, closed Sun; late May-mid-Sept Mon-Sat 10:00-20:00, Sun 10:00-until start of play on performance days only; order tickets online after mid-Jan or by phone Mon-Sun 9:00-21:00; £1 booking fee by phone, no fee if ordering online or in person; toll tel. 0844-826-4242, www.open airtheatre.org; grounds open 1.5 hours prior to evening performances, one hour prior to 14:30 matinee, and 30 minutes prior to earlier matinees; 10-minute walk north of Baker Street Tube, near Queen Mary's Gardens within Regent's Park; detailed directions and more info at www.openairtheatre.org).

Fringe Theater: London's rougher evening-entertainment

scene is thriving, filling pages in *Time Out*. Choose from a wide range of fringe theater and comedy acts (generally £5).

Classical Music

Concerts at Churches—For easy, cheap, or free concerts in historic churches, ask the TI (or check *Time Out*) about **lunch concerts,** especially:

- St. Bride's Church, with free lunch concerts twice a week at 13:15 (generally Tue, Wed, or Fri—confirm by phone or online, church tel. 020/7427-0133, www.stbrides.com).
- St. James's at Piccadilly, with 50-minute concerts on Monday, Wednesday, and Friday at 13:10 (suggested £3.50 donation, info tel. 020/7381-0441, www.st-james-piccadilly.org).
- St. Martin-in-the-Fields, offering free concerts on Monday, Tuesday, and Friday at 13:00 (suggested £3.50 donation, church tel. 020/7766-1100, www.smitf.org).

St. Martin-in-the-Fields also hosts fine **evening concerts** by candlelight (£6-26, several nights a week at 19:30,) and live jazz in its underground Café in the Crypt (£5.50-9 tickets, Wed at 20:00).

Evensong and Organ Recitals at Churches—Evensong services are held at several churches, including:

- St. Paul's Cathedral (Mon-Sat at 17:00, Sun at 15:15).
- Westminster Abbey (Mon-Tue and Thu-Fri at 17:00, Sat-Sun at 15:00; there's a service on Wed, but it may be spoken, not sung).
- Southwark Cathedral (Mon-Tue and Thu-Fri at 17:30, Sat at 16:00, Sun at 15:00, no service on Wed or alternate Mon, tel. 020/7367-6700, www.southwark.anglican.org/cathedral).

Free **organ recitals** are often held on Sunday at 17:45 in Westminster Abbey (30 minutes, tel. 020/7222-5152). Many other churches have free concerts; ask for the *London Organ Concerts Guide* at the TI.

Prom Concerts, Opera, and Dance—For a fun classical event (mid-July–mid-Sept), attend a **Prom Concert** (shortened from "Promenade Concert") during the annual festival at the Royal Albert Hall. Nightly concerts are offered at give-a-peasant-some-culture prices to "Promenaders"—those willing to stand throughout the performance (£5 standing-room spots sold at the door, £7 restricted-view seats, most £20-54 but depends on performance, Tube: South Kensington, toll tel. 0845-401-5045, www.bbc.co.uk/proms).

Some of the world's best **opera** is belted out at the prestigious Royal Opera House, near Covent Garden (box office tel. 020/7304-4000, www.roh.org.uk), and at the London Coliseum (English National Opera, St. Martin's Lane, Tube: Leicester

Square, box office toll tel. 0871-911-0200, www.eno.org).

For **dance,** try Sadler's Wells Theatre (Rosebery Avenue, Islington, Tube: Angel, info tel. 020/7863-8198, box office toll tel. 0844-412-4300, www.sadlerswells.com).

Other Nightlife

Tours—Guided walks are offered several times a day. **London Walks** is the most established company. Daytime walks vary by theme: ancient London, museums, legal London, Dickens, Beatles, Jewish quarter, Christopher Wren, and so on. In the evening, expect a more limited choice: ghosts, Jack the Ripper, pubs, or literary-themed. Get the latest from their brochure or website, or call for a recorded listing of that day's walks. Show up at the listed time and place, pay the guide, and enjoy the two-hour tour (£8, cash only, tel. 020/7624-3978, recorded info tel. 020/7624-9255, www.walks.com).

To see the city illuminated at night, consider a bus tour. A two-hour **London by Night Sightseeing Tour** leaves every evening from Victoria Station and other points (see page 724).

Summer Evenings Along the South Bank—If you're visiting London in summer, consider the South Bank.

Take a trip around the **London Eye** while the sun sets over the city (the wheel spins until late—last ascent at 21:30 July-Aug, 21:00 in June and Sept). Then cap your night with an evening walk along the pedestrian-only **Jubilee Walkway,** which runs east-west along the river. It's where Londoners go to escape the heat. This pleasant stretch of the walkway—lined with pubs and casual eateries—goes from the London Eye past Shakespeare's Globe to Tower Bridge (you can walk in either direction).

If you're in the mood for a movie, take in a flick at the **BFI Southbank,** located just across the river, alongside Waterloo Bridge. Run by the British Film Institute, the state-of-the-art theater shows mostly classic films, as well as art cinema (£9, £5 on Tue and weekday matinees, Tube: Waterloo or Embankment, box office tel. 020/7928-3232, check www.bfi.org.uk for schedules).

Farther east along the South Bank is **The Scoop**—an outdoor amphitheater next to City Hall. It's a good spot for outdoor movies, concerts, dance, and theater productions throughout the summer—with Tower Bridge as a scenic backdrop. These events are free, nearly nightly, and family-friendly. For the latest event schedule, see www.morelondon.com and click on "The Scoop" (next to City Hall, Riverside, The Queen's Walkway, Tube: London Bridge).

Cruises—During the summer, boats sail as late as 19:00 between Westminster Pier (near Big Ben) and the Tower of London. (For details, see page 728.)

LONDON

A handful of outfits run Thames River evening cruises with four-course meals and dancing. **London Showboat** offers the best value (£75, April-Oct Wed-Sun, March and Nov-Dec Thu-Sat, Jan-Feb Fri-Sat, 3.5 hours, departs at 19:30 from Westminster Pier and returns by 23:00, reservations necessary, tel. 020/7740-0400, www.citycruises.com). Dinner cruises are also offered by **Bateaux London** (£75-125, tel. 020/7695-1800, www.bateauxlondon.com). For more on cruising, get the *River Thames Boat Services* brochure from a London TI.

Sleeping in London

London is an expensive city for rooms. Cheaper rooms are relatively dumpy. Don't expect £130 cheeriness in an £80 room. For £70, you'll get a double with breakfast in a safe, cramped, and dreary place with minimal service and the bathroom down the hall. For £90, you'll get a basic, clean, reasonably cheery double in a usually cramped, cracked-plaster building with a private bath, or a soulless but comfortable room without breakfast in a huge Motel 6–type place. My London splurges, at £160-260, are spacious, thoughtfully appointed places good for entertaining or romancing. Off-season, it's possible to save money by arriving late without a reservation and looking around. Competition softens prices, especially for multinight stays. Check hotel websites for special deals. Remember, all of Britain's accommodations are now non-smoking.

Reserve your London room as soon as you can commit to a date. To call a London hotel from the US or Canada, dial 011-44-

LONDON

Sleep Code

(£1 = about $1.60, country code: 44, area code: 020)
S = Single, **D** = Double/Twin, **T** = Triple, **Q** = Quad, **b** = bathroom, **s** = shower only. Unless otherwise noted, credit cards are accepted and prices include breakfast.

To help you sort through these listings easily, I've divided the rooms into three categories, based on the price for a double room with bath:

$$$ **Higher Priced**—Most rooms £115 or more.
$$ **Moderately Priced**—Most rooms between £70-115.
$ **Lower Priced**—Most rooms £70 or less.

Prices can change without notice; verify the hotel's current rates online or by email. For other updates, see www.ricksteves.com/update.

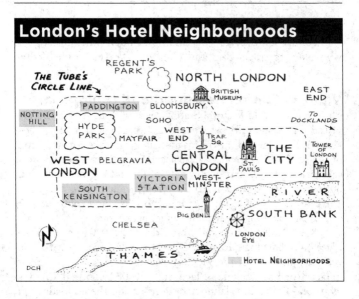

London's Hotel Neighborhoods

20 (London's area code without the initial zero), then the local eight-digit number.

Looking for Hotel Deals Online

Given London's high hotel prices, consider using the Internet to help score a hotel deal. Various websites list rooms in high-rise, three- and four-star business hotels. You'll give up the charm and warmth of a family-run establishment, and breakfast will probably not be included, but you might find that the price is right.

Start by checking the websites of several chains to get an idea of typical rates and to check for online-only deals. Big London hotel chains include the following: Millennium/Copthorne (www.millenniumhotels.com), Thistle (www.thistle.com), Intercontinental/Holiday Inn (www.ichotelsgroup.com), Radisson (www.radisson.com), Hilton (www.hilton.com), and Red Carnation (www.redcarnationhotels.com). For information on no-frills, Motel 6–type chains, see "Big, Good-Value, Modern Hotels," later.

Auction-type sites (such as www.priceline.com or www.hotwire.com) can be great for matching flexible travelers with empty hotel rooms, often at prices well below the hotel's normal rates.

Other favorite accommodation discount sites mentioned by my readers include www.londontown.com (an informative site with a discount booking service), http://athomeinlondon.co.uk and www.londonbb.com (both list central B&Bs), www.lastminute.com, www.visitlondon.com, http://roomsnet.com, and www.eurocheapo.com. Read candid reviews of London hotels at www.tripadvisor.com. And check the "Graffiti Wall" at

LONDON

www.ricksteves.com for the latest tips and discoveries.

For a good overview on finding London hotel deals, go to www.smartertravel.com and click on "Travel Guides," then "London."

Victoria Station Neighborhood (Belgravia)

The streets behind Victoria Station teem with little, moderately-priced-for-London B&Bs. It's a safe, surprisingly tidy, and decent area without a hint of the trashy, touristy glitz of the streets in front of the station. I've divided these accommodations into two broad categories: west or east of the station. Decent eateries abound in both areas (see page 808). All the recommended hotels are within a five-minute walk of the Victoria Tube, bus, and train stations. On hot summer nights, request a quiet back room.

Near the hotels on the west side is the 400-space Semley Place NCP **parking garage** (£32/day, possible discounts with hotel voucher, just west of the Victoria Coach Station at Buckingham Palace Road and Semley Place, toll tel. 0845-050-7080, www .ncp.co.uk). The best laundry options are on the east side: The handy **Pimlico Launderette** is about five blocks southwest of Warwick Square (daily 8:00-19:00, self- or full service, south of Sutherland Street at 3 Westmoreland Terrace, tel. 020/7821-8692), and **Launderette Centre** is a block northeast of Warwick Square (Mon-Fri 8:00-22:00, Sat 8:00-20:00, Sun 9:00-20:00, last wash 2 hours before closing, about £7 wash and dry, £9 full-service, 31 Churton Street, tel. 020/7828-6039).

West of Victoria Station

Here in Belgravia, the prices are a bit higher and your neighbors include Andrew Lloyd Webber and Margaret Thatcher (her policeman stands outside 73 Chester Square). All of these places line up along tranquil Ebury Street, two blocks over from Victoria Station.

$$$ Lime Tree Hotel, enthusiastically run by Charlotte and Matt, comes with 25 spacious, stylish, comfortable, thoughtfully decorated rooms and a fun-loving breakfast room (Sb-£85-95, Db-£120-140, larger superior Db-£140-160, Tb-£150-185, family room-£170-200, free Internet access and Wi-Fi, small lounge opens onto quiet garden, 135 Ebury Street, tel. 020/7730-8191, www.limetreehotel.co.uk, info@limetreehotel.co.uk, trusty Alan covers the night shift).

$$$ B+B Belgravia has done its best to make a tight-and-tangled old guest house sleek and mod. While the 17 rooms are small, the young, can-do staff takes good care of guests, the coffee is always on in the lobby, and the location is unbeatable (Sb-£99, Db-£125, Db twin-£135, Tb-£155, Qb-£165, free Internet access and Wi-Fi, DVD library, loaner bikes, 64-66 Ebury Street—enter at #66, tel. 020/7259-8570, www.bb-belgravia.com, info@bb -belgravia.com). A few doors down, at #82, they rent eight larger "apartments" with basic kitchenettes and a do-it-yourself continental breakfast in the fridge (Db-£120-160 depending on size, reception at main building).

$$ Cartref House B&B offers rare charm on Ebury Street, with 10 delightful rooms and a warm welcome (Sb-£73, Db-£102, Tb-£133, Qb-£164, fans, free Wi-Fi, 129 Ebury Street, tel. 020/7730-6176, www.cartrefhouse.co.uk, info@cartrefhouse.co .uk, Sharon and Derek).

$$ Morgan House rents 11 good rooms and is entertainingly run, with lots of travel tips and friendly chat from owner Rachel Joplin and her staff, Danilo and Fernanda (S-£58, D-£78, Db-£98, T-£98, family suites-£138-148 for 3-4 people, Wi-Fi, 120 Ebury Street, tel. 020/7730-2384, www.morganhouse.co.uk, morgan house@btclick.com).

$$ Lynton Hotel B&B is a well-worn place renting 13 inexpensive rooms with small prefab WCs. It's a fine value run by brothers Mark and Simon Connor (D-£80, Db-£95, ask for best Rick Steves price, free Wi-Fi, 113 Ebury Street, tel. 020/7730-4032, www.lyntonhotel.co.uk, mark-and-simon@lyntonhotel .co.uk).

East of Victoria Station

This area is a bit less genteel-feeling than the neighborhood west of the station, but still plenty inviting. Most of these are on or near Warwick Way, the main drag through this area.

$$ Luna Simone Hotel rents 36 fresh, spacious, well-maintained rooms with modern bathrooms. It's a smartly managed place, run for more than 40 years by twins Peter and Bernard and son Mark, and they still seem to enjoy their work (Sb-£70, Db-£100, Tb-£120, Qb-£150, ask about discount with cash and this book, free Internet access and Wi-Fi, near the corner of Charlwood Street and Belgrave Road at 47 Belgrave Road, handy bus #24 to Victoria Station and Trafalgar Square stops out front, tel. 020/7834-5897, www.lunasimonehotel.com, stay@lunasimone hotel.com).

$$ New England Hotel, run by Jay and the Patel family, has slightly worn but well-priced rooms in a tight old corner building (small Sb-£59, Db-£89, Tb-£109, Qb-£119, pay Internet access and Wi-Fi, 20 Saint George's Drive, tel. 020/7834-1595, fax 020/7834-9000, www.newenglandhotel.com, stay@newenglandhotel.com).

$$ Best Western Victoria Palace offers modern business-class comfort compared to the other creaky old hotels listed here. Choose between the 43 rooms in the main building (Db-£120,

Victoria Station Neighborhood

1 Lime Tree Hotel

2 B+B Belgravia

3 Cartref House & Lynton Hotel B&Bs

4 Morgan House

5 Luna Simone Hotel

6 New England Hotel

7 Best Western Victoria Palace

8 Cherry Court Hotel

9 Jubilee Hotel

10 Bakers Hotel

11 easyHotel Victoria

12 To Vandon House Hotel

13 Ebury Wine Bar

14 Jenny Lo's Tea House

15 La Bottega Deli

16 To The Duke of Wellington Pub

17 The Thomas Cubitt Pub

18 Grumbles Restaurant

19 Seafresh Fish Restaurant

20 The Jugged Hare Pub

21 St. George's Tavern

22 Grocery Stores (4)

23 Launderettes (2)

24 Bus Tours – Day (2)

25 Bus Tours – Night

26 Tube, Taxis, City Buses

27 Green Line Coach Terminal

28 Buses to Luton & Stansted Airports

29 Apollo Victoria Theatre

30 Victoria Palace Theatre

LONDON

100 YARDS

100 METERS

GROSV. PL.

LWR.

ECCLES

STREET

ELIZABETH

ECC. PL.

BUCKINGHAM

TO 16

EBURY

SEMLEY

P

COACH (BUS) STN.

FOUNTAIN SQUARE

P PARKING

⊖ TUBE STATION

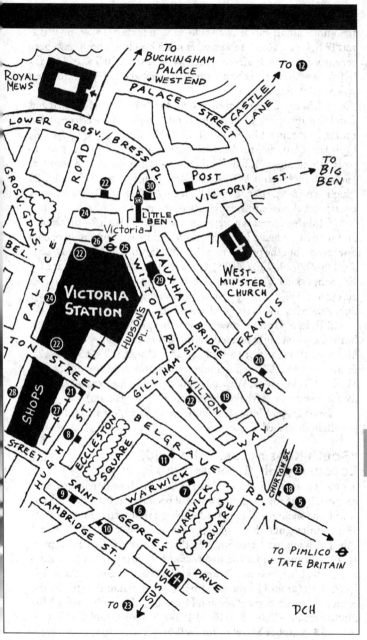

Royal Mews

TO BUCKINGHAM PALACE & WEST END

TO 12

PALACE STREET

CASTLE LANE

LOWER GROSV. / BRESS

GROSV. GDNS.

ROAD

PALACE

PL.

Post

VICTORIA ST.

TO BIG BEN

22

30

Little Ben

24

Victoria

26

25

WEST-MINSTER CHURCH

FRANCIS

22

24

VICTORIA STATION

WILTON

HUDSON'S PL.

VAUXHALL BRIDGE

29

ST.

20

ROAD

22

STREET

GILL'HAM

WILTON

WAY

WILTON

22

19

28

SHOPS

21

27

ST.

8

ECCLESTON SQUARE

BELGRAVE

11

CHURTON ST.

23

18

STREET

SAINT

9

WARWICK

7

5

CAMBRIDGE ST.

6

GEORGE'S

WARWICK SQUARE

R.D.

TO PIMLICO & TATE BRITAIN

10

SUSSEX DRIVE

TO 23

SUSSEX

DCH

LONDON

includes breakfast, elevator, 60-64 Warwick Way), or 22 rooms in the annex a half-block away (Db-£89, breakfast-£8.50, no elevator, 17 Belgrave Road, reception at main building); both have been recently renovated (air-con, free Wi-Fi, tel. 020/7821-7113, fax 020/7630-0806, www.bestwesternvictoriapalace.co.uk, info@best westernvictoriapalace.co.uk).

$ Cherry Court Hotel, run by the friendly and industrious Patel family, rents 12 very small but bright and well-designed rooms in a central location (Sb-£50, Db-£55, Tb-£80, Qb-£95, Quint/b-£110, ask for best Rick Steves price, 5 percent fee to pay with credit card, fruit-basket breakfast in room, air-con, free Internet access and Wi-Fi, laundry, peaceful garden patio, 23 Hugh Street, tel. 020/7828-2840, fax 020/7828-0393, www.cherry courthotel.co.uk, info@cherrycourthotel.co.uk).

$ Jubilee Hotel is a well-run slumbermill with 24 tiny rooms and many tiny beds. It's a bit musty and its windows only open a few inches, but the price is right (S-£39-45, Sb-£59-65, tiny D-£55-59, Db-£69-79, Tb-£79-95, Qb-£99-109, higher prices are for Fri-Sun, ask for Rick Steves discount when booking, pay Internet access and Wi-Fi, 31 Eccleston Square, tel. 020/7834-0845, www .jubileehotel.co.uk, stay@jubileehotel.co.uk, Bob Patel).

$ Bakers Hotel is a well-worn cheapie, with 11 tight rooms, but it's conveniently located and offers near–youth-hostel prices and a small breakfast (S-£40, D-£55, Db-£65, T-£65, Tb-£75, family room-£85, less for longer stays and on weeknights, pay Wi-Fi, 126 Warwick Way, tel. 020/7834-0729, www.bakershotel .co.uk, reservations@bakershotel.co.uk, Amin Jamani).

$ easyHotel Victoria, at 36 Belgrave Road, is part of the budget chain described on page 796.

"South Kensington," She Said, Loosening His Cummerbund

To stay on a quiet street so classy it doesn't allow hotel signs, surrounded by trendy shops and colorful restaurants, call "South Ken" your London home. Shoppers like being a short walk from Harrods and the designer shops of King's Road and Chelsea. When I splurge, I splurge here. Sumner Place is just off Old Brompton Road, 200 yards from the handy South Kensington Tube station (on Circle Line, two stops from Victoria Station; and on Piccadilly Line, direct from Heathrow). There's a handy **launderette** on the corner of Queensberry Place and Harrington Road (Mon-Fri 7:30-21:00, Sat 9:00-20:00, Sun 10:00-19:00, bring 50p and £1 coins).

$$$ Number Sixteen, for well-heeled travelers, packs over-the-top formality and class into its 42 rooms, plush lounges, and tranquil garden. It's in a labyrinthine building, with modern decor—perfect for an urban honeymoon (Db-from £200—but soft,

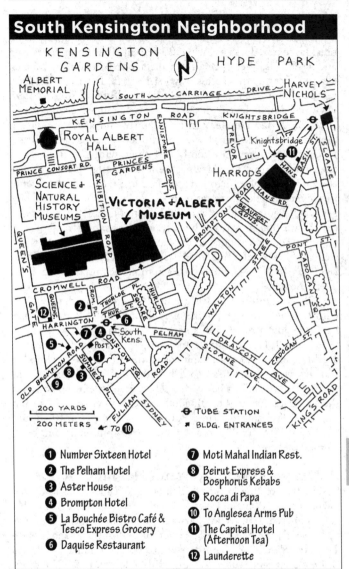

South Kensington Neighborhood

KENSINGTON GARDENS

HYDE PARK

ALBERT MEMORIAL

SOUTH CARRIAGE DRIVE

HARVEY NICHOLS

KENSINGTON ROAD

KNIGHTSBRIDGE

ROYAL ALBERT HALL

Knightsbridge

PRINCE CONSORT RD.

PRINCES GARDENS

HARRODS

SCIENCE & NATURAL HISTORY MUSEUMS

VICTORIA & ALBERT MUSEUM

BEAUFORT GDNS.

QUEEN'S GATE

CROMWELL ROAD

THURLOE PL.
THURLOE SQUARE
THUR. ST.

WALTON STREET

PONT ST.
CADOGAN

HARRINGTON

South Kens.

PELHAM

DRAYCOTT

CADOGAN

Post

SLOANE

SLOANE AVE.

KING'S ROAD

OLD BROMPTON ROAD

SUMNER PL.

FULHAM
SYDNEY

200 YARDS
200 METERS

TO ➓

⊖ TUBE STATION
✳ BLDG. ENTRANCES

❶ Number Sixteen Hotel	❼ Moti Mahal Indian Rest.
❷ The Pelham Hotel	❽ Beirut Express & Bosphorus Kebabs
❸ Aster House	❾ Rocca di Papa
❹ Brompton Hotel	❿ To Anglesea Arms Pub
❺ La Bouchée Bistro Café & Tesco Express Grocery	⓫ The Capital Hotel (Afternoon Tea)
❻ Daquise Restaurant	⓬ Launderette

ask for discounted "seasonal rates," especially on weekends and in Aug—subject to availability, does not include 20 percent VAT, breakfast buffet in the garden-£17, elevator, 16 Sumner Place, tel. 020/7589-5232, fax 020/7584-8615, US tel. 800-553-6674, www .firmdalehotels.com, sixteen@firmdale.com).

$$$ The Pelham Hotel, a 52-room business-class hotel with a pricey mix of pretense and style, is not quite sure which investment company owns it. It's genteel, with low lighting and a pleasant drawing room among the many perks (Db-£180-260, breakfast extra, does not include 20 percent VAT, lower prices Aug and weekends, Web specials can include free breakfast, air-con, elevator, free Internet access, pay Wi-Fi, gym, 15 Cromwell Place, tel. 020/7589-8288, fax 020/7584-8444, US tel. 1-888-757-5587, www.pelhamhotel.co.uk, reservations@pelhamhotel.co.uk).

$$$ Aster House, run by friendly and accommodating Simon and Leonie Tan, has a cheerful lobby, lounge, and breakfast room. Its rooms are comfy and quiet, with TV, phone, and air-conditioning. Enjoy breakfast or just lounging in the whisper-elegant Orangery, a Victorian greenhouse. Simon and Leonie offer free loaner mobile phones to their guests (Sb-£120, Db-£180, bigger Db-£225, rates do not include 20 percent VAT, ask about discount with this book if you book three or more nights, 25 percent off for five or more nights, additional 5 percent off with cash, check website for specials, free Wi-Fi, 3 Sumner Place, tel. 020/7581-5888, fax 020/7584-4925, www.asterhouse.com, asterhouse@bt internet.com).

$$ Brompton Hotel is a humble, borderline-dreary place with 17 rooms above a jumble of cafés and clubs. There's a noisy bar and some street noise, so ask for a room in the back if you want quiet. It has old carpets and no public spaces, and they serve breakfast in your room. In spite of all this, it's cheap for London and very well-located (Sb-£85, Db-£90, Tb-£130, "deluxe" rooms are just like the others but with a tub, save a little by booking via their website, includes continental breakfast, Wi-Fi, across from the South Kensington Tube station at 30 Brompton Road, tel. 020/7584-4517, fax 020/7823-9936, www.bromhotel.com, book @bromhotel.com).

Notting Hill and Bayswater Neighborhoods

Residential Notting Hill has quick bus and Tube access to downtown, and, for London, is very "homely" (Brit-speak for cozy). It's also peppered with trendy bars and restaurants, and is home to the famous Portobello Road Market (offbeat antiques shops open daily are enlivened on Saturdays with 2,000 additional stalls until 17:00, closed Sun, Tube: Notting Hill Gate, tel. 020/7229-8354, www.portobelloroad.co.uk).

Popular with young international travelers, Bayswater's Queensway street is a multicultural festival of commerce and eateries. The neighborhood does its dirty clothes at **Galaxy Launderette** (£6 self-service, £8-10 full-service, daily 8:00-20:00, staff on hand with soap and coins, 65 Moscow Road, at corner of St. Petersburgh Place and Moscow Road, tel. 020/7229-7771). For **Internet access,** you'll find several stops along busy Queensway,

Notting Hill & Bayswater Neighborhoods

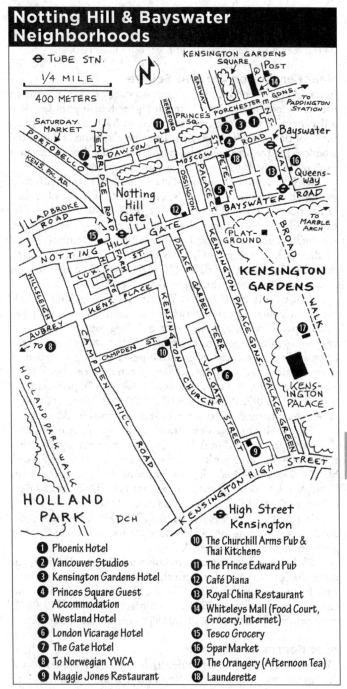

LONDON

1. Phoenix Hotel
2. Vancouver Studios
3. Kensington Gardens Hotel
4. Princes Square Guest Accommodation
5. Westland Hotel
6. London Vicarage Hotel
7. The Gate Hotel
8. To Norwegian YWCA
9. Maggie Jones Restaurant
10. The Churchill Arms Pub & Thai Kitchens
11. The Prince Edward Pub
12. Café Diana
13. Royal China Restaurant
14. Whiteleys Mall (Food Court, Grocery, Internet)
15. Tesco Grocery
16. Spar Market
17. The Orangery (Afternoon Tea)
18. Launderette

and a self-serve bank of computer terminals on the food circus level—third floor—of Whiteleys Shopping Centre (daily 8:30-24:00, corner of Queensway and Porchester Gardens).

Near Kensington Gardens Square

Several big, old hotels line the quiet Kensington Gardens Square (not to be confused with the much bigger Kensington Gardens adjacent to Hyde Park), a block west of bustling Queensway, north of Bayswater Tube station. These hotels are quiet for central London, but the area feels a bit sterile, and (aside from Vancouver Studios) the hotels here tend to be quite impersonal.

$$$ Vancouver Studios offers 45 modern rooms with fully equipped kitchenettes (utensils, stove, microwave, and fridge) rather than breakfast (Sb-£89, Db-£130, Tb-£170, extra bed-£20, can be more at busy times, discount for week-long stay or more, pay Internet access, free Wi-Fi, welcoming lounge and wonderful garden, near Kensington Gardens Square at 30 Prince's Square, tel. 020/7243-1270, fax 020/7221-8678, www.vancouverstudios .co.uk, info@vancouverstudios.co.uk).

$$ Phoenix Hotel, a Best Western modernization of a 125-room hotel, offers American business-class comforts; spacious, plush public spaces; and big, fresh, modern-feeling rooms. Its prices—which range from fine value to rip-off—are determined by a greedy computer program, with huge variations according to expected demand. Book online to save money (flexible prices, but usually Sb-£65, Db-£90, elevator, free Wi-Fi, 1-8 Kensington Gardens Square, tel. 020/7229-2494, fax 020/7727-1419, US tel. 800-528-1234, www.phoenixhotel.co.uk, info@phoenixhotel.co.uk).

$$ Kensington Gardens Hotel, an annex of Phoenix Hotel down the street (see above), laces 17 pleasant rooms together in a tall, skinny building with lots of stairs and no elevator (Ss-£57, Sb-£64, Db-£86, Tb-£105; book by phone or email, rather than through the pricier website, and ask for best Rick Steves price; continental breakfast served at Phoenix Hotel, free Wi-Fi, 9 Kensington Gardens Square, tel. 020/7243-7600, fax 020/7792-8612, www.kensingtongardenshotel.co.uk, info@kensington gardenshotel.co.uk, Rowshanak).

$$ Princes Square Guest Accommodation is a big 50-room place that's well-located, practical, and a good value, especially with its online discounts (Sb-£50-60, Db-£60-80, Tb-£80-100, elevator, pay Wi-Fi, 23-25 Princes Square, tel. 020/7229-9876, www.princessquarehotel.co.uk, info@princessquarehotel.co.uk).

Near Kensington Gardens

$$$ Westland Hotel, conveniently located on a busy street a five-minute walk from the Notting Hill neighborhood, feels like a wood-paneled hunting lodge with a fine lounge. The 32 spacious rooms are comfortable, with old-fashioned charm. Their £130 doubles are the best value, but check their website for specials. It's been run by the Isseyegh family for three generations (Sb-£110, deluxe Sb-£124, Db-£130, deluxe Db-£152, cavernous premier Db-£172, sprawling Tb-£165-193, gargantuan Qb-£186-220, Quint/b-£234, elevator, pay Wi-Fi, garage-£12/day, between Notting Hill Gate and Queensway Tube stations at 154 Bayswater Road, tel. 020/7229-9191, fax 020/7727-1054, www.westlandhotel .co.uk, reservations@westlandhotel.co.uk, Shirley and Bertie).

$$$ **London Vicarage Hotel** is family-run, understandably popular, and elegantly British in a quiet, classy neighborhood. It has 17 rooms furnished with taste and quality, a TV lounge, a grand staircase, and facilities on each floor. Mandy and Monika maintain a homey atmosphere (S-£56, Sb-£95, D-£95, Db-£125, T-£120, Tb-£160, Q-£130, Qb-£176, 20 percent less in winter—check website, no elevator, free Wi-Fi; 8-minute walk from Notting Hill Gate and High Street Kensington Tube stations, near Kensington Palace at 10 Vicarage Gate; tel. 020/7229-4030, fax 020/7792-5989, www.londonvicaragehotel.com, vicaragehotel@btconnect .com).

$$ **The Gate Hotel** has seven cramped, tired rooms on a delightful curved street near the start of the Portobello Road Market, in the heart of the characteristic Notting Hill neighborhood. While the lodgings are basic, the location is wonderful (Sb-£60, Db-£85, bigger "luxury" Db-£95, Tb-£115, each room £10 more Fri-Sat, 5 percent more if paying with credit card, continental breakfast in room, no elevator, pay Wi-Fi, 6 Portobello Road, Tube: Noting Hill Gate, tel. 020/7221-0707, fax 020/7221-9128, www.gatehotel.co.uk, bookings@gatehotel.co.uk, Jasmine).

Near Holland Park

$ **Norwegian YWCA (Norsk K.F.U.K.)**—where English is definitely a second language—is open to any Norwegian woman, and to non-Norwegian women under 30. (Men must be under 30 with a Norwegian passport.) Located on a quiet, stately street, it offers a study, TV room, piano lounge, and an open-face Norwegian ambience (goat cheese on Sundays!). They have mostly quads, so those willing to share with strangers are most likely to get a bed (July-Aug: Ss-£37.50, shared double-£36.50/bed, shared triple-£31.50/bed, shared quad-£28/bed, includes breakfast year-round plus sack lunch and dinner Sept-June, £20 key deposit and £2 membership fee required, pay Wi-Fi, 52 Holland Park, Tube: Holland Park, tel. 020/7727-9346 or 020/7727-9897, www.kfukhjemmet.org.uk, kontor@kfukhjemmet.org.uk). With each visit, I wonder which is easier to get—a sex change or a Norwegian passport?

Paddington Station Neighborhood

The neighborhood near Paddington Station—while a bit less charming than the other areas I've recommended—is pleasant enough, and very convenient to the Heathrow Express airport train. The area is flanked by the Paddington and Lancaster Gate Tube stops. Most of my recommendations circle Norfolk Square, just two blocks in front of Paddington Station, yet still quiet and comfortable. Its main drag, London Street, is lined with handy eateries—pubs, Indian, Italian, Greek, Lebanese, and more—plus convenience stores and an Internet café. To reach this area, exit the station toward Praed Street (with your back to the tracks, it's to the left). Once outside, continue straight across Praed Street and down London Street; Norfolk Square is a block ahead on the left.

On Norfolk Square

These places (and many more on the same street) are essentially interchangeable; all offer small rooms at a reasonable price, in tall buildings with lots of stairs and no elevator. I've chosen the ones that offer the most reasonable prices and the warmest welcome.

$$ St. David's Hotels, run by the hospitable Neokleous family, has 60 tight rooms in several adjacent buildings (S-£60, Sb-£70, D-£70, Db-£90, Tb-£100, free Wi-Fi, 14-20 Norfolk Square, tel. 020/7723-3856, fax 020/7402-9061, www.stdavids hotels.com, info@stdavidshotels.com).

$$ Tudor Court Hotel has 38 rooms run by the Gupta family (S-£39, Sb-£82, Db-£89, Tb-£108, family room-£132, 10-12 Norfolk Square, tel. 020/7723-5157, fax 020/7723-0727, www .tudorcourtpaddington.co.uk, reservations@tudorcourtpaddington .co.uk).

$$ Falcon Hotel has 19 small rooms wrapped around a tight staircase (S-£50, Sb-£55, D-£69, Db-£75, pay Wi-Fi, 11 Norfolk Square, tel. 020/7723-8603, fax 020/7402-7009, www.falcon-hotel .com, info@falcon-hotel.com).

$$ Ashley Hotel, next door, is a classic old place with 54 rooms (S-£35-40, Sb-£50-60, Db-£70-80, pay Wi-Fi, 15-17 Norfolk Square, tel. 020/7723-3375, fax 020/7723-0173, www.ashley hotellondon.com, info@ashleyhotellondon.com).

$ easyHotel, the budget chain described on page 796, has a branch at 10 Norfolk Place.

Elsewhere near Paddington Station

To reach these hotels, follow the earlier Paddington Station directions, but continue past Norfolk Square to the big intersection with Sussex Gardens; the Royal Park is to the right, and Springfield Hotel is immediately to the left.

$$$ The Royal Park is the neighborhood's classy splurge, with 48 plush rooms, polished service, a genteel lounge (free champagne for guests nightly 19:00-20:00), and all the little extras (standard Db-£139-149, bigger "executive" Db-£169-179, prices vary with demand and do not include 20 percent VAT or breakfast, free Internet access and Wi-Fi, 3 Westbourne Terrace, tel. 020/7479-6600, fax 020/7479-6601, www.theroyalpark.com, info@theroyalpark.com).

$$ Springfield Hotel is efficiently run and old-school simple, with 17 well-worn rooms. It sits on the wide, busy street called Sussex Gardens (request a quieter back room), with several other similar hotels nearby if you're in a pinch (Sb-£60, Db-£80-90, Tb-£100, check online for deals, extra fee for paying with credit card, 154 Sussex Gardens, tel. 020/7723-9898, fax 020/7723-0874, www.springfieldhotellondon.co.uk, info@springfieldhotellondon.co.uk).

Other Neighborhoods

North of Marble Arch: **$$$ The 22 York Street B&B** offers a casual alternative in the city center, renting 10 traditional, hardwood, comfortable rooms (Sb-£89, Db-£120, free Internet access and Wi-Fi, inviting lounge; from Baker Street Tube station, walk 2 blocks down Baker Street and take a right to 22 York Street—since there's no sign, just look for #22; tel. 020/7224-2990, www.22yorkstreet.co.uk, mc@22yorkstreet.co.uk, energetically run by Liz and Michael Callis).

$$$ The Sumner Hotel, renting 19 rooms in a 19th-century Georgian townhouse, is located a few blocks north of Hyde Park and Oxford Street, a busy shopping destination. Decorated with fancy modern Italian furniture, this swanky place packs in all the extras (Db-£160-190 depending on size, ask about discount with this book, extra bed-£30, air-con, elevator, free Wi-Fi, 54 Upper Berkeley Street just off Edgware Road, Tube: Marble Arch, tel. 020/7723-2244, fax 0870-705-8767, www.thesumner.com, hotel@thesumner.com, manager Peter).

Near Buckingham Palace: **$$ Vandon House Hotel,** run by Central College in Iowa, is packed with students most of the year, but rents its 32 rooms to travelers from late May through August at great prices. The rooms, while institutional, are comfy, and the location is excellent (S-£46, D-£70, Db-£90, Tb-£99, Qb-£119, only twin beds, elevator, pay Internet access and Wi-Fi; 3-minute walk west of St. James's Park Tube station or 7-minute walk from Victoria Station, near west end of Petty France Street on a tiny road, 1 Vandon Street; tel. 020/7799-6780, www.vandonhouse.com, info@vandonhouse.com).

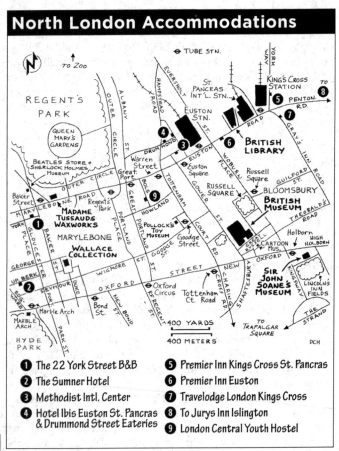

North London Accommodations

- ❶ The 22 York Street B&B
- ❷ The Sumner Hotel
- ❸ Methodist Intl. Center
- ❹ Hotel Ibis Euston St. Pancras & Drummond Street Eateries
- ❺ Premier Inn Kings Cross St. Pancras
- ❻ Premier Inn Euston
- ❼ Travelodge London Kings Cross
- ❽ To Jurys Inn Islington
- ❾ London Central Youth Hostel

LONDON

Near Euston Station and the British Library: The **$$$ Methodist International Centre (MIC),** a modern, youthful Christian hotel and conference center, fills its lower floors with international students and its top floor with travelers. The 28 rooms are modern and sleek yet comfortable, with fine bathrooms, phones, and desks. The atmosphere is friendly, safe, clean, and controlled; it also has a spacious lounge and game room (Sb-£117 on Fri-Sun, £137 on Mon-Thu; Db-£130 on Fri-Sun, £149 on Mon-Thu; pricier "deluxe" rooms also available, buying a £100 annual membership saves you £30-40 per night—do the math to see if it's worth paying for, check website for specials, elevator, pay Wi-Fi, on a quiet street a block west of Euston Station, 81-103 Euston Street—not Euston Road, Tube: Euston, tel. 020/7380-0001, www.micentre .com, reservations@micentre.com). In addition to the rooms in the main building, they have several "annex" rooms—three rooms in one house that share a single bathroom; this could work well for families (S-£85, D-£95). In June through August, when the students are gone, they also rent simpler twin rooms in the main building (S or D-£75, includes one breakfast, extra breakfast-£13).

Big, Good-Value, Modern Hotels

London has an abundance of modern, impersonal, American-style chain hotels. While they lack the friendliness and funkiness of a memorable B&B, the value they provide is undeniable; doubles generally go for around £90-100 (or less—often possible with promotional rates). As these hotels are often located on busy streets in dreary train-station neighborhoods, use common sense after dark and wear your money belt.

Premier Inn

For any of these, call their reservations toll line at 0870-242-8000 or—the best option—book online at www.premierinn.com.

$$ Premier Inn London County Hall, literally down the hall from a $400-a-night Marriott Hotel, fills one end of London's massive former County Hall building. This family-friendly place is wonderfully located near the base of the London Eye and across the Thames from Big Ben. Its 313 efficient rooms come with all the necessary comforts, though it's quite anonymous—rather than a real reception desk, you'll find self-service check-in kiosks with a couple of clerks standing by to help (Db-£109-150 for 2 adults and up to 2 kids under age 16, elevator, pay Wi-Fi, some easy-access rooms, 500 yards from Westminster Tube stop and Waterloo Station, Belvedere Road, central reservations toll tel. 0870-242-8000, reception desk toll tel. 0870-238-3300, easiest to book online at www.premierinn.com).

$$ Premier Inn London Southwark, with 59 rooms, is near Shakespeare's Globe on the South Bank (Db for up to 2 adults and 2 kids-£91-150, elevator, pay Wi-Fi, Bankside, 34 Park Street, Tube: London Bridge, toll tel. 0870-990-6402, www.premierinn .com).

$$ Premier Inn Kings Cross St. Pancras, with 276 rooms, is across the street from the east end of King's Cross Station and near the Eurostar terminus at St. Pancras Station (Db-£96-150, air-con, elevator, pay Wi-Fi, 26-30 York Way, Tube: King's Cross St. Pancras, toll tel. 0870-990-6414, www.premierinn.com).

Other **$$ Premier Inns** charging £90-150 per room include **London Euston** (big, blue Lego-type building packed with vacationing families, on handy but noisy street at corner of Euston Road and Dukes Road, Tube: Euston, toll tel. 0870-238-3301), **London Kensington Earl's Court** (11 Knaresborough Place, Tube: Earl's Court or Gloucester Road, toll tel. 0870-238-3304),

London Victoria (82-83 Eccleston Square, Tube: Victoria, toll tel. 0870-423-6494), and **London Putney Bridge** (farther out, 3 Putney Bridge Approach, Tube: Putney Bridge, toll tel. 0870-238-3302). Avoid the **Tower Bridge** location, which is an inconvenient 15-minute walk from the nearest Tube stop.

Other Chains

Travelodge: **$$ Travelodge London Kings Cross** is another typical chain hotel with 140 cookie-cutter rooms, just 200 yards south (in front) of King's Cross Station (Db-usually £85, family rooms, can be noisy, elevator, pay Wi-Fi, Grays Inn Road, Tube: King's Cross St. Pancras, tel. 020/7278-5179). Other convenient Travelodge London locations are nearby **Kings Cross Royal Scot, Euston, Marylebone, Covent Garden, Liverpool Street,** and **Farringdon.** For details on all Travelodge hotels, see www.travelodge.co.uk.

Ibis: **$$$ Hotel Ibis London Euston St. Pancras** rents 380 rooms on a quiet street a block west of Euston Station (Db-£89-149, usually £129, no family rooms, elevator, pay Internet access and Wi-Fi, 3 Cardington Street, Tube: Euston, tel. 020/7388-7777 or 020/7304-7712, fax 020/7388-0001, www.ibishotel.com, h0921 @accor.com). There's also an **Ibis London City** (5 Commercial Street, Tube: Aldgate East, tel. 020/7422-8400), but the other Ibis locations are far from the center.

Jurys Inn: **$$ Jurys Inn Islington** rents 200-plus compact, comfy rooms near King's Cross Station (Db/Tb-£109-169, some discounted rooms available online, 2 adults and 2 kids under age 12 can share one room, 60 Pentonville Road, Tube: Angel, tel. 020/7282-5500, fax 020/7282-5511, www.jurysinns.com). You'll also find Jurys Inns at **Chelsea** (Imperial Road, Tube: Imperial Wharf, tel. 020/7411-2200) and near **Heathrow Airport** (see "Heathrow and Gatwick Airports," later).

easyHotel

With several hotels in good neighborhoods around London, easyHotel is a radical concept—offering what you need to sleep well and safe, and nothing more. Most of them are fitted into old buildings, so the rooms are all odd shapes, from tiny windowless closets to others that are quite spacious. All rooms are well-ventilated and come with an efficient "bathroom pod" that looks like it was popped out of a plastic mold—just big enough to take care of business. While they do have a 24-hour reception, everything else is spartan: you get two towels, liquid soap, and a clean bed—no breakfast, no fresh towels, and no daily cleaning. The base rate ranges from £21 to £65, depending on the room size and when you book—"The earlier you book, the less you pay." Prices are the same for one person or two, but then you're nickel-and-dimed with optional charges for the TV, Wi-Fi, luggage storage, and so on.

If you go with the basic package, it's like hosteling with privacy—a hard-to-beat value. But you get what you pay for; in my experience, easyHotels are cheap in every sense of the word (no elevator, thin walls, noisy halls filled with loud travelers seeking bargain beds, flimsy construction that often results in broken things in the room). And they're only a good deal if you book far enough ahead to get a good price, and skip the many extras...which can add up fast. Regardless of the location, reserve through their website (www.easyhotel.com).

$ easyHotel Victoria is well-located in an old building near Victoria Station (77 rooms, 36 Belgrave Road—for location, see map on pages 784-785, Tube: Victoria, tel. 020/7834-1379, enquiries @victoria.easyhotel.com). They also have branches at **South Kensington** (34 rooms, 14 Lexham Gardens, Tube: Earl's Court or Gloucester Road, tel. 020/7136-2870, enquiries@southken.easy hotel.com), **Earl's Court** (80 rooms, 44-48 West Cromwell Road, Tube: Earl's Court, tel. 020/7373-4546, enquiries@earlscourt.easy hotel.com), **Paddington** (47 rooms, 10 Norfolk Place, Tube: Paddington, tel. 020/7706-9911, enquiries@paddington.easyhotel .com), and **Heathrow** and **Luton** airports (Heathrow location described on page 799).

Hostels

$ London Central Youth Hostel is the flagship of London's hostels, with 300 beds and all the latest in security and comfortable efficiency. Families and travelers of any age will feel welcome in this wonderful facility. You'll pay the same price for any bed in a 4- to 8-bed single-sex dorm—with or without private bathroom—so try to grab one with a bathroom (£20-30 per bunk bed—fluctuates with demand, £3/night extra for nonmembers, breakfast-£4; includes sheets, towel, and locker; families welcome to book an entire room, free Wi-Fi, members' kitchen, laundry, book long in advance, between Oxford Street and Great Portland Street Tube stations at 104 Bolsover Street, toll tel. 0870-770-6144 or 0845-371-9154, www.yha.org.uk, londoncentral@yha.org.uk).

$ St. Paul's Youth Hostel, near St. Paul's, is clean, modern, friendly, and well-run. Most of the 190 beds are in shared, single-sex 3- to 11-bunk rooms (bed-around £20 depending on demand, twin D-£60, includes locker and sheets but not breakfast, nonmembers pay £3 extra, cheap meals, open 24 hours, 36 Carter Lane, Tube: St. Paul's, tel. 020/7236-4965 or toll tel. 0845-371-9012, www.yha.org.uk, stpauls@yha.org.uk).

$ A cluster of three **St. Christopher's Inn** hostels, south of the Thames near London Bridge, have cheap dorm beds; one branch is for women only (£22-32, 161-165 Borough High Street, Tube: Borough or London Bridge, reservations tel. 020/8600-7500, www.st-christophers.co.uk).

Dorms

$ The **University of Westminster** opens its dorm rooms to travelers during summer break, from mid-June through late September. Located in several high-rise buildings scattered around central London, the rooms—some with private bathrooms, others with shared bathrooms nearby—come with access to well-equipped kitchens and big lounges (S-£25-35, Sb-£35-54, D-£40-60, Db-£50-95, apartment Sb-£43-71, apartment Db-£56-82, weekly rates, tel. 020/7911-5181, www.westminster.ac.uk/business, unilet vacations@westminster.ac.uk).

$ **University College London** also has rooms for travelers, from mid-June until mid-September (S-£30-32, D-£55-65, breakfast extra, pay Internet access, tel. 020/7278-3895, www.ucl.ac.uk/residences).

$ **Ace Hotel,** a budget hotel within four townhouses set in a residential neighborhood, has contemporary decor (£21-32 per bed in 3- to 8-bed dorms, bunk-bed D-£53-58, bunk-bed Db-£57-68, Db with patio-£105, pay Internet access, lounge and garden, 16-22 Gunterstone Road, Tube: Baron's Court or West Kensington, tel. 020/7602-6600, www.ace-hotel.co.uk, reception@ace-hotel.co.uk).

$ The **London School of Economics** has openings in its dorms from late July through September (S-£33-43, Sb-£59-65, D-£52-60, Db-£76-94, tel. 020/7955-7575, www.lsevacations.co.uk, vacations@lse.ac.uk).

Heathrow and Gatwick Airports

At or near Heathrow Airport

It's so easy to get to Heathrow from central London, I see no reason to sleep there. But if you do, here are some options. The Yotel is actually inside the airport, while the rest are a short bus or taxi ride away. In addition to public buses, the cleverly named £4 "Hotel Hoppa" shuttle bus connects the airport to many nearby hotels (different routes serve the various hotels and terminals).

$$ **Yotel,** at the airport, has small sleep dens that offer a place to catch a quick nap (£37-64/4 hours), or to stay overnight (tiny "standard cabin"—£60/8 hours, "premium cabin"—£82/8 hours; cabins sleep 1-2 people; price is per cabin not person, reserve online for free or by phone for small fee). Prices vary by day, week, and time of year, so check their website. All rooms are only slightly larger than a double bed, and have private bathrooms and free Internet access and Wi-Fi. These windowless rooms have oddly

purplish lighting (Heathrow Terminal 4, tel. 020/7100-1100, www
.yotel.com, customer@yotel.com).

$ easyHotel, your cheapest bet, is in a low-rent residential
neighborhood a £5 taxi ride from the airport. Its 53 no-frills, pod-
like rooms are on two floors. Before booking at this very basic
place, read the explanation on page 796 (Db-£25-45, no breakfast,
no elevator, pay Internet access and Wi-Fi, Brick Field Lane; take
local bus #140 from airport's Central Bus Station or the "Hotel
Hoppa" #H8 from Terminals 1 or 3, or the hotel can arrange a
£5 taxi to the airport; tel. 020/8897-9237, www.easyhotel.com,
enquiries@heathrow.easyhotel.com).

$$ Hotel Ibis London Heathrow is a chain hotel offering
predictable value (Db-£77, Db-£52 on Fri-Sun, check website for
specials as low as £45, breakfast-£7, pay Internet access and Wi-Fi;
112-114 Bath Road, take local bus #105, #111, #140, #285, #423,
or #555 from airport's Central Bus Station or #555 direct from
Terminal 4, or the "Hotel Hoppa" #H6 from Terminals 1 or 3, or
#H56 from Terminals 4 or 5; tel. 020/8759-4888, fax 020/8564-
7894, www.ibishotel.com, h0794@accor.com).

$$ Jurys Inn, another hotel chain, tempts tired travelers with
300-plus cookie-cutter rooms (Db-£89-105, check website for
deals, breakfast extra; on Eastern Perimeter Road, Tube: Hatton
Cross plus 5-minute walk; take the Tube one stop from Terminals
1, 2, or 3; or two stops from Terminals 4 or 5; or the "Hotel Hoppa"
#H9 from Terminals 1 or 3, or #H53 from Terminals 4 or 5; or buses
#285, #482, #490, or #555; tel. 020/8266-4664, fax 020/8266-4665,
www.jurysinns.com).

At or near Gatwick Airport

$$ Yotel, with small rooms, has a branch right at the airport
(Gatwick South Terminal; see prices and contact info in Heathrow
listing, earlier).

$$ Gatwick Airport Central Premier Inn rents cheap rooms
350 yards from the airport (Db-£40-75, breakfast-£8, £2 shuttle
bus from airport—must reserve in advance, Longbridge Way,
North Terminal, toll tel. 0871-527-8406, frustrating phone tree,
www.premierinn.com). Four more Premier Inns are within a five-
mile radius from the airport.

$$ Barn Cottage, a converted 16th-century barn flanked by a
tennis court and swimming pool, sits in the peaceful countryside,
with a good pub just two blocks away. Its two wood-beamed rooms,
antique furniture, and large garden makes you forget Gatwick is
10 minutes away (S-£55, D-£75, cash only, Church Road, Leigh,
Reigate, Surrey, tel. 01306/611-347, www.a1tourism.com/uk/barn
cott.html, warmly run by Pat and Mike Comer). Don't confuse
this place with others of the same name. A taxi from Gatwick to

here runs about £15; the Comers can take you back to the airport or train station for about £10.

$ Gatwick Airport Travelodge has budget rooms about two miles from the airport (Db-£39-57, breakfast extra, pay Wi-Fi, Church Road, Lowfield Heath, Crawley, £3 shuttle bus from airport, toll tel. 0871-984-6031, www.travelodge.co.uk).

For Longer Stays

Staying a week or longer? Consider the advantages that come with renting a furnished apartment—or "flat," as the British say. Complete with a small, equipped kitchen and living room, this option can also work for families or groups on shorter visits. Among the many organizations ready to help, the following have been recommended by local guides and readers: www.perfect placeslondon.co.uk, www.homefromhome.co.uk, www.london33 .com, www.london-house.com, www.gowithit.co.uk, www.aplace likehome.co.uk, www.regentsuites.com, and www.airbnb.com /travel/london/gb.

Sometimes you can save money by renting directly from the apartment owner (check www.vrbo.com). Readers also report success using Craigslist (http://london.craigslist.co.uk; search within "vacation rentals").

Read the rental conditions carefully and ask lots of questions. If a certain amenity is important to you (such as Wi-Fi or a washing machine in the unit), ask specifically about it and what to do if it stops working. Plot the location carefully (plug the address into http://maps.google.com), and remember to factor in travel time and costs from outlying neighborhoods to central London. Finally, it's a good idea to buy trip cancellation/interruption insurance, as many weekly rentals are nonrefundable.

Eating in London

In London, the sheer variety of foods—from every corner of its former empire and beyond—is astonishing. You'll be amazed at the number of hopping, happening new restaurants of all kinds.

If you want to dine (as opposed to eat), drop by a London newsstand to get a weekly entertainment guide or an annual restaurant guide (both have extensive restaurant listings). Visit www .london-eating.co.uk or www.squaremeal.co.uk for more options.

The thought of a £50 meal in Britain generally ruins my appetite, so my London dining is limited mostly to easygoing, fun, moderately priced alternatives. I've listed places by neighborhood—handy to your sightseeing or hotel. Considering how expensive London can be, if there's any good place to cut corners to stretch your budget, it's by eating cheaply. Pub grub (at one of

London's 7,000 pubs) and ethnic restaurants (especially Indian and Chinese) are good low-cost options. Of course, picnicking is the fastest and cheapest way to go. Good grocery stores and sandwich shops, fine park benches, and polite pigeons abound in Britain's most expensive city.

Remember, London (and all of Britain) is smoke-free. Expect restaurants and pubs that sell food to be non-smoking indoors, with smokers occupying patios and doorways outside.

Central London
Near Trafalgar Square
These places are within about 100 yards of Trafalgar Square.

St. Martin-in-the-Fields Café in the Crypt is just right for a tasty meal on a monk's budget—maybe even on a monk's tomb. You'll dine sitting on somebody's gravestone in an ancient crypt. Their enticing buffet line is kept stocked all day, serving breakfast, lunch, and dinner (£6-10 cafeteria plates, hearty traditional desserts, free jugs of water). They also serve a restful cream tea (£6, daily 14:00-17:00). You'll find it directly under the St. Martin-in-the-Fields Church, facing Trafalgar Square (Mon-Wed 8:00-20:00, Thu-Sat 8:00-21:00, Sun 11:00-18:00, profits go to the church, Tube: Charing Cross, tel. 020/7766-1158 or 020/7766-1100). Wednesday evenings at 20:00 come with a live jazz band (£6-9 tickets). While here, check out the concert schedule for the busy church upstairs (or visit www.smitf.org).

The Chandos Pub's Opera Room floats amazingly apart from the tacky crush of tourism around Trafalgar Square. Look for it opposite the National Portrait Gallery (corner of William IV Street and St. Martin's Lane) and climb the stairs (to the right of the pub entrance) to the Opera Room. This is a fine Trafalgar rendezvous point and wonderfully local pub. They serve traditional, plain-tasting £6-7 pub meals—meat pies and fish-and-chips are their specialty. The ground-floor pub is stuffed with regulars and offers snugs (private booths), the same menu, and more serious beer drinking. Chandos proudly serves the local Samuel Smith beer at £2 a pint (kitchen open daily 11:00-19:00, order and pay at the bar, 29 St. Martin's Lane, Tube: Leicester Square, tel. 020/7836-1401).

Gordon's Wine Bar, with a simple, steep staircase leading into a candlelit 15th-century wine cellar, is filled with dusty old bottles, faded British memorabilia, and nine-to-fivers. At the "English rustic" buffet, choose a hot meal or cold meat dish with a salad, or a hearty (and splittable) plate of cheeses, bread, and pickles (£7.75)—or share four plates for £12. Then step up to the wine bar and consider the many varieties of wine and port available by the glass. This place is passionate about port. The low carbon-crusted vaulting deeper in the back seems to intensify the

LONDON

Central London Eateries

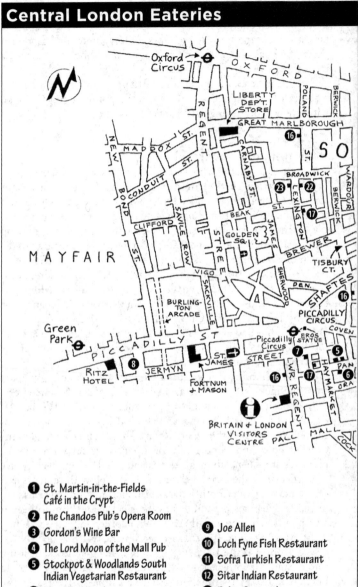

1. St. Martin-in-the-Fields Café in the Crypt
2. The Chandos Pub's Opera Room
3. Gordon's Wine Bar
4. The Lord Moon of the Mall Pub
5. Stockpot & Woodlands South Indian Vegetarian Restaurant
6. West End Kitchen
7. Criterion Restaurant
8. The Wolseley
9. Joe Allen
10. Loch Fyne Fish Restaurant
11. Sofra Turkish Restaurant
12. Sitar Indian Restaurant
13. Belgo Centraal
14. Neal's Yard Eateries
15. Food for Thought Café

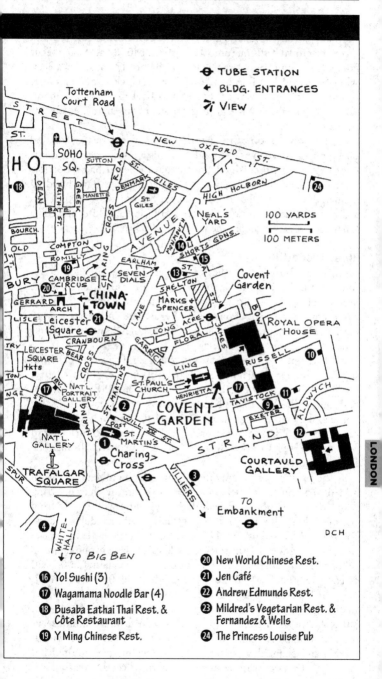

- ⊖ TUBE STATION
- ← BLDG. ENTRANCES
- 🗺 VIEW

100 YARDS
100 METERS

⑯ Yo! Sushi (3)
⑰ Wagamama Noodle Bar (4)
⑱ Busaba Eathai Thai Rest. &
   Côte Restaurant
⑲ Y Ming Chinese Rest.
⑳ New World Chinese Rest.
㉑ Jen Café
㉒ Andrew Edmunds Rest.
㉓ Mildred's Vegetarian Rest. &
   Fernandez & Wells
㉔ The Princess Louise Pub

LONDON

DCH

Hogarth-painting atmosphere. Although it's crowded, you can normally corral two chairs and grab the corner of a table. On hot days, the crowd spills out onto a leafy back patio, where a barbecue cooks for a long line of tables (arrive before 17:00 to get a seat, Mon-Sat 11:00-23:00, Sun 12:00-22:00, 2 blocks from Trafalgar Square, bottom of Villiers Street at #47, Tube: Embankment, tel. 020/7930-1408, www.gordonswinebar.com, manager Gerard Menan).

The **Lord Moon of the Mall** pub, with real ales on tap and cheap pub grub such as fish-and-chips, is a good place to experience retro English cuisine from the days when it had a horrible reputation. The pub fills a great old former Barclays Bank building a block down Whitehall from Trafalgar Square (daily 9:00-22:00, kid-friendly menu but no kids after 20:00, 16-18 Whitehall, Tube: Charing Cross or Embankment, tel. 020/7839-7701).

Near Piccadilly

Hungry and broke in the theater district? Head for Panton Street (off Haymarket, two blocks southeast of Piccadilly Circus), where several hardworking little places compete, all seeming to offer a three-course meal for about £8.50. Peruse the entire block (vegetarian, Pizza Express, Moroccan, Thai, Chinese, and two famous diners) before making your choice.

Stockpot is a meat, potatoes, gravy, and mushy-peas kind of place, famous and rightly popular for its edible, cheap English meals (Mon-Sat 7:00-23:30, Sun 7:00-22:00, 38-40 Panton Street, cash only). The **West End Kitchen** (across the street at #5, same hours and menu) is a direct competitor that's also well-known and just as good. Vegetarians may prefer the **Woodlands South Indian Vegetarian Restaurant,** which serves an impressive £18 *thali* (37 Panton Street).

The palatial **Criterion** offers grand-piano ambience beneath gilded tiles and chandeliers in a dreamy Byzantine church setting from 1880. It's right on Piccadilly Circus but a world away from the punk junk. It's a deal for the visual experience during lunch and before 19:00—but after 19:00, the menu becomes really expensive...and, at any hour, the service could care less. Anyone can drop in for coffee or a drink (£17-20 fixed-price meals, daily 12:00-14:30 & 17:30-19:00 & 22:00-23:30, 224 Piccadilly, tel. 020/7930-0488).

The **Wolseley** is the grand 1920s showroom of a long-defunct British car. The last Wolseley drove out with the Great Depression, but today this old-time bistro bustles with formal waiters serving traditional Austrian and French dishes in an elegant black-marble-and-chandeliers setting fit for its location next to the Ritz. Although the food can be unexceptional, prices are reasonable, and the presentation and setting are grand. Reservations are a must (£16.50 plates; cheaper soup, salad, and sandwich menu available; Mon-Fri 7:00-24:00, Sat 8:00-24:00, Sun 8:00-23:00, 160 Piccadilly, tel. 020/7499-6996). They're popular for their fancy cream or afternoon tea (£10 cream teas, £20 afternoon tea, served Sun-Fri 15:30-18:30, Sat 15:30-17:30).

Near Covent Garden

Covent Garden bustles with people and touristy eateries. The area feels overrun, but if you must eat around here, there are some good options.

Joe Allen, tucked in a basement a block away, serves modern international and American cuisine with both style and hubbub. Downstairs off a quiet street with candles and white tablecloths, it's comfortably spacious and popular with the theater crowd (meals for about £30, £16 two-course specials and £18 three-course specials 17:00-18:45, open daily 11:30-23:00, piano music after 21:00, 13 Exeter Street, tel. 020/7836-0651).

Loch Fyne Fish Restaurant is part of a Scottish chain that grows its own oysters and mussels. It offers an inviting atmosphere with a fine fishy energy and no pretense (£10-15 entrées, £12.50 two-course early dinner served until 18:30, open daily, a couple of blocks behind Covent Garden at 2 Catherine Street, tel. 020/7240-4999).

Sofra Turkish Restaurant is good for quality Turkish with a touch of class. They have several menus: *meze* (Turkish tapas), vegetarian, and set (£8 before 18:00, £10 after 18:00, open long hours daily, 36 Tavistock Street, tel. 020/7240-3773).

Sitar Indian Restaurant is a well-respected Indian/Bangladeshi place serving dishes from many regions, fine fish, and a tasty £17 vegetarian *thali*. It's small and dressy, with snappy service (£15 entrées, daily 12:00-24:00, next to Somerset House at 149 Strand, tel. 020/7836-3730).

Belgo Centraal serves hearty Belgian specialties in a vast 400-seat underground lair. It's a mussels, chips, and beer emporium dressed up as a mod-monastic refectory—with noisy acoustics and waiters garbed as Trappist monks. The classy restaurant section is more comfortable and less rowdy, but usually requires reservations. It's often more fun just to grab a spot in the boisterous beer hall, with its tight, communal benches (no reservations accepted). Both sides have the same menu and specials. Belgians claim they eat as well as the French and as heartily as the Germans. Belgo, which offers a stunning array of dark, blond, and fruity Belgian beers, actually makes Belgian things trendy—a formidable feat (£10-14 meals, open daily 12:00-23:00; Mon-Fri £5-6.30 "beat the clock" meal specials 17:00-18:30—the time you order is the price you pay—including main dishes and fries; no meal-splitting after 18:30, and you must buy food with beer; daily £8 lunch special 12:00-17:00; 1 kid eats free for each parent ordering a regular entrée; 1 block north of Covent Garden Tube station at 50 Earlham Street, tel. 020/7813-2233).

Neal's Yard is *the* place for cheap, hip, and healthy eateries near Covent Garden. The neighborhood is a tabouli of fun, hippie-type cafés. One of the best is the venerable and ferociously vegetarian **Food for Thought,** packed with local health nuts (good £5 vegetarian meals, £7.50 dinner plates, Mon-Sat 12:00-20:30, Sun 12:00-17:00, 2 blocks north of Covent Garden Tube station, 31 Neal Street, near Neal's Yard, tel. 020/7836-0239).

Near Soho and Chinatown

London has a trendy scene that most Beefeater-seekers miss entirely. These restaurants are scattered throughout the hipster, gay, and strip-club district, teeming each evening with fun-seekers and theatergoers. Even if you plan to have dinner elsewhere, it's a treat just to wander around this lively area.

Beware of the extremely welcoming women standing outside the strip clubs (especially on Great Windmill Street). Enjoy the sales pitch—but only fools fall for the "£5 drink and show" lure. They don't get back out without emptying their wallet...literally.

Yo! Sushi is a futuristic Japanese-food-extravaganza experience, complete with thumping rock, Japanese cable TV, and a 195-foot-long conveyor belt. For £1.25, you get unlimited green tea or water. Snag a bar stool and grab dishes as they rattle by (priced by color of dish; check the chart: £1.75-5 per dish, daily 12:00-23:00, 2 blocks south of Oxford Street, where Lexington Street becomes Poland Street, 52 Poland Street, tel. 020/7287-0443). If you like Yo!, there are about 40 other locations around town, including a handy branch a block from the London Eye on Belvedere Road, as well as outlets within Selfridges, Harvey Nichols department stores, Victoria train station, and Whiteleys Mall on Queensway.

Wagamama Noodle Bar is a noisy, pan-Asian, organic slurpa-thon. As you enter, check out the kitchen and listen to the roar of the basement, where benches rock with happy eaters. Everybody sucks. Portions are huge and splitting is allowed (£7-10 meals, Mon-Sat 11:30-23:00, Sun 12:00-22:00, crowded after 19:00, 10A Lexington Street, tel. 020/7292-0990 but no reservations taken). If you like this place, handy branches are all over town, including one near the British Museum (4 Streatham Street), Kensington (26 High Street), in Harvey Nichols (109 Knightsbridge), Covent Garden (1 Tavistock Street), Leicester Square (14 Irving Street), Piccadilly Circus (8 Norris Street), Fleet Street (#109), and next to the Tower of London (Tower Place).

Busaba Eathai Thai Restaurant is a hit with locals for its snappy service, casual-yet-high-energy ambience, and good, inexpensive Thai cuisine. You'll sit communally around big, square 16-person hardwood tables or in two-person tables by the window—with everyone in the queue staring at your noodles. They don't take reservations, so arrive by 19:00 or line up (£7-10 meals, Mon-Thu 12:00-23:00, Fri-Sat 12:00-23:30, Sun 12:00-22:00, 106 Wardour Street, tel. 020/7255-8686). They have three other handy locations: on nearby Panton Street, just below Piccadilly Circus; at 22 Store Street, near the British Museum and Goodge Street Tube; and at 8-13 Bird Street, just off Oxford Street and across from the Bond Street Tube.

Côte Restaurant is a contemporary French bistro chain, serving good-value French cuisine with no pretense at the right prices (£9-13 mains, £12 three-course early dinner specials if you order by 19:00, open Mon-Wed 8:00-23:00, Thu-Fri 8:00-24:00, Sat 10:00-24:00, Sun 10:00-22:30, 124-126 Wardour Street, tel. 020/7287-9280).

Y Ming Chinese Restaurant—across Shaftesbury Avenue from the ornate gates, clatter, and dim sum of Chinatown—has dressy European decor, serious but helpful service, and authentic Northern Chinese cooking (good £10 meal deal offered 12:00-18:00, £7-10 plates, open Mon-Sat 12:00-23:45, closed Sun, 35-36 Greek Street, tel. 020/7734-2721).

New World Chinese Restaurant is a sprawling old-fashioned Chinese diner that just feels real. It's a fixture in Chinatown, serving cheap Cantonese food, including dim sum lunch and a similar dinner menu with an array of little £3 dishes (daily 11:00-24:00, 1 Gerrard Place, tel. 020/7734-0677).

Jen Café, across the street, is a humble Chinese corner eatery much loved for its homemade dumplings (£3-5 plates, long hours daily, 4 Newport Place, tel. 020/7287-9708).

On Lexington Street, in the Heart of Soho

Andrew Edmunds Restaurant is a tiny, candlelit place where you'll want to hide your camera and guidebook and not act like a tourist. This little place—with a jealous and loyal clientele—is the closest I've found to Parisian quality in a cozy restaurant in London. The modern European cooking and creative seasonal menu are worth the splurge (£6-8 starters, £11-18 entrées, Mon-Sat 12:30-15:00 & 18:00-22:45, Sun 13:00-15:30 & 18:00-22:30, come early or call ahead, request ground floor rather than basement, 46 Lexington Street, tel. 020/7437-5708).

Mildred's Vegetarian Restaurant, across from Andrew Edmunds, has cheap prices, an enjoyable menu, and a pleasant interior filled with happy eaters (£7-9 meals, Mon-Sat 12:00-23:00, closed Sun, vegan options, 45 Lexington Street, tel. 020/7494-1634).

Fernandez & Wells is a delightfully simple little wine, cheese, and ham bar. Drop in and grab a stool as you belly up to the big wooden bar. Share a plate of top-quality cheeses and/or Spanish or French hams with fine bread and oil, while sipping a nice glass of wine and talking with Dean or his staff (Mon-Sat 11:00-22:00, Sun 12:00-19:00, quality sandwiches at lunch, wine/cheese/ham bar after 16:00, 43 Lexington Street, tel. 020/7734-1546).

West London
Near Victoria Station Accommodations
These restaurants are within a few blocks of Victoria Station—and all are places I've enjoyed eating at. As with the accommodations in this area, I've grouped them by location: east or west of the station (see the map on pages 784-785).

Cheap Eats: For groceries, a handy **M&S Simply Food** is inside Victoria Station (Mon-Sat 7:00-24:00, Sun 8:00-22:00), along with a **Sainsbury's Market** (daily 6:00-23:00, at rear entrance, on Eccleston Street). A second Sainsbury's is just north of the station on Victoria Street, and a larger Sainsbury's is on Wilton Road near Warwick Way, a couple of blocks southeast of the station (Mon-Fri 7:00-23:00, Sat 7:00-22:00, Sun 11:00-17:00). A string of good ethnic restaurants lines Wilton Road (near the recommended Seafresh Fish Restaurant). For affordable if forgettable meals, try the row of cheap little eateries on Elizabeth Street.

West of Victoria Station
Ebury Wine Bar, filled with young professionals, provides a cut-above atmosphere, delicious £13-18 entrées, and a £21 three-course and £16 two-course special anytime (it includes a glass of champagne, but you're welcome to swap it for wine). In the delightful back room, the fancy menu features modern European cuisine with a French accent; at the wine bar, find a cheaper bar menu that's better than your average pub grub. This is emphatically a "traditional wine bar," with no beers on tap (daily 11:00-23:00, reserve after 20:00, at intersection of Ebury and Elizabeth Streets, 139 Ebury Street, tel. 020/7730-5447).

Jenny Lo's Tea House is a simple budget place serving up reliably tasty £7-9 eclectic Chinese-style meals to locals in the know. While the menu is small, everything is high quality. Jenny clearly learned from her father, Ken Lo, one of the most famous Cantonese chefs in Britain, whose fancy place is just around the corner (Mon-Fri 11:30-15:00 & 18:00-22:00, closed Sat-Sun, cash only, 14 Eccleston Street, tel. 020/7259-0399).

LONDON

La Bottega is an Italian delicatessen that fits its upscale Belgravia neighborhood. It offers tasty, freshly cooked pastas (£6), lasagnas, and salads (lasagna and salad meal-£8), along with great sandwiches (£3) and a good coffee bar with pastries. While not cheap, it's fast (order at the counter), and the ingredients would please an Italian chef. Grab your meal to go, or enjoy the Belgravia good life with locals, either sitting inside or on the sidewalk (Mon-Fri 8:00-19:00, Sat 9:00-18:00, Sun 10:00-17:00, on corner of Ebury and Eccleston Streets, tel. 020/7730-2730).

The Duke of Wellington Pub is a classic neighborhood place with forgettable grub, woodsy sidewalk seating, and an inviting interior (dinner served Mon-Sat 18:00-21:00, 63 Eaton Terrace, tel. 020/7730-1782).

The Thomas Cubitt Pub, packed with young professionals, is a trendy neighborhood gastropub, great for a drink or pricey meal (44 Elizabeth Street, tel. 020/7730-6060).

East of Victoria Station

Grumbles brags it's been serving "good food and wine at nonscary prices since 1964." Offering a delicious mix of "modern eclectic French and traditional English," this unpretentious little place with cozy booths inside (on two levels, including a cellar) and four nice sidewalk tables is *the* spot to eat well in this otherwise workaday neighborhood. Their traditional dishes are their forte (£9-18 plates, £10 early-bird specials 18:00-19:00, open daily 12:00-14:30 & 18:00-23:00, reservations wise, half a block north of Belgrave Road at 35 Churton Street, tel. 020/7834-0149, Alex).

Seafresh Fish Restaurant is the neighborhood place for plaice—and classic and creative fish-and-chips cuisine. You can either take out on the cheap or eat in, enjoying a white fish ambience. Though Mario's father started this place in 1965, it feels like the chippie of the 21st century (meals-£5 to go, £10-14 to sit, Mon-Sat 12:00-15:00 & 17:00-22:30, closed Sun, 80-81 Wilton Road, tel. 020/7828-0747).

The Jugged Hare pub, a 10-minute walk from Victoria Station, sits in a lavish old bank building, with vaults replaced by tankards of beer and a fine kitchen. They have a fun, traditional menu with more fresh veggies than fries, and a plush, vivid pub scene good for a meal or just a drink (£6.25 sandwiches, £8-10 meals, food served daily 12:00-21:30, drinks served daily 11:00-23:00, 172 Vauxhall Bridge Road, tel. 020/7828-1543).

St. George's Tavern is *the* pub for a meal in this neighborhood. They serve dinner from the same fun menu in three zones: on the sidewalk to catch the sun and enjoy some people-watching, in the sloppy pub, and in a classier back dining room. They're proud of their sausages and "toad in the hole." The scene is inviting for just a beer, too (£7-10 meals, Mon-Sat 10:00-22:00, Sun until 21:00, corner of Hugh Street and Belgrave Road, tel. 020/7630-1116).

Near Notting Hill and Bayswater Accommodations

For locations, see the map on page 789.

Maggie Jones, a Charles Dickens-meets-Ella Fitzgerald splurge, is exuberantly rustic and very English, with a 1940s-jazz soundtrack. You'll get solid English cuisine, including huge plates of crunchy vegetables, served by a young and casual staff. It's pricey, but the portions are huge (especially the meat-and-fish pies, their specialty). You're welcome to save lots by splitting your main course. The candlelit upstairs is the most romantic, while the basement is kept lively with the kitchen, tight seating, and lots of action. If you eat well once in London, eat here—and do it quick, before it burns down (lunch—£5 starters, £7 entrées; dinner—£6-9 starters, £13-19 entrées; Mon-Sat 12:30-14:30 & 18:30-23:00, Sun 12:30-16:00 & 18:30-22:30, reservations recommended, 6 Old Court Place, just east of Kensington Church Street, near High Street Kensington Tube stop, tel. 020/7937-6462).

The Churchill Arms pub and **Thai Kitchens** (same location) are local hangouts, with good beer and a thriving old-English ambience in front, and hearty £6.50 Thai plates in an enclosed patio in the back. You can eat the Thai food in the tropical hide-away (table service) or in the atmospheric pub section (order at the counter and they'll bring it to you). They also serve basic English pub food (£3 sandwiches, £6 meals). The place is festooned with Churchill memorabilia and chamber pots (including one with Hitler's mug on it—hanging from the ceiling farthest from Thai Kitchen—sure to cure the constipation of any Brit during World War II). Arrive by 18:00 or after 21:00 to avoid a line. During busy times, diners are limited to an hour at the table (daily 12:00-22:00, 119 Kensington Church Street, tel. 020/7792-1246).

The Prince Edward serves good grub in a quintessential pub setting (£7-12 meals, Mon-Wed 10:00-23:00, Thu-Sat 10:00-23:30, Sun 10:00-22:30, plush-pubby indoor seating or sidewalk tables, family-friendly, pay Wi-Fi, 2 blocks north of Bayswater Road at the corner of Dawson Place and Hereford Road, 73 Prince's Square, tel. 020/7727-2221).

Café Diana is a healthy little eatery serving sandwiches, salads, and Middle Eastern food. It's decorated—almost shrine-like—with photos of Princess Diana, who used to drop by for pita sandwiches. You can dine in the simple interior, or order some food from the counter to go (£3-4 sandwiches, £6-8 meat dishes, daily 8:00-23:00, 5 Wellington Terrace, on Bayswater Road, opposite Kensington Palace Garden Gates, where Di once lived, tel. 020/7792-9606, Abdul).

On Queensway: The road called Queensway is a multiethnic food circus, lined with lively and inexpensive eateries—browse the options along here and choose your favorite. For a cut above, head for **Royal China Restaurant**—filled with London's Chinese, who consider this one of the city's best eateries. It's dressed up in black, white, and gold, with candles and brisk waiters. While it's pricier than most neighborhood Chinese restaurants, the food is noticeably better (£9-13 dishes, Mon-Thu 12:00-23:00, Fri-Sat 12:00-23:30, Sun 11:00-22:00, dim sum until 17:00, 13 Queensway, tel. 020/7221-2535). For a lowbrow alternative, **Whiteleys Mall Food Court**—at the top end of Queensway—offers a fun selection of ethnic and fast-food chain eateries among Corinthian columns, and a multiscreen theater in a delightful mall (daily 9:00-23:00; options include Yo! Sushi, good salads at Café Rouge, pizza, Starbucks, and a coin-op Internet place; third floor, corner of Porchester Gardens and Queensway).

Supermarkets: **Tesco** is a half-block from the Notting Hill Gate Tube stop (Mon-Sat 7:00-23:00, Sun 12:00-18:00, near intersection with Pembridge Road, 114-120 Notting Hill Gate). The smaller **Spar Market** is at 18 Queensway (Mon-Sat 7:00-24:00, Sun 9:00-24:00), and **Marks & Spencer** can be found in Whiteleys Mall (Mon-Sat 10:00-20:00, Sun 12:00-18:00).

Near South Kensington Accommodations

Popular eateries line Old Brompton Road and Thurloe Street (Tube: South Kensington), and a good selection of cheap eateries are clumped around the Tube station. For locations, see the map on page 787.

La Bouchée Bistro Café is a classy hole-in-the-wall touch of France. This candlelit and woody bistro, with very tight seating, serves a two-course, £11.50 special on weekdays during lunch and from 17:30-18:30, and £17 *plats du jour* all *jour*. Reservations are smart in the evening (daily 12:00-15:00 & 17:30-23:30, 56 Old Brompton Road, tel. 020/7589-1929).

Daquise, run by a well-established Warsaw restaurateur, is ideal if you're in the mood for kielbasa and kraut (£12 meals, weekday lunch special, daily 12:00-23:00, 20 Thurloe Street, tel. 020/7589-6117).

Moti Mahal Indian Restaurant, with minimalist-yet-classy mod ambience and attentive service, serves mostly Bangladeshi cuisine that's delicious. Consider chicken *jalfrezi* if you like spicy food, and buttery chicken if you don't (£10 dinners, daily 12:00-14:30 & 17:30-23:00, 3 Glendower Place, tel. 020/7584-8428).

Beirut Express has fresh, well-prepared Lebanese cuisine. In the front, you'll find take-away service as well as barstools for quick service (£4 sandwiches). In the back is a sit-down restaurant with £14 plates (daily 12:00-23:00, 65 Old Brompton Road, tel. 020/7591-0123).

Bosphorus Kebabs is the student favorite for a quick, fast, and hearty Turkish dinner. While mostly for take-away, they have a few tight tables indoors and on the sidewalk (£5 meals, Turkish kebabs, daily until 24:00, 59 Old Brompton Road, tel. 020/7584-4048).

Rocca di Papa is a bright and dressy Italian place with a heated terrace (£8 pizza, pasta, and salads; open daily, 73 Old Brompton Road, tel. 020/7225-3413).

The Anglesea Arms, with a great terrace surrounded by classy South Kensington buildings, is a destination pub that feels like the classic neighborhood favorite. It's a thriving and happy place, with a woody ambience and a mellow back dining room a world away from any tourism. Chef Julian Legge freshens up traditional English cuisine and prints up a daily menu listing his creative meals. While it'd be a shame to miss his cooking, this is also a fine place for simply a beer (£6 starters, £13 entrées, meals served daily 12:00-15:00 & 18:00-22:00, a couple of blocks off Old Brompton Road at 15 Selwood Terrace, tel. 020/7373-7960).

Supermarket: **Tesco Express** is handy for picnics (daily 7:00-24:00, 50-52 Old Brompton Road).

Elsewhere in London

Between St. Paul's and the Tower: **The Counting House,** formerly an elegant old bank, offers great £8-10 meals, nice homemade meat pies, fish, and fresh vegetables. The fun "nibbles menu" is available starting in the early evening until 22:00 (or until 21:00 on Mon-Tue; open Mon-Fri 11:00-23:00, closed Sat-Sun, gets really busy with the buttoned-down 9-to-5 crowd after 12:15, near Mansion House in The City, 50 Cornhill, tel. 020/7283-7123).

Near St. Paul's: **De Gustibus Sandwiches** is where a top-notch artisan bakery meets the public, offering fresh, you-design-it sandwiches, salads, and soups. Just one block below St. Paul's, it has simple seating or take-out picnic sacks for lugging to one of the great nearby parks (Mon-Fri 7:00-17:00, closed Sat-Sun, from church steps follow signs to youth hostel a block downhill, 53-55 Carter Lane, tel. 020/7236-0056; another outlet is inside the Borough Market in Southwark).

Near the British Library: Drummond Street (running just west of Euston Station) is famous in London for cheap and good Indian vegetarian food (£5-10 dishes). Consider **Chutneys** (124 Drummond, tel. 020/7388-0604) and **Ravi Shankar** (133-135 Drummond, tel. 020/7388-6458) for a good *thali* (both open long hours daily).

London's Airports

AIRPORTS

ENGLAND

50 MILES
50 KM

LUTON

CAMBRIDGE

STANSTED

LONDON

LONDON CITY

BATH

WINDSOR

GREENWICH

NORTH SEA

HEATHROW

GATWICK

CHANNEL TUNNEL

DCH

ENGLISH CHANNEL

TO PARIS & BRUSSELS

London Connections

Airports

Heathrow Airport

Heathrow Airport is one of the world's busiest airports. Think about it: 68 million passengers a year on 470,000 flights from 180 destinations riding 90 airlines, like some kind of global maypole dance. Read signs and ask questions. For Heathrow's airport, flight, and transfer information, call the switchboard at toll tel. 0844-335-1801, or visit the helpful website at www.heathrow airport.com.

Heathrow has five terminals: T-1 (mostly domestic and Irish flights, with some service to Europe and the US); T-2 (closed for renovation, should reopen in 2013); T-3 (North and South American, Asian, and some European flights); T-4 (European and US flights); and T-5 (British Airways flights only). You can walk between T-1 and T-3. To travel between the other terminals, you can take the Heathrow Express trains (free), buses (free), or the Tube (requires a ticket). Unlike most American airports, there is no train that links all the terminals together on one line, so you may have to transfer if you're going to T-4 or T-5.

If you're flying out of Heathrow, it's critical to confirm which terminal your flight will use (check the Web or call your airline in advance)—because if it's T-4 or T-5, you'll need to allow extra time. Taxi drivers generally know which terminal you'll need, but bus drivers may not.

Each terminal has an airport information desk (generally daily 6:00-22:00), car-rental agencies, exchange bureaus, ATMs, a pharmacy, a **VAT refund desk** (tel. 020/8910-3682; you must present the VAT claim form from the retailer here to get your tax rebate on items purchased in Britain), and **baggage storage** (£8/item for 24 hours, hours vary by terminal but generally daily 5:30-23:00, www.left-baggage.co.uk). Get online 24 hours a day at Heathrow's **Internet access points** (at each terminal—T-4's is up on the mezzanine level) or with your laptop (pay Wi-Fi provided by Boingo, www.boingo.com). There's a **post office** on the first floor of T-3. Each terminal has cheap **eateries.**

Heathrow's small **"TI"** (tourist info shop), even though it's a for-profit business, is worth a visit to pick up free information: a simple map, the *London Planner,* and brochures (daily 6:30-22:00, 5-minute walk from T-3 in Tube station, follow signs to Underground; bypass queue for transit info to reach window for London questions).

Getting to London from Heathrow Airport

You have five basic options for traveling the 14 miles between Heathrow Airport and downtown London: Tube (£4.50/person), bus (£5/person), direct shuttle bus (£21.50/person), express train with connecting Tube or taxi (about £20/person), or taxi (about £55 per group).

By Tube (Subway): For £4.50, the Tube takes you from any Heathrow terminal to downtown London in 50-60 minutes on the Piccadilly Line (6/hour; depending on your destination, may require a transfer, buy ticket at the Tube station ticket window). If you plan to use the Tube for transport in London, it may make sense to buy a Travelcard or pay-as-you-go Oyster card at the Tube station ticket window at the airport. (For information on these passes, see page 716.) If your Travelcard covers only Zones 1-2, it does not include Heathrow (Zone 6); however, you can pay a small supplement for the initial trip from Heathrow to downtown.

If you're taking the Tube from downtown London *to* the airport, note that the Piccadilly Line trains don't stop at every terminal. Trains either stop at T-4, then T-1/T-3 (also called Heathrow Central), in that order; or T-1/T-3 and T-5. When leaving central London on the Tube, allow extra time if going to T-4 or T-5, since you have to be sure you get on a train going to your terminal; carefully check the destination information before you board.

By Bus: Most buses depart from the outdoor common area in the heart of the Heathrow complex called the Central Bus Station. It serves T-1 and T-3, and is a 5-minute walk from these terminals. To get to T-4 or T-5 from the Central Bus Station, go inside, downstairs, and follow signs to take Heathrow Express trains to your terminal (free, but only runs every 15-20 minutes to those terminals); or catch one of the free buses that circulate between terminals.

National Express has regular service from Heathrow's Central Bus Station to Victoria Coach Station in downtown London, near several of my recommended hotels. While slow, the bus is affordable and convenient for those staying near Victoria Station (£5, 1-2/hour, less frequent from Victoria Station to Heathrow, 45-60 minutes depending on time of day, toll tel. 0871-781-8181, www.nationalexpress.com).

By Shuttle: SkyShuttle operates buses about every half hour between all Heathrow terminals and hotels in central London (£21.50/person one-way, £34.40/person round-trip; reservations toll tel. 0845-481-0960, call between 6:00-22:00; www.skyshuttle.co.uk).

By Train: Two different trains (slow for £8, fast for £18) run between Heathrow Airport and London's Paddington Station. At Paddington Station, you're in the thick of the Tube system, with easy access to any of my recommended neighborhoods—my Paddington hotels are just outside the front door, and Notting Hill Gate is just two Tube stops away. The **Heathrow Connect** train is the slightly slower, much cheaper option, serving T-1 and T-3 at one station called Heathrow Central; use free transfers if you're coming from either T-4 or T-5 (£8 one-way, 2/hour, 30 minutes, toll tel. 0845-678-6975, www.heathrowconnect.com). The **Heathrow Express** train is fast (15 minutes to downtown from T-1 and T-3; 21 minutes from T-5; transfer required from T-4) and runs more frequently (4/hour), but it's pricey (£18 "express class" one-way, £32 round-trip, ask about discount promos at ticket desk, buy ticket before you board or pay a £3 surcharge to buy it on the train, covered by BritRail pass, daily 5:10-23:25, toll tel. 0845-600-1515, www.heathrowexpress.co.uk). At the airport, you can use Heathrow Express as a free transfer between terminals.

By Taxi: Taxis from the airport cost about £45-70 to west and central London (one hour). For four people traveling together, this can be a deal. Hotels can often line up a cab back to the airport for about £30-40. For the cheapest taxi to the airport, don't order one from your hotel. Simply flag down a few and ask them for their best "off-meter" rate. Locals refer to hired cars that do the trip off-meter as "mini-cabs." These are reliable and generally cost about what you'd pay for a taxi in good traffic, but—with a fixed price—they can save you money when taxis are snarled in congestion with the meter running.

Getting to Bath from Heathrow Airport

By Bus: Direct buses run daily from Heathrow to Bath (£19.10, 10/day direct, 2-3 hours, more frequent but slower with transfer in London, toll tel. 0871-781-8181, www.nationalexpress.com). BritRail passholders may prefer the 2.5-hour Heathrow-Bath bus/train connection via Reading (BritRail passholders just pay £15 for bus; otherwise £46-65 depending on time of day, about £20 cheaper when bought in advance; tel. 0118-957-9425, buy bus ticket from www.railair.com, train ticket from www.firstgreatwestern.co.uk). First catch the RailAir Link shuttle bus (2/hour, 45 minutes) to Reading (RED-ding), then hop on the express train (2/hour, 1 hour) to Bath. Factoring in the connection in Reading—which can add at least an hour to the trip—the train is a less convenient option than the direct bus to Bath. For more bus information, see "By Bus—To Bath," page 822.

Gatwick Airport

More and more flights land at Gatwick Airport, halfway between London and the South Coast (toll tel. 0844-335-1802, www.gatwickairport.com). Gatwick has two terminals, North and South, which are easily connected by a free monorail (2-minute trip, runs 24 hours daily). Note that boarding passes say "Gatwick N" or "Gatwick S" to indicate your terminal. British Airways flights generally use Gatwick North. The Gatwick Express trains (described next) stop only at Gatwick South. Schedules in each terminal show only arrivals and departures from that terminal.

Getting to London: Gatwick Express trains are clearly the best way into London from this airport. They shuttle conveniently between Gatwick South and London's Victoria Station, with many of my recommended hotels (£17, £29 round-trip, 4/hour, 30 minutes, runs 5:00-24:00 daily, purchase tickets on train at no extra charge, toll tel. 0845-850-1530, www.gatwickexpress.com). If you buy your tickets at the station before boarding, ask about their deal where three adults travel for the price of two, or four for the price of three. (If you see others in the ticket line, suggest buying your tickets together—you'll save more than £5 each.)

You can save a few pounds by taking Southern Railway's slower and less frequent **shuttle train** between Gatwick South and Victoria Station (£10.90, up to 4/hour, 45 minutes, toll tel. 0845-127-2920, www.southernrailway.com).

A train also runs from Gatwick South to **St. Pancras International Station** (£8.90, 8/hour, 1 hour, www.firstcapitalconnect.co.uk)—useful for travelers taking the Eurostar train (to Paris or Brussels) or staying in the St. Pancras/King's Cross neighborhood.

Even slower, but cheap and handy to the Victoria Station neighborhood, you can take the **bus** from Gatwick to Victoria (£7.50, hourly, 1.5 hours, toll tel. 0871-781-8181, www.nationalexpress.com).

Getting to Bath: To get to Bath from Gatwick, you can catch a bus to Heathrow and take the bus to Bath from there (10/day, 4-5 hours total, £25 one-way, transfer at Heathrow Airport, www.nationalexpress.com—see "Getting to Bath from Heathrow Airport," earlier). By train, the best Gatwick-Bath connection involves a transfer in Reading (£45-54 one-way depending on time of day, £12 in advance, hourly, 2.5 hours, www.firstgreatwestern .co.uk; avoid transfer in London, where you'll have to change stations).

London's Other Airports

Stansted Airport: If you're using Stansted (toll tel. 0870-0000-303, www.stanstedairport.com), you have several options for getting into or out of London. Two different **buses** connect the airport and downtown London's Victoria Station neighborhood: National Express (£10, £17 round-trip, every 20 minutes, 1.75 hours, runs 24 hours a day, picks up and stops throughout London, ends at Victoria Coach Station, toll tel. 0871-781-8181, www.national express.com) and Terravision (£9, 2-3/hour, 1.25 hours, ends at Green Line Coach Station just south of Victoria Station). Or you can take the faster, pricier Stansted Express **train** (£18-20 one-way, £25-27 round-trip, connects to London's Tube system at Tottenham Hale and Liverpool Street, 4/hour, 45 minutes, 5:00-23:00, toll tel. 0845-850-0150, www.stanstedexpress.com). Stansted is expensive by **cab**; figure £120 one-way from central London.

Luton Airport: For Luton (airport tel. 01582/405-100, www .london-luton.co.uk), there are two choices into or out of London. The fastest way to go is by **rail** to London's St. Pancras International Station (£12 one-way, 1-5/hour, 25-45 minutes—check schedule to avoid the slower trains, toll tel. 0845-712-5678, www.eastmidlands trains.co.uk); catch the 10-minute shuttle bus (£1) from outside the terminal to the Luton Airport Parkway Station. The Green Line express **bus** #757 runs to Buckingham Palace Road, just south of London's Victoria Station (£13 one-way, £16 round-trip, small discount for easyJet passengers who buy online, 2-4/hour, 1.25-1.5 hours, 24 hours a day, toll tel. 0844-801-7261, www.greenline .co.uk). If you're sleeping at Luton, consider easyHotel (see listing on page 796).

London City Airport: There's a slim chance you might use London City Airport (tel. 020/7646-0088, www.londoncity airport.com). To get into London, take the Docklands Light Railway (DLR) to the Bank Tube station, which is one stop east of St. Paul's on the Central Line (£4 one-way, covered by Travelcard, £2.20-2.70 on Oyster card, 22 minutes, tel. 020/7222-1234, www .tfl.gov.uk/dlr).

LONDON

Connecting London's Airports by Bus

More and more travelers are taking advantage of cheap flights out of London's smaller airports. A handy **National Express bus** runs between Heathrow, Gatwick, Stansted, and Luton airports—easier than having to cut through the center of London—although traffic can be bad and increase travel times (toll tel. 0871-781-8181, www.nationalexpress.com).

From Heathrow Airport to: Gatwick Airport (1-4/hour, 1.25-1.5 hours, £19.50 one-way, £36.50 round-trip, allow at least three hours between flights), **Stansted Airport** (1-2/hour, 1.5-1.75 hours, £22.50 one-way, £29.30 round-trip), **Luton Airport** (hourly, 1-1.5 hours, £20.30 one-way, £25.60 round-trip).

Trains and Buses

Britain is covered by a myriad of rail systems (owned by different companies), which together are called National Rail. London, the country's major transportation hub, has a different train station for each region. There are nine main stations:

Euston—Serves northwest England, North Wales, and Scotland.

King's Cross—Serves northeast England and Scotland, including York and Edinburgh.

Liverpool Street—Serves east England, including Essex and Harwich.

London Bridge—Serves south England, including Brighton.

Marylebone—Serves southwest and central England, including Stratford-upon-Avon.

Paddington—Serves south and southwest England, including Heathrow Airport, Windsor, Bath, South Wales, and the Cotswolds.

St. Pancras International—Serves north and south England, plus the Eurostar to Paris or Brussels.

Victoria—Serves Gatwick Airport, Canterbury, Dover, and Brighton.

Waterloo—Serves southeast England, including Salisbury.

In addition, there are other, smaller train stations in London that you are not likely to use, such as **Charing Cross** or **Blackfriars.**

Any train station has schedule information, can make reservations, and can sell tickets for any destination. Most stations offer a baggage-storage service (£8/bag for 24 hours, look for *left luggage* signs); because of long security lines, it can take a while to check or pick up your bag (www.excess-baggage.com). For more details on the services available at each station, see www.nationalrail.co.uk/stations.

London's Train Stations

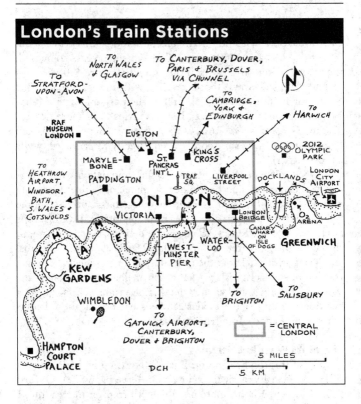

TO
NORTH WALES
& GLASGOW

TO CANTERBURY, DOVER,
PARIS & BRUSSELS
VIA CHUNNEL

TO
STRATFORD-
UPON-AVON

TO
CAMBRIDGE,
YORK &
EDINBURGH

TO
HARWICH

RAF
MUSEUM
LONDON

EUSTON

2012
OLYMPIC
PARK

MARYLE-
BONE

ST.
PANCRAS
INT'L.

KING'S
CROSS

DOCKLANDS

LONDON
CITY
AIRPORT

TO
HEATHROW
AIRPORT,
WINDSOR,
BATH,
S. WALES &
COTSWOLDS

PADDINGTON

TRAF.
SQ.

LIVERPOOL
STREET

LONDON

VICTORIA

LONDON
BRIDGE

O2
ARENA

CANARY
WHARF
ON
ISLE
OF DOGS

GREENWICH

WEST-
MINSTER
PIER

WATER-
LOO

KEW
GARDENS

WIMBLEDON

TO
BRIGHTON

TO
SALISBURY

HAMPTON
COURT
PALACE

TO
GATWICK AIRPORT,
CANTERBURY,
DOVER & BRIGHTON

= CENTRAL
LONDON

DCH

5 MILES

5 KM

Buying Tickets: For general information, call 0845-748-4950 (or visit www.nationalrail.co.uk or www.eurostar.com; £5 booking fee for telephone reservations). If you book far enough ahead, you might find discounted train tickets on certain routes at www .megatrain.com (toll tel. 0871-266-3333; as they also sell bus tickets, be careful to specify that you want to take the train).

By Train
To Paris or Brussels via Eurostar Train
From St. Pancras International Station to: Paris (15/day, 2.5 hrs), **Bruges** (via Brussels: 10/day, 2.5 hrs to Brussels Midi; then transfer, backtracking to Bruges: 2/hr, 1 hr, entire trip just a few dollars more with Eurostar ticket). Arrive at least 30 min early; security procedures for the Eurostar are similar to airport check-in.

Eurostar Fares: Channel fares are reasonable but complicated. Prices vary depending on how far ahead you reserve, whether you can live with restrictions, and whether you're eligible for any discounts (children, youths, seniors, round-trip travelers, and railpass holders all qualify).

Fares can change without notice, but typically a **one-way, full-fare ticket** (with no restrictions on refundability) runs about $425 first-class and $300 second-class. **Cheaper seats** come with more restrictions and can sell out quickly (figure $100-160 for second-class, one-way). Those traveling with a railpass that covers France or Britain should look first at the **passholder** fare ($85-130 for second-class, one-way Eurostar trips). For more details, visit my *Guide to Eurail Passes* (www.ricksteves.com/eurostar), Rail Europe (www.raileurope.com), or go directly to Eurostar (www.eurostar.com).

Once you're confident about the time and date of your crossing, you can check and book fares by phone or online. Ordering online through Eurostar or major agents offers a print-at-home e-ticket option. You can also order by phone through Rail Europe at US tel. 800-EUROSTAR for home delivery before you go, or through Eurostar (French toll tel. 08 92 35 35 39, priced in euros) and pick up your ticket at the train station. In continental Europe, you can buy your Eurostar ticket at any major train station in any country or at any travel agency that handles train tickets (expect a booking fee). In Britain, tickets can be issued only at the Eurostar office in St. Pancras International Station.

To Points West in Britain
From Paddington Station to: Bath (2/hour, 1.5 hours; also consider a guided Evan Evans tour by bus—see page 822), **Oxford** (2/hour direct, 1 hour, more possible with transfer in Reading, 1 hour), **Penzance** (every 1-2 hours, 5-5.5 hours, possible change in Plymouth), and **Cardiff** (2/hour, 2 hours).

To Points North in Britain
From King's Cross Station: Trains run at least hourly, stopping in **York** (2 hours), **Durham** (3 hours), and **Edinburgh** (4.5 hours). Trains to **Cambridge** also leave from here (3/hour, 45-60 minutes).

From Euston Station to: Conwy (nearly hourly, 3.25 hours, transfer in Chester), **Liverpool** (hourly, 2 hours, more with transfer), **Blackpool** (hourly, 3 hours, transfer at Preston), **Keswick** (hourly, 4.5 hours, transfer to bus at Penrith), and **Glasgow** (1-2/hour, 4.5-5 hours).

From London's Other Stations
Trains run between London and **Canterbury,** leaving from St. Pancras International Station and arriving in Canterbury West (1-2/hour, 1 hour), as well as from London's Victoria Station and arriving in Canterbury East (2/hour, 1.5 hours).

Direct trains leave for **Stratford-upon-Avon** from Maryle-

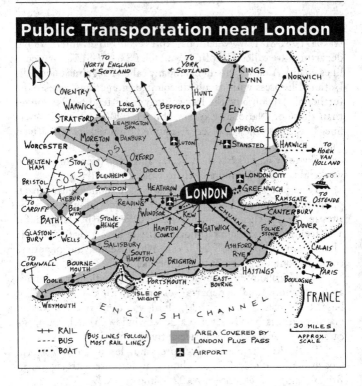

Public Transportation near London

TO NORTH ENGLAND & SCOTLAND · TO YORK & SCOTLAND · KING'S LYNN · NORWICH · COVENTRY · WARWICK · STRATFORD · LONG BUCKBY · BEDFORD · HUNT. · ELY · CAMBRIDGE · WORCESTER · MORETON · LEAMINGTON SPA · BANBURY · LUTON · STANSTED · HARWICH · TO HOEK VAN HOLLAND · CHELTENHAM · STOW · COTSWOLDS · OXFORD · DIDCOT · BRISTOL · BLENHEIM · LONDON CITY · SWINDON · HEATHROW · LONDON · GREENWICH · TO CARDIFF · AVEBURY · BEDWYN · READING · KEW · CHANNEL · RAMSGATE · TO OSTENDE · CANTERBURY · BATH · STONEHENGE · WINDSOR · HAMPTON COURT · GATWICK · FOLKESTONE · DOVER · GLASTONBURY · WELLS · SALISBURY · ASHFORD · RYE · CALAIS · TO CORNWALL · BOURNEMOUTH · SOUTHAMPTON · BRIGHTON · EASTBOURNE · HASTINGS · TO PARIS · POOLE · PORTSMOUTH · BOULOGNE · FRANCE · ISLE OF WIGHT · WEYMOUTH

ENGLISH CHANNEL

┼┼ RAIL
---- BUS
•••• BOAT
(BUS LINES FOLLOW MOST RAIL LINES)
✈ AIRPORT
AREA COVERED BY LONDON PLUS PASS
30 MILES
APPROX. SCALE

bone Station, located near the southwest corner of Regents Park (5/day direct, more with transfers, 2.25 hours).

To Other Destinations: Windsor (2/hour, 1 hour, direct from Waterloo Station; also 3/hour, 35 minutes, from Paddington Station with change in Slough), **Greenwich** (from Bank Tube stop take the DLR—Docklands Light Railway—to Cutty Sark Station), **Dover** (hourly, 1 hour, direct from St. Pancras International Station; also hourly, 2 hours, direct from Victoria Station or Charing Cross Station), **Brighton** (4-5/hour, 1 hour, from Victoria Station and London Bridge Station), **Portsmouth** (3/hour, 1.5-2 hours, most from Waterloo Station, a few from Victoria Station), and **Salisbury** (1-2/hour, 1.5 hours, from Waterloo Station).

By Bus

Buses are slower but considerably cheaper than trains for reaching destinations around Britain, and beyond. Most depart from **Victoria Coach Station,** which is one long block south of Victoria Station (near many recommended accommodations and Tube: Victoria). Inside the station, you'll find basic eateries, kiosks, and a helpful information desk stocked with schedules and ready to point you to your bus or answer any questions.

Most domestic buses are operated by **National Express** (toll tel. 0871-781-8181, www.nationalexpress.com); their international departures are called **Eurolines** (toll tel. 0871-781-8177, www.euro lines.co.uk). A newer, smaller company called **Megabus** undersells National Express with deeply discounted promotional fares—the further ahead you buy, the less you pay (trips tend to take longer than those on National Express, toll tel. 0900-160-0900, www .megabus.com). They also sell discounted train tickets on selected routes.

Try to avoid bus travel on Friday and Sunday evenings, when weekend travelers are more likely to make buses sell out.

To ensure getting a ticket—and to save money with special promotions—you can book your ticket in advance online (see websites above). The cheapest pre-purchased tickets can be changed (for a £5 fee), but they're nonrefundable. If you have a British mobile phone, you can buy an "M-Ticket," which sends your paperless confirmation number right to your phone.

If you're planning to buy your ticket at the station, try to arrive an hour before the bus departs—or drop by the day before. (For buses to Stansted Airport and Oxford, you can buy the ticket on board; otherwise you'll buy it at a ticket window.) Watch your bags carefully—luggage thieves thrive at the station.

To Bath: The National Express bus leaves from Victoria Coach Station (9/day, 2.75-3.75 hours, avoid those with layover in Bristol, sample fares: one-way-£22, round-trip-£29).

To get to Bath via Stonehenge, consider taking a guided bus tour from London to Stonehenge, Salisbury, and Bath, and abandoning the tour in Bath (be sure to confirm that Bath is the last stop on that particular tour). **Evan Evans'** tour is £69 and includes admissions. The tour leaves from Victoria Coach Station every morning at 8:45 (you can stow your bag under the bus), stops in Salisbury (for a look at its magnificent cathedral) and Stonehenge, and then stops in Bath for a city tour before returning to London (offered year-round; they also offer another tour to Stonehenge and Bath via Windsor Castle). You can book the tour at the Victoria Coach Station or the Evan Evans office (258 Vauxhall Bridge Road, near Victoria Coach Station, tel. 020/7950-1777, US tel. 866-382-6868, www.evanevans.co.uk). **Golden Tours** also runs a Stonehenge-Bath tour (£59, check website for seasonal tour days; departs from Fountain Square, located across from Victoria Coach Station, US tel. 800-548-7083, toll tel. 0844-880-6981, www .goldentours.co.uk).

To Other Destinations: Oxford (2-4/hour, about 1.5 hours), **Cambridge** (hourly, 2-2.5 hours), **Canterbury** (about hourly, 2-2.5 hours), **Dover** (about hourly, 2.5-3.25 hours), **Penzance** (5/day, 8.5-10 hours, overnight available), **Cardiff** (hourly, 3.25

hours), **Liverpool** (8/day direct, 5.25-6 hours, overnight available), **Blackpool** (4/day direct, 6.25-7 hours, overnight available), **York** (4/day direct, 5.25 hours), **Durham** (4/day direct, 6.5-7.5 hours), **Glasgow** (3/day direct, 8-9 hours, train is a much better option), **Edinburgh** (2/day direct, 8.75-9.75 hours, go by train instead).

BATH

The best city to visit within easy striking distance of London is Bath—just a 1.5-hour train ride away. Two hundred years ago, this city of 85,000 was the trendsetting Hollywood of Britain. If ever a city enjoyed looking in the mirror, Bath's the one. It has more "government-listed" or protected historic buildings per capita than any other town in England. The entire city, built of the creamy warm-tone limestone called "Bath stone," beams in its cover-girl complexion. An architectural chorus line, it's a triumph of the Georgian style. Proud locals remind visitors that the town is routinely banned from the "Britain in Bloom" contest to give other towns a chance to win. Bath's narcissism is justified. Even with its mobs of tourists (2 million per year) and greedy prices, Bath is a joy to visit.

Bath's fame began with the allure of its (supposedly) healing hot springs. Long before the Romans arrived in the first century, Bath was known for its warm waters. Romans named the popular spa town Aquae Sulis, after a local Celtic goddess. The town's importance carried through Saxon times, when it had a huge church on the site of the present-day abbey and was considered the religious capital of Britain. Its influence peaked in 973 with King Edgar's sumptuous coronation in the abbey. Later, Bath prospered as a wool town.

Bath then declined until the mid-1600s, wasting away to just a huddle of huts around the abbey, with hot, smelly mud and 3,000 residents, oblivious to the Roman ruins 18 feet below their dirt floors. In fact, with its own walls built upon ancient ones, Bath was no bigger than that Roman town. Then, in 1687, Queen Mary, fighting infertility, bathed here. Within 10 months she gave birth to a son...and a new age of popularity for Bath.

The revitalized town boomed as a spa resort. Ninety percent of the buildings you'll see today are from the 18th century. A father-and-son team of local architects—both named John Wood (the Elder and the Younger)—were inspired by the Italian architect Andrea Palladio to build a "new Rome." The town bloomed in the Neoclassical style, and streets were lined not with scrawny sidewalks but with wide "parades," upon which the women in their stylishly wide dresses could spread their fashionable tails.

Beau Nash (1673-1762) was Bath's "master of ceremonies." He organized both the daily regimen of aristocratic visitors and the city, lighting the streets, improving security, banning swords, and opening the Pump Room. Under his fashionable baton, Bath became a city of balls, gaming, and concerts—the place to see and be seen in England. This most civilized place became even more so with the great Neoclassical building spree that followed.

These days, modern tourism has stoked the local economy, as has the fast morning train to London. (A growing number of Bath professionals catch the 7:13 train to Paddington Station every morning.) With renewed access to Bath's soothing hot springs at the Thermae Bath Spa, the venerable waters are in the spotlight again, attracting a new generation of visitors in need of a cure or a soak.

Planning Your Time

Bath deserves two nights even on a quick trip. Here's how I'd spend a busy day in Bath: 9:00-Tour the Roman Baths; 10:30-Catch the free city walking tour; 12:30-Picnic on the open deck of a Bath tour bus; 14:00-Free time in the shopping center of old Bath; 15:30-Tour the Fashion Museum or Museum of Bath at Work, 20:00-Take the evening walking tour, enjoy the Bizarre Bath comedy walk, see a play, or go for a nighttime soak at the Thermae Bath Spa.

Orientation to Bath

(area code: 01225)

Bath's town square, three blocks in front of the bus and train station, is a cluster of tourist landmarks, including the abbey, Roman and Medieval Baths, and the Pump Room. Bath is hilly. In general, you'll gain elevation as you head north from the town center.

Tourist Information

The TI is in the abbey churchyard (Mon-Sat 9:30-18:00, Sun 10:00-16:00, closes one hour earlier Mon-Sat Oct-May, pricey toll tel. 0906-711-2000—50p/minute, www.visitbath.co.uk). The TI

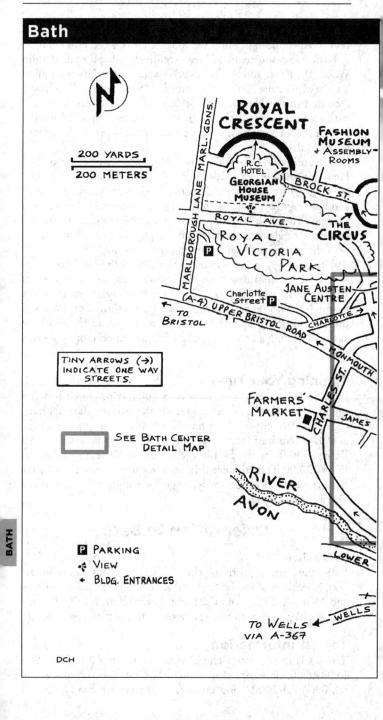

Bath

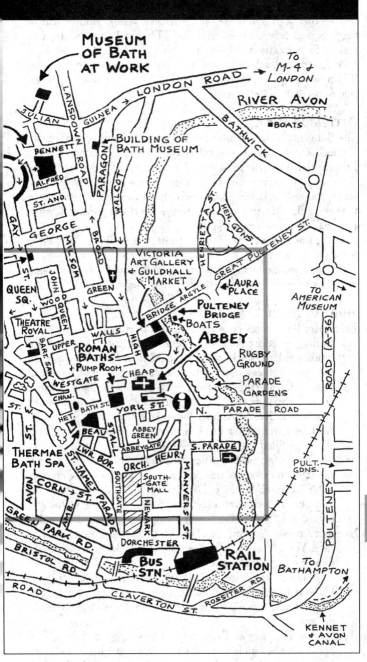

sells various visitor guides and maps—survey your options before buying one (£1-1.50). Only the most basic visitor guide—with a very rudimentary map—is free. The TI books rooms and theater tickets for no extra fee (booking tel. 0844-847-5256). If you're a Jane Austen fan, ask about the walking tours that leave from the TI on weekends. Entertainment listings from the local paper are posted on their bulletin board.

Arrival in Bath

The Bath Spa **train station** has a national and international tickets desk and a privately run travel agency masquerading as a TI. Directly in front of the train station is Bath's brand-new SouthGate Bath shopping center. To get from the train station to the TI, exit straight ahead, walk two blocks up Manvers Street, and turn left at the triangular "square" overlooking the riverfront park, following the small TI arrow on a signpost.

The **bus station** is west of the train station, along Dorchester Street.

My recommended B&Bs are all within a 10- to 15-minute walk or a £4-5 taxi ride from the train and bus stations.

Helpful Hints

Festivals: Bath hosts book, music, and theater festivals in the spring, including the **Bath Literature Festival** (www.bathlit fest.org.uk), the **Bath International Music Festival** (classical, folk, jazz, contemporary; www.bathmusicfest.org.uk), and the eclectic **Bath Fringe Festival** (theater, walks, talks, bus trips; www.bathfringe.co.uk). The **Jane Austen Festival** unfolds genteelly in late September (www.janeausten.co.uk/festival). And for three weeks in December, the squares around the abbey are filled with a **Christmas market.**

Bath's festival **box office** sells tickets for most events and can tell you exactly what's on tonight (a block down from the TI at 2 Church Street, tel. 01225/463-362, www.bathfestivals .org.uk). The city's weekly local paper, the *Bath Chronicle*, publishes a "What's On" event listing (www.thisisbath.com).

Internet Access: Ask your hotel or the TI for the closest Internet café. You can also get online at the Bath **library** (£1.20/20 minutes, slightly cheaper with free library membership, Mon 9:30-18:00, Tue-Thu 9:30-19:00, Fri-Sat 9:30-17:00, Sun 13:00-16:00, in the Podium Shopping Centre on Northgate Street near Pulteney Bridge, tel. 01225/394-041, www.bath nes.gov.uk).

Bookstore: Topping & Company, an inviting bookshop, has posters in the windows advertising frequent author readings, free coffee and tea for browsers, and tables filled with tidy stacks of carefully selected volumes (daily 9:00-20:00, near the bottom of the street called "The Paragon"—where it meets George Street, tel. 01225/428-111, www.toppingbooks.co.uk).

Laundry: The **Spruce Goose Launderette** is between the Circus and the Royal Crescent, on the pedestrian lane called Margaret's Buildings. Bring lots of £1 coins for washing and £0.20 coins for drying, as there are no change machines (self-service: about £4-5/load, daily 8:00-20:00, last load at 19:00; full-service: £12/load, Mon-Fri 8:00-12:00; tel. 01225/483-309). **Speedy Wash** can pick up your laundry anywhere in town on weekdays before 11:00 for same-day service (£12/small bag, Mon-Fri 7:30-17:30, Sat 8:30-13:00 but no pickup, closed Sun, no self-service, most hotels work with them, 4 Mile End, London Road, tel. 01225/427-616).

Car Rental: Enterprise provides a pickup service for customers to and from their hotels (extra fee for one-way rentals, at Lower Bristol Road outside Bath, tel. 01225/443-311, www.enterprise.com). Others include **Thrifty** (pickup service and one-way rentals available, in the Burnett Business Park in Keynsham—between Bath and Bristol, tel. 01179/867-997, www.thrifty.co.uk), **Hertz** (one-way rentals possible, at Windsor Bridge, tel. 0870-850-2691, www.hertz.co.uk), and **National/Europcar** (one-way rentals available, £7 by taxi from the train station, at Brassmill Lane—go west on Upper Bristol Road, tel. 01225/481-982 or 01761/479-205). Skip **Avis**—it's a mile from the Bristol train station; you'd need to rent a car to get there. Most offices close Saturday afternoon and all day Sunday, which complicates weekend pickups. Ideally, take the train or bus from downtown London to Bath, and rent a car as you leave Bath.

Parking: Parking in the city center is difficult. Short-term street parking is available but pricey (about £2.50/hour, 2-hour maximum, buy pay-and-display tickets from machine). You'll pay less per hour in long-stay lots (figure £9/24 hours; the Charlotte Street car park is handy). For more info on parking, visit www.bathnes.gov.uk/bathnes.

Tours in Bath

▲▲▲**Walking Tours**—Free two-hour tours are offered by **The Mayor's Corps of Honorary Guides,** led by volunteers who want to share their love of Bath with its many visitors (as the city's mayor first did when he took a group on a guided walk back in the 1930s). Their chatty, historical, and gossip-filled walks are essential for your understanding of this town's amazing Georgian social scene. How else would you learn that the old "chair ho" call for your sedan chair evolved into today's "cheerio" farewell? Tours leave from outside the Pump Room in the abbey churchyard (free, no tips, year-round Sun-Fri at 10:30 and 14:00, Sat at 10:30 only; additional evening walks May-Sept Tue and Fri at 19:00; tel. 01225/477-411, www.bathguides.co.uk). Tip for theatergoers: When your guide stops to talk outside the Theatre Royal, skip out for a moment, pop into the box office, and see about snaring a great deal on a play for tonight.

For a **private tour,** call the local guides' bureau, Bath Parade Guides (£60/2 hours, tel. 01225/337-111, www.bathparadeguides .co.uk, bathparadeguides@yahoo.com). For **Ghost Walks** and **Bizarre Bath** tours, see "Nightlife in Bath," later.

▲▲**City Bus Tours**—City Sightseeing's hop-on, hop-off bus tours zip through Bath. Jump on a bus anytime at one of 17 signposted pickup points, pay the driver, climb upstairs, and hear recorded commentary about Bath. City Sightseeing has two 45-minute routes: a city tour (unintelligible audio recording on half the buses, live guides on the other half—choose the latter), and a "Skyline" route outside town (all live guides, stops near the American Museum—15-minute walk). On a sunny day, this is a multitasking tourist's dream come true: You can munch a sandwich, work on a tan, snap great photos, and learn a lot, all at the same time. Save money by doing the bus tour first—ticket stubs get you minor discounts at many sights (£11.50, ticket valid for 2 days and both tour routes, generally 4/hour daily in summer 9:30-18:30, in winter 10:00-15:00, tel. 01225/330-444, www.city-sightseeing.com).

Taxi Tours—Local taxis, driven by good talkers, go where big buses can't. A group of up to four can rent a cab for an hour (about £20) and enjoy a fine, informative, and—with the right cabbie—entertaining private joyride. It's probably cheaper to let the meter run than to pay for an hourly rate, but ask the cabbie for advice.

Sights in Bath

In the Town Center

▲▲▲**Roman and Medieval Baths**—In ancient Roman times, high society enjoyed the mineral springs at Bath. From Londinium—and throughout the empire—Romans traveled so often to Aquae Sulis, as the city was called, to "take a bath" that finally it became known simply as Bath. Today, a fine museum surrounds the ancient bath. With the help of a great audioguide, you'll wander past well-documented displays, Roman artifacts, a temple pediment with an evocative bearded face, a bronze head of the goddess Sulis Minerva, excavated ancient foundations, and the actual mouth of the spring. At the end you'll have a chance to walk around the big pool itself, where Romans once lounged, splished,

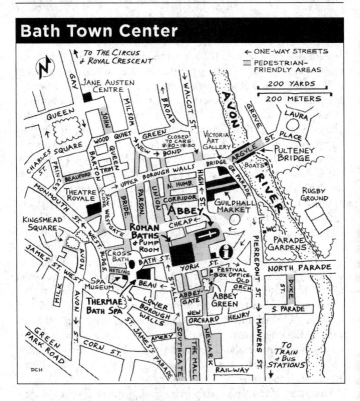

Bath Town Center

splashed, and thanked the gods for the gift of naturally hot water.

After touring the Roman Baths, stop by the attached Pump Room for a spot of tea, or to gag on the water.

Cost and Hours: £11.50, £0.75 more in July-Aug, includes audioguide, £15 combo-ticket includes Fashion Museum—a £3.50 savings, family ticket available, daily July-Aug 9:00-22:00, March-June and Sept-Oct 9:00-18:00, Nov-Feb 9:30-17:30, last entry one hour before closing, tel. 01225/477-785, www.romanbaths.co.uk.

Tours: Take advantage of the included, essential **audioguide,** which will make your visit easy and informative. In addition to the basic commentary, look for posted numbers to key into your audioguide for specialty topics—including a kid-friendly tour and insightful musings from American expat writer Bill Bryson. For those with a big appetite for Roman history, in-depth **guided tours** leave from the end of the museum at the edge of the actual bath (included with ticket, on the hour, a poolside clock is set for the next departure time, 20-40 minutes depending on the guide). You can revisit the museum after the tour.

▲**Pump Room**—For centuries, Bath was forgotten as a spa. Then, in 1687, the previously barren Queen Mary bathed here, became pregnant, and bore a male heir to the throne. A few years later, Queen Anne found the water eased her painful gout. Word of its wonder waters spread, and Bath earned its way back on the aristo-cratic map. High society soon turned the place into one big pleasure palace. The Pump Room, an elegant Georgian hall just above the Roman Baths, offers visitors their best chance to raise a pinky in this Chippendale grandeur. Above the newspaper table and sedan chairs, a statue of Beau Nash himself sniffles down at you. Drop by to sip coffee or tea or to enjoy a light meal (daily 9:30–12:00 for cof-fee and £6–9 breakfast, 12:00–14:30 for £6–16 lunches, 14:30–16:30 for £17.50 traditional afternoon tea, tea/coffee and pastries also available in the afternoons; open for dinner July-Aug, during Bath International Music Festival, and Christmas holidays only; live music daily—string trio or piano, times vary; tel. 01225/444-477). For just the price of a coffee (£3), you're welcome to drop in any-time—except during lunch—to enjoy the music and atmosphere.

The Spa Water: This is your chance to eat a famous (but for-gettable) "Bath bun" and split a drink of the awful curative water (£0.50 or free with your Roman and Medieval Baths ticket). The water comes from the King's Spring and is brought to you by an appropriately attired server, who explains that the water is 10,000 years old, pumped up from nearly 100 yards deep, and marinated in 43 wonderful minerals. Convenient public WCs (which use plain old tap water) are in the entry hallway that connects the Pump Room with the baths.

▲**Thermae Bath Spa**—After simmering unused for a quarter-century, Bath's natural thermal springs once again offer R&R for the masses. The state-of-the-art spa is housed in a complex of three buildings that combine historic structures with controversial (and expensive) new glass-and-steel architecture.

Is the Thermae Bath Spa worth the time and money? The expe-rience is pretty pricey and humble compared to similar German and Hungarian spas. Because you're in a tall, modern building in the city center, it lacks a certain old-time elegance. Jets are very lim-ited, and the only water toys you'll see are big foam noodles. There's no cold plunge—the only way to cool off between steam rooms is to step onto a small, unglamorous balcony. The Royal Bath's two pools are essentially the same, and the water isn't particularly hot in either—in fact, the main attraction is the rooftop view from the top one (best with a partner or as a social experience).

That said, this is the only natural thermal spa in the UK, and a chance to bathe in Bath. If you visit, bring your own swimsuit and come for a couple of hours (Fri night and all day Sat-Sun are most crowded). Or consider an evening visit, when—on a chilly day—Bath's twilight glows through the steam from the rooftop pool.

Cost: The cheapest spa pass is £24 for two hours, which gains you access to the Royal Bath's large, ground-floor "Minerva Bath"; the four steam rooms and the waterfall shower; and the view-filled, open-air, rooftop thermal pool. If you want to stay longer, it's £34/4 hours and £54/day (towel, robe, and slippers-£9). The much-hyped £39 Twilight Package includes three hours and a meal (one plate, drink, robe, towel, and slippers). The appeal of this package is not the mediocre meal, but being on top of the building at a magical hour (which you can do for less money at the regular rate).

Thermae also has all the "pamper thyself" extras: massages, mud wraps, and various healing-type treatments, including "watsu"—water shiatsu (£40-70 extra). Book treatments at www.thermaebathspa.com.

Hours: Daily 9:00-22:00, last entry at 19:30. No kids under 16 are allowed. It's 100 yards from the Roman and Medieval Baths, on Beau Street. Tel. 01225/331-234. There's a salad-and-smoothies café for guests.

The Cross Bath: This renovated, circular Georgian structure across the street from the main spa provides a simpler and less-expensive bathing option. It has a hot-water fountain that taps directly into the spring, making its water temperature higher than the spa's (£14/1.5 hours, daily 10:00-20:00, last entry at 18:30, check in at the bath's main office across the street and you'll be escorted to the Cross Bath, changing rooms, no access to Royal Bath, no kids under 12).

Spa Visitor Centre: Also across the street, in the Hetling Pump Room, this free, one-room exhibit explains the story of the spa (Mon-Sat 10:00-17:00, Sun 10:00-16:00, £2 audioguide).

▲**Abbey**—The town of Bath wasn't much in the Middle Ages, but an important church has stood on this spot since Anglo-Saxon times. King Edgar I was crowned here in 973, when the church was much bigger (before the bishop packed up and moved to Wells). Dominating the town center, today's abbey—the last great medieval church of England—is 500 years old and a fine example of Late Perpendicular Gothic, with breezy fan vaulting and enough stained glass to earn it the nickname "Lantern of the West."

The **facade** (c. 1500, but mostly restored) is interesting for some of its carvings. Look for the angels going down the ladder. The statue of Peter (to the left of the door) lost his head to mean iconoclasts; it was re-carved out of his once supersized beard. Take a moment to appreciate the abbey's architecture from the Abbey Green square.

Going **inside** is worth the £2.50 suggested donation (April-Oct Mon-Sat 9:00-18:00, Sun 13:00-14:30 & 16:30-17:30; Nov-March Mon-Sat 9:00-16:30, Sun 13:00-14:30 & 16:30-17:30; handy flier narrates a self-guided 19-stop tour, tel. 0122/422-462, www.bathabbey.org). The glass, red-iron gas-powered lamps, and heating grates on the floor are all remnants of the 19th century. The window behind the altar shows 52 scenes from the life of Christ. A window to the left of the altar shows Edgar's coronation.

Posted on the door (and on the abbey website) is the schedule for **events,** including concerts, services, and evensong.

Climbing to the top of the **tower** is only possible with an official 50-minute guided tour. You'll climb 212 steps for views across the rooftops of Bath and down into the Roman and Medieval Baths complex (£5, sporadic schedule but generally at the top of each hour Mon-Sat April-Oct 10:00-16:00, Nov-March 11:00-14:00, more often during busy times, no tours Sun, buy tickets in abbey gift shop).

A small but worthwhile exhibit, the abbey's **Heritage Vaults** tell the story of Christianity in Bath since Roman times (free, Mon-Sat 10:00-17:30, until 16:30 Nov-March, closed Sun, entrance just outside church, south side).

▲**Pulteney Bridge, Parade Gardens, and Cruises**—Bath is inclined to compare its shop-lined Pulteney Bridge to Florence's Ponte Vecchio. That's pushing it. But to best enjoy a sunny day, pay £1 to enter the Parade Gardens below the bridge (Easter-Sept daily 11:00-17:00, shorter hours off-season, includes deck chairs, ask about concerts held some Sun at 15:00 in summer, entrance a block south of bridge, www.bathnes.gov.uk). Taking a siesta to relax peacefully at the riverside provides a wonderful break (and memory).

Across the bridge at Pulteney Weir, tour boat companies run **cruises** (£8 round-trip, £4 one-way, up to 7/day if the weather's good, one hour to Bathampton and back, WCs on board, tel. 01225/312-900). Just take whatever boat is running—all stop in Bathampton (allowing you to hop off and walk back—about 45-60 minutes). Boats come with picnic-friendly sundecks.

Guildhall Market—The little, old-school shopping mall located across from Pulteney Bridge is a frumpy time warp in this affluent town. It's fun for browsing and picnic-shopping. Its cheap Market Café is recommended in "Eating in Bath," later.

Victoria Art Gallery—This gallery, next to Pulteney Bridge, has two parts: the ground floor houses temporary exhibits, while the upstairs is filled with paintings from the late 17th century to the present, along with a small collection of decorative arts (free, Tue-Sat 10:00-17:00, Sun 13:30-17:00, closed Mon, WC, tel. 01225/477-233, www.victoriagal.org.uk).

Northwest of the Town Center

Several worthwhile public spaces and museums can be found a slightly-uphill 10-minute walk away.

▲▲The Circus and the Royal Crescent—If Bath is an architectural cancan, these are its knickers. These first Georgian "condos"—built by the John Woods (the Circus by the Elder, the Royal Crescent by the Younger)—are well-explained by the city walking tours. "Georgian" is British for "Neoclassical," or dating from the 1770s. These two building complexes, conveniently located a block apart from each other, are quintessential Bath.

Circus: True to its name, this is a circular housing complex. Picture it as a coliseum turned inside out. Its Doric, Ionic, and Corinthian capital decorations pay homage to its Greco-Roman origin, and are a reminder that Bath (with its seven hills) aspired to be "the Rome of England." The frieze above the first row of columns has hundreds of different panels, each representing the arts, sciences, and crafts. The first floor was high off the ground, to accommodate aristocrats on sedan chairs and women with sky-high hairdos. The tiny round windows on the top floors were the servants' quarters. While the building fronts are uniform, the backs are higgledy-piggledy, infamous for their "hanging loos." Stand in the middle of the Circus among the grand plane trees, on the capped old well. Imagine the days when there was no indoor plumbing, and the servant girls gathered here to fetch water—this was gossip central. If you stand on the well, your clap echoes three times around the circle (try it).

Royal Crescent: A long, graceful arc of buildings—impossible to see in one glance unless you step way back to the edge of the big park in front—evokes the wealth and gentility of Bath's glory days. As you cruise the Crescent, pretend you're rich. Then pretend you're poor. Notice the "ha ha fence," a drop-off in the front yard that acted as a barrier, invisible from the windows, for keeping out sheep and peasants. The refined and stylish **Royal Crescent Hotel** sits unmarked in the center of the Crescent (with the giant rhododendron growing over the door). You're welcome to (politely) drop in to explore its fine ground-floor public spaces and back garden. A gracious and traditional tea is served in the garden out back (£12.50 cream tea, £22.50 afternoon tea, daily 15:00-17:00, sharing is OK, reserve a day in advance in summer, tel. 01225/823-333).

▲Georgian House at No. 1 Royal Crescent—This museum (corner of Brock Street and Royal Crescent) offers your best look into a period house. Your visit is limited to four roped-off rooms, but if you take your time and talk to the docents stationed in each room, it's worth the £6 admission to get behind one of those classy Georgian facades. The docents are determined to fill you in on all the fascinating details of Georgian life...like how high-class women shaved their eyebrows and pasted on carefully trimmed strips of furry mouse skin in their place. On the bedroom dresser sits a bowl of black beauty marks and a head-scratcher from those pre-shampoo days. Fido spent his days in the kitchen treadmill powering the rotisserie (mid-Feb-Oct Tue-Sun 10:30-17:00, Nov Tue-Sun 10:30-16:00, last entry 30 minutes before closing, closed Mon and Dec-mid-Feb, £2 guidebook available, no photos, "no stiletto heels, please," tel. 01225/428-126, www.bath-preservation-trust.org.uk). Its WC is accessible from the street (under the entry steps, across from the exit and shop).

▲▲Fashion Museum—Housed underneath Bath's Assembly Rooms, this museum displays four centuries of fashion on one floor. It's small, but the fact-filled, included audioguide can stretch a visit to an informative and enjoyable hour. Like fashion itself, the collection changes all the time. A major feature is usually the museum's choices for "Dress of the Year" dating back to 1963—a fascinating opportunity to see nearly a half-century's fashion trends in one sweep of the head. (The menswear version—awarded sporadically—shows a bit less variation, but has flashes of creativity.) Many of the exhibits are organized by theme (bags, shoes, underwear, wedding dresses, and so on). You'll see how fashion evolved—just like architecture and other arts—from one historical period to the next: Georgian, Regency, Victorian, the Swinging '60s, and so on. If you're intrigued by all those historic garments, take a chance to lace up your own trainer corset (which looks more like a lifejacket) and try on a hoop underdress (£7, £15 combo-ticket covers Roman Baths—saving you £3.50, family ticket available, daily March-Oct 10:30-18:00, Nov-Feb 10:30-17:00, last entry one hour before closing, on-site self-service café, tel. 01225/477-789, www.fashionmuseum.co.uk).

Assembly Rooms: Whether or not you're touring the Fashion Museum, poke into the building that houses it, where you can wander the big, grand, empty Assembly Rooms. Card games, concerts, tea, and dances were held here in the 18th century, before the advent of fancy hotels with grand public spaces made them obsolete. Note the extreme symmetry (pleasing to the aristocratic eye) and the high windows (assuring privacy). After the Allies bombed the historic and well-preserved German city of Lübeck, the Germans picked up a Baedeker guide and chose a similarly lovely city to bomb: Bath. The Assembly Rooms—gutted in this wartime tit-for-tat by WWII bombs—have since been restored to their original splendor. (Only the chandeliers are original.)

Nearby: Below the Fashion Museum (to the left as you leave, 20 yards away, at the door marked *14* and *Alfred House*) is one of the few surviving sets of **iron house hardware.** "Link boys" carried torches through the dark streets, lighting the way for big shots in their sedan chairs as they traveled from one affair to the next. The link boys extinguished their torches in the black conical "snuffers." The lamp above was once gaslit. The crank on the left was used to hoist bulky things to various windows (see the hooks). Few of these sets survived the dark days of the WWII Blitz, when most were collected and melted down, purportedly to make weapons to feed the British war machine. (Not long ago, these well-meaning Brits finally found out that all of their patriotic extra commitment to the national struggle had been for naught, since the metal ended up in junk heaps.)

Shoppers head down **Bartlett Street,** just below the Fashion Museum, to browse the antique shops.

▲▲**Museum of Bath at Work**—This modest but lovable place explains the industrial history of Bath. The museum is more interesting than it sounds, serving as a vivid reminder that there's always been a grimy, workaday side to this spa town. The core of the museum is the well-preserved, circa-1900 fizzy-drink business of Mr. Bowler, which includes a Dickensian office, engineer's shop, brass foundry, and factory floor. It's just a pile of meaningless old gadgets—until the included audioguide resurrects Mr. Bowler's creative genius. You'll find that each item has its own story. Upstairs are display cases featuring other Bath creations through the years, including a 1914 Horstmann car, wheeled sedan chairs (this *is* Bath, after all), and the versatile plasticine (colorful proto-Play-Doh—still the preferred medium of Aardman Studios, creators of the stop-motion animated *Wallace & Gromit* movies). At the snack bar, you can buy your own historic fizzy drink (a descendant of the ones once made here). On your way out, don't miss the small collection of exhibits on the ground floor, featuring cabinetmaking, the traditional methods for cutting the local "Bath Stone," a locally produced six-stroke engine, and more (£5, people over 60 pay £3.50, April-Oct daily 10:30-17:00, Nov-March weekends only except closed in Dec, last entry at 16:00, Julian Road, 2 steep blocks up Russell Street from Assembly Rooms, tel. 01225/318-348, www.bath-at-work.org.uk).

Sightseeing Tip: Notice the proximity of this museum to the very different Fashion Museum (described earlier). Museum attendants told me that—while open-minded spouses appreciate both places—it's standard for husbands to visit the Museum of Bath at Work while their wives are touring the Fashion Museum. Maybe it's time to divide and conquer?

Jane Austen Centre—This exhibition focuses on Jane Austen's tumultuous, sometimes-troubled five years in Bath (circa 1800, during which time her father died), and the influence the city had on her writing. There's little of historic substance here; you'll walk through a Georgian townhouse that she didn't live in (one of her real addresses in Bath was a few houses up the road, at 25 Gay Street), and you'll see mostly enlarged reproductions of things associated with her writing. The museum describes various places from two novels set in Bath (*Persuasion* and *Northanger Abbey*). After a live intro (15 minutes, 2/hour, starts at :15 and :45 past the hour) explaining how this romantic but down-to-earth woman dealt with the silly, shallow, and arrogant aristocrats' world, where "the doing of nothings all day prevents one from doing anything," you'll see a 15-minute video and wander through the rest of the exhibit. The well-stocked gift shop—with "I love Mr. Darcy" tote bags and Colin Firth's visage emblazoned on teacups, postcards, and more—is worthy of a shopping spree for Jane Austen fans (£7; mid-March-mid-Nov daily 9:45-17:30, July-Aug Thu-Sat until 19:00; mid-Nov-mid-March Sun-Fri 11:00-16:30, Sat 9:45-17:30; between Queen's Square and the Circus at 40 Gay Street, tel. 01225/443-000, www.janeausten.co.uk).

Upstairs, the award-winning **Regency Tea Rooms** hits the spot for Austenites, with costumed waitstaff and themed teas (£6-10), including the all-out "Tea with Mr. Darcy" for £11.50 (also £6 sandwiches, open same hours as the Centre, last orders 45 minutes before closing).

Jane Austen–themed **walking tours** of the city begin at the TI and end at the Centre (£5, 1.5 hours, Sat-Sun at 11:00, July-Aug also Fri-Sat at 16:00, no reservation necessary).

Building of Bath Collection—This offers an intriguing behind-the-scenes look at how the Georgian city was actually built (£4, mid-Feb-Nov Sat-Mon 10:30-17:00, last entry 30 minutes before closing, closed Tue-Fri and Dec-mid-Feb, a short walk north of the city center on a street called "The Paragon," tel. 01225/333-895, www.bath-preservation-trust.org.uk).

Outer Bath

▲**American Museum**—I know, you need this in Bath like you need a Big Mac. The UK's only museum dedicated to American history, this may be the only place that combines Geronimo and Groucho Marx. It has thoughtful exhibits on the history of Native Americans and the Civil War, but the museum's heart is with the decorative arts and cultural artifacts that reveal how Americans lived from colonial times to the mid-19th century. Each of the 18 completely furnished rooms (from a plain 1600s Massachusetts dining/living room to a Rococo Revival explosion in a New Orleans bedroom) is hosted by eager guides, waiting to fill you in on the everyday items that make domestic Yankee history surprisingly interesting. (In the Lee Room, look for the original mouse holes, lovingly backlit, in the floor boards.) One room is a quilter's nirvana. You could easily spend an afternoon here, enjoying the surrounding gardens, arboretum, and trails (£8, mid-March-Oct Tue-Sun 12:00-17:00, closed Mon and Nov-mid-March, last entry one hour before closing, at Claverton Manor, tel. 01225/460-503, www.americanmuseum.org). The museum is outside of town and a headache to reach if you don't have a car (10-15-minute walk from bus #18 or the hop-on, hop-off bus stop).

Activities in Bath

Walking—The Bath Skyline Walk is a six-mile wander around the hills surrounding Bath (leaflet at TI). Plenty of other scenic paths are described in the TI's literature. For additional options, get *Country Walks around Bath*, by Tim Mowl (£4.50 at TI or bookstores).

Hiking the Canal to Bathampton—An idyllic towpath leads two miles from the Bath Spa train station, along the Kennet and Avon Canal, to the sleepy village of Bathampton. Immediately behind the station in Bath, cross the footbridge, turn left, and find where the canal hits the River Avon. Head northeast along the small canal, noticing the series of Industrial Age locks and giving thanks that you're not a horse pulling a barge. After the path criss-crosses the canal a few times, you'll mostly walk with the water on your right. You'll be in Bathampton in less than an hour, where The George, a classic pub, awaits with a nice meal and cellar-temp beer (reservations smart, tel. 01225/425-079).

Boating—The Bath Boating Station, in an old Victorian boat-house, rents rowboats, canoes, and punts (£7 per person/first hour, then £3/additional hour, Easter-Sept daily 10:00-18:00, closed off-season, Forester Road, one mile northeast of center, tel. 01225/312-900, www.bathboating.co.uk).

Swimming and Kids' Activities—The Bath Sports and Leisure Centre has a fine pool for laps as well as lots of waterslides. Kids have entertaining options in the mini-gym "Active Club" area, which includes a rock wall and a "Zany Zone" indoor playground (swimming: £3.70 for adults, £2.30 for kids; kids and their parents pay £4 each to use "Active Club" plus pool; Mon-Fri 6:30-22:00, Sat 6:30-19:00, Sun 8:00-20:00, kids' hours limited, call for open-swim times, just across North Parade Bridge, tel. 01225/486-905, www.aquaterra.org).

Shopping—There's great browsing between the abbey and the Assembly Rooms (Fashion Museum). Shops close at about 17:30, and many are open on Sunday (11:00-16:00). Explore the antique shops lining Bartlett Street, below the Fashion Museum.

Nightlife in Bath

For an up-to-date list of events, pick up the local weekly newspaper, the *Bath Chronicle*, which includes a "What's On" schedule (www.thisisbath.com). Younger travelers may enjoy the party-ready bar, club, and nightlife recommendations at www.itchybath.co.uk.

▲▲Bizarre Bath Street Theater—For an entertaining walking-tour comedy act "with absolutely no history or culture," follow Dom, J. J., or Noel Britten on their creative and lively Bizarre Bath walk. This 1.5-hour "tour," which combines stand-up comedy with cleverly executed magic tricks, plays off unsuspecting passersby as well as tour members. It's a belly laugh a minute (£8, or £7 if you show your Rick Steves book, April-Oct nightly at 20:00, smaller groups Mon-Thu, promises to insult all nationalities and sensitivities, just racy enough but still good family fun, leaves from The Huntsman pub near the abbey, confirm at TI or call 01225/335-124, www.bizarrebath.co.uk).

▲Theatre Royal Performance—The 18th-century, 800-seat Theatre Royal, newly restored and one of England's loveliest, offers a busy schedule of London West End–type plays, including many "pre-London" dress-rehearsal runs (£15-39, shows generally start at 19:30 or 20:00, matinees at 14:30, box office open Mon-Sat 10:00-20:00, Sun 12:00-20:00, £3 extra to book online or by phone with a credit card, tel. 01225/448-844, www.theatreroyal.org.uk).

Forty nosebleed spots on a bench (misnamed "standbys") go on sale at noon Monday through Saturday for that day's evening performance (£5, 2 tickets maximum). If the show is sold out, same-day "standing places" go on sale at 18:00 (12:00 for matinees) for £3 (2 tickets maximum). For either of these cheap options, it's better to pay cash at the box office (£3 fee for online or phone purchases). Also at the box office, you can snatch up any "last minute" seats for £10-15 a half-hour before "curtain up."

A handy, cheap sightseers' tip: During the free Bath walking tour, your guide stops here. Pop into the box office, ask what's playing tonight, and see if there are many seats left. If the play sounds good and plenty of seats remain unsold, you're fairly safe to come back 30 minutes before curtain time to buy a ticket at that cheaper price. Oh...and if you smell jasmine, it's the ghost of Lady Grey, a mistress of Beau Nash.

Evening Walks—Take your choice: comedy (Bizarre Bath, described earlier), history, or ghost tour. The free **city history walks** (a daily standard described on page 829) are offered on some summer evenings (2 hours, May-Sept Tue and Fri at 19:00, leave from Pump Room). **Ghost Walks** are a popular way to pass the after-dark hours (£7, cash only, 1.5 hours, year-round Thu-Sat at 20:00, leave from The Garrick's Head pub to the left and behind Theatre Royal as you face it, tel. 01225/350-512, www.ghostwalks ofbath.co.uk).

Pubs—Most pubs in the center are very noisy, catering to a rowdy twentysomething crowd. But on the top end of town, you can still find some classic old places with inviting ambience and live music.

These are listed in order from closest to farthest away:

The Old Green Tree, the most convenient of all these pubs, is a rare traditional pub right in the town center (locally brewed real ales, no children, 12 Green Street; also recommended for lunch—see "Eating in Bath," later).

The Star Inn is much appreciated by local beer-lovers for its fine ale and "no machines or music to distract from the chat." It's a "spit 'n' sawdust" place, and its long bench, nicknamed "death row," still comes with a complimentary pinch of snuff from tins on the ledge. Try the Bellringer Ale, made just up the road (Mon-Fri 12:00-14:30 & 17:30-24:00, Sat-Sun 12:00-24:00, no food served, 23 The Vineyards, top of The Paragon/A4 Roman Road, tel. 01225/425-072, generous and friendly welcome from Paul, who runs the place).

The Bell has a jazzy, pierced-and-tattooed, bohemian feel, but with a mellow older crowd. There's some kind of activity nearly every night, usually involving live music (the only food served is £2.50 sandwiches, Mon-Sat 11:30-23:00, Sun 12:00-22:30, 103 Walcot Street, tel. 01225/460-426, www.walcotstreet.com).

Summer Nights at the Baths—In July and August, you can stretch your sightseeing day at the Roman Baths, open nightly until 22:00 (last entry 21:00), when the gas lamps flame and the baths are far less crowded and more atmospheric. To take a dip yourself, consider popping in to the Thermae Bath Spa (last entry at 19:30).

Sleeping in Bath

Bath is a busy tourist town. Accommodations are expensive, and low-cost alternatives are rare. By far the best budget option is the YMCA—it's central, safe, simple, very well-run, and has plenty of twin rooms available. To get a good B&B, make a telephone reservation in advance. Competition is stiff, and it's worth asking any of these places for a weekday, three-nights-in-a-row, or off-season deal. Friday and Saturday nights are tightest (with many rates going up by about 25 percent)—especially if you're staying only one night, since B&Bs favor those lingering longer. If staying only Saturday night, you're very bad news to a B&B hostess. If you're driving to Bath, stowing your car near the center will cost you (though some less-central B&Bs have parking)—see "Parking" on page 829, or ask your hotelier. Almost every place provides Wi-Fi at no charge to its guests.

B&Bs near the Royal Crescent

These listings are all a 15-minute uphill walk or an easy £4-5 taxi ride from the train station. Or take any hop-on, hop-off bus tour from the station, get off at the stop nearest your B&B (likely Royal

Sleep Code

(£1 = about $1.60, country code: 44, area code: 01225)
S = Single, **D** = Double/Twin, **T** = Triple, **Q** = Quad, **b** = bathroom,
s = shower only. Unless otherwise noted, credit cards are accepted.

To help you sort easily through these listings, I've divided the rooms into three categories based on the price for a standard double room with bath:

$$$ Higher Priced—Most rooms £100 or more.
$$ Moderately Priced—Most rooms between £60-100.
$ Lower Priced—Most rooms £60 or less.

Prices can change without notice; verify the hotel's current rates online or by email. For other updates, see www.ricksteves.com/update.

Avenue—confirm with driver), check in, then finish the tour later in the day. The Marlborough Lane places have easier parking, but are less centrally located.

$$$ Marlborough House, exuberantly run by Peter, is the most mod-and-trendy B&B I've seen in Bath. Each of the six rooms comes with a sip of brandy (Sb-£70-95, standard Db-£70-110, superior Db-£85-125, Tb-£95-135, organic breakfasts and toiletries, free Wi-Fi, free parking, some street noise, 1 Marlborough Lane, tel. 01225/318-175, fax 01225/466-127, www.marlborough-house.net, mars@manque.dircon.co.uk).

$$ Brocks Guest House has six rooms in a Georgian townhouse built by John Wood in 1765. Located between the prestigious Royal Crescent and the courtly Circus, it was redone in a way that would make the great architect proud (standard Db-£79-85, superior Db-£87-95, Tb-£99-125, Qb-£115-125, higher rates are for Fri-Sat, free Wi-Fi, little top-floor library, 32 Brock Street, tel. 01225/338-374, fax 01225/334-245, www.brocksguesthouse.co.uk, brocks@brocksguesthouse.co.uk, Richard).

$$ Parkside Guest House has five thoughtfully appointed Edwardian rooms. It's a bit older, but it's tidy, clean, homey, and well-priced—and has a spacious back garden (Sb-£60, Db-£80, ask for best Rick Steves price, free Wi-Fi, limited free parking, 11 Marlborough Lane, tel. & fax 01225/429-444, www.parksidebandb.co.uk, post@parksidebandb.co.uk, kind Inge Lynall).

$$ Cornerways B&B, located on a noisy street, is simple and well-worn, with three rooms and old-fashioned homey touches (Sb-£45-55, Db-£65-75, ask about discount with this book and 3-night stay, free Wi-Fi, DVD library, free parking, 47 Crescent

Gardens, tel. 01225/422-382, www.cornerwaysbath.co.uk, info @cornerwaysbath.co.uk, Sue Black).

B&Bs East of the River

These listings are a 10-minute walk from the city center. While generally a better value, they are not quite as conveniently located.

$$$ Villa Magdala rents 18 stately, hotelesque rooms in a freestanding Victorian townhouse opposite a park. In a city that's so insistently Georgian, it's fun to stay in a mansion that's decorated so enthusiastically Victorian (Db-£95-130 depending on size and demand, family rooms, inviting lounge, free Wi-Fi, free parking, in quiet residential area on Henrietta Street, tel. 01225/466-329, fax 01225/483-207, www.villamagdala.co.uk, enquiries @villamagdala.co.uk, Roy and Lois).

$$$ The Kennard, immaculately maintained by proud owners Giovanni and Mary Baiano, rents 12 rooms a short walk through a genteel neighborhood from the Pulteney Bridge. Each of the rooms is different, but all are colorfully and elaborately decorated (prices are for Sun-Thu/Fri-Sat: S-£58/£65, Sb-£79/£120, Db-£98/£120, Tb-£138/£160, free Wi-Fi, free street parking permits, thoughtfully planned Georgian garden out back, 11 Henrietta Street, tel. 01225/310-472, fax 01225/460-054, www.kennard.co.uk, reception@kennard.co.uk).

$$$ The Ayrlington, next door to a lawn-bowling green, has 16 attractive rooms with Asian decor and hints of a more genteel time. Though this well-maintained hotel fronts a busy street, it's quiet and tranquil. Rooms in the back have pleasant views of sports greens and Bath beyond. For the best value, request a standard top-floor double with a view of Bath (twin Db-£80-100, standard Db-£100-125, superior Db-£120-150, big deluxe Db-£130-170, higher price is for Fri-Sun, free Wi-Fi, fine garden, free and easy parking, 24-25 Pulteney Road, tel. 01225/425-495, fax 01225/469-029, www.ayrlington.com, mail@ayrlington.com, Ling Roper).

$$ 14 Raby Place is another good value, mixing Georgian glamour with homey warmth and modern, artistic taste within its five rooms. Muriel Guy—a no-high-tech Luddite—keeps things simple and endearingly friendly. She's a fun-loving live wire who serves organic food for breakfast (S with private bathroom on the hall-£35, Db-£70-75, Tb-£80, cash only; 14 Raby Place—go over bridge on North Parade Road, left on Pulteney Road, cross to church, Raby Place is first row of houses on hill; tel. 01225/465-120).

In the Town Center

You'll pay a premium to sleep right in the center. And, since Bath is so pleasant and manageable by foot, a downtown location isn't

Bath Accommodations

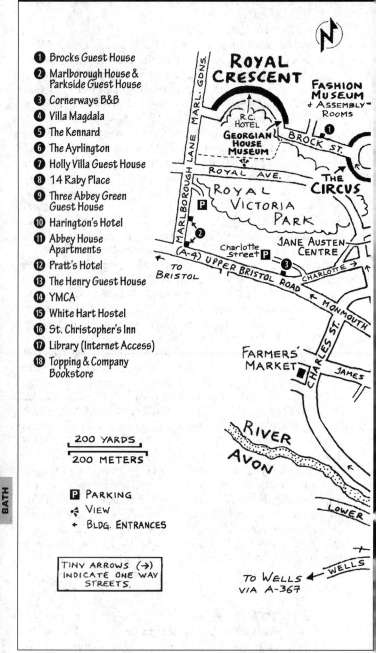

1. Brocks Guest House
2. Marlborough House & Parkside Guest House
3. Cornerways B&B
4. Villa Magdala
5. The Kennard
6. The Ayrlington
7. Holly Villa Guest House
8. 14 Raby Place
9. Three Abbey Green Guest House
10. Harington's Hotel
11. Abbey House Apartments
12. Pratt's Hotel
13. The Henry Guest House
14. YMCA
15. White Hart Hostel
16. St. Christopher's Inn
17. Library (Internet Access)
18. Topping & Company Bookstore

200 YARDS
200 METERS

P PARKING
VIEW
BLDG. ENTRANCES

TINY ARROWS (→) INDICATE ONE WAY STREETS.

ROYAL CRESCENT
FASHION MUSEUM & ASSEMBLY ROOMS
MARL. GDNS.
MARLBOROUGH LANE
R.C. HOTEL
GEORGIAN HOUSE MUSEUM
BROCK ST.
ROYAL AVE.
THE CIRCUS
ROYAL VICTORIA PARK
JANE AUSTEN CENTRE
Charlotte street
(A-4) UPPER BRISTOL ROAD
TO BRISTOL
CHARLOTTE
MONMOUTH
CHARLES ST.
FARMERS' MARKET
JAMES
RIVER AVON
LOWER
WELLS
TO WELLS VIA A-367

BATH

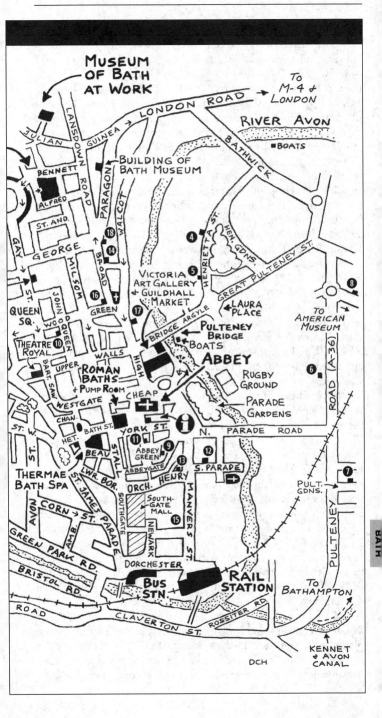

essential. Still, these are particularly well-located.

$$$ Three Abbey Green Guest House, with seven rooms, is bright, cheery, and located in a quiet, traffic-free courtyard only 50 yards from the abbey and the Roman Baths. Its spacious rooms are a fine value (Db-£95-145, four-poster Db-£145-175, family rooms-£135-195, price depends on season and size of room, 2-night minimum on weekends, free Internet access and Wi-Fi, tel. 01225/428-558, www.threeabbeygreen.com, stay@threeabbeygreen.com, Sue and Derek). They also rent self-catering apartments (Db-£135-165, Qb-£160-195, 2-night minimum).

$$$ Harington's Hotel rents 13 fresh, modern rooms on a quiet street in the town center. This stylish place feels like a boutique hotel, but with a friendlier, laid-back vibe (Sb-£79-155, standard Db-£88-135, superior Db-£98-145, large superior Db-£108-155, Tb-£138-185, prices vary substantially depending on demand, free Wi-Fi, attached bistro for guests only, 10 Queen Street, tel. 01225/461-728, fax 01225/444-804, www.haringtons hotel.co.uk, post@haringtonshotel.co.uk). Melissa and Peter offer a discount with this book for two-night stays except on Fridays, Saturdays, and holidays. They also rent two self-catering apartments down the street—one can sleep up to three (Db-£130, Tb-£145), and the other can sleep up to nine (prices on request; for apartments: 2-night minimum on weekdays, 3-night minimum on weekends).

$$$ Abbey House Apartments consist of three flats on Abbey Green and several others scattered around town—all tastefully restored by Laura (who, once upon a time, was a San Francisco rock musician). The apartments called Abbey View and Abbey Green (which comes with a washer and dryer) both have views of the abbey from their nicely equipped kitchens. These are especially practical and economical if you plan on cooking. Laura provides everything you need for simple breakfasts, and it's fun and cheap to stock the fridge or get take-away for a meal in your flat. When Laura meets you to give you the keys, you become a local (Sb-£90, Db-£100-175, price depends on size, 2-night minimum, rooms can sleep four with Murphy and sofa beds, apartments clearly described on website, free Wi-Fi, Abbey Green, tel. 01225/464-238, www.laurastownhouseapartments.co.uk, laura @laurastownhouseapartments.co.uk).

$$$ Pratt's Hotel is as proper and olde English as you'll find in Bath. Its creaks and frays are aristocratic, and even its public places make you want to sip a brandy. The 46 rooms show their age a bit, but are comfy and spacious. Since it's near a busy street, occasionally it can get noisy—request a quiet room, away from the street (Sb-£60-100, Db-£90-140, price depends on demand, check website for current rates and specials, dogs-£7.50 but children under 15 free with 2 adults, elevator, pay Wi-Fi, attached restaurant-bar, 4-6 South Parade, tel. 01225/460-441, fax 01225/448-807, www.forestdale.com, pratts@forestdale.com).

$$ The Henry Guest House is a simple, vertical place, renting eight clean rooms. It's friendly, well-run, and just two blocks in front of the train station (Sb-£55-65, Db-£85-105, higher prices are for bigger "premier" rooms, extra bed-£15, family room-£135, 2-night minimum on weekends, free Wi-Fi, 6 Henry Street, tel. 01225/424-052, www.thehenry.com, stay@thehenry.com). Steve and Liz also rent two self-catering apartments nearby that sleep up to eight with cots and a sleeper couch (email them for rates).

Bargain Accommodations

Bath's Best Budget Beds: **$** The **YMCA,** centrally located on a leafy square, has 210 beds in industrial-strength rooms—all with sinks and prison-style furnishings. The place is a godsend for budget travelers—safe, secure, quiet, and efficiently run. With lots of twin rooms and no double beds, this is the only easily accessible budget option in downtown Bath (rates for Sun-Thu/Fri-Sat: S-£28/£32, twin D-£44/£52, T-£60/£69, Q-£72/£84, dorm beds-£16/£19, WCs and showers down the hall, includes continental breakfast, cooked breakfast-£2.30, cheap lunches, free linens, rental towels, lockers, pay Internet access, free Wi-Fi, laundry facilities, down a tiny alley off Broad Street on Broad Street Place, tel. 01225/325-900, fax 01225/462-065, www.bathymca.co.uk, stay@bathymca .co.uk).

Sloppy Backpacker Dorms: **$** **White Hart Hostel** is a simple nine-room place offering adults and families good, cheap beds in two- to six-bed dorms (£15/bed, S-£25, D-£40, Db-£50-70, kitchen, fine garden out back, 5-minute walk behind train station at Widcombe—where Widcombe Hill hits Claverton Street, tel. 01225/313-985, www.whitehartbath.co.uk). The White Hart also has a pub with a reputation for decent food. **$** **St. Christopher's Inn,** in a prime, central location, is part of a chain of low-priced, high-energy hubs for backpackers looking for beds and brews. Their beds are so cheap because they know you'll spend money on their beer. It sits above the lively, youthful Belushi's pub, which is also where you'll find the reception (54 beds in 6- to 12-bed rooms-£15-21, D-£52-58, higher prices are for weekends and walk-ins—it's always cheaper to book online, check website for specials, pay Internet access, free Wi-Fi, laundry facilities, lounge, 9 Green Street, tel. 01225/481-444, www.st-christophers .co.uk).

BATH

Eating in Bath

Bath is bursting with eateries. There's something for every appetite and budget—just stroll around the center of town. A picnic dinner of deli food or take-out fish-and-chips in the Royal Crescent Park or down by the river is ideal for aristocratic hoboes. The restaurants I recommend are small and popular—reserve a table on Friday and Saturday evenings. Most pricey little bistros offer big savings with their two- and three-course lunches and "pre-theatre" specials. In general, you can get two courses for £10 at lunch or £12 in the early evening (compared to £15 for a main course after 18:30 or 19:00). Restaurants advertise their early-bird specials, and as long as you order within the time window, you're in for a cheap meal.

Romantic, Upscale French and English

Tilleys Bistro serves healthy French, English, and vegetarian meals with candlelit ambience. Owners Dawn and Dave make you feel as if you are guests at a dinner party in their elegant living room. Their fun menu lets you build your own meal, and there's an interesting array of £6-9 starters. If you cap things off with the cheese plate and a glass of the house port, you'll realize that's a passion of Dave's. While it's pricey and the portions are modest, this is a memorable splurge (£10-19 entrées; lunch specials: £12.50/2 courses, £15/3 courses; Mon-Sat 12:00-14:30 & 18:00-22:30, Sun 18:00-21:00 only, reservations smart, 3 North Parade Passage, tel. 01225/484-200).

The Garrick's Head is an elegantly simple gastropub right around the corner from the Theatre Royal, with a pricey restaurant on one side and a bar serving affordable snacks on the other. You're welcome to eat from the bar menu, even if you're in the fancy dining room or outside enjoying some great people-watching (£6-10 pub grub, £11-16 entrées on the fancier menu, Mon-Sat 11:00-22:00, Sun 12:00-22:00, drinks until later, 8 St. John's Place, tel. 01225/318-368).

The Circus Café and Restaurant is a relaxing little eatery serving well-executed English cuisine with European flair. Choose between the interior—with a clean, minimalist modern atmosphere either on the main floor or in the cellar—and the four tables on the peaceful street connecting the Circus and the Royal Crescent (£8 lunches, £7 starters and £13 entrées at dinner, open Mon-Sat 12:00-15:00 & 18:00-20:00, closed Sun, reservations smart, 34 Brock Street, tel. 01225/466-020).

Casanis French Bistro-Restaurant is a local hit. Chef Laurent, who hails from Nice, cooks "authentic Provençal cuisine" from the south of France, while his wife Jill serves. The decor matches the cuisine—informal, relaxed, simple, and top-quality. The intimate Georgian dining room upstairs is a bit nicer and more spacious than the ground floor (lunch specials: £13.50/2 courses, £17/3 courses; dinner special available 18:00-19:00: £17/2 courses, £21/3 courses; open Tue-Sat 12:00-14:00 & 18:00-22:00, closed Sun-Mon, immediately behind the Assembly Rooms at 4 Saville Row, tel. 01225/780-055).

Casual, Non-Traditional Alternatives

Whether ethnic food or vegetarian, there are plenty of ways to get some fun culinary variation in this town.

Demuths Vegetarian Restaurant is highly rated and ideal for the well-heeled vegetarian. Its tight, stark, understated interior comes with a vegan vibe (£6-11 lunches, £7 starters and £13-15 entrées at dinner, daily 10:00-16:00 & 17:30-21:00, later on weekends, 2 North Parade Passage, tel. 01225/446-059).

Yen Sushi is your basic little sushi bar—plain and sterile, with stools facing a conveyor belt that constantly tempts you with a variety of freshly made delights on color-coded plates. When you're done, they tally your plates and give you the bill (£1.50-4 plates, you can fill up for £12 or so, daily 12:00-15:00 & 17:30-22:30, 11 Bartlett Street, tel. 01225/333-313).

Martini Restaurant, a hopping, purely Italian place, has class and jovial waiters (£9-12 pastas and pizzas, £14-19 meat and fish dishes, daily 12:00-14:30 & 18:00-22:30—except open all day long on Sat, plenty of veggie options, daily fish specials, extensive wine list, reservations smart on weekends, 9 George Street, tel. 01225/460-818; Nunzio, Franco, and chef Luigi).

Rajpoot Tandoori serves—by all assessments—the best Indian food in Bath. You'll hike down deep into a sprawling cellar, where the plush Indian atmosphere and award-winning cooking make paying the extra pounds palatable. The seating is tight and the ceilings low, but it's air-conditioned (£8.25 three-course lunch special, £9-11 entrées; figure £20 per person with rice, naan, and drink; daily 12:00-14:30 & 18:00-23:00, 4 Argyle Street, tel. 01225/466-833, Ali).

Thai Balcony Restaurant's open, spacious interior is so plush, it'll have you wondering, "Where's the Thai wedding?" While locals debate which of Bath's handful of Thai restaurants serves the best food or offers the lowest prices, there's no doubt that Thai Balcony's fun and elegant atmosphere makes for a memorable and enjoyable dinner (£9 two-course lunch special, £8-9 plates, daily 12:00-14:00 & 18:00-22:00, reservations smart on weekends, Saw Close, tel. 01225/444-450).

Yak Yeti Yak is a fun Nepalese restaurant, with both Western

Bath Restaurants

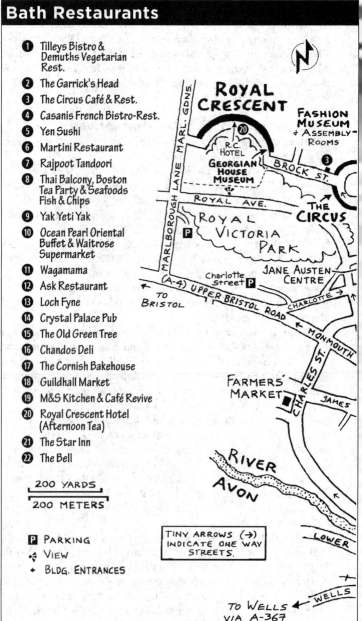

1. Tilleys Bistro & Demuths Vegetarian Rest.
2. The Garrick's Head
3. The Circus Café & Rest.
4. Casanis French Bistro-Rest.
5. Yen Sushi
6. Martini Restaurant
7. Rajpoot Tandoori
8. Thai Balcony, Boston Tea Party & Seafoods Fish & Chips
9. Yak Yeti Yak
10. Ocean Pearl Oriental Buffet & Waitrose Supermarket
11. Wagamama
12. Ask Restaurant
13. Loch Fyne
14. Crystal Palace Pub
15. The Old Green Tree
16. Chandos Deli
17. The Cornish Bakehouse
18. Guildhall Market
19. M&S Kitchen & Café Revive
20. Royal Crescent Hotel (Afternoon Tea)
21. The Star Inn
22. The Bell

200 YARDS

200 METERS

P PARKING
⚬ VIEW
✦ BLDG. ENTRANCES

ROYAL CRESCENT

FASHION MUSEUM & ASSEMBLY-ROOMS

MARL. GDNS.

R.C. HOTEL

GEORGIAN HOUSE MUSEUM

BROCK ST.

3

THE CIRCUS

ROYAL AVE.

MARLBOROUGH LANE

P

ROYAL VICTORIA PARK

JANE AUSTEN CENTRE

Charlotte Street

P

(A-4) UPPER BRISTOL ROAD

TO BRISTOL

CHARLOTTE

MONMOUTH

CHARLES ST.

FARMERS' MARKET

JAMES

RIVER AVON

LOWER

TINY ARROWS (→) INDICATE ONE WAY STREETS.

WELLS

TO WELLS VIA A-367

BATH

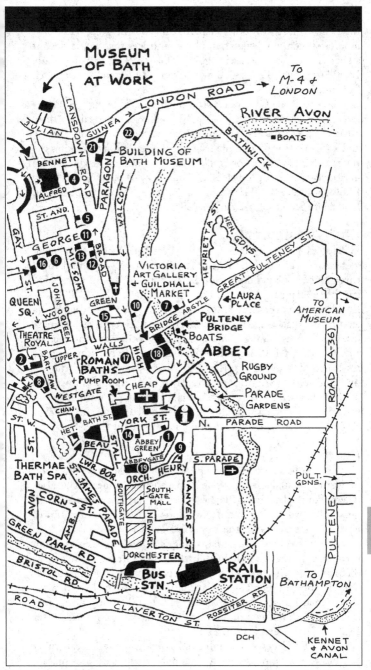

MUSEUM OF BATH AT WORK

To M-4 & LONDON

LONDON ROAD

RIVER AVON

BOATS

JULIAN

LANSDOWN ROAD

GUINEA

BATHWICK

21

22

BENNETT

PARAGON

Building of Bath Museum

4

ALFRED

ST. AND.

5

WALCOT

HEN. GDNS.

HENRIETTA ST.

GREAT PULTENEY ST.

GAY

GEORGE

11

BROAD

Victoria Art Gallery & Guildhall Market

LAURA PLACE

16 6

13

MILSOM

12

To AMERICAN MUSEUM

ST.

JOHN

WOOD

QUEEN

GREEN

15

10

7

ARGYLE

BRIDGE

QUEEN SQ.

THEATRE ROYAL

WALLS

Pulteney Bridge

Boats

ABBEY

2

BART. SAW

UPPER

Roman Baths + Pump Room

17

18

HIGH

Rugby Ground

ROAD (A-36)

8

WESTGATE

CHEAP

Parade Gardens

CHAN.

HET.

BATH ST.

YORK ST.

i

N. PARADE ROAD

ST. W.

STALL

14

Abbey Green

1

9

ST.

BEAU.

ABBEYGATE

S. PARADE

PULTENEY

THERMAE BATH SPA

LWR. BOR.

19

ORCH.

HENRY

PULT. GDNS.

AVON

ST. JAMES PARADE

SOUTHGATE

MANVERS ST.

CORN ST.

SOUTH-GATE MALL

GREEN PARK RD.

BLY.

NEWARK

BRISTOL RD.

DORCHESTER

BUS STN

RAIL STATION

To BATHAMPTON

ROAD

CLAVERTON ST.

ROSSITER RD.

DCH

KENNET & AVON CANAL

BATH

and sit-on-the-floor seating. Sera and his wife Sarah, along with their cheerful, hardworking Nepali team, cook up great traditional food (and plenty of vegetarian plates) at prices that would delight a sherpa (£7-9 lunches, £5 veggie plates, £8-9 meat plates, daily 12:00-14:30 & 17:00-22:30, downstairs at 12 Pierrepont Street, tel. 01225/442-299).

Ocean Pearl Oriental Buffet is famous for being the restaurant Asian tourists eat at repeatedly. It offers a practical, 40-dish, all-you-can-eat buffet in the modern Podium Shopping Centre and spacious seating in a high, bright dining hall overlooking the river. You'll pay £6.50 for lunch, £11.50 for dinner, or you can fill up a take-away box for just £3.50 at lunch or £4.50 at dinner (daily 12:00-15:00 & 18:00-22:30, in the Podium Shopping Centre on Northgate Street, tel. 01225/331-238).

Chain Restaurants

With so many homegrown favorites, I see little reason to frequent a chain restaurant in Bath. But if you're a fan, you'll find these three places: **Wagamama Noodle Bar** specializes in pan-Asian cuisine (£7-9 meals, Mon-Sat 12:00-23:00, Sun 12:00-22:00, 1 York Buildings, George Street, tel. 01225/337-314, www.wagamama .com); **Ask** dishes up Italian comfort food (£8-10 pizzas and pastas, good salads, daily 12:00-23:00, George Street but entrance on Broad Street, tel. 01225/789-997); and **Loch Fyne,** which serves fresh fish at reasonable prices, fills what was once a lavish bank building with a bright, airy, youthful, high-energy atmosphere (£10-18 meals, £10 two-course special from lunch until 19:00 on weekdays, daily 12:00-22:30, 24 Milsom Street, tel. 01225/750-120). All of these chains are found all over Britain.

Pubs

With so many other tempting options (and since this is not a good pub-grub town), eating at a pub in Bath isn't as appealing as elsewhere. For the best pub grub, head for **The Garrick's Head** gastropub (described earlier). But if you're looking for a more traditional, lowbrow place, consider these options.

Crystal Palace Pub is an inviting place just a block away from the abbey, facing the delightful little Abbey Green. With a focus on food rather than drink, they serve "pub grub with a Continental flair" in three different spaces, including a picnic-table back patio (£9-12 meals, food served Mon-Fri 11:00-21:00, Sat 11:00-20:00, Sun 12:00-20:00, last orders for drinks at 23:00, no kids after 16:30, Abbey Green, tel. 01225/482-666).

The Old Green Tree, in the old town center, serves satisfying lunches to locals in a characteristic pub setting (real ales on tap,

£6-7 sandwiches, £9 meals, food served for lunch Mon-Sat 12:00-15:00 only, open daily for drinks, no children, can be crowded on weekend nights, 12 Green Street, tel. 01225/448-259).

If you're looking for a pub to drink and hang out in, rather than eat at, check out **The Star Inn** and **The Bell** (both described on page 841).

Simple Options

These are excellent options for a fast, handy, and tasty meal on the go. If you get take-away (possible at most of these), you can munch your picnic while watching street musicians from a bench on the Abbey Square.

Boston Tea Party feels like a Starbucks—if there were only one. It's fresh and healthy, serving extensive breakfasts, light lunches, and salads. The outdoor seating overlooks a busy square. They also host musical events, and their walls are decorated with works by local artists (£3-7 breakfasts, £5-7 lunches, Mon-Sat 7:30-19:00, Sun 9:00-19:00, free Wi-Fi, 19 Kingsmead Square, tel. 01225/313-901).

Chandos Deli has good coffee and tasty £3-5 sandwiches made on artisan breads. This upscale but casual five-table place serves breakfast pastries and lunch to dedicated foodies who don't want to pay too much (Mon-Sat 9:00-17:00, Sun 11:00-17:00, 12 George Street, tel. 01225/314-418).

Seafoods Fish & Chips is respected by lovers of greasy fried fish in Bath. There's diner-style and outdoor seating, or you can get your food to go for a bit cheaper (£4-5 meals, Mon-Sat 11:30-22:00, closed Sun, 38 Kingsmead Square, tel. 01225/465-190).

The Cornish Bakehouse, tucked down a shopping gallery across from the Guildhall Market, has freshly baked £3 take-away pasties (Mon-Sat 8:30-17:30, Sun 10:00-17:00, off High Street at 11A The Corridor, tel. 01225/426-635).

Produce Market and Café: **Guildhall Market,** across from Pulteney Bridge, has produce stalls with food for picnickers. At its inexpensive **Market Café,** you can slurp a curry or sip a tea while surrounded by stacks of used books, bananas on the push list, and honest-to-goodness old-time locals (£3-5 traditional English meals including fried breakfasts all day, Mon-Sat 8:00-17:00, closed Sun, tel. 01225/461-593 a block north of the abbey, on High Street).

Supermarkets: **Waitrose,** at the Podium Shopping Centre, is great for picnics, with a good salad bar (Mon-Fri 8:30-20:00, Sat 8:30-19:00, Sun 11:00-17:00, just west of Pulteney Bridge and across from post office on High Street). **Marks & Spencer,** near the train station, has a grocery at the back of its department store and two eateries: **M&S Kitchen** on the ground floor and the

BATH

pleasant, inexpensive **Café Revive** on the top floor (Mon-Fri 8:30-19:00, Sat 8:30-18:00, Sun 11:00-17:00, 16-18 Stall Street).

Bath Connections

Bath's train station is called Bath Spa (toll tel. 0845-748-4950). The National Express bus station is just west of the train station (bus info toll tel. 0871-781-8181, www.nationalexpress.com). For all public bus services in southwestern England, see www.travelinesw.com.

From London to Bath: To get from London to Bath and see Stonehenge to boot, consider an all-day organized **bus tour** from London (and skip out of the return trip; see page 822).

From Bath to London: You can catch a **train** to London's Paddington Station (2/hour, 1.5 hours, best deals for travel after 9:30 and when purchased in advance, www.firstgreatwestern.co.uk), or save money—but not time—by taking the National Express **bus** to Victoria Coach Station (9/day direct, 2.75-3.75 hours, one-way-£22, round-trip-£29).

From Heathrow to Bath: See page 815.

From Bath to London's Airports: You can reach **Heathrow** directly and easily by National Express bus (10/day, 2-3 hours, £19.10 one-way, toll tel. 0871-781-8181, www.nationalexpress.com) or by a train-and-bus combination (take twice-hourly train to Reading, catch twice-hourly airport shuttle bus from there, allow 2.5 hours total, £46-65 depending on time of day, about £20 cheaper when bought in advance, BritRail passholders just pay £15 for bus).

You can get to **Gatwick** by train (about hourly, 2.5 hours, £45-54 one-way depending on time of day, cheaper in advance, transfer in Reading) or by bus (10/day, 4-5 hours, £25 one-way, transfer at Heathrow Airport).

Between Bristol Airport and Bath: Located about 20 miles west of Bath, this airport is closer than Heathrow, but they haven't worked out good connections to Bath yet. From Bristol Airport, your most convenient options are to take a taxi (£35) or take a tour with Alan Price (http://celtichorizons.com). Otherwise, at the airport you can hop aboard the Bristol Airport Flyer (bus #A1), which takes you to the Temple Meads train station in Bristol (£7, 2-6/hour, 30 minutes, buy bus ticket at airport info counter or from driver, tell driver you want the Temple Meads train station). At the Temple Meads Station, check the departure boards for trains going to the Bath Spa train station (4/hour, 15 minutes, £6). To get from Bath to Bristol Airport, just reverse these directions: Take the train to Temple Meads, then catch the Bristol Airport Flyer bus.

From Bath by Train to: Salisbury (1-2/hour, 1 hour), **Portsmouth** (hourly, 2.25 hours), **Exeter** (1-2/hour, 1.5-2 hours, transfer in Bristol or Westbury), **Penzance** (1-2/hour, 4.5-5 hours, one direct, most 1-2 transfers), **Moreton-in-Marsh** (hourly, 2.5-3 hours, 2-3 transfers), **York** (2/hour, 4.25-4.5 hours, 1-2 transfers in Birmingham, Bristol, and/or London), **Oxford** (hourly, 1.25 hours, transfer in Didcot.

ITALY

ROME

Roma

Rome is magnificent and brutal at the same time. It's a showcase of Western civilization, with astonishingly ancient sights and a modern vibrancy. But if you're careless, you'll be run down or pickpocketed. And with the wrong attitude, you'll be frustrated by the kind of chaos that only an Italian can understand. On my last visit, a cabbie struggling with the traffic said, *"Roma chaos."* I responded, *"Bella chaos."* He agreed.

While Paris is an urban garden, Rome is a magnificent tangled forest. If your hotel provides a comfortable refuge; if you pace yourself; if you accept—and even partake in—the siesta plan; if you're well-organized for sightseeing; and if you protect yourself and your valuables with extra caution and discretion, you'll love it. (And Rome is much easier to live with if you avoid the midsummer heat.)

For me, Rome is in a three-way tie with Paris and London as Europe's greatest city. Two thousand years ago, the word "Rome" meant civilization itself. Everything was either civilized (part of the Roman Empire, Latin- or Greek-speaking) or barbarian. Today, Rome is Italy's political capital, the capital of Catholicism, and the center of the ancient world, littered with evocative remains. As you peel through its fascinating and jumbled layers, you'll find Rome's buildings, cats, laundry, traffic, and 2.6 million people endlessly entertaining. And then, of course, there are its stupendous sights.

Visit St. Peter's, the greatest church on earth, and scale Michelangelo's 448-foot-tall dome, the world's tallest. Learn something about eternity by touring the huge Vatican Museum. You'll find the story of creation—bright as the day it was painted—in the restored Sistine Chapel. Do the "Caesar Shuffle" through ancient

Rome's Neighborhoods

VATICAN MUSEUM

VATICAN CITY

ST. PETER'S

PIAZZA DEL POPOLO

NORTH ROME

VILLA BORGHESE

BORGHESE GALLERY

"SHOPPING TRIANGLE"

SPANISH STEPS

TERMINI

NAT'L. MUSEUM

TRAIN STATION

PANTHEON NEIGHBORHOOD

PIAZZA VENEZIA

CAPITOL HILL

FORUM

ANCIENT ROME

PILGRIM'S ROME

SAN GIOVANNI IN LATERANO

TIBER RIVER

STA. MARIA

TRASTEVERE

COLOSSEUM

TESTACCIO

SOUTH OF TESTACCIO

SOUTH ROME

APPIAN WAY

E.U.R.

NOT TO SCALE

DCH

Rome's Forum and Colosseum. Savor Europe's most sumptuous building, the Borghese Gallery, and take an early-evening "Dolce Vita Stroll" down Via del Corso with Rome's beautiful people. Enjoy an after-dark walk from Campo de' Fiori to the Spanish Steps, lacing together Rome's Baroque and bubbly nightspots. Dine well at least once.

Planning Your Time

Rome is wonderful, but it's huge and exhausting. On a first-time visit, many travelers find that Rome is best done quickly—Italy is more charming elsewhere. But whether you're here for a day or a week, you won't be able to see all of Rome's attractions, so don't try—you'll keep coming back to Rome. After several dozen visits, I still have a healthy list of excuses to return.

Rome in a Day: Some people actually try to "do" Rome in a day. Crazy as that sounds, if all you have is a day, it's one of the most exciting days Europe has to offer. Start at 8:30 at the Colosseum. Then explore the Forum, hike over Capitol Hill, and cap your "Caesar Shuffle" with a visit to the Pantheon. After a quick lunch, taxi to the Vatican Museum (the lines usually die down mid-afternoon). See the Vatican Museum and take a shortcut from the

Sistine Chapel directly into St. Peter's Basilica (open until 19:00 April-Sept). Taxi back to Campo de' Fiori to find dinner. Finish your day lacing together all the famous floodlit spots (follow my self-guided "Night Walk Across Rome"). Note: If you only want a day in Rome, consider side-tripping in from Florence, or maybe before the night train to Venice.

Rome in Two to Three Days: On the first day, do the "Caesar Shuffle" from the Colosseum to the Forum, then over Capitol Hill to the Pantheon. After a siesta, join the locals strolling from Piazza del Popolo to the Spanish Steps (follow my self-guided "Dolce Vita Stroll"). On the second day, see Vatican City (St. Peter's, climb the dome, tour the Vatican Museum). Have dinner on the atmospheric Campo de' Fiori, then walk to the Trevi Fountain and Spanish Steps (following my "Night Walk Across Rome"). With a third day, add the Borghese Gallery (reservations required) and the National Museum of Rome.

Orientation to Rome

Sprawling Rome actually feels manageable once you get to know it. The old core, with most of the tourist sights, sits in a diamond formed by Termini train station (in the east), the Vatican (west), Villa Borghese Gardens (north), and the Colosseum (south). The Tiber River runs through the diamond from north to south. In the center of the diamond sits Piazza Venezia, a busy square and traffic hub. It takes about an hour to walk from Termini train station to the Vatican.

Think of Rome as a series of neighborhoods, huddling around major landmarks.

Ancient Rome: In ancient times, this was home for the grandest buildings of a city of a million people. Today, the best of the classical sights stand in a line from the Colosseum to the Forum to the Pantheon.

Pantheon Neighborhood: The Pantheon anchors the neighborhood I like to call the heart of Rome. It stretches eastward from the Tiber River through Campo de' Fiori and Piazza Navona, past the Pantheon to the Trevi Fountain.

North Rome: With the Spanish Steps, Villa Borghese Gardens, and trendy shopping streets (Via Veneto and the "shopping triangle"), this is a more modern, classy area.

Vatican City: Located west of the Tiber, it's a compact world of its own, with two great, huge sights: St. Peter's Basilica and the Vatican Museum.

Trastevere: This seedy, colorful wrong-side-of-the-river neighborhood is village Rome. It's the city at its crustiest—and perhaps most "Roman."

Rick Steves' Free Audio Tours

I've produced free, self-guided audio versions of my tours of the major sights in Rome (download them via www.ricksteves .com/audioeurope, iTunes, or the Rick Steves Audio Europe smartphone app). These user-friendly, easy-to-follow, fun, and enlightening audio tours are available for the Colosseum, Roman Forum, Pantheon, St. Peter's Basilica, Sistine Chapel, Trastevere, Jewish Ghetto, Ostia Antica, and Pompeii. If you don't mind me in your ear, these audio tours are hard to beat: Nobody will stand you up, the quality is reliable, you can take the tour exactly when you like, and they're free.

Termini: Though light on sightseeing highlights, the train-station neighborhood has many recommended hotels and public-transportation connections.

Pilgrim's Rome: Several prominent churches dot the area south of Termini train station.

Southeast Rome: Southeast of the city center, you'll find the Appian Way, home of the catacombs.

Within each of these neighborhoods, you'll find elements from the many layers of Rome's 2,000-year history: the marble ruins of ancient times; tangled streets of the medieval world; early Christian churches; grand Renaissance buildings and statues; Baroque fountains and church facades; 19th-century apartments; and 20th-century boulevards choked with traffic.

Since no one is allowed to build taller than St. Peter's dome, and virtually no buildings have been constructed in the city center since Mussolini got distracted in 1938, Rome has no modern skyline. The Tiber River is basically ignored—after the last floods (1870), the banks were built up very high, and Rome turned its back on its naughty river.

Tourist Information

Rome has two tourist information offices and numerous kiosks (generally open daily 9:30-19:00). The TI offices are at the airport (terminal 3) and Termini train station (open until 20:30, way down track 24, look for signs). Little kiosks are near the Forum (on Piazza del Tempio della Pace), in Trastevere (on Piazza Sonnino), on Via Nazionale (at Palazzo delle Esposizioni), near Castel Sant'Angelo (at Piazza Pia), at the Church of Santa Maria Maggiore (on Via dell'Olmata), near Piazza Navona (at Piazza delle Cinque Lune), and near the Trevi Fountain (at Via del Corso and Via Minghetti). The TI's website is http://en.turismoroma.it.

At any TI, ask for a city map, a listing of sights and hours (in

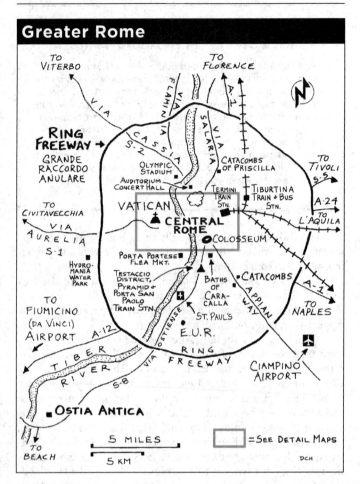

Greater Rome

TO VITERBO

TO FLORENCE

N

VIA FLAMINIA

VIA CASSIA S-2

VIA SALARIA

VIA A-H

RING FREEWAY →
GRANDE RACCORDO ANULARE

OLYMPIC STADIUM

CATACOMBS OF PRISCILLA

AUDITORIUM CONCERT HALL

TERMINI TRAIN STN.

TIBURTINA TRAIN & BUS STN.

TO TIVOLI S-5

VATICAN

CENTRAL ROME

COLOSSEUM

TO L'AQUILA

A-24

TO CIVITAVECCHIA

VIA AURELIA S-1

HYDRO-MANIA WATER PARK

PORTA PORTESE FLEA MKT.

TESTACCIO DISTRICT, PYRAMID & PORTA SAN PAOLO TRAIN STN.

BATHS OF CARACALLA

CATACOMBS

APPIAN WAY

A-1

TO NAPLES

TO FIUMICINO (DA VINCI) AIRPORT

A-12

ST. PAUL'S

E.U.R.

VIA OSTIENSE

RING FREEWAY

CIAMPINO AIRPORT

TIBER RIVER

S-8

OSTIA ANTICA

TO BEACH

5 MILES

5 KM

☐ = SEE DETAIL MAPS

DCH

the free *Museums of Rome* booklet), and the free *Evento* booklet, with English-language pages listing the month's cultural events. The TIs don't offer room-booking services. If a commercial info-center offers to book you a room, just say no—you'll save money by booking direct.

If all you need is a **map,** skip the TI and pick up a freebie map at your hotel. The best map I found is published by Rough Guide (€8 in bookstores).

Rome's single best source of up-to-date tourist information is its **call center,** with English-speakers on staff. Dial 06-0608 (answered daily 9:00-21:00, press 2 for English). You can call to buy museum tickets, sightseeing passes (see page 866), and theater tickets using your credit card. There's usually only a €1.50 fee.

Several English-oriented **websites** provide insight into events and daily life in the city: www.inromenow.com (light tourist info on lots of topics), www.wantedinrome.com (events and accommodation rentals), and http://rome.angloinfo.com (on living in and moving to Rome).

Arrival in Rome

By Train at Termini Station: Termini, Rome's main train station, is a buffet of tourist services. While information desks are jammed with travelers, very handy red info kiosks at the head of the tracks can answer your simple questions.

Along track 24, about 100 yards down, you'll find the **TI** (daily 8:00-20:30), a **post office** (Mon-Fri 8:30-14:00, Sat 8:30-13:00, closed Sun), a **hotel booking** office, and **car rental** desks. The **baggage storage** *(deposito bagagli)* is downstairs (€4/5 hours, then cheaper, daily 6:00-24:00).

The **"Leonardo Express" train** to Fiumicino Airport runs from track 25; access is at the very far end of track 24. A good self-service **cafeteria,** Ciao, is near the head of track 24, upstairs, with fine views (daily 11:00-22:30).

Near track 1, you'll find a **pharmacy** (daily 7:30-22:00); along the same track is a **waiting room** and **train information** office (daily 6:00-24:00). The handy **Drugstore Conad,** selling everything from groceries to electronics, is just downstairs (daily 6:00-24:00).

Elsewhere in the station are **ATMs,** late-hours banks, and 24-hour thievery. In the station's main entrance lobby, **Borri Books** sells books in English, including popular fiction, Italian history and culture, and kids' books, plus maps upstairs (daily 7:00-23:00).

Termini is also a local transportation hub. The city's two Metro lines (A and B) intersect at Termini Metro station (downstairs). Buses (including Rome's hop-on, hop-off bus tours—see "Tours in Rome," later) leave across the square directly in front of the main station hall. The Metro and bus areas were under construction in 2011 and may still be torn up—look for signs directing you to the Metro platform or bus stop. Taxis queue in front; avoid con men hawking "express taxi" services in unmarked cars (only use ones marked with the word *taxi* and a phone number). To avoid the long taxi line, simply hike out past the buses to the main street and hail one.

From Termini, most of my recommended hotels are easily accessible by foot (for those near this train station) or by Metro (for those in the Colosseum and Vatican neighborhoods).

The station has some sleazy sharks with official-looking business cards; avoid anybody selling anything unless they're in a legitimate shop at the station.

By Train or Bus at Tiburtina Station: Tiburtina, Rome's second-largest train station, is located in the city's northeast corner. In general, slower trains (from Milan, Bolzano, Bologna, Udine, and Reggio di Calabria) and some night trains (from Munich, Milan, Venice, Innsbruck, and Udine) use Tiburtina, as does the night bus to Fiumicino Airport. Direct night trains from Paris and Vienna use Termini Station instead. However, as Tiburtina is being redeveloped for high-speed rail, it's likely that additional major trains will soon begin using the station.

Tiburtina is better known as a hub for bus service to destinations all across Italy. Buses depart from the piazza in front of the station. Ticket offices are located in the piazza and around the corner on Circonvallazione Nomentana.

Within the train station are a **currency-exchange office** and a 24-hour **grocery.** Tiburtina Station is on Metro line B, with easy connections to Termini (a straight shot, four stops away) and the entire Metro system. Or take bus #492 from Tiburtina to various city-center stops (such as Piazza Barberini, Piazza Venezia, and Piazza Cavour) and the Vatican neighborhood.

By Car: The Grande Raccordo Anulare circles greater Rome. This ring road has spokes that lead you into the center. Entering from the north, leave the autostrada at the Settebagni exit. Following the ancient Via Salaria (and the black-and-white *Centro* signs), work your way doggedly into the Roman thick of things. This will take you along the Villa Borghese Gardens and dump you right on Via Veneto in downtown Rome. Avoid rush hour and drive defensively: Roman cars stay in their lanes like rocks in an avalanche.

Parking in Rome is dangerous. Park near a police station or get advice at your hotel. The Villa Borghese underground garage is handy (Metro: Spagna). Garages charge about €24 per day.

Consider this: Your car is a worthless headache in Rome. Avoid a pile of stress and save money by parking at the huge, easy, and relatively safe lot behind the train station in the hill town of Orvieto (follow *P* signs from autostrada) and catching the train to Rome (hourly, 60-90 minutes).

If you absolutely must drive and park a car in Rome, try to avoid commuter traffic by arriving Friday evening, or anytime during the weekend, and by leaving town during the weekend. Park your car at Tiburtina station (€1/hour, www.atac.roma.it) and take a 10-minute ride on the Metro line B into the center.

By Plane: For information on Rome's airports and connections into the city, see "Rome Connections—By Plane" at the end of this chapter.

Helpful Hints

Sightseeing Tips: Avid sightseers can save money by buying the Roma Pass (see "Tips on Sightseeing in Rome" sidebar), available at TIs and participating sights—buy one before visiting the Colosseum or Forum, and you can skip the long lines there. If you want to see the Borghese Gallery, remember to reserve ahead (see page 919). To bypass the long Vatican Museum line, reserve an entry time online (see page 925 for details).

Internet Access: If your hotel doesn't offer free or cheap Internet access, your hotelier can point you to the nearest Internet café. Remember to bring your passport, which you may be asked to show before going online.

Bookstores: These stores (all open daily except Anglo American and Open Door) sell travel guidebooks, including mine. The first two are chains, while the others have a more personal touch. **Borri Books** is at Termini train station, and **Feltrinelli International** has two branches (at Largo Argentina, and just off Piazza della Repubblica at Via Vittorio Emanuele Orlando 84, tel. 06-482-7878). **Anglo American Bookshop** has great art and history sections (closed Sun and Mon morning, a few blocks south of Spanish Steps at Via della Vite 102, tel. 06-679-5222). **Libreria Fanucci** is centrally located (a block toward the Pantheon from Piazza Navona at Piazza Madama 8, tel. 06-686-1141). In Trastevere, Irishman Dermot at the **Almost Corner Bookshop** stocks an Italian-interest section (Via del Moro 45, tel. 06-583-6942), and the **Open Door Bookshop** carries the only used books in English in town (closed Sun, Via della Lungaretta 23, tel. 06-589-6478).

Laundry: Your hotelier can direct you to the nearest launderette. The **ondablu** chain usually comes with Internet access; one of their more central locations is near Termini train station (€2/hour, about €8 to wash and dry a 15-pound load, usually open daily 8:00-22:00, Via Principe Amedeo 70b, tel. 06-474-4647).

Travel Agencies: You can get train tickets and railpass-related reservations and supplements at travel agencies (at little or no additional cost), avoiding a trip to a train station. Your hotelier will know of a convenient agency nearby.

Dealing with (and Avoiding) Problems

Theft Alert: While violent crime is rare in the city center, petty theft is rampant. With sweet-talking con artists meeting you at the station, well-dressed pickpockets on buses, and thieving gangs of children at the ancient sites, Rome is a gauntlet

Tips on Sightseeing in Rome

These tips will help you use your time and money efficiently, making the Eternal City seem less eternal and more entertaining.

Roma Pass: Rome offers several sightseeing passes to help you save money. For most visitors, the Roma Pass (www .romapass.it) is the clear winner. The Roma Pass costs €25 and is valid for three days, covering public transportation and free or discounted entry to Roman sights. You get free admission to your first two sights (where you also get to skip the ticket line), and then a discount on the rest within the three-day window. Sights covered (or discounted) by the pass include the following: Colosseum/Palatine Hill/Roman Forum, Borghese Gallery (though you still must make a reservation and pay the €2-3 booking fee), Capitoline Museums, Castel Sant'Angelo, Montemartini Museum, Ara Pacis, Museum of Roman Civilization, Etruscan Museum, Baths of Caracalla, Trajan's Market, and some of the Appian Way sights. The pass also covers all four branches of the National Museum of Rome, considered as a single "sight": Palazzo Massimo (clearly the most important of the lot), Museum of the Bath at the Baths of Diocletian (Roman inscriptions), Crypta Balbi (medieval art), and Palazzo Altemps (sculpture collection).

If you'll be visiting any two of the major sights in a three-day period, get the pass. It's sold at participating sights, TIs, and even the Colosseum *tabacchi* shop. Try to buy it at a less-crowded TI or sight. Don't bother to order it online because you have to physically pick up the pass in Rome, negating any time-saving advantage.

Validate your Roma Pass by writing your name and validation date on the card. Then insert it directly into the turnstile at your first two (free) sights. At other sights, show it at the ticket office to get your reduced *(ridotto)* price—about 30 percent off.

To get the most out of your pass, visit the two most expensive sights first—for example, the Colosseum (€12) and the National Museum (€10). Definitely use it to bypass the long ticket line at the Colosseum. For sights that normally sell a combined ticket (such as the Colosseum/Palatine Hill/Roman Forum or the four National Museum branches), visiting the combined sight counts as a single entry.

The Roma Pass comes with a three-day transit pass. Write your name and birth date on the transit pass, validate it on your first bus or Metro ride by passing it over a sensor at a turnstile or validation machine (look for a yellow circle), and you can take unlimited rides within Rome's city limits until midnight of the third day.

The TI's other passes—Roma and Pui Pass ("Rome and More") and the Archeologia Card—are generally not worth the trouble for most tourists.

Combo-Ticket for Colosseum, Forum, and Palatine Hill: A €12 combo-ticket covers these three adjacent sights (no individual tickets are sold per sight). The combo-ticket allows one entry per sight, and is valid for two days. Note that these sights are also covered by the Roma Pass. To avoid ticket-buying lines at the Colosseum and Forum, purchase your combo-ticket or Roma Pass at the lesser-visited Palatine Hill. If you're deciding between the combo-ticket or Roma Pass, the pass is the better deal, unless you're planning on seeing only the sights covered by the combo-ticket.

Museum Reservations: The marvelous Borghese Gallery requires reservations well in advance (for specifics, see page 919). You can reserve online to avoid long lines at the Vatican Museum (see page 925).

Opening Hours: Rome's sights have notoriously variable hours from season to season. Get a current listing of opening times from one of Rome's TIs—ask for the free booklet *Museums of Rome*. Or check online at www.060608.it (click on "Culture and Leisure"; although the pages are in English, search by using the Italian names of sights). On holidays, expect shorter hours or closures.

Churches: Many churches, which have divine art and free entry, open early (around 7:00-7:30), close for lunch (roughly 12:00-15:00), and close late (about 19:00). Kamikaze tourists maximize their sightseeing hours by visiting churches before 9:00 or late in the day, and during the siesta, seeing major sights that stay open all day (St. Peter's, Colosseum, Forum, Capitoline Museums, and National Museum of Rome). Many churches have "modest dress" requirements, which means no bare shoulders, miniskirts, or shorts—for men, women, or children. This dress code is enforced at the Vatican Museum, St. Peter's Basilica, and St. Paul's Outside the Walls. Elsewhere, you may see many tourists in shorts (but not skimpy shorts) touring churches.

Picnic Discreetly: Public drinking and eating is no longer allowed at major sights, though the ban is proving difficult to enforce. To avoid the risk of being fined, choose an empty piazza for your picnic, or keep a low profile.

Miscellaneous Tips: I carry a plastic water bottle and refill it at Rome's many public drinking spouts. Because public restrooms are scarce, use toilets at museums, restaurants, and bars.

of rip-offs. While it's not as bad as it was a few years ago, and pickpockets don't want to hurt you—they usually just want your money—green or sloppy tourists will be scammed. Thieves strike when you're distracted. Don't trust kind strangers. Keep nothing important in your pockets. Be most on guard while boarding and leaving buses and subways. Thieves crowd the door, then stop and turn while others crowd and push from behind. You'll find less crowding and commotion—and less risk—waiting for the end cars of a subway rather than the middle cars. The sneakiest thieves pretend to be well-dressed businessmen (generally with something in their hands), or tourists wearing fanny packs and toting cameras and even Rick Steves guidebooks.

Scams abound: Don't give your wallet to self-proclaimed "police" who stop you on the street, warn you about counterfeit (or drug) money, and ask to see your cash. If a bank machine eats your ATM card, see if there's a thin plastic insert with a tongue hanging out that thieves use to extract it.

If you know what to look out for, fast-fingered moms with babies and gangs of children picking the pockets and handbags of naive tourists are not a threat, but an interesting, albeit sad, spectacle. Pickpockets troll through the tourist crowds around the Colosseum, Forum, Piazza della Repubblica, and train and Metro stations. Watch them target tourists who are overloaded with bags or distracted with a video camera. The kids look like beggars and hold up newspapers or cardboard signs to confuse their victims. They scram like stray cats if you're on to them.

Reporting Losses: To report lost or stolen passports and documents, or to make an insurance claim, you must file a police report (at Termini train station, with *polizia* at track 11 or with carabinieri at track 20; offices are also at Piazza Venezia). To replace a passport, file the police report, then call your embassy to make an appointment (US embassy: tel. 06-46741, Via Vittorio Veneto 121, www.usembassy.it). To report lost or stolen credit cards, see page 1438.

Emergency Numbers: Police—tel. 113. Ambulance—tel. 118.

Pedestrian Safety: Your main safety concern in Rome is crossing streets safely, using extreme caution. Scooters don't need to stop at red lights, and even cars exercise what drivers call the "logical option" of not stopping if they see no oncoming traffic. As noisy gasoline-powered scooters are replaced by electric ones, they'll be quieter (hooray) but more dangerous for pedestrians. Follow locals like a shadow when you cross a street (or spend a good part of your visit stranded on curbs). When you do cross alone, don't be a deer in the headlights.

Find a gap in the traffic and walk with confidence while making eye contact with approaching drivers—they won't hit you if they can tell where you intend to go.

Staying/Getting Healthy: The siesta is a key to survival in summertime Rome. Lie down and contemplate the extraordinary power of gravity in the Eternal City. I drink lots of cold, refreshing water from Rome's many drinking fountains (the Forum has three).

There's a pharmacy (marked by a green cross) in every neighborhood. Several pharmacies stay open late in Termini train station (daily 7:30-22:00) and at Piazza dei Cinquecento 51 (open 24 hours daily, next to Termini train station on the corner of Via Cavour, tel. 06-488-0019).

Embassies can recommend English-speaking doctors. Consider MEDline, a 24-hour home-medical service; doctors speak English and make calls at hotels for €150-180 (tel. 06-808-0995). Anyone is entitled to free emergency treatment at public hospitals. The hospital closest to Termini train station is Policlinico Umberto 1 (entrance for emergency treatment on Via Lancisi, translators available, Metro: Policlinico). The American Hospital, a private hospital on the edge of town, is accustomed to helping Yankees (Via Emilio Longoni 69, tel. 06-22-551).

Getting Around Rome

Sightsee on foot, by city bus, by Metro, or by taxi. I've grouped your sightseeing into walkable neighborhoods. Make it a point to visit sights in a logical order. Needless backtracking wastes precious time.

The public-transportation system, which is cheap and efficient, consists primarily of buses, a few trams, and the two underground subway (Metro) lines. Consider it part of your Roman experience.

Buying Tickets

All public transportation uses the same ticket (€1, valid for one Metro ride—including transfers underground—plus unlimited city buses and *elettrico* buses during a 75-minute period). Passes good on buses and the Metro are sold in increments of one day (€4, good until midnight), three days (€11), and one week (€16, about the cost of two taxi rides).

You can purchase tickets and passes at some newsstands, tobacco shops (*tabacchi,* marked by a black-and-white *T* sign), and major Metro stations and bus stops, but not onboard. It's smart to stock up on tickets early, or to buy a pass or a Roma Pass (which includes a three-day transit pass—see page 866). That way, you don't have to run around searching for an open *tabacchi* when you

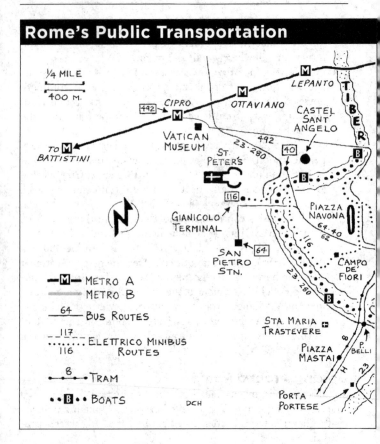

Rome's Public Transportation

1/4 MILE
400 M.

LEPANTO

CIPRO
OTTAVIANO

TO M
BATTISTINI

VATICAN
MUSEUM

ST.
PETER'S

CASTEL
SANT
ANGELO

TIBER

492
23 280

40

116

GIANICOLO
TERMINAL

PIAZZA
NAVONA

64 40
62

SAN
PIETRO
STN.

64

116

23 280

CAMPO
DE'
FIORI

—M— METRO A
METRO B

STA. MARIA
TRASTEVERE

64
——— BUS ROUTES

117
116 ELETTRICO MINIBUS
ROUTES

8
•—•—• TRAM

••B•• BOATS

PIAZZA
MASTAI

P.
BELLI

8

23

DCH

PORTA
PORTESE

spot your bus approaching. Metro stations rarely have human ticket-sellers, and the machines are often either broken or require exact change (it helps to insert your smallest coin first).

Validate your ticket by sticking it in the Metro turnstile (magnetic strip-side up, arrow-side first) or in the machine when you board the bus (magnetic strip-side down, arrow-side first)—watch others and imitate. To get through a Metro turnstile with a transit pass or Roma Pass, use it just like a ticket (on buses, however, you only need to validate your pass if that's your first time using it). If the validation machine won't work, you can ride with your ticket unstamped, but you must write the date, time, and bus number on it, or risk getting fined. For more information, visit www.atac .roma.it (which has a useful route planner in English), or call 800-431-784 or 06-57-003.

By Metro

The Roman subway system (Metropolitana, or "Metro") is simple,

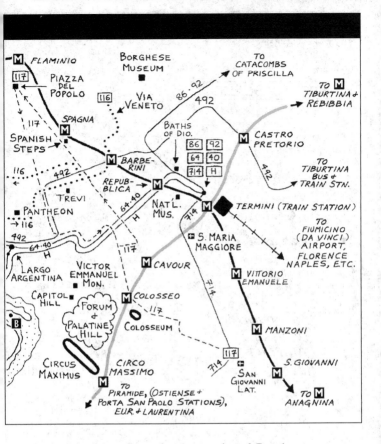

with two clean, cheap, fast lines—A and B—that intersect at Termini train station. The Metro runs from 5:30 to 23:30 (Fri-Sat until 1:30 in the morning). The subway's first and last compartments are generally the least crowded (and the least likely to harbor pickpockets).

You'll notice lots of big holes in the city as a new line is built. Line C, from the Colosseum to Largo Argentina, will likely be done in 2020.

While much of Rome is not served by its skimpy subway, the following stops are helpful:

Termini (intersection of lines A and B): Termini train station, shuttle train to airport, National Museum of Rome, and recommended hotels

Repubblica (line A): Baths of Diocletian/Octagonal Hall, Via Nazionale, and recommended hotels

Barberini (line A): Cappuccin Crypt, Trevi Fountain, and Villa Borghese

Rome's Metro

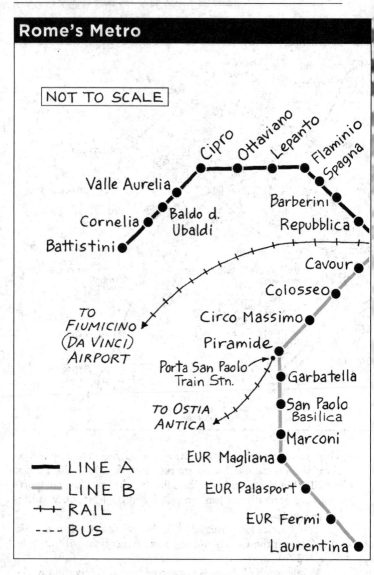

NOT TO SCALE

Cipro
Ottaviano
Lepanto
Flaminio
Spagna
Valle Aurelia
Baldo d. Ubaldi
Cornelia
Barberini
Repubblica
Battistini
Cavour
Colosseo
Circo Massimo
TO FIUMICINO (DA VINCI) AIRPORT
Piramide
Porta San Paolo Train Stn.
Garbatella
San Paolo Basilica
TO OSTIA ANTICA
Marconi
EUR Magliana
EUR Palasport
EUR Fermi
Laurentina

—— LINE A
—— LINE B
++ RAIL
---- BUS

Spagna (line A): Spanish Steps, and classy shopping area

Flaminio (line A): Piazza del Popolo, start of recommended "Dolce Vita Stroll" down Via del Corso

Ottaviano (line A): St. Peter's and Vatican City

Cipro (line A): Vatican Museum and recommended hotels

Tiburtina (line B): Tiburtina train and bus station

Colosseo (line B): Colosseum, Roman Forum, bike rental, and recommended hotels

ROME

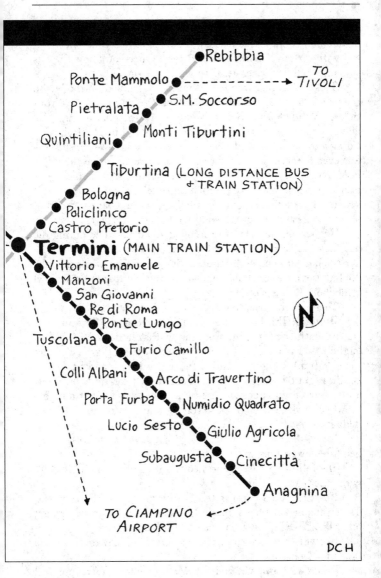

Rebibbia
Ponte Mammolo — — — — → TO TIVOLI
S.M. Soccorso
Pietralata
Monti Tiburtini
Quintiliani
Tiburtina (LONG DISTANCE BUS & TRAIN STATION)
Bologna
Policlinico
Castro Pretorio
Termini (MAIN TRAIN STATION)
Vittorio Emanuele
Manzoni
San Giovanni
Re di Roma
Ponte Lungo
Tuscolana
Furio Camillo
Colli Albani
Arco di Travertino
Porta Furba
Numidio Quadrato
Lucio Sesto
Giulio Agricola
Subaugusta
Cinecittà
Anagnina
TO CIAMPINO AIRPORT

DCH

By Bus

The Metro is handy, but it won't get you everywhere—take the bus. Bus routes are clearly listed at the stops. TIs usually don't have bus maps, but with some knowledge of major stops, you won't necessarily need one (though if you do want a route map, buy it from *tabacchi* shops; bus info: www.atac.roma.it with good route planner in English, or tel. 06-57003, usually not in English).

Buses (especially the touristy #40 and #64) are havens for

thieves and pickpockets. Assume any commotion is a thief-created distraction. If one bus is packed, there's likely a second one on its tail with far fewer crowds and thieves. Once you know the bus system, you'll find it's easier than searching for a cab.

Tickets have a barcode and must be stamped on the bus in the yellow box with the digital readout (be sure to retrieve your ticket). Validate your ticket as you board (magnetic strip-side down, arrow-side first), or you are cheating. While relatively safe, riding without a stamped ticket on the bus is stressful. Inspectors fine even innocent-looking tourists €50. Remember that there's no need to validate a transit pass or Roma Pass on the bus, unless your pass is new and hasn't yet been stamped elsewhere in the transit system. Bus etiquette (not always followed) is to board at the front or rear doors and exit out the middle.

Regular bus lines start running at about 5:30, and during the day they run every 5-10 minutes. After 23:30, and sometimes earlier (such as on Sundays), buses are less frequent but dependable. Night buses are also reliable, and are marked with an *N* and an owl symbol on the bus-stop signs.

These are the major bus routes:

Bus #64: This bus cuts across the city, linking Termini train station with the Vatican, stopping at Piazza della Repubblica (sights), Via Nazionale (recommended hotels), Piazza Venezia (near Forum), Largo Argentina (near Pantheon), and St. Peter's Basilica (get off just past the tunnel). Ride it for a city overview and to watch pickpockets in action. The #64 can get horribly crowded, awkward for female travelers uncomfortably close to male strangers.

Bus #40: This express bus following the #64 route is especially helpful—fewer stops and crowds.

The following three routes conveniently connect Trastevere with other parts of Rome:

Bus #H: This express bus, linking Termini Station and Trastevere, makes a few stops on Via Nazionale (for Trastevere, get off at Piazza Belli, just after crossing the Tiber River).

Bus #8: This tram connects Largo Argentina with Trastevere (get off at Piazza Belli).

Buses #23 and #280: Link Vatican with Trastevere and Testaccio, stopping at the Vatican Museum (nearest stop is Via Leone IV), Castel Sant'Angelo, Trastevere (Piazza Belli), Porta Portese (Sunday flea market), and Piramide (Metro and gateway to Testaccio).

Here are other useful routes:

Bus #62: Largo Argentina to St. Peter's Square.

Bus #81: San Giovanni in Laterano, Largo Argentina, and Piazza Risorgimento (Vatican).

Buses #85 and #87: Piazza Venezia, Colosseum, San Clemente, and San Giovanni in Laterano.

Bus #492: Travels east-west across the city, connecting Tiburtina (train and bus stations), Piazza Barberini, Piazza Venezia, Piazza Cavour (Castel Sant'Angelo), and Piazza Risorgimento (Vatican).

Bus #714: Termini train station, Santa Maria Maggiore, San Giovanni in Laterano, and Terme di Caracalla (Baths of Caracalla).

Elettrico **Minibuses:** Two cute *elettrico* minibuses wind through the narrow streets of old and interesting neighborhoods, and are great for transport or simple joyriding:

Elettrico **#116:** Through the medieval core of Rome: Ponte Vittorio Emanuele II (near Castel Sant'Angelo) to Campo de' Fiori, Pantheon, Piazza Barberini, and the southern edge of the scenic Villa Borghese Gardens.

Elettrico **#117:** San Giovanni in Laterano, Colosseo, Via dei Serpenti, Trevi Fountain, Piazza di Spagna, and Piazza del Popolo.

By Taxi

I use taxis in Rome more often than in other cities. They're reasonable and useful for efficient sightseeing in this big, hot metropolis. Taxis start at €2.80, then charge about €1.30 per kilometer (surcharges: €1 on Sun, €3 for nighttime hours of 22:00-7:00, one regular suitcase or bag rides free, tip by rounding up to the nearest euro). Sample fares: Termini train station to Vatican-€10; Termini train station to Colosseum-€6; Colosseum to Trastevere-€7 (or look up your route at www.worldtaximeter.com). Three or four companions with more money than time should taxi almost everywhere.

It's tough to wave down a taxi in Rome, especially at night. Find the nearest taxi stand by asking a passerby or a clerk in a shop, *"Dov'è una fermata dei taxi?"* (doh-VEH OO-nah fehr-MAH-tah DEHee TAHK-see). Some taxi stands are listed on my maps. To save time and energy, have your hotel or restaurant call a taxi for you; the meter starts when the call is received (generally adding a euro or two to the bill). To call a cab on your own, dial 06-4994 or 06-6645. It's routine for Romans to ask the waiter in a restaurant to call a taxi when they ask for the bill. The waiter will tell you how many minutes you have to enjoy your coffee.

Beware of corrupt taxis. A common cabbie scam is to take your €20 note, drop it, and pick up a €5 note (similar color), claiming that's what you gave him. To avoid this scam, pay in small bills; if you only have a large bill, show it to the cabbie as you state its face value.

If hailing a cab on the street, be sure the meter is restarted when you get in (should be around €2.80, or around €5 if you or your hotelier phoned for the taxi). Many meters show both the fare and the time elapsed during the ride—and some tourists pay €10 for an eight-and-a-half-minute trip (more than the fair meter rate).

When you arrive at the train station or airport, beware of hustlers conning naive visitors into unmarked rip-off "express taxis." Only use official taxis, with a *taxi* sign and phone number marked on the door. By law, they must display a multilingual official price chart. If you have any problems with a taxi, point to the chart and ask the cabbie to explain it to you. Making a show of writing down the taxi number (to file a complaint) can motivate a driver to quickly settle the matter.

If you take a Rome city cab from the airport to anywhere in central Rome within the old city walls, the cost should be €45 (covering up to four people and their bags); however, every year some readers report being ripped off. The catch is that cabbies not based in Rome can charge €60. At the airport, look specifically for a Rome city cab, with the "SPQR" shield on the door. By law, they can charge only €45 for the ride.

Tired travelers arriving at the airport will likely find it less stressful to take the airport shuttle van to their hotel, or catch the train to Termini train station and take the Metro or a cheaper taxi from there (for details on getting from the airport to downtown Rome via taxi, shuttle, or train, see "Rome Connections," near the end of this chapter).

By Bike

Biking in the big city of Rome can speed up sightseeing or simply be an enjoyable way to explore. Though Roman traffic can be stressful, Roman drivers are respectful of cyclists. The best rides are on small streets in the city center. A bike path along the banks of the Tiber River makes a good 20-minute ride (easily accessed from the ramps at Porta Portese and Ponte Regina Margherita near Piazza del Popolo). Get a bike with a well-padded seat—the little stones that pave Roman streets are unforgiving.

Top Bike Rental and Tours is professionally run by Roman bike enthusiasts who want to show off their city. Your rental comes with a handy map that suggests a route and indicates less-trafficked streets. Ciro and Marta also offer four-hour-long English-only guided tours around the city and the Ancient Appian Way; check their website for days and times (rental: €8/half-day, €13/day, discount with this book, best to reserve in advance via email; bike tours: start at €29, reservations required; daily 9:30-19:00, leave ID for deposit, from Santa Maria Maggiore TI kiosk take Via dell'Olmata and turn left one block down, Via dei Quattro

Cantoni 40, tel. 06-488-2893, www.topbikerental.com, info@top bikerental.com).

Cool Rent, near the Colosseo Metro stop, is cheaper but less helpful (€3/hour, €10/day, 3-person bike cart-€10/hour, daily 9:30-20:00, driver's license or other ID for deposit, 10 yards to the right as you exit the Metro). A second outlet is just off Via del Corso (on Largo di Lombardi, near corner of Via del Corso and Via della Croce).

By Car with Driver

You can hire your own private car with driver through Autoservizi Monti Concezio, run by gentle, capable, and English-speaking Ezio (car-€35/hour, minibus-€40/hour, 3-hour minimum for city sightseeing, long rides outside Rome are more expensive, mobile 335-636-5907 or 349-674-5643, www.montitours.com, concezio monti@gmail.com).

Tours in Rome

Walking Tours

Finding the best guided tours in Rome is challenging. Local guides are good but pricey. Tour companies are cheaper, but quality and organization are unreliable. You have several main tour options: Download my audio tours to your mobile device (easy, perfectly reliable, and free—see page 1444); hire a private Italian guide (around €150-180 for a half-day tour—those listed here are excellent and worth every euro, if you can afford it); organize a group of 4-6 people from your hotel to split the cost of hiring a private guide (this ends up costing about the same as joining a tour from one of the companies listed here); or go on a scheduled walking tour with one of the companies listed below (about €25, generally expat guides).

Local Guides—Consider hiring your own personal tour guide. I've worked with each of these licensed independent local guides. They speak excellent English, and enjoy tailoring tours to your interests. Their prices (roughly €50/hour, €180/half-day) flex with the day, season, and demand. Arrange your date and price by email.

Francesca Caruso loves to teach and share her appreciation of her city, and has contributed generously to this chapter (francesca inroma@gmail.com). Popular with my readers, Francesca understandably books up quickly; if she's busy, she'll recommend one of her colleagues. **Carla Zaia** is an engaging expert on all things Roman (mobile 349-759-0723, carlaromeguide@gmail.com). **Cristina Giannicchi** has an archaeology background (mobile 338-111-4573, www.crisacross.com, crisgiannicchi@gmail.com).

Sara Magister is a Roman with a doctorate in art history, who wrote a book on Renaissance Rome (tel. 06-583-6783, mobile 339-379-3813, a.magister@iol.it). **Giovanna Terzulli** is a personable, knowledgeable art historian (terzulli@tiscali.it).

Walking-Tour Companies—Rome has many highly competitive tour companies, each offering a series of themed walks through various slices of Rome. Three-hour guided walks generally cost €25-30 per person. Guides are usually native English-speakers, often American expats. Tours are limited to small groups, geared to American tourists, and given in English only. I've listed some here, but without a lot of details on their offerings. Before your trip, spend some time on these companies' websites to get to know your options, as each company has a particular teaching and guiding personality. Some are highbrow, and others are less scholarly. It's sometimes required, and always smart, to book a spot in advance (easy online). I must add that we get a lot of negative feedback on some of these tour companies. Readers report that their advertising can be misleading, and that scheduling mishaps are not uncommon.

Context Rome's walking tours are more intellectual than most, designed for travelers with longer-than-average attention spans. They are more expensive than others, and are led by "docents" rather than guides (tel. 06-9762-5204, US tel. 800-691-6036, www.contextrome.com). **Enjoy Rome** offers five different walks and a website filled with helpful information (Via Marghera 8a, tel. 06-445-1843, www.enjoyrome.com, info@enjoyrome.com). **Rome Walks** has put together several particularly creative itineraries (mobile 347-795-5175, www.romewalks.com, info@romewalks.com, Annie). **Roman Odyssey** offers a Rick Steves discount on their walks and private tours (tel. 06-580-9902, mobile 328-912-3720, www.romanodyssey.com, Rahul). **Through Eternity** offers travelers with this book a discount on most tours; book through their website for the best discount (tel. 06-700-9336, mobile 347-336-5298, www.througheternity.com, info@througheternity.com, Rob).

Hop-on, Hop-off Bus Tours

Several different agencies, including the ATAC public bus company, run hop-on, hop-off tours around Rome. These tours are constantly evolving and offer varying combinations of sights. You can grab one (and pay as you board) at any stop; Termini train station and Piazza Venezia are handy hubs. Although the city is perfectly walkable and traffic jams can make the bus dreadfully slow, these open-top bus tours remain popular.

Trambus #110 seems to be the best. It's operated by the ATAC city-bus lines, and offers an orientation tour on big red double-decker buses with an open-air upper deck. In less than two hours, you'll have 80 sights pointed out to you (with a next-to-worthless recorded narration). While you can hop on and off, the service can be erratic (mobbed midday, not ideal in bad weather) and it can be very slow in heavy traffic. It's best to think of this as a two-hour quickie orientation with scant information and lots of images. The stops include Ara Pacis, Piazza Cavour, St. Peter's Square, Corso Vittorio Emanuele (for Piazza Navona), Piazza Venezia, Colosseum, and Via Nazionale. Bus #110 departs every 20 minutes (runs daily 8:30-20:30, tel. 06-684-0901, www.trambusopen.com). Buy the €15 ticket as you board.

Archeobus is an open-top bus, also operated by ATAC, that runs twice hourly from Termini train station out to the Appian Way (with stops at the Colosseum, Baths of Caracalla, San Callisto, San Sebastiano, and the Tomb of Cecilia Metella). This is a handy way to see the sights down this ancient Roman road, but it can be frustrating for various reasons—sparse narration, sporadic service, and not ideal for hopping on and off (€15, €30 combo-ticket with Trambus 110, ticket valid 24 hours, 1.5-hour loop, daily 8:30-16:30, from Termini train station and Piazza Venezia, tel. 06-684-0901, www.trambusopen.com). A similar bus laces together all the Christian sights.

Self-Guided Walks

Here are three walks that give you a moving picture of Rome, an ancient yet modern city. You'll walk through history ("Roman Forum Walk"), take a refreshing early-evening stroll ("Dolce Vita Stroll"), and enjoy the thriving night scene ("Night Walk Across Rome").

Roman Forum Walk

The Forum was the political, religious, and commercial center of the city. Rome's most important temples and halls of justice were here. This was the place for religious processions, political demonstrations, elections, important speeches, and parades by conquering generals. As Rome's empire expanded, these few acres of land became the center of the civilized world.

Cost: €12 combo-ticket also includes Colosseum and Palatine Hill; ticket valid two consecutive days—one entry per sight; also covered by Roma Pass. If the line at the Forum is long, buy a combo-ticket or Roma Pass nearby at the less-crowded Palatine Hill entrance on Via di San Gregorio. The Roma Pass is also sold at the *tabacchi* shop at the Colosseum Metro stop.

Hours: The Roman Forum, Colosseum, and Palatine Hill are all open daily 8:30 until one hour before sunset: April-Sept until

Roman Forum Walk

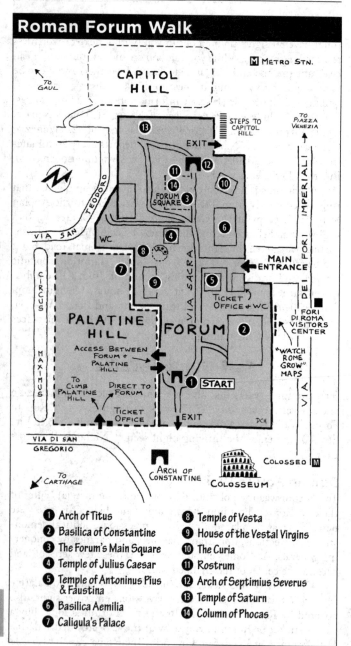

CAPITOL HILL

TO GAUL

M METRO STN.

TO PIAZZA VENEZIA

STEPS TO CAPITOL HILL

EXIT

(13)

(11) (12)

(14)

FORUM SQUARE (3)

(10)

VIA SAN TEODORO

WC

(4)

(8)

(6)

MAIN ENTRANCE

CIRCUS MAXIMUS

(7)

(9)

VIA SACRA

(5)

TICKET OFFICE & WC

I FORI DI ROMA VISITORS CENTER

PALATINE HILL

FORUM

(2)

"WATCH ROME GROW" MAPS

ACCESS BETWEEN FORUM + PALATINE HILL

TO CLIMB PALATINE HILL

DIRECT TO FORUM

(1) START

TICKET OFFICE

EXIT

DEI FORI IMPERIALI

VIA

DCH

VIA DI SAN GREGORIO

TO CARTHAGE

ARCH OF CONSTANTINE

COLOSSEUM

COLOSSEO M

1. Arch of Titus
2. Basilica of Constantine
3. The Forum's Main Square
4. Temple of Julius Caesar
5. Temple of Antoninus Pius & Faustina
6. Basilica Aemilia
7. Caligula's Palace
8. Temple of Vesta
9. House of the Vestal Virgins
10. The Curia
11. Rostrum
12. Arch of Septimius Severus
13. Temple of Saturn
14. Column of Phocas

ROME

19:15, Oct until 18:30, off-season closes as early as 16:30; last entry one hour before closing.

Getting There: The closest Metro stop is Colosseo. The Forum has two entrances. The main entrance is on Via dei Fori Imperiali ("Road of the Imperial Forums"). From the Colosseum Metro stop, walk away from the Colosseum on Via dei Fori Imperiali to find the low-profile Forum ticket office, located where Via Cavour spills into Via dei Fori Imperiali.

The other entrance is at the Palatine Hill ticket office on Via di San Gregorio—after buying your ticket, take the path to the right (not up the hill), and wind around to enter the Forum at the Arch of Titus.

Information: A free visitors center (called I Fori di Roma), located across Via dei Fori Imperiali from the Forum's main entrance, has a TI, bookshop, small café, WCs, and a film (daily 9:30-18:30). A bookstore is at the Forum entrance. Vendors at the Forum sell small *Rome: Past and Present* books with plastic overlays that restore the ruins (includes DVD, smaller book marked €15, prices soft, so offer €10). Info office tel. 06-3996-7700.

Tours: An unexciting yet informative **audioguide** helps decipher the rubble (€4, €6 version includes Palatine Hill, must leave ID), but you'll have to return it to one of the Forum entrances instead of being able to exit directly to Capitol Hill or the Colosseum. Official **guided tours** in English run Monday through Friday at around 13:00 (€4, 45 minutes, confirm time at ticket office). You can download a free Rick Steves **audio tour** of the Roman Forum for your mobile device via www.ricksteves .com/audioeurope, iTunes, or the Rick Steves Audio Europe smartphone app.

• *Start at the Arch of Titus (Arco di Tito). It's the white triumphal arch that rises above the rubble on the east end of the Forum (closest to the Colosseum). Stand at the viewpoint alongside the arch and gaze over the valley known as the Forum.*

❶ **Arch of Titus (Arco di Tito):** This arch commemorated the Roman victory over the province of Judaea (Israel) in A.D. 70. The Romans had a reputation as benevolent conquerors who tolerated the local customs and rulers. All they required was allegiance to the empire, shown by worshipping the emperor as a god. No problem for most conquered people, who already had half a dozen gods on their prayer lists anyway. But Israelites believed in only one god, and it wasn't the emperor. Israel revolted. After a short but bitter war, the Romans defeated the rebels, took Jerusalem, destroyed their temple (leaving only the foundation wall—today's revered "Wailing Wall"), and brought home 50,000 Jewish slaves... who were forced to build this arch (and the Colosseum).

• *Walk down Via Sacra into the Forum. After about 50 yards, turn right and follow a path uphill to the three huge arches of the...*

❷ **Basilica of Constantine (a.k.a. Basilica Maxentius):** Yes, these are big arches. But they represent only one-third of the original Basilica of Constantine, a mammoth hall of justice. The arches were matched by a similar set along the Via Sacra side (only a few squat brick piers remain). Between them ran the central hall, which was spanned by a roof 130 feet high—about 55 feet higher than the side arches you see. (The stub of brick you see sticking up began an arch that once spanned the central hall.) The hall itself was as long as a football field, lavishly furnished with colorful inlaid marble, a gilded bronze ceiling, and statues, and filled with strolling Romans. At the far (west) end was an enormous marble statue of Emperor Constantine on a throne. (Pieces of this statue, including a hand the size of a man, are on display in Rome's Capitoline Museums.)

The basilica was begun by the emperor Maxentius, but after he was trounced in battle (see page 900), the victor Constantine completed the massive building. No doubt about it, the Romans built monuments on a more epic scale than any previous Europeans, wowing their "barbarian" neighbors.

• *Now stroll deeper into the Forum, downhill along Via Sacra, through the trees. Many of the large basalt stones under your feet were walked on by Caesar Augustus 2,000 years ago. Pass by the only original bronze door still swinging on its ancient hinges (the green door at the Tempio di Romolo, on the right) and continue between ruined buildings until Via Sacra opens up to a flat, grassy area.*

❸ **The Forum's Main Square:** The original Forum, or main square, was this flat patch about the size of a football field, stretching to the foot of Capitol Hill. Surrounding it were temples, law courts, government buildings, and triumphal arches.

Rome was born right here. According to legend, twin brothers Romulus (Rome) and Remus were orphaned in infancy and raised by a she-wolf on top of Palatine Hill. Growing up, they found it hard to get dates. So they and their cohorts attacked the nearby Sabine tribe and kidnapped their women. After they made peace, this marshy valley became the meeting place and then the trading center for the scattered tribes on the surrounding hillsides.

The square was the busiest and most crowded—and often the seediest—section of town. Besides the senators, politicians, and currency exchangers, there were even sleazier types—souvenir hawkers, pickpockets, fortune-tellers, gamblers, slave marketers, drunks, hookers, lawyers, and tour guides.

The Forum is now rubble, but imagine it in its prime: blinding white marble buildings with 40-foot-high columns and shining bronze roofs; rows of statues painted in realistic colors; processional chariots rattling down Via Sacra. Mentally replace tourists in T-shirts with tribunes in togas. Imagine the buildings towering and the people buzzing around you while an orator gives a rabble-rousing speech from the Rostrum. If things still look like just a pile of rocks, at least tell yourself, "But Julius Caesar once leaned against these rocks."

• *At the near (east) end of the main square (the Colosseum is to the east) are the foundations of a temple now capped with a peaked wood-and-metal roof.*

❹ **The Temple of Julius Caesar (Tempio del Divo Giulio, or "Ara di Cesare"):** Julius Caesar's body was burned on this spot (under the metal roof) after his assassination. Peek behind the wall into the small apse area, where a mound of dirt usually has fresh flowers—given to remember the man who, more than any other, personified the greatness of Rome.

Caesar (100-44 B.C.) changed Rome—and the Forum—dramatically. He cleared out many of the wooden market stalls and began to ring the square with even grander buildings. Caesar's house was located behind the temple, near that clump of trees. He walked right by here on the day he was assassinated ("Beware the Ides of March!" warned a street-corner Etruscan preacher).

Though he was popular with the masses, not everyone liked Caesar's urban design or his politics. When he assumed dictatorial powers, he was ambushed and stabbed to death by a conspiracy of senators, including his adopted son, Brutus *("Et tu, Brute?")*.

The funeral was held here, facing the main square. The citizens gathered, and speeches were made. Mark Antony stood up to say (in Shakespeare's words), "Friends, Romans, countrymen, lend me your ears. I come to bury Caesar, not to praise him." When Caesar's body was burned, the citizens who still loved him threw anything at hand on the fire, requiring the fire department to come put it out. Later, Emperor Augustus dedicated this temple in his name, making Caesar the first Roman to become a god.

• *Behind and to the left of the Temple of Julius Caesar are the 10 tall columns of the...*

❺ **Temple of Antoninus Pius and Faustina:** The Senate built this temple to honor Emperor Antoninus Pius (A.D. 138-161) and his deified wife, Faustina. The 50-foot-tall Corinthian (leafy) columns must have been awe-inspiring to out-of-towners who grew up in thatched huts. Although the temple has been inhabited by a church, you can still see the basic layout—a staircase led to a shaded porch (the columns), which admitted you to the main building (now a church), where the statue of the god sat. Originally, these columns supported a triangular pediment decorated with sculptures.

Picture these columns, with gilded capitals, supporting brightly painted statues in the pediment, and the whole building capped with a gleaming bronze roof. The stately gray rubble of today's Forum is a faded black-and-white photograph of a 3-D Technicolor era.

The building is a microcosm of many of the changes that occurred after Rome fell. In medieval times, the temple was pillaged. Note the diagonal cuts high on the marble columns—a failed attempt by scavengers to cut through the pillars to pull them down for their precious stone. (They used vinegar and rope to cut the marble...but because vinegar also eats through rope, they abandoned the attempt.) In 1550, a church was housed inside the ancient temple. The door shows the street level at the time of Michelangelo. The long staircase was underground until excavated in the 1800s.

• *There's a ramp next to the Temple of A. and F. Walk halfway up it and look to the left to view the...*

❻ **Basilica Aemilia:** A basilica was a covered public forum, often serving as a Roman hall of justice. In a society that was as legal-minded as America is today, you needed a lot of lawyers—and a big place to put them. Citizens came here to work out matters such as inheritances and building permits, or to sue somebody.

Notice the layout. It was a long, rectangular building. The stubby columns all in a row form one long, central hall flanked by two side aisles. Medieval Christians required a larger meeting hall for their worship services than Roman temples provided, so they used the spacious Roman basilica as the model for their churches. Cathedrals from France to Spain to England, from Romanesque to Gothic to Renaissance, all have the same basic floor plan as a Roman basilica.

• *Return again to the Temple of Julius Caesar. To the right of the temple are the three tall Corinthian columns of the Temple of Castor and Pollux. Beyond that is Palatine Hill—the corner of which may have been...*

❼ **Caligula's Palace (a.k.a. the Palace of Tiberius):** Emperor Caligula (ruled A.D. 37-41) had a huge palace on Palatine Hill overlooking the Forum. It actually sprawled down the hill into the Forum (some supporting arches remain in the hillside).

Caligula was not a nice person. He tortured enemies, stole senators' wives, and parked his chariot in handicap spaces. But Rome's luxury-loving emperors only added to the glory of the Forum, with each one trying to make his mark on history.

• *To the left of the Temple of Castor and Pollux, find the remains of a small white circular temple.*

❽ **The Temple of Vesta:** This is perhaps Rome's most sacred spot. Rome considered itself one big family, and this temple represented a circular hut, like the kind that Rome's first families lived in. Inside, a fire burned, just as in a Roman home. And back in the days before lighters and butane, you never wanted your fire to go out. As long as the sacred flame burned, Rome would stand. The

ROME

flame was tended by priestesses known as Vestal Virgins.

• *Around the back of the Temple of Vesta, you'll find two rectangular brick pools. These stood in the courtyard of the...*

❾ House of the Vestal Virgins: The Vestal Virgins lived in a two-story building surrounding a long central courtyard with these two pools at one end. Rows of statues depicting leading Vestal Virgins flanked the courtyard. This place was the model—both architecturally and sexually—for medieval convents and monasteries.

Chosen from noble families before they reached the age of 10, the six Vestal Virgins served a 30-year term. Honored and revered by the Romans, the Vestals even had their own box opposite the emperor in the Colosseum.

As the name implies, a Vestal took a vow of chastity. If she served her term faithfully—abstaining for 30 years—she was given a huge dowry, and allowed to marry. But if they found any Virgin who wasn't, she was strapped to a funeral car, paraded through the streets of the Forum, taken to a crypt, given a loaf of bread and a lamp...and buried alive. Many women suffered the latter fate.

• *Return to the Temple of Julius Caesar and head to the Forum's west end (opposite from the Colosseum). As you pass alongside the big open space of the Forum's main square, consider how the piazza is still a standard part of any Italian town. It has reflected and accommodated the gregarious and outgoing nature of the Italian people since Roman times.*

Stop at the big, well-preserved brick building (on right) with the triangular roof and look in.

❿ The Curia (Senate House): The Curia was the most important political building in the Forum. While the present building dates from A.D. 283, this was the site of Rome's official center of government since the birth of the republic. (Note that ongoing archaeological work may restrict access to the Curia, as well as the Arch of Septimius Severus—described later—and the exit to Capitol Hill.) Three hundred senators, elected by the citizens of Rome, met here to debate and create the laws of the land. Their wooden seats once circled the building in three tiers; the Senate president's podium sat at the far end. The marble floor is from ancient times. Listen to the echoes in this vast room—the acoustics are great.

Rome prided itself on being a republic. Early in the city's history, its people threw out the king and established rule by elected representatives. Each Roman citizen was free to speak his mind and have a say in public policy. Even when emperors became the supreme authority, the Senate was a power to be reckoned with. The Curia building is well-preserved, having been used as a church since early Christian times. In the 1930s, it was restored and opened to the public as a historic site. (Note: Although Julius Caesar was assassinated in "the Senate," it wasn't here—the Senate was temporarily meeting across town.)

A statue and two reliefs inside the Curia help build our mental image of the Forum. The statue, made of porphyry marble in about A.D. 100 (with its head, arms, and feet now missing), was a tribute to an emperor, probably Hadrian or Trajan. The two relief panels may have decorated the Rostrum. Those on the left show people (with big stone tablets) standing in line to burn their debt records following a government amnesty. The other shows the distribution of grain (Rome's welfare system), some buildings in the background, and the latest fashion in togas.

• *Go back down the Senate steps and find the 10-foot-high wall just to the left of the big arch, marked...*

⓫ Rostrum (Rostra): Nowhere was Roman freedom more apparent than at this "Speaker's Corner." The Rostrum was a raised platform, 10 feet high and 80 feet long, decorated with statues, columns, and the prows of ships (rostra).

On a stage like this, Rome's orators, great and small, tried to draw a crowd and sway public opinion. Mark Antony rose to offer Caesar the laurel-leaf crown of kingship, which Caesar publicly (and hypocritically) refused while privately becoming a dictator. Men such as Cicero railed against the corruption and decadence that came with the city's newfound wealth. In later years, daring citizens even spoke out against the emperors, reminding them that Rome was once free. Picture the backdrop these speakers would have had—a mountain of marble buildings piling up on Capitol Hill.

In front of the Rostrum are trees bearing fruits that were sacred to the ancient Romans: olives (provided food, light, and preservatives), figs (tasty), and wine grapes (made a popular export product).

• *The big arch to the right of the Rostrum is the...*

⓬ Arch of Septimius Severus: In imperial times, the Rostrum's voices of democracy would have been dwarfed by images of the empire, such as the huge six-story-high Arch of Septimius Severus (A.D. 203). The reliefs commemorate the African-born emperor's battles in Mesopotamia. Near ground level, see soldiers marching captured barbarians back to Rome for the victory parade. Despite Severus' efficient rule, Rome's empire was crumbling under the weight of its own corruption, disease, decaying infrastructure, and the constant attacks by foreign "barbarians."

• *Pass underneath the Arch of Septimius Severus and turn left. On the slope of Capitol Hill are the eight remaining columns of the...*

⓭ Temple of Saturn: These columns framed the entrance to the Forum's oldest temple (497 B.C.). Inside was a humble, very old wooden statue of the god Saturn. But the statue's pedestal held the gold bars, coins, and jewels of Rome's state treasury, the booty collected by conquering generals.

• *Standing here, at one of the Forum's first buildings, look east at the lone, tall...*

🎱 **Column of Phocas:** This is the Forum's last monument (A.D. 608), a gift from the powerful Byzantine Empire to a fallen empire—Rome. Given to commemorate the pagan Pantheon's becoming a Christian church, it's like a symbolic last nail in ancient Rome's coffin. After Rome's 1,000-year reign, the city was looted by Vandals, the population of a million-plus shrank to about 10,000, and the once-grand city center—the Forum—was abandoned, slowly covered up by centuries of silt and dirt. In the 1700s, an English historian named Edward Gibbon overlooked this spot from Capitol Hill. Hearing Christian monks singing at these pagan ruins, he looked out at the few columns poking up from the ground, pondered the "Decline and Fall of the Roman Empire," and thought, "Hmm, that's a catchy title...."

• *There are several ways to exit the Forum:*

1. Exiting past the Arch of Titus lands you at the Colosseum.

2. Exiting near the Arch of Septimius Severus leads you to the stairs up to Capitol Hill.

3. The Forum's main entrance spills you back out onto Via dei Fori Imperiali.

4. From the Arch of Titus, you can climb Palatine Hill to the top—see page 902.

Dolce Vita Stroll

This is the city's chic stroll, from Piazza del Popolo (Metro: Flaminio) down a wonderfully traffic-free section of Via del Corso, and up Via Condotti to the Spanish Steps each evening around 18:00. Saturdays and Sundays are best; leave earlier than 18:00 if you plan to visit the Ara Pacis, which closes at 19:00 (and is closed Mon).

Shoppers, people-watchers, and flirts on the prowl fill this neighborhood of some of Rome's most fashionable stores (some open after siesta 16:30-19:30). While both the crowds and the shops along Via del Corso have gone downhill recently, elegance survives in the grid of streets between this street and the Spanish Steps.

To get to **Piazza del Popolo,** where the stroll starts, take Metro line A to Flaminio and walk south to the square. Delightfully car-free, Piazza del Popolo is marked by an obelisk that was brought to Rome by Augustus after he conquered Egypt. (It used to stand in the Circus Maximus.) In medieval times, this area was just inside Rome's main entry (for more background on the square, see page 921).

Dolce Vita Stroll

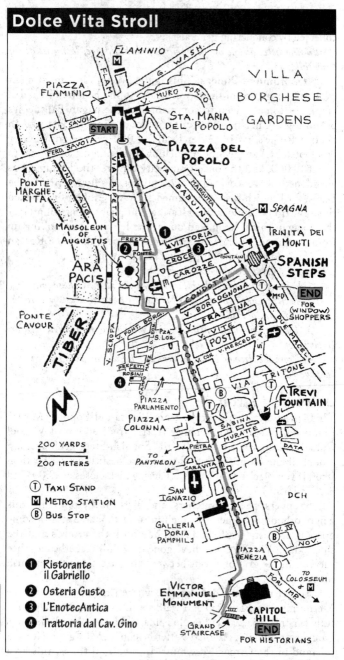

T Taxi Stand
M Metro Station
B Bus Stop

❶ Ristorante il Gabriello
❷ Osteria Gusto
❸ L'EnotecAntica
❹ Trattoria dal Cav. Gino

The Baroque church of **Santa Maria del Popolo** is worth popping into (Mon-Sat until 19:00, Sun until 19:30, next to gate in old wall on north side of square). Inside, look for Raphael's Chigi Chapel (KEE-gee, second chapel on left) and two paintings by Caravaggio (the side paintings in the Cerasi Chapel, left of altar; see listing on page 922).

From Piazza del Popolo, shop your way down **Via del Corso.** Historians side-trip right down Via Pontefici past the fascist architecture to see the massive rotting round-brick **Mausoleum of Augustus,** topped with overgrown cypress trees. Beyond it, next to the river, is Augustus' **Ara Pacis** (Altar of Peace), now enclosed within a protective glass-walled museum (described on page 924).

From the mausoleum, return to Via del Corso and the 21st century, continuing straight until **Via Condotti.** Window-shoppers should take a left to join the parade to the **Spanish Steps.** The streets that parallel Via Condotti to the south (Borgognona and Frattini) are more elegant, and filled with high-end boutiques.

Historians: Ignore Via Condotti and forget the Spanish Steps. Stay on Via del Corso, which has been straight since Roman times, a half-mile down to the Victor Emmanuel Monument. Climb Michelangelo's stairway to his glorious (especially when floodlit) square atop Capitol Hill. Stand on the balcony (just past the mayor's palace on the right), which overlooks the Forum. As the horizon reddens and cats prowl the unclaimed rubble of ancient Rome, it's one of the finest views in the city.

Night Walk Across Rome:
Campo de' Fiori to the Spanish Steps

Rome can be grueling. But taking an after-dark walk is a fine way to mix romance into all the history, enjoy the cool of the evening, and enliven everything with some of Europe's best people-watching. My favorite nighttime stroll laces together Rome's floodlit nightspots and fine urban spaces with real-life theater vignettes.

Sitting so close to a Bernini fountain that traffic noises evaporate; jostling with local teenagers to see all the gelato flavors; observing lovers straddling more than the bench; jaywalking past *polizia* in flak-proof vests; and marveling at the ramshackle elegance that softens this brutal city for those who were born here and can imagine living nowhere else—these are the flavors of Rome best tasted after dark.

Start this mile-long walk at the great, colorful **Campo de' Fiori,** my favorite outdoor dining room after dark (see page 962 of "Eating in Rome"). The center of the square is marked with a statue of Giordano Bruno, an intellectual heretic who was burned on this spot in 1600. Bruno overlooks this "Field of Flowers," the site of a busy produce market in the morning and a favorite of strollers after

Night Walk Across Rome

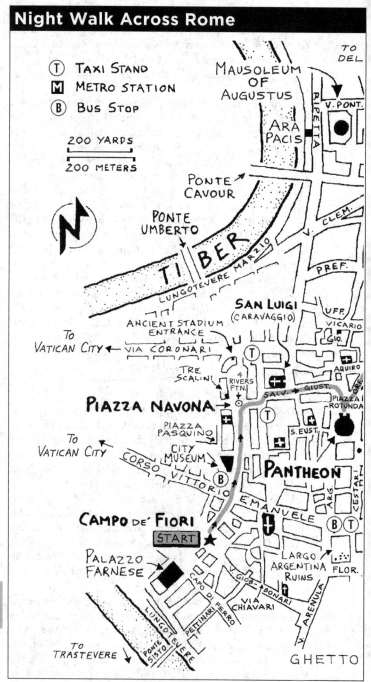

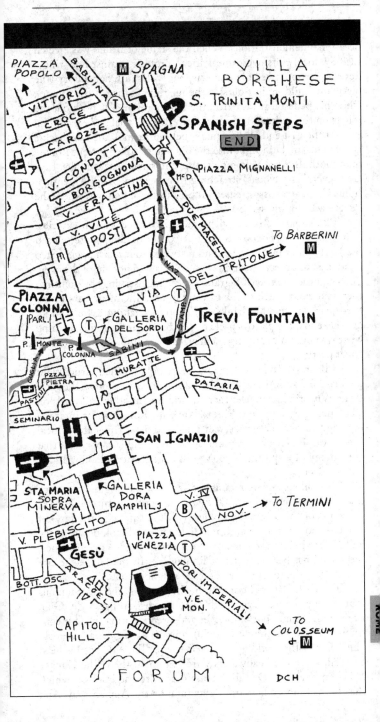

sundown. This neighborhood is still known for its free spirit and occasional demonstrations. When the statue of Bruno was erected in 1889, local riots overcame Vatican protests against honoring a heretic. Bruno faces his nemesis, the Vatican Chancellory (the big white building just outside the far-right corner of the square), while his pedestal reads, "And the flames rose up." Check out the reliefs on the pedestal for scenes from Bruno's trial and execution.

At the east end of the square (behind Bruno), the ramshackle apartments are built right into the old outer wall of ancient Rome's mammoth Theater of Pompey. This entertainment complex covered several city blocks, stretching from here to Largo Argentina. Julius Caesar was assassinated in the Theater of Pompey, where the Senate was renting space.

The square is lined with and surrounded by fun eateries. Bruno faces the **Forno** (in the left corner of the square, closed Sun), a popular place for hot and tasty take-out *pizza bianco*. Step in, at least to observe the frenzy as pizza is sold hot out of the oven. You can order *un etto* (100 grams, an average serving) by pointing, then take your snack to the counter to pay. The many bars lining the square are fine for drinks and people-watching. Late at night on weekends, the place is packed with beer-drinking kids, turning what was once a charming medieval square into one vast Roman street party.

If Bruno did a hop, step, and jump forward, then turned right on Via dei Baullari and marched 200 yards, he'd cross the busy Corso Vittorio Emanuele; then, continuing another 150 yards on Via Cuccagna, he'd find **Piazza Navona**. Rome's most interesting night scene features street music, artists, fire-eaters, local Casanovas, ice cream, fountains by Bernini, and outdoor cafés that are worthy of a splurge if you've got time to sit and enjoy Italy's human river.

This oblong square retains the shape of the original racetrack that was built around A.D. 80 by the emperor Domitian. (To see the ruins of the original entrance, exit the square at the far—or north—end, then take an immediate left, and look down to the left 25 feet below the current street level.) Since ancient times, the square has been a center of Roman life. In the 1800s, the city would flood the square to cool off the neighborhood.

The **Four Rivers Fountain** in the center is the most famous fountain by the man who remade Rome in Baroque style, Gian Lorenzo Bernini. Four burly river gods (representing the four continents that were known in 1650) support an Egyptian obelisk. The water of the world gushes everywhere. The Nile has his head covered, since the headwaters were unknown then. The Ganges holds an oar. The Danube turns to admire the obelisk, which Bernini had moved here from a stadium on the Appian Way. And

Uruguay's Río de la Plata tumbles backward in shock, wondering how he ever made the top four. Bernini enlivens the fountain with horses plunging through the rocks and exotic flora and fauna from these newly discovered lands. Homesick Texans may want to find the armadillo. (It's the big, weird armor-plated creature behind the Plata river statue.)

The Plata river god is gazing upward at the church of St. Agnes, worked on by Bernini's former student-turned-rival, Francesco Borromini. Borromini's concave facade helps reveal the dome and epitomizes the curved symmetry of Baroque. Tour guides say that Bernini designed his river god to look horrified at Borromini's work. Or maybe he's shielding his eyes from St. Agnes' nakedness, as she was stripped before being martyred. But either explanation is unlikely, since the fountain was completed two years before Borromini even started work on the church.

Leave Piazza Navona directly across from Tre Scalini (famous for its rich chocolate ice cream), and go east down Corsia Agonale, past rose peddlers and palm readers. Jog left around the guarded building (where Italy's senate meets), and follow the brown sign to the Pantheon, which is straight down Via del Salvatore.

Sit for a while under the floodlit and moonlit portico of the **Pantheon.** The 40-foot single-piece granite columns of the Pantheon's entrance show the scale the ancient Romans built on. The columns support a triangular Greek-style roof with an inscription that says "M. Agrippa" built it. In fact, it was built *(fecit)* by Emperor Hadrian (A.D. 120), who gave credit to the builder of an earlier structure. This impressive entranceway gives no clue that the greatest wonder of the building is inside—a domed room that inspired later domes, including Michelangelo's St. Peter's and Brunelleschi's Duomo (in Florence).

With your back to the Pantheon, veer to the right, uphill toward the yellow sign that reads *Casa del Caffè* on Via Orfani. **Tazza d'Oro Casa del Caffè,** one of Rome's top coffee shops, dates back to the days when this area was licensed to roast coffee beans. Locals come here for its fine *granita di caffè con panna* (coffee slush with cream).

Continue up Via Orfani to **Piazza Capranica**—home to the big, plain Florentine Renaissance–style Palazzo Capranica (directly opposite as you enter the square). Big shots, like the Capranica family, built towers on their palaces—not for any military use, but just to show off. Leave the piazza to the right of the palace, heading down Via in Aquiro.

The street leads to a sixth-century B.C. **Egyptian obelisk** taken as a trophy by Augustus after his victory in Egypt over Mark Antony and Cleopatra. The obelisk was set up as a sundial. Walk the zodiac markings to the well-guarded front door. This is Italy's

Parliament building, where the lower house meets, and you may see politicians, political demonstrations, and TV cameras.

To your right is Piazza Colonna, where we're heading next—unless you like gelato...

A two-block detour to the left (past Albergo Nazionale) brings you to Rome's most famous *gelateria.* **Giolitti's** is cheap for take-out or elegant and splurge-worthy for a sit among classy locals (open daily until past midnight, Via Uffici del Vicario 40); get your gelato in a cone *(cono)* or cup *(coppetta).*

Piazza Colonna features a huge second-century column. Its reliefs depict the victories of Emperor Marcus Aurelius over the barbarians. When Marcus died in A.D. 180, the barbarians began to get the upper hand, beginning Rome's long three-century fall. The big, important-looking palace houses the headquarters for the deputies (or cabinet) of the prime minister.

Noisy **Via del Corso** is Rome's main north-south boulevard. It's named for the Berber horse races—without riders—that took place here during Carnevale. This wild tradition continued until the late 1800s, when a series of fatal accidents (including, reportedly, one in front of Queen Margherita) led to its cancellation. Historically the street was filled with meat shops. When it became one of Rome's first gaslit streets in 1854, these butcher shops were banned and replaced by classier boutiques, jewelers, and antiques dealers. Nowadays most of Via del Corso is closed to traffic for a few hours every evening and becomes a wonderful parade of Romans out for a stroll (see my "Dolce Vita Stroll," earlier).

Cross Via del Corso to enter a big palatial building with columns, which houses the Galleria del Sordi shopping mall. Inside, take the fork to the right and exit out the back. (If you're here after 22:00, when the mall is closed, circle around the right side of the Galleria on Via dei Sabini.) Once out the back, head up Via de Crociferi, to the roar of the water, lights, and people of the Trevi Fountain.

The **Trevi Fountain** shows how Rome took full advantage of the abundance of water brought into the city by its great aqueducts. This watery Baroque avalanche by Nicola Salvi was completed in 1762. Salvi used the palace behind the fountain as a theatrical backdrop for the figure of "Ocean," who represents water in every form. The statue surfs through his wet kingdom—with water gushing from 24 spouts and tumbling over 30 different kinds of plants—while Triton blows his conch shell.

The magic of the square is enhanced by the fact that no streets directly approach it. You can hear the excitement as you approach, and then—*bam!*—you're there. The scene is always lively, with lucky Romeos clutching dates while unlucky ones clutch beers. Romantics toss a coin over their shoulder, thinking it will give

ROME

them a wish and assure their return to Rome. That may sound silly, but every year I go through this tourist ritual...and it actually seems to work.

Take some time to people-watch (whisper a few breathy *bellos* or *bellas*) before leaving. There's a peaceful zone at water level on the far right.

Facing the Trevi Fountain, go forward, walking along the right side of the fountain on Via della Stamperia. Cross the busy Via del Tritone. Continue 100 yards and veer right at Via delle Fratte, a street that changes its name to Via Propaganda before ending at **Piazza di Spagna,** with the very popular Spanish Steps. The piazza is named for the Spanish Embassy to the Vatican, which has been here for 300 years. It's been the hangout of many Romantics over the years (Keats, Wagner, Openshaw, Goethe, and others). In the 1700s, British aristocrats on the "Grand Tour" of Europe came here to ponder Rome's decay. The British poet John Keats pondered his mortality, then died of tuberculosis at age 25 in the pink building on the right side of the steps. Fellow Romantic Lord Byron lived across the square at #66.

The Sinking Boat Fountain at the foot of the steps, built by Bernini or his father, Pietro, is powered by an aqueduct. Actually, all of Rome's fountains are aqueduct-powered; their spurts are determined by the water pressure provided by the various aqueducts. This one, for instance, is much weaker than Trevi's gush.

The piazza is a thriving night scene. It's clear that the main sight here is not the famous steps, but the people who sit on them. Window-shop along Via Condotti, which stretches away from the steps. This is where Gucci and other big names cater to the trendsetting jet set. Facing the Spanish Steps, you can walk right, about a block, to tour one of the world's biggest and most lavish McDonald's (salad bar, WC).

Our walk is finished. If you'd like to reach the top of the steps sweat-free, there's a free elevator just outside the Spagna Metro stop (elevator closes at 21:00; Metro stop is to the left of the Spanish Steps). Afterward, you can zip home on the Metro (usually open until 22:00) or grab a taxi at either the north or south side of the piazza.

Sights in Rome

I've clustered Rome's sights into walkable neighborhoods, some quite close together (see the "Rome's Neighborhoods" map, earlier). For example, the Colosseum and the Forum are a few minutes' walk from Capitol Hill; a 10-minute walk beyond that is the Pantheon. I like to group these sights into one great day, starting at the Colosseum and ending at the Pantheon.

Rome

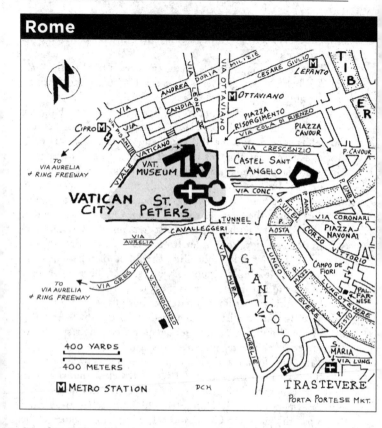

Ancient Rome

The core of the ancient city, where the grandest monuments were built, is between the Colosseum and Capitol Hill. To the north, this ancient area flows into the Renaissance at Capitol Hill, then into the modern era at Piazza Venezia.

The Colosseum and Nearby

▲▲▲**Colosseum (Colosseo)**—This 2,000-year-old building is the classic example of Roman engineering. The Romans pioneered the use of concrete and the rounded arch, which enabled them to build on this tremendous scale. While the essential structure of the Colosseum is Roman, the four-story facade is decorated with mostly Greek columns—Doric-like Tuscan columns on the ground level, Ionic on the second story, Corinthian on the next level, and at the top, half-columns with a mix of all three. Built when the Roman Empire was at its peak in A.D. 80, the Colosseum represents Rome at its grandest. The Flavian Amphitheater (the Colosseum's real name) was an arena for gladiator contests and

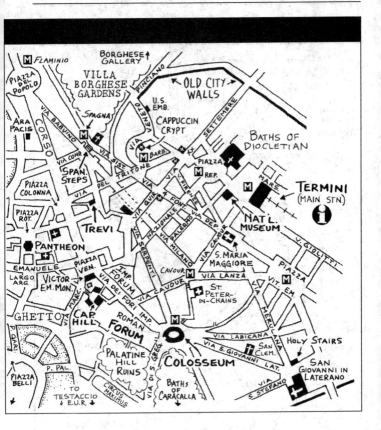

public spectacles. When killing became a spectator sport, the Romans wanted to share the fun with as many people as possible, so they stuck two semicircular theaters together to create a freestanding amphitheater. The outside (where slender cypress trees stand today) was decorated with a 100-foot-tall bronze statue of Nero that gleamed in the sunlight. In a later age, the colossal structure was nicknamed a "coloss-eum," the wonder of its age. It could accommodate 50,000 roaring fans (100,000 thumbs). This was where ancient Romans—whose taste for violence was the equal of modern America's—enjoyed their *Dirty Harry* and *Terminator*. Gladiators, criminals, and wild animals fought to the death in every conceivable scenario. The bit of reconstructed Colosseum floor gives you an accurate sense of the original floor and the subterranean warren where animals were held, then lifted up in elevators. Released at floor level, the animals would pop out from behind blinds into the arena—the gladiator didn't know where, when, or by what he'd be attacked.

Cost and Hours: €12 combo-ticket also includes Roman

Colosseum

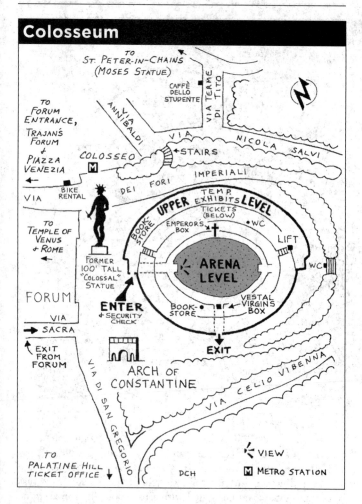

Forum and Palatine Hill; ticket valid two consecutive days—one entry per sight; also covered by the Roma Pass. Open daily 8:30 until one hour before sunset: April-Sept until 19:15, Oct until 18:30, off-season closes as early as 16:30; last entry one hour before closing; tel. 06-3996-7700.

Getting There: Metro: Colosseo. Bus #60 is handy for hotels near Via Firenze and Via Nazionale. Bus #87 links Largo Argentina with the Colosseum.

Sightseeing Strategy: It makes sense to see the Colosseum, Forum, and Palatine Hill in succession on a single visit. If you're getting a Roma Pass (you could buy it at the *tabacchi* shop in the Colosseo Metro station), this order works best: See the blockbuster Colosseum first, when you're freshest, then the Forum, then the

Palatine if you have energy left over. But if you're getting a combo-ticket, this is the most efficient order: Buy your combo-ticket at the (less-crowded) Palatine entrance and sightsee the Palatine, ending at the Forum's Arch of Titus. From there, do the Forum. Then exit the Forum at the east end (Colosseum), and finish with the Colosseum.

Avoiding Lines: The lines in front of the Colosseum are for buying tickets and for security checks, not for actually entering the sight. Everyone has to wait in the security line to go through the metal detectors first, but once you're through that—if you have your ticket or pass already—stay to the left and muscle your way past the ticket-buying crowd to go directly to the turnstile, which never has a line. Enter by inserting your ticket in the turnstile or flashing your pass. You'll likely save lots of time if you get your ticket or pass in advance using one of these alternatives:

1. If you're planning on getting a €25 Roma Pass, buy it at a less-crowded place to bypass the ticket-buying line at the Colosseum. You can purchase the pass at the *tabacchi* shop in the Colosseo Metro station, or at the entrance to Palatine Hill on Via di San Gregorio (facing the Forum, with Colosseum at your back, go left down the street). Avoid buying it at the Forum, which also tends to have lines.

2. If you're buying a combo-ticket, get it at the less-crowded Palatine Hill entrance. Or buy and print it online in advance at www.ticketclic.it (€1.50 booking fee, good for two consecutive days, not changeable). Note that the "free tickets" you'll see listed are valid only for EU citizens with ID.

3. Pay to join an official guided tour (€4 plus €12 combo-ticket, see "Tours," below). Once past the security check, tell one of the guards that you want to purchase a guided tour and he will usher you toward the ticket booth marked *Visite Guidate* (you'll also pay for your ticket here).

Private walking-tour guides (or their American assistants) linger outside the Colosseum, offering tours that include the admission fee and allow you to skip the line. This will cost you a few extra euros (€22 for two-hour tours of the Colosseum, Palatine Hill, and Forum, including the €12 ticket), but can save time; however, see the warning below.

Warnings: It can be hard to judge the length of the ticket line because it's tucked into the Colosseum arcade. Unscrupulous private guides tell tourists that there's a long line, when there really might be no line at all. If you do sign up with a private guide, confirm that your tour will start right away, and look at your ticket to make sure that it includes admission to Palatine Hill and Forum (some guides, claiming to cover all three sights, will purchase a group Colosseum-only ticket, then say "ciao" after the Colosseum tour).

ROME

Also beware of the **greedy gladiators.** For a fee, the incredibly crude modern-day gladiators snuff out their cigarettes and pose for photos. They take easy-to-swindle tourists for too much money. Watch out if you tangle with these guys (they're accustomed to getting as much as €100 from naive tourists). If you go for it, €4-5 for one photo usually keeps them appeased.

And finally, look out for **pickpockets.** The Colosseum's exterior is traditionally a happy hunting ground for pickpockets and con artists.

Tours: A dry but fact-filled **audioguide** is available just past the turnstiles (€4.50 for 2 hours of use). A handheld **videoguide** senses where you are in the site and plays related video clips (€5.50, pick up after turnstiles). Guided **tours** in English (which let you skip the ticket line) depart nearly hourly between 10:00 and 17:00, and last 45 minutes to one hour (€4 plus your €12 ticket, purchase inside the Colosseum near the ticket booth marked *Visite Guidate*). You can download a free Rick Steves **audio tour** of the Colosseum for your mobile device via www.ricksteves.com/audioeurope, iTunes, or the Rick Steves Audio Europe smartphone app.

▲**Arch of Constantine**—If you are a Christian, were raised a Christian, or simply belong to a so-called "Christian nation," ponder this arch. It marks one of the great turning points in history—the military coup that made Christianity mainstream. In A.D. 312, Emperor Constantine defeated his rival Maxentius in the crucial Battle of the Milvian Bridge. The night before, he had seen a vision of a cross in the sky. Constantine—whose mother and sister were Christians—became sole emperor and legalized Christianity. With this one battle, a once-obscure Jewish sect with a handful of followers was now the state religion of the entire Western world. In A.D. 300, you could be killed for being a Christian; a century later, you could be killed for not being one. Church enrollment boomed.

The restored arch is like an ancient museum. It's decorated entirely with recycled carvings originally made for other buildings. By covering it with exquisite carvings of high Roman art—works that glorified previous emperors—Constantine put himself in their league. Hadrian is featured in the round reliefs, with Marcus Aurelius in the square reliefs higher up. The big statues on top are of Trajan and Augustus. Originally, Augustus drove a chariot similar to the one topping the modern Victor Emmanuel II monument. Fourth-century Rome may have been in decline, but Constantine clung to its glorious past.

▲**St. Peter-in-Chains Church (San Pietro in Vincoli)**—Built in the fifth century to house the chains that held St. Peter, this church is most famous for its Michelangelo statue. Check out the much-venerated chains under the high altar, then focus on mighty

Ancient Rome Sights

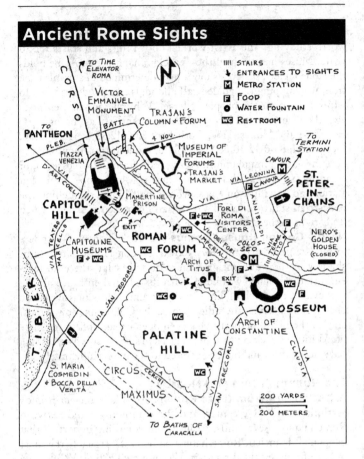

Moses. (Note that this isn't the famous St. Peter's Basilica, which is at Vatican City.)

Pope Julius II commissioned Michelangelo to build a massive tomb, with 48 huge statues, crowned by a grand statue of this egomaniacal pope. The pope had planned to have his tomb placed in the center of St. Peter's Basilica. When Julius died, the work had barely been started, and no one had the money or necessary commitment to Julius to finish the project.

In 1542, some of the remnants of the tomb project were brought to St. Peter-in-Chains and pieced together by Michelangelo's assistants. Some of the best statues ended up elsewhere, like the *Prisoners* in Florence, and the *Slaves* in the Louvre. *Moses* and the Louvre's *Slaves* are the only statues Michelangelo personally completed for the project. Flanking *Moses* are the Old Testament sister-wives of Jacob, Leah (to our right) and Rachel, both begun by Michelangelo but probably finished by pupils.

ROME

This powerful statue of Moses—mature Michelangelo—is worth studying. The artist worked on it in fits and starts for 30 years. Moses has received the Ten Commandments. As he holds the stone tablets, his eyes show a man determined to stop his tribe from worshipping the golden calf and idols...a man determined to win salvation for the people of Israel. Why the horns? Centuries ago, the Hebrew word for "rays" was mistranslated as "horns."

Cost and Hours: Free, April-Sept 8:00-12:30 & 15:30-19:00, Oct-March 8:00-12:30 & 15:00-18:00, modest dress required; the church is a 15-minute uphill, zigzag walk from the Colosseum, or a shorter, simpler walk from the Cavour Metro stop—from that station, go downhill on Via Cavour a half-block, then climb the pedestrian staircase called Via di San Francesco di Paola, which leads right to the church.

Nero's Golden House (Domus Aurea)—The sparse underground remains of Emperor Nero's "Golden House" are a faint shadow of their ancient grandeur. In its heyday, the gold leaf-encrusted residence was huge, with its original entrance all the way over at the Arch of Titus in the Forum. Nero's massive estate once sprawled across the valley (where the Colosseum now stands) and up the hill—the part that's been open on-and-off to the public. While it's exciting to think that Nero's house survives, it's in a sad state of ruin, and has been closed to the public indefinitely.

The Roman Forum and Nearby

▲▲▲Roman Forum (Foro Romano)—This is ancient Rome's birthplace and civic center, and the common ground between Rome's famous seven hills. As just about anything important that happened in ancient Rome happened here, it's arguably the most important piece of real estate in Western civilization. While only a few fragments of that glorious past remain, history-seekers find plenty to ignite their imaginations amid the half-broken columns and arches.

Cost and Hours: €12 combo-ticket includes Colosseum and Palatine Hill—see page 866, audioguide available; open daily 8:30 until one hour before sunset: April-Sept until 19:15, Oct until 18:30, off-season closes as early as 16:30; last entry one hour before closing, Metro: Colosseo, tel. 06-3996-7700. See my "Roman Forum Walk," earlier.

▲▲Palatine Hill (Monte Palatino)—The hill overlooking the Forum is jam-packed with history—"the huts of Romulus," the huge Imperial Palace, a view of the Circus Maximus—but there's only the barest skeleton of rubble left to tell the story.

We get our word "palace" from this hill, where the emperors chose to live. The Palatine Hill was once so filled with palaces that

ROME

later emperors had to build out. (Looking up at it from the Forum, you see the substructure that supported these long-gone palaces.)

The Palatine museum contains statues and frescoes that help you imagine the luxury of the imperial Palatine. From the pleasant garden, you'll get an overview of the Forum. On the far side, look down into an emperor's private stadium and then beyond at the dusty Circus Maximus, once a chariot course. Imagine the cheers, jeers, and furious betting.

While many tourists consider the Palatine Hill just extra credit after the Forum, it offers an insight into the greatness of Rome that's well worth the effort. (And, if you're visiting the Colosseum or Forum, you've got a ticket whether you like it or not.)

Cost and Hours: €12 combo-ticket also includes Roman Forum and Colosseum—see page 866; open same hours as Roman Forum and Colosseum, Metro: Colosseo. Audioguides cost €4 (€6 version includes Roman Forum, must leave ID). Guided tours in English are offered once daily at 11:30 (€4, 45 minutes, not always available off-season); ask for information at the ticket booth. The entrance is on Via di San Gregorio (facing the Forum with the Colosseum at your back, it's down the street to your left). You can also enter the Palatine from within the Roman Forum—just climb the hill from the Arch of Titus.

Mamertine Prison—This 2,500-year-old cistern-like prison, where—according to tradition—the Romans imprisoned Saints Peter and Paul, isn't worth a visit, as its artifacts have been replaced by a "multi-media" walk-through. If you do go in, ignore the modern floor and look up at the hole in the ceiling, through which prisoners were lowered. Then take the stairs down to the level of the actual prison floor. Downstairs was once the column to which Peter was chained. It's said that a miraculous fountain sprang up in this room so that Peter could convert and baptize his jailers, who were also subsequently martyred. The upside-down cross commemorates Peter's upside-down crucifixion (€10, daily 9:00-19:00, at the foot of Capitol Hill, near Forum's Arch of Septimius Severus, Metro: Colosseo, tel. 06-679-2902).

Imagine humans, amid fat rats and rotting corpses, awaiting slow deaths. On the walls near the entry were once lists of notable prisoners (Christian and non-Christian) and the ways they were executed: *strangolati, decapitato, morto per fame* (died of hunger). The sign by the Christian names read, "Here suffered, victorious for the triumph of Christ, these martyr saints."

▲Trajan's Column, Market, and Imperial Forums—This grand column is the best example of "continuous narration" that we have from antiquity. More than 2,500 figures scroll around the 140-foot-high column, telling of Trajan's victorious Dacian campaign (circa A.D. 103, in present-day Romania), from the assembling of the army at the bottom to the victory sacrifice at the top. The ashes of Trajan and his wife were once held in the base, and the sun once glinted off a polished bronze statue of Trajan at the top. (Today, St. Peter is on top.) Study the propaganda that winds up the column like a scroll, trumpeting Trajan's wonderful military exploits. Viewing balconies once stood on either side, but it seems likely that Trajan fans came away only with a feeling that the greatness of their emperor and empire was beyond comprehension. This column marked "Trajan's Forum," which was built to handle the shopping needs of a wealthy city of more than a million people. Commercial, political, religious, and social activities all mixed in the forum.

Nestled into the cutaway curve of Quirinal Hill is the semicircular brick complex of **Trajan's Market.** It was likely part shopping mall, part warehouse, and part administration building. Or, as some archaeologists have recently suggested, it may have contained mostly government offices.

Paying the admission fee gets you inside Trajan's Market, Trajan's Forum, and the **Museum of the Imperial Forums.** The museum takes you through discoveries from the forums of emperors Julius Caesar, Augustus, Nerva, and Trajan, with fragments of statues and a slideshow that reconstructs how the forum looked in each emperor's time.

Trajan's Column is just a few steps off Piazza Venezia (a hub for major bus routes #40, #64, and #87), on Via dei Fori Imperiali, across the street from the Victor Emmanuel Monument. Trajan's Market can be entered only through the Museum of the Imperial Forums at Via IV Novembre 94. Trajan's Forum stretches southeast of the column toward the Colosseo Metro stop and the Colosseum itself.

Cost and Hours: €6.50, includes entry to the market ruins, Tue-Sun 9:00-19:00, closed Mon, last entry 30 minutes before closing, Via IV Novembre 94, up the staircase from Trajan's Column; tel. 06-0608, ww.mercatiditraiano.it.

Bocca della Verità—The legendary "Mouth of Truth" at the Church of Santa Maria in Cosmedin draws a playful crowd. Stick your hand in the mouth of the gaping stone face in the porch wall. As the legend goes (and was popularized by the 1953 film *Roman Holiday,* starring Gregory Peck and Audrey Hepburn), if you're a liar, your hand will be gobbled up. The mouth is only accessible when the church gate is open.

Cost and Hours: €0.50, daily 9:30-17:50, closes earlier offseason, Piazza Bocca della Verità, near the north end of Circus Maximus.

Capitol Hill and Nearby

Of Rome's famous seven hills, this is the smallest, tallest, and most famous—home of the ancient Temple of Jupiter and the center of city government for 2,500 years. There are several ways to get to the top of Capitol Hill. (While I call it "Capitol Hill" for simplicity, it's correctly called "Capitoline Hill.") If you're coming from the north (from Piazza Venezia), take Michelangelo's impressive stairway to the right of the big, white Victor Emmanuel Monument. Coming from the southeast (the Forum), take the steep staircase near the Arch of Septimius Severus. From near Trajan's Forum along Via dei Fori Imperiali, take the winding road. All three converge at the top, in the square called Campidoglio (kahm-pee-DOHL-yoh).

Shortcut: A clever little "back door" gives you access from the top of Capitol Hill directly to the top of the Victor Emmanuel Monument and the Santa Maria in Aracoeli church, saving lots of uphill stair-climbing. To find the back door, locate the She-Wolf statue (to the left of the mayoral palace). Climb the wide set of stairs near the statue (the highest set of stairs you see). To reach the church, turn left at the column in the middle of the staircase, following signs to *Aracoeli*. To reach the Victor Emmanuel Monument, continue up to the top of the steps, pass through the iron gate, and enter the small unmarked door at #13 on the right. You'll soon emerge on a café terrace midway up the monument with vast views. The Rome from the Sky elevator to the top is just around the corner (see page 909).

▲**Capitol Hill Square (Campidoglio)**—This square atop the hill, once the religious and political center of ancient Rome, is still the home of the city's government. In the 1530s, the pope called on Michelangelo to re-establish this square as a grand center. Michelangelo placed the ancient equestrian statue of Marcus Aurelius as the square's focal point. Effective. (The original statue is now in the adjacent museum.) The twin buildings on either side are the Capitoline Museums. Behind the replica of the statue is the mayoral palace (Palazzo Senatorio).

Michelangelo intended that people approach the square from his grand stairway off Piazza Venezia. From the top of the stairway, you see the new Renaissance face of Rome, with its back to the Forum. Michelangelo gave the buildings the "giant order"—huge pilasters make the existing two-story buildings feel one-storied and more harmonious with the new square. Notice how the statues atop these buildings welcome you and then draw you in.

The terraces just downhill (past either side of the mayor's palace) offer grand views of the Forum. To the left of the mayor's palace is a copy of the famous She-Wolf statue on a column. Farther down is *il nasone* ("the big nose"), a refreshing water fountain. Block the spout with your fingers, and water spurts up for

Capitol Hill & Piazza Venezia

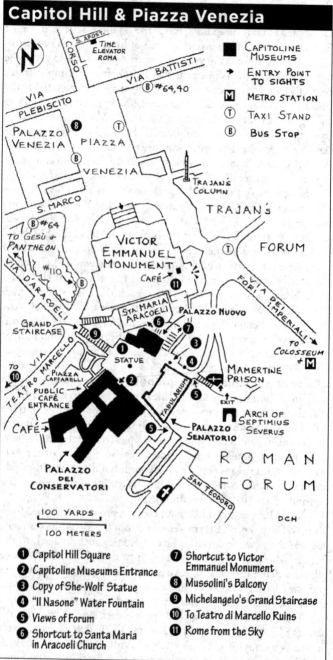

100 YARDS

100 METERS

1 Capitol Hill Square
2 Capitoline Museums Entrance
3 Copy of She-Wolf Statue
4 "Il Nasone" Water Fountain
5 Views of Forum
6 Shortcut to Santa Maria in Aracoeli Church

7 Shortcut to Victor Emmanuel Monument
8 Mussolini's Balcony
9 Michelangelo's Grand Staircase
10 To Teatro di Marcello Ruins
11 Rome from the Sky

drinking. Romans joke that a cheap Roman boy takes his date out for a drink at *il nasone*. Near the She-Wolf statue is the staircase leading to a shortcut to the Victor Emmanuel Monument (for details, see "Shortcut," above).

▲▲**Capitoline Museums (Musei Capitolini)**—This museum encompasses two buildings (Palazzo dei Conservatori and Palazzo Nuovo), connected by an underground passage that leads to the vacant Tabularium and panoramic views of the Roman Forum.

Cost and Hours: €8-11 depending on cost of temporary exhibit, €8.50-13 combo-ticket with Montemartini Museum, Tue-Sun 9:00-20:00, closed Mon, last entry one hour before closing, tel. 06-8205-9127, www.museicapitolini.org.

Overview: The museum's layout—with two different buildings connected by an underground passage—can be confusing. To identify the museum's two buildings, face the equestrian statue (with your back to the grand stairway). You'll enter at the Palazzo dei Conservatori (on your right), cross underneath the square (beneath the Palazzo Senatorio, or mayoral palace, not open to public), and exit from the Palazzo Nuovo (on your left).

At the Palazzo dei Conservatori entrance, buy your ticket and consider renting the good €5 audioguide (€6.20/2 people).

The **Palazzo dei Conservatori** claims to be one of the world's oldest museums, founded in 1471 when a pope gave ancient statues to the citizens of Rome. In the courtyard, enjoy the massive chunks of Constantine: his head, hand, and foot. When intact, this giant held the place of honor in the Basilica of Constantine in the Forum. The museum is worthwhile, with lavish rooms and several great statues. You'll see the 13th-century *Capitoline She-Wolf* (the little statues of Romulus and Remus were added in the Renaissance). Don't miss the *Boy Extracting a Thorn* and the enchanting *Commodus as Hercules*. Behind Commodus is a statue of his dad, Marcus Aurelius, on a horse. The greatest surviving equestrian statue of antiquity, this was the original centerpiece of the square (where a copy stands today). Christians in the Dark Ages thought that the statue's hand was raised in blessing, which probably led to their misidentifying him as Constantine, the first Christian emperor. While most pagan statues were destroyed by Christians, "Constantine" was spared.

The second-floor café, Caffè Capitolino, has a splendid patio offering city views. It's lovely at sunset (public entrance for non-museum-goers off Piazza Caffarelli and through door #4).

Go downstairs to the **Tabularium**. Built in the first century B.C., these sturdy vacant rooms once held the archives of ancient Rome. The word Tabularium comes from "tablet," on which Romans wrote their laws. You won't see any tablets, but you will see a superb head-on view of the Forum from the windows.

Leave the Tabularium and enter the **Palazzo Nuovo,** which houses mostly portrait busts of forgotten emperors. But it also has two must-see statues: the *Dying Gaul* and the *Capitoline Venus* (both on the first floor up).

Santa Maria in Aracoeli—This church is built on the site where Emperor Augustus (supposedly) had a premonition of the coming of Mary and Christ standing on an "altar in the sky" *(ara coeli).* The church is Rome in a nutshell, where you can time-travel across 2,000 years by standing in one spot.

Cost and Hours: Daily 9:00-12:30 & 15:00-18:30. It's atop Capitol Hill, squeezed between the Victor Emmanuel Monument and the square called Campidoglio. While dedicated pilgrims climb up the long, steep staircase from street level (the right side of Victor Emmanuel Monument, as you face it), savvy sightseers prefer to enter through the "back door" atop Capitol Hill (see "Shortcut," page 905).

Piazza Venezia

This vast square, dominated by the big, white Victor Emmanuel Monument, is a major transportation hub and the focal point of modern Rome. (The square will be dug up for years—Metro line C is under construction, and when anything of archaeological importance is uncovered, progress is interrupted.) Stand with your back to the monument and look down Via del Corso, the city's axis, surrounded by Rome's classiest shopping district. In the 1930s, Benito Mussolini whipped up Italy's nationalistic fervor from a balcony above the square (with your back to Victor Emmanuel Monument, it's the less-grand balcony on the left). Fascist masses filled the square screaming, "Four more years!"—or something like that. Mussolini created boulevard Via dei Fori Imperiali (to your right) to open up views of the Colosseum in the distance to impress his visiting friend Adolf Hitler. Mussolini lied to his people, mixing fear and patriotism to push his country to the right and embroil the Italians in expensive and regrettable wars. In 1945, they shot and hung Mussolini from a meat hook in Milan.

Circling around the right side of the Victor Emmanuel Monument, look down into the ditch on your left to see the ruins of an ancient apartment building from the first century A.D.; part of it was transformed into a tiny church (faded frescoes and bell tower). Rome was built in layers—almost everywhere you go, there's an earlier version beneath your feet. (The hop-on, hop-off Trambus 110 stops just across the busy intersection from here.)

Continuing on, you reach two staircases leading up Capitol Hill. One is Michelangelo's grand staircase up to the Campidoglio. The longer of the two leads to the Santa Maria in Aracoeli church, a good example of the earliest style of Christian churches (described earlier). The contrast between this climb-on-your-knees ramp to God's house and Michelangelo's elegant stairs illustrates the changes Renaissance humanism brought civilization.

From the bottom of Michelangelo's stairs, look right several blocks down the street to see a condominium actually built upon the surviving ancient pillars and arches of Teatro di Marcello.

Victor Emmanuel Monument—This oversize monument to Italy's first king, built to celebrate the 50th anniversary of the country's unification in 1870, was part of Italy's push to overcome the new country's strong regionalism and create a national identity. The scale of the monument is over-the-top. The 43-foot-long statue of the king on the horse is the biggest equestrian statue in the world. The king's moustache is over five feet wide, and a person could fit into the horse's hoof. Open to the public, the structure offers a grand view of the Eternal City (free, 242 punishing steps to the highest viewpoint accessible on foot—unless you take the shortcut from Capitol Hill described on page 905).

Locals love to hate the "Altar of the Nation." Romans think of the 200-foot-high, 500-foot-wide monument not as an altar of the fatherland, but as "the wedding cake," "the typewriter," or "the dentures." (For short, they call it "the Vittoriano.") It wouldn't be so bad if it weren't sitting on a priceless acre of ancient Rome and if they had chosen better marble (the in-your-face white picks up the pollution horribly, requiring frequent cleaning). Soldiers guard Italy's Tomb of the Unknown Soldier as the eternal flame flickers.

The Victor Emmanuel Monument also houses a little-visited **Museum of the Risorgimento,** which explains the movement and war that led to the unification of Italy in 1870 (free, daily 9:30-18:30, tel. 06-679-3598, café).

▲**Rome from the Sky**—This elevator, located near the top of the Victor Emmanuel Monument next to the outdoor café, zips you to the rooftop for the grandest 360-degree view of the center of Rome (even better than from the top of St. Peter's dome). Helpful panoramic diagrams describe the skyline, with powerful binoculars available for zooming in on particular sights. Go in late afternoon, when it's beginning to cool off and Rome glows.

Cost and Hours: €7, Mon-Thu 9:30-18:30, Fri-Sun 9:30-19:30, ticket office closes 45 minutes earlier, tel. 06-6920-2049, follow signs inside the Victor Emmanuel Monument to *ascensori panoramici* or take the shortcut from Capitol Hill.

Pantheon Neighborhood

The area around the Pantheon is the heart of Rome. This neighborhood stretches eastward from the Tiber River through Campo de' Fiori and Piazza Navona, past the Pantheon to the Trevi Fountain. Besides being home to ancient sights and historic churches, it's also the place that gives Rome its urban-village feel. Wander narrow streets, sample the many shops and eateries, and gather with the locals in squares marked by a bubbling fountain. Exploring is especially good in the evening, when the restaurants bustle and streets are jammed with foot traffic. For more on nocturnal sightseeing, see my "Night Walk Across Rome," earlier.

Getting There: To reach the Pantheon neighborhood, you can walk (it's a 20-minute walk from Capitol Hill), take a taxi, or catch a bus. Buses #64 and #40 carry tourists and pickpockets frequently between Termini train station and Vatican City, stopping at a chaotic square called Largo Argentina, located a few blocks south of the Pantheon. (Take either Via dei Cestari or Via di Torre Argentina north to the Pantheon.) The *elettrico* minibus #116 runs between Campo de' Fiori and Piazza Barberini via the Pantheon. The most dramatic approach is on foot coming from Piazza Navona along Via Giustiniani, which spills directly into Piazza della Rotunda, offering the classic Pantheon view.

▲▲▲**Pantheon**—For the greatest look at the splendor of Rome, antiquity's best-preserved interior is a must. Because the Pantheon became a church dedicated to the martyrs just after the fall of Rome, the barbarians left it alone, and the locals didn't use it as a quarry. The portico is called "Rome's umbrella"—a fun local gathering in a rainstorm. Walk past its one-piece granite columns (biggest in Italy, shipped from Egypt) and through the original bronze doors. Sit inside under the glorious skylight and enjoy classical architecture at its best.

The dome, 142 feet high and wide, was Europe's biggest until the Renaissance. Michelangelo's dome at St. Peter's, while much higher, is about three feet narrower. The brilliance of this dome's construction astounded architects through the ages. During the Renaissance, Brunelleschi was given permission to cut into the dome (see the little square hole above and to the right of the entrance) to analyze the material. The concrete dome gets thinner and lighter with height—the highest part is volcanic pumice.

This wonderfully harmonious architecture greatly inspired Raphael and other artists of the Renaissance. Raphael, along with Italy's first two kings, chose to be buried here.

The Pantheon is the only ancient building in Rome continuously used since its construction. When you leave, notice that the building is sunken below current street level, showing how the rest of the city has risen on 20 centuries of rubble.

Cost and Hours: Free, Mon-Sat 8:30-19:30, Sun 9:00-18:00, holidays 9:00-13:00, closed for Mass Sat at 17:00 and Sun at 10:30, tel. 06-6830-0230.

Audio Tour: You can download a free Rick Steves audio tour

Pantheon Neighborhood

of the Pantheon for your mobile device via www.ricksteves.com
/audioeurope, iTunes, or the Rick Steves Audio Europe smartphone app.

Nearby: The nearest WCs are at bars and downstairs in the
McDonald's on the Pantheon's square. Several reasonable eateries
are a block or two north up Via del Pantheon. Some of Rome's
best gelato and coffee are nearby. For dining recommendations, see
page 962.

▲▲**Churches near the Pantheon**—The **Church of San Luigi
dei Francesi** has a magnificent chapel painted by Caravaggio (free,
daily 10:00-12:30 & 16:00-19:00). The only Gothic church in Rome
is **Santa Maria sopra Minerva**, with a little-known Michelangelo
statue, *Christ Bearing the Cross* (free, Mon-Fri 7:00-19:00, Sat-Sun
8:00-13:00 & 15:30-19:00, on a little square behind Pantheon, to
the east). The **Church of San Ignazio,** several blocks east of the
Pantheon, is a riot of Baroque illusions with a false dome (free, daily

7:30-12:30 & 15:00-19:15). A few blocks away, across Corso Vittorio Emanuele, is the rich and Baroque **Gesù Church,** headquarters of the Jesuits in Rome (free, daily 7:00-12:30 & 16:00-19:45).

▲**Galleria Doria Pamphilj**—This underappreciated gallery, tucked away in the heart of the old city, fills a palace on Piazza del Collegio Romano. It offers a rare chance to wander through a noble family's lavish rooms with the prince who calls this downtown mansion home. Well, almost. Through an audioguide, the prince lovingly narrates his family's story, including how the Doria Pamphilj (pahm-FEEL-yee) family's cozy relationship with the pope inspired the word "nepotism." Highlights include paintings by Caravaggio, Titian, and Raphael, and portraits of Pope Innocent X by Diego Velázquez (on canvas) and Gian Lorenzo Bernini (in marble). The fancy rooms of the palace are interesting, with a mini–Versailles-like hall of mirrors and paintings lining the walls to the ceiling in the style typical of 18th-century galleries.

Cost and Hours: €9.50, includes worthwhile audioguide, daily 10:00-17:00, last entry 45 minutes before closing, café, from Piazza Venezia walk 2 blocks up Via del Corso to #305, tel. 06-679-7323, www.dopart.it/roma.

Time Elevator Roma—This cheesy, overpriced show is really just for kids. The 45-minute multiscreen show jolts you through the centuries. Equipped with headphones, you get nauseous in a comfortable, air-conditioned theater as the history of Rome unfolds before you—from the founding of the city, through its rise and fall, to its Renaissance rebound, and up to the present.

Cost and Hours: €12, children 5-12-€9, daily 10:30-19:30, shows at the bottom of each hour, last showing at 19:30, no kids under 39 inches, just off Via del Corso, a 3-minute walk from Piazza Venezia, across from Galleria Doria Pamphilj at Via dei S.S. Apostoli 20, tel. 06-9774-6243, www.timeelevator.it.

Piazza di Pietra (Piazza of Stone)—The square was actually a quarry set up to chew away at the abandoned Roman building. You can still see the holes that hungry medieval scavengers chipped into the columns to steal the metal pins that held the slabs together (two blocks toward Via del Corso from Pantheon).

▲**Trevi Fountain**—The bubbly Baroque fountain, worth ▲▲ by night, is a minor sight to art scholars...but a major nighttime gathering spot for teens on the make and tourists tossing coins. The coins tourists deposit daily are collected to feed Rome's poor. (For more information, see page 894.)

Near Termini Train Station

These sights are within a 10-minute walk of the train station. By Metro, use the Termini stop for the National Museum and the Repubblica stop for the rest.

Near Termini Train Station

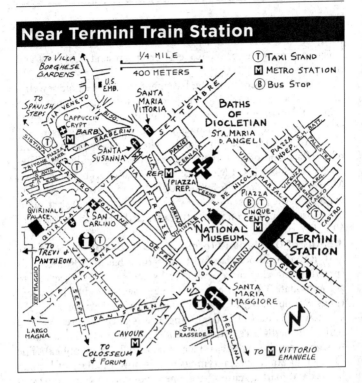

▲▲▲**National Museum of Rome (Museo Nazionale Romano Palazzo Massimo alle Terme)**—The National Museum's main branch, at Palazzo Massimo, houses the greatest collection of ancient Roman art anywhere. It's a historic yearbook of Roman marble statues with some rare Greek originals. On the ground floor alone, you can look eye-to-eye with Julius and Augustus Caesar, Alexander the Great, and Socrates.

On the first floor, along with statues and busts showing such emperors as Trajan and Hadrian, you'll see the best-preserved Roman copy of the Greek *Discus Thrower*. Statues of athletes like this commonly stood in the baths, where Romans cultivated healthy bodies, minds, and social skills, hoping to lead well-rounded lives. Other statues on this floor originally stood in the pleasure gardens of the Roman rich—surrounded by greenery, with the splashing sound of fountains, the statues all painted in bright, lifelike colors. Though executed by Romans, the themes are mostly Greek, with godlike humans and human-looking gods.

The second floor features a collection of frescoes and mosaics that once decorated the walls and floors of Roman villas. They're remarkably realistic and unstuffy, featuring everyday people, animals, flowery patterns, and geometrical designs. The Villa Farnese frescoes—in black, red, yellow, and blue—are mostly architectural designs, with fake columns, friezes, and garlands. The Villa di Livia frescoes immerse you in a leafy green garden full of birds and fruit trees.

Finally, descend into the basement to see fine gold jewelry, dice, an abacus, and vault doors leading into the best coin collection in Europe, with fancy magnifying glasses maneuvering you through cases of coins from ancient Rome to modern times.

Cost and Hours: €10 combo-ticket covers nearby Museum of the Bath and other forgettable branches, audioguide-€4, Tue-Sun 9:00-19:45, closed Mon, last entry 45 minutes before closing, Metro: Termini, tel. 06-3996-7700). The museum is about 100 yards from the train station—as you leave the station, it's the sandstone-brick building on your left. Enter at the far end, at Largo di Villa Peretti.

▲**Baths of Diocletian (Terme di Diocleziano)**—Around A.D. 300, Emperor Diocletian built the largest baths in Rome. This sprawling meeting place—with baths and schmoozing spaces to accommodate 3,000 bathers at a time—was a big deal in ancient times. While much of it is still closed, three sections are open: The Church of Santa Maria degli Angeli was once the great central hall of the baths (free, Mon-Sat 7:00-18:30, Sun 7:00-19:30, closed to sightseers during Mass, faces Piazza della Repubblica). The Octagonal Hall, once a gymnasium, is now a gallery of Roman bronze and marble statues (free, open sporadically Sun 9:00-13:00 only, faces Piazza della Repubblica). The skippable Museum of the Bath, despite its name, has nothing on the baths (€10 combo-ticket covers National Museum of Rome and more, Tue-Sun 9:00-19:45, closed Mon, last entry 45 minutes before closing, audioguide-€4, Viale Enrico de Nicola 79, entrance faces Termini train station, tel. 06-3996-7700).

Santa Maria degli Angeli: From noisy Piazza della Repubblica, step through the curved brick wall of the ancient baths and into the vast and cool church built upon the remains of a vast and steamy Roman bath complex. The church we see today was (at least partly) designed by Michelangelo (1561), who used the baths' main hall as the nave. Later, when Piazza della Repubblica became an important Roman intersection, another architect renovated the church. To allow people to enter from the grand new piazza, he spun it 90 degrees, turning Michelangelo's nave into a long transept. The eight red granite columns are original, from ancient Rome—stand next to one and feel its five-foot girth. (Only the eight in the transept proper are original. The others are made of plastered-over brick.) In Roman times, this hall was covered with mosaics, marble, and gold, and lined with statues.

Octagonal Hall: Open only on occasional Sunday mornings, this octagonal building, capped by a dome with a hole in the top, may have served as a cool room *(frigidarium)*, with small pools of cold water for plunging into. Or, because of its many doors, it may simply have been a large intersection, connecting other parts of the baths. Originally, the floor was 25 feet lower—as you can see through the glass-covered hole in the floor. The graceful iron grid overhead supported the canopy of a 1928 planetarium.

▲**Santa Maria della Vittoria**—This church houses Bernini's statue, the swooning *St. Teresa in Ecstasy.*

The statue is to the left of the altar. Teresa has just been stabbed with God's arrow of fire. Now, the angel pulls it out and watches her reaction. Teresa swoons, her eyes roll up, her hand goes limp, she parts her lips...and moans. The smiling, cherubic angel understands just how she feels. Teresa, a 16th-century Spanish nun, later talked of the "sweetness" of "this intense pain," describing her oneness with God in ecstatic, even erotic, terms.

Bernini, the master of multimedia, pulls out all the stops to make this mystical vision real. Actual sunlight pours through the alabaster windows, bronze sunbeams shine on a marble angel holding a golden arrow. Teresa leans back on a cloud and her robe ripples from within, charged with her spiritual arousal. Bernini has created a little stage-setting of heaven. And watching from the "theater boxes" on either side are members of the family that commissioned the work.

Cost and Hours: Free, pay €0.50 for light, Mon-Sat 8:30-12:00 & 15:30-18:00, Sun 15:30-18:00, about 5 blocks northwest of Termini train station on Largo Susanna, Metro: Repubblica.

Santa Susanna Church—The home of the American Catholic Church in Rome, Santa Susanna holds Mass in English daily at 18:00 and on Sunday at 9:00 and 10:30. They arrange papal audiences (see page 929), and their excellent website contains tips for travelers and a list of convents that rent out rooms.

Cost and Hours: Free, Mon-Fri 9:00-12:00 & 16:00-18:00, closed Sat-Sun, Via XX Settembre 15, near recommended Via Firenze hotels, Metro: Repubblica, tel. 06-4201-4554, www.santa susanna.org.

Pilgrim's Rome

East of the Colosseum (and south of Termini train station) are several venerable churches that Catholic pilgrims make a point of visiting. Near one of the churches is a small WWII museum.

Church of San Giovanni in Laterano—Built by Constantine, the first Christian emperor, this was Rome's most important church through medieval times. A building alongside the church houses the Holy Stairs (Scala Santa) said to have been walked up by Jesus, which today are ascended by pilgrims on their knees.

Pilgrim's Rome

Cost and Hours: Free, audioguide—€5; church—daily 7:00-18:30; Holy Stairs—daily April-Sept 6:15-12:00 & 15:30-18:30, Oct-March 6:15-12:00 & 15:00-18:00; Piazza San Giovanni in Laterano, Metro: San Giovanni, or bus #85 or #87; tel. 06-6988-6409.

Museum of the Liberation of Rome (Museo Storico della Liberazione di Roma)—This small memorial museum, near the Church of San Giovanni in Laterano, is housed in the prison wing of the former Nazi police headquarters of occupied Rome. Other than a single printed sheet to help, there's little in English. Still, for those interested in resistance movements and the Nazi occupation, it's a stirring visit. You'll see a few artifacts, many photos of heroes, and a couple of cells preserved as they were found on June 4, 1944, when the city was liberated.

Cost and Hours: Free, Tue-Sun 9:30-12:30, Tue and Thu-Fri also 15:30-19:00, closed Mon and Aug, just behind the Holy Stairs at Via Tasso 145, tel. 06-700-3866.

Church of Santa Maria Maggiore—Some of Rome's best-surviving mosaics line the nave of this church built as Rome was falling. The nearby Church of Santa Prassede has still more early mosaics.

Cost and Hours: Free, daily 8:30-18:00, Piazza Santa Maria Maggiore, Metro: Termini or Vittorio Emanuele, tel. 06-6988-6802.

▲**Church of San Clemente**—Besides visiting the church itself, with frescoes by Masolino, you can also descend into the ruins of an earlier church. Descend yet one more level and enter the eerie remains of a pagan temple to Mithras.

Cost and Hours: Upper church—free, lower church—€5, both open Mon-Sat 9:00-12:30 & 15:00-18:00, Sun 12:00-18:00, last entry for lower church 20 minutes earlier; Via di San Giovanni in Laterano, Metro: Colosseo, or bus #85 or #87; tel. 06-774-0021, www.basilicasanclemente.com.

North Rome

Borghese Gardens and Via Veneto

▲**Villa Borghese Gardens**—Rome's scruffy three-square-mile "Central Park" is great for its shade and people-watching (plenty of modern-day Romeos and Juliets). The best entrance is at the head of Via Veneto (Metro: Barberini, then 10-minute walk up Via Veneto and through the old Roman wall at Porta Pinciana). There you'll find a cluster of buildings with a café, a kiddie arcade, and bike rental (€4/hour). Rent a bike (or, for romantics, a pedaled rickshaw—*riscio*) and follow signs to discover the park's cafés, fountains, statues, lake, great viewpoint over Piazza del Popolo, and prime picnic spots.

▲▲▲**Borghese Gallery (Galleria Borghese)**—This plush museum, filling a cardinal's mansion in the park, was recently restored and offers one of Europe's most sumptuous art experiences. You'll enjoy a collection of world-class Baroque sculpture, including Bernini's *David* and his excited statue of Apollo chasing Daphne, as well as paintings by Caravaggio, Raphael, Titian, and Rubens. The museum's slick, mandatory reservation system keeps crowds to a manageable size.

The essence of the collection is the connection of the Renaissance with the classical world. As you enter, notice the second-century Roman reliefs with Michelangelo-designed panels above either end of the portico. The villa was built in the early 17th century by the great art collector Cardinal Scipione Borghese, who wanted to prove that the glories of ancient Rome were matched by the Renaissance.

In the main entry hall, opposite the door, notice the thrilling

North Rome

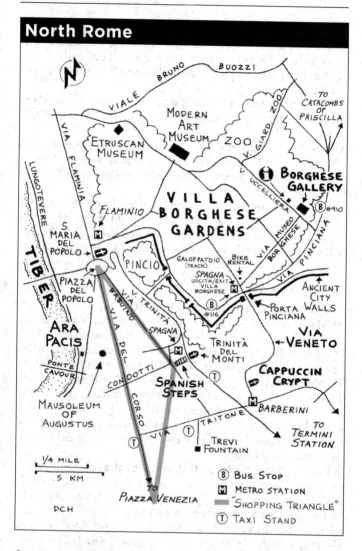

first-century Greek sculpture of a horse falling. The Renaissance-era rider was added by Pietro Bernini, father of the famous Gian Lorenzo Bernini.

Each room seems to feature a Baroque masterpiece. The best of all is in Room III: Bernini's *Apollo and Daphne*. It's the perfect Baroque subject—capturing a thrilling, action-filled moment. In the mythological story, Apollo races after Daphne. Just as he's about to catch her, she calls to her father to save her. Magically, her fingers begin to sprout leaves, her toes become roots, her skin turns to bark, and she transforms into a tree. Frustrated Apollo will end

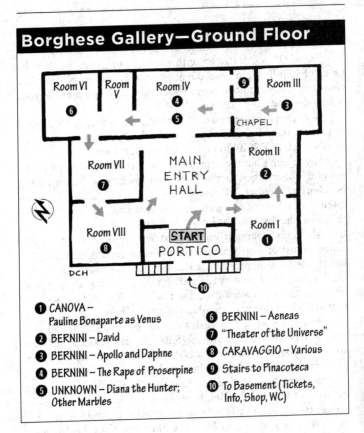

Borghese Gallery—Ground Floor

Room VI — ⑥
Room V
Room IV — ④ ⑤
⑨ Room III — ③
CHAPEL
Room II — ②
Room VII — ⑦
MAIN ENTRY HALL
Room I — ①
Room VIII — ⑧
START
PORTICO
DCH
⑩

① CANOVA –
Pauline Bonaparte as Venus

② BERNINI – David

③ BERNINI – Apollo and Daphne

④ BERNINI – The Rape of Proserpine

⑤ UNKNOWN – Diana the Hunter;
Other Marbles

⑥ BERNINI – Aeneas

⑦ "Theater of the Universe"

⑧ CARAVAGGIO – Various

⑨ Stairs to Pinacoteca

⑩ To Basement (Tickets,
Info, Shop, WC)

up with a handful of leaves. Walk slowly around the statue. It's more air than stone.

Cost, Hours, and Reservations: €8.50, €12.50 during special exhibits, both prices include basic €2 reservation fee, credit cards accepted, Tue-Sun 9:00-19:00, ticket office closes one hour earlier, closed Mon. Reservations are mandatory and easy to get in English online (www.ticketeria.it, €1 extra booking fee, user-friendly website) or by calling 06-32810 (if you get an Italian recording, wait for the English translation to get the most up-to-date information, or press 2 for their standard information in English; office hours Mon-Fri 9:00-18:00, Sat 9:00-13:00, office closed Sat in Aug and Sun year-round, www.galleriaborghese.it). Reserve a minimum of several days in advance for a weekday visit, at least a week ahead for weekends. Reservations are tightest at 11:00 and 15:00, on Tuesdays, and on weekends. For off-season weekdays (but not weekends), your chances of getting a same-day reservation are fairly high, if you're flexible about the entry time.

When you reserve, request a day and time, and you'll get a

claim number. You'll be advised to pick up your ticket 30 minutes before your appointed time. The ticket office is located on the lower level. If you're paying with a credit card, you can skip the ticket pickup line and head directly to the computer kiosks, enter your reservation number, swipe your credit card, and *pronto*—your tickets are ready.

If you're planning to use a Roma Pass for entry, you still need to make a reservation and pay the €2 fee. Call the reservations number (tel. 06-32810) to make your appointment.

If you don't have a reservation, you can try arriving near the top of the hour, when they sell unclaimed tickets to those standing by. Generally, out of 360 reservations, a few will fail to show (but more than a few may be waiting to grab them). You're most likely to land a standby ticket at 13:00 or 17:00.

Museum Strategy: Visits are strictly limited to two hours. Budget most of your time for the more interesting ground floor, but set aside 30 minutes for the paintings of the Pinacoteca upstairs (highlights are marked by the audioguide icons). Avoid the crowds by seeing the Pinacoteca first. The fine bookshop and cafeteria are best visited outside your two-hour entry window.

Tours: €6 guided English tours are offered at 9:10 and 11:10 (may also be offered at 13:10 and 15:10). You can't book a tour when you make your museum reservation—sign up as soon as you arrive. Or consider the excellent 1.5-hour audioguide tour for €5.

Getting There: The museum is set idyllically but inconveniently in the vast Villa Borghese Gardens. To avoid missing your appointment, allow yourself plenty of time to find the place. A taxi drops you 100 yards from the museum. Your destination is the Galleria Borghese (gah-leh-REE-ah bor-GAY-zay). Be sure *not* to tell the cabbie "Villa Borghese"—which is the park, not the museum.

The best public-transportation service is bus #910, which goes from Termini train station to the Via Pinciana stop (a few steps from the villa). Coming from Campo de' Fiori or Via del Corso (at Via Minghetti), bus #116 drops you off at the southern edge of the park. From Largo Argentina, bus #63 takes you to the American Embassy on Via Veneto; walk uphill on Via Veneto to the southern edge of the park.

By Metro, you have two options. From the Spagna Metro stop (or the Spanish Steps), it's a 15-minute walk: From inside the Metro station, follow signs to *Via Veneto* (not *Villa Borghese*). You'll continue along an underground labyrinth of escalators and moving sidewalks. Once you hit the supermarket, take a right up the stairs of the exit marked *uscita Villa Borghese*. At the top, turn left and head straight—you'll see signs to the gallery.

From the Barberini Metro stop, walk up Via Veneto, enter the park, and turn right, following signs.

Etruscan Museum (Villa Giulia Museo Nazionale Etrusco)—The fascinating Etruscan civilization thrived in this part of Italy around 600 B.C., when Rome was an Etruscan town. The Villa Giulia (a fine Renaissance palace) hosts a museum that tells the story. Aficionados of all things Etruscan come here for the famous "husband and wife sarcophagus"—a dead couple seeming to enjoy an everlasting banquet from atop their tomb (sixth century B.C. from Cerveteri); the *Apollo from Veii* statue (of textbook fame); and an impressive room filled with gold sheets of Etruscan printing and temple statuary from the Sanctuary of Pyrgi.

Cost and Hours: €4, Tue-Sun 8:30-19:30, closed Mon, last entry one hour before closing, scant English information, 20-minute walk from Borghese Gallery, Piazzale di Villa Giulia 9, tel. 06-322-6571.

Via Veneto—In the 1960s, movie stars from around the world paraded down curvy Via Veneto, one of Rome's glitziest nightspots. Today it's still lined with the city's poshest hotels and the American Embassy, but any hint of local color has faded to bland.

▲Cappuccin Crypt—If you want to see artistically arranged bones, this is the place. The crypt is below the church of Santa Maria della Immacolata Concezione on Via Veneto, just up from Piazza Barberini.

The bones of more than 4,000 friars who died between 1528 and 1870 are in the basement, all lined up in a series of six crypts for the delight—or disgust—of the always-wide-eyed visitor. The dirt in the crypt was brought from Jerusalem 400 years ago, and the monastic message on the wall explains that this is more than just a macabre exercise: "We were what you are...you will become what we are now."

Cost and Hours: €1 donation, daily 9:00-12:00 & 15:00-18:00, modest dress required, no photos, turn off mobile phones, Metro: Barberini, tel. 06-487-1185. As you leave, pick up a few of Rome's most interesting postcards (proceeds support Capuchin mission work) and head back outside, where it's not just the bright light that provides contrast with the crypt. Within a few steps are the American Embassy, Hard Rock Cafe, and fancy Via Veneto cafés, filled with the poor and envious keeping an eye out for the rich and famous.

Piazza del Popolo—This vast oval square marks the traditional north entrance to Rome (its oval shape dates from the early 19th century). Today the square, known for its symmetrical design and its art-filled churches, is the starting point for the city's evening *passeggiata* (see my "Dolce Vita Stroll," earlier).

From the Flaminio Metro stop, pass through the third-century A.D. Aurelian Wall via the Porta del Popolo, and look south. The

10-story obelisk in the center of the square once graced the temple of Ramses II in Egypt and the Roman Circus Maximus racetrack. The obelisk was brought here in 1589 as one of the square's beautification projects. At the south side of the square, twin domed churches mark the spot where three main boulevards exit the square and form a trident. The central boulevard (running between the churches) is Via del Corso, which since ancient times has been the main north-south drag through town, running to Capitol Hill (the governing center) and the Forum. Along the north side of the square (flanking the Porta del Popolo) are two more buildings, which give the square a pleasant symmetry: the Carabinieri station and the church of Santa Maria del Popolo.

From the square, the *Tridente* of roads takes people south to the city center (along Via del Corso), to the Spanish Steps (Via Babuino), and to the Tiber River (Via Ripetta). Two large fountains grace the sides of the square—Neptune to the west and Roma to the east (marking the base of Pincio Hill). Though the name Piazza del Popolo means "Square of the People" (and it is a popular hangout), the word was probably derived from the Latin *populus,* after the poplar trees along the square's northeast side.

Santa Maria del Popolo—One of Rome's most overlooked churches, this features two chapels with top-notch art and a facade built of travertine scavenged from the Colosseum. The church is brought to you by the Rovere family, which produced two popes, and you'll see their symbol—the oak tree and acorns—throughout.

Go inside. The Chigi Chapel (second on the left) was designed by Raphael and inspired (as Raphael was) by the Pantheon. Notice the Pantheon-like dome, pilasters, and capitals. Above in the oculus, God looks in, aided by angels who power the eight known planets. Raphael built the chapel for his wealthy banker friend Agostino Chigi, buried in the pyramid-shaped tomb in the wall to the right of the altar. Later, Chigi's great-grandson hired Bernini to make two of the four statues, and Bernini delivered a theatrical episode. In one corner, Daniel straddles a lion and raises his praying hands to God for help. Kitty-corner across the chapel, an angel grabs Habbakuk's hair and tells him to go take some food to poor Daniel.

In the Cerasi Chapel (left of altar), Caravaggio's *The Conversion on the Way to Damascus* shows Paul sprawled on his back beside his horse while his servant looks on. The startled future saint is blinded by the harsh light as Jesus' voice asks him, "Why do you persecute me?" In the style of the Counter-Reformation, Paul receives his new faith with open arms.

In the same chapel, Caravaggio's *Crucifixion of St. Peter* is shown as a banal chore; the workers toil like faceless animals. The light and dark are in high contrast. Caravaggio liked to say,

"Where light falls, I will paint it."

Cost and Hours: Free, Mon-Sat 7:00-12:00 & 16:00-19:00, Sun 8:00-13:30 & 16:30-19:30; on north side of Piazza del Popolo—as you face gate in old wall from the square, church entrance is to your right.

▲▲Catacombs of Priscilla (Catacombe di Priscilla)— While most tourists and nearly all tour groups go out to the ancient Appian Way to see the famous catacombs of San Sebastiano and San Callisto, the Catacombs of Priscilla (on the other side of town) are less commercialized and crowded, and just feel more intimate, as catacombs should.

You enter from a convent and explore the result of 250 years of tunneling that occurred from the second to the fifth centuries, most likely to hold tombs for early Christians. As poorer Christians couldn't generally afford a nice plot in a cemetery, they would dig graves at a generous person's home...and dig and dig. You'll see a few thousand of the 40,000 niches carved here, along with some beautiful frescoes, including what is considered the first depiction of Mary nursing the baby Jesus.

Cost and Hours: €8, Tue-Sun 8:30-12:00 & 14:30-17:00, closed Mon, last entry 30 minutes before closing, closed one random month a year—check website or call first, tel. 06-8620-6272, www.catacombepriscilla.com. Visits are by 30-minute guided tour only (English-language tours go whenever a small group gathers—generally every 20 minutes or so).

Getting There: The catacombs are northeast of Termini Station (at Via Salaria 430), far from the center but well-served by buses (20-30 minutes). From Termini, take bus #92 or #86 from Piazza Cinquecento; from Piazza Venezia and along Via del Corso take bus #63. Tell the driver "kah-tah-KOHM-bay" and he'll let you off near Piazza Crati, which is close to the catacombs.

From the Spanish Steps to Ara Pacis

▲Spanish Steps—The wide, curving staircase, culminating with an obelisk between two Baroque church towers, makes for one of Rome's iconic sights. Beyond that, it's a people-gathering place. By day, the area hosts shoppers looking for high-end fashions; on warm evenings, it attracts young people in love with the city. For more, see my "Night Walk Across Rome" earlier.

"Shopping Triangle"—The triangular-shaped area between the Spanish Steps, Piazza Venezia, and Piazza del Popolo (along Via del Corso) contains Rome's highest concentration of upscale boutiques and fashion stores (see triangle at bottom of map on page 918).

▲▲Ara Pacis (Altar of Peace)—On January 30, 9 B.C., soon-to-be-emperor Augustus led a procession of priests up the steps and into this newly built "Altar of Peace." They sacrificed an animal on the altar and poured an offering of wine, thanking the gods for helping Augustus pacify barbarians abroad and rivals at home. This marked the dawn of the Pax Romana (c. A.D. 1-200), a Golden Age of good living, stability, dominance, and peace (pax). The Ara Pacis (AH-rah PAH-chees) hosted annual sacrifices by the emperor until the area was flooded by the Tiber River. Buried under silt, it was abandoned and forgotten until the 16th century, when various parts were discovered and excavated. Mussolini gathered the altar's scattered parts and reconstructed them here in 1938. In 2006, the Altar of Peace reopened to the public in a striking modern building. As the first new building allowed to be built in the old center since 1938, it's been controversial, but its quiet, air-conditioned interior may signal the dawn of another new age in Rome.

The Altar of Peace was originally located east of here, along today's Via del Corso. The model shows where it stood in relation to the Mausoleum of Augustus (now next door) and the Pantheon. Approach the Ara Pacis and look through the doorway to see the raised altar. This simple structure has just the basics of a Roman temple: an altar for sacrifices surrounded by cubicle-like walls that enclose a consecrated space.

The reliefs on the north and south sides probably depict the parade of dignitaries who consecrated the altar, while reliefs on the west side (near the altar's back door) celebrate the two things Augustus brought to Rome: peace (goddess Roma as a conquering Amazon, right side) and prosperity (fertility goddess). Imagine the altar as it once was, standing in an open field, painted in bright colors—a mingling of myth, man, and nature.

Cost and Hours: €9, tightwads can look in through huge windows for free; Tue-Sun 9:00-19:00, closed Mon, last entry one hour before closing; €3.50 audioguide also available as free podcast at www.arapacis.it, good WC downstairs. The Ara Pacis is a long block west of Via del Corso on Via di Ara Pacis, on the east bank of the Tiber near Ponte Cavour, Metro: Spagna; a 10-minute walk down Via dei Condotti. Tel. 06-0608.

Vatican City

Vatican City, a tiny independent country, contains the Vatican Museum (with Michelangelo's Sistine Chapel) and St. Peter's Basilica (with Michelangelo's exquisite *Pietà*). A helpful **TI** is just to the left of St. Peter's Basilica as you're facing it (Mon-Sat 8:30-19:00, closed Sun, tel. 06-6988-1662, Vatican switchboard tel. 06-6982, www.vatican.va). The entrances to St. Peter's and to the Vatican Museum are a 15-minute walk apart (follow the outside of the Vatican wall, which links the two sights). The nearest Metro stops still involve a 10-minute walk to either sight: For St. Peter's, the closest stop is Ottaviano; for the Vatican Museum, it's Cipro.

▲▲▲Vatican Museum (Musei Vaticani)

The four miles of displays in this immense museum—from ancient statues to Christian frescoes to modern paintings—culminate in the Raphael Rooms and Michelangelo's glorious Sistine Chapel. (If you have binoculars, bring them.) This is one of Europe's top three or four houses of art. It can be exhausting, so plan your visit carefully, focusing on a few themes. Allow two hours for a quick visit, three or four hours for enough time to enjoy it.

Cost and Hours: €15 plus optional €4 reservation fee, Mon-Sat 9:00-18:00, last entry at 16:00 (though the official closing time is 18:00, the staff starts ushering you out at 17:30), closed on religious holidays and Sun except last Sun of the month (when it's free, more crowded, and open 9:00-14:00, last entry at 12:30). Hours are subject to constant change and frequent holidays; check http://mv.vatican.va for current times. Lines are extremely long in the morning—go in the afternoon, or skip the ticket-buying line altogether by reserving an entry time on their website for €19 (€15 ticket plus €4 booking fee, pay with credit card). Guided tours and audioguides are available.

The museum is closed on many holidays (mainly religious ones) including, for 2012: Jan 1 (New Year's), Jan 6 (Epiphany), Feb 11 (Vatican City established), March 19 (St. Joseph), April 8 and 9 (Easter Sunday and Monday), May 1 (Labor Day), June 29 (Saints Peter and Paul), Aug 15 plus either Aug 14 or 16—it varies year to year (Assumption of the Virgin), Nov 1 (All Saints' Day), Dec 8 (Immaculate Conception), and Dec 25 and 26 (Christmas). Other holidays and changes in opening hours may pop up—check the hours and calendar at http://mv.vatican.va.

The Sistine Chapel closes before the museum. Individual rooms may close at odd hours, especially in the afternoon. The rooms described here are usually open.

Dress Code: Modest dress (no shorts, above-knee skirts, or bare shoulders) is required. This dress code is strictly enforced here and at St. Peter's Basilica (which you can visit after leaving the Sistine Chapel).

Avoiding Lines: You can buy a ticket and **reserve an entry time online** at http://mv.vatican.va for €19 (€15 ticket plus €4 booking fee, pay with credit card). You choose your day and time, they email you a confirmation immediately, and you print out the voucher with its reservation bar code. At the Vatican Museum, bypass the ticket-buying line and queue up at the "Entrance with Reservations" line (to the right). Show your voucher to the guard, who will scan it and let you in. Once inside the museum, go to

Vatican Museum Overview

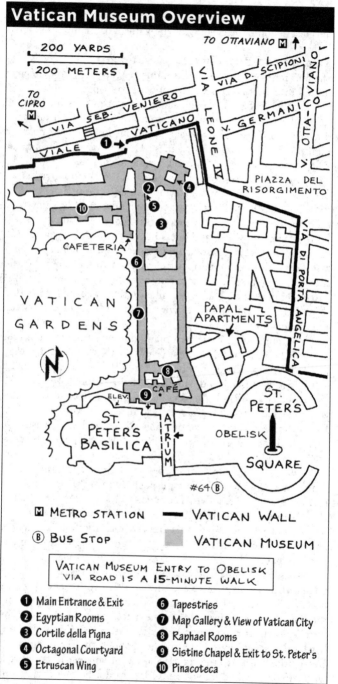

Vatican Museum Entry to Obelisk via road is a 15-minute walk

1 Main Entrance & Exit
2 Egyptian Rooms
3 Cortile della Pigna
4 Octagonal Courtyard
5 Etruscan Wing
6 Tapestries
7 Map Gallery & View of Vatican City
8 Raphael Rooms
9 Sistine Chapel & Exit to St. Peter's
10 Pinacoteca

a ticket window (either in the lobby or upstairs), present your voucher and ID, and they'll issue your ticket.

If you book a **guided tour through the Vatican Museum** (see below), you can also skip the ticket-buying line and approach the guard with your voucher. If you book with a private tour company, you may still have a short wait at crowded times.

If you don't have a reservation, **try arriving after 14:00,** when crowds subside somewhat. Another good time is during the papal audience on Wednesday after 10:30, when many tourists are at St. Peter's Basilica.

Make sure you get in the right line. Generally, individuals without tickets line up against the Vatican City wall (to the left of the entrance as you face it), and individuals with reservations enter on the right.

Tours: The Vatican offers English tours that are easy to book online (€31, includes admission, http://mv.vatican.va). As with individual ticket reservations, present your confirmation voucher to a guard to the right of the entrance, then, once inside, go to the Guided Tours desk (in the lobby, up a few stairs).

Both private tour companies and private guides offer guided English tours of the museum, usually allowing you to skip the long ticket-buying line. For a listing of several companies, see page 877.

Audio Tours: If you rent an **audioguide** (€7 plus passport, available at the top of the ramp/escalator), you lose the option of taking the shortcut from the Sistine Chapel to St. Peter's (since audioguides must be returned to the museum entrance/exit). You can download a free Rick Steves **audio tour** of the Sistine Chapel for your mobile device via www.ricksteves.com/audioeurope, iTunes, or the Rick Steves Audio Europe smartphone app.

○ Self-Guided Tour: Start, as Western civilization did, in **Egypt and Mesopotamia.** Next, the Pio Clementino collection features **Greek and Roman statues.** Decorating its courtyard are some of the best Greek and Roman statues in captivity, including the *Laocoön* group (first century B.C., Hellenistic) and the *Apollo Belvedere* (a second-century Roman copy of a Greek original). The centerpiece of the next hall is the *Belvedere Torso* (just a 2,000-year-old torso, but one that had a great impact on the art of Michelangelo). Finishing off the classical statuary are two fine fourth-century porphyry sarcophagi. These royal purple tombs were made (though not used) for the Roman emperor Constantine's mother and daughter. They were Christians—and therefore outlaws—until Constantine made Christianity legal in A.D. 312. Both sarcophagi were quarried and worked in Egypt. The technique for working this extremely hard stone (a special tempering of metal was required) was lost after this, and porphyry was

Vatican City

This tiny independent country of little more than 100 acres, contained entirely within Rome, has its own postal system, dress code (dress modestly—even if you're just wandering through the square), armed guards, helipad, mini-train station, and radio station (KPOP). Politically powerful, the Vatican is the religious capital of 1.1 billion Roman Catholics. If you're not a Catholic, become one for your visit.

The pope is both the religious and secular leader of Vatican City. For centuries, locals referred to him as "King Pope." Italy and the Vatican didn't always have good relations. In fact, after unification (in 1870), when Rome's modern grid plan was built around the miniscule Vatican, it seemed as if the new buildings were designed to be just high enough so no one could see the dome of St. Peter's from street level. Modern Italy was created in 1870, but the Holy See didn't recognize it as a country until 1929, when the pope and Mussolini signed the Lateran Pact, giving sovereignty to the Vatican and a few nearby churches.

Like every European country, Vatican City has its own versions of the euro coin (with a portrait of the pope). You're unlikely to find one in your pocket, though, as they are snatched up by collectors before falling into actual circulation.

Small as it is, Vatican City has two huge sights: St. Peter's Basilica (with Michelangelo's *Pietà*) and the Vatican Museum (with the Sistine Chapel). The Vatican post office, with offices on St. Peter's Square (next to TI) and in the Vatican Museum, is famous for its stamps (Mon-Sat 8:30-18:30, closed Sun). Vatican stamps are good throughout Rome, but to use the Vatican's mail service, you need to mail your cards from the Vatican; write your postcards ahead of time. (Note that the Vatican won't mail cards with Italian stamps.)

Seeing the Pope: Your best chances for a sighting are on Sunday and Wednesday. The pope usually gives a blessing at noon on Sunday from his apartment on St. Peter's Square (except in July and August, when he speaks at his summer residence at Castel Gandolfo, 25 miles from Rome, reachable by train from Rome's Termini Station). St. Peter's is easiest (just show up) and, for most, enough of a "visit." Those interested in a more formal appearance (though not more intimate) can get a ticket for the Wednesday general audience (at 10:30) when the pope, arriving in his bulletproof Popemobile, greets and blesses the crowds at St. Peter's from a balcony or canopied platform on the square (except in winter, when he speaks at 10:30 in the 7,000-seat Paolo VI Auditorium, next to St. Peter's Basilica). If you only want to see St. Peter's—but not the pope—avoid these times (the basilica closes during papal audiences and crowds are substantial).

For the Wednesday audience, while anyone can observe from a distance, you need a (free) ticket to actually get close to the papal action (and get a seat). To find out the pope's schedule, call 06-6982-3114.

Vatican City

CIPRO Ⓜ

VIA CANDIA

VIA LEONE IV

VIA OTTAVIANO Ⓜ OTTAVIANO

TO TERMINI

VIALE GIULIO CESARE

N

VIALE VATICANO ENTER

VATICAN MUSEUM →

PIAZZA RISORGIMENTO

SISTINE CHAPEL

PAPAL APT.

EXIT

TO CASTEL SANT'ANGELO + BUS #40 →

Ⓣ

VIA CONCILIAZIONE

ST. PETER'S →

ⓘ **

ST. PETER'S SQUARE + OBELISK

VATICAN BOUNDARY

Ⓑ #64

↓ To SAN PIETRO STATION

NOT TO SCALE: VATICAN MUSEUM ENTRY TO OBELISK IS A 15-MINUTE WALK

Ⓣ TAXI STAND
Ⓜ METRO STATION
Ⓑ BUS STOP

ⓘ INFO, WC + POST
* POPE VIEWING TICKET PICK-UP

DCH

Santa Susanna Church lets you order tickets online (free, with no booking charge). Pick up your reserved tickets, or check for last-minute availability, at the church the Tuesday before the audience between 17:00 and 18:30, and consider staying for the 18:00 English Mass (Via XX Settembre 15, near recommended Via Firenze hotels, Metro: Repubblica, tel. 06-4201-4554—charming Rosanna speaks English, get all the details at www.santasusanna.org).

Probably less convenient—because of the long line—is getting a ticket at St. Peter's Square from the Vatican guard at their station at the bronze doors (open Tue 12:00-19:30; last-minute tickets may be available Wed morning—just join the line). It's under the "elbow" of Bernini's colonnade, on the right side of the square as you face the basilica.

While many visitors come hoping for a more intimate audience, private audiences ended with the death of Pope John Paul II. Pope Benedict doesn't do them.

not chiseled again until Renaissance times in Florence.

Overachievers may first choose to pop into the **Etruscan wing**—labeled *Museo Etrusco*—located a few steps up from this level. Others have permission to save their aesthetic energy for the Sistine.

After long halls of tapestries, old maps, broken penises, and fig leaves, you'll come to what most people are looking for: the Raphael Rooms (or *stanza*) and Michelangelo's Sistine Chapel.

These outstanding works are frescoes. A fresco (meaning "fresh" in Italian) is technically not a painting. The color is mixed into wet plaster, and, when the plaster dries, the painting is actually part of the wall. This is a durable but difficult medium, requiring speed and accuracy, as the work is built one patch at a time.

After fancy rooms illustrating the "Immaculate Conception of Mary" (in the 19th century, the Vatican codified this hard-to-sell doctrine, making it a formal part of the Catholic faith) and the triumph of Constantine (with divine guidance, which led to his conversion to Christianity), you enter rooms frescoed by **Raphael** and his assistants. The highlight is the restored *School of Athens*. This is remarkable for its blatant pre-Christian classical orientation, especially since it originally wallpapered the apartments of Pope Julius II. Raphael honors the great pre-Christian thinkers—Aristotle, Plato, and company—who are portrayed as the leading artists of Raphael's day. The bearded figure of Plato is Leonardo da Vinci. Diogenes, history's first hippie, sprawls alone in bright blue on the stairs, while Michelangelo broods in the foreground—supposedly added later. Apparently, Raphael snuck a peek at the Sistine Chapel and decided that his arch-competitor was so good that he had to put their personal differences aside and include him in this tribute to the artists of his generation. Today's St. Peter's was under construction as Raphael was working. In the *School of Athens*, he gives us a sneak preview of the unfinished church.

Next is the brilliantly restored **Sistine Chapel.** This is the pope's personal chapel and also the place where, upon the death of the ruling pope, a new pope is elected (as in April 2005).

The Sistine Chapel is famous for Michelangelo's pictorial culmination of the Renaissance, showing the story of creation, with a powerful God weaving in and out of each scene through that busy first week. This is an optimistic and positive expression of the High Renaissance and a stirring example of the artistic and theological maturity of the 33-year-old Michelangelo, who spent four years on this work.

Later, after the Reformation wars had begun and after the Catholic army of Spain had sacked the Vatican, the reeling Church began to fight back. As part of its Counter-Reformation, a much older Michelangelo was commissioned to paint the *Last Judgment* (behind the altar). Beautifully restored, the message is as clear as the day Michelangelo finished it: Christ is returning, some will go to hell and some to heaven, and some will be saved by the power of the rosary.

In the controversial restoration project, no paint was added. Centuries of dust, soot (from candles used for lighting and Mass), and glue (added to make the art shine) were removed, revealing the bright original colors of Michelangelo. Photos are allowed (without a flash) elsewhere in the museum, but as part of the deal with the company who did the restoration, no photos are allowed in the Sistine Chapel.

For a **shortcut,** a small door at the far-right corner of the Sistine Chapel allows groups and individuals (without an audio-guide) to escape directly to St. Peter's Basilica. If you exit here, you're done with the museum. The Pinacoteca is the only important part left. Consider doing it at the start. Otherwise it's a 15-minute heel-to-toe slalom through tourists from the Sistine Chapel to the entry/exit. Be prepared for the odd chance that the shortcut is simply closed (which sometimes happens).

If you take the long march back, you'll find the **Pinacoteca** (the Vatican's small but fine collection of paintings, with Raphael's *Transfiguration,* Leonardo's unfinished *St. Jerome,* and Caravaggio's *Deposition*), a cafeteria (long lines, uninspired food), and the underrated early Christian art section, before you exit via the souvenir shop.

▲▲▲St. Peter's Basilica (Basilica San Pietro)

There is no doubt: This is the richest and grandest church on earth. To call it vast is like calling Einstein smart. Plaques on the floor show where other, smaller churches would end if they were placed inside. The ornamental cherubs would dwarf a large man. Birds roost inside, and thousands of people wander about, heads craned heavenward, hardly noticing each other. Don't miss Michelangelo's *Pietà* (behind bulletproof glass) to the right of the entrance. Bernini's altar work and seven-story-tall bronze canopy are brilliant.

Dress Code: No shorts or bare shoulders (applies to men, women, and children), and no miniskirts. This dress code is strictly enforced.

Hours: Daily April-Sept 7:00-19:00, Oct-March 7:00-18:00. The church closes on Wednesday mornings during papal audiences. The best time to visit the church is early or late; at 17:00, when the church is fairly empty, sunbeams can work their magic, and the late-afternoon Mass fills the place with spiritual music.

Tours: The Vatican TI conducts free 1.5-hour tours of St.

Peter's (depart Mon-Fri from TI, generally at 9:45 and 14:15, confirm schedule at TI, tel. 06-6988-1662). Audioguides can be rented near the checkroom (€5 plus ID, daily 9:00-17:00). You can download a free Rick Steves audio tour of St. Peter's Basilica for your mobile device via www.ricksteves.com/audioeurope, iTunes, or the Rick Steves Audio Europe smartphone app.

If you want to see the **Vatican Gardens,** you must book a tour online at least a week in advance at http://biglietteriamusei .vatican.va. No response means they're booked up (€31, 2 hours, usually daily except Wed and Sat, includes entry to Vatican Museum; tours start at 9:30 or 10:00 at Vatican Museum tour desk).

To see St. Peter's original grave, you can take a **Scavi "Excavations"** tour into the Necropolis (€12, 1.5 hours, ages 15 and older only, no photos). Book at least a month in advance by email (scavi @fsp.va) or fax (06-6987-3017), following the detailed instructions at www.vatican.va; no response means they're booked up.

Dome Climb (Cupola): Daily April-Sept 8:00-18:00, Oct-March 8:00-17:00. Allow one hour for the round-trip to the top of the dome (or a half-hour to the roof). You can take the elevator or stairs to the roof (231 steps up), then climb another 323 steps to the top of the dome. The entry to the elevator is just outside the basilica on the north side of St. Peter's (near the secret exit from the Sistine Chapel). Look for signs to the cupola.

◐ Self-Guided Tour: For a quick walk through the basilica, follow these points:

❶ The atrium is itself bigger than most churches. The huge white columns on the portico date from the first church (fourth century). Notice the historic doors (the Holy Door, on the right, won't be opened until just before the next Jubilee Year, in 2025).

❷ The purple, circular porphyry stone marks the site of Charlemagne's coronation in A.D. 800 (in the first St. Peter's church that stood on this site). From here, get a sense of the immensity of the church, which can accommodate 60,000 worshippers standing on its six acres.

❸ Michelangelo planned a Greek-cross floor plan, rather than the Latin-cross standard in medieval churches. A Greek cross, symbolizing the perfection of God, and by association the goodness of man, was important to the humanist Michelangelo. But accommodating large crowds was important to the Church in the fancy Baroque age, which followed Michelangelo, so the original nave length was doubled. Stand halfway up the nave and imagine the stubbier design that Michelangelo had in mind.

❹ View the magnificent dome from the statue of St. Andrew. See the vision of heaven above the windows: Jesus, Mary, a ring of saints, rings of angels, and, on the very top, God the Father.

St. Peter's Basilica

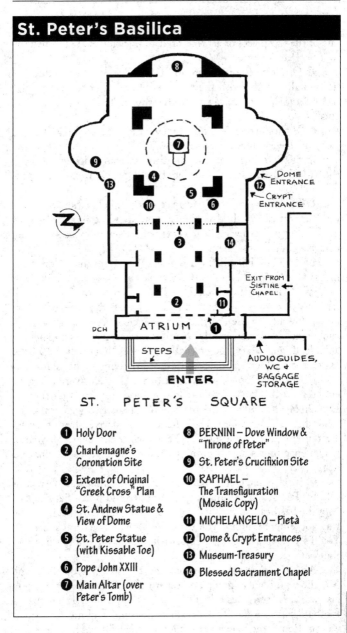

ST. PETER'S SQUARE

1. Holy Door
2. Charlemagne's Coronation Site
3. Extent of Original "Greek Cross" Plan
4. St. Andrew Statue & View of Dome
5. St. Peter Statue (with Kissable Toe)
6. Pope John XXIII
7. Main Altar (over Peter's Tomb)
8. BERNINI – Dove Window & "Throne of Peter"
9. St. Peter's Crucifixion Site
10. RAPHAEL – The Transfiguration (Mosaic Copy)
11. MICHELANGELO – Pietà
12. Dome & Crypt Entrances
13. Museum-Treasury
14. Blessed Sacrament Chapel

❺ The statue of St. Peter, with an irresistibly kissable toe, is one of the few pieces of art that predate this church. It adorned the first St. Peter's church.

❻ Circle to the right around the statue of Peter to find the lighted glass niche with the red-robed body of Pope John XXIII (r. 1958-1963), who oversaw major reforms in the Vatican II conference.

❼ The main altar sits directly over St. Peter's tomb and under Bernini's seven-story bronze canopy.

❽ St. Peter's throne and Bernini's starburst dove window is the site of a daily Mass (Mon-Sat at 17:00, Sun at 17:45—after vespers at 17:00).

❾ St. Peter was crucified here when this location was simply "the Vatican Hill." The obelisk now standing in the center of St. Peter's square marked the center of a Roman racecourse long before a church stood here.

❿ The church is filled with mosaics, not paintings. Notice the mosaic version of Raphael's *Transfiguration*.

⓫ Michelangelo sculpted his *Pietà* when he was 24 years old. (A *pietà* is a work that represents Mary with the body of Christ taken down from the cross.) Michelangelo's mastery of the body is obvious in this powerfully beautiful masterpiece. Jesus is believably dead, and Mary, the eternally youthful "handmaiden" of the Lord, accepts God's will...even if it means giving up her son.

The Holy Door (to the right of the *Pietà*, covered in gray concrete with a gold cross) won't be reopened until Christmas Eve, 2024, the dawn of the next Jubilee Year. Every 25 years, the Church celebrates an especially festive year derived from the Old Testament idea of the Jubilee Year (originally every 50 years), which encourages new beginnings and the forgiveness of sins and debts.

⓬ Visitors can go down to the Crypt within the foundations of Old St. Peter's, containing tombs of popes and memorial chapels. Exit the basilica and turn left to head down the steps (back out the way you entered, unless you took the Vatican Museum shortcut). You'll see people here lined up to visit the Crypt, and to ride up to the roof.

An elevator leads to the roof and the stairway up the dome (€7, allow an hour to go up and down). The dome, Michelangelo's last work, is (you guessed it) the biggest anywhere. Taller than a football field is long, it's well worth the sweaty climb for a great view of Rome, the Vatican grounds, and the inside of the basilica—particularly heavenly while there is singing. Look around—Rome has no modern skyline. No building in Rome is allowed to exceed the height of St. Peter's. The elevator takes you to the rooftop of the nave. From there, a few steps take you to a balcony at the base of the dome looking down into the church interior. After that, the one-way, 323-step climb (for some people, it's claustrophobic) to the cupola begins. The rooftop level (below the dome) has a gift shop, WC, drinking fountain, and a commanding view.

⓭ For most, the museum (in the sacristy) is not worth the admission.

⓮ Blessed Sacrament Chapel. You're welcome to step through the metalwork gates into this oasis of peace reserved for prayer and meditation.

Near Vatican City

▲Castel Sant'Angelo—Built as a tomb for the emperor, used through the Middle Ages as a castle, prison, and place of last refuge for popes under attack, and today a museum, this giant pile of ancient bricks is packed with history.

Ancient Rome allowed no tombs—not even the emperor's—within its walls. So Emperor Hadrian grabbed the most commanding position just outside the walls and across the river and built a towering tomb (c. A.D. 139) well within view of the city. His mausoleum was a huge cylinder (210 by 70 feet) topped by a cypress grove and crowned by a huge statue of Hadrian himself riding a chariot. For nearly a hundred years, Roman emperors (from Hadrian to Caracalla, in A.D. 217) were buried here.

In the year 590, the Archangel Michael appeared above the mausoleum to Pope Gregory the Great. Sheathing his sword, the angel signaled the end of a plague. The fortress that was Hadrian's mausoleum eventually became a fortified palace, renamed for the "holy angel."

Castel Sant'Angelo spent centuries of the Dark Ages as a fortress and prison, but was eventually connected to the Vatican via an elevated corridor at the pope's request (1277). Since Rome was repeatedly plundered by invaders, Castel Sant'Angelo was a handy place of last refuge for threatened popes. In anticipation of long sieges, rooms were decorated with papal splendor (you'll see paintings by Carlo Crivelli, Luca Signorelli, and Andrea Mantegna). In 1527, during a sack of Rome by troops of Charles V of Spain, the pope lived inside the castle for months with his entourage of hundreds (an unimaginable ordeal, considering the food service at the top-floor bar).

Touring the place is a stair-stepping workout. After you walk around the entire base of the castle, take the small staircase down to the original Roman floor (following the route of Hadrian's funeral procession). In the atrium, study the model of the mausoleum as it was in Roman times. Imagine being surrounded by a veneer of marble, and the niche in the wall filled with a towering "welcome to my tomb" statue of Hadrian. From here, a ramp leads to the right, spiraling 400 feet. While some of the fine original brickwork and bits of mosaic survive, the marble veneer is long gone (notice the holes in the wall that held it in place). At the end of the ramp, a bridge crosses over the room where the ashes of the emperors were kept. From here, the stairs continue out of the ancient section and into the medieval structure (built atop the mausoleum) that housed the papal apartments. Don't miss the Sala del Tesoro (Treasury), where the wealth of the Vatican was locked up in a huge chest. (*Do* miss the 58 rooms of the military museum.) From the pope's piggy bank, a narrow flight of stairs leads to the rooftop and perhaps the finest view of Rome anywhere (pick out landmarks as you stroll around). From the safety of this dramatic vantage point, the pope surveyed the city in times of siege. Look down at the bend of the Tiber, which for 2,700 years has cradled the Eternal City.

Cost and Hours: €8, more for special exhibits, Tue-Sun 9:00-19:30, closed Mon, last entry one hour before closing, near Vatican City, Metro: Lepanto or bus #64, tel. 06-681-9111, www.castel santangelo.beniculturali.it.

Ponte Sant'Angelo—The bridge leading to Castel Sant'Angelo was built by Hadrian for quick and regal access from downtown to his tomb. The three middle arches are actually Roman originals, and a fine example of the empire's engineering expertise. The statues of angels (each bearing a symbol of the passion of Christ—nail, sponge, shroud, and so on) are Bernini-designed and textbook Baroque. In the Middle Ages, this was the only bridge in the area that connected St. Peter's and the Vatican with downtown Rome. Nearly all pilgrims passed this bridge to and from the church. Its shoulder-high banisters recall a tragedy: During a Jubilee Year festival in 1450, the crowd got so huge that the mob pushed out the original banisters, causing nearly 200 to fall to their deaths.

Trastevere

Trastevere is the colorful neighborhood across *(tras)* the Tiber *(Tevere)* River. Trastevere (trahs-TAY-veh-ray) offers the best look at medieval-village Rome. The action unwinds to the chime of the church bells. Go there and wander. Wonder. Be a poet. This is Rome's Left Bank.

This proud neighborhood was long a working-class area. Now that it's becoming trendy, high rents are driving out the source of so much color. Still, it's a great people scene, especially at night. Stroll the back streets (for restaurant recommendations, see "Eating in Rome," later.)

To reach Trastevere by foot from Capitol Hill, cross the Tiber on Ponte Cestio (over Isola Tiberina). You can also take tram #8 from Largo Argentina, or bus #H from Termini and Via Nazionale (get off at Piazza Belli). From the Vatican (Piazza Risorgimento), it's bus #23 or #271.

Linking Trastevere with my "Night Walk Across Rome": You can walk from Trastevere to Campo de' Fiori to link up with the beginning of my "Night Walk Across Rome" (described earlier): From Trastevere's church square (Piazza di Santa Maria), take Via del Moro to the river and cross at Ponte Sisto, a pedestrian bridge that has a good view of St. Peter's dome. Continue straight ahead for one block. Take the first left, which leads down Via di Capo di Ferro through the scary and narrow darkness to Piazza Farnese, with the imposing Palazzo Farnese. Michelangelo contributed to the facade of this palace, now the French Embassy. The fountains on the square feature huge one-piece granite hot tubs from the ancient Roman Baths of Caracalla. One block from there (opposite the palace) is the atmospheric square Campo de' Fiori.

▲**Santa Maria in Trastevere Church**—One of Rome's oldest churches, this was made a basilica in the fourth century, when Christianity was legalized (free, daily 7:30-21:00). It was the first church dedicated to the Virgin Mary. Its portico (covered area just outside the door) is decorated with fascinating fragments of stone—many of them lids from catacomb burial niches—and filled with early Christian symbolism. The church is on Piazza di Santa Maria, the Trastevere neighborhood's most important meeting place. During major soccer games, a large screen is set up here so that everybody can share in the tension and excitement. At other times, children gather here with a ball and improvise matches of their own.

▲**Villa Farnesina**—Here's a unique opportunity to see a sumptuous Renaissance villa in Rome decorated with Raphael paintings. It was built in the early 1500s for the richest man in Renaissance Europe, Siennese banker Agostino Chigi. Architect Baldassare Peruzzi's design—a U-shaped building with wings enfolding what used to be a vast garden—successfully blended architecture and nature in a way that both ancient and Renaissance Romans loved. Orchards and flower beds flowed down in terraces from the palace to the riverbanks. Later construction of modern embankments and avenues robbed the garden of its grandeur, leaving it with a more melancholy charm.

In the **Loggia of Galatea,** find Raphael's painting of the nymph Galatea (on the wall by the entrance door). Galatea is considered Raphael's vision of female perfection—not a portrait of an individual woman, but a composite of his many lovers in an idealized vision. Raphael and his assistants also painted the subtly erotic **Loggia of Psyche.**

Cost and Hours: €5; April-June and mid-Sept-Oct Mon-Sat

Trastevere

Hotel/Restaurants

1. Hotel Santa Maria
2. Residenza Arco dei Tolomei & Arco del Lauro B&B
3. Relais le Clarisse
4. Casa San Giuseppe
5. Trattoria da Lucia
6. Trattoria da Olindo
7. Dar Poeta Pizzeria
8. Osteria Ponte Sisto da Oliviero
9. Ristorante Checco er Carettiere
10. Pizzeria "Ai Marmi"
11. To Cantina Paradiso
12. Gelateria alla Scala

DCH

100 YARDS

100 METERS

9:00–16:00, closed Sun; July–mid-Sept and Nov–March Mon-Sat 9:00–13:00, closed Sun; across the river from Campo de' Fiori, a short walk from Ponte Sisto on Via della Lungara, tel. 06-6802-7268.

Gianicolo Hill Viewpoint—From this park atop a hill, the city views are superb, and the walk to the top holds a treat for architecture buffs. Start at Trastevere's Piazza di San Cosimato, and follow Via Luciano Manara to Via Garibaldi, at the base of the hill. Via Garibaldi winds its way up the side of the hill to the church of San Pietro in Montorio. To the right of the church, in a small court-

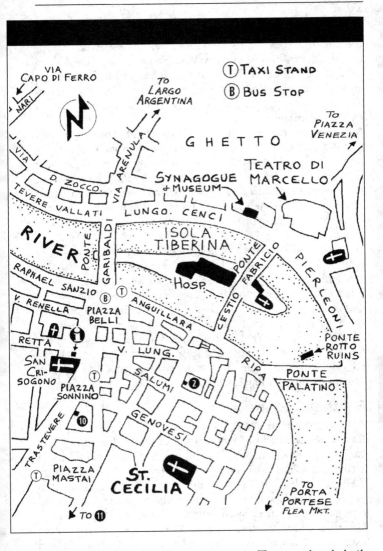

yard, is the Tempietto by Donato Bramante. This tiny church, built to commemorate the martyrdom of St. Peter, is considered a jewel of Italian Renaissance architecture.

Continuing up the hill, Via Garibaldi connects to Passeggiata del Gianicolo. From here, you'll find a pleasant park with panoramic city views. Ponder the many Victorian-era statues, including that of baby-carrying, gun-wielding, horse-riding Anita Garibaldi. She was the Brazilian wife of the revolutionary General Giuseppe Garibaldi, who helped forge a united Italy in the late 19th century.

Near Trastevere: Jewish Quarter

From the 16th through the 19th centuries, Rome's Jewish population was forced to live in a cramped ghetto at an often-flooded bend of the Tiber River. While the medieval Jewish ghetto is long gone, this area—just across the river and toward Capitol Hill from Trastevere—is still home to Rome's synagogue and fragments of its Jewish heritage.

Synagogue (Sinagoga) and Jewish Museum (Museo Ebraico)—Rome's modern synagogue stands proudly on the spot where the medieval Jewish community lived in squalor for more than 300 years. The site of a historic visit by Pope John Paul II, this synagogue features a fine interior and a museum filled with artifacts of Rome's Jewish community. The only way to visit the synagogue—unless you're here for daily prayer service—is with a tour.

Cost and Hours: €7.50 ticket includes museum and guided hourly tour of synagogue; June-Sept Sun-Thu 10:00-19:00, Fri 10:00-16:00, closed Sat; Oct-May Sun-Thu 10:00-17:00, Fri 9:00-14:00, closed Sat; last entry 45 minutes before closing, modest dress required, English tours usually at :15 past the hour, 30 minutes, check schedule at ticket counter; on Lungotevere dei Cenci, tel. 06-6840-0661, www.museoebraico.roma.it. Walking tours of the Jewish Ghetto are conducted at least once a day except Saturday (€8, usually at 13:15, sign up at museum 30 minutes before departure, minimum of 3 required).

Southeast Rome

Ancient Appian Way

Baths of Caracalla (Terme di Caracalla)—Inaugurated by Emperor Caracalla in A.D. 216, this massive bath complex could accommodate 1,600 visitors at a time. Today it's just a shell—a huge shell—with all of its sculptures and most of its mosaics moved to museums. You'll see a two-story roofless brick building surrounded by a garden, bordered by ruined walls. The two large rooms at either end of the building were used for exercise. In between the exercise rooms was a pool flanked by two small mosaic-floored dressing rooms. Niches in the walls once held statues. (The statues are displayed elsewhere: for example, the immense *Toro Farnese*—a marble sculpture of a bull surrounded by people—snorts in Naples' Archaeological Museum.)

In its day, this was a remarkable place to hang out. For ancient Romans, bathing was a social experience. The Baths of Caracalla functioned until Goths severed the aqueducts in the sixth century. In modern times, grand operas are performed here.

Cost and Hours: €6; Tue-Sun 9:00 until one hour before sunset: 19:00 in summer, 16:30 in winter; Mon 9:00-14:00, last

The Ancient Appian Way

TO
SAN SEBASTIANO GATE,
MUSEUM OF THE WALLS
& DOWNTOWN ROME

Ⓐ Bus #660 Stop

Ⓑ Bus #118 Stops

Ⓒ Bus #118 (South-
bound Stop Only)

Ⓓ Bus #218 Stop

Ⓔ Archeobus Stops

DOMINE QUO
VADIS CHURCH

ARDEATINA

PEDESTRIAN
WALKWAY
(CLOSED WED)

VIA APPIA

COLUMBARIUM
SECOND
MILESTONE

VICOLO
DELLA
BASILICA

CATACOMBS
OF SAN
CALLISTO
& WC

VIA D. SETTE CHIESE

VILLA
OF
MAXENTIUS

FOSSE
ARDEANTINE

CATACOMBS
OF
SAN SEBASTIANO
& WC

VIA DI
SAN SEB.

CIRCUS
OF
MAXENTIUS

VIA APPIA ANTICA

TOMB OF
CECILIA
METELLA

THIRD
MILESTONE

VIA CECILIA METELLA

TO
AQUEDUCT
PARK

APPIA ANTICA CAFFÈ
& BIKE RENTAL

ALIMENTARI

TORRE DI
CAPO DI BOVE

SCENIC
SECTION

VIA CAPO
DI BOVE

¼ MILE

.5 KM

DCH

TO
4TH THROUGH 11TH
MILESTONES & BRINDISI

entry one hour before closing.

Information: Audioguide-€4, free downloadable audio tour at www.pierreci.it—choose English and search for "terme di cara-calla," good €8 guidebook can be read in shaded garden while sit-ting on a chunk of column.

Getting There: Take the Metro to Circus Maximus, then walk five minutes south along Via delle Terme di Caracalla; bus

#714 from Termini Station or bus #118 from the Appian Way—see "Getting There" under next listing; tel. 06-3996-7700.

▲**Appian Way**—For a taste of the countryside around Rome and more wonders of Roman engineering, take the four-mile trip from the Colosseum out past the wall to a stretch of the ancient Appian Way, where the original pavement stones are lined by several interesting sights. Ancient Rome's first and greatest highway, the Appian Way once ran from Rome to the Adriatic port of Brindisi, the gateway to Greece. Today you can walk (or bike) some stretches of the road, rattling over original paving stones, past crumbling monuments that once lined the sides.

The wonder of its day, the Appian Way (named after Appius Claudius Caecus, a Roman official) was the largest, widest, fastest road ever, called the "Queen of Roads." Built in 312 B.C., it connected Rome with Capua (near Naples), running in a straight line for much of the way, ignoring the natural contour of the land. Eventually, this most important of Roman roads stretched 430 miles to the port of Brindisi—the gateway to the East—where boats sailed for Greece and Egypt. Twenty-nine such roads fanned out from Rome. Just as Hitler built the Autobahn system in anticipation of empire maintenance, the expansion-minded Roman government realized the military and political value of a good road system.

Today the road and the landscape around it are preserved as a cultural park. For the tourist, the ancient Appian Way offers three attractions: the road itself, with its ruined monuments; the two major Christian catacombs open to visitors; and the peaceful atmosphere, which provides a respite from the city. Be aware, however, that the road today is busy with traffic—and actually quite treacherous in spots.

The road starts at the massive **San Sebastiano Gate and Museum of the Walls,** about two miles south of the Colosseum (€3, Tue-Sun 9:00-14:00, closed Mon, last entry 30 minutes before closing, tel. 06-7047-5284). The stretch that's of most interest to tourists starts another two miles south of the gate. I like to begin near the Tomb of Cecilia Metella, at the far (southern) end of the key sights, and work northward (mostly downhill) toward central Rome.

Getting There: To get to the Tomb of Cecilia Metella on **public bus #660,** take Metro line A from central Rome to the Colli Albani stop, where you catch bus #660 (along Via Appia Nuova) and ride 10 minutes to the last stop—Cecilia Metella/Via Appia Antica. This drops you off right at the intersection of Via Appia Antica and Via Cecilia Metella. As it can be frustrating to buy a bus ticket on the Appian Way, have one in hand for your return trip.

A **taxi** will get you from Rome to the Tomb of Cecilia Metella for about €20. However, to return by taxi, you'll have to phone for one, as there are no taxi stands on the Appian Way (or just take handy bus #118 back to Rome).

If you want to visit just a few sights, consider **bus #118.** In Rome, catch #118 from either the Piramide or Circo Massimo Metro stops; going away from the city center, it stops at the San Sebastiano Gate, Domine Quo Vadis Church, Catacombs of San Callisto, and Catacombs of San Sebastiano. Although bus #118 does not stop at the Tomb of Cecilia Metella, the Tomb is only 500 yards away from the bus stop at the Catacombs of San Sebastiano. Going back to Rome, bus #118 takes a somewhat different route (skipping the Catacombs of San Sebastiano); catch this north-bound bus just up the road at the Catacombs of San Callisto.

Bus #218 goes from San Giovanni in Laterano to Domine Quo Vadis Church and the west entrance of the Catacombs of San Callisto, but isn't handy for other Appian Way sights.

The handy, but much more expensive, **Archeobus** runs from Termini train station to the Appian Way sights (see page 879 of the "Tours in Rome" section). It stops at all the key attractions—you can hop off, tour the sights, and pick up a later bus (officially runs hourly, but service can be spotty).

Getting Back: No matter how you arrive at the Appian Way, **bus #118** is the easiest and cheapest way to return to Rome (get off at the end of the line, the Piramide Metro stop).

▲▲**Catacombs of San Sebastiano**—A guide leads you underground through the tunnels where early Christians were buried. You'll see faded frescoes and graffiti by early Christian tag artists. Besides the catacombs themselves, there's a historic fourth-century basilica with holy relics.

Cost and Hours: €8, includes 25-minute tour, 2/hour, Mon-Sat 9:00-12:00 & 14:00-17:00, last tour leaves at 17:00, closed Sun and mid-Nov-mid-Dec, Via Appia Antica 136, tel. 06-785-0350, www.catacombe.org.

▲▲**Catacombs of San Callisto**—The larger of the two sets of catacombs, San Callisto also is the more prestigious, having been the burial site for several early popes.

Cost and Hours: €8, includes 30-minute tour, at least 2/hour, Thu-Tue 9:00-12:00 & 14:00-17:00, closed Wed and Feb, Via Appia Antica 110, tel. 06-5130-1580 or 06-5130-151, www.catacombe.roma.it.

Near Rome

▲▲**Ostia Antica**—For an exciting day trip, pop down to the Roman port of Ostia, which is similar to Pompeii but a lot closer and, in some ways, more interesting. Because Ostia was a working port town, it shows a more complete and gritty look at Roman life than wealthier Pompeii. Wandering around today, you'll see warehouses, apartment flats, mansions, shopping arcades, and baths that served a once-thriving port of 60,000 people. Later, Ostia became a ghost town, and it's now excavated. Buy a map, then explore the town, including the 2,000-year-old theater. Finish with its fine little museum.

Getting There: Getting to Ostia Antica from downtown Rome is a snap—it's a 45-minute combination Metro/train ride. (Since the train is part of the Metro system, it only costs one Metro ticket each way—€2 total round-trip.)

From Rome, take Metro line B to the Piramide stop, which is also the Roma Porta San Paolo train station, so the train tracks are just a few steps from the Metro tracks. Follow signs to *Lido*—go up the escalator, turn left, and go down the steps into the Roma-Lido station. All trains depart in the direction of *Lido*, leave every 15 minutes, and stop at Ostia Antica along the way. The lighted schedule reads something like, "*Treno in partenza alle ore 13.25, bin 3*," meaning, "Train departing at 13:25 from track 3." Look for the next train, hop on, ride for about 30 minutes (keep your Metro ticket handy), and get off at the Ostia Antica stop. (If you don't have a ticket to get back, purchase one at the ticket window at the station, or from the nearby snack bar.)

Leaving the train station in Ostia Antica, cross the road via the blue skybridge and walk straight down Via della Stazione di Ostia Antica, continuing straight until you reach the parking lot. The entrance is to your left.

Cost and Hours: €6.50 for the site and museum, Tue-Sun April-Oct 8:30-19:00, Nov-Feb 8:30-17:00, March 8:30-18:00, last entry one hour before closing, closed Mon. The museum closes from 13:30 to 14:15 for lunch. Tel. 06-5635-8099; www.itnw.roma.it/ostia/scavi (Italian website), www.ostiaantica.info (English summary), or www.ostia-antica.org. A map of the site with suggested itineraries is available for €2 from the ticket office. Although you'll see little audioguide markers throughout the site, there are no audioguides. However, you can download a free Rick Steves audio tour of the site for your mobile device via www.ricksteves.com/audioeurope, iTunes, or the Rick Steves Audio Europe smartphone app.

Sleeping in Rome

Double rooms listed in this chapter will range from about €65 (very simple, toilet and shower down the hall) to €480 (maximum plumbing and more), with most clustering around €150 (with private bathrooms). I've favored these pricier options, because intense

Sleep Code

(€1 = about $1.40, country code: 39)
S = Single, **D** = Double/Twin, **T** = Triple, **Q** = Quad, **b** = bathroom,
s = shower only. Unless otherwise noted, breakfast is
included, hotel staff speak basic English, and credit cards are
accepted.

To help you sort easily through these listings, I've divided
the rooms into three categories based on the price for a
standard double room with bath (or for a bunk at a hostel):

$$$ Higher Priced—Most rooms €180 or more.
 $$ Moderately Priced—Most rooms between €130-180.
  $ Lower Priced—Most rooms €130 or less.

Prices can change without notice; verify the hotel's
current rates online or by email. For other updates, see www
.ricksteves.com/update.

and grinding Rome is easier to enjoy with a welcoming oasis to call
home.

Hotels, B&Bs, and vacation rentals are required to charge a
tax of €2 per person per night upon check-out (maximum of 10
nights). The tax does not apply to children under 10.

It's common for hotels in Rome to lower their prices 10-35
percent off-season, although prices at hostels and the cheaper
hotels won't fluctuate much. Room rates are lowest in sweltering
August. Easter, September, and Christmas are the most crowded
and expensive. Particularly on Easter (April 8 in 2012) and Saint
Peter and Paul's Day (June 29), the entire city gets booked up.

Traffic in Rome roars. With the arrival of double-paned windows and air-conditioning, night noise is not the problem it once
was. Even so, light sleepers who ask for a *tranquillo* room will likely
get a room in the back...and sleep better.

Most hotels are eager to connect you with a shuttle service to
the airport. It's reasonable and easy for departure, but upon arrival,
I just catch a cab or the train into the city.

Almost no hotels have parking, but nearly all have a line on
spots in a nearby garage (about €24/day).

Convents: Although I list only four, Rome has many convents that rent out rooms. At convents, the beds are twins and
English is often in short supply, but the price is right. Consider
these nun-run places, all listed in this chapter: the expensive but
divine **Casa di Santa Brigida** (near Campo de' Fiori), the **Suore
di Santa Elisabetta** (near Santa Maria Maggiore), the **Casa Il
Rosario** (near Piazza Venezia), and the user-friendly **Casa per**

Ferie Santa Maria alle Fornaci (near the Vatican). For more options, see the Church of Santa Susanna's website for a list (www.santasusanna.org, select "Coming to Rome").

Hostels and Dorms: For easy communication with young, friendly entrepreneurs, €20-30 dorm beds, and some inexpensive doubles—within a 10-minute hike of Termini train station—consider the various hostels I've listed, or check www.backpackers.it for more listings.

Near Termini Train Station

While not as atmospheric as other areas of Rome, the hotels near Termini train station are less expensive, restaurants are plentiful, and the many public-transportation options link it easily with the entire city. The city's two Metro lines intersect at the station, and most buses leave from here. Piazza Venezia is a 20-minute walk down Via Nazionale.

Via Firenze

Via Firenze is safe, handy, central, and relatively quiet. It's a 10-minute walk from Termini Station and the airport train, and two blocks beyond Piazza della Repubblica and the TI. The Defense Ministry is nearby, so you've got heavily armed guards watching over you all night.

The neighborhood is well-connected by public transportation (with the Repubblica Metro stop nearby). Virtually all the city buses that rumble down Via Nazionale (#64, #70, #115, #640, and the #40 express) take you to Piazza Venezia (Forum) and Largo Argentina (Pantheon). From Largo Argentina, both the #64 bus (jammed with people and thieves) and the #40 express bus continue to the Vatican. Or, at Largo Argentina, you can transfer to electric trolley #8 to Trastevere (get off at first stop after crossing the river).

Phone and Internet Center is a cute and handy little hole-in-the-wall cybercafé within a block or so of several recommended hotels (€3/hour, daily 8:30-20:30, Via Modena 48, tel. 06-482-8850). To stock your closet pantry, pop over to **Despar Supermarket** (daily 8:00-21:00, Via Nazionale 211, at the corner of Via Venezia). A 24-hour **pharmacy** near the recommended hotels is Farmacia Piram (Via Nazionale 228, tel. 06-488-4437).

$$$ Residenza Cellini feels like the guest wing of a gorgeous Neoclassical palace. It offers 11 rooms, "ortho/anti-allergy beds," four-star comforts and service, and a breezy breakfast terrace (Db-€185, larger Db-€205, extra bed-€25, show this book and ask for best Rick Steves price if paying with cash, air-con, elevator, Internet access and Wi-Fi, Via Modena 5, tel. 06-4782-5204, fax 06-4788-1806, www.residenzacellini.it, residenzacellini@tin.it,

Hotels near Termini Train Station

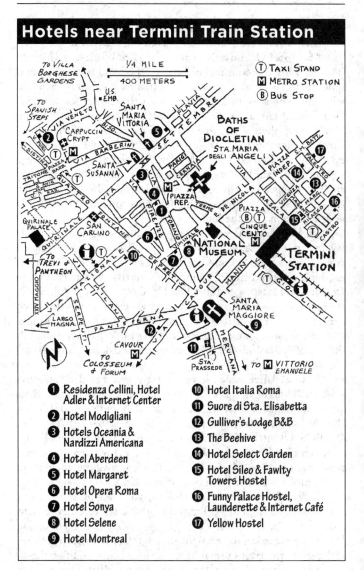

- ① TAXI STAND
- Ⓜ METRO STATION
- Ⓑ BUS STOP

① Residenza Cellini, Hotel Adler & Internet Center

② Hotel Modigliani

③ Hotels Oceania & Nardizzi Americana

④ Hotel Aberdeen

⑤ Hotel Margaret

⑥ Hotel Opera Roma

⑦ Hotel Sonya

⑧ Hotel Selene

⑨ Hotel Montreal

⑩ Hotel Italia Roma

⑪ Suore di Sta. Elisabetta

⑫ Gulliver's Lodge B&B

⑬ The Beehive

⑭ Hotel Select Garden

⑮ Hotel Sileo & Fawlty Towers Hostel

⑯ Funny Palace Hostel, Launderette & Internet Café

⑰ Yellow Hostel

Barbara, Gaetano, and Donato).

$$$ Hotel Modigliani, a delightful 23-room place, is energetically run in a clean, bright, minimalist yet in-love-with-life style that its artist namesake would appreciate. There's a very generous lounge, a garden, and a newsletter introducing you to each of the staff (Db-€195, but check website for deals and ask about additional Rick Steves discount; air-con, Wi-Fi; northwest of Via Firenze—from Tritone Fountain on Piazza Barberini, go 2 blocks up Via della Purificazione to #42; tel. 06-4281-5226, www.hotel modigliani.com, info@hotelmodigliani.com, Giulia and Marco).

$$ Hotel Oceania is a peaceful slice of air-conditioned heaven. This 23-room manor house–type hotel is spacious and quiet, with spotless, tastefully decorated rooms, run by Stefano, who still maintains his father Armando's tradition of serving delicious "world-famous" coffee. He works hard to maintain a caring family atmosphere with a fine staff, and provides lots of thoughtful extra touches (Sb-€125, Db-€158, Tb-€190, Qb-€212, show this book and ask for best Rick Steves price if paying with cash, large roof terrace, family suite, Internet access and Wi-Fi, videos in the TV lounge, Via Firenze 38, third floor, tel. 06-482-4696, fax 06-488-5586, www.hoteloceania.it, info@hoteloceania.it, Anna and Radu round out the staff).

$$ Hotel Aberdeen, which perfectly combines high quality and friendliness, is warmly run by Annamaria, with support from cousins Sabrina and Cinzia and sister Laura. The 37 comfy, modern, air-conditioned rooms are a terrific value. Enjoy the frescoed breakfast room (Sb-€102, Db-€160, Tb-€170, Qb-€200, for these rates—or better—book direct via email or use the "Rick Steves reader reservations" link on their website, much cheaper rates off-season, Internet access and Wi-Fi, Via Firenze 48, tel. 06-482-3920, fax 06-482-1092, www.hotelaberdeen.it, info@hotel aberdeen.it).

$ Hotel Adler, which serves breakfast on its garden patio, has wide halls and eight quiet, simple rooms in a good location (plus six more rooms in their slightly pricier Bellesuite wing). It's run the old-fashioned way by a charming family (Db-€130, Tb-€170, Qb-€195, Quint/b-€220, ask about discount with this book, air-con, elevator, Internet access and Wi-Fi, Via Modena 5, second floor, tel. 06-484-466, fax 06-488-0940, www.hoteladler-roma .com, info@hoteladler-roma.com, Alessandro).

$ Hotel Nardizzi Americana, with 33 pleasant, air-conditioned rooms and a delightful rooftop terrace, is an excellent value (Sb-€95, Db-€125, Tb-€155, Qb-€175, email them or use "Rick Steves readers reservations" link on their website to get special rates, normal website may have even lower rates, additional cash discount, air-con, elevator, Internet access and Wi-Fi, Via Firenze 38, fourth floor, tel. 06-488-0035, fax 06-488-0368, www.hotel nardizzi.it, info@hotelnardizzi.it, Stefano, Fabrizio, Mario, and Samy).

$ Hotel Margaret, basic but welcoming, fills its walls with Impressionist prints and offers 12 decent rooms at a good price (Db-€95, big Db-€120, Tb-€140, Qb-€170, mention this book for their best rate, air-con, elevator, Wi-Fi, northeast of Via Firenze at Via Antonio Salandra 6, fourth floor, tel. 06-482-4285, fax

06-482-4277, www.hotelmargaretrome.com, info@hotelmargaret
.net, friendly Monica).

Between Via Nazionale and Santa Maria Maggiore

$$ Hotel Opera Roma, with contemporary furnishings and
marble accents, boasts 15 fresh and spacious but somewhat dark
rooms. It's located a stone's throw from the Opera House (Db-
€165, Tb-€190, show this book and ask for best Rick Steves price,
5 percent less with cash, air-con, elevator, Internet access and
loaner laptop on request, Via Firenze 11, tel. 06-487-1787, www
.hoteloperaroma.com, info@hoteloperaroma.com, Rezza and
Federica).

$$ Hotel Sonya offers 28 well-equipped, high-tech rooms,
a central location, and decent prices. Farhad, a member of the
multi-talented staff, bakes cakes and other goodies daily for the
better-than-usual breakfast (Sb-€90, Db-€150, Tb-€165, Qb-€185,
Quint/b-€200, show this book and ask for best Rick Steves price
if paying cash, air-con, elevator, loaner laptops in room and Wi-Fi,
faces the Opera House at Via Viminale 58, Metro: Repubblica or
Termini, tel. 06-481-9911, fax 06-488-5678, www.hotelsonya.it,
info@hotelsonya.it, Francesca and Ivan).

$$ Hotel Selene spreads its rooms out on a few floors of a
big palazzo. With elegant furnishings and room to breathe, its 40
rooms are a good value (Db-€145, Tb-€165, €10 less with cash,
air-con, elevator, Via del Viminale 8, tel. 06-482-4460, www.hotel
seleneroma.it, reception@hotelseleneroma.it).

$ Hotel Montreal, run with care, is a bright, solid business-
class place with 27 rooms on a big street a block southeast of Santa
Maria Maggiore (Sb-€95, Db-€120, Tb-€150, may be less if you
email direct and ask for a Rick Steves discount, air-con, eleva-
tor, Internet access, communal garden terrace, good security, Via
Carlo Alberto 4, 1 block from Metro: Vittorio Emanuele, 3 blocks
west of Termini train station, tel. 06-445-7797, fax 06-446-5522,
www.hotelmontrealroma.com, info@hotelmontrealroma.com,
Pasquale).

$ Hotel Italia Roma, in a busy, interesting, and handy locale,
is located safely on a quiet street next to the Ministry of the Interior.
Thoughtfully run by Andrea, Sabrina, Nadine, and Gabriel, it
has 35 comfortable, clean, and bright rooms (Sb-€80, Db-€120,
Tb-€160, Qb-€180, 30 percent cheaper July-Aug, air-con-€10
extra per day, elevator, Internet access and Wi-Fi, Via Venezia 18,
just off Via Nazionale, Metro: Repubblica, tel. 06-482-8355, fax
06-474-5550, www.hotelitaliaroma.it, info@hotelitaliaroma.com).
Request one of the four "residenza" rooms upstairs on the third
floor, which are newer, quiet, and the same price. They also have
eight decent annex rooms across the street.

$ Suore di Santa Elisabetta is a heavenly Polish-run convent with a peaceful garden and 70 beds in tidy twin-bedded (only) rooms. Often booked long in advance, with such tranquility it's a super value (S-€40, Sb-€48, D-€66, Db-€85, Tb-€106, Qb-€128, Quint/b-€142, no air-con, elevator serves top floors only, fine view roof terrace and breakfast hall, 23:00 curfew, a block southwest of Santa Maria Maggiore at Via dell'Olmata 9, Metro: Termini or Vittorio Emanuele, tel. 06-488-8271, fax 06-488-4066, www .elzbietanki-roma.eu, ist.it.s.elisabetta@libero.it).

$ Gulliver's Lodge B&B has four fun, colorful rooms on the ground floor of a large, secure building. Well-located on a busy street, the rooms are nevertheless quiet. Although the public spaces are few, in-room extras like DVD players (and DVDs, including my Italy shows) make it a nice home base (Db-€110, Tb-€120, cash only, air-con, Internet access and Wi-Fi, a 15-minute walk southwest of Termini train station at Via Cavour 101, Metro: Cavour, tel. 06-9727-3789, www.gulliverslodge.com, stay@gulliverslodge .com, Sara and Mary).

Sleeping Cheaply, Northeast of Termini Train Station

The cheapest beds in town are northeast of Termini train station (Metro: Termini). Some travelers feel this area is weird and spooky after dark, but these hotels feel plenty safe. With your back to the train tracks, turn right and walk two blocks out of the station. **Splashnet** launderette/Internet café is handy if you're staying in this area (€6 full-serve wash and dry, Internet access-€1.50/hour, €2 luggage storage per day—or free if you wash and go online, daily 8:30-24:00, just off Via Milazzo at Via Varese 33, tel. 06-4470-3523).

$ The Beehive gives vagabonds—old and young—a cheap, clean, and comfy home in Rome, thoughtfully and creatively run by Steve and Linda, a friendly young American couple. They offer six great-value artsy-mod double rooms (D-€80, T-€105) and an eight-bed dorm (€25 bunks, Internet access and Wi-Fi, private garden terrace, 2 blocks north of Termini train station at Via Marghera 8, tel. 06-4470-4553, www.the-beehive.com, info@the -beehive.com).

$ Hotel Select Garden, a modern and comfortable 19-room hotel run by the cheery Picca family, boasts lively modern art adorning the walls and a beautiful lemon-tree garden. It's a welcome refuge from the bustling Eternal City, located on a quiet street just a couple of blocks from the train station (Sb-€85, Db-€100, Tb-€120, show this book and ask for best Rick Steves price, air-con, Wi-Fi, Via V. Bachelet 6, tel. 06-445-6383, fax

06-444-1086, www.hotelselectgarden.com, info@hotelselect garden.com, Armando).

$ Hotel Sileo, with shiny chandeliers in dim rooms, has a contract to house train conductors who work the night shift—so two of its doubles are rentable only from 18:30 to 9:00 for €60. The rest of their 10 rooms are available any time of day (Db-€75, Tb-€90, air-con, elevator, Via Magenta 39, fourth floor, tel. & fax 06-445-0246, www.hotelsileo.com, info@hotelsileo.com). Friendly Alessandro and Maria Savioli don't speak English, but daughter Anna does.

$ Funny Palace Hostel, adjacent to Splashnet and run by its entrepreneurial owner Mabri, rents dorm beds in quiet four-person rooms and 18 stark-but-clean private rooms (dorm beds-€30, Db-€100, cash only, reception in the launderette—described earlier, Via Varese 33/31, tel. 06-4470-3523, www.hostelfunny.com).

$ Yellow Hostel rents 130 beds in 4-, 6-, and 12-bed coed dorms to 18- through 39-year-olds only. Hip yet sane, it's well-run with fine facilities, including lockers. There's no curfew, and a late-night bar is next door (€24-34 per bed depending on plumbing, size, and season; reserve via email—no telephone reservations accepted, no breakfast, Wi-Fi and laptop rental available, 6 blocks from station, just past Via Vicenza at Via Palestro 44, tel. 06-493-82682, www.the-yellow.com).

$ Fawlty Towers Hostel is all right, and works for backpackers arriving by train. It offers 50 beds and lots of fun, games, and extras (4-bed dorms-€25 per person, S-€55, D-€65, Db-€80, Q-€90, includes sheets, elevator, free Internet access, kitchenette, peaceful sun terrace, from station walk a block down Via Marghera and turn right to Via Magenta 39, tel. 06-445-0374, fax 06-4543-5942, www.fawltytowers.org, info@fawltytowers.org). Their nearby annex, **Bubbles,** offers similar beds and rates and shares the same reception desk.

Near Ancient Rome

Stretching from the Colosseum to Piazza Venezia, this area is central. Sightseers are a short walk from the Colosseum, Roman Forum, and Trajan's Column.

Near the Colosseum

$$$ Hotel Lancelot is a comfortable yet elegant refuge—a 60-room hotel with the ambience of a B&B. It's quiet and safe, with a shady courtyard, restaurant, bar, and tiny communal sixth-floor terrace. Well-run by Faris and Lubna Khan, it's popular with returning guests (Sb-€125, Db-€196, Tb-€222, Qb-€260, €20 extra for sixth-floor terrace room with a Colosseum view, discount

Hotels near Ancient Rome

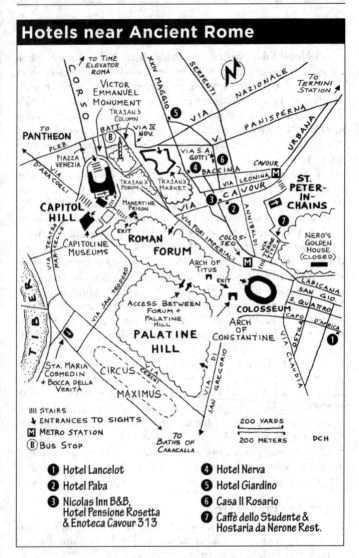

● Hotel Lancelot
● Hotel Paba
● Nicolas Inn B&B,
  Hotel Pensione Rosetta
  & Enoteca Cavour 313

● Hotel Nerva
● Hotel Giardino
● Casa Il Rosario
● Caffè dello Studente &
  Hostaria da Nerone Rest.

with this book, air-con, elevator, wheelchair-accessible, Wi-Fi, parking–€10/day, 10-minute walk behind Colosseum near San Clemente Church at Via Capo d'Africa 47, tel. 06-7045-0615, fax 06-7045-0640, www.lancelothotel.com, info@lancelothotel.com). Faris and Lubna speak the Queen's English.

$$ Hotel Paba has seven fresh rooms, chocolate box–tidy and lovingly cared for by Alberta Castelli. Though it overlooks busy Via Cavour just two blocks from the Colosseum, it's quiet enough (Db–€135, extra bed–€40, cash discount, huge beds, breakfast

ROME

served in room, air-con, elevator, Wi-Fi, Via Cavour 266, Metro: Cavour, tel. 06-4782-4902, fax 06-4788-1225, www.hotelpaba .com, info@hotelpaba.com).

$$ Nicolas Inn Bed & Breakfast, a delightful little four-room place with thoughtful touches, is spacious and bright. It's run by François and American expat Melissa, who make you feel like you have caring friends in Rome (Db-€100-170, extra bed-€30, cash discount with this book, included breakfast served at neigh-boring bar, air-con, Wi-Fi, Via Cavour 295, tel. 06-976-18483, www.nicolasinn.com, info@nicolasinn.com).

$ Hotel Pensione Rosetta, homey and family-run, rents 20 rooms. It's pretty minimal, with no lounge and no breakfast, but has a good location and reasonable prices (Sb-€65, Db-€90, Tb-€105, air-con, Wi-Fi, Via Cavour 295, tel. 06-478-23069, www.rosettahotel.com, info@rosettahotel.com).

Near Piazza Venezia

$$$ Hotel Nerva is a three-star slice of tranquility with 19 small, overpriced (but often discounted) rooms on a surprisingly quiet back street just steps away from the Roman Forum (Sb-€140, Db-€190, extra bed-€45, ask for Rick Steves discount, rates very soft—especially off-season, air-con, elevator, Via Tor de' Conti 3, tel. 06-678-1835, fax 06-6992-2204, www.hotelnerva.com, info @hotelnerva.com, Antonio, Paolo, Anna).

$ Hotel Giardino, true to its name, has a small garden area and offers 11 pleasant rooms in a central location three blocks northeast of Piazza Venezia. With a tiny central lobby and a small breakfast room, it suits travelers who prize location over big-hotel amenities (Sb-€85, Db-€130, one smaller Db for 15 percent less; show this book and ask for best Rick Steves price, cash only, check website for specials, air-con, effective double-paned windows, on a busy street off Piazza di Quirinale at Via XXIV Maggio 51, tel. 06-679-4584, fax 06-679-5155, www.hotel-giardino-roma.com, info@hotel-giardino-roma.com, helpful Gianluca).

$ Casa Il Rosario is a peaceful, well-run Dominican con-vent renting 40 rooms with monastic simplicity to both pilgrims and tourists in a good neighborhood (reserve several months in advance, S-€42, Sb-€54, Db-€94, Tb-€120, single beds only, fans, free Internet access, roof-terrace picnics welcome, 23:00 curfew, midway between the Quirinale and Colosseum near bottom of Via Nazionale at Via Sant'Agata dei Goti 10, bus #40 or #170 from Termini, tel. 06-679-2346, fax 06-6994-1106, irodopre@tin.it).

In the Pantheon Neighborhood

Winding, narrow lanes filled with foot traffic and lined with bou-tique shops and tiny trattorias...this is village Rome at its best.

You'll pay for the atmosphere, but this is where you want to be—especially at night, when Romans and tourists gather in the flood-lit piazzas for the evening stroll, the *passeggiata*.

Near Campo de' Fiori

You'll pay a premium (and endure a little extra night noise) to stay in the old center. But each of these places is romantically set deep in the tangled back streets near the idyllic Campo de' Fiori and, for many, worth the extra money.

$$$ Casa di Santa Brigida overlooks the elegant Piazza Farnese. With soft-spoken sisters gliding down polished hallways and pearly gates instead of doors, this lavish 20-room convent makes exhaust-stained Roman tourists feel like they've died and gone to heaven. If you don't need a double bed, it's worth the splurge (Sb-€110, twin Db-€190, 3 percent extra if you pay with credit card, can pay with personal check for no extra charge, book well in advance, air-con, elevator, Internet access, tasty €25 dinners, roof garden, plush library, Monserrato 54, tel. 06-6889-2596, fax 06-6889-1573, piazzafarnese@brigidine.org, many of the sisters are from India and speak English). If you get no response to your fax or email within three days, consider that a "no."

$ Hotel Smeraldo, with 50 rooms, is strictly run, clean, and a great deal (Sb-€100, Db-€130, Tb-€160, rooms €30 less off-season, air-con, elevator, flowery roof terrace, midway between Campo de' Fiori and Largo Argentina at Vicolo dei Chiodaroli 9, tel. 06-687-5929, fax 06-6880-5495, www.smeraldoroma.com, albergo smeraldoroma@tin.it, Massimo and Walter). Their **Dipendenza Smeraldo,** 10 yards around the corner at Via dei Chiavari 32, has 16 similar rooms (same price and free breakfast, same reception and contact info).

In the Jewish Ghetto

$$ Hotel Arenula, with 50 decent rooms, is the only hotel in Rome's old Jewish ghetto. While it has the ambience of a gym and attracts lots of students, it's a good value in the thick of old Rome (Sb-€75-98, Db-€133, €100 July-Aug, ask about high-season discount with this book, extra bed-€21, air-con, no elevator, Wi-Fi, opposite the fountain in the park on Via Arenula at Via Santa Maria de' Calderari 47, tel. 06-687-9454, fax 06-689-6188, www .hotelarenula.com, info@hotelarenula.com, Rosanna).

Close to the Pantheon

These places are buried in the pedestrian-friendly heart of ancient Rome, each within a four-minute walk of the Pantheon. You'll pay more here—but you'll save time and money by being exactly where you want to be for your early and late wandering.

ROME

Hotels in the Pantheon Neighborhood

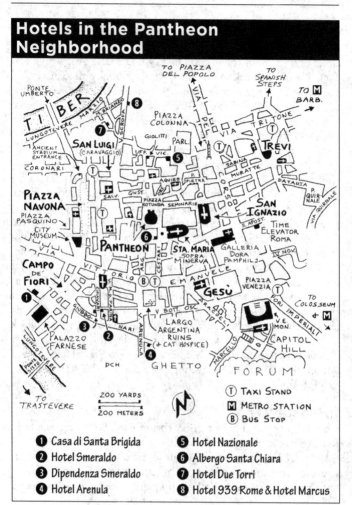

- ❶ Casa di Santa Brigida
- ❷ Hotel Smeraldo
- ❸ Dipendenza Smeraldo
- ❹ Hotel Arenula
- ❺ Hotel Nazionale
- ❻ Albergo Santa Chiara
- ❼ Hotel Due Torri
- ❽ Hotel 939 Rome & Hotel Marcus

$$$ Hotel Nazionale, a four-star landmark, is a 16th-century palace that shares a well-policed square with the Parliament building. Its 100 rooms are accentuated by lush public spaces, fancy bars, a uniformed staff, and a marble-floored restaurant. It's a big, stuffy hotel with a revolving front door, but it's a worthy splurge if you want security, comfort, and ancient Rome at your doorstep (Sb-€220, Db-€350, giant deluxe Db-€480, extra person-€70, ask for Rick Steves discount, check online for summer and weekend discounts, air-con, elevator, Piazza Montecitorio 131, tel. 06-695-001, fax 06-678-6677, www.hotelnazionale.it, info@hotelnazionale.it).

$$$ Albergo Santa Chiara is big, solid, and hotelesque. Flavia, Silvio, and their fine staff offer marbled elegance (but basic furniture) and all the hotel services in the old center. Its ample public lounges are dressy and professional, and its 99 rooms are quiet and spacious (Sb-€138, Db-€190, Db-€215 April-June and Oct, Tb-€262, check website for discounts, book online direct and request special Rick Steves rates, elevator, behind Pantheon at Via di Santa Chiara 21, tel. 06-687-2979, fax 06-687-3144, www.albergo santachiara.com, info@albergosantachiara.com).

$$$ **Hotel Due Torri,** hiding out on a tiny quiet street, is beautifully located. It feels professional yet homey, with an accommodating staff, generous public spaces, and 26 small rooms. While the location and lounge are great, the rooms are overpriced (Sb-€125, Db-€195, family apartment-€230 for 3 and €260 for 4, check website for frequent discounts, air-con, elevator, pay Internet access, a block off Via della Scrofa at Vicolo del Leonetto 23, tel. 06-6880-6956, fax 06-686-5442, www.hotelduetorriroma.com, info@hotelduetorriroma.com, Cinzia).

$**Hotel 939 Rome** and **Hotel Marcus** are two hotels that seem like one (same entrance, lobby, and contact info). The 939 has renovated rooms, while the Marcus is more utilitarian. Together they offer 17 rooms on the second floor in the old center of Rome above noisy Via della Scrofa (Db-€100-140, extra bed-€30, check website for frequent discounts, air-con, elevator; from Via della Scrofa, turn right at Piazza Nicosia and head to Via del Clementino 94; tel. 06-6830-0312, www.hotel939.com, hotel939@hotmail.it, helpful Aurora).

In Trastevere

Colorful and genuine in a gritty sort of way, Trastevere is a treat for travelers looking for a less touristy and more bohemian atmosphere. Choices are few here, but by trekking across the Tiber, you can have the experience of being comfortably immersed in old Rome. To locate the following places, see the map on pages 938-939.

$$$ **Hotel Santa Maria** sits like a lazy hacienda in the midst of Trastevere. Surrounded by a medieval skyline, you'll feel as if you're on some romantic stage set. Its 18 small but well-equipped, air-conditioned rooms—former cells in a cloister—are all on the ground floor, as are a few suites for up to six people. The rooms circle a gravelly courtyard of orange trees and stay-awhile patio furniture (Db-€180, Tb-€220; show this book and ask for best Rick Steves price, higher rates for stays shorter than three nights, cash preferred, family rooms, free loaner bikes, Internet access and Wi-Fi, face church on Piazza Maria Trastevere and go right down Via della Fonte d'Olio 50 yards to Vicolo del Piede 2, tel. 06-589-4626, fax 06-589-4815, www.hotelsantamaria.info, info@hotel santamaria.info, Stefano). Some rooms come with family-friendly

fold-down bunks for €30 extra per person. Their freshly renovated six-room **Residenza Santa Maria** is a couple of blocks away (same prices and contact info).

$$$ Residenza Arco dei Tolomei has six small, unique, antique-filled rooms in a quiet and elegant setting—you can pretend you're visiting aristocratic relatives (Db-€200, discounts for cash and for stays of 3 days or more, reserve well in advance, Internet access and Wi-Fi, from Piazza Piscinula a block up Via dell'Arco de' Tolomei at #27, tel. 06-5832-0819, www.bbarcodei tolomei.com, info@bbarcodeitolomei.com, Marco, Gianna Paola, and dog Pixel).

$$$ Relais le Clarisse retains the tranquil feel of its former life as a convent. Its five tastefully furnished rooms, which vary in size and amenities, surround a leafy courtyard—a little slice of the countryside in the city (Db-€205, Db suite-€195-220, Tb suite-€220-250, Qb suite-€260-290, prices vary with season, just off Viale Trastevere at Via Cardinale Merry del Val 20, tel. & fax 06-5833-4437, www.leclarisse.com, info@leclarisse.com, Maria and Toy).

$$ Casa San Giuseppe is down a characteristic laundry-strewn lane with views of Aurelian Walls. While convent-owned, it's a secular place renting 29 plain but peaceful, spacious, and spotless rooms (Sb-€115, Db-€155, Tb-€185, Qb-€215, garden-facing rooms are quiet, air-con, elevator, Internet access, parking-€15, just north of Piazza Trilussa at Vicolo Moroni 22, tel. 06-5833-3490, fax 06-5833-5754, www.casasangiuseppe.it, info @casasangiuseppe.it, Germano).

$$ Arco del Lauro B&B rents six white, minimalist rooms in a good location. Facing a courtyard (no views but little noise), the friendly welcome and good value make up for the lack of public spaces (Db-€135, Qb-€185, prices good if booked direct, cash only, included breakfast served in a café, Internet access and Wi-Fi, from Piazza Piscinula a block up Via dell'Arco de' Tolomei at #27, tel. 06-9784-0350, www.arcodellauro.it, info@arcodellauro.it, Lorenza and Daniela).

Near Vatican City

Sleeping near the Vatican is expensive, but some enjoy calling this neighborhood home. Even though it's handy to the Vatican (when the rapture hits, you're right there), everything else is a long way away.

$$$ Hotel Alimandi Vaticano, facing the Vatican Museum, is beautifully designed. Run by the Alimandi family (Enrico, Irene, Germano), it features four stars, 24 spacious rooms, and all the modern comforts you can imagine (Sb-€170, standard Db-€170-200, big Db with 2 double beds-€240-260, Tb-€230-260,

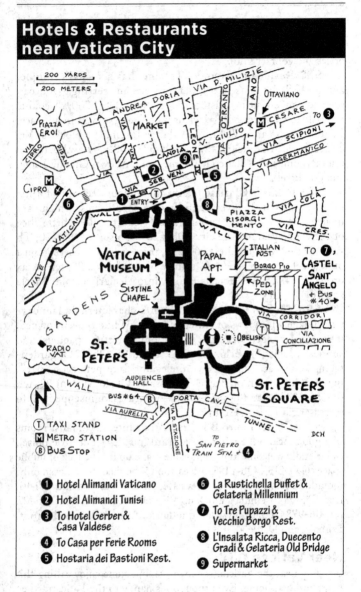

Hotels & Restaurants near Vatican City

Legend:

- (T) TAXI STAND
- (M) METRO STATION
- (B) BUS STOP

1. Hotel Alimandi Vaticano
2. Hotel Alimandi Tunisi
3. To Hotel Gerber & Casa Valdese
4. To Casa per Ferie Rooms
5. Hostaria dei Bastioni Rest.
6. La Rustichella Buffet & Gelateria Millennium
7. To Tre Pupazzi & Vecchio Borgo Rest.
8. L'Insalata Ricca, Duecento Gradi & Gelateria Old Bridge
9. Supermarket

cash discount, air-con, elevator, Viale Vaticano 99, Metro: Cipro, tel. 06-397-45562, fax 06-397-30132, www.alimandi.it, alimandi vaticano@alimandi.com).

$$ Hotel Alimandi Tunisi is a good value, run by other members of the friendly and entrepreneurial Alimandi family—Paolo, Grazia, Luigi, Marta, and Barbara. Their 27 perfumed rooms are air-conditioned, modern, and marbled in white (Sb-

€90, Db-€130-175, cash discount, grand buffet breakfast served in great roof garden, elevator, small gym, pool table, piano lounge, down the stairs directly in front of Vatican Museum, Via Tunisi 8, Metro: Cipro, reserve by phone at tel. 06-3972-3941, fax 06-3972-3943, www.alimandi.it, alimandi@tin.it). They offer a €15/person airport shuttle.

$$ Hotel Gerber, set in a quiet residential area, is family-run with 27 well-polished, businesslike, air-conditioned rooms (Sb-€120, Db-€170, Tb-€190, Qb-€200, ask about discount with this book when you reserve direct, elevator, Wi-Fi, leafy terrace, Via degli Scipioni 241, at intersection with Via Ezio, a block from Metro: Lepanto, tel. 06-321-6485, fax 06-321-7048, www.hotel gerber.it, info@hotelgerber.it, Peter, Simonetta, and friendly dog Kira).

$ Casa Valdese is an efficient, well-managed church-run hotel just over the Tiber River and near the Vatican, with 35 big, quiet rooms. It feels safe if a bit institutional, with the bonus of two breezy communal roof terraces with incredible views (two external Sb-€58, Db-€130, Tb-€180, Qb-€210, discounts for 3-night stays, Internet access and Wi-Fi; from Lepanto Metro station, go one block down Via M. Colonna, turn left on Via degli Scipioni, then continue for a block to the intersection with Via Alessandro Farnese 18; tel. 06-321-5362, fax 06-321-1843, www .casavaldeseroma.it, reception@casavaldeseroma.it).

$ Casa per Ferie Santa Maria alle Fornaci houses pilgrims and secular tourists with simple class just a short walk south of the Vatican in 54 identical stark, utilitarian, mostly twin-bedded rooms. This is the most user-friendly convent-type place I've found. Reserve at least three months in advance (Sb-€70, Db-€98, Tb-€130, air-con, elevator; take bus #64 from Termini train station to San Pietro train station, then walk 100 yards north along Via della Stazione di San Pietro to Piazza Santa Maria alle Fornaci 27; tel. 06-393-67632, fax 06-393-66795, www.trinitaridematha.it, cffornaci@tin.it).

Eating in Rome

I've listed a number of restaurants I enjoy. While most are in quaint and therefore pricey and touristy areas (Piazza Navona, the Pantheon neighborhood, Campo de' Fiori, and Trastevere), many are tucked away just off the tourist crush.

In general, I'm impressed by how small the price difference is from a mediocre restaurant to a fine one. You can pay about 20 percent more for double the quality. If I had $90 for three meals in Rome, I'd spend $50 for one and $20 each for the other two, rather than $30 on all three. For splurge meals, I'd consider Gabriello,

Fortunato, and Al Bric (in that order).

Rome's fabled nightspots (most notably Piazza Navona, near the Pantheon, and Campo de' Fiori) are lined with the outdoor tables of touristy restaurants with enticing menus and formal-vested waiters. The atmosphere is super-romantic: I, too, like the idea of dining under floodlit monuments, amid a constantly flowing parade of people. But you'll likely be surrounded by tourists, and noisy English-speakers can kill the ambience of the spot...leaving you with just a forgettable and overpriced meal. Restaurants in these areas are notorious for surprise charges, forgettable food, microwaved ravioli, and bad service.

I enjoy the view by savoring just a drink or dessert on a famous square, but I dine with locals on nearby low-rent streets, where the proprietor needs to serve a good-value meal and nurture a local following to stay in business. If you're set on eating—or just drinking and snacking—on a famous piazza, you don't need a guidebook listing to choose a spot; enjoy the ritual of slowly circling the square, observing both the food and the people eating it, and just sit where the view and menu appeals to you.

Note that Rome discourages people from picnicking or drinking at historic monuments (such as on the Spanish Steps) in the old center. Technically violators can be fined, though it rarely happens. You'll be fine if you eat *with* a view rather than *on* the view.

In Trastevere

Colorful Trastevere is now pretty touristy. Still, Romans join the tourists to eat on the rustic side of the Tiber River. Start at the central square (Piazza Santa Maria). Then choose: Eat with tourists enjoying the ambience of the famous square, or wander the back streets in search of a mom-and-pop place with barely a menu. My recommendations are within a few minutes' walk of each other (between Piazza Santa Maria Trastevere and Ponte Sisto; see map on pages 938-939).

Trattoria da Lucia lets you enjoy simple, traditional food at a good price in a great scene. It's the quintessential rustic, 100 percent Roman Trastevere dining experience, and has been family-run since World War II. You'll meet four generations of the family, including Giuliano and Renato, their uncle Ennio, and Ennio's mom—pictured on the menu in the 1950s. The family specialty is *spaghetti alla Gricia*, with pancetta (€9 pastas, €11 *secondi*, Tue-Sun 12:30-15:00 & 19:30-23:00, closed Mon, cash only, comfy indoor or evocative outdoor seating, just off Via del Mattonato on Vicolo del Mattonato 2, tel. 06-580-3601, some English spoken).

Trattoria da Olindo takes homey to extremes. You really feel like you dropped in on a family that cooks for the neighborhood to supplement their income. Don't expect any smiles here (€7 pastas,

€9 *secondi,* Mon-Sat dinner served 20:00-22:30, closed Sun, cash only, indoor and funky outdoor seating, on the corner of Vicolo della Scala and Via del Mattonato at #8, tel. 06-581-8835).

Dar Poeta Pizzeria, tucked in a back alley, cranks out some of the best wood-fired pizza I've had in Rome. It's run by four friends—Marco, Paolo, Enrico, and another Marco—who welcome you into the informal restaurant beneath exposed brick arches. If you're in a spicy mood, order *lingua di fuoco* (tongue of fire). If you're extra hungry, pay an extra euro for *pizza alto* (thicker crust). Choose between their classic, cramped interior and lively tables outside on the cobblestones. Their chocolate dessert calzone is a favorite (€6-9 pizzas, daily 12:00-24:00, Vicolo del Bologna 45, tel. 06-588-0516).

Osteria Ponte Sisto da Oliviero, small and Mediterranean, specializes in traditional Roman cuisine, but has frequent Neapolitan specials as well. Just outside the tourist zone, it caters mostly to Romans and offers beautiful desserts and a fine value (€10 pastas, €14 *secondi,* Thu-Tue 12:30-15:30 & 19:30-24:00, closed Wed, Via Ponte Sisto 80, tel. 06-588-3411, Oliviero). Crossing Ponte Sisto (pedestrian bridge) toward Trastevere, continue across the little square (Piazza Trilussa) and you'll see it on the right.

Ristorante Checco er Carettiere is a big family-run place that's been a Trastevere fixture for four generations. With white tablecloths, well-presented food, and dressy local diners, this is *the* place for a special meal in Trastevere. While it's overpriced, you'll eat well amidst lots of fun commotion. Reservations are smart, especially on weekends (€16 pastas, €22 *secondi,* daily 12:30-15:00 & 19:30-23:15, Via Benedetta 10, tel. 06-580-0985). Their *osteria* next door (#13) shares the same kitchen and offers less ambience, lower prices, and a more basic menu that changes daily (€11 pastas). Romans consider their *gelateria* (next door at #7) to be among the best on this side of the river.

Pizzeria "Ai Marmi" is a bright and noisy festival of pizza, where the oven and pizza-assembly line are surrounded by marble-slab tables (hence the nickname "the Morgue"). It's a classic Roman scene, with famously good €8 pizzas and very tight seating. Expect a long line between 20:00 and 22:00 (Thu-Tue 18:30-24:00, closed Wed, cash only, outdoor seating on busy Viale Trastevere, tram #8 from Largo Argentina to first stop over bridge, just beyond Piazza Sonnino at Viale Trastevere 53, tel. 06-580-0919).

Cantina Paradiso Wine and Cocktail Bar, a block over Viale Trastevere from the touristy action, has a simple romantic charm. During happy hour (18:00-21:00), the €6 drinks come with a well-made little buffet that can turn into a cheap, light dinner (€8 pastas, daily 12:00-24:00, lunch buffet, vegetarian options, Via San Francesco a Ripa 73, tel. 06-5899-799, Kiki).

And for Dessert: **Gelateria alla Scala** is a terrific little ice-cream shop that dishes up delightful cinnamon *(cannella)* and oh-wow pistachio (daily 12:00–24:00, Piazza della Scala 51, across from church on Piazza della Scala).

In the Jewish Ghetto

The Jewish Ghetto sits just across the river from Trastevere.

Sora Margherita, hiding without a sign on a cluttered square, has been a rustic neighborhood favorite since 1927. Amid a picturesque commotion, families chow down on old-time Roman and Jewish dishes for a decent price. As it's technically not a real restaurant (it avoids red tape by being officially designated as an *associazione culturale*), you'll need to sign a card to join the "cultural association" when you order (don't worry; membership has no obligations except that you enjoy your meal). The menu's crude term for the fettuccini gives you some idea of the mood of this place: *nazzica culo* ("shaky ass"—what happens while it's made). Reservations are almost always necessary (June-Aug Mon-Fri 12:30–15:00, dinner seatings on Thu and Fri only at 20:00 and 21:30, closed Sat-Sun; Sept-May Mon-Sat 12:30–15:00, dinner seatings on Fri and Sat at 20:00 and 21:30, closed Sun; just south of Via del Portico d'Ottavia at Piazza delle Cinque Scole 30—look for the red curtain, tel. 06-687-4216, Ivan doesn't speak English).

In the Pantheon Neighborhood

For the restaurants in this central area, I've listed them based on which landmark they're closest to: Campo de' Fiori, Piazza Navona, the Trevi Fountain, or the Pantheon itself.

On and near Campo de' Fiori

While it is touristy, Campo de' Fiori offers a sublimely romantic setting. And, since it's so close to the collective heart of Rome, it remains popular with locals, even though its restaurants offer greater atmosphere than food value. The square is lined with popular and interesting bars, pizzerias, and small restaurants—all great for people-watching over a glass of wine. Later at night it's taken over by a younger clubbing crowd.

Osteria da Giovanni ar Galletto is nearby, on the more elegant and peaceful Piazza Farnese. Angelo entertains an upscale Roman crowd and has magical outdoor seating. Regrettably, service can be horrible, you need to double-check the bill, and single diners aren't treated very well. Still, if you're in no hurry and ready to savor my favorite al fresco setting in Rome (while humoring the waiters), this is a good bet (€10 pastas, €15 *secondi*, Mon-Sat 12:15–15:00 & 19:30–23:00, closed Sun, reservations smart for outdoor seating, tucked in corner of Piazza Farnese at #102, tel. 06-686-1714).

Osteria Enoteca al Bric is a mod bistro-type place run by Roberto and Barbara, who love to cook, serve good wine, and listen to jazz. With only the finest ingredients, and an ambience elegant in its simplicity, they've created the perfect package for a romantic night out. Wine-case lids decorate the wall like happy memories. With candlelit grace, it's perfect for the wine snob in the mood for pasta and fine cheese. Aficionados choose their bottle from the huge selection lining the walls near the entrance. Beginners order fine wine by the glass with help from the waiter when they order their meal (daily from 19:30 for dinner, closed Mon, reserve if dining after 20:30, 100 yards off Campo de' Fiori at Via del Pellegrino 51, tel. 06-687-9533). While Al Bric can be pricey, feel free to establish a price limit (e.g., €40 per person without wine) and trust them to feed you royally within that price.

Filetti di Baccalà is a cheap and basic Roman classic, where nostalgic regulars cram into wooden tables savoring their old-school favorites—fried cod finger-food fillets (€5 each) and raw *puntarelle* greens (slathered with anchovy sauce in spring and winter). Study what others are eating, and order from your grease-stained server by pointing at what you want. Sit in the fluorescently lit interior or try to grab a seat out on the little square, a quiet haven a block east of Campo de' Fiori (Mon-Sat 17:30-23:00, closed Sun, cash only, Largo dei Librari 88, tel. 06-686-4018).

Trattoria der Pallaro, an eccentric and well-worn eatery that has no menu, has a slogan: "Here, you'll eat what we want to feed you." Paola Fazi—with a towel wrapped around her head turban-style—and her gang dish up a rustic five-course meal of typically Roman food for €25, including wine and coffee, and capped with a thimble of mandarin juice. While the service is odd and the food is forgettable, the experience can be fun (Tue-Sun 12:00-15:30 & 19:00-24:00, closed Mon, cash only, indoor/outdoor seating on quiet square, a block south of Corso Vittorio Emanuele, down Largo del Chiavari to Largo del Pallaro 15, tel. 06-6880-1488).

Pizzeria da Baffetto 2 makes pizza Roman-style: thin crust, crispy, and wood-fired. Eat in the cramped informal interior, or outside on the busy square (€7-9 pizzas, Wed-Mon 12:00-15:30 & 18:30-24:00, closed Tue, a block north of Campo de' Fiori at Piazza del Teatro di Pompeo 18, tel. 06-6821-0807).

Near Piazza Navona

Piazza Navona is the most quintessential setting for dining on a Roman square. Whether you eat here or not, you'll want to stroll the piazza before or after your evening meal. This is where many people fall in love with Rome. The tangled streets just to the west are lined with popular eateries of many stripes.

Pizzeria da Baffetto, buried deep in the old quarter behind

Restaurants in the

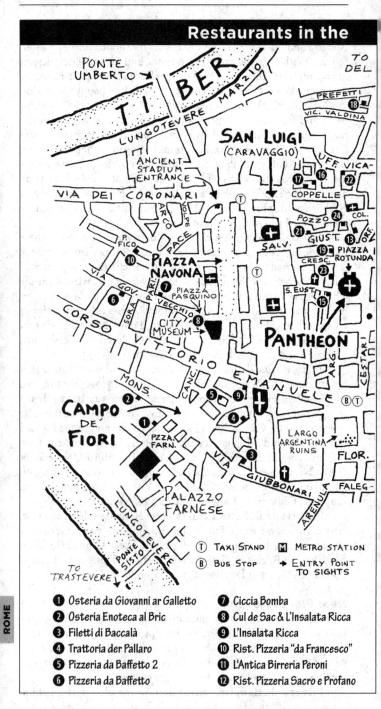

PONTE UMBERTO →

TIBER

LUNGOTEVERE MARZIO

TO DEL

PREFETTI ⑱

VIC. VALDINA

SAN LUIGI
(CARAVAGGIO)

UFF. VICA-

ANCIENT STADIUM ENTRANCE

VIA DEI CORONARI

⑰ ⑯

COPPELLE

ARCO VOLPE

PACE

Ⓣ

POZZO ㉔ COL.

⑬

⑤ SALV.

GIUST. ㉑

P. FICO

⑩

PIAZZA NAVONA →

⑲ PIAZZA ROTUNDA

CRESC.

㉓

S. EUST.

PIAZZA PASQUINO ⑦

Ⓣ

VIA GOV.

⑥ SORA

PARI.

VECCHIO

⑧

Ⓣ

⑮

PANTHEON

CORSO

CITY MUSEUM →

VITTORIO

EMANUELE

ARG.

CESTARI

MONS.

CAMPO DE' FIORI

②

①

⑤ ⑨

④

Ⓑ Ⓣ

PZZA. FARN.

③

LARGO ARGENTINA RUINS

FLOR.

VIA

GIUBBONARI

FALEG-

PALAZZO FARNESE

LUNGOTEVERE

ARENULA

PONTE SISTO

TO TRASTEVERE

Ⓣ TAXI STAND   Ⓜ METRO STATION
Ⓑ BUS STOP   → ENTRY POINT TO SIGHTS

❶ Osteria da Giovanni ar Galletto
❷ Osteria Enoteca al Bric
❸ Filetti di Baccalà
❹ Trattoria der Pallaro
❺ Pizzeria da Baffetto 2
❻ Pizzeria da Baffetto
❼ Ciccia Bomba
❽ Cul de Sac & L'Insalata Ricca
❾ L'Insalata Ricca
❿ Rist. Pizzeria "da Francesco"
⓫ L'Antica Birreria Peroni
⓬ Rist. Pizzeria Sacro e Profano

ROME

Pantheon Neighborhood

13 Ristorante da Fortunato
14 Ristorante Enoteca Corsi
15 Miscellanea
16 Osteria da Mario
17 Le Coppelle Taverna
18 Trattoria dal Cav. Gino
19 Antica Salumeria
20 Super Market Di per Di
21 Supermercato Despar
22 Gelateria Caffè Pasticceria Giolitti
23 Crèmeria Monteforte
24 Gelateria San Crispino

Piazza Navona, is a Roman favorite, famous for its rustic charm and tasty pizza. Its tables are tightly arranged amid the commotion of photos and sketches littering the walls. The pizza-assembly kitchen keeps things energetic, and the pizza oven keeps the main room warm (you can opt for a table on the cobbled street). Come early or late, or be prepared to wait (€7 pizzas, cash only, daily from 18:30, order "P," "M," or "D"—small, medium, or large; west of Piazza Navona on the corner of Via Sora at Via del Governo Vecchio 114, tel. 06-686-1617).

Ciccia Bomba is a traditional trattoria where Gianpaolo and crew serve up well-priced homemade pasta, wood-fired pizza, and other Roman specialties. With a name like "Fatso," this place had better have good food...and it does (€7 pastas, €9 *secondi,* Mon-Sat 12:00-15:00 & 19:00-24:00, closed Sun, off-season open Sun and closed Wed, Via del Governo Vecchio 76, a block west of Piazza Navona, just north from Piazza Pasquino, tel. 06-6880-2108).

Cul de Sac is a corridor-wide trattoria lined with wine bottles and packed with enthusiastic locals. Come early for an excellent tasting plate of salami and one of their many bottles of wine (they've got more than 1,000), or come later for a full meal of nicely cooked Roman dishes (daily 12:00-16:00 & 18:00-24:00, tel. 06-6880-1094, a block off Piazza Navona on Piazza Pasquino).

L'Insalata Ricca is a popular chain that specializes in hearty and healthy €8 salads and less-healthy pastas (daily 12:00-15:45 & 18:45-24:00). They have a handy branch on Piazza Pasquino (next to Cul de Sac, tel. 06-6830-7881), and a more spacious and enjoyable location a few blocks away, on a bigger square next to busy Corso Vittorio Emanuele (near Campo de' Fiori at Largo dei Chiavari 85, tel. 06-6880-3656).

Ristorante Pizzeria "da Francesco" is a bustling, unpretentious place with hardworking young waitstaff, great indoor seating, and classic outdoor seating on a cluttered little square that makes you want to break out a sketch pad. Their blackboard explains the daily specials (€7 pizzas, €8 pastas, €10 *secondi,* open daily, 3 blocks west of Piazza Navona at Piazza del Fico 29, tel. 06-686-4009).

Near the Trevi Fountain

L'Antica Birreria Peroni is Rome's answer to a German beer hall. Serving hearty mugs of the local Peroni beer and lots of just plain fun beer-hall food and Italian classics, the place is a hit with Romans for a cheap night out (Mon-Sat 12:00-24:00, closed Sun, midway between Trevi Fountain and Capitol Hill, a block off Via del Corso at Via di San Marcello 19, tel. 06-679-5310).

Ristorante Pizzeria Sacro e Profano fills an old church with spicy southern Italian (Calabrian) cuisine and satisfied tourists. Run with enthusiasm by Francesco and friends, this is just far enough away from the Trevi mobs. Their pizza oven is wood-fired, and their hearty €15 *antipasti* plate is a filling montage of Calabrian taste treats (daily 12:00-15:00 & 18:00-24:00, a block off Via del Tritone at Via dei Maroniti 29, tel. 06-679-1836).

Close to the Pantheon

Eating on the square facing the Pantheon is a temptation (there's even a McDonald's that offers some of the best outdoor seating in town), and I'd consider it just to relax and enjoy the Roman scene. But if you walk a block or two away, you'll get less view and better value. Here are some suggestions.

Ristorante da Fortunato is an Italian classic, with fresh flowers on the tables and waiters in white coats and black ties politely serving good meat and fish to politicians, foreign dignitaries, and tourists with good taste. Don't leave without perusing the photos of their famous visitors—everyone from former Iraqi Foreign Minister Tariq Aziz to Bill Clinton seems to have eaten here. All are pictured with the boss, Fortunato, who, since 1975, has been a master of simple edible elegance. The outdoor seating is fine for watching the river of Roman street life flow by, but the atmosphere is inside. For a dressy night out, this is a reliable and surprisingly reasonable choice—but be sure to reserve ahead (plan to spend €45 per person, Mon-Sat 12:30-15:00 & 19:30-23:30, closed Sun, a block in front of the Pantheon at Via del Pantheon 55, tel. 06-679-2788).

Ristorante Enoteca Corsi is a wine shop that grew into a thriving lunch-only restaurant. The Paiella family serves straightforward, traditional cuisine at great prices to an appreciative crowd of office workers. Check the blackboard for daily specials (gnocchi on Thursday, fish on Friday, and so on). Friendly Giuliana and Manuela welcome eaters to step into their wine shop and pick out a bottle. For the cheap take-away price, plus €2-4 (depending on the wine), they'll uncork it at your table. With €8 pastas, €11 main dishes, and fine wine at a third of the price you'd pay in normal restaurants, this can be a superb value. Consider finishing with a glass of the family's homemade *limoncello* (Mon-Sat 12:00-15:00, closed Sun, a block toward the Pantheon from the Gesù Church at Via del Gesù 87, no reservations possible, tel. 06-679-0821).

Miscellanea is run by much-loved Mikki, who's on a mission to keep foreign students well-fed. You'll find hearty and fresh €4 sandwiches and a long list of €6 salads, along with pasta and other staples. Mikki (and his son, Romero) often tosses in a fun little extra, including—if you have this book on the table—a free glass of Mikki's "sexy wine" (homemade from *fragoline*—strawberry-flavored grapes). This place is popular with American students on foreign-study programs (daily 8:00-24:00, indoor/outdoor seating, facing the rear of the Pantheon at Via della

Palombella 34, tel. 06-6813-5318).

Osteria da Mario, a homey little mom-and-pop joint with a no-stress menu, serves traditional favorites in a fun dining room or on tables spilling out onto a picturesque old Roman square (€8 pastas, €10 *secondi,* Mon-Sat 13:00-15:30 & 19:00-23:00, closed Sun, from the Pantheon walk 2 blocks up Via Pantheon, go left on Via delle Coppelle, take first right to Piazza delle Coppelle 51, tel. 06-6880-6349, Marco).

Le Coppelle Taverna is simple, basic, family-friendly, and inexpensive—especially for pizza—with a checkered-tablecloth ambience (€9 pizzas, daily 12:30-15:00 & 19:30-23:30, Via delle Coppelle 39, tel. 06-6880-6557, Alfonso).

Trattoria dal Cav. Gino, tucked away on a tiny street behind the Parliament, has been a favorite since 1963. Photos on the wall recall the days when it was the haunt of big-time politicians. Grandpa Gino shuffles around grating the parmesan cheese while his sister and son serve up traditional Roman favorites and make sure things run smoothly. Reserve ahead, even for lunch (€8 pastas, €11 *secondi,* cash only, Mon-Sat 13:00-14:45 & 20:00-22:30, closed Sun, fish on Friday, behind Piazza del Parlamento and just off Via di Campo Marzio at Vicolo Rosini 4, tel. 06-687-3434, Fabrizio and Carla—Gino's son and daughter—both speak English).

Picnicking Close to the Pantheon

It's fun to munch a picnic with a view of the Pantheon. (Remember to be discreet.) Here are some options.

Antica Salumeria is an old-time *alimentari* (grocery store) on the Pantheon square. Eduardo speaks English and will help you assemble your picnic: artichokes, mixed olives, bread, cheese, meat (they're proud of their Norcia prosciutto), and wine (with plastic glasses). Just set a price (figure €10 per person), and Eduardo will assemble it. Their pastries are fresh from their own bakery. While you can create your own sandwiches (sold by the weight, more fun, and cheaper), they also sell quality ready-made sandwiches for around €5 (daily 8:00-21:00, mobile 334-340-9014).

Supermarkets near the Pantheon: Food is relatively cheap at Italian supermarkets. **Super Market Di per Di** is a convenient place for groceries a block from Gesù Church (Mon-Sat 8:00-21:00, Sun 9:00-19:30, 50 yards off Via del Plebiscito at Via del Gesù 59). Another place, **Supermercato Despar,** is a half a block from the Pantheon toward Piazza Navona (daily 9:00-22:00, Via Giustiniani 18).

Gelato Close to the Pantheon

Three fine *gelaterie* are within a two-minute walk of the Pantheon. **Gelateria Caffè Pasticceria Giolitti,** Rome's most famous

ROME

and venerable ice-cream joint, has reasonable take-away prices and elegant Old World seating (daily 7:00-24:00, just off Piazza Colonna and Piazza Monte Citorio at Via Uffici del Vicario 40, tel. 06-699-1243).

Crèmeria Monteforte is known for its traditional, quality gelato and super-creamy sorbets *(cremolati)*. The fruit flavors are especially refreshing—think gourmet slushies (Tue-Sun 10:00-24:00, off-season closes earlier, closed Mon and Dec, faces the west side of the Pantheon at Via della Rotonda 22, tel. 06-686-7720).

Gelateria San Crispino, well-respected by Romans, serves small portions of particularly tasty gourmet gelato using creative ingredients. Because of their commitment to natural ingredients, the colors are muted; gelato purists consider bright colors a sign of unnatural chemicals used to attract children. They serve cups, but no cones (daily 12:00-24:00, a block in front of the Pantheon on Piazza della Maddalena, tel. 06-6889-1310).

In North Rome:
Near the Ara Pacis and Spanish Steps

To locate these restaurants, see the map on page 888.

Ristorante il Gabriello is inviting and small—modern under medieval arches—and provides a peaceful and local-feeling respite from all the top-end fashion shops in the area. Claudio serves with charisma, while his brother Gabriello cooks creative Roman cuisine using fresh, organic products from his wife's farm. Italians normally just trust the waiter and say, "Bring it on." Tourists are understandably more cautious, but you can be trusting here. Simply close your eyes and point to anything on the menu. Or invest €45 in "Claudio's Extravaganza" (not including wine), and he'll shower you with edible kindness. Specify whether you'd prefer fish, meat, or both. (Note that Romans think raw shellfish is the ultimate in fine dining. If you disagree, make that clear.) When finished, I stand up, hold my belly, and say, *"Ahhh, la vita è bella"* (€10 pastas, €15 *secondi,* dinner only, Mon-Sat 19:00-23:00, closed Sun, reservations smart, air-con, dress respectfully—no shorts please, 3 blocks from Spanish Steps at Via Vittoria 51, tel. 06-6994-0810).

Osteria Gusto is thriving with trendy locals. While pricey, it's untouristy, gives a glimpse of today's Roman scene, and is fine for a glass of good wine over an artisanal cheese plate or a complete dinner (€13 pastas, €20 *secondi,* daily 12:30-15:30 & 19:00-24:00, opens at 18:30 for drinks and appetizers only, reservations recommended after 20:00 and on weekends, on the corner of Via Soderini at Via della Frezza 16, tel. 06-3211-1482).

L'EnotecAntica, an upbeat, atmospheric 200-plus-year-old *enoteca,* has around 60 Italian-only wines by the glass (€4 to €10), and a fresh €14 *antipasti* plate of veggies, salami, and cheese. It's very crowded on summer evenings (daily 11:00–24:00, Via della Croce 76b, tel. 06-679-0896).

In Ancient Rome: Eating Cheaply near the Colosseum

You'll find good views but poor value at the restaurants directly behind the Colosseum. To get your money's worth, eat at least a block away. Here are three handy eateries, all shown on the map on page 952: one at the foot of Via Cavour, and two at the top of Terme di Tito (a long block uphill from the Colosseum, near St. Peter-in-Chains church—of Michelangelo's *Moses* fame; for directions, see page 902).

Enoteca Cavour 313 is a wine bar with a mission: to offer good wine and quality food with an old-fashioned commitment to value and friendly service. It's also a convenient place for a good lunch near the Forum and Colosseum. Angelo and his three partners enjoy creating a mellow ambience under lofts of wine bottles (daily specials and fine wines by the glass, daily 12:30–14:45 & 19:30–24:00, 100 yards off Via dei Fori Imperiali at Via Cavour 313, tel. 06-6785-496).

Caffè dello Studente is popular with engineering students attending the nearby University of Rome. Pina, Mauro, and their perky daughter Simona (speaks English) give my readers a royal welcome and serve typical *bar gastronomia* fare—toasted sandwiches, salads, and pizzas (stick to any of the aforementioned fare to avoid frozen dishes). If they have a "Rick Steves menu," give it a miss. You can get your food to go *(da portar via)*, eat standing at the crowded bar, or wait for table service outside. If it's not busy, show this book when you order at the bar and sit without paying extra at a table (Mon-Sat 7:30–22:30, April-Oct Sun 9:00–22:30, Nov-March closed Sun, Via delle Terme di Tito, tel. 06-488-3240).

Hostaria da Nerone, next door, is a more formal restaurant with much better food and homemade pasta dishes. Their €9 *antipasti* plate—with a variety of veggies, fish, and meat—is a good value for a quick lunch. While the *antipasti* menu indicates specifics, you can have a plate of whatever's out—just direct the waiter to assemble the €9 *antipasti* plate of your lunchtime dreams (Mon-Sat 12:00–15:00 & 19:00–23:00, closed Sun, indoor/outdoor seating, Via delle Terme di Tito 96, tel. 06-481-7952, run by Teo and Eugenio).

Near Termini Train Station

You have several eating options near my recommended hotels on Via Firenze.

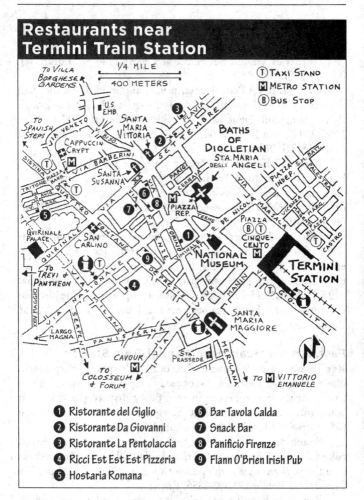

Restaurants near Termini Train Station

TO VILLA BORGHESE GARDENS
¼ MILE
400 METERS

Ⓣ TAXI STAND
Ⓜ METRO STATION
Ⓑ BUS STOP

TO SPANISH STEPS

U.S. EMB.

SANTA MARIA VITTORIA

CAPPUCCIN CRYPT

BATHS OF DIOCLETIAN
STA. MARIA DEGLI ANGELI

VIA VENETO

SANTA SUSANNA

VIA BARBERINI

PIAZZA REP.

QUIRINALE PALACE

SAN CARLINO

TO TREVI & PANTHEON

NATIONAL MUSEUM

PIAZZA CINQUE-CENTO

TERMINI STATION

LARGO MAGNA

SANTA MARIA MAGGIORE

CAVOUR

STA. PRASSEDE

TO COLOSSEUM & FORUM

TO Ⓜ VITTORIO EMANUELE

❶ Ristorante del Giglio
❷ Ristorante Da Giovanni
❸ Ristorante La Pentolaccia
❹ Ricci Est Est Est Pizzeria
❺ Hostaria Romana
❻ Bar Tavola Calda
❼ Snack Bar
❽ Panificio Firenze
❾ Flann O'Brien Irish Pub

Dining

Ristorante del Giglio is an elegant circa-1900 place with a long tradition of serving traditional Roman dishes. You'll eat pricey dishes in a big hall of about 20 tables with dressy locals and tourists following the recommendations of nearby hotels. While not a particularly good value, the space is nice and it's stress-free (€12 pastas, €15 *secondi*, Mon 19:00-23:00, Tue-Sat 12:15-15:00 & 19:00-23:00, closed Sun, alluring dessert cart, Via Torino 137, tel. 06-488-1606, Fiorella).

Ristorante Da Giovanni is a well-worn old-time eatery that makes no concessions to tourism or the modern world—just hard-working cooks and waiters serving standard dishes at great prices to a committed clientele. It's simply fun to eat in the middle of this high-energy, old-school diner (€6-9 pastas and *secondi*, daily specials, Mon-Sat 12:00-15:00 & 19:00-22:00, closed Sun and Aug, corner of Via XX Settembre at Via Antonio Salandra 1, tel. 06-485-950).

Ristorante La Pentolaccia, pricier and more romantic than the nearby Da Giovanni, is a dressy, tourist-friendly place with tight seating and classic Roman cooking (Mon-Sat 12:00-15:00 & 17:30-23:00, Sun 17:30-23:00, a block off Via XX Settembre at Via Flavia 38, tel. 06-483-477).

Ricci Est Est Est Pizzeria, a venerable family-run pizzeria, has plenty of historical ambience, good €8 pizzas, and dangerously tasty *fritti,* such as fried *baccalà* (cod) and zucchini flowers (Tue-Sun 19:00-24:00, closed Mon and Aug, Via Genova 32, tel. 06-488-1107).

Hostaria Romana is a busy bistro with a hustling and fun-loving gang of waiters and noisy walls graffitied by happy eaters. While they specialize in fish and traditional Roman dishes, their €10 *antipasti* plate can make a good meal in itself (Mon-Sat 12:15-15:00 & 19:15-23:00, closed Sun, a block up the lane just past the entrance to the big tunnel near the Trevi Fountain at Via de Boccaccio 1, tel. 06-474-5284).

Fast, Simple Meals near Termini Train Station

Bar Tavola Calda is a workers' favorite for a quick, cheap lunch. They have good, fresh hot dishes ready to go for a fine price. Head back past the bar to peruse their enticing display, point at what you want, then grab a seat and the young waitstaff will serve you (Mon-Fri 6:00-18:00, closed Sat-Sun, Via Torino 40).

Snack Bar puts out a lunchtime display of inexpensive pastas, colorful sandwiches, fresh fruit, and salad. Their loyal customers love the *caffè con crema* whipped with sugar (daily 6:00-24:00, Via Firenze 33, mobile 339-393-1356, Enrica).

Panificio Firenze has take-out pizza, sandwiches, and an old-fashioned *alimentari* (grocery) with everything you'd need for a picnic (Mon-Fri 7:00-19:00, Sat 7:00-14:00, closed Sun, Via Firenze 51-52, tel. 06-488-5035).

Flann O'Brien Irish Pub is an entertaining place for a light meal of pasta...or something *other* than pasta, such as grilled meats and giant salads, served early and late, when other places are closed. They have Irish beer, live sporting events on TV, and perhaps the most Italian crowd of all. Walk way back before choosing a table (daily 7:00-24:00, Via Nazionale 17, at intersection with Via Napoli, tel. 06-488-0418).

Near Vatican City

Avoid the restaurant-pushers handing out fliers near the Vatican: bad food and expensive menu tricks. Try any of these instead (see map on page 958).

Hostaria dei Bastioni, run by Emilio, is conveniently located midway on your hike from St. Peter's to the Vatican Museum, with noisy street-side seating and a quiet interior (€7 pastas, €12 *secondi*, no cover charge, Mon-Sat 12:00-15:30 & 19:00-23:00, closed Sun, Via Leone IV 29, at corner of Vatican wall, tel. 06-3972-3034).

La Rustichella serves tasty wood-fired pizza and the usual pasta in addition to their famous and sprawling *antipasti* buffet (€8 for a single plate). Arrive when it opens at 19:30 to avoid a line and have the pristine buffet to yourself. Do like the Romans do—take a moderate amount and make one trip only (Tue-Sun 12:30-15:00 & 19:30-24:00, closed Mon, near Metro: Cipro, opposite church at end of Via Candia, Via Angelo Emo 1, tel. 06-3972-0649). Consider the fun and fruity **Gelateria Millennium** next door.

L'Insalata Ricca is another branch of the popular chain that serves salads and pastas (daily 12:30-15:30 & 18:30-23:45, across from Vatican walls at Piazza Risorgimento 5, tel. 06-3973-0387).

Duecento Gradi is a good bet for fresh and creative €5 sandwiches (daily 12:00-23:00, Piazza Risorgimento 3, tel. 06-3975-4239).

Viale Giulio Cesare: This street is lined with cheap *pizza rustica* shops, self-serve places, and inviting eateries.

Along Borgo Pio: The pedestrian-only Borgo Pio—a block from Piazza San Pietro—has restaurants worth a look, such as **Tre Pupazzi** (Mon-Sat 12:00-15:00 & 19:00-23:00, closed Sun, at corner of Via Tre Pupazzi and Borgo Pio, tel. 06-686-8371). At **Vecchio Borgo,** across the street, you can get pasta, pizza slices, and veggies to go (Mon-Sat 9:00-21:00, closed Sun, Borgo Pio 27a, tel. 06-8117-3585).

Picnic Supplies: Turn your nose loose in the wonderful **Mercato Trionfale** covered market, one of the best in the city, three blocks north of the Vatican Museum (Mon-Sat roughly 7:00-14:00, closed Sun, corner of Via Tunisi and Via Andrea Doria). If the market is closed, try several nearby supermarkets; the most convenient is **GS Di per Di** (Mon-Sat 8:00-20:00, Sun 9:00-20:00, Via Sebastiano Veniero 16).

Gelato: **Gelateria Old Bridge** scoops up hearty portions of fresh gelato for tourists and nuns alike. The quality, quantity, and value can't be beat (daily 10:00-23:00, just off Piazza Risorgimento across from Vatican walls at Via Bastioni 3).

Rome Connections

Rome is well-connected with the rest of the planet, by train, bus, plane, and cruise ship. This section addresses your arrival and departure from the city. It explains the various options and gives a rundown on their points of departure.

By Train

Rome's main train station is the centrally located **Termini** Station, which has connections to the airport. Rome's other major station is **Tiburtina** bus/train station, which is starting to get a few high-speed rail connections. For in-depth descriptions of both Termini and Tiburtina stations, see page 863. Smaller stations include **Ostiense** (useful for going to South Rome and Testaccio) and its neighbor, **Porta San Paolo** (with connections to Ostia Antica). If you're staying near the Vatican and taking a regional train, it saves time to get off at **San Pietro** Station rather than at Termini.

Since virtually all of the most convenient connections for travelers depart from Termini, I've listed those below. In 30 years of visits, I've never had occasion to use Tiburtina, but that may change—Tiburtina is currently being redeveloped for high-speed rail. At least one Eurostar Italia train stops here already, and a new company—Nuovo Trasporto Viaggiatori (NTV)—has said it will begin running its Italo high-speed trains from Tiburtina in late 2011 (for details, see www.ntvspa.it). As a precaution, it's always smart to confirm whether your train departs from Termini or Tiburtina.

From Rome's Termini Station by Train to: Venice (roughly hourly, 3.5 hours, overnight possible), **Florence** (at least hourly, 1.5 hours), **La Spezia Centrale** (8/day direct, more with transfers in Pisa, 4 hours), **Milan** (hourly, 3.5-8 hours, overnight possible), **Amsterdam** (6/day, 20 hours), **Interlaken** (5/day, 7-9 hours, 2-3 changes, no direct overnight option), **Frankfurt** (7/day, 12 hours, several overnight options), **Munich** (4/day, 11 hours, several overnight options), **Nice** (6/day, 10 hours), **Paris** (4/day, 11-13 hours, several overnight options, important to reserve ahead), **Vienna** (3/day, 12-13 hours, several overnight options).

By Plane

Rome's two airports—**Fiumicino** (a.k.a. Leonardo da Vinci) and the small **Ciampino**—share the same website (www.adr.it). For budget flights within Europe, easyJet uses both airports, while Ryanair only uses Ciampino. Vueling and Blue Express only use Fiumicino.

Fiumicino Airport

Rome's major airport has a TI (in terminal 3, daily 8:00-19:00), ATMs, banks, luggage storage, shops, and bars. The Rome Walks website (www.romewalks.com) has a useful video on options for getting into the city from the airport.

A slick, direct **"Leonardo Express" train** connects the airport and Rome's central Termini train station in 30 minutes for €15. Trains run twice hourly in both directions from roughly 6:00 to 23:00 (leaving the airport at :06 and :36). From the airport's arrival gate, follow signs to *Stazione/Railway Station*. Buy your ticket from a machine, the Biglietteria office, or a newsstand at the platform, then validate it in a yellow machine near the track. Make sure the train you board is going to the central "Roma Termini" station, not "Roma Orte" or others.

Going from Termini train station to the airport, trains depart at about :22 and :52 past the hour, from track 25 (located way down at the far end of track 24; allow 10 minutes for the hike, moving walkways downstairs). Check the departure boards for "Fiumicino Aeroporto"—the local name for the airport—and confirm with an official or a local on the platform that the train is indeed going to the airport (€15, buy ticket from any *tabacchi* or newsstand in the station, or at the self-service machines, Termini-Fiumicino trains run 5:52-22:52). Read your ticket: If it requires validation, stamp it in the yellow machine near the platform before boarding. From the train station at the airport, you can access all of the terminals. Most American airlines flying to the US depart from Terminal 5 (some Delta flights leave from T3—call Delta at 848-780-376).

Allow lots of time going in either direction; there's a fair amount of transportation involved, including moving walkways, escalators, and walking (e.g., getting from your hotel to Termini, from Termini to the train platform, the ride to the airport, getting from the airport train station to check-in, etc.). Flying to the US involves an extra level of security—plan on getting to the airport even earlier (I like to arrive 2.5 hours ahead of my flight).

Shuttle van services run to and from the airport and can be economical for one or two people. Consider Rome Airport Shuttle (€25/1 person, extra people-€6 each, by reservation only, tel. 06-4201-4507 or 06-4201-3469, www.airportshuttle.it).

A **taxi** between Fiumicino and downtown Rome takes 45 minutes in normal traffic (for tips on taxis, see page 875). If you're catching a taxi at the airport, be sure to wait at the taxi stand. Avoid unmarked, unmetered taxis; these guys will try to tempt you away from the taxi-stand lineup by offering an immediate (rip-off) ride. Rome's official taxis have a fixed rate to and from the airport (€45 for up to four people with bags). If your cab driver tries to charge you more than €45 from the airport into town, say,

"Quarantacinque euro—È la legge" (kwah-RAHN-tah CHEENG-kway AY-oo-roh—ay lah LEJ-jay; which means, "Forty-five euros—It's the law"), and they should back off.

A new law allows cabbies not based in Rome to charge €60 for the ride. That sign is posted next to the €45-fare sign—confusing many tourists and allowing dishonest cabbies to overcharge. Only use a Rome city cab (with the "SPQR" shield on the door). They can only charge €45 for the ride to anywhere in the historic center (within the old city walls, where most of my recommended hotels are located).

To get from the airport into town cheaply by taxi, try teaming up with any tourist also just arriving (most are heading for hotels near yours in the center). When you're departing Rome, your hotel can arrange a taxi to the airport at any hour.

For **airport information,** call 06-65951. To inquire about flights, call 06-6595-3640 (Alitalia: tel. 06-2222; British Airways: tel. 199-712-266; Continental: tel. 06-6605-3030; Delta: tel. 848-780-376; Swiss International: tel. 848-868-120; United: tel. 848-800-692).

The local tour company Rome Walks has created a helpful **video** explaining how to get from Fiumicino to the city center. You can find it online on Rome Walks' YouTube channel (click "Fiumicino International Airport to Rome Centre").

Ciampino Airport

Rome's smaller airport (tel. 06-6595-9515) handles charter flights and some budget airlines (including all Ryanair and some easyJet flights).

To get to downtown Rome from the airport, you can take the Cotral bus, which leaves every 40 minutes (€1.20, 20-minute ride, toll-free tel. 800-174-471, www.cotralspa.it), to the Anagnina Metro stop, where you can connect by Metro to the stop nearest your hotel. Rome Airport Shuttle (listed earlier) also offers service to and from Ciampino. The Terravision Express Shuttle connects Ciampino and Termini, leaving every 20 minutes (€4 one-way, €8 round-trip, www.terravision.eu). The SIT Bus Shuttle also connects Termini train station to Ciampino (€6, about 2/hour, 30-60 minutes, runs 7:45-23:15 Ciampino to Termini, 4:30-21:30 Termini to Ciampino, pickup on Via Marsala just outside the train exit closest to track 1, tel. 06-591-7844, www.sitbusshuttle.it). A taxi should cost €35 to downtown (within the old city walls, including most of my recommended hotels).

VENICE

Venezia

Soak all day in this puddle of elegant decay. Venice is Europe's best-preserved big city. This car-free urban wonderland of a hundred islands—laced together by 400 bridges and 2,000 alleys—survives on the artificial respirator of tourism.

Born in a lagoon 1,500 years ago as a refuge from barbarians, Venice is overloaded with tourists and is slowly sinking (unrelated facts). In the Middle Ages, the Venetians became Europe's clever middlemen for East-West trade and created a great trading empire. By smuggling in the bones of St. Mark (San Marco) in A.D. 828, Venice gained religious importance as well. With the discovery of America and new trading routes to the Orient, Venetian power ebbed. But as Venice fell, her appetite for decadence grew. Through the 17th and 18th centuries, Venice partied on the wealth accumulated through earlier centuries as a trading power.

Today, Venice is home to just over 60,000 people in its old city, down from a peak population of nearly 200,000. While there are about 500,000 in greater Venice (counting the mainland, not counting tourists), the old town has a small-town feel. Locals seem to know everyone. To see small-town Venice away from the touristic flak, escape the Rialto-San Marco tourist zone and savor the town early and late without the hordes of vacationers day-tripping in from cruise ships and nearby beach resorts. A 10-minute walk from the madness puts you in an idyllic Venice that few tourists see.

Venice Overview

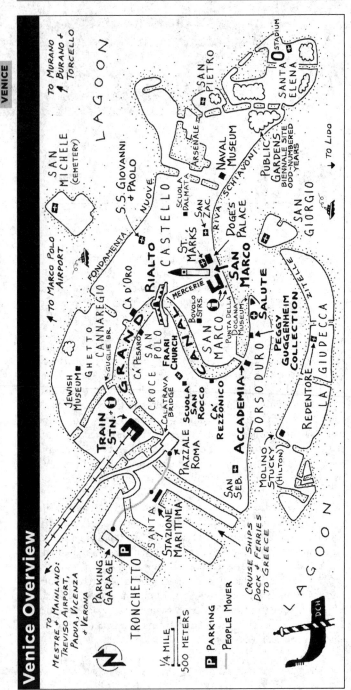

Planning Your Time

Venice is worth at least a day on even the speediest tour. Hyper-efficient train travelers take the night train in and/or out. Sleep in the old center to experience Venice at its best: early and late. For a one-day visit, cruise the Grand Canal, do the major sights on St. Mark's Square (the square itself, Doge's Palace, Correr Museum, and St. Mark's Basilica), see the Frari Church for art, and wander the back streets on a pub crawl. Enjoy an evening gondola ride. Venice's greatest sight is the city itself. While doable in a day, Venice is worth two. It's a medieval cookie jar, and nobody's looking. Make time to simply wander.

Orientation to Venice

The island city of Venice is shaped like a fish. Its major thoroughfares are canals. The Grand Canal winds through the middle of the fish, starting at the mouth where all the people and food enter, passing under the Rialto Bridge, and ending at St. Mark's Square (Piazza San Marco). Park your 21st-century perspective at the mouth and let Venice swallow you whole.

Venice is a car-less kaleidoscope of people, bridges, and odorless canals. The city has no major streets, and addresses are hopelessly confusing. There are six districts (shown on map on opposite page): San Marco (most touristy), Castello (behind San Marco), Cannaregio (from the train station to the Rialto), San Polo (other side of the Rialto), Santa Croce (the "eye" of the fish, east of the train station), and Dorsoduro (the "belly" of the fish and southernmost district of the city). Each district has about 6,000 address numbers.

To find your way, navigate by landmarks, not streets. Many street corners have a sign pointing you to *(per)* the nearest major landmark, such as San Marco, Accademia, Rialto, and Ferrovia (train station). Obedient visitors stick to the main thoroughfares as directed by these signs...and miss the charm of back-street Venice.

Beyond the city's core lie several other islands, including San Giorgio (with great views of Venice), Giudecca (more views), San Michele (old cemetery), Murano (famous for glass), Burano (lace-making), Torcello (old church), and the skinny Lido beach.

Tourist Information

With this book, a free city map from your hotel, and the *Shows & Events* entertainment guide (described on next page), there's little need to visit a tourist office in Venice. That's fortunate, because the city's TIs are crowded and clunky. If you need to check or confirm something, visit one of its four offices: at the **train station** (daily 8:00-21:00), **St. Mark's Square** (daily 9:00-15:30, opposite

Rick Steves' Free Audio Tours

I've produced free, self-guided audio versions of my tours of the major sights in Venice (download them via www.rick steves.com/audioeurope, iTunes, or the Rick Steves Audio Europe smartphone app). These user-friendly, easy-to-follow, fun, and enlightening audio tours are available for St. Mark's Basilica, St. Mark's Square, Frari Church, and my Grand Canal Cruise. If you don't mind me in your ear, these audio tours are hard to beat: Nobody will stand you up, the quality is reliable, you can take the tour exactly when you like, and they're free.

end from church), nearby at the **San Marco-Vallaresso vaporetto stop** (daily 10:00-18:00), and at the **airport** (daily 9:00-21:00). You can save time by phoning 041-529-8711 or visiting www.turismo venezia.it.

At the TI—or at many hotels—pick up the free *Shows and Events* pamphlet. It lists upcoming events and nightlife, as well as list museum hours, train and vaporetto schedules, emergency telephone numbers, and so on (www.turismovenezia.it, click on "venezia").

For a creative travel guide written by young Venetians, consider *My Local Guide Venice,* for its neighborhood histories, self-guided walking tours, and recommendations on sights and activities (sold at TIs for €10).

Maps: In Venice of all places, you need a good map. Hotels give away freebies (no better than the small color one at the front of this book). The TI sells a decent €2.50 map and miniguide—but you can find a wider range at bookshops, newsstands, and postcard stands. The cheap maps are pretty bad, but if you spend €5, you'll get a map that shows you everything. Investing in a good map can be the best €5 you'll spend in Venice. Don't take street names too seriously—spellings change with the dialect. Also, keep in mind that many street names change midway.

Arrival in Venice

A two-mile-long causeway (with highway and train lines) connects Venice to the mainland. Mestre, the sprawling mainland transportation hub, has fewer crowds, cheaper hotels, and plenty of inexpensive parking lots, but zero charm. Don't stop in Mestre unless you're parking your car or transferring trains.

By Train: All trains to "Venice" stop at Venezia Mestre (on the mainland). Most continue on to Santa Lucia Station on the island of Venice itself. If your train only stops at Mestre, worry

Arrival in Venice

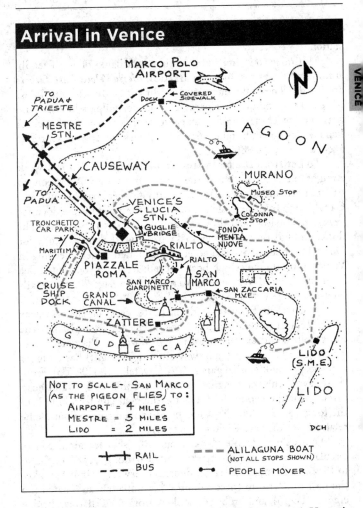

not. Shuttle trains regularly connect Mestre's station with Venice's Santa Lucia Station (6/hour, 10 minutes, €1).

Venice's **Santa Lucia train station** plops you right into the old town on the Grand Canal, an easy vaporetto ride or fascinating 40-minute walk to St. Mark's Square. Upon arrival, skip the station's crowded TI, because the two TIs at St. Mark's Square are better, and it's not worth a long wait for a minimal map (buy a good one from a newsstand or pick up a free one at your hotel). Confirm your departure plan (stop by train info desk or just study the *partenze*/departures posters on walls).

Consider storing unnecessary heavy bags, although lines for **baggage check** may be very long (at track 1, €4/5 hours, daily 6:00-24:00, no lockers, 45-pound weight limit on bags). **WCs** are at track 1 and in the back of the big bar-cafeteria area inside the station.

Minimize your time in the station—the banks of user-friendly automated ticket machines (marked *Biglietto Veloce/Fast Ticket*) are handy. They take euros and credit cards, display schedules, issue tickets, and even make reservations for railpass-holders. The gray-only machines are for tickets to nearby destinations such as Padua. Or you could take care of these tasks at downtown travel agencies (see page 986).

To get from the train station to downtown Venice, walk straight out of the station to the canal. On your left is a vaporetto ticket booth and the dock for vaporetto #2 (fast boat down Grand Canal, catch from right side of dock). To your right is the dock for *vaporetti* #1 (slow boat down Grand Canal, catch from far right dock) and #51 (goes counterclockwise around Venice, handy for Dorsoduro hotels). See the hotel listings (later, under "Sleeping in Venice") to find out which boat to catch to get to your hotel. See "Getting Around Venice—By Vaporetto," on page 987 for details on vaporetto tickets and passes.

By Car: The freeway dead-ends after crossing the causeway at Venice, near several parking lots on the edge of the island. The most central and expensive lot is San Marco on Piazzale Roma. Tronchetto (across the causeway and on the right) has a bigger and cheaper multistoried garage (€20/day, tel. 041-520-7555). From there, avoid the travel agencies masquerading as TIs, and head directly for the vaporetto docks for the boat connection (#2) to the town center. Don't let water-taxi boatmen con you out of the relatively inexpensive €6.50 vaporetto ride.

Venice's new **People Mover** monorail, a shuttle train fixed to a circular cable, carries passengers from the parking lot at Tronchetto to Piazzale Roma. It costs €1, departs every few minutes, makes the half-mile trip in three minutes, is completely automated (no crew on board), and drops you a block from the Calatrava Bridge on Piazzale Roma (across the Grand Canal from Santa Lucia train station).

Parking in **Mestre** (on the mainland) is simple and cheap (open-air lots cost €8/day Mon-Fri, €10/day Sat-Sun, across from Mestre train station, easy shuttle-train connections to Venice's Santa Lucia Station—6/hour, 10 minutes, €1).

By Plane: For information on Venice's airport and connections into the city, see "Venice Connections," at the end of this chapter.

Passes for Venice

The sights you probably care the most about (Accademia, Peggy Guggenheim Collection, Scuola San Rocco, Campanile, and the three sights within St. Mark's Basilica that charge admission) are not covered on any pass. To see the Doge's Palace, you must also pay for the less-visited Correr Museum (both on St. Mark's Square). While this €13 ticket is called a "pass" (described next), think of it as just a combo-ticket. Venice offers various other cards and passes that cover multiple sights few visitors want to see; these are generally not worth the trouble.

Doge's Palace/Correr Museum Tickets: The **San Marco Museum Plus Pass** (€13) covers admission to the Doge's Palace and Correr Museum (including two other museums within the Correr—the National Archaeological Museum and the Monumental Rooms of Marciana National Library), plus your choice of **one** of these seven museums: Ca' Rezzonico (Museum of 18th-Century Venice); Palazzo Mocenigo Costume Museum; Casa Goldoni (home of the Italian playwright); Ca' Pesaro (modern art); Museum of Natural History in the Santa Croce district; the Glass Museum on the island of Murano; or the Lace Museum on the island of Burano (www.museiciviciveneziani.it). To bypass the long line at the Doge's Palace, purchase this pass at the less-crowded Correr Museum (or any other included museum).

The San Marco Museum Plus Pass is available only from April through October. Off-season (Nov-March), it's replaced by the **Museum Card of the Museums of St. Mark's Square** (€12), which covers only the Doge's Palace and Correr Museum (includes the two museums inside the Correr).

Museum Pass: Busy sightseers may prefer the more expensive Museum Pass. This pass covers the Doge's Palace and Correr Museum, plus entry to **all** of the museums listed above for the San Marco Museum Plus Pass (€18, www.museiciviciveneziani.it). In general, this pass saves you money only if you visit five or more sights; before you buy, make sure they're sights you really want to see.

Chorus Pass: Church-lovers can get admission to 16 of Venice's churches and their art (generally €3 each)—including the Frari—for €10 (€20 for Family Pass, www.chorusvenezia.org).

Transportation Passes: Venice also sells transit-only passes covering *vaporetti* and buses that arrive on the edge of town. For a rundown on these, see "Getting Around Venice," later.

Helpful Hints

Get Lost: Accept the fact that Venice was a tourist town 400 years ago. It was, is, and always will be crowded. While 80 percent of Venice is, in fact, not touristy, 80 percent of the tourists never notice. Hit the back streets. Venice is the ideal town to explore on foot. Walk and walk to the far reaches of the town. Don't worry about getting lost. In fact, get as lost as possible.

Keep reminding yourself, "I'm on an island, and I can't get off." When it comes time to find your way, just follow the directional arrows on building corners or simply ask a local, *"Dov'è San Marco?"* ("Where is St. Mark's?") People in the tourist business (that's most Venetians) speak some English. If they don't, listen politely, watch where their hands point, say, *"Grazie,"* and head off in that direction. If you're lost, refer to your map, or pop into a hotel and ask for their business card—it comes with a map and a prominent "You are here."

Be Prepared to Splurge: Venice is expensive for residents as well as tourists. Demand is huge, supply is limited, and running a business is costly. Things just cost more here; everything must be shipped in and hand-trucked to its destination. Perhaps the best way to enjoy Venice is just to succumb to its charms and blow a lot of money.

Warning: The dark, late-night streets of Venice are safe. Even so, pickpockets (often elegantly dressed) work the crowded main streets, docks, and *vaporetti* (wear your money belt, zip up your valuables, and watch your purse or day bag). Your biggest risk of pickpockets is inside St. Mark's Basilica.

A handy Polizia station is on the right side of St. Mark's Square (near Caffè Florian). A service called Counter of Tourist Mediation at the Venice Complaint Office handles complaints about local crooks—including gondolier, restaurant, or hotel rip-offs (tel. 041-529-8710, fax 041-523-0399, complaint.apt@turismovenezia.it).

Immigrants selling items such as knock-off handbags on the streets are doing so illegally—if you buy goods from them, you'll risk getting a big fine.

Crowd Control: The city is inundated with cruise-ship crowds and tours from mainland hotels daily from 10:00 to about 17:00. Crowds can be a serious problem at **St. Mark's Basilica.** Try going early or late, or even better, you can bypass the line if you have a bag to check (see page 1006). At the **Doge's Palace,** avoid the long line by purchasing your ticket at the less-crowded Correr Museum. You can also visit late in the day, buy your ticket online, or book a tour. For the **Campanile,** ascend late (it's open until 21:00 July-Sept), or skip it entirely if you're going to the similar San Giorgio Maggiore bell tower. For the **Accademia,** go early or late—or reserve a ticket in advance by phone or online.

Sights that have crowd problems get even more crowded when it rains.

Medical Help: Venice's S.S. Giovanni e Paolo hospital (tel. 118) is a 10-minute walk from both the Rialto and San Marco neighborhoods, located on Fondamenta dei Mendicanti toward

Fondamenta Nuove. You can take vaporetto #41 from San Zaccaria-Jolanda to the Ospedale stop.

Take Breaks: Venice's endless pavement, crowds, and tight spaces are hard on the tourist. Schedule breaks in your sightseeing. Grab a cool place to sit down, relax, and recoup—meditate on a pew in an uncrowded church, or stop in a café.

Etiquette: Walk on the right and don't loiter on bridges. On St. Mark's Square, a "decorum patrol" admonishes snackers and sunbathers. Picnicking is forbidden (keep a low profile). The only place for a legal picnic is in Giardinetti Reali, the small park along the waterfront west of the Piazzetta near St. Mark's Square.

Dress Modestly: Men should keep their shirts on. When visiting St. Mark's Basilica or other major churches, men, women, and even children must cover their shoulders and knees (or risk being turned away). Remove hats when entering a church.

Public Toilets: Handy public WCs (€1.50) are near major landmarks, including: St. Mark's Square (one is behind the Correr Museum, to the left of the post office; another is at the waterfront park, Giardinetti Reali), Rialto, and at the Accademia Bridge. Use free toilets whenever you can—in a museum you're visiting or a café you're eating in. Like Mom always said, "Just try."

Best Views: While the best views of Venice may be from water level, there are several upper-altitude viewing spots: On St. Mark's Square, try the soaring Campanile, St. Mark's Basilica (specifically the balcony of the San Marco Museum, requires admission), or the St. Mark's Square clock tower (requires tour). The Rialto and Accademia bridges provide free, expansive views of the Grand Canal, along with a cooling breeze. Or get off the main island for a view of the Venetian skyline: Ascend the Church of San Giorgio Maggiore's bell tower, or venture to La Giudecca island to visit the swanky bar of the Molino Stucky Hilton Hotel (free shuttle boat from San Zaccaria-M.V.E. vaporetto stop).

Pigeon Poop: If your head is bombed by a pigeon, resist the initial response to wipe it off immediately—it'll just smear into your hair. Wait until it dries, and it should flake off cleanly. But if the poop splatters on your clothes, wipe it off immediately to avoid a stain.

Water: I carry a water bottle to refill at public fountains. Venetians pride themselves on having pure, safe, and tasty tap water piped in from the foothills of the Alps. You can actually see the mountains from Venice's bell towers on crisp, clear winter days.

Street Lingo: *Campo* means square, *campiello* is a small square, *calle* is street, *fondamenta* is the road running along a canal, *rio* is a small canal, *rio terra* is a street that was once a canal and has been filled in, and *ponte* is a bridge.

Services

Internet Access: You'll find handy, if pricey (up to €8/hour), little Internet places all over town. They are usually on back streets: Ask your hotelier for the nearest place. Most hotels provide both free Internet access and Wi-Fi for guests.

Post Office: The main P.O. is on the Mercerie, between St. Mark's and the Rialto, at #5016 (Mon-Fri 8:30-18:30, Sat 8:30-13:00, closed Sun). Use post offices only as a last resort, as simple transactions can take 45 minutes if you get in the wrong line. You can buy stamps from tobacco shops and mail postcards at any of the red postboxes around town.

Bookstores: In keeping with its literary heritage, Venice has classy and inviting bookstores. The small **Libreria Studium,** a block behind St. Mark's Basilica, has a carefully chosen selection of new English books, including my guidebooks (Mon–Sat 9:00–19:30, Sun 9:30–13:30 & 14:00–18:00, on Calle de la Canonica at #337, tel. 041-522-2382). Used-bookstore lovers shouldn't miss the funky **Acqua Alta** bookstore, where Luigi has prepared for the next flood by displaying his wares in a selection of vessels, including bathtubs and a gondola (daily 9:00–21:00, just beyond Campo Santa Maria Formosa on Calle Longa Santa Maria Formosa at #5176, tel. 041-296-0841, mobile 340-680-0704) or **Marco Polo,** which has a solid selection of used books in English (Mon-Sat 10:00-19:00, closed Sun, on Calle del Teatro Malibran at #5886a, close to St. Mark's side of Rialto Bridge, mobile 348-569-1125).

Laundry: I've listed launderettes near some of my recommended hotels. For more options, ask your hotelier to direct you to one nearby.

Travel Agencies: If you need to get train tickets, make seat reservations, or arrange a *cuccetta* (koo-CHET-tah—a berth on a night train) avoid a time-consuming trip to the crowded train station by using a downtown travel agency. Most trains between Venice, Florence, and Rome require reservations, even for railpass-holders. A travel agency can also give advice on cheap flights (book at least a week in advance for the best fares).

    Near St. Mark's Square, **Oltrex Change and Travel** sells train and plane tickets and books train reservations for a €3.50 fee (tickets sold daily May-Oct 9:00-18:00, Nov-April 9:00-16:30, one bridge past the Bridge of Sighs, Riva degli Schiavoni 4192, tel. 041-524-2828, Luca and Beatrice).

Near Rialto, **Kele & Teo Travel** sells train tickets for about a 10 percent service charge (Mon-Fri 9:00-18:00, Sat 9:00-12:00, closed Sun; leaving the Rialto Bridge heading for St. Mark's, it's half a block away, tucked down a side street on the right; tel. 041-520-8722).

English Church Services: The **San Zulian Church**—the only church in Venice that you can actually walk around—offers a Mass in English (generally May-Sept Mon-Fri at 9:30 and Sun at 11:30, Sun only Oct-April, 2 blocks toward Rialto off St. Mark's Square). **St. George's Anglican Church** welcomes all Christians to its English-speaking Eucharist (Sun at 10:30, located in Dorsoduro, midway between Accademia and Peggy Guggenheim Collection).

Haircuts: I've been getting my hair cut at **Coiffeur Benito** for nearly two decades. Benito has been keeping local men and women trim for 27 years. He's an artist—actually a "hair sculptor"—and a cut here is a fun diversion from the tourist grind (about €20 for women, €18 for men, Tue-Fri 8:30-13:00 & 15:30-19:30, Sat 8:30-13:00 only, closed Sun-Mon, behind San Zulian Church near St. Mark's Square, Calle S. Zulian Già del Strazzariol 592a, tel. 041-528-6221).

Getting Around Venice

On Foot: Navigate by major landmarks. There are signs on street corners all over town pointing to *San Marco, Accademia, Ferrovia* (train station), and *Piazzale Roma* (the bus stop behind the train station). Determine whether your destination is in the direction of a major signposted landmark, then follow the signs through the maze of squares, lanes, and bridges.

By Vaporetto: The public-transit system is a fleet of motor-ized bus-boats called *vaporetti*. They work like city buses except that they never get a flat, the stops are docks, and if you get off between stops, you might drown.

For most travelers, only two vaporetto lines matter: line #1 and line #2. These lines leave every 10 minutes (less off-season) and go up and down the Grand Canal, between the "mouth" of the fish at one end and San Marco at the other. Line #1 is the slow boat, taking 45 minutes and making every stop along the way. Line #2 is the fast boat that zips down the Grand Canal in 25 minutes, stop-ping only at Tronchetto (parking lot), Piazzale Roma (bus station), Ferrovia (train station), San Marcuola, Rialto Bridge, San Tomà (Frari Church), Accademia Bridge, San Marco (west end of St. Mark's Square), and San Zaccaria (east end of St. Mark's Square).

Catching a vaporetto is very much like catching a city bus. Helpful charts at the docks show a map of the lines and stops. At one end of the Grand Canal are Tronchetto, Piazzale Roma (Ple.

Venice

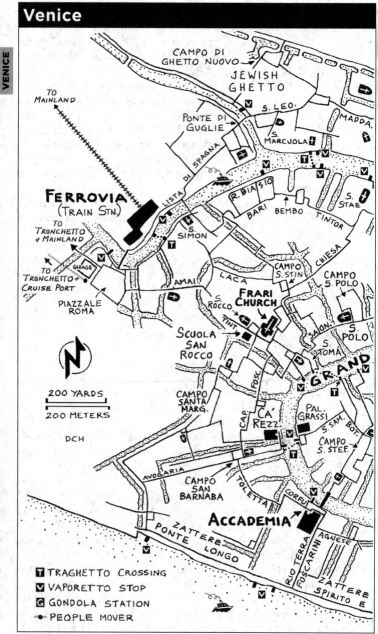

VENICE

TRAGHETTO CROSSING
VAPORETTO STOP
GONDOLA STATION
PEOPLE MOVER

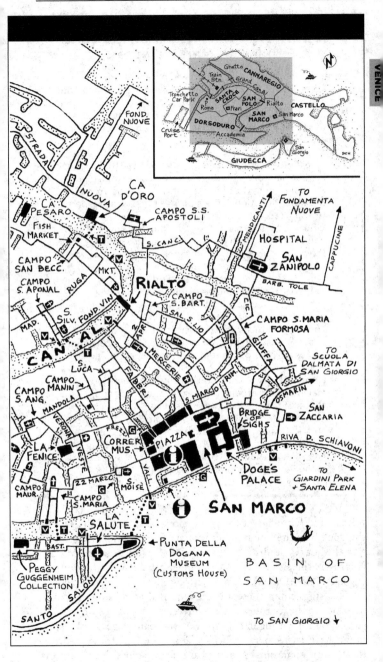

Handy *Vaporetti* from San Zaccaria, near St. Mark's Square

Several *vaporetti* leave from the San Zaccaria docks, located 150 yards east of St. Mark's Square. There are four separate San Zaccaria docks spaced about 70 yards apart: Danieli, Jolanda, M.V.E., and Pietà. (Note: Although I list which specific dock these lines leave from, they often change from season to season—be prepared.)

- Line #1 goes up the Grand Canal, making all the stops, including San Marco-Vallaresso, Rialto, Ferrovia (train station), and Piazzale Roma (but it does not go as far as Tronchetto). In the other direction, it goes to the Lido. Line #1 departs from the San Zaccaria-Danieli dock.
- Line #2 zips over to San Giorgio Maggiore, the island church across from St. Mark's Square (5 minutes, €2 ride). From there, it continues on to the parking lot at Tronchetto (departs from San Zaccaria-M.V.E.).
- Line #41 goes to San Michele and Murano in 45 minutes (departs from San Zaccaria-Jolanda).
- The "LN" heads to Burano (70 minutes, from San Zaccaria-Pietà dock).
- The Molino Stucky shuttle boat takes even non-guests to the Hilton Hotel, with its popular view bar (free, 20-minute ride, leaves at 0:20 past the hour from near the San Zaccaria-M.V.E. dock).
- Lines #51 and #52 are the *circulare* (cheer-koo-LAH-ray), making a loop around the perimeter of the island, with a stop at the Lido—perfect if you just like riding boats. Line #51 goes counterclockwise (departs from San Zaccaria-Danieli), and #52 goes clockwise (departs from San Zaccaria-Jolanda).
- The Alilaguna airport shuttle to and from the airport stops at the San Zaccaria-Jolanda dock.

Roma), and Ferrovia. At the other end is San Marco. The sign on the dock lists the line number that stops there and which direction the boat is headed, for example: "#2—Direction San Marco." Nearby is the sign for line #2 going in the other direction, for example: "#2—Direction Tronchetto."

It's simple, but there are a few quirks. Some stops have just one dock for boats going in both directions, so make sure the boat you get on is pointing in the direction you want to go. Larger stops might have two separate docks side by side (one for each direction), while some smaller stops have docks across the canal from each other (one for each direction). Electronic reader boards on busy docks display which boats are coming next, and when.

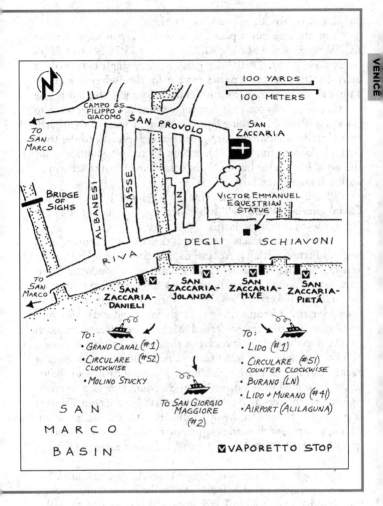

To clear up any confusion, ask a ticket-seller or conductor (there's often one stationed on the dock to help confused tourists), or pick up the most current ACTV timetable (free at ticket booths, in English and Italian, tel. 041-2424, www.hellovenezia.com or www.actv.it).

A **single ticket** costs a whopping €6.50. (Don't worry—much cheaper passes are described below.) Tickets are good for one hour in one direction; you can hop on and off at stops during that time. Technically, you're not allowed a round-trip (though in practice, a round-trip is allowed if you can complete it within a one-hour span). Note that you'll pay only €2 for a few shorter runs, including the route from San Marco to La Salute or from

San Zaccaria-M.V.E. to San Giorgio Maggiore.

You can also buy a **pass** for unlimited use of *vaporetti* and ACTV buses: €16/12 hours, €18/24 hours, €23/36 hours, €28/48 hours, €33/72 hours, €50/7-day pass). Because single tickets cost a hefty €6.50 a pop, these passes can pay for themselves in a hurry. Think through your Venice itinerary before you step up to the ticket booth to pay for your first vaporetto trip. It makes sense to get a pass if you'll be taking four rides or more (e.g., to your hotel, on a Grand Canal joyride, into the lagoon and back, to the train station). And it's fun to be able to hop on and off spontaneously, and avoid long ticket lines. On the other hand, many tourists just walk and rarely use a boat.

Those settling in can ride like a local by buying the **CartaVenezia** ID card (€40, which lets you ride for about €1 per trip; see www.actv.it for details).

Buy vaporetto tickets or passes at ticket booths at main stops (such as Ferrovia, Rialto, Accademia, and San Marco-Vallaresso). You can buy individual tickets on board from a conductor (do it immediately upon boarding or you risk a €50 fine). Plan your travel so you'll have tickets or a pass handy when you need them—not all stops have ticket booths. Passes are validated and start with your first swipe. The pass system (called iMob) is electronic—just touch your card to the electronic reader on the dock to validate it.

For fun, take my Grand Canal Cruise. Boats can be literally packed during the tourist rush hour. Morning rush hour (8:00-10:00) is headed in the direction of St. Mark's Square, as tourists and commuters arrive. Afternoon rush hour (about 17:00) is when they're headed in the other direction for the train station. Riding at night, with nearly empty boats and chandelier-lit palace interiors viewable from the Grand Canal, is an entirely different experience.

By *Traghetto*: Only four bridges cross the Grand Canal, but *traghetti* (gondolas) shuttle locals and in-the-know tourists across the Grand Canal at eight handy locations (marked on the color map of Venice at the front of this book). Venetians stand while riding, but you shouldn't (€0.50, don't tip—literally). Note that *traghetti* generally don't run in the evening.

By Water Taxi: Venetian taxis, like speedboat limos, hang out at busy points along the Grand Canal. Prices, which average €65, are soft (about €70 to train station or €110 to airport for up to four people, extra fees for very early or late runs). Negotiate and settle on the price before stepping in. For travelers with lots of luggage or small groups who can split the cost, taxi-boat rides can be a worthwhile and time-saving convenience—and skipping across the lagoon in a classic wooden motorboat is a cool indulgence. For €90 an hour, you can have a private unguided taxi-boat tour.

By Gondola: To hire a gondolier for your own private cruise, see page 1018.

Tours in Venice

Avventure Bellissime Venice Tours—This company offers a selection of two-hour walks, including a basic St. Mark's Square introduction called the "Original Venice Walking Tour" (€21, includes church entry, most days at 11:00, Sun at 14:00; 45 minutes on the square, 15 minutes in the church, one hour along back streets). Other walks include Cannaregio/Jewish Ghetto, San Polo/Dorsoduro, and ghost stories and legends (€20, group size 8-22, English-language only, tel. 041-520-8616, see www.tours -italy.com for details, info@tours-italy.com, Monica or Jonathan). Their 70-minute Grand Canal boat tour (€40, daily at 16:30, limited to eight people) is timed for good late-afternoon light. To get a discount on any tour, say "Rick sent me."

Classic Venice Bars Tour—Debonair guide Alessandro Schezzini is a connoisseur of Venetian *bacari*—classic old bars serving wine and traditional *cicchetti* snacks. He organizes two-hour Venetian pub tours (€30, any night on request at 18:00, depart from the top of the Rialto Bridge, reserve by phone or email, mobile 335-530-9024, www.schezzini.it, alessandro@schezzini .it). Alessandro's tours include sampling *cicchetti* with wines at three different *bacari*, plus he'll answer all of your questions about Venice. (If you think of this tour as a light dinner with a local friend, you can consider it part of your eating budget.)

Venicescapes—Michael Broderick's private theme tours of Venice are intellectually demanding and beyond the attention span of most mortal tourists. But those with a keen interest in learning and a desire to gain a solid understanding of Venice find him passionate and engaging. Rather than a "sightseeing tour," your time with Michael is more like a rolling graduate-level lecture. For a description of his various itineraries, see his website (book well in advance, tours last 4-6 hours: $275 for 2 people, $50/person after that, pay in dollars or the current euro equivalent, admissions and transportation are extra, tel. 041-520-6361, www.venicescapes.org, info@venicescapes.org).

Artviva: The Original and Best Walking Tours—This company offers a number of tours, including a Venice in One Glorious Day Special and four theme tours (Grand Canal, Venice Walk, Doge's Palace, Gondola Tour). The two-hour "Learn to Be a Gondolier" tour teaches the ancient craft of rowing Venetian-style (€80, 4 people maximum). See the tour details and Rick Steves readers' discounts on their website (book in advance, tours run March-Nov, tel. 055-264-5033, www.italy.artviva.com, staff@artviva.com).

Local Guides—Licensed guides are carefully trained and love explaining Venice to visitors. If you organize a small group at breakfast at your hotel to split the cost (figure on roughly €70/hour with a 2-hour minimum), the fee becomes more reasonable. The following companies and guides give excellent tours to individuals, families, and small groups.

Elisabetta Morelli (€65/hour, show this book and ask for best Rick Steves price, 2-hour minimum, tel. 041-526-7816, mobile 328-753-5220, bettamorelli@inwind.it).

Walks Inside Venice is a group of three women enthusiastic about teaching (€70/hour per group, 3-hour minimum; Roberta: mobile 347-253-0560; Cristina: mobile 348-341-5421; Sara: mobile 335-522-9714; www.walksinsidevenice.com, info@walksinside venice.com).

Venice with a Guide is a co-op of 10 equally good guides (www.venicewithaguide.com).

Alessandro Schezzini, mentioned earlier for his Classic Venice Bars Tour, isn't a licensed Italian guide and therefore can't take you into sights. But his relaxed two-hour back-streets "Rick Steves" tour does a great job of getting you beyond the clichés and into offbeat Venice (€15/person, book by email—alessandro @schezzini.it, mobile 335-530-9024, www.schezzini.it).

Self-Guided Cruise

▲▲▲Welcome to Venice's Grand Canal Cruise

Take a joyride and introduce yourself to Venice by boat. Cruise the Canal Grande all the way to San Marco, starting at Ferrovia (the train station).

If it's your first trip down the Grand Canal, you might want to stow this book and just take it all in—Venice is a barrage on the senses that hardly needs a narration. But these notes give the cruise a little meaning and help orient you to this great city.

This tour is designed to be done on the slow boat #1 (which takes about 45 minutes). The express boat #2 travels the same route, but it skips many stops and takes only 25 minutes, making it hard to sightsee.

To help you enjoy the visual parade of canal wonders, I've organized this tour by boat stop. I'll point out both what you can see from each stop, and what to look forward to as you cruise to the next stop. You can download a free audio version of this tour for your mobile device via www.ricksteves.com/audioeurope, iTunes, or the Rick Steves Audio Europe smartphone app.

Overview

The Grand Canal is Venice's "Main Street." At more than two

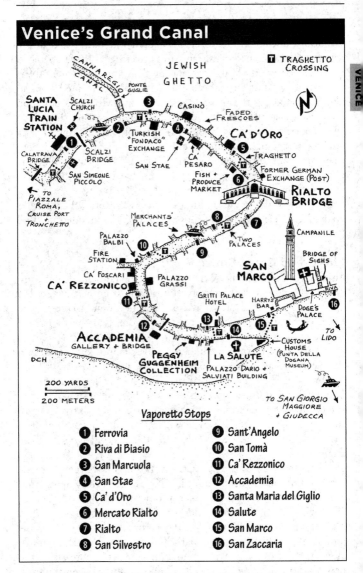

Venice's Grand Canal

T TRAGHETTO CROSSING

JEWISH GHETTO

CANNAREGIO CANAL

PONTE GUGLIE

SANTA LUCIA TRAIN STATION

SCALZI CHURCH

CASINÒ

FADED FRESCOES

CA' D'ORO

CALATRAVA BRIDGE

SCALZI BRIDGE

TURKISH "FONDACO" EXCHANGE

TRAGHETTO

FORMER GERMAN EXCHANGE (POST)

SAN SIMEONE PICCOLO

SAN STAE

CA' PESARO

FISH + PRODUCE MARKET

RIALTO BRIDGE

TO PIAZZALE ROMA, CRUISE PORT + TRONCHETTO

MERCHANTS' PALACES

PALAZZO BALBI

FIRE STATION

CA' FOSCARI

CA' REZZONICO

PALAZZO GRASSI

TWO PALACES

CAMPANILE

BRIDGE OF SIGHS

SAN MARCO

GRITTI PALACE HOTEL

HARRY'S BAR

DOGE'S PALACE

RIVA

ACCADEMIA GALLERY + BRIDGE

PEGGY GUGGENHEIM COLLECTION

LA SALUTE

PALAZZO DARIO + SALVIATI BUILDING

CUSTOMS HOUSE (PUNTA DELLA DOGANA MUSEUM)

TO LIDO

DCH

200 YARDS
200 METERS

TO SAN GIORGIO MAGGIORE + GIUDECCA

Vaporetto Stops

1. Ferrovia
2. Riva di Biasio
3. San Marcuola
4. San Stae
5. Ca' d'Oro
6. Mercato Rialto
7. Rialto
8. San Silvestro
9. Sant'Angelo
10. San Tomà
11. Ca' Rezzonico
12. Accademia
13. Santa Maria del Giglio
14. Salute
15. San Marco
16. San Zaccaria

miles long, nearly 150 feet wide, and nearly 15 feet deep, the Grand Canal is the city's largest, lined with its most impressive palaces. It's the remnant of a river that once spilled from the mainland into the Adriatic. The sediment it carried formed barrier islands that cut Venice off from the sea, forming a lagoon. Venice was built on the marshy islands of the former delta, sitting on pilings driven nearly 15 feet into the clay (alder was the preferred wood). About 25 miles of canals drain the city, dumping like streams into the

VENICE

Grand Canal. Technically, Venice has only three canals: Grand, Giudecca, and Cannaregio. The 45 small waterways that dump into the Grand Canal are referred to as rivers (e.g., Rio Nuovo).

Venice is a city of palaces, dating from the days when it was the world's richest city. The most lavish palaces formed a grand chorus line along the Grand Canal. Once frescoed in reds and blues, with black-and-white borders and gold-leaf trim, they made Venice a city of dazzling color. This cruise is the only way to truly appreciate the palaces, approaching them at water level, where their main entrances were located. Today, strict laws prohibit any changes in these buildings, so while landowners gnash their teeth, we can enjoy Europe's best-preserved medieval city—slowly rotting. Many of the grand buildings are now vacant. Others harbor chandeliered elegance above mossy, empty (often flooded) ground floors.

The Grand Canal Cruise Begins

This tour starts at the Ferrovia vaporetto stop (at Santa Lucia train station). It also works if you board upstream from Ferrovia, either at Tronchetto (where cars arrive) or Piazzale Roma (where airport buses and the People Mover monorail from Tronchetto arrive). Just start the tour when your vaporetto reaches Ferrovia.

A few tips: You're more likely to find an empty seat if you catch the vaporetto at Piazzale Roma, which is just a short walk from Ferrovia over the Calatrava Bridge. If you start at Tronchetto, your only choice is boat #2—which really rushes this tour. Wherever you catch your vaporetto, confirm that you're on a boat that goes all the way to San Marco, by way of Rialto *("San Marco via Rialto")*. If the conductor announces *"Solo Rialto!,"* the boat only goes as far as Rialto.

Ferrovia: The **Santa Lucia train station,** one of the few modern buildings in town, was built in 1954. It's been the gateway into Venice since 1860, when the first station was built. "F.S." stands for "Ferrovie dello Stato," the Italian state railway system.

More than 20,000 people a day commute in from the mainland, making this the busiest part of Venice during rush hour. To alleviate some of the congestion and make the commute easier, the new **Calatrava Bridge** spans the Grand Canal between the train station and Piazzale Roma upstream (described on page 1017).

Opposite the train station, atop the green dome of **San Simeone Piccolo** church, St. Simeon waves *ciao* to whoever enters or leaves the "old" city. The pink church with the white Carrara-marble facade, just beyond the train station, is the **Church of the Scalzi** (Church of the Barefoot, named after the shoeless Carmelite monks), where the last doge (Venetian ruler) rests. It looks relatively new because it was partially rebuilt after being bombed in

1915 by Austrians aiming (poorly) at the train station.

Riva de Biasio: Venice's main thoroughfare is busy with all kinds of **boats:** taxis, police boats, garbage boats, ambulances, construction cranes, and even brown-and-white UPS boats. Somehow they all manage to share the canal in relative peace.

About 25 yards past the Riva de Biasio stop, you'll look left down the broad **Cannaregio Canal** to see what was the **Jewish Ghetto** (see page 1017). The twin pale-pink six-story "skyscrapers"—the tallest buildings you'll see at this end of the canal—are reminders of how densely populated the world's original ghetto was. Set aside as the local Jewish quarter in 1516, this area became extremely crowded. This urban island developed into one of the most closely knit business and cultural quarters of all the Jewish communities in Italy, and gave us our word "ghetto" (from *geto*, the copper foundry located here).

San Marcuola: At this stop, facing a tiny square just ahead, stands the unfinished church of San Marcuola, one of only five churches fronting the Grand Canal. Centuries ago, this canal was a commercial drag of expensive real estate in high demand by wealthy merchants. About 20 yards ahead on the right stands the stately gray **Turkish "Fondaco" Exchange,** one of the oldest houses in Venice. Its horseshoe arches and roofline of triangles and dingleballs are reminders of its Byzantine heritage. Turkish traders in turbans docked here, unloaded their goods into the warehouse on the bottom story, then went upstairs for a home-style meal and a place to sleep. Venice in the 1500s was very cosmopolitan, welcoming every religion and ethnicity, so long as they carried cash. (Today the building contains the city's Museum of Natural History—and Venice's only dinosaur skeleton.)

Just 100 yards ahead on the left, Venice's **Casinò** is housed in the palace where German composer Richard *(The Ring)* Wagner died in 1883. See his distinct strong-jawed profile in the white plaque on the brick wall. In the 1700s, Venice was Europe's Vegas, with casinos and prostitutes everywhere. Casinòs ("little houses") have long provided Italians with a handy escape from daily life. Today they're run by the state to keep Mafia influence at bay. Notice the fancy front porch, rolling out the red carpet for high rollers arriving by taxi or hotel boat.

San Stae: The San Stae Church sports a delightful Baroque facade. Opposite the San Stae stop, look for the peeling plaster that once made up **frescoes** (scant remains on the lower floors). Imagine the facades of the Grand Canal at their finest. As colorful as the city is today, it's still only a faded, sepia-toned remnant of a long-gone era, a time of lavishly decorated, brilliantly colored palaces.

Just ahead, jutting out a bit on the right, is the ornate white facade of **Ca' Pesaro.** "*Ca'*" is short for *casa* (house). Because only the house of the doge (Venetian ruler) could be called a palace (*palazzo*), all other Venetian palaces are technically "*Ca'*."

In this city of masks, notice how the rich marble facades along the Grand Canal mask what are generally just simple, no-nonsense brick buildings. Most merchants enjoyed showing off. However, being smart businessmen, they only decorated the side of the buildings that would be seen and appreciated. But look back as you pass Ca' Pesaro (which houses the International Gallery of Modern Art—see page 1015). It's the only building you'll see with a fine side facade. Ahead, on the left, with its glorious triple-decker medieval arcade (just before the next stop) is Ca' d'Oro.

Ca' d'Oro: The lacy **Ca' d'Oro** (House of Gold) is the best example of Venetian Gothic architecture on the canal. Its three stories offer different variations on balcony design, topped with a spiny white roofline. Venetian Gothic mixes traditional Gothic (pointed arches and round medallions stamped with a four-leaf clover) with Byzantine styles (tall, narrow arches atop thin columns), filled in with Islamic frills. Like all the palaces, this was originally painted and gilded to make it even more glorious than it is now. Today the Ca' d'Oro is an art gallery (listed on page 1018).

Look at the Venetian chorus line of palaces in front of the boat doing an architectural cancan. On the right is the arcade of the covered **fish market,** with the open-air **produce market** just beyond. It bustles in the morning but is quiet the rest of the day. This is a great scene to wander through—even though European Union hygiene standards have made it cleaner, but less colorful, than it once was. Find the *traghetto* gondola ferrying shoppers—standing like Washington crossing the Delaware—back and forth. There are eight *traghetto* crossings along the Grand Canal, each one marked by a classy low-key green-and-black sign. Make a point to use them. At €0.50 a ride, they are one of the best deals in Venice.

Mercato Rialto: This stop was opened in 2007 to serve the busy market (boats only stop here between 8:00 and 20:00). The long and officious-looking building at this stop is the Venice courthouse. Straight ahead in the distance, rising above the huge post office, is the tip of the Campanile (bell tower) crowned by its golden angel at St. Mark's Square, where this tour will end. The former post office (100 yards directly ahead, on left side) will soon be a shopping center. It was once the German Exchange—the trading center for German metal merchants in the early 1500s.

You'll cruise by some trendy and beautifully situated wine bars on the right, but look ahead as you round the corner and see the impressive Rialto Bridge come into view.

A major landmark of Venice, the **Rialto Bridge** is lined with shops and tourists. Constructed in 1588, it's the third bridge built on this spot. Until the 1850s, this was the only bridge crossing the Grand Canal. With a span of 160 feet and foundations stretching 650 feet on either side, the Rialto was an impressive engineering feat in its day. Earlier Rialto Bridges could open to let big ships in, but not this one. When this new bridge was completed, much of the Grand Canal was closed to shipping and became a canal of palaces.

Rialto: Rialto, a separate town in the early days of Venice, has always been the commercial district, while San Marco was the religious and governmental center. Today, a winding street called the Mercerie connects the two, providing travelers with human traffic jams and a mesmerizing gauntlet of shopping temptations. This is the only stretch of the historic Grand Canal with landings upon which you can walk. They unloaded the city's basic necessities here: oil, wine, charcoal, iron. Today, the quay is lined with tourist-trap restaurants.

Venice's sleek, graceful black **gondolas** are a symbol of the city (for more on gondolas, see page 1018). With about 500 gondoliers joyriding amid the churning *vaporetti*, there's a lot of congestion on the Grand Canal. Pay attention—this is where most of the gondola and vaporetto accidents take place. While the Rialto is the highlight of many gondola rides, gondoliers understandably prefer the quieter small canals. Watch your vaporetto driver curse the better-paid gondoliers.

Ahead 100 yards on the left, two gray-colored **palaces** stand side by side (the City Hall and the mayor's office). Their horseshoe-shaped arched windows are similar and their stories are the same height, lining up to create the effect of one long balcony.

San Silvestro: We now enter a long stretch of important **merchants' palaces,** each with proud and different facades. Because ships couldn't navigate beyond the Rialto Bridge, the biggest palaces—with the major shipping needs—line this last stretch of the navigable Grand Canal.

Palaces like these were multifunctional: ground floor for the warehouse, offices and showrooms upstairs, and the living quarters above the offices on the "noble floors" (with big windows designed to allow in maximum light). Servants lived and worked on the top floors (with the smallest windows). For fire safety reasons, the kitchens were also located on the top floors. Peek into the noble floors to catch a glimpse of their still-glorious chandeliers of Murano glass.

Sant'Angelo: Notice how many buildings have a foundation of waterproof white stone *(pietra d'Istria)* upon which the bricks sit high and dry. Many canal-level floors are abandoned as the rising water level takes its toll. The **posts**—historically painted gaily with the equivalent of family coats of arms—don't rot under water. But the wood at the waterline, where it's exposed to oxygen, does. On the smallest canals, little blue gondola signs indicate that these docks are for gondolas only (no taxis or motor boats).

San Tomà: Fifty yards ahead, on the right side (with twin obelisks on the rooftop) stands **Palazzo Balbi,** the palace of an early-17th-century captain general of the sea. These Venetian equivalents of five-star admirals were honored with twin obelisks decorating their palaces. This palace, like so many in the city, flies three flags: Italy (green-white-red), the European Union (blue with ring of stars), and Venice (a lion on a field of red and gold). Today it houses the administrative headquarters of the regional government.

Just past the admiral's palace, look immediately to the right, down a side canal. On the right side of that canal, before the bridge, see the traffic light and the **fire station** (with four arches hiding fireboats parked and ready to go).

The impressive **Ca' Foscari,** with a classic Venetian facade (on the corner, across from the fire station), dominates the bend in the canal. This is the main building of the University of Venice, which has about 25,000 students. Notice the elegant lamp on the corner.

The grand heavy white **Ca' Rezzonico,** just before the Ca' Rezzonico stop, houses the Museum of 18th-Century Venice (listed on page 1014). Across the canal is the cleaner and leaner **Palazzo Grassi,** the last major palace built on the canal, erected in the late 1700s. It was recently purchased by a French tycoon and now displays his contemporary art collection.

Ca' Rezzonico: Up ahead, the Accademia Bridge leads over the Grand Canal to the **Accademia Gallery** (right side), filled with the best Venetian paintings. The bridge was put up in 1934 as a temporary structure. Locals liked it, so it stayed.

Accademia: From here, look through the graceful bridge and way ahead to enjoy a classic view of **La Salute Church,** topped by a crown-shaped dome supported by scrolls (see page 1014). This Church of Saint Mary of Good Health was built to thank God for delivering Venetians from the devastating plague of 1630 (which had killed about a third of the city's population).

The low white building among greenery (100 yards ahead, on the right, between the Accademia Bridge and the church) is the **Peggy Guggenheim Collection.** The American heiress "retired" here, sprucing up a palace that had been abandoned in mid-construction. Peggy willed the city her fine collection of modern art (described on page 1013).

As you approach the next stop, notice on the right how the fine line of higgledy-piggledy palaces evokes old-time Venice. Two doors past the Guggenheim, Palazzo Dario has a great set of characteristic **funnel-shaped chimneys.** These forced embers through a loop-the-loop channel until they were dead—required in the days when stone palaces were surrounded by humble wooden buildings, and a live spark could make a merchant's workforce homeless. Notice this early Renaissance building's flat-feeling facade with "pasted-on" Renaissance motifs. Three doors later is the **Salviati building** (with the fine mosaics), which was once a glassworks.

Santa Maria del Giglio: Back on the left stands the fancy Gritti Palace hotel. Hemingway and Woody Allen both stayed here (but not together).

Take a deep whiff of Venice. What's all this nonsense about stinky canals? All I smell is my shirt. By the way, how's your captain? Smooth dockings? To get to know him, stand up in the bow and block his view.

Salute: The huge La Salute Church towers overhead as if squirted from a can of Catholic Reddi-wip. Like Venice itself, the church rests upon pilings. To build the foundation for the city, more than a million trees were piled together, reaching beneath the mud to the solid clay. Much of the surrounding countryside was deforested by Venice. Trees were exported and consumed locally to fuel the furnaces of Venice's booming glass industry, to build Europe's biggest merchant marine, and to prop up this city in the mud.

As the Grand Canal opens up into the lagoon, the last building on the right with the golden ball is the 17th-century **Customs House,** which now houses the Punta della Dogana Museum of Contemporary Art (listed on page 1014). Its two bronze Atlases hold a statue of Fortune riding the ball. Arriving ships stopped here to pay their tolls.

San Marco: Up ahead on the left, the green pointed tip of the Campanile marks **St. Mark's Square,** the political and religious center of Venice...and the final destination of this tour. You could get off at the San Marco stop and go straight to St. Mark's Square. But I'm staying on the boat for one more stop, just past St. Mark's Square (it's a quick walk back).

Survey the lagoon. Opposite St. Mark's Square, across the water, the ghostly white church with the pointy bell tower is **San Giorgio Maggiore,** with great views of Venice. Next to it is the residential island Giudecca, stretching from close to San Giorgio Maggiore past the Venice youth hostel (with a nice view, directly across) to the Hilton Hotel (good nighttime view, far right end of island).

Still on board? If you are, as we leave the San Marco stop, prepare for a drive-by view of St. Mark's Square. First comes the bold white facade of the old mint (where Venice's golden ducat, the "dollar" of the Venetian Republic, was made) and the library facade. Then the twin columns, topped by St. Theodore and St. Mark, who've welcomed visitors since the 15th century. Between the columns, catch a glimpse of two giant figures atop the **Clock Tower**—they've been whacking their clappers every hour since 1499. The domes of **St. Mark's Basilica** are soon eclipsed by the lacy facade of the **Doge's Palace.** Next you'll see the **Bridge of Sighs** (currently under scaffolding), and then the grand harborside promenade—the **Riva.**

Follow the Riva with your eye, past elegant hotels to the green area in the distance. This is the largest of Venice's few **parks,** which hosts the Biennale art show every odd year. Much farther in the distance is the **Lido,** the island with Venice's beach. Its sand and casinos are tempting, but its car traffic disrupts the medieval charm of Venice.

San Zaccaria: OK, you're at your last stop. Quick—muscle your way off this boat! (If you don't, you'll eventually end up at the Lido.)

At San Zaccaria, you're right in the thick of the action. A number of other *vaporetti* depart from here (see page 987). Otherwise, it's a short walk back along the Riva to St. Mark's Square. Ahoy!

Sights in Venice

San Marco District

For information on the San Marco Museum Plus Pass and the pricier Museum Pass, which cover most of the sights on the square, see page 982.

▲▲▲**St. Mark's Square (Piazza San Marco)**—This grand square is surrounded by splashy, historic buildings and sights: St. Mark's Basilica, the Doge's Palace, the Campanile bell tower, and the Correr Museum. The square is filled with music, lovers, pigeons, and tourists by day, and is your private rendezvous with the Venetian past late at night, when Europe's most magnificent dance floor is *the* romantic place to be.

With your back to the church, survey one of Europe's great urban spaces, and the only square in Venice to merit the title "Piazza." Nearly two football fields long, it's surrounded by the offices of the republic. On the right are the "old offices" (16th-century Renaissance). At left are the "new offices" (17th-century High Renaissance). Napoleon called the piazza "the most beautiful drawing room in Europe," and added to the intimacy by building the final wing, opposite the basilica, that encloses the square.

For a slow and pricey evening thrill, invest about €12-20 (including the cover charge for the music) in a glass of wine or coffee at one of the elegant cafés with the dueling orchestras. For an unmatched experience that offers the best people-watching, it's worth the small splurge.

The **Clock Tower** (Torre dell'Orologio), built during the Renaissance in 1496, marks the entry to the main shopping drag, called the Mercerie, which connects St. Mark's Square with the Rialto. From the piazza, you can see the bronze men (Moors) swing their huge clappers at the top of each hour. In the 17th century, one of them knocked an unsuspecting worker off the top and to his death—probably the first-ever killing by a robot. Notice one of the world's first "digital" clocks on the tower facing the square (with dramatic flips every five minutes). You can go inside the Clock Tower only with a pre-booked guided tour that takes you close to the clock's innards and out to a terrace with good views over the square and city rooftops. Reserve in person at the Correr Museum, by calling 848-082-000, or online at www.museicivici veneziani.it (€12 combo-ticket includes Correr Museum; tours in English Mon-Wed at 10:00 and 11:00; also Thu-Sun at 14:00 and 15:00, plus 17:00 in peak season). Book a day in advance or show up at the Correr Museum prior to a scheduled tour to see if space is available.

A good **TI** is on the square (with your back to the basilica, it's in the far-left, southwest corner of the square; daily 9:00-15:30), and a €1.50 WC is 30 yards beyond St. Mark's Square (see Albergo Diorno sign marked on pavement, WC open daily 9:00-17:30). Another **TI** is on the lagoon (daily 10:00-18:00, walk toward the water by the Doge's Palace and go right, €1.50 WCs nearby). You can download a free Rick Steves **audio tour** of St. Mark's Square for your mobile device via www.ricksteves.com/audioeurope, iTunes, or the Rick Steves Audio Europe smartphone app.

▲▲▲**St. Mark's Basilica (Basilica di San Marco)**—Built in the 11th century to replace an earlier church, this basilica's distinctly Eastern-style architecture underlines Venice's connection with Byzantium (which protected it from the ambition of Charlemagne and his Holy Roman Empire). It's decorated with booty from returning sea captains—a kind of architectural Venetian trophy chest. The interior glows mysteriously with gold mosaics and colored marble. Since about A.D. 830, the saint's bones have been housed on this site.

Cost and Hours: Basilica entry is free, open Mon-Sat 9:45-17:00, Sun 14:00-17:00 (Sun until 16:00 Nov-March), St. Mark's Square, vaporetto stops: San Marco or San Zaccaria, tel. 041-270-8311, www.basilicasanmarco.it. The dress code is strictly enforced for everyone (no bare shoulders or bare knees). Lines can be long, and bag check is mandatory, free, and can save you time in line. No photos are allowed inside.

Three separate exhibits within the church charge admission: the **Treasury** (€3, includes free audioguide), **Golden Altarpiece**

VENICE

St. Mark's Square

TO RIALTO

SAN ZULIAN

TO RIALTO

ST. MARK'S BAG CHECK

MERCERIE

S. MARCO

SPADARIA

FABBRI

C. FIUBERA

6

TRON

OLD OFFICES

PIAZZETTA D. LEONCINI

CLOCK TOWER

ST. MARK'S BASILICA

10

RAMO SELVA

G

9

12

CAMPA-NILE

FRENZERIA

PIAZZA SAN MARCO

DOGE'S PALACE

CORRER MUSEUM
←Napoleon's Wing

13

PIAZZETTA

Post WC

8

11

NEW OFFICES

SAL

SAN

CALLE VALLARESSO

MOISÈ

SAN

S. MARCO COLUMN

7

SAN MOISÈ

i

GIARDINETTI REALI

G

S. THEODORE COLUMN

→ TO ACCADEMIA

WC

i

V SAN MARCO - GIARDINETTI

V SAN MARCO - VALLARESSO

SAN MARCO

T

TO SALUTE

← ENTRANCES TO SIGHTS

V VAPORETTO STOP

T TRAGHETTO CROSSING

G GONDOLA STATION

☙ VIEW

100 YARDS

100 METERS

DCH

VENICE

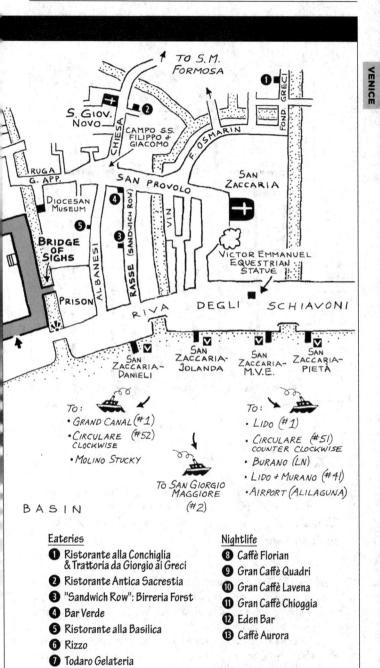

Eateries

1 Ristorante alla Conchiglia
   & Trattoria da Giorgio ai Greci
2 Ristorante Antica Sacrestia
3 "Sandwich Row": Birreria Forst
4 Bar Verde
5 Ristorante alla Basilica
6 Rizzo
7 Todaro Gelateria

Nightlife

8 Caffè Florian
9 Gran Caffè Quadri
10 Gran Caffè Lavena
11 Gran Caffè Chioggia
12 Eden Bar
13 Caffè Aurora

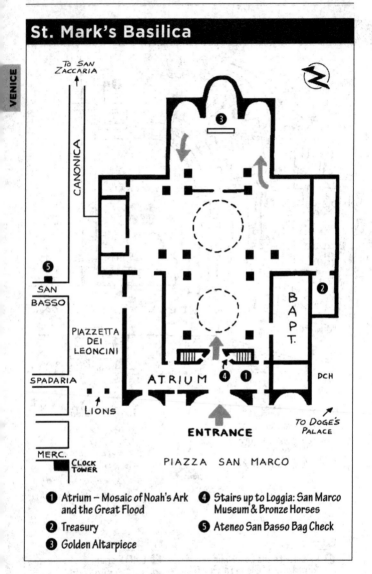

St. Mark's Basilica

To San Zaccaria

CANONICA

SAN BASSO

PIAZZETTA DEI LEONCINI

SPADARIA

LIONS

ATRIUM

B A P T.

DCH

To Doge's Palace

ENTRANCE

MERC.

CLOCK TOWER

PIAZZA SAN MARCO

VENICE

1 Atrium – Mosaic of Noah's Ark and the Great Flood

2 Treasury

3 Golden Altarpiece

4 Stairs up to Loggia: San Marco Museum & Bronze Horses

5 Ateneo San Basso Bag Check

(€2), and **San Marco Museum** (€4). The San Marco Museum has the original bronze horses (copies of these overlook the square), a balcony offering a remarkable view over St. Mark's Square, and various works related to the church.

Bag Check (and Skipping the Line): Small purses and shoulder-slung bags may be allowed inside the church, but larger bags and backpacks are not. Check them for free for up to one hour at the nearby Ateneo San Basso, 30 yards to the left of the basilica, down narrow Calle San Basso (see map on previous page for location; open Mon-Sat 9:30-17:30, Sun 14:00-16:30).

Those with a bag to check actually get to skip the line. Leave your bag at Ateneo San Basso and pick up your claim tag. Two people per tag are allowed to enter the basilica. Take your tag to the basilica's tourist entrance. Keep to the left of the railing where the line forms and show your tag to the gatekeeper. He'll let you in, ahead of the line. After touring the church, come back and pick up your bag. (Note: Ateneo San Basso may not let you check small bags that would be allowed inside.)

Dress Code: Modest dress (no shorts or bare shoulders) is strictly enforced, even for kids.

Theft Alert: St. Mark's Basilica is the most dangerous place in Venice for pickpocketing—inside, it's always a crowded jostle.

Tours: Free hour-long English tours (heavy on the mosaics' religious symbolism) are generally offered daily at 11:00; meet in the atrium. But the schedule varies, so see the schedule board in the atrium. You can download a free Rick Steves audio tour of St. Mark's Basilica for your mobile device via www.ricksteves.com /audioeurope, iTunes, or the Rick Steves Audio Europe smartphone app.

The Mosaics: St. Mark's Basilica has 4,750 square yards of Byzantine mosaics, the best and oldest of which are in the atrium (turn right as you enter and stop under the last dome—this may be roped off, but dome is still visible). Facing the church, gape up (it's OK, no pigeons) and read the story of Adam and Eve that rings the bottom of the dome. Now, facing the piazza, look domeward for the story of Noah, the ark, and the flood (two by two, the wicked being drowned, Noah sending out the dove, a happy rainbow, and a sacrifice of thanks).

Step inside the church and notice how the marble floor is richly decorated in mosaics. As in many Venetian buildings, because the best foundation pilings were made around the perimeter, the floor rolls. As you shuffle under the central dome, look up for the Ascension. Follow the one-way tourist route and consider stopping off at the Treasury and Golden Altarpiece.

Additional Sights: The Treasury (ask for the included and informative audioguide when you buy your ticket) and Golden Altarpiece give you the best chance outside of Istanbul or Ravenna to see the glories of the Byzantine Empire. Venetian crusaders looted the Christian city of Constantinople and brought home piles of lavish loot (perhaps the lowest point in Christian history until the advent of TV evangelism). Much of this plunder is stored in the Treasury (tesoro) of San Marco. As you view these treasures, remember that most were made in about A.D. 500, while Western Europe was stuck in the Dark Ages. Beneath the high altar lies the body of St. Mark ("Marce") and the Golden Altarpiece (Pala d'Oro), made of 250 blue-backed enamels with religious scenes, all set in a gold frame and studded with 15 hefty rubies, 300 emeralds, 1,500 pearls, and assorted sapphires, amethysts, and topaz (c. 1100).

In the San Marco Museum (Museo di San Marco) upstairs you can see an up-close mosaic exhibition, a fine view of the church interior, a view of the square from the balcony with bronze horses, and (inside, in their own room) the original horses. These well-traveled horses, made during the days of Alexander the Great (fourth century B.C.), were taken to Rome by Nero, to Constantinople/Istanbul by Constantine, to Venice by crusaders, to Paris by Napoleon, back "home" to Venice when Napoleon fell, and finally indoors and out of the acidic air. The staircase up to the museum is in the atrium, near the basilica's main entrance, marked by a sign that says *Loggia dei Cavalli, Museo.*

▲▲▲**Doge's Palace (Palazzo Ducale)**—The seat of the Venetian government and home of its ruling duke, or doge, this was the most powerful half-acre in Europe for 400 years. The Doge's Palace was built to show off the power and wealth of the Republic. The doge lived with his family on the first floor near the halls of power. From his once-lavish (now sparse) quarters, you'll follow the one-way tour through the public rooms of the top floor, finishing with the Bridge of Sighs and the prison. The place is wallpapered with masterpieces by Veronese and Tintoretto. Don't worry much about the great art. Enjoy the building.

You'll see the restored facades from the **courtyard.** Notice a grand staircase (with nearly naked Moses and Paul Newman at the top). Even the most powerful visitors climbed this to meet the doge. This was the beginning of an architectural power trip.

In the **Senate Hall,** the 120 senators met, debated, and passed laws. Tintoretto's large *Triumph of Venice* on the ceiling (central painting, best viewed from the top) shows the city in all its glory. Lady Venice is up in heaven with the Greek gods, while barbaric lesser nations swirl up to give her gifts and tribute.

The **Armory**—a dazzling display originally assembled to intimidate potential adversaries—shows remnants of the military might that the empire employed to keep the East-West trade lines open (and the local economy booming).

The giant **Hall of the Grand Council** (175 feet by 80 feet, capacity 2,600) is where the entire nobility met to elect the senate and doge. It took a room this size to contain the grandeur of the Most Serene Republic. Ringing the room are portraits of the first 76 doges (in chronological order). The one at the far end that's blacked out is the notorious Doge Marin Falier, who opposed the will of the Grand Council in 1355. He was tried for treason, beheaded, and airbrushed from history.

On the wall over the doge's throne is Tintoretto's monster-piece, *Paradise*, the largest oil painting in the world. Christ and Mary are surrounded by a heavenly host of 500 saints. The painting leaves you feeling that you get to heaven not by being a good Christian, but by being a good Venetian.

Cross the covered **Bridge of Sighs** over the canal to the **prisons.** Circle the cells. Notice the carvings made by prisoners—from olden days up until 1930—on some of the stone windowsills of the cells, especially in the far corner of the building.

Cross back over the Bridge of Sighs, pausing to look through the marble-trellised windows at all of the tourists.

Cost and Hours: Covered by €13 San Marco Museum Plus Pass, which also includes admission to the Correr Museum (both sights also covered by €18 Museum Pass); no individual tickets are sold to this sight. If the line is long at the Doge's Palace, buy your pass at the Correr Museum across the square; then you can go directly through the Doge's turnstile without waiting in line. Open daily April-Oct 8:30-18:30, Nov-March 8:30-17:30, last entry one hour before closing.

Location: Next to St. Mark's Basilica, just off St. Mark's Square. Vaporetto stops: San Marco or San Zaccaria.

Tours: The audioguide costs €5. For a live guided tour, consider the Secret Itineraries Tour, which takes you into palace rooms otherwise not open to the public (€18, or €12 with San Marco Museum Plus Pass; two or three English-language tours each morning). Reserve ahead for this tour in peak season—they can fill up as much as a month in advance. Book online at www .museiciviciveneziani.it, reserve by phone (tel. 848-082-000, or from the US dial 011-39-041-4273-0892), or ask at the info desk.

▲▲**Correr Museum (Museo Civico Correr)**—This uncrowded museum gives you a good overview of Venetian history and art. In the Napoleon Wing, you'll see fine Neoclassical sculpture by Antonio Canova. Then peruse armor, banners, and paintings that re-create festive days of the Venetian republic. The upper floor lays out a good overview of Venetian art, including several paintings by the Bellini family. There are English descriptions and breathtaking views of St. Mark's Square throughout.

Cost and Hours: Covered by €13 San Marco Museum Plus Pass, which also includes the Doge's Palace—both also covered by €18 Museum Pass, daily April-Oct 10:00-19:00, Nov-March 9:00-17:00, last entry one hour before closing, enter at far end of square directly opposite basilica, tel. 041-240-5211, www.museicivici veneziani.it.

Avoid long lines at the crowded Doge's Palace by buying either of the museum passes listed above at the Correr Museum.

For €12 you can get a combo-ticket for the Correr Museum and a tour of the Clock Tower on St. Mark's Square, but your ticket won't include the Doge's Palace. For more on reserving a Clock Tower tour, see page 1003.

▲**Campanile (Campanile di San Marco)**—This dramatic bell tower replaced a shorter lighthouse, once part of the original fortress that guarded the entry of the Grand Canal. The lighthouse crumbled into a pile of bricks in 1902, a thousand years after it was built. You'll see construction work being done to strengthen the base of the tower. Ride the elevator 300 feet to the top of the bell tower for the best view in Venice (especially at sunset). For an ear-shattering experience, be on top when the bells ring. The golden archangel Gabriel at the top always faces into the wind.

Cost and Hours: €8, daily April-June and Oct 9:00-19:00, July-Sept 9:00-21:00, Nov-March 9:30-15:45, closed from Christmas to mid-Jan, tel. 041-522-4064. Lines are longest at midday; beat the crowds and enjoy the crisp morning air at 9:00 or the cool evening breeze at 18:00.

La Fenice Opera House (Gran Teatro alla Fenice)—During Venice's glorious decline in the 18th century, this was one of seven opera houses in the city, and one of the most famous in Europe. For 200 years, great operas and famous divas debuted here, applauded by ladies and gentlemen in their finery. Then in 1996, an arson fire completely gutted the theater. But La Fenice ("The Phoenix") has risen from the ashes, thanks to an eight-year effort to rebuild the historic landmark according to photographic archives of the interior. To see the results at their most glorious, attend an evening performance.

You can also tour the opera house during the day. All you really see is the theater itself; there's no "backstage" tour of dressing rooms, or an opera museum. The auditorium, ringed with box seats, is impressive: pastel blue with sparkling gold filigree, muses depicted on the ceiling, and a starburst chandelier. It's also a bit saccharine and brings sadness to Venetians who remember the place before the fire. Other than a minor exhibit of opera scores and Maria Callas memorabilia, there's little to see from the world of opera. The dry audioguide recounts two centuries of construction.

Cost and Hours: €7, includes 45-minute audioguide, generally open daily 10:00-19:30, but schedule varies greatly depending on rehearsal and performance schedule, concert box office open daily 9:30-18:30, call center open daily 7:30-20:00, on Campo San Fantin between St. Mark's Square and Accademia Bridge, vaporetto stop: Santa Maria del Giglio, tel. 041-2424, www.teatro lafenice.it.

Behind St. Mark's Basilica

▲**Bridge of Sighs**—Connecting two wings of the Doge's Palace high over a canal, this enclosed bridge is currently surrounded by scaffolding for restoration. Travelers popularized this bridge in the Romantic 19th century. Supposedly, a condemned man would be led over this bridge on his way to the prison, take one last look at the glory of Venice, and sigh. Though overhyped, when it's uncovered the bridge is undeniably tingle-worthy—especially after dark, when the crowds have dispersed and it's just you and floodlit Venice. A local legend says that lovers will be assured eternal love if they kiss on a gondola at sunset under the bridge. The bridge is around the corner from the Doge's Palace: Walk toward the waterfront, turn left along the water, and look up the first canal on your left. You can walk across the bridge (from the inside) by visiting the Doge's Palace.

Church of San Zaccaria—This historic church is home to a sometimes-waterlogged crypt, a Bellini altarpiece, a Tintoretto painting, and the final resting place of St. Zechariah, the father of John the Baptist.

Cost and Hours: Free, €1 to enter crypt, €0.50 coin to light up Bellini's altarpiece, Mon-Sat 10:00-12:00 & 16:00-18:00, Sun 16:00-18:00 only, 2 canals behind St. Mark's Basilica.

Across the Lagoon from St. Mark's Square

▲**San Giorgio Maggiore**—This is the dreamy church-topped island you can see from the waterfront by St. Mark's Square. The striking church, designed by Palladio, features art by Tintoretto, Sunday Mass, a bell tower, and good views of Venice.

Cost and Hours: Free entry to church; May-Sept Mon-Sat 9:30-12:30 & 14:30-18:00, Sun 8:30-11:00 & 14:30-18:00; Oct-April until 16:30.

The bell tower costs €3 and is accessible by elevator (runs from 30 minutes after the church opens until 30 minutes before the church closes).

Getting There: To reach the island from St. Mark's Square, take the five-minute ride on vaporetto #2 (€2, 6/hour, ticket valid for one hour; leaves from San Zaccaria-M.V.E. stop located east of Bridge of Sighs by equestrian statue; catch boat in direction: Tronchetto).

Dorsoduro District

▲▲**Accademia (Gallerie dell'Accademia)**—Venice's top art museum, packed with highlights of the Venetian Renaissance, features paintings by the Bellini family, Titian, Tintoretto, Veronese, Tiepolo, Giorgione, Canaletto, and Testosterone. It's just over the wooden Accademia Bridge from the San Marco action.

VENICE

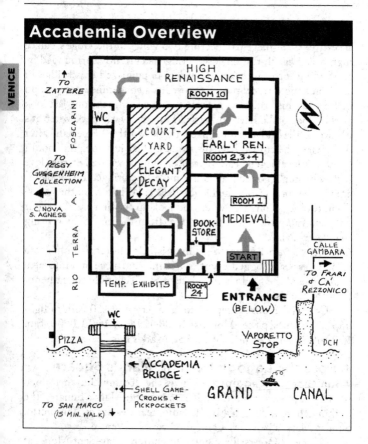

Accademia Overview

The Accademia is the greatest museum anywhere for Venetian Renaissance art and a good overview of painters whose works you'll see all over town. Venetian art is underrated and, I think, misunderstood. It's nowhere near as famous today as the work of the florescent Florentines, but—with historical slices of Venice, ravishing nudes, and very human Madonnas—it's livelier, more colorful, and simply more fun. The Venetian love of luxury shines through in this collection, which starts in the Middle Ages and runs to the 1700s. Look for grand canvases of colorful, spacious settings, peopled with happy locals in extravagant clothes having a great time.

Medieval highlights include elaborate altarpieces and golden-haloed Madonnas, all painted at a time when realism, depth of field, and emotion were considered beside the point. Medieval Venetians, with their close ties to the East, borrowed techniques such as gold-leafing, frontal poses, and "iconic" faces from the religious icons of Byzantium (modern-day Istanbul).

Among early masterpieces of the Renaissance are Mantegna's studly *St. George* and Giorgione's mysterious *The Tempest*. As the Renaissance reaches its heights, so do the paintings, such as Titian's magnificent *Presentation of the Virgin*, a religious scene, yes, but it's really just an excuse to display secular splendor (Titian was the most famous painter of his day—perhaps even more famous than Michelangelo). Veronese's sumptuous *Feast in the House of Levi* also has an ostensibly religious theme (in the middle, find Jesus eating his final meal)—but it's outdone by the luxury and optimism of Renaissance Venice. Life was a good thing and beauty was to be enjoyed. (Veronese was hauled before the Inquisition for painting such a bawdy Last Supper...so he fine-tuned the title). End your tour with Guardi's and Canaletto's painted "postcards" of the city—landscapes for visitors who lost their hearts to the romance of Venice.

Cost and Hours: €6.50, Mon 8:15-14:00, Tue-Sun 8:15-19:15, last entry 45 minutes before closing, no photos allowed. The dull audioguide costs €5 (€7/2 people). One-hour guided tours in English are €5 (€7/2 people, Sat-Sun at 11:00). At Accademia Bridge, vaporetto stop: Accademia. Tel. 041-522-2247, www.gallerieaccademia.org.

Avoiding Crowds: Expect long lines in the late morning, because they allow only 300 visitors in at a time; visit early or late to miss the crowds. Better yet, reserve an entry time at least a day in advance (€1 fee, calling 041-520-0345 is easier than reserving online at their clunky website; calls answered Mon-Fri 9:00-18:00, Sat 9:00-14:00, closed Sun; pick up tickets at least 20 minutes before entry time).

There's a decent canalside pizzeria (Pizzeria Accademia Foscarini, closed Tue) at the base of the Accademia Bridge.

▲▲**Peggy Guggenheim Collection**—The popular museum of far-out art, housed in the American heiress' former retirement palazzo, offers one of Europe's best reviews of the art of the first half of the 20th century. Stroll through styles represented by artists whom Peggy knew personally—Cubism (Picasso, Braque), Surrealism (Dalí, Ernst), Futurism (Boccioni), American Abstract Expressionism (Pollock), and a sprinkling of Klee, Calder, and Chagall. The place is staffed by international interns working on art-related degrees.

Cost and Hours: €12, generally includes temporary exhibits, Wed-Mon 10:00-18:00, closed Tue, last entry 15 minutes before closing, audioguide-€7, mini-guidebook-€6, free and mandatory baggage check for anything bigger than a small purse, pricey café, photos allowed only in garden and terrace—a fine and relaxing perch overlooking Grand Canal; near Accademia, Dorsoduro 704, a five-minute walk from the Accademia Bridge (vaporetto:

Accademia) or from La Salute Church (vaporetto: Salute); tel. 041-240-5411, www.guggenheim-venice.it.

▲**La Salute Church (Santa Maria della Salute)**—This impressive church with a crown-shaped dome was built and dedicated to the Virgin Mary by grateful survivors of the 1630 plague.

Cost and Hours: Church—free, daily 9:00-12:00 & 15:00-17:30; sacristy—€2, may have shorter hours than church; tel. 041-274-3928. It's a 10-minute walk from the Accademia Bridge; the Salute vaporetto stop is at its doorstep (the hop from San Marco-Vallaresso to Salute on vaporetto #1 is €2).

▲**Ca' Rezzonico (Museum of 18th-Century Venice)**—This grand Grand Canal palazzo offers the best look in town at the life of Venice's rich and famous in the 1700s. Wander under ceilings by Tiepolo, among furnishings from that most decadent century, enjoying views of the canal and paintings by Guardi, Canaletto, and Longhi.

Cost and Hours: €7, covered by passes, April-Oct Wed-Mon 10:00-18:00, Nov-March Wed-Mon 10:00-17:00, closed Tue, last entry one hour before closing, audioguide-€4 or €6/2 people, free and mandatory baggage check, at Ca' Rezzonico vaporetto stop, tel. 041-241-0100, www.museiciviciveneziani.it.

▲**Punta della Dogana**—This new museum of contemporary art, housed in the former Customs House at the end of the Grand Canal, features cutting-edge 21st-century art in spacious rooms. This isn't Picasso and Matisse, or even Pollock and Warhol—those guys are ancient history. But if you're into the likes of Jeff Koons, Rachel Whiteread, and a host of newer artists, the museum is world-class. The displays change completely about every year, drawn from the museum's large collection. In fact, the art spreads over two locations—the triangular Customs House and Palazzo Grassi.

Cost and Hours: €15 for one locale, €20 for both, Wed-Mon 10:00-19:00, closed Tue, last entry one hour before closing, audioguide-€5 or €8/2 people, small café. The Customs House is near La Salute Church (Dogana *traghetto* or vaporetto: Salute). Palazzo Grassi is a bit upstream, on the east side of the Grand Canal (vaporetto: San Samuele). Tel. 199-139-139, www.palazzograssi.it.

Santa Croce District

▲▲▲**Rialto Bridge**—One of the world's most famous bridges, this distinctive and dramatic stone structure crosses the Grand Canal with a single confident span. The arcades along the top of the bridge help reinforce the structure...and offer some enjoyable shopping diversions, as does the **market** east of the bridge (souvenir stalls open daily, produce market closed Sun-Mon, fish market closed Sun).

▲**Ca' Pesaro International Gallery of Modern Art**—This museum features 19th- and early-20th-century art in a 17th-century canalside palazzo. The collection is strongest on Italian (especially Venetian) artists, but also presents a broad array of other well-known artists. The highlights are in one large room: Klimt's beautiful/creepy *Judith II*, with eagle-talon fingers; Kandinsky's *White Zig Zags* (plus other recognizable shapes); the colorful *Nude in the Mirror* by Bonnard, which flattens the 3-D scene into a 2-D pattern of rectangles; and Chagall's surprisingly realistic portrait of his hometown rabbi, *The Rabbi of Vitebsk*. The adjoining Room VII features small-scale works by Matisse, Max Ernst, Mark Tobey, and a Calder mobile. Admission also includes an Oriental Art wing.

Cost and Hours: €5.50, covered by passes, Tue-Sun 10:00-17:00, closed Mon, last entry one hour before closing, 2-minute walk from San Stae vaporetto stop, tel. 041-524-0662.

Palazzo Mocenigo Costume Museum—The Museo di Palazzo Mocenigo offers a walk through six rooms of a fine 17th-century mansion with period furnishings, family portraits, ceilings painted (c. 1790) with family triumphs (the Mocenigos produced seven doges), Murano glass chandeliers in situ, and a paltry collection of costumes with sparse descriptions.

Cost and Hours: €6, covered by passes, Tue-Sun 10:00-16:00, closed Mon, a block in from San Stae vaporetto stop, tel. 041-721-798.

San Polo District

▲▲**Frari Church (Chiesa dei Frari)**—My favorite art experience in Venice is seeing art in the setting for which it was designed—as it is at the Frari Church. The Franciscan "Church of the Brothers" and the art that decorates it is warmed by the spirit of St. Francis. It features the work of three great Renaissance masters: Donatello, Giovanni Bellini, and Titian—each showing worshippers the glory of God in human terms.

In **Donatello's wood carving of St. John the Baptist** (just to the right of the high altar), the prophet of the desert—dressed in animal skins and nearly starving from his diet of bugs 'n' honey—announces the coming of the Messiah. Donatello was a Florentine working at the dawn of the Renaissance.

Bellini's *Madonna and Child with Saints and Angels* painting (in the sacristy farther to the right) came later, done by a Venetian in a more Venetian style—soft focus without Donatello's harsh realism. While Renaissance humanism demanded Madonnas and saints that were accessible and human, Bellini places them in a physical setting so beautiful that it creates its own mood of serene holiness. The genius of Bellini, perhaps the greatest Venetian painter, is obvious in the pristine clarity, rich colors (notice Mary's clothing), believable depth, and reassuring calm of this three-paneled altarpiece.

Finally, glowing red and gold like a stained-glass window over the high altar, **Titian's** *The Assumption of Mary* sets the tone of exuberant beauty found in the otherwise sparse church. Titian the Venetian—a student of Bellini—painted steadily for 60 years... you'll see a lot of his art. As stunned apostles look up past the swirl of arms and legs, the complex composition of this painting draws you right to the radiant face of the once-dying, now-triumphant Mary as she joins God in heaven.

Feel comfortable to discreetly freeload off passing tours. For many, these three pieces of art make a visit to the Accademia Gallery unnecessary (or they may whet your appetite for more). Before leaving, check out the Neoclassical pyramid-shaped Canova monument and (opposite that) the grandiose tomb of Titian. Compare the carved marble *Assumption* behind Titian's tombstone portrait with the painted original above the high altar.

Cost and Hours: €3, Mon-Sat 9:00-18:00, Sun 13:00-18:00, last entry 15 minutes before closing, no visits during services, modest dress recommended. On Campo dei Frari, near San Tomà vaporetto and *traghetto* stops.

Audio Tours: Audioguides are available (€2, €3/2 people). You can download a free Rick Steves audio tour of the Frari Church for your mobile device via www.ricksteves.com/audioeurope, iTunes, or the Rick Steves Audio Europe smartphone app.

Concerts: The church occasionally hosts evening concerts (€15, buy ticket at church). For concert details, look for fliers, check www.basilicadeifrari.it, or call the church at 041-272-8611.

▲▲**Scuola San Rocco**—Sometimes called "Tintoretto's Sistine Chapel," this lavish meeting hall (next to the Frari Church) has some 50 large, colorful Tintoretto paintings plastered to the walls and ceilings. The best paintings are upstairs, especially the *Crucifixion* in the smaller room. View the neck-breaking splendor with one of the mirrors available at the entrance.

Cost and Hours: €7, audioguide-€1, daily 9:30-17:30, last entry 30 minutes before closing, tel. 041-523-4864, www.scuola grandesanrocco.it.

Church of San Polo—This nearby church, which pales in comparison to the two sights just listed, is only worth a visit for art-lovers. One of Venice's oldest churches (from the ninth century), San Polo features works by Tintoretto, Veronese, and Tiepolo and son.

Cost and Hours: €3, Mon-Sat 10:00-17:00, closed Sun, last entry 15 minutes before closing.

Cannaregio District

Jewish Ghetto—In medieval times, Jews were grudgingly allowed to do business in Venice, but they weren't permitted to live there until 1385 (subject to strict laws and special taxes). Anti-Semitic forces tried to oust them from the city, but in 1516, the doge compromised by restricting Jews to a special (undesirable) neighborhood. It was located on an easy-to-isolate island near the former foundry *(geto),* coining the word "ghetto" for a segregated neighborhood.

The population swelled with immigrants from elsewhere in Europe, reaching 5,000 in the 1600s, the Golden Age of Venice's Jews. Restricted within their tiny neighborhood (the Ghetto Nuovo, or "New Ghetto"), they expanded upward, building six-story "skyscrapers" that still stand today. The community's five synagogues were built atop the high-rise tenements. (As space was very tight and you couldn't live above a house of worship, this was the most practical use of precious land.) Only two synagogues are still active. You can spot them (with their five windows) from the square, but to visit them you have to book a tour through the Jewish Museum.

This original Ghetto becomes most interesting after touring the **Jewish Museum** (Museo Ebraico), which consists of two parts: a museum and a synagogue. The humble two-room museum has silver menorahs, cloth covers for the Torah scrolls, various religious objects, artifacts from the old community, and scant English explanations (€3, June-Sept Sun-Fri 10:00-17:00, Oct-May Sun-Fri 10:00-16:30, closed Sat and Jewish holidays, Campo di Ghetto Nuovo, vaporetto stop: San Marcuola, tel. 041-715-359, small café and bookstore). To see the **synagogue,** you must sign up for a half-hour English tour (€8.50, tours run hourly on the half-hour June-Sept Sun-Fri 10:00-19:00, Oct-May Sun-Fri 10:00-17:30, closed Sat and Jewish holidays). Group sizes are limited (the 11:30 tour is often booked full), so show up 20 minutes early to be sure you get in.

Calatrava Bridge (a.k.a. Ponte della Costituzione)—This controversial bridge, officially called "Constitution Bridge," is just upstream and around the bend from the train station. Only the fourth bridge to cross the Grand Canal, it carries foot traffic between the train station and Piazzale Roma. A modern structure of glass, steel, and stone, the bridge finally opened in 2008 after delays, cost overruns, and questions about its stability.

The bridge was designed by Spanish architect Santiago Calatrava, whose other projects include a museum in his hometown of Valencia, Spain; the twisting torso skyscraper in Malmö, Sweden; and the Olympic Sports complex in Athens, Greece.

The bridge draws snorts from Venetians. With an original

price tag of €4 million, the cost rose to around €11 million. The modern design of the bridge is also a sore point for a city with such rich medieval and Renaissance architecture. And, to add practical insult to aesthetic injury, the heavy bridge is crushing the centuries-old foundations at either end, threatening nearby buildings.

Interestingly, Calatrava's modern structure harkens back to the past, employing the same low-arch design of many older Venetian bridges. Pedestrians walk over similar shallow stair steps, and the bridge uses local Istrian stone.

Ca' d'Oro—This "House of Gold" palace, fronting the Grand Canal, is quintessential Venetian Gothic (Gothic seasoned with Byzantine and Islamic accents—see "Ca' d'Oro" on page 998). Inside, the permanent collection includes a few big names in Renaissance painting—Ghirlandaio, Signorelli, and Mantegna; a glimpse at a lush courtyard; and a grand view of the Grand Canal.

Cost and Hours: €5, slow and dry audioguide-€4, Mon 8:15-14:00, Tue-Sun 8:15-19:15, free peek through hole in door of courtyard, vaporetto stop: Ca' d'Oro, Calle Ca' d'Oro 3932.

Castello District

▲Scuola Dalmata di San Giorgio—This little-visited "school" (which means "meeting place") features an exquisite wood-paneled chapel decorated with the world's best collection of paintings by Vittorio Carpaccio (1465-1526).

The Scuola, a reminder that cosmopolitan Venice was once Europe's melting pot, was one of a hundred such community centers for various ethnic, religious, and economic groups, supported by the government partly to keep an eye on foreigners. It was here that the Dalmatians (from the southern coast of present-day Croatia) worshipped in their own way, held neighborhood meetings, and preserved their culture.

Cost and Hours: €3, Mon 14:45-18:00, Tue-Sat 9:15-13:00 & 14:45-18:00, Sun 9:15-13:00, on Calle dei Furlani, tel. 041-522-8828.

Santa Elena—For a pleasant peek into a completely non-touristy, residential side of Venice, walk or catch vaporetto #1 from St. Mark's Square to the neighborhood of Santa Elena (at the fish's "tail"). This 100-year-old suburb lives as if there were no tourism. You'll find a kid-friendly park, a few lazy restaurants, and beautiful sunsets over San Marco.

Experiences in Venice

Gondola Rides

Gondolas cost lots more after 19:00 but are also more romantic and relaxing under the moon (although this may not be an option in winter—gondoliers go home early in cold weather). A rip-off for some, this is a traditional must for romantics. Gondoliers charge about €80 for a 40-minute ride during the day; from 19:00 on, figure on €100. To add music (a singer and an accordionist), it'll cost an additional €110 before 19:00, or €130 after 19:00. You can divide the cost—and the romance—among up to six people per boat, but you'll need to save two seats for the musicians if you choose to be serenaded. Only two seats (the ones in back) are next to each other. If you want to haggle, you'll find softer prices during the day. (Note that gondoliers have a trick where one guy says "No," and another, acting secretive, comes to you a bit later and says, "OK, but don't let my friend know I'm offering you this incredible price.") Establish the price and duration before boarding, enjoy your ride, and pay only when you're finished.

If you've hired musicians and want to hear a Venetian song *(un canto Veneziano)*, try requesting *"Venezia La Luna e Tu."* Asking to hear *"O Sole Mio"* (which comes from Naples) is like asking a bartender in Cleveland to sing *"The Eyes of Texas."*

Glide through nighttime Venice with your head on someone's shoulder. Follow the moon as it sails past otherwise unseen buildings. Silhouettes gaze down from bridges while window glitter spills onto the black water. You're anonymous in the city of masks, as the rhythmic thrust of your striped-shirted gondolier turns old crows into songbirds. This is extremely relaxing (and, I think, worth the extra cost to experience at night). Because you might get a narration plus conversation with your gondolier, talk with several and choose one you like who speaks English well. Women, beware...while gondoliers can be extremely charming, local women say that anyone who falls for one of these Romeos "has slices of ham over her eyes."

For cheap gondola thrills during the day, stick to the €0.50 one-minute ferry ride on a Grand Canal *traghetto*. At night, *vaporetti* are nearly empty, and it's a great time to cruise the Grand Canal on the slow boat #1. Or hang out on a bridge along the gondola route and wave at romantics.

Nightlife in Venice

You must experience Venice after dark. The city is quiet at night, as tour groups stay in the cheaper hotels of Mestre on the mainland, and the masses of day-trippers return to their beach resorts and cruise ships. **Gondolas** cost more, but are worth the extra expense (described earlier). At night, *vaporetti* are nearly empty, and it's a great time to cruise the Grand Canal on the slow boat #1.

Venice has a busy schedule of events, festivals, and entertainment. Check at the TI for listings, and keep an eye out for publications such as the free *Shows & Events* magazine (monthly, bilingual, available at top-end hotels and the TI, www.turismo venezia.it).

Baroque Concerts—Venice is a city of the powdered-wig Baroque era. For about €25 (prices vary), you can take your pick of traditional Vivaldi concerts in churches throughout town. Homegrown Vivaldi is as trendy here as Strauss is in Vienna and Mozart is in Salzburg. In fact, you'll find frilly young Vivaldis hawking concert tickets on many corners. The TI has a list of this week's Baroque concerts. Shows start at 21:00 and generally last 1.5 hours. You'll see posters in hotels all over town (hotels sell tickets at face-value). A one-stop shop for concerts is the Vivaldi Store, at the east end of Rialto Bridge (5537 Salizada del Fontego dei Tedeschi). Tickets for Baroque concerts in Venice can usually be bought the same day as the concert, so don't bother with websites that sell tickets with a surcharge.

Consider the venue carefully. The general rule of thumb: Musicians in wigs and tights offer better spectacle; musicians in black-and-white suits are better performers. **San Vitale Church** (at the north end of Accademia Bridge) and the **Interpreti Veneziani orchestra** (which often plays there) are reliably top-notch (tel. 041-277-0561, www.interpretiveneziani.com). For the latest on church concerts, check any TI or visit www.turismovenezia.it.

Other Performances—Venice's most famous theaters are **La Fenice** (grand old opera house, box office tel. 041-786-5111, see page 1010), **Teatro Goldoni** (mostly Italian live theater), and **Teatro della Fondamenta Nuove** (theater, music, and dance).

Musica a Palazzo is a unique evening of opera at the Doge's Palace. You'll spend about 45 minutes in three sumptuous rooms as eight musicians (generally four instruments and four singers) perform. With these kinds of surroundings, under Tiepolo frescoes, you'll be glad you dressed up. As there are only 70 seats, you must book by phone or online in advance. Opera-lovers find this to be a wonderful evening (€50, nightly shows at 20:30, Palazzo Barbarigo-Minotto, Fondamenta Duodo o Barbarigo—on the Grand Canal next to the Santa Maria del Giglio vaporetto stop, mobile 340-971-7272, www.musicapalazzo.com).

Venezia is advertised as "the show that tells the great story of Venice" and "simply the best show in town." I found the performance to be slow-moving and a bit cheesy, and the venue to be disappointing (€40, nightly at 19:00, 80 minutes, ticket includes a 30-minute video on Venice at 18:00, Teatro San Gallo, just off St. Mark's Square on Campo San Gallo, tel. 041-241-2002, www.teatrosangallo.net).

St. Mark's Square—For tourists, St. Mark's Square is the highlight, with lantern light and live music echoing from the cafés. Just being here after dark is a thrill, as **dueling café orchestras**

entertain. Every night, enthusiastic musicians play the same songs, creating the same irresistible magic. Hang out for free behind the tables (allowing you to move easily on to the next orchestra when the musicians take a break), or spring for a seat and enjoy a fun and gorgeously set concert. If you sit a while, it can be €12-20 well spent (for a drink and the cover charge for music). Dancing on the square is free (and encouraged). Streetlamp halos, live music, floodlit history, and a ceiling of stars make St. Mark's magic at midnight. You're not a tourist, you're a living part of a soft Venetian night... an alley cat with money. In the misty light, the moon has a golden hue. Shine with the old lanterns on the gondola piers, where the sloppy lagoon splashes at the Doge's Palace...reminiscing.

Sleeping in Venice

For hassle-free efficiency and the sheer magic of being close to the action, I favor hotels that are handy to sightseeing activities. I've listed rooms in four neighborhoods: St. Mark's bustle, the Rialto action, the quiet Dorsoduro area behind the Accademia art museum, and near the train station (handy for train travelers, but far from the action). I also mention several apartment rentals, big fancy hotels, cheap dorms, and places on the mainland.

Hotels in Venice can be tricky to locate. While I've tried to give clear directions, you'll do best by following the arrival instructions provided on your hotel's website.

Book a room as soon as you know when you'll be in town. Venice gets booked up during its festivals, religious holidays such

---

Sleep Code

(€1 = about $1.40, country code: 39)
S = Single, **D** = Double/Twin, **T** = Triple, **Q** = Quad, **b** = bathroom, **s** = shower only. Unless otherwise noted, credit cards are accepted, breakfast is included, and English is generally spoken.

To help you easily sort through these listings, I've divided the rooms into three categories based on the price for a standard double room with bath:

$$$ Higher Priced—Most rooms €180 or more.
$$ Moderately Priced—Most rooms between €130-180.
$ Lower Priced—Most rooms €130 or less.

Prices can change without notice; verify the hotel's current rates online or by email. For other updates, see www.ricksteves.com/update.

VENICE

Hotels near St. Mark's Square

TO RIALTO

TO RIALTO

RT. COLONNE

10

C. FIUBERA

FABBRI

MERCERIE

SPADARIA

San Zulian

LARGA S. MARCO

9

8

PIAZZETTA D. LEONCINI

TRON

OLD OFFICES

CLOCK TOWER

ST. MARK'S BASILICA

RAMO SELVA

G

CAMPA-NILE

PIAZZA SAN MARCO

DOGE'S PALACE

FRENNARIA

POST WC

CORRER MUSEUM + NAPOLEON'S WING

i   NEW OFFICES

PIAZZETTA

S. MARCO COLUMN

SAL

SAN MOISÈ

CALLE VALLARESSO

GIARDINETTI REALI

WC   i

G   S. THEODORE COLUMN

San Moisè

TO ACCADEMIA

V   San Marco - Giardinetti

V   San Marco - Vallaresso

SAN   MARCO

T

TO SALUTE

- **ENTRANCES TO SIGHTS**
- V **VAPORETTO STOP**
- T **TRAGHETTO CROSSING**
- G **GONDOLA STATION**

100 YARDS

100 METERS

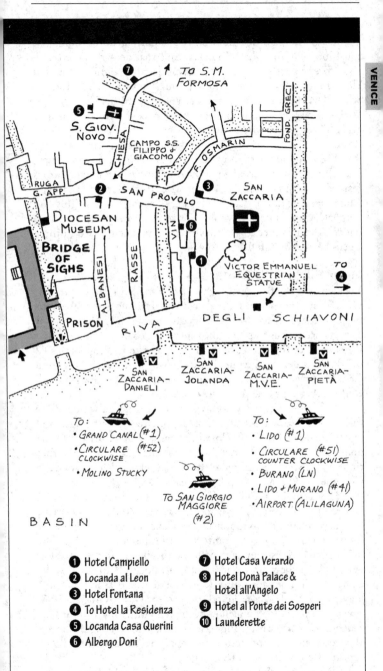

To:
- GRAND CANAL (#1)
- CIRCULARE (#52) CLOCKWISE
- MOLINO STUCKY

To:
- LIDO (#1)
- CIRCULARE (#51) COUNTER CLOCKWISE
- BURANO (LN)
- LIDO & MURANO (#41)
- AIRPORT (ALILAGUNA)

TO SAN GIORGIO MAGGIORE (#2)

BASIN

1. Hotel Campiello
2. Locanda al Leon
3. Hotel Fontana
4. To Hotel la Residenza
5. Locanda Casa Querini
6. Albergo Doni
7. Hotel Casa Verardo
8. Hotel Donà Palace & Hotel all'Angelo
9. Hotel al Ponte dei Sosperi
10. Launderette

as Easter, and Fridays and Saturdays year-round.

Over the past decade, Venice's supply of hotel rooms has mushroomed. This glut of hotels means that demand is soft and, therefore, so are prices. Hotels have tossed straight pricing out the window. Smart travelers will email several places and see who offers the best rates. It's important to email the hotel directly (rather than going through a booking service) and to say you are a Rick Steves reader who expects their best price. Then survey your results, and pick what you think is the best value for that day.

I've done my best to predict prices for peak season: April, May, June, September, and October. Prices will be higher during festivals, and almost all places drop prices from November through March (except during Carnevale and Christmas) and in July and August. Many hotels in Venice list rooms on www.venere.com, which is worth checking for last-minute vacancies (two to three weeks before the date).

Near St. Mark's Square

Located near the Bridge of Sighs, just off the Riva degli Schiavoni waterfront promenade, these places rub drainpipes with Venice's most palatial five-star hotels. To get here from the train station or Piazzale Roma bus stop, ride the vaporetto to San Zaccaria—either the slow #1 or the fast #2 (from the Tronchetto parking lot, it's #2 only). Consider using your ride to follow my tour of the Grand Canal (see page 994); to make sure you arrive via the Grand Canal, confirm that your boat goes "*via Rialto.*"

The nearest laundry is **Lavanderia Gabriella,** which offers full service a few streets north of the square (€15/load wash and dry, Mon-Fri 8:00-12:30, closed Sat-Sun; with your back to the door of San Zulian Church, go over Ponte dei Ferali, take first right down Calle dei Armeni, then first left on Rio Terra de le Colonne to #985; tel. 041-522-1758, Elisabetta).

$$$ Hotel Campiello, lacy and bright, was once part of a 19th-century convent. Ideally located 50 yards off the waterfront, on a tiny square, its 16 rooms offer a tranquil, friendly refuge for travelers who appreciate comfort and professional service (Sb-€130, Db-€180, discount with cash and this book, air-con, elevator, Wi-Fi; from the waterfront street—Riva degli Schiavoni—take Calle del Vin, between pink Hotel Danieli and Hotel Savoia e Jolanda, to #4647, Castello; tel. 041-520-5764, fax 041-520-5798, www.hcampiello.it, campiello@hcampiello.it; family-run for four generations, currently by Thomas, Monica, Nicoletta, and Marco). They also rent three modern family apartments, under rustic timbers just steps away (up to €380/night).

$$ Locanda al Leon is a basic place renting 14 decent rooms just off Campo S.S. Filippo e Giacomo (Db-€135-150, Tb-€170,

Qb-€220, ask for best Rick Steves price and show this book if paying cash, air-con, Internet access and Wi-Fi, Campo S.S. Filippo e Giacomo 4270, Castello, tel. 041-277-0393, fax 041-521-0348, www.hotelalleon.com, leon@hotelalleon.com, Giuliano and Marcella). From the San Zaccaria-Danieli vaporetto stop, take Calle dei Albanesi (two streets left of pink Hotel Danieli) to its far end.

$$ Hotel Fontana is a two-star family-run place with 15 rooms near a school, two bridges behind St. Mark's Square. Their annex across the street has much lower ceilings and slightly lower prices (Sb-€110, Db-€140-170, family rooms, cash discount, quieter rooms on garden side, 2 rooms have terraces for €10 extra, air-con, elevator, Internet access and Wi-Fi, Campo San Provolo 4701, Castello, tel. 041-522-0579, fax 041-523-1040, www.hotelfontana.it, info@hotelfontana.it, Diego and Gabriele). From the San Zaccaria vaporetto dock, take Calle delle Rasse—to the left of pink Hotel Danieli—then turn right at the end, and continue to the first square.

$$ Hotel la Residenza is a grand old palace facing a peaceful square. It has 15 great rooms on three levels and a huge, luxurious old lounge. This is a great value for romantics—you'll feel like you're in the Doge's Palace after-hours. Hang out in the living room and you become royalty (Sb-€100, Db-€130-165, air-con, Wi-Fi, Campo Bandiera e Moro 3608, Castello, tel. 041-528-5315, fax 041-523-8859, www.venicelaresidenza.com, info@venicelaresidenza.com, Giovanni). From the Bridge of Sighs, walk east along Riva degli Schiavoni, cross three bridges, and take the first left up Calle del Dose to Campo Bandiera e Moro.

$$ Locanda Casa Querini rents six bright, high-ceilinged rooms on a quiet square tucked away behind St. Mark's. You can enjoy your breakfast or a sunny picnic/happy hour sitting at their tables right on the sleepy little square (Db-€150, third person-€20-25, one cheaper small double, ask for cash discount, air-con, Wi-Fi, halfway between San Zaccaria vaporetto stop and Campo Santa Maria Formosa at Campo San Giovanni in Oleo 4388, Castello, tel. 041-241-1294, fax 041-523-6188, www.locandaquerini.com, casaquerini@hotmail.com, Patrizia and Silvia). From the San Zaccaria vaporetto stop, take the street to the right of the Bridge of Sighs to Campo S.S. Filippo e Giacomo, continue on Calle drio la Chiesa, take the second left, and curl around to the left into the little square, Campo San Giovanni Novo.

$ Albergo Doni is dark, clean, and quiet—a bit of a time warp—with 13 dim but once-classy rooms run by a likable smart aleck named Gina, her niece Tessa, and her nephew, an Italian stallion named Nikos (D-€90, Db-€115, T-€120, Tb-€155, reserve with credit card but pay in cash, ceiling fans, three Db rooms have air-con, avoid their overflow apartment, Fondamenta del

VENICE

Hotels near the Rialto Bridge

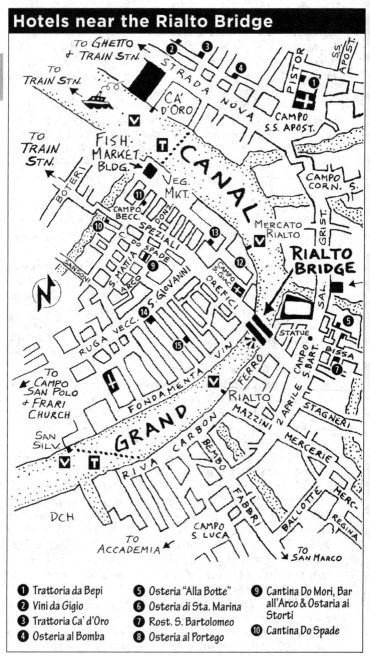

1 Trattoria da Bepi
2 Vini da Gigio
3 Trattoria Ca' d'Oro
4 Osteria al Bomba

5 Osteria "Alla Botte"
6 Osteria di Sta. Marina
7 Rost. S. Bartolomeo
8 Osteria al Portego

9 Cantina Do Mori, Bar all'Arco & Ostaria ai Storti
10 Cantina Do Spade

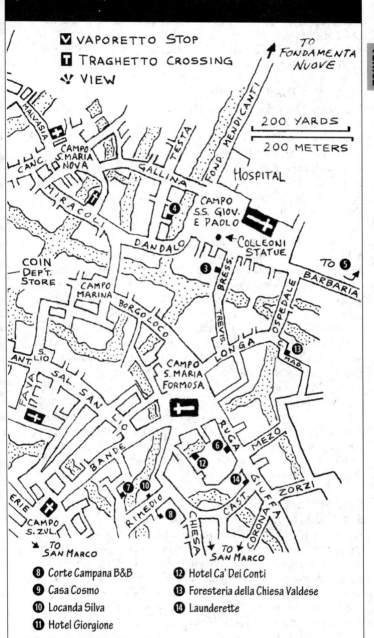

VENICE

✓ VAPORETTO STOP
T TRAGHETTO CROSSING
↯ VIEW

TO FONDAMENTA NUOVE

200 YARDS
200 METERS

MALVASIA
CAMPO S. MARIA NOVA
CANC.
MIRACOLI
TESTA
GALLINA
FOND. MENDICANTI
HOSPITAL
CAMPO S.S. GIOV. E PAOLO
④
← COLLEONI STATUE
COIN DEP'T. STORE
DANDALO
③
BRESS.
TO ⑤ BARBARIA
CAMPO MARINA
BORGOLOCO
TREVIS.
LONGA
OSPEDALE
C. MAP.
⑬
ANT. LIO
FAVA
SAL. SAN
LIO
BANDE
CAMPO S. MARIA FORMOSA
T
RUGA
MEZO
⑥
⑫
⑭
GIUFFA
ZORZI
ERIE
CAMPO S. ZUL.
RIMEDIO
⑦ ⑩
⑧
CHIESA
CAST.
CORONA
↘ TO SAN MARCO
↓ TO SAN MARCO

⑧ Corte Campana B&B
⑨ Casa Cosmo
⑩ Locanda Silva
⑪ Hotel Giorgione
⑫ Hotel Ca' Dei Conti
⑬ Foresteria della Chiesa Valdese
⑭ Launderette

Vin 4656, Castello, tel. & fax 041-522-4267, www.albergodoni.it, albergodoni@hotmail.it). From the San Zaccaria vaporetto stop, cross one bridge to the right and take the first left (marked Calle del Vin), then turn left at the little square named Ramo del Vin, jog left, and find the hotel ahead on Fondamenta del Vin.

Near the Rialto Bridge

Vaporetto #2 quickly connects the Rialto with the train station, the Piazzale Roma bus stop, and the Tronchetto parking lot. The slower vaporetto #1 connects everything but Tronchetto.

You can do your laundry at **Effe Erre,** a modern self-service *lavanderia* near recommended Hotel al Piave at Ruga Giuffa 4826 (open daily 6:30-23:00, €11/small load wash and dry; full-service for just a couple euros more, 9:00-13:00, winter hours may be shorter, mobile 349-058-3881, Massimo).

West of the Rialto Bridge

$ Pensione Guerrato, above the colorful Rialto produce market and just two minutes from the Rialto Bridge, is run by friendly, creative, and hardworking Roberto and Piero. Their 800-year-old building—with 24 spacious, air-conditioned, and charming rooms—is simple, airy, and wonderfully characteristic (D-€90, Db-€130, Tb-€150, Qb-€170, Quint/b-€185, check website for special discounts, ask for Rick Steves discount below Web specials or with this book and cash, Wi-Fi, Calle drio la Scimia 240a, San Polo, tel. & fax 041-528-5927, www.pensioneguerrato.it, hguerrat @tin.it, Monica and Rosanna). From the train station, take vaporetto #1 to the Mercato Rialto stop (comes before the "Rialto" stop), exit the boat to your right, and follow the waterfront. Calle drio la Scimia (not simply Scimia, the block before), is on the left—you'll see the hotel sign. My tour groups book this place for 50 nights each year. Sorry. The Guerrato also rents family apartments in the old center (great for groups of 4-8) for around €55 per person.

East of the Rialto Bridge

$$$ Hotel al Ponte Antico is exquisite, professional, and small. With nine plush rooms and a velvety royal living/breakfast room, it's perfect for a romantic anniversary. Because its wonderful terrace overlooks the Grand Canal, Rialto Bridge, and market action, its non-canal-view rooms may be a better value (Db-€290, superior Db-€380, deluxe canal-front Db-€450, air-con, Wi-Fi; 100 yards from Rialto Bridge, follow Salizzada S. Grisostomo behind post office and past Coin department store, turn left down the dark and empty Calle del Aseo to #5768, Cannaregio; tel. 041-241-1944, fax 041-241-1828, www.alponteantico.com, info @alponteantico.com).

$ Locanda la Corte, a three-star hotel, is perfumed with elegance. Its 19 attractive high-ceilinged wood-beamed rooms—done in earthy pastels—circle a small, quiet courtyard (Sb-€100, standard Db-€120, superior Db-€150, cash discount, ask for Rick Steves discount, suites and family rooms available, air-con, Wi-Fi, Castello 6317, tel. 041-241-1300, fax 041-241-5982, www.locanda lacorte.it, info@locandalacorte.it, Marco, Raffaela, and Tommy the cat). Take vaporetto #52 from the train station to Fondamenta Nuove, exit the boat to your left, follow the waterfront, and turn right after the second bridge to reach S.S. Giovanni e Paolo. Facing the Rosa Salva bar, take the street to the left (Calle Bressana); the hotel is a short block away at #6317, before the bridge.

$ Casa Pisani Canal Hotel is a sweet little place renting five rooms (Db-€100-120, huge Db suite overlooking canal-€240, air-con, Wi-Fi, Calle de le Erbe 6105, Cannaregio, tel. 041-724-1030, www.casapisanicanal.it, info@casapisanicanal.it, Tortorelle family). It's just off Campo S.S. Giovanni e Paolo, on Calle de le Erbe.

$ Alloggi Barbaria rents eight quiet, spacious backpacker-type rooms on one floor around a bright and institutional-feeling common area. Beyond Campo S.S. Giovanni e Paolo, this IKEA-style place is a long walk from the action but a good value and a chance to see the real Venice (Db-€90-100, third or fourth person-€25 each, pay cash for best price, family deals, air-con, tel. 041-522-2750, fax 041-277-5540, www.alloggibarbaria.it, info @alloggibarbaria.it, Giorgio and Fausto). Take vaporetto #52 to Ospedale stop, turn left as you get off the boat, then right down Calle de le Capucine to #6573.

Southeast of the Rialto Bridge

$$ Hotel al Piave, with 27 fine air-conditioned rooms above a bright and classy lobby, is fresh, modern, and comfortable. You'll enjoy the neighborhood and always get a cheery welcome (Db-€150, Tb-€200; family suites-€280 for 4, €300 for 5, or €320 for 6; cash discount, Internet access and Wi-Fi, Ruga Giuffa 4838/40, Castello, tel. 041-528-5174, fax 041-523-8512, www.hotelalpiave .com, info@hotelalpiave.com, Mirella, Paolo, and Ilaria speak English). From the San Zaccaria vaporetto stop, take the street to the right of the Bridge of Sighs to Campo S.S. Filippo e Giacomo, and continue on Calle drio la Chiesa. Cross the bridge, continue straight, then turn left onto Ruga Giuffa; find the hotel on your left at #4838.

$ Hotel Riva, with gleaming marble hallways, big exposed beams, fine antique furnishings, and bright rooms, is romantically situated on a canal along the gondola serenade route. You could actually dunk your breakfast rolls in the canal (but don't). Ten of the 30 rooms come with air-conditioning for the same price—request one when you reserve. Or, if you prefer lots of light but no air-conditioning, you can ask Sandro to hold a corner *(angolo)* room for you (Sb-€90, D-€100, Db-€120, Tb-€170, €20 extra for view, reserve with credit card but pay with cash only, Ponte dell'Angelo, tel. 041-522-7034, fax 041-528-5551, www.hotelriva .it, info@hotelriva.it, Daniella). Facing St. Mark's Basilica, walk behind it on the left along Calle de la Canonica, take the first left (at blue *Pauly & C* mosaic in street), continue straight, go over the bridge, and angle right to the hotel at Ponte dell'Angelo.

$ Corte Campana B&B, run by enthusiastic and helpful Riccardo, rents three quiet and characteristic rooms just behind St. Mark's Square, plus two apartments (Db-€125, Tb or Tb apartment-€165, Qb-€190, prices are soft, cash only, 2-night minimum, €10/night less for stays of 4 nights, air-con, Internet access, Calle del Remedio 4410, Castello, tel. & fax 041-523-3603, mobile 389-272-6500, www.cortecampana.com, info@cortecampana.com). From nearby Locanda Silva—described below—go 30 yards down the canal, turn right onto Calle del Remedio, follow it to #4410, and ring the bell at the black gate.

$ Casa Cosmo is a humble little five-room place run by Davide and his parents. While it comes with minimal services and no public spaces, it's air-conditioned, very central, inexpensive, and quiet (Db-€110, cash discount, no breakfast, Calle di Mezo 4976, San Marco, tel. & fax 041-296-0710, www.casacosmo.com, info @casacosmo.com). From the Rialto vaporetto stop, head inland on Larga Mazzini (which becomes Merceria). Turn right onto San Salvador, then immediately left onto tiny Calle di Mezo to #4976 (it's just behind Foot Locker).

$ Locanda Silva is a big, basic, beautifully located, institutional-feeling place renting 23 decent old-school rooms (S-€65, Sb-€80, D-€85, weekday Db-€110, weekend Db-€130, substantially less during slow times, request Rick Steves discount, closed Dec-Jan, Fondamenta del Remedio 4423, tel. 041-522-7643, fax 041-528-6817, www.locandasilva.it, info@locandasilva.it, Sandra and Massimo). From San Marco, head north toward Campo Santa Maria Formosa, go down Calle del Remedio, and turn left at the canal to Fondamenta del Remedio.

Near the Accademia Bridge

When you step over the Accademia Bridge, the commotion of touristy Venice is replaced by a sleepy village laced with canals. This quiet area, next to the best painting gallery in town, is a 15-minute walk from the Rialto or St. Mark's Square.

The fast vaporetto #2 connects the Accademia Bridge with the train station (15 minutes), Piazzale Roma bus stop (20 minutes),

Tronchetto parking lot (25 minutes), and St. Mark's Square (5 minutes). For hotels south of the Accademia Bridge, vaporetto #51 to Zattere (or the Alilaguna speedboat from the airport to Zattere) are good options.

South of the Accademia Bridge

$$$ Hotel Belle Arti has a grand entry and a formal, stern staff. With the ambience of a modern American hotel, its 64 rooms feel out of place in musty Old World Venice (Sb-€130, Db-€240, Tb-€280, air-con, elevator; 100 yards behind Accademia art museum: facing museum, jog left, then right, down Via Dorsoduro to #912, Dorsoduro; tel. 041-522-6230, fax 041-528-0043, www .hotelbellearti.com, info@hotelbellearti.com).

$$$ Pensione Accademia fills the 17th-century Villa Mara- vege like a Bellini painting. Its 27 rooms are comfortable, elegant, and air-conditioned. You'll feel aristocratic gliding through its grand public spaces and lounging in its wistful, breezy gardens (Sb- €145, standard Db-€235, bigger "superior" Db-€280, Qb-€330, ask for discount when you book; facing Accademia art museum, go right, cross the bridge, go right to where the small canal hits the big one, Dorsoduro 1058; tel. 041-521-0188, fax 041-523-9152, www .pensioneaccademia.it, info@pensioneaccademia.it).

$$$ Hotel Agli Alboretti is a cozy family-run 23-room place in a quiet neighborhood a block behind the Accademia art museum. With red carpeting and wood-beamed ceilings, it feels classy (Sb-€115, Db-€200, Tb-€225, Qb-€250, air-con, elevator, 100 yards from the Accademia vaporetto stop on Rio Terra A. Foscarini at #884, Dorsoduro, tel. 041-523-0058, fax 041-521-0158, www.aglialboretti.com, info@aglialboretti.com, Anna).

$$ Pensione la Calcina, the home of English writer John Ruskin in 1876, maintains a 19th-century formality. It comes with all the three-star comforts in a professional yet intimate package. Its 32 rosy, perfumed rooms are squeaky clean, with nice wood furniture, hardwood floors, and a peaceful canalside setting fac- ing Giudecca Island (Sb-€140, Sb with view-€150, Db-€150-310 depending on size and view, Qb-€280, air-con, Wi-Fi, rooftop terrace, floating buffet-breakfast terrace, near Zattere vaporetto stop at south end of Rio di San Vio at #780, Dorsoduro, tel. 041- 520-6466, fax 041-522-7045, www.lacalcina.com, info@lacalcina .com). Guests get discounted meals at their La Piscina restaurant.

$$ Casa Rezzonico is a silent getaway far from the mad- ding crowds. Its private garden terrace has perhaps the lushest grass in Italy, and its seven spacious, very Venetian rooms have garden/canal views (Sb-€120, Db-€160, Tb-€190, Qb-€220, ask for discount when you book, air-con, Wi-Fi, Fondamenta Gherardini 2813, Dorsoduro, tel. 041-277-0653, fax 041-277-5435,

VENICE

Hotels near the Accademia Bridge

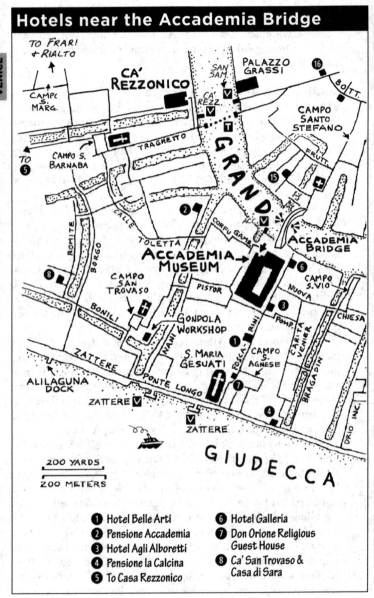

1 Hotel Belle Arti
2 Pensione Accademia
3 Hotel Agli Alboretti
4 Pensione la Calcina
5 To Casa Rezzonico
6 Hotel Galleria
7 Don Orione Religious Guest House
8 Ca' San Trovaso & Casa di Sara

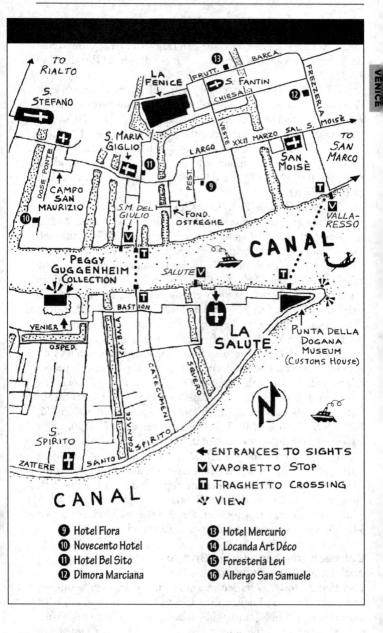

www.casarezzonico.it, info@casarezzonico.it). Take vaporetto #1 to Ca' Rezzonico, head up Calle del Traghetto, cross Campo San Barnaba to the canal, and continue on Fondamenta Gherardini to #2813.

$$ Hotel Galleria has nine tight, velvety rooms, most with views of the Grand Canal. Some rooms are quite narrow. It's run with a family feel by Luciano and Stefano (S-€85, D-€120, skinny Grand Canal view Db-€150, palatial Grand Canal view Db-€180, includes breakfast in room, fans, 30 yards from Accademia art museum, next to recommended Foscarini pizzeria, Dorsoduro 878a, tel. 041-523-2489, fax 041-520-4172, www.hotelgalleria.it, galleria@tin.it).

$$ Don Orione Religious Guest House is a big cultural center dedicated to the work of a local man who became a saint in modern times. Filling an old monastery, it feels institutional, like a modern retreat center—clean, peaceful, and strictly run, with 74 rooms. It's beautifully located, comfortable, and a fine value (Sb-€84, Db-€140, Tb-€180, profits go to mission work in the developing world, groups welcome, air-con, Dorsoduro, tel. 041-522-4077, fax 041-528-6214, www.donorione-venezia.it, info@donorione-venezia.it). From the Zattere vaporetto stop, turn right, then turn left. It's just after the church at #909a.

$ Ca' San Trovaso rents seven simple, spacious rooms split between the main hotel and a nearby annex. The location is peaceful, on a small canal (Sb-€90, Db-€115, Db with bigger canal view and air-con-€130, Tb-€145, pay cash for best prices, includes breakfast in your room, air-con, small roof terrace, Dorsoduro 1350/51, tel. 041-277-1146, mobile 339-445-8821, fax 041-277-7190, www.casantrovaso.com, s.trovaso@tin.it, Mark and his son Alessandro). From the Zattere vaporetto stop, exit left, and cross a bridge. Turn right at tiny Calle Trevisan, cross another bridge, cross the adjacent bridge, take an immediate right, and then the first left. Nearby, Mama Cristina's **Casa di Sara** is a brightly colored B&B with quiet rooms, a tiny roof terrace, and the same prices (mobile 345-070-8547, www.casadisara.com, info@casadisara.com).

Between the Accademia Bridge and St. Mark's Square

$$$ Hotel Flora sits buried in a sea of fancy designer boutiques and elegant hotels almost on the Grand Canal. It's formal, with uniformed staff and grand public spaces, yet the 43 rooms have a homey warmth and the garden oasis is a sanctuary for foot-weary guests (generally Db-€260, check website for special discounts or email Sr. Romanelli for Rick Steves discount off standard prices, air-con, elevator, Calle dei Bergamaschi 2283a, San Marco, tel. 041-520-5844, fax 041-522-8217, www.hotelflora.it, info@hotel flora.it). It's at the end of Calle dei Bergamaschi, a long, skinny dead-end lane just off Calle Larga XXII Marzo.

$$$ Novecento Hotel rents nine plush rooms. Owned by Hotel Flora (described above), this boutique hotel is decorated circa-1900 throughout, with a big lounge and an elegant living room (Db-€240-260, air-con, Wi-Fi, Calle del Dose 2683, off Campo San Maurizio, San Marco, tel. 041-241-3765, fax 041-521-2145, www.novecento.biz, info@novecento.biz).

$$$ Hotel Bel Sito offers pleasing yet well-worn Old World character, 38 rooms, generous public spaces, a peaceful courtyard, and a picturesque location—facing a church on a small square between St. Mark's Square and the Accademia (Sb-€110, Db-€185, air-con, Wi-Fi, elevator; catch vaporetto #1 to Santa Maria del Giglio stop, take street inland to square, hotel is at far end to your right at Santa Maria del Giglio 2517, San Marco; tel. 041-522-3365, fax 041-520-4083, www.hotelbelsito.info, info@hotelbelsito.info, manager Rossella).

$$ Dimora Marciana, a mod place furnished in a traditional Venetian style, has seven rooms in a quiet alley just a two-minute walk from St. Mark's Square (Db-€165, Tb-€190, 2-room Qb-€230, mention Rick Steves when you book to get the best prices, cash discount, air-con, Wi-Fi, small bar, tel. 041-522-0755, www.dimoramarciana.com, info@dimoramarciana.com, Daniel). From behind the Correr Museum, turn right on Frezzeria, then take Calle Bognolo—the second street on the left—to #1604.

$$ Hotel Mercurio offers 19 peaceful, comfortable, and recently renovated rooms near La Fenice Opera House. Some rooms offer canal views (Sb-€130, Db-€170, Tb-€200, €10 less with cash, less mid-June-Aug and Nov-Feb except Christmas week, air-con, Wi-Fi, Calle del Fruttariol 1848, San Marco, tel. 041-522-0947, fax 041-582-5270, www.hotelmercurio.com, info @hotelmercurio.com, Monica, Vittorio, and Natale). From the San Marco-Vallaresso vaporetto stop, follow Calle Vallaresso to Calle Frezzaria, turn right, and follow it over a bridge as it becomes Calle del Frutariol. The hotel is on the left just before La Fenice Opera House.

$$ Locanda Art Déco is a charming little place. While the Art Deco theme is scant, a wrought-iron staircase leads from the inviting lobby to six thoughtfully decorated rooms (Db-€150-170, Tb-€200, 3-night minimum on weekends, cash discount, air-con, free Wi-Fi, just north of the Accademia Bridge off Campo Santo Stefano at Calle delle Botteghe 2966, San Marco, tel. 041-277-0558, fax 041-270-2891, www.locandaartdeco.com, info@locanda artdeco.com). They also rent loft apartments.

$$ Foresteria Levi, run by a foundation that promotes research on Venetian music, offers 35 quiet, institutional yet

VENICE

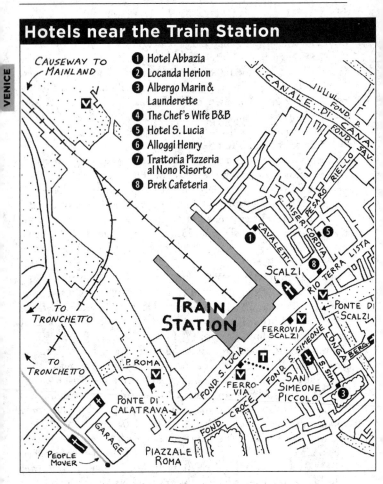

Hotels near the Train Station

1. Hotel Abbazia
2. Locanda Herion
3. Albergo Marin & Launderette
4. The Chef's Wife B&B
5. Hotel S. Lucia
6. Alloggi Henry
7. Trattoria Pizzeria al Nono Risorto
8. Brek Cafeteria

CAUSEWAY TO MAINLAND

CANALE DI CANA

FOND. SAV.

RIELLO

PESARO

C. MISERICORDIA

FOND. P.

CAVALETI

SCALZI

RIO TERRA LISTA

PONTE DI SCALZI

TRAIN STATION

TO TRONCHETTO

FERROVIA SCALZI

LONGA BERG.

S. SIM.

TO TRONCHETTO

P. ROMA

FOND. S. LUCIA

FERRO-VIA

FOND. S. SIMEONE

SAN SIMEONE PICCOLO

PONTE DI CALATRAVA

FOND. CROCE

GARAGE

PEOPLE MOVER

PIAZZALE ROMA

comfortable and spacious rooms (Sb-€100, Db-€190, Tb-€210, Qb-€240; ask for Rick Steves discount—10-20 percent in high season, 20-50 percent in low season; fans, elevator, free Wi-Fi, laundry, on Calle Giustinian at San Marco 2893, tel. 041-786-711, fax 041-786-766, www.foresterialevi.it, info@foresterialevi.it). It's 80 yards from the Accademia Bridge on the St. Mark's side. Leaving the bridge (opposite the Accademia vaporetto stop), take an immediate left, cross the bridge, and go down Calle Giustinian straight to the Fondazione Levi building. Buzz the *Foresteria* door to the right.

$ Albergo San Samuele's is a backpacker place: dumpy but in a great locale. It rents 12 basic rooms in a crumbling old palace near Campo Santo Stefano. Sleep here only if their price is far less than other listings (S-€60, D-€80, Db-€100, extra bed-€30, no

VENICE

breakfast, Salizada San Samuele 3358, San Marco, tel. 041-520-5165, fax 041-522-8045, www.albergosansamuele.it, info@albergo sansamuele.it).

Near the Train Station

I don't recommend the train station area. It's crawling with noisy, disoriented tourists with too much baggage and people whose life's calling is to scam visitors out of their money. It's so easy just to hop a vaporetto upon arrival and sleep in the Venice of your dreams. Still, for those who like to park their bags near the station, these places work well. The nearest self-service laundry is **Orange** (daily 7:30-22:30, €5/small load; across the Grand Canal from the station—follow directions to recommended Albergo Marin, on the right at Ramo delle Chioverete 665a/b).

$$$ Hotel Abbazia, in the dreary hotel zone near the train station, fills a former abbey with both history and class. The refectory makes a grand living room for guests, a garden fills the old courtyard, and the halls leading to 50 rooms are monkishly wide (Db-€180-200, larger superior rooms-€25 extra—choose Venetian or modern style, ask for Rick Steves discount when you book direct, air-con, Wi-Fi, no elevator but plenty of stairs, fun-loving staff, 2 blocks from the station on the very quiet Calle Priuli dei Cavaletti 68, tel. 041-717-333, fax 041-717-949, www.abbaziahotel .com, info@abbaziahotel.com).

$ Locanda Herion rents 17 basic rooms for a decent price (Db-€100-120, cash discount, air-con, tel. 041-275-9426, fax 041-275-6647, www.locandaherion.com, info@locandaherion.com). Exiting the train station, turn left to follow Rio Terra Lista de Spagna. Cross the Ponte di Guglie and turn right at the yellow *San Marcuola traghetto* sign to find Campiello Picutti o del Magazen 1697a.

$ Albergo Marin and its staff offers 17 good-value quiet rooms handy to the train station (Sb-€110, D-€90, Db-€120, Tb-€150, cash discount, fans on request, Ramo delle Chioverete #670b, Santa Croce, tel. 041-718-022, fax 041-721-485, www.albergo marin.it, info@albergomarin.it). From the station, cross the Grand Canal and turn immediately right. Take the first left, then the first right, then right again to Ramo delle Chioverete.

$ The Chef's Wife B&B is run by American Stacy Gibboni. The "chef" is her Venetian husband, who runs a restaurant next door. Together they rent one sprawling and very cozy apartment for two to four people (Db-€100, Qb-€150, ask for Rick Steves rate, 2-night minimum, huge living room, no air-con, Wi-Fi, adjacent to Stacy's art studio, Corte del Pegoloto 1801, Cannaregio, mobile 328-365-8753, www.thechefswife.eu, stacysguesthouse @hotmail.it). It's near the San Marcuola vaporetto stop—see Stacy's website for directions.

$ Hotel S. Lucia, 150 yards from the train station, is oddly modern and sterile, with bright and spacious rooms and tight showers. Its 15 rooms are simple and clean. Guests enjoy their sunny garden area out front (S-€60, Db-€105, Tb-€145, discounts for three or more nights, cash discount, breakfast-€5, air-con, Calle della Misericordia 358, Cannaregio, tel. 041-715-180, fax 041-710-610, www.hotelslucia.com, info@hotelslucia.com, Gianni and Alessandra). Exit the station, head left, then take the second left onto Calle della Misericordia. The hotel is 100 yards ahead on the right.

$ Alloggi Henry, a homey little family-owned hotel, rents 15 simple and flowery rooms in a quiet residential neighborhood. It's a 10-minute walk from the train station (D-€80, Db-€100,

Tb-€130, show this book and ask for best Rick Steves price if paying cash, no breakfast, air-con, Calle Ormesini 1506e, Cannaregio, tel. 041-523-6675, fax 041-715-680, www.alloggihenry.com, info @alloggihenry.com, Manola and Henry). From the station, follow Lista de Spagna, San Leonardo, and Farsetti. Turn left on Calle Ormesini, then turn right into tiny Campiello Briani. They also rent a three-room apartment that sleeps up to nine.

Big, Fancy Hotels that Discount Shamelessly

Here are several big, plush four-star places with greedy sky-high rack rates (around Db-€300) that often have great discounts (as low as Db-€120) for drop-ins, off-season travelers, or online booking through their websites. If you want sliding-glass-door, uniformed-receptionist kind of comfort and formality in the old center, these are worth considering: **$$$ Hotel Giorgione** (big, garish, shiny, near Rialto Bridge, www.hotelgiorgione.com, see map on pages 1026-1027); **$$$ Hotel Casa Verardo** (elegant and quietly parked on a canal behind St. Mark's, more stately, www.casaverardo.it, see map on pages 1022-1023); **$$$ Hotel Donà Palace** (sitting like Las Vegas in the touristy zone a few blocks behind St. Mark's Basilica, works with neighbors **$$$ Hotel all'Angelo** and **$$$ Hotel al Ponte dei Sosperi** to rent 100 overpriced but often discounted rooms, all on Calle Larga San Marco, www.donapalace .it, see map on pages 1022-1023); and **$$$ Hotel Ca' Dei Conti** (five minutes northeast of St. Mark's Square, palatial and perfectly located but €500 rooms worth it only when deeply discounted, www.cadeiconti.com, see map on pages 1026-1027).

Cheap Dormitory Accommodations

$ Foresteria della Chiesa Valdese, run by the Methodist Church, offers 60 beds in doubles and 6- to 8-bed dorms, halfway between St. Mark's Square and the Rialto Bridge. This chilly run-down yet charming old place has elegant ceiling paintings (dorm bed-€28, Db-€92, Tb-€111, Qb-€136, discount for stays of 2 nights or more; includes breakfast, sheets, towels, and lockers; room lock-out 10:00-13:30, must check in and out when office is open— 8:30-20:00, reservations by phone only—no email, Fondamenta Cavagnis 5170, Castello, tel. 041-528-6797, fax 041-241-6238, www .foresteriavenezia.it, info@foresteriavenezia.it). From Campo Santa Maria Formosa, walk past Bar all'Orologio to the end of Calle Longa and cross the bridge onto Fondamenta Cavagnis.

    $ Venice's youth hostel, on Giudecca Island with 260 beds and grand views across the Bay of San Marco, is a godsend for backpackers shell-shocked by Venetian prices (€25 beds with sheets and breakfast in 8- to 20-bed dorms, cheaper for hostel members, lockers, room lock-out 10:30-13:30, office open daily 7:00-24:30, catch vaporetto #2 from station to Zittele, tel. 041-523-8211, can reserve online at www.ostellovenezia.it).

On the Mainland

$ Villa Dolcetti, about 12 miles from Marco Polo Airport, is a 1635 building with nine comfortable rooms. Art-lovers Diego and Tatiana provide a buffet breakfast, free parking, and lots of sight-seeing advice (Db-€70, superior Db-€80, Tb-€90-110, request discount, Internet access and Wi-Fi, tel. 041-563-1077, fax 041-563-1139, www.villadolcetti.com, info@villadolcetti.com). It's on the Venice-Padua road in the Venetian suburb of Oriago di Mira, at Via Venezia 85. Email them for driving and bus directions (buses run to/from Piazzale Roma, 2/hour, 25 minutes).

$ Villa Mocenigo Agriturismo, about 10 miles from Marco Polo Airport, is a working family-run farm in a peaceful rural location between Venice and Padua. Its 10 rooms are furnished with antiques, and regional specialties are served for dinner (Sb-€40-60, Db-€60-80, extra bed-€15-25, dinner and wine-€15-25 per person, air-con, Via Viasana 59 in Mirano-Venezia, tel. & fax 041-433-246, mobile 335-547-4728, www.villamocenigo.com, info@villamocenigo.com). Email them for directions by car or bus. Buses to Venice leave directly from the villa (3/hour, 45 minutes).

Eating in Venice

While touristy restaurants are the scourge of Venice, the following places are still popular with Venetians and respect the tourists who happen in. First trick: Walk away from triple-language menus. Second trick: Order the daily special. Third trick: For freshness, eat fish. Most seafood dishes are the catch-of-the-day. Remember that seafood can be sold by weight rather than a set price (if you see "100 g" or "*l'etto*" by a too-good-to-be-true price on the menu, that's the cost per 100 grams—about a quarter pound). The abbreviation *s.q.* is similar, meaning according to quantity (you pay for the weight of the particular piece). If you want a meal with a canal view, it generally comes with lower quality or a higher price. I've listed a few better-value places below.

Unique to Venice, *cicchetti* bars specialize in finger foods and appetizers that can combine to make a quick and tasty meal. The selection and ambience are best on workdays (Mon-Sat lunch and early dinner).

Near the Rialto Bridge

Venetians are embarrassed by the lousy food and aggressive "service" at the string of joints dominating the best romantic, Grand

Canal-fringing real estate in town. Still, if you want to linger over dinner with a view of the most famous bridge and the songs of gondoliers oaring by (and don't mind eating with other tourists), this can be enjoyable. Don't trust the waiter's recommendations for special meals. The budget ideal would be to get a simple pizza or pasta and a drink for €15, and savor the ambience without getting ripped off. But few restaurants will allow you to get off that easy. To avoid a dispute over the bill, ask if there's a minimum charge— before you sit down (most places have one).

North of the Bridge

These restaurants are located between Campo S.S. Apostoli and Campo Santa Maria Nova.

Trattoria da Bepi, bright and alpine-paneled, feels like a classic. Owner Loris scours the market for only the best ingredients— especially seafood—and takes good care of the hungry clientele. Ask for his seasonal specialties—the crab dishes are excellent. There's good seating inside and out (€10 pastas, €15 *secondi*, Fri-Wed 12:00-14:30 & 19:00-22:00, closed Thu, near Rialto Bridge, half a block north of Campo Santi Apostoli on Salizada Pistor, tel. 041-528-5031).

Little **Vini da Gigio** has a passion for good food, serving traditional Venetian dishes (€13 pastas, €20 *secondi*, no cover, Wed-Sun 19:00-late, last order at 22:30, closed Mon-Tue, 4 blocks from Ca' d'Oro vaporetto stop, behind the church on Campo San Felice, tel. 041-528-5140).

Trattoria Ca' d'Oro, while a little less accessible and inviting to the tourist, is a venerable favorite with a small, appealing menu and an enthusiastic following. Just to sip a wine and enjoy *cicchetti* at the bar is a treat—their *polpette* (tuna and potato meatballs) are famous, and the house wine will set you back just €0.50. It's also fine for a meal (€9 pastas, €10 *secondi*, closed Thu, reservations recommended; from the Ca' d'Oro vaporetto dock, walk 100 yards directly away from the canal, cross Strada Nuova, and you'll hit it; tel. 041-528-5324).

Osteria al Bomba is a *cicchetti* bar with a female touch, thanks to Giovanna. It's unusual (clean, no toothpicks, no cursing) and quite good, with lots of veggies. You can stand and eat at the bar—try a little €3 *crostino* with polenta and cod—or oversee the construction of the house *"antipasto misto di cicchetti"* plate (€15, enough fish and vegetables for two) and choose your wine by the glass from the posted list. A seat at the long table comes with a €2 *coperto* (daily 12:00-15:00 & 18:00-23:00, near Campo S.S. Apostoli, go a block off Strada Nuova down a small alley, then take the first right on Calle dell'Oca, tel. 041-520-5175).

VENICE

Restaurants near the Rialto Bridge

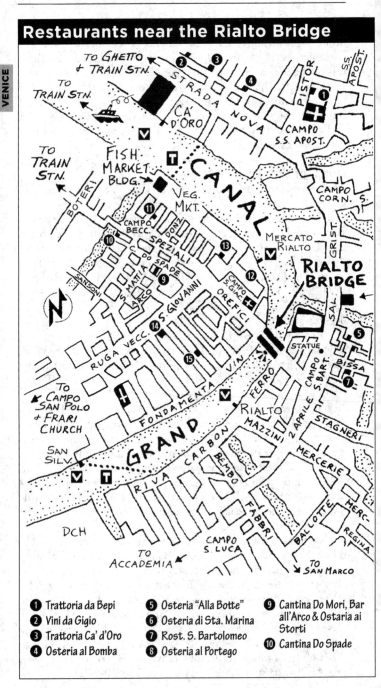

1 Trattoria da Bepi
2 Vini da Gigio
3 Trattoria Ca' d'Oro
4 Osteria al Bomba
5 Osteria "Alla Botte"
6 Osteria di Sta. Marina
7 Rost. S. Bartolomeo
8 Osteria al Portego
9 Cantina Do Mori, Bar all'Arco & Ostaria ai Storti
10 Cantina Do Spade

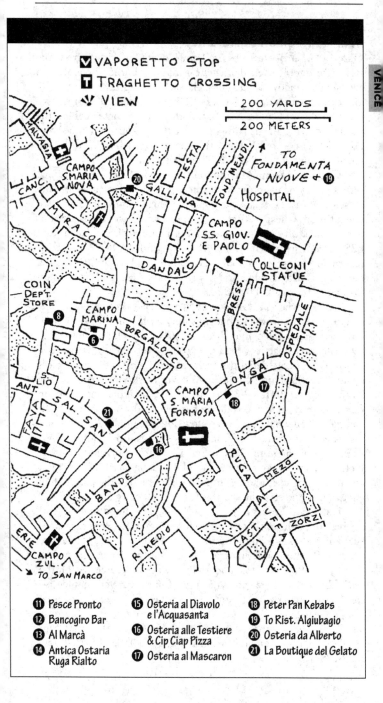

✓ VAPORETTO STOP
T TRAGHETTO CROSSING
↯ VIEW

200 YARDS
200 METERS

TO FONDAMENTA NUOVE & **⑲**
HOSPITAL

CAMPO S. MARIA NOVA
MALVASIA
CANC.
MIRACOLI
COIN DEP'T. STORE
CAMPO MARINA
⑳ GALLINA
TESTA
FOND. MEND.
CAMPO S.S. GIOV. E PAOLO
DANDALO
COLLEONI STATUE
BRESS.
OSPEDALE
BORGALOCCO
⑧
⑥
S. LIO
ANT.
FAVA
SAL. SAN
㉑
CAMPO S. MARIA FORMOSA
LONGA
⑰
⑱
RUGA
MEZO
GIUFFA
ZORZI
CAST.
LIO
BANDE
⑯
RIMEDIO
ERIE
CAMPO ZUL.
↯ TO SAN MARCO

⑪ Pesce Pronto
⑫ Bancogiro Bar
⑬ Al Marcà
⑭ Antica Ostaria Ruga Rialto
⑮ Osteria al Diavolo e l'Acquasanta
⑯ Osteria alle Testiere & Cip Ciap Pizza
⑰ Osteria al Mascaron
⑱ Peter Pan Kebabs
⑲ To Rist. Algiubagio
⑳ Osteria da Alberto
㉑ La Boutique del Gelato

East of the Rialto Bridge, near Campo San Bartolomeo

Osteria "Alla Botte," despite being located a minute from the Rialto Bridge, is packed with a casual neighborhood clientele in two simple woody rooms. For a classic Venetian taste, try the €18 all-seafood *antipasto misto* (daily 12:00-15:00 & 19:00-23:00, two short blocks off Campo San Bartolomeo in the corner behind the statue—down Calle de la Bissa, notice the "day after" photo showing a debris-covered Venice after the notorious 1989 Pink Floyd open-air concert, tel. 041-520-9775, Cristiano).

Osteria di Santa Marina, on the wonderful Campo Marina, serves pricey near-gourmet cuisine in a dressy dining room. The presentation is impressive, but you feel there's more pretense than love of food. Cheap-eating tricks are frowned on in this elegant, borderline stuffy restaurant (enticing menu with €15 pastas and €25 *secondi,* Mon-Sat 12:30-14:30 & 19:30-22:00, closed Sun, reserve for dinner, eat indoors or outdoors on pleasant little square, between Rialto Bridge and Campo Santa Maria Formosa on Campo Marina, tel. 041-528-5239).

Rosticceria San Bartolomeo is a cheap—if confusing—self-service diner, a throwback budget eatery with a likeably surly staff. Take out, grab a table, munch at the bar, or pay a bit more to eat at the restaurant upstairs (good €6-7 pasta, great fried *mozzarella al prosciutto* for €1.50, delightful fruit salad, €1 glasses of wine, prices listed on wall behind counter, no cover or service charge, daily 9:00-21:30, tel. 041-522-3569). To find it, imagine the statue on Campo San Bartolomeo walking backward 20 yards, turning left, and going under a passageway—now, follow him.

If you're pub crawling from Rosticceria San Bartolomeo, continue over a bridge to Campo San Lio. Here, turn left, passing Hotel Canada on your right, and follow Calle Carminati straight about 50 yards over another bridge. On the left is the pastry shop *(pasticceria),* and straight ahead is Osteria al Portego (at #6015).

Osteria al Portego is a friendly neighborhood bar—one of the best in town. Carlo serves good meals and excellent *cicchetti*—best enjoyed early, around 18:00 (from 19:00 to 21:00, tables are reserved for those ordering from the menu; the *cicchetti* are picked over by 21:00). Prices for food and wine are posted clearly on the wall. The *cicchetti* here can make a great meal, but you should also consider sitting down for a dinner from their fine menu. This place can get very busy, so reserve ahead if you want a table (€13 pastas, €2 glasses of wine, Mon-Sat 10:30-15:00 & 18:00-21:30, Sun 18:00-21:30, near Campo Marina at Calle Malvasia 6015, tel. 041-522-9038).

West of the Rialto Bridge

All of these places are informal, serving *cicchetti* and/or light meals. The first group of bars are within 200 yards of each other, a few steps behind the Rialto fish market; the rest are a short walk from this hive of eateries (see map on pages 1042-1043). This area is very crowded by day, nearly empty early in the evening, and crowded with young Venetians later.

Cicchetti and Light Meals West of the Rialto

Most bars are closed 15:00-18:00 (though Cantina Do Mori and Ostaria ai Storti stay open all day), and offer glasses of house wine for under a euro, better wine for around €2, and *cicchetti* for €1-2. At each place, look for the list of snacks and wine by the glass at the bar or on the wall. If you're ready for desert, try dipping a Burano biscuit in a glass of strawberry-flavored *fragolino* or another sweet dessert wine.

Cantina Do Mori has been famous with locals (since 1462) and savvy travelers (since 1982) as a convivial place for fine wine. You'll choose from a forest of little edibles on toothpicks and *francobolli* (a spicy selection of 20 tiny mayo-soaked sandwiches nicknamed "stamps"). Go here to be abused in a fine atmosphere—the frowns are part of the shtick (Mon-Sat 8:00-20:00, closed Sun, stand-up only, arrive early before the *cicchetti* are gone, San Polo 429, tel. 041-522-5401). From the Rialto Bridge, walk 200 yards down Ruga degli Orefici, away from St. Mark's Square—then turn left on Ruga Vecchia S. Giovanni, then right at Sotoportego Do Mori.

Bar all'Arco, a bustling one-room joint across from Cantina Do Mori, is particularly enjoyable for its tiny open-face sandwiches (closed Sun, tel. 041-520-5666).

Ostaria ai Storti serves lots of veggies and a few homemade pastas (check the daily specials) at great prices. With a homey feel, it's a fun place to congregate. Check out the photo of the market in 1909, below the bar. Alessandro speaks English and enjoys helping educate travelers while serving *fragolino* (daily 9:00-22:30, 20 yards from Cantina Do Mori on Calle delle Do Spade 819, tel. 041-523-6861).

Cantina Do Spade is run by Sebastiano, who clearly lists the *cicchetti* and wines of the day (daily 11:00-15:00 & 18:00-21:00, 30 yards down Calle delle Do Spade from Ostaria ai Storti at Calle delle Do Spade 19, tel. 041-521-0583).

At **Pesce Pronto,** you can actually sample fish while watching the market action. Bruno and Umberto serve artful fish hors d'oeuvres, *sfornato con pesce* (a savory baked pastry), and many other fresh fish tidbits—all at a fair price. This fancy hole-in-the-wall is fun for a quick bite—eat standing up or take it to go. At 12:30, they serve €10-12 "express plates" of pasta and other choices (Tue-Sat 9:00-14:30 & 17:00-19:30, closed Sun-Mon, facing the fish market at Calle de le Beccarie o Panataria 319, tel. 041-822-0298).

Youthful *Cicchetti* Bars near Campo San Giacometto

A strip of bars between Campo San Giacometto and the Grand Canal, several with canal-front tables, together make a thriving youth *spritz* scene that's worth a look even if you don't eat or drink there.

The **Bancogiro Bar** is good for strong cheese and its canalside tables (€3.50/person cover, €15 cheese plate, wine by glass is listed on board, Tue-Sun 12:00-23:00, closed Mon, tel. 041-523-2061).

Al Marcà, a few steps away and off the canal, is an even livelier little nook with a happy crowd, where young locals gather to grab drinks and little snacks. The price list is clear, and I've found the crowd to be welcoming to tourists interested in connecting (Mon-Sat 9:00-15:00 & 18:00-21:00, closed Sun, on Campo Cesare Battisti).

More *Cicchetti* Bars West of the Rialto Bridge

Antica Ostaria Ruga Rialto, a.k.a. "the Ruga," is a neighborhood fixture where Giorgio and Marco serve great bar snacks and wine to a devoted clientele. Treats here are their polenta, sardine with onions, and veggies. Bar or table, no problem—they're happy to make you a €3, €6, or €10 mixed plate (daily 11:00-14:30 & 19:00-24:00, easy to find—just past the Chinese restaurant at Ruga Vecchia San Giovanni 692, tel. 041-521-1243).

Osteria al Diavolo e l'Acquasanta, three blocks west of the Rialto Bridge, serves good—if pricey—Venetian-style pasta, and makes a handy lunch stop for sightseers and gondola riders. Though they list *cicchetti* and wine by the glass on the wall, I'd come here for a light meal rather than for appetizers (Mon 12:00-14:30, Wed-Sun 12:00-21:30, closed Tue, hiding on Calle della Madonna—a quiet street just off Ruga Vecchia San Giovanni, tel. 041-277-0307).

Pizza and Pasta Farther West of the Rialto Bridge

Antica Birraria la Corte is an everyday eatery on the delightful Campo San Polo, between the Rialto Bridge and the Frari Church. Popular with locals for its pizza, calzones, and salads, it fills the far side of this cozy, family-filled square. While the interior is a sprawling beer hall, it's a joy to eat on the square, where metal tables teeter on the cobbles, the wind plays with the paper mats, and children run free (daily 12:00-14:30 & 19:00-22:30, Campo San Polo 2168; tel. 041-275-0570).

Trattoria Pizzeria al Nono Risorto is unpretentious, inexpensive, youthful, and famous for serving some of the best pizza in town. You'll sit in a gravelly garden under a leafy canopy, surrounded by an enthusiastic waitstaff and Italians enjoying huge €8 salads, pastas, and pizzas, and €12 grilled meat or fish dishes (Thu-Tue 12:00-14:30 & 19:00-22:30, closed Wed, reservations smart on weekends; from Rialto fish market, walk 3 minutes to Campo San Cassiano—it's just over the bridge on Sotoportego de Siora Bettina; see map on pages 1036-1037; tel. 041-524-1169).

Near Campo Santa Maria Formosa

Campo Santa Maria Formosa is one of my favorite community scenes. While the restaurants fronting the square aren't much, several good options for dining lie a short walk away. For locations, see the map on pages 1042-1043.

Osteria alle Testiere is my top dining recommendation in Venice. Hugely respected, they are dedicated to quality, serving up creative, artfully presented market-fresh seafood (there's no meat on the menu), homemade pastas, and fine wine in what the chef calls a "Venetian Nouvelle" style. With only 22 seats, it's tight and homey, yet elegant. They have daily specials, 10 wines by the glass, and one agenda: a great dining experience. Luca, the owner-host, is gracious and passionate about his food. This is one place to let loose and trust your host. Reservations are required for their three seatings: 12:30, 19:00, and 21:30 (€19 pastas, €25 *secondi*, plan on spending €50 for dinner, closed Sun-Mon, just off Campo Santa Maria Formosa at Calle del Mondo Novo 5801, tel. 041-522-7220).

Osteria al Mascaron is where I've gone for years to watch Gigi, Momi, and their food-loving band of ruffians dish up rustic-yet-sumptuous pastas with steamy seafood to salivating foodies. The pastas, while pricey, are for two (it's OK to ask for single portions). The €16 *antipasto misto* plate—have fun pointing—and two glasses of wine make a terrific light meal, and their seafood pastas make beautiful memories (Mon-Sat 12:00-15:00 & 19:00-23:00, closed Sun, reservations smart Fri-Sat, a block past Campo Santa Maria Formosa at Calle Longa Santa Maria Formosa 5225, tel. 041-522-5995).

Fast and Cheap Eats: The Campo Santa Maria Formosa area has plenty of ways to sit and munch cheap. The veggie stand on the square is a fixture. For *döner kebabs* to go, head down Calle Longa to **Peter Pan** (€3.50). For pizza to go, it's **Cip Ciap** (next to Osteria alle Testiere at the bridge).

Near St. Mark's Square

For locations, see the map on page 1005.

Dining near St. Mark's Square

The following three places are a few blocks east of St. Mark's Square and offer classy dining experiences. The first two listings are the best canalside dining values I've found in Venice. Both specialize in fish, and have a reasonable-for-the-romantic-setting menu; if you want a canalside seat for dinner, call to reserve it (make sure you're seated at the right restaurant—the two are close together and easily confused). To reach these from St. Mark's Square, head behind the basilica to Campo San Provolo, then follow Calle Osmarin to Fondamenta dei Greci. To get to the third, head up Chiesa from Campo San Provolo.

Ristorante alla Conchiglia seats its guests at lovely tables that line the sleepy canal (€10 pizzas, big €14 salads, €15 fixed-price meals, daily specials, daily, closed Dec and Jan, Fondamenta dei Greci, tel. 041-528-9095).

Trattoria da Giorgio ai Greci, right next door, is enthusiastically run by Giorgio and sons Davide and chatty Roberto (€17-21 fixed-price meals, daily 12:00-22:30, Ponte dei Greci 4988, tel. 041-528-9780).

Ristorante Antica Sacrestia is a classic restaurant where the owner, Pino, takes a hands-on approach to greeting guests. His staff serve a delightful antipasto spread (€18), are proud of their fish, and offer €20-45 fixed-price meals of fish, meat, or vegetarian dishes. It's also a local favorite for pizza. This is the kind of place where you are best off going with the waiters' suggestions. My readers are welcome to a free *sgroppino* (lemon vodka after-dinner drink) upon request (Tue-Sun 11:30-15:00 & 18:00-22:30, closed Mon, immediately behind San Giovanni Novo Church at Calle della Sacrestia 4442, Castello, tel. 041-523-0749).

Budget Eateries near St. Mark's Square

Picnicking isn't allowed on St. Mark's Square, but you can legally take your snacks to the nearby Giardinetti Reali, the small park along the waterfront west of the Piazzetta.

"Sandwich Row": On Calle delle Rasse, just steps away from the tourist intensity at St. Mark's Square, is a strip I call "Sandwich Row." Lined with sandwich bars, it's the closest place to St. Mark's to get a decent sandwich at an affordable price with a place to sit down (most places open daily 7:00-24:00, €1 extra to sit; from the Bridge of Sighs, head down the Riva and take the second lane on the left). I particularly like **Birreria Forst,** which serves a selection of meaty €2.70 sandwiches with tasty sauce on wheat bread, or made-to-order sandwiches for around €3.50 (daily 10:00-20:30, air-con, rustic wood tables, Calle delle Rasse 4540, tel. 041-523-0557) and **Bar Verde,** a more modern sandwich bar with fun people-watching views from its corner tables (big €4 sandwiches,

splittable €8 salads, fresh pastries including Sicilian cannoli, at the end of Calle delle Rasse, facing Campo S.S. Filippo e Giacomo).

Ristorante alla Basilica, just one street behind St. Mark's Basilica, is a church-run institutional-feeling place serving a solid €13 three-course lunch daily from 11:45 to 15:00 (modern, air-con, Calle degli Albanesi 4255, tel. 041-522-0524).

Rizzo is a convenient bar/*alimentari* market located north of St. Mark's Square on the main drag of Calle dei Fabbri. Grab €4.50 homemade lasagna and other reasonably priced snacks, such as yogurt, sautéed spinach, or fried sandwiches. It's stand-and-eat only—there's no seating (Mon-Sat 8:00-20:00, closed Sun, Calle dei Fabbri 933A, tel. 041-522-3388).

In Dorsoduro
Near the Accademia Bridge
For locations, see next page.

Ristorante/Pizzeria Accademia Foscarini, next to the Accademia Bridge and Galleria, offers decent €8-11 pizzas in a great canalside setting. Their toasted *fareiti* sandwich is a local favorite (€6.50 at the table). Though the pizzas may be forgettable, this place is both scenic and practical—on each visit to Venice, I grab a pizza lunch here while I ponder the Grand Canal bustle (May-Oct Wed-Mon 7:00-21:30, Nov-April until 20:00, closed Tue, Dorsoduro 878C, tel. 041-522-7281).

Enoteca Cantine del Vino Già Schiavi is much-loved for its €1 *cicchetti* and €3.50 sandwiches (order from list on board). It's also a good place for a €2 glass of wine and appetizers (Mon-Sat 8:00-20:30, closed Sun, 100 yards from Accademia art museum on San Trovaso canal; facing Accademia, take a right and then a forced left at the canal to the second bridge—S. Trovaso 992, tel. 041-523-0034). You're welcome to enjoy your wine and finger food hanging out at the bar, sitting on the bridge out front, or in the nearby square—which actually has grass. This is primarily a wine shop with great prices for bottles to go—and plastic glasses for picnickers.

Terrazza del Casin dei Nobili, located in Zattere (on the Venice side of the Giudecca Canal), takes full advantage of the warm, romantic evening sun. They serve finely crafted regional specialties with creativity at reasonable prices. The canalside seating is breezy and beautiful, but comes with the rumble of *vaporetti* from the nearby stop. The interior is bright and hip (good €10 pizzas, €10 pastas, €15 *secondi*, €2 cover, Fri-Wed 12:00-23:00, closed Thu, exit vaporetto at Zattere stop and turn left to Zattere 924/5, tel. 041-520-6895). The canal-front Zattere district has a fun youthful vibe, with bars that do a good job of entertaining.

VENICE

Restaurants near the

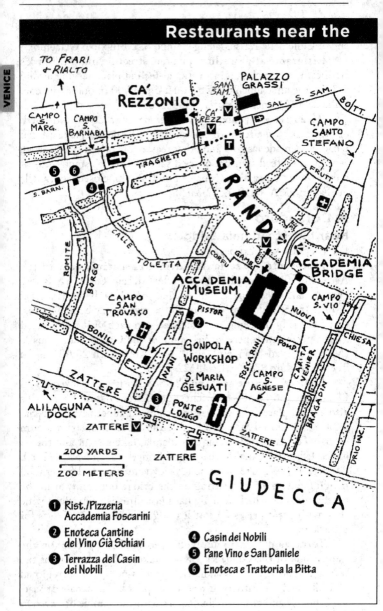

TO FRARI + RIALTO

CA' REZZONICO

PALAZZO GRASSI

SAN. SAM.

SAL. S. SAM.

BO TT.

CAMPO S. MARG.

CAMPO S. BARNABA

CA' REZZ.

CAMPO SANTO STEFANO

S. BARN.

TRAGHETTO

FRUTT.

GRAND

CALLE

ROMITE

BORGO

TOLETTA

CORFU

GAMB.

ACC.

ACCADEMIA BRIDGE

ACCADEMIA MUSEUM

CAMPO SAN TROVASO

PISTOR

CAMPO S. VIO

NUOVA

BONILI

NANI

GONDOLA WORKSHOP

FOSCARINI

POMP.

CARITA VENIER

CHIESA

ZATTERE

S. MARIA GESUATI

CAMPO S. AGNESE

BRAGADIN

ALILAGUNA DOCK

PONTE LONGO

ZATTERE

DRIO INC.

ZATTERE

ZATTERE

200 YARDS

200 METERS

GIUDECCA

❶ Rist./Pizzeria Accademia Foscarini

❷ Enoteca Cantine del Vino Già Schiavi

❸ Terrazza del Casin dei Nobili

❹ Casin dei Nobili

❺ Pane Vino e San Daniele

❻ Enoteca e Trattoria la Bitta

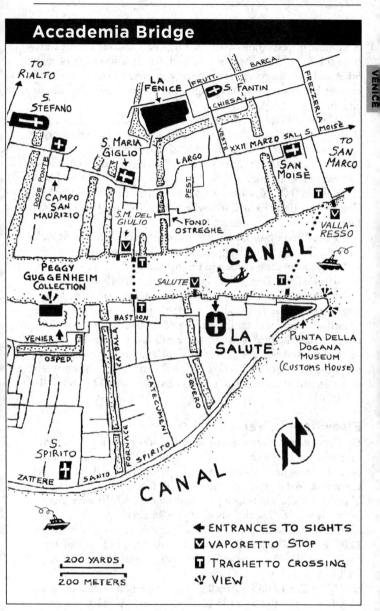

Accademia Bridge

TO RIALTO

S. STEFANO

LA FENICE

FRUTT.

BARCA

S. FANTIN

CHIESA

FREZZERIA

VESTE

XXII MARZO

SAL. S.

MOISÈ

TO SAN MARCO

S. MARIA GIULIO

LARGO

PEST

SAN MOISÈ

DOSE PONTE

CAMPO SAN MAURIZIO

S.M. DEL GIULIO

FOND. OSTREGHE

VALLA-RESSO

CANAL

PEGGY GUGGENHEIM COLLECTION

SALUTE

BASTION

CA BALA

VENIER

OSPED.

LA SALUTE

PUNTA DELLA DOGANA MUSEUM (CUSTOMS HOUSE)

CATECUMENI

SQUERO

S. SPIRITO

FORNACE

SPIRITO

ZATTERE

SANTO

CANAL

N

← ENTRANCES TO SIGHTS

☑ VAPORETTO STOP

🇹 TRAGHETTO CROSSING

☇ VIEW

200 YARDS

200 METERS

Near Campo San Barnaba

A number of restaurants are near this small square, a short walk from the Accademia. As these are each within a few steps of each other and the energy and atmosphere can vary, I like to survey the options before choosing (although reservations may be necessary later in the evening).

Casin dei Nobili ("Pleasure Palace of Nobles")—related to the Terrazza del Casin dei Nobili, listed above—has a high-energy, informal, modern setting. The patio is filled with simple tables, happy tourists, and inviting €11 daily lunch specials (€12 pastas, €20 *secondi,* good pizzas, and "fantasy salads," Tue-Sun 12:00-15:00 & 19:00-23:00, closed Mon, cash only, a half-block south of Campo San Barnaba at Calle delle Casin 2765, tel. 041-241-1841, Damiano).

Pane Vino e San Daniele is a busy little place that feels real, with the TV on, an enticing blackboard listing the day's specials, and the kitchen action filling its dining room (€7 pastas, €10 salads and *secondi,* Calle Longa San Barnaba 2861, tel. 041-243-9865).

Enoteca e Trattoria la Bitta is dark and woody, with a soft-jazz bistro feel and a small, forgettable back patio. They serve beautifully presented traditional Venetian food with—proudly—no fish. Their helpful waitstaff and small menu is clearly focused on quality. Reservations are required (€10 pastas, €15 *secondi,* dinner only, Mon-Sat 18:30-23:00, closed Sun, cash only, between previous two listings at Calle Longa San Barnaba 2753, tel. 041-523-0531).

Elsewhere in Venice

On Fondamente Nuove: **Ristorante Algiubagio** is a good opportunity to eat well overlooking the lagoon. The name is a combination of the owners' four names—Alberto, Giulio, Barbara, and Giovanna—who strive to impress visitors with quality, creative Venetian cuisine made using the best ingredients. Reserve a table on the lagoon facing the island of San Michele or in their classy cantina dining room (€16 pastas, €25 *secondi,* €3 cover, Wed-Mon 12:00-15:00 & 19:00-22:30, closed Tue, to the left of the vaporetto dock as you face the water at Fondamenta Nuove 5039, Cannaregio, tel. 041-523-6084).

Near Campo Santa Maria Nova: **Osteria da Alberto,** with excellent daily specials, €13 seafood plates, €10 pastas, a good house wine, and a woody and characteristic interior, is one of my standbys. It's smart to reserve at night—I'd request a table in the front (Mon-Sat 12:00-15:00 & 18:00-23:00, closed Sun, midway between Campo S.S. Apostoli and Campo S.S. Giovanni e Paolo, next to Ponte de la Panada on Calle Larga Giacinto Gallina, tel. 041-523-8153, run by Graziano and Giovanni).

Near the Train Station: There are piles of eateries near the station. The **train station food circus** in the station is quite good, with peaceful garden seating out back. A block away is the efficient and economic **Brek,** a popular chain self-service cafeteria (daily 11:30-22:00, head left as you leave the station and walk about 50 yards past the bridge to Rio Terra Lista di Spagna 124).

Cheap Meals

The keys to eating affordably in Venice are pizza, bars/cafés, and picnics. *Panini* and *tramezzini* (sandwiches) are sold fast and cheap at bars everywhere and can stave off midmorning hunger. There's a great "sandwich row" of cheap cafés near St. Mark's Square (see page 1048). For speed, value, and ambience, you can get a filling plate of typically Venetian appetizers at nearly any bar. For budget eating, I like stand-up mini-meals at *cicchetti* **bars** best.

Picnics

The **produce market** that sprawls for a few blocks just past the Rialto Bridge is a fun place to assemble a picnic (best Mon-Sat 8:00-13:00, closed Sun). The adjacent fish market is wonderfully slimy (closed Sun-Mon). Side lanes in this area are speckled with fine little hole-in-the-wall munchie bars, bakeries, and cheese shops. Remember that the only legal place to picnic in public in Venice is Giardinetti Reali, the waterfront park near St. Mark's Square.

Gelato

La Boutique del Gelato, as lines attest, is considered the best *gelateria* in Venice. They dish up generous €1.20 scoops (daily 10:00-22:00, closed Dec-Jan, located on map on pages 1042-1043, leave Campo Santa Maria Formosa from the corner with the bell tower, cross the bridge, turn right on Salizada San Lio, and find it next to Hotel Bruno at #5727).

On St. Mark's Square, there are two venerable *gelaterie:* **Gran Caffè Lavena** (daily until 24:00, first café to left of the Clock Tower, behind the first orchestra) and **Todaro Gelateria** (on the corner of the Piazzetta, near the Grand Canal and just under St. Theodore slaying the dragon, tel. 041-528-5165).

Venice Connections

From Venice by Train to: Florence (hourly, 2-3 hours, may transfer in Bologna; often crowded so make reservations), **Milan** (hourly, 2.5 hours), **Cinque Terre/Monterosso** (almost hourly, 6-7 hours, with 1-3 changes), **Cinque Terre/La Spezia** (almost hourly, 5-6 hours, with 1-3 changes), **Rome** (hourly, 3.5 hours, may transfer in Bologna, overnight possible), **Interlaken** (7/day, 6-7.5 hours, 2-5 changes, no pleasant overnight option), **Munich** (4-6/day, 7 hours, change in Verona; 1 direct night train, 8 hours), **Salzburg** (4/day, 6-7 hours, 1-2 changes, 1 direct night train), **Paris** (3/day, 10-12 hours with change in Milan, may also transfer in Basel or Zürich; 1 direct night train, 13.5 hours, important to reserve ahead, 2 more night trains with changes), **Ljubljana** (3/day, 7.5 hours—take bus from Piazzale Roma to Villach in Austria, then transfer to train; 1 direct night train, 4 hours, but arrives at 2:00 in the morning), and **Vienna** (3/day, 8 hours—take bus from Piazzale Roma to Villach in Austria, then transfer to train; 1 direct night train, 11 hours).

Airports

Venice has two airports—Marco Polo and the small Treviso. For budget flights within Europe, easyJet uses Marco Polo, while Ryanair, Wizz Air, and Blue use Treviso.

Marco Polo Airport

Venice's modern airport is on the mainland, six miles north of the city. It's a sleek wood beam-and-glass terminal, with a TI (daily 9:00-21:00), ATMs, car-rental agencies, a bank, a post office, and a few shops and eateries. For flight information, call tel. 041-260-9260, visit www.veniceairport.com, or ask at your hotel for help.

There are three ways to get between the airport (which is on the mainland) and downtown Venice (on an island):

- Alilaguna water bus—medium in speed and cost
- Water taxis—fastest and most expensive
- Buses to Piazzale Roma—slowest and least expensive

Each of these options is explained in detail below. The Alilaguna water buses are the simplest way to reach most of this chapter's recommended hotels—except those near the train station, in which case the bus to Piazzale Roma may be the better choice.

When flying out of Venice, travelers are advised to get to the airport two hours before departure (even for flights within Europe), so allow yourself plenty of time.

Alilaguna Water Bus

These boats make the scenic (if slow) journey across the lagoon, shuttling passengers between the airport and a number of different stops on the island of Venice (€13, 60-90-minute trip depending on your destination; boats leave every 30-60 minutes). There are several lines (blue, red, orange), and it can get confusing. But if you know what stop you want, it's easy to find the line that goes there.

Here are some key stops in Venice:
- San Marco-Giardinetti—Hotels west of St. Mark's Square
- San Zaccaria—Hotels east of St. Mark's Square
- Zattere—Dorsoduro hotels
- Guglie—Hotels near Santa Lucia train station
- Rialto—Hotels near the Rialto Bridge
- Fondamenta Nuove—Hotels on the north side of the city, on the fish's "back"

From the Airport to Venice: The airport's boat dock is an eight-minute walk from the terminal. Exit the arrivals terminal and turn left, following signs along a paved, level covered sidewalk (easy for wheeled bags). You can buy tickets at the airport's TI or the "Public Transport" window (often crowded), at vending machines inside the airport terminal (cash only), or simply at the ticket booth at the dock. Any ticket-seller can tell you which line to catch to get to your destination. Boats from the airport run from roughly 7:00 to midnight.

From Venice to the Airport: Give yourself plenty of time to make your flight. Ask your hotelier what dock and what line is best. Boats start leaving Venice as early as 3:40 so that passengers can catch early flights.

For a full schedule, see the Alilaguna website (www.alilaguna .it), call 041-523-5775, ask your hotelier, scan the schedules posted at Alilaguna docks, or ask at the TI. Note that the Alilaguna water bus is not part of the ACTV vaporetto system, so it is not covered by city transit passes.

Water Taxi

Luxury taxi speedboats zip directly between the airport and your hotel, getting you within steps of your final destination in about 30 minutes. The official price is €100 for up to four people, though you may get a higher quote (around €110)—talk them down. A taxi can be a smart investment for small groups and those with an early departure. From the airport, arrange your ride at the airport's water-taxi desk or at the dock (next to the Alilaguna dock). From Venice, book your taxi trip through your hotel the day before you leave.

Airport Shuttle Buses

Buses take you across the bridge from the mainland to the island, dropping you at the "mouth" of the fish, on a square called Piazzale Roma. From there, you can catch a vaporetto down the Grand Canal—convenient for hotels near the Rialto Bridge and St. Mark's Square.

Two companies compete for the airport shuttle business. The ATVO "Venezia Express" and the ACTV bus #5 both connect the airport and Piazzale Roma (€2.50-3, 20-40 minutes, 2/hour, 5:00-24:00, www.atvo.it or www.actv.it). The ATVO is slightly faster and pricier.

From the Airport to Venice: Both buses leave from just outside the arrivals terminal. Buy tickets at the TI, from ticket machines in the terminal or outside next to the buses, or sometimes directly from the driver. Check which ticket you are buying—ATVO tickets are not valid on ACTV buses and vice versa.

When you arrive at Piazzale Roma, you'll find the vaporetto dock by walking to the six-story white building, then taking a right. To go down the Grand Canal, catch either the slow vaporetto #1 or faster #2 toward St. Mark's Square (€6.50 for either boat; for more info, see "Getting Around Venice," page 987). To reach Zattere (and the Dorsoduro hotels), go the other direction on #51. If you're confused, a local commuter or the ticket-seller can help you.

If your hotel is near the train station, you can walk there from Piazzale Roma across the Calatrava Bridge.

From Venice to the Airport: Buses leave Piazzale Roma between 5:00 and 20:40, departing from the northeast corner of the lot near Hotel Santa Chiara.

Other Services

Private Shuttle Bus: Treviso Car Service offers a private minivan service between Marco Polo Airport and Piazzale Roma (€50 per minivan, seats up to 8, tel. 338-204-4390, www.trevisocarservice.com, Andrea).

Treviso Airport

Several budget airlines, such as Ryanair and Blue, use Treviso Airport, 12 miles northwest of Venice (www.trevisoairport.it). Regular ATVO buses take you to Piazzale Roma (€6, 2-3/hour, 1.25 hours, www.atvo.it). Buy your tickets at the ATVO desk in the airport and stamp them on the bus. The buses also stop at Mestre's train station. Treviso Car Service offers minivan service to Piazzale Roma (€55 per minivan; see "Private Shuttle Bus" listing above).

FLORENCE

Firenze

Florence, the home of the Renaissance and birthplace of our modern world, has the best Renaissance art in Europe. Get your bearings with a Renaissance walk. Florentine art goes beyond paintings and statues—there's food, fashion, and handicrafts. You can lick Italy's best gelato while enjoying some of Europe's best people-watching.

Planning Your Time

If you're in Italy for three weeks, Florence deserves at least a well-organized day: see the Accademia, tour the Uffizi Gallery, visit the underrated Bargello (best statues), and do the Renaissance ramble (explained on page 1070; to avoid heat and crowds, do this walk in the morning or late afternoon). Art lovers will want to chisel out another day of their itinerary for the many other Florentine cultural treasures. Shoppers and ice-cream lovers may need to do the same.

Plan your sightseeing carefully: Opening hours can be erratic, and crowds can cause long lines. Before heading into Florence, carefully check all the opening and closing times of your must-see museums at the TI, by phone, or online. This is especially true if you'll be in town for only a day or two during the crowded summer months.

The Uffizi Gallery and Accademia (starring Michelangelo's *David*) nearly always have long ticket-buying lines, especially in peak season (April-Oct) and on holiday weekends. Crowds thin out weekdays in the off-season. Whatever time of year you visit, you can easily avoid the wait by making reservations (see page 1068). Note that both of these major sights are closed on Monday.

FLORENCE

Rick Steves' Free Audio Tours

I've produced free, self-guided audio versions of my tours of the major sights in Florence (download them via www.rick steves.com/audioeurope, iTunes, or the Rick Steves Audio Europe free smartphone app). These user-friendly, easy-to-follow, fun, and enlightening audio tours are available for my Renaissance Walk, the Accademia, and the Uffizi Gallery. If you don't mind me in your ear, these audio tours are hard to beat: Nobody will stand you up, the quality is reliable, you can take the tour exactly when you like, and they're free.

The Museum of San Marco closes at 13:50 on weekdays and at 16:50 on weekends. Other museums close early only on certain days (e.g., the first Sunday of the month, second and fourth Monday, etc.). In general, Sundays and Mondays are bad, with many museums either closed or with shorter hours.

Connoisseurs of smaller towns should consider taking the bus to Siena for a day or evening trip (75 minutes one-way, confirm when last bus returns).

Orientation to Florence

The best of Florence lies on the north bank of the Arno River. The main historical sights cluster around the red-brick dome of the cathedral (Duomo). Everything is within a 20-minute walk of the train station, cathedral, or Ponte Vecchio (Old Bridge). The less impressive but more characteristic Oltrarno area (south bank) is just over the bridge. Though small, Florence is intense. Prepare for scorching summer heat, kamikaze motor scooters, slick pickpockets, few WCs, steep prices, and long lines.

Tourist Information

There are three TIs in Florence: across from the train station, near Santa Croce Church, and on Via Cavour.

The TI across the square from the train station is most crowded—expect long lines (Mon-Sat 8:30-19:00, Sun 8:30-14:00; with your back to tracks, exit the station—it's 100 yards away, across the square in wall near corner of church at Piazza Stazione 4; tel. 055-212-245, www.firenzeturismo.it). In the train station, avoid the Hotel Reservations "Tourist Information" window (marked *Informazioni Turistiche Alberghiere*) near the McDonald's; it's not a real TI but a hotel-reservation business instead.

The TI near Santa Croce Church is pleasant, helpful, and uncrowded (Mon-Sat 9:00-19:00, Sun 9:00-14:00, shorter hours off-season, Borgo Santa Croce 29 red, tel. 055-234-0444, turismo2 @comune.fi.it).

Another winner is the TI three blocks north of the Duomo (Mon-Sat 8:30-18:30, Sun 8:30-13:30, Via Cavour 1 red, tel. 055-290-832, international bookstore across street).

At any TI, pick up these free, handy resources:

- a city map (ask for the "APT" map, which has bus routes of interest to tourists on the back)
- a current museum-hours listing (extremely important, since no guidebook—including this one—has ever been able to accurately predict the hours of Florence's sights for the coming year). Also check www.comune.fi.it (select "Museums," then "Museums' Opening Hours").
- information on entertainment, including the TI's monthly *Florence and Tuscany News* (good for events and entertainment listings)
- the ad-driven monthly *Florence Concierge Information* magazine (which lists museums, plus concerts, markets, sporting events, church services, shopping ideas, some bus and train connections, and an entire similar section on Siena)
- *The Florentine* newspaper (published every other Thu in English, for expats and tourists, with great articles giving cultural insights; download latest issue at www.theflorentine.net).

These English freebies are available at TIs and hotels all over town.

Arrival in Florence

By Train: Florence's main train station is called **Santa Maria Novella** (*Firenze S.M.N.* on schedules and signs). Built in Mussolini's "Rationalism" style back between the wars, in some ways the station seems to have changed little—notice the 1930s-era lettering and architecture.

Florence also has two suburban train stations: **Firenze Rifredi** and **Firenze Campo di Marte.** Note that some trains don't stop at the main station—before boarding, confirm that you're heading for S.M.N., or you may overshoot the city. (If this happens, don't panic; the other stations are a short taxi ride from the center.)

Minimize time in the main station—doing business here is generally intense, crowded, and overpriced. It's also rife with pickpockets. The banks of user-friendly automated ticket machines are handy. They take euros and credit cards, display schedules, issue tickets, and even make reservations for railpass-holders. Still, it can be quicker to get tickets and train info from travel agencies in town.

With your back to the tracks, look left to see a 24-hour pharmacy (*Farmacia*, near McDonald's), the fake "Tourist Information"

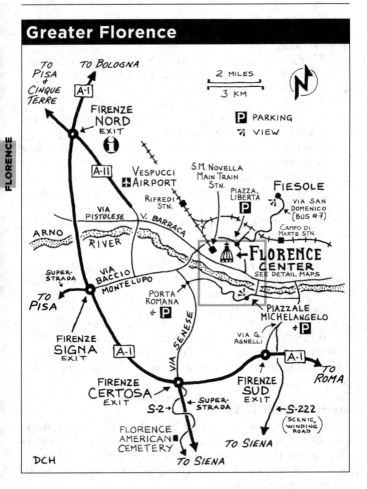

Greater Florence

TO PISA & CINQUE TERRE

TO BOLOGNA

A-1

FIRENZE NORD EXIT

2 MILES / 3 KM

N

P PARKING

VIEW

A-11

VESPUCCI AIRPORT

S.M. NOVELLA MAIN TRAIN STN.

RIFREDI STN.

PIAZZA LIBERTÀ

FIESOLE

VIA SAN DOMENICO (BUS #7)

VIA PISTOLESE

V. BARRACA

CAMPO DI MARTE STN.

ARNO RIVER

FLORENCE CENTER

SEE DETAIL MAPS

SUPERSTRADA

VIA BACCIO

MONTELUPO

PORTA ROMANA

PIAZZALE MICHELANGELO

TO PISA

VIA SENESE

VIA G. AGNELLI

FIRENZE SIGNA EXIT

A-1

TO ROMA

A-1

FIRENZE CERTOSA EXIT

S-2

SUPERSTRADA

FIRENZE SUD EXIT

S-222 (SCENIC WINDING ROAD)

FLORENCE AMERICAN CEMETERY

TO SIENA

TO SIENA

DCH

office (funded by hotels), city buses, bus ticket booth, the taxi stand (fast-moving line, except on holidays), and the entrance to the Galleria S.M. Novella underground mall/passage that leads from the station under the square to the Church of Santa Maria Novella. (Warning: Pickpockets—often dressed as tourists—frequent this tunnel, especially the surface point near the church.) Baggage check is near track 16 (€4/5 hours, then €0.60/hour for 6-12 hours and €0.20/hour for 13-plus, daily 6:00-23:50, passport required, maximum 40 pounds, no explosives—sorry).

To get to the TI, walk away from the tracks and exit the train station to the left (going straight out of the station leads you to an uninviting wasteland of construction). The real TI is 100 yards away, across the square from the station, by the stone church (see "Tourist Information"). Pick up picnic supplies at the Conad

Florence Overview

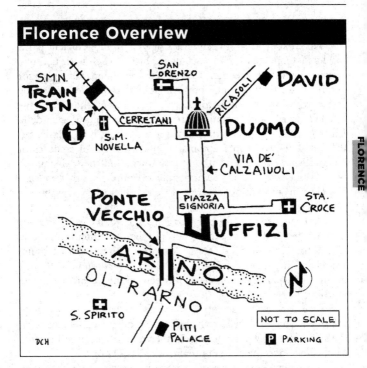

supermarket, located along the west side of the station on Via Luigi Alamanni (Mon-Sat 8:00-20:00, closed Sun).

Most recommended hotels are within a 10- or 15-minute walk of the station. The Duomo, though not visible from here, is located to the left (east) down busy Via dei Panzani, a 10-minute walk away.

By Bus: The bus station is next to the train station, with the TI across the square. For more information on buses, see page 1066.

By Car: The autostrada has several exits for Florence. Get off at the Nord, Sud, or Certosa exits and follow signs toward—but not into—the *Centro*.

Don't even attempt driving into the city center. Florence has a traffic-reduction system that's complicated and confusing even to locals. Every car passing into the *Zona Traffico Limitato (ZTL)* is photographed; those who haven't jumped through bureaucratic hoops to get a permit can expect to receive a €100 ticket in the mail. If you get lost and cross the line several times...you get several fines. The no-go zone (defined basically by the old medieval wall, now a boulevard circling the historic center of town—watch for *Zona Traffico Limitato* signs) is roughly the area between the river, main train station, Piazza della Libertà, Piazza Donatello, and Piazza Beccaria.

Fortunately, the city center is ringed with big, efficient parking lots (signposted with the standard big *P*), each with taxi and bus service into the center. Check www.firenzeparcheggi.it for details on all their parking lots, availability, and prices. From the freeway, follow the signs to *Centro*, then *Stadio*, then *P*. I usually head for "Parcheggio del Parterre," just beyond Piazza della Libertà (€1.50/hour, €18/day, €65/week, open 24 hours daily, tel. 055-500-1994, 600 spots, automated, pay with cash or credit card, never fills up completely). To get into town, find the taxi stand at the elevator exit, or ride one of the *elettrico* minibuses that connect all of the major parking lots with the city center (see www.ataf.net for routes).

You can also park for free along any suburban curb near a bus stop that feels safe, and take the bus into the city center from there. Check for signs that indicate parking restrictions—for example, a circle with a slash through it and "*dispari giovedi*, 0,00-06,00" means don't park on Thursdays between midnight and six in the morning.

Free parking is easy up at Piazzale Michelangelo (see page 1089), but don't park where the buses drop off passengers; park on the side of the piazza farthest from the view. To get from Piazzale Michelangelo to the center of town, take bus #12 or #13.

If you're picking up a rental car upon departure, don't struggle with driving into the center. Taxi with your luggage to the car-rental office, and head out from there.

By Plane: For information on Florence's Amerigo Vespucci Airport, see page "Florence Connections," near the end of this chapter.

Helpful Hints

Theft Alert: Florence has particularly hardworking thief gangs who hang out where you do: near the train station, the station's underpass (especially where the tunnel surfaces), and major sights. American tourists—especially older ones—are considered easy targets. Some thieves even dress like tourists to fool you. Be on guard at two squares frequented by drug pushers (Santa Maria Novella and Santo Spirito). Bus #7 (to the nearby town of Fiesole, with great Florence views) is a favorite with tourists and, therefore, with thieves.

Medical Help: There's no shortage of English-speaking medical help in Florence. To reach a doctor who speaks English, call **Medical Service Firenze** at 055-475-411; the phone is answered 24/7. Rates are reasonable. For a doctor to come to your hotel within an hour of your call, you'd pay €100-200 (higher rates apply on Sun, holidays, or late visits). You pay only €50 if you go to the clinic when the doctor's in (Mon-Fri 11:00-12:00 & 17:00-18:00, Sat 11:00-12:00, closed Sun, no appointment necessary, Via L. Magnifico 59, near Piazza della Libertà). A second clinic is available at Via Porta Rossa 1 (Mon-Sat 13:00-15:00, closed Sun).

Dr. Stephen Kerr is an English doctor specializing in helping sick tourists (clinic open for drop-ins Mon-Fri 15:00-17:00, other times by appointment, €50 per visit, Piazza Mercato Nuovo 1, between Piazza della Repubblica and Ponte Vecchio, tel. 055-288-055, mobile 335-836-1682, www.dr-kerr.com). The TI has a list of other English-speaking doctors.

There are 24-hour **pharmacies** at the train station and on Borgo San Lorenzo (near the Baptistery).

Reservations: To avoid standing in long lines, book ahead to visit the Accademia and Uffizi Gallery (see page 1068 for details); you'll pay about a €4 booking fee, but it's worth it for the efficiency and peace of mind of having an assured entry time. One sight, the Brancacci Chapel, requires reservations, though these are free and easy to make; just call at least a day in advance (see page 1068).

Price Hike Alert: Some of Florence's museums have found a clever way to squeeze more money out of visitors. They host a special exhibit that few tourists really care to see, and require you to pay extra for your ticket, even if all you want to see is the permanent collection.

Churches: Many churches now operate like museums, charging an admission fee to see their art treasures. Modest dress for men, women, and even children is required in some churches, and recommended for all of them—no bare shoulders, short shorts, or short skirts. Be respectful of worshippers and the paintings; don't use a flash. Churches usually close from 12:00 or 12:30 to 15:00 or 16:00.

Freebies: Many of Florence's sights and activities are free. There is no charge for entry to the Duomo, Orsanmichele Church, Santo Spirito Church, and San Miniato Church. It's free to visit the leather school at Santa Croce Church and the perfumery near the Church of Santa Maria Novella, and fun to browse at the three markets (Centrale for produce, Nuovo and San Lorenzo for goods).

Free public spaces include the Uffizi and Palazzo Vecchio courtyards; the art-filled loggia on Piazza della Signoria; and Piazzale Michelangelo, with glorious views over Florence. A walk across the picturesque Ponte Vecchio costs nothing at all—unless you succumb to temptation at one of the many shops along the way. A stroll anywhere in Florence with a gelato in hand is an inexpensive treat.

Addresses: Street addresses list businesses in red and residences in black (color-coded on the actual street number and indicated by a letter following the number in printed addresses: "r" = red; no indication or "n" = black, for *nero*). *Pensioni* are usually black but can be either. The red and black numbers each appear in roughly consecutive order on streets but bear no apparent connection with each other. I'm lazy and don't concern myself with the distinction (if one number's wrong, I look for the other) and can easily find my way around.

Internet Access: In bustling, tourist-filled Florence, you'll see small Internet cafés on virtually every street (remember to bring your passport). **V.I.P. Internet** has cheap rates, numerous terminals, and long hours (€1.50/hour, daily 9:00-24:00, near recommended hotel Katti House at Via Faenza 49 red, tel. 055-264-5552). **Internet Train,** the dominant chain, is pricier, with bright and cheery rooms, speedy computers, and decent hours (€4.30/hour, cheaper for students, reusable card good for any other Internet Train location, open daily roughly 9:00-20:00, www.internettrain.it). Find branches near Piazza della Repubblica (Via Porta Rossa 38 red), behind the Duomo (Via dell'Oriolo 40), on Piazza Santa Croce (Via de Benci 36 red), near *David* and recommended hotels (Via Guelfa 54 red), and near Ponte Vecchio (Borgo San Jacopo 30 red). Internet Train also offers Wi-Fi, phone cards, CD-burning, and other related services.

Bookstores: Local guidebooks (sold at kiosks) are cheap, and give you a map and a decent commentary on the sights. For brandname guidebooks in English, try **Feltrinelli International** (Mon-Sat 9:00-19:30, closed Sun, a few blocks north of the Duomo and across the street from TI and Medici-Riccardi Palace at Via Cavour 12 red, tel. 055-219-524); **Edison Bookstore** (also has CDs, plus novels on the Renaissance and much more on its four floors; Mon-Sat 9:00-24:00, Sun 10:00-24:00, facing Piazza della Repubblica, tel. 055-213-110); **Paperback Exchange** (cheaper, all books in English, bring in your used book for a discount on a new one, Mon-Fri 9:00-19:30, Sat 10:30-19:30, closed Sun, just south of the Duomo on Via delle Oche 4 red, tel. 055-293-460); or **BM Bookshop** (with perhaps the city's largest collection of English books and guidebooks—including mine; Mon-Sat 9:30-19:30, closed Sun, near Ponte alla Carraia at Borgognissanti 4 red, tel. 055-294-575).

Maps: While the city is awash in free tourist maps, which work fine for most visits, if you want to invest in a durable, detailed, and smartly designed map, consider Rough Guide's *Map of Florence & Siena* (€9).

Florence

TO FORTEZZA DI BASSO

TO PIAZZA D. LIBERTA

MUSEUM OF SAN MARCO

ACCADEMIA

SMN. TRAIN STATION

PIAZZA S.S. ANNUNZIATA

MERCATO CENTRALE

MEDICI CHAPELS

SAN LORENZO

MEDICI-RICCARDI PALACE

HOSPITAL OF THE INNOCENTS

STA. MARIA NOVELLA

BUS STN.

PRECIOUS STONES MUSEUM

LEONARDO MUSEUM

PERF. MUS.

CERRETANI

BAPT.

DUOMO

DUOMO MUSEUM

CAMPANILE

CASA DI DANTE

PZZA. REP.

Post

STROZZI

BARGELLO

Post

STA. TRINITA

ORSANMICH.

CASA BUONARROTI

ARNO

PORTA ROSSA

PIAZZA SIGNORIA

GOLD.

VIGNA NUOVA

PONTE VECCHIO

PALAZZO VECCHIO

SANTA CROCE

TO SANTO SPIRITO & BRAN. CHAPEL

UFFIZI GALLERY

GALILEO SCIENCE MUSEUM

RIVER

OLTRARNO

BACCHUS FOUNTAIN

GROTTO

PITTI PALACE

BOBOLI GARDENS

BARDINI GARDENS

CITY WALLS

TO PORTA ROMANA

FORTE DI BELVEDERE

PIAZZALE MICHELANGELO

PORCELAIN MUSEUM

SAN MINIATO

200 YARDS
200 METERS

⤢ VIEW
◆ ENTRY POINT TO SIGHTS

DCH

Services: WCs are scarce. Use them when you can, in cafés or museums you patronize.

Laundry: The **Wash & Dry Lavarapido** chain offers long hours and efficient, self-service launderettes at several locations (about €7 for wash and dry, daily 8:00-22:00, tel. 055-580-480 or toll-free 800-231-172). These are close to recommended hotels: Via dei Servi 105 red (and a rival launderette at Via Guelfa 55, off Via San Zanobi; both near *David*), Via del Sole 29 red and Via della Scala 52 red (between train station and

FLORENCE

river), Via Ghibellina 143 red (Palazzo Vecchio), Via Faenza 26 (near station), and Via dei Serragli 87 red (across the river in Oltrarno neighborhood).

Travel Agency: Get train tickets, reservations, and supplements at travel agencies rather than at the congested train station. The cost is either the same or the charge is minimal. Ask your hotel for the nearest travel agency.

Water: Carry a water bottle to refill at Florence's twist-the-handle public fountains.

Chill Out: Schedule several cool breaks into your sightseeing where you can sit, pause, and refresh yourself with a sandwich, gelato, or coffee.

Getting Around Florence

I organize my sightseeing geographically and do it all on foot. I think of Florence as a Renaissance treadmill—it requires a lot of walking.

Buses: The city's full-size buses don't cover the old center well, especially now that the whole area around the Duomo has been declared off-limits to motorized traffic. Of the many bus lines, I found these of most value for seeing outlying sights: Lines #12 and #13 go from the train station to Porta Romana, up to San Miniato Church and Piazzale Michelangelo, and on to Santa Croce. Most other lines leave from Piazza San Marco (near the Accademia and Museum of San Marco), including bus #7, which goes to Fiesole, a small town with big views of Florence. To get from the train station to Piazza San Marco, either walk or take bus #1, #6, #14, or #23.

Fun little *elettrico* **minibuses** wind through the tangled old center of town and up and down the river—just €1.20 gets you a 90-minute joyride. These buses, which run every 10 minutes, are popular with sore-footed sightseers and eccentric local seniors. *Elettrico* #C2 twists through the congested old center from the train station to Piazza Beccaria. *Elettrico* #C3 goes up and down the Arno River from Ognissanti to Santa Croce Church and beyond; #C1 winds around Piazza Repubblica, then heads north up to Piazza Libertà. *Elettrico* #D goes from the train station to Ponte Vecchio, cruising through Oltrarno, and finishing at Ponte San Niccolò. The minibuses connect many major parking lots with the historical center (tickets sold at machines at lots). Routes are shown on the free TI map (see the handy inset) and the "La Rete dei Bussini Potenziata" leaflet, free at the ATAF bus office, located just east of the train station, on Piazza della Stazione.

Buy bus tickets at *tabacchi* (tobacco) shops, newsstands, or the ATAF bus office (€1.20/90 minutes, €4.50/4 tickets, €5/24 hours, €12/3 days, 1-day and 3-day passes aren't always available in *tabacchi*, validate in machine on the bus, tel. 800-424-500, www.ataf.net). You can buy tickets on board, but you'll pay more (€2) and you'll need exact change. Follow general bus etiquette: Board at front or rear doors, exit out the center.

Hop-on, hop-off bus tours stop at the major sights (see "Hop-on, Hop-off Bus Tours" in the following section).

Taxi: The minimum cost for a taxi ride is €5, or €6 after 22:00 and on Sundays (rides in the center of town should be charged as tariff #1). A taxi ride from the train station to Ponte Vecchio costs about €9. Taxi fares and supplements (e.g., €2 extra if you call a cab rather than hail one) are clearly explained on signs in each taxi.

Tours in Florence

Tour companies big and small offer plenty of tours that go out to smaller towns in the Tuscan countryside (the most popular day trips: Siena, San Gimignano, Pisa, and into Chianti country for wine-tasting). They also do city tours, but for most people, the city is really best on foot (and the book you're holding provides as much information as you'll get with a generic bus tour).

For extra insight with a personal touch, consider the tour companies and individual Florentine guides listed here. They are hardworking, creative, and offer a worthwhile array of organized sightseeing activities. Study their websites for details. If you're taking a city tour, remember that individuals save money with a scheduled public tour (such as those offered daily by Artviva Tours of Florence, listed next). If you're traveling as a family or small group, however, you're likely to save money by booking a private guide (since rates are based on roughly €55/hour for any size of group).

Artviva Walking Tours—This company offers a variety of tours (up to 12/day year-round) featuring downtown Florence, museum highlights, and Tuscany day trips. Their guides are native English-speakers. The three-hour "Original Florence" walk hits the main sights but gets offbeat to weave a picture of Florentine life in medieval and Renaissance times. Tours go rain or shine with as few as four participants (€25, daily at 9:15). Museum tours include the Uffizi (€39, includes admission, 2 hours), Accademia (called "Original *David*" tour, €35, includes admission, 1 hour), and "Original Florence in One Day" (€94, includes admission to Uffizi and Accademia, 6 hours). Their "Florence Orientation" talk starts in their office and is followed by a wine-tasting in an atmospheric bar (€10, daily at 17:00). They also offer talks by artists, writers, and wine and culinary experts (usually €20/person, late April-Oct Mon-Fri at 17:50, one hour, reserve at least one day ahead, dress is "elegant casual"—do your best).

Reservations are necessary for all tours and talks. For specifics

FLORENCE

Make Reservations to Avoid Lines

Florence has an optional reservation system for its state-run sights, which include the Accademia, Uffizi Gallery, Bargello, Medici Chapels, and Pitti Palace. I highly recommend getting reservations for the Accademia (Michelangelo's *David*) and the Uffizi (Renaissance paintings), but not the others.

The Brancacci Chapel is the only sight in Florence that requires reservations. These are free and simple to make. Call at least a day in advance and sign up for the film, too. Sometimes same-day reservations are available (tel. 055-276-8224 or 055-276-8558, English spoken, call center open daily 9:00-17:00). For more information, see page 1088.

The Uffizi and Accademia

Your best strategy is to get reservations for these two top sights as soon as you know when you'll be in town. Although you can generally get an entry time for the Accademia within a few days, the Uffizi can be booked more than a month in advance.

There are several ways to make a reservation: Have your hotelier arrange it, call the reservation number directly, book online, take a tour, or go in person in advance to the museums or the Orsanmichele Church ticket window. Here are details on the options:

- When you make your **hotel** reservation, ask if they can book your museum reservations for you (some hoteliers will do this for free; others charge a €3-5 fee). This is your easiest option.
- Reserve by **phone** before you leave the States (from the US, dial 011-39-055-294-883, or within Italy call 055-294-883; €4/ticket reservation fee; booking office open Mon-Fri 8:30-18:30, Sat 8:30-12:30, closed Sun). The reservation line is often busy, and even if you get through, you may be disconnected while on hold. Be persistent and try again. When you do get through, an English-speaking operator walks you through the process, and a few minutes later you say *grazie*,

and schedules, pick up their extensive brochure in your hotel lobby or their office (Mon-Sat 8:00-18:00, Sun 8:30-13:30 but off-season closed Sun and for lunch, near Piazza della Repubblica at Via dei Sassetti 1, second floor, above Odeon Cinema, tel. 055-264-5033 during day or mobile 329-613-2730 18:00-20:00, www.italy.art viva.com, staff@artviva.com).

Florentia—Top-notch private walking tours—geared for thoughtful, well-heeled travelers with longer-than-average attention spans—are led by Florentine scholars. The tours range from introductory city walks and museum visits to in-depth thematic walks, such as the Oltrarno neighborhood, "Unusual Florence," and side-trips into Tuscany (tours €175/half-day, €350/day, reserve having received an appointment and a six-digit confirmation number. Bring the confirmation(s) with you and pay cash at the sight(s). The advantage to phoning versus booking online is that you pay nothing upfront when you phone.

- Using a credit card, you can reserve your visit **online.** Pricey middleman sites—such as www.uffizi.com and www.tickitaly .com—are reliable, but their booking fees are exorbitant, running about €10 per ticket. Or you could take your chances with the city's troublesome official site (www.firenzemusei .it) in the hopes that its glitches have been fixed. It's the cheapest place to make reservations online (€4/ticket reservation fee), but even when it's working, the site often reverts to Italian-only (*"Annulia Operazione"* means "cancel"), you can't book a time before noon, and some readers report not receiving vouchers they've paid for.

- Take a **tour** that includes your museum admission. Artviva Walking Tours offers tours of the Uffizi (€39/person, 2 hours), Accademia (€35/person, 1 hour), and both museums (€94/person, 6 hours; see listing on page 1067, or visit www .italy.artviva.com).

- To **reserve in Florence,** here are your choices: call the reservation number (see above); ask your hotelier for help; or head to the booking window at Orsanmichele Church (€4 reservation fee, daily 10:00-17:00, along Via Calzaiuoli—see location on map on page 1072). For another Uffizi option, go to its ticket office and pay cash (Tue-Sun 8:15-18:50, use the *Main Entrance*—door #2, enter to the left of the line).

Off-Season: If you're in Florence off-season (Oct-March), you can probably get into the Uffizi or Accademia without a reservation in the late afternoon (after 16:00). At worst, you can make a reservation for later that day or the next day. But why hassle with it when you can make a reservation in advance? After seeing hundreds of bored, sweaty tourists waiting in lines without reservations, it's hard not to be amazed at their cluelessness.

in advance, tel. 338-890-8625, www.florentia.org, info@florentia .org).

Context Florence—This scholarly group of graduate students and professors leads "walking seminars," such as a three-hour study of Michelangelo's work and influence (€85/person, includes Accademia admission) and a two-hour evening orientation stroll (€35/person). I enjoyed the fascinating three-hour fresco workshop (€75/person, you take home a fresco you make yourself). See their website for other innovative offerings: Medici walk, lecture series, food walks, kids' tours, and programs in Venice, Rome, Naples, London, and Paris (tel. 069-762-5204, US tel. 888-467-1986, www .contexttravel.com, info@contexttravel.com).

Local Guides—Good guides include **Paola Barubiani** and her art historian partners at Walks Inside Florence (€55/hour for up to 4 people, €50/person for small-group 3-hour tour, €165/group of 2-6 people for private 3-hour tour, special rates for family tours, ask about Rick Steves discount, mobile 335-526-6496, www.walks insideflorence.com, paola@walksinsideflorence.it). **Alessandra Marchetti,** a Florentine who has lived in the US, gives private walking tours of Florence and driving tours of Tuscany (€60-75/ hour, mobile 347-386-9839, aleoberm@tin.it). **Paola Migliorini** and her partners at Tuscany Tours offer museum tours, city walking tours, private cooking classes, wine tours, and Tuscan excursions by van—you can tailor tours as you like (€55/hour without car, €65/hour in an 8-seat van, tel. 055-472-448, mobile 347-657-2611, www.florencetour.com, info@florencetour.com).

Hop-on, Hop-off Bus Tours—Around town, you'll see big double-decker sightseeing buses double-parking near major sights. Tourists on the top deck can listen to brief recorded descriptions of the sights, snap photos, and enjoy an effortless drive-by look at the major landmarks. Tickets cost €22, are valid for two days, and include two bus lines. Line A takes one hour with a trip up to Piazzale Michelangelo; Line B takes two hours with a side-trip to Fiesole (first bus at 9:30, last bus at 18:00, pay as you board, www .firenze.city-sightseeing.it). As the name implies, you can hop off when you want and catch the next bus (usually every 30 minutes, depending on the season). Hop-on stops include the train station and Pitti Palace. As most sights are buried in the old center where big buses can't go, Florence doesn't really lend itself to this kind of tour bus. Look at the route map before committing.

Self-Guided Walk

A Renaissance Ramble Through Florence

During the Dark Ages, it was especially obvious to the people of Italy—sitting on the rubble of Rome—that there had to be a brighter age before them. The long-awaited rebirth, or Renaissance, began in Florence for good reason. Wealthy because of its cloth industry, trade, and banking; powered by a fierce city-state pride (locals would pee into the Arno with gusto, knowing rival city-state Pisa was downstream); and fertile with more than its share of artistic genius (imagine guys like Michelangelo and Leonardo attending the same high school)—Florence was a natural home for this cultural explosion.

Take a two-hour walk through the core of Renaissance Florence by starting at the Accademia (home of Michelangelo's *David)* and cutting through the heart of the city to Ponte Vecchio on the Arno River (see map on page 1074). You can download a free audio version of this walk for your mobile device via www .ricksteves.com/audioeurope, iTunes, or the Rick Steves Audio Europe smartphone app.

At the Accademia, you'll see *David,* the ultimate Renaissance Man. Then walk to the cathedral (Duomo) to marvel at the dome that kicked off the architectural Renaissance. Step inside the Baptistery to view a ceiling covered with preachy 2-D medieval mosaic art. Then, to learn what happened when art met math, check out the realistic 3-D reliefs on the doors. The painter Giotto designed the bell tower—an early example of a Renaissance genius who could excel in many areas.

Continue toward the river on Florence's great pedestrian mall, Via de' Calzaiuoli—part of the original grid plan given to the city by the ancient Romans. Stop by any gelato shop for some cool refreshment. Down a few blocks, compare medieval and Renaissance statues on the exterior of the Orsanmichele Church.

Via de' Calzaiuoli connects the cathedral with the central square (Piazza della Signoria), the city palace (Palazzo Vecchio), and the Uffizi Gallery, which contains the greatest collection of Italian Renaissance paintings in captivity. Finally, walk through the Uffizi courtyard—a statuary think tank of Renaissance greats—to the Arno River and Ponte Vecchio.

Sights in Florence

North of the Arno River
North of the Duomo (Cathedral)
▲▲▲**Accademia (Galleria dell'Accademia)**—When you look into the eyes of Michelangelo's magnificent sculpture of *David,* you're looking into the eyes of Renaissance Man.

In 1501, Michelangelo Buonarroti, a 26-year-old Florentine, was commissioned to carve a large-scale work. The figure comes from a Bible story. The Israelites are surrounded by barbarian warriors led by a brutish giant named Goliath. When the giant challenges the Israelites to send out someone to fight him, a young shepherd boy steps forward. Armed only with a sling, David defeats the giant. This 17-foot-tall symbol of divine victory over evil represents a new century and a whole new Renaissance outlook.

Originally, *David* was meant to stand on the roofline of the Duomo, but was placed more prominently at the entrance of Palazzo Vecchio (where a copy stands today). In the 19th century, *David* was moved indoors for his own protection, and stands under a wonderful Renaissance-style dome designed just for him.

Nearby are some of the master's other works, including his powerful (unfinished) *Prisoners,* *St. Matthew,* and a *Pietà* (possibly

Heart of Florence

by one of his disciples). Michelangelo, who would work tirelessly through the night, believed that the sculptor was a tool of God, responsible only for chipping away at the stone until the intended sculpture emerged. Beyond the magic marble are some mildly interesting pre-Renaissance and Renaissance paintings, including a couple of lighter-than-air Botticellis, the plaster model of Giambologna's *Rape of the Sabines*, and a musical instrument collection with an early piano.

Cost and Hours: €6.50, plus €4 fee for recommended reservation (see pages 1068-1069 for details), Tue-Sun 8:15-18:50, closed Mon, last entry 45 minutes before closing (Via Ricasoli 60, tel. 055-238-8609 or 055-294-883, www.polomuseale.firenze.it).

Audio Tour: You can download a free audio tour of the Accademia for your mobile device via www.ricksteves.com/audio europe, iTunes, or the Rick Steves Audio Europe smartphone app.

Nearby: Piazza S.S. Annunziata, behind the Accademia, displays lovely Renaissance harmony. Facing the square are two fine buildings: the 15th-century Santissima Annunziata church (worth a peek) and Filippo Brunelleschi's Hospital of the Innocents (Spedale degli Innocenti, not worth going inside), with terra-cotta medallions by Luca della Robbia. Built in the 1420s, the hospital is considered the first Renaissance building. I love sleeping on this square (at the recommended Hotel Loggiato dei Serviti) and picnicking here during the day (with the riffraff, who remind me of the persistent gap—today as in Renaissance times—between those who appreciate fine art and those just looking for some cheap wine).

▲▲Museum of San Marco (Museo di San Marco)—Located one block north of the Accademia, this 15th-century monastery houses the greatest collection anywhere of frescoes and paintings by the early Renaissance master Fra Angelico. The ground floor features the monk's paintings, along with some works by Fra Bartolomeo. Upstairs are 43 cells decorated by Fra Angelico and his assistants. While the monk-painter was trained in the medieval religious style, he also learned and adopted Renaissance techniques and sensibilities, producing works that blended Christian symbols and Renaissance realism. Don't miss the cell of Savonarola, the charismatic monk who rode in from the Christian right, threw out the ruling Medici family, turned Florence into a theocracy, sponsored "bonfires of the vanities" (burning books, paintings, and so on), and was finally burned himself when Florence decided to change channels.

Cost and Hours: €4, Tue-Fri 8:15-13:50, Sat 8:15-16:50; also open 8:15-16:50 on second and fourth Sun and 8:15-13:50 on first, third, and fifth Mon of each month; last entry 30 minutes before

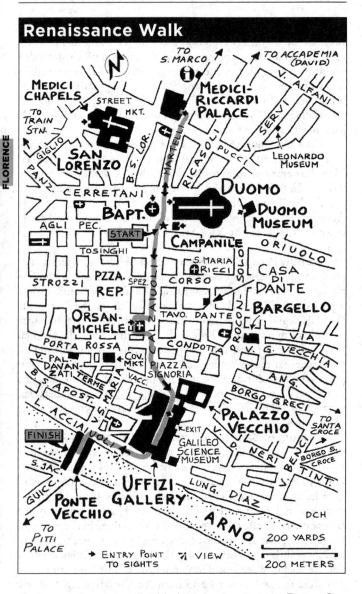

Renaissance Walk

closing, reservations possible but unnecessary, on Piazza San Marco, tel. 055-238-8608, www.polomuseale.firenze.it.

Museum of Precious Stones (Museo dell'Opificio delle Pietre Dure)—This unusual gem of a museum features room after room of exquisite mosaics of inlaid marble and stones. Upstairs, you'll see remnants of a workshop (funded by the art-patron Medici family) from 1588, including 500 different precious stones and the tools used to cut and inlay them. The helpful loaner booklet available next to the ticket window describes it all in English.

Cost and Hours: €4, Mon-Sat 8:15-14:00, closed Sun, around corner from Accademia at Via degli Alfani 78, tel. 055-265-1357.

Church of San Lorenzo—This red-brick dome—which looks like the Duomo's little sister—marks the burial place of Giovanni di Bicci de' Medici (1360-1429), founder of the influential Medici family. Part *Sopranos*, part Kennedys, part John-D-and-Catherine-T art patrons, the Medicis dominated Florentine politics for 300 years (c. 1434-1737). Immeasurably wealthy from their cloth, silk, and banking businesses, the family rose to the ranks of Europe's nobility, producing popes and queens.

The facade of the church is big, ugly, and unfinished, because Pope Leo X (also a Medici) pulled the plug on the project due to dwindling funds—after Michelangelo had labored on it for four years (1516-1520). Inside, though, is the spirit of Florence in the 1420s, with gray-and-white columns and arches in perfect Renaissance symmetry and simplicity. The Brunelleschi-designed church is lit by an even, diffused light. The Medici coat of arms (with the round pills of these "medics") decorates the ceiling, and everywhere are images of St. Lawrence, the Medici patron saint who was martyred on a grill.

Highlights of the church include two finely sculpted Donatello pulpits (in the nave). In the Martelli Chapel (left wall of the left transept), Filippo Lippi's *Annunciation* features a smiling angel greeting Mary in a sharply 3-D courtyard. Light shines through the vase in the foreground, like the Holy Spirit entering Mary's womb. The Old Sacristy (far left corner), designed by Brunelleschi, was the burial chapel for the Medicis. Bronze doors by Donatello flank the sacristy's small altar. Overhead, the dome above the altar shows the exact arrangement of the heavens on July 4, 1442, leaving scholars to hypothesize about why that particular date was used. Back in the nave, the round inlaid marble in the floor before the main altar marks where Cosimo the Elder is buried. Assistants in the church provide information on request, and the information brochure is free and in English.

Cost and Hours: €3.50, Feb-Oct Mon-Sat 10:00-17:00, Sun 13:30-17:00, closed Nov-Jan, www.basilicasanlorenzo.it.

Nearby: Outside the church, along the left side, is a cloister with peek-a-boo Duomo views and two sights: The San Lorenzo Museum (of fancy reliquaries) is included in your church admission, but is hardly worth the walk, except to see Donatello's grave. Next door is the Laurentian Library (Biblioteca Laurenziana, not included in church entry), starring Michelangelo's impressive staircase entrance. The library is worthwhile if it's open (€3, only opens during special exhibits, generally 9:30-13:00). A street market bustles outside the church (listed after the Medici Chapels, below).

Around the back end of the church is the entrance to the Medici Chapels and the New Sacristy, designed by Michelangelo for a later generation of dead Medicis.

▲▲Medici Chapels (Cappelle Medicee)—The burial site of the ruling Medici family in the Church of San Lorenzo includes the dusky Crypt; the big, domed Chapel of Princes; and the magnificent all-Michelangelo New Sacristy, featuring the master's architecture, tombs, and statues. The Medicis made their money in textiles and banking and patronized a dream team of Renaissance artists that put Florence on the cultural map. Michelangelo, who spent his teen years living with the Medicis, was commissioned for the family's final tribute.

Cost and Hours: €6, Tue-Sat April-Oct 8:15-16:50, Nov-March 8:15-13:50; also open first, third, and fifth Sun and second and fourth Mon of each month; last entry 30 minutes before closing, confirm latest hours at TI or chapel, tel. 055-238-8602, www.polomuseale.firenze.it. Don't waste money on a reservation to visit this sight.

▲San Lorenzo Market—Florence's vast open-air market sprawls around the Church of San Lorenzo. Most of the leather stalls are run by Iranians selling South American leather that was tailored in Italy. Prices are soft (daily 9:00-19:00, closed Mon in winter, between the Duomo and train station).

▲Mercato Centrale (Central Market)—Florence's giant iron-and-glass-covered central market, a wonderland of picturesque produce, is fun to explore. While the nearby San Lorenzo Market—with its garment stalls in the streets—feels like a step up from a haphazard flea market, the Mercato Centrale retains a Florentine elegance. Wander around. You'll see parts of the cow you'd never dream of eating (no, that's not a turkey neck), enjoy generous free samples, watch pasta-making, and have your pick of plenty of fun eateries sloshing out cheap and tasty pasta to locals (Mon-Sat 7:00-14:00, in winter open Sat until 17:00, closed Sun). For eating ideas in and around the market, see "Eating in Florence," later.

▲Medici-Riccardi Palace (Palazzo Medici-Riccardi)—Lorenzo the Magnificent's home is worth a look for its art. The tiny Chapel of the Magi contains colorful Renaissance gems like the *Procession of the Magi* frescoes by Benozzo Gozzoli. The former library has a Baroque ceiling fresco by Luca Giordano, a prolific artist from Naples known as "Fast Luke" *(Luca fa presto)* for his ambidextrous painting abilities. While the Medicis originally occupied this 1444 house, in the 1700s it became home to the Riccardi family, who added the Baroque flourishes.

Cost and Hours: €5, €7 with mandatory special exhibits, Thu-Tue 9:00-19:00, closed Wed, last entry 30 minutes before closing; kitty-corner from Church of San Lorenzo, one long block north of Duomo, ticket entrance is north of the main gated entrance, Via Cavour 3, tel. 055-276-0340.

Leonardo Museum (Museo Leonardo da Vinci)—This small entrepreneurial venture is fun for anyone who wants to crank the shaft and spin the ball bearings of Leonardo's genius inventions. While there are no actual historic artifacts, it shows about 30 of Leonardo's inventions and experiments made into models. You'll see a full-size armored tank, walk into a chamber of mirrors, operate a rotating crane, and watch experiments in flying. Each is described in English. What makes this exhibit special is that you're encouraged to touch and play with the models—it's great for kids.

Cost and Hours: €6, daily 10:00-19:00, closes at 18:00 in winter, Via dei Servi 66 red, tel. 055-282-966, www.mostredileonardo .com.

Duomo and Nearby

▲▲Duomo (Cattedrale di Santa Maria del Fiore)—Florence's Gothic cathedral has the third-longest nave in Christendom. The church's noisy Neo-Gothic facade from the 1870s is covered with pink, green, and white Tuscan marble. In the interior, you'll see a huge *Last Judgment* by Giorgio Vasari and Federico Zuccari (inside the dome). Much of the church's great art is stored in the Duomo Museum behind the church.

The cathedral's claim to artistic fame is Brunelleschi's magnificent dome—the first Renaissance dome and the model for domes to follow. Think of the confidence of the age: The Duomo was built with a big hole in its roof awaiting a dome. This was before the technology to span it with a dome was available. No *problema*. They knew that someone soon could handle the challenge...and the local architect Filippo Brunelleschi did. First, he built the grand white skeletal ribs, which you can see, then filled them in with interlocking bricks in a herringbone pattern. The dome grew upward like an igloo, supporting itself as it proceeded from the base. At the top, Brunelleschi arched the ribs in and fixed them in place with the lantern. His dome, built in only 14 years, was the largest since Rome's Pantheon.

Massive crowds line up to see the huge church. The church is a major sight, but not worth a long wait. Either go late (the crowds subside by late afternoon), or take the Terraces tour mentioned below.

Cost and Hours: Free entry, Mon-Fri 10:00-17:00, Thu until 15:30 in May and Oct and until 16:30 in winter, Sat 10:00-16:45,

Sun 13:30-16:45, modest dress code enforced, tel. 055-230-2885, www.operaduomo.firenze.it.

Crowd-Beating Tip: Taking the "**Terraces of the Cathedral and Dome**" tour allows you to skip the long lines to enter the cathedral and to climb the dome. After a short guided tour of the interior, you'll climb up onto the exterior terrace, where great views reward the stair hike (see "Climbing the Duomo's Dome," next). When the tour is finished on the terrace, you can continue on your own up to the top of the dome (€15, 45 minutes; offered Mon-Fri at 10:30, 12:00, and 15:00; at 10:30 and 12:00 on Sat, no tours on Sun, buy tickets at nearby Duomo Museum and they'll tell you where to meet your guide). If you're planning to climb the dome anyway (€8), the tour is a fine value.

▲**Climbing the Duomo's Dome**—For a grand view into the cathedral from the base of the dome, a peek at some of the tools used in the dome's construction, a chance to see Brunelleschi's "dome-within-a-dome" construction, a glorious Florence view from the top, and the equivalent of 463 plunges on a Renaissance StairMaster, climb the dome. Michelangelo, setting out to construct the dome of St. Peter's in Rome, drew inspiration from the dome of Florence. He said, "I'll make its sister...bigger, but not more beautiful." To avoid the long, dreadfully slow-moving line, arrive by 8:30 or drop by very late. Those taking the "Terraces" tour of the Duomo (see above) can skip the line.

Cost and Hours: €8, Mon-Fri 8:30-19:00, Sat 8:30-17:40, closed Sun, last entry 40 minutes before closing, enter from outside church on north side, tel. 055-230-2885.

▲**Campanile (Giotto's Tower)**—The 270-foot bell tower has 50 fewer steps than the Duomo's dome (but that's still 413 steps—no elevator); offers a faster, less-crowded climb; and has a view of the Duomo to boot, but the cage-like top makes taking good photographs difficult.

Cost and Hours: €6, daily 8:30-19:30, last entry 40 minutes before closing.

▲**Baptistery**—Michelangelo said its bronze doors were fit to be the gates of paradise. Check out the gleaming copies of Lorenzo Ghiberti's bronze doors facing the Duomo. Making a breakthrough in perspective, Ghiberti used mathematical laws to create the illusion of receding distance on a basically flat surface.

The doors on the north side of the building were designed by Ghiberti when he was young; he'd won the honor and opportunity by beating Brunelleschi in a competition (the rivals' original entries are in the Bargello).

Inside, sit and savor the medieval mosaic ceiling, where it's always Judgment Day and Jesus is giving the ultimate thumbs-up and thumbs-down. The rest of the ceiling mosaics tell the history of the world, from Adam and Eve (over the north/entrance doors, top row) to Noah and the Flood (over south doors, top row), to the life of Christ (second row) to the beheading of John the Baptist (bottom row), all bathed in the golden glow of pre-Renaissance heaven.

Cost and Hours: €4, interior open Mon-Sat 12:15-19:00 except first Sat of month 8:30-14:00, Sun 8:30-14:00, last entry 30 minutes before closing, audioguide-€2, photos allowed inside, tel. 055-230-2885; bronze doors are on the outside, so always "open"; original panels are in the Duomo Museum.

▲▲▲**Duomo Museum (Museo dell'Opera del Duomo)**—The underrated cathedral museum, behind the church (at Via del Proconsolo 9), is great if you like sculpture. On the ground floor, look for a late Michelangelo *Pietà*, the eight restored panels of Ghiberti's north doors for the Baptistery, and statues from the original Baptistery facade. Upstairs, you'll find Brunelleschi's models for his dome, as well as Donatello's anorexic *Mary Magdalene* and playful choir loft. The museum features most of Ghiberti's original "Gates of Paradise" panels (under renovation through early 2012); the panels on the Baptistery's doors today are copies.

Cost and Hours: €6, Mon-Sat 9:00-19:30, Sun 9:00-13:40, last entry 40 minutes before closing, one of the few museums in Florence always open on Mon, Via del Proconsolo 9, tel. 055-230-2885. At this museum, you can purchase €15 tickets for the "Terraces of the Cathedral and Dome" tour mentioned on the previous page, which allows you to bypass the long cathedral-entry and dome-climbing lines.

Nearby: If you find this church art intriguing, head to the left around the back of the Duomo to find Via dello Studio (near the south transept), then walk a block toward the river to #23a. You can look through the open doorway of the Opera del Duomo art studio and see workers sculpting new statues, restoring old ones, or making exact copies. They're carrying on an artistic tradition that dates back to the days of Brunelleschi.

Between the Duomo and Piazza della Signoria

▲▲▲**Bargello (Museo Nazionale)**—This underappreciated sculpture museum is in a former police station-turned-prison that looks like a mini-Palazzo Vecchio. It has Donatello's painfully beautiful *David* (the very influential first male nude to be sculpted in a thousand years), works by Michelangelo, and rooms of Medici treasures explained only in Italian (politely suggest to the staff that English descriptions would be wonderful). Moody Donatello, who embraced realism with his lifelike statues, set the personal and artistic style for many Renaissance artists to follow. The best works are in the ground-floor room at the foot of the outdoor staircase and in the room directly above.

Cost and Hours: €4, but mandatory special exhibitions often increase the price to €7, Tue-Sat April-Oct 8:15-16:50, Nov-March 8:15-13:50; also open first, third, and fifth Mon and the second and fourth Sun of each month; last entry 40 minutes before closing, reservations possible but unnecessary, Via del Proconsolo 4, reservation tel. 055-238-8606, www.polomuseale.firenze.it.

Casa di Dante (Dante's House)—Dante Alighieri (1265-1321), the poet who gave us *The Divine Comedy*, is the Shakespeare of Italy, the father of the modern Italian language, and the face on the country's €2 coin. However, most Americans know little of him, and this museum is not the ideal place to start. Even though it has English information, this small museum (in a building near where he likely lived) assumes visitors have prior knowledge of the poet. Dante lovers can trace his interesting life and works through pictures, models, and artifacts. And because the exhibits are as much about medieval Florence as they are about the man, novices can learn a little about Dante and the city he lived in.

Cost and Hours: €4, summer daily 10:00-18:00; winter Tue-Sun 10:00-17:00, closed Mon; last entry 30 minutes before closing, near the Bargello at Via Santa Margherita 1, tel. 055-219-416, www.museocasadidante.it.

▲**Orsanmichele Church**—In the ninth century, this loggia (covered courtyard) was a market used for selling grain (stored upstairs). Later, it was enclosed to make a church.

Outside are dynamic statue-filled niches, some with accompanying symbols from the guilds that sponsored the art. Donatello's *St. Mark* and *St. George* (on the northeast and northwest corners) step out boldly in the new Renaissance style.

The interior has a glorious Gothic tabernacle (1359) housing the painted wooden panel that depicts *Madonna delle Grazie* (1346). The iron bars spanning the vaults were the Italian Gothic answer to the French Gothic external buttresses. Look for the rectangular holes in the piers—these were once wheat chutes that connected to the upper floors.

Cost and Hours: Free entry, Tue-Sun 10:00-17:00, closed Mon, niche sculptures always viewable from the outside.

Concerts and Ticket Office: You can give the *Madonna della Grazie* a special thanks if you're in town when an evening concert is held inside the Orsanmichele (tickets sold on day of concert from door facing Via de' Calzaiuoli; also books Uffizi and Accademia tickets, ticket window open daily 10:00-17:00).

A block away, you'll find the...

▲**Mercato Nuovo (a.k.a. the Straw Market)**—This market loggia is how Orsanmichele looked before it became a church. Originally a silk and straw market, Mercato Nuovo still functions as a rustic yet touristy market (at the intersection of Via Calimala and Via Porta Rossa). Prices are soft, but the San Lorenzo Market (listed earlier) is much better for haggling. Notice the circled X in the center, marking the spot where people hit after being hoisted up to the top and dropped as punishment for bankruptcy. You'll also find *Porcellino* (a statue of a wild boar nicknamed "little pig"), which people rub and give coins to in order to ensure their return to Florence. This new copy, while only a few years old, already has a polished snout. At the back corner, a wagon sells tripe (cow innards) sandwiches—a local favorite (daily 9:00-20:00).

▲**Piazza della Repubblica and Nearby**—This large square sits on the site of Florence's original Roman Forum. The lone column—nicknamed "the belly button of Florence"—once marked the intersection of the two main Roman roads. All that survives of Roman Florence is its grid street plan and this column. Look at any map of Florence today (there's one by the benches—where the old boys hang out to talk sports and politics), and you'll see the ghost of Rome in its streets: a grid-plan city center surrounded by what was the Roman wall. Roman Florence was a garrison town, a rectangular fort with this square marking the intersection of the two main roads (Via Corso and Via Roma).

Today's piazza, framed by a triumphal arch, is a nationalistic statement celebrating the unification of Italy. Florence, the capital of the country (1865-1870) until Rome was "liberated" (from the Vatican), lacked a square worthy of this grand new country. So the neighborhood here—once the Jewish quarter—was razed to open up an imposing, modern forum surrounded by stately circa-1890 buildings.

Venerable cafés and stores line the square. The La Rinascente department store, facing Piazza della Repubblica, is one of the city's mainstays (WC on fourth floor, continue up the stairs from there to the bar with a view terrace).

▲**Palazzo Davanzati**—This five-story late-medieval tower house offers a rare look at a noble dwelling built in the 14th century. Currently only the ground and first floors are open to visitors, though the remaining floors can be visited by appointment. Like other buildings of the age, the exterior is festooned with 14th-century horse-tethering rings made out of iron, torch holders, and poles upon which to hang laundry and fly flags. Inside, though the furnishings are pretty sparse, you'll see richly painted walls, a long chute that functioned as a well, plenty of fireplaces, a lace display, and even a modern toilet.

Cost and Hours: €2, Tue-Sat 8:15-13:50; also open second and fourth Mon and first, third, and fifth Sun; Via Porta Rossa 13, tel. 055-238-8610.

On and near Piazza della Signoria

Piazza della Signoria, the main civic center of Florence, is dominated by Palazzo Vecchio, the Uffizi Gallery, and the marble greatness of old Florence littering the cobbles. This square still vibrates with the echoes of Florence's past—executions, riots, and great celebrations. Today, it's a tourist's world with pigeons, postcards, horse buggies, and tired hubbies. If it would make your weary companion happy, stop in at the recommended but expensive **Rivoire** café to enjoy its fine desserts, pudding-thick hot chocolate, and the best view seats in town.

▲▲▲**Uffizi Gallery**—This greatest collection of Italian paintings anywhere features works by Giotto, Leonardo, Raphael, Caravaggio, Titian, and Michelangelo, and a roomful of Botticellis, including the *Birth of Venus*. German, Dutch, and Flemish masters are well represented by works by Dürer, Rembrandt, and Rubens.

The museum is nowhere near as big as it is great. Few tourists spend more than two hours inside. The paintings are displayed on one comfortable U-shaped floor in chronological order from the 13th through 17th centuries. The left wing, starring the Florentine Middle Ages to the Renaissance, is the best. The connecting corridor contains sculpture, and the right wing focuses on the High Renaissance and Baroque.

Medieval (1200-1400): Paintings by **Duccio, Cimabue,** and **Giotto** show the baby steps being made from the flat Byzantine style toward realism. In his *Madonna and Child,* Giotto created a "stage" and peopled it with real beings. The triumph here is Mary herself—big and monumental, like a Roman statue. Beneath her robe, she has knees and breasts that stick out at us. This three-dimensionality was revolutionary, a taste of the Renaissance a century before it began.

Early Renaissance (mid-1400s): Paolo Uccello's *Battle of San Romano* is an early study in perspective with a few obvious flubs (recently restored but likely back on display in 2012). Piero della Frencesca's *Duke and Duchess of Urbino* heralds the era of humanism and the new centrality of ordinary people in art, warts and all. Fra Filippo Lippi's radiantly beautiful Madonnas are light years away from the generic Marys of the medieval era.

Renaissance (1450-1500) and High Renaissance (1500-1550): The Botticelli room is filled with masterpieces and classical fleshiness—the famous *Birth of Venus* and the *Allegory of Spring.* Here is the Renaissance in its first bloom, its "springtime" of innocence. Madonna is out, Venus is in. This is a return to the pre-Christian pagan world of classical Greece, where things of the flesh are not sinful.

Don't miss Michelangelo's *Holy Family,* the only surviving completed easel painting by the greatest sculptor in history;

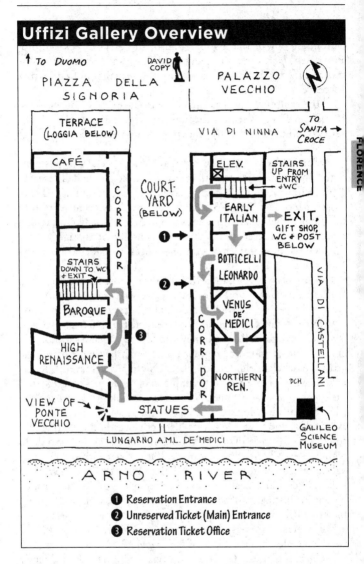

Uffizi Gallery Overview

TO DUOMO

DAVID COPY

PIAZZA DELLA SIGNORIA

PALAZZO VECCHIO

TERRACE (LOGGIA BELOW)

CAFÉ

VIA DI NINNA

TO SANTA CROCE

ELEV.

STAIRS UP FROM ENTRY & WC

COURT-YARD (BELOW)

CORRIDOR

EARLY ITALIAN

EXIT, GIFT SHOP, WC & POST BELOW

STAIRS DOWN TO WC & EXIT

❶➡

BOTTICELLI LEONARDO

❷➡

BAROQUE

VENUS DE' MEDICI

CORRIDOR

❸

HIGH RENAISSANCE

NORTHERN REN.

VIA DI CASTELLANI

VIEW OF PONTE VECCHIO

STATUES

DCH

LUNGARNO A.M.L. DE' MEDICI

GALILEO SCIENCE MUSEUM

ARNO RIVER

❶ Reservation Entrance
❷ Unreserved Ticket (Main) Entrance
❸ Reservation Ticket Office

FLORENCE

Raphael's *Madonna of the Goldfinch,* with Mary and the Baby Jesus brought down from heaven into the real world of trees, water, and sky; and Titan's voluptuous *Venus of Urbino.*

Classical sculpture: If the Renaissance was the foundation of the modern world, the foundation of the Renaissance was classical sculpture. Sculptors, painters, and poets alike turned for inspiration to ancient Greek and Roman works as the epitome of balance, 3-D perspective, human anatomy, and beauty.

In the octagonal classical sculpture room (which may be under renovation when you visit), the highlight is the *Venus de' Medici*, a Roman copy of the lost original of the great Greek sculptor Praxiteles' *Aphrodite*. Balanced, harmonious, and serene, this statue was considered the epitome of beauty and sexuality in Renaissance Florence.

The sculpture hall has the best view in Florence of the Arno River and Ponte Vecchio through the window, dreamy at sunset. Wrap up your visit by enjoying Duomo views from the café terrace.

Cost and Hours: €6.50 but mandatory special exhibits generally bump the price to €10, extra €4 for recommended reservation, cash required to pick up reserved tickets, Tue-Sun 8:15-18:50, closed Mon, last entry 45 minutes before closing, museum info tel. 055-238-8651, www.polomuseale.firenze.it. To avoid the long ticket lines, get reservations at least a month ahead in high season. For details on making reservations, check the sidebar on pages 1068-1069.

Audio Tour: You can download a free audio tour of the Uffizi Gallery for your mobile device via www.ricksteves.com/audio europe, iTunes, or the Rick Steves Audio Europe smartphone app.

In the Uffizi Courtyard: Enjoy the courtyard (free), full of artists and souvenir stalls. (Swing by after dinner when it's completely empty.) The surrounding statues honor earthshaking Florentines: artists (Michelangelo), philosophers (Niccolò Machiavelli), scientists (Galileo), writers (Dante), explorers (Amerigo Vespucci), and the great patron of so much Renaissance thinking, Lorenzo "the Magnificent" de' Medici.

▲**Palazzo Vecchio**—With its distinctive castle turret, this fortified palace—the Town Hall, officially called the Palazzo della Signoria—is a Florentine landmark. But if you're visiting only one palace interior in town, the Pitti Palace is better. The interior of Palazzo Vecchio is best for fans of coffered and gilded ceilings, of Florentine history, or of the artist Giorgio Vasari, who wallpapered the place with mediocre magnificence.

The museum's most famous statues are Michelangelo's *Victory* and Donatello's bronze statue of *Judith and Holofernes*.

Cost and Hours: €6, €8 combo-ticket with Brancacci Chapel, skippable audioguide, tours are free and in English but require reservation, Fri-Wed 9:00-19:00, Thu 9:00-14:00, ticket office closes one hour earlier, tel. 055-276-8224.

Nearby: Even if you don't go to the museum, do step into the **free courtyard** behind the fake *David* just to feel the essence of the Medicis. Until 1873, Michelangelo's *David* stood at the entrance, where the copy is today. While the huge statues in the square are important only as the whipping boys of art critics and as rest stops for pigeons, the nearby **loggia** has several important statues. Look for Benvenuto Cellini's bronze statue of Perseus holding the head of Medusa. The plaque on the pavement in front of the fountain marks the spot where the monk Savonarola was burned in MCDXCVIII, or 1498.

▲▲**Galileo Science Museum (Museo Galilei e Istituto di Storia della Scienza)**—When we think of the Florentine Renaissance, we think of visual arts: painting, mosaics, architecture, and sculpture. But when the visual arts declined in the 1600s (abused and co-opted by political powers), music and science flourished in Florence. The first opera was written here. And Florence hosted many scientific breakthroughs, as you'll see in this fascinating collection of Renaissance and later clocks, telescopes, maps, and ingenious gadgets. Trace the technical innovations as modern science emerges from 1000 to 1900. One of the most talked-about bottles in Florence is the one here that contains Galileo's finger. Exhibits include various tools for gauging the world, from a compass and thermometer to Galileo's telescopes. Other displays delve into clocks, pumps, medicine, and chemistry. Some English information is available, and the docents are helpful. It's friendly, comfortably cool, never crowded, and just a block east of the Uffizi on the Arno River.

Cost and Hours: €8, €20 family ticket, Wed-Mon 9:30-18:00, Tue 9:30-13:00, Piazza dei Giudici 1, tel. 055-265-311, recorded info tel. 055-293-493, www.museogalileo.it.

▲**Ponte Vecchio**—Florence's most famous bridge is lined with shops that have traditionally sold gold and silver. A statue of Benvenuto Cellini, the master goldsmith of the Renaissance, stands in the center, ignored by the flood of tacky tourism. This is a very romantic spot late at night (when lovers gather, and a top-notch street musician performs).

Notice the "prince's passageway" above the bridge, called the **Vasari Corridor.** In less secure times, the city leaders had a fortified passageway connecting Palazzo Vecchio and the Uffizi with the mighty Pitti Palace, to which they could flee in times of attack. This passageway is sometimes open to the public, but a visit is almost impossible to arrange, and if you do manage it, it's usually a disappointment (you could check at the Uffizi to see if it's open or try a private tour company such as Artviva Walking Tours; see page 1067).

East of Piazza della Signoria

▲▲**Santa Croce Church**—This 14th-century Franciscan church, decorated with centuries of precious art, holds the tombs of great Florentines.

The loud 19th-century Victorian Gothic facade faces a huge square ringed with tempting shops and littered with tired tourists.

Escape into the church and admire its sheer height and spaciousness. Start at the back of the nave (farthest from the altar). On the left wall (as you face the altar) is the **tomb of Galileo Galilei** (1564-1642), the Pisan who lived his last years under house arrest near Florence for having defied the Church by saying that the earth revolved around the sun. His heretical remains were only allowed in the church long after his death. Directly opposite (on the right wall) is the **tomb of Michelangelo Buonarroti** (1475-1564).

The first chapel to the right of the main altar features the famous fresco by Giotto of the *Death of St. Francis*. With simple but eloquent gestures, Francis' brothers bid him a sad farewell. One folds his hands and stares longingly at Francis' serene face. Another bends to kiss Francis' hand, while others raise their arms in grief. It's one of the first expressions of human emotion in modern painting. It's also one of the first to create a real three-dimensional grouping of figures.

At the end of the right transept, a left turn at the first door leads into the sacristy, where you'll find a rumpled bit of **St. Francis' tunic** (*Parte della Tonaca*, scrunched up in a small gold frame). In the hallway near the bookstore, notice the photos of the devastating flood of 1966. Beyond that is the leather school, the first shop of what is now a popular leather district. Wander through the former dorms for monks, watch the leatherworking in action, and browse the finished products—for sale, of course.

Exit between the Rossini and Machiavelli tombs into the cloister (open-air courtyard). On the left, enter Brunelleschi's Pazzi Chapel, which captures the Renaissance in miniature.

Cost and Hours: €5 includes the church, Pazzi Chapel, and museum; Mon-Sat 9:30-17:30, Sun 13:00-17:30, last entry 30 minutes before closing, modest dress code enforced, 10-minute walk east of Palazzo Vecchio along Borgo de' Greci, tel. 055-246-6105. The leather school is free and sells tickets to the church. If the church has a long line, come here to avoid the line (daily 10:00-18:00, has own entry behind church plus an entry within the church, www.leatherschool.com).

▲**Casa Buonarroti (Michelangelo's House)**—Fans enjoy a house standing on property once owned by Michelangelo. The house was built after Michelangelo's death by the artist's grand-nephew, who turned it into a little museum honoring his famous relative. You'll see some of Michelangelo's early, less-than-monumental statues and a few sketches. Be warned: Michelangelo's descendants attributed everything they could to their famous relative, but very little here (beyond two marble relief panels and a couple of sketches) is actually by Michelangelo.

Cost and Hours: €6.50, Wed-Mon 9:30-14:00, closed Tue, English descriptions, Via Ghibellina 70, tel. 055-241-752.

Near the Train Station

▲▲**Church of Santa Maria Novella**—This 13th-century Dominican church is rich in art. Along with crucifixes by Giotto and Brunelleschi, there's every textbook's example of the early Renaissance mastery of perspective: *The Holy Trinity* by Masaccio. The exquisite chapels trace art in Florence from medieval times to early Baroque. The outside of the church features a dash of Romanesque (horizontal stripes), Gothic (pointed arches), Renaissance (geometric shapes), and Baroque (scrolls). Step in and look down the 330-foot nave for a 14th-century optical illusion.

Cost and Hours: €3.50, Mon-Thu 9:00-17:30, Fri 11:00-17:30, Sat 9:00-17:00, Sun 13:00-17:00, last entry 30 minutes before closing, tel. 055-219-257.

Nearby: A palatial **perfumery** (Farmacia di Santa Maria Novella) is a block from Piazza Santa Maria Novella, 100 yards down Via della Scala at #16 (free but shopping encouraged, inconsistent hours but likely daily 9:30-19:30, see map on page 1065, tel. 055-216-276, www.smnovella.com). Thick with the lingering aroma of centuries of spritzes, it started as the herb garden of the Santa Maria Novella monks. Well-known even today for its top-quality products, it is extremely Florentine. Pick up the history sheet at the desk, and wander deep into the shop. From the back room, you can peek at one of Santa Maria Novella's cloisters with its dreamy frescoes and imagine a time before Vespas and tourists.

You can get a closer look inside the **Museum and Cloisters,** adjacent to the church, but they're definitely lesser sights (€2.70, entry to the left of the church's facade; Mon-Thu and Sat 9:00-17:00, closed Fri and Sun).

South of the Arno River

To locate these sights, see the map on page 1065.

▲▲**Pitti Palace**—The imposing Pitti Palace, several blocks southwest of Ponte Vecchio, is not only home to the second-best collection of paintings in town, the **Palatine Gallery,** but also happens to be the most sumptuous palace you can tour in Florence. The building itself is mammoth, holding several different museums and anchoring two gardens. Stick primarily to the gallery, forget about everything else, and the palace becomes a little less exhausting.

You'll walk through one palatial room after another, walls sagging with masterpieces by 16th- and 17th-century masters, including Rubens, Titian, and Rembrandt. Its Raphael collection is the second-biggest anywhere—the Vatican beats it by one. Each room has some descriptions in English, though the paintings themselves have limited English labels.

The collection is all on one floor. To see the highlights, walk straight down the spine through a dozen or so rooms. Before you exit, consider a visit to the Royal Apartments. These 14 rooms (of which only a few are open at any one time) are where Florence's aristocrats lived in the 18th and 19th centuries. Each room features a different color and time period. Here, you get a real feel for the splendor of the dukes' world.

The Rest of the Pitti Palace: If you've got the energy and interest, it'd be a Pitti to miss the palace's other offerings.

The **Modern Art Gallery,** on the second floor, features Romantic, Neoclassical, and Impressionist works by 19th- and 20th-century Tuscan painters.

The **Argenti Museum** (on the ground and mezzanine floors) is the Medici treasure chest, with jeweled crucifixes, exotic porcelain, and gilded ostrich eggs, made to entertain fans of the applied arts.

The **Boboli and Bardini Gardens,** located behind the palace, offer a pleasant and shady refuge from the city heat. Enter the Boboli Gardens from the Pitti Palace courtyard. The less-visited Bardini Gardens are behind the Boboli, rising in terraces toward Piazzale Michelangelo.

Cost and Hours: The main reason to visit is to see the Palatine Gallery, but you can't buy a ticket for the gallery alone; to see it you'll need to buy ticket #1, which includes the Palatine Gallery, Royal Apartments, and Modern Art Gallery (€8.50 but often €12 with mandatory special exhibits, cash only, Tue-Sun 8:15-18:50, closed Mon, tel. 055-238-8614, www.polomuseale. firenze.it). Ticket #2 covers the Boboli and Bardini Gardens, Argenti Museum, Costume Gallery, and Porcelain Museum (€6, more with special exhibits, daily 8:15-18:30, until 19:30 June-Aug, same phone and website as above). An €11.50 combo-ticket covers the whole palace complex (valid 3 days). If there's a long line, you can bypass it by buying a reservation for immediate entry at the ticket window (€3 reservation fee).

▲▲**Brancacci Chapel**—For the best look at works by Masaccio (one of the early Renaissance pioneers of perspective in painting), see his restored frescoes here. Instead of medieval religious symbols, Masaccio's paintings feature simple, strong human figures with facial expressions that reflect their emotions. The accompanying works of Masolino and Filippino Lippi provide illuminating contrasts.

Reservations are free and required (see below). Your ticket includes a 40-minute film in English on the church, the frescoes, and Renaissance Florence (reserve a viewing time when you book your entry). The film starts promptly at the top of the hour. Computer animation brings the paintings to life—making them appear to move and giving them 3-D depth—while narration describes the events depicted in the panels. Yes, it's a long time commitment, and the film takes liberties with the art. But it's visually interesting and your best way to see the frescoes close up. The film works great either before or after you visit the frescoes.

Cost and Hours: €4, free reservations required (see below), €8 combo-ticket with Palazzo Vecchio, both tickets include worthwhile 40-minute film in English—reserve film when you book entry, limit of 30 visitors every 15 minutes, Mon and Wed-Sat 10:00-17:00, Sun 13:00-17:00, closed Tue, ticket office closes at 16:30; in Church of Santa Maria del Carmine—cross Ponte Vecchio and turn right on Borgo San Jacopo, walk 10 minutes, then turn left into Piazza del Carmine; tel. 055-276-8224 or 055-276-8558.

Reservations: Call the chapel at least a day ahead for free, mandatory reservations; tickets are sometimes available for the same day (tel. 055-276-8224 or 055-276-8558, English spoken, call center open daily 9:00-17:00). If the line is busy, keep trying—it's best to call around 14:00-15:00 or just before the ticket office closes at 16:30. Reservation times begin every 15 minutes, with a maximum of 30 visitors per time slot (you have 15 minutes inside the chapel). When you call to reserve, you can also book a time to see the film.

Santo Spirito Church—This church has a classic Brunelleschi interior and a painted, carved wooden crucifix attributed to 17-year-old Michelangelo. The sculptor donated this early work to the monastery in appreciation for allowing him to dissect and learn about bodies. The Michelangelo *Crocifisso* is displayed in the sacristy, through a door midway down the left side of the nave (if it's closed, ask someone to let you in). Copies of Michelangelo's *Pietà* and *Risen Christ* flank the nave. Beer-drinking, guitar-playing rowdies decorate the church steps.

Cost and Hours: Free entry, Mon-Tue and Thu-Sat 9:30-12:30 & 16:00-17:30, Sun 15:00-17:30 only, closed Wed, Piazza Santo Spirito, tel. 055-211-716.

▲**Piazzale Michelangelo**—Overlooking the city from across the river (look for the huge statue of *David*), this square has a superb view of Florence and the stunning dome of the Duomo.

It's worth the 30-minute hike, drive (free parking), or bus ride (either #12 or #13 from the train station—takes a long time). It makes sense to take a taxi or ride the bus up, and then enjoy the easy downhill walk back into town. An inviting café with great views is just below the overlook. The best photos are taken from the street immediately below the overlook (go around to the right and down a few steps). Off the west side of the piazza is a somewhat hidden terrace, an excellent place to retreat from the mobs. After dark, the square is packed with school kids licking ice cream and each other. About 200 yards beyond all the tour groups and teenagers is the stark, beautiful, crowd-free Romanesque San Miniato Church (next listing).

The hike down is quick and enjoyable. Take the steps between the two bars on the San Miniato Church side of the parking lot (Via San Salvatore al Monte), and in a couple of minutes you walk through the old wall (Porta San Miniato) and emerge in the delightful little Oltrarno neighborhood of San Niccolò.

▲▲**San Miniato Church**—According to legend, the martyred St. Minias—this church's namesake—was beheaded on the banks of the Arno in A.D. 250. He picked up his head and walked here (this was before the #12 bus), where he died and was buried in what became the first Christian cemetery in Florence. In the 11th century, this church was built to house Minias' remains. Imagine this fine church all alone—without any nearby buildings or fancy stairs—a peaceful refuge where white-robed Benedictine monks could pray and work (their motto: *ora et labora*). The church's green-and-white marble facade (12th century) is classic Florentine Romanesque. The church has wonderful 3-D paintings, a plush ceiling of glazed terra-cotta panels by Luca della Robbia, and a sumptuous Renaissance chapel (located front and center). The highlight for me is the brilliantly preserved art in the sacristy (behind altar in the room on right) showing scenes from the life of St. Benedict (circa 1350, by a follower of Giotto). Drop a euro into the box to light the room for five minutes.

Cost and Hours: Free entry, daily April-Oct 8:00-19:30, Nov-March 8:00-13:00 & 14:30-18:00, Gregorian chants April-Sept daily at the 17:30 Mass (17:00 in winter), 200 yards above Piazzale Michelangelo, bus #12 or #13 from train station, tel. 055-234-2731.

Sleeping in Florence

Nearly all of my recommended accommodations are located in the center of Florence, within minutes of the great sights.

The accommodations scene varies wildly with the season. Spring and fall are very tight and expensive, while mid-July through August is wide open and discounted. November through February is also generally empty. I've listed prices for peak season: April, May, June, September, and October.

In Florence, you can snare a stark, clean, and comfortable double with breakfast and a private bath for about €100 (less in smaller towns). You get elegance in peak season for €160.

Florence is notorious for its mosquitoes. If your hotel lacks air-conditioning, request a fan and don't open your windows, especially at night. Many hotels furnish a small plug-in bulb *(zanzariere)*—

Sleep Code

(€1 = about $1.40, country code: 39)
S = Single, **D** = Double/Twin, **T** = Triple, **Q** = Quad, **b** = bathroom,
s = shower only.

You can assume a hotel takes credit cards unless you see "cash only" in the listing. Unless otherwise noted, hotel staff speak basic English and breakfast is included.

To help you easily sort through these listings, I've divided the rooms into three categories based on the price for a standard double room with bath during high season:

$$$ Higher Priced—Most rooms €160 or more.
$$ Moderately Priced—Most rooms between €100-160.
$ Lower Priced—Most rooms €100 or less.

Prices can change without notice; verify the hotel's current rates online or by email. For other updates, see www .ricksteves.com/update.

usually set in the ashtray—that helps keep the bloodsuckers at bay. If not, you can purchase one cheaply at any pharmacy *(farmacia)*.

Museumgoers take note: When you book your room, ask if your hotelier will reserve entry times for you to visit the popular Uffizi Gallery and the Accademia (Michelangelo's *David*). This service is fast, easy, and offered free or for a small fee by most hotels—the only requirement is advance notice. Ask them to book your visits for any time the day after your arrival. If you'd rather make the reservations yourself, see pages 1068-1069 for details.

North of the Arno River
Between the Duomo and the Train Station

$$ Hotel Accademia, which comes with marble stairs, parquet floors, and attractive public areas, has 21 pleasant rooms and a floor plan that defies logic (Db-€150, Tb-€180, cash discount with this book, air-con, Internet access and Wi-Fi, Via Faenza 7, tel. 055-293-451, fax 055-219-771, www.hotelaccademiafirenze.com, info @hotelaccademiafirenze.com, Tea, Francesca, and Paolo).

$$ Hotel Centrale, with 20 spacious rooms, is indeed central (Db-€150, superior Db-€176, Tb-€182, discount with this book, ask for Rick Steves rate when you reserve, air-con, elevator, Internet access and Wi-Fi, Via dei Conti 3, tel. 055-215-761, fax 055-215-216, www.hotelcentralefirenze.it, info@hotelcentrale firenze.it, Margherita and Roberto).

$ Katti House and the nearby **Soggiorno Annamaria** are run by house-proud mama-and-daughter team Maria and Katti,

FLORENCE

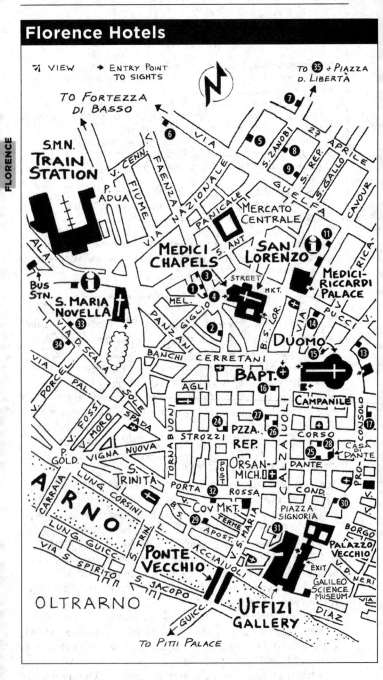

Florence Hotels

① Hotel Accademia
② Hotel Centrale
③ Katti House & Soggiorno Annamaria
④ Hotel Lorena
⑤ Galileo Hotel
⑥ Hotel Il Bargellino
⑦ Hotel Enza
⑧ Casa Rabatti
⑨ Soggiorno Magliani
⑩ Hotel Loggiato dei Serviti
⑪ Hotel Dei Macchiaioli & Hotel Europa
⑫ To Athenaeum Personal Hotel
⑬ Palazzo Niccolini al Duomo
⑭ Residenza dei Pucci
⑮ Hotel Duomo
⑯ Soggiorno Battistero
⑰ La Residenza del Proconsolo B&B
⑱ Hotel Morandi alla Crocetta
⑲ Panella's Residence
⑳ Residenza il Villino
㉑ B&B Il Bargello
㉒ Hotel Cardinal of Florence &
   Oblate Sisters of the Assumption
㉓ Hotel Dalí
㉔ Hotel Pendini
㉕ B&B Dei Mori
㉖ Hotel Axial & Hotel Maxim
㉗ Residenzia Giotto B&B
㉘ Albergo Firenze
㉙ Hotel Torre Guelfa &
   Hotel Alessandra
㉚ In Piazza della Signoria B&B
㉛ Relais Ufizzi
㉜ Hotel Davanzati
㉝ Hotel Alba Palace
㉞ Bellevue House
㉟ To Villa Camerata & Hostel 7 Santi

who keep their 15 rooms spotless, inviting, and well-maintained. While both offer equal comfort, Soggiorno Annamaria has a more historic setting, with frescoed ceilings, unique tiles, timbered beams, and quieter rooms (Db-€70-100, air-con, Internet access and Wi-Fi, Via Faenza 21, tel. & fax 055-213-410, www.kattihouse .com, info@kattihouse.com).

$ **Hotel Lorena,** just across from the Medici Chapels, has 19 rooms (six of which share a bathroom) and a tiny, cramped lobby. Though it's a bit like a youth hostel, it's cheap and conveniently located. Roberto speaks little English, but seems eager to please (Sb-€40, D-€55, Db-€65, Tb-€90, air-con, Wi-Fi, curfew from 2:00 in the morning to 7:00, Via Faenza 1, tel. 055-282-785, fax 055-288-300, www.hotellorena.com, info@hotellorena.com).

North of the Duomo
North of the Mercato Centrale
After dark, this neighborhood can feel a little sketchy, but I've never heard of anyone running into harm here. It's a short walk from the train station and an easy stroll to all the sightseeing action. Plenty of good budget restaurants and markets are nearby.

$$ **Galileo Hotel,** a classy business hotel of 31 rooms, is run with familial warmth (Db-€130, Tb-€150, ask for Rick Steves discount when you book direct, quadruple-pane windows effectively shut out street noise, Wi-Fi, Via Nazionale 22a, tel. 055-496-645, fax 055-496-447, www.galileohotel.it, info@galileohotel.it, Rhuna).

$ **Hotel Il Bargellino,** run by Bostonian Carmel and her Italian husband Pino, is a bit farther out and consequently feels like it's in a residential neighborhood. They rent 10 summery rooms decorated with funky antique furniture and Pino's modern paintings. Guests enjoy relaxing with Carmel and Leopoldo the parrot on the big, breezy momentum-slowing terrace adorned with lemon shrubs (S-€45, D-€80, Db-€90, extra bed-€25, no breakfast, Wi-Fi, north of the train station at Via Guelfa 87, tel. & fax 055-238-2658, www.ilbargellino.com, carmel@ilbargellino .com).

$ **Hotel Enza** rents 19 relaxing rooms (Sb-€55, Db-€80, show this book and ask for best Rick Steves price, extra bed-€20, optional €5 breakfast by request only, air-con, Internet access and Wi-Fi, Via San Zanobi 45 black, tel. 055-490-990, fax 055-473-672, www.hotelenza.it, info@hotelenza.it, Diana).

$ **Casa Rabatti** is the ultimate if you always wanted to have a Florentine mama. Its four simple, clean rooms are run with warmth by Marcella. This is a great place to practice your Italian, since Marcella loves to chat and speaks minimal English. Seeing nearly two decades of my family Christmas cards on the walls,

I'm reminded of how long she has been keeping budget travelers happy (D-€50, Db-€60, €25 extra per bed in shared quad or quint, show this book and ask for best Rick Steves price, cash only but secure reservation with credit card, no breakfast, fans available, 5 blocks from station at Via San Zanobi 48 black, tel. 055-212-393, casarabatti@inwind.it).

If Marcella's booked, she'll put you up in her daughter's place nearby, at Via Nazionale 20 (five big, airy family-friendly rooms; €25/person, fans, no breakfast, closer to the station). While daughter Patrizia works, her mom runs the place. Getting bumped to Patrizia's gives you slightly more comfort and slightly less personality...certainly not a net negative.

$ Soggiorno Magliani is central and humble, with six no-frills rooms (sharing two baths) that feel and smell like a great-grandmother's home. It's run by the friendly duo Vincenza and her English-speaking daughter Cristina, and the price is right (S-€36, D-€46, T-€63, cash only but secure reservation with credit card, no breakfast, near Via Guelfa at Via Santa Reparata 1, tel. 055-287-378, hotel-magliani@libero.it).

Between the Duomo and the Accademia

$$$ Hotel Loggiato dei Serviti, at the most prestigious address in Florence on the most Renaissance square in town, gives you Old World romance with hair dryers. Stone stairways lead you under open-beam ceilings through this 16th-century monastery's monumental public rooms—it's so artful, you'll be snapping photos everywhere. The 33 cells—with air-conditioning, TVs, mini-bars, and telephones—would be unrecognizable to their original inhabitants. The hotel staff is both professional and warm (Sb-€120, Db-€160-170, superior Db-€180, family suites from €263, ask for Rick Steves rate when you book, elevator, Piazza S.S. Annunziata 3, tel. 055-289-592, fax 055-289-595, www.loggiato deiservitihotel.it, info@loggiatodeiservitihotel.it, Fabio, Chiara, and Simonetta). When full, they rent five spacious and sophisticated rooms in a 17th-century annex a block away. While it lacks the monastic mystique, the annex rooms are bigger, gorgeous, and cost the same.

$$$ Hotel Dei Macchiaioli, which opened in 2010, is managed by the same friendly team as the recommended Hotel Accademia. With 15 rooms, the hotel is located in a restored *palazzo* owned for generations by a noble Florentine family. You'll eat breakfast under original frescoed ceilings while enjoying modern comforts (Sb-€100, Db-€180, Tb-€220, ask for the Rick Steves discount if you book direct, air-con, Wi-Fi, Via Cavour 21, tel. 055-213-154, www.hoteldeimacchiaioli.com, info@hoteldei macchiaioli.com, helpful Tea).

$$ Hotel Europa, run by cheery Miriam, Roberto, and daughter Priscilla since 1970, has a welcoming atmosphere. The breakfast room is spacious, and some of the 20 rooms have views of the Duomo (Sb-€89, Db-€140, Tb-€165, cash discount, elevator, Wi-Fi, Via Cavour 14, tel. 055-239-6715, fax 055-268-984, www.webhoteleuropa.com, firenze@webhoteleuropa.com)

$$ Athenaeum Personal Hotel is a classy, ultramodern place with 60 rooms located a block from the Accademia and a 10-minute walk from the Duomo. It has a comfy lounge, modern art on the walls, and a spacious courtyard with a miniature waterfall where you can dine al fresco (Sb-€128, Db-€150, Tb-€180, check website for seasonal price variations, elevator, Wi-Fi, Via Cavour 88, tel. 055-589-456, fax 055-561-408, www.hotelathenaeum florence.com, info@hotelathenaeum.com).

Near the Duomo

All of these places are within a block of Florence's biggest church and main landmark.

$$$ Palazzo Niccolini al Duomo, one of five elite Historic Residence Hotels in Florence, is run by Niccolini da Camugliano. The lounge is palatial (free chamomile tea served in the evenings), and the 12 rooms are big and splendid, with original 16th-century frescoes. If you have the money and want a Florentine palace to call home, this is a very good bet, located just one block from the Duomo (Db-€150 and up, fancier and pricier suites with DVD players, ask for the Rick Steves discount when you book, check online to choose a room and consider last-minute deals, Via dei Servi 2, tel. 055-282-412, fax 055-290-979, www.niccolinidome palace.com, info@niccolinidomepalace.com).

$$ Residenza dei Pucci rents 12 tastefully decorated rooms (each one different) spread over three floors. The decor is a mix of soothing earth tones and aristocratic furniture (Sb-€135, Db-€150, Tb-€170, Qb-€238, cash discount with this book, air-con, no elevator, reception open 9:00-20:00—let them know if you'll arrive late, Via dei Pucci 9, tel. 055-281-886, fax 055-264-314, www .residenzadeipucci.com, residenzadeipucci@residenzadeipucci .com, Mirella).

$$ Hotel Duomo, big and venerable, rents 24 rooms four floors up. The Duomo looms like a monster outside the hotel's windows. The rooms, while pretty forgettable, are comfortable enough, and the location can't be beat (Db-€100-170, cash discount with this book, Internet access, Piazza del Duomo 1, tel. 055-219-922, www.hotelduomofirenze.it, info@hotelduomofirenze.it, Alberto).

$$ Soggiorno Battistero rents seven simple, airy rooms, most with great views, literally overlooking the Baptistery and the Duomo square. Choose a view or a quieter room in the back when you book by email. It's a pristine, fresh, and minimalist little place run by Italian Luca and his American wife Kelly, who makes the hotel particularly welcoming (Sb-€78, Db-€103, Tb-€140, Qb-€150, show this book and ask for best Rick Steves price, cash discount, breakfast served in room, air-con, Wi-Fi, Piazza San Giovanni 1, third floor—no elevator, tel. 055-295-143, fax 055-268-189, www.soggiornobattistero.it, info@soggiornobattistero.it).

$$ La Residenza del Proconsolo B&B, run by helpful Mariano, has five pleasantly appointed rooms a minute from the Duomo (three rooms have Duomo views). The place lacks public spaces, but the rooms are quite large—perfect for eating breakfast, which is served in your room (Sb-€90, Db-€140, Tb-€160, Wi-Fi, Via del Proconsolo 18n, tel. 055-264-5657, mobile 335-657-4840, www.proconsolo.com, info@proconsolo.com).

East of the Duomo

$$ Hotel Morandi alla Crocetta, a former convent, envelops you in a 16th-century cocoon. Located on a quiet street with 12 rooms, period furnishings, parquet floors, and wood-beamed ceilings, it takes you back a few centuries (Sb-€70-100, Db-€100-140, breakfast included if you book direct, air-con, a block off Piazza S.S. Annunziata at Via Laura 50, tel. 055-234-4747, fax 055-248-0954, www.hotelmorandi.it, welcome@hotelmorandi.it, well-run by Maurizio, Rolando, and Frank).

$$ Panella's Residence, once a convent and today part of owner Graziella's extensive home, is a classy B&B, with six chic and romantic rooms, antique furnishings, and historic architectural touches (Db-€140, superior Db-€165, more if paying by credit card, discounts for 3 or more nights, air-con, Wi-Fi, Via della Pergola 42, tel. 055-234-7202, fax 055-247-9669, www.panella residence.com, panella_residence@yahoo.it).

$$ Residenza il Villino, popular and friendly, aspires to offer a Florentine home. It has 10 rooms and a picturesque, peaceful little courtyard (small Db-€110, Db-€130, family suite that sleeps up to six—price upon request, discount with cash and this book, ask for special Rick Steves rates in low season, air-con, Internet access and Wi-Fi, just north of Via degli Alfani at Via della Pergola 53, tel. 055-200-1116, fax 055-200-1101, www.ilvillino.it, info@il villino.it, Sergio, Elisabetta, and son Lorenzo).

$ B&B Il Bargello is a home away from home, run by friendly and helpful Canadian expat Gabriella. Hike up three long flights to reach six smart, relaxing rooms. Gabriella offers a cozy communal living room, kitchen access, book exchange, and an inviting rooftop terrace with close-up views of Florence's towers (Db-€100, ask for Rick Steves rate when you book direct and pay cash, air-con, Internet access and Wi-Fi, 20 yards off Via

Proconsolo at Via de' Pandolfini 33 black, tel. 055-215-330, mobile 339-175-3110, www.firenze-bedandbreakfast.it, info@firenze-bed andbreakfast.it).

$ Hotel Cardinal of Florence is a third-floor walk-up with 17 new, tidy, and sun-splashed rooms overlooking either a silent courtyard (many with views of Brunelleschi's dome) or quiet street. Relax and enjoy Florence's rooftops from the sun terrace (Sb-€60, Db-€95, ask for best Rick Steves rate, cash discount, €15/day limited parking—request when you reserve, Borgo Pinti 5, tel. 055-234-0780, fax 055-234-3389, www.hotelcardinalofflorence.com, info@hotelcardinalofflorence.com, Mauro and Ida).

$ Hotel Dalí has 10 decent, basic rooms with new baths in a nice location for a great price. Samanta and Marco run this guest house with a charming passion; they offer no Wi-Fi "because it burns your brains" (S-€40, D-€65, Db-€80, extra bed-€25, no breakfast, fans but no air-con, request quiet room when you book, free parking, 2 blocks behind the Duomo at Via dell'Oriuolo 17, tel. & fax 055-234-0706, hoteldali@tin.it).

$ Oblate Sisters of the Assumption run an institutional 30-room hotel in a Renaissance building with a dreamy garden, great public spaces, appropriately simple rooms, and a quiet, prayerful ambience (S-€40, Db-€80, Tb-€120, Qb-€160, cash only, single beds only, optional breakfast-€5, air-con, elevator, €10/day limited parking—request when you book, Borgo Pinti 15, tel. 055-248-0582, fax 055-234-6291, sroblateborgopinti@virgilio.it, sisters are likely to speak French but not English—Sister Theresa is very helpful).

Between the Duomo and Piazza della Signoria

These are the most central of my accommodations recommendations (and therefore a little overpriced). They're worth the extra cost for many, but given Florence's walkable core, nearly every hotel can be considered central.

$$ Hotel Pendini, with three tarnished stars, fills the top floor of a grand building constructed to celebrate Italian unification in the late 19th century. It overlooks Piazza della Repubblica, and as you walk into the lobby, you feel as if you are walking back in time. Its 40 rooms are well worn and pretty stodgy, though a few have been redecorated recently. The place is memorable—and a good value (Db-€89-155, Internet access and Wi-Fi, Via Strozzi 2, tel. 055-211-170, www.hotelpendini.it, info@hotelpendini.it).

$$ B&B Dei Mori, a peaceful haven, has five newly remodeled rooms ideally located on a quiet pedestrian street near the Casa di Dante. Accommodating hostess Suzanne offers lots of tips on dining and sightseeing in Florence (D-€100, Db-€120, discount for my readers—ask when you book, air-con €5 extra, reception

open 8:00-19:00, Via Dante Alighieri 12, tel. 055-211-438, www
.deimori.com, deimori@bnb.it).

$$ Hotel Axial (run by the same folks who own Hotel
Maxim—see next listing) offers 14 soundproofed, tidy, and plain
rooms on Florence's main pedestrian drag (Sb-€89-109, Db-€139,
book on their website for best price, cash discount, check for web-
site promotions, air-con, elevator, Wi-Fi, Via de' Calzaiuoli 11,
tel. 055-218-984, fax 055-211-733, www.hotelaxial.it, info@hotel
axial.it).

$$ Hotel Maxim, right on Via de' Calzaiuoli, is a big and
institutional-feeling place warmly run by a family team: father
Paolo, son Nicola, and daughter Chiara. Its halls are narrow, but
the 26 basic rooms are comfortable and well-maintained (Sb-€75,
Db-€110, Tb-€138, Qb-€155, discount with cash and this book,
air-con, elevator, Internet access and Wi-Fi, Via de' Calzaiuoli
11, tel. 055-217-474, fax 055-283-729, www.hotelmaximfirenze.it,
reservation@hotelmaximfirenze.it).

$$ Residenzia Giotto B&B offers you the chance to stay on
Florence's upscale shopping drag, Via Roma. Occupying the top
floor of a 19th-century building, this place has six bright rooms
and a terrace with knockout views of the Duomo's tower (Sb-€90,
Db-€140, extra bed €25, discount for stays of more than 3 nights,
elevator, Via Roma 6, tel. 055-214-593, fax 055-264-8568, www
.residenzagiotto.it, info@residenzagiotto.it, Giorgio speaks good
English). Let them know your arrival time in advance.

$$ Albergo Firenze, a big, efficient place, offers 58 basic
rooms in a central locale two blocks behind the Duomo. It's
institutional and often busy with big groups (Sb-€84, Db-€114,
Tb-€147 but these are the hotel's wishful-thinking prices—ask for
a discount, air-con, elevator, noisy, at Piazza Donati 4 across from
Via del Corso 8, tel. 055-214-203, fax 055-212-370, www.albergo
firenze.net, info@albergofirenze.net, Enrico).

Near Piazza della Signoria and Ponte Vecchio

$$$ Hotel Torre Guelfa is topped by a fun medieval tower with
a panoramic rooftop terrace and a huge living room. Its 24 pricey
rooms vary wildly in size. Room 15, with a private terrace (€245), is
worth reserving several months in advance (standard Db-€170-190,
Db junior suite-€235, family deals, cash discount, air-con, elevator,
a couple blocks northwest of Ponte Vecchio, Borgo S.S. Apostoli
8, tel. 055-239-6338, fax 055-239-8577, www.hoteltorreguelfa.com,
info@hoteltorreguelfa.com, Sabina, Giancarlo, and Sandro).

$$$ In Piazza della Signoria B&B, overlooking Piazza della
Signoria, is peaceful, refined, and homey at the same time. Fit for
a honeymoon, the 10 rooms come with all the special touches and
little extras you'd expect in a top-end American B&B—such as

being served fresh-squeezed orange juice for breakfast (viewless Db-€220, view Db-€250, Tb-€280, ask for discount when you book direct with this book, family apartments, lavish bathrooms, air-con, tiny elevator, Internet access and Wi-Fi, Via dei Magazzini 2, tel. 055-239-9546, mobile 348-321-0565, fax 055-267-6616, www.inpiazzadellasignoria.com, info@inpiazzadellasignoria.com, Sonia and Alessandro).

$$$ Relais Uffizi is a peaceful little gem, with 15 classy rooms tucked away down a tiny alleyway off Piazza della Signoria. The lounge has a huge window overlooking the action in the square below (Sb-€140, Db-€180, Tb-€220, buffet breakfast, elevator, Wi-Fi, Chiasso de Baroncelli/Chiasso del Buco 16, tel. 055-267-6239, fax 055-265-7909, www.relaisuffizi.it, info@relaisuffizi.it, charming Alessandro).

$$$ Hotel Davanzati, bright and shiny with artistic touches, has 19 cheerful rooms with all the comforts. The place is a family affair, thoughtfully run by friendly Tommaso and father Fabrizio, who offer drinks and snacks each evening at their candlelit happy hour (Sb-€122, Db-€189, Tb-€259, show this book and ask for best Rick Steves rate, prices soft off-season, cash discount; PlayStation 2, DVD player, and laptop with free Wi-Fi in every room; air-con, next to Piazza Davanzati at Via Porta Rossa 5, tel. 055-286-666, fax 055-265-8252, www.hoteldavanzati.it, info @hoteldavanzati.it).

$$ Hotel Alessandra is 16th-century, tranquil, and sprawling, with 27 big, tasteful rooms (S-€67, Sb-€110, D-€110, Db-€150, Tb-€195, Qb-€215, cash discount, air-con, Internet access and Wi-Fi, Borgo S.S. Apostoli 17, tel. 055-283-438, fax 055-210-619, www.hotelalessandra.com, info@hotelalessandra.com, Anna and son Andrea).

Near the Train Station

As with any big Italian city, the area around the train station is a magnet for hardworking pickpockets on the alert for lost, vulnerable tourists with bulging money belts hanging out of their khakis.

$$ Hotel Alba Palace is a three-star hotel with a welcoming reception, cushy red leather sofas, and a piano in the lounge. Breakfast is served in a glass-roofed patio area, and the rooms have been tastefully redone in traditional Florentine style (Sb-€90, Db-€150, Tb-€170, check website for price fluctuations, elevator, Wi-Fi, Via della Scala 22/38 red, tel. 055-282-610, fax 055-288-358, www.hotelalbafirenze.it, info@hotelalbafirenze.it).

$ Bellevue House is a third-floor (no elevator) oasis of tranquility, with six spacious rooms flanking a long mellow-yellow lobby. It's a peaceful time warp thoughtfully run by Rosanna and Antonio di Grazia (Db-€70-90, family deals, cash discount, optional €3 breakfast in street-level bar, Via della Scala 21, tel. 055-260-8932, mobile 333-612-5973, fax 055-265-5315, www.belle vuehouse.it, info@bellevuehouse.it).

Hostels Away from the Center

These two hostels, northeast of the downtown, are a bus ride from the action. A far more central hostel is in Oltrarno (see end of next section).

$ Villa Camerata, classy for an IYHF hostel, is in a pretty villa three miles northeast of the train station, on the outskirts of Florence (€20/bed with breakfast, 4- to 6-bed rooms, must have hostel membership card or pay additional €3/night, self-serve laundry; take bus #17 from the train station to Salviatino stop; Via Righi 2, tel. 055-601-451, fax 055-610-300, www.aighostels.com, firenze@aighostels.com).

$ Hostel 7 Santi calls itself a "travelers' haven." It fills a former convent, but you'll feel like you're in an old school. Still, it offers some of the best cheap beds in town; is friendly to older travelers; and comes with the services you'd expect in a big, modern hostel, including free Wi-Fi and a self-serve laundry. It's in a more residential neighborhood near the Campo di Marte stadium, about a 10-minute bus ride from the center (200 beds in 60 rooms, mostly 4- or 6-bed dorms with a floor of doubles and triples, €20/dorm bed, Sb-€40, Ds-€60, Db-€70; includes breakfast, sheets, and towels; no curfew; from the station, take bus #17 direction: Campo di Marte to bus stop Chiesa dei Sette Santi; Viale dei Mille 11, tel. 055-504-8452, www.7santi.com, info@7santi.com).

South of the Arno River, in the Oltrarno

Across the river in the Oltrarno area, between the Pitti Palace and Ponte Vecchio, you'll still find small, traditional crafts shops, neighborly piazzas, and family eateries. The following places are an easy walk from Ponte Vecchio. Only the first one is a real hotel—the rest are a ragtag gang of budget alternatives.

$$$ Hotel Silla is a classic three-star hotel with 35 cheery, spacious, pastel, and modern rooms. It faces the river and overlooks a park opposite the Santa Croce Church (Db-€180, Tb-€220, ask for Rick Steves rate when you book, air-con, elevator, Wi-Fi, Via dei Renai 5, tel. 055-234-2888, fax 055-234-1437, www.hotelsilla.it, hotelsilla@hotelsilla.it, Laura, Chiara, Massimo, and Stefano).

$ Istituto Gould is a Protestant Church–run place with 40 clean and spartan rooms that have twin beds and modern facilities (Sb-€45, Db-€56-68, Tb-€75, Qb-€92, breakfast €5 extra, quieter rooms in back, no air-con but rooms have fans, Via dei Serragli 49, tel. 055-212-576, fax 055-280-274, www.istitutogould.it, foresteria firenze@diaconiavaldese.org). You must arrive when the office is

Oltrarno Hotels

● To Hotel Silla
● Istituto Gould
● Soggiorno Alessandra
● Casa Santo Nome di Gesù
● Ostello Santa Monaca

open (Mon-Fri 8:45-13:00 & 15:00-19:30, Sat 9:00-13:30 & 14:30-18:00, no check-in Sun or holidays).

$ Soggiorno Alessandra has five bright, comfy, and small-ish rooms. Because of its double-paned windows, you'll hardly notice the traffic noise (D-€58-73, Db-€78, Tb-€98, Qb-€128, ask about discount with 2-night stay, air-con-€8, just past the Carraia Bridge at Via Borgo San Frediano 6, tel. 055-290-424, fax 055-218-464, www.soggiornoalessandra.it, info@soggiornoalessandra .it, Alessandra).

$ Casa Santo Nome di Gesù is a grand 29-room convent whose sisters—Franciscan Missionaries of Mary—are thankful to rent rooms to tourists. Staying in this 15th-century palace, you'll be immersed in the tranquil atmosphere created by a huge, peaceful garden, generous and prayerful public spaces, and smiling nuns (D-€70, Db-€85, elevator, no air-con but rooms have fans, twin beds only, memorable convent-like breakfast room, strict 23:29 curfew, Piazza del Carmine 21, tel. 055-213-856, fax 055-281-835, www.fmmfirenze.it, info@fmmfirenze.it).

Hostel: **$ Ostello Santa Monaca,** a long block south of the Brancacci Chapel, is well run and attracts a young backpacking crowd (€15-24/bed with sheets, 2- to 20-bed dorms, 10:00-14:00 lock-out, 2:00 in the morning curfew, free Internet access and Wi-Fi, self-serve laundry, kitchen, Via Santa Monaca 6—see map on next page, tel. 055-268-338, fax 055-280-185, www.ostellodi firenze.it, info@ostello.it).

Eating in Florence

To save money and time for sights, keep lunches fast and simple, eating in one of the countless pizzerias and self-service cafeterias (or picnicking your way though the Mercato Centrale).

For good sit-down meals, consider the following listings. Remember, restaurateurs like to serve what's fresh. If you're into flavor, go for the seasonal best bets—featured in the *piatti del giorno* ("special of the day") section of menus.

For dessert, it's gelato (see the sidebar on pages 1112-1113).

North of the Arno River
Near the Train Station

Trattoria al Trebbio serves traditional food with simple Florentine elegance in its candlelit interior. Tables spill out onto a romantic little square—an oasis of Roman Trastevere-like charm (€8 pastas, €13 *secondi,* daily 12:00-15:00 & 19:15-23:00, reserve for outdoor seating, half a block off Piazza Santa Maria Novella at Via delle Belle Donne 47, tel. 055-287-089, Antonio).

Trattoria "da Giorgio" is a family-style diner serving up piping-hot, delicious home cooking to happy locals and tourists alike. Their three-course fixed-price meal is a great value for €12, including water and a drink. Choose from among the daily specials or the regular menu (Mon-Sat 12:00-14:30 & 18:00-22:00, closed Sun, Via Palazzuolo 100 red, tel. 055-284-302, Silvano).

Osteria Belle Donne makes you feel like you're eating dinner in a crowded terrarium piled high with decorative knickknacks. Old-fashioned Tuscan food is served on tight tables, with a few spilling onto a tiny deck outside. They take no reservations and tend to steamroll tourists; arrive early or wait (€10 pastas, €12 *secondi,* daily 12:00-15:00 & 19:00-23:00, Via delle Belle Donne 16 red, tel. 055-238-2609, run by sprightly Giacinto).

Trattoria Marione serves sincerely home-cooked–style meals to a mixed group of tourists and Florentines in a happy, crowded, food-loving, and steamy ambience (€8 pastas, €10 *secondi,* daily

Florence Restaurants

FLORENCE

1. Trattoria al Trebbio
2. Trattoria "da Giorgio"
3. Osteria Belle Donne
4. Trattoria Marione
5. Trattoria Sostanza-Troia
6. Trattoria 13 Gobbi
7. Trattoria Zà-Zà & Trattoria Mario's
8. Trattoria la Burrasca
9. Osteria la Congrega
10. Trattoria Lo Stracotto
11. Osteria Vineria i'Brincello
12. Trattoria Nerone Pizzeria
13. Mercato Centrale & Nerbone in the Market
14. Casa del Vino
15. Il Pirata
16. Pasticceria Robiglio
17. La Mescita Fiaschetteria
18. Il Centro Supermercati
19. Self-Service Rist. Leonardo
20. The Oil Shoppe
21. Rivoire Café
22. Frescobaldi Rist. & Wine Bar
23. Ristorante Paoli & Cantinetta dei Verrazzano
24. Trattoria Nella
25. Osteria Vini e Vecchi Sapori
26. I Fratellini
27. L'Antico Trippaio
28. 'Ino Bottega di Alimentari e Vini
29. Trattoria Icche C'è C'è
30. Ristorante del Fagioli
31. Boccadama Enoteca Rist.
32. Trattoria Anita
33. Gelateria Grom
34. Gelateria Carrozze
35. Gelateria Carabè
36. Festival del Gelato
37. Perchè No! Gelateria
38. Vivoli's Gelateria
39. Gelateria de' Neri
40. La Congrega Lounge Bar

12:00-17:30 & 19:00-23:00, Via della Spada 27 red, tel. 055-214-756, Fabio).

Trattoria Sostanza-Troia, characteristic and well established, is famous for its beef. Hearty steaks and pastas are splittable. Whirling ceiling fans and walls strewn with old photos evoke earlier times, while the artichoke pies remind locals of Grandma's cooking. Crowded, shared tables with paper tablecloths give this place a bistro feel. They offer two dinner seatings, at 19:30 and 21:00, which require reservations (dinners for about €30 plus wine, cash only, lunch Mon-Sat 12:30-14:00, closed Sun, closed Sat in off-season, Via del Porcellana 25 red, tel. 055-212-691).

Trattoria 13 Gobbi ("13 Hunchbacks") is a trendy favorite, glowing with candles around a tiny garden. Romantic in front and kid-friendly in back, it serves beautifully presented Tuscan food on big, fancy plates to a mostly tourist crowd (€8.50 pastas, €15 *secondi,* daily 12:00-15:00 & 19:30-23:00, Via del Porcellana 9 red, tel. 055-284-015, Enrico).

Near the Mercato Centrale

The following market-neighborhood eateries are distinct but within a hundred yards of each other. Scout around and choose your favorite.

Dining near the Mercato Centrale

Trattoria Zà-Zà is a fun, characteristic, high-energy place facing the Mercato Centrale. It's a family-friendly festival of standard Tuscan dishes such as *ribollita* and *bistecca alla fiorentina,* plus a variety of big, splittable salads. Florentines lament the invasion of tourists, but everyone's happy, and the food is still great. Arrive early or make a reservation, especially for the wonderful outdoor piazza seating. Understand your itemized bill (as they are reportedly math-challenged), and don't mistake their outside seating with the neighboring restaurant's (daily 11:00-23:00, Piazza del Mercato Centrale 26 red, tel. 055-215-411).

Trattoria la Burrasca is Flintstone-chic. Friendly duo Elio and Simone offer a limited menu with daily specials of rib-stickin' Tuscan home cooking. It's small—10 tables—and often filled with my readers. If Archie Bunker were Italian, he'd eat at this trattoria for special nights out (€7 pastas, €10 *secondi,* no cover or service charge, Tue-Sun 12:00-15:30 & 19:00-23:00, closed Mon, Via Panicale 6, north corner of Mercato Centrale, tel. 055-215-827).

Osteria la Congrega brags that it's "a Tuscan wine bar designed to help you lose track of time." In a fresh, imaginative, two-level setting, chef-owner Mahyar takes pride in his fun, easy menu, which features modern Tuscan cuisine, top-notch meat, and seasonal produce. He offers quality vegetarian dishes, creative

FLORENCE

salads, and an inexpensive but excellent house wine. There are just 10 tables, and reservations are required for dinner (€8 pastas, €12 nightly specials, Mon-Sat 12:00-15:00 & 19:00-23:00, closed Sun, a block from Mercato Centrale, Via Panicale 43 red, tel. 055-264-5027). Mahyar offers fine wines by the glass (see list on blackboard) and occasional live jazz. Between meals, he's busy teaching cooking classes here (www.osterialacongrega.it).

Trattoria Lo Stracotto is a stylish new truffle-colored eatery just steps away from the Medici Chapels. It's run with enthusiasm and flair by two cousins, who serve up tasty traditional dishes such as *bistecca alla fiorentina* and *ribollita* (based on grandfather's recipe), and good chocolate soufflé. Enjoy the candlelit ambience and soft music as you sit either in the dining room or out on the terrace (€7 pastas, €10 *secondi*, daily 11:00-23:00, Piazza Madonna degli Aldobrandi 16/17, tel. 055-230-2062, Francesco and Tomasso).

Osteria Vineria i'Brincello—a bright, happy no-frills diner with lots of spirit and friendly service—is great for a simple lunch. Notice the list of Tuscan daily specials on the blackboard hanging from the ceiling (€7 pastas, daily 12:00-15:00 & 19:00-23:00, corner of Via Nazionale and Via Chiara at Via Nazionale 110 red, tel. 055-282-645, Shahid cooks while Claudia serves).

Trattoria Nerone Pizzeria serves up cheap, hearty Tuscan dishes and decent pizzas. The lively, flamboyantly outfitted space (once the garden courtyard of a convent) feels like a good but kitschy American-Italian chain restaurant (€7 pizzas, €7 pastas, €10 *secondi*, daily 12:00-15:00 & 18:30-23:00, just north of Via Nazionale at Via Faenza 95 red, tel. 055-291-217, Tulio).

Eating Cheaply in or near the Mercato Centrale

Notice that all of these eateries, except the last one, are open only for lunch.

Mercato Centrale (Central Market) is great for an ad-lib lunch. It offers colorful piles of picnic produce, people-watching, and rustic sandwiches (Mon-Sat 7:00-14:00, Sat in winter until 17:00, closed Sun, a block north of San Lorenzo street market). Meat, fish, and cheese are sold on the ground level, with fruit and veggies mostly upstairs. The thriving ground-level eateries within the market (such as Nerbone, described next) serve some of the cheapest hot meals in town. The fancy deli, Perini, is famous for its quality products and generous free samples. Buy a picnic of fresh mozzarella cheese, olives, fruit, and crunchy bread to munch on the steps of the nearby Church of San Lorenzo, overlooking the bustling street market.

Nerbone in the Market is a venerable café and the best place for a sit-down meal within Mercato Centrale. Join the shoppers and workers who crowd up to the bar to grab their €5 plates—tripe is very big here—and then find an informal table to eat at nearby. Of the several cheap market diners, this feels the most authentic (lunch only, cash only, inside Mercato Centrale on the side closest to the Church of San Lorenzo, mobile 339-648-0251).

Trattoria Mario's, around the corner from Trattoria Zà-Zà (listed earlier), has been serving hearty lunches to marketgoers since 1953 (Fabio and Romeo are the latest generation). Their simple formula: bustling service, old-fashioned good value, a lunch-only fixed-price meal, and shared tables. It's *cucina casalinga*—home cooking *con brio*. This place is extremely popular, and their best dishes often sell out first, so go early. If there's a line, put your name on the list (€5 pastas, €8 *secondi*, cash only, Mon-Sat 12:00-15:30, closed Sun and Aug, no reservations, Via Rosina 2, tel. 055-218-550).

Casa del Vino, Florence's oldest operating wine shop, offers glasses of wine from among 25 open bottles. Owner Gianni, whose family has owned the Casa for more than 70 years, is a class act. Gianni's *carta dei panini* lists many delightful €3.50 sandwiches (the crostini are notable). Some opened bottles behind the counter are marked with prices for wine by the glass; otherwise, see the list tacked to the bar. During busy times, it's a mob scene. You'll eat standing outside, with workers on a quick lunch break (Mon-Sat 9:30-17:00, closed Sat in summer and Sun year-round, hidden behind stalls of San Lorenzo Market at Via dell'Ariento 16 red, tel. 055-215-609).

Il Pirata, a deli and rotisserie, puts out a €7.50 all-you-can-eat buffet each evening (18:00-22:00, includes water). They offer budget travelers an array of homemade Italian dishes and roasted meats for takeout or to dine in at the counter. Pick up a plastic plate, fill it, get it microwaved if you like, grab a stool, and chow down (closed Sun, 2 blocks from the Accademia at Via de' Ginori 56 red, tel. 055-218-625). You don't want to linger here (and the owner is a bit of a smart aleck)—but at least you'll fill your stomach.

Budget Lunches Between the Duomo and the Accademia

Pasticceria Robiglio, a smart little café, opens up its stately dining area and sets out a few tables on the sidewalk for lunch on workdays. They have a small menu of daily pasta and *secondi* specials, and seem determined to do things like they did in the elegant pre-tourism days (generous €8 plates, a great €7.50 *niçoise*-like "fantasy salad," pretty pastries, good wines by the glass, smiling service, daily 12:00-15:00, longer hours as a café, a block toward the Duomo off Piazza S.S. Annunziata at Via dei Servi 112 red, tel. 055-212-784). Before you leave, be tempted by their pastries—famous among Florentines.

La Mescita Fiaschetteria is a characteristic hole-in-the-wall just around the corner from *David*—but a world away from all the tourism. It's where locals and students enjoy daily pasta specials and hearty sandwiches with good €1 house wine. You can trust Mirco—just point to what looks good (such as the €5 pasta plate), and you'll soon be eating well and inexpensively. The place can either be mobbed by students or in a peaceful time warp, depending on when you stop by (Mon-Sat 12:00-16:00, closed Sun, Via degli Alfani 70 red, mobile 347-795-1604).

Picnic on the Ultimate Renaissance Square: Il Centro Supermercati, a handy supermarket across from the Accademia *(David)*, happily makes sandwiches to your specs (Mon-Sat 8:00-20:00, Sun 10:00-19:00, Via Ricasoli 109). Choose your fresh bread and tasty meat and cheese (assembled and sold by the weight); embellish with some veggies, milk, yogurt, or juice; and hike around the block to Piazza S.S. Annunziata, the first Renaissance square in Florence. There's a fountain for washing fruit on the square. Grab a stony seat anywhere you like, and savor one of my favorite cheap Florence eating experiences. (Or, drop by either of the two places listed earlier for a sandwich and juice to go.)

Fast and Cheap near the Duomo

Self-Service Ristorante Leonardo is inexpensive, air-conditioned, quick, and handy. Eating here, you'll get the sense that they're passionate about the quality of their food. Stefano and Luciano (like Pavarotti) run the place with enthusiasm, and put out free pitchers of tap water. It's just a block from the Duomo, southwest of the Baptistery (tasty €4 pastas, €5 main courses, Sun-Fri 11:45-14:45 & 18:45-21:45, closed Sat, upstairs at Via Pecori 11, tel. 055-284-446).

The Oil Shoppe cobbles together huge gourmet hot and cold sub sandwiches *all'Italiana* from creative ingredients (€3.50). You can get a sandwich plus fries and water (€5), or build your own salad and pair it with a homemade soup of the day for a fast, cheap, and hearty lunch. Eat at the skinny counter or take your food to go (generally Mon-Fri 10:30-18:00 or until the bread runs out, closed Sat-Sun, 2 long blocks east of the Duomo at Via S. Egidio 22 red, cheery Alberto runs the show).

Near Piazza della Signoria and Ponte Vecchio

Dining

Piazza della Signoria, the scenic square facing Palazzo Vecchio, is ringed by beautifully situated yet touristy eateries serving overpriced, bad-value, and probably microwaved food. If you're determined to eat on the square, have pizza at Ristorante il Cavallino or bar food from the Irish pub next door. The Piazza della Signoria's saving grace is **Rivoire** café, famous for its fancy desserts and thick hot chocolate. While obscenely expensive, it has the best view tables on the square (Tue-Sun 7:30-24:00, closed Mon, tel. 055-214-412).

Frescobaldi Ristorante and Wine Bar, the showcase of Italy's aristocratic wine family, is a good choice for a formal dinner in Florence. Candlelight reflects on glasses, and high-vaulted ceilings complement the sophisticated dishes and fine wines. They offer the same menu in three different dining areas: cozy interior, woody wine bar, and breezy terrace. If coming for dinner, make a reservation, dress up, and hit an ATM (€12 appetizers and pastas, €20 *secondi,* lunch salads, Tue-Sat 12:00-14:30 & 19:00-22:30, Mon 19:00-22:30, closed Sun and Aug, air-con, half a block north of Palazzo Vecchio at Via dei Magazzini 2-4 red, tel. 055-284-724). Don't let them railroad you into ordering things you don't want.

Ristorante Paoli dishes up wonderful traditional cuisine to loads of cheerful eaters being served by jolly little old men under a richly frescoed Gothic vault. Because of its fame and central location, it's filled mostly with tourists, but for a sophisticated, traditional Tuscan splurge meal, this is a fine choice. Salads are dramatically cut and mixed from a trolley right at your table. The walls are sweaty with memories that go back to 1824, and the service is flamboyant and fun-loving (but don't get taken—confirm prices). Woodrow Wilson slurped spaghetti here—his bust looks down on you as you eat (€11 pastas, €15 *secondi,* €25 tourist fixed-price meal, daily 12:00-15:00 & 19:00-23:00, reserve for dinner, between Piazza della Signoria and the Duomo at Via dei Tavolini 12 red, tel. 055-216-215).

Trattoria Nella serves good typical Tuscan cuisine at affordable prices. Twin brothers Federico and Lorenzo carry on their father Sergio's tradition of keeping their clientele well-fed and happy. Their ravioli with walnuts is a hit with regulars (daily specials, €9 pastas, €14 *secondi,* daily 12:00-15:00 & 19:00-22:00, reserve for dinner, 3 blocks northwest of Ponte Vecchio, Via delle Terme 19 red, tel. 055-218-925).

Cheap and Simple near Piazza della Signoria

Cantinetta dei Verrazzano, a long-established bakery-café-wine bar, serves delightful sandwich plates in an old-time setting. Their *specialità Verrazzano* is a fine plate of four little crostini (like mini-bruschetta) proudly featuring different breads, cheeses, and meats from the Chianti region (€7.50). The *tagliere di focacce,* a sampler plate of mini-focaccia sandwiches, is also fun (price depends on quantity). Add a glass of Chianti to either of these dishes to make a fine light meal. Office workers pop in for a quick lunch, and it's traditional to share tables (Mon-Sat 8:00-21:00, closed Sun, just off Via de' Calzaiuoli on a side street across from Orsanmichele

Church at Via dei Tavolini 18, tel. 055-268-590). They also have benches and tiny tables for eating at "take-out" prices. Simply step to the back and point to the hot *focacce* sandwich (€3) you'd like, order a drink at the bar, and take away your food or sit with locals and watch the action while you munch.

Osteria Vini e Vecchi Sapori, half a block north of Palazzo Vecchio, is a colorful 16-seat hole-in-the-wall serving Tuscan food, including plates of mixed crostini (€1 each—step right up and choose at the bar) and €10 daily specials. Be sure to try their raspberry *(lampone)* tiramisu. In the evening, it becomes a little restaurant with a fun, accessible menu of delicious €8 pastas and €10 *secondi* (Tue-Sat 12:30-15:00 & 19:30-22:00, Sun 12:30-15:00, closed Mon, reserve for dinner; facing the bronze equestrian statue in Piazza della Signoria, go behind its tail into the corner and to your left; Via dei Magazzini 3 red, tel. 055-293-045, run by Mario while wife Rosanna cooks and son Thomas serves).

I Fratellini is an informal little eatery where the "little brothers" have served peasants 29 different kinds of sandwiches and cheap glasses of Chianti wine (see list on wall) since 1875. Join the local crowd to order, then sit on a nearby curb or windowsill to munch, placing your glass on the wall rack before you leave (€4 for sandwich and wine, daily 9:00-20:00 or until the bread runs out, closed Sun in winter, 20 yards in front of Orsanmichele Church on Via dei Cimatori, tel. 055-239-6096). Be adventurous with the menu (easy-order by number). Consider *finocchiona* (a special Tuscan salami), *lardo di Colonnata* (lard aged in Carrara marble), and *cinghiale piccante* (spicy wild boar) sandwiches. Order the most expensive wine they're selling by the glass (Brunello for €4; bottles are labeled).

L'Antico Trippaio, an antique tripe stand, is a fixture in the town center (daily 9:00-20:00, on Via Dante Alighieri, mobile 339-742-5692). Cheap and authentic as can be, this is where Florentines come daily for €3.50 sandwiches *(panini)* featuring specialties like *trippa alla fiorentina* (tripe), *lampredotto* (cow's stomach), and a list of more appetizing sandwiches. Roberto offers a free plastic glass of his Chianti with each sandwich for travelers with this book. The best people-watching place to munch your sandwich is three blocks away, on Piazza della Signoria.

'Ino Bottega di Alimentari e Vini is a mod little shop filled with gifty edibles. Serena and Alessandro serve sandwiches and wine—you'll get your €5-7 sandwich on a napkin with an included glass of their wine of the day as you perch on a tiny stool. They can also make a fine *piatto misto* of cheeses and meats; just say how much you'd like to spend (daily 11:00-17:00, immediately behind Uffizi Gallery on Ponte Vecchio side, Via dei Georgofili 3 red, tel. 055-219-208).

FLORENCE

Gelato

Gelato is an edible art form. Italy's best ice cream is in Florence—one souvenir that can't break and won't clutter your luggage. But beware of scams at touristy joints on busy streets that turn a simple request for a cone into a €10 "tourist special" rip-off. To avoid this, survey the size options and be very clear in your order (for example, "a €3 cone").

A key to gelato appreciation is sampling liberally and choosing flavors that go well together. Ask, as Italians do, for *"Un assaggio, per favore?"* (A taste, please?; oon ah-SAH-joh pehr fah-VOH-ray) and *"Che si sposano bene?"* (What marries well?; kay see spoh-ZAH-noh BEN-ay).

Artiginale, nostra produzione, and *produzione propia* mean gelato is made on the premises; also, gelato displayed in covered metal tins (rather than white plastic) is more likely to be homemade. Gelato aficionados avoid colors that don't appear in nature—for fewer chemicals and real flavor, go for mellow hues (bright colors attract children). These places are open daily for long hours.

Near the Duomo: The recent favorite in town, **Grom** uses organic ingredients and seasonal fresh fruit, along with biodegradable spoons and tubs. Their traditional approach and quality give locals déjà vu, reminding them of the good old days and the ice cream of their childhood. Mario, who really cares, sees "gelato as cuisine," and adjusts the menu monthly to fit what's in season (daily 10:30-24:00, Via delle Oche 24 red). Their *liquirizia* (licorice) flavor is worth a sample.

Near Ponte Vecchio: **Gelateria Carrozze** is a longtime favorite (daily 11:00-20:00, until 1:00 in the morning in summer,

East of Piazza della Signoria

Trattoria Icche C'è C'è (EE-kay chay chay; dialect for "whatever there is, there is") is a small family-style restaurant where fun-loving Gino and his wife Mara serve quality local food, including a €13 three-course fixed-price meal (€6 pastas, €10 *secondi*, Tue-Sun 12:30-14:30 & 19:30-22:30, closed Mon and two weeks in Aug, midway between Bargello and river at Via Magalotti 11 red, tel. 055-216-589).

Ristorante del Fagioli is an enthusiastically run eatery where you feel the heritage. The dad, Gigi, commands the kitchen, while family members Antonio, Maurizio, and Simone keep the throngs of loyal customers returning. The cuisine: home-style bread soups, hearty steaks, and Florentine classics. Don't worry—while *fagioli* means "beans," that's the family name, not the extent of the menu (€9 pastas, €9 *secondi*, closed Sat-Sun, reserve for dinner, cash only, between Santa Croce Church and the Alle Grazie bridge at Corso dei Tintori 47, tel. 055-244-285).

on riverfront 30 yards from Ponte Vecchio toward the Uffizi at Piazza del Pesce 3).

Near the Accademia: A Sicilian choice on a tourist thoroughfare, **Gelateria Carabè** is particularly famous for its luscious *granite*—Italian ices made with fresh fruit. Antonio, whose family has made ice cream the Sicilian way for more than 100 years, can tell you why that's important (daily 11:00-20:00; from the Accademia, it's a block toward the Duomo at Via Ricasoli 60 red).

Near Orsanmichele Church: For gelato served in a brash, neon environment, it's **Festival del Gelato** or **Perchè No!,** both located just off the busy main pedestrian drag (Via de' Calzaiuoli). They serve a stunning array of brightly colored kid-pleasing flavors (Festival del Gelato is at Via del Corso 75; Perchè No! is at Via dei Tavolini 19).

Near the Church of Santa Croce: The venerable favorite, **Vivoli's** still serves great gelato—but it's more expensive and stingy in its servings. Before ordering, try a free sample of their rice flavor—*riso* (closed Mon, Aug, and Jan; opposite the Church of Santa Croce, go down Via Torta a block and turn right on Via Stinche). Locals flock to **Gelateria de' Neri** (Via de' Neri 26 red), also owned by Vivoli's.

Across the River: If you want an excuse to check out the little village-like neighborhood across the river from Santa Croce, enjoy a gelato at the tiny **Il Gelato di Filo** (named for Filippo and Lorenzo) at Via San Miniato 5 red, a few steps toward the river from Porta San Miniato. Gelato chef Edmir is proud of his fruity sorbet as well.

Boccadama Enoteca Ristorante is a stylish shabby-chic wine bistro serving creative Tuscan fare based on seasonal produce. Eat in the intimate candlelit dining room or at a few tables lining tranquil Piazza Santa Croce. Reservations are smart (€9 *primi*, €14 *secondi,* daily 11:00-16:00 & 18:30-24:00, on south side of Piazza Santa Croce at 25-26 red, tel. 055-243-640).

Trattoria Anita, midway between the Uffizi and Santa Croce, offers a good lunch special: three hearty Tuscan courses—pasta, *secondo,* and *contorno* (side dish)—for €8 (Mon-Sat 12:00-14:30 & 19:00-22:15, closed Sun, on the corner of Via Vinegia and Via del Parlagio at #2 red, tel. 055-218-698, Gianni and Maurizio).

South of the River, in the Oltrarno
Dining with a Ponte Vecchio View
Golden View Open Bar is a lively, trendy bistro, good for a romantic meal or just a salad, pizza, or pasta with fine wine and a fine view of Ponte Vecchio and the Arno River. Reservations for

window tables are essential (reasonable prices, €10 pizzas and big salads, daily 11:30-24:00, impressive wine bar, 50 yards upstream from Ponte Vecchio at Via dei Bardi 58, tel. 055-214-502, run by Antonio, Marco, and Tomaso). They have four seating areas (with the same menu and prices) for whatever mood you're in: a riverside pizza place, a classier restaurant, a jazzy lounge, and a wine bar (they also serve a buffet of appetizers free with your drink from 19:00 to 22:00). Mixing their fine wine, river views, and live jazz makes for a wonderful evening (jazz nightly at 21:00 except Tue and Thu off-season).

In the Heart of the Oltrarno

Of the many good and colorful restaurants in the Oltrarno, these are my favorites. Reservations are a good idea in the evening.

Dining in the Oltrarno

Ristorante Enoteca le Barrique, with eight tables, offers a delightful, quiet, intimate break from traditional Italian cuisine. The Japanese chef fuses Tuscan and Asian with a fun, inviting menu. The list is short, as everything is fresh and seasonal. While the candlelit interior is calm and sweet, the garden out back is a welcome option on a hot summer night (€10 homemade pastas, €14 *secondi,* €2 cover, Tue-Sun 21:00-late, closed Mon, two blocks beyond Piazza del Carmine at Via del Leone 40, tel. 055-224-192, mobile 338-963-2334, Allessandro). If Le Barrique doesn't work for you, **Ristorante Pandemonio,** a block farther down the street, is also good (closed Sun, Via del Leone 50, tel. 055-224-002).

Trattoria 4 Leoni creates the quintessential Oltrarno dinner scene. The Tuscan-style food is made with an innovative twist and an appreciation for vegetables. You'll enjoy the fun energy and characteristic seating, both inside and on the colorful square, Canto ai Quattro Pagoni (informally known as Piazza della Passera). While the wines by the glass are pricey, the house wine is very good (€10 pastas, €15 *secondi,* daily 12:00-24:00; from Ponte Vecchio walk four blocks up Via de' Guicciardini, turn right on Via dello Sprone, then slightly left to Via de' Vellutini 1; tel. 055-218-562).

Olio & Convivium Gastronomia started as an elegant deli whose refined oil-tasting room morphed into a romantic, aristocratic restaurant. Their three intimate rooms are surrounded by fine *prosciutti,* cheeses, and wine shelves. It's an intimidating place and a little pretentious, but one that foodies will appreciate for its quiet atmosphere. Use it for a special evening. Their list of €13-20 *gastronomia* plates offers an array of taste treats and fine wines by the glass (€14 pastas, €18 *secondi,* stylish €18 lunches, €3 cover, Tue-Sat 12:00-14:30 & 19:00-22:30, Mon lunch only, closed Sun,

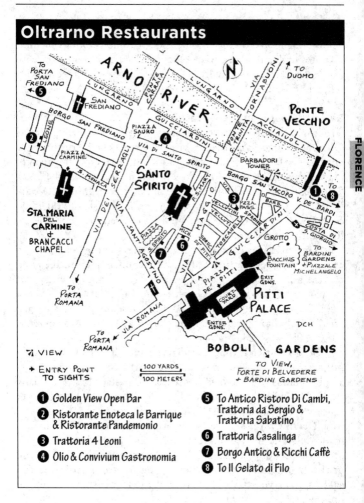

Oltrarno Restaurants

1 Golden View Open Bar
2 Ristorante Enoteca le Barrique & Ristorante Pandemonio
3 Trattoria 4 Leoni
4 Olio & Convivium Gastronomia
5 To Antico Ristoro Di Cambi, Trattoria da Sergio & Trattoria Sabatino
6 Trattoria Casalinga
7 Borgo Antico & Ricchi Caffè
8 To Il Gelato di Filo

strong air-con, Via di Santo Spirito 4, tel. 055-265-8198, Monica).

Antico Ristoro Di' Cambi is a meat-lover's dream—thick with Tuscan traditions, rustic touches, and T-bone steaks. The bustling scene has a memorable beer-hall energy. As you walk in, you'll pass a glass case filled with red chunks of Chianina beef that's priced by weight (and splittable by two or even more). This is a good chance to enjoy the famous *bistecca alla fiorentina*, sitting inside the convivial woody interior or outside on a square (€8 pastas, €12 *secondi*, closed Sun, reserve on weekends and to sit outside, Via Sant'Onofrio 1 red, one block south of Ponte Amerigo Vespucci, tel. 055-217-134, run by Stefano and Fabio, the Cambi cousins).

Trattoria da Sergio, a tiny eatery about a block before Porta

San Frediano, has charm and a strong following—reservations are a must. The food is on the gourmet side of home-cooking—mama's favorites with a modern twist—and therefore a bit more expensive (€10 pastas, €15 *secondi*, daily 19:30-23:00, Borgo San Frediano 145 red, tel. 055-223-449, Sergio and Marco).

Eating Cheaply in the Oltrarno

Trattoria Sabatino, farthest away and least touristy of my Oltrarno listings, is a spacious, brightly lit mess hall—disturbingly cheap—with family character and a simple menu. It's a super place to watch locals munch. You'll find it just outside the Porta San Frediano, one of Florence's medieval gates, a 15-minute walk from Ponte Vecchio (€4 pastas, €5 *secondi*, Mon-Fri 12:00-15:00 & 19:15-22:00, closed Sat-Sun, Via Pisana 2 red, tel. 055-225-955, little English spoken).

Trattoria Casalinga, an inexpensive standby, comes with aproned women bustling around the kitchen. Florentines and tourists alike pack the place and leave full and happy, with euros to spare for gelato (€6 pastas, €7 *secondi*, Mon-Sat 12:00-14:30 & 19:00-21:45, after 20:00 reserve or wait, closed Sun and Aug, just off Piazza Santo Spirito, near the church at Via de' Michelozzi 9 red, tel. 055-218-624, Andrea).

Borgo Antico is the hit of Piazza Santo Spirito, with enticing pizzas, big deluxe plates of pasta, a delightful setting, and a trendy and boisterous young crowd (€9 pizza and pasta, €16 *secondi*, daily 12:00-24:00, best to reserve for a seat on the square, Piazza Santo Spirito 6 red, tel. 055-210-437, Andrea).

Ricchi Caffè, next to Borgo Antico, has fine gelato, home-made desserts, shaded outdoor tables, and pasta dishes at lunch (daily 7:00-24:00, tel. 055-215-864). After noting the plain facade of the Brunelleschi church facing the square, step inside the café and pick your favorite picture of the many ways it might be finished.

Florence Connections

Florence is Tuscany's transportation hub, with fine train, bus, and plane connections to virtually anywhere in Italy. The city has several train stations, a bus station (next to the main train station), and an airport (plus Pisa's airport nearby). Livorno, on the coast west of Florence, is a major cruise-ship port for passengers visiting Florence, Pisa, and other nearby destinations.

Trains

From Florence by Train to: Livorno—port of call for many cruise ships (hourly, 1.5 hours, some change in Pisa, Lucca connection possible), **La Spezia** (for the Cinque Terre, 5/day direct, 1.75 hours, otherwise nearly hourly with change in Pisa, €9.20), **Milan** (hourly, 1.75 hours), **Milan Malpensa Airport** (2/day express, 2.75 hours), **Venice** (hourly, 2-3 hours, may transfer in Bologna; often crowded—reserve ahead), **Rome** (at least hourly, 1.5 hours, most connections require seat reservations, €44), **Interlaken** (8/day, 6-7 hours, 2-3 changes), **Frankfurt** (1/day, 12 hours, 1-3 changes), **Paris** (3/day, 10-15 hours, 1-2 changes, important to reserve overnight train ahead), **Vienna** (1 direct overnight train, or 5/day with 1-3 changes, 10-16 hours).

Buses

The SITA bus station (100 yards west of the Florence train station on Via Santa Caterina da Siena) is traveler-friendly—a big old-school lot with numbered stalls and all the services you'd expect. Schedules for regional trips are posted everywhere, and TV monitors show imminent departures. Bus service drops dramatically on Sunday.

By Bus to: San Gimignano (hourly, 1.25-2 hours, change in Poggibonsi, less frequent on Sat-Sun, €6.25), **Siena** (2/hour, 1.25-hour *corse rapide* buses are fastest—even faster than the train, €7), **Volterra** (4/day, 2/day Sun, 2 hours, change in Colle Val d'Elsa, €7.60), Florence's **Amerigo Vespucci Airport** (2/hour, 30 minutes, €5). Buy tickets in the station if possible, as you'll pay 30 percent more if you buy tickets on the bus (except for the airport bus). Bus info: www.sitabus.it or tel. 800-373-760 (Mon-Fri 8:30-18:30, Sat 8:30-12:30, closed Sun); some schedules are listed in the *Florence Concierge Information* magazine.

Taxis

For small groups with more money than time, zipping to nearby towns by taxi can be a good value (e.g., €120 from your Florence hotel to your Siena hotel).

A more comfortable alternative is to hire a private car service. Florence-based **Transfer Chauffeur Service** has a fleet of modern vehicles with drivers who can whisk you between cities, to and from the cruise-ship port, and through the Tuscan countryside for around the same price as a cab (€130 for Florence to Siena, tel. 055-614-2182, mobile 338-862-3129, www.transfercs.com, marco.masala@transfercs.com, Marco).

Airports

Florence's Amerigo Vespucci Airport, also called Peretola Airport, is about five miles northwest of Florence (open 5:10-24:00, no overnighting allowed, TI, cash machines, car-rental agencies, airport info tel. 055-306-1630, flight info tel. 055-306-1700—domestic only, www.aeroporto.firenze.it). Shuttle buses (far right of airport as you exit arrivals hall) connect the airport with Florence's SITA bus station, 100 yards west of the train station on Via Santa Caterina da Siena (2/hour, 30 minutes, daily 6:00-23:30, €5, first bus leaves for airport from Florence at 5:30). Allow about €20 and 30 minutes for a taxi.

Pisa's **Galileo Galilei Airport** also handles international and domestic flights (TI open daily 11:00-23:00, cash machine, car-rental agencies, baggage storage, cafeteria, tel. 050-849-300, www.pisa-airport.com). You can connect to **Florence** easily by train (2/hour, 1.5 hours, €5.50, most transfer at Pisa Centrale) or by Terravision bus (about hourly, 1.25 hours, €10 one-way, ticket kiosk is at the right end of the arrivals hall as you're facing the exits, catch bus outside and to the far right of the bus parking lot, www.terravision.eu).

THE CINQUE TERRE

The Cinque Terre (CHINK-weh TAY-reh), a remote chunk of the Italian Riviera, is the traffic-free, lowbrow, underappreciated alternative to the French Riviera. There's not a museum in sight. Just sun, sea, sand (pebbles), wine, and pure, unadulterated Italy. Enjoy the villages, swimming, hiking, and evening romance of one of God's great gifts to tourism. For a home base, choose among five *(cinque)* villages, each of which fills a ravine with a lazy hive of human activity—callused locals, sunburned travelers, and no Vespas. While the Cinque Terre is now discovered (and can be quite crowded midday, when tourist boats drop by), I've never seen happier, more relaxed tourists.

The chunk of coast was first described in medieval times as "the five lands." In the feudal era, this land was watched over by castles. Tiny communities grew up in their protective shadows, ready to run inside at the first hint of a Turkish Saracen pirate raid. Marauding pirates from North Africa were a persistent problem until about 1400. Many locals were kidnapped and ransomed or sold into slavery, and those who remained built fires on flat-roofed watchtowers to relay warnings—alerting the entire coast to imminent attacks. The last major raid was in 1545.

As the threat of pirates faded, the villages prospered, catching fish and growing grapes. Churches were enlarged with a growing population. But until the advent of tourism in this generation, the towns remained isolated. Even today, traditions survive, and each of the five villages comes with a distinct dialect and its own proud heritage.

Sadly, a few ugly, noisy Americans give tourism a bad name here. Even hip, young residents are put off by loud, drunken tourists. They say—and I agree—that the Cinque Terre is an exceptional place. It deserves a special dignity. Party in Viareggio or Portofino, but be mellow in the Cinque Terre. Talk softly. Help keep it clean. In spite of the tourist crowds, it's still a real community, and we are its guests.

In this chapter, I cover the five towns in order from east to west, from Riomaggiore to Monterosso. Since I still get the names of the towns mixed up, I think of them by number: #1 Riomaggiore (a workaday town), #2 Manarola (picturesque), #3 Corniglia (on a hilltop), #4 Vernazza (the region's cover girl, the most touristy and dramatic), and #5 Monterosso al Mare (the closest thing to a beach resort of the five towns).

Arrival in the Cinque Terre

Big, fast trains from elsewhere in Italy speed past the Cinque Terre (though some stop in Monterosso and Riomaggiore). Unless you're coming from a nearby town, you'll have to change trains at least once to reach Manarola, Corniglia, or Vernazza.

Generally, if you're coming from the north, you'll change trains in Sestri Levante or Genoa (specifically, Genoa's Piazza Principe station). If you're coming from the south or east, you'll most likely have to switch trains in La Spezia (change at La Spezia Centrale station). No matter where you're coming from, it's best to check in the station before you leave to see your full schedule and route options (use the computerized kiosks or ask at a ticket window). Don't forget to validate your ticket by stamping it— ka-CHUNK!—in the yellow machines located on train platforms and elsewhere in the station. Conductors here are notorious for levying stiff fines on forgetful tourists. For more information on riding the train between Cinque Terre towns, see "Getting Around the Cinque Terre," later in this chapter.

If the Cinque Terre is your first, last, or only stop on this trip, consider flying into Pisa or Genoa, rather than Milan. These airports are less confusing than Milan's, and closer to the Cinque Terre.

Planning Your Time

The ideal stay is two or three full days; my recommended minimum stay is two nights and a completely uninterrupted day. The Cinque Terre is served by the local train from Genoa and La Spezia. Speed demons arrive in the morning, check their bags in La Spezia, take the five-hour hike through all five towns, laze away the afternoon on the beach or rock of their choice, and zoom away on the overnight train to somewhere back in the real world. But be warned: The Cinque Terre has a strange way of messing up your momentum. (The evidence is the number of Americans who

have fallen in love with the region and/or one of its residents...and are still here.) Frankly, staying fewer than two nights is a mistake that you'll likely regret.

The towns are just a few minutes apart by hourly train or boat. There's no checklist of sights or experiences—just a hike, the towns themselves, and your fondest vacation desires. Study this chapter in advance and piece together your best day, mixing hiking, swimming, trains, and a boat ride. For the best light and coolest temperatures, start your hike early.

Market days perk up the towns from 8:00 to 13:00 on Tuesday in Vernazza, Wednesday in Levanto, Thursday in Monterosso and Sestri Levante, and Friday in La Spezia.

The winter is really dead—most hotels and some restaurants close in December and January. The long Easter weekend (April 6-9 in 2012) and July and August are peak of peak, the toughest times to find rooms. In spring, the towns can feel inundated with Italian school groups day-tripping on spring excursions (they can't afford to sleep in this expensive region). For more information on the region, see www.cinqueterre.it.

The Cinque Terre National Park

The creation of the Cinque Terre National Marine Park in 1999 has brought lots of money (all visitors pay a fee to hike the trails), new restrictions on land and sea to protect wildlife, and lots of concrete bolstering walkways, trails, beaches, breakwaters, and docks. Each village has a park-sponsored information center, and two towns have tiny, nearly worthless folk museums. The park is run by its president, Franco Bonanini, a powerful man—nicknamed "The Pharaoh" for his grandiose visions—who used to be Riomaggiore's mayor. For the latest on the park, see www.parconazionale5terre.it.

Cinque Terre Cards

Visitors hiking between the towns need to pay a park entrance fee. This fee keeps the trails safe and open, and pays for viewpoints, picnic spots, WCs, and more. The popular coastal trail generates enough revenue to subsidize the development of trails and outdoor activities higher in the hills.

You have three options for covering the park fee: the Cinque Terre Card (the best deal), the Cinque Terre Treno Card, or the Cinque Terre Treno e Batello Card. All are valid until midnight on the expiration date. Write your name on your card or risk a big fine (see www.parconazionale5terre.it).

The **Cinque Terre Card,** good for one day of hiking, costs €5 (includes map; €8/2 days, €10/3 days, €20/7 days). It covers all trails, shuttle buses, and park museums, but not trains or boats, and a three-hour bike rental. Buy it at trailheads, at national park offices, and at most train stations (no validation required).

The **Cinque Terre Treno Card** covers what the Cinque Terre Card does, plus the use of the local trains (from Levanto to La Spezia, including all Cinque Terre towns). It's sold at TIs inside train stations—but not at trailheads—and comes with a map, information brochure, and train schedule (€9/1 day, €15/2 days, €20/3 days, €37/week, validate card at train station by punching it in the yellow machine). This card is not a good value, because you'd have to hike and take three train trips every day just to break even.

The **Cinque Terre Treno e Batello Card,** valid for one day, covers the same things as the Cinque Terre Treno Card, plus boats between Monterosso and Riomaggiore (€19.50). It's a poor value unless you plan to hike and take several boat or train rides all in one day—determine the individual cost for each leg of your trip before buying this pass.

Getting Around the Cinque Terre

Within the Cinque Terre, you'll get around the villages more cheaply by train, but more scenically by boat. And any way you do it, a visit here comes with lots of stairs and climbing.

By Train

Along the coast here, trains go in only two directions: "per [to] Genova" (the Italian spelling of Genoa) or "per La Spezia." Assuming you're on vacation, accept the unpredictability of Cinque Terre trains (they're often late...unless you are, too—in which case they're on time). Relax while you wait—buy a cup of coffee at a station bar. When the train comes (know which direction to look for: La Spezia or Genova), casually walk over and hop on. This is especially easy in Monterosso, with its fine café-with-a-view on track #1 (direction: Milano/Genova).

Use the handy TV monitors in the station to make sure you're headed for the right platform. Most of the northbound trains that stop at all Cinque Terre towns and are headed toward Genova will list Sestri Levante as the *destinazione*.

By train, the five towns are just a few minutes apart. Know your stop. After the train leaves the town before your destination, go to the door and get ready to slip out before the mob packs in. Words to the wise for novice tourists, who often miss their stop: The stations are small and the trains are long, so (especially in Vernazza) you might have to get off deep in a tunnel. Also, the doors don't open automatically—you may have to flip open the handle of the door yourself. If a door isn't working, go quickly to the next car to leave. (When leaving a town by train, if you find the platform jammed with people, walk down the platform into the tunnel where things quiet down.)

It's cheap to buy individual train tickets to travel between the towns (€1.80, good for 75 minutes). Stamp the ticket at the station machine before you board. Riding without a validated ticket can be expensive ("minimum €25 fine" means they charge what they want—usually €50) if you meet a conductor. If you have a Eurailpass, don't spend one of your valuable flexi-days on the cheap Cinque Terre.

In general, I'd skip the train from Riomaggiore to Manarola (the trains are unreliable, and the 15-minute Via dell'Amore stroll is a delight—see page 1126 for more on this path).

Cinque Terre Train Schedule: Since the train is the Cinque Terre's lifeline, many shops and restaurants post the current schedule, and most hotels offer copies of it. Carry a schedule with you—it'll come in handy (one comes with the Cinque Terre Card). Note that fast trains leaving La Spezia zip right through the Cinque Terre; some stop only in Monterosso (town #5) and Riomaggiore (town #1). But any train that stops in Manarola, Corniglia, and Vernazza (towns #2, #3, and #4) will stop in all five towns (including the trains on the schedule below).

All of the times listed below were accurate as of this printing; most are daily and a few run Monday through Saturday, while others (not listed here) operate only on Sundays. Confirm times locally.

Trains leave La Spezia Centrale for all or most of the Cinque Terre villages at 7:12, 8:12, 10:07, 11:10, 12:00, 13:17, 13:27, 14:06, 15:10, 15:27, 16:01, 17:05, 17:13, 17:27, 18:06, 19:10, 19:29, 20:18, 21:23, 23:10, and 00:50.

Going back to La Spezia, trains leave Monterosso at 6:20, 7:12, 8:15, 9:29, 10:20, 11:00, 11:58 12:19, 13:26, 14:09, 14:20, 15:24, 16:07, 16:17, 17:30, 18:08, 18:20, 19:24, 20:20, 20:32, 20:43, 21:32, 22:24, 23:11, and 23:44 (same trains depart Vernazza about four minutes later).

Convenient TV monitors posted at several places in each station clearly show exactly what times the next trains are leaving in each direction (and if they're late, how late they are expected to be). I trust these monitors much more than my ability to read any printed schedule.

By Boat

From Easter through October, a daily boat service connects Monterosso, Vernazza, Manarola, Riomaggiore, and Portovenere. Boats provide a scenic way to get from town to town and survey what you just hiked. And boats offer the only efficient way to visit the nearby resort of Portovenere (the alternative is a tedious train-bus connection via La Spezia). In peaceful weather, the boats can be more reliable than the trains, but if seas are rough, they don't run at all. Because the boats nose in and tourists have to gingerly disembark onto little more than a plank, even a small chop can cancel some or all of the stops.

I see the tour boats as a syringe, injecting each town with a boost of euros. The towns are addicted, and they shoot up hourly through the summer. (Between 10:00-15:00—especially on weekends—masses of gawkers unload from boats, tour buses, and cruise ships, inundating the villages and changing the tenor of the region.)

Boats depart Monterosso about hourly (10:30-17:00), stopping at the Cinque Terre towns (except at Corniglia) and ending up an hour later in Portovenere. (Portovenere-Monterosso boats run 9:00-17:00.) The ticket price depends on the length of the boat ride (short hops-€5-6, longer hops-€8-10, five-town all-day pass-€15). Round-trip tickets are slightly cheaper than two one-way trips. You can buy tickets at little stands at each town's harbor (tel. 0187-732-987 and 0187-818-440). Another all-day boat pass for €23 extends to Portovenere and includes a 40-minute scenic ride around three small islands (2/day). Boats are not covered by the Cinque Terre Card, but are included in the Cinque Terre Treno e Batello Card. Boat schedules are posted at docks, harbor bars,

Cinque Terre park offices, and hotels (www.navigazionegolfodei poeti.it).

By Shuttle Bus

Shuttle buses connect each Cinque Terre town with its distant parking lot and various points in the hills (for example, from Corniglia's beach and train station to its hilltop town center). Note that these shuttle buses do not connect the towns with each other. Most rides cost €1.50 (and are covered by the Cinque Terre Card)—pick up bus schedules from a Cinque Terre park office or note the times posted on bus doors and at bus stops. Some (but not all) departures from Vernazza, Manarola, and Riomaggiore go beyond the parking lots and high into the hills. Pay for a round-trip ride and just cruise both ways to soak in the scenery (round-trip 30-45 minutes).

Hiking the Cinque Terre

All five towns are connected by good trails, marked with red-and-white paint, white arrows, and some signs. You'll experience the area's best by hiking all the way from one end to the other. While you can detour to dramatic hilltop sanctuaries, I'd keep it simple by following trail #2—the low route between the villages. The entire seven-mile hike can be done in about four hours, but allow five for dawdling. Germans (with their task-oriented *Alpenstock* walking sticks) are notorious for marching too fast through the region. Take it slow...smell the cactus flowers and herbs, notice the lizards, listen to birds singing in the olive groves, and enjoy vistas on all sides.

Trails can be closed in bad weather or because of landslides. Remember that hikers need to pay a fee to enter the trails (see "Cinque Terre Cards," earlier in this chapter). If you're hiking the entire five-town route, consider that the trail between Riomaggiore (#1) and Manarola (#2) is easiest. The hike between Manarola and Corniglia (#3) has minor hills. The trail from Corniglia to Vernazza (#4) is challenging, while the path from Vernazza to Monterosso (#5) is the most challenging. For that hike, you might want to start in Monterosso in order to tackle the toughest section while you're fresh—and to enjoy the region's most dramatic scenery as you approach Vernazza.

Other than the wide, easy Riomaggiore-Manarola segment, the trail is generally narrow, rocky, and comes with lots of steps. Be warned that I get many emails from readers who say the trail was tougher than they expected. The rocks and metal grates can be slippery in the rain. Some readers wish they had brought their walking sticks or trekking poles, since there aren't any for sale here. While the trail is a bit of a challenge, it's perfectly doable for any fit hiker...and worth the sweat.

Maps aren't necessary for the basic coastal hikes described here. But for the expanded version of this hike (12 hours, from Portovenere to Levanto) and more serious hikes in the high country, pick up a good hiking map (about €5, sold everywhere). To leave the park cleaner than when you found it, bring a plastic bag *(sacchetto di plastica)* and pick up a little trail trash along the way. It would be great if American visitors—who get so much joy out of this region—were known for this good deed.

Riomaggiore-Manarola (20 minutes): Facing the front of the train station in Riomaggiore (#1), go up the stairs to the right, following signs for *Via dell'Amore.* The photo-worthy promenade—wide enough for baby strollers—winds along the coast to Manarola (#2). It's primarily flat, and it's even wheelchair accessible since there are elevators at each end (elevators at Riomaggiore included in pass, elevator at Manarola for disabled use only). While there's no beach along the trail, stairs lead down to sunbathing rocks. A long tunnel and mega-nets protect hikers from mean-spirited rocks. The classy park-run Bar & Vini A Pie de Ma wine bar—located at the Riomaggiore trailhead—offers light meals, awesome town views, and clever boat storage under the train tracks (for more info, see page 1137). There's also the scenic, peaceful cliffside Bar Via dell'Amore, serving homemade hot meals, closer to the Manarola end of the trail (daily in summer 9:00-24:00, until 20:00 off-season, light meals any time, full meals 12:00-15:00 & 19:30-21:30). The official park picnic area steeply rises above Bar Via dell'Amore on several terraces, with shaded picnic tables and a WC.

Manarola-Corniglia (45 minutes): The walk from Manarola (#2) to Corniglia (#3) is a little longer and more rugged and steep than the Via dell'Amore. It's also less romantic. To avoid the last stretch (switchback stairs leading up to the hill-capping town of Corniglia), end your hike at Corniglia's train station and catch the shuttle bus to the town center (2/hour, €1.50, free with Cinque Terre Card, usually timed to meet the trains).

Corniglia-Vernazza (1.5 hours): The hike from Corniglia (#3) to Vernazza (#4)—the wildest and greenest section of the coast—is very rewarding but very hilly (going the other direction from Vernazza to Corniglia is steeper). From the Corniglia station and beach, zigzag up to the town (via the steep stairs, the longer road, or the shuttle bus). Ten minutes past Corniglia, toward Vernazza, you'll see Guvano beach far beneath you (once the region's nude beach). The scenic trail leads past a bar and picnic tables, through lots of fragrant and flowery vegetation, into Vernazza. If you need a break before reaching Vernazza, stop by Franco's Ristorante and Bar La Torre; it has a small menu but big views (between meal times only drinks are served; see listing on page 1157).

Vernazza-Monterosso (1.5 hours): The trail from Vernazza (#4) to Monterosso (#5) is a scenic up-and-down-a-lot trek. Trails are narrow and rough with a lot of steps (some readers report "very dangerous"), but easy to follow. Locals frown on camping at the picnic tables located midway. The views just out of Vernazza, looking back at the town, are spectacular.

Longer Hikes: Above the trails that run between the towns, higher-elevation hikes crisscross the region. Shuttle buses make the going easier, connecting coastal villages and trailheads in the hills. Ask locally about the more difficult six-mile inland hike to Volastra. This tiny village, perched between Manarola and Corniglia, hosts lots of Germans and Italians in the summertime. Just below its town center, in the hamlet of Groppo, is the Cinque Terre Cooperative Winery (see page 1141). For the whole trip on the high road between Manarola and Corniglia, allow two hours one-way. In return, you'll get sweeping views and a closer look at the vineyards. Shuttle buses run from Manarola to Volastra (€2.50 or free with Cinque Terre Card, pick up schedule from park office, 8/day, more departures in summer, 15 minutes); consider taking the bus up and hiking down.

Swimming, Kayaking, and Biking

Every town in the Cinque Terre has a beach or a rocky place to swim. Monterosso has the biggest and sandiest, with beach umbrellas and beach-use fees (but it's free where there are no umbrellas). Vernazza's is tiny—better for sunning than swimming. Manarola and Riomaggiore have the worst beaches (no sand), but Manarola offers the best deep-water swimming.

Wear your walking shoes and pack your swim gear. Several of the beaches have showers (no shampoo, please). Underwater sightseeing is full of fish—goggles are sold in local shops. Sea urchins can be a problem if you walk on the rocks, and sometimes jellyfish wash up on the pebbles. If you have swim shoes, this is the place to wear them.

You can rent kayaks in Riomaggiore, Vernazza, and Monterosso. (For details, see individual town listings in this chapter.) Some readers say kayaking can be dangerous—the kayaks tip easily, training is not provided, and lifejackets are not required.

Mountain biking is also possible (park info booths in each town have details on rentals and maps of trails high above the coast). A free three-hour bike rental is included with the Cinque Terre Card (note that these bikes can be used only on specific bike trails, not the standard hiking trails).

Sleeping in the Cinque Terre

If you think too many people have my book, avoid Vernazza. You get fewer crowds and better value for your money in other towns. Monterosso is a good choice for sun-worshipping softies, those who prefer the ease of a real hotel, and the younger crowd (more nightlife). Hermits, anarchists, wine-lovers, and mountain goats like Corniglia. Sophisticated Italians and Germans choose Manarola. Riomaggiore is bigger than Vernazza and less resorty than Monterosso.

While the Cinque Terre is too rugged for the mobs that ravage the Spanish and French coasts, it's popular with Italians, Germans, and in-the-know Americans. Hotels charge more and are packed on holidays (including Easter), in July and August, and on Fridays and Saturdays all summer. August weekends are worst. But €65-70 doubles are available May-June and September-October—you'll end up paying at least €10-20 extra for July and August. The prices I've listed are the maximum for July-August. For a terrace or view, you might pay an extra €20 or more. Apartments for four can be economical for families—figure on €100-120.

In general, you'll pay the most for the comforts of a hotel in Monterosso, and the cheapest rooms are in Corniglia. Prices in Riomaggiore and Manarola are comparable (a double averages around €75). Rooms in Vernazza are smaller, and for a recently remodeled room, expect to pay €15-25 more.

Book ahead if you'll be visiting in June, July, August, on a weekend, or around a holiday. At other times, you can land a double room on any day by just arriving in town (ideally by noon) and asking around at bars and restaurants, or simply by approaching locals on the street. Many travelers enjoy the opportunity to shop around a bit and get the best price by bargaining. Private rooms—called *affitta camere*—are no longer an intimate stay with a family. They are generally comfortable apartments (often with small kitchens) where you get the key and come and go as you like, rarely seeing your landlord. Many landowners rent the buildings by the year to local managers, who then attempt to make a profit by filling them night after night with tourists.

For the best value, visit two private rooms and snare the best. Going direct cuts out a middleman and softens prices. Staying more than one night gives you bargaining leverage. Plan on paying cash. Private rooms are generally bigger and more comfortable than those offered by the pensions and offer the same privacy as a hotel room.

If you want the security of a reservation, make it at a hotel long in advance (smaller places generally don't take reservations very far ahead). Query by email, not fax. If you do reserve, honor your reservation (or, if you must cancel, do it as early as possible).

Since people renting rooms usually don't take deposits, they lose money if you don't show up. Cutthroat room hawkers at the train stations might try to lure you away from a room that you've already reserved with offers of cheaper rates. Don't do it. You owe it to your hosts to stick with your original reservation.

Some hoteliers and individuals renting rooms in the Cinque Terre take advantage of the demand by artificially bumping up prices. This problem seems most prevalent in Vernazza and Riomaggiore. Shop around before you commit. Due to the global economic slump, travelers will have more negotiating power this year.

Eating in the Cinque Terre

Hanging out at a seaview restaurant while sampling local specialties could become one of your favorite memories.

Tegame alla Vernazza is the most typical main course in Vernazza: anchovies, potatoes, tomatoes, white wine, oil, and herbs. Anchovies (*acciughe;* ah-CHOO-gay) are ideally served the day they're caught. If you've always hated anchovies (the harsh, cured-in-salt American kind), try them fresh here. *Pansotti* are ravioli with ricotta and a mixture of greens, often served with a walnut sauce...delightful and filling.

While antipasto means cheese and salami in Tuscany, here you'll get *antipasti frutti di mare*, a plate of mixed "fruits of the sea" and a fine way to start a meal. Many restaurants are particularly proud of their *antipasti frutti di mare*. Splitting one of these and a pasta dish can be plenty.

This region is the birthplace of pesto. Basil, which loves the temperate Ligurian climate, is ground with cheese (half parmigiano cow cheese and half pecorino sheep cheese), garlic, olive oil, and pine nuts, and then poured over pasta. Try it on spaghetti, *trenette*, or *trofie* (made of flour with a bit of potato, designed specifically for pesto to cling to). Many also like pesto lasagna, always made with white sauce, never red. If you become addicted, small jars of pesto are sold in the local grocery stores and gift shops. If it's refrigerated, it's fresh; this is what you want if you're eating it today. For taking home, get the jar-on-a-shelf pesto.

Focaccia, the tasty pillowy bread, also originates here in Liguria. Locals say the best focaccia is made between the Cinque Terre and Genoa. It's simply flatbread with olive oil and salt. The baker roughs up the dough with finger holes, then bakes it. Focaccia comes plain or with onions, sage, or olive bits, and is a local favorite for a snack on the beach. Bakeries sell it in rounds or slices by the weight (a portion is about 100 grams, or *un etto*).

Farinata, a humble fried bread snack, is made from chickpea meal, water, oil, and pepper, and baked on a copper tray in a wood-burning stove. *Farinata* is sold at pizza and focaccia places.

The *vino delle Cinque Terre*, while not one of Italy's top wines, flows cheap and easy throughout the region. It's white—great with seafood. For a sweet dessert wine, the *sciacchetrà* wine is worth the splurge (€4 per small glass, often served with a cookie). You could order the fun dessert, *torta della nonna* (grandmother's cake), and dunk chunks of it into your glass. Aged *sciacchetrà* is dry and costly (up to €12/glass). While 10 kilos of grapes yield seven liters of local wine, *sciacchetrà* is made from near-raisins, and 10 kilos of grapes make only 1.5 liters of *sciacchetrà*. The word means "push and pull"—push in lots of grapes, pull out the best wine. If your room is up a lot of steps, be warned: *Sciacchetrà* is 18 percent alcohol, while regular wine is only 11 percent.

In the cool, calm evening, sit on Vernazza's breakwater with a glass of wine and watch the phosphorescence in the waves.

Nightlife in the Cinque Terre

While the Cinque Terre is certainly not noted for bumping beach-town nightlife like nearby Viareggio, you'll find some sort of travel-tale-telling hub in Monterosso, Vernazza, and Riomaggiore (Manarola and Corniglia are sleepy). Monterosso has a lively scene, especially in the summertime—but no discoteca yet. In Vernazza the nightlife centers in the bars on the waterfront piazza, which is the small-town-style place to "see and be seen." Bar Centrale in Riomaggiore is, well, the central place for cocktails and meeting fellow travelers (see "Nightlife" in each village for more details). Wherever your night adventures take you, have fun, but please remember that residents live upstairs.

Helpful Hints for the Cinque Terre

Tourist and Park Information: Each town (except Corniglia) has a well-staffed TI and park office (listed throughout this chapter).

Money: Banks and ATMs are plentiful throughout the region.

Baggage Storage: You can store bags at La Spezia's train station and the National Park kiosk at Riomaggiore's train station (but not overnight).

Services: Every train station has a handy public WC. Otherwise, pop into a bar or restaurant.

Taxi: Cinqueterre Taxi covers all five towns (mobile 328-583-4969, www.cinqueterretaxi.com, info@cinqueterretaxi.com).

Local Guides: Andrea Bordigoni (€110/half-day, €175/day, mobile 347-972-3317, bordigo@inwind.it) and **Paola Tommarchi** (€120/half-day, €175/day, mobile 334-109-7887, paola tomma@alice.it) both offer good tours.

Booking Agency: Miriana and Filippo at **Cinque Terre Riviera**

book rooms in the Cinque Terre towns, Portovenere, and La Spezia for a 10 percent markup over the list price (can also arrange transportation, cooking classes, and weddings; Via Picedi 18 in La Spezia; tel. 0187-520-702, Miriana—mobile 340-794-7358, Filippo—mobile 393-939-1901, www.cinqueterreriviera.com, info@cinqueterreriviera.com, English spoken).

Cheap Tricks: Consider arriving without a reservation and bargaining with locals for a private room; staying more than one night and paying cash should get you a double for around €65 (this is possible anytime, but safest on weekdays Sept-May). Many rooms come with kitchenettes, and bakeries and food shops make meals to go. Picnic tables along the trail come with a first-class view. Even hobos can afford the major delights of the Cinque Terre: hiking, nursing a drink at the harbor, strolling with the locals through town, and enjoying the beach.

Riomaggiore (Town #1)

The most substantial non-resort town of the group, Riomaggiore is a disappointment from the train station. But once you leave that neighborhood, you'll discover a fascinating tangle of pastel homes leaning on each other like drunken sailors. Just walk through the tunnel next to the train tracks (or ride the elevator through the hillside to the top of town). You'll find the rooms are priced right.

Orientation to Riomaggiore

Tourist Information

The TI is in the train station at the ticket desk (daily 6:30-20:00, tel. 0187-920-633). If the TI in the station is crowded, buy your hiking pass at the Cinque Terre park shop/information office next door by the mural (daily 8:00-19:30, tel. 0187-760-515, netpointrio maggiore@parconazionale5terre.it). For a less-formal information source, try Ivo and Alberto, who run Bar Centrale (described later in this section).

Arrival in Riomaggiore

The bus shuttles locals and tourists up and down Riomaggiore's steep main street and continues to the parking lot outside of town (€1.50 one-way, €2.50 round-trip, free with Cinque Terre Card, 2/hour, main stop at the fork of Via Colombo and Via Malborghetto, or flag it down as it passes). If you park at the lot (€3/hour or

€22/day), use cash—some readers have been overcharged on their credit cards. About seven buses a day head into the hills, where you'll find the region's top high-country activities (for details, see "Sights in Riomaggiore," later).

Helpful Hints

Internet Access: The **park shop** and information office has eight Internet terminals upstairs and Wi-Fi (€5/hour, daily May-Sept 8:00-22:00, Oct-April until 19:30). **Hotel Zorzara** has two terminals in town and charges about the same (daily 11:00-21:30, under the archway just past the first Co-op grocery store).

Baggage Storage: The attendant at the train station park office will open the kiosk next door to store your bags (€0.50/hour per piece, €6 surcharge if left longer than 6 hours, daily 8:00-19:45, no overnight storage, passport required).

Laundry: A self-service launderette is on the main street (€3.50 wash, €3.50 dry, daily 8:30-20:00, run by Edi's Rooms next door, Via Colombo 111).

Bike Rental: Ask at the TI about where to go to pick up a bike (first 3 hours free with Cinque Terre Card, then €1.50/hour, passport or €50 deposit required).

Self-Guided Walk

Welcome to Riomaggiore

Here's an easy loop trip that maximizes views and minimizes uphill walking.

• *Start at the train station. (If you arrive by boat, cross beneath the tracks and take a left, then hike through the tunnel along the tracks to reach the station.) You'll come to some...*

Colorful Murals: These murals, with subjects modeled after real-life Riomaggiorians, glorify the nameless workers who constructed the nearly 300 million cubic feet of dry stone walls (without cement). These walls run throughout the Cinque Terre, giving the region its characteristic *muri a secco* terracing for vineyards and olive groves. These murals, done by Argentinean artist Silvio Benedetto, are well-explained in English but may be covered for restoration on your visit.

• *Head to the railway tunnel entrance, and ride the elevator to the top of town (€0.50 or €1 family ticket, free with Cinque Terre Card, daily 8:00-19:45). You're at the...*

Top o' the Town: Here you're treated to spectacular sea views. To continue the view-fest, go right and follow the walkway (ignore the steps marked *Marina Seacoast* that lead to the harbor). It's a five-minute level stroll to the church. You'll pass under the city

Riomaggiore

VIA DELL' AMORE TO MANAROLA

MURALS

SAN GIOVANNI CHURCH

ELEVATOR

ELEVATOR TO HIGH ROAD

TRAIN STATION

VIA GASPERI

SIGNORINI

TO 19

CINQUE TERRE INFO

PED. TUNNEL

VIA

VIA SANT.

V. MALB

COLOMBO

VIA

LIGURIAN SEA

NOT TO SCALE

HARBOR + BOAT DOCK

BOAT TICKETS

TO 20

N

"BEACH" SWIMMING + SHOWERS

STAIRS

DCH

1 Locanda del Sole
2 Locanda Ca' dei Duxi
3 Mar Mar/Il Grifone Rooms
4 La Dolce Vita Rooms
5 Locanda dalla Compagnia
6 Edi's Rooms & Launderette
7 Villa Argentina
8 Ristorante la Lampara
9 La Lanterna Restaurant
10 Ristorante Ripa del Sole
11 Te La Do Io La Merenda Snack Bar
12 Enoteca & Ristorante Dau Cila
13 Bar & Vini A Pie de Ma
14 Co-op Groceries (2)
15 Bar Centrale & Gelateria
16 Bar dell'Amore
17 Internet Access (Hotel Zorzara)
18 Boat Dock
19 To Madonna di Montenero Trail
20 To Torre Guardiola Pathway & WWII Bunkers
21 Park Office Kiosk (Bag Storage)

THE CINQUE TERRE

hall (flying two flags) with murals celebrating the heroic grape pickers and fishermen of the region (also by Silvio Benedetto).
• *Before reaching the church, pause to enjoy the...*

Town View: The major river of this region once ran through this valley, as implied by the name Riomaggiore (local dialect for "river" and "major"). As in the other Cinque Terre towns, the river ravine is now paved over, and the romantic arched bridges that once connected the two sides have been replaced by a practical modern road.

Notice the lack of ugly aerial antennae. In the 1980s, every residence got cable. Now, the TV tower on the hilltop behind the church steeple brings the modern world into each home. While the church was rebuilt in 1870, it was first built in 1340. It's dedicated to St. John the Baptist, the patron saint of Genoa, a maritime republic that dominated the region. The elevator next to the church may be completed by the time you get here. It's to help seniors get around the steep town, and also to link to the elevator near the Via dell'Amore trailhead.

• *Continue past the church down to Riomaggiore's main street, named...*

Via Colombo: Walk about 30 feet after the WC, go down the stairs, and pop into the tiny Cinque Terre Antiche museum (€0.50, free with Cinque Terre Card, daily 9:30-13:00 & 14:00-18:00). Sit down for a few minutes to watch a circa-1950 video of the Cinque Terre.

Continuing down Via Colombo, you'll pass a bakery, a couple of grocery shops, and the self-service laundry. There's homemade gelato next to the Bar Centrale. When Via Colombo dead-ends, to the left you'll find the stairs down to the Marina neighborhood, with the harbor, the boat dock, a 200-yard trail to the beach *(spiaggia),* and an inviting little art gallery. To the right of the stairs is the tunnel, running alongside the tracks, which takes you directly back to the station and the trail to the other towns. From here, you can take a train, hop a boat, or hike to your next destination.

Sights in Riomaggiore

Beach—Riomaggiore's rugged and tiny "beach" is rocky, but it's clean and peaceful. Take a two-minute walk from the harbor: Face the harbor, then follow the path to your left. Passing the rugged boat landing, stay on the path to the beach.

Kayaks and Water Sports—The town has a diving center (scuba, snorkeling, kayaks, and small motorboats; office down the stairs and under the tracks on Via San Giacomo, daily May-Sept 9:00-18:00, tel. 0187-920-011, www.5terrediving.it).

Hikes—Consider the cliff-hanging Torre Guardiola trail that leads from the beach up to old WWII bunkers and a hilltop botanical pathway of native flora and fauna with English information (free with Cinque Terre Card, daily 10:00-18:30, steep 20-minute climb, take the stairs between the boat dock and the beach). Another trail rises scenically to the 14th-century Madonna di Montenero sanctuary, high above the town (45 minutes, take the main road inland until you see signs, or ride the green shuttle bus 12 minutes from the town center to the sanctuary trail, then walk uphill five minutes, details at park office next to the train station, park center at the sanctuary offers bike rental).

Nightlife in Riomaggiore

Bar Centrale, run by sociable Ivo, Alberto, and the gang, offers "nightlife" any time of day—making it a good stop for Italian breakfast and music. Ivo, who lived in San Francisco and speaks good English, fills his bar with San Franciscan rock and a fun-loving vibe. During the day, this is a shaded place to relax with other travelers. At night, it offers the younger set the liveliest action (and best *mojitos*) in town. They also serve €5 fast-food pastas and microwaved pizzas (daily 7:30-24:00 or later, closed Mon in winter, in the town center at Via Colombo 144, tel. 0187-920-208). There's a good *gelateria* next door.

Enoteca & Ristorante Dau Cila, a cool little hideaway down at the miniscule harbor with a mellow jazz-and-Brazilian-lounge ambience, is a counterpoint to wild Bar Centrale (snacks and meals, fine wine by the glass; see "Eating in Riomaggiore," page 1137).

Bar & Vini A Pie de Ma, at the beginning of Via dell'Amore, has piles of charm, often music, and stays open until midnight in the summer.

The marvelous **Via dell'Amore** trail, lit only with subtle ground lighting so that you can see the stars, welcomes romantics after dark. The trail is free after 19:30.

Sleeping in Riomaggiore

Riomaggiore has arranged its private-room rental system better than its neighbors. Several agencies—with regular office hours, English-speaking staff, and email addresses—line up within a few yards of each other on the main drag. Each manages a corral of local rooms for rent. These offices can close unexpectedly, so it's smart to settle up the day before you leave in case they're closed when you need to depart. Expect lots of stairs. If you don't mind the hike, the street above town has safe overnight parking (free 20:00-8:00).

Room-Finding Services

$$$ Locanda del Sole has seven modern, basic, and overpriced rooms with a shared and peaceful terrace. Located at the utilitarian top end of town, it's a five-minute walk downhill to the center. Easy parking makes it especially appealing to drivers (Db-€130, free parking with this book, Via Santuario 114, tel. & fax 0187-920-773, mobile 340-983-0090, www.locandadelsole.net, info@locandadelsole.net, Enrico).

Sleep Code

(€1 = about $1.40, country code: 39)
S = Single, **D** = Double/Twin, **T** = Triple, **Q** = Quad, **b** = bathroom, **s** = shower only. Unless otherwise noted, credit cards are accepted, English is spoken, and breakfast is included (except in Vernazza).

To help you sort easily through these listings, I've divided the rooms into three categories based on the price for a standard double room with bath:

$$$ Higher Priced—Most rooms €100 or more.
$$ Moderately Priced—Most rooms between €50-100.
$ Lower Priced—Most rooms €50 or less.

Prices can change without notice; verify the hotel's current rates online or by email. For other updates, see www.ricksteves.com/update.

$$$ Locanda Ca' dei Duxi rents 10 good rooms from an efficient little office on the main drag (Db-€100-130 depending on view and season, extra person-€20, air-con; parking-€10/day, book when you reserve; open year-round, Via Colombo 36, tel. & fax 0187-920-036, mobile 329-825-7836, www.duxi.it, info@duxi.it, Samuele).

$$ Mar Mar/Il Grifone Rooms offers 12 rooms and 15 apartments, with American expats Amy and Maddy smoothing communications (Db-€60-90 depending on view, Db suite with top view-€120, cash only, reception open 9:00-17:00 in season, Via Colombo 181, tel. & fax 0187-920-932, www.5terre-marmar.com, info@5terre-marmar.com). Try calling if you don't get a return email. They also run a mini-hostel in a fine communal apartment with a cool living room, terrace, and kitchen in a good, quiet location. Take care of this little treasure so it survives (9 beds in 3 rooms, €22/bed).

$$ La Dolce Vita offers three rooms on the main drag and two apartments around town (Db-€60-80, open daily 9:30-19:30; if they're closed, they're full; Via Colombo 120, tel. & fax 0187-760-044, mobile 349-326-6803, agonatal@interfree.it, helpful Giacomo and Simone).

$$ Locanda dalla Compagnia rents five modern rooms at the top of town, just 300 yards below the parking lot and the little church. All rooms—nice but rather dim—are on the same ground floor, sharing an inviting lounge. Franca runs it with Giovanna's help (Db-€70, cash only, air-con, mini-fridge, no view, Via del

Santuario 232, tel. 0187-760-050, fax 0187-920-586, lacomp
@libero.it).

$$ Edi's Rooms rents 20 rooms and apartments. You pay
extra for views (Db-€70-120 depending on room, apartment
Qb-€100-160, reserve with credit card, office open daily 8:30-
20:00 in summer, winter 10:30-12:30 & 14:30-19:00, some rooms
involve climbing a lot of steps—ask before viewing or reserving,
Via Colombo 111, tel. 0187-760-842, tel. & fax 0187-920-325, www
.lancoracinqueterre.com, edi-vesigna@iol.it).

For Drivers: **$$$ Villa Argentina** has 16 plain rooms, many
with views overlooking the town. It makes up for its sterility with
friendly staff, easy access to the elevator to San Giovanni Church,
and a sunny, communal terrace (Db-€130 with view, fans, park-
ing-€15/day, Via de Gasperi 170, tel. 0187-920-213, fax 0187-760-
531, www.villargentina.com, villaargentina@libero.it).

Eating in Riomaggiore

Ristorante la Lampara serves a *frutti di mare* pizza, *trenette al
pesto,* and the aromatic *spaghetti al cartoccio*—€11 oven-cooked spaghetti with seafood in foil (daily 7:00-24:00, closed Tue in winter,
just above tracks off Via Colombo at Via Malborghetto 10, tel.
0187-920-120).

La Lanterna, dressier than the Lampara, is wedged into
a niche in the Marina, overlooking the harbor under the tracks
(daily 12:00-22:00, Via San Giacomo 10, tel. 0187-920-589).

Ristorante Ripa del Sole is the local pick for an elegant night
out, with the same prices and better quality than the Lampara and
Lanterna. The €13 antipasto "Cinque Terre" gives you five tastes of
anchovy specialties (Tue-Sun 12:00-14:00 & 18:30-21:30, closed
Mon, closed Jan-Feb, 10-minute hike above town, Via de Gasperi
282, tel. 0187-920-143).

Te La Do Io La Merenda ("I'll Give You a Snack") is good
for a snack, pizza, or takeout. Their counter is piled with an assortment of munchies, and they have pastas, roasted chicken, and
focaccia sandwiches to go (daily 9:00-21:00, Via Colombo 161, tel.
0187-920-148).

Enoteca & Ristorante Dau Cila is the *nuovo chic* of the
Cinque Terre, decked out like a black-and-white movie set in a
centuries-old boat shed. Try their antipasto specialty of several
seafood appetizers, and listen to jazz with the waves lapping at
the harbor below (€12 pastas, €18 *secondi,* March-Oct daily until
24:00, Via San Giacomo 65, tel. 0187-760-032, Luca).

Bar & Vini A Pie de Ma, at the trailhead on the Manarola
end of town, is a nice place for a scenic light bite or quiet drink

at night. Enjoying a meal at a table on its dramatically situated terrace provides an indelible Cinque Terre memory (daily 10:00-20:00, until 24:00 in summer, tel. 0187-921-037).

Picnics: Groceries and delis on Via Colombo sell food to go, including pizza slices, for a picnic at the harbor or beach. The two **Co-op groceries,** one at the top and one at the bottom of the main street, are the least expensive and will make sandwiches to go (daily 7:30-13:00 & 17:00-19:30, Via Colombo 55 and 205).

Manarola (Town #2)

Like Riomaggiore, Manarola is attached to its station by a 200-yard-long tunnel. During WWII air raids, these tunnels provided refuge and a safe place for rattled villagers to sleep. The town itself fills a ravine, bookended by its wild little harbor to the west and a diminutive church square inland to the east. A delightful and gentle stroll, from the church down to the harborside park, provides the region's easiest little vineyard walk (described in my "Self-Guided Walk," next page).

Orientation to Manarola

Arrival in Manarola

The TI next to the train station is open daily 7:00-20:00. A shuttle bus runs between the low end of Manarola's main street (at the *tabacchi* shop and newsstand) and the parking lot (€1.50 one-way, €2.50 round-trip, free with Cinque Terre Card, 2/hour, just flag it down). Shuttle buses also run about hourly from Manarola to Volastra, near the Cinque Terre Cooperative Winery (see "Sights in Manarola," later).

To get to the dock and the boats that connect Manarola with the other Cinque Terre towns, find the steps to the left of the harbor view—they lead down to the ticket kiosk. Continue around the left side of the cliff (as you're facing the water) to catch the boats.

Note that the Cassa di Risparmio della Spezia ATM at the bottom of the main street (near the entrance to the train-station tunnel) is notorious for running out of euros, especially in summer. It's been known to charge users' accounts without spitting out the *soldi* (cash)—avoid using it.

Manarola

NOT TO SCALE

ıllı STAIRS ↓ VIEW

TO CORNIGLIA

SWIMMING

CEMETERY PIAZZA

PUNTA BONFIGLIO

SAN LORENZO CHURCH

TO PARKING, ♦ CINQUE TERRE CO-OP WINERY ♦

MAIN ST.

BELL TOWER

CHAPEL

SWIMMING ♦ SHOWER

BOAT DOCK

PEDESTRIAN TUNNEL

TRAIN STATION

LIGURIAN SEA

VIA dell'AMORE TRAIL

TO RIOMAGGIORE

❶ La Torretta Rooms
❷ Marina Piccola Rooms & Restaurant
❸ Albergo Ca' d'Andrean
❹ Carugiu B&B & Casa Capellini
❺ Michela Rooms
❻ Ariadmare Rooms
❼ Ostello 5-Terre
❽ To Hotel il Saraceno
❾ Trattoria Il Porticciolo
❿ Trattoria Dal Billy
⓫ Shuttle Bus to Parking Lot & Volastra
⓬ Manarola Vineyard Walk

THE CINQUE TERRE

Self-Guided Walk

Welcome to Manarola

From the harbor, this 30-minute circular walk shows you the town and surrounding vineyards, and ends at a fantastic viewpoint, perfect for a picnic.

• *Start down at the waterfront.*

The Harbor: Manarola is tiny and picturesque, a tumble of buildings bunny-hopping down its ravine to the fun-loving waterfront. Notice how the I-beam crane launches the boats. Facing the harbor, look to the right, at the hillside Punta Bonfiglio cemetery and park (where this walk ends).

The town's swimming hole is just below. Manarola has no sand, but offers the best deep-water swimming in the area. The first "beach" has a shower, ladder, and wonderful rocks. The second has tougher access and no shower, but feels more remote and pristine (follow the paved path toward Corniglia, just around the point). For many, the tricky access makes this beach dangerous.

• *Hiking inland up the town's main drag, you'll come to the train tracks covered by Manarola's new square, called...*

Piazza Capellini: Built in 2004, this square is an all-around great idea, giving the town a safe, fun zone for kids. Locals living near the tracks also enjoy a little less noise. Check out the mosaic that displays the varieties of local fish in colorful enamel.

• *Fifty yards uphill, you'll find the...*

Sciacchetrà Museum: Run by the national park, it's hardly a museum. But pop in to its inviting room to see a tiny exhibit on the local wine industry (€0.50, free with Cinque Terre Card, daily 9:30-13:00 & 13:30-18:00, 15-minute video in English by request, 100 yards uphill from train tracks, across from the post office).

• *Hiking farther uphill, you can still hear...*

Manarola's Stream: As in Riomaggiore, Monterosso, and Vernazza, Manarola's stream was covered over by a modern sewage system after World War II. Before that time, romantic bridges arched over its ravine. A modern waterwheel recalls the origin of the town's name—local dialect for "big wheel" (one of many possible derivations). Mills like this once powered the local olive oil industry.

• *Keep climbing until you come to the square at the...*

Top of Manarola: The square is faced by a church, an oratory—now a religious and community meeting place—and a bell tower, which served as a watch tower when pirates raided the town (the cupola was added once the attacks ceased). Behind the church is Manarola's well-run youth hostel—originally the church's schoolhouse. To the right of the oratory, a lane leads to Manarola's sizable tourist-free zone.

While you're here, check out the church. According to the white marble plaque in its facade, the Parish Church of St. Lawrence dates from "MCCCXXXVIII" (1338). Step inside to see two paintings from the unnamed "Master of the Cinque Terre," the only painter of any note from the region (left wall and above main altar). While the style is Gothic, the work dates from the late 15th century, long after Florence had entered the Renaissance.

• *Walk 20 yards below the church and find a wooden railing. It marks the start of a delightful stroll around the high side of town, and back to the seafront. This is the beginning of the...*

Manarola Vineyard Walk: Don't miss this experience. Simply follow the wooden railing, enjoying lemon groves and wild red valerian (used for insomnia since the days of the Romans). Along the path, which is primarily flat, you'll get a close-up look at the region's famous dry-stone walls and finely crafted vineyards (with dried-heather thatches to protect the grapes from the southwest winds). Smell the rosemary. Study the structure of the town, and pick out the scant remains of an old fort. Notice the S-shape of the main road—once a riverbed—that flows through town. The town's roofs are traditionally made of locally quarried slate, rather than tile, and are held down by rocks during windstorms. As the harbor comes into view, you'll see the breakwater, added just a decade ago.

Out of sight above you on the right are simple wooden religious scenes, the work of local resident Mario Andreoli. Before his father died, Mario promised him he'd replace the old cross on the family's vineyard. Mario has been adding figures ever since. After recovering from a rare illness, he redoubled his efforts. On religious holidays, everything's lit up: the Nativity, the Last Supper, the Crucifixion, the Resurrection, and more. Some of the scenes are left up year-round.

• *This trail ends at a T-intersection, where it hits the main coastal trail. Turn left. (A right takes you to the trail to Corniglia.) Before descending back into town, take a right, detouring into...*

The Cemetery: Ever since Napoleon—who was king of Italy in the early 1800s—decreed that cemeteries were health risks, Cinque Terre's burial spots have been located outside of town. The result: The dearly departed generally get first-class sea views. Each cemetery—with its evocative yellowed photos and finely carved Carrara marble memorial reliefs—is worth a visit. (The basic structure for all of them is the same, but Manarola's is most easily accessible.)

In cemeteries like these, there's a hierarchy of four places to park your mortal remains: a graveyard, a spacious death condo *(loculo)*, a mini bone-niche *(ossario)*, or the communal ossuary. Because of the tight space, a time limit is assigned to the first three options (although many older tombs are grandfathered in). Bones go into the ossuary in the middle of the chapel floor after about a generation. Traditionally, locals make weekly visits to loved ones here, often bringing flowers. The rolling stepladder makes access to top-floor *loculi* easy.

• *The Manarola cemetery is on Punta Bonfiglio. Walk just below it, farther out through a park (playground, drinking water, WC, and picnic benches). Your Manarola finale: the bench at the tip of the point, offering one of the most commanding views of the entire region. The easiest way back to town is to take the stairs at the end of the point.*

Sights in Manarola

Wine Tasting—Hike or ride the green shuttle bus to the Cinque Terre Cooperative Winery (La Cantina Sociale) in the village of Groppo for a tour and wine tasting. Depending on the weather, a guide will take you around the vineyards as well as the winery, where they produce a dry white and the prized *sciacchetrà* sweet wine (€5-11, English may be spotty, Mon-Sat 7:00-19:00, Sun 9:00-12:30 & 14:30-19:00, tel. 0187-920-076).

Getting There: To hike, follow the road past the Manarola parking lot, look for trail markers, stay straight when trail #2 splits to the right, and then go uphill once the trail hits the street. It takes about 30 minutes. By bus, catch the shuttle at the lower end of the main street or flag it down. Ask the driver to drop you off at La Cantina or it might not stop (€1.50 one-way, €2.50 round-trip, free with Cinque Terre Card, 8/day, more in summer, 10 minutes).

Sleeping in Manarola

(€1 = about $1.40, country code: 39)

Manarola has plenty of private rooms. Ask in bars and restaurants. There's a modern three-star place halfway up the main drag, a seaview hotel on the harbor, a big modern hostel, and a cluster of options around the church at the peaceful top of the town (a 5-minute hike from the train tracks).

$$$ La Torretta is a trendy, upscale 13-room place that caters to a demanding clientele. It's a peaceful refuge with all the comforts for those happy to pay, including a communal hot tub with a view. Enjoy a complimentary snack and glass of prosecco on arrival and free wine tastings during your stay (smaller Db-€135, regular Db-€180, Db suite-€250, cash discount, book several months in advance as it is justifiably popular, Wi-Fi, on Piazza della Chiesa beside the bell tower at Vico Volto 20, tel. 0187-920-327, fax 0187-760-024, www.torrettas.com, torretta@cdh.it, Gabriele).

$$$ Marina Piccola offers 13 bright, slick rooms on the water—so they figure a warm welcome is unnecessary (Db-€115, buffet breakfast, air-con, Via Birolli 120, tel. 0187-920-103, fax 0187-920-966, www.hotelmarinapiccola.com, info@hotelmarina piccola.com).

$$$ Albergo Ca' d'Andrean, run by Simone, is quiet, comfortable, and modern—except for its antiquated reservation system. While the welcome is formal at best, it has 10 big, sunny air-conditioned rooms and a cool garden oasis complete with lemon trees (Sb-€72, Db-€100, breakfast-€6, cash only, send personal or traveler's check to reserve from US—or call if you're reserving from the road, closed Nov-Christmas, up the hill at Via A. Discovolo 101, tel. 0187-920-040, fax 0187-920-452, www.cadandrean.it, ca dandrean@libero.it).

$$ Carugiu B&B rents two no-view rooms at the top of town (Db-€65, Db suite-€80, €5/day less with 3-night stay, Via Ettore Cozzani 42, tel. 0187-920-359, English-speaking daughter-in-law

Cristina's mobile 349-346-9208, www.carugiu.com, info@carugiu .com).

$$ Casa Capellini rents four rooms: One has a view balcony, another a 360-degree terrace—book long in advance (Sb-€40, Db-€70; €90 for the *alta camera* on the top, with a kitchen, private terrace, and knockout view; two doors down the hill from the church—with your back to the church, it's at 2 o'clock; Via Ettore Cozzani 12, tel. 0187-920-823 or 0187-736-765, www.casa capellini-5terre.it, casa.capellini@tin.it, Gianni and Franca don't speak English).

$$ Michela Rooms has two spacious, modern rooms—one is an apartment (Db-€75) and the other is a simple double (Db-€65). You trek up the hill for the good prices, not for good views (no breakfast, air-con, located near recommended Trattoria Dal Billy at Via Rollando 221, she'll meet you at the station, mobile 320-184-0930, www.michelarooms5terre.com).

$$ Ariadmare Rooms rents four modern, sunny rooms and an apartment 20 yards beyond Trattoria Dal Billy at the very top of town. Three rooms have spacious terraces with knockout views (Db-€80, 2 adults and 1 child-€80, Db apartment-€90, ask for best Rick Steves price, Wi-Fi, up stairs on the left at Via Aldo Rollandi 137, tel. 0187-920-367, mobile 349-058-455, http://ariadimare.info, ask at Billy's if no one's home). Maurizio speaks a little English, while Mamma Franca communicates with lots of Italian and toothy smiles.

$ Ostello 5-Terre, Manarola's modern and pleasant hostel, occupies the former parochial school above the church square and offers 48 beds in four- to six-bed rooms. Nicola and Riccardo run a calm and peaceful place—it's not a party hostel—and quiet is greatly appreciated. They rent dorm rooms as doubles. Reserve well in advance. Full means full—they don't accommodate the desperate on the floor (Easter-mid-Oct: dorm beds-€23, Db-€65, Qb-€100; off-season: dorm beds-€20, Db-€55, Qb-€88; closed Nov-Feb; not co-ed except for couples and families; no membership necessary; optional €5 breakfast and €5-6 pasta; in summer, office closed 13:00-17:00, rooms closed 10:00-17:00, 1:00 curfew; off-season, office and rooms closed until 16:00, strict midnight curfew; open to all ages, laundry, safes, phone cards, Internet access, book exchange, elevator, great roof terrace and sunset views, Via B. Riccobaldi 21, tel. 0187-920-215, fax 0187-920-218, www.hostel5terre.com, info@hostel5terre.com). Book online with your credit-card number; note that you'll be charged for one night if you cancel with fewer than three days' notice.

For Drivers: **$$$ Hotel il Saraceno,** with seven spacious, modern rooms, is a deal for drivers. Located above Manarola in the tiny town of Volastra (chock full of vacationing Germans and

THE CINQUE TERRE

Italians in summer), it's serene, clean, and right by the shuttle bus to Manarola (Db-€100, buffet breakfast, Wi-Fi, free parking, Via Volastra 8, tel. 0187-760-081, fax 0187-760-791, www.thesaraceno .com, hotel@thesaraceno.com, friendly Antonella).

Eating in Manarola

Many hardworking places line the main drag. I like the Scorza family's friendly **Trattoria Il Porticciolo** (€7 pastas, tasty seafood-based dishes, free glass of *sciacchetrà* dessert wine with this book, Thu-Tue 10:30-22:30, closed Wed, reservations smart for dinner, just below the train tracks at Via R. Birolli 92, tel. 0187-920-083, Davide).

For harborside dining, **Marina Piccola** is the winner. While less friendly and a little more expensive, the setting is memorable (€10 pastas, Wed-Mon 11:30-16:30 & 18:30-22:00, closed Tue, tel. 0187-920-923).

Trattoria Dal Billy is a hidden gem, high on the hill but well worth the climb, with impressive views over the valley. It's run by two friends, Edoardo and Dario; the original "Billy"—a retired sea captain—still helps out and will regale you with fisherman's tales as you survey the photo gallery of impressive catches. Among your choices are black pasta with seafood and squid ink, green pasta with artichokes, mixed seafood starters, and homemade desserts. Dinner reservations are a must (€11 pastas, €14 *secondi*, generally daily 8:00-10:00, 12:00-15:00 & 19:00-23:30, sometimes closed Thu, Via Aldo Rollandi 122, tel. 0187-920-628). Exit the church square at the top of Manarola right at the back by the dry-stone wall, follow the steps, and continue ahead.

Corniglia (Town #3)

This is the quiet town—the only one of the five not on the water—with a mellow main square. According to a (likely fanciful) local legend, the town was originally settled by a Roman farmer who named it for his mother, Cornelia (how Corniglia is pronounced). The town and its ancient residents produced a wine so famous that—some say—vases found at Pompeii touted its virtues. Regardless of the veracity of the legends, wine remains Corniglia's lifeblood today. Follow the pungent smell of ripe grapes into an alley cellar and get a local to let you dip a straw into a keg. Remote and less visited than the other Cinque Terre towns, Corniglia has fewer tourists, cooler temperatures, a few restaurants, a windy overlook on its promontory, and plenty of

THE CINQUE TERRE

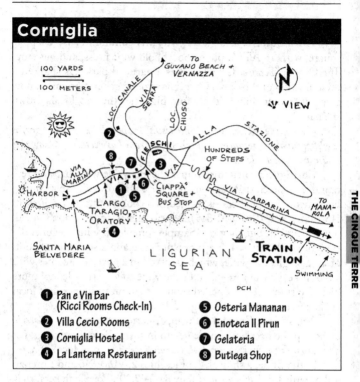

Corniglia

- **①** Pan e Vin Bar (Ricci Rooms Check-In)
- **②** Villa Cecio Rooms
- **③** Corniglia Hostel
- **④** La Lanterna Restaurant
- **⑤** Osteria Mananan
- **⑥** Enoteca Il Pirun
- **⑦** Gelateria
- **⑧** Butiega Shop

THE CINQUE TERRE

private rooms for rent (ask at any bar or shop, no cheaper than other towns).

Orientation to Corniglia

Arrival in Corniglia

From the station, a footpath zigzags up nearly 400 steps to the town. Or take the green shuttle bus, generally timed to meet arriving trains (€1.50 one-way, €2.50 round-trip, free with Cinque Terre Card, 2/hour). Before leaving for the bus, confirm departure times at the TI in the train station or consult the schedule posted at the stop (daily 6:30-19:30). If you're driving, be aware that only residents can park on the main road between the recommended Villa Cecio and the point where the steep switchback staircase meets the road. Beyond that area, parking is €1.50 per hour.

Self-Guided Walk

Welcome to Corniglia

We'll explore this tiny town—population 240—and end at a scenic viewpoint.

• *Begin near the bus stop, located at a...*

Town Square: The gateway to this community is "Ciappà" square, with an ATM, phone booth, old wine press, and bus stop. The Cinque Terre's designation as a national park has sparked a revitalization of the town. Corniglia's young generation might now stay put, rather than migrate into big cities the way locals did in the past.

• *Stroll the spine of Corniglia, Via Fieschi. In the fall, the smell of grapes (on their way to becoming wine) wafts from busy cellars. Along this main street, you'll see...*

Corniglia's Enticing Shops: The enjoyable wine bar and restaurant, Enoteca Il Pirun—named for a type of oddly shaped old-fashioned wine pitcher—is located in a cool cantina at Via Fieschi 115 (daily, tel. 0187-812-315). Mario and Marilena don't speak much English, but they try. Sample some local wines—generally free for small tastes. For a fun experience and a souvenir to boot, order a €3 glass of wine, which is served in a *pirun* and comes with a bib to keep. The *pirun* aerates the wine to give the alcohol more kick. Mario's recently opened small restaurant upstairs offers local cuisine (see "Eating in Corniglia," later).

Across from Enoteca Il Pirun, Alberto and Cristina's *gelateria* dishes up the best homemade gelato in town. Before ordering, get a free taste of Alberto's *miele di Corniglia*, made from local honey.

In the Butiega shop at Via Fieschi 142, Vincenzo and Lorenzo sell organic local specialties (daily 8:00-19:30). For picnickers, they offer €2.50 made-to-order ham-and-cheese sandwiches and a fun €3.50 *antipasto misto* to go. (There are good places to picnic farther along on this walk.)

• *Following Via Fieschi, you'll end up at the...*

Main Square: On Largo Taragio, tables from two bars and a trattoria spill around a WWI memorial and the town's old well. It once piped in natural spring water from the hillside to locals living without plumbing. What looks like a church is the Oratory of Santa Caterina. (An oratory is a kind of a spiritual clubhouse for a service group doing social work in the name of the Catholic Church. For more information, see "Oratory of the Dead" on page 1171.) Behind the oratory, you'll find a clearing that local children have made into a soccer field. The stone benches and viewpoint make this a peaceful place for a picnic (less crowded than the end-of-town viewpoint, described below).

• *Opposite the oratory, notice how steps lead steeply down on Via alla Marina to Corniglia's non-beach. It's a five-minute paved climb to sunning rocks, a shower, and a small deck (with a treacherous entry into the water). From the square, continue up Via Fieschi to the...*

End-of-Town Viewpoint: The Santa Maria Belvedere, named for a church that once stood here, marks the scenic end of

Corniglia. This is a super picnic spot. From here, look high to the west, where the village and sanctuary of San Bernardino straddle a ridge (a good starting point for a hike; accessible by shuttle bus from Monterosso or a long uphill hike from Vernazza). Below is the tortuous harbor, where locals hoist their boats onto the cruel rocks.

Sights in Corniglia

Beaches—This hilltop town has rocky sea access below its train station (toward Manarola). Once a beach, it's all been washed away and offers no services. Look for signs that say *al mare* or *Marina*.

Guvano beach is in the opposite direction (toward Vernazza). Guvano (GOO-vah-noh) was created by an 1893 landslide that cost the village a third of its farmland. The big news is that after decades as a nude beach, Guvano has been sold to the national park, which plans to improve access (and keep sunbathers clothed). Look for upgrades to what has been a dark, uneven walk through a long tunnel to reach the beach, and avoid the steep, overgrown, unofficial trail.

Sleeping in Corniglia

(€1 = about $1.40, country code: 39)
Perched high above the sea on a hilltop, Corniglia has plenty of private rooms (generally Db-€65). To get to the town from the station, catch the shuttle bus or make the 15-minute uphill hike. The town is riddled with humble places that charge too much and have meager business skills and a limited ability to converse with tourists—so it's almost never full.

$$ Cristiana Ricci is an exception to the rule. She communicates well and is reliable, renting four small, clean, and peaceful rooms—two with kitchens and one with a terrace and sweeping view—just inland from the bus stop (Db-€60-70, Qb-€90, €10/day less when you stay 2 or more nights, free Internet access, check in at the Pan e Vin bar at Via Fieschi 123, mobile 338-937-6547, cri_affittacamere@virgilio.it, Stefano). Her mom rents a big, modern apartment (€90 for 2-4 people).

$$ Villa Cecio feels like an abandoned hotel. They offer eight well-worn rooms on the outskirts of town, with saggy beds and little character or warmth (Db-€65, ask for best Rick Steves price, cash preferred, great views, on main road 200 yards toward Vernazza at Via Serra 58, tel. 0187-812-043, fax 0187-812-138, mobile 334-350-6637, www.cecio5terre.com, info@cecio5terre.com, Giacinto). They also rent eight similar rooms in an annex on the square where the bus stops.

$ Corniglia Hostel was formerly the town's schoolhouse. It's in a pastel-yellow building up some steps from the main square where the bus stops. The playground in front is often busy with happy kids. Despite its institutional atmosphere, the hostel's prices, central location, and bright and clean rooms ensure its popularity (€24/bed in two 8-bed dorms, €27 with minimal breakfast; four Db-€55, €60 with breakfast; air-con, self-serve laundry, lockers, no public spaces except lobby, office open 7:00-13:00 & 15:00-24:00, rooms closed 13:00-15:00, 1:30 curfew, Via alla Stazione 3, tel. 0187-812-559, fax 0187-763-984, www.ostellocorniglia.com but reserve at www.hostelworld.com, ostellocorniglia@gmail.com, helpful Daniele).

Eating in Corniglia

Corniglia has few restaurants. **Cecio,** above the town, has terrace seating with a view of the sea. The trattoria **La Lantera,** on the main square, is the most atmospheric. (Neither comes with particularly charming service.)

Restaurant **Osteria Mananan**—between the Ciappà bus stop and the main square on Via Fieschi—serves the best food in town in its small stony and elegant interior (Fri-Wed 12:15-14:30 & 19:45-21:15, closed Thu, no outdoor seating, tel. 0187-821-166). **Enoteca Il Pirun,** on Via Fieschi, has a small restaurant above the wine bar, where Mario serves typical local dishes (€28 fixed-price meal includes homemade wine, daily 12:00-16:00 & 19:30-23:30, tel. 0187-812-315).

Vernazza (Town #4)

With the closest thing to a natural harbor—overseen by a ruined castle and a stout stone church—Vernazza is the jewel of the Cinque Terre. Only the occasional noisy slurping up of the train by the mountain reminds you of the modern world.

The action is at the harbor, where you'll find outdoor restaurants, a bar hanging on the edge of the castle, a breakwater with a promenade, and a tailgate-party street market every Tuesday morning. In the summer, the beach becomes a soccer field, where teams fielded by local bars and restaurants provide late-night entertainment. In the dark, locals fish off the promontory, using glowing bobbers that shine in the waves.

Proud of their Vernazzan heritage, the town's 500 residents like to brag: "Vernazza is locally owned. Portofino has sold out." Fearing the change it would bring, keep-Vernazza-small proponents stopped the construction of a major road into the town and region. Families are tight and go back centuries; several generations stay together. In the winter, the population shrinks, as many people return to their more comfortable big-city apartments to spend the money they reaped during the tourist season.

Leisure time is devoted to taking part in the *passeggiata*—strolling lazily together up and down the main street. Sit on a bench and study the passersby doing their *vasche* (laps). Explore the characteristic alleys, called *carugi*. Learn—and live—the phrase *"la vita pigra di Vernazza"* (the lazy life of Vernazza).

Orientation to Vernazza

Tourist Information

The TI and park information booths are both at the train station. The park office is more of a souvenir shop, while the combination TI/train-ticket desk sells Cinque Terre Cards (park office—daily April-Oct 9:30-20:00, Nov-March until 19:30, tel. 0187-812-524, TI/train-ticket desk—daily 7:00-19:30, tel. 0187-812-533 but often busy). Some of the staff at the TI/train desk will ring the owner of the room you have reserved so that he or she can meet you, but they cannot make reservations. Public WCs are nearby in the station.

Arrival in Vernazza

By Train: Vernazza's train station is only about three cars long, but the trains are much longer, so most of the cars come to a stop in a long, dark tunnel. Get out anyway, and walk through the tunnel to the station.

By Car: There's a non-resident parking lot, but be aware that parking is tough—the lot fills up quickly from May through September (€2/hour, €12/24 hours, cash only, about 500 yards above town, pay first at the parking stand before getting your spot). A hardworking shuttle service, generally with friendly English-speaking Beppe or Simone behind the wheel, connects the lot to the top of town (€1.50, free with Cinque Terre Card, 3-4/hour, runs 7:00-19:00). Yellow lines mark parking spots for residents. The highest lot (a side-trip uphill) is for overnight stays.

Helpful Hints

Internet Access: The **Blue Marlin Bar,** run by Massimo and Carmen, has the lowest prices and longest hours (€0.10/minute, open earlier but Internet available Fri-Wed 9:30-22:30, closed Thu, see listing on page 1162). The slick six-terminal **Internet Point,** run by Alberto and Isabella, is in the village center (€0.15/minute, €0.10/minute after 30 minutes, daily June-Oct 9:30-23:00, until 20:00 Nov-May, Wi-Fi, will burn your digital photos to a CD or DVD for €6, sells international phone cards, ask about the Rick Steves discount in their **Cantina Del Molo Enoteca** across the street, tel. 0187-812-949).

Laundry: Lavanderia il Carugetto is completely self-serve (coin-op, wash-€6, dry-€5, daily 8:00-22:00, on a narrow lane a block off the main drag opposite the Internet Point, operated by the fish shop).

Massage: Kate offers one-hour holistic massage (€50), hot stone massage (€60), and reflexology (€40, tel. 0187-812-537, mobile 333-568-4653, http://vernazzamassage5terre.com, katarina allen@hotmail.com). Stephanie, an American expat, gives a good, strong therapeutic massage in a neat little studio at the top of town (€50/hour, mobile 338-9429-494, stephsette @gmail.com).

Best Views: A steep 10-minute hike in either direction from Vernazza gives you a classic village photo op (for the best light, head toward Corniglia in the morning, and toward Monterosso in the evening). Franco's **Bar La Torre,** with a panoramic terrace, is uphill from his restaurant on the trail toward Corniglia (listed in "Eating in Vernazza," later).

Self-Guided Walks

Welcome to Vernazza

This tour includes Vernazza's characteristic town squares, and ends on its scenic breakwater.

• *From the train station, walk uphill until you hit the parking lot, with a bank, a post office, and a barrier that keeps out all but service vehicles. Vernazza's shuttle buses run from here to the parking lot and into the hills. Walk to the tidy, modern square called...*

Fontana Vecchia: Named after a long-gone fountain, this is where older locals remember the river filled with townswomen doing their washing. Now they enjoy checking on the baby ducks. The trail leads up to the cemetery. Imagine the entire village sadly trudging up here during funerals. (The cemetery is peaceful and evocative at sunset, when the fading light touches each crypt.)

• *Glad to be here in happier times, begin your saunter downhill to the harbor. Just before the* Pensione Sorriso *sign, on your right (big brown wood doors), you'll see the...*

Ambulance Barn: A group of volunteers is always on call for a dash to the hospital, 40 minutes away in La Spezia. Opposite the barn is a big empty lot. Like many landowners, the owner of Pensione Sorriso had plans to expand, but since the 1980s, the government said no. While some landowners are frustrated, the old character of these towns survives.

• *A few steps farther along (past the town clinic and library), you'll see a...*

World Wars Monument: Look for a marble plaque in the wall to your left, dedicated to those killed in the World Wars. Not a family in Vernazza was spared. Listed on the left are soldiers *morti in combattimento,* who died in World War I; on the right is the World War II section. Some were deported to *Germania;* others—labeled *Part* (stands for *partigiani,* or partisans)—were killed while fighting against Mussolini. Cynics considered partisans less than heroes. After 1943, Hitler called up Italian boys over 15. Rather than die on the front for Hitler, they escaped to the hills. They became "resistance fighters" in order to remain free.

The path to Corniglia leaves from here (behind and above the plaque). Behind you is a small square and playground, decorated with three millstones, once used to grind local olives into oil. There's a good chance you'll see an expat mom here at the village playground with her kids. I've met many American women who fell in love with a local guy, stayed, and are now happily raising families here. (But I've never met an American guy who moved in with a local girl.)

From here, Vernazza's tiny river goes underground. Until the 1950s, Vernazza's river ran openly through the center of town. Old-timers recall the days before the breakwater, when the river cascaded down and the surf crashed along Vernazza's main drag. Back then, the town was nicknamed "Little Venice" for the series of romantic bridges that arched over the stream, connecting the two sides of the town before the main road was built.

Before the tracks (on the left), the wall has 10 spaces, one reserved for each party's political ads during elections—a kind of local pollution control. The map on the right, under the railway tracks, shows the region's hiking trails. Trail #2 is the basic favorite. The second set of tracks (nearer the harbor) was recently renovated to lessen the disruptive noise, but locals say it made no difference.

• *Follow the road downhill to...*

Vernazza's "Business Center": Here, you'll pass many locals doing their *vasche* (laps). At Enoteca Sotto l'Arco, Gerry and Paola sell wine—they can uncork it and throw in plastic glasses—and delightful jars of local pesto, which goes great on bread (Wed-Mon 9:00-21:00, Tue 12:30-21:00, Via Roma 70). Next, you'll pass the Blue Marlin Bar (Vernazza's top nightspot) and the tiny Chapel of Santa Marta (the small stone chapel with iron grillwork over the window), where Mass is celebrated only on special Sundays. Farther down, you'll walk by a grocery, *gelateria,* bakery, pharmacy, another grocery, and another *gelateria.* There are plenty of fun and cheap food-to-go options here.

Vernazza

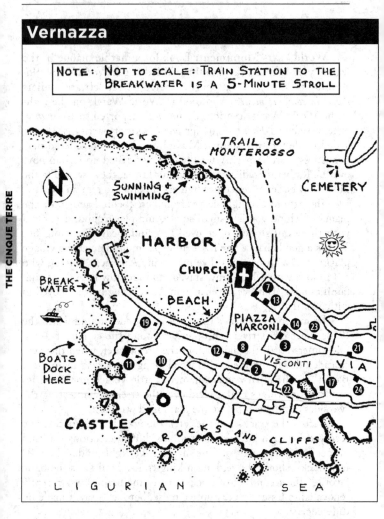

NOTE: NOT TO SCALE: TRAIN STATION TO THE BREAKWATER IS A 5-MINUTE STROLL

ROCKS

TRAIL TO MONTEROSSO

CEMETERY

SUNNING & SWIMMING

HARBOR

CHURCH

BREAK-WATER

ROCKS

BEACH

PIAZZA MARCONI

BOATS DOCK HERE

VISCONTI

VIA

CASTLE

ROCKS AND CLIFFS

LIGURIAN   SEA

• *On the left, in front of the second* gelateria, *an arch (with a peaceful little sitting perch atop it) leads to what was a beach, where the town's stream used to hit the sea back in the 1970s. Continue down to the...*

Harbor Square and Breakwater: Vernazza, with the only natural harbor of the Cinque Terre, was established as the sole place boats could pick up the fine local wine. The two-foot-high square stone at the foot of the stairs by the recommended Burgus Wine Bar is marked *Sasso del Sego* (stone of tallow). Workers crushed animal flesh and fat in its basin to make tallow, which drained out of the tiny hole below. The tallow was then used to waterproof boats or wine barrels. For more town history, step into the Burgus to see fascinating old photos of Vernazza on the wall.

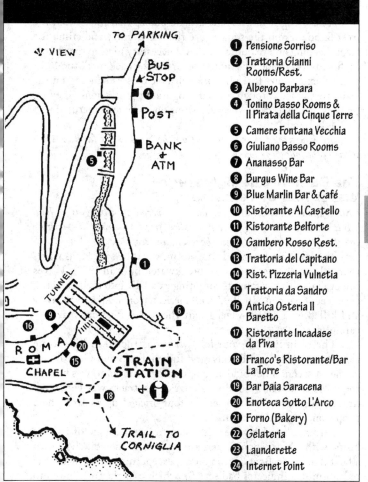

On the far side (behind the recommended Ristorante Pizzeria Vulnetia), peek into the tiny street with its commotion of arches. Vernazza's most characteristic side streets, called *carugi,* lead up from here. The trail (above the church, toward Monterosso) leads to the classic view of Vernazza (see "Best Views," under "Helpful Hints" earlier in this section).

Located in front of the harborside church, the tiny piazza—decorated with a river-rock mosaic—is a popular hangout spot. It's where Vernazza's old ladies soak up the last bit of sun, and kids enjoy a patch of level ball field.

Vernazza's harborfront church is unusual for its strange entryway, which faces east (altar side). With relative peace and prosperity in the 16th century, the townspeople doubled the church in size, causing it to overtake a little piazza that once faced the west facade. From the square, use the "new" entry and climb the steps, keeping an eye out for the level necessary to keep the church high and dry. Inside, the lighter pillars in the back mark the 16th-century extension. Three historic portable crosses hanging on the walls are carried through town during Easter processions. They are replicas of crosses that Vernazza ships once carried on crusades to the Holy Land.

• *Finish your town tour seated out on the breakwater (and consider starting the following tour).*

The Burned-Out Sightseer's Visual Tour of Vernazza

• *Sit at the end of the harbor breakwater (perhaps with a glass of local white wine or something more interesting from a nearby bar—borrow the glass, they don't mind), face the town, and see...*

The Harbor: In a moderate storm, you'd be soaked, as waves routinely crash over the *molo* (breakwater, built in 1972). Waves can even wash away tourists squinting excitedly into their cameras. (I've seen it happen.) In 2007, an American woman was swept away and killed by a rogue wave. Enjoy the new waterfront piazza—carefully.

The train line (to your left) was constructed in 1874 to tie together a newly united Italy, and linked Turin and Genoa with Rome. A second line (hidden in a tunnel at this point) was built in the 1920s. The yellow building alongside the tracks was Vernazza's first train station. You can see the four bricked-up alcoves where people once waited for trains.

Vernazza's fishing fleet is down to just a couple of fishing boats (with the net spools). Vernazzans are still more likely to own a boat than a car. Boats are on buoys, except in winter or when the red storm flag indicates bad seas (in which case they're allowed to be pulled up onto the square—which is usually reserved for restaurant tables). In the 1970s, tiny Vernazza had one of Italy's top water polo teams, and the harbor was their "pool." Later, when the league required a real pool, Vernazza dropped out.

The Castle: On the far right, the castle, which is now a grassy park with great views (and nothing but stones), still guards the town (€1.50 donation supports the local Red Cross, daily 10:00-19:00; from harbor, take stairs by Trattoria Gianni and follow *Ristorante Al Castello* signs, tower is a few steps beyond). It was the town's lookout back in pirate days. The highest umbrellas mark the recommended Ristorante Al Castello. The squat tower on the water is great for a glass of wine or a meal. From the breakwater, you could follow the rope to the Ristorante Belforte, and pop inside, past the submarine-strength door. A photo of a major storm showing the entire tower under a wave (not uncommon in the winter) hangs near the bar.

The Town: Vernazza has two halves. *Sciuiu* (Vernazzan dialect for "flowery") is the sunny side on the left, and *luvegu* (dank) is the shady side on the right. Houses below the castle were connected by an interior arcade—ideal for fleeing attacks. The "Ligurian pastel" colors are regulated by a commissioner of good taste in the regional government. The square before you is locally famous for some of the area's finest restaurants. The big red central house—on the site where Genoan warships were built in the 12th century—used to be a guardhouse.

In the Middle Ages, there was no beach or square. The water went right up to the buildings, where boats would tie up, Venetian-style. Imagine what Vernazza looked like in those days, when it was the biggest and richest of the Cinque Terre towns. There was no pastel plaster, just fine stonework (traces of which survive above the Trattoria del Capitano). Apart from the added plaster, the general shape and size of the town has changed little in five centuries. Survey the windows and notice inhabitants quietly gazing back.

Above the Town: The small, round tower above the red guardhouse—another part of the city fortifications—reminds us of Vernazza's importance in the Middle Ages, when it was a key ally of Genoa (whose archenemies were the other maritime republics, especially Pisa). Franco's Ristorante and Bar La Torre, just behind the tower, welcomes hikers who are finishing, starting, or simply contemplating the Corniglia-Vernazza hike, with great town views. Vineyards fill the mountainside beyond the town. Notice the many terraces. Someone—probably after too much of that local wine—calculated that the roughly 3,000 miles of dry-stone walls built to terrace the region's vineyards have the same amount of stonework as the Great Wall of China.

Wine production is down nowadays, as the younger residents choose less physical work. But locals still maintain their tiny plots and proudly serve their family wines. The patchwork of local vineyards is atomized and complex because of inheritance traditions. Historically, families divided their land between their children. Parents wanted each child to get some good land. Because some lots were "kissed by the sun" while others were shady, the lots were split into increasingly tiny and eventually unviable pieces.

A single steel train line winds up the gully behind the tower. It is for the vintner's *trenino*, the tiny service train. Play "Where's *trenino?*" and see if you can find two trains. The vineyards once stretched as high as you can see, but since fewer people sweat in the fields these days, the most distant terraces have gone wild again.

The Church, School, and City Hall: Vernazza's Ligurian

Gothic church, built with black stones quarried from Punta Mesco (the distant point behind you), dates from 1318. Note the gray stone that marks the church's 16th-century expansion. The gray-and-red house above the spire is the local elementary school (about 25 children attend). High-schoolers go to the "big city": La Spezia. The red building to the right of the schoolhouse, a former monastery, is the City Hall. Vernazza and Corniglia function as one community. Through most of the 1990s, the local government was Communist. In 1999, they elected a coalition of many parties working to rise above ideologies and simply make Vernazza a better place. Finally, on the top of the hill, with the best view of all, is the town cemetery.

Sights in Vernazza

Tuesday-Morning Market—Vernazza's meager business community is augmented Tuesday mornings (8:00-13:00) when a gang of cars and trucks pull into town for a tailgate market.

Beach—The harbor's sandy cove has sunning rocks and showers by the breakwater. There's also a ladder on the breakwater for deep-water access.

Boat Rental—Nord Est rents canoes and small motorboats from their stand on the harbor. With a rental boat, you can reach a tiny *acqua pendente* (waterfall) cove between Vernazza and Monterosso; locals call it their *laguna blu* (motorboats-€60/2 hours, €80/4 hours; plus gas, usually about €15; includes snorkeling gear; May-Oct only, mobile 338-700-0436, manuelamoggia@tiscali.it).

Shuttle Bus Joyride—For a cheap and scenic joyride, with a chance to chat about the region with friendly Beppe or Simone, ride the shuttle bus for the entire route for the cost of a round-trip ticket. Some buses also head to two sanctuaries in the hills above town (4/day—usually at 7:00, 9:45, 12:00, and 15:00; schedule posted at park office, train station, and bus stop in front of post office; €2.50 one-way, free with Cinque Terre Card, churches at sanctuaries usually closed). The high-country 40-minute loop—buses are marked *Drignana*—gives you lots of scenery without having to hike (don't take buses marked *No panoramic*, as these won't take scenic routes).

Nightlife in Vernazza

Vernazza's younger generation of restaurant workers lets loose after-hours. They work hard through the tourist season, travel in the winter, speak English, and enjoy connecting with international visitors. After the restaurants close down, the town is quiet except for a couple of nightspots. For more information on the Blue

Marlin, Ananasso, Il Pirata, and Ristorante Incandase, see their listings under "Eating in Vernazza," later.

Blue Marlin Bar dominates the late-night scene with a mix of locals and tourists, home-cooked food until 22:00, good drinks, and piano jam sessions. If you're young and hip, this is *the* place to hang out.

Ananasso Bar offers early-evening happy-hour fun and cocktails (called *"aperitivi"*) that both locals and visitors enjoy. Its harborfront tables get the last sunshine of the day.

Burgus Wine Bar, chic and cool with a jazz ambience, is a popular early-evening and after-dinner harborside hangout. Sip local wine or a cocktail, and sample Lorenza's artful complimentary snack foods, available 18:00-20:30. Let her explain the historic town photos and museum cases of artifacts (Tue-Sun 6:45-24:00, closed Mon, also handy for early breakfast, Piazza Marconi 4, tel. 0187-812-556).

Il Pirata delle Cinque Terre, at the top of the town, features the entertaining Canoli brothers, who fill a happy crowd of tourists with wonderful Sicilian pastries and drinks each evening. Many come for dinner and end up staying because of these two wild and crazy guys and the camaraderie they create among their diners.

Ristorante Incadase da Piva (tucked up the lane behind the pharmacy) is the haunt of Piva, Vernazza's troubadour. Piva often gets out his guitar and sings traditional local songs as well as his own compositions. If you're looking for a local Hemingway, check here.

Franco's **Bar La Torre,** clinging to the terraces above Ristorante La Torre, has more evening life than nightlife—it closes around 22:00. Wine bottles are reasonably priced around €12, and the soaring view is intoxicating.

Really Late: There's a little cave on the beach just under the church that lends itself to fun in the wee hours, when everything else is closed.

Sleeping in Vernazza

(€1 = about $1.40, country code: 39)
Vernazza, the spindly and salty essence of the Cinque Terre, is my top choice for a home base. Off-season (Oct-March), you can generally arrive without a reservation and find a place, but at other times, it's smart to book ahead (especially for June-Aug, any weekend, and holidays such as Easter).

People recommended here are listed for their communication skills (they speak English, have email, are reliable with bookings) and because they rent several rooms. Consequently, my recommendations charge more than comparable rooms you'll find if you shop around. Comparison-shopping will likely save you €10-20 per double per night—and often get you a better place and view to boot. The real Vernazza gems are stray single rooms with owners who have no interest in booking in advance or messing with email. Arrive by early afternoon and drop by any shop or bar and ask; most locals know someone who rents rooms.

Anywhere you stay here requires some climbing, but keep in mind that more climbing means better views. Most do not include breakfast. Cash is preferred or required almost everywhere. Night noise can be a problem if you're near the station. Rooms on the harbor come with church bells (but only between 7:00 and 22:00).

Pensions

These pensions are located on the Vernazza map.

$$$ Pensione Sorriso is the oldest pension in town (and where I stayed on my first visit in 1975). Above the train station, it's run by Aldo and Francesca—the local Sonny and Cher—who welcome guests to their 19 rooms. While the main building has the charm, it comes with train noise and saggy beds; the annex, up the street, is in a quieter apartment that feels forgotten (Sb-€70, D-€85, Db-€110 without air-con, Db-€125 with air-con, Tb-€130, includes breakfast, peaceful garden, Via Gavino 4, tel. 0187-812-224, fax 0187-821-198, www.pensionesorriso.com, info@pensione sorriso.com).

$$$ Trattoria Gianni rents 27 small rooms and three apartments just under the castle. The rooms are in three buildings—one funky, two modern—up a hundred tight, winding spiral stairs. The funky ones, which may or may not have private baths, are artfully decorated à la shipwreck, with tiny balconies and grand sea views *(con vista sul mare)*. The comfy new *(nuovo)* rooms lack views. Both have modern bathrooms and access to a super-scenic cliff-hanging guests' garden. Steely Marisa requires check-in before 16:00 or a phone call to explain when you're coming. Emanuele (Gianni's son, who now runs the restaurant), Simona, and the staff speak a little English (S-€45, D-€80, Db-€120, Tb-€140, for best prices pay cash and mention this book when you reserve, cancellations required a week in advance or you'll be charged one night's deposit, breakfast-€5, closed Jan-Feb, Piazza Marconi 5, tel. & fax 0187-812-228, tel. 0187-821-003, on Wed call mobile 393-9008-155 instead, www.giannifranzi.it, info@giannifranzi.it). Pick up your keys at Trattoria Gianni's restaurant/reception on the harbor square. If they're booked up, Simona may show you a room in a friend's place (no Rick Steves discount).

$$ Albergo Barbara rents nine simple but clean and modern rooms overlooking the harbor square—most with small windows and small views. It's run by English-speaking Giuseppe and his no-nonsense Swiss wife, Patricia (D-€55, Db-€65-70, big Db with nice harbor view-€110, 2-night stay preferred, free Wi-Fi, closed Dec-Feb, Piazza Marconi 30, tel. & fax 0187-812-398, mobile 338-793-3261, reserve online with credit card but pay cash, www .albergobarbara.it, info@albergobarbara.it).

Private Rooms *(Affitta Camere)*

Vernazza is honeycombed with private rooms year-round, offering the best values in town. Owners may be reluctant to reserve rooms far in advance. It's easiest to call a day or two ahead or simply show up in the morning and look around. Doubles cost €55-90, depending on the view, season, and plumbing—you get what you pay for. Most places accept only cash. Some have killer views, come with lots of stairs, and cost the same as a small, dark place on a back lane over the train tracks. Little English is spoken at many of these places. If you call to let them know your arrival time (or call when you arrive, using your mobile phone or the pay phone just below the station), they'll meet you at the train station.

Well-Managed and Well-Appointed Rooms in the Inland Part of Town

$$$ Tonino Basso rents four super clean, modern rooms—at a steep price. Each room has its own computer for free Internet access. He's in the only building in Vernazza with an elevator. You get tranquility and air-conditioning, but no views (Sb-€65, Db-€120, Tb-€150, Qb-€180, prices go down Nov-March, call Tonino's mobile number upon arrival and he'll meet you, tel. 0187-821-264, mobile 335-269-436, fax 0187-812-807, toninobasso @libero.it). If you can't locate Tonino, ask his friends at Enoteca Sotto L'Arco at Via Roma 70.

$$ Camere Fontana Vecchia is a delightful place, with four bright, spacious, quiet rooms and an apartment near the post office (no view). As the only place in Vernazza with almost no stairs to climb and the sound of a babbling brook outside your window, it's perhaps the best value in town (D-€70, Db-€80, T-€95, Tb-€110, super-trendy 2-person apartment-€100, fans and heat, open all year, Via Gavino 15, tel. 0187-821-130, mobile 333-454-9371, fax 0187-812-261, m.annamaria@libero.it, youthful and efficient Anna speaks English). If no one answers, ask at Enoteca Sotto L'Arco on the main drag.

$$ Giuliano Basso rents four pleasant rooms, crafted with care, just above town in the terraced wilds (sea views from terraces). Straddling a ravine among orange trees, it's an artfully decorated Robinson Crusoe–chic wonderland, proudly built out of stone by Giuliano himself (Db-€80, Db suite with air-con-€100, Db suite with private rooftop balcony-€100, extra bed-€25, fridge access, free Internet access; above train station, take the ramp just before Pensione Sorriso, more train noise than others, mobile 333-341-4792, or have Enoteca Sotto L'Arco contact him or his American partner Michele, www.cdh.it/giuliano, giuliano@cdh.it).

Other Reliable Places Scattered Through Town and the Harborside

These places are not identified on this book's map; ask for directions when you reserve.

$$$ La Malà is Vernazza's jetsetter pad. Four pristine white rooms boast four-star-hotel-type extras, a common terrace looking out over the rocky shore, and air-conditioning (Db-€150, Db suite-€210, includes breakfast at a designated bar, tel. 334-287-5718, fax 0187-812-218, www.lamala.it, info@lamala.it, Giamba and Armanda). It's a climb—way, way up to the top of town. They also rent the simpler "Armanda's Room" nearby (no view, Db-€70) and an apartment (€150/2 people, extra bed-€20, ring bell at Piazza Marconi 15).

$$ Monica Lercari rents several classy rooms with modern comforts, perched at the top of town (Db-€80, seaview D-€100, grand seaview terrace D-€120, "honeymoon suite" Db-€180 also covers your choice of bike or rowboat rental; includes breakfast, air-con, next to recommended Ristorante Al Castello, tel. 0187-812-296, alcastellovernazza@yahoo.it).

$$ Antonio and Ingrid Fenelli Camere rent three very central, comfy, and fairly priced rooms that are an excellent value. You'll meet friendly Antonio—a hulking man in a huge white T-shirt and bathing suit who's a fixture on the village streets—and his charming petite English-speaking wife Ingrid (small Db-€55, Db-€70, Tb-€80, two-person apartment with terrace-€95, air-con, 10 steps above pharmacy at Via Carattino 2, tel. 0187-812-183). They have no email, but getting a room by phone or in person is worth the trouble.

$$ Memo Rooms has three clean and spacious rooms that offer good value. They overlook the main street, in what feels like a miniature hotel. Enrica will meet you if you call upon arrival (Db-€70, Via Roma 15, tel. 0187-812-360, mobile 338-285-2385).

$$ Martina Callo's four air-conditioned rooms overlook the square; they're up plenty of steps near the silent-at-night church tower (room #1: Tb-€100 or Qb-€115 with harbor view; room #2: huge Qb family room with no view-€110; room #3: Db with grand view terrace-€75; room #4: roomy Db with no view-€60; ring bell at Piazza Marconi 26, tel. & fax 0187-812-365, mobile 329-435-5344, www.roomartina.com, roomartina@roomartina.com).

$$ Nicolina rents five recently renovated units with double-paned windows. Two rooms are in the center over the pharmacy, up a few steep steps, one has only sleeper sofas (Db-€80); another two are in a different building with great views (Db-€100, Tb-€120, Qb-€150); and the last unit is a two-bedroom quadruple with even better views (€200). Inquire at Pizzeria Vulnetia on the harbor square (Piazza Marconi 29, tel. & fax 0187-821-193, www.camere nicolina.it, camerenicolina.info@cdh.it).

$$ Rosa Vitali rents two four-person apartments across from the pharmacy overlooking the main street. One has a terrace and fridge (top floor); the other has windows and a full kitchen (Db-€85, Tb-€110, Qb-€130, reception at Via Visconti 10 between the grotto and Piazza Marconi, tel. 0187-821-181, mobile 340-267-5009, www.rosacamere.it, rosa.vitali@libero.it).

$$ Francamaria and her kind husband Andrea rent eight sharp, comfortable, and creatively renovated but expensive rooms—all described in detail on her website (small no-view Db-€75, big and modern no-view Db-€90, larger view Db-up to €115, Qb-€125-160, family apartments, prices depend on view and size, few steps, reception at Piazza Marconi 30, don't confuse with Albergo Barbara at same address, tel. & fax 0187-812-002, mobile 328-711-9728, www.francamaria.com, francamaria@francamaria .com).

More Private Rooms in Vernazza

$$ Maria Capellini rents a couple of simple, clean rooms, including one on the ground floor right on the harbor (Db with kitchen-€85, Tb-€110, cash only, fans, mobile 338-436-3411, www.mariacapellini.com, mariacapellini@hotmail.it, Maria and Giacomo).

$$ Il Pirata delle Cinque Terre has a few big, basic rooms with the sounds of the river below. Managed by Noelia and Leyla, wives of the drink-slinging Canoli brothers (see listing under "Eating in Vernazza"), it's a two-minute walk from the bar and a five-minute walk to the sea (Db-€90, Tb-€130, Qb-€160; includes breakfast with this book at the Il Pirata bar—which also functions as the reception; 2-night minimum, cash only, guaranteed hot water, convenient to parking; from the Il Pirata, hike up 100 yards to the yellow building that was the old mill; tel. 0187-812-047, mobile 338-596-2503, www.ilpiratarooms.com, ilpiratarooms @libero.it).

$$ Ivo's Camere rents two simple rooms high above the main street (Db-€75, Via Roma 6, includes breakfast at a nearby bar, reception at Pizzeria Fratelli Basso, free Internet access, Via Roma 1, tel. 0187-821-042, mobile 333-477-5521, www.ivocamere.com, post@ivocamere.com). They also rent a studio apartment (€100).

$$ Daria Bianchi rents 12 clean, spacious, and comfortable rooms near the station. Four rooms are above the Blue Marlin looking down on the main street, and eight are near the City Hall (Db-€70, Qb-€100-120, fans, reception next to Blue Marlin Bar, tel. 0187-812-151, mobile 338-581-4688, www.vernazzarooms.com).

$$ Emanuela Colombo has two rooms—one spacious and basic on the main square, the other *molto* chic and located in a quiet side street (Db-€90, Tb-€110, check in at Enoteca Sotto L'Arco, tel. 339-834-2486, www.vacanzemanuela.it, manuela@libero.it).

More Options: **$$ Affitta Camere Alberto Basso** (a clean, modern room with a noisy harbor/piazza view, Db-€75, check in at Internet Point, albertobasso@hotmail.com), **$$ Capitano Rooms** (3 recently remodeled rooms above the main drag, Db-€90, ask for Paolo or Barbara at the recommended Trattoria del Capitano restaurant, tel. 0187-812-201), **$$$ Eva's Rooms** (3 rooms, Db-€60-80, overlooking main street with some train noise, ring at Via Roma 56, tel. 0187-821-134, www.evasrooms.it, massimoeva@libero.it), **$$$ Manuela Moggia** (Db-€80, Tb-€95, Qb with kitchen-€125, top of the town at Via Gavino 22, tel. 0187-812-397, mobile 333-413-6374, www.manuela-vernazza.com, manuelamoggia@tiscali.it), **$$$ Villa Antonia** (2 nice rooms sharing 1 bathroom, D-€70, on the main drag, mobile 320-372-4570 or 333-971-5602), and **$$$ Elisabetta Rooms** (3 rooms that need updating but have fantastic views, Db-€65, fans, Via Carattino 62, mobile 347-451-1834, www.elisabettacarro.it, carroelisabetta@hotmail.com).

Eating in Vernazza

Breakfast

Locals take breakfast about as seriously as flossing. A cappuccino and a pastry or a piece of focaccia from a bar or bakery does it. Most of my recommended accommodations don't come with breakfast (when they do, I've noted so in my listings). Instead, you have several fun options. The first two, on the harborfront square, have the best ambience.

Ananasso Bar feels Old World, with youthful energy and a great location. They offer toasted *panini*, pastries, and designer cappuccino. You can eat a bit cheaper at the bar (you're welcome to picnic on the nearby bench or seawall rocks with a Mediterranean view) or enjoy the best-situated tables in town (Fri-Wed 8:00-late, closed Thu).

Burgus Wine Bar, described earlier in "Nightlife in Vernazza," serves a continental breakfast by the harbor for early birds (€4, from 6:45).

Blue Marlin Bar (mid-town, just below the train station) serves a good array of clearly priced à la carte items including eggs and bacon, adding up to the priciest breakfast in town (likely to total €10). It's run by Massimo and Carmen (Fri-Wed 7:00-24:00, closed Thu, tel. 0187-821-149). If you're awaiting a train any time of day, the Blue Marlin's outdoor seats beat the platform.

Il Pirata delle Cinque Terre is located at the top of the town, where the dynamic Sicilian duo Gianluca and Massimo (twins, a.k.a. the Canoli brothers) enthusiastically offer a great assortment of handcrafted authentic Sicilian pastries. Their fun and playful service makes up for the lack of a view. Gianluca is a pastry artist, hand-painting fanciful sculptured marzipan. Their sweet pastry breakfasts are a hit, with a stunning array of hot-out-of-the-oven treats like *panzerotto* (made of ricotta, cinnamon, and vanilla, €2.50) and hot meat-and-cheese bruschetta (€3). Other favorites include their *granite* (slushees made from fresh fruit), but, proudly, they serve no bacon and eggs (since "this is Italy"). While the atmosphere of the place seems like suburban Milan, it has a curious charisma among its customers—bringing Vernazza a welcome bit of Sicily (daily 6:30-24:00, also simple lunches and tasty dinners, Via Gavino 36, tel. 0187-812-047).

Lunch and Dinner

If you enjoy Italian cuisine and seafood, Vernazza's restaurants are worth the splurge. All take pride in their cooking. Wander around at about 20:00 and compare the ambience, but don't wait too late to eat—many kitchens close at 22:00. To get an outdoor table on summer weekends, reserve ahead. Expect to spend €10 for pastas, €12-16 for *secondi*, and €2-3 for a cover charge. Harborside restaurants and bars are easygoing. You're welcome to grab a cup of coffee or glass of wine and disappear somewhere on the breakwater, returning your glass when you're done. If you dine in Vernazza but are staying in another town, be sure to check train schedules before dining, as trains run less frequently in the evening. While kitchens are generally closed 15:00-19:00, snacks and drinks are served all day.

Above the Harbor, by the Castle

Ristorante Al Castello is run by gracious and English-speaking Monica, her husband Massimo, kind Mario, and the rest of her family (you won't see mamma—she's busy personally cooking each home-style *secondo*). Hike high above town to just below the castle for commanding views. Their *lasagne al pesto* and scampi crêpes are time-honored family specialties. For simple fare and a special evening, reserve one of the dozen romantic cliffside seaview tables for two (Thu-Tue 12:00-15:00 for lunch, 19:00-22:00 for dinner, closed Wed and Nov-April, tel. 0187-812-296).

Ristorante Belforte's experimental and creative cuisine includes a hearty *zuppa Michela* (€21 for a boatload of seafood), fishy *spaghetti Bruno* (€13), and *trofie al pesto* (hand-rolled noodles with pesto). Their classic *antipasto del nostro chef* (€36 for six plates) is designed to be plenty for two people. From the breakwater, follow either the stairs or the rope that leads up and around to the restaurant. You'll find a tangle of tables embedded in four levels of the lower part of the old castle. For the ultimate seaside perch, call and reserve one of four tables on the *terrazza con vista* (terrace with view). Most of Belforte's seating is outdoors—if the weather's bad, the interior can get crowded (€13 pastas, €23 *secondi*, Wed-Mon 12:00-22:00, limited menu 15:00-19:00, closed Tue and Nov-March, tel. 0187-812-222, Michela).

Harborside

Gambero Rosso ("red prawn," the same name as Italy's top restaurant guide) is considered Vernazza's most venerable restaurant. It feels classy and costs more than the others. Try Chef Claudio's namesake risotto (€15 pastas, €20 *secondi*, €3 cover, Tue-Sun 12:00-15:00 & 19:00-22:00, closed Mon and Dec-Feb, Piazza Marconi 7, tel. 0187-812-265).

Trattoria del Capitano might serve the best food for the money, including *spaghetti con frutti di mare* (pasta entangled with various types of seafood) and *grigliata mista*—a mix of seasonal Mediterranean fish (€10 pastas, €16 *secondi*, €2 cover, Wed-Mon 12:00-15:00 & 19:00-22:00, closed Tue except in Aug, closed Nov-Dec, tel. 0187-812-201, while Paolo speaks English, grandpa Giacomo doesn't need to).

Trattoria Gianni is an old standby for locals and tourists who appreciate the best prices on the harbor. You'll enjoy well-prepared seafood and receive steady, reliable, and friendly service from Emanuele and Alessandro (€10 pastas, €13 *secondi*, €3 cover, check their *menù cucina tipica Vernazza*, Thu-Tue 12:00-15:00 & 19:00-22:00, closed Wed except July-Aug, tel. 0187-812-228).

Ristorante Pizzeria Vulnetia is simpler, serving regional specialties such as prizewinning *tegame alla Vernazza*—anchovies, tomatoes, and potatoes baked in the oven (€8 pizzas, €10 pastas, €15 *secondi*, €2 cover, Tue-Sun 12:00-15:30 & 18:30-22:00, closed Thu, Piazza Marconi 29, tel. 0187-821-193).

Inland, on or near the Main Street

Several of Vernazza's inland eateries manage to compete without the harbor ambience, but with slightly cheaper prices.

Trattoria da Sandro, on the main drag, mixes Genovese and Ligurian cuisine with friendly service. It can be a peaceful alternative to the harborside scene, plus they dish up award-winning stuffed mussels (Wed-Mon 12:00-15:00 & 18:30-22:00, closed Tue, Via Roma 62, tel. 0187-812-223, Gabriella and Alessandro).

Antica Osteria Il Baretto is another solid bet for homey, reasonably priced traditional cuisine, run by Simone and Jenny. As it's off the harbor and a little less glitzy than the others, it's favored by locals who prefer less noisy English while they eat (Tue-Sat 8:00-16:00 & 18:00-24:00, closed Mon, indoor and outdoor seating, Via Roma 31).

Ristorante Incadase da Piva is a rare bit of old Vernazza. For 25 years, charismatic Piva has been known for his *tegame alla Vernazza,* his *risotto con frutti di mare* (seafood risotto), and his love of music. The town troubadour, he often serenades his guests when the cooking's done (€13 pastas, €16 *secondi,* Fri-Wed 10:30-15:00 & 18:00-22:30, closed Thu, tucked away 20 yards off the main drag, up a lane behind the pharmacy).

Other Eating Options

Il Pirata delle Cinque Terre, popular for breakfast, is also a favorite for lunch and dinner (€9 pastas, salads, Sicilian specialties), and its homemade desserts and drinks. The Canoli twins entertain while they serve, as diners enjoy delicious meals while laughing out loud in this simple café/pastry shop (at the top of town; for complete description, see listing under "Breakfast," earlier).

Franco's Ristorante La Torre, sitting humbly above Vernazza on the trail to Corniglia, offers family-run warmth, a spectacular view, perfect peace, and especially romantic dinners at sunset. Hours can be sporadic, so confirm that he's open before hiking up (Wed-Mon 12:00-21:30, sometimes also open Tue, kitchen closed 15:00-19:30 but drinks served all day, cash only, tel. 0187-821-082, mobile 338-404-1181).

Bar Baia Saracena ("Saracen Bay") serves decent pizza and microwaved pastas out on the breakwater. Eat here for the economy and the view (€5-7 salads, €9 pizza, closed Wed July-Aug, closed Fri Sept-June, tel. 0187-812-113, Luca).

Pizzerias, Sandwiches, and Groceries: Vernazza's main street creatively fills tourists' needs. Two pizzerias stay busy, and while they mostly do take-out, each will let you sit and eat for the same cheap price. One has tables on the street, and the other **(Ercole)** hides a tiny terrace and a few tables out back (it's the only pizzeria in town with a wood-fired oven). **Rosticceria Ar Tian** sells pasta and cooked dishes by weight for a cheap meal to go (at bottom of Via Roma across from Gelateria Stalin). **Forno Bakery** has good focaccia and veggie tarts, and several bars sell sandwiches and pizza by the slice. **Grocery stores** also make inexpensive sandwiches to order (generally Mon-Tue and Thu-Sat 8:00-13:00 & 17:00-19:30, Wed 8:00-13:00, closed Sun). Tiny jars of pesto spread give elegance to picnics.

Gelato: The town's three *gelaterias* are good. What looks like Gelateria Amore Mio (near the grotto, mid-town), is actually Gelateria Stalin—founded in 1968 by a pastry chef with that unfortunate name. His niece Sonia, who speaks "ice cream," and nephew Francesco now run the place, and are generous with free tastes. They have a neat little licking zone with tiny benches hidden above the crowds; look for it on the little bridge a few steps past their door (daily 8:00-24:00, closes at 19:00 off-season, 24 flavors, sit there or take it to go).

Monterosso al Mare (Town #5)

This is a resort with a few cars and lots of hotels, rentable beach umbrellas, crowds, and a thriving late-night scene. Monterosso al Mare—the only Cinque Terre town built on flat land—has two parts: A new town (called Fegina) with a parking lot, train station, and TI; and an old town (Centro Storico), which cradles Old World charm in its small, crooked lanes. In the old town, you'll find hole-in-the-wall shops, pastel townscapes, and a new generation of creative small-businesspeople eager to keep their visitors happy.

A pedestrian tunnel connects the old with the new—but take a small detour around the point for a nicer walk. It offers a close-up view of two sights: a 16th-century lookout tower, built after the last serious pirate raid in 1545; and a Nazi "pillbox," a small, low concrete bunker where gunners hid. (During World War II, nearby La Spezia was an important Axis naval base, and Monterosso was bombed while the Germans were here.)

Strolling the waterfront promenade, you can pick out each of the Cinque Terre towns decorating the coast. After dark, they sparkle. Monterosso is the most enjoyable of the five for young travelers wanting to connect with other young travelers and looking for a little evening action. Even so, Monterosso is not a full-blown Portofino-style resort—and locals appreciate quiet, sensitive guests.

Orientation to Monterosso

Tourist Information

The TI Proloco is next to the train station (April-Oct daily 9:00-19:00, closed Nov-March, exit station and go left a few doors, tel. 0187-817-506, www.prolocomonterosso.it, info@prolocomonte rosso.it, Annamaria). The Cinque Terre has park offices on Piazza Garibaldi in the old town and in the train station in the new town (daily 8:00-20:00, tel. 0187-817-059, www.parconazionale5terre.it, parcoragazze@hotmail.com). If you arrive late on a summer day, head to the Internet café for tourist information (see below).

Arrival in Monterosso

By Train: Train travelers arrive in the new town, from which it's a scenic, flat 10-minute stroll to all the old-town action (leave station to the left; but for hotels in the new town, turn right out of station).

Shuttle buses run along the waterfront between the old town (Piazza Garibaldi, just beyond the tunnel), the train station, and the parking lot at the end of Via Fegina (*Campo Sportivo* stop). While the buses can be convenient, saving you a 10-minute schlep with your bags, they only go once an hour, and are likely not worth the trouble (€1.50, free with Cinque Terre Card).

The other alternative is to take a **taxi** (certain vehicles have permission to drive in the old city center). They usually wait outside the train station, but you may have to call (€7 from station to the old town, mobile 335-616-5842 or 335-628-0933).

By Car: Monterosso is 30 minutes off the freeway (exit: Levanto-Carrodano). Note that about three miles above Monterosso, a fork directs you to Centro Storico (old part of town—Via Roma parking lot with a few spots) or Fegina (the new town and beachfront parking, most likely where you want to go). You have to choose which area, because you can't drive directly from the new town to the old center, which is closed to cars without special permits.

Parking is easy (except July-Aug and summer weekends) in the huge beachfront guarded lot in the new town (€12/24 hours). If you're heading to the old town, the lot is on Via Roma, a 10-minute downhill walk to the main square (€1.50/hour, €15/24 hours in the parking structure). Near the lot you can parallel park along the road, but you pay €1.50 per hour and there's no daily limit. For the cheapest Monterosso rates, park at blue lines (5 minutes further uphill from Via Roma parking structure) for €8 per day.

Helpful Hints

Medical Help: The town's bike-riding, leather bag-toting, English-speaking doctor is Dr. Vitone, who charges €50-80 for a simple visit (less for poor students, mobile 338-853-0949).

Internet Access: The Net, a few steps off the main drag (Via Roma), has 10 high-speed computers (€1.50/10 minutes) and Wi-Fi. Enzo happily provides information on the Cinque Terre, has a line on local accommodations, and can burn your photos onto a CD for €6 (daily 9:30-23:00, off-season

Monterosso

NOTE: NOT TO SCALE—
TRAIN STATION TO
PIAZZA GARIBALDI
IS A 5-MINUTE STROLL

TO LEVANTO & AUTOSTRADA
EXIT: CARRODANO OR BRUGNATO

THE CINQUE TERRE

VIA MESCO

VIA IV NOV

VIA PADRE SEM

VIA MOLINELLI

NEW TOWN
(FEGINA)

TRAIN
STATION

TO
TRAIL TO
LEVANTO

VIA E. MONTALE

B E A C

VIA FE

FREE BEACH
IL GIGANTE STATUE

P

FREE
BEACH

L I G U R I A N

1. Hotel Villa Steno
2. Albergo Pasquale
3. La Poesia Rooms
4. Locanda il Maestrale
5. Albergo Marina
6. Hotel la Colonnina
7. Il Giardino Incantato
   & Rist. L'Alta Marea
8. L'Antica Terrazza
9. Manuel's Guesthouse
10. Buranco Agriturismo
11. Hotel Souvenir
12. Albergo al Carugio
13. Il Timone Rooms
14. A Cà du Gigante
15. Hotel Baia
16. Hotel Punta Mesco
17. Pensione Agavi
18. Ristorante Belvedere
19. Ciak Restaurant

closes for lunch and dinner breaks, Via Vittorio Emanuele 55, tel. 0187-817-288, mobile 335-778-5085, www.monterossonet .com).

Laundry: Lavarapido, in the new part of town, will return your laundry to your hotel for you (€12/13 pounds, daily 8:30-22:00, Via Molinelli 17, mobile 339-484-0940, Lucia).

Massage: Giorgio Moggia, the local physiotherapist, gives good massages at your hotel or in his studio (€60/hour, tel. 339-314-6127, giomogg@tin.it).

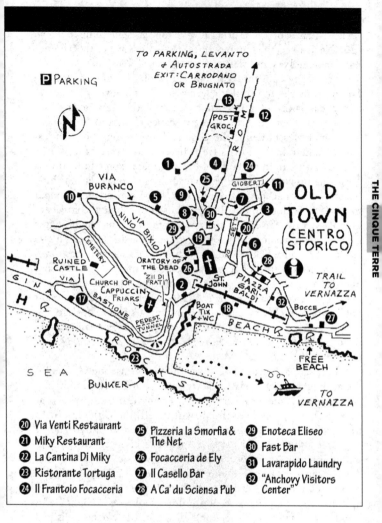

20 Via Venti Restaurant
21 Miky Restaurant
22 La Cantina Di Miky
23 Ristorante Tortuga
24 Il Frantoio Focacceria

25 Pizzeria la Smorfia & The Net
26 Focacceria de Ely
27 Il Casello Bar
28 A Ca' du Sciensa Pub

29 Enoteca Eliseo
30 Fast Bar
31 Lavarapido Laundry
32 "Anchovy Visitors Center"

Self-Guided Walk

Welcome to Monterosso

• *Hike out from the dock in the old town and climb a few rough steps to the very top of the...*

Breakwater: If you're visiting by boat, you'll start here anyway. From this point, you can survey the old town and the new town (stretching to the left, with train station and parking lot). The little fort above is a private home. The harbor now hosts more paddleboats than fishing boats. Sand erosion is a major problem. The partial breakwater is designed to save the beach from washing away. While old-timers remember a vast beach, their grandchildren truck in sand each spring to give tourists something to lie on. (The Nazis liked the Cinque Terre, too—find two of their bomb-hardened bunkers, near left and far right.)

The fancy €300-a-night four-star Hotel Porto Roca (on the far right) marks the trail to Vernazza. High above, you see the costly road built in the 1980s to connect Cinque Terre towns with the freeway over the hills. The two capes (Punta di Montenero and Punta Mesco) define the Cinque Terre region—you can just about make out the towns from here. The closer cape, Punta Mesco, marks an important sea-life sanctuary, home to a rare sea grass that provides an ideal home for fish eggs. Buoys keep fishing boats away. The cape was once a quarry, providing employment to locals who chipped out the stones used to cobble the streets of Genoa. On the far end of the new town, marking the best free beach around, you can just see the statue named *Il Gigante*. It's 45 feet tall and once held a trident. While it looks as if it was hewn from the rocky cliff, it's actually made of reinforced concrete and dates from the beginning of the 20th century, when it supported a dancing terrace for a *fin de siècle* villa. A violent storm left the giant holding nothing but memories of Monterosso's glamorous age.

• *From the breakwater, walk to the old-town square (just past the train tracks and beyond the beach). Find the statue of a dandy holding what looks like a box cutter in...*

Piazza Garibaldi: The statue honors Giuseppe Garibaldi, the dashing firebrand revolutionary who, in 1870, helped unite the people of Italy into a modern nation. Facing Garibaldi, with your back to the sea, you'll see (from right to left) the City Hall (with the now-required European Union flag aside the Italian one), a big home and recreation center for poor and homeless elderly, and a park information center (in a building bombed in 1945 by the Allies, who were attempting to take out the train line). You'll also see the A Ca' du Sciensa pub (with historic town photos inside and upstairs, you're welcome to pop in for a look—see "Nightlife in Monterosso," later in this section). There's a little "anchovy visitors center" behind the City Hall, in case you've got a hankering for a salty little snack.

Just under the bell tower (with back to the sea, it's on your left), a set of covered arcades facing the sea is where the old-timers hang out (they see all and know all). The crenellated bell tower marks the church.

• *Go to church (the entrance is on the inland side).*

Church of St. John the Baptist: This black-and-white church, with marble from Carrara, is typical of this region's Romanesque style. Note the lacy stone rose window above the entrance. The church dates from 1307—the proud inscription on the middle column inside reads "MilleCCCVII." Outside the church, on the side facing the main street, find the high-water mark from a November 1966 flood (the same month as the flood that devastated Florence).

• *Leaving the church, turn left immediately and go to church again.*

Oratory of the Dead: During the Counter-Reformation, the Catholic Church offset the rising influence of the Lutherans by creating brotherhoods of good works. These religious Rotary clubs were called "confraternities." Monterosso had two, nicknamed White and Black. This building is the oratory of the Black group, whose mission—as the macabre decor indicates—was to arrange for funerals and take care of widows, orphans, the shipwrecked, and the souls of those who ignore the request for a €1 donation. It dates from the 16th century, and membership has passed from father to son for generations. Notice the fine 17th-century carved choir stalls just inside the door. Look up on the ceiling to find the symbol of the confraternity: a skull, crossbones, and an hourglass... death awaits us all.

• *Return to the beach and find the brick steps that lead up to the hill-capping convent (starting between the train tracks and the pedestrian tunnel).*

The Switchbacks of the Friars: Follow the yellow brick road (OK, it's orange...but I couldn't help singing as I skipped sky-ward). Go constantly uphill until you reach a convent church, then a cemetery, in a ruined castle at the summit. The lane *(Salita dei Cappuccini)* is nicknamed *Zii di Frati* ("switchbacks of the friars"). Midway up the switchbacks, you'll see a statue of St. Francis and a wolf enjoying a grand view.

• *From here, backtrack 20 yards and continue uphill. When you reach a gate marked* Convento e Chiesa Cappuccini, *you have arrived.*

Church of the Capuchin Friars: The former convent (until recently a hotel) now accommodates friars. Before stepping inside, notice the church's striped Romanesque facade. It's all fake. Tap it—no marble, just cheap 18th-century stucco. Sit in the rear pew. The high altarpiece painting of St. Francis can be rolled up on special days to reveal a statue of Mary, which stands behind it. Look at the statue of St. Anthony to the right and smile (you're on convent camera). Wave at the security camera—they're nervous about the precious painting to your left.

This fine painting of the Crucifixion is attributed to Antony Van Dyck, the Flemish master who lived and worked for years in nearby Genoa (though art historians suspect that, at best, it was painted by someone in the artist's workshop). When Jesus died, the earth went dark. Notice the eclipsed sun in the painting, just to the right of the cross. Do the electric candles work? Pick one up, pray for peace, and plug it in. (Leave €0.50, or unplug it and put it back.)

• *Leave and turn left to hike uphill to the cemetery that fills the remains of the castle, capping the hill. Look out from the gate and enjoy the view.*

Cemetery and Ruined Castle: In the Dark Ages, the village huddled within this castle. Slowly it expanded. Notice the town view from here—no sea. You're looking at the oldest part of Monterosso, huddled behind the hill, out of view of 13th-century pirates. Explore the cemetery, but remember that cemeteries are sacred and treasured places (as is clear by the abundance of fresh flowers). Ponder the black-and-white photos of grandparents past. *Q.R.P.* is *Qui Riposa in Pace* (a.k.a. R.I.P.). Rich families had their own little tomb buildings. See if you can find the Odoardo family tomb—look to the wall on the left (apparently, February 30 happened in Monterosso). Climb to the very summit—the castle's keep, or place of last refuge. Priests are buried in a line of graves closest to the sea, but facing inland—the town's holy sanctuary high on the hillside (above the road, hiding behind trees). Each Cinque Terre town has a lofty sanctuary, dedicated to Mary and dear to the village hearts.

• *From here, your tour is over—any trail leads you back into town.*

Sights in Monterosso

Beaches—Monterosso's beaches, immediately in front of the train station, are easily the Cinque Terre's best and most crowded. This town is a sandy resort with rentable beach extras: Figure €20 to rent two chairs and an umbrella for the day. Light lunches are served by beach cafés to sunbathers at their lounge chairs. It's often worth the euros to enjoy a private beach. Beaches are free (and marked on the Monterosso al Mare map) only where you see no umbrellas. Don't use your white hotel towels; most hotels will give you beach towels—sometimes for a fee. The local hidden beach, which is free and generally less crowded, is tucked away under Il Casello restaurant at the east end of town, near the trailhead to Vernazza. The beach is gravelly, and for some, best enjoyed with water shoes. The bocce ball court (next to Il Casello) is busy with the old boys enjoying their favorite pastime.

Kayaks—**Samba** rents kayaks on the beach (€7/hour for 1-person kayak, €12/hour for 2-person kayak, to the right of train station as you exit, mobile 339-681-2265, Domenico). The paddle to Vernazza is a favorite.

Shuttle Buses for High-Country Hikes—Monterosso's bus service (described earlier in "Arrival in Monterosso") continues beyond the town limits, but check the schedules—only one or two departures a day head into the high country. Some buses go to the Sanctuary of Soviore, where you can hike back down to Monterosso (1.5 hours, moderately steep). Rides cost €1.50 (free with Cinque Terre Card, pick up schedule from park office). Or you can hike to Levanto (no Cinque Terre card necessary, not as stunning as the rest of the coastal trail, 2.5 hours, straight uphill and then easy decline, follow signs at west end of the new town). For hiking details, ask at either park info booth (at the train station or Piazza Garibaldi).

Wine Tasting—Buranco Agriturismo offers visits to their vineyard and cantina daily at 12:00. You'll taste two of their wines plus a grappa and a *limoncino*—along with home-cooked food (€25/person with snacks, €40/person for full lunch, reservations required at least three days in advance, English may be limited, follow Via Buranco uphill to path, 10 minutes above town, tel. 0187-817-677, www.burancocinqueterre.it). They also rent apartments; see "Sleeping in Monterosso," on the next page.

Boat Rides—From the old-town harbor, boats run nearly hourly (10:30-17:00) to Vernazza, Manarola, Riomaggiore, and Portovenere. Schedules are posted in Cinque Terre park offices (for details, see "Getting Around the Cinque Terre: By Boat," on page 1124).

Angelo's Boat Tours—Local fisherman Angelo and his American wife Paula are now fishers of tourists who'd love to take you out for a scenic cruise. You'll swim, explore the coast, snorkel in a private cove below a waterfall, and lunch on freshly caught fish. Paula enjoys cooking for guests (4-10 people: €500/4-hour cruise, €600/5 hours; 1-3 people: €85/hour for the boat plus €35/person for the meal—no meal charge for kids 13 and under; €85/person for 2-hour sunset tapas cruise, mobile 333-318-2967, angelosboattours@yahoo.com).

Nightlife in Monterosso

A Ca' du Sciensa has nothing to do with science—it's the last name of the town moneybags who owned this old mansion. The antique dumbwaiter is still in use—a remnant from the days when servants toiled downstairs while the big shots wined and dined up top. This classy yet laid-back pub offers breezy square seating, bar action on the ground level, an intimate lounge upstairs, and discreet balconies overlooking the square to share with your best travel buddy. It's a good place for light meals such as salads (until 24:00) and plenty of drinks. Luca encourages you to wander around the place and enjoy the old Cinque Terre photo collection (daily 10:00-2:00 in the morning, serves late-night sandwiches and microwaved pasta, closed Nov-March, Piazza Garibaldi 17, tel. 0187-818-233).

Enoteca Eliseo, the first wine bar in town, comes with operatic ambience. Eliseo and his wife, Mary, love music and wine. You can select a fine bottle from their shop shelf, and for €7 extra, enjoy it and the village action from their cozy tables. Wines sold by the glass *(bicchiere)* are posted (Wed-Mon 9:00-24:00, closed Tue, Piazza Matteotti 3, a few blocks inland behind church, tel. 0187-817-308).

Fast Bar, the best bar in town for young travelers and night owls, is located on Via Roma in the old town. Customers mix travel tales with big, cold beers, and the crowd (and the rock 'n' roll) gets noisier as the night rolls on. Come here to watch Italian or American sporting events on their TV any time of day (sandwiches and snacks usually served until midnight, open nightly until 2:00, closed Thu Nov-March).

La Cantina Da Miky, in the new town just beyond the train station, is a trendy downstairs bar-restaurant with an extensive cocktail and grappa menu. Run by Manuel, son of well-known local restaurateur Miky, it sometimes hosts live music. Take advantage of its outdoor seating by the beach. This could be just the place to meet your future well-heeled Ligurian *amore* (daily until well after 24:00, Via Fegina 90, tel. 0187-802-525).

Sleeping in Monterosso

(€1 = about $1.40, country code: 39)

Monterosso, the most beach-resort-y of the five Cinque Terre towns, offers maximum comfort and ease. The TI Proloco just outside the train station can give you a list of €70-80 double rooms. Rooms in Monterosso are a better value for your money than similar rooms in crowded Vernazza, and the proprietors seem more genuine and welcoming. To locate the hotels, see the Monterosso map.

In the Old Town

$$$ Hotel Villa Steno is lovingly managed and features great view balconies, private gardens off some rooms, air-conditioning, and the friendly help of English-speaking Matteo and his wife Carla. Of their 16 rooms, 12 have view balconies (Sb-€100, Db-€165, Tb-€190, Qb-€220, includes hearty buffet breakfast, ask about Rick Steves discount with cash and this book, Internet access and Wi-Fi in lobby, laundry, Via Roma 109, tel. 0187-817-028 or 0187-818-336, fax 0187-817-354, www.villasteno.com, steno@pasini .com). It's a 10-minute hike (or €7 taxi ride) from the train station to the top of the old town. Readers get a free Cinque Terre info packet and a glass of the local sweet wine, *sciacchetrà,* when they check in—ask for it. The Steno has a tiny parking lot for guests (€5/day, reserve in advance).

$$$ Albergo Pasquale is a modern, comfortable place, run by the same family as the Hotel Villa Steno (above). It's conveniently located just a few steps from the beach, boat dock, tunnel entrance to the new town, and train tracks. While there is some traffic and train noise, it's located right on the harbor and has an elevator, offering easier access than most (same prices and welcome drink as Villa Steno; air-con, all rooms with sea view, Via Fegina 8, tel. 0187-817-550 or 0187-817-477, fax 0187-817-056, www.hotel pasquale.com, pasquale@pasini.com, Felicita and Marco).

$$$ La Poesia has four warmly colored rooms that share a peaceful garden terrace, where you'll enjoy a complimentary *aperitivo* upon arrival. A shuttle to/from the train station is also included (Db-€150, suite not worth €40 extra, air-con, Via Genova 4, tel. 0187-817-283, www.lapoesia-cinqueterre.com, info@lapoesia -cinqueterre.com, mamma Nicoletta speaks little English, daughter Veronica speaks more).

$$$ Locanda il Maestrale rents six small, stylish rooms in a sophisticated and peaceful little inn. While renovated with all the modern comforts, it retains centuries-old character under frescoed ceilings. Its peaceful sun terrace overlooking the old town and Via Roma action is a delight (small Db-€110, Db-€140, suite-€170, less off-season, ask about Rick Steves discount with cash and this book, air-con, Wi-Fi, Via Roma 37, tel. 0187-817-013, mobile 338-4530-531, fax 0187-817-084, www.locandamaestrale.net, maestrale @monterossonet.com, Stefania).

$$$ Albergo Marina, creatively run by enthusiastic husband-and-wife team Marina and Eraldo, has 23 thoughtfully appointed rooms and a garden with lemon trees. With a free, delicious buffet featuring local specialties from 14:00 to 19:00 daily, they offer a great value (standard Db-€115, big Db-€128, ask about Rick Steves discount with cash and this book, elevator, air-con; free use of bikes, kayak, and snorkel equipment; two-person wine-barrel hot tub costs extra; Via Buranco 40, tel. 0187-817-613, fax 0187-817-242, www.hotelmarina5terre.com, marina@hotelmarina5terre .com).

$$$ Hotel la Colonnina, a comfy, modern place with 21 big and pretty rooms, is buried in the town's fragrant and sleepy back streets with no sea views (Db-€142, Tb-€200, Qb-€225, €15 more for bigger rooms with viewless terrace, cash or traveler's checks only, air-con, Internet access and Wi-Fi, fridges, elevator, inviting rooftop terrace with sun beds, garden, Via Zuecca 6, tel. 0187-817-439, fax 0187-817-788, www.lacolonninacinqueterre.it, info@lacolonninacinqueterre.it, Christina). The hotel is in the old town behind the statue of Garibaldi (take street to left of A Ca' du Sciensa one block up).

$$$ Il Giardino Incantato ("The Enchanted Garden") is a charming four-room B&B in a tastefully renovated 16th-century Ligurian home in the heart of the old town. Breakfast is served in a hidden garden (choose from an extensive list the night before), and the garden is illuminated with candles in the evening (Db-€170, Db suite-€200, air-con, free minibar and tea and coffee service, Via Mazzini 18, tel. 0187-818-315, mobile 333-264-9252, www.ilgiardinoincantato.net, giardino_incantato@libero.it, kind and eager to please Fausto and Mariapia).

$$$ L'Antica Terrazza rents four classy rooms right in town. With a pretty terrace overlooking the pedestrian street and minimal stairs, Raffaella offers a good deal (Db-€110, 5 percent discount with cash, air-con, Wi-Fi and Internet access, Vicolo San Martino 1, tel. 0187-817-499, mobile 347-132-6213, anticaterrazza @libera.it).

$$$ Manuel's Guesthouse, perched among terraces, is a garden getaway ruled by disheveled artist Manuel and run by his nephew Lorenzo. They have seven big, bright rooms and a grand view. Their killer terrace is hard to leave—especially after a few drinks (Db-€120, Db suite with view-€140, ask for best Rick Steves price, cash only, air-con, Wi-Fi and Internet access, in old town, up about 100 steps behind church at top of town, Via San Martino 39, mobile 333-439-0809 or 329-547-3775, www.manuels guesthouse.com, info@manuelsguesthouse.com).

$$$ Buranco Agriturismo, a 10-minute walk from the old town, has wonderful gardens and views over the vine-covered valley. Its primary business is wine and olive-oil production (their wine is judged among the 100 best in Italy), but they offer three apartments for a great value. It's a rare opportunity to stay in a farmhouse but still be able to get to town on foot (2-6 people-€60/person including breakfast, €30/child under 12, dinner on request, air-con, free shuttle from station, bottle of their wine included, open year-round, tel. 0187-817-677, mobile 349-434-8046, fax 0187-802-084, www.burancocinqueterre.it, info@buranco.it, informally run by Loredana, Mary, and Giulietta).

$$ Hotel Souvenir is Monterosso's cash-only backpacker's hotel. Family-run, it has two buildings, each utilitarian but comfortable (one more stark than the other). Both share a lounge and pleasant leafy courtyard. The first is for students (S-€30, Sb-€35, D-€55, Db-€70, T-€105, breakfast-€5); the other is nicer and pricier (Sb-€45, Db-€80, Tb-€120, includes breakfast; guests receive discount at La Pineta beach-chair rental near the train station). Walk three blocks inland from the main old-town square to Via Gioberti 24 (tel. 0187-817-822, tel. & fax 0187-817-595, hotel _souvenir@yahoo.com, helpful Beppe).

$$ Albergo al Carugio is a simple, practical nine-room place in a big apartment-style building at the top of the old town. It's quiet, comfy, yet forgettable, with no discernable management, and run in a crooked-painting-on-the-wall way (Db-€90 July-

Aug, otherwise €65-80, air-con, Via Roma 100, tel. 0187-817-453, alcarugio@virgilio.it).

$$ Il Timone Rooms, a little B&B by the post office, has three tidy, modern rooms. Francesco also rents a few rooms near the cemetery, but they aren't worth the hike (Db-€90, breakfast at a bar, air-con, Via Roma 75, tel. 349-870-8666, www.iltimonedi monterosso.it).

In the New Town

$$$ A Cà du Gigante, despite its name, is a tiny yet stylish refuge with nine rooms. About 100 yards from the beach (and surrounded by blocky apartments on a modern street), the interior is done with taste and modern comfort in mind (Db-€160, Db seaview suite-€180, includes parking, air-con, ask about Rick Steves discount with 3-night stay and this book, occasional last-minute deals, Via IV Novembre 11, tel. 0187-817-401, fax 0187-817-375, www.il gigantecinqueterre.it, gigante@ilgigantecinqueterre.it, Claudia).

$$$ Hotel Baia (by-yah), overlooking the beach near the station, has clean high-ceilinged dimly lit rooms, dark hallways, and impersonal staff. Of the hotel's 28 rooms, half have views. The best little two-chair view balconies are on top floors (Db-€180, non-view Db in back-€150, elevator only for baggage and guests with disabilities, minimum 2-night stay May-Sept, Via Fegina 88, tel. 0187-817-512, fax 0187-818-322, www.baiahotel.it, info@baiahotel.it).

$$$ Hotel Punta Mesco is a tidy and well-run little haven renting 17 quiet, modern rooms without views, but 10 have small terraces. For the price, it's perhaps the best comfort in town (Db-€126, Tb-€170, cash discount, air-con, Wi-Fi, free bike loan, free parking, Via Molinelli 35, tel. & fax 0187-817-495, www.hotelpunta mesco.it, info@hotelpuntamesco.it, Diego).

$$$ Pensione Agavi has 10 bright, airy, quiet, and overpriced rooms, about half overlooking the beach near the big rock. This is not a place to party—it feels like an old hospital with narrow hallways (D-€80, Db-€110, Tb-€140, no breakfast, cash only, refrigerators, turn left out of station to Fegina 30, tel. 0187-817-171, mobile 333-697-4071, fax 0187-818-264, hotel.agavi@libero.it).

Eating in Monterosso

Ristorante Belvedere is *the* place for a good-value meal indoors or outdoors on the harborfront. Their *amfora belvedere*—mixed seafood stew—is huge, and can easily be shared by up to four (€45). Share with your group and add pasta for a fine meal. Mussel fans will enjoy the *tagliolini della casa* (€8). It's energetically run by Federico and Roberto (€9 pastas, €12 *secondi*, €2 cover, Wed-Mon

12:00-14:30 & 19:00-22:00, usually closed Tue, on the harbor in the old town, tel. 0187-817-033).

L'Alta Marea offers special fish ravioli, the catch of the day, and huge crocks of fresh, steamed mussels. Young chef Marco cooks with charisma, while his wife, Anna, takes good care of the guests. This place is quieter, buried in the old town two blocks off the beach, and has covered tables out front for people-watching. This is a good opportunity to try rabbit (€9 pastas, €12-15 *secondi*, €2 cover, ask about Rick Steves discount with cash and this book, Thu-Tue 12:00-15:00 & 18:00-22:00, closed Wed, Via Roma 54, tel. 0187-817-170).

Ciak—a cut above its neighbors in elegance and also a little higher in price—is known for their huge sizzling terra-cotta crocks for two, crammed with the day's catch and either accompanied by risotto or spaghetti, or swimming in a soup *(zuppa)*. Another popular choice is the seafood *antipasto Lampara*. Stroll a couple of paces past the outdoor tables up Via Roma to see what Ciak's got on the stove (Thu-Tue 12:00-15:00 & 19:00-22:30, closed Wed, tel. 0187-817-014).

Via Venti is a fun little trattoria, buried in an alley deep in the heart of the old town, where Papa Ettore creates imaginative seafood dishes using the day's catch and freshly made pasta. Ilaria and her partner Michele serve up delicate and savory gnocchi (tiny potato dumplings) with crab sauce, tender ravioli stuffed with fresh fish in a swordfish sauce, and pear-and-cheese pasta. There's nothing pretentious here...just good cooking, service, and prices (€11 pastas, €16 *secondi*, Fri-Wed 12:00-15:30 & 18:30-22:00, closed Thu, tel. 0187-818-347). From the bottom of Via Roma, with your back to the sea and the church to your left, head to the right down Via XX Settembre and follow it to the end, to #32.

Miky is packed with well-dressed locals who know their seafood and want to eat it in a classy environment, but don't want to spend a fortune. For elegantly presented, top-quality food, this is my Cinque Terre favorite. It's clearly a proud family operation: Miky (dad), Simonetta (mom), and charming Sara (daughter) all work hard. All their pasta is "pizza pasta"—cooked normally but finished in a bowl that's encased in a thin pizza crust. They cook the concoction in a wood-fire oven to keep in the aroma. Miky's has a fine wine list with many available by the glass if you ask. If I was ever to require a dessert, it would be their mixed sampler plate, *dolce mista*—€10 and plenty for two (€15 pastas, €22 *secondi*, €8 sweets, Wed-Mon 12:00-15:00 & 19:00-23:00, closed Tue, reservations wise in summer, diners tend to dress up a bit; in the new town 100 yards north of train station at Via Fegina 104; tel. 0187-817-608).

La Cantina Di Miky, a few doors down toward the station, serves Ligurian specialties, following in Miky's family tradition of quality (it's run by son Manuel). It's more trendy and informal than Miky's, and you can sit downstairs or on the outdoor terrace (€15 anchovy tasting plate, €12 pastas, €15 *secondi*, creative desserts, daily 11:00-24:00 or later, Via Fegina 90, tel. 0187-802-525). This place doubles as a cocktail bar in the evenings—see "Nightlife in Monterosso," earlier in this section.

Ristorante Tortuga is the top option in Monterosso for seaview elegance, with gorgeous outdoor seating on a bluff and an elegant white tablecloth-and-candles interior. If you're out and about, drop by to consider which table you'd like to reserve for later (€15 pastas, €20 *secondi*, closed Mon, just outside the tunnel that connects the old and new town, daily 12:00-14:30 & 18:00-22:00, tel. 0187-800-065, mobile 333-240-7956, Silvia and Giamba).

Light Meals, Take-Out Food, and Breakfast

Lots of shops and bakeries sell pizza and focaccia for an easy picnic at the beach or on the trail. At **Il Frantoio,** Simone makes tasty pizza to go or to munch perched on a stool (Fri-Wed 9:00-14:00 & 16:00-19:30, closed Thu, just off Via Roma at Via Gioberti 1, tel. 0187-818-333). **Pizzeria la Smorfia** also cooks up good pizza to eat in or take out (Tue-Sun 11:30-15:00 & 18:00-23:00, closed Mon, 73 Via Vittorio Emanuele, tel. 0187-818-395). **Focacceria de Ely** makes airy focaccia and thick-crust pizzas for casual seating or take-out (daily 10:30-20:00, until 24:00 in summer, Emigliano).

Il Casello is the only place for a fun meal on a terrace overlooking the old town beach. With outdoor tables on a rocky outcrop, it's a good bet for a salad or a sandwich, or a well-prepared pasta or *secondi*. For an economic meal with romance, reserve the balcony upstairs (daily June-Aug, meals from 11:30 and 22:30, closed Nov-March, tel. 333-492-7629, Bacco).

Cinque Terre Connections

By Train

The five towns of the Cinque Terre are on a pokey milk-run train line (described in "Getting Around the Cinque Terre," on page 1122). Erratically timed but roughly hourly trains connect each town with the others, plus La Spezia, Genoa, and Riviera towns to the north. While a few of these local trains go to more distant points (Milan or Pisa), it's much faster to change in La Spezia, Monterosso, or Sestri Levante to a bigger train (local train info tel. 0187-817-458).

From La Spezia Centrale by Train to: Rome (8/day direct, 4 hours, more with changes, €45), **Pisa** (about hourly, 1-1.5 hours, €5), **Florence** (4/day direct, otherwise nearly hourly, 2.5 hours, €10), **Milan** (about hourly, 3 hours direct or with change in Genoa,

€22), **Venice** (about hourly, 5-6 hours, 1-3 changes, €50).

From **Monterosso by Train to: Venice** (about hourly, 6-7 hours, 1-3 changes, €52), **Milan** (8/day direct, otherwise hourly, 3-4 hours, more with change in Genoa, €22), **Genoa** (hourly, 1.2-2 hours, €8), **La Spezia** (hourly, 20-30 minutes), **Rome** (hourly, 4.5 hours, change in La Spezia, €50). For destinations in **France,** change trains in Genoa.

THE NETHERLANDS

AMSTERDAM

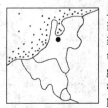

Amsterdam is a progressive way of life housed in Europe's most 17th-century city. Physically, it's built upon millions of pilings. But more than that, it's built on good living, cozy cafés, great art, street-corner jazz, stately history, and a spirit of live-and-let-live. It has 765,000 people and almost as many bikes. It also has more canals than Venice...and about as many tourists.

During the Dutch Golden Age in the 1600s, Amsterdam was the world's richest city, an international sea-trading port, and the cradle of capitalism. Wealthy, democratic burghers built a planned city of canals lined with trees and townhouses topped with fancy gables. Immigrants, Jews, outcasts, and political rebels were drawn here by its tolerant atmosphere, while painters such as young Rembrandt captured that atmosphere on canvas.

The Dutch are unique. They are among the world's most handsome people—tall, healthy, and with good posture—and the most open, honest, and refreshingly blunt. They like to laugh. As connoisseurs of world culture, they appreciate Rembrandt paintings, Indonesian food, and the latest French film—but with an un-snooty, blue-jeans attitude.

Approach Amsterdam as an ethnologist observing a strange culture. Stroll through any neighborhood and see things that are commonplace here but rarely found elsewhere. Carillons chime quaintly in neighborhoods selling sex, as young professionals smoke pot with impunity next to old ladies in bonnets selling flowers. Observe the neighborhood's "social control," where an elderly man feels safe in his home knowing he's being watched by the prostitutes next door.

Be warned: Amsterdam, a bold experiment in freedom, may

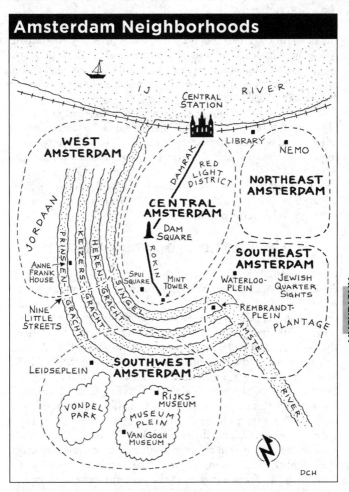

Amsterdam Neighborhoods

box your Puritan ears. Take it all in, then pause to watch the clouds blow past stately old gables—and see the Golden Age reflected in a quiet canal.

Planning Your Time

Amsterdam is worth a full day of sightseeing on even the busiest itinerary. While the city has a couple of must-see museums, its best attraction is its own carefree ambience. The city's a joy on foot—and a breezier and faster delight by bike.

In the morning, see the city's two great art museums: the Van Gogh and the Rijksmuseum (cafeteria lunch). Walk from the museums to the Singel canal flower market, then take a relaxing hour-long, round-trip canal cruise from the dock at Spui (described later, under "Tours in Amsterdam"). After the cruise, stroll through the peaceful Begijnhof courtyard and tour the nearby Amsterdam Museum. Visiting the Anne Frank House after 18:00 may save you an hour in line in summer (see page 1204 for last-entry times). Have a memorable dinner: Try Dutch pancakes or a *rijsttafel*—an Indonesian smorgasbord.

On a balmy evening, Amsterdam has a Greek-island ambience. Stroll through the Jordaan neighborhood for the idyllic side of town and wander down Leidsestraat to Leidseplein for the roaring café and people scene. Tour the Red Light District while you're at it.

With extra time: With two days in the Netherlands, I'd side-trip by bike, bus, or train to Haarlem. With a third day, I'd do the other great Amsterdam museums.

Orientation to Amsterdam

(area code: 020)

Amsterdam's Central Train Station (Amsterdam Centraal), on the north edge of the city, is your starting point, with the TI, bike rental, and trams branching out to all points. Damrak is the main north-south axis, connecting Central Station with Dam Square (people-watching and hangout center) and its Royal Palace. From this main street, the city spreads out like a fan, with 90 islands, hundreds of bridges, and a series of concentric canals—named Herengracht (Gentleman's Canal), Keizersgracht (Emperor's Canal), and Prinsengracht (Prince's Canal)—that were laid out in the 17th century, Holland's Golden Age. Amsterdam's major sights are within walking distance of Dam Square.

To the east of Damrak is the oldest part of the city (today's Red Light District), and to the west is the newer part, where you'll find the Anne Frank House and the peaceful Jordaan neighborhood. Museums and Leidseplein nightlife cluster at the southern edge of the city center.

Tourist Information

"VVV" (pronounced "fay fay fay") is Dutch for "TI," a tourist information office. Amsterdam's tourist offices are crowded and inefficient—avoid them if you can. You can save yourself a trip by calling the TI at 020/201-8800 (Mon-Fri 8:00-18:00) or try 0900-400-4040 (Mon-Fri 9:00-17:00). From the US dial 011-31-20-551-2525.

The main TI at Central Station is busy, but is convenient when arriving by train (daily July-Aug 8:00-20:00, Sept-June 9:00-18:00). An affiliated office is in the AUB/Last Minute Ticket Shop on Leidseplein, tucked into the side of the giant Stadsschouwburg

Theater (Mon-Fri 10:00-19:30, Sat 10:00-18:00, Sun 12:00-18:00; doesn't book hotel rooms). These TIs outside of Amsterdam are helpful and less crowded: at Schiphol Airport (daily 7:00-22:00) and in the town of Haarlem (next chapter).

Tickets: Although Amsterdam's main TI sells tickets to the Anne Frank House (€1 extra per ticket, same-day tickets available) and the Rijks, Van Gogh, and Stedelijk museums (no fee), it's quicker to get tickets in advance online (see below).

Maps and Brochures: Given the city's maze of streets and canals, I'd definitely get a good city map (€2.50 at Central Station TI, same map given away free at the TI in the AUB/Last-Minute Ticket Shop—go figure). Also consider picking up any of the walking-tour brochures (€3 each, including tours covering city center, former Jewish Quarter, Jordaan, and funky De Pijp neighborhood). For entertainment, get a copy of *Time Out Amsterdam* (€3, €1.50 if bought with city map); for additional entertainment ideas, see the free papers listed later (under "Helpful Hints" and "Entertainment in Amsterdam").

Currency Exchange: At Central Station, **GWK Currency Exchange** offices have hotel reservation windows where clerks sell local and international phone cards and mobile-phone SIM cards, and answer basic tourist questions, with shorter lines than the TI (daily 8:00-22:00, near front of station in both the east and west corridors, tel. 020/627-2731).

Resources for Gay Travelers: A short walk from Central Station down Damrak is **GAYtic,** a TI specifically oriented to the needs of LGBT travelers. The office stocks maps, magazines, and brochures, and dispenses advice on nightlife as well as general tourist information (Mon-Sat 11:00-20:00, Sun 12:00-20:00, Spuistraat 44, tel. 020/330-1461, www.gaytic.nl, info@gaytic.nl). **Pink Point**, in a kiosk outside Westerkerk, next to the Homomonument, is less of a resource, but has advice about nightlife, and sells gay-themed souvenirs (usually daily 10:00-18:00, 11:00-17:00 in winter, closed Tue-Wed Jan-Feb).

Advance Tickets and Sightseeing Cards

Advance Tickets for Major Sights: Avoid long ticket lines during high season (late March through October) by buying tickets online for the Anne Frank House, Rijksmuseum, Van Gogh Museum, and Stedelijk modern-art museum.

It's easy to buy tickets through each museum's website: www.annefrank.org (€0.50 surcharge per ticket, but worth it), www.rijksmuseum.nl, www.vangoghmuseum.com, and www.stedelijk.nl (no extra fee for Rijks, Van Gogh, or Stedelijk). Print out your ticket and bring it to the ticket-holder's line for a quick entry.

You can also buy tickets for these sights in advance at

Amsterdam's TIs, but the lines at the TIs seem almost as long as the ones you're trying to avoid at the sights.

Tips if You Don't Have Advance Tickets: Use a Museum-kaart to get in quickly at covered sights (details in "Sightseeing Cards," next). If you haven't reserved a ticket for the Anne Frank House, trim your wait in line by arriving the minute it opens, or late in the day; this works better in early spring and fall than in summer, when even after-dinner lines can be long. Visit the Van Gogh Museum on a Friday evening, when it's open until 22:00, with no lines and few crowds, even in peak season.

Sightseeing Cards: Two cards merit consideration for heavy-duty sightseers. If your trip includes Haarlem or any other Dutch city, you're more likely to save more money with the Museumkaart, which covers many sights throughout the Netherlands, than the overpriced I amsterdam City Card, which is valid only in Amsterdam. (There's no reason to buy both.) However, if Amsterdam's your only stop in the Netherlands, and if you plan to get around on transit (rather than by bike), the I amsterdam City Card makes sense, as it includes a transit pass. Both cards allow free entry to most of the sights in Amsterdam (including the Rijks and Van Gogh museums), but neither card covers the Heineken Brewery, Westerkerk tower, or any sights dealing with sex or mari-juana. The Anne Frank House is covered by the Museumkaart but not the I amsterdam City Card.

The **Museumkaart,** which costs €45 and is valid for a year throughout the Netherlands, is a no-brainer for anyone visiting at least six museums (for example, an itinerary that includes these museums, for a total of €59.50: Rijksmuseum-€12.50, Van Gogh Museum-€14, Anne Frank House-€8.50, Amsterdam Museum-€10, Amstelkring Museum-€7, and the Dutch Resistance Museum-€7.50). The Museumkaart is sold at all participating museums, and—except at the Anne Frank House—you can use it to skip the ticket-buying line (though everyone has to go through security). If you plan to buy a Museumkaart, get it at a smaller, less-crowded museum (such as the Amsterdam Museum). You'll see ads for the **Holland Pass,** but it's not worth it—the Museumkaart is a much better deal.

The **I amsterdam City Card,** which focuses on Amsterdam and includes most transportation, is not worth the cost unless you're planning on a day or two of absolutely non-stop sightseeing, and connecting it all by public transit. Along with many sights and discounts, this pass includes one free canal boat tour and unlim-ited use of trams, buses, and metro—but not trains (and except for the canal tour, all of these public-transit options are covered by a normal transit pass anyway—see "Getting Around Amsterdam," later). You have a set number of consecutive hours to use it (for example: Visit your first museum at 14:00 Mon with a 24-hour pass, and it's good until 13:59 on Tue). This pass doesn't allow you to skip lines at major sights, except at the Van Gogh Museum (€38/24 hours, €48/48 hours, or €58/72 hours; sold at major museums, TIs, and with shorter lines at the GVB transit office across from Central Station, next to TI; www.iamsterdamcard.com).

Arrival in Amsterdam

By Train

The portal connecting Amsterdam to the world is its aptly named Central Station (Amsterdam Centraal). Through at least 2014, expect the station and the plaza in front of it to be a chaotic construction zone—the station is being completely reworked, and the locations of things described here may change before your visit.

Trains arrive on a level above the station. Go down the stairs or the escalator (at the "A" end of the platform). Descending from the platforms, you'll find yourself in one of the corridors leading to the street exit for the city center (Centrum).

The station is fully equipped for the traveler. You'll find GWK Travelex counters (described earlier) in both the east and west corridors, and international ticket offices near the exit of both corridors. Luggage lockers are in the east corridor, under the "B" end of the platforms (€5-7/24 hours, depending on size of bag, always open, can fill up on busy summer weekends). The station has plenty of shops and places to grab a bite to eat. On the train level, platform 2 is lined with eateries, including the tall, venerable, 1920s-style **First Class Grand Café.** Handy **Albert Heijn** supermarkets are easy to find at the ends of both the east and west corridors.

Exiting the station, you're in the heart of the city. Straight ahead, just past the canal, is Damrak street, leading to Dam Square. To your left are the TI and GVB public-transit offices. Farther to your left are bike rentals (**MacBike** is located in the station building, and **Star Bikes** is a five-minute walk past it, both listed on page 1192). To the right of the station are the postcard-perfect neighborhoods of West Amsterdam; some of my recommended hotels are within walking distance (see map on pages 1220-1221).

Just beyond the taxis are the platforms for the city's blue trams, which come along frequently, ready to take you anywhere your feet won't (buy ticket or pass from conductor). Trams #1, #2, and #5 (which run to nearly all my recommended hotels) leave from in front of the station's west (main) entrance. All trams leaving Central Station stop at Dam Square along their route. For more on the transit system, see page 1190.

By Plane

For details on getting from Schiphol Airport into downtown

Amsterdam, see "Amsterdam Connections," at the end of this chapter.

Helpful Hints

Theft Alert: Tourists are considered green and rich, and the city has more than its share of hungry thieves—especially on trams and at the many hostels. Wear your money belt.

Emergency Telephone Number: Throughout the Netherlands, dial 112.

Street Smarts: Beware of silent transportation—trams and bicycles—when walking around town. Don't walk on tram tracks or pink/maroon bicycle paths. Before you step off any sidewalk, do a double- or triple-check in both directions to make sure all's clear.

Sightseeing Strategies: To beat the lines at Amsterdam's most popular sights, plan ahead. You can bypass the main ticket-buyers' line at the Anne Frank House, and the Rijks, Van Gogh, and Stedelijk museums by buying online tickets before you go (see page 1185 for details). Friday night is a great time to visit the Van Gogh Museum, which is open until 22:00 (far smaller crowds then).

Shop Hours: Most shops are open Tuesday through Saturday 10:00-18:00, and Sunday and Monday 12:00-18:00. Some shops stay open later (21:00) on Thursdays. Supermarkets are generally open Monday through Saturday 8:00-20:00 and are closed on Sundays.

Festivals: Every year, **Queen's Day** (Koninginnedag, April 30) and **Gay Pride** (Aug 3-5 in 2012) bring crowds, fuller hotels, and higher room prices.

Cash Only: Thrifty Dutch merchants hate paying the unusually high fees charged by credit-card companies here; expect to pay cash in unexpected places, including grocery stores, cafés, budget hotels, train station machines and windows, and at some museums.

Internet Access: It's easy at cafés all over town, but the best place for serious surfing and email is the towering **Central Library,** which has hundreds of fast, free terminals (Openbare Biblio-theek Amsterdam, daily 10:00-22:00, free Wi-Fi, a 10-minute walk from train station, described on page 1209). "Coffee-shops," which sell marijuana, usually also offer Internet access—letting you surf with a special bravado.

English Bookstores: For fiction and guidebooks—including mine—try the **American Book Center** at Spui 12, right on the square (Mon 11:00-20:00, Tue-Sat 10:00-20:00 except Thu until 21:00, Sun 11:00-18:30, tel. 020/535-2575, www.abc.nl). The huge and helpful **Selexyz Scheltema** is at Koningsplein

20 near the Leidsestraat (store open Mon 11:00-18:00, Tue-Sat 9:30-18:00 except Thu until 21:00, Sun 12:00-18:00; lots of English novels, guidebooks, and maps; tel. 020/523-1411). **Waterstone's Booksellers,** a UK chain, also sells British newspapers (near Spui at 152 Kalverstraat, Mon-Sat 10:00-18:30 except Mon until 18:00 and Thu until 21:00, Sun 11:00-18:00, tel. 020/638-3821).

Free Publications: Hefty, hip, and helpful *Amsterdam Magazine* ("Beyond Windmills, Wooden Shoes, and Weed") includes a city map, and is available all over the city. Boom Chicago's magazine, aimed at the hostelling crowd, is handed out on Leidseplein and available in some spots across town. You may find one or both of these in your hotel room: *Visitors Guide Amsterdam,* sort of a mini-yellow-pages for tourists, with a fairly crummy map but good tips and (paid) listings; and *Rush on Amsterdam,* a glossy quarterly magazine that has current info on what's on at the city's museums, and even includes a pretty good map.

Entertainment: Pick up a copy of *Time Out Amsterdam* at either TI or the bookstores listed above (€3), check out this chapter's "Entertainment in Amsterdam" section, or call the **AUB/Last Minute Ticket Shop** (theater, classical music, and major rock shows, tickets sold only at shop, Leidseplein 26, tel. 0900-0191, calls costs €0.40/minute, www.amsterdamsuitburo.nl, www.lastminuteticketshop.nl).

Maps: The free tourist maps can be confusing, except for *Amsterdam Museums: Guide to 37 Museums* (includes tram info and stops, ask for it at the big museums, such as the Van Gogh). Several free magazines, listed above, include decent and detachable maps. If you want a top-notch map, buy one (about €2.50). I like the *Carto Studio Centrumkaart Amsterdam*. Amsterdam Anything's virtual "Go Where the Locals Go" city map is worth checking out, especially if you have mobile Internet access (www.amsterdamanything.nl).

Pharmacy: The shop named **DA** (Dienstdoende Apotheek) has all the basics—shampoo and toothpaste—as well as a pharmacy counter hidden in the back (Mon-Sat 9:00-22:00, Sun 11:00-22:00, Leidsestraat 74-76 near where it meets Keizersgracht, tel. 020/627-5351).

Laundry: Try **Clean Brothers Wasserij** in the Jordaan (daily 8:00-20:00 for €7 self-service, €9 drop-off—ready in an hour—Mon-Fri 9:00-17:00, Sat 9:00-18:00, no drop-off Sun, Westerstraat 26, one block from Prinsengracht, tel. 020/627-9888) or **Powders** near Leidseplein (daily 7:00-22:00, €6.50 self-service, €10 drop-off available Mon-Wed and Fri 8:00-17:00, Sat-Sun 9:00-15:00, no drop-off Thu, Kerkstraat 56, one block south of Leidsestraat, mobile 06-2630-6057).

Best Views: While the **Westerkerk** offers fine views from its tower (and is convenient if you're visiting the Anne Frank House), the best city views are from the **Central Library** (Openbare Bibliotheek Amsterdam; see page 1209). Other good views are from the Oude Kerk tower and the rooftop terrace at the NEMO Science Museum.

Getting Around Amsterdam

Amsterdam is big, and you'll find the trams handy. The longest walk a tourist would make is an hour from Central Station to the Rijksmuseum. When you're on foot, be extremely vigilant for silent but potentially painful bikes, trams, and crotch-high curb posts.

If you've got a car, park it—all you'll find are frustrating one-way streets, terrible parking, and meter maids with a passion for booting cars parked incorrectly. You'll pay €55 a day to park safely in a central garage, about €27 for a "day ticket" to park on the street (9:00-19:00), and about €3.50/hour in a parking lot. If you must bring a car to Amsterdam, it's best to leave it at one of the city's supervised park-and-ride lots (follow *P&R* signs from freeway, €6/24 hours, includes round-trip transit into city center for up to five people, 4-day maximum).

By Tram, Bus, and Metro

Amsterdam's public transit system includes trams, buses, and an underground metro; of these, trams are most useful for most tourists.

Tickets: The entire country's public transit network operates on a single ticket system called the OV-Chipkaart (for "Openbaar Vervoer"—public transit). For locals, it couldn't be easier. With a single pre-paid card, they can hop on any form of public transit in the country, scan their card, and the fare is immediately deducted. Cards can be reloaded automatically, straight from residents' bank accounts.

But travelers—who generally stay only a few days—must still rely on either single tickets or multiday passes. (While officially classified as "OV-Chipkaarten," these tickets and passes with electronic chips are nothing like the reloadable, valid-nationwide, plastic cards locals use.)

Within Amsterdam, a single transit ticket costs €2.60 and is good for one hour on the tram, bus, and metro, including transfers. Passes good for unlimited transportation are available for 24 hours (€7), 48 hours (€11.50), 72 hours (€15.50), and 96 hours (€19.50). (The I amsterdam City Card, described on page 1186, includes a transit pass.) Given how expensive single tickets are, consider buying a pass or renting a bike for your stay before you buy that first ticket.

The easiest way to buy a ticket or transit pass is to simply board a tram or bus and pay the conductor (no extra fee). Tickets and passes are also available at metro station vending machines (there's one just outside Central Station), at GVB public-transit offices, and at TIs.

The helpful GVB public-transit information office in front of Central Station can answer questions (next to TI, Mon-Fri 7:00-21:00, Sat-Sun 10:00-18:00). Its free, multilingual *Public Transport Amsterdam Tourist Guide* includes a transit map and explains ticket options and tram connections to all the sights. For more public transit information, visit www.gvb.nl.

Trams: Board the tram at any entrance not marked with a red/white "do not enter" sticker. If you need a ticket or pass, pay the conductor (in a booth at the back); if there's no conductor, pay the driver in front. You must always "check in" as you board by scanning your ticket or pass at the pink-and-white scanner, and "check out" by scanning it again when you get off. The scanner will beep and flash a green light after a successful scan. Be careful not to accidentally scan your ticket or pass twice while boarding, or it becomes invalid. Checking in and out is very important, as controllers do pass through and fine violators. When you reach your stop, to open the door, press a green button on one of the poles near an exit.

Trams #2 *(Nieuw Sloten)* and #5 *(A'veen Binnenhof)* travel the north-south axis, from Central Station to Dam Square to Leidseplein to Museumplein (Van Gogh and Rijks museums). Tram #1 (marked *Osdorp*) also runs to Leidseplein. At Central Station, these three trams depart from the west side of Stationsplein (with the station behind you, they're to your right).

Tram #14—which doesn't connect to Central Station—goes east-west (Westerkerk-Dam Square-Muntplein-Waterlooplein-Plantage). If you get lost in Amsterdam, don't sweat it—10 of the city's 17 trams take you back to Central Station.

Buses and Metro: Tickets and passes work on buses and the metro just as they do on the trams—scan your ticket or pass to "check in" as you enter and again to "check out" when you leave. The metro system is scant—used mostly for commuting to the suburbs—but it does connect Central Station with some sights east of Damrak (Nieuwmarkt-Waterlooplein-Weesperplein). The glacial speed of the metro-expansion project is a running joke among cynical Amsterdammers.

By Bike

Everyone—bank managers, students, pizza delivery boys, and police—uses this mode of transport. It's by far the smartest way to travel in a city where 40 percent of all traffic rolls on two wheels.

You'll get around town by bike faster than you can by taxi. On my last visit, I rented a bike for five days, chained it up outside my hotel at night, and enjoyed wonderful mobility. I highly encourage this for anyone who wants to get maximum fun per hour in Amsterdam. One-speed bikes, with *"brrringing"* bells, rent for about €10 per day (cheaper for longer periods) at any number of places—hotels can send you to the nearest spot.

Rental Shops: Star Bikes Rental has cheap rates, long hours, and inconspicuous black bikes. They're happy to arrange an after-hours drop-off if you give your credit-card number and pre-pay (€5/4 hours, €7/day, €9/24 hours, €12/2 days, €17/3 days, daily 9:00-19:00, requires ID but no monetary deposit, 5-minute walk from east end of Central Station at De Ruyterkade 127, tel. 020/620-3215, www.starbikesrental.com).

MacBike, with 900 bikes and counting, is the bike-rental powerhouse—you'll see their bright red bikes all over town (they do stick out a bit). It has a huge and efficient outlet at Central Station (€7/3 hours, €9.50/24 hours, €14/48 hours, €19/72 hours, more for 3 gears, 25 percent discount with I amsterdam City Card, €50 deposit plus passport or credit-card imprint, no helmets, daily 9:00-17:45; at east end of station—on the left as you're leaving; tel. 020/620-0985, www.macbike.nl). They have two smaller, satellite stations at Leidseplein (Weteringschans 2) and Waterlooplein (Nieuwe Uilenburgerstraat 116). Return your bike to the station where you rented it. MacBike sells several pamphlets outlining bike tours with a variety of themes in and around Amsterdam for €1-2.

Frederic Rent-a-Bike, a 10-minute walk from Central Station, has quality bikes and a helpful staff (€10/24 hours, €16/48 hours, €40/week, 10 percent discount on multiday rental with this book, daily 9:00-17:30, no after-hours drop-off, Brouwersgracht 78, tel. 020/624-5509, www.frederic.nl).

Lock Your Bike: Bike thieves are bold and brazen in Amsterdam. Bikes come with two locks and stern instructions to use both. The wimpy ones go through the spokes, and the industrial-strength chains are meant to be wrapped around the actual body of the bike and through the front wheel, and connected to something stronger than any human. Do this diligently. If you're sloppy, it's an expensive mistake and one that any "included" theft insurance won't cover.

More Tips: No one wears a helmet. For safety, use arm signals, follow the bike-only traffic signals, stay in the obvious and omnipresent bike lanes, and yield to traffic on the right. Fear oncoming trams and tram tracks. Carefully cross tram tracks at a perpendicular angle to avoid catching your tire in the rut. Warning: Police ticket cyclists the same as they do drivers. Obey all traffic signals, and walk your bike through pedestrian zones. Fines for biking through pedestrian zones are reportedly €30-50. A handy bicycle route-planner can be found at www.routecraft.com (select "bikeplanner," then click British flag at far right for English). For a "Do-It-Yourself Bike Tour of Amsterdam" and for bike tours, see page 1196.

By Boat

While the city is great on foot, bike, or tram, you can also get around Amsterdam by boat. **Rederij Lovers** boats shuttle tourists on a variety of routes covering different combinations of the city's top sights. Their Museum Line, for example, costs €12.50, includes museum discounts, and stops near the Hermitage, Rijksmuseum/Van Gogh Museum, and Central Station (at least every 45 minutes, 4 stops, 1.5 hours). Sales booths in front of Central Station (and the boats) offer free brochures listing museum hours and admission prices. Most routes come with recorded narration and run daily 10:00-17:30 (tel. 020/530-1090, www.lovers.nl).

The similar **Canal Bus** is actually a boat, offering 14 stops on four different boat routes (€22/24-hour pass, departures daily 10:00-18:00, until 22:00 April-Oct, leaves near Central Station and Rederij Lovers dock, tel. 020/623-9886, www.canal.nl). They also run smaller tour boats with live commentary (see next page).

If you're simply looking for a floating, nonstop tour, the regular canal tour boats (without the stops) give more information, cover more ground, and cost less (see "Tours in Amsterdam," next page).

For do-it-yourself canal tours and lots of exercise, Canal Bus also rents "canal bikes" (a.k.a. paddleboats) at several locations: near the Anne Frank House, near the Rijksmuseum, near Leidseplein, and where Leidsestraat meets Keizersgracht (€8/hour per person, daily July-Aug 10:00-22:00, Sept-June 10:00-18:00).

By Taxi

For short rides, Amsterdam is a bad town for taxis. Given the fine tram system and ease of biking, I use taxis less in Amsterdam than in just about any other city in Europe. The city's taxis have a high drop charge (€7.50) for the first two kilometers (e.g. from Central Station to the Mint Tower), after which it's €2.30 per kilometer (no extra fee for luggage; it's worth trying to bargain a lower rate, as competition among cabbies is fierce). You can wave them down, find a rare taxi stand, or call one (tel. 020/677-7777). You'll also see **bike taxis,** particularly near Dam Square and Leidseplein. Negotiate a rate for the trip before you board (no meter), and they'll wheel you wherever you want to go (€1/3 minutes, no surcharge for baggage or extra weight, sample fare from Leidseplein to Anne Frank House: about €6).

Tours in Amsterdam

By Boat

▲▲Canal Boat Tours—These long, low, tourist-laden boats leave continually from several docks around town for a relaxing, if uninspiring, one-hour introduction to the city (with recorded headphone commentary). Select a boat tour for convenience based on the starting point, or if a particular tour is free and included with the I amsterdam City Card (which covers Blue Boat Company and Holland International boats). Tip: Boats leave only when full, so jump on a full boat to avoid waiting at the dock. Choose from one of these three companies:

Rondvaart Kooij is cheapest (€8.50, 3/hour in summer 10:00-22:00, 2/hour in winter 10:00-17:00, at corner of Spui and Rokin streets, about 10 minutes from Dam Square, tel. 020/623-3810, www.rederijkooij.nl).

Blue Boat Company's boats depart from near Leidseplein (€13; every half-hour April-Sept 10:00-18:00, also at 19:00; hourly Oct-March 10:00-17:00, 1.25 hours, Stadhouderskade 30, tel. 020/679-1370, www.blueboat.nl). Their 90-minute evening cruise has a live English-speaking guide (€15, nightly at 20:00, April-Sept also at 21:00 and 22:00, reservations required).

Holland International offers a standard one-hour trip and a variety of longer tours (€13, 1-hour "100 Highlights" tour with recorded commentary, 4/hour daily 9:00-22:00, 2/hour after 18:00; tel. 020/625-3035, www.hir.nl). Their €18, 90-minute "ultimate" tour with a live guide leaves twice daily (at 11:00 and 13:00).

No fishing allowed—but bring your camera. Some prefer to cruise at night, when the bridges are illuminated.

Hop-On, Hop-Off Canal Boats—Small, 12-person electric Canal Hopper boats leave every 20-30 minutes with live commentary on two different hop-on, hop-off routes (€22 day pass, €17 round-trip ticket, July-Aug daily 10:00-17:00, Sept-June Fri-Sun only, "yellow" west route runs 2/hour and stops near Anne Frank House and Rijksmuseum, less-frequent "orange" east route runs 3/hour and stops near Red Light District and Damrak, tel. 020/535-3303, www.canal.nl).

Wetlands Safari, Nature Canoe Tours near Amsterdam—If you want some exercise and a dose of village life, consider this five-hour tour. Majel Tromp, a friendly villager who speaks great English, takes groups limited to 15 people. The program: Meet at the bus stops behind Central Station (leave the station from the west corridor and take the escalator up to the buses) at 9:30, catch a public bus, stop for coffee, take a 3.5-hour canoe trip (2-3 people per canoe) with several stops, tour a village by canoe, munch a rural canalside picnic lunch (included), then canoe and bus back into Amsterdam by 15:00 (€43, discount with this book, May-mid-Sept Sun-Fri, reservations required, tel. 020/686-3445, mobile 06-5355-2669, www.wetlandssafari.nl, info@wetlandssafari.nl).

On Foot

Red Light District Tours—Randy Roy's Red Light Tours consists of one expat American woman, Kimberley. She lived in the Red Light District for years and gives fun, casual, yet informative 90-minute walks through this fascinating and eye-popping neighborhood. While the actual information is light, you'll walk through various porn and drug shops and have an expert to answer your questions. Call or email to reserve (€12.50 includes a drink in a colorful bar at the end, nightly at 20:00, Fri and Sat also at 22:00, no tours Dec-Feb, tours meet in front of Victoria Hotel—in front of Central Station, mobile 06-4185-3288, www.randyroysredlight tours.com, kimberley@randyroysredlighttours.com).

Free City Walk—New Europe Tours "employs" native, English-speaking students to give these irreverent and entertaining three-hour walks (using the same "free tour, ask for tips, sell their other tours" formula popular in so many great European cities). This long walk covers a lot of the city with an enthusiasm for the contemporary pot-and-prostitution scene (free, daily at 11:15 and 13:15, just show up at the National Monument on Dam Square, www .neweuropetours.eu).

Adam's Apple Tours—This walking tour offers a two-hour, English-only look at the historic roots and development of Amsterdam. You'll have a small group of generally 5-6 people and a caring guide, starting off at Central Station and ending up at Dam Square (€25; May-Sept daily at 10:00, 12:30, and 15:00 based on demand; call 020/616-7867 to confirm times and book, www .adamsapple.nl, Frank).

Private Guide—Albert Walet is a likeable, hardworking, and knowledgeable local guide who enjoys personalizing tours for Americans interested in knowing his city. "Ab" specializes in history and architecture, and exudes a passion for Amsterdam (€59/2 hours, €99/4 hours, up to 4 people, on foot or by bike, mobile 06-2069-7882, abwalet@yahoo.com). Ab also takes travelers to nearby towns, including Haarlem, Leiden, and Delft.

By Bike

The **Yellow Bike Guided Tours** company offers city bike tours of either two hours (€18.50, daily at 10:30) or three hours (€21.50, daily at 13:30), which both include a 20-minute break. They also offer a four-hour, 15-mile tour of the dikes and green pastures of the countryside (€27.50, lunch extra, includes 45-minute break, April-Oct daily at 19:30). All tours leave from Nieuwezijds Kolk

29, three blocks from Central Station (reservations smart, tel. 020/620-6940, www.yellowbike.nl). If you take one of their tours, you can rent the bike for the rest of the day at a 50 percent discount (€10/24 hours, ID and either €100 deposit or credit-card imprint required). If you'd prefer a private guide, see Albert Walet, above.

Do-It-Yourself Bike Tour of Amsterdam—A day enjoying the bridges, bike lanes, and sleepy, off-the-beaten-path canals on your own one-speed is an essential Amsterdam experience. The real joys of Europe's best-preserved 17th-century city are the countless intimate glimpses it offers: the laid-back locals sunning on their porches under elegant gables, rusted bikes that look as if they've been lashed to the same lamppost since the 1960s, wasted hedonists planted on canalside benches, and happy sailors permanently moored, but still manning the deck.

For a good day trip, rent a bike at or near Central Station (see "By Bike" on page 1191). Head west down Haarlemmerstraat, working your wide-eyed way down the Prinsengracht (drop into Café 't Papeneiland at Prinsengracht 2) and detouring through the small, gentrified streets of the Jordaan neighborhood before popping out at Westerkerk under the tallest spire in the city.

Pedal south to the lush and peaceful Vondelpark, then cut back through the center of town (Leidseplein to the Mint Tower, along Rokin street to Dam Square). From there, cruise the Red Light District, following Oudezijds Voorburgwal past the Old Church (Oude Kerk) to Zeedijk street, and return to the train station.

By Public Minibus

For a quick, do-it-yourself public-bus tour along scenic Prinsengracht, catch Amsterdam's cute little Stop/Go minibus (€1, tickets valid one hour, buy from driver, transit passes valid, daily 9:00-17:30, 8 seats, can be muggy on hot days, www.gvb.nl).

It arcs along the city's longest canal, offering clever budget travelers a very cheap and fun 20-minute experience that's faster than a touristy canal tour. The scenic bus ride goes where normal big buses can't fit (along the bumpy and cobbled canalside lanes), giving you a delightful look at the workaday city. The high ride, comfortable seats, and big windows show you Amsterdam well.

The Stop/Go route follows the outside of the canal counterclockwise and returns clockwise along the inside. The buses have only four set stops (in front of the Central Library, at the river docks behind Central Station, at the main/west entrance of Central Station, and near the opera house/City Hall—Stopera—on Waterlooplein)—but you can just wave one down from anywhere on the route. Grab a seat in the back for the best view. If you see something fun, just jump out—there's another bus in 12 minutes.

If the bus hits construction on Prinsengracht, it veers to the next street over, then heads back to the canal as soon as possible.

For this short tour, catch the bus at Central Station. From the station, the minibus passes characteristic cafés in the Jordaan district, countless houseboats, and the whole gamut of gables (under a parade of leaning, Golden Age buildings complete with all the hooks and pulleys). Rolling along the Prinsengracht, you'll see the long line at the Anne Frank House just before the towering Westerkerk. You'll pass within a block of the thriving Leidseplein and Rijksmuseum (look to the right at Spiegelgracht) before passing Rembrandtplein (with its fun 3-D *Night Watch* statues) and crossing the Amstel River to finish at the Waterlooplein flea market, near Rembrandt's House, Gassan Diamonds, and the metro station (subway trains run every 2 minutes, returning you to Central Station in 3 minutes).

From the bus, watch for these little bits of Amsterdam:

- green, metal public urinals
- late 19th-century lamp poles
- bikes chained to anything unmovable (including the practical new "staple" design bike racks)
- *amsterdammertjes* ("little Amsterdammers," referring to the countless, little, dark-red bollards—bearing the city's emblem of three diagonal crosses—that protect walkers from passing traffic)
- underground recycling and garbage bins designed to keep workers from having to dump out bins into trucks (a law prohibits employees from lifting anything over 25 kilos—about 55 pounds)
- "*ja*" and "*nee*" stickers on mail slots, indicating whether residents accept junk mail and advertising. (The cool people of the Jordaan are mostly "*nee nee*.")

Sights in Amsterdam

One of Amsterdam's delights is that it has perhaps more small specialty museums than any other city its size. From houseboats to sex, from marijuana to Old Masters, you can find a museum to suit your interests.

For tips on how to save time otherwise spent in the long ticket-buying lines of the big three museums—the Anne Frank House, Van Gogh Museum, and Rijksmuseum—see "Advance Tickets and Sightseeing Cards" on page 1185. Admission prices are high: A sightseeing card such as the Museumkaart, or I amsterdam City Card, can pay for itself quickly. Entry to most sights is free with a card (I've noted those that aren't covered).

Most museums require baggage check (usually free, often in

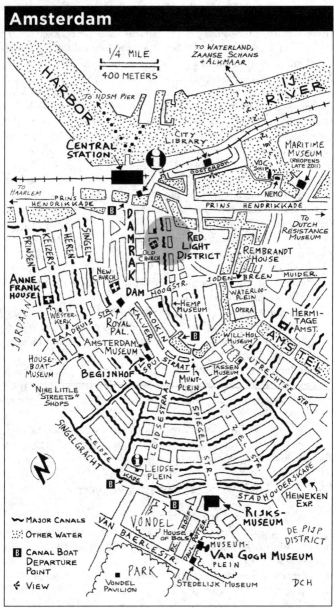

Amsterdam

coin-op lockers where you get your coin back).

The following sights are arranged by neighborhood for handy sightseeing.

Southwest Amsterdam

▲▲▲**Rijksmuseum**—At the Rijksmuseum ("Rijks" rhymes with "bikes"), Holland's Golden Age shines with the best collection anywhere of the Dutch Masters—from Vermeer's quiet domestic scenes, to Steen's raucous family meals, to Hals' snapshot portraits, to Rembrandt's moody brilliance.

The 17th century saw the Netherlands at the pinnacle of its power. The Dutch had won their independence from Spain, trade and shipping boomed, wealth poured in, the people were understandably proud, and the arts flourished. This era was later dubbed the Dutch Golden Age. With no church bigwigs or royalty around to commission big canvases in the Protestant Dutch republic, artists had to find different patrons—and they discovered the upper-middle-class businessmen who fueled Holland's capitalist economy. Artists painted their portraits and decorated their homes with pretty still lifes and non-preachy, slice-of-life art.

Dutch art is meant to be enjoyed, not studied. It's straightforward, meat-and-potatoes art for the common man. The Dutch love the beauty of everyday things painted realistically and with exquisite detail.

Gaze into the eyes of the men who made Amsterdam the richest city on earth in the 1600s.

The main core of the Rijksmuseum is closed until 2013 for a massive renovation. Thankfully, the most famous masterpieces—nearly everything on the typical tourist's hit list—are on display in the wonderful and easy-on-the-feet Philips Wing (southwest corner of the museum, the part of the building nearest the Van Gogh Museum). This delightful exhibit offers one of the most exciting and enjoyable art experiences in Europe.

Cost and Hours: €12.50, audioguide-€5, no photos, daily 9:00-18:00, last entry 30 minutes before closing, tram #2 or #5 from Central Station to Hobbemastraat. Info tel. 020/674-7047 or switchboard tel. 020/674-7000, www.rijksmuseum.nl. The Philips Wing entrance is near the corner of Hobbemastraat and Jan Luijkenstraat, on the south side of the Rijksmuseum—the part of the huge building nearest the Van Gogh Museum.

Avoiding Crowds: The museum is most crowded from April to September (especially April to June), on weekends, and during morning hours. Avoid waits in the ticket-buying line by buying your ticket or pass in advance. No one can completely avoid the security line.

You can buy and print your ticket online at www.rijksmuseum .nl. The ticket is good anytime (no entry time specified). Buying online has the added advantage of letting you enter through the "fast lane," scooting you to the front of the security line.

You can also buy tickets at the TI, Keytours (near the museum at Paulus Potterstraat 8), at the AUB/Last Minute Ticket Shop on Leidseplein, and even at many hotels (may change with renovation).

▲▲▲Van Gogh Museum—Near the Rijksmuseum, the Van Gogh Museum (we say "van GO," the Dutch say "van HHHOCK") is a cultural high even for those not into art. This remarkable museum features works by the troubled Dutch artist whose art seemed to mirror his life. Vincent, who killed himself in 1890 at age 37, is best known for sunny, Impressionist canvases that vibrate and pulse with vitality. The museum's 200 paintings—a stroll through the artist's work and life—were owned by Theo, Vincent's younger, art-dealer brother. If you like brightly colored landscapes in the Impressionist style, you'll like this museum. If you enjoy finding deeper meaning in works of art, you'll really love it. The mix of Van Gogh's creative genius, his tumultuous experiences, and the traveler's determination to connect to it makes this museum as much a walk with Vincent as with his art.

The main collection of Van Gogh paintings on the first floor is arranged chronologically, taking you through the changes in Vincent van Gogh's life and styles. The paintings are divided into five periods of Vincent's life—the Netherlands, Paris, Arles, St. Rémy, and Auvers-sur-Oise—proceeding clockwise around the floor. Highlights include *Sunflowers, The Bedroom, The Potato Eaters,* and many brooding self-portraits.

The third floor shows works that influenced Vincent, from Monet and Pissarro to Gauguin, Cézanne, and Toulouse-Lautrec. The worthwhile audioguide includes insightful commentaries and quotes from Vincent himself. Temporary exhibits fill the new wing, down the escalator from the ground floor lobby.

Cost and Hours: €14, more for special exhibits, audioguide-€5, kids' audioguide-€2.50, no photos, daily 10:00-18:00, Fri until 22:00—with no crowds in evening, Paulus Potterstraat 7, tram #2 or #5 from Central Station to Van Baerlestraat stop, tel. 020/570-5200, www.vangoghmuseum.nl.

Avoiding Lines: Skip the 15-30-minute wait in the ticket-buying line by getting your ticket in advance. You can buy and print your ticket online at www.vangoghmuseum.nl. The ticket is good anytime (no entry time specified). You can also buy tickets at the TI or Keytours (just up the street at Paulus Potterstraat 8). Advance-ticket and pass holders can go right in.

Southwest Amsterdam

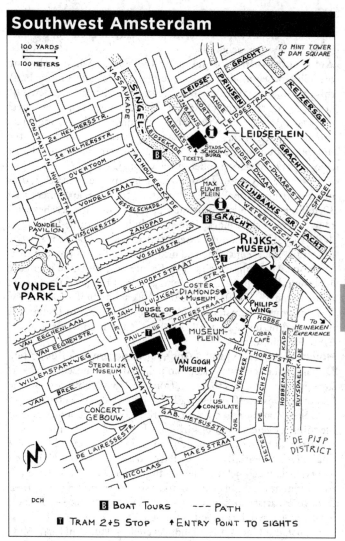

100 YARDS
100 METERS

TO MINT TOWER & DAM SQUARE

LEIDSEPLEIN

TICKETS

MAX EUWE-PLEIN

RIJKS-MUSEUM

VONDEL PAVILION

VONDEL-PARK

COSTER DIAMONDS + MUSEUM

PHILIPS WING

HOUSE OF BOLS

MUSEUM-PLEIN

COBRA CAFÉ

To HEINEKEN EXPERIENCE

VAN GOGH MUSEUM

STEDELIJK MUSEUM

US CONSULATE

CONCERT-GEBOUW

DE PIJP DISTRICT

DCH

B BOAT TOURS   - - - PATH

T TRAM 2 & 5 STOP   ◆ ENTRY POINT TO SIGHTS

AMSTERDAM

▲▲**Stedelijk Museum**—After a long renovation project, the Stedelijk (STAYD-eh-lik) reopens in late 2011 in its spiffed-up building, which now flaunts an architecturally daring new entry facing Museumplein (near the Van Gogh Museum). The Netherlands' top modern-art museum, its fun, far-out, and refreshing collection includes post-1945 experimental and conceptual art, and works by Picasso, Chagall, Cézanne, Kandinsky, and Mondrian.

Cost and Hours: Likely €12, Tue-Sun 10:00-17:00, possibly Thu until 22:00, possibly open Mon, check website for reopening date and exact price and hours, café with outdoor seating, top-notch shop, Paulus Potterstraat 13/Museumplein 10, tel. 020/573-2911, www.stedelijk.nl.

▲Museumplein—Bordered by the Rijks, Van Gogh, and Stedelijk museums, and the Concertgebouw (classical music hall), this park-like square is interesting even to art-haters. Amsterdam's best acoustics are found underneath the Rijksmuseum, where street musicians perform everything from chamber music to Mongolian throat singing. Mimes, human statues, and crafts booths dot the square. Skateboarders career across a concrete tube, while locals enjoy a park bench or a coffee at the Cobra Café.

Nearby is **Coster Diamonds,** a handy place to see a diamond-cutting and polishing demo (free, frequent, and interesting 30-minute tours followed by sales pitch, popular for decades with tour groups, prices marked up to include tour guide kickbacks, daily 9:00-17:00, Paulus Potterstraat 2, tel. 020/305-5555, www.costerdiamonds.com). The end of the tour leads straight into their Diamond Museum, which is worthwhile only for those who have a Museumkaart (which covers entry) or feel the need to see even more diamonds (€7.50, daily 10:00-17:00, tel. 020/305-5300, www.diamantmuseumamsterdam.nl). The tour at **Gassan Diamonds** is free and better (see page 1212), but Coster is convenient to the Museumplein scene.

House of Bols: Cocktail & Genever Experience—This leading Dutch distillery runs a pricey and polished little museum/marketing opportunity across the street from the Van Gogh Museum. The "experience" is a self-guided walk through what is essentially an ad for Bols—"four hundred years of working on the art of mixing and blending...a celebration of gin"—with some fun sniffing opportunities and a drink at a modern, mirrored-out cocktail bar for a finale. (It's essentially the gin-flavored version of the Heineken Experience, listed below.) The highlight is a chance to taste up to five different local gins with a talkative expert guiding you. Then have your barista mix up the cocktail of your dreams—based on what you learned during your sniffing.

Cost and Hours: €11.50, not covered by Museumkaart, Wed-Mon 12:00-18:45, Fri until 22:45, closed Tue, last entry 45 minutes before closing, must be 18, Paulus Potterstraat 14, tel. 020/570-8575, www.houseofbols.com. If you like the booze and hang out and talk, this can be a good deal (but do it after the Van Gogh Museum).

Heineken Experience—This famous old brewery welcomes visitors to a slick and entertaining beer-appreciation fest. It's a fun trip, if you can ignore the fact that you're essentially paying for an hour of advertising (€15, includes two drinks, daily 11:00-19:00, last entry at 17:30; tram #16, #24, or #25 to Heinekenplein; an easy walk from Rijksmuseum, tel. 020/523-9222, www.heineken experience.com).

De Pijp District—This former working-class industrial and residential zone (behind the Heineken Experience, near the Rijksmuseum) is emerging as a colorful, vibrant district. Its spine is Albert Cuypstraat, a street taken over by a long, sprawling produce market packed with interesting people. The centerpiece is **Restaurant Bazar** (marked by a roof-capping golden angel), a church turned into a Middle Eastern food circus (see listing on page 1236).

▲**Leidseplein**—Brimming with cafés, this people-watching mecca is an impromptu stage for street artists, accordionists, jugglers, and unicyclists. It's particularly bustling on sunny afternoons. The Boom Chicago theater fronts this square (see "Entertainment in Amsterdam," later). Stroll nearby Lange Leidsedwarsstraat (one block north) for a taste-bud tour of ethnic eateries, from Greek to Indonesian.

▲▲**Vondelpark**—This huge and lively city park is popular with the Dutch—families with little kids, romantic couples, strolling seniors, and hippies sharing blankets and beers. It's a favored venue for free summer concerts. On a sunny afternoon, it's a hedonistic scene that seems to say, "Parents...relax."

Rembrandtplein and Tuschinski Theater—One of the city's premier nightlife spots is the leafy Rembrandtplein (the artist's statue stands here, along with a jaunty group of statues giving us *The Night Watch* in 3-D) and the adjoining Thorbeckeplein. Several late-night dance clubs keep the area lively into the wee hours. Utrechtsestraat is lined with upscale shops and restaurants. Nearby Reguliersdwarsstraat (a street one block south of Rembrandtplein) is a center for gay and lesbian nightclubs.

The **Tuschinski Theater,** a movie palace from the 1920s (a half-block from Rembrandtplein down Reguliersbreestraat), glitters inside and out. Still a working theater, it's a delightful old place to see first-run movies. The exterior is an interesting hybrid of styles, forcing the round peg of Art Nouveau into the square hole of Art Deco. The stone-and-tile facade features stripped-down, functional Art Deco squares and rectangles, but is ornamented with Art Nouveau elements—Tiffany-style windows, garlands, curvy iron lamps, Egyptian pharaohs, and exotic gold lettering over the door. Inside (lobby is free), the sumptuous decor features red carpets, nymphs on the walls, and semi-abstract designs. Grab a seat in the lobby and watch the ceiling morph (Reguliersbreestraat 26-28).

Houseboat Museum (Woonbootmuseum)—In the 1930s, modern cargo ships came into widespread use—making small, sail-powered cargo boats obsolete. In danger of extinction, these little vessels found new life as houseboats lining the canals of Amsterdam. Today, 2,500 such boats—their cargo holds turned into classy, comfortable living rooms—are called home. For a peek into this *gezellig* (cozy) world, visit this tiny museum. Captain Vincent enjoys showing visitors around the houseboat, which feels lived-in because, until 1997, it was.

Cost and Hours: €3.50, not covered by Museumkaart; March-Oct Tue-Sun 11:00-17:00, closed Mon; Nov-Dec and Feb Fri-Sun 11:00-17:00, closed Mon-Thu; closed most of Jan; on Prinsengracht, opposite #296 facing Elandsgracht, tel. 020/427-0750, www.houseboatmuseum.nl.

West Amsterdam

▲▲▲**Anne Frank House**—A pilgrimage for many, this house offers a fascinating look at the hideaway of young Anne during the Nazi occupation of the Netherlands. Anne, her parents, an older sister, and four others spent a little more than two years in a "Secret Annex" behind her father's business. While in hiding, 13-year-old Anne kept a diary chronicling her extraordinary experience. Acting on a tip, the Nazis arrested the group in August of 1944 and sent them to concentration camps in Poland and Germany. Anne and her sister died of typhus in March of 1945, only weeks before their camp was liberated. Of the eight inhabitants of the Secret Annex, only Anne's father, Otto Frank, survived. He returned to Amsterdam and arranged for his daughter's diary to be published in 1947. It was followed by many translations, a play, and a movie.

Pick up the English pamphlet at the door. The thoughtfully designed exhibit offers thorough coverage of the Frank family, the diary, the stories of others who hid, and the Holocaust. The Franks' story was that of Holland's Jews. The seven who died were among the more than 100,000 Dutch Jews killed during the war years. (Before the war, 135,000 Jews lived in the Netherlands.) Of Anne's school class of 87 Jews, only 20 survived. When her father returned to Amsterdam, he fought to preserve this house, wanting it to become, in his words, "more than a museum." It was his dream that visitors come away from the Anne Frank House with an indelible impression—and a better ability to apply the lessons of the Holocaust to our contemporary challenges.

Cost and Hours: €8.50, covered by Museumkaart but not by I amsterdam City Card; March 15-Sept 14 daily 9:00-21:00, Sat and July-Aug until 22:00; Sept 15-March 14 daily 9:00-19:00, Sat until 21:00; last entry 30 minutes before closing, no baggage check, no large bags allowed inside, Prinsengracht 267, near Westerkerk, tel. 020/556-7100, www.annefrank.org.

Avoiding Lines: Skip the long ticket-buying line (especially in the daytime during summer) by reserving an entry time and buying a ticket at the main TI or online at www.annefrank.org (€0.50/ticket fee). With your ticket in hand, you can skip the line and ring the buzzer at the low-profile door marked *Entrance: Reservations Only.* Without an advance ticket try arriving when the museum opens (at 9:00) or after 18:00. A Museumkaart does not allow you to skip the line here.

Westerkerk—Located near the Anne Frank House, this landmark church (free, generally open April-Sept Mon-Sat 11:00-15:00, closed Sun) has a barren interior, Rembrandt's body buried somewhere under the pews, and Amsterdam's tallest steeple.

The tower is open only for tours and offers a grand city view. The tour guide, who speaks in English and Dutch, tells of the church and its carillon. Only six people are allowed at a time (it's first-come, first-served), so lines can be long (€6, 30-minute tour; departures on the half hour April-Sept Mon-Sat 10:00-18:00, July-Aug until 20:00, last tour leaves at 30 minutes before closing, closed Sun; Oct-March tourable only with a private tour—call 020/689-2565 or email anna@buscher-malocca.nl).

Central Amsterdam, near Dam Square

Royal Palace (Koninklijk Huis)—This palace was built as a lavish city hall (1648-1655), when Holland was a proud new republic and Amsterdam was the richest city on the planet—awash in profit from trade. The building became a "Royal Palace" when Napoleon installed his brother Louis as king (1806). After Napoleon's fall, it continued as a royal residence for the Dutch royal family, the House of Orange. Today, it's one of four of Queen Beatrix's official residences. You can tour the interior and see several lavishly decorated rooms of chandeliers, paintings, statues, and furniture that reflect Amsterdam's former status as the center of global trade.

Cost and Hours: €7.50, daily 12:00-17:00 but often closed for official business—check calendar on website, tel. 020/620-4060, www.paleisamsterdam.nl.

New Church (Nieuwe Kerk)—Barely newer than the "Old" Church (located in the Red Light District), this 15th-century sanctuary has an intentionally dull interior, after the decoration was removed by 16th-century iconoclastic Protestants seeking to unclutter their communion with God. This is where many Dutch royal weddings and all coronations take place. There's usually a steep entrance fee due to popular temporary exhibitions (€8; daily 10:00-17:00, Thu until 22:00, on Dam Square, info tel. 020/353-8168, tel. 020/638-6909, www.nieuwekerk.nl).

▲**Begijnhof**—Stepping into this tiny, idyllic courtyard in the city center, you escape into the charm of old Amsterdam. (Please be considerate of the people who live around the courtyard, and don't photograph the residents or their homes.) Notice house #34,

Central Amsterdam

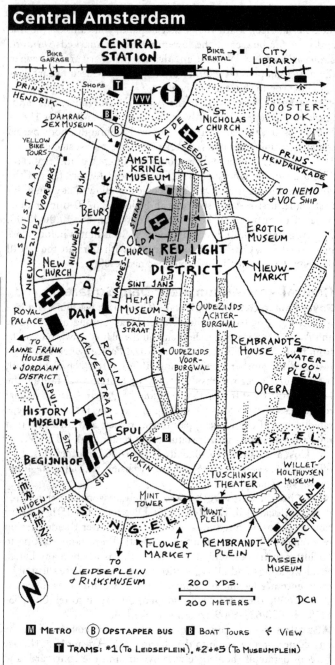

AMSTERDAM

CENTRAL STATION

BIKE GARAGE

BIKE RENTAL

CITY LIBRARY

Shops

T

VVV

i

PRINS-HENDRIK-

DAMRAK SEX MUSEUM

Yellow Bike Tours

SPUISTRAAT

NIEUWEZIJDS VOORBURG.

DIJK

B

B

KADE

ZEEDIJK

ST. NICHOLAS CHURCH

OOSTER-DOK

PRINS-HENDRIKKADE

TO NEMO & VOC SHIP

AMSTEL-KRING MUSEUM

BEURS

STRAAT

Old Church

RED LIGHT DISTRICT

EROTIC MUSEUM

NIEUW-MARKT

NEW CHURCH

DAMRAK

WARMOES.

SINT JANS

HEMP MUSEUM

OudeZijds Achter-Burgwal

ROYAL PALACE

DAM

DAM STRAAT

OudeZijds Voor-Burgwal

REMBRANDT'S HOUSE

WATER-LOO-PLEIN

TO ANNE FRANK HOUSE & JORDAAN DISTRICT

KALVERSTRAAT

ROKIN

SPUI

OPERA

HISTORY MUSEUM

SPUI

B

AMSTEL

BEGIJNHOF

STR.

ROKIN

TUSCHINSKI THEATER

WILLET-HOLTHUYSEN MUSEUM

HEREN-

HUIDEN-STRAAT

SINGEL

Mint TOWER

MUNT-PLEIN

REMBRANDT-PLEIN

HEREN-GRACHT

N

TO LEIDSEPLEIN & RIJKSMUSEUM

FLOWER MARKET

TASSEN MUSEUM

200 YDS.

200 METERS

DCH

M METRO   B OPSTAPPER BUS   B BOAT TOURS   View

T TRAMS: #1 (TO LEIDSEPLEIN), #2 & #5 (TO MUSEUMPLEIN)

a 500-year-old wooden structure (rare, since repeated fires taught city fathers a trick called brick). Peek into the hidden Catholic church, dating from the time when post-Reformation Dutch Catholics couldn't worship in public. It's opposite the English Reformed church, where the Pilgrims worshipped while waiting for their voyage to the New World—marked by a plaque near the door.

Cost and Hours: Free, open to visitors Mon-Tue and Thu-Sat—see website for sporadic hours—and Sun for church service in English at 10:30, closed Wed, on Begijnensteeg lane, just off Kalverstraat between #130 and #132, pick up flier at office near entrance, www.ercadam.nl.

▲▲**Amsterdam Museum**—Follow the city's growth from fishing village to world trade center to hippie haven. Housed in a 500-year-old former orphanage, this creative and hardworking museum features Rembrandt's paintings, fine English descriptions, and a carillon loft. The loft comes with push-button recordings of the town bell tower's greatest hits and a self-serve carillon "keyboard" that lets you ring a few bells yourself. The museum's free pedestrian corridor—lined with old-time group portraits—is a powerful teaser. This museum is a fine place to buy the Museumkaart, and then use it to skip long lines at the Van Gogh Museum (for details, see page 1186).

Cost and Hours: €10, good audioguide-€4.50, Mon-Fri 10:00-17:00, Sat-Sun 11:00-17:00, pleasant restaurant, next to Begijnhof, Kalverstraat 92, tel. 020/523-1822, www.ahm.nl.

Red Light District

▲▲**Amstelkring Museum (Our Lord in the Attic/Museum Ons' Lieve Heer op Solder)**—While Amsterdam has long been known for its tolerant attitudes, 16th-century politics forced Dutch Catholics to worship discreetly. Near the train station, in the Red Light District, you'll find a fascinating, hidden Catholic church filling the attic of three 17th-century merchants' houses.

For two centuries (1578-1795), Catholicism in Amsterdam was illegal, but tolerated (like pot in the 1970s). When hard-line Protestants took power in 1578, Catholic churches were vandalized and shut down, priests and monks were rounded up and kicked out of town, and Catholic kids were razzed on their way to school. The city's Catholics were forbidden to worship openly, so they gathered secretly to say Mass in homes and offices. In 1663, a wealthy merchant built this church, one of a handful of places in Amsterdam that served as a secret parish church until Catholics were once again allowed to worship in public.

This unique church comes with a little bonus: a rare glimpse inside a historic Amsterdam home straight out of a Vermeer painting. Don't miss the silver collection and other exhibits of daily life from 300 years ago.

Cost and Hours: €7, Mon-Sat 10:00-17:00, Sun and holidays 13:00-17:00, no photos, Oudezijds Voorburgwal 40, tel. 020/624-6604, www.opsolder.nl.

▲▲**Red Light District**—Europe's most touristed ladies of the night tease and tempt here, as they have for centuries, in 400 display-case windows around Oudezijds Achterburgwal and Oudezijds Voorburgwal, surrounding the Old Church (Oude Kerk, see below). Drunks and druggies make the streets uncomfortable late at night after the gawking tour groups leave (about 22:30), but it's a fascinating walk earlier in the evening.

The neighborhood, one of Amsterdam's oldest, has hosted prostitutes since 1200. Prostitution is entirely legal here, and the prostitutes are generally entrepreneurs, renting space and running their own businesses, as well as filling out tax returns and even paying union dues. Popular prostitutes net about €500 a day (for what's called "S&F" in its abbreviated, printable form, costing €25-50 per customer).

Sex Museums—Amsterdam has two sex museums: one in the Red Light District and another one a block in front of Central Station on Damrak street. While visiting one can be called sightseeing, visiting both is harder to explain. The one on Damrak is cheaper and more interesting. Here's a comparison:

The **Erotic Museum** in the Red Light District is five floors of uninspired paintings, videos, old photos, and sculpture (€7, not covered by Museumkaart, daily 11:00-1:00 in the morning, along the canal at Oudezijds Achterburgwal 54, tel. 020/624-7303).

The **Damrak Sex Museum** tells the story of pornography from Roman times through 1960. Every sexual deviation is revealed in various displays. The museum includes early French pornographic photos; memorabilia from Europe, India, and Asia; a Marilyn Monroe tribute; and some S&M displays (€4, not covered by Museumkaart, daily 9:30-23:30, Damrak 18, a block in front of Central Station, tel. 020/622-8376).

Old Church (Oude Kerk)—This 14th-century landmark—the needle around which the Red Light District spins—has served as a reassuring welcome-home symbol to sailors, a refuge to the downtrodden, an ideological battlefield of the Counter-Reformation, and today, a tourist sight with a dull interior (€5, more for temporary exhibits, Mon-Sat 11:00-17:00, Sun 13:00-17:00, tel. 020/625-8284, www.oudekerk.nl). It's 167 steps to the top of the church tower (€6, April-Sept Mon-Sat 13:00-17:00, closed Oct-March).

▲**Hash, Marijuana, and Hemp Museum**—This is a collection of dope facts, history, science, and memorabilia. While small, it has a very memorable finale: the high-tech grow room, in which dozens of varieties of marijuana are grown in optimal hydroponic (among other) environments. Some plants stand five feet tall and shine under the intense grow lamps. The view is actually through glass walls into the neighboring **Sensi Seed Bank Grow Shop** (at #150), which sells carefully cultivated seeds and all the gear needed to grow them (€9, not covered by Museumkaart, daily 10:00-23:00, Oudezijds Achterburgwal 148, tel. 020/623-5961, www.hashmuseum.com).

The nearby **Cannabis College** is "dedicated to ending the global war against the cannabis plant through public education" (free, daily 11:00-19:00, Oudezijds Achterburgwal 124, tel. 020/423-4420, www.cannabiscollege.com). For more, see "Smoking" on page 1237.

Northeast Amsterdam

Central Library (Openbare Bibliotheek Amsterdam)—This huge, multistory glass building holds almost 1,400 seats—many with wraparound views of the city—and hundreds of free Internet terminals (and free Wi-Fi, which requires signing up at the desk). It's the classiest possible place to check email. This library, which opened in 2007, demonstrates the Dutch people's dedication to a freely educated populace (the right to information, they point out, is enshrined in the UN's Universal Declaration of Human Rights). This being Amsterdam, the library has almost twice as many bike racks as parking places. Everything's relaxed and inviting, from the fun kids' zone and international magazine and newspaper section on the ground floor to the cafeteria with its dramatic view-terrace dining on the top (La Place, €10 meals, salad bar, daily 10:00-21:00). The library is a 10-minute walk from the east end of Central Station (daily 10:00-22:00, tel. 020/523-0900, www.oba.nl).

NEMO (National Center for Science and Technology)—This kid-friendly science museum is a city landmark. Its distinctive copper-green building, jutting up from the water like a sinking ship, has prompted critics to nickname it the *Titanic*. Designed by Italian architect Renzo Piano (known for Paris' Pompidou Center and Berlin's Sony Center complex on Potsdamer Platz), the building's shape reflects its nautical surroundings as well as the curve of the underwater tunnel it straddles.

Several floors feature permanent and rotating exhibits that allow kids (and adults) to explore topics such as light, sound, and gravity, and play with bubbles, topple giant dominoes, and draw with lasers. The museum's motto: "It's forbidden NOT to touch!" Whirring, room-size pinball machines reputedly teach kids about physics. English explanations are available.

Up top is a restaurant with a great city view, as well as a sloping terrace that becomes a popular "beach" in summer, complete with lounge chairs, a sandbox, and a lively bar. On the bottom floor is an inexpensive cafeteria offering €3-5 sandwiches.

Cost and Hours: €12.50, combo-ticket with VOC Ship *Amsterdam*-€15.50, July-Aug daily 10:00-17:00, Sept-June generally closed Mon, Oosterdok 2, above entrance to IJ tunnel. Tel. 0900-919-1100—€0.35/minute, www.e-nemo.nl. It's a 15-minute walk from Central Station or bus #22, #42, or #43 to the Kadijksplein stop. The roof terrace—open until 19:30 in the summer—is generally free.

VOC Ship *Amsterdam*—While the nearby Maritime Museum is closed for renovation (see below), the good ship *Amsterdam* moors near the NEMO, welcoming kids (and kids at heart) to join its crew. (Once the Maritime Museum is open, expect to find the *Amsterdam* back there).

The *Amsterdam* is a replica of a type of ship called an East Indiaman, which had its heyday during the 17th and 18th centuries, sailing for the Dutch East India Company (abbreviated VOC, for Vereenigde Oostindische Compagnie—you'll see it on insignias throughout the boat). Even though trade was the name of the game, with scurvy thieves in the waters, ships such as the *Amsterdam* had to be prepared to defend themselves. You'll see plenty of muskets, as well as cannons and gunpowder kegs.

Wander the decks, then duck your head and check out the captain's and surgeon's quarters, packed with items they would have used. Don't forget to climb down into the hold. While the ship is a little light on good historical information (be sure to pick up the free flier, which explains terminology like the difference between the poop deck and the quarterdeck), it's still a shipshape sight that entertains naval history buffs as well as *Pirates of the Caribbean* fans.

Cost and Hours: €6, combo-ticket with NEMO-€15.50, same hours as NEMO, docked just to the west of NEMO at Oosterdok 2, tel. 020/523-2222, www.scheepvaartmuseum.nl.

Netherlands Maritime Museum (Nederlands Scheepvaart-museum)—This huge collection of model ships, maps, and sea-battle paintings—reopening in late 2011 after major renovations—fills the 300-year-old Dutch Navy Arsenal. Given the Dutch seafaring heritage, I expected a more interesting museum; let's hope the renovations perk up the place (price and hours likely to change, but roughly €9; Tue-Sun 10:00-17:00, may be open Mon in summer; English explanations, bus #22 or #42 to Kattenburgerplein 1, tel. 020/523-2222, www.scheepvaartmuseum.nl).

Southeast Amsterdam

To reach the following sights from the train station, take tram #9 or #14. All of these sights (except the Tropical Museum) are

Southeast Amsterdam

TO RED LIGHT DISTRICT

TO NEMO, VOC SHIP, MARITIME MUSEUM & IJ TUNNEL

REMBRANDT'S HOUSE

GASSAN DIAMONDS

UILENBURGERGRACHT

VALKENBURGERSTRAAT

ENTREPOTDOK

FLEA MARKET

MOSES + AARON CHURCH

WATERLOO-PLEIN

TO ❶

OPERA

MR. VISSER-PLEIN

HERENGRACHT

WERT-HEIM PARK

RESISTANCE MUSEUM

❸

KERKLAAN

PLANTAGE

JEWISH HISTORY MUSEUM

M B

DOCK WORKER STATUE

MUIDERSTRAAT

NIEUWE

PLANTAGE-MIDDEN.

❹

ARTIS ZOO

M

A M...

BLAUWBRUG

DRAW-BRIDGE

WEESPER

HORTUS BOTANICAL GARDEN

DUTCH THEATER MEMORIAL

PLANTAGE

LAAN

TO REMBRANDT-PLEIN

HERMITAGE AMSTERDAM

STRAAT

NIEUWE KEIZERSGR.

TO TROPICAL MUSEUM + ❷

TO MAGERE (SKINNY) BRIDGE

DCH

200 YARDS
200 METERS

Ⓜ METRO   Ⓑ STOP/GO BUS
⬆ ENTRY POINT TO SIGHTS

❶ To Stayokay Stadsdoelen Hostel
❷ To Stayokay Zeeburg Hostel
❸ Restaurant Plancius
❹ Café Koosje

close to each other and can easily be connected into an interesting walk, or better yet, a bike ride. Several of the sights in southeast Amsterdam cluster near the large square, Waterlooplein, dominated by the modern opera house.

Waterlooplein Flea Market—For more than a hundred years, the Jewish Quarter flea market has raged daily except Sunday (at the Waterlooplein metro station, behind Rembrandt's House). The long, narrow park is filled with stalls selling cheap clothes, hippie stuff, old records, tourist knickknacks, and garage-sale junk.

▲**Rembrandt's House (Museum Het Rembrandthuis)**—A middle-aged Rembrandt lived here from 1639 to 1658 after his wife's death, as his popularity and wealth dwindled down to obscurity and bankruptcy. As you enter, ask when the next etching demonstration is scheduled and pick up the fine, included audioguide. Tour the place this way: Explore Rembrandt's reconstructed house (filled with exactly what his bankruptcy inventory of 1656 said he owned); imagine him at work in his reconstructed studio; marvel at his personal collection of exotic objects, many of which he included in paintings; attend the etching demonstration and ask the printer to explain the etching process (drawing in soft wax on a metal plate that's then dipped in acid, inked up, and printed); and then, for the finale, enjoy several rooms of original Rembrandt etchings. You're not likely to see a single painting, but the master's etchings are marvelous and well-described. I came away wanting to know more about the man and his art.

Cost and Hours: €9, includes audioguide, daily 10:00-17:00, etching demonstrations almost hourly, Jodenbreestraat 4, tel. 020/520-0400, www.rembrandthuis.nl.

▲**Diamonds**—Many shops in this "city of diamonds" offer tours. These tours come with two parts: a chance to see experts behind magnifying glasses polishing the facets of precious diamonds, followed by a visit to an intimate sales room to see (and perhaps buy) a mighty shiny yet very tiny souvenir.

The handy and professional **Gassan Diamonds** facility fills a huge warehouse a block from Rembrandt's House. A visit here plops you in the big-tour-group fray (notice how each tour group has a color-coded sticker so they know which guide gets the commission on what they buy). You'll get a sticker, join a free 15-minute tour to see a polisher at work, and hear a general explanation of the process. Then you'll have an opportunity to sit down and have color and clarity described and illustrated with diamonds ranging in value from $100 to $30,000. Before or after, you can have a free cup of coffee in the waiting room across the parking lot (daily 9:00-17:00, Nieuwe Uilenburgerstraat 173, tel. 020/622-5333, www.gassandiamonds.com, handy WC). Another company, **Coster,** also offers diamond demos, not as good as Gassan's, but convenient if you're near the Rijksmuseum (described on page 1202).

▲**Willet-Holthuysen Museum (a.k.a. Herengracht Canal Mansion)**—This 1687 townhouse is a must for devotees of Hummel-topped sugar bowls and Louis XVI–style wainscoting. For others, it's a pleasant look inside a typical (rich) home with much of the original furniture and decor. Forget the history and just browse through a dozen rooms of beautiful and saccharine objects from the 19th century.

Cost and Hours: €7, Mon-Fri 10:00-17:00, Sat-Sun 11:00-17:00; take tram #4, #9, or #14 to Rembrandtplein—it's a 2-minute walk southeast to Herengracht 605. Tel. 020/523-1870, www.willetholthuysen.nl. The museum lacks audioguides, but ask for a free blue notebook to learn more about the house's history.

Tassen Museum (Hendrikje Museum of Bags and Purses)— This hardworking little museum fills an elegant 1664 canal house with 500 years of bag and purse history—from before the invention of pockets through the 20th century. The collection, with lots of artifacts, is well-described in English and gives a fascinating insight into fashion through the ages that fans of handbags will love, and their partners might even enjoy. The creative and surreal bag styles of the 1920s and 1930s are particularly interesting (€7.50, not covered by Museumkaart, daily 10:00-17:00, three floors—one houses temporary exhibits and two hold the permanent collection, start on top floor, behind Rembrandtplein at Herengracht 573, tel. 020/524-6452, www.tassenmuseum.nl).

▲**Hermitage Amsterdam**—The famous Hermitage Museum in St. Petersburg, Russia, loans art to Amsterdam for display in the Amstelhof, a 17th-century former nursing home that takes up a whole city block along the Amstel River.

Why is there Russian-owned art in Amsterdam? The Hermitage collection in St. Petersburg is so vast that they can only show about 5 percent of it at any one time. Therefore, the Hermitage is establishing satellite collections around the world. The one here in Amsterdam is the biggest, filling the large Amstelhof. By law, the great Russian collection can only be out of the country for six months at a time, so the collection is always rotating. Curators in Amsterdam make a point to display art that complements—rather than just repeats—what the city's other museums show so well.

Cost and Hours: Generally €15, but price varies with exhibit; audioguide-€3, daily 10:00-17:00, Wed until 20:00; come later in the day to avoid crowds, mandatory free bag check, café, Nieuwe Herengracht 14, tram #4 to Rembrandtplein or #9 or #14 to Waterlooplein. Recorded info tel. 020/530-7488, www.hermitage.nl.

De Hortus Botanical Garden—This is a unique oasis of tranquility within the city (no mobile phones are allowed, because "our collection of plants is a precious community—treat it with respect"). One of the oldest botanical gardens in the world, it dates from 1638, when medicinal herbs were grown here. Today, among its 6,000 different kinds of plants—most of which were collected by the Dutch East India Company in the 17th and 18th centuries—you'll find medicinal herbs, cacti, several greenhouses (one with a fluttery butterfly house—a hit with kids), and a tropical palm house. Much of it is described in English: "A Dutch merchant snuck a coffee plant out of Ethiopia, which ended up in this garden in 1706. This first coffee plant in Europe was the literal granddaddy of the coffee cultures of Brazil—long the world's biggest coffee producer."

Cost and Hours: €7.50, not covered by Museumkaart; Mon-Fri 9:00-17:00, Sat-Sun 10:00-17:00, July-Aug until 19:00, Dec-Jan until 16:00; Plantage Middenlaan 2A, tel. 020/625-9021, www.dehortus.nl. The inviting Orangery Café serves tapas.

▲**Jewish Historical Museum (Joods Historisch Museum)**—This interesting museum tells the story of the Netherlands' Jews through three centuries, serving as a good introduction to Judaism and Jewish customs and religious traditions.

Originally opened in 1932, the museum was forced to close

during the Nazi years. Recent renovations have brought it into the 21st century. Its current location comprises four historic former synagogues that have been joined by steel and glass to make one modern complex.

The highlight is the Great Synagogue. Upstairs (in the women's gallery), displays tell Amsterdam's Jewish history from 1600 to 1900. From here, a skyway leads to the New Synagogue and the 20th century. The new, worthwhile exhibit on the "Jews of the Netherlands" uses personal artifacts and touch-screen computers to tell the devastating history of the Nazi occupation. By purposefully showing everyday objects such as chairs and clothes, the museum helps make an inconceivable period of time meaningful and real.

Cost and Hours: €9, more for special exhibits, daily 11:00-17:00, last entry 30 minutes before closing, free audioguide, displays all have English explanations, children's museum and kosher-style café on site, Jonas Daniel Meijerplein 2. Tel. 020/531-0310, www.jhm.nl.

▲Dutch Theater (Hollandsche Schouwburg)—Once a lively theater in the Jewish neighborhood, and today a moving memorial, this building was used as an assembly hall for local Jews destined for Nazi concentration camps. On the wall, 6,700 family names pay tribute to the 104,000 Jews deported and killed by the Nazis. Some 70,000 victims spent time here, awaiting transfer to concentration camps. Upstairs is a small history exhibit with a model of the ghetto, plus photos and memorabilia (such as shoes and letters) of some victims, putting a human face on the staggering numbers. Television monitors show actual footage of the rounding-up of Amsterdam's Jews by the Nazis. You can also see a few costumes from the days when the building was a theater. All in all, the place offers relatively little to see but plenty to think about. Back in the ground floor courtyard, notice the hopeful messages that visiting school groups attach to the wooden tulips.

Cost and Hours: Free, daily 11:00-16:00, Plantage Middenlaan 24, tel. 020/531-0340, www.hollandscheschouwburg.nl.

▲▲Dutch Resistance Museum (Verzetsmuseum)—This is an impressive look at how the Dutch resisted their Nazi occupiers from 1940 to 1945. You'll see propaganda movie clips, study forged ID cards under a magnifying glass, and read about ingenious and courageous efforts—big and small—to hide local Jews from the Germans and undermine the Nazi regime.

The museum does a good job of presenting the Dutch people's struggle with a timeless moral dilemma: Is it better to collaborate with a wicked system to effect small-scale change—or to resist violently, even if your efforts are doomed to fail? You'll learn why some parts of Dutch society opted for the former, and others for the latter. While proudly describing acts of extraordinary courage, it doesn't shy away from the less-heroic side of the story (for example, the fact that most of the population—while troubled by the persecution of their Jewish countrymen—only became actively anti-Nazi after gentile Dutch men were deported to forced-labor camps).

Cost and Hours: €7.50 includes audioguide; Tue-Fri 10:00-17:00, Sat-Mon 11:00-17:00, English descriptions, no flash photos, mandatory and free bag check, tram #9 from station or #14 from Dam Square, Plantage Kerklaan 61. Tel. 020/620-2535, www .verzetsmuseum.org.

Nearby: Two recommended eateries—Restaurant Plancius and Café Koosje—are on the same block as the museum (see listings on page 1236), and Amsterdam's famous zoo is just across the street.

▲**Tropical Museum (Tropenmuseum)**—As close to the Third World as you'll get without lots of vaccinations, this imaginative museum offers wonderful re-creations of tropical life and explanations of Third World problems (largely created by Dutch colonialism and the slave trade). Ride the elevator to the top floor, and circle your way down through this immense collection, opened in 1926 to give the Dutch people a peek at their vast colonial holdings. Don't miss the display case where you can see and hear the world's most exotic musical instruments. The Ekeko cafeteria serves tropical food.

Cost and Hours: €9, daily 10:00-17:00, tram #9 to Linnaeusstraat 2, tel. 020/568-8200, www.tropenmuseum.nl.

Entertainment in Amsterdam

Many Amsterdam hotels serve breakfast until 11:00 because so many people—visitors and locals—live for nighttime in this city.

On summer evenings, people flock to the main squares for drinks at outdoor tables. Leidseplein is the liveliest, surrounded by theaters, restaurants, and nightclubs. The slightly quieter Rembrandtplein (with adjoining Thorbeckeplein and nearby Reguliersdwarsstraat) is the center of gay clubs and nightlife. Spui features a full city block of bars. And Nieuwmarkt, on the east edge of the Red Light District, is a bit rough, but is probably the most local.

The Red Light District (particularly Oudezijds Achterburgwal) is less sleazy in the early evening, and almost carnival-like as the neon comes on and the streets fill with tour groups. But it starts to feel scuzzy after about 22:30.

Information

Pick up one of these free papers for listings of festivals and performances of theater, film, dance, cabaret, and live rock, pop, jazz, and classical music. The hip monthly *Amsterdam Magazine* is made for tourists, but savvy enough to appeal to locals; its "upcoming" section has a solid listing of entertainment options (available all over, includes good map). The irreverent *Boom!* has the basics on the youth and nightlife scene, and is packed with practical tips and countercultural insights (includes €5 discount on Boom Chicago comedy theater act described on next page; available at TIs and many bars). *Unfold Amsterdam* is a biweekly fold-out with tips on current art-scene events (available at bookstores). *Uitkrant* is in Dutch, but it's just a calendar of events, and anyone can figure out the name of the event and its date, time, and location (available at TIs, bars, and bookstores).

Newsstands sell *Time Out Amsterdam*, Dutch papers (Thursday editions generally list events), and the *International Herald Tribune* (has special Netherlands insert).

Box Office: The **AUB/Last Minute Ticket Shop** at Stadsschouwburg Theater is the best one-stop-shopping box office for theater, classical music, and major rock shows. The Last Minute window sells half-price, same-day tickets to certain shows (Mon-Sat 10:00-19:30, Sun 12:00-18:00, Leidseplein 26, tel. 0900-0191—€0.40/minute, www.lastminuteticketshop.nl).

Music

You'll find classical music at the Concertgebouw (free 12:30 lunch concerts on Wed; arrive at 12:00 for best first-come, first-served seating; at far south end of Museumplein, tel. 0900-671-8345, www.concertgebouw.nl) and at the former Beurs (on Damrak). For opera and dance, try the opera house in the Stopera building (Waterlooplein 22, tel. 020/625-5455). In the summer, Vondelpark hosts open-air concerts.

Two rock music (and hip-hop) clubs near Leidseplein are **Melkweg** (Lijnbaansgracht 234a, tel. 020/531-8181, www.melkweg.nl) and **Paradiso** (Weteringschans 6, tel. 020/626-4521, www.paradiso.nl). They present big-name acts that you might recognize if you're younger than I am.

Jazz has a long tradition at the **Bimhuis** nightclub, east of the Red Light District (Oude Schans 73-77, tel. 020/788-2188, www.bimhuis.nl).

The nearby town of Haarlem offers free pipe organ concerts on Tuesday evenings in summer at its 15th-century church, the **Grote Kerk** (at 20:15 mid-May-mid-Oct, additional concerts Thu at 15:00 July-Aug, see next chapter).

Comedy

Boom Chicago, an R-rated comedy improv act, was started 15 years ago by a group of Americans on a graduation tour. They have been entertaining tourists and locals ever since. The two-hour, English-only show is a series of rude, clever, and high-powered improvisational skits offering a raucous look at Dutch culture and local tourism (€20 weekdays, generally €24 Fri-Sat; Sun-Fri shows at 20:15, sometimes also Fri at 23:30, Sat at 19:30 and discounted show at 22:30; confirm times when you buy your ticket, ticket office open daily from 13:00 until 15 minutes after curtain time, no Mon shows Jan-March, tel. 020/423-0101, www.boomchicago.nl). It all happens at the 300-seat Leidseplein Theater at Leidseplein 12; enter through the skinny Boom Bar (optional meal and drink service).

They do *Best of Boom* (a collection of their greatest hits over the years) as well as new shows for locals and return customers. When sales are slow, ticket-sellers on the street out front offer steeply discounted tickets, with a drink included. Drop by that afternoon and see what's up.

Theater

Amsterdam is one of the world centers for experimental live theater (much of it in English). Many theaters cluster around the street called the Nes, which stretches south from Dam Square.

Movies

It's not unusual for movies at many cinemas to be sold out—consider buying tickets during the day. Catch modern movies in the 1920s setting of the classic **Tuschinski Theater** (between Muntplein and Rembrandtplein, described on page 1203).

Museums

Several museums stay open late. The **Anne Frank House** always stays open until at least 19:00 year-round; it's open daily until 22:00 in July and August, and closes late on Saturdays year-round (22:00 peak-season, 21:00 off-season). The **Hermitage Amsterdam** stays open until 20:00 on Wednesdays. The **Van Gogh Museum** is open on Fridays until 22:00 and sometimes has music and a wine bar in the lobby.

The **Hash, Marijuana, and Hemp Museum** is open daily until 23:00. And the **sex museums** always stay open late (Damrak Sex Museum until 23:30, Erotic Museum until 1:00 in the morning).

Skating After Dark

Amsterdammers get their skating fix on wheels every Friday night in summer and early fall in Vondelpark. Huge groups don inline skates and meet at the round bench near the Vondel Pavilion (around 20:15, www.fridaynightskate.com). Anyone can join in. You can rent skates at the shop at the far end of the park (Vondeltuin Rental, daily 11:00-20:00 in good weather; first hour-€5, then €2.50/hour; price includes helmet, wrist guards, and knee guards; at southeastern edge of park, mobile 0627-565-576, www.vondeltuin.nl).

Sleeping in Amsterdam

Greeting a new day by descending steep stairs and stepping into a leafy canalside scene—graceful bridges, historic gables, and bikes clattering on cobbles—is a fun part of experiencing Amsterdam. But Amsterdam is a tough city for budget accommodations, and any hotel room under €140 (or B&B room under €100) will have rough edges. Still, you can sleep well and safely in a great location for €100 per double.

I've grouped my hotel listings into three neighborhoods, each of which has its own character.

West Amsterdam (which includes the Jordaan) has Old World ambience, with quiet canals, old gabled buildings, and candlelit restaurants. It's also just minutes on foot to Dam Square. Many of my hotels are charming, friendly, gabled mansions. The downside here is that you'll pay more.

Southwest Amsterdam has two main areas for accommodations: near Leidseplein (more central) and near Vondelpark (farther away). The streets near the bustling Leidseplein have restaurants, tourist buzz, nightlife, canalside charm, B&B coziness, and walkable (or easy tram) access to the center of town. Farther afield is the quieter semi-suburban neighborhood around Vondelpark and Museumplein, close to the Rijks and Van Gogh museums. You'll find good hotel values and ready access to Vondelpark and the art museums, but you're a half-hour walk (or 10-minute tram ride) to Dam Square.

Staying in **Central Amsterdam** is ideal for people who like shopping, tourist sights, and easy access to public transportation (including Central Station). On the downside, the area has traffic noise, concrete, and urban grittiness, and the hotels can lack character.

Some national holidays merit your making reservations far in advance. Amsterdam is jammed during tulip season (late March-mid-May), conventions, festivals, and on summer weekends. During peak season, some hoteliers will not take weekend bookings for people staying fewer than two or three nights.

Around just about every corner in downtown Amsterdam, you'll see construction: cranes for big transportation projects and

Sleep Code

(€1 = about $1.40, country code: 31, area code: 020)
S = Single, **D** = Double/Twin, **T** = Triple, **Q** = Quad, **b** = bathroom, **s** = shower only. Nearly everyone speaks English. Credit cards are accepted, and prices include breakfast and tax unless otherwise noted.

To help you easily sort through these listings, I've divided the rooms into three categories, based on the price for a standard double room with bath:

$$$ Higher Priced—Most rooms €140 or more.
 $$ Moderately Priced—Most rooms between €80-140.
  $ Lower Priced—Most rooms €80 or less.

Prices can change without notice; verify the hotel's current rates online or by email. For other updates, see www .ricksteves.com/update.

small crews of bricklayers repairing the wobbly, cobbled streets that line the canals. Canalside rooms can come with great views—and early-morning construction-crew noise. If you're a light sleeper, ask the hotelier for a quiet room in the back. Smoking is illegal in hotel rooms throughout the Netherlands. Parking in Amsterdam is even worse than driving—if you must park a car, ask your hotelier for advice.

If you'd rather trade big-city action for small-town coziness, consider sleeping in Haarlem, 20 minutes away by train (see next chapter).

West Amsterdam
Stately Canalside Hotels

These hotels, a half-mile apart, both face historic canals. They come with fine lobbies (some more ornate than others) and rooms that can feel like they're from another century. This area oozes elegance and class, and it is fairly quiet at night.

$$$ The Toren is a chandeliered, historic mansion with a pleasant, canalside setting and a peaceful garden out back for guests. Run by Eric and Petra Toren, this smartly renovated, super-romantic hotel is classy yet friendly, with 38 rooms in a great location on a quiet street two blocks northeast of the Anne Frank House. The capable staff is a great source of local advice. The gilt-frame, velvet-curtained rooms are an opulent splurge (tiny Sb-€115, Db-€200, deluxe Db-€250, third person-€40, prices bump way up during conferences and decrease in winter, rates do not include 5 percent tax, breakfast buffet-€12, air-con, elevator, Internet access

Hotels & Restaurants

in West Amsterdam

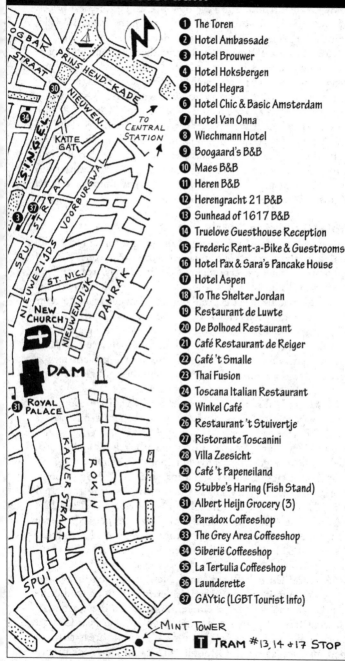

1. The Toren
2. Hotel Ambassade
3. Hotel Brouwer
4. Hotel Hoksbergen
5. Hotel Hegra
6. Hotel Chic & Basic Amsterdam
7. Hotel Van Onna
8. Wiechmann Hotel
9. Boogaard's B&B
10. Maes B&B
11. Heren B&B
12. Herengracht 21 B&B
13. Sunhead of 1617 B&B
14. Truelove Guesthouse Reception
15. Frederic Rent-a-Bike & Guestrooms
16. Hotel Pax & Sara's Pancake House
17. Hotel Aspen
18. To The Shelter Jordan
19. Restaurant de Luwte
20. De Bolhoed Restaurant
21. Café Restaurant de Reiger
22. Café 't Smalle
23. Thai Fusion
24. Toscana Italian Restaurant
25. Winkel Café
26. Restaurant 't Stuivertje
27. Ristorante Toscanini
28. Villa Zeesicht
29. Café 't Papeneiland
30. Stubbe's Haring (Fish Stand)
31. Albert Heijn Grocery (3)
32. Paradox Coffeeshop
33. The Grey Area Coffeeshop
34. Siberië Coffeeshop
35. La Tertulia Coffeeshop
36. Launderette
37. GAYtic (LGBT Tourist Info)

AMSTERDAM

and Wi-Fi, Keizersgracht 164, tel. 020/622-6033, fax 020/626-9705, www.thetoren.nl, info@thetoren.nl). To get the best prices, check their website for their "daily rate," and in the "remarks" field, ask for the 10 percent Rick Steves cash discount.

$$$ Hotel Ambassade, lacing together 59 rooms in a maze of connected houses, is elegant and fresh, sitting aristocratically on Herengracht. The staff is top-notch, and the public areas (including a library and breakfast room) are palatial, with antique furnishings and modern art (Sb-€195, Db-€195-245, spacious "deluxe" Db with canal view-€295, Db suite-€345, Tb-€245-295, extra bed-€40, ask for Rick Steves discount when booking, see website for specials, rates do not include 5 percent tax, breakfast-€17, air-con, elevator, free Internet access and Wi-Fi, Herengracht 341, for location see map on previous page, tel. 020/555-0222, www.ambassade-hotel .nl, info@ambassade-hotel.nl, Roos—pronounced "Rose").

Simpler Canalside Hotels

These places have basic rooms—some downright spare, none at all plush—and most do without an elevator or other extras. Each of them, however, offer a decent night's sleep in a lovely area of town.

$$ Hotel Brouwer is a woody and homey old-time place. It's situated tranquilly yet centrally on the Singel canal and rents eight rooms with canal views, old furniture, and soulful throw rugs (Sb-€60, Db-€95, Tb-€120, rates don't include 5 percent tax, cash only, small elevator, free Wi-Fi and Internet access, located between Central Station and Dam Square, near Lijnbaanssteeg at Singel 83, tel. 020/624-6358, www.hotelbrouwer.nl, akita@hotel brouwer.nl).

$$ Hotel Hoksbergen is a welcoming, well-run canalside place in a peaceful location where helpful, hands-on owners Tony and Bert rent 14 rooms (Db-€98, Tb-€143, five Qb apartments-€165-198, fans, free Wi-Fi, Singel 301, tel. 020/626-6043, www.hotelhoksbergen.com, info@hotelhoksbergen.nl).

$$ Hotel Hegra is cozy and affordable, with 11 tight rooms filling a 17th-century merchant's house overlooking the canal (S-€50, D-€79, Ds-€89-€109, Db-€105-€119, Ts-€115-€125, Tb-€130, some rooms with canal view, pay Internet access, free Wi-Fi, bike rental, just north of Wolvenstraat at Herengracht 269, tel. 020/623-7877, www.hotelhegra.nl, info@hotelhegra.nl, Robert).

$$ Hotel Chic & Basic Amsterdam has a boutique-hotel feel, even though it's part of a Spanish chain. With its mod utilitarian design and younger clientele, it provides a break from all the lace curtains. Located in a quiet neighborhood near Central Station, it offers 25 minimalist rooms and public areas that are bathed in space-age white. Rooms with canal views are pricier and breezier (Sb-€95-130, Db-€120-155, €20 more on holiday weekends, less in winter, cheaper prices are for less-sleek "vintage" rooms without canal views, free coffee, continental breakfast, fans on request, tangled floor plan connecting three canalside buildings, free Internet access and Wi-Fi, Herengracht 13, tel. 020/522-2345, www.chicandbasic.com, amsterdam@chicandbasic.com, manager Bernardo Campo).

$$ Hotel Van Onna has 41 simple, industrial-strength rooms, some with canal views. The price is right, and the leafy location makes you want to crack out your easel. The popular top-floor attic rooms are cozy hideaways (Sb-€45-65, Db-€80-100, Tb-€125-135, Qb-€170-190, price depends on season, cash only, cot-like beds are sufficient, no phones or TVs, free Internet access and Wi-Fi, in the Jordaan at Bloemgracht 104, tel. 020/626-5801, www.hotel vanonna.nl, info@hotelvanonna.nl, Leon and Tsibo).

$$ Wiechmann Hotel's 37 rooms are sparsely furnished with just the dark-wood essentials, but they're spacious, and the *gezellig* public areas are chock-full of Old World charm (Sb-€65-105, Db-€125-165, Tb-€205, Qb-€230, Db suite-€260, prices lower in winter, check online for best price, 15 percent cheaper for 3 or more nights if booking through their website, some canal views, back rooms are quiet, free Internet access and Wi-Fi, nicely located at Prinsengracht 328-332, tel. 020/626-3321, www.hotelwiechmann .nl, info@hotelwiechmann.nl, John and Taz the welcome dog).

B&Bs and Private-Room Rentals

B&Bs offer a chance to feel like a local during your visit. The first and third listings here are in a residential and peaceful neighborhood that's a short walk from Central Station; the second and fourth are in slightly busier areas. The last two listings are services that manage and rent many apartments and rooms in West Amsterdam.

$$ Boogaard's B&B is a delightful pad on a narrow lane right out of Mister Rogers' neighborhood. The B&B, which has four comfortable rooms and an inviting public living room, is run by Peter, an American expat opera singer. Peter, who clearly enjoys hosting Americans in his home, serves his fresh-baked goodies at breakfast and treats you royally. As his place is popular with my readers, it's smart to book well in advance (Db-€120, 2-night minimum; furnished family apartment with kitchen-€240 for 4 people, 3-night minimum; prices don't include 5 percent tax, aircon, free Wi-Fi, DVD library, free laundry, loaner cell phones and laptops, Langestraat 34, tel. 064/358-6835, www.boogaardsbnb .com, info@boogaardsbnb.com).

$$ Maes B&B (pronounced "mahss") is a dynamite value, renting tastefully cozy rooms for much less than you'd pay at a

AMSTERDAM

hotel. Instead of a reception desk, you get antique-filled rooms, the use of a full kitchen, and a warm welcome from Ken and Vlad. They also run **Heren B&B**, a crisply modern space around the corner from Maes, with large rooms—one with a canal view (both locations: Sb-€95, Db-€105, bigger Db-€115-125, extra bed-€30, suites and full apartments also available, free Internet access and Wi-Fi, if street noise bothers you ask for room in back, Herenstraat 26, tel. 020/427-5165, www.bedandbreakfastamsterdam.com, maes info@xs4all.nl).

$$ Herengracht 21 B&B has two stylish, tiny, intimate rooms filled with art and run by lovely Loes Olden (2-floor Db-€125, canal-view Db-€135, air-con, free Wi-Fi, Herengracht 21, tel. 020/625-6305, mobile 06-2812-0962, www.herengracht21 .nl, loes@herengracht21.nl).

$$ Sunhead of 1617 B&B justifiably calls itself a "bed and delicious breakfast," but you're just as likely to remember the thoughtfully decorated, flower-filled rooms and the personality of owner Carlos (rear Db-€119, front Db-€129, Db apartment-€169, Tb apartment-€210, more on holidays, free Wi-Fi, mobile 06-2865-3572, Herengracht 152, www.sunhead.com, carlos@sunhead.com).

$$ With **Truelove Guesthouse,** a room-rental service, you'll feel like you're staying at your Dutch friends' house while they're out of town. Sean and Paul—whose tiny antique store on Prinsenstraat doubles as the reception desk for their rental service—have 15 rooms and apartments in houses sprinkled throughout the northern end of the Jordaan neighborhood. The apartments are stylish and come with kitchens and pull-out beds (Db-€90-105, Db apartment-€100-120, Qb apartments-€140-220, prices soft in off-season and midweek, 10 percent more with credit card, 2-night minimum on weekends, no breakfast, pick up keys in store at Prinsenstraat 4, store tel. 020/320-2500, mobile 06-2480-5672, fax 084-711-4950, www.cosyandwarm-amsterdam.com, trueloveantiek@zonnet.nl).

$ Frederic Rent-a-Bike & Guestrooms, with a bike-rental shop as the reception, is a collection of private rooms on a gorgeous canal just outside the Jordaan, a five-minute walk from Central Station. Frederic has amassed about 100 beds, ranging from dumpy €70 doubles behind the bike-rental shop, to spacious and elegant apartments (from €46/person; these places require a 2-night minimum, occasionally more). Some places are ideal for families and groups of up to six. He also rents houseboat apartments. All are displayed on his website (phone bookings preferred, book with credit card but pay with cash, no breakfast, Brouwersgracht 78, tel. 020/624-5509, www.frederic.nl, info @frederic.nl, Frederic and Marjolijn). His excellent bike shop is open daily 9:00-17:30 (€10/24 hours).

Southwest Amsterdam
Charming B&Bs near Leidseplein

The area around Amsterdam's rip-roaring nightlife center (Leidseplein) is colorful, comfortable, and convenient. These canalside mom-and-pop places are within a five-minute walk of rowdy Leidseplein, but are in generally quiet and typically Dutch settings. Within walking distance of the major museums, and steps off the tram line, this neighborhood offers a perfect mix of charm and location.

$$ Hotel de Leydsche Hof is a hidden gem located on a canal. Its two large rooms are a symphony in white, overlooking a tree-filled backyard. Frits and Loes give their big, elegant, old building a stylish air. Breakfast is served in the grand canal-front room (Db-€120, cash only, 2-night minimum, free Internet access and Wi-Fi, Leidsegracht 14, tel. 020/638-2327, mobile 06-5125-8588, www.freewebs.com/leydschehof, loespiller@planet.nl).

$$ Wildervanck B&B, run by Helene and Sjoerd Wildervanck, offers two tasteful rooms in an elegant, 17th-century canal house (big Db on first floor-€135, Db with twin beds on ground floor-€120, extra bed-€30, 2-night minimum, breakfast in their pleasant dining room, free Wi-Fi, family has three girls, Keizersgracht 498, on Keizersgracht canal just west of Leidsestraat, tel. 020/623-3846, www.wildervanck.com, info@wildervanck.com).

$$ Hotel Keizershof is wonderfully Dutch, with six bright, airy rooms—some with canal views—in a 17th-century canal house with a lush garden and a fine living room. A very steep spiral staircase leads to rooms named after old-time Hollywood stars. The enthusiastic hospitality of Mrs. de Vries and her daughter, Hanneke, give this place a friendly, almost small-town charm (S-€70, D-€90, Ds-€100, Db-€115, 2-night minimum, reserve with credit card but pay with cash, free Internet access and Wi-Fi; tram #16, #24, or #25 from Central Station, Keizersgracht 618, where Keizers canal crosses Nieuwe Spiegelstraat; tel. 020/622-2855, www.hotelkeizershof.nl, info@hotelkeizershof.nl).

Near Vondelpark and Museumplein

These options cluster around Vondelpark in a safe neighborhood. Though they don't have a hint of Old Dutch or romantic canalside flavor, they're reasonable values and only a short walk from the action. Unless noted, the places below have elevators. Many are in a pleasant nook between rollicking Leidseplein and the park, and most are a 5- to 15-minute walk to the Rijks and Van Gogh museums. They are easily connected with Central Station by trams #1, #2, and/or #5.

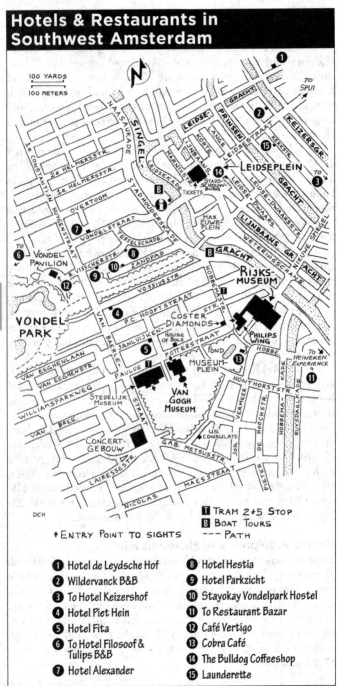

Hotels & Restaurants in Southwest Amsterdam

AMSTERDAM

100 YARDS
100 METERS

N

TO SPUI

TO

LEIDSEPLEIN

RIJKS-MUSEUM

VONDEL PAVILION

VONDEL PARK

COSTER DIAMONDS

PHILIPS WING

To Heineken Experience

MUSEUM-PLEIN

Van Gogh Museum

Stedelijk Museum

House of Bols

U.S. CONSULATE

CONCERT-GEBOUW

MAX EUWE-PLEIN

STADS-SCHOUW-BURG

TICKETS

DCH

T TRAM 2 & 5 STOP
B BOAT TOURS
--- PATH

↟ ENTRY POINT TO SIGHTS

❶ Hotel de Leydsche Hof
❷ Wildervanck B&B
❸ To Hotel Keizershof
❹ Hotel Piet Hein
❺ Hotel Fita
❻ To Hotel Filosoof & Tulips B&B
❼ Hotel Alexander
❽ Hotel Hestia
❾ Hotel Parkzicht
❿ Stayokay Vondelpark Hostel
⓫ To Restaurant Bazar
⓬ Café Vertigo
⓭ Cobra Café
⓮ The Bulldog Coffeeshop
⓯ Launderette

$$$ Hotel Piet Hein offers 81 stylishly sleek yet comfortable rooms as well as a swanky lounge, good breakfast, and pleasant garden, all on a quiet street (Sb-€115, Db-€175, extra-posh Db-€200-250, Tb-€205, extra bed-€30, specials on website, air-con in some rooms, free Wi-Fi and Internet access, Vossiusstraat 51-53, tel. 020/662-7205, www.hotelpiethein.nl, info@hotelpiethein.nl).

$$$ Hotel Fita has 15 bright rooms in a great location—100 yards from the Van Gogh Museum, an even shorter hop from the tram stop, and on a corner with no car traffic. The decor may not be the latest, but all the amenities are there—including espresso machines in every room—and the welcome is very warm (Sb-€105, two small ground-floor Db-€135, Db-€145-165 depending on size, Tb-€205, free Wi-Fi and Internet access in lobby, free laundry service, Jan Luijkenstraat 37, tel. 020/679-0976, fax 020/664-3969, www.fita.nl, info@fita.nl, joking and colorful owner Hans).

$$ Hotel Filosoof greets you with Aristotle and Plato in the foyer and classical music in its generous lobby. Its 38 rooms, some across the street from reception, are decorated with themes; the Egyptian room has a frieze of hieroglyphics. Philosophers' sayings hang on the walls, and thoughtful travelers wander down the halls or sit in the garden, rooted in deep discussion. The rooms are small, but the hotel is endearing (Db-€110-130 weeknights, €130-150 Fri-Sat, bigger "deluxe" rooms-€20 extra, suites-€60 extra, prices depend on season and don't include tax; no breakfast, free Internet access and Wi-Fi, 3-minute walk from tram line #1, get off at Jan Pieter Heijestraat, Anna van Den Vondelstraat 6, tel. 020/683-3013, fax 020/685-3750, www.hotel filosoof.nl, reservations@hotelfilosoof.nl).

$$ Hotel Alexander is a modern, newly renovated, 32-room hotel on a quiet street. Some of the rooms overlook the garden patio out back (Db-€135, prices soft in winter—call or check their website for best deal, Internet access, pay Wi-Fi, tel. 020/589-4020, fax 020/589-4025, Vondelstraat 44-46, www.hotelalexander .nl, info@hotelalexander.nl).

$$ Tulips B&B, with a bunch of cozy rooms—some on a canal—is run by a friendly Englishwoman, Karen, and her Dutch husband, Paul. Rooms are clean, white, and bright, with red carpeting, plants, and flowers (D-€85, Db-€120, suite-€150, extra bed-€30, discounts for longer stays, cash only, prefer 3-night stays on weekends, includes milk-and-cereal breakfast, no shoes, no elevator but not a lot of stairs, free Wi-Fi, south end of Vondelpark at Sloterkade 65, 7-minute walk from trams #1 and #2, directions sent when you book, tel. 020/679-2753, rooms@bedandbreakfast amsterdam.net, www.bedandbreakfastamsterdam.net).

$$ Hotel Hestia, on a safe and sane street, is efficient and family-run, with 18 clean, airy, and generally spacious rooms

(Sb-€83-93, very small Db-€101-107, standard Db-€128-148, Tb-€158-176, Qb-€188-206, Quint/b-€218-236, can be less in winter—check website for best price, Roemer Visscherstraat 7, tel. 020/618-0801, fax 020/685-1382, www.hotel-hestia.nl, info@hotel -hestia.nl, Arnaud).

$$ Hotel Parkzicht, an old-fashioned, no-frills, dark-wood place with extremely steep stairs, rents 13 big, plain, and somewhat frayed rooms on a street bordering Vondelpark (S-€49, Sb-€59, Db-€79-92, Tb-€140, closed Nov-March, no elevator, free Wi-Fi, some noise from neighboring youth hostel, Roemer Visscherstraat 33, tel. 020/618-1954, fax 020/618-0897, www.parkzicht.nl, hotel @parkzicht.nl).

Central Amsterdam
Basic Hotels in the City Center
You won't get a warm welcome at either of the two following hotels. But if you're looking for a no-nonsense room that's convenient to plenty of tram lines, these hotels fit the bill.

$$$ Hotel Ibis Amsterdam Centre, located next door to the Central Station, is a modern, efficient, 187-room place. It offers a central location, comfort, and good value, without a hint of charm (Db-€140-160 Nov-Aug, Db-€200 Sept-Oct, breakfast-€15, check website for deals, book long in advance—especially for Sept-Oct, air-con, pay Internet access; facing Central Station, go left toward the multistory bicycle garage to Stationsplein 49; tel. 020/522-2899, fax 020/522-2889, www.ibishotel.com, h1556@accor.com). When business is slow, usually in mid-summer, they occasionally rent rooms to same-day drop-ins for around €100.

$$ Hotel Résidence Le Coin offers 42 larger-than-average rooms complete with small kitchenettes. Located near the Mint Tower, this hotel is a two-minute walk to the Flower Market and a five-minute walk to Rembrandtplein (Sb-€119, small Db-€139, bigger Db-€154, Qb-€230, extra bed-€37, breakfast-€12, pay Wi-Fi, by the University at Nieuwe Doelenstraat 5, tel. 020/524-6800, fax 020/524-6801, www.lecoin.nl, hotel@lecoin.nl).

Budget Hotels Between Dam Square and the Anne Frank House: Inexpensive, well-worn hotels line the convenient but noisy and unromantic main drag, Raadhuisstraat. Expect a long, steep, and depressing stairway, with noisy rooms in the front and quieter rooms in the back. Though neither of the places below serve breakfast, they're both steps from a recommended pancake house. For locations, see the map on pages 1220-1221.

$ Hotel Pax has 11 large, plain, but airy rooms with IKEA furniture—a lot like a European dorm room (S-€35-45, D-€65, Db-€80, T-€85, Tb-€100, prices drop dramatically in winter, no breakfast, six rooms share two showers and two toilets,

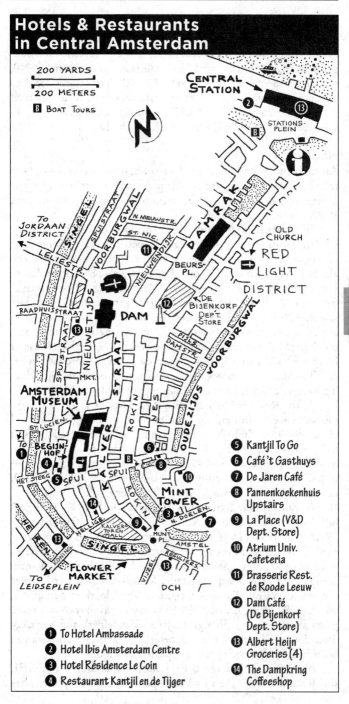

Hotels & Restaurants in Central Amsterdam

200 YARDS
200 METERS
B Boat Tours

CENTRAL STATION

STATIONSPLEIN

TO JORDAAN DISTRICT

SINGEL
SPUISTRAAT
VOORBURGWAL
N. NIEUWSTR.
ST. NIC.
NIEUWENDIJK
LELIESTR.
DAMRAK

OLD CHURCH
RED LIGHT DISTRICT

RAADHUISSTRAAT
BEURS-PL.

DE BIJENKORF DEP'T. STORE

DAM
SPUISTRAAT
NIEUWE ZIJDS
KALVER STRAAT
MKT.

PLS.
DAM STR.
VOORBURGWAL

AMSTERDAM MUSEUM

ROKIN
NES
OUDEZIJDS

ST. LUCIEN.
TO
BEGIJN-HOF
HET STEEG
SPUI
SPUI
B

MINT TOWER

HEREN
HELLIGE
KONING
KALVER TOREN MALL

FORTIN
N. DOELEN.
MUNT PL.
AMSTEL

SINGEL

FLOWER MARKET
TO LEIDSEPLEIN

VIJZEL
REGULIERS.
DCH

5 Kantjil To Go
6 Café 't Gasthuys
7 De Jaren Café
8 Pannenkoekenhuis Upstairs
9 La Place (V&D Dept. Store)
10 Atrium Univ. Cafeteria
11 Brasserie Rest. de Roode Leeuw
12 Dam Café (De Bijenkorf Dept. Store)
13 Albert Heijn Groceries (4)
14 The Dampkring Coffeeshop

1 To Hotel Ambassade
2 Hotel Ibis Amsterdam Centre
3 Hotel Résidence Le Coin
4 Restaurant Kantjil en de Tijger

AMSTERDAM

Raadhuisstraat 37, tel. 020/624-9735, hotelpax@tiscali.nl, run by go-getters Philip and Pieter).

$ Hotel Aspen, a few doors away and a great value for a budget hotel, has eight tidy, stark, and well-maintained rooms (S-€40, tiny D-€55-65, Db-€75-80, Tb-€95, Qb-€110, prices same 365 days a year, no breakfast, free Wi-Fi and Internet access, Raadhuisstraat 31, tel. 020/626-6714, fax 020/620-0866, www.hotelaspen.nl, info @hotelaspen.nl, run by kindhearted Rudy and Esam).

Hostels

Amsterdam has a world of good, cheap hostels located throughout the city. Most are designed for the party crowd, but here are a few quieter options. They all offer dorm beds; Stayokay Vondelpark also has some basic doubles.

In the Jordaan: **$ The Shelter Jordan** is a scruffy, friendly, Christian-run, 100-bed place in a great neighborhood. While most of Amsterdam's hostels are pretty wild, this place is drug-free and alcohol-free, with boys on one floor and girls on another. These are Amsterdam's best budget beds (bunks in 12-20-bed dorms-€23.50, €28 Fri-Sat and around holidays, same bunks in shoulder season-€20.50, less in off-season; bunks in 6-8-bed dorms-€1.50 extra; bunks in 4-5-bed rooms-€4 extra; includes sheets and breakfast, Internet access in lobby, near Anne Frank House at Bloemstraat 179, tel. 020/624-4717, www.shelter.nl, jordan@shelter .nl). The Shelter serves hot meals, runs a snack bar in its big, relaxing lounge, offers lockers, and leads nightly Bible studies.

In the Red Light District: **$ The Shelter City** is Shelter Jordan's sister—similar, but definitely not preaching to the local choir. While its 180 beds are buried in the heart of the red lights, it feels very well-run and perfectly safe (same prices as Shelter Jordan, bunks in Qb-€6 extra, D-€49 for spouses or single-sex; same amenities, rules, and Bible study; Barndesteeg 21, tel. 020/625-3230, fax 020/623-2282, www.shelter.nl, city@shelter.nl).

In Vondelpark: **$ Stayokay Vondelpark (IYHF),** with 530 beds in 130 rooms, is one of Amsterdam's top hostels for the under-25 set (€20-37/bed in 4- to 20-bed dorms, D-€60-95—most with bunk beds, higher prices are for March-Oct, members save €2.50, price depends on demand—cheapest when booked in advance, family rooms, lots of school groups, lockers, laundry, pay Internet access and Wi-Fi, bike rental, right on Vondelpark at Zandpad 5, tel. 020/589-8996, fax 020/589-8955, www.stayokay.com, vondel park@stayokay.com). Though Stayokay Vondelpark and Stayokay Stadsdoelen (listed next) are generally booked long in advance, occasionally a few beds open up each day at 11:00.

Near Waterlooplein: **$ Stayokay Stadsdoelen (IYHF),** smaller and simpler than its Vondelpark sister (listed above), has only large dorms and no private bathrooms, but is free of large school groups (€17-32/bed with sheets and breakfast in 10-bed dorms, members save €2.50, price depends on demand—cheapest when booked in advance, lockers, pay Internet access, bike rental, Kloveniersburgwal 97, see map on page 1226, tel. 020/624-6832, fax 020/639-1035, www.stayokay.com, stadsdoelen@stayokay .com).

Farthest East: **$ Stayokay Zeeburg (IYHF)** is a 500-bed hostel with all the modern services. While it's pretty far from the center, by tram or bike you're just 15 minutes from Damrak street (€20-30/bed in 6- to 14-bed dorms, price depends on demand— cheapest when booked in advance, pay Internet access and Wi-Fi, lockers, games, restaurant, bike rental, tram #14 to Timorplein 21, tel. 020/551-3190, fax 020/623-4986, www.stayokay.com, zeeburg @stayokay.com).

Eating in Amsterdam

Of Amsterdam's thousand-plus restaurants, no one knows which are best. I'd pick an area and wander. The rowdy food ghetto thrives around Leidseplein; if you don't mind eating in a touristy area, wander along Leidsedwarsstraat, Restaurant Row. The area around Spui canal and that end of Spuistraat is also trendy and not as noisy. For fewer crowds and more charm, find something in the Jordaan district. Most hoteliers keep a reliable eating list for their neighborhood and know which places keep their travelers happy. I've listed some handy places to consider.

To dine cheaply yet memorably alongside the big spenders, grab a meal to go, then find a bench on a lively neighborhood square or along a canal. Sandwiches *(broodjes)* of delicious cheese on fresh bread are cheap at snack bars, delis, and *broodjes* restaurants. Ethnic restaurants serve cheap, splittable carryout meals. Ethnic fast-food stands abound, offering a variety of meats wrapped in pita bread. Easy to buy at grocery stores, yogurt in the Netherlands (and throughout northern Europe) is delicious and often drinkable right out of its plastic container.

In Central Amsterdam

For the locations of these eateries, see the "Hotels and Restaurants in Central Amsterdam" map on page 1229.

On and near Spui

Restaurant Kantjil en de Tijger is a thriving place with a plain and noisy ambience, full of happy eaters who know a good value. The food is purely Indonesian; the waiters are happy to explain your many enticing options. Their three *rijsttafels* (traditional "rice tables" with about a dozen small courses) range from €20 to €30 per person. While they are designed for two people, three people can make a meal by getting a *rijsttafel* for two and ordering a soup or light dish for the third person. A good budget alternative to the full-blown *rijsttafel* is a *nasi rames*—10 small dishes on one big plate for €13 (daily 12:00-23:00, early-bird €10 dinner daily 16:30-18:45, reservations smart, mostly indoor with a little outdoor seating, Spuistraat 291, tel. 020/620-0994).

Kantjil to Go, run by Restaurant Kantjil, is a tiny take-out bar serving up inexpensive but delicious Indonesian fare (€5 for 300 grams, €6.50 for 600 grams, vegetarian specials, daily 12:00-21:00, Thu-Sat until 22:00, storefront at Nieuwezijds Voorburgwal 342, around the back of the sit-down restaurant listed above, tel. 020/620-3074). Split a large box (they'll happily give you an empty extra box for your dining pleasure), grab a bench on the charming Spui Square around the corner, and you've got perhaps the cheapest hot meal in town.

Near the Mint Tower

Café 't Gasthuys, one of Amsterdam's many brown cafés (so called for their smoke-stained walls), has a busy dumbwaiter cranking out light lunches, sandwiches, and reasonably priced, if uncreative, dinners. It offers a long bar, a fine secluded back room, peaceful canalside seating, and sometimes slow service (€5-9 lunch plates, €11-15 dinner plates, daily 12:00-16:30 & 17:30-21:30, Thu-Sat until 22:00; Grimburgwal 7—from the Rondvaart Kooij boat dock, head down Langebrugsteeg, and it's one block down on the left; tel. 020/624-8230).

De Jaren Café ("The Years Café") is a chic yet inviting place—clearly a favorite with locals. Upstairs is the minimalist restaurant with a top-notch salad bar and a canal-view deck (serving €14-20 dinners after 17:30, including fish, meat, and veggie dishes, and salad bar, or €12 for salad bar only). Downstairs is a modern Amsterdam café, great for light lunches (soups, salads, and sandwiches served all day and evening), or just coffee over a newspaper. On a sunny day, the café's canalside patio is a fine spot to nurse a drink; this is also a nice place to go just for a drink in the evening and to enjoy the spacious Art Deco setting (daily 10:00-24:00, Nieuwe Doelenstraat 20-22, a long block up from Muntplein, tel. 020/625-5771).

Pannenkoekenhuis Upstairs is a tiny and characteristic perch up some extremely steep stairs, where Arno Jakobs cooks and serves delicious €7 pancakes to four tables throughout the afternoon (Fri-Sat 12:00-18:00, Sun 12:00-17:00, closed Mon-Thu, Grimburgwal 2, tel. 020/626-5603).

La Place, on the ground floor of the V&D department store, has an abundant, colorful array of fresh, appealing food served cafeteria-style. A multistory eatery that seats 300, it has a small outdoor terrace upstairs. Explore before you make your choice. This bustling spot has a lively market feel, with everything from made-on-the-spot beef stir-fry, to fresh juice, to veggie soups (€3 pizza and €4 sandwiches, Sun-Mon 11:00-20:00, Tue-Sat 10:00-20:00, Thu until 21:00, at the end of Kalverstraat near Mint Tower, tel. 020/622-0171). For fast and healthy take-out food (sandwiches, yogurt, fruit cups, and more), try the bakery on the department store's ground floor. (They run another branch, which has the city's ultimate view terrace, on the top floor of the **Central Library**—Openbare Bibliotheek Amsterdam—near Central Station.)

Atrium University Cafeteria, a three-minute walk from Mint Tower, feeds travelers and students from Amsterdam University for great prices, but only on weekdays (€6 meals, Mon-Fri 11:00-15:00 & 17:00-19:30, closed Sat-Sun; from Spui, walk west down Landebrug Steeg past canalside Café 't Gasthuys three blocks to Oudezijds Achterburgwal 237, go through arched doorway on the right; tel. 020/525-3999).

Between Central Station and Dam Square

Brasserie Restaurant de Roode Leeuw (*roode leeuw* means "red lion") offers a peaceful, calm respite from the crush of Damrak. During the day, the whole restaurant shares the same menu, but after 18:00, it's split roughly in half, with finer service, cloth table-cloths, and higher prices in back, and a more casual setup (and better people-watching on Damrak street) up front. Either way, you'll get a menu filled with traditional Dutch food, good service, and the company of plenty of tourists. Call ahead to reserve a window seat (restaurant: €15-20 entrées, €30 three-course fixed-price meal with traditional Dutch choices; brasserie: €10-15 entrées; daily 12:00-22:00, Damrak 93-94, tel. 020/555-0666).

Dam Café, on the first floor of the Bijenkorf department store on Dam Square, has a small lineup of inexpensive salads, sandwiches, and desserts. Enjoying views of busy Damrak, comfortable seating, and an upscale café vibe, you'll feel miles above the chaotic streets below (€8-11 salads, Mon 11:00-18:00, Tue-Fri 10:30-18:00, Thu until 21:00, Sat 9:30-18:00, Sun 12:00-18:00, Dam 1, tel. 088-245-9080). For a much wider range of dishes but no Dam views, head up to **Kitchen,** the store's swanky fifth-floor self-service restaurant (similar prices and hours as café).

Munching Cheap

Traditional fish stands sell €3 herring sandwiches and other salty treats, usually from easy-to-understand photo menus. **Stubbe's Haring,** where the Stubbe family has been selling herring for 100 years, is handy and well-established, a few blocks from Central Station (Tue-Fri 10:00-18:00, Sat 10:00-17:00, closed Sun-Mon, at the locks where Singel canal boat arrives at the train station, see map on pages 1220-1221). Grab a sandwich and have a picnic canalside.

Supermarkets: You'll see **Albert Heijn** grocery stores (daily 8:00-22:00) all over town. Four helpful, central locations are: Dam Square (Nieuwezijds Voorburgwal 226), Mint Tower (Koningsplein 4), Leidsestraat (at Konigsplein, on the corner of Leidsestraat and Singel), and Central Station (far end of passage under the tracks).

West Amsterdam
Near the Anne Frank House and in the Jordaan District

Nearly all of these places are within a few scenic blocks of the Anne Frank House, providing handy lunches and atmospheric dinners in Amsterdam's most characteristic neighborhood. For locations, see the map on pages 1220-1221.

Restaurant de Luwte is romantic, located on a picturesque street overlooking a canal. It has lots of candles, a muted but fresh modern interior, spacious seating, a few cool outdoor canalside tables, and French Mediterranean cuisine. Ask about their specials (€20 entrées, €30 three-course fixed-price meal, big dinner salads for €18, daily 18:00-22:00, Leliegracht 26-28, tel. 020/625-8548, manager Maarten).

De Bolhoed has serious vegetarian and vegan food in a colorful setting that Buddha would dig, with a clientele that appears to dig Buddha (big splittable portions, €15 dinners, light lunches, daily 12:00-22:00, dinner starts at 17:00, Prinsengracht 60, tel. 020/626-1803).

Café Restaurant de Reiger must offer the best cooking of any *eetcafé* in the Jordaan. Famous for its fresh ingredients and delightful bistro ambience, it's part of the classic Jordaan scene. In addition to an English menu, ask for a translation of the €17.50-20 daily specials on the chalkboard. They're proud of their fresh fish and French-Dutch cuisine. The café, which is crowded late and on weekends, takes no reservations, but you're welcome to have a drink (€3 house wine and fun little bar munchies menu) at the bar while you wait (Tue-Sun 17:00-24:00, closed Mon, veggie options, Nieuwe Leliestraat 34, tel. 020/624-7426).

Café 't Smalle is extremely charming, with three zones where you can enjoy a light lunch or a drink: canalside, inside around the bar, and up some steep stairs in a quaint little back room. The café is open daily until midnight, and simple meals (salads, soup, and fresh sandwiches) are served 11:00-17:30 (plenty of fine €2-3 Belgian beers on tap and interesting wines by the glass, at Egelantiersgracht 12 where it hits Prinsengracht, tel. 020/623-9617).

Thai Fusion, despite the name, serves straight-up top-quality Thai food in a sleekly modern, black-and-white room wedged neatly in the middle of the Nine Little Streets action (€15-20 main courses, €25-30 two-course meals, Mon-Fri 16:30-22:30, Sat-Sun 12:00-22:30, good veggie options, Berenstraat 8, tel. 020/320-8332).

Toscana Italian Restaurant is the Jordaan's favorite place for good, inexpensive Italian cuisine, including pizza, in a woody, Dutch-beer-hall setting (€6-8 pizza and pastas, €16 main courses, daily 16:00-23:30, fast service, Haarlemmerstraat 130, tel. 020/622-0353).

Winkel, the North Jordaan's cornerside hangout, serves appetizing French-Dutch meals at its plentiful outside tables and easy-going interior. It really gets hopping on Monday mornings when the Noordermarkt flea market is underway, but Amsterdammers come from across town all week for the *appeltaart* (€11-14 dinner plates, €5 snacks served after 16:00, daily 8:00-24:00 except Sun from 10:00, Noordermarkt 43, tel. 020/623-0223).

Sara's Pancake House is a basic pancake diner where extremely hardworking Sara cranks out sweet and savory €8-10 flapjacks made from fresh, organic ingredients (daily until 22:30, later on weekends, breakfast served until noon, Raadhuisstraat 45, tel. 020/320-0662).

Restaurant 't Stuivertje is a small, family-run neighborhood eatery tucked away in the Jordaan, serving French-inspired Dutch cuisine in an elegantly cozy but unpretentious atmosphere (€15-25 main courses, dinner salads, Wed-Sun 17:30-22:00, closed Mon-Tue, Hazenstraat 58 near Elandsgracht, tel. 020/623-1349).

Ristorante Toscanini is an up-market Italian place that's always packed. It's so popular that the staff can be a bit arrogant, but the lively, spacious ambience and great Italian cuisine more than make up for that—if you can get a seat. Reservations are essentially required (the staff recommends two-weeks notice for Fri and Sat). Otherwise your best bet is to arrive when they open at 18:00 (€14 first courses, €20 main courses, Mon-Sat 18:00-22:30, closed Sun, deep in the Jordaan at Lindengracht 75, tel. 020/623-2813).

Villa Zeesicht has all the romantic feel of a classic European café. The cozy interior is crammed with tiny tables topped by tall candlesticks, and wicker chairs outside gather under a wisteria-covered awning. The menu is uninventive—come here instead for the famous *appeltaart*, and for the great people-watching on Torensluis bridge (€11-16 plates, daily 9:00-21:30, Torensteeg 7, tel. 020/626-7433).

Drinks Only: **Café 't Papeneiland** is a classic brown café with Delft tiles, an evocative old stove, and a stay-awhile perch overlooking a canal with welcoming benches. It's been the neighborhood hangout since the 17th century (drinks but no food, overlooking northwest end of Prinsengracht at #2, tel. 020/624-1989). It feels a little exclusive; patrons who come here to drink and chat aren't eager to see it overrun by tourists. The café's name means "Papists' Island," since this was once a refuge for Catholics; there used to be an escape tunnel here for priests on the run.

Southwest Amsterdam
Near Leidseplein
Stroll through the colorful cancan of eateries on Leidsedwarsstraat, Restaurant Row, just off Leidseplein, and choose your favorite. Nearby, the busy Leidsestraat offers plenty of starving-student options (between the Prinsengracht and the Herengracht) offering fast and fun food for around €5 a meal.

Beyond the Rijksmuseum
Restaurant Bazar offers one of the most memorable and fun budget eating experiences in town. Converted from a church, it has spacious seating and mod belly-dance music, and is filled with young locals enjoying good, cheap Middle Eastern and North African cuisine. Reservations are a good idea if you plan to eat after 20:00 (fill up with the €8.50 daily plate, delicious €13 couscous, or €16 three-course meal of the day; daily 11:00-23:00, until 24:00 on weekends, Albert Cuypstraat 182, tel. 020/675-0544). Restaurant Bazar marks the center of the thriving Albert Cuyp market, which is wrapped up by about 17:00, though the restaurant is open late.

In Vondelpark
Café Vertigo offers a fun selection of excellent soups, salads, and sandwiches. It's a surprisingly large complex of outdoor tables, an indoor pub, and an elegant, candlelit, back-room restaurant beneath the grand, Italian Renaissance Vondel Pavilion. The service can be slow, but if you grab an outdoor table, you can watch the world spin by (daily 10:00-24:00 except off-season weekdays from 11:00, Vondelpark 3, tel. 020/612-3021).

Southeast Amsterdam
Near the Dutch Resistance Museum
For locations of the following eateries, see the map on page 1211.

Restaurant Plancius, adjacent to the Dutch Resistance Museum, is a modern and handy spot for lunch. Its good indoor and outdoor seating make it popular with the museum staff and broadcasters from the nearby local TV studios (creative breakfasts, hearty fresh sandwiches, light €5-9 lunches and €16-19 dinners, daily 10:00-22:00, Plantage Kerklaan 61a, tel. 020/330-9469).

Café Koosje, located halfway between the Dutch Resistance Museum and the Dutch Theater, is a corner lunchtime pub/bar ringed with outdoor seating. Inside, casual wooden tables and benches huddle under chandeliers, and the hip, young waitstaff serves beer and salads big enough for two (€5 sandwiches, €11 salads, food served daily 9:00-22:00, Plantage Middenlaan 37, on the corner of Plantage Kerklaan, tel. 020/320-0817).

Smoking

Tobacco

A quarter of Dutch people smoke tobacco. Holland has a long tradition as a smoking culture, being among the first to import the tobacco plant from the New World.

Tobacco shops glorify the habit, yet the Dutch people are among the healthiest in the world. Tanned, trim, firm, 60-something Dutch people sip their beer, take a drag, and ask me why Americans murder themselves with Big Macs.

Still, their version of the Surgeon General has finally woken up to the drug's many potential health risks. Warning stickers bigger than America's are required on cigarette packs, and some of them are almost comically blunt, such as: "Smoking will make you impotent...and then you die." (The warnings have prompted gag stickers like, "Life can kill you.")

Since 2008, a Dutch law has outlawed smoking tobacco almost everywhere indoors: on trains, and in hotel rooms, restaurants, cafés, and bars.

Marijuana (a.k.a. Cannabis)

Throughout the Netherlands, you'll see "coffeeshops"—cafés selling marijuana, with display cases showing various joints or baggies for sale. The minimum age for purchase is 18, and coffeeshops can sell up to five grams of marijuana per person per day. However, the newly conservative Dutch government is floating a proposal to ban tourists from buying marijuana—only Dutch citizens with a *wietpas* (weed pass) would be able to buy a joint. It's unclear if the proposal will be formally put into law, but be aware that the high times may be a changin'.

The Dutch buy marijuana by asking, "Can I see the cannabis menu?" Because it's illegal to advertise marijuana, the buyer has to take the initiative and request a menu. In some places there's actually a button you must push and hold down to see an illuminated menu, the contents of which look like the inventory of a drug bust.

The Netherland's indoor-smoking ban pertains to tobacco smoke, not pot smoke. But the Dutch, like the rest of Europe, mix their marijuana with tobacco. It might seem strange to an American, but these days, if a coffeeshop is busted, it's for tobacco. Coffeeshops with a few outdoor seats have a huge advantage, as their customers can light up outside. Shops without the outdoor option are in for an extra challenge, as many local smokers would rather get their weed to-go than smoke it without tobacco at their neighborhood coffeeshop. As a substitute for tobacco, shops have started mixing a kind of herb tea into joints. Pre-rolled joints are now sold three ways: pure, with the non-tobacco "hamburger helper" herb mix, or with tobacco. If you like your joint tobacco-free anyway, pure marijuana joints are much easier to find than they used to be.

Shops sell marijuana and hashish both in pre-rolled joints and in little baggies. Some places sell individual joints (€2-5). Others sell only small packs of three or four joints. Baggies of marijuana usually cost €10-15. Some shops charge per gram. The better pot, while costlier, is actually a better value, as it takes less to get high—and it's a better high. Shops have loaner bongs and inhalers, and they dispense cigarette papers like toothpicks. As long as you're a paying customer (e.g., buy a cup of coffee), you can pop into any coffeeshop and light up, even if you didn't buy your pot there.

Don't ever buy pot on the street in Amsterdam, and don't smoke marijuana openly while walking down the street. Well-established coffeeshops are considered much safer, and coffeeshop owners have an interest in keeping their trade safe and healthy. They warn Americans—unused to the strength of the local stuff—to try a lighter leaf. In fact, they are generally very patient in explaining the varieties available.

Coffeeshops

Most of downtown Amsterdam's coffeeshops feel grungy and fore-boding to American travelers who aren't part of the youth-hostel crowd. The neighborhood places (and those in small towns around the countryside) are much more inviting to people without pierc-ings, tattoos, and favorite techno artists. I've listed a few places with a more pub-like ambience for Americans wanting to go local, but within reason. For locations, see the maps under "Sleeping in Amsterdam," earlier.

Paradox is the most *gezellig* (cozy) coffeeshop I found—a mellow, graceful place. The managers, Ludo and Wiljan, and their staff are patient with descriptions and happy to walk you through all your options. This is a rare coffeeshop that serves light meals. The juice is fresh, the music is easy, and the neighborhood is charming (single tobacco-free joints–€3, loaner bongs, games, daily 10:00-20:00, two blocks from Anne Frank House at Eerste Bloemdwarsstraat 2, tel. 020/623-5639, www.paradoxcoffeeshop.com).

The Grey Area coffeeshop—a hole-in-the-wall spot with three tiny tables—is a cool, welcoming, and smoky place appreciated among local aficionados as a perennial winner of Amsterdam's Cannabis Cup awards. Judging by the autographed photos on the wall, many famous Americans have dropped in (say hi to Willie Nelson). You're welcome to just nurse a bottomless cup of coffee. The Grey Area is run by two friendly Americans, Adam and Jon. They are helpful and even have a vaporizer if you want to "smoke" without smoking (daily 12:00-20:00, they close relatively early out of consideration for their neighbors, between Dam Square and Anne Frank House at Oude Leliestraat 2, tel. 020/420-4301, www.greyarea.nl).

Siberië Coffeeshop is a short walk from Central Station, but feels cozy, with a friendly canalside ambience. Clean, big, and bright, this place has the vibe of a not-too-far-out Starbucks (daily 11:00-23:00, Fri-Sat until 24:00, free Wi-Fi for customers, helpful staff, English menu, Brouwersgracht 11, tel. 020/623-5909, www.siberie.nl).

La Tertulia is a sweet little mother-and-daughter–run place with pastel decor and a cheery terrarium atmosphere (Tue-Sat 11:00-19:00, closed Sun-Mon, sandwiches, brownies, games, Prinsengracht 312, www.coffeeshopamsterdam.com).

The Bulldog is the high-profile, leading touristy chain of coffeeshops. These establishments are young but welcoming, with reliable selections. They're pretty comfortable for green tourists wanting to just hang out for a while. The flagship branch, in a former police station right on Leidseplein, is very handy, offering alcohol upstairs, pot downstairs, and fun outdoor seating where you can watch the world skateboard by. There's a chance it may close because it's considered too near a school, but it will likely stay open (daily 10:00-1:00 in the morning, Fri-Sat until 3:00, Leidseplein 17, tel. 020/625-6278, www.bulldog.nl). They opened their first café (on the canal near the Old Church in the Red Light District) in 1975.

The Dampkring is a rough-and-ready constant party. It's a high-profile and busy place, filled with a young clientele and loud music, but the owners still take the time to explain what they offer. Scenes from the movie *Ocean's Twelve* were filmed here (daily 10:00-1:00 in the morning, close to Spui at Handboogstraat 29, tel. 020/638-0705, www.dampkring.nl).

Smartshops

These business establishments sell "natural" drugs that are legal. Many are harmless nutritional supplements, but they also sell stimulants similar to Ecstasy and strange drug cocktails rolled into joints. It's all perfectly legal, but if you've never taken drugs recreationally, don't start here.

Amsterdam Connections

The Netherlands is so small, level, and well-covered by trains and buses that transportation is a snap. The easy-to-navigate airport is well-connected to Amsterdam and other destinations by bus and train.

By Train

Amsterdam Central Station

Amsterdam's Central Station is being renovated—a messy construction project that's expected to last through 2014 (see "Arrival in Amsterdam" on page 1187 for more details on the station). The station's train-information center can require a long wait. Save lots of time by getting train tickets and information at a small-town station (such as Haarlem), the airport upon arrival (wonderful service), or a travel agency. You can buy tickets ahead of time for the next day.

If you have a railpass, it's quicker to validate it when you arrive at Schiphol Airport than in Amsterdam's Central Station where ticket-counter lines are long; you can stretch your railpass by buying an inexpensive ticket from the airport into Amsterdam and using your first "flexi" day for a longer trip.

From Amsterdam Central Station by Train to: Schiphol Airport (4-6/hour, 15 minutes, €3.70, have coins handy to buy from a machine to avoid lines), **Haarlem** (6/hour, 20 minutes, €3.70 one-way, €7.10 same-day round-trip), **Delft** (2/hour direct, 1 hour, more with transfer in Leiden or The Hague), **Bruges/Brugge** (hourly, 3.25-3.75 hours, transfer at Antwerp Central or Brussels Midi; transfer can be tight—be alert and check with conductor), **Brussels** (Intercity trains hourly, 2.75 hours), **Ostend** (for ferries to UK; hourly, 4 hours, 3 changes), **London** (6/day, 4.75-5.5 hours, with transfer to Eurostar Chunnel train in Brussels; Eurostar discounted with railpass, www.eurostar.com), **Copenhagen** (2/day, 11.25 hours, multiple transfers; one direct night train), **Frankfurt** (every 2 hours, 4 hours direct), **Munich** (roughly hourly, 7.5-8.75 hours, 1-2 transfers; night train possible via Hamburg, 15.5 hours), **Bern** (5/day, 8-9 hours, fastest trains change once in Frankfurt), **Paris** (nearly hourly, 3.25 hours direct via fast Thalys train or 5 hours with change to Thalys train in Brussels, www.thalys.com).

When booking Thalys trains, even railpass-holders need to buy a seat reservation (generally €26-33 in second-class or €41-54 in first class—the first-class reservation generally gets you a meal on board). If your railpass covers France but not BeNeLux, the reservation will cost more. (Railpasses that don't include France are not accepted on Thalys trains.) Save money by taking a bus to Paris—described next.

By Bus

To Paris by Bus: If you don't have a railpass, the cheapest way to get to Paris is by Eurolines bus (about 6/day, 8 hours, €46 one-way, €86 round-trip; price depends on demand—nonrefundable, advance-purchase one-way tickets as cheap as €17 and round-trip as cheap as €28, check online for deals, Julianaplein 5, Amstel Station, five stops by metro from Central Station, tel. 020/560-8788, www.eurolines.com).

By Plane

Amsterdam's Schiphol Airport

Schiphol (SKIP-pol) Airport is located about 10 miles southwest of Amsterdam's city center.

Information: Schiphol flight information can give you flight times and your airline's Amsterdam phone number for flight reconfirmation (tel. 0900-0141, from other countries dial +31-20-794-0800, www.schiphol.nl). To reach the airlines directly, call: KLM and Northwest—tel. 020/474-7747; Delta—tel. 020/201-3536; United—tel. 020/201-3708; US Airways—tel. 020/201-3550; Continental—tel. 020/346-9381; Martinair—tel. 020/601-1767; SAS—toll tel. 0900-7466-3727; Lufthansa—toll tel. 0900-123-4777; British Airways—tel. 020/346-9559; and easyJet—toll tel. 0900-265-8022.

Orientation: Schiphol has four terminals. Terminal 1 is for flights to most European countries (not including the UK); Terminals 2 and 3 are for flights to the UK, US, and other non-European countries; and the new, smaller Terminal 4 (attached to Terminal 3) is for low-cost carriers. Inside the airport, the terminal waiting areas are called lounges; an inviting shopping and eating zone called Holland Boulevard runs between Lounges 2 and 3.

Arrival at Schiphol: Baggage claim areas for all terminals empty into the same arrival zone, called Schiphol Plaza—with ATMs, shops, eateries, a busy **TI** (near Terminal 2), a train station, and bus stops for getting into the city. You can validate your Eurailpass and hit the rails immediately, or, to stretch your railpass, buy an inexpensive ticket into Amsterdam today and start the pass later.

Airport Services: The ABN/AMRO **banks** offer fair

exchange rates (in both arrivals and lounge areas). The **GWK Travelex** currency-exchange office is located in Arrivals 3 and sells SIM cards for mobile phones. **Jill and James,** in Schiphol Plaza, near Terminal 4, is a useful all-purpose service counter that sells SIM cards, has an ATM, and ships packages. The **Orbitel** mobile shop just outside Terminal 2 sells only one brand of SIM cards.

You can surf the **Internet** (for a price) and make phone calls at the Communication Centres (one on the top level of Lounge 2, another on the ground floor of Lounge 1; both are behind customs and not available once you've left the security checkpoint). Convenient luggage **lockers** are at various points around the airport—allowing you to leave your bag here on a lengthy layover (both short-term and long-term lockers; biggest bank of lockers near the train station at Schiphol Plaza).

Airport Train Ticket Counter: To get train information, buy a ticket, or validate your railpass, take advantage of the fantastic "Train Tickets and Services" counter (Schiphol Plaza ground level, just past Burger King). They have an easy info desk, almost no lines (much quicker than the ticket desk at the Amsterdam train station downtown), and issue tickets for a fee (€0.50 for domestic tickets, €3.50 for tickets to Belgium, Luxembourg, and nearby German cities; up to €10 for other international tickets).

Time-Killing Tips: If you have extra time at Schiphol, check out the Rijksmuseum Amsterdam Schiphol, a little art gallery and museum store on Holland Boulevard, the lively shopping/eating zone between Lounges 2 and 3. The Rijksmuseum loans a dozen or so of its minor masterpieces from the Dutch Golden Age to this unique airport museum, including actual Dutch Masters by Rembrandt, Vermeer, and others (free, daily 5:15-21:30).

To escape the airport crowds, follow signs for the Panorama Terrace to the third floor of Terminal 2, where you'll find a quieter, full-of-locals cafeteria, a kids' play area, and a view terrace where you can watch planes come and go while you nurse a coffee. If you plan to visit the terrace on arrival, stop there before you pass through customs.

From Schiphol Airport to Amsterdam: Direct **trains** to Amsterdam's Central Station run frequently (4-6/hour, 15 minutes, €3.70). The Connexxion **shuttle bus** takes you to your hotel neighborhood; since there are three different routes, ask the attendant which one works best for your hotel (2/hour, 20 minutes, €15 one-way, €24.50 round-trip, one route stops at Westerkerk near Anne Frank House and many recommended hotels, other routes may cost a couple euros more, departs from lane A7 in front of airport, reserve at least 2 hours ahead for shuttles to airport, tel. 088-339-4741, www.airporthotelshuttle.nl). Allow about €40 for a **taxi**

HAARLEM

Cute and cozy, yet authentic and handy to the airport, Haarlem is a fine home base, giving you small-town warmth overnight, with easy access (20 minutes by train) to wild and crazy Amsterdam during the day.

Bustling Haarlem gave America's Harlem its name back when New York was New Amsterdam, a Dutch colony. For centuries, Haarlem has been a market town, buzzing with shoppers heading home with fresh bouquets, nowadays by bike.

Enjoy the market on Monday (clothing) or Saturday (general), when the town's atmospheric main square bustles like a Brueghel painting, with cheese, fish, flowers, and families. Make yourself at home; buy some flowers to brighten your hotel room.

Orientation to Haarlem

(area code: 023)
Tourist Information

Haarlem's TI (VVV), in the town center, is friendlier, more helpful, and less crowded than Amsterdam's, so ask your Amsterdam questions here (Mon-Fri 9:30-17:30, Sat 10:00-17:00, closed most Sun but may be open 12:00-16:00, across from V&D department store at Verwulft 11, toll tel. 0900-616-1600—€0.50/minute, www.haarlem.nl, info@vvvhaarlem.nl).

The TI offers a good selection of maps and sightseeing and walking tour brochures, and sells discounted tickets (€1-2 off) for the Frans Hals Museum and the Teylers Museum.

The little yellow computer terminal on the curb outside the

west entrance of the train station prints out free maps anytime. (It's fun...just dial the street and hit "print." Drivers will also find these terminals stationed at roads coming into town.)

Arrival in Haarlem

By Train: Lockers are available at the station on platform 3a (€3.65/day, no coins—use a credit card or buy a "Chipknip" prepaid debit card at a ticket window). Two parallel streets flank the train station (Kruisweg and Jansweg). Head up either street, and you'll reach the town square and church within 10 minutes. If you need help, ask a local person to point you toward Grote Markt (Market Square).

By Bus: Buses from Schiphol Airport stop both in the center (Centrum/Verwulft stop, a short walk from Grote Markt) and at the train station. For more on bus connections from the airport, see "Haarlem Connections," at the end of this chapter.

By Car: Parking is expensive on the streets (€2.50/hour). It's cheaper (€1/30 minutes; €2.50 overnight—19:00-8:00) in these central garages: at the train station, at the southern end of Gedempte Oude Gracht (the main thoroughfare), near the recommended Die Raeckse Hotel, and near the Frans Hals Museum. The most central garage, near the Teylers Museum, is pricier (€1.50 every 40 minutes—essentially, €2.75/hour).

By Plane: For details on getting from Schiphol Airport to Haarlem, see "Haarlem Connections," at the end of this chapter.

Helpful Hints

Blue Monday and Early Closures: Most sights are closed on Monday, except the church. Two sights close early the rest of the week: **Corrie Ten Boom House** (15:30) and **De Adriaan windmill** (16:00).

Internet Access: Try **Hotel Amadeus** (overlooking Grote Markt, €1/30 minutes), **High Times Coffeeshop** (free if you buy some pot, Lange Veerstraat 47), or **Suny Teletechniques** (€2/hour, daily 10:00-24:00, near train station at Lange Herenstraat 4, tel. 023/551-0037).

Post Office: There isn't one. To buy stamps, head to a newsstand with the orange *TNT* logo; if you need to send a package, ask your hotelier for help.

Laundry: My Beautiful Launderette is handy and fairly central (€6 self-service wash and dry, daily 8:30-20:30, €9 full service available Mon-Fri 9:00-17:00, near V&D department store at Boter Markt 20).

Bike Rental: You can rent bikes from **Pieters Fietsverhuur** at the train station (fixed-gear bike-€6.50/day, more for 3-speed bike, €50 deposit and passport number required, Mon-Sat

6:00-24:00, Sun 8:00-24:00, Stationsplein 7, tel. 023/531-7066). They have only 50 bikes to rent and often run out by midmorning—especially when the weather's good. **Rent a Bike Haarlem** charges more, but is friendly and efficient, and carries plenty of new, good-quality bikes. If you're renting for less than a full day, negotiate a cheaper price (fixed-gear bike-€10/day, 3-speed bike-€13.50/day, mountain bikes available, after-hours drop-off possible, ID but no money required for deposit; April-Sept daily 9:00-18:00; Oct-March Tue-Fri 10:00-17:30, Thu until 18:00, Sat 10:00-17:00, closed Sun-Mon; near station at Lange Herenstraat 36, tel. 023/542-1195, www.rentabikehaarlem.nl).

Taxi: The drop charge of €7.50 gets you a little over a mile.

Local Guide: Consider hiring **Walter Schelfhout,** a bearded repository of Haarlem's historical fun facts. If you're into beer lore, Walter's your guy (€75/2 hours, also leads a beer walk, tel. 023/535-5715, mobile 06-1258-9299, schelfhout@dutch.nl).

Best View: At **La Place** (top-floor cafeteria of the V&D department store—see page 1256), you get wraparound views of the city as you sip your €2 self-serve tea.

Best Ice Cream: Gelateria Bartoli (on the south side of the Grote Kerk) is the local favorite (daily April-Sept 12:00-22:00, March and Oct-Dec 12:00-17:30 in good weather, closed Jan-Feb).

Sights in Haarlem

▲▲**Grote Markt (Market Square)**—Haarlem's Grote Markt, where 10 streets converge, is the town's delightful centerpiece...as it has been for 700 years. To enjoy a coffee or beer here, simmering in Dutch good living, is a quintessential European experience. Observe. Sit and gaze at the church, appreciating essentially the same scene that Dutch artists captured centuries ago in oil paintings that now hang in museums.

Just a few years ago, trolleys ran through the square, and cars were parked everywhere. But today, it's a pedestrian zone, with market stalls filling the square on Mondays and Saturdays, and café tables dominating on other days.

This is a fun place to build a picnic with Haarlem finger foods and enjoy great seating on the square. Look for pickled herring (take-away stand on the square), local cheese (Gouda and Edam—tasty shop a block away on Barteljorisstraat), french fries with mayonnaise (recommended old-time fries place behind the church on Warmoesstraat), and, in the summer, *stroopwafels* (waffles with built-in syrup) and *poffertjes* (little sugar doughnuts, cooked on the spot).

Haarlem

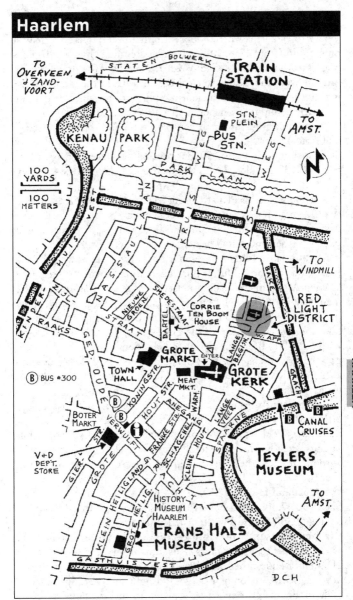

TO OVERVEEN & ZANDVOORT

STATEN BOLWERK

TRAIN STATION

TO AMST.

STN. PLEIN

BUS STN.

KENAU PARK

PARK LAAN

N

100 YARDS
100 METERS

HUIS VEST

TO WINDMILL

KINDER-ZIJL

RAAKS

GED. OUDE

NIEUWE GROEN

SMEDESTRAAT

BARTEL

Corrie Ten Boom House

RED LIGHT DISTRICT

W. APP.

BAKE

LANGE BEGIN

GROTE MARKT

ENTER

GROTE KERK

GRACHT

B BUS #300

TOWN HALL

KONINGSTR

MEAT MKT.

LANGE VEER

B CANAL CRUISES

BOTER MARKT

B

VERWULFT

HOUT STR

ANEGANG

FRANKESTR

SCHAGCHEL

WARM

KLEINE HOUT

SPAARNE

TEYLERS MUSEUM

V & D DEPT. STORE

GIER STR

GROTE HEILIGLAND

KLEIN HEILIGLAND

GROTE HEILIG.

KLEIN HEILIG.

HISTORY MUSEUM HAARLEM

FRANS HALS MUSEUM

TO AMST.

GASTHUIS VEST

DCH

HAARLEM

▲**Church (Grote Kerk)**—This 15th-century Gothic church (now Protestant) is worth a look, if only to see Holland's greatest pipe organ (from 1738, 100 feet high). Its more than 5,000 pipes impressed both Handel and Mozart. Note how the organ, which fills the west end, seems to steal the show from the altar. Quirky highlights of the church include a replica of Foucault's pendulum, the "Dog-Whipper's Chapel," and a 400-year-old cannonball.

To enter, find the small *Entrée* sign behind the Coster statue on Grote Markt.

Cost and Hours: €2.50, not covered by Museumkaart, Mon-Sat 10:00-17:00, closed Sun to tourists, tel. 023/553-2040, www.bavo.nl.

Concerts: Consider attending (even part of) a **concert** to hear the Oz-like pipe organ (regular free concerts Tue at 20:15 mid-May-mid-Oct, additional concerts Thu at 15:00 July-Aug; bring a sweater—the church isn't heated).

▲▲**Frans Hals Museum**—Haarlem is the hometown of Frans Hals, the foremost Dutch portrait painter of the 17th-century Golden Age. This refreshing museum, once an almshouse for old men back in 1610, displays many of Hals' greatest paintings, done in his nearly Impressionistic style. You'll see group portraits and take-me-back paintings of old-time Haarlem. Stand eye-to-eye with life-size, lifelike portraits of Haarlem's citizens—brewers, preachers, workers, bureaucrats, and housewives. Take a close look at the people who built the Dutch Golden Age, and then watched it start to fade.

Along with Frans Hals' work, the museum features a copy of Pieter Brueghel the Younger's *Flemish Proverbs*, a fun painting that shows 72 charming Flemish scenes representing different folk sayings. Pick up the chart to identify these clever bits of everyday wisdom. It's near the 250-year-old dollhouse on display in a former chapel.

Cost and Hours: €7.50, often €10 with special exhibits, Tue-Sat 11:00-17:00, Sun 12:00-17:00, closed Mon, Groot Heiligland 62, tel. 023/511-5775, www.franshalsmuseum.nl.

History Museum Haarlem—This small museum, across the street from the Frans Hals Museum, offers a glimpse of old Haarlem. Request the English version of the 10-minute video, low-key Haarlem's version of a sound-and-light show. Study the large-scale model of Haarlem in 1822 (when its fortifications were still intact), and wander the three rooms without English descriptions (overpriced at €4, Tue-Sat 12:00-17:00, Sun 13:00-17:00, closed Mon, Groot Heiligland 47, tel. 023/542-2427, www.historisch museumhaarlem.nl). The adjacent architecture center (free) may be of interest to architects.

▲**Corrie ten Boom House**—Haarlem was home to Corrie ten Boom, popularized by her inspirational book (and the movie that followed), *The Hiding Place*. Both tell about the Ten Boom family's experience protecting Jews from the Nazis. Corrie ten Boom gives the other half of the Anne Frank story—the point of view of those who risked their lives to hide Dutch Jews during the Nazi occupation (1940-1945).

The clock shop was the Ten Boom family business. The elderly father and his two daughters—Corrie and Betsy, both in their 50s—lived above the store and in the brick building attached in back (along Schoutensteeg alley). Corrie's bedroom was on the top floor at the back. This room was tiny to start with, but then the family built a second, secret room (less than a yard deep) at the very back—"the hiding place," where they could hide six Jews at a time. Devoutly religious, the family had a long tradition of tolerance, having hosted prayer meetings here in their home for both Jews and Christians for generations.

The Gestapo, tipped off that the family was harboring Jews, burst into the Ten Boom house. Finding a suspicious number of ration coupons, the Nazis arrested the family, but failed to find the six Jews (who later escaped) in the hiding place. Corrie's father and sister died while in prison, but Corrie survived the Ravensbrück concentration camp to tell her story in her memoir.

The Ten Boom House is open only for English tours—check the sign on the door for the next start time. The gentle and loving one-hour tours come with a little evangelizing that some may find objectionable.

Cost and Hours: Free, but donations accepted; April-Oct Tue-Sat first tour at 10:00, last tour at 15:30; Nov-March Tue-Sat first tour at 11:00, last tour around 14:30; closed Sun-Mon; 50 yards north of Grote Markt at Barteljorisstraat 19; the clock-shop people get all wound up if you go inside—wait in the little side street at the door, where tour times are posted; tel. 023/531-0823, www.corrietenboom.com.

▲**Teylers Museum**—Famous as the oldest museum in Holland, Teylers is a time-warp experience, filled with all sorts of fun curios for science buffs: fossils, minerals, primitive electronic gadgetry, and examples of 18th- and 19th-century technology (it also has two lovely painting galleries and hosts good temporary exhibits). The science-oriented sections of this place feel like a museum of a museum. They're serious about authenticity here: The presentation is perfectly preserved, right down to the original labels. Since there was no electricity in the olden days, you'll find little electric lighting...if it's dark outside, it's dark inside. The museum's benefactor, Pieter Teyler van der Hulst, was a very wealthy merchant who willed his estate, worth the equivalent of €80 million today, to a foundation whose mission was to "create and maintain a museum to stimulate art and science." The museum opened in 1784, six years after Teyler's death (his last euro was spent in 1983—now it's a national museum). Add your name to the guest book, which goes back to before Napoleon's visit here. The freshly renovated oval room—a temple of science and learning—is the core of the museum; in the art salons paintings are hung in the old style. An excellent (and, I'd say, essential) audioguide is included.

Cost and Hours: Overpriced at €9, Tue-Sat 10:00-17:00, Sun 12:00-17:00, closed Mon, Spaarne 16, tel. 023/516-0960, www.teylersmuseum.eu. The museum's modern café has good prices and faces a delightful garden.

▲**De Adriaan Windmill**—Haarlem's old-time windmill, located just a 10-minute walk from the station and Teylers Museum, welcomes visitors with a short video, little museum, and fine town views (€3, not covered by Museumkaart; March-Oct Wed-Fri 13:00-16:00, Sat-Sun 10:00-16:00, closed Mon-Tue; same hours in winter except only open Fri-Sun, Papentorenvest 1, tel. 023/545-0259, www.molenadriaan.nl).

Canal Cruise—Making a scenic 50-minute loop through and around Haarlem with a live guide who speaks Dutch and sometimes English, **Post Verkade Cruise**'s little trips are more relaxing than informative (€9.50; April-Oct daily departures at the top of the hour 12:00-16:00; also evening cruises, across canal from Teylers Museum at Spaarne 11a, tel. 023/535-7723, www.postverkadecruises.nl). For a similar experience in an open boat, find **Haarlem Canal Tours,** nearby on Korte Spaarne (€12.50, leaves every 1.5 hours daily 10:00-19:00, may not run in bad weather and off-season, www.haarlemcanaltours.com).

▲**Red Light District**—Wander through a little Red Light District that's as precious as a Barbie doll—and legal since the 1980s (2 blocks northeast of Grote Markt, off Lange Begijnestraat, no senior or student discounts). Don't miss the mall on Begijnesteeg marked by the red neon sign reading *'t Steegje* ("free"). Just beyond that, the nearby 't Poortje ("office park") costs €6 to enter. Jog to the right to pop into the much more inviting "Red Lantern" (window-shopping welcome, at Korte Begijnestraat 27). As you wander through this area, remember that the people here don't condone prostitution any more than your own community back home probably does; they just find it practical not to criminalize it and drive it underground, but instead to regulate it and keep the practice as safe as possible.

Nightlife in Haarlem

Haarlem's evening scene is great. Consider four basic zones: Grote Markt in the shadow of the Grote Kerk; Lange Veerstraat; Boter Grote Markt; and Vijfhoek (Five Corners).

Grote Markt is lined with trendy bars that seem made for nursing a drink—**Café Studio** is generally the hot spot for a drink here (at Grote Markt 25); I'd also duck into the dark interior of **In Den Uiver** (near the Grote Kerk entry at Riviervischmarkt 13, live jazz Thu and Sun). Lange Veerstraat (behind the Grote Kerk) is colorful and bordered with lively spots. Boter Grote Markt is more convivial and local, as it's less central and away from the tourists. Vijfhoek, named for the five lanes that converge here, is incredibly charming, although it has only one pub (with plenty of drinks, bar snacks, a relaxed crowd, and fine indoor or outdoor seating). Also worth exploring is the area from this cutest corner in town to the New Church (Nieuwe Kerk), a couple of blocks away. If you want a more high-powered scene, Amsterdam is just 20 minutes away by train.

Sleeping in Haarlem

The helpful Haarlem TI can nearly always find you a €27.50 bed in a private home (but for a €5.50-per-person fee, plus a cut of your host's money; two-night minimum, €30-35 for single room). Avoid this if you can; it's cheaper to reserve by calling direct. Nearly every Dutch person you'll encounter speaks English.

Haarlem is most crowded on Easter weekend (April 6-8 in 2012), in April (particularly the flower parade—April 21 in 2012—and Queen's Day, on April 30), May, July, and August (especially during Haarlem's jazz festival on the third weekend of Aug).

The prices listed here include breakfast (unless otherwise noted) and usually include the €2-per-person-per-day tourist tax. To avoid this town's louder-than-normal street noises, forgo views for a room in the back. Hotels and the TI have a useful parking brochure.

In the Center
Hotels and B&Bs

$$$ Hotel Lion D'Or is a classy, 34-room business hotel with all the professional comforts, pleasingly posh decor, and a handy but less-than-quaint location (Db-€150, Fri-Sat Db-€125, extra bed-€15, check website for special deals, ask for Rick Steves discount with 2-night stay when you book direct, air-con, elevator, pay Internet access and Wi-Fi, across the street from train station

HAARLEM

Sleep Code

(€1 = about $1.40, country code: 31, area code: 023)
S = Single, D = Double/Twin, T = Triple, Q = Quad, b = bathroom, s = shower only. Nearly everyone speaks English. Credit cards are accepted and breakfast is included unless otherwise noted.

To help you easily sort through these listings, I've divided the rooms into three categories, based on the price for a standard double room with bath:

$$$ Higher Priced—Most rooms €85 or more.
 $$ Moderately Priced—Most rooms between €60-85.
  $ Lower Priced—Most rooms €60 or less.

Prices can change without notice; verify the hotel's current rates online or by email. For other updates, see www.ricksteves.com/update.

at Kruisweg 34, tel. 023/532-1750, fax 023/532-9543, www.hotel liondor.nl, reservations@hotelliondor.nl, friendly Dirk Pauw).

$$$ Stempels Hotel, modern yet elegant, is located in a reno-vated, 250-year-old building. With bare floors, comfy high-quality beds, and minimalist touches in its 17 rooms, what it lacks in warmth it makes up for in style and value. Double-paned windows help keep down the noise, since it's a block east of Grote Markt, with a bustling brasserie and bar downstairs (standard Sb-€90, standard Db-€105-110, pricier rooms and suites available, break-fast-€12, in-room computers with free Internet access and Wi-Fi, Klokhuisplein 9, tel. 023/512-3910, www.stempelsinhaarlem.nl, info@stempelsinhaarlem.nl).

$$$ Hotel Amadeus, on Grote Markt, has 15 small, bright, and basic rooms, some with views of the square. This characteris-tic hotel, ideally located above an early 20th-century dinner café, is relatively quiet, especially if you take a room in the back. Its lush old lounge/breakfast room on the second floor overlooks the square, and Mike and Inez take good care of their guests (Sb-€60, Db-€85, Tb-€110, check website for special deals, 5 percent Rick Steves discount off full price with 2-night stay and cash, pay Internet access and Wi-Fi, Grote Markt 10—from square it's a steep climb to lounge and then an elevator, tel. 023/532-4530, fax 023/532-2328, www.amadeus-hotel.com, info@amadeus-hotel.com). The Hotel Amadeus' breakfast room overlooking the main square is a great place to watch the town greet a new day—one of my favorite Haarlem moments.

Haarlem Hotels & Restaurants

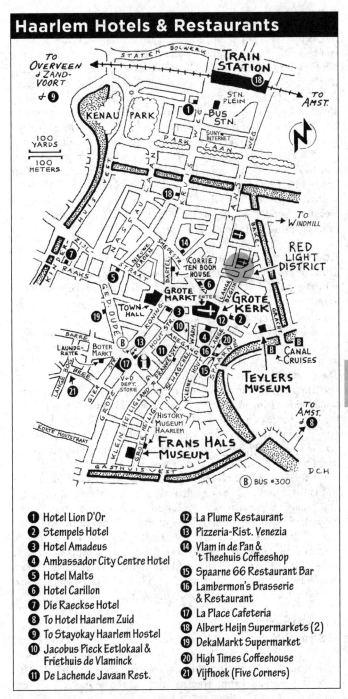

1. Hotel Lion D'Or
2. Stempels Hotel
3. Hotel Amadeus
4. Ambassador City Centre Hotel
5. Hotel Malts
6. Hotel Carillon
7. Die Raeckse Hotel
8. To Hotel Haarlem Zuid
9. To Stayokay Haarlem Hostel
10. Jacobus Pieck Eetlokaal & Friethuis de Vlaminck
11. De Lachende Javaan Rest.
12. La Plume Restaurant
13. Pizzeria-Rist. Venezia
14. Vlam in de Pan & 't Theehuis Coffeeshop
15. Spaarne 66 Restaurant Bar
16. Lambermon's Brasserie & Restaurant
17. La Place Cafeteria
18. Albert Heijn Supermarkets (2)
19. DekaMarkt Supermarket
20. High Times Coffeehouse
21. Vijfhoek (Five Corners)

$$$ Ambassador City Centre Hotel, with 29 comfortable rooms in a big, plain hotel, is located just behind the Grote Kerk. If you're willing to trade some street noise for amazing church views, ask for a room in the front (Db-€100, often less off-season, breakfast buffet-€14, free Internet access and Wi-Fi, Oude Groenmarkt 20, tel. 023/512-5300, www.acc-hotel.nl, info@acc-hotel.nl). They also run **Hotel Joops**, with 32 rooms, a block away (rooms are €10 cheaper; studios and apartments with kitchenettes for 2-4 people-€120-150 depending on season and number of people).

$$ Hotel Malts is well-located and rents 12 bright, simple, and fresh rooms for a good price. The rooms in front are big, but not recommended for light sleepers (small D-€69, small Db-€79, standard Db-€85, big Db-€95, check website for best prices, no elevator, free Wi-Fi, Zijlstraat 56, tel. 023/551-2385, www.malts hotel.nl, info@maltshotel.nl, Marco).

Rooms in Restaurants

These places are all run as sidelines by restaurants, and you'll know it by the style of service and rooms. Lobbies are in the restaurant, and there are no public spaces. Still, they are handy and—for Haarlem—inexpensive.

$$ Hotel Carillon overlooks the town square and comes with a little traffic and bell-tower chimes. With run-down public spaces and st-e-e-e-p stairs, it's an old-school, over-the-restaurant place. The rooms themselves, however, are freshly updated and pleasant. The front rooms come with more street noise and great town-square views (tiny loft S-€40, Db-€80-90, Tb-€102, Qb-€110, ask for Rick Steves discount when you reserve—must show book on arrival, no elevator, free Wi-Fi, Grote Markt 27, tel. 023/531-0591, fax 023/531-4909, www.hotelcarillon.com, info@hotelcarillon .com, owners Kelly Kuo, Andres Haas, and June).

$$ Die Raeckse Hotel, family-run and friendly, is not as central as the others and has less character and more traffic noise—but its 21 rooms are decent and comfortable. Quiet rooms in back cost more than the noisy rooms on the street—but they're worth it (Sb-€55, smaller Db-€80-85, big Db-€85-90, Tb-€120, Qb-€130-145, €5/night discount for 2-night stay, ask for Rick Steves discount with this book Nov-March, free but time-limited Internet access, free Wi-Fi, Raaks Straat 1, tel. 023/532-6629, fax 023/531-7937, www.die-raeckse.nl, dieraeckse@zonnet.nl).

Near Haarlem

$$$ Hotel Haarlem Zuid, with 300 modern rooms, is sterile but a good value for drivers. It sits in an industrial zone a 20-minute walk from the center, on the road to the airport (Db-€88-110, breakfast-€13, elevator, free parking, laundry service, fitness center-€5, reasonable hotel restaurant, Toekanweg 2, tel. 023/536-7500, fax 023/536-7980, www.hotelhaarlemzuid.nl, haarlemzuid @valk.com). Bus #300 conveniently connects the hotel with the train station, Grote Markt, and the airport (every 10 minutes, stop: Europaweg).

$ Stayokay Haarlem Hostel, completely renovated and with all the youth-hostel comforts, charges €25-30 for beds in four- and six-bed dorms. They also rent simple €60-80 doubles (€2.50 less for members, includes sheets and breakfast, save by booking on their website, pay Internet access and Wi-Fi, laundry service, reception open 8:00-20:30 but late arrivals OK, Jan Gijzenpad 3, two miles from Haarlem station—take bus #2 from station, or a 10-minute walk from Santpoort Zuid train station, tel. 023/537-3793, www .stayokay.com/haarlem, haarlem@stayokay.com).

Eating in Haarlem

Restaurants

Jacobus Pieck Eetlokaal is popular with locals for its fine-value "global cuisine," good salads, and unpretentious flair. Sit in the peaceful garden courtyard, at a sidewalk table, or in the romantically cozy interior. The Oriental Peak Salad is a perennial favorite, and the dish of the day (*dagschotel*, €12.50) always sells out (great €7 sandwiches at lunch, Mon 11:00-16:00 only, Tue-Sat 10:00-22:00, closed Sun, cash only, Warmoesstraat 18, behind church, tel. 023/532-6144).

De Lachende Javaan ("The Laughing Javanese") is a long-established Indonesian place serving a memorable *rijsttafel* (€20-24, Tue-Sun 17:00-22:00, closed Mon, Frankestraat 27, tel. 023/532-8792).

La Plume Restaurant steakhouse is noisy, with a happy, local, and carnivorous crowd enjoying the candlelit scene (€15-20 meals, daily 17:30-23:00, Fri-Sat until 24:00, *satay* and ribs are favorites, Lange Veerstraat 1, tel. 023/531-3202). The relaxing outdoor seating faces the church and a lively pedestrian street.

Pizzeria-Ristorante Venezia, run for 25 years by the same Italian family from Bari, is the place to go for pizza or pasta (€8-10 choices, daily 13:00-23:00, facing V&D department store at Verwulft 7, tel. 023/531-7753). You'll feel like you're in Rome at a good indoor table, or sit outdoors in a busy people-zone.

At **Vlam in de Pan,** a dynamo named Femke serves vegetarian delights: soup, salad, veggie sushi, quiches, and other fresh, mostly organic foods. Enjoy the small, funky dining area, or get your food to take away (€10-15 plates, Tue-Fri 16:00-21:00, closed Sat-Mon, Smedestraat 13, tel. 023/551-1738).

Lange Veerstraat Restaurant Row: If you don't know what

you want to eat, stroll the delightful Lange Veerstraat behind the church and survey a fun range of restaurants (from cheap falafels to Cuban, and much more).

On the Spaarne River Canal: Haarlem seems to turn its back on its river with most of the eating energy a couple of blocks away. To enjoy a meal with a fine canal view, consider the **Spaarne 66 Restaurant Bar.** The Lemmers girls (a mom and her daughters) run this cozy eatery, with a woody, old-time interior and fine, outdoor canalside seating (light €7 lunches, €20 Mediterranean/Dutch dinner plates, €30 three-course fixed-price meal, Wed-Mon 11:00-24:00, closed Tue, Spaarne 66, tel. 023/551-3800).

Dressy Splurge: At **Lambermon's,** expert chef Michèl Lambermon serves chichi pan-European cuisine in a suave, modern, corner restaurant. The brasserie on the ground floor offers €25 two-course lunches and €35 three-course dinners (€23-28 main courses, Mon-Sat 12:00-15:00 & 18:00-22:00, Sun 14:00-22:00; pricier restaurant upstairs open Wed-Sat 18:00-22:00 only, closed Sun-Tue; Korte Veerstraat 1, tel. 023/542-7804).

Budget Options

La Place is a snazzy chain cafeteria that dishes up fresh, healthy, budget food with Haarlem's best view. Sit on the top floor or roof garden of the V&D department store (Mon 11:00-18:00, Tue-Sat 9:30-18:00, Thu until 21:00, closed Sun except for first Sun of month 12:00-17:00, Grote Houtstraat 70, on corner of Gedempte Oude Gracht, tel. 023/515-8700).

Friethuis de Vlaminck is your best bet for a cone of old-fashioned, fresh Flemish-style fries (€2, daily 11:00-18:30, Warmoesstraat 3, behind church, tel. 023/532-1084). Winnie offers a dazzling array of sauces. With his help, you can be adventurous.

Supermarkets: **Albert Heijn** has two convenient locations. One is in the train station (Mon-Fri 6:30-21:00, Sat 7:00-21:00, Sun 8:00-21:00, cash only) and the other is at Kruisstraat 10 (Mon-Sat 8:00-20:00, closed Sun, cash only). The **DekaMarkt** is a few blocks east of Grote Markt (Mon-Sat 8:00-20:00, Thu-Fri until 21:00, Sun 16:00-21:00, Gedempte Oude Gracht 54, between V&D department store and post office).

Haarlem Connections

From Haarlem by Train to: Amsterdam (6/hour, 20 minutes, €3.70 one-way, €7.10 same-day round-trip), **Delft** (2/hour, 40 minutes), **Brussels** (hourly, 2.75 hours, transfer in Rotterdam), **Bruges/Brugge** (hourly, 3.5 hours, 2-3 changes—avoid Thalys connections if traveling with a railpass).

   To Schiphol Airport: Your best option is the **bus** (4-10/hour,

40 minutes, €4—buy ticket from driver, bus #300). To catch the bus from the middle of Haarlem, head to the Centrum/Verwulft stop, near the V&D department store. To catch it from the train station, look for the stop marked "Zuidtangent." (Construction of a new underground bike-parking lot near the train station may temporarily move this bus stop a block or two from the station, most likely to the tree-lined street called Parklaan). You can also get there by **train** (6/hour, 30-40 minutes, transfer at Amsterdam-Sloterdijk station, €5.40 one-way), or **taxi** (about €45).

SPAIN

BARCELONA

Barcelona is Spain's second city, and the capital of the proud and distinct region of Catalunya. With Franco's fascism now ancient history, Catalan flags wave once again. And the local language and culture are on a roll in Spain's most cosmopolitan and European corner.

Barcelona bubbles with life in its narrow Barri Gòtic alleys, along the grand boulevards, and throughout the chic, grid-planned, new part of town, called Eixample. While Barcelona had an illustrious past as a Roman colony, Visigothic capital, 14th-century maritime power, and—in more modern times—a top Mediterranean textile and manufacturing center, you'll have more fun if you throw out the history books and just drift through the city. If you're in the mood to surrender to a city's charms, let it be in Barcelona.

Planning Your Time

Located in the far northeast corner of Spain, Barcelona makes a good first or last stop for your trip. With the fast AVE train, Barcelona is three hours away from Madrid. Or you could sandwich Barcelona between flights. From the US, it's as easy to fly into Barcelona as it is to land in Madrid, Lisbon, or Paris. Those who plan on renting a car at some point during their trip can start here first, fly or train to Madrid, and sightsee Madrid and Toledo, all before picking up their car—cleverly saving on several days' worth of rental fees.

On the shortest visit, Barcelona is worth one night, one day, and an evening flight or train ride out. The Ramblas is two different streets by day and by night. Stroll it from top to bottom in the evening and again the next morning, grabbing breakfast on a stool

Barcelona Overview

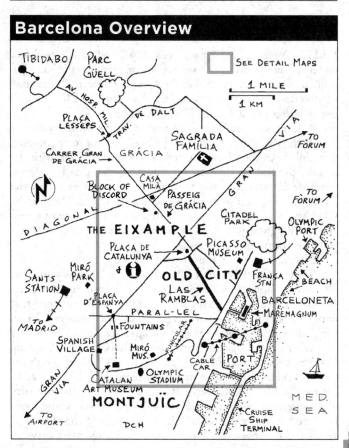

in a market café. Wander the Barri Gòtic (BAH-ree GOH-teek), see the cathedral, and have lunch in the Eixample (eye-SHAM-plah). The top two sights in town, Antoni Gaudí's Sagrada Família church and the Picasso Museum, are usually open until 20:00 during the summer (Picasso closed Mon). Note that if you want to tour the Catalan Concert Hall, with its oh-wow Modernista interior, you'll need to reserve at least two days in advance (see page 1286). The illuminated Magic Fountains on Montjuïc make a good finale for your day.

Of course, Barcelona in a day is insane. To better sample the city's ample charm, spread your visit over two or three days. With two days, you could divide and conquer the town geographically: one day for the Barri Gòtic (Ramblas, cathedral area, Picasso Museum); and another for the Eixample and Gaudí sights (Casa Milà, Sagrada Família, Parc Güell). Do Montjuïc on whichever day you're not exhausted (if any).

Orientation to Barcelona

Like Los Angeles, Barcelona is a basically flat city that sprawls out under the sun between the sea and the mountains. It's huge (1.6 million people, with about 4 million people in greater Barcelona), but travelers need only focus on four areas: the Old City, the harbor/Barceloneta, the Eixample, and Montjuïc.

A large square, Plaça de Catalunya, sits at the center of Barcelona, dividing the older and newer parts of town. Sloping downhill from the Plaça de Catalunya is the Old City, with the boulevard called the Ramblas running down to the harbor. Above Plaça de Catalunya is the modern residential area called the Eixample. The Montjuïc hill overlooks the harbor. Outside the Old City, Barcelona's sights are widely scattered, but with a map and a willingness to figure out the sleek Metro system (or a few euros for taxis), all is manageable.

Here are more details per neighborhood:

The **Old City** is where you'll probably spend most of your time. This is the compact soul of Barcelona—your strolling, shopping, and people-watching nucleus. It's a labyrinth of narrow streets that once were confined by the medieval walls. The lively pedestrian drag called the **Ramblas**—one of Europe's great people-watching streets—runs through the heart of the Old City from Plaça de Catalunya down to the harbor. The Old City is divided into thirds by the Ramblas and another major thoroughfare, Via Laietana. To the west of the Ramblas is the **Raval,** enlivened by its university and modern-art museum. The Raval is of least interest to tourists (and, in fact, some parts of it are quite seedy and should be avoided). Far better is the **Barri Gòtic** (Gothic Quarter), between the Ramblas and Via Laietana, with the cathedral as its navel. To the east of Via Laietana is the trendy **Ribera** district (a.k.a. "El Born"), centered on the Picasso Museum and the Church of Santa Maria del Mar.

The **harborfront** has been energized since the 1992 Olympics. A pedestrian bridge links the Ramblas with the modern Maremagnum shopping/aquarium complex. On the peninsula across the harbor is **Barceloneta,** a traditional fishing neighborhood that's home to some good seafood restaurants and a string of sandy beaches. Beyond Barceloneta, a man-made beach, several miles long, leads east to the commercial and convention district called the **Fòrum.**

North of the Old City, beyond the bustling hub of Plaça de Catalunya, is the elegant **Eixample** district—its grid plan is softened by cut-off corners. Much of Barcelona's Modernista architecture is found here. To the north is the **Gràcia** district and, beyond that, Antoni Gaudí's **Parc Güell.**

Cheap Tricks in Barcelona

- Arriving by train? Save time, hassle, and the cost of a Metro ride by finding out if your train stops at any of the handy downtown stations (such as Passeig de Gràcia or Plaça de Catalunya). But remember that AVE trains from Madrid stop only at Sants Station.
- For getting around the city, skip taxis and the Tourist Bus, and instead use the excellent network of Metro and buses. The T10 Card (10 rides for €8.25) makes the system super-cheap—each ride costs €0.83 instead of €1.45 for an individual ticket.
- Use the T10 Card on bus #50, which is cheaper than the hop-on, hop-off bus and gives you a local's tour of Gràcia and Montjuïc (see page 1270).
- If visiting only the cathedral, go when it's free, 8:00-12:45 (until 13:45 on Sun) or 17:15-19:30. But if you want to see the elevator (€2.50), choir (€2.20), and museum (€2), it's better to go when those sights are covered by the €5 cathedral entry. Several interesting sights around the cathedral (such as the Deacon's House and the Roman Temple) are also free to enter, as well as the nearby Church of Santa Maria del Mar in La Ribera.
- One of Barcelona's most delightful Modernista sights, Antoni Gaudí's Parc Güell, is free and an enjoyable place to relax. Some expensive Gaudí sights (such as Casa Milà, Casa Batllò, and the Sagrada Família) can be just as interesting from the outside, without paying the entry fee.
- Some museums have certain days and times when they don't charge admission: the Picasso and City History museums (first Sun of month and Sun afternoon), Catalan Art Museum (first Sun of month), and Frederic Marès Museum.
- When tapas-hopping, note that trendy, upscale neighborhoods—such as the Eixample and La Ribera—come with higher prices. For a cheaper and more characteristic meal, find a blue-collar neighborhood (such as Carrer de la Mercè).

The large hill overlooking the city to the southwest is **Montjuïc,** home to a variety of attractions, including some excellent museums (Catalan Art, Joan Miró) and the Olympic Stadium.

Apart from your geographical orientation, you'll need to orient yourself linguistically to a language distinct from Spanish. Although Spanish ("Castilian"/*castellano*) is widely spoken, the native tongue in this region is Catalan—nearly as different from Spanish as Italian.

Tourist Information

Barcelona's TI has several branches. The main one is at **Plaça de Catalunya** (daily 9:00-21:00, under the main square near recommended hotels—look for red sign, tel. 932-853-832). Other convenient branches include at the top of the **Ramblas** (daily 9:00-21:00, at #115); **Plaça de Sant Jaume,** just south of the cathedral (Mon-Fri 8:30-20:00, Sat 9:00-19:00, Sun 10:00-14:00); **Plaça d'Espanya** (daily July-Sept 10:00-20:00, Oct-June 10:00-16:00); the **airport** (daily 9:00-21:00, offices in both sections A and B of terminal 2); **Sants train station** (Mon-Fri 8:00-20:00, Sat-Sun 8:00-14:00, near track 6); **Nord bus station** (daily July-Sept 9:00-21:00, Oct-June 9:00-15:00); and more. Throughout the summer, young red-jacketed tourist-info helpers appear in the most touristy parts of town. The central information number for all TIs is 932-853-834 (www.barcelonaturisme.cat).

At any TI, pick up the free city map (although the free Corte Inglés map provided by most hotels is better), the small Metro map, and the free quarterly *See Barcelona* guide (practical information on museum hours, restaurants, transportation, history, festivals, and so on). The monthly *Barcelona Metropolitan* magazine and quarterly *What's On Barcelona* (both free and in English) have timely and substantial coverage of topics and events. The *Metro Walks* booklet (€2) details seven city walks combined with Metro rides, including a few interesting outlying neighborhoods. The TI is a handy place to buy tickets for the Tourist Bus (described later, under "Getting Around Barcelona"). Some TIs (at Plaça de Catalunya, Plaça de Sant Jaume, and the airport) also provide a room-booking service.

The TIs at Plaça de Catalunya and Plaça de Sant Jaume offer guided walks (described later, under "Tours in Barcelona"). The Plaça de Catalunya TI's Modernisme desk gives out a handy route map showing all the Modernista buildings and offers a sightseeing discount package (€12 for a great guidebook and 20 percent discounts to many Modernisme sites—worthwhile if going beyond my big three; for €18 you'll also get a guidebook to Modernista bars and restaurants).

The **all-Catalunya TI** works fine for the entire region, and even Madrid (Mon-Sat 10:00-19:00, Sun 10:00-14:00, on Plaça de Joan Carlos I, at the intersection of Diagonal and Passeig de Gràcia, Passeig de Gràcia 107, tel. 932-388-091).

Articket Card: This ticket includes admission to seven art museums and their temporary exhibits, including the recommended Picasso Museum, Casa Milà, Catalan Art Museum, and Fundació Joan Miró (€22, valid for six months, sold at TIs and participating museums, www.articketbcn.org). If you're planning to go to three or more of the museums, this time-saver pays for itself. To skip the ticket-buying line at a museum, show your

Articket Card (to the ticket-taker, at the info desk, or at the group entrance), and you'll get your entrance ticket pronto.

Barcelona Card: This card covers public transportation (buses, Metro, Montjuïc funicular, and *golondrina* harbor tour) and includes free admission to minor sights and discounts on major sights (€27.50/2 days, €33.50/3 days, €38/4 days, €45/5 days, sold at TIs and El Corte Inglés department store).

Arrival in Barcelona

By Train: Virtually all trains end up at Barcelona's Sants train station (described below). But be aware that many trains also pass through other stations en route, such as **França Station** (between the Ribera and Barceloneta neighborhoods), or the downtown **Passeig de Gràcia** or **Plaça de Catalunya** stations (which are also Metro stops—and very close to most of my recommended hotels). Figure out which stations your train stops at, and get off at the one most convenient to your hotel. (AVE trains from Madrid go only to Sants Station.)

Sants Station is vast and sprawling, but manageable. In the large lobby area under the upper tracks, you'll find a TI; ATMs; a world of handy shops and eateries; and a classy, quiet Sala Euromed lounge for travelers with first-class reservations (TV, free drinks, study tables, and coffee bar). Sants is the only Barcelona station with luggage storage (small bag-€3/day, big bag-€4.50/day, requires security check, daily 5:30-23:00, follow signs to *consigna*, at far end of hallway from tracks 13-14).

There's also a long wall of ticket windows. Figure out which is right for you before you wait in line (all are labeled in English). Generally, the first stretch (on the left, windows 1-10) is for local trains, such as to Sitges; the next group (windows 11-21) handles advance tickets for long-distance trains; farther to the right are information windows (23-26)—go here first if you're not sure which window you want; and those at the right end (windows 27-31) sell tickets for long-distance trains leaving today. Attendants are often standing by to help you find the right line. You can use the ticket machines to buy tickets *(media distancia),* but they don't work for long-distance tickets (though you can print out pre-reserved tickets at the purple ATM-like machines).

To get into downtown Barcelona from Sants Station, simply follow signs for the Metro. The L3 (green) line zips you directly to a number of useful points in town, including all of my recommended hotels. You also can save time by taking the *cercanías* local trains to Plaça de Catalunya, just five minutes away. Lines C1, C3, C4, or C7, departing from track 8, all take you there. Or when a train is pulling in, look at the red letter board listing the stops— Plaça de Catalunya is the first stop on the list. You can purchase tickets (€1.45) at touch-screen machines near the tracks, or use your T10 Card (explained on page 1268).

If departing from the downtown **Passeig de Gràcia Station,** where three Metro lines converge with the rail line, you might find the underground tunnels confusing. You can't access the RENFE Station directly from some of the entrances. Use the northern entrances to this station (rather than the southern "Consell de Cent" entrance, which is closest to Plaça de Catalunya).

By Plane: Barcelona's **El Prat de Llobregat Airport,** eight miles southwest of town, has two large terminals: 1 and 2. Terminal 2 is divided into sections A, B, and C. Terminal 1 and the bigger sections of terminal 2 (A and B) each have a post office, a pharmacy, a left-luggage office, plenty of good cafeterias in the gate areas, and ATMs (avoid the gimmicky machines before the baggage carousels; instead, use the bank-affiliated ATMs at the far-left end of the arrivals hall as you face the street). Airport info tel. 913-211-000.

You have two options for getting downtown cheaply and quickly: The **Aerobus** (#A1 and #A2, corresponding with terminals 1 and 2) stops immediately outside the arrivals lobby of both terminals (and in each section of terminal 2). In about 30 minutes, it takes you to downtown, where it makes several stops, including Plaça d'Espanya and Plaça de Catalunya—near many of my recommended hotels (departs every 6 minutes, from airport 6:00-1:00 in the morning, from downtown 5:30-24:15, €5 one-way, €8.65 round-trip, buy ticket from machine or from driver, tel. 934-156-020). The line to board the bus can be very long, but—thanks to the high frequency of buses—it moves fast.

The second option from terminal 2 is the RENFE *cercanías* **train,** which involves more walking. Head down the long orange-roofed overpass between sections A and B to reach the station (line 2, 2/hour at about :08 and :38 past the hour, 20 minutes to Sants Station, 25 minutes to Passeig de Gràcia Station—near Plaça de Catalunya and many recommended hotels, 30 minutes to França Station; €3 or covered by T10 Card, which you can purchase at automated machines at the airport train station). Long-term plans call for the RENFE *cercanías* train and eventually the AVE to be extended to terminal 1, and for the Metro's line 9 to be extended to both terminals 1 and 2. Stay tuned.

A **taxi** between the airport and downtown costs about €30.

Some budget airlines, including Ryanair, use **Girona-Costa Brava Airport,** located 60 miles north of Barcelona near Girona. Sagalés buses link to Barcelona (departures timed to meet flights, 1.25 hours, €12, tel. 935-931-300 or 902-361-550, www.sagales .com). You can also go to Girona on a Sagalés bus (hourly, 25 minutes, €3) or a taxi (€25), then catch a train to Barcelona (at least hourly, 1.25 hours, €15-20). A taxi between the Girona airport and Barcelona costs at least €120. Airport info tel. 972-186-600.

By Car: Barcelona's parking fees are outrageously expensive (the lot behind La Boquería market charges upward of €25/day). You won't need a car in Barcelona, because the taxis and public transportation are so good.

By Cruise Ship: Several major cruise lines (including Royal Caribbean, Norwegian, Princess, and Disney) come into Barcelona's Puerto del Muelle Adosado. Each of its four terminals (A-D) has a café, security checkpoint, waiting room, check-in desks, bus stop, and taxi stand. It's about 1.5 miles to the city center—easiest by taxi (10-15 minutes, €10 to the Ramblas, €15 to Plaça de Catalunya). Legal supplements are posted on the taxi window: €2.10 port fee and €1/bag. Taxis meet each arriving ship and are waiting as you exit the terminal building. During high season (May-Sept), when as many as six ships dock on the same day, the ride can take twice as long and cost €10 more.

An alternative is to take the blue port-run Lanzadera bus from the terminal parking lot (follow *Public Bus* signs) to the Columbus Monument at the bottom of the Ramblas, near the Metro Drassanes stop (€3 round-trip, €2 one-way, buses leave every 20-30 minutes, timed to cruise ship arrival, tel. 932-986-000). From there you can walk or Metro to your destination.

Helpful Hints

Theft Alert: You're more likely to be pickpocketed here—especially on the Ramblas—than about anywhere else in Europe. Most of the crime is nonviolent, but muggings do occur. Leave valuables in your hotel and wear a money belt.

Street scams are easy to avoid if you recognize them. Most common is the too-friendly local who tries to engage you in conversation by asking for the time, talking sports, asking whether you speak English, and so on. Beware of thieves posing as lost tourists who ask for your help. A typical street gambling scam is the pea-and-carrot game, a variation on the shell game. The people winning are all ringers, and you can be sure that you'll lose if you play. Also beware of groups of women aggressively selling carnations, people offering to clean off a stain from your shirt, and people picking things up in front of you on escalators. If you stop for any commotion or show on the Ramblas, put your hands in your pockets before someone else does. Assume any scuffle is simply a distraction by a team of thieves. Crooks are inventive, so keep your guard up. Don't be intimidated...just be smart.

Some areas feel seedy and can be unsafe after dark; I'd avoid the southern part of the Barri Gòtic (basically the two or three blocks directly south and east of Plaça Reial—though the strip near the Carrer de la Mercè tapas bars is better), and I wouldn't venture too deep into the Raval (just west of the Ramblas). One block can separate a comfy tourist zone from the junkies and prostitutes.

US Consulate: It's at Passeig Reina Elisenda 23 (passport services Mon-Fri 9:00-13:00, closed Sat-Sun, tel. 932-802-227).

Emergency Phone Numbers: General emergencies—112, police—092, ambulance—061 or 112.

Internet Access: Navega Web has hundreds of computers for accessing the Internet and burning pictures onto a disk. It's conveniently located across from La Boquería market, downstairs in the bright Centre Comercial New Park (daily 10:00-24:00, Ramblas 88-94, tel. 933-179-193).

Pharmacy: A 24-hour pharmacy is near La Boquería market at #98 on the Ramblas.

Laundry: Several self-service launderettes are located around the Old City. **Wash 'n Dry** is on the edge of the tourist zone, near a seedy neighborhood just down the street past the Palau Güell (self-service: wash-€5/load, dry-€2/load, daily 7:00-22:00; full-service: €15/load, daily 9:00-22:00; Carrer Nou de la Rambla 19, tel. 934-121-953).

Getting Around Barcelona

By Metro: Barcelona's Metro, among Europe's best, connects just about every place you'll visit. Rides cost €1.45. The T10 Card is a great deal—€8.25 gives you 10 rides (cutting the per-ride cost nearly in half), and the card is shareable. It's good on all Metro and local bus lines as well as the RENFE train lines (including rides to the airport and train station) and the suburban FGC lines. Full- and multiday passes are also available (€6.20/1 day, €11.50/2 days, €16.50/3 days, €21/4 days, €25/5 days, www.tmb.cat). Automated machines at the Metro entrance have English instructions and sell all types of tickets (these can be temperamental about accepting bills, so try to have change on hand).

Pick up the free Metro map (at any TI) and study it to get familiar with the system. There are several color-coded lines, but most useful for tourists is the **L3 (green) line;** if you're sticking to my recommended sights and neighborhoods, you'll barely have use for any other. Handy city-center stops on this line include (in order):

Sants Estació—Main train station

Espanya—Plaça d'Espanya, with access to the lower part of Montjuïc and trains to Montserrat

Paral-lel—Funicular to top of Montjuïc

Drassanes—Bottom of the Ramblas, near Maritime Museum, Maremagnum mall, and the cable car up to Montjuïc

Liceu—Middle of the Ramblas, near the heart of the Barri Gòtic and cathedral

Plaça de Catalunya—Top of the Ramblas and main square with TI, airport bus, and lots of transportation connections

Passeig de Gràcia—Classy Eixample street at the Block of Discord; also connection to L2 (purple) line to Sagrada Família and L4 (yellow) line (described below)

Diagonal—Gaudí's Casa Milà

Lesseps—Walk or catch bus #24 to Gaudí's Parc Güell

The **L4 (yellow) line,** which crosses the L3 (green) line at Passeig de Gràcia, is also useful. Helpful stops include **Jaume I** (between the Barri Gòtic/cathedral and La Ribera/Picasso Museum) and **Barceloneta** (at the south end of the Ribera, near the harbor action).

When you enter the Metro, first look for your line number and color, then follow signs to take that line in the direction you're going. Insert your ticket into the turnstile (with the arrow pointing in), then reclaim it. On board, most trains have handy Metro-line diagrams with dots that light up next to upcoming destinations. Because the lines cross one another multiple times, there can be several ways to make any one journey. (It's a good idea to keep a general map with you—especially if you're transferring.) Watch your valuables. If I were a pickpocket, I'd set up shop along the made-for-tourists L3/green line.

By Public Bus: Given the excellent Metro service, it's unlikely you'll take a local bus (also €1.45 or covered by T10 Card, insert ticket in machine behind driver), although I've noted places where the bus makes sense. In particular, bus #50 is good for a tour of Gràcia and Montjuïc (see page 1270).

By Tourist Bus: The handy hop-on, hop-off Tourist Bus (Bus Turístic) offers three multi-stop circuits in colorful double-decker buses that go topless in sunny weather. The two-hour blue route covers north Barcelona (most Gaudí sights); the two-hour red route covers south Barcelona (Barri Gòtic, Montjuïc); and the shorter, 40-minute green route covers the beaches and modern Fòrum complex. All have headphone commentary (44 stops, daily 9:00-22:00 in summer, 9:00-21:00 in winter, buses run every 5-25 minutes, most frequent in summer, no green route Oct-March). Ask for a brochure (includes city map) at the TI or at a pick-up point. One-day (€22) and two-day (€29) tickets, which you can buy on the bus or at the TI, offer 10-20 percent discounts on the city's major sights and walking tours, which will likely save you about the equivalent of half the cost of the Tourist Bus (www .barcelonabusturistic.cat).

By Taxi: Barcelona is one of Europe's best taxi towns. Taxis are plentiful (there are more than 10,000) and honest (whether they like it or not—the light on top shows which tariff they're charging). They're also reasonable (€2 drop charge, €1/kilometer, these "*Tarif 2*" rates are in effect 7:00-21:00, pay higher "*Tarif 1*" rates off-hours, luggage-€1/piece, other fees posted in window). Save time by hopping a cab (figure €10 from Ramblas to Sants Station).

Tours in Barcelona

Walking Tours—The TI at Plaça de Sant Jaume offers great guided walks through the **Barri Gòtic** in English only (€12.50, daily at 10:00, 2 hours, groups limited to 35, buy your ticket 15 minutes early at the TI desk—not from the guide, in summer call ahead to reserve, tel. 932-853-832, www.barcelonaturisme.cat). A local guide will explain the medieval story of the city as you walk from Plaça de Sant Jaume through the cathedral neighborhood, finishing at City Hall. The Plaça de Catalunya TI offers a **Picasso** walk, taking you through the streets of his youth and early career and finishing in the Picasso Museum (€18, includes museum admission; Tue, Thu, and Sat at 16:00; 2 hours plus museum visit). There are also **gourmet** walks (€19, Fri and Sat at 10:00, 2 hours) and **Modernisme** walks (€12.50, Fri and Sat June-Sept at 18:00, Oct-May at 16:00, 2 hours); both depart from the TI at Plaça de Catalunya.

Guided Bus Tours—The Barcelona Guide Bureau offers several sightseeing tours leaving from Plaça de Catalunya. Departure times can vary—confirm locally. The **Gaudí** tour visits the facades of Casa Batlló and Casa Milà, as well as Parc Güell and the Sagrada Família (€45, includes Sagrada Família admission, daily at 9:00, also at 15:15 mid-April-Oct, 3 hours). Other tours offered year-round include the **Montjuïc** tour (€33, includes Spanish Village admission, daily at 12:00, 3 hours) and the **All Barcelona Highlights** tour (€60, includes Sagrada Família and Spanish Village admissions, daily at 9:00, 6 hours). From April through October, there's also the **Gaudí Beyond the City** tour of "off-the-beaten-path masterpieces" (€30, daily at 12:30, 3 hours); and—for soccer fans—the **Barça** tour, which takes you to the Camp Nou stadium (€35, daily at 15:15, 3 hours). You can get detailed information and book tickets at a TI, on their website, or simply by showing up at their departure point on Plaça de Catalunya in front of the Hard Rock Cafe—look for the guides holding orange umbrellas. Buying tickets online can save you a few euros—usually about 10 percent (tel. 933-152-261, www.barcelonaguidebureau.com).

Bus #50 Self-Guided Tour—Combining public bus #50 with a T10 Card (see page 1268) gives you an inexpensive tour through Gràcia and Montjuïc. You can catch bus #50 at the Sagrada Família stop (on the Nativity facade side). Once aboard, you'll wind through Gràcia's streets down to the Gran Via de les Corts Catalanes, crossing the Passeig de Gràcia (a block away from Plaça de Catalunya). Enjoy the long blocks of Gràcia until you reach Plaça d'Espanya, where on the right you'll see Barcelona's bullring (which is being turned into a mall). You'll go through the two towers of Plaça d'Espanya, with the Catalan Art Museum on the hill in front of you. Then you'll loop through the hills of Montjuïc, passing the Spanish Village, the site of the '92 Olympics (with the communications tower and stadium), the Fundació Joan Miró, and the funicular and cable car up to the Castle of Montjuïc. The end of the line is about a block away from the funicular. From here you can walk back to the Joan Miró or Catalan Art museums; or continue in the direction of the bus route down the hill to a different cable car, which takes you to the Barceloneta area.

Bike Tours—Several companies run bike tours around Barcelona. **Un Cotxe Menys** ("One Car Less") organizes three-hour English-only bike tours daily at 11:00 (April-mid-Sept also Fri-Mon at 16:30). Your guide leads you from sight to sight, mostly on bike paths and through parks, with a stop-and-go commentary (€22 includes bike rental and drink, no reservations needed—just show up at Plaça de Sant Jaume, next to the TI, tel. 932-682-105, www.biketoursbarcelona.com.

Local Guides—The Barcelona Guide Bureau is a co-op with about 20 local guides who give personalized four-hour tours (weekdays-€208, per-person price drops as group gets bigger; weekends and holidays-€248, no price break with size of group); **Joana Wilhelm** and **Carles Picazo** are excellent (Via Laietana 54, tel. 932-682-422 or 933-107-778, www.bgb.es). **Jose Soler** is a great and fun-to-be-with local guide who enjoys tailoring a walk through his hometown to your interests (€195/half-day per group, mobile 615-059-326, www.pepitotours.com, info@pepitotours.com).

Self-Guided Walks

Most visitors to Barcelona spend much of their time in the twisty, atmospheric Old City. These two walks will give meaning to your wandering. The first begins at Barcelona's main square and leads you down the city's main drag through one of Europe's best public spaces: the Ramblas. The second walk starts at the same square but guides you into the heart of the Barri Gòtic, to the neighborhood around Barcelona's impressive cathedral.

▲▲▲The Ramblas Ramble: From Plaça de Catalunya down the Ramblas

Barcelona's central square and main boulevard exert a powerful pull. Many visitors spend the majority of their time doing laps on

The Ramblas Ramble

RAMBLAS
Ⓜ METRO STATION
Ⓑ BUS STOP

NOT TO SCALE-
PLAÇA DE CATALUNYA TO COLUMBUS
MONUMENT IS A 30 MIN. WALK

TO BLOCK
OF DISCORD

PASSEIG
DE GRÀCIA

RED TOURIST BUS

RAMBLA DE CATALUNYA

FNAC DEP'T. STORE

FGC TRAIN INFO

CAFÉ ZÜRICH

PLAÇA DE CATALUNYA
Catalunya

EL CORTE INGLÉS
DEP'T. STORE

CANALETES FOUNTAIN

Catalunya Ⓜ

❶

BIRDS

SANTA ANNA

AV. PORTAL DE L'ANGEL

AEROBUS, BLUE TOURIST BUS & TAXIS

ACADEMY OF SCIENCE

❷

CANUDA

ROMAN NECROPOLIS

CAFÉ GRANJA VIADER

BAROQUE CHURCH

❸

CARME

PORTAFERRISSA

CULTURAL INFO PALAU DE LA VIRREINA

Liceu Ⓜ

FLOWER

PHARMACY
CIGARS

EROTIC MUSEUM

LA BOQUERÍA MARKET

❹

CARDENAL

"UMBRELLA" BLDG.

HOSP.

BOQ.

S. PAV

MIRÓ MOSAIC

BARRI XINES

FERRAN

TO PLAÇA DE S. JAUME

LICEU OPERA HOUSE

Liceu Ⓜ

PLAÇA REIAL

NOU RAMBLA

Drassanes Ⓜ

❺

PALAU GÜELL

L'ARC

❻

ESCUDELLERS

HERBOLARI FERRAN

MARITIME MUSEUM

COLUMBUS MONUMENT

TO BARCELO-NETA

PASSEIG COLÓM

PICNIC SPOT

DCH

GOLONDRINAS BOATS

RAMBLA DE MAR

TO MAREMAGNUM

HARBOR

BARCELONA

❶ The Top of the Ramblas
❷ Rambla of the Little Birds
❸ Baroque Church
❹ La Boquería
❺ Plaça Reial
❻ Bottom of the Ramblas

the Ramblas. While the allure of the Ramblas is fading (as tacky tourist shops and fast-food joints replace its former elegance), this is still a fun people zone that offers a good introduction to the city. See it, but be sure to venture farther afield. Here's a top-to-bottom orientation walk.

Plaça de Catalunya: This vast central square divides old and new Barcelona. It's also the hub for the Metro, bus, airport shuttle, and Tourist Bus (blue northern route leaves from El Corte Inglés; red southern route leaves from the west, or Ramblas, side of the square). Overlooking the square, the huge **El Corte Inglés** department store offers everything from bonsai trees to a travel agency, plus one-hour photo developing, haircuts, and cheap souvenirs (Mon-Sat 10:00-22:00, closed Sun, pick up English directory flier, supermarket in basement, ninth-floor terrace cafeteria/restaurant has great city view—take elevator from entrance nearest the TI, tel. 933-063-800). Across the square from El Corte Inglés is **FNAC,** a French department store popular for electronics, music, and books (on west side of square—behind red Tourist Bus stop; Mon-Sat 10:00-22:00, closed Sun).

Four great boulevards radiate from Plaça de Catalunya: the Ramblas; the fashionable Passeig de Gràcia (top shops, noisy with traffic); the cozier, but still fashionable, Rambla de Catalunya (most pedestrian-friendly); and the stubby, shop-filled and delightfully traffic-free Avinguda Portal de l'Angel. Homesick Americans can even find a Hard Rock Cafe. Locals traditionally start or end a downtown rendezvous at the venerable Café Zürich (at the corner near the Ramblas).

• *Cross the street from the café to…*

❶ **The Top of the Ramblas:** Begin your ramble 20 yards down at the ornate fountain (near #129). More than a Champs-Elysées, this grand boulevard takes you from rich (at the top) to rough (at the port) in a one-mile, 30-minute stroll. You'll raft the river of Barcelonan life past a grand opera house, elegant cafés, retread prostitutes, brazen pickpockets, power-dressing con men, artists, street mimes, an outdoor bird market, great shopping, and people looking to charge more for a shoeshine than what you paid for the shoes.

Grab a bench and watch the scene. Open up your map and read some history into it: You're about to walk right across medieval Barcelona, from Plaça de Catalunya to the harbor. Notice how the higgledy-piggledy street plan of the medieval town was contained within the old town walls—now gone, but traced by a series of roads named Ronda (meaning "to go around"). Find the Roman town, occupying about 10 percent of what became the medieval town—with tighter roads yet around the cathedral. The sprawling modern grid plan beyond the Ronda roads is from the

19th century. Breaks in this urban waffle show where a little town was consumed by the growing city. The popular Passeig de Gràcia was literally the "Road to Gràcia" (once a separate town, now a characteristic Barcelona neighborhood).

Rambla means "stream" in Arabic. The Ramblas used to be a drainage ditch along the medieval wall that once defined what's now called the Barri Gòtic (Gothic Quarter). "Ramblas" is plural, a succession of five separately named segments, but address numbers treat it as a single long street. (In fact, street signs label it as "La Rambla," singular.) Because no streets cross the Ramblas, it has a great pedestrian feel.

You're at Rambla Canaletes, named for the fountain. The black-and-gold **Fountain of Canaletes** is the starting point for celebrations and demonstrations. Legend says that a drink from the fountain ensures that you'll return to Barcelona one day. All along the Ramblas, you'll see newspaper stands (open 24 hours, selling phone cards) and ONCE booths (selling lottery tickets that support Spain's organization of the blind, a powerful advocate for the needs of people with disabilities).

Got some change? As you wander downhill, drop coins into the cans of the human statues (the money often kicks them into entertaining gear). If you take a photo, it's considered good etiquette to drop in a coin. Warning: Wherever people stop to gawk, pickpockets are at work.

• *Walk 100 yards downhill to #115 and the...*

❷ **Rambla of the Little Birds:** Traditionally, kids bring their parents here to buy pets, especially on Sundays. Apartment-dwellers find birds, turtles, and fish easier to handle than dogs and cats. If you're walking by at night, you'll hear the sad sounds of little tweety birds locked up in their collapsed kiosks.

Along the Ramblas, buildings with balconies that have flowers are generally living spaces; balconies with air-conditioners generally indicate offices. The Academy of Science's clock (at #115) marks official Barcelona time—synchronize. The Carrefour Express supermarket has cheap groceries (at #113, Mon-Sat 10:00-22:00, closed Sun, shorter checkout lines in back of store).

A recently discovered **Roman necropolis** is in a park across the street from the bird market, 50 yards behind the big, modern Citadines Hotel (go through the passageway at #122). Local apartment-dwellers blew the whistle on contractors, who hoped they could finish their building before anyone noticed the antiquities they had unearthed. Imagine the tomb-lined road leading into the Roman city of Barcino 2,000 years ago.

• *Another 50 yards takes you to Carrer del Carme (at #105), and a...*

❸ **Baroque Church:** The big Betlem church fronting the boulevard is Baroque, unusual in Barcelona. Note the Baroque-style sloping roofline, ball-topped pinnacles, and the scrolls above the entrance. And though Barcelona's Gothic age was rich (with buildings to prove it), the Baroque age hardly left a mark. (The city's importance dropped when New World discoveries shifted lucrative trade to ports on the Atlantic.)

For a sweet treat, head down the narrow lane behind the church (going uphill parallel to the Ramblas about 30 yards) to the recommended **Café Granja Viader,** which has specialized in baked and dairy delights since 1870. (For more sugary treats, follow "A Short, Sweet Walk" on page 1321, which begins at the intersection in front of the church.)

• *Continue down the boulevard and stroll through the Ramblas of Flowers to the Metro stop marked by the red* M *(near #96), where you'll find...*

❹ **La Boquería:** This lively produce market is an explosion of chicken legs, bags of live snails, stiff fish, delicious oranges, and sleeping dogs (Mon-Sat 8:00-20:00, best mornings after 9:00, closed Sun, at #91). Originally outside the walls (as many medieval markets were), it expanded into the colonnaded courtyard of a now-gone monastery. Wander around—as local architect Antoni Gaudí used to—and gain inspiration. The Francesc Conserves shop sells 25 kinds of olives (straight in, near back on right, 100-gram minimum). Full legs of ham *(jamón serrano)* abound; *Paleta Ibérica de Bellota* hams are the best, and cost about €120 each. Beware: *Huevos del toro* are bull testicles—surprisingly inexpensive...and oh so good. Drop by a café for an *espresso con leche* or breakfast *tortilla española* (potato omelet).

For a quick bite, visit the recommended **Pinotxo Bar** (just to the right as you enter the market), where animated Juan and his family are busy feeding shoppers. (Getting Juan to crack a huge smile and a thumbs-up for your camera makes a great shot...and he loves it.) The stools nearby are a fine perch for enjoying both your coffee and the people-watching. The market and lanes nearby are busy with tempting little eateries (several are listed on page 1312).

• *Now turn your attention across the boulevard.*

The **Museum of Erotica** is your standard European sex museum (€9, daily 10:00-20:00, across from market at #96).

To the left, at #100, **Gimeno** sells cigars (appreciate the dying art of cigar boxes). Go ahead, do something forbidden in America but perfectly legal here...buy a Cuban (little singles for less than €1). Tobacco shops sell stamps and phone cards—and plenty of bongs and marijuana gear (the Spanish approach to pot is very casual).

Fifty yards farther, underfoot in the center of the Ramblas, find the much-trod-upon **anchor mosaic**—a reminder of the city's attachment to the sea. Created by noted abstract artist Joan Miró, it marks the midpoint of the Ramblas. (The towering Columbus Monument in the distance—hidden by trees—is at the end of this walk.)

Continue a few more steps down to the **Liceu Opera House.** From the Opera House, cross the Ramblas to Café de l'Opera for a beverage (#74). This bustling café, with Modernista decor and a historic atmosphere, boasts that it's been open since 1929, even during the Spanish Civil War.

• *Continue down the Ramblas to #46; turn left down an arcaded lane (Correr de Colom) to a square filled with palm trees.*

❺ **Plaça Reial:** This elegant Neoclassical square has a colonial (or maybe post-colonial) ambience. It comes complete with old-fashioned taverns, modern bars with patio seating, a Sunday coin-and-stamp market (10:00-14:00), Gaudí's first public works (the two colorful helmeted lampposts), and characters who don't need the palm trees to be shady. **Herbolari Ferran** is a fine and aromatic shop of herbs, with fun souvenirs such as top-quality saffron, or *safra* (Mon-Fri 9:30-14:00 & 16:30-20:00, closed Sat-Sun, downstairs at Plaça Reial 18—to the right as you enter the square). The small streets stretching toward the water from the square are intriguing, but less safe.

Back on the other side of the Ramblas, **Palau Güell** offers an enjoyable look at a Gaudí interior (Carrer Nou de la Rambla 3, may be partly closed for renovation, see page 1292). This apartment was the first of Gaudí's innovative buildings, with a parabolic front doorway that signaled his emerging nonrectangular style.

• *Continue farther downhill on the Ramblas.*

❻ **Bottom of the Ramblas:** The neighborhood on the right-hand side, Barri Xines, is the world's only Chinatown with nothing even remotely Chinese in or near it. Named for the prejudiced notion that Chinese immigrants go hand-in-hand with poverty, prostitution, and drug dealing, the neighborhood's actual inhabitants are poor Spanish, North African, and Roma (Gypsy) people. At night, the Barri Xines is frequented by prostitutes, many of them transvestites, who cater to sailors wandering up from the port. Prostitution is nothing new here. Check out the thresholds at #22 and #24 (along the left side of the Ramblas)—with holes worn in long ago by the heels of anxious ladies.

The bottom of the Ramblas is marked by the city's giant medieval shipyards (on the right, now the Maritime Museum—partly closed for restoration through 2013) and the Columbus Monument (they are described on page 1281). Just beyond the Columbus Monument, **La Rambla del Mar** ("Rambla of the Sea") is a modern extension of the boulevard into the harbor. A popular wooden pedestrian bridge—with waves like the sea—leads to Maremagnum, a soulless Spanish mall with a cinema, a huge aquarium, restaurants, and piles of people. Late at night, it's a rollicking youth hangout. It's a worthwhile stroll.

▲▲The Barri Gòtic:
From Plaça de Catalunya to the Cathedral

Barcelona's Barri Gòtic, or Gothic Quarter, is a bustling world of shops, bars, and nightlife packed between otherwise uninteresting 14th- and 15th-century buildings. The section near the port is generally dull and seedy. But the area around the cathedral is a tangled-yet-inviting grab bag of undiscovered courtyards, grand squares, schoolyards, Art Nouveau storefronts, baby flea markets (on Thursdays), musty junk shops, classy antiques shops (on Carrer de la Palla), street musicians strumming Catalan folk songs, and balconies with domestic jungles behind wrought-iron bars. Go on a cultural scavenger hunt. Write a poem. This self-guided walk gives you a structure, covering the main sights and offering a historical overview before you get lost.

• *Start on Barcelona's bustling main square.*

Plaça de Catalunya: This square is the center of the world for seven million Catalan people. The square (described on page 1273) is decorated with the likenesses of important Catalans. From here, walls that contained the city until the 19th century arc around in each direction to the sea. Looking at your map of Barcelona, you'll see a regimented waffle design—except for the higgledy-piggledy old town corralled by these walls.

The city grew with its history. Originally a Roman town, Barcelona was ruled by the Visigoths from the fall of Rome until 714, when the Moors arrived (they were, in turn, sent packing by the French in 801—because their stay was cut so short, there are few Moorish-style buildings here). Finally, in the 10th century, the Count of Barcelona unified the region, and the idea of Catalunya came to be. The area between Plaça de Catalunya and the old Roman walls (circling the smaller ancient town, down by the cathedral) was settled by churches, each a magnet gathering a small community outside the walls (or "extra muro"). Around 1250, when these "extra muro" communities became numerous and strong enough, the king agreed to invest in a larger wall, and Barcelona expanded. This outer wall was torn down in the 1850s and replaced by a series of circular boulevards (named Rondas).

• *From Plaça de Catalunya's TI, head downhill, crossing the busy street (Calle Fontanella) into a broad pedestrian boulevard called...*

Avinguda Portal de l'Angel: This boulevard is named "Gate of the Angel" for the gate in the medieval wall—crowned by an angel—that once stood here. The angel kept the city safe from plagues and bid voyagers safe journey as they left the security of the city. Imagine the fascinating scene here at the Gate of the

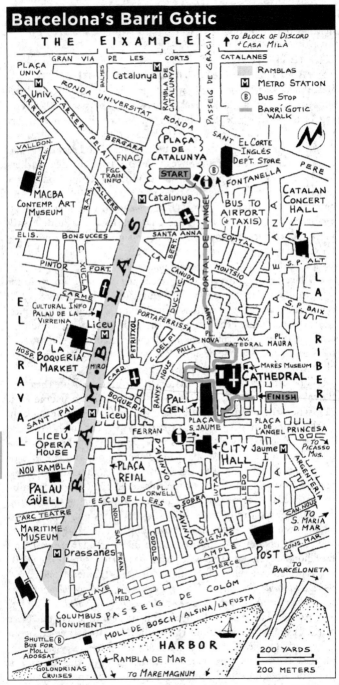

Barcelona's Barri Gòtic

THE EIXAMPLE

GRAN VIA
DE LES CORTS
CATALANES

→ To BLOCK OF DISCORD / CASA MILÀ

PLAÇA UNIV.
Ⓜ Univ.

	Ramblas
Ⓜ	Metro Station
Ⓑ	Bus Stop
	Barri Gotic Walk

RONDA UNIVERSITAT

BALMES

Catalunya

RAMBLA DE CATALUNYA

PASSEIG DE GRACIA

RONDA

SANT

EL CORTE INGLÉS DEPT. STORE

PERE

CARRER PELAI

BERGARA

FNAC

FGC TRAIN INFO

PLAÇA DE CATALUNYA

START Ⓑ ℹ FONTANELLA

Catalan Concert Hall

VALLDON.

MONTAL.

MACBA CONTEMP. ART MUSEUM

TALLERS

RAM·BLAS

Ⓜ Catalunya

BUS TO AIRPORT (+TAXIS)

COMTAL

MONTSIO

S.P. ALT

ELIS.
BONSUCCES

SANTA ANNA

PINTOR

XUCLA FORT.

CARME

PORTAFERRISSA

CANUDA

DUC.VIC.

ARCS

PL. NOVA

AV. CATEDRAL

PL. MAURA

S.P. BAIX

LA RIBERA

EL RAVAL

CULTURAL INFO PALAU DE LA VIRREINA

Liceu Ⓜ

LA BOQUERIA MARKET

MIRO

PETRITXOL

CARD.

BANYS NOUS

C. DEL PI

PALLA

PORTAL DE L'ANGEL

MARÈS MUSEUM

CATHEDRAL

FINISH ←

HOSP.

SANT PAU

Ⓜ Liceu

BOQUERIA

FERRAN

D'AVINYO

PAL GEN.

PLAÇA S. JAUME

PLAÇA DE L'ANGEL

PRINCESA

TO PICASSO MUS.

LICEU OPERA HOUSE

NOU RAMBLA

PALAU GÜELL

PLAÇA REIAL

PL. ORWELL

CITY HALL

Jaume I Ⓜ

ARGENTERIA

L'ARC TEATRE

MARITIME MUSEUM

ESCUDELLERS

D'AVINYO

CIUTAT

LLEDO

CAN NOUS

TO S. MARIA D. MAR

NOU SAN FRAN.

CODOLS

D'SOBRA

GIGNAS

AMPLE

MERCE

POST

CONS. MAR.

TO BARCELONETA

Ⓜ Drassanes

CLAVE

PL. MED.

COLUMBUS MONUMENT

PASSEIG DE COLÓM

MOLL DE BOSCH / ALSINA / LA FUSTA

HARBOR

200 YARDS
200 METERS

SHUTTLE BUS FOR MOLL ADOSSAT Ⓑ

GOLONDRINAS CRUISES

RAMBLA DE MAR

TO MAREMAGNUM

BARCELONA

Angel, where Barcelona stopped and the wilds began.

While walking down the Avinguda Portal de l'Angel, consider an optional detour a half-block right on **Carrer de Santa Anna,** where a lane on the right leads into a courtyard facing one of those "extra muro" churches, with a fine cloister and simple, typically Romanesque facade.

Continuing down the main boulevard (Avinguda Portal de l'Angel), you reach a fork in the road with a blue-and-yellow-tiled **fountain.** This was once a freestanding well—in the 17th century, it was the last watering stop for horses before leaving town. Take the left fork to the cathedral (past the Architects' House, with its Picasso-inspired frieze).

Enter the square, where you'll stand before two bold **towers**—the remains of the old Roman wall that protected a smaller Barcino, as the city was called in ancient times. The big stones that make up the base of the towers are actually Roman. The wall stretches left of the towers, incorporated into the Deacon's House, which you'll enter from the other side later).

• *The sights from here on are located on the map on page 1283. Walk around—past the modern bronze letters* BARCINO *and the mighty facade of the cathedral (which we'll enter momentarily)—and go inside the...*

Deacon's House (Casa de l'Ardiaca): Visitors are welcome inside this mansion, which today functions as the city archives (its front door faces the wall of the church). It's free to enter and a good example of a Renaissance nobleman's palace. Notice how the century-old palm tree seems to be held captive by urban man. Inside you can see the Roman stones up close. Upstairs affords a good view of the cathedral's exterior—textbook Catalan Gothic (plain and practical, like this merchant community) next to textbook Romanesque (the smaller, once freestanding, more humble church adjacent on the right, which you'll visit entering from its cloister later).

• *Exit the house to the left and follow the lane. You'll emerge at the entrance to the...*

Cathedral of Barcelona (Catedral de Barcelona): This huge house of worship is worth a look. Its vast size, peaceful cloister, and many ornate chapels—each one sponsored by a local guild—are impressive. For a self-guided tour, see "Sights in Barcelona," later.

• *After visiting the cathedral's cloister, exit and walk to the tiny lane ahead on the right (far side of the statue, Carrer de Montjuïc del Bisbe). This leads to the cute...*

Plaça Sant Felip Neri: This square serves as the playground of an elementary school bursting with youthful energy. The Church of Sant Felip Neri, which Gaudí attended, is still pocked with bomb damage from the Civil War. As a stronghold of democratic, anti-Franco forces, Barcelona saw a lot of fighting. The shrapnel that damaged this church was meant for the nearby Catalan government building (Palau de la Generalitat, described next).

Study the medallions on the wall. Guilds powered the local economy, and the carved reliefs here show that this building must have housed the shoemakers. In fact, on this square you'll find a fun little Shoe Museum (described on page 1284).

• *Circle the block back to the cathedral's cloister and take a right, walking along Carrer del Bisbe next to the huge building (on the right), which stretches all the way to the next square.*

Palau de la Generalitat: For more than 600 years, this place has been the home of the Catalan government. Through good times and bad, the Catalan spirit has survived, and this building has housed its capital.

• *Continue along Carrer del Bisbe to...*

Plaça de Sant Jaume (jow-mah): This stately central square of the Barri Gòtic, once the Roman forum, has been the seat of city government for 2,000 years. Today the two top governmental buildings in Catalunya face each other: the Barcelona City Hall (Ajuntament; free but only open to the public Sun 10:00-13:30) and the seat of the autonomous government of Catalunya (Palau de la Generalitat). It always flies the Catalan flag (red and yellow stripes) next to the obligatory Spanish one. From these balconies, the nation's leaders (and soccer heroes) greet the people on momentous days.

• *Take two quick left turns from the corner of Carrer Bisbe (just 10 yards away), and climb Carrer del Paridís. Follow this street as it turns right, but pause when it swings left, at the summit of...*

"Mont" Tàber: A millstone in the corner marks ancient Barcino's highest elevation, a high spot in the road called Mount Tàber. A plaque on the wall says it all: "Mont Tàber, 16.9 meters." Step into the courtyard for a peek at a surviving corner of the imposing **Roman temple** (Temple Roma d'August) that once stood here on Mont Tàber, keeping a protective watch over Barcino (free, well-explained on wall in English, daily 10:00-14:00 & 16:00-20:00).

• *Continue down Carrer del Paridís back to the cathedral, take a right, and go downhill about 100 yards to...*

Plaça del Rei: The Royal Palace sat on this "King's Square" (a block from the cathedral) until Catalunya became part of Spain in the 15th century. Then it was the headquarters of the local Inquisition. In 1493, a triumphant Christopher Columbus, accompanied by six New World natives (whom he called "Indians") and several pure-gold statues, entered the Royal Palace. King Ferdinand and Queen Isabel rose to welcome him home, and they honored him with the title "Admiral of the Oceans."

• *Your tour is over. Nearby, just off Plaça del Rei, is the City History Museum. The Frederic Marès Museum is just up the street (toward the cathedral entrance; both described later). Or simply wander and enjoy Barcelona at its Gothic best.*

Sights in Barcelona

Barcelona's Old City

I've divided Barcelona's Old City sights into three neighborhoods: near the harbor, at the bottom of the Ramblas; the cathedral and nearby (Barri Gòtic); and the Picasso Museum and nearby (La Ribera).

On the Harborfront, at the Bottom of the Ramblas

▲**Maritime Museum (Museu Marítim)**—Barcelona's medieval shipyard, the best preserved in the entire Mediterranean, has an impressive collection covering the salty history of ships and navigation from the 13th to the 20th centuries. Riveting for nautical types, and interesting for anyone, its modern and beautifully presented exhibits will put you in a seafaring mood. The museum is undergoing a major renovation, closing off large sections one at a time through 2013, so what you see will depend on when you visit. The museum's cavernous halls evoke the 14th-century days when Catalunya was a naval and shipbuilding power, cranking out 30 huge galleys a winter. As in the US today, military and commercial ventures mixed and mingled as Catalunya built its trading empire. The excellent included audioguide tells the story and explains the various seafaring vessels displayed—including an impressively huge and richly decorated royal galley (€2.50, prices may change as more exhibits reopen, daily 10:00-20:00, last entry at 19:30, breezy courtyard café, Avinguda de la Drassanes, tel. 933-429-920, www.mmb.cat).

▲**Columbus Monument (Monument a Colóm)**—Marking the point where the Ramblas hits the harbor, this 200-foot-tall monument built for an 1888 exposition offers an elevator-assisted view from its top. The tight four-person elevator takes you to the glassed-in observation area at the top for congested but sweeping views (€3, daily May-Oct 9:00-20:30, Nov-April 10:00-18:30). It was here in Barcelona that Ferdinand and Isabel welcomed Columbus home after his first trip to America. It's ironic that Barcelona would so honor the man whose discoveries ultimately led to its downfall as a great trading power.

***Golondrinas* Cruises**—At the harbor near the foot of the Columbus Monument, tourist boats called *golondrinas* offer two different unguided trips. The shorter version goes around the harbor in 35 minutes (€6.50, daily on the hour 11:30-19:00, every 30 minutes mid-June-mid-Sept, may not run Nov-April—call ahead, tel. 934-423-106). The longer 1.5-hour trip goes up the coast to the Fòrum complex and back (€13.50, can disembark at Fòrum in summer only, about 7/day, daily 11:30-19:30, shorter hours in winter).

▲Cathedral of Barcelona

Most of the construction on Barcelona's vast cathedral (Catedral de Barcelona) took place in the 14th century, during the glory days of the Catalan nation. The facade was humble, so in the 19th century the proud local bourgeoisie redid it in a more ornate Neo-Gothic style.

Cost and Hours: Strangely, even though the cathedral is free to enter daily 8:00-12:45 (until 13:45 on Sun) and 17:15-19:30, you must pay €5 to enter between 12:45 and 17:15 (tel. 933-151-554). The dress code is strictly enforced; don't wear tank tops, short shorts, or short skirts.

Getting There: The huge can't-miss-it cathedral is in the center of the Barri Gòtic, on Plaça de la Seu. For an interesting way to reach the cathedral from Plaça de Catalunya, and some commentary on the surrounding neighborhood, see my self-guided walk of the Barri Gòtic, described earlier.

❍ Self-Guided Tour: Though the cathedral is Gothic and supported by buttresses, it has smooth outside walls. That's because the supporting buttresses are on the inside, providing walls for 28 richly ornamented chapels. This, along with the interior's open and spacious feeling, is characteristic of Catalan Gothic. Typical of all medieval churches, the cathedral has an "ambulatory" plan, allowing worshippers to amble around to the chapel of their choice.

Although the main part of the church is fairly plain, the **chapels,** sponsored by local guilds, show great wealth. Located in the community's most high-profile space, they provided a kind of advertising to illiterate worshippers. The Native Americans that Columbus brought to town were supposedly **baptized** in the first chapel on the left.

The chapels ring a finely carved 15th-century **choir** *(coro)*. For €2.20 (no charge if you paid church entry fee), you can enter and get a close-up look (with the lights on) of the ornately carved stalls and the emblems representing the various Knights of the Golden Fleece who once sat here. The chairs were folded up, giving VIPs stools to lean on during the standing parts of the Mass. Each was creatively carved and—since you couldn't sit on sacred things—the artists were free to enjoy some secular and naughty fun here. Study the upper tier of carvings.

The **high altar** sits upon the **tomb** of Barcelona's patron saint, Eulàlia. She was a 13-year-old local girl tortured 13 times by

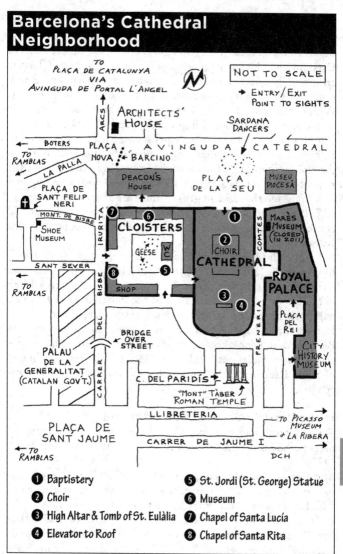

Barcelona's Cathedral Neighborhood

TO PLAÇA DE CATALUNYA VIA AVINGUDA DE PORTAL L'ANGEL

NOT TO SCALE

→ ENTRY/EXIT POINT TO SIGHTS

ARCS

ARCHITECTS' HOUSE

SARDANA DANCERS

BOTERS

PLAÇA NOVA

AVINGUDA CATEDRAL

TO RAMBLAS

LA PALLA

BARCINO

DEACON'S HOUSE

PLAÇA DE LA SEU

MUSEU DIOCESÀ

PLAÇA DE SANT FELIP NERI

MONT. DE BISBE

IRURITA

⑦

⑥

CLOISTERS

MARÈS MUSEUM (CLOSED IN 2011)

SHOE MUSEUM

GEESE WC

①

②

CHOIR

CATEDRAL

COMTES

SANT SEVER

⑧

⑤

ROYAL PALACE

TO RAMBLAS

BISBE

SHOP

③

④

FRENERIA

PLAÇA DEL REI

DEL

BRIDGE OVER STREET

CITY HISTORY MUSEUM

PALAU DE LA GENERALITAT (CATALAN GOV'T.)

CARRER

C. DEL PARIDÍS

"MONT" TÀBER ROMAN TEMPLE

LLIBRETERIA

TO PICASSO MUSEUM & LA RIBERA

PLAÇA DE SANT JAUME

CARRER DE JAUME I

DCH

TO RAMBLAS

① Baptistery

② Choir

③ High Altar & Tomb of St. Eulàlia

④ Elevator to Roof

⑤ St. Jordi (St. George) Statue

⑥ Museum

⑦ Chapel of Santa Lucía

⑧ Chapel of Santa Rita

Romans for her faith before finally being crucified on an X-shaped cross. Her X symbol is carved on the pews. Climb down the stairs for a close look at her exquisite marble sarcophagus. Many of the sarcophagi in this church predate the present building.

You can ride the **elevator** to the roof for a view (€2.50, no charge if you paid church entry fee, Mon-Fri 10:30-18:00, Sat 10:00-12:00, closed Sun, start from chapel left of high altar).

Enter the **cloisters** (through arch, right of high altar). Once inside, look back at the arch, an impressive mix of Romanesque and Gothic. Nearby, a tiny **statue** of St. George slaying the dragon stands in the garden. Jordi (George) is one of the patron saints of Catalunya and by far the most popular boy's name here. Cloisters are generally found in monasteries, but this church has one because it needed to accommodate more chapels—to make more money. With so many wealthy merchants in town who believed that their financial generosity would impress God and win them favor, the church needed more private chapel space. Merchants wanted to be buried close to the altar, and their tombs also spill over into the cloister. Notice on the pavement stones, as in the chapels, the symbols of the trades or guilds: scissors, shoes, bakers, and so on.

Long ago the resident **geese**—there are always 13, in memory of Eulàlia—functioned as an alarm system. Any commotion would get them honking, alerting the monk in charge. They honk to this very day.

From the statue of St. Jordi, circle to the right (past a WC hidden on the left). The skippable little €2 **museum** (far corner; no charge if you paid church entry fee) is one plush room with a dozen old religious paintings. Just beyond the museum, in the corner, built into the outside wall of the cloister, is the dark, barrel-vaulted Romanesque **Chapel of Santa Lucía,** a small church that predates the cathedral. People hoping for good eyesight (Santa Lucía's specialty) leave candles outside. Farther along the cloister, the **Chapel of Santa Rita** (her forte: impossible causes) usually has the most candles.

In the Barri Gòtic, near the Cathedral

For an interesting route from Plaça de Catalunya to the cathedral neighborhood, see my self-guided walk of the Barri Gòtic (page 1277).

Shoe Museum (Museu del Calçat)—Shoe-lovers enjoy this two-room shoe museum, watched over by an earnest attendant. The huge shoes at the entry are designed to fit the foot of the Columbus Monument at the bottom of the Ramblas (€2.50, Tue-Sun 11:00-14:00, closed Mon, one block beyond outside door of cathedral cloister, behind Plaça de G. Bachs on Plaça Sant Felip Neri, tel. 933-014-533).

▲▲City History Museum (Museu d'Història de la Ciutat)—Walk through the history of the city with the help of an included audioguide. First watch the nine-minute introductory video in the small theater (playing alternately in Catalan, Spanish, and English)—it's worth viewing in any language. Then take an elevator down 65 feet (and 2,000 years—see the date spin back while you descend) to stroll the streets of Roman Barcelona. You'll see sewers, models of domestic life, and bits of an early-Christian church. Finally, an exhibit in the 11th-century count's palace shows you Barcelona through the Middle Ages (€7, free all day first Sun of month and other Sun from 15:00 in summer; Tue-Sat April-Oct 10:00-19:00, Nov-March 10:00-17:00, Sun 10:00-20:00, last entry 30 minutes before closing, closed Mon; Plaça del Rei, enter on Vageur street, tel. 932-562-122).

Frederic Marès Museum (Museu Frederic Marès)—This museum, which has been closed for renovation, may be open by the time you visit—call first. When open, its eclectic collection of local artist (and packrat) Frederic Marès sprawls around a peaceful courtyard through several old Barri Gòtic buildings. The biggest part of the collection is sculpture, hailing from ancient times to the early 20th century. But even more interesting is Marès' vast collection of items he found representative of everyday life in the 19th century—rooms upon rooms of fans, stamps, pipes, and other bric-a-brac, all lovingly displayed. There are also several sculptures by Frederic Marès himself, and temporary exhibits (€4.20 admission may change after renovation, but hours and free days will stay the same: free Wed and Sun from 15:00; open Tue-Sat 10:00-19:00, Sun 10:00-20:00, closed Mon; Plaça de Sant Iu 5-6, tel. 932-563-500, www.museumares.bcn.cat). The delightfully tranquil courtyard café offers a nice break, even when the museum is closed.

▲▲▲Picasso Museum (Museu Picasso)

This is the best collection in the country of the work of Spaniard Pablo Picasso (1881-1973), and—since he spent his formative years (age 14-21) in Barcelona—it's the best collection of his early works anywhere. By seeing his youthful, realistic art, you can more fully appreciate the artist's genius and better understand his later, more challenging art. The collection is scattered through several connected Gothic palaces, six blocks from the cathedral in the Ribera district (for more on this area, see page 1286).

Cost and Hours: €9, free all day first Sun of month and other Sun from 15:00, open Tue-Sun 10:00-20:00, closed Mon, Montcada 15-23, ticket office at #21, Metro: Jaume I, tel. 932-563-000, www.museupicasso.bcn.cat. The ground floor has a required bag check, as well as a handy array of other services (bookshop, WC, and cafeteria).

Crowd-Beating Tips: There's almost always a line, but it moves quickly (you'll rarely wait more than an hour to get in). The busiest time is from when it opens until about 13:00 (worst on Tuesdays), as well as on free days; generally the later in the afternoon you visit, the fewer the crowds. If you have an Articket Card (see page 1264), skip the line by going to the group entrance.

Eating: The museum itself has a good **café.** Nearby, the **Textil Café,** hiding in a beautiful and inviting museum courtyard across the street, is a decent place to sip a *café con leche* or eat a light meal (Tue-Sun 12:00-24:00, closed Mon, 30 yards from Picasso Museum at Montcada 14-14, tel. 932-954-657; also hosts jazz concerts Sunday nights 20:30-23:00, weather permitting—usually not in winter, no cover, but you have to order something). And just down the street is a neighborhood favorite for tapas, the recommended **El Xampanyet** (closed Mon).

In La Ribera, near the Picasso Museum

There's more to the Ribera neighborhood than just the Picasso Museum. While the nearby waterfront Barceloneta district was for the working-class sailors, La Ribera housed the wealthier shippers and merchants. Its streets are lined with their grand mansions—which, like the much-appreciated Church of Santa Maria del Mar, were built with shipping wealth.

La Ribera (also known as "El Born") is separated from the Barri Gòtic by Via Laietana, a four-lane highway built through the Old City in the early 1900s to alleviate growing traffic problems. From the Plaça de l'Angel (nearest Metro stop—Jaume I), cross this busy street to enter an up-and-coming zone of lively and creative restaurants and nightlife. The Carrer de l'Argenteria ("Goldsmiths Street"—streets in La Ribera are named after the workshops that used to occupy them) runs diagonally from the Plaça de l'Angel straight down to the Church of Santa Maria del Mar. The Catalan Concert Hall is to the north.

▲▲Catalan Concert Hall (Palau de la Música Catalana)— This concert hall, finished in 1908, features my favorite Modernista interior in town (by Lluís Domènech i Muntaner). Inviting arches lead you into the 2,138-seat hall. A kaleidoscopic skylight features a choir singing around the sun, while playful carvings and mosaics celebrate music and Catalan culture. You can only get in by tour, which starts with a relaxing 12-minute video (€12, 50-minute tours in English run daily every hour 10:00-15:00, may have longer hours on weekends and holidays, tour times may change based on performance schedule, about 6 blocks northeast of cathedral, tel. 932-957-200, www.palaumusica.org).

The Catch: You must buy your ticket in advance to get a spot on an English guided tour (tickets available up to 7 days in advance—ideally buy yours at least 2 days before, though they're sometimes available the same day or day before). You can buy the ticket in person at the concert hall box office (open daily 9:30-15:30); by phone with your credit card (toll tel. 902-485-475); or online at the concert hall website (€1 fee, www.palaumusica.org).

It might be easier to get tickets for a **concert** (300 per year, tickets for some performances as cheap as €7, see website for details).

Barcelona's La Ribera

TO CATALAN CONCERT HALL

TO CATHEDRAL + RAMBLAS

M METRO STATION

CHOCOLATE MUSEUM

PL. PONS I CLERCH

PLAÇA DE L'ANGEL

C. DE LA BORIA

CARDERS

BOUGER

ASSAONADORS

CARRER DE LA PRINCESA

M Jaume I

COTONERS

BARRA DE FERRO

CARRER DE

PICASSO MUSEUM

VIGATANS

GRUNYÍ

BROSOLÍ

D'EN ROSIC

MANRESA

L'ARGENTERIA

C. DE LA NAU

ABAIX

CARRER DE BANYS VELLS

MIRALLERS

SOMBRERERS

FLASSADERS

C. DEL REC

CARRER DE MONTCADA

MOSQUES

PASSEIG DEL BORN

FUSINA

DEL

BORN MARKET

COMERC

SANTA MARIA DEL MAR

PL. STA. MARIA

STA. MARIA

VIDRIERA

RIBERA

CANVIS NOUS

AGULLERS

ESPASERIA

CANVIS VELLS

ASES

PL. OLLES

PESCATERIA

RERA PAL.

SANT JUAN

REC

CARRER

POST

CONSOLAT DE MAR

LA LLOTJA

PLAÇA DEL PALAU

MARQUÈS DE L'ARGENTERIA

FRANÇA TRAIN STN.

PLAÇA ANTONI LOPEZ

AVINGUDA DEL

TO MAREMAGNUM + BARCELONETA

TO M Barceloneta

❶ Gothic Point Hostel
❷ Sagardi Euskal Taberna Rest. & Bar
❸ Taller de Tapas
❹ El Xampanyet Bar
❺ Textil Café
❻ 1714 Massacre Monument
❼ Un Cotxe Menys Bike Rental

▲**Church of Santa Maria del Mar**—This church is the proud centerpiece of La Ribera. "Del Mar" means "of the sea," and that's where the money came from. The proud shippers built this church in only 55 years, so it has a harmonious style that is considered pure Catalan Gothic. As you step in, notice the figures of workers carved into the big front doors. During the Spanish Civil War (1936-1939), the Church sided with the conservative forces of Franco against the people. In retaliation, the working class took their anger out on this church, burning all of its wood furnishings and decor (carbon still blackens the ceiling). Today it's stripped down—naked in all its Gothic glory. The tree-like columns inspired Gaudí (their influence on the columns inside his Sagrada Família church is obvious). Sixteenth-century sailors left models of their ships at the foot of the altar for Mary's protection. Even today there remains a classic old Catalan ship at Mary's feet. As within Barcelona's cathedral, here you can see the characteristic Catalan Gothic buttresses flying inward, defining the chapels that ring the nave (free entry, daily 9:00-13:30 & 16:30-20:00).

Exit the church from the side, and you arrive at a square with a modern **monument** to a 300-year-old massacre that's still part of the Catalan consciousness. On September 11, 1714, the Bourbon king ruling from Madrid massacred Catalan patriots, who were buried in a mass grave on this square. From that day on, the king outlawed Catalan culture and its institutions (no speaking the language, no folk dances, no university, and so on). The eternal flame burns atop this monument, and 9/11 is still a sobering anniversary for the Catalans.

To the Picasso Museum: From behind the church, the Carrer de Montcada leads two blocks to the Picasso Museum (described earlier). The street's mansions—built by rich shippers centuries ago—now house galleries, shops, and even museums. The Picasso Museum itself consists of five such mansions laced together.

Passeig del Born—Just behind the church, this long square was formerly a jousting square (as its shape indicates). This is the neighborhood center and a popular springboard for exploring tapas bars, fun restaurants, and nightspots in the narrow streets all around. Wandering around here at night, you'll find piles of inviting and intriguing little restaurants (I've listed my favorites on page 1317). Enjoy a glass of wine on the square facing the church, or consider renting a bike here for a pedal down the beach promenade.

Chocolate Museum (Museu de la Xocolata)—This museum, only a couple of blocks from the Picasso Museum, is a delight for chocolate-lovers. Operated by the local confectioners' guild, it tells the story of chocolate from Aztecs to Europeans via the port of Barcelona, where it was first unloaded and processed. But the history lesson is just an excuse to show off a series of remarkably ornate candy sculptures. These works of edible art—which change every year but often include such Spanish themes as Don Quixote or bullfighting—begin as store-window displays for Easter or Christmas. Once the holiday passes, the confectioners bring the sculptures here to be enjoyed (€4.30, Mon and Wed-Sat 10:00-19:00, Sun 10:00-15:00, closed Tue, Carrer Comerç 36, tel. 932-687-878, www.museuxocolata.com).

The Eixample: Modernisme and Antoni Gaudí

Wide sidewalks, hardy shade trees, chic shops, and plenty of Art Nouveau fun make the Eixample a refreshing break from the Old City. For the best Eixample example, ramble Rambla de Catalunya (unrelated to the more famous Ramblas) and pass through Passeig de Gràcia (Metro for Block of Discord: Passeig de Gràcia, or Metro for Casa Milà: Diagonal).

The 19th century was a boom time for Barcelona. By 1850 the city was busting out of its medieval walls. A new town was planned to follow a grid-like layout. The intersection of three major thoroughfares—Gran Via, Diagonal, and Meridiana—would shift the city's focus uptown. But uptown Barcelona is a unique variation on the common grid-plan city: Barcelona snipped off the building corners to create light and spacious eight-sided squares at every intersection.

The Eixample, or "Expansion," was a progressive plan in which everything was made accessible to everyone. Each 20-block-square district would have its own hospital and large park, each 10-block-square area would have its own market and general services, and each five-block-square grid would house its own schools and day-care centers. The hollow space found inside each "block" of apartments would form a neighborhood park.

Although much of that vision never quite panned out, the Eixample was an urban success. Rich and artsy big shots bought plots along the grid. The richest landowners built as close to the center as possible. For this reason, the best buildings are near the Passeig de Gràcia. While adhering to the height, width, and depth limitations, they built as they pleased—often in the trendy new Modernista style.

For many visitors, Modernista architecture is Barcelona's main draw. (The TI even has a special desk set aside just for Modernisme-seekers.) And one name tops them all: **Antoni Gaudí** (1852-1926). Barcelona is an architectural scrapbook of Gaudí's galloping gables and organic curves. A devoted Catalan and Catholic, he immersed himself in each project, often living on-site. At various times, he called Parc Güell, Casa Milà, and the Sagrada Família home.

First I've covered the main Gaudí attractions close to the Old City. The Sagrada Família and Parc Güell are farther afield, but worth the trip. And since many visitors do those two sights together, I've included tips on how to connect them.

Gaudí Sights near the Old City

▲▲**Casa Milà (La Pedrera)**—This Gaudí exterior laughs down on the crowds filling Passeig de Gràcia. Casa Milà, also called La Pedrera ("The Quarry"), has a much-photographed roller coaster of melting-ice-cream eaves. This is Barcelona's quintessential

Modernista Sights

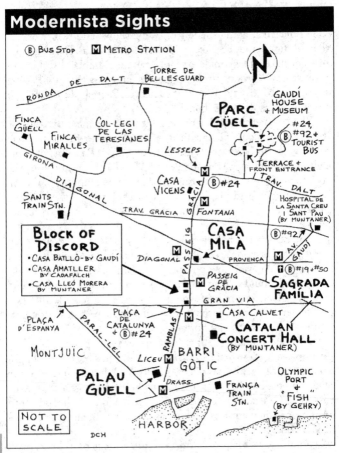

Ⓑ BUS STOP   Ⓜ METRO STATION

TORRE DE BELLESGUARD

RONDA DE DALT

GAUDÍ HOUSE & MUSEUM

PARC GÜELL

FINCA GÜELL

COL-LEGI DE LAS TERESIANES

FINCA MIRALLES

GIRONA

DIAGONAL

LESSEPS

#24, Ⓑ #92 + TOURIST BUS

TERRACE + FRONT ENTRANCE

TRAV. DALT

SANTS TRAIN STN.

CASA VICENS

Ⓑ #24

TRAV. GRACIA

FONTANA

HOSPITAL DE LA SANTA CREU I SANT PAU (BY MUNTANER)

BLOCK OF DISCORD
- CASA BATLLÓ · BY GAUDÍ
- CASA AMATLLER BY CADAFALCH
- CASA LLEÓ MORERA BY MUNTANER

DIAGONAL

PASSEIG DE GRACIA

CASA MILA

PROVENÇA

Ⓑ #92

AV. GAUDÍ

Ⓜ

Ⓑ #19 + #50

SAGRADA FAMÍLIA

PASSEIG DE GRACIA

GRAN VIA

CASA CALVET

PLAÇA D'ESPANYA

PARAL·LEL

PLAÇA DE CATALUNYA + Ⓑ #24

CATALAN CONCERT HALL (BY MUNTANER)

MONTJUÏC

RAMBLAS

LICEU

BARRI GÒTIC

DRASS.

FRANÇA TRAIN STN.

OLYMPIC PORT + "FISH" (BY GEHRY)

PALAU GÜELL

NOT TO SCALE

HARBOR

DCH

BARCELONA

Modernista building and was Gaudí's last major work (1906-1910) before dedicating his final years to the Sagrada Família.

You can visit three sections of Casa Milà: the apartment, the attic, and the rooftop (€14, good audioguide-€4, daily March-Oct 9:00-20:00, Nov-Feb 9:00-18:30, last entry 30 minutes before closing, Passeig de Gràcia 92, Metro: Diagonal, toll tel. 902-400-973). If you pay for an audioguide, you can choose between the 1.25-hour tour, which offers more listening options, or the 30-minute version.

After entering, head upstairs. Two elevators take you up to either the apartment or the attic. Normally you're directed to the apartment, but if you arrive late in the day, go to the attic elevator first, then climb right up to the rooftop to make sure you have enough time to enjoy Gaudí's works and the views.

The typical fourth-floor **apartment** is decorated as it might have been when the building was first occupied by middle-class urbanites (a seven-minute video explains Barcelona society at the time). Notice Gaudí's clever use of the atrium to maximize daylight in all of the apartments.

The **attic** houses a sprawling multimedia "Gaudí Space," tracing the history of the architect's career with models, photos, and videos of his work. It's all displayed under distinctive parabola-shaped arches. While evocative of Gaudí's style in themselves, the arches are formed this way partly to support the multilevel roof above. This area was also used for ventilation, helping to keep things cool in summer and warm in winter. Tenants had storage spaces and did their laundry up here.

From the attic, a stairway leads to the fanciful, undulating, jaw-dropping **rooftop,** where 30 chimneys play volleyball with the clouds.

Back at the **ground level** of Casa Milà, poke into the dreamily painted original entrance courtyard. The first floor hosts free art exhibits.

Concerts: During July, a rooftop concert series called "Pedrera by Night" features live music—jazz, flamenco, tango—and gives you the chance to see the rooftop illuminated (around €13, 22:00-24:00, toll tel. 902-400-973, http://obrasocial.caixacatalunya.es).

Eating: Stop by the recommended **La Bodegueta,** a long block away (daily lunch special).

▲**Block of Discord**—Four blocks from Casa Milà, you can survey a noisy block of competing late-19th-century facades. Several of Barcelona's top Modernista mansions line Passeig de Gràcia (Metro: Passeig de Gràcia). Because the structures look as though they are trying to outdo each other in creative twists, locals nicknamed the block between Consell de Cent and Arago the "Block of Discord."

First (at #43) and most famous is Gaudí's **Casa Batlló,** with skull-like balconies and a tile roof that suggests a cresting dragon's back; Gaudí based the work on the popular legend of St. Jordi (George) slaying the dragon. You can tour the house—a rival of Casa Milà (€17.80, includes audioguide, daily 9:00-20:00, may close early for special events—closings posted in advance at entrance, tel. 932-160-306, www.casabatllo.cat). You'll see the main floor (with a funky mushroom-shaped fireplace nook), the blue-and-white-ceramic–slathered atrium, the attic (more parabolic arches), and the rooftop, all with the help of the good audioguide. Because preservation of the place is privately funded, the entrance fee is steep—but the interior is even more fanciful and over-the-top than Casa Milà's. There's barely a straight line in the house. By the way, if you're tempted to snap photos from the middle of the street, be careful—Gaudí died under a streetcar.

Next door, at **Casa Amatller** (#41), check out architect Josep Puig i Cadafalch's creative mix of Moorish- and Gothic-inspired architecture and iron grillwork, which decorates a step-gable like those in the Netherlands. Pop inside for a peek at the elaborate entrance hall.

On the corner (at #35), **Casa Lleó Morera** has a wonderful interior highlighted by the dining room's fabulous stained glass. The architect, Lluís Domènech i Muntaner, also designed the Catalan Concert Hall (you'll notice similarities).

The recommended **La Rita** restaurant, just around the corner on Carrer Arago, serves a fine three-course lunch for a great price (Mon-Fri from 13:00).

▲**Palau Güell**—Just as the Picasso Museum reveals a young genius on the verge of a breakthrough, this early Gaudí building (completed in 1890) shows the architect taking his first tentative steps toward what would become his trademark curvy style. The parabolic-arch doorways, viewable from the outside, are the first clue that this is not a typical townhouse. Until the extensive renovation is complete, only part of the house is open to the public: the main floor and the Neo-Gothic cellar, which was used as a stable—notice the big carriage doors in the back and the rings on some of the posts used to tie up the horses (free while under renovation, may charge an entry fee after completion, Tue-Sat 10:00-14:30, closed Sun-Mon, a half-block off the Ramblas at Carrer Nou de la Rambla 3-5, tel. 933-173-974, www.palauguell.cat). Even if the rooftop—with its fanciful mosaic chimneys (visible from the street if you crane your neck)—is open, I'd skip it if you plan to see the more interesting one at Casa Milà.

▲▲▲Sagrada Família (Holy Family Church)

Gaudí's most famous and persistent work is this unfinished landmark church. He worked on the Sagrada Família from 1883 until his death in 1926. Since then, construction has moved forward in fits and starts. Even today, the half-finished church is not expected to be completed for another quarter-century. (But over 30 years of visits, I've seen considerable progress.) The temple is funded exclusively by private donations and entry fees, which is another reason its completion has taken so long. Your admission helps pay for the ongoing construction.

Cost and Hours: €12, daily April-Sept 9:00-20:00, Oct-March 9:00-18:00, Metro: Sagrada Família puts you right on the doorstep—exit toward *Pl de la Sagrada Família,* tel. 932-073-031, www.sagradafamilia.cat.

Crowd-Beating Tips: The ticket line can be very long (up to about 30-45 minutes at peak times). In summer, it's generally least crowded during lunch and after 18:30, and most crowded right when the church opens. To skip the ticket-buying line, purchase tickets in advance online (www.servicaixa.com, pick up at ServiCaixa terminal outside the Passion Facade) or at any ServiCaixa machine (located throughout the city).

Tours: The 45-minute English tours cost €4 (May-Oct daily at 11:00 and 13:00, Nov-April usually Fri-Mon only, same times). Or rent the good 70-minute audioguide (also €4).

Elevators: Two different elevators take you partway up the towers for a great view of the city and a gargoyle's-eye perspective of the loopy church. Each one costs €2.50 (pay as you board elevator). The **Passion facade elevator** takes you 215 feet up, where you can climb higher if you want; then an elevator takes you back down. The **Nativity facade elevator** is similar, but you can also cross the dizzying bridge between the towers—and you must walk all the way down. (Some people prefer the Nativity elevator despite the additional steps because it offers close views of the facade that Gaudí actually worked on.) For the climbing sections, expect the spiral stairs to be tight, hot, and congested. Lines for both elevators can be very long (up to a 2-hour wait at the busiest times); signs along the stanchions give you an estimated wait time. To avoid long lines, follow the "Crowd-Beating Tips" (listed earlier) and go directly to the elevators when you arrive. The Nativity facade elevator generally has a shorter line.

The Construction Project: There's something powerful about an opportunity to feel a community of committed people with a vision, working on a church that will not be finished in their lifetime (as was standard in the Gothic age). Local craftsmen often cap off their careers by spending a couple of years on this exciting construction site. The church will trumpet its completion with 18 spires: A dozen "smaller" 330-foot spires (representing the apostles) will stand in groups of four and mark the three entry facades of the building. Four taller towers (dedicated to the four Evangelists) will surround the two tallest, central towers: a 400-foot-tall tower of Mary and the grand 550-foot Jesus tower, which will shine like a spiritual lighthouse—visible even from out at sea. A unique exterior ambulatory will circle the building, like a cloister turned inside out. If there's any building on earth I'd like to see, it's the Sagrada Família...finished.

○ **Self-Guided Tour:** To get a good rundown, follow this commentary.

• *Begin by facing the western side of the church (where you'll enter).*

Passion Facade: It seems strange to begin with something that Gaudí had nothing to do with...but that's where they put the entrance. When Gaudí died in 1926, only the stubs of four spires stood above the building site. The rest of the church has been inspired by Gaudí's vision but designed and executed by others.

Gaudí knew he wouldn't live to complete the church and recognized that later architects and artists would rely on their own muses for inspiration. This artistic freedom was amplified in 1936, when Civil War shelling burned many of Gaudí's blueprints. Judge for yourself how the recently completed and controversial Passion facade by Josep María Subirachs (b. 1927) fits with Gaudí's original formulation (which you'll see downstairs in the museum).

Subirachs' facade is full of symbolism from the Bible. The story of Christ's Passion unfolds in the shape of a Z, from bottom to top. Find the stylized Alpha and Omega over the door; Jesus—hanging on the cross—with an open book (the word of God) for hair; and the grid of numbers adding up to 33 (Jesus' age at the time of his death). The distinct face of the man below and just left of Christ is a memorial to Gaudí.

Now look high above: The figure perched on the bridge between the towers is the soul of Jesus, ascending to heaven. The colorful ceramic caps of the towers symbolize the miters (formal hats) of bishops.

Grand and impressive as this seems, keep in mind it's only the *side* entry to the church. The nine-story apartment building to the right will be torn down to accommodate the grand front entry. The three facades—Passion, Nativity, and Glory—will chronicle Christ's life from birth to death to resurrection.

• *We'll enter the church later. For now, look right to find the...*

School: Gaudí erected this school for the children of the workers building the church. Now it houses an exhibit focusing on the architect's use of geometric forms. You'll also see a classroom and a replica of Gaudí's desk as it was the day he died, and a model for the proposed Glory facade...the next big step.

• *Leaving the school, turn right and go down the ramp under the church, into the...*

Museum: Housed in what is someday intended to be the church's crypt, the museum runs underground from the Passion facade to the Nativity facade. The first section tells the chronological story of the Sagrada Família. Look for the replicas of the pulpit and confessional that Gaudí, the micro-manager, designed for his church. As you wander through the plaster models used for the church's construction, you'll notice that they don't always match the finished product—these are ideas, not blueprints set in stone. Photos show the construction work as it was when Gaudí died in 1926 and how it's progressed over the years. See how the church's design is a fusion of nature, architecture, and religion. The columns seem light, with branches springing forth and capitals that look like palm trees.

Walking down the long passage to the other side of the church, you'll pass under a giant plaster model of the nave (you'll see the real thing soon). Find the hanging model showing how Gaudí used gravity to calculate the perfect parabolas incorporated into the church design (the mirror above this model shows how the right-side-up church is derived from this). Nearby, you'll find some original Gaudí architectural sketches in a dimly lit room and a worthwhile 20-minute movie (generally shown in English at :50 past each hour).

Then you'll peek into a busy workshop for making plaster models of the planned construction, just like what Gaudí used—he found these helpful for envisioning the final product in 3-D. The museum wraps up with an exhibit on the design and implementation of the Passion facade.

• *Climb up the ramp and hook left to see the...*

Nativity Facade (east side): This, the only part of the church essentially finished in his lifetime, shows Gaudí's original vision. (Cleverly, this facade was built and finished first to inspire financial support, which Gaudí knew would be a challenge.) Mixing Gothic-style symbolism, images from nature, and Modernista asymmetry, it is the best example of Gaudí's unmistakable cake-in-the-rain style. The sculpture shows a unique twist on the Nativity, with Jesus as a young carpenter and angels playing musical instruments.

• *From here you have two options:*

To take the elevator up the Nativity facade, go through the small door to the right of the main door. The line stretches through an area called the Rosary Cloister.

To enter the church (where you'll also find the Passion facade elevator entrance), go in the door to the left of the main entry. First you'll pass the Montserrat Cloister, with the **Gaudí and Nature** *exhibition that compares nature, waves, shells, mushrooms, the ripple of a leaf, and so on to Gaudí's work. Then you'll enter the...*

Construction Zone (the Nave): The cranking cranes, rusty forests of rebar, and scaffolding require a powerful faith, but the Sagrada Família offers a fun look at a living, growing bigger-than-life building. Part of Gaudí's religious vision was a love for nature. He said, "Nothing is invented; it's written in nature." His columns blossom with life, and little windows let light filter in like the canopy of a rain forest, giving both privacy and an intimate connection with God. The U-shaped choir hovers above the nave, tethered halfway up the columns. A relatively recent addition—hanging out in the middle of the back wall—is a statue of Barcelona's patron saint, St. Jordi (George of dragon-slaying fame). The nave's roof was just completed in 2010. At the far end of the nave, you'll see the line to take the elevator up the Passion facade.

Finishing the floors in the nave was a priority before Pope Benedict XVI's visit on November 7, 2010, to consecrate of the church. Currently, the construction is focused on a few major tasks: stabilizing the existing nave (which has been rattled by vibrations from the Metro and AVE train lines underground) and eventually adding the third, biggest entry—the Glory facade. They're also in the process of replacing the temporary clear windows with stained-glass ones. The final phase is the central tower (550 feet tall), which, it's estimated, will require four underground support pylons, each consisting of 8,000 tons of cement.

Gaudí lived on the site for more than a decade, and is buried in a Neo-Gothic 19th-century crypt (which is where the church began). His tomb is viewable for free from the small church around the corner from the main ticket entrance (during Mass—Mon-Sat 8:30-10:00 & 18:30-21:00, longer hours on Sun). There's a move afoot to make Gaudí a saint. Perhaps someday his tomb will be a place of pilgrimage. Gaudí—a faithful Catholic whose medieval-style mysticism belied his Modernista architecture career—was certainly driven to greatness by his passion for God. When undertaking a lengthy project, he said, "My client"—meaning God—"is in no hurry."

Scenic Connection to Parc Güell: If your next stop is Parc Güell (described next), and you don't want to spring for a taxi, try this route: With the Nativity facade at your back, walk to the near-left corner of the park across the street. Then cross the street to reach the diagonal Avinguda Gaudí (between the Repsol gas station and the KFC). From here you'll follow the funky lampposts four blocks gradually uphill (about 10 minutes) along Avinguda Gaudí, a pleasantly shaded, café-lined pedestrian street. When you reach the striking Modernista-style Hospital de la Santa Creu i Sant Pau (designed by Lluís Domènech i Muntaner), cross the street and go up one block (left) on St. Antonio Maria Claret street to catch bus #92, which will take you to the side entrance of Parc Güell.

From the Sagrada Família, you could also get to Parc Güell by taking the Metro to Lesseps, then bus #24 (described under "Getting There" for Parc Güell), but that involves two changes... and less scenery.

More Bus Connections: From the Sagrada Família, bus #19 makes an easy 15-minute journey to the Old City (stops near the cathedral and La Ribera district); bus #50 goes from the Sagrada Família, to the corner of Gran Via de les Corts Catalanes and Passeig de Gràcia, and to Montjuïc, skipping the funicular but taking you past all the sights (see "Getting to Montjuïc" on page 1298).

▲Parc Güell

Gaudí fans enjoy the artist's magic in this colorful park. Gaudí intended this 30-acre garden to be a 60-residence housing project—a kind of gated community. As a high-income housing development, it flopped; but as a park, it's a delight, offering another peek into Gaudí's eccentric genius. Notice the mosaic medallions that say "park" in English, reminding folks that this is modeled on an English garden.

Cost and Hours: Free, daily 10:00-20:00, tel. 932-130-488.

Getting There: From Plaça de Catalunya, the blue Tourist Bus or bus #24 will leave you at the park's side entrance, or a €8 taxi will drop you off at the main entrance. From elsewhere in the city, do a Metro-plus-bus combination: Go by Metro to the Lesseps stop. To avoid the tiring uphill 20-minute walk to the park, don't follow the *Parc Güell 1300 metros* sign; instead, exit the Metro station, cross the streets Princep d'Astúries and Gran de Grácia, and catch bus #24 (on Gran de Grácia), which takes you to the park's side entrance in less than 10 minutes. For a more scenic approach (on bus #92) from the Sagrada Família, see the previous listing.

❷ Self-Guided Tour: This tour assumes you're arriving at the front/main entrance (by taxi). If you're instead arriving by bus at the side entrance, walk straight ahead through the gate to find the terrace with colorful mosaic benches, then walk down to the stairway and front entrance.

As you wander the park, imagine living here a century ago—if this gated community had succeeded and was filled with Barcelona's wealthy.

Front Entrance: Entering the park, you walk by Gaudí's wrought-iron gas lamps (1900-1914). His dad was a blacksmith, and he always enjoyed this medium. Two gate houses made of gingerbread flank the entrance. One houses a good bookshop; the other is home to the skippable Center for Interpretation of Parc Güell (Centre d'Interpretació), which shows Gaudí's building methods plus maps, photos, and models of the park (€2.30, daily 11:00-15:00, tel. 933-190-222). The Gaudí House and Museum, described later, is better.

Stairway and Columns: Climb the grand stairway, past the famous ceramic dragon fountain. At the top, dip into the "Hall of 100 Columns," designed to house a produce market for the neighborhood's 60 mansions. The fun columns—each different, made from concrete and rebar, topped with colorful ceramic, and studded with broken bottles and bric-a-brac—add to the market's vitality.

As you continue up (on the left-hand staircase), look left, down the playful "pathway of columns" that supports a long arcade. Gaudí drew his inspiration from nature, and this arcade is like a surfer's perfect tube.

Terrace: Once up top, sit on a colorful bench—designed to fit your body ergonomically—and enjoy one of Barcelona's best views. Look for the Sagrada Família church in the distance. Gaudí was an engineer as well. He designed a water-catchment system by which rain hitting this plaza would flow into and through the columns from the market below, and power the park's fountains.

When considering the failure of Parc Güell as a community development, also consider that it was an idea a hundred years ahead of its time. Back then, high-society ladies didn't want to live so far from the cultural action. Today, the surrounding neighborhoods are some of the wealthiest in town, and a gated community here would be a big hit.

Gaudí House and Museum: This pink house with a steeple, standing in the middle of the park (near the side entrance), was actually Gaudí's home for 20 years, until his father died. His humble artifacts are mostly gone, but the house is now a museum with some quirky Gaudí furniture and a chance to wander through a model home used to sell the others. Though small, it offers a good taste of what could have been (€5.50, daily April-Sept 10:00-20:00, Oct-March 10:00-18:00).

Montjuïc

Montjuïc ("Mount of the Jews"), overlooking Barcelona's hazy port, has always been a show-off. Ages ago it had an impressive fortress. In 1929 it hosted an international fair, from which most of today's sights originated. And in 1992 the Summer Olympics directed the world's attention to this pincushion of attractions once again.

I've listed these sights by altitude, from highest to lowest; if you're visiting all of them, do them in this order so that most of your walking is downhill (for selective sightseers, the Fundació Joan Miró and Catalan Art Museum are the most worthwhile). Note that if you want to visit only the Catalan Art Museum, you can just take the Metro to Plaça d'Espanya and ride the escalators up (with some stair-climbing as well) to the museum.

Getting to Montjuïc: You have several options. The simplest is to take a **taxi** directly to your destination (about €7 from downtown).

Buses from various points in the city take you up to Montjuïc, including public bus #50 (from the corner of Gran Via and Passeig de Gràcia, or from the Sagrada Família), public bus #55 (from Plaça de Catalunya, next to Caja de Madrid building), and the red Tourist Bus.

A **funicular** takes visitors from the Paral-lel Metro stop up to Montjuïc (covered by a Metro ticket, every 10 minutes, 9:00-22:00). To reach the funicular, take the **Metro** to the Paral-lel stop, then follow signs for *Parc Montjuïc* and the little funicular icon—you can enter the funicular directly without using another ticket (number of minutes until next departure posted at start of entry tunnel). From the top of the funicular, turn left and walk

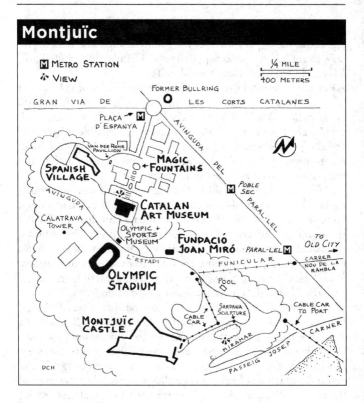

Montjuïc

M METRO STATION
⚑ VIEW

¼ MILE
400 METERS

FORMER BULLRING

GRAN VIA DE LES CORTS CATALANES

PLAÇA D'ESPANYA

AVINGUDA DEL

VAN DER ROHE PAVILLION

MAGIC FOUNTAINS

SPANISH VILLAGE

AVINGUDA

POBLE SEC

PARAL-LEL

CATALAN ART MUSEUM

CALATRAVA TOWER

OLYMPIC + SPORTS MUSEUM

FUNDACIÓ JOAN MIRÓ

PARAL-LEL

TO OLD CITY

L'ESTADI

FUNICULAR

CARRER NOU DE LA RAMBLA

OLYMPIC STADIUM

POOL

SARDANA SCULPTURE

CABLE CAR

CABLE CAR TO PORT

MONTJUÏC CASTLE

C. MIRAMAR

CARNER

PASSEIG JOSEP

DCH

two minutes to the Joan Miró museum, six minutes to the Olympic Stadium, or ten minutes to the Catalan Art Museum.

From the port, the most scenic way to Montjuïc is on the **cable car,** called the 1929 Transbordador Aereo (€9 one-way, €12.50 round-trip, 3/hour, daily 10:45-19:00, until 20:00 in June-Sept, closed in high wind, tel. 932-252-718).

Getting Around Montjuïc: Up top, the bus marked *Parc de Montjuïc* (#PM) loops between the sights. This circular line starts at Plaça d'Espanya and goes to the Catalan Art Museum, the Joan Miró museum, the funicular, and the Castle of Montjuïc. Public bus #50 and the red Tourist Bus also do circuits around the top of Montjuïc.

Castle of Montjuïc—The castle offers great city views from its fortress. The castle itself has a fascist past rife with repression. It was built in the 18th century by the central Spanish government to keep an eye on Barcelona and stifle citizen revolt. When Franco was in power, the castle was the site of hundreds of political executions (free, daily April-Sept 9:00-21:00, Oct-March 9:00-19:00, tel. 932-564-445, www.bcn.cat/castelldemontjuic).

Getting There: To spare yourself the hike up to the castle,

BARCELONA

and to catch some great views of the city, take the **cable car** from just above the upper station of the Montjuïc funicular (€6.30 one-way, €9 round-trip, June-Sept daily 10:00-21:00, until 19:00 April-May and Oct, until 18:00 Nov-March).

▲**Fundació Joan Miró**—Showcasing the talents of yet another Catalan artist, this museum has the best collection of Joan Miró art anywhere. You'll also see works by other Modern artists (such as *Mercury Fountain* by American sculptor Alexander Calder). If you don't like abstract art, you'll leave here scratching your head. But those who love this place are not faking it...they understand the genius of Miró and the fun of abstract art.

As you wander, consider this: Miró believed that everything in the cosmos is linked—colors, sky, stars, love, time, music, dogs, men, women, dirt, and the void. He mixed childlike symbols of these things creatively, as a poet uses words. It's as liberating for the visual artist to be abstract as it is for the poet: Both can use metaphors rather than being confined to concrete explanations. Miró would listen to music and paint. It's interactive, free interpretation. He said, "For me, simplicity is freedom."

Here are some tips to help you enjoy and appreciate Miró's art: first meditate on it, then read the title (for example, *The Smile of a Tear*), then meditate on it again. Repeat the process until you have an epiphany. There's no correct answer—it's pure poetry. Devotees of Miró say they fly with him and don't even need drugs. You're definitely much less likely to need drugs if you take advantage of the wonderful audioguide, well worth the €4 extra charge (€8.50, Tue-Sat July-Sept 10:00-20:00, Oct-June 10:00-19:00, Thu until 21:30, Sun 10:00-14:30, closed Mon, 200 yards from top of funicular, Parc de Montjuïc, tel. 934-439-470, www.bcn.fjmiro.es). The museum has a cafeteria, a café, and a bookshop.

Olympic and Sports Museum (Museu Olímpic i de l'Esport)—This museum, opened in 2007, rides the coattails of the stadium across the street (see next listing). You'll twist down a timeline-ramp that traces the history of the Olympic Games, interspersed with random exhibits about various sports. Downstairs you'll find exhibits designed to test your athleticism, a play-by-play rehash of the '92 Barcelona Olympiad, a commemoration of Spaniard Juan Antonio Samaranch (the influential president of the IOC for two decades), a sports media exhibit, and a schmaltzy movie collage. High-tech but hokey, the museum is worth the time and money only for those nostalgic for the '92 Games (€4, Tue-Sat April-Sept 10:00-20:00, Oct-March 10:00-18:00, Sun 10:00-14:30, closed Mon, Avinguda de l'Estadi 60, tel. 932-925-379, www.fundaciobarcelonaolimpica.es).

Olympic Stadium (Estadi Olímpic)—For two weeks in the summer of 1992, the world turned its attention to this stadium (between the Catalan Art Museum and the Fundació Joan Miró at Passeig Olímpic 17). Redesigned from an earlier 1929 version, the stadium was updated, expanded, and officially named for Catalan patriot Lluís Companys i Jover. The XXV Olympiad kicked off here on July 25, when an archer dramatically lit the Olympic torch—which still stands high at the end of the stadium overlooking the city skyline—with a flaming arrow. Over the next two weeks, Barcelona played host to the thrill of victory (most memorably at the hands of Michael Jordan, Magic Johnson, Larry Bird, and the rest of the US basketball "Dream Team") and the agony of defeat (i.e., the nightmares of the Dream Team's opponents). Hovering over the stadium is the futuristic Montjuïc Communications Tower, designed by Santiago Calatrava and used to transmit Olympic highlights and lowlights around the world. Aside from the memories of the medals, Olympic Stadium offers little to see today...except when it's hosting a match for Barcelona's soccer team, RCD Espanyol.

Spanish Village (Poble Espanyol)—This tacky five-acre model village uses fake traditional architecture from all over Spain as a shell to contain gift shops. Craftspeople do their clichéd thing only in the morning (not worth your time or €8.90, www.poble -espanyol.com). After hours, it's a popular local nightspot.

▲▲Catalan Art Museum (Museu Nacional d'Art de Catalunya)—The big vision for this wonderful museum is to showcase Catalan art from the 10th century through about 1930. Often called "the Prado of Romanesque art" (and "MNAC" for short), it holds Europe's best collection of Romanesque frescoes (€8.50, ticket valid for two days within one month, audioguide-€3.10, free first Sun of month, open Tue-Sat 10:00-19:00, Sun 10:00-14:30, closed Mon, last entry 30 minutes before closing; in massive National Palace building above Magic Fountains, near Plaça d'Espanya—take escalators up; tel. 936-220-376, www .mnac.es).

As you enter, pick up a map (helpful for such a big and confusing building). The left wing is Romanesque, and the right wing is Gothic, exquisite Renaissance, and Baroque. Upstairs is more Baroque, plus modern art, photography, coins, and more.

The MNAC's rare, world-class collection of **Romanesque** art came mostly from remote Catalan village churches in the Pyrenees (saved from unscrupulous art dealers, including many Americans). The Romanesque wing features frescoes, painted wooden altar fronts, and ornate statuary. This classic Romanesque art—with flat 2-D scenes, each saint holding his symbol, and Jesus (easy to identify by the cross in his halo)—is impressively displayed on replicas of the original church ceilings and apses.

Across the way, in the **Gothic** wing, fresco murals give way to vivid 14th-century wood-panel paintings of Bible stories. A roomful of paintings (Room 34) by the Catalan master Jaume Huguet (1412-1492) deserves a look, particularly his altarpiece of Barcelona's patron saint, George.

For a break, glide under the huge dome (which once housed an ice-skating rink) over to the air-conditioned cafeteria. This was the prime ceremony room and dance hall for the 1929 International Exposition. Then, from the big ballroom, ride the glass elevator upstairs, where the **Modern** section takes you on a delightful walk from the late 1800s to about 1930. It's kind of a Catalan Musée d'Orsay, offering a big chronological clockwise circle covering Spain's Golden Age (Zurbarán, heavy religious scenes, Spanish royals with their endearing underbites), Symbolism and Modernisme (furniture complements the empty spaces you likely saw in Gaudí's buildings), Impressionists, *fin de siècle* fun, and Art Deco.

Upstairs you'll also find photography (with a bit on how photojournalism came of age covering the Spanish Civil War), seductive sofas, and the chic Oleum restaurant, with vast city views (and €20 meals).

▲**Magic Fountains (Font Màgica)**—Music, colored lights, and huge amounts of water make an artistic and coordinated splash on summer nights at Plaça d'Espanya (20-minute shows start on the half-hour; almost always May-Sept Thu-Sun 21:00-23:30, no shows Mon-Wed; Oct-April Fri-Sat 19:00-21:00, no shows Sun-Thu; from the Espanya Metro station, walk toward the towering National Palace).

Nightlife in Barcelona

Refer to the *See Barcelona* guide (free from TI) and ask about the latest at a TI. Major sights open until 20:00 include the Picasso Museum (closed Mon), Gaudí's Sagrada Família (daily, until 18:00 Oct-March), Casa Milà (daily, until 18:30 Nov-Feb), and Parc Güell (daily). On Thursday, Montjuïc's Joan Miró museum stays open until 21:30 (otherwise open July-Sept Tue-Sat until 20:00).

Many lesser sights also stay open at least until 20:00, such as La Bouquería market (Mon-Sat), Columbus Monument (May-Oct daily), City History Museum (April-Sept Tue-Sun), Church of Santa Maria del Mar (daily), Casa Batlló (daily), Parc Güell's Gaudí House and Museum (April-Sept daily), and Castle of Montjuïc (April-Sept daily). The Magic Fountains on Plaça d'Espanya make a splash on weekend evenings (Fri-Sat, plus Thu and Sun in summer). The Tourist Bus runs until 22:00 every day in summer.

Music and Entertainment: The weekly *Guía del Ocio*, sold at newsstands for €1 (or free in some hotel lobbies), is a Spanish-language entertainment listing (with guidelines for English-speakers inside the back cover; www.guiadelocio.com). The monthly *Barcelona Metropolitan* magazine and quarterly *What's On Barcelona* are also helpful (free from the TI). For music, consider a performance at Casa Milà ("Pedrera by Night" July concert series, see page 1291), the Liceu Opera House (on the Ramblas), or the Catalan Concert Hall (page 1286). There are many nightspots around Plaça Reial (such as the popular Jamboree).

Palau de la Virreina, an arts-and-culture TI, offers information on Barcelona cultural events—music, opera, and theater (daily 10:00-20:00, Ramblas 99, see map on page 1272).

Sleeping in Barcelona

Book ahead. Barcelona is Spain's most expensive city. Still, it has reasonably priced rooms. Cheap places are more crowded in summer; fancier business-class hotels fill up in winter and offer discounts on weekends and in summer. When considering relative hotel values, in summer and on weekends you can often get modern comfort in business-class hotels for about the same price (€100) as you'll pay for ramshackle charm (and only a few minutes' walk from the Old City action). Some TI branches (including those at Plaça de Catalunya, Plaça de Sant Jaume, and the airport)

Sleep Code

(€1 = about $1.40, country code: 34)
S = Single, **D** = Double/Twin, **T** = Triple, **Q** = Quad, **b** = bathroom, **s** = shower only. Unless otherwise noted, credit cards are accepted, English is spoken, and prices listed generally include the 7-8 percent tax. Hotel breakfasts can range from free to simple €3 spreads to €25 buffets.

To help you easily sort through these listings, I've divided the rooms into three categories, based on the price for a standard double room with bath (during high season):

$$$ Higher Priced—Most rooms €150 or more.
$$ Moderately Priced—Most rooms between €100-150.
$ Lower Priced—Most rooms €100 or less.

Prices can change without notice; verify the hotel's current rates online or by email. For other updates, see www.ricksteves.com/update.

While many of my recommendations are on pedestrian streets, night noise can be a problem (especially in cheap places, which have single-pane windows). For a quiet night, ask for "*tranquilo*" rather than "*con vista.*"

BARCELONA

offer a room-finding service, though it's cheaper to go direct. Note that prices at the Hotel Continental Barcelona and the Hotel Continental Palacete include great all-day snack-and-drink bars.

Business-Class Comfort near Plaça de Catalunya

These hotels have sliding-glass doors leading to plush reception areas, air-conditioning, and perfectly sterile modern bedrooms. Most are on big streets within two blocks of Barcelona's exuberant central square. As business-class hotels, they have hard-to-pin-down prices that fluctuate wildly. I've listed the average rate you'll pay. But in summer and on weekends, supply often far exceeds the demand, and many of these places cut prices to around €100—always ask for a deal.

$$$ **Hotel Catalonia Duques de Bergara** has four stars, an elegant old entryway, splashy public spaces, slick marble and hardwood floors, 150 comfortable but simple rooms, and a garden courtyard with a pool a world away from the big-city noise (Db-€200 but can drop to as low as €100, extra bed-€35, breakfast-€16, non-smoking rooms available on request, air-con, elevator, free Internet access and Wi-Fi, a half-block off Plaça de Catalunya at Carrer de Bergara 11, tel. 933-015-151, fax 933-173-442, www.hoteles-catalonia.com, duques@hoteles-catalonia.es).

$$$ **Nouvel Hotel,** in an elegant, Victorian-style building on a handy pedestrian street, is less business-oriented and offers more character than the others listed here. It boasts royal lounges and 78 comfy rooms (Sb-€110, Db-€192, includes breakfast; ask about discount with this book—you must reserve direct by email, not their website; extra bed-€35, deposit for TV remote-€20, air-con, elevator, pay Wi-Fi, Carrer de Santa Ana 20, tel. 933-018-274, fax 933-018-370, www.hotelnouvel.com, info@hotelnouvel.com, Roberto).

$$ **Hotel Reding,** on a quiet street a five-minute walk west of the Ramblas and Plaça de Catalunya action, is a slick and sleek place renting 44 mod rooms at a good price (Db-€120, ask about free breakfast with this book but only if you book direct, prices go up during trade fairs, extra bed-€38, breakfast-€14, online deals don't include breakfast, non-smoking rooms, air-con, elevator, free Internet access and Wi-Fi, near Metro: Universitat, Gravina 5-7, tel. 934-121-097, fax 932-683-482, www.hotelreding.com, recepcion@hotelreding.com).

$$ **Hotel Duc de la Victoria,** with 156 rooms, is professional yet friendly, buried in the Barri Gòtic just three blocks off the Ramblas (Db-€140, bigger "superior" rooms on a corner with windows on 2 sides-€25 extra, breakfast-€15, non-smoking, air-con, elevator, Internet access, pay Wi-Fi, Duc 15, tel. 932-703-410, fax

934-127-747, www.nh-hotels.com, nhducdelavictoria@nh-hotels
.com).

$$ Hotel Lleó (YEH-oh) is well-run, with 89 big, bright,
and comfortable rooms; a great breakfast room; and a generous
lounge (Db-€130 but flexes way up with demand, can be cheaper
in summer, extra bed-about €30, breakfast-€13, non-smoking
rooms, air-con, elevator, small rooftop pool, free Internet access
and Wi-Fi, 2 blocks west of Plaça de Catalunya at Carrer de Pelai
22, tel. 933-181-312, fax 934-122-657, www.hotel-lleo.com, info
@hotel-lleo.com).

$$ Hotel Atlantis is solid, with 50 big, homey-yet-mod rooms
and great prices for the location (Sb-€90, Db-€107, Tb-€125,
breakfast-€9, non-smoking rooms, air-con, elevator, free Internet
access and Wi-Fi, older windows let in a bit more street noise
than other hotels in this category—request a room with double-
paned windows or a quieter room in back, Carrer de Pelai 20, tel.
933-189-012, fax 934-120-914, www.hotelatlantis-bcn.com, inf
@hotelatlantis-bcn.com).

Hotels with "Personality" on or near the Ramblas

These recommended places are generally family-run, with ad-lib
furnishings, more character, and lower prices. Only the Jardí offers
a quaint square buried in the Barri Gòtic ambience—but you're
definitely paying for the location.

$ Hotel Continental Barcelona, in a building overlook-
ing the top of the Ramblas, offers an inviting lounge and classic,
tiny-view balcony opportunities if you don't mind the noise. Its
comfortable rooms come with double-thick mattresses, wildly
clashing carpets and wallpaper, and perhaps one too many clever
ideas (they're laden with microwaves, fridges, a "command center"
of light switches, and Tupperware drawers). Choose between your
own little Ramblas-view balcony (where you can eat your breakfast)
or a quieter back room (Sb-€90, Db-€100, twin Db-€110, Db with
Ramblas balcony-€120, extra bed-€40, mention this book for best
price, prices include breakfast, non-smoking, air-con, elevator, free
Internet access and Wi-Fi, Ramblas 138, tel. 933-012-570, fax 933-
027-360, www.hotelcontinental.com, barcelona@hotelcontinental
.com). J. M.'s (José María) free breakfast and all-day snack-and-
drink bar make this a better deal than the price suggests.

$ Hostería Grau is homey, family-run, and almost alpine. Its
25 cheery, garden-pastel rooms are a few blocks off the Ramblas in
the colorful university district. The first two floors have seven-foot-
high ceilings, then things get tall again (S-€35, D-€65, Db-€90,
extra bed-€15; 2-bedroom family suites: Db-€95, Tb-€130,
Qb-€160; slippery prices jump during fairs and big events, ask

Hotels near the Ramblas

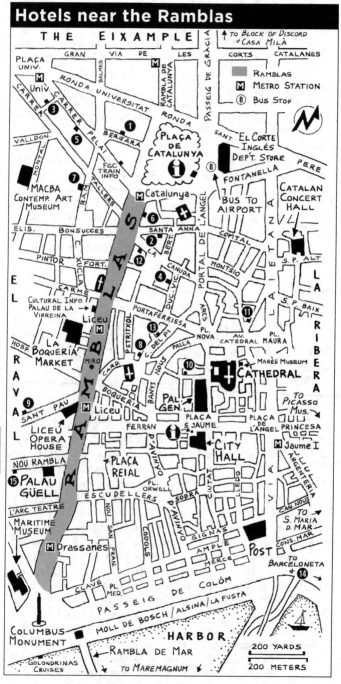

about free breakfast when you book direct and show this book, air-con, elevator, free Internet access and Wi-Fi, 200 yards up Carrer dels Tallers from the Ramblas at Ramelleres 27, tel. 933-018-135, fax 933-176-825, www.hostalgrau.com, reservas@hostalgrau.com, Monica). Before booking, confirm the hotel's strict cancellation policy—generally if canceling a room less than 48 hours in advance (or a suite less than five days in advance), you'll pay for the first night.

$ Hotel Jardí offers 40 clean, remodeled rooms on a breezy square in the Barri Gòtic. Many of the tight, plain, comfy rooms come with petite balconies (for an extra charge) and enjoy an almost Parisian ambience. It's a good deal only if you value the cute square location. Book well in advance, as this family-run place has an avid following (small basic interior Db-€70, nicer interior Db-€85, outer Db with balcony or twin with window-€90, large outer Db with balcony or square-view terrace-€100, add €5 to these rates on weekends, extra bed-€12, breakfast-€6, non-smoking, air-con, elevator, some stairs, free Wi-Fi in lobby, halfway between Ramblas and cathedral at Plaça Sant Josep Oriol 1, tel. 933-015-900, fax 933-425-733, www.hoteljardi-barcelona.com, reservations@hotel jardi-barcelona.com).

$ Hostal Opera, with 70 stark rooms 20 yards off the Ramblas, is clean, institutional, and modern. The street can feel seedy at night, but it's safe, and the hotel is very secure (Sb-€39-60, Db-€59-90, no breakfast, air-con only in summer, elevator, fee for Internet access and free Wi-Fi in lobby, Carrer Sant Pau 20, tel. 933-188-201, www.operaramblas.com, info@operaramblas .com).

Deep in the Barri Gòtic

$$$ Hotel Neri is chic, posh, and sophisticated, with 22 rooms spliced into the ancient stones of the Barri Gòtic, overlooking an overlooked square (Plaça Sant Felip Neri) a block from the cathedral. It has big plasma-screen TVs, pricey modern art on the bedroom walls, and dressed-up people in its gourmet restaurant (Db-€265, suites-€360-425, generally cheaper on weekdays, breakfast-€21, air-con, elevator, free Wi-Fi, rooftop tanning deck, St. Sever 5, tel. 933-040-655, fax 933-040-337, www.hotelneri.com, info@hotelneri.com).

$$ Hotel Regencia Colón, one block in front of the cathedral square, offers 50 solid, well-priced rooms in a handy location (Db-€105, more on weekends, breakfast-€12, air-con, elevator, Carrer Sagristans 13-17, tel. 933-189-858, fax 933-172-822, www.hotelregenciacolon.com, info@hotelregenciacolon.com).

Humble, Cheaper Places Buried in the Old City

$ Hostal Campi is big, subdued, and ramshackle, but offers simple class. This easygoing old-school spot rents 24 rooms a few doors off the top of the Ramblas (S-€33, D-€56, Db-€65, T-€75, Tb-€85, no breakfast, non-smoking rooms, lots of stairs with no elevator, pay Internet access, Canuda 4, tel. & fax 933-013-545, www.hostalcampi.com, reservas@hostalcampi.com, friendly Margarita and Nando).

$ Hostal Maldá rents the best cheap beds I've found in the old center. With 25 rooms above a small shopping mall near the cathedral, it's a time-warp—quiet and actually charming—but does not take reservations (though you can try calling a day before). It generally remains full through the summer, but it's worth a shot (S-€15, D-€30, T-€45, cash only, lots of stairs with no elevator, 100 yards up Carrer del Pi from delightful Plaça Sant Josep Oriol, Carrer del Pi 5, tel. 933-173-002). Good-natured Aurora doesn't speak English, but Delfi, who works only half the year, does.

Hostels in the Center of Town

Barcelona has a wonderful chain of well-run and centrally located hostels (www.equity-point.com), providing €21-26 dorm beds in 4- to 14-bed coed rooms with €2 sheets and towels, free Internet access, Wi-Fi, breakfast, lockers (B.Y.O. lock, or buy one there), and plenty of opportunities to meet other backpackers. They're open 24 hours but aren't party hostels, so they enforce quiet after 23:00. There are three locations to choose from: Eixample, Barri Gòtic, or near the beach.

$ Centric Point Hostel is a huge place renting 430 cheap beds at what must be the best address in Barcelona (bar, kitchen, Passeig de Gràcia 33, see map on page 1310, tel. 932-151-796, fax 932-461-552, www.centricpointhostel.com).

$ Gothic Point Hostel rents 150 beds a block from the Picasso Museum (roof terrace, Carrer Vigatans 5, see map on page

1287, tel. 932-687-808, www.gothicpoint.com).

$ Sea Point Hostel has 70 beds on the beach nearby (Plaça del Mar 4, tel. 932-247-075, www.seapointhostel.com).

In the Eixample

For an uptown, boulevard-like neighborhood, sleep in the Eixample, a 10-minute walk from the Ramblas action.

$$ Hotel Granvía, filling a palatial 1870s mansion, offers Botticelli and chandeliers in the public areas; a sprawling, peaceful sun patio; and 54 spacious, comfy rooms. Its salon is plush and royal, making the hotel an excellent value for romantics. To reduce street noise, ask for a quiet interior room or a room overlooking the courtyard in the back of the building (Sb-€60-114, Db-€76-162, Tb-€103-200, includes breakfast and taxes, ask for Rick Steves rates when you book direct, can be cheaper in slow times, breakfast-€11, non-smoking, air-con, elevator, free Internet access and Wi-Fi, Gran Via de les Corts Catalanes 642, tel. 933-181-900, fax 933-189-997, www.hotelgranvia.com, hgranvia@nnhotels.com, manager Asun Pareja).

$$ Hotel Continental Palacete, with 19 rooms, fills a 100-year-old chandeliered mansion. With flowery wallpaper and ornately gilded stucco, it's gaudy in the city of Gaudí, but it's also friendly, clean, quiet, and well-located. Most of the rooms are recently updated, there's an outdoor terrace, and guests have unlimited access to the extravagant "cruise-inspired" fruit, veggie, and drink buffet—worth factoring into your comparison-shopping (Sb-€102, Db-€137, €35-45 more for bigger and brighter view rooms, extra bed-€55, ask about discount with this book, prices include breakfast, non-smoking, air-con, free Internet access and Wi-Fi, 2 blocks north of Plaça de Catalunya at corner of Carrer Diputació, Rambla de Catalunya 30, tel. 934-457-657, fax 934-450-050, www .hotelcontinental.com, palacete@hotelcontinental.com).

$ Hostal Residencia Neutral, with a central Eixample address and 28 very basic rooms, is a family-run time warp and a fine value (tiny S-€38, Ds-€65, Db-€70, Ts-€80, Tb-€85, Qb-€89, €6 continental breakfast in pleasant breakfast room, request a back room to avoid street noise, thin walls, fans, elevator, free Internet access and Wi-Fi, elegantly located 2 blocks north of Gran Via at Rambla de Catalunya 42, tel. 934-876-390, fax 934-876-848, www .hostalneutral.es, info@hostalneutral.es, Julia and Anna).

$ Hotel Ginebra is minimal, clean, and quiet considering its central location. The Herrera family rents 12 rooms in a dated apartment building overlooking the main square (Db-€75-80, extra bed-€15, breakfast-€3, air-con, elevator, free Wi-Fi, Rambla de Catalunya 1/3, tel. 933-171-063, www.hotelginebra.net, info @hotelginebra.net, Juan speaks English).

Hotels & Restaurants in Barcelona's Eixample

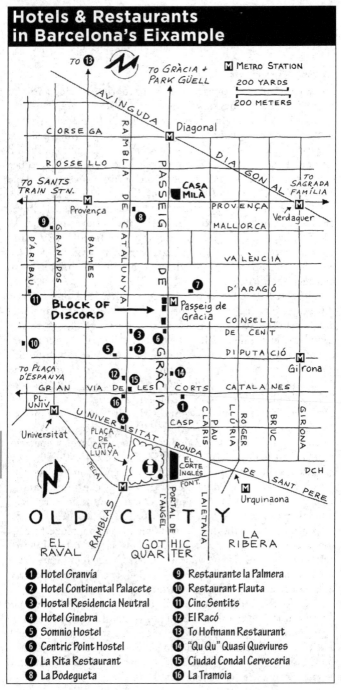

BARCELONA

Metro Station

200 YARDS
200 METERS

TO GRÀCIA & PARK GÜELL

TO SANTS TRAIN STN.

CASA MILÀ

BLOCK OF DISCORD

Passeig de Gràcia

TO PLAÇA D'ESPANYA

Universitat

PLAÇA DE CATALUNYA

EL CORTE INGLÉS

Urquinaona

OLD CITY

EL RAVAL   GOTHIC QUARTER   LA RIBERA

- ❶ Hotel Granvía
- ❷ Hotel Continental Palacete
- ❸ Hostal Residencia Neutral
- ❹ Hotel Ginebra
- ❺ Somnio Hostel
- ❻ Centric Point Hostel
- ❼ La Rita Restaurant
- ❽ La Bodegueta
- ❾ Restaurante la Palmera
- ❿ Restaurant Flauta
- ⓫ Cinc Sentits
- ⓬ El Racó
- ⓭ To Hofmann Restaurant
- ⓮ "Qu Qu" Quasi Queviures
- ⓯ Ciudad Condal Cerveceria
- ⓰ La Tramoia

$ Somnio Hostel, an innovative newer place run by a pair of American expats, has both dorm beds and private rooms (dorm bed-€25, S-€42, D-€77, Db-€85; prices include sheets, towels, and lockers; air-con, elevator, free Internet access and Wi-Fi, Carrer de la Diputació 251, second floor, tel. 932-725-308, www.somnio hostels.com, info@somniohostels.com).

Apartments in Barceloneta

$ BCNflats rents 40 renovated apartments with kitchens right near the beach in the lively Barceloneta quarter, the former fishermen's neighborhood that's become increasingly gentrified (Db-€100 in June-Aug, €80 Sept-May, up to 2 kids stay free, prices vary with size—see photos on website, €40 cleaning fee, no minimum-stay requirement, 10 percent less for 7-night stay, 25 percent deposit required to reserve online, €150 refundable cash security deposit collected at check-in, no breakfast, complimentary bottle of *cava* when you mention this book, Frederick or an associate will meet you to check in—arrange when you reserve, mobile 620-585-594, www.bcnflats.net, info@bcnflats.net). They also have 12 more units in the somewhat seedy Barri Gòtic near the Ramblas (larger, higher prices, same website).

Eating in Barcelona

Barcelona, the capital of Catalan cuisine—featuring seafood—offers a tremendous variety of colorful eateries, ranging from basic and filling to chic and trendy. Because of their common struggles, Catalans seem to have an affinity for Basque culture, so you'll find a lot of Basque tapas places here, too. Most of my listings are lively spots with a busy tapas scene at the bar, along with restaurant tables for *raciones*. A regional specialty is *pa amb tomaquet* (pah ahm too-MAH-kaht), bread topped with a mix of crushed tomato and olive oil.

I've listed mostly practical, characteristic, colorful, and affordable restaurants. My recommendations are grouped by neighborhood—along the Ramblas; in the Barri Gòtic; in the Ribera neighborhood (best for foodies); and in the Eixample—followed by some budget options scattered throughout the city. Note that many restaurants close in August (or July), when the owners take a vacation.

Restaurants generally serve lunch from 13:00 to 16:00 and dinner from 20:00 until very late (Spaniards don't start dinner until about 21:00). It's deadly to your Barcelona experience to eat too early—if a place feels touristy, come back later and it may be a thriving local favorite. For an afternoon sweet treat, I've suggested "A Short, Sweet Walk" (see page 1321).

Along the Ramblas

Within a few steps of the Ramblas you'll find handy lunch places, an inviting market hall, and a slew of vegetarian options.

Lunching Simply yet Memorably near the Ramblas

Although these places are enjoyable for a lunch break during your Ramblas sightseeing, many are also open for dinner. For locations, see the map on page 1316.

Taverna Basca Irati serves 40 kinds of hot and cold Basque *pintxos* for €1.80 each. These are open-faced sandwiches—like sushi on bread. Muscle in through the hungry local crowd, get an empty plate from the waiter, and then help yourself. Every few minutes, waiters prance proudly by with a platter of new, still-warm munchies. Grab one as they pass by...it's addictive. You pay on the honor system: You're charged by the number of toothpicks left on your plate when you're done. Wash it down with €2-3 glasses of Rioja (full-bodied red wine), Txakolí (sprightly Basque white wine) or *sidra* (apple wine) poured from on high to add oxygen and bring out the flavor (daily 11:00-24:00, a block off the Ramblas, behind arcade at Carrer Cardenal Casanyes 15, Metro: Liceu, tel. 933-023-084).

Restaurant Elisabets is a happy little neighborhood eatery packed with antique radios, and is popular with locals for its €11 "home-cooked" three-course lunch special. Stop by for lunch, survey what those around you are enjoying, and order what looks best (Mon-Sat 7:30-23:00, closed Sun and Aug, lunch special served 13:00-16:00, otherwise only €3 tapas—not full meals, 2 blocks west of Ramblas on far corner of Plaça Bonsucces at Carrer Elisabets 2, tel. 933-175-826, run by Pilar).

Café Granja Viader is a quaint time capsule, family-run since 1870. They boast about being the first dairy business to bottle and distribute milk in Spain. This feminine-feeling place—specializing in baked and dairy delights, toasted sandwiches, and light meals—is ideal for a traditional breakfast. Or indulge your sweet tooth: Try a glass of *orxata* (or *horchata*—chufa-nut milk, summer only), *llet mallorquina* (Majorca-style milk with cinnamon, lemon, and sugar), *crema catalana* (crème brûlée, their specialty), or *suis* ("Swiss"—hot chocolate with a snowcap of whipped cream). *Mel y mato* is fresh cheese with honey...very Catalan (Tue-Sat 9:00-13:45 & 17:00-20:45, Mon 17:00-20:45 only, closed Sun, a block off the Ramblas behind El Carme church at Xucla 4, tel. 933-183-486).

Picnics: Shoestring tourists buy groceries at **El Corte Inglés** (Mon-Sat 10:00-22:00, closed Sun, supermarket in basement, Plaça de Catalunya) and **Carrefour Express supermarket** (Mon-Sat 10:00-22:00, closed Sun, Ramblas 113).

In and near La Boquería Market

Try eating at La Boquería market at least once (#91 on the Ramblas). Like all farmers markets in Europe, this place is ringed by colorful, good-value eateries. Lots of stalls sell fun take-away food—especially fruit salads and fresh-squeezed fruit juices. There are several good bars around the market busy with shoppers munching at the counter (breakfast, tapas all day, coffee). The market, and most of the eateries listed here (unless noted), are open Monday through Saturday from 8:00 until 20:00 (though things get very quiet after about 16:00) and are closed on Sunday.

Pinotxo Bar is just to the right as you enter the market. It's a great spot for coffee, breakfast (spinach tortillas, or whatever's cooking with toast), or tapas. Fun-loving Juan and his family are La Boquería fixtures. Grab a stool across the way to sip your drink with people-watching views. Have a Chucho?

Kiosko Universal is popular for its great prices on wonderful fish dishes. As you enter the market from the Ramblas, it's all the way to the left in the first alley. If you see people waiting, ask who's last in line *("¿El último?")*. You'll eat immersed in the spirit of the market (€14 fixed-price lunches with different fresh-fish options 12:00-16:00, always packed but better before 12:30, tel. 933-178-286).

Restaurant la Gardunya, at the back of the market, offers tasty meat and seafood meals made with fresh ingredients bought directly from the market (€13 fixed-price lunch includes wine and bread, €16 three-course dinner specials don't include wine, €10-20 à la carte dishes, Mon-Sat 13:00-16:00 & 20:00-24:00, closed Sun, mod seating indoors or outside watching the market action, Carrer Jerusalem 18, tel. 933-024-323).

Bar Terrace Restaurant Ra is a lively terrace immediately behind the market (at the right end of the big parking lot) with outdoor tables filled by young, trendy, happy eaters. At lunch they serve one great salad/pasta/wine meal for €11. If you feel like eating a big salad under an umbrella...this is the place (€9-15 à la carte dishes, daily 10:00-12:30 & 13:30-16:00 & 21:00-24:00, fancier menu at night, mobile 615-959-872). Warning: Major renovation work may mean that Ra is closed during your visit.

Vegetarian Eateries near
Plaça de Catalunya and the Ramblas

Biocenter, a Catalan soup-and-salad restaurant popular with local vegetarians, takes its cooking very seriously and feels a bit more like a real restaurant than most (€6-9.75 weekday lunch specials include soup or salad and plate of the day, €15 dinner specials, Mon-Sat 13:00-23:00, Sun 13:00-16:00, 2 blocks off the Ramblas at Pintor Fortuny 25, Metro: Catalunya, tel. 933-014-583).

Juicy Jones is a tutti-frutti vegan/vegetarian eatery with colorful graffiti decor, a hip veggie menu (served downstairs), groovy laid-back staff, and a stunning array of fresh-squeezed juices served at the bar. Pop in for a quick €3 "juice of the day." For lunch you can get the Indian-inspired €6 *thali* plate, the €6.25 plate of the day, or an €8.50 meal including one of the two plates plus soup or salad and dessert (daily 12:30-23:30, also tapas and salads, Carrer Cardenal Casanyes 7, tel. 933-024-330). There's another location on the other side of the Ramblas (Carrer Hospital 74).

In Barceloneta
La Mar Salada is a traditional seafood restaurant with a slight modern twist, located on the strip leading to the Barceloneta beach. Their à la carte menu includes seafood-and-rice dishes, fresh fish, and homemade deserts. A nice meal will run you about €30-35 per person (€14 fixed-price weekday meal, Wed-Mon 13:00-16:00 & 20:00-23:00, Sat-Sun 13:00-23:00, closed Tue, indoor and outdoor seating, Passeig Joan de Borbó 59, tel. 932-212-127).

In the Barri Gòtic
These eateries populate Barcelona's atmospheric Gothic Quarter, near the cathedral. Choose between a sit-down meal at a restaurant or a string of very old-fashioned tapas bars.

Restaurants in the Barri Gòtic
Café de l'Academia is a delightful place on a pretty square tucked away in the heart of the Barri Gòtic—but patronized mainly by the neighbors. They serve "honest cuisine" from the market with Catalan roots. The candlelit, air-conditioned interior is rustic yet elegant, with soft jazz, flowers, and modern art. And if you want to eat outdoors on a convivial, mellow square...this is the place (€10-12 first courses, €12-15 second courses, fixed-price lunch for €10 at the bar or €14 at a table, Mon-Fri 13:30-16:00 & 20:30-23:30, closed Sat-Sun, near the City Hall square, off Carrer de Jaume I up Carrer Dagueria at Carrer Lledo 1, tel. 933-198-253).

Popular Chain Restaurants: Barcelona enjoys a chain of several bright, modern restaurants. These five are a hit for their modern, artfully presented Spanish and Mediterranean cuisine, crisp ambience, and unbeatable prices. Because of their three-course €9 lunches and €16-20 dinners (both with wine), all are crowded with locals and in-the-know tourists (all open daily 13:00-15:45 & 20:30-23:30, unless otherwise noted). My favorite of the bunch is **La Crema Canela,** which feels cozier than the others and is the only one that takes reservations (opens at 20:00 for dinner, 30 yards north of Plaça Reial at Passatge de Madoz 6, tel. 933-182-744). The rest are notorious for long lines at the door—arrive 30 minutes

BARCELONA

before opening, or be prepared to wait. Like La Crema Canela, the next two are also within a block of the Plaça Reial: **La Fonda** (opens at 19:00 for dinner, Carrer dels Escudellers 10, very close to a seedy stretch of street—approach it from the Ramblas rather than from Plaça Reial, tel. 933-017-515) and **Les Quinze Nits** (on Plaça Reial at #6—you'll see the line, tel. 933-173-075). The fourth place, **La Dolça Herminia,** is near the Catalan Concert Hall (2 blocks toward Ramblas from Catalan Concert Hall at Carrer de les Magdalenes 27, tel. 933-170-676). The fifth restaurant in the chain, **La Rita,** is described later, under "Restaurants in the Eixample."

Tapas on Carrer de la Mercè in the Barri Gòtic

Barcelona boasts great *tascas*—colorful local tapas bars. Get small plates (for maximum sampling) by asking for "tapas," not the bigger *"raciones."* Glasses of *vino tinto* go for about €0.50. And though trendy uptown restaurants are safer, better-lit, and come with English menus and less grease, these places will stain your journal. The neighborhood's dark, the regulars are rough-edged, and you'll get a glimpse of a crusty Barcelona from before the affluence hit. Try *pimientos de padrón*—Russian roulette with peppers that are lightly fried in oil and salted...only a few are jalapeño-spicy. At the cider bars, it's traditional to order *queso de cabrales* (a traditional, very moldy bleu cheese) and spicy chorizo (sausage), ideally prepared *al diablo* ("devil-style")—soaked in wine, then flambéed at your table. Several places serve *leche de pantera* (panther milk)—liquor mixed with milk.

From the bottom of the Ramblas (near the Columbus Monument), hike east along Carrer Clave. Then follow the small street that runs along the right side of the church (Carrer de la Mercè), stopping at the *tascas* that look fun. For a montage of edible memories, wander Carrer de la Mercè west to east and consider these spots, stopping wherever looks most inviting. I've listed ye olde dives, but there are many trendy places here as well. Most of these places close down around 23:00.

La Pulpería (at #16) has a bit less character than the others, but eases you into the scene with fried fish, octopus, and *patatas bravas,* all with Galician Ribeiro wine. Farther down at the corner (#28), **La Plata** keeps things wonderfully simple, serving extremely cheap plates of sardines (€1.70), little salads (€1.50), and small glasses of keg wine (less than €1). **Tasca el Corral** (#17) serves mountain favorites from northern Spain by the half-*ración* (see their list), such as *queso de cabrales* and chorizo *al diablo* with *sidra* (apple wine sold by the €5 bottle). **Sidrería Tasca La Socarrena** (#21) offers hard cider from Asturias in €5 bottles with *queso de cabrales* and chorizo. At the end of Carrer de la Mercè, **Cerveceria Vendimia** slings tasty clams and mussels (hearty *raciones* for €4-6

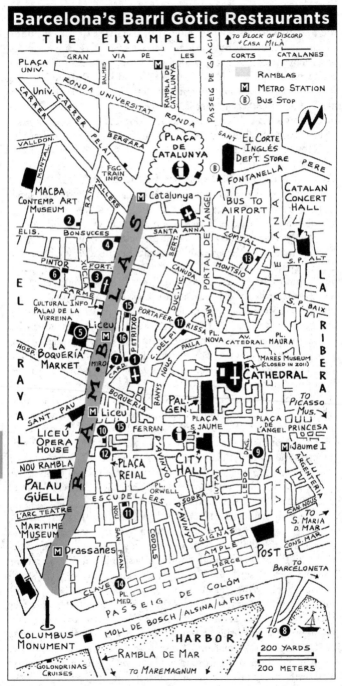

Barcelona's Barri Gòtic Restaurants

Restaurants Key

1. Taverna Basca Irati
2. Restaurant Elisabets
3. Café Granja Viader
4. Supermarket
5. La Bouquería Market Eateries
6. Biocenter Veggie Rest.
7. Juicy Jones
8. To La Mar Salada
9. Café de l'Academia
10. La Crema Canela
11. La Fonda
12. Les Quinze Nits
13. La Dolça Herminia
14. Carrer de la Mercè Tapas Bars
15. Casa Colomina
16. Granja La Pallaresa
17. Fargas Chocolate Shop

a plate—they don't do smaller portions, so order sparingly). Sit at the bar and point to what looks good. Their *pulpo* (octopus) is more expensive and is the house specialty. Carrer Ample and Carrer Gignas, the streets parallel to Carrer de la Mercè inland, have more refined bar-hopping possibilities.

In the Ribera District, near the Picasso Museum

La Ribera, the hottest neighborhood in town, sparkles with eclectic and trendy as well as subdued and classy little restaurants hidden in the small lanes surrounding the Church of Santa Maria del Mar. While I've listed a few well-established tapas bars that are great for light meals, to really dine, simply wander around for 15 minutes and pick the place that tickles your gastronomic fancy. I think those who say they know what's best in this area are kidding themselves—it's changing too fast and the choices are too personal. One thing's for sure: There are a lot of talented and hardworking restaurateurs with plenty to offer. Consider starting your evening off with a glass of fine wine at one of the *enotecas* on the square facing the Church of Santa Maria del Mar. Sit back and admire the pure Catalan Gothic architecture. My first three listings are all on the main drag, Carrer de l'Argenteria. For locations, see the map on page 1287.

Sagardi offers a wonderful array of Basque goodies—tempting *pinchos* and *montaditos* at €1.80 each—along its huge bar. Ask for a plate and graze (just take whatever looks good). You can sit on the square with your plunder for 20 percent extra. Wash it down with Txakolí, a Basque white wine poured from the spout of a huge wooden barrel into a glass as you watch. When you're done, they'll count your toothpicks to tally your bill (daily 12:00-24:00, Carrer de l'Argenteria 62-64, tel. 933-199-993).

Sagardi Euskal Taberna, hiding behind the thriving Sagardi

BARCELONA

tapas bar (described above), is a mod, rustic, and minimalist woody restaurant committed to serving Basque T-bone steaks and grilled specialties with only the best ingredients. Crisp, friendly service and a big open kitchen with sizzling grills contribute to the ambience. Reservations are smart (€10-20 first courses, €20-30 second courses, plan on €45 for dinner, daily 13:00-16:00 & 20:00-24:00, Carrer de l'Argenteria 62, tel. 933-199-993).

Taller de Tapas ("Tapas Workshop") is an upscale, trendier tapas bar and restaurant that dishes up well-presented, sophisticated morsels and light meals in a medieval-stone yet mod setting. Pay 10 percent more to sit on the square. Elegant, but a bit stuffy, it's favored by local office workers who aren't into the Old World Gothic stuff. Four plates will fill a hungry diner for about €20 (daily 8:30-24:00, Carrer de l'Argenteria 51, tel. 932-688-559).

El Xampanyet, a colorful family-run bar with a fun-loving staff (Juan Carlos, his mom, and the man who may be his father), specializes in tapas and anchovies. Don't be put off by the seafood from a tin: Catalans like it this way. A *sortido* (assorted plate) of *carne* (meat) or *pescado* (fish) with *pa amb tomaquet* (bread with crushed-tomato spread) makes for a fun meal. It's filled with tourists during the sightseeing day, but this is a local favorite after dark. The scene is great but—especially during busy times—it's tough without Spanish skills. When I asked about the price, Juan Carlos said, "Who cares? The ATM is just across the street." Plan on spending €20 for a meal with wine (same price at bar or table, Tue-Sat 12:00-16:00 & 19:00-23:30, Sun 12:00-16:00 only, closed Mon, a half-block beyond the Picasso Museum at Montcada 22, tel. 933-197-003).

In the Eixample

The people-packed boulevards of the Eixample (Passeig de Gràcia and Rambla de Catalunya) are lined with appetizing eateries featuring breezy outdoor seating. Choose between a real restaurant or an upscale tapas bar. For locations, see the map on page 1310.

Restaurants in the Eixample

La Rita is a fresh and dressy little restaurant serving Catalan cuisine near the Block of Discord. Their lunches (three courses with wine for €8, Mon-Fri 13:00-15:45) and dinners (€15, à la carte, daily 20:30-23:30) are a great value. Like most of its sister restaurants—described under "Eating in Barcelona—In the Barri Gòtic," earlier—it takes no reservations and its prices attract long lines, so arrive just before the doors open...or wait (a block from Metro: Passeig de Gràcia, near corner of Carrer de Pau Claris and Carrer Arago at Arago 279, tel. 934-872-376).

La Bodegueta is an atmospheric below-street-level bodega serving hearty wines, homemade vermouth, *anchoas* (anchovies), tapas, and *flautas*—sandwiches made with flute-thin baguettes. Its daily €12 lunch special of three courses with wine is served 13:00-16:00. A long block from Gaudí's Casa Milà, this makes a fine sightseeing break (Mon-Sat 8:00-24:00, Sun 19:00-24:00, at intersection with Provenza, Rambla de Catalunya 100, Metro: Provença, tel. 932-154-894).

Restaurante la Palmera serves a mix of Catalan, Mediterranean, and French cuisine in an elegant yet smoky room with bottle-lined walls. The smoke keeps out the tourists. This place offers great food, service, and value—for me, a very special meal in Barcelona. They have three zones: the classic main room, a more forgettable adjacent room, and a few outdoor tables. I like the classic room. Reservations are smart (€12 plates, creative €16 six-plate *degustation* lunch, Tue-Sat 13:00-15:45 & 20:30-23:15, closed Sun-Mon, Enric Granados 57, at the corner with Mallorca, tel. 934-532-338).

Restaurant Flauta fills two floors with enthusiastic eaters (I prefer the ground floor). It's fresh and modern, with a fun, no-stress menu featuring €5 small plates, creative €4 *flauta* sandwiches, and a €12.50 three-course lunch deal including a drink. Good €2.30 wines by the glass are listed on the blackboard. This is a place to order high on the menu for a satisfying, moderately priced meal (Mon-Sat 13:00-24:00, closed Sun, fun-loving and helpful staff recommends the fried vegetables, no reservations, just off Via Diputació at d'Aribau 23, tel. 933-237-038).

Cinc Sentits ("Five Senses"), with only about 30 seats, is my gourmet recommendation. It's a chic, minimalist, smoke-free, but slightly snooty place where all the attention goes to the fine service and elegantly presented dishes. It's run by Catalans who lived in Canada (so there's absolutely no language barrier) and serve avant-garde cuisine inspired by Catalan traditions and ingredients. Their €49 and €69 *degustation menus* are unforgettable extravaganzas. Reservations are required (Tue-Sat 13:30-15:00 & 20:30-23:00, closed Sun-Mon, near Carrer d'Aragó at d'Aribau 58, tel. 933-239-490).

El Racó is a local favorite for "creative Mediterranean cuisine"—pasta, pizza, crêpes, and salads (about €7-9 each) in a modern, lively, cavernous-but-bright, air-conditioned setting (daily 13:00-24:00, Rambla de Catalunya 25, tel. 933-175-688).

A Bit Farther Out: **Hofmann** is a renowned cooking school with an excellent if pricey restaurant serving modern Mediterranean market cuisine. Dress up and dine in intimate rooms papered with photos of famous patrons. The four-course €40 lunches are made up of just what the students are working on that day—so there's no choice (watch the students as they cook). Dinners can easily cost twice as much (à la carte). Save room (and euros) for the incredible desserts. Reserve long in advance, because locals love this place (Mon-Fri 13:30-15:15 & 21:00-23:15, closed Sat-Sun and Aug, 4 blocks northwest of Casa Milà at La Granada del Penedès 14-16, tel. 932-187-165, www.hofmann-bcn.com).

Tapas Bars in the Eixample

Many trendy and touristic tapas bars in the Eixample offer a cheery welcome and slam out the appetizers. These three are my favorites.

Quasi Queviures ("**Qu Qu**" for short) serves upscale tapas, sandwiches, or the whole nine yards—classic food served fast from a fun menu with modern decor and a high-energy sports-bar ambience. It's bright, clean, and not too crowded. Walk through their enticing kitchen to get to the tables in back. Committed to developing a loyal following, they claim, "We fertilize our local customers with daily specialties" (€2-5 tapas, €5 dinner salads, €8 plates, prices 17 percent higher on the terrace, daily 8:00-24:00, between Gran Via and Via Diputació at Passeig de Gràcia 24, tel. 933-174-512).

Ciudad Condal Cerveceria brags that it serves the best *montaditos* (€2-3 little open-faced sandwiches) and beers in Barcelona. It's an Eixample favorite, with an elegant bar and tables plus good seating out on the Rambla de Catalunya for all that people-watching action. It's classier than Qu Qu and packed after 21:00, when you'll likely need to put your name on a list and wait. While it has no restaurant-type menu, the list of tapas and *montaditos* is easy, fun, and comes with a great variety (including daily specials). This place is a cut above your normal tapas bar, but with reasonable prices (most tapas around €4-5, daily until 24:00, facing the intersection of Gran Via and Rambla de Catalunya at Rambla de Catalunya 18, tel. 933-181-997).

La Tramoia, at the opposite corner from Ciudad Condal Cerveceria, serves piles of cheap *montaditos* and tapas at its ground-floor bar and at nice tables inside and out. If Ciudad Condal Cerveceria is jammed, you're more likely to find a seat here. The brasserie-style restaurant upstairs bustles with happy local eaters enjoying grilled meats (€6-15 plates), but I'd stay downstairs for the €4-8 tapas (open daily, also facing the intersection of Gran Via and Rambla de Catalunya at Rambla de Catalunya 15, tel. 934-123-634).

Budget Options Around Town

Bright, clean, and inexpensive sandwich shops proudly hold the cultural line against the fast-food invasion hamburgerizing the rest of Europe. Catalan sandwiches are made to order with crunchy

French bread. Rather than butter, locals prefer *tomaquet* (a spread of crushed tomatoes). You'll see two big local chains (Pans & Company and Bocatta) everywhere, but these serve mass-produced McBaguettes ordered from a multilingual menu. I've had better luck with hole-in-the-wall sandwich shops—virtually as numerous as the chains—where you can see exactly what you're getting. Kebab places are another good, super-cheap standby.

A Short, Sweet Walk

Let me propose this three-stop dessert (or, since these places close well before the traditional Barcelona dinnertime, a late-afternoon snack). You'll try a refreshing glass of *orxata*, munch some *churros con chocolate*, and visit a fine *xocolateria*, all within a three-minute walk of one another in the Barri Gòtic just off the Ramblas. Start at the corner of Carrer Portaferrissa midway down the Ramblas. For the best atmosphere, begin your walk at about 18:00 (note that the last place is closed on Sun). For locations, see the map on page 1316.

Turrón **at Casa Colomina:** Walk down Carrer Portaferrissa to #8 (on the right). Casa Colomina, founded in 1908, specializes in homemade *turróns*—a variation of nougat made with almond, honey, and sugar, brought to Spain by the Moors 1,200 years ago. Three different kinds are sold in big €12 slabs: *blando*, *duro*, and *yema*—soft, hard, and yolk (€2 smaller chunks also available). In the summer, the shop also sells ice cream and the refreshing *orxata* (or *horchata*—a drink made from the *chufa* nut). Order a glass and ask to see and eat a *chufa* nut (a.k.a. earth almond or tiger nut; Mon-Sat 10:00-20:30, Sun 12:30-20:30, tel. 933-122-511).

Churros con Chocolate **at Granja La Pallaresa:** Continue down Carrer Portaferrissa, taking a right at Carrer Petritxol to this fun-loving *xocolateria*. Older, elegant ladies gather here for the Spanish equivalent of tea time—dipping their greasy *churros* into pudding-thick cups of hot chocolate (€4.10 for five *churros con chocolate*, Mon-Fri 9:00-13:00 & 16:00-21:00, Sat-Sun 9:00-13:00 & 17:00-21:00, Carrer Petritxol 11, tel. 933-022-036).

Homemade Chocolate at Fargas: For your last stop, head for the ornate Fargas chocolate shop. Continue down Carrer Petritxol to the square, hook left through the two-part square, and then left up Carrer del Pi—it's on the corner of Portaferrissa and Carrer del Pi. Since the 19th century, gentlemen with walking canes have dropped by here for their chocolate fix. Founded in 1827, this is one of the oldest and most traditional chocolate shops in Barcelona. If they're not too busy, ask to see the old chocolate mill *("¿Puedo ver el molino?")* to the right of the counter. They sell even tiny quantities (one little morsel) by the weight, so don't be shy. A delicious chunk of the crumbly semi-sweet house specialty costs €0.45 (tray by the mill). The tempting bonbons in the window cost about €1 each (Mon-Fri 9:30-13:30 & 16:00-20:00, Sat 10:00-14:00 & 16:00-20:00, closed Sun, tel. 933-020-342).

Barcelona Connections

By Train

Unless otherwise noted, all of these trains depart from the Sants Station; however, some trains also stop at other stations more convenient to the downtown tourist zone: França Station, Passeig de Gràcia, or Plaça de Catalunya. Figure out if your train stops at these stations (and board there) to save yourself the trip to Sants.

The **AVE train to Madrid** has shaved hours off that journey, making it faster than flying (when you consider that you're zipping from downtown to downtown). The train departs almost hourly. The nonstop train is a little more expensive (€135, 2.5-3 hours) than the slightly slower train that makes a few stops and adds about a half-hour (€115, 3.5 hours). Regular reserved AVE tickets can be prepurchased at www.renfe.com and picked up at the station. If you have a railpass, you'll pay only a reservation fee of €25 for first class, which includes a meal (€15 second class, buy at any train station in Spain). Passholders can't reserve online through RENFE but can make the reservation at www.raileurope.com for delivery before leaving the US ($17 in second class, $40 in first class).

From Barcelona by Train to: Sevilla (3/day—two fast, 5.5 hours, €140; one slow, 12 hours, €62), **Granada** (1/day Wed, Fri, and Sun only, 11.5 hours, €61; also 1 night train/day, 12 hours, €63), **Lisbon** (no direct trains, head to Madrid and then catch night train to Lisbon, 17 hours, about €100), **Nice** (1/day via Montpelier, about €100; cheaper connections possible with multiple changes including Cerbère), **Paris** (3/day, 9 hours, 1-2 changes; 1 night train/day, 12 hours, about €200, or €50 with railpass, reservation mandatory). Train info: toll tel. 902-320-320, www.renfe.com.

By Bus

Destinations include **Madrid** (14/day, 8 hours, €28—a fraction of the AVE train price, departs from Nord bus station at Metro: Arc de Triomf on line 1, bus info toll tel. 902-260-606, Alsa bus company toll tel. 902-422-242). For bus schedules, see www.barcelonanord.com.

By Plane

Check the reasonable flights from Barcelona to Sevilla or Madrid. Vueling is Iberia's most popular discount airline (e.g., Barcelona-Madrid flights as low as €40 if booked in advance, toll tel. 902-

333-933, www.vueling.com). Iberia (toll tel. 902-400-500, www
.iberia.com) and Air Europa (toll tel. 902-401-501 or 932-983-907,
www.aireuropa.com) offer €80 flights to Madrid. Also, for flights
to other parts of Europe, consider British Airways (toll tel. 902-
111-333, www.britishairways.com), easyJet (toll tel. 902-299-992,
www.easyjet.com), and Ryanair (www.ryanair.com).

Most flights use Barcelona's **El Prat de Llobregat Airport**
(tel. 913-211-000). Its two terminals serve both domestic and
international flights and are linked by shuttle buses. Air France,
Air Europa, American, British, Continental, Iberia, Lufthansa,
Spanair, US Airways, Vueling, and others use the newer terminal 1. EasyJet, Delta, and minor airlines use terminal 2. Ryanair
uses a smaller airstrip 60 miles away, called **Girona-Costa Brava
Airport** (tel. 972-186-600). Information on both airports can be
found on the official Spanish airport website, www.aena.es.

For details on getting between either airport and downtown
Barcelona, see "Arrival in Barcelona—By Plane" on page 1266.

BARCELONA

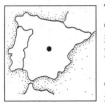

MADRID

Today's Madrid is upbeat and vibrant, still enjoying a post-Franco renaissance. You'll feel it. Even the living-statue street performers have a twinkle in their eyes.

Madrid is the hub of Spain. This modern capital—Europe's highest, at more than 2,000 feet—has a population of 3.2 million. Like its people, the city is relatively young. In 1561, when Spain ruled the world's most powerful empire, King Philip II decided to move his capital from Toledo to Madrid. One hundred years ago, Madrid had only 400,000 people—so the majority of today's Madrid is modern sprawl surrounding an intact, easy-to-navigate historic core.

To support their bids to host the 2012 and 2016 Olympics, Madrid began some massive city-improvement building projects. Although they lost both bids (to London and then Rio de Janeiro), the construction continues as if they'd won. Politicians who back these projects have been rewarded both financially (locals claim some corrupt officials are getting kickbacks) and politically— residents love to see all the new squares, pedestrian streets, belt-way tunnels, parks, and Metro stations popping up. Optimists are eyeing other Olympics bids for 2020 or 2024, which gives them an excuse to keep up the construction.

Madrid's ambitious improvement plans brought about the creation of a wonderful pedestrian street crossing the city from the Prado to the Royal Palace. Strolling along Calle de las Huertas (from Plaza Mayor to the Prado) or the recently pedestrianized Calle del Arenal (from Puerta del Sol toward the Royal Palace), you'll see how the investment is turning ramshackle zones into trendy ones. The macro-Metro station in Puerta del Sol, with a

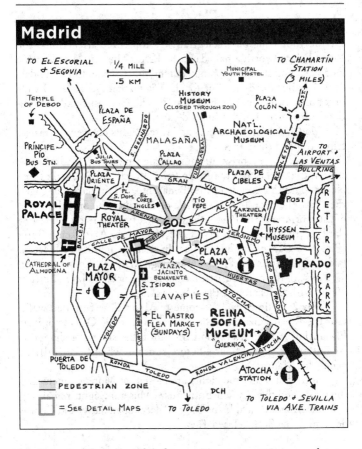

Madrid

big hyper-modern glass fish for a main entrance, accommodates a super-efficient commuter line that connects the two train stations and the main square. By installing posts to keep cars off sidewalks, making the streets safer after dark, and restoring old buildings, Madrid is working hard to make itself more livable...and fun to visit.

Tourists are the real winners. Dive headlong into the grandeur and intimate charm of Madrid. The lavish Royal Palace, with its gilded rooms and frescoed ceilings, rivals Versailles. The Prado has Europe's top collection of paintings. The city's huge Retiro Park invites you to take a shady siesta and hopscotch through a mosaic of lovers, families, skateboarders, pets walking their masters, and expert bench-sitters. Save time for Madrid's elegant shops and people-friendly pedestrian zones. On Sundays, cheer for the bull at a bullfight or bargain like mad at a mega-size flea market. Lively Madrid has enough street-singing, bar-hopping, and people-watching vitality to give any visitor a boost of youth.

Planning Your Time

Divide your time between Madrid's top three attractions: the Royal Palace (worth a half-day), the Prado Museum (also worth a half-day), and its bar-hopping contemporary scene. On a Sunday, consider allotting extra time for the flea market (year-round) and/or a bullfight (some Sundays March-mid-Oct, especially during San Isidro festival mid-May-mid-June).

Madrid is worth two days and three nights on even the fastest trip. I'd spend them this way:

Day 1: Take a brisk 20-minute good-morning-Madrid walk from Puerta del Sol to the Prado (from Puerta del Sol, walk three blocks south to Plaza de Jacinto Benavente, left to Plaza del Ángel, then take the pedestrianized Calle de las Huertas). Spend the rest of the morning at the Prado, then take an afternoon siesta in Retiro Park, or tackle modern art at the Centro de Arte Reina Sofía (Picasso's *Guernica*) and/or the Thyssen-Bornemisza Museum. Ride bus #27 from the Prado out through Madrid's modern section for a dose of the non-touristy, no-nonsense big city. Have dinner at 20:00, with tapas around Plaza Santa Ana.

Day 2: Follow my "Welcome to Madrid" self-guided walk, tour the Royal Palace, and have lunch at Café de Oriente or near Plaza Mayor. Your afternoon is free for other sights, or shopping. Be out at the magic hour—before sunset—when beautifully lit people fill Madrid.

Note that many top sights are closed on Monday, including the Prado and the Thyssen-Bornemisza Museum; sights remaining open on Monday include the Royal Palace (open daily) and Centro de Arte Reina Sofía (closed Tue).

Orientation to Madrid

Puerta del Sol marks the center of Madrid. No major sight is more than a 20-minute walk or a €4 taxi ride from this central square. The Royal Palace (to the west) and the Prado Museum and Retiro Park (to the east) frame Madrid's historic center. This zone can be covered on foot. Southwest of Puerta del Sol is a 17th-century district with the slow-down-and-smell-the-cobbles Plaza Mayor and memories of preindustrial Spain. North of Puerta del Sol runs Calle de Gran Vía, and between the two are lively pedestrian shopping streets. Gran Vía, bubbling with shops and cinemas, leads to the modern Plaza de España. From the Prado, the Paseo de la Castellana is a straight boulevard cutting north through the modern town to the "gateway to Europe" towers. Between Puerta del Sol and the Atocha train station stretches the colorful, up-and-coming multiethnic Lavapiés district.

Tourist Information

Madrid's many TIs share a phone number (tel. 915-881-636) and website (www.esmadrid.com).

The best TI is on **Plaza Mayor** (daily 9:30-20:30, air-con, limited free Internet access). It's centrally located and innovative, offering several €4 English guided walks a day (described later in "Tours in Madrid") and a free downloadable MP3 self-guided tour. They also provide the SATE police service to aid foreigners who've run into trouble.

Madrid's other TIs have the same hours (Mon-Sat 8:00-20:00, Sun 9:00-14:00): near the **Prado Museum** (Duque de Medinaceli 2, behind Palace Hotel); **Chamartín train station** (near track 20); **Atocha train station** (in AVE side); and **airport** (Terminals 1 and 4). Small info kiosks are in **Plaza de Callao** and in **Plaza de Cibeles** (daily 9:30-20:30).

At any TI, pick up a map, the handy *Traveler's Tips* booklet, the *Es Madrid* English-language monthly, and confirm your sightseeing plans. The TI's free *Public Transport* map is very well-designed to meet travelers' needs and has the most detailed map of the center. Get this and use it. TIs have the latest on bullfights and zarzuela (light Spanish opera). Energetic travelers can save money buying the **Madrid Card,** which covers most of the city's museums (€32/24 hours, €42/48 hours, €52/72 hours).

For entertainment listings, the TI's printed material is not very good. Pick up the Spanish-language weekly entertainment guide ***Guía del Ocio*** (€1, sold at newsstands) or check their complete website: www.guiadelocio.com. It lists daily live music *("Conciertos"),* museums *("Museos"*—with the latest times and special exhibits), restaurants (an exhaustive listing), TV schedules, and movies ("V.O." means original version, *"V.O. en inglés sub"* means a movie is played in English with Spanish subtitles rather than dubbed). For listings of activities for kids, see www.guiadelnino.com.

For tips on sightseeing, hotels, and more, visit www.madridman.com, run with passion by American Scott Martin.

Arrival in Madrid
By Train

Madrid's two train stations, Chamartín and Atocha, are both on Metro lines with easy access to downtown Madrid. (For Atocha Station, use the "Atocha RENFE" Metro stop; the stop named simply "Atocha" is farther from the station.) Chamartín handles most international trains and the AVE train to Segovia. Atocha generally covers southern Spain, as well as the AVE trains to Barcelona, Córdoba, Sevilla, and Toledo. Both stations offer long-distance trains *(largo recorridos)* as well as smaller local trains (*regionales* and *cercanías*) to nearby destinations.

Greater Madrid

N

1 MILE
1 KM

CHAMARTÍN
TRAIN STATION

Chamartín

PLAZA DE
CASTILLA

Bernabéu
Stadium

Santiago
Bernabéu

M-30 FREEWAY

TO BARAJAS
AIRPORT,
BARCELONA 4

A-2

TO EL ESCORIAL
& SEGOVIA

A-6

FERNANDEZ

J. COSTA

AMÉRICA

CLOTHING
MUSEUM

ARCO
VICTORIA

MUSEUM
OF THE
AMERICAS

SAN BERNARDO

SOROLLA
MUSEUM

Iglesia

Ventas

VENTAS
BULLRING

Moncloa

PRINCESA

MALA-
SAÑA

RECOLETOS

PLAZA
COLÓN

ALCALÁ

CASA
DE
CAMPO

PLAZA
ESPAÑA

Norte

GRAN

VÍA

Sol

RETIRO
PARK

PRÍNCIPE
PÍO
TRAIN & BUS
STATIONS

Royal
Palace

SOL

Prado

PLAZA
MAYOR

Atocha
RENFE

MEDITERRANEO

A-3

MANZANARES

CALLE
TOLEDO

CABEZA

ATOCHA
TRAIN STN.

ROYAL
TAPESTRY
FACTORY

Menéndez
Pelajo

MÉNDEZ ALVARO

Méndez
Álvaro

DCH

TO 5 & TOLEDO VIA N·401

TO TOLEDO & SEVILLA
VIA: A.V.E. TRAINS

1 Estación Sur de Autobuses

2 Principe Pío Station
(Sepulvedana Buses)

3 Intercambiador de Moncloa

4 To Intercambiador de Avenida
de América

5 To Plaza Elíptica Station

☐ = HISTORIC CITY CENTER
SEE DETAIL MAPS

M METRO STATION - NOT ALL SHOWN

→ BUS #27 SELF-GUIDED TOUR

MADRID

Buying Tickets: You can buy tickets at the stations, at travel agencies, or online. Convenient travel agencies for buying tickets in Madrid include the El Corte Inglés Travel Agency at Atocha (Mon-Fri 8:00-22:00, Sat-Sun 10:00-18:00, on ground floor of AVE side at the far end) and the El Corte Inglés department store at Puerta del Sol (see "Travel Agencies" on page 1332).

Traveling Between Chamartín and Atocha Stations: To travel between the two stations, you can take the Metro (line 1, 30-40 minutes, €1, see "Getting Around Madrid" on page 1332), but the *cercanías* trains are faster (6/hour, 13 minutes, Atocha-Sol-Chamartín lines C3 and C4 are the most convenient, €1.25, free with railpass or any train ticket to Madrid—show it at ticket window in the middle of the turnstiles, depart from Atocha's track 2 and generally Chamartín's track 1, 3, 8, or 9—but check the *Salidas Inmediatas* board to be sure).

Chamartín Station

The TI is opposite track 19. The impressively large information, tickets, and customer-service office is at track 11. You can relax in the Sala VIP Club if you have a first-class railpass and first-class seat or sleeper reservations (between tracks 13 and 14, cooler of free drinks). Luggage storage *(consignas)* is across the street, opposite track 17. The station's Metro stop is also called Chamartín (not "Pinar de Chamartín").

Atocha Station

The station is split in two: an AVE side (mostly long-distance trains) and a *cercanías* side (mostly local trains to the suburbs or *cercanías* and the Metro for connecting into downtown). These two parts are connected by a corridor of shops. Each side of the station has separate schedules and customer-service offices. The TI, which is in the AVE side, offers tourist info, but no train info (Mon-Sat 8:00-20:00, Sun 9:00-14:00, tel. 915-284-630).

Atocha has three ticket offices: The *cercanías* side has a small office for local trains and a big office for major trains (such as AVE). The AVE side has a pleasant, airy ticket office that also sells tickets for AVE and other long-distance trains (there are two lines: "Advance Sale" or "Selling Out Today"/"Departures Today"). If the line at one office is long, check the other offices. Grab a number ("Su turno") from a machine to get your turn in line.

Atocha's **AVE side,** which is in the towering old-station building, is remarkable for the lush, tropical garden filling its grand hall. It has the slick AVE trains, other fast trains (Grandes Líneas), a pharmacy (daily 8:00-22:00, facing garden), and the wicker-elegant Samarkanda—both an affordable cafeteria (daily 13:00-20:00) and a pricey restaurant (daily from 21:00, tel. 915-309-746). Luggage

Cheap Tricks in Madrid

- Instead of expensive city tour buses, take bus #27 on a €1 sightseeing joyride past some major Madrid landmarks. Catch the bus in front of the Royal Botanical Garden on the Paseo del Prado and ride it to Plaza Castilla (the end of the line). This ride is described on page 1354.
- You can enter some major sights for free at certain times (for example, the Prado is free Tue-Sat 18:00-20:00 and Sun 17:00-20:00, while the Centro de Arte Reina Sofía is free Mon-Fri after 19:00, Sat after 14:30 and all day Sun). These Madrid sights are always free: CaixaForum, Naval Museum, Chapel of San Antonio de la Florida, Bullfighting Museum, Caja Madrid, and the Temple de Debod.
- The Plaza Mayor TI organizes cheap 1.5-hour English-language guided walks. Called Discover Madrid, they have different themes, run several times a day, and cost only €4.

storage *(consigna)* is below Samarkanda (daily 6:00-22:20). In the departure lounge on the upper floor, TV monitors announce track numbers. For information, try the *Información* counter (daily 6:30-22:30), next to Centro Servicios AVE (which handles only AVE changes and problems). The *Atención al Cliente* office deals with problems on Grandes Líneas (daily 6:30-23:30). Also on the AVE side is the Club AVE/Sala VIP, a lounge reserved solely for AVE business-class travelers and for first-class ticket-holders or Eurailers with a first-class reservation (upstairs, past the security check on right; free drinks, newspapers, showers, and info service).

On the **cercanías side** of Atocha Station you'll find the local *cercanías* trains, *regionales* trains, some eastbound faster trains, and the "Atocha RENFE" Metro stop. The *Atención al Cliente* office in the *cercanías* section has information only on trains to destinations near Madrid.

Terrorism Memorial: The terrorist bombings of March 11, 2004, took place in Atocha and on local lines going into and out of the station. Security is understandably tight here. A moving memorial is in the *cercanías* part of the station near the Atocha RENFE Metro stop. Walk inside and under the cylinder to read the thousands of condolence messages in many languages (daily 11:00-14:00 & 17:00-19:00). Its 36-foot cylindrical glass memorial towers are visible from outside on the street.

By Plane

For information on Madrid's Barajas Airport, see the end of this chapter.

Helpful Hints

Theft Alert: Be wary of pickpockets—anywhere, anytime. Areas of particular risk are Puerta del Sol (the central square), El Rastro (the flea market), Gran Vía (the paseo zone: Plaza del Callao to Plaza de España), the Ópera Metro station (or anywhere on the Metro), bus #27, the airport, and any crowded streets. Be alert to the people around you: Someone wearing a heavy jacket in the summer is likely a pickpocket. Lately, Romanian teenagers dress like American teens and work the areas around the three big art museums; being under 18, they can't be arrested by the police. Assume a fight or any commotion is a scam to distract people about to become victims of a pickpocket. Wear your money belt. The small streets north of Gran Vía are particularly dangerous, even before nightfall. Muggings occur, but are rare. For help, see the next listing.

Tourist Emergency Aid: SATE is a centrally located police office offering emergency aid to victims of theft. Help ranges from canceling stolen credit cards to assistance in reporting a crime (daily 9:00-22:00, near Plaza de Santo Domingo at Calle Leganitos 19, 24-hour tel. 902-102-112, English spoken once you get connected to a person). It's best to call in your report to the SATE line in English, then go to the police station (where they'll likely speak only Spanish) to sign your statement.

The Plaza Mayor TI also serves as a SATE branch of sorts. You may see a police station in the Sol Metro station; this office handles only Metro theft.

Prostitution: Diverse by European standards, Madrid is spilling over with immigrants from South America, North Africa, and Eastern Europe. Many young women come here, fall on hard times, and end up on the streets. While it's illegal to make money from someone else selling sex (i.e., pimping), prostitutes over 18 can solicit legally (€30, FYI). Calle de la Montera (leading from Puerta del Sol to Plaza Red de San Luis) is lined with what looks like a bunch of high-school girls skipping out of school for a cigarette break. Again, don't stray north of Gran Vía around Calle de la Luna and Plaza Santa María Soledad—while the streets may look inviting... this area is a meat-eating flower.

Embassies: The US Embassy is at Serrano 75 (tel. 915-872-200); the Canadian Embassy is at Paseo de la Castellana 259 D (tel. 913-828-400).

One-Stop Shopping: The dominant department store is **El Corte Inglés,** which takes up several huge buildings in the commercial pedestrian zone just off Puerta del Sol (Mon-Sat 10:00-22:00, Sun 11:00-21:00, navigate with the help of the info desk near the door of the main building—the tallest

MADRID

building with the biggest sign, Preciados 3, tel. 913-798-000). They give out good, free Madrid maps. In the main building you'll find two handy travel agencies (see listing at end of this section), a post office, a modern cafeteria (seventh floor), and a supermarket with a fancy "Club del Gourmet" section in the basement. Across the street is its Librería branch—a huge bookstore. The second building fronting Puerta del Sol contains six floors of music, computers, home electronics, and SIM cards for mobile phones, with a box office on the top floor selling tickets to whatever's on in town. Locals figure you'll find anything you need at El Corte Inglés. Salespeople wear flag pins indicating which languages they can speak.

Internet Access: There are plenty of centrally located places to check your email. Any *locutorio* call center should have a few computers and is generally the cheapest Internet option in the neighborhood. Near Plaza Santa Ana, **La Bolsa de Minutos** has plenty of fast terminals, offers a disc-burning service, and is a productive place to kill time if you're waiting for the tapas-crawl action to heat up (daily 9:30-24:00, Calle Espoz y Mina 17, tel. 915-322-622).

Phone Cards: You can buy cheap international phone cards at some newsstands, at Internet cafés, or at the easy-to-find *locutorio* call centers (but these are generally uncomfortable places to sit and make calls). When choosing a phone card, remember that toll-free numbers start with 900, whereas 901 and 902 numbers can be expensive. Ask your hotel if they charge for the 900 number before making calls.

Bookstores: For books in English, try **FNAC Callao** (Calle Preciados 28, tel. 915-956-100), **Casa del Libro** (English on ground floor, Gran Vía 29, tel. 915-212-219), and **El Corte Inglés** (guidebooks and some fiction, in its Librería branch kitty-corner from main store, fronting Puerta del Sol—see "One-Stop Shopping," earlier).

Travel Agencies: The grand department store **El Corte Inglés** has two travel agencies (air and rail tickets, but not reservations for railpass-holders, €2 fee, on first and seventh floors, for hours and contact info see "One-Stop Shopping," earlier).

Getting Around Madrid

If you want to use Madrid's excellent public transit, my two best tips are these: Pick up and study the fine *Public Transit* map/flier (available at TIs), and take full advantage of the cheap 10-ride Metrobus ticket deal.

By Metro: The city's broad streets can be hot and exhausting. A subway trip of even a stop or two saves time and energy. Madrid's Metro is simple, speedy, and cheap (€1/ride within zone

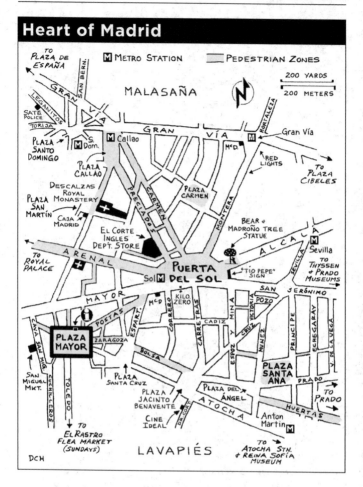

Heart of Madrid

M METRO STATION ▨ PEDESTRIAN ZONES

200 YARDS
200 METERS

TO PLAZA DE ESPAÑA

MALASAÑA

GRAN VÍA

Gran Vía

LEGANITOS
SAN BERN.

SATE POLICE
TORIJA

GRAN VÍA

M Callao

PLAZA SANTO DOMINGO

M S. Dom.

PLAZA CALLAO

RED LIGHTS

TO PLAZA CIBELES

DESCALZAS ROYAL MONASTERY

PLAZA SAN MARTÍN

Caja Madrid

El Corte Ingles Dept. Store

PRECIADOS

CARMEN

PLAZA CARMEN

MONTERA

BEAR & MADROÑO TREE STATUE

ALCALÁ

M Sevilla

TO THYSSEN + PRADO MUSEUMS

TO ROYAL PALACE

ARENAL

PUERTA DEL SOL

Sol M

"TIO PEPE" SIGN

SAN JERÓNIMO

MAYOR

PLAZA MAYOR

POSTAS

ESPARTEROS

ZARAGOZA

MCD

KILO ZERO

CORREOS

CARRETAS

CAPIZ

MINA

POZO

VICTORIA

CRUZ

NUÑEZ

PRINCIPE

ECHEGARAY

N VEGA

BOLSA

ESPOZ

PLAZA SANTA ANA

PRADO

TO PRADO

SAN MIGUEL MKT.

CAVA SAN MIG.

CUCHILLEROS

TOLEDO

PLAZA SANTA CRUZ

PLAZA JACINTO BENAVENTE

CINE IDEAL

DRCOR.

PLAZA DEL ÁNGEL

ATOCHA

HUERTAS

Anton Martín M

TO EL RASTRO FLEA MARKET (SUNDAYS)

LAVAPIÉS

TO ATOCHA STN. + REINA SOFÍA MUSEUM

DCH

A—which covers most of the city, but not trains out to the airport; runs 6:00-1:30 in the morning, www.metromadrid.es or www .ctm-madrid.es). The 10-ride Metrobus ticket can be shared by several travelers and works on both the Metro and buses (€9—or €0.90 per ride, sold at kiosks, tobacco shops, and in Metro). Insert your Metrobus ticket in the turnstile (it usually shows how many rides remain on it), then retrieve it as you pass through. Stations offer free system maps. Navigate by Metro stops (shown on city maps). To transfer, follow signs to the next Metro line (numbered and color-coded). The names of the end stops are used to indicate directions. Green *salida* signs point to the exit. Using neighborhood maps and street signs to exit smartly saves lots of walking. And watch out for thieves.

By Bus: City buses, though not as easy as the Metro, can be

Madrid Metro

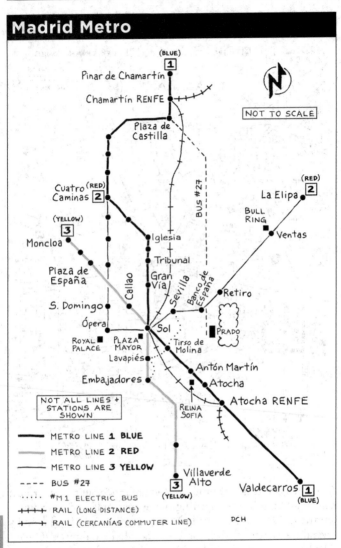

useful (€1 tickets sold on bus, or €9 for a 10-ride Metrobus ticket—see above; bus maps at TI or info booth on Puerta del Sol, poster-size maps are usually posted at bus stops, buses run 6:00-24:00, much less frequent *Buho* buses run all night).

By Taxi: Madrid's 15,000 taxis are reasonably priced and easy to hail. Foursomes travel as cheaply by taxi as by Metro. A ride from the Royal Palace to the Prado costs about €4. After the €2.05 drop charge, the per-kilometer rate depends on the time: *Tarifa 1* (€1/kilometer) should be charged Mon-Fri 6:00-22:00; *Tarifa 2*

(€1.17/kilometer) is valid after 21:00 and on Saturdays, Sundays, and holidays. If your cabbie uses anything rather than *Tarifa 1* on weekdays (shown as an isolated "1" on the meter), you're being cheated. Rates can be higher if you go outside Madrid. Other legitimate charges include the €5.50 supplement for the airport, the €3 supplement for train or bus stations, and €18 per hour for waiting. Make sure the meter is turned on as soon as you get into the cab so the driver can't tack anything onto the official rate. If the driver starts adding up "extras," look for the sticker detailing all legitimate surcharges (which should be on the passenger window).

Tours in Madrid

Discover Madrid—The Plaza Mayor TI organizes a daily schedule of cheap, interesting guided walks. Tours last about 1.5 hours, are in English only, cost €4, and depart daily from the Plaza Mayor TI. Check their detailed booklet or online for specifics and departure times, which change frequently (www.esmadrid.com /descubremadrid_en). Groups can be very small, so you almost feel like you have a private guide. Buy your ticket at the TI, over the phone at 902-221-424, or online at www.entradas.com (search for "Descubre Madrid" within the site). Tours can fill up, so booking at least a few hours in advance is a good idea.

Madrid Vision Hop-On, Hop-Off Bus Tours—Madrid Vision offers two different hop-on, hop-off circuits of the city: historic and modern. Buy a ticket from the driver (€17/1 day, €21/2 days) and you can hop from sight to sight and route to route as you like, listening to a recorded English commentary along the way. Each route has about 15 stops and takes about 1.5 hours, with buses departing every 10 or 20 minutes. The two routes intersect at the south side of Puerta del Sol and in front of Starbucks across from the Prado (daily 9:30-24:00 in summer, 10:00-19:00 in winter, tel. 917-791-888, www.madridvision.es).

LeTango Tours—Carlos Galvin, a Spaniard who speaks flawless English (and has led tours for my groups since 1998), and his wife from Seattle, Jennifer, run city tours and more. Carlos mixes a market walk in the historic center with a culinary-and-tapas crawl to get close to the Madrileños, their culture, and their food. His walk gives a good three-hour orientation and introduction to the fascinating and tasty culture of Madrid, plus travel tips (€98 per person, €120 for gourmet version, 10 percent cash discount, includes light tapas, minimum 2 people, family-friendly, price goes down with more people).

Carlos also offers customized tours (whether city-, regional-, or country-wide), event and hotel bookings, and Madrid apartment rentals (about €189/night for 5 people, €15 per additional person;

tel. 913-694-752, mobile 661-752-458, www.letango.com, info @letango.com).

Local Guides—**Frederico and Cristina** are licensed guides who lead city walks through the pedestrian streets of the historic core of Madrid. Fred, Cris, and their team offer all-ages tours of the big museums, including the Prado, Royal Palace, and Thyssen-Bornemisza and Reina Sofía museums, as well as a tapas tour. If you're looking to get outside Madrid, consider their guided tour to surrounding towns, available on either public or private transit (per-group costs: Mon-Fri €185, Sat-Sun €235, ask for best Rick Steves price; admissions, transportation, and tapas not included; 4 hours, 2- and 6-hour tours also available, tel. 913-102-974, mobile 649-936-222, www.spainfred.com, spainfred@gmail.com).

Inés Muñiz Martin is a good, licensed guide for Madrid and the region. She has led my tour groups in the city for years (€105-175 for 2-5 hours, 25 percent more on weekends and holidays, ask for best Rick Steves price, mobile 629-147-370, www.immguided tours.com, info@immguidedtours.com).

Susana Jarabo, with a master's in art history, is another excellent independent guide (mobile 667-027-722, susanjarabo @yahoo.es).

Hernán Amaya Satt directs a group of licensed guides who take individuals around Madrid, including its museums, on 18 personalized tours (rates vary according to tour and number of people, ask about discount off official rates for Rick Steves readers, family rates, mobile 680-450-231, www.madrid-museum-tours .com, info@madrid-museum-tours.com).

Stephen Drake-Jones, a British expat, gives walks of historic old Madrid almost daily. A historian with a passion for the Duke of Wellington (the general who stopped Napoleon), Stephen founded Madrid's Wellington Society and has been its chairman for over 30 years. For €50, you become a member and get a three-hour tour with three stops for drinks and tapas (morning or afternoon). Eccentric Stephen sorts out Madrid's Habsburg and Bourbon history. He likes his wine—if that's a problem, skip the tour. He also does day trips in the countryside (from €275 per couple) and a four-hour wine-tasting tour that lets you sample regional cheese and ham (€85 per person; mobile 609-143-203, www.wellsoc.org, chairman@wellsoc.org).

Big-Bus City Sightseeing Tours—Julia Travel offers standard guided bus tours departing from Plaza de España 7 (office open Mon-Fri 8:00-19:00, Sat-Sun 8:00-15:00, tel. 915-599-605). Their city tours include a three-hour Madrid tour with a live guide in two or three languages (€21, one stop for a drink at Hard Rock Cafe, one shopping stop, no museum visits, daily at 9:45 and 15:00, no reservation required—just show up 15 minutes before departure).

Julia Travel also runs tours to destinations near Madrid. The Valley of the Fallen and El Escorial tour is particularly efficient, given the lousy bus connections for this route (€50, 5 hours, makes the day trip easy—blitzing both sights with a commentary en route and no time-stealing shopping stops, Tue-Sun at 8:45, none Mon). Three trips include Toledo: one of the city itself (€41/5 hours, daily at 8:45 and 15:00, or €55/8 hours, daily at 9:45); one of Madrid and Toledo together (€52, half-day in Toledo plus panoramic 3-hour Madrid tour, daily at 9:00); and a marathon tour of El Escorial, Valley of the Fallen, and Toledo (€84, full day, Tue-Sun at 9:00, none Mon). Note that only the Toledo-only full-day tours include the cathedral. The half-day Toledo and combo-tours skip this town's one must-see sight...but not the long shopping stops, because the shops give kickbacks to the guides. See their website for other tours and services (www.juliatravel.com/en).

Self-Guided Walk

Welcome to Madrid:
From Puerta del Sol to the Royal Palace

Connect the sights with the following commentary. Allow an hour for this half-mile walk. Begin at Madrid's central square, Puerta del Sol (Metro: Sol).

▲▲Puerta del Sol

The bustling Puerta del Sol is named for a long-gone medieval gate with the sun carved onto it. It's a hub for the Metro, *cercanías* trains, political demonstrations, and pickpockets. In recent years it has undergone a facelift to become a mostly pedestrian, wide-open, cement-filled space without benches or trees (making it pretty darn hot in summer).

• *Stand by the statue of King Charles III and survey the square.*

Because of his enlightened urban policies, King Charles III (who ruled until 1788) is affectionately called "the best mayor of Madrid." He decorated the city squares with beautiful fountains, got those meddlesome Jesuits out of city government, established the public school system, mandated underground sewers, made the Retiro a public park rather than a royal retreat, and generally cleaned up Madrid.

Turn left and take a short walk away from the king. Just beyond the Metro entrances you'll see a statue of a bear pawing the berry bush—a symbol of Madrid. Bears used to live in the royal hunting grounds outside Madrid. And the *madroño* trees produce a berry that makes the traditional *madroño* liqueur.

Walk back toward the king, past the glass-fish entrance to the *cercanías* trains and Metro. Look left to a red-and-white building

From Puerta del Sol to the Royal Palace

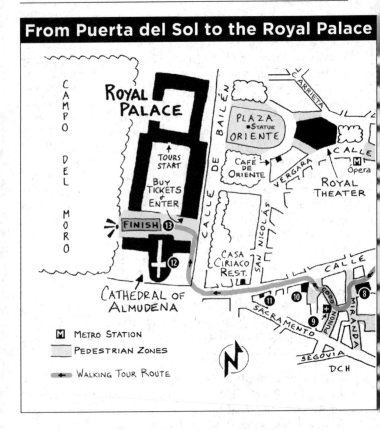

with a bell tower. This was Madrid's first post office, founded by Charles III in the 1760s. Today it's the county **governor's office,** though it's notorious for having been Francisco Franco's police headquarters. An amazing number of those detained and interrogated by the Franco police tried to "escape" by jumping out its windows to their deaths. Notice the hats of the civil guardsmen at the entry. It's said the hats have square backs, cleverly designed so that the men can lean against the wall while enjoying a cigarette.

Appreciate the harmonious architecture of the buildings that circle the square. Crowds fill the square on New Year's Eve as the rest of Madrid watches the action on TV. As Spain's "Big Ben" atop the governor's office chimes 12 times, Madrileños eat one grape for each ring to bring good luck through each of the next 12 months.

• *Cross the square, walking to the governor's office.*

Look at the curb directly in front of the entrance to the governor's office. The scuffed-up marker is **"kilometer zero,"** the very

① Puerta del Sol
② Governor's Office
③ La Mallorquina Pastry Shop
④ Calle de Postas
⑤ Plaza Mayor
⑥ Torre del Oro Bar Andalú
⑦ Mesones (Cave Bars)
⑧ Mercado de San Miguel
⑨ Convent Pastries
⑩ City Hall
⑪ Real-Estate Office
⑫ Cathedral of Almudena
⑬ Royal Palace

center of Spain (with its six main highways indicated). Near the entrance are two plaques expressing thanks from the regional government to its citizens for assisting in times of dire need. To the left of the entrance, a plaque on the wall honors those who helped during the terrorist bombings of March 11, 2004.

A similar plaque on the right marks the spot where the war against Napoleon started in 1808. Napoleon wanted his brother to be king of Spain. Trying to finagle this, he brought nearly the entire Spanish royal family to France for negotiations. An anxious crowd gathered outside this building awaiting word of the fate of their royals. This was just after the French Revolution, and there was a general nervousness between France and Spain. When the people of Madrid heard that Napoleon had appointed his own brother as the new king of Spain, they gathered angrily in the streets. The French guard simply massacred the mob. Painter Francisco de Goya, who worked just up the street, observed the event and captured the tragedy in his paintings *Second of May, 1808* and *Third of May, 1808*, now in the Prado.

From Puerta del Sol to Plaza Mayor

On the corner of Calle Mayor and Puerta del Sol (downhill end of Puerta del Sol, across from McDonald's) is the busy *confitería* **La Mallorquina** (daily 9:00-21:00, closed mid-July-Aug). Go inside for a tempting peek at racks with goodies hot out of the oven. Enjoy observing the churning energy at the bar lined with Madrileños popping in for a fast coffee and a sweet treat. The shop is famous for its cream-filled *Napolitana* pastry (€1). Or sample Madrid's answer to doughnuts, *rosquillas* (*tontas* means "silly"—plain, and *listas* means "all dressed up and ready to go"—with icing, €0.50 each). The room upstairs is more genteel.

From inside the shop, look back toward the entrance and notice the tile above the door with the 18th-century view of Puerta del Sol. Compare this with today's view out the door. This was before the square was widened, when a church stood where the *Tío Pepe* sign stands today. The French used this church to detain Spanish patriots awaiting execution. (The venerable *Tío Pepe* sign, advertising a famous sherry for more than 100 years, was Madrid's first billboard, and today it's the only such ad allowed on the square.)

• *Cross busy Calle Mayor, round McDonald's, and veer up the pedestrian alley called **Calle de Postas.***

The street sign shows the post coach heading for that famous first post office. Medieval street signs included pictures so the illiterate could "read" them. Fifty yards up the street, at Calle San Cristóbal, is Pans & Company, a popular Catalan sandwich chain offering lots of healthy choices. While Spaniards consider American fast food unhealthy—both culturally and physically—they love it. (The McDonald's and Burger Kings in Spain are thriving.)

• *From here, hike up Calle San Cristóbal.*

Within two blocks you'll pass the local feminist bookshop (Librería Mujeres) and reach a small square. At the square, notice the big brick 17th-century Ministry of Foreign Affairs building (with the pointed spire)—originally a jail for aristocratic prisoners, since even the black sheep of fine families were given special treatment.

• *Turn right, and walk down Calle de Zaragoza under the arcade into...*

▲Plaza Mayor

This square, built in 1619, is a vast cobbled traffic-free chunk of 17th-century Spain. Each side of the square is uniform, as if a grand palace were turned inside-out. The statue is of Philip III, who ordered the square's construction. Before the statue stood here, this site served as the city's 17th-century theater/multimedia center. Upon this stage, much Spanish history has been played out: bullfights, fires, royal pageantry, and events of the gruesome Inquisition. Reliefs serving as seatbacks under the lampposts tell the story. During the Inquisition, many were tried here—suspected heretics, Protestants, Jews, tour guides without a local license, and Muslims whose "conversion" to Christianity was dubious. The guilty were paraded around the square before their execution, wearing billboards listing their many sins (bleachers were built for bigger audiences, while the wealthy rented balconies). Some were slowly strangled as they held a crucifix, hearing the reassuring words of a priest as this life was squeezed out of them with a garrote. Others were burned.

The square is painted a democratic shade of burgundy—the result of a citywide vote. Since Franco's death in 1975, there's been a passion for voting here. Three different colors were painted as samples on the walls of this square, and the city voted for its favorite.

A stamp-and-coin market bustles here on Sundays from 10:00 to 14:00; on any given day it's a colorful and affordable place to enjoy a cup of coffee. (Skip the overpriced food.) Throughout Spain, lesser *plazas mayores* provide peaceful pools in the whitewater river of Spanish life. The TI (daily 9:30-20:30, wonderfully air-conditioned and with free but limited Internet access) is under the building on the north side of the square, the Casa de la Panadería, decorated with painted figures (it once housed the Bakers' Guild). The TI is also a meeting point for cheap daily walking tours—consider dropping by to reserve a spot (see "Tours in Madrid," earlier).

• For some interesting, if gruesome, bullfighting lore, drop by the...

Torre del Oro Bar Andalú

This bar is a good spot for a drink to finish off your Plaza Mayor visit (northwest corner of square, to the left of the Bakers' Guild). The bar has *Andalú* (Andalusian) ambience and an entertaining staff. Warning: They push expensive tapas on tourists. But buying a beer is safe and painless—just order a *caña* (small beer, shouldn't cost more than €2.50). The price list posted outside the door makes your costs perfectly clear (*mostrador* indicates the price at the bar).

The interior of the Torre del Oro bar is a temple to bullfighting, festooned with gory decor. Notice the breathtaking action captured in the many photographs. Look under the stuffed head of Barbero the bull. At eye level you'll see a *puntilla*, the knife used to put a bull out of his misery at the arena. This was the knife used to kill Barbero. The plaque explains: weight, birth date, owner, date of death, which matador killed him, and the location. Just to the left of Barbero, there's a photo of Franco with a very famous

MADRID

bullfighter. This is Manuel Benítez Pérez—better known as El Cordobés, the Elvis of bullfighters and a working-class hero. At the top of the stairs to the WC, find the photo of El Cordobés and Robert Kennedy—looking like brothers. At the end of the bar in a glass case is the "suit of lights" the great El Cordobés wore in his ill-fated 1967 fight. With Franco in attendance, El Cordobés went on and on, long after he could have ended the fight, until finally the bull gored him. El Cordobés survived; the bull didn't. Find another photo of Franco with El Cordobés at the far end, to the left of Segador the bull. Under the bull (to the left, over the counter) is a photo of El Cordobés' illegitimate son kissing a bull. Disowned by El Cordobés senior, yet still using his dad's famous name after a court battle, the junior El Cordobés is one of this generation's top fighters.

Consider taking a break at one of their sidewalk tables (or at any café/bar terrace facing Madrid's grandest square). Cafetería Margerit (nearby) occupies the sunniest corner of the square and is a good place to enjoy a coffee with the view. The scene is easily worth the extra euro you'll pay for the drink.

From Plaza Mayor to the Royal Palace

Leave Plaza Mayor on Calle Ciudad Rodrigo (to your right as you exit the bull bar). You'll pass a series of solid turn-of-the-20th-century storefronts and sandwich joints, such as Casa Rúa, famous for their cheap *bocadillos de calamares*—fried squid rings on a roll.

From the archway, head toward the covered market hall. Before you reach it, look left down the street called Cava de San Miguel. If you like singing and sangria, come back after 22:00 on a Friday or Saturday night, and visit one of the *mesones* that line the street. These cave-like bars, stretching far back from the street, get packed with Madrileños out on tacky dates who—emboldened by sangria, the setting, and Spain—are prone to suddenly break out in song. It's a lowbrow, electric-keyboard, karaoke-type ambience, best on Friday and Saturday nights. The odd shape of these bars isn't a contrivance for the sake of atmosphere—Plaza Mayor was built on a slope, and these underground vaults are part of a structural system that braces the leveled plaza.

To wash down those *calamares* in a more refined setting, pop into the covered **Mercado de San Miguel** (ornate iron posts, on left) for a glass of wine (daily 10:00-24:00). This historic structure, originally built in the early 1900s, has high-end food vendors. The market is frequented by tourists and locals alike looking for refreshment or gourmet picnic supplies.

• *From the archway, walk past the market and follow the pedestrian lane left. At the first corner, turn right and cross the small plaza to the modern brick* **convent** *(on left).*

MADRID

Notice the proud coat of arms over the convent's main entry. In 17th-century Spain, the most prestigious thing a noble family could do was build and maintain a convent. To harvest all the goodwill created in your community, you'd want your family's insignia right there for all to see.

In the alley across the plaza, a big brown door on the left has a sign: *Venta de Dulces* (Sweets for Sale). To buy goodies from the cloistered nuns, buzz the *monjas* button, then wait patiently for the sister to respond over the intercom. Say *"dulces"* (DOOL-thays), and she'll let you in (Mon-Sat 9:30-13:00 & 16:00-18:30, closed Sun). When the lock buzzes, push open the door and follow the sign to *torno,* the lazy Susan that lets the sisters sell their baked goods without being seen (smallest quantity: *medio* kilo— around €8). Of the many choices listed, *galletas* (shortbread cookies) are the least expensive. Or try the *pastas de almendra* (almond cookies).

• *Follow Calle del Codo (where those in need of bits of armor shopped— see the street sign) uphill around the convent to Plaza de la Villa, the square where the* **City Hall** *is located. Stop at the gate before entering the square to notice (on your left) what's considered the oldest door in town on Madrid's oldest building—made of flint and inhabited since 1480.*

Imagine how Philip II took this city by surprise when he decided to move the capital of Europe's largest empire—in the 17th century, it was even bigger than ancient Rome—from Toledo to humble Madrid. With no great edifices to administer their empire, the Habsburgs went on a building spree. But because their empire was drained of its riches by prolonged religious wars, they built Madrid with cheap brick instead of elegant granite.

The statue in the garden is of Don Alvaro de Bazán— mastermind of the Christian victory over the Turkish Ottomans at the naval battle of Lepanto in 1571. This pivotal battle, fought off the coast of Greece, slowed the Ottoman threat to Christian Europe. This square was the heart of medieval Madrid, though little remains of the 14th-century town.

From here, busy Calle Mayor leads downhill for a couple more blocks to the Royal Palace. Halfway down (on the left), at #75, a **real-estate office** *(inmobiliaria)* advertises apartments for rent (apartments or condos, priced by the month, are in the hundreds or low thousands of euros) and condos for sale (with six-digit prices). To roughly convert square meters to square feet, multiply by 10. Notice how, for expensive items, Spaniards still think in terms of pesetas ("pts"), the Spanish currency before euros took over in 2002.

A few steps farther down, on a tiny square opposite the recommended Casa Ciriaco restaurant (at #84, closed Wed and Aug), a statue memorializes the 1906 anarchist bombing. The target was the royal couple as they paraded by on their wedding day. While the crowd was throwing flowers, an anarchist (what terrorists used to be called) threw a bouquet lashed to a bomb from a balcony of #84, which was a hotel at the time. He missed the royal newly-weds, but killed 23 people. Gory photos of the event hang inside the restaurant (to the right of the entrance).

• *Continue down Calle Mayor. Within a couple of blocks you'll come to a busy street, Calle de Bailén.*

Across the busy street is Madrid's **Cathedral of Almudena** (built 1883-1993). While it faces the Royal Palace, you'll enter on the side from Calle de Bailén. Before entering (€1 donation requested), notice the central door featuring a relief of the cathedral's 1993 consecration with Pope John Paul II, King Juan Carlos, Queen Sofía, and Princess María Mercedes (the king's mom, in a wheelchair). While the exterior is a contemporary mix of styles, the interior is Neo-Gothic, with a refreshingly modern and colorful ceiling, glittering 5,000-pipe organ, and a grand 15th-century painted altarpiece—striking in the otherwise modern interior. The historic highlight is the 12th-century coffin (empty, painted leather on wood, in a chapel behind the altar) of Madrid's patron saint, Isidro. A humble peasant, Isidro loved the handicapped and performed miracles. Forty years after he died, this coffin was opened and his body was found miraculously preserved, which convinced the pope to canonize him as the patron saint of Madrid and of farmers, with May 15 as his feast day.

• *This is a good time to tour the **Royal Palace** (next to the cathedral, described later, under "Sights in Madrid"). Or you could...*

Return to Puerta del Sol

With your back to the palace, face the equestrian statue of Philip IV and (beyond the statue) the Neoclassical **Royal Theater** (Teatro Real, rebuilt in 1997). On your left, the once-impressive **Madrid Tower** skyscraper marks Plaza de España. Walk behind the Royal Theater (on the right, passing Café de Oriente—a favorite with theatergoers) to another square, where you'll find the Ópera Metro stop and the wonderfully pedestrianized Calle del Arenal, which leads back to Puerta del Sol.

Sights in Madrid

▲▲▲Royal Palace (Palacio Real)

Europe's third-greatest palace (after Versailles and Vienna's Schönbrunn), with arguably the most sumptuous original interior, is packed with tourists and royal antiques.

After a fortress burned down on this site in the 18th century,

King Philip V commissioned this huge palace as a replacement. Though he ruled Spain for 40 years, Philip V was very French. (The grandson of Louis XIV, he was born in Versailles and preferred speaking French.) He ordered this palace to be built as his own Versailles (although his wife's Italian origin had a tremendous impact on the style). It's big—more than 2,000 rooms, with tons of luxurious tapestries, a king's ransom of chandeliers, priceless porcelain, and bronze decor covered in gold leaf. While these days the royal family lives in a mansion a few miles away, this place still functions as a royal palace, and is used for formal state receptions, royal weddings, and tourists' daydreams.

The lions you'll see throughout were symbols of power. The Bourbon kings considered previous royalty not up to European par, and this palace—along with their establishment of a Spanish porcelain works and tapestry works—was their effort to raise the bar.

Cost and Hours: €8 without a tour, €10 with a one-hour tour (explained later); April-Sept Mon-Sat 9:00-18:00, Sun 9:00-15:00; Oct-March Mon-Sat 9:30-17:00, Sun 9:00-15:00; last entry one hour before closing. The palace can close if needed for a royal function; call a day ahead to check (tel. 914-548-800).

Crowd-Beating Tips: The palace is most crowded on Wednesdays, when it's free for locals. To minimize lines, either arrive early, or go late any day except Wednesday.

Getting There: To get to the palace from Puerta del Sol, walk down the pedestrianized Calle del Arenal. If arriving by Metro, get off at the Ópera stop.

Services: At the palace, there are free lockers and a WC just past the ticket booth. Upstairs you'll find a refreshing air-conditioned cafeteria (with salad bar) and a more serious bookstore.

Nearby: For eating options in the neighborhood, see page 1372.

Photography: Not allowed.

Touring the Palace: A simple one-floor, 24-room one-way circuit is open to the public. You can wander on your own or join an English-language tour (check time of next tour and decide as you buy your ticket; the English-language tours depart sporadically, not worth a long wait). The tour guides, like the museum guidebook, show a passion for meaningless data. The €4 audioguides are much more interesting. If you enjoy sightseeing cheek-to-cheek, share the audioguide with your companion. The armory and the pharmacy (included in your ticket) are in the courtyard.

In the Throne Room you'll find a Rococo riot of red velvet walls, lions, and frescoes of Spanish scenes symbolizing the monarchy. The 12 mirrors, impressive in their day, each represent a different month. The chandeliers (silver and crystal from Venice's island of Murano) are the best in the house. Be sure to look up. The ceiling fresco (1764) is the last great work by G. B. Tiepolo, who died in Madrid in 1770. This painting celebrates the days of the vast Spanish empire—upon which the sun also never set. Find the Native American (hint: follow the rainbow to the macho red-caped conquistador who motions to someone he conquered).

Other highlights are four paintings of King Charles IV (looking a bit like a dim-witted George Washington) and his wife, María Luisa (who wore the pants in the palace)—all originals by Francisco de Goya. The Gasparini Room was the royal dressing room. It's a triumph of the Rococo style, with exotic motifs that were in vogue during that period. The tapestries in the Hall of Columns are 17th-century Belgian, from designs by Raphael.

As you leave the palace, walk around the corner to the left, along the palace exterior, to the grand yet people-friendly Plaza de Oriente (with my recommended lunch spot, Café de Oriente).

Madrid's Museum Neighborhood

Three great museums, all within a 10-minute walk of one another, cluster in east Madrid: El Prado (Europe's top collection of paintings), the Thyssen-Bornemisza Museum (a baron's collection of European art, from the old masters to the moderns), and the Centro de Arte Reina Sofía (modern art, including Picasso's famous *Guernica*).

If visiting all three museums, save a few euros by buying the *Paseo del Arte* **combo-ticket** (€17.60, buy at any of the three museums, good for a year). Note that the Prado and Reina Sofía have free-admission evenings throughout the week (Prado: Tue-Sat 18:00-20:00, Sun 17:00-20:00; Reina Sofía: Mon and Wed-Fri 19:00-21:00, Sat 14:30-21:00, all day Sun). The Prado and Thyssen-Bornemisza are closed Monday, and the Reina Sofía is closed Tuesday.

▲▲▲Prado Museum

With more than 3,000 canvases, including entire rooms of masterpieces by superstar painters, the Prado (PRAH-doh) is overwhelming. The Prado is *the* place to enjoy the great Spanish painter Francisco de Goya, and it's also the home of Diego Velázquez's *Las Meninas,* considered by many to be the world's finest painting, period. In addition to Spanish works you'll find paintings by Italian and Flemish masters, including Hieronymous Bosch's fantastical *Garden of Earthly Delights* altarpiece.

Cost and Hours: €8, free Tue-Sat 18:00-20:00 and Sun 17:00-20:00, and free anytime to anyone under 18. Open Tue-Sun 9:00-20:00, closed Mon, last entry 30 minutes before closing.

Location: It's at the Paseo del Prado. The Banco de España

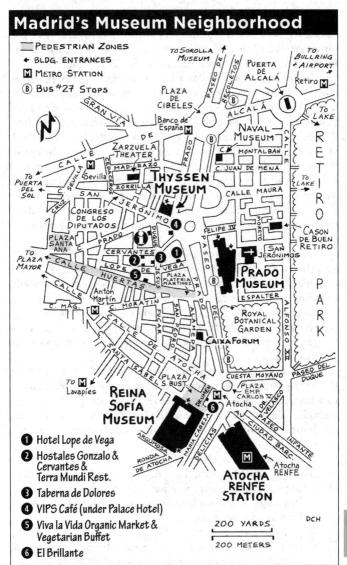

Madrid's Museum Neighborhood

- PEDESTRIAN ZONES
- ◆ BLDG. ENTRANCES
- Ⓜ METRO STATION
- Ⓑ BUS #27 STOPS

TO SOROLLA MUSEUM
TO BULLRING + AIRPORT
PUERTA DE ALCALÁ
Retiro Ⓜ
PLAZA DE CIBELES
GRAN VIA
Banco de España Ⓜ
ALCALÁ
NAVAL MUSEUM
TO LAKE
RETIRO
CALLE DE
ZARZUELA THEATER
MAD·RAZO
C. MONTALBAN
C. JUAN DE MENA
SAN SEVILLA Ⓜ
ZORRILLA
THYSSEN MUSEUM
CALLE MAURA
TO LAKE
SAN JERÓNIMO
CRUZ
CONGRESO DE LOS DIPUTADOS
FELIPE IV
CASON DE BUEN RETIRO
PLAZA SANTA ANA
CERVANTES
LOPE DE VEGA
SAN JERÓNIMOS
PLAZA PLATERIA MARTINEZ
PRADO MUSEUM
TO PLAZA MAYOR
CALLE
HUERTAS
PLAZA JESÚS
ESPALTER
Antón Martín Ⓜ
C. MORATIN
ROYAL BOTANICAL GARDEN
C. MAG.
CALLE
SANTA ISABEL
DE ATOCHA
CAIXAFORUM
ALFONSO XII
PASEO DEL DUQUE
TO Ⓜ Lavapiés
REINA SOFIA MUSEUM
PLAZA S. BUST.
CUESTA MOYANO
PLAZA EMP. CARLOS V
Atocha
DR VELASCO
ARGUMOSA
RONDA DE ATOCHA
MARIA CABEZA
DEL·ICIAS
ATOCHA RENFE STATION
Ⓜ Atocha RENFE
PASEO INFANTE
CIUDAD BARC

1 Hotel Lope de Vega
2 Hostales Gonzalo & Cervantes & Terra Mundi Rest.
3 Taberna de Dolores
4 VIPS Café (under Palace Hotel)
5 Viva la Vida Organic Market & Vegetarian Buffet
6 El Brillante

200 YARDS
200 METERS

DCH

(line 2) and Atocha Metro (line 1) stops are each a five-minute walk from the museum.

The Prado Expansion: The first extension, inaugurated in 2007, added a sculpture gallery and temporary exhibits, as well as a café and gift shop. In 2009 more space opened on the ground floor, with 12 new galleries showing nearly 200 works, all from the 19th century, ranging from Goya to Joaquín Sorolla.

Crowd-Beating Tips: Lunchtime (14:00-16:00) and weekdays are generally less crowded. It's always packed when free and on weekends; it's worth paying the entry price on other days to have your space. Free tickets are issued only after 18:00.

Entrances: You can buy your ticket at the Goya entrance, either from the ticket office or from the two machines just outside it (the machines only take credit cards and sell regularly priced tickets for the permanent collection). See which has a shorter line. At free-entrance times, you'll still need a ticket to enter, which you can only get at the Goya entrance. Then go around the corner to the left and into the big service-filled Jerónimos entrance. If there's a really long line here, go back around the building to the Velázquez entrance (The Murillo entrance, the one across from the Royal Botanical Garden, is for advance bookings such as school groups). Pick up a detailed floor plan and consider renting an audioguide.

Tours: Take a tour, rent the €3.50 audioguide, or buy a guidebook. Given the ever-changing locations of paintings, the audioguide (with 120 paintings described) is a good investment, allowing you to wander. When you see a painting of interest, simply punch in the number and enjoy the description. You can return the audioguide at any of the exits. And, if you're on a tight budget, remember that two can listen cheek-to-cheek and share one machine.

Services and Information: Your bags will be scanned (just like at the airport) before you leave them at the free and mandatory baggage storage (no water bottles, food, backpacks, or large umbrellas allowed inside). A cafeteria is in the extension area near the Jerónimos entrance. Tel. 913-302-800, http://museoprado .mcu.es.

Photography: Not allowed.

Touring the Museum: This huge museum is not laid out chronologically; make sure you have a map (free, available at entry). Paintings are moved around frequently—if you can't find a particular painting, ask a guard.

Highlights include the world's finest collection of works by Francisco de Goya. Follow this complex man through the stages of his life—from dutiful court painter, to political rebel and scandal-maker, to the disillusioned genius of his "black paintings."

Just as impressive are the works by Diego Velázquez, who was the photojournalist of court painters, capturing the Spanish king and his court with a blend of formal portrait and candid snapshot. Be sure to see *The Maids of Honor (Las Meninas)*, a peek at nannies caring for Princess Margarita and, at the same time, a behind-the-scenes look at Velázquez at work.

MADRID

Other masterpieces include works by El Greco, who was born in Greece (his name is Spanish for "The Greek"), trained in Venice, and settled in Toledo—60 miles from Madrid. His paintings are like Byzantine icons drenched in Venetian color and fused in the fires of Spanish mysticism. Don't miss the cryptic triptych by Hieronymous Bosch, *The Garden of Earthly Delights (El Jardín de las Delicias)*. It sends the message that the pleasures of life are fleeting, and we'd better avoid them or we'll wind up in hell.

▲▲Thyssen-Bornemisza Museum

Locals call this stunning museum simply the Thyssen (TEE-sun). It displays the impressive collection that Baron Thyssen (a wealthy German married to a former Miss Spain) sold to Spain for $350 million. The museum offers a unique chance to enjoy the sweep of all art history—including a good sampling of the "isms" of the 20th century—in one collection. It's basically minor works by major artists and major works by minor artists. (Major works by major artists are in the Prado.) But art-lovers appreciate how the good baron's art complements the Prado's collection by filling in where the Prado is weak—such as Impressionism, which is the Thyssen's forte.

Cost and Hours: €8 (€7 online, up to €8 more for optional special exhibits); children under 12 free, Tue-Sun 10:00-19:00, closed Mon, last entry 30 minutes before closing.

Location: The museum is kitty-corner from the Prado at Paseo del Prado 8 in Palacio de Villahermosa (Metro: Banco de España).

Services and Information: Free baggage storage, €4 audio-guide, café, shop, tel. 914-203-944, www.museothyssen.org.

Photography: Not allowed.

Touring the Museum: After purchasing your ticket, continue down the wide main hall past larger-than-life paintings of King Juan Carlos and Queen Sofía, and then paintings of the baron (who died in 2002) and his art-collecting baroness, Carmen. At the info desk, pick up two museum maps (one for numbered rooms, another for lettered rooms): Each floor is divided into two separate areas: the permanent collection (blue-numbered rooms) and additions from the baroness since the 1980s (red-lettered rooms). Most visitors stick to the permanent collection.

Ascend to the top floor and work your way down, taking a delightful walk through art history. Visit the rooms on each floor in numerical order, from Primitive Italian (Room 1) to Surrealism and Pop Art (Room 48).

Temporary exhibits at the Thyssen often parallel those at the free **Caja Madrid** exhibit hall (Tue-Sat 10:00-20:00, closed Mon, tel. 913-792-050, www.fundacioncajamadrid.es), across from the Descalzas Royal Monastery on Plaza San Martín, a short walk from Puerta del Sol.

Afterward, if you're heading to the Reina Sofía and you're tired, hail a cab at the gate to zip straight there, or take bus #27, which stops in the square with the Neptune fountain, in front of the Starbucks (ride to the end of the Paseo del Prado, get off at the McDonald's and cross the street, going away from the Botanical Gardens, to Plaza Sánchez Bustillo and the museum).

▲▲▲Centro de Arte Reina Sofía

Perhaps Europe's most enjoyable modern art museum, the Reina Sofía shows off an exceptional collection of 20th-century art in what was Madrid's first public hospital (notice the iron-barred windows—facing the courtyard—for the mentally ill ward).

The current curator, who has a passion for cinema, has paired paintings with films from each decade throughout the museum. This provides a fascinating insight into the social context that inspired the art of Spain's tumultuous 20th century. Make a point to understand why a particular film was chosen, in order to gain an insight into Spain's 20th-century scars.

Cost and Hours: €6, free Mon and Wed-Fri after 19:00, Sat afternoon after 14:30 (less crowded after 15:00), and all day Sun, always free to those under 18 and over 65. Even if admission is free when you visit, grab a ticket. The museum is open Mon and Wed-Sat 10:00-21:00, Sun 10:00-14:30, closed Tue.

Location: It's across from the Atocha Metro station, on Plaza Sánchez Bustillo (at Calle de Santa Isabel 52). In the Metro station, follow signs for Reina Sofía. At the opening into a square, look for the exterior glass elevators. There are two entrances: the old entrance (leads to permanent collection first; on Plaza Sánchez Bustillo, on a big square close to the Metro stop) and the newer entrance (mostly for tour groups).

Services and Information: Good information sheets, no tours in English, hardworking €4 audioguide, no *Guernica* photos allowed, free baggage storage. The *librería* just outside the new addition has a larger selection of Picasso and Surrealist reproductions than the main gift shop at the entrance. The museum's café is a standout for its surprisingly good food. Tel. 914-675-062, www.museoreinasofia.es.

Touring the Museum: The permanent collection is on the second and fourth floors; temporary exhibits are on the first and third floors. Ride the fancy glass elevator to the second floor and follow the room numbers for art chronologically displayed from 1900 to 1940. The fourth floor continues the collection, from 1940 to 1980.

The museum is most famous for Pablo Picasso's *Guernica* (second floor, Room 6), an epic painting showing the horror of modern war. Notice the two rooms of studies Picasso did for *Guernica,* filled with iron-nail tears and screaming mouths. *Guernica* was displayed at the Museum of Modern Art in New York City until Franco's death, and now it reigns as Spain's national piece of art. After pondering the destruction of war, check out the photos of Picasso creating this masterpiece.

Don't miss the model of the Spanish Pavilion at the 1937 Paris Expo. Picasso was readying to paint something light and "typically Spanish," such as flamenco and matadors, for the Expo. But the bombing of Guernica jolted him into the realization that "the real Spain" was a country torn by civil war. The pavilion was a vessel for anti-Franco propaganda and its centerpiece was *Guernica.*

The museum houses an easy-to-enjoy collection by other modern artists, including more of Picasso and a mind-bending room of works by Salvador Dalí. The early Dalí is in Room 3; the signature Dalí works are in Room 5. *The Great Masturbator* is exhausting psychologically, depicting in its surrealism a lonely, highly sexual genius, in love with his muse, Gala, while she is still married to a French poet.

Near the Prado

▲**Retiro Park (Parque del Buen Retiro)**—Once the private domain of royalty, this majestic park has been a favorite of Madrid's commoners since Charles III decided to share it with his subjects in the late 18th century. Siesta in this 300-acre green-and-breezy escape from the city. At midday on Saturday and Sunday, the area around the lake becomes a street carnival, with jugglers, puppeteers, and lots of local color. These peaceful gardens offer great picnicking and people-watching (closes at dusk). From the Retiro Metro stop, walk to the big lake (El Estanque), where you can rent a rowboat. Past the lake, a grand boulevard of statues leads to the Prado.

▲**Royal Botanical Garden (Real Jardín Botánico)**—After your Prado visit, you can take a lush and fragrant break in this sculpted park. Wander among trees from around the world. The flier in English explains that this is actually more than a park—it's a museum of plants.

Cost and Hours: €2.50, daily 10:00-21:00, until 18:00 in winter, entry opposite Prado's Murillo/south entry, Plaza de Murillo 2.

▲**Naval Museum (Museo Naval)**—This museum tells the story of Spain's navy, from the Armada to today, in a plush and fascinating-to-boat-lovers exhibit. Given Spain's importance in maritime history, there's quite a story to tell. Because this is a military facility, you'll need to show your passport to get in.

Cost and Hours: Free, good English brochure, Tue-Sun 10:00-14:00, closed Mon and Aug, a block north of the Prado across boulevard from Thyssen-Bornemisza Museum, Paseo del Prado 5, tel. 915-239-884, www.museonavalmadrid.com.

CaixaForum—Across the street from the Prado and Royal Botanical Garden, you'll find this impressive exhibit hall with sleek architecture and an outdoor hanging garden—a bushy wall festooned with greens designed by a French landscape artist. The forum, funded by La Caixa Bank, features world-class art exhibits—generally 20th-century art, well-described in English and changing three times a year. Ride the elevator to the top, where you'll find a chic café with €12 lunch specials and sperm-like lamps swarming down from the ceiling, and explore your way down.

Cost and Hours: Free, daily 10:00-20:00, Paseo del Prado 36, tel. 913-307-300, www.obrasocial.lacaixa.es.

Elsewhere in Madrid

Descalzas Royal Monastery (Monasterio de las Descalzas Reales)—Madrid's most visit-worthy monastery was founded in the 16th century by Philip II's sister, Joan of Habsburg (known to Spaniards as Juana, and to Austrians as Joanna). She's buried here. The monastery's chapels are decorated with fine art, Rubens-designed tapestries, and the heirlooms of the wealthy women who joined the order (the nuns were required to give a dowry). Because this is still a working Franciscan monastery, tourists can visit only when the nuns vacate the cloister, and the number of daily visitors is limited. The scheduled tours often sell out—come in the morning to buy your ticket, even if you want an afternoon tour.

Cost and Hours: €5, visits guided in Spanish or English depending on demand, Tue-Thu and Sat 10:30-12:30 & 16:00-17:30, Fri 10:30-12:30, Sun 11:00-13:30, closed Mon, Plaza de las Descalzas Reales 3, near the Ópera Metro stop and just a short walk from Puerta del Sol, tel. 914-548-800. The free **Caja Madrid** exhibit hall is across the street from the monastery (see page 1349).

▲**Museum of the Americas (Museo de América)**—Thousands of pre-Colombian and colonial artworks and artifacts make up the bulk of this worthwhile museum. Covering the cultures of the Americas (North and South), its exhibits focus on language, religion, and art, and provide a new perspective on the cultures of our own hemisphere. Highlights include one of only four surviving Mayan codices (ancient books), and a section about the voyages of the Spanish explorers, with their fantastical imaginings of mythical creatures awaiting them in the New World. Don't save the museum for later in the day—it closes at 15:00.

Cost and Hours: €3, free Sun, Tue-Sat 9:00-15:00, Sun

10:00-15:00, closed Mon, northwest of the city center at Avenida de los Reyes Católicos 6, Metro: Moncloa, tel. 915-492-641, http://museodeamerica.mcu.es.

Getting There: The museum is a 10-minute walk from the Moncloa Metro stop: Take the Calle de Isaac Peral exit, cross Plaza de Moncloa, and veer right to Calle de Fernández de los Ríos. Follow that street (toward the shiny Faro de Moncloa tower), and turn left on Avenida de los Reyes Católicos. Head around the base of the tower, which stands at the museum's entrance.

▲**National Archaeological Museum (Museo Arqueológico Nacional)**—This good museum has been under major renovation, so it's likely only about 300 of its most noteworthy pieces will be on display during your visit. If you're here after all of its rooms have reopened, you'll follow a chronological walk through the story of Iberia. With a rich collection of artifacts, the walk shows off the wonders of each age: Celtic pre-Roman, Roman, a fine and rare Visigothic section, Moorish, Romanesque, and beyond.

Cost and Hours: Always free; open Tue-Sat 9:30-20:00, Sun 9:30-15:00, closed Mon; Calle Serrano 13, Metro: Serrano or Colón, tel. 915-777-912.

Sorolla Museum (Museo Sorolla)—Joaquín Sorolla (1863-1923) is known for his portraits, landscapes, and use of light. It's a relaxing experience to stroll through the rooms of his former house and studio, especially to see the lazy beach scenes of his hometown Valencia. Take a break after your visit to reflect in the small garden in front of his house.

Cost and Hours: €3, free on Sun, open Tue-Sat 9:30-20:00, Sun 10:00-15:00, closed Mon, General Martínez Campos 37, Metro: Iglesia, tel. 913-101-584, http://museosorolla.mcu.es.

History Museum (Museo de Historia)—The museum, which covers the history of Madrid, is closed for a major renovation until sometime in 2012. If open, you can trace the city's history in old paintings and models (but no English). As you enter, notice Pedro de Ribera's fine Baroque door featuring "St. James the Moor-Slayer." (Calle Fuencarral 78, Metro: Tribunal or Bilbao, tel. 917-011-863).

▲**Clothing Museum (Museo del Traje)**—This museum shows the history of clothing from the 18th century until today. In a cool and air-conditioned chronological sweep, the museum's one floor of exhibits includes regional ethnic costumes, a look at how bullfighting and the French influenced styles, accessories through the ages, and Spanish flappers. The only downside of this marvelous modern museum is that it's a long way from anything else of interest.

Cost and Hours: €3, free Sat 14:00-19:00 and all day Sun, open Tue-Sat 9:30-19:00, Sun 10:00-15:00, closed Mon, last entry 30 minutes before closing, Avenida de Juan Herrera 2; Metro: Moncloa and a longish walk, bus #46, or taxi; tel. 915-497-150.

▲**Chapel of San Antonio de la Florida**—In this simple little Neoclassical chapel from the 1790s, Francisco de Goya's tomb stares up at a splendid cupola filled with his own proto-Impressionist frescoes. He frescoed this using the same unique technique that he employed for his "black paintings." Use the mirrors to enjoy the drama and energy he infused into this marvelously restored masterpiece.

Cost and Hours: Free, Tue-Fri 9:30-20:00, Sat-Sun 10:00-14:00, closed Mon, Glorieta de San Antonio de la Florida, tel. 915-420-722. This chapel is a five-minute walk down Paseo de San Antonio de la Florida from Metro: Príncipe Pío (and its bus station, serving Segovia).

Royal Tapestry Factory (Real Fábrica de Tapices)—Have a look at traditional tapestry-making. You can actually order a tailor-made tapestry (starting at $10,000).

Cost and Hours: €3.50, by tour only, on the half-hour, Mon-Fri 10:00-14:00, closed Sat-Sun and Aug, some English tours, Calle Fuenterrabia 2, Metro: Menendez Pelayo, take Gutenberg exit, tel. 914-340-550.

Temple de Debod—In 1968 Egypt gave Spain its own ancient temple. It was a gift of the Egyptian government, which was grateful for Franco's help in rescuing monuments that had been threatened by the rising Nile waters above the Aswan Dam. Consequently, Madrid is the only place I can think of in Europe where you can actually wander through an intact original Egyptian temple—complete with fine carved reliefs from 200 B.C. Set in a romantic park that locals love for its great city views (especially at sunset), the temple—as well as its art—is well-described. Popular as the view may be, the uninspiring "grand Madrid view" only causes me to wonder why anyone would build a city here.

Cost and Hours: Temple free; April-Sept Tue-Fri 10:00-14:00 & 18:00-20:00, Sat-Sun 10:00-14:00, closed Mon; Oct-March Tue-Fri 9:45-13:45 & 16:15-18:15, Sat-Sun 10:00-14:00, closed Mon, in Parque de Montaña, north of the Royal Palace.

Experiences in Madrid

▲▲**Self-Guided Bus Tour: Paseo de la Castellana**—Tourists risk leaving Madrid without ever seeing the modern "Manhattan" side of town. But it's easy to do. From the Prado Museum, bus #27 makes the trip straight north along Paseo del Prado and then Paseo de la Castellana, through the no-nonsense skyscraper part of this city of more than three million. The line ends at the leaning towers of Puerta de Europa (Gate of Europe). This trip is simple and cheap (€1, buses run every 10 minutes, sit on the right if possible, beware of pickpockets). You just joyride for 30 minutes to the last stop (longer if it's rush hour), get out when everyone else does, ogle the skyscrapers, and catch the Metro for a 20-minute ride back to the city's center. At twilight, when fountains and facades are floodlit, the ride is particularly enjoyable.

Bus #27 rumbles from Atocha Station past the Royal Botanical Garden (opposite McDonald's) and the Velázquez entrance to the Prado (if you're starting from here, catch the bus from the museum side to head north).

Look out for these landmarks: the Prado Museum (right); a square with a fountain of Neptune (left); an obelisk and war memorial to those who have died for Spain (right, with the stock market behind it); the Naval Museum (right); Plaza de Cibeles (with the fancy City Hall, the Bank of Spain, and other huge buildings); and then the National Library (right).

When you come to a square with a statue of Columbus, it marks the end of the historic town and the beginning of the modern city. At this point the boulevard changes its name. It used to be named for Franco; now it's named for the people he no longer rules—*la Castellana* (Castilians). Next comes the American Embassy (hard to see behind its fortified wall, right) and Franco's ministries (left, typical fascist architecture, c. 1940s, some still used). Continuing up the boulevard, look left to see the Picasso Tower (which looks like one of New York's former World Trade Center towers, because both buildings were designed by the same architect), the huge Bernabéu soccer stadium (right, home of Real Madrid, Europe's most successful soccer team, see page 1357), and the Ministry of Defense (left).

Your trip ends at Plaza de Castilla, where you can't miss the avant-garde Puerta de Europa, consisting of the twin "Torres Kios," office towers designed to lean at a 15-degree angle, one with the big green logo of the Bank of Madrid. In the distance you can see four of the tallest buildings in Spain. The plaza sports a futuristic obelisk by contemporary Spanish architect Santiago Calatrava.

It's the end of the line for the bus—and for you. You can return directly to Puerta del Sol on the Metro, or cross the street and ride bus #27 along the same route back to the Prado or Atocha Station.

▲**Electric Minibus Joyride Through Lavapiés**—For a relaxing ride through the characteristic old center of Madrid, hop little electric minibus #M1 (€1, 5/hour, 20-minute trip, Mon-Sat 8:00-20:00, none on Sun). These are designed mostly for seniors who could use a lift (offer your seat if there's a senior standing). Catch the minibus at the Sevilla Metro stop and simply ride it to the end (Metro: Embajadores). Enjoy this gritty slice of workaday Madrid—both people and architecture—as you roll slowly through

Plaza Santa Ana, down a bit of the pedestrianized Calle de las Huertas, past gentrified Tirso de Molina (its junkies now replaced by a family-friendly flower market), through Plaza de Lavapiés and a barrio of African and Bangladeshi immigrants, until you get to Embajadores. From there you can catch the next #M1 minibus (which returns to the Sevilla Metro stop along a different route) or descend into the subway system.

▲▲**Bullfight**—Madrid's Plaza de Toros hosts Spain's top bullfights on some Sundays and holidays from March through mid-October, and nearly every day during the San Isidro festival (mid-May through mid-June—often sold out long in advance). Fights start between 17:00 and 21:00 (early in spring and fall, late in summer). The bullring is at the Ventas Metro stop (a 25-minute Metro ride from Puerta del Sol, tel. 913-562-200, www.las-ventas.com).

Bullfight tickets range from €5 to €150. There are no bad seats at Plaza de Toros; paying more gets you in the shade and/or closer to the gore. (The action often intentionally occurs in the shade to reward the expensive-ticket holders.) To be close to the bullring, choose areas 8, 9, or 10; for shade: 1, 2, 9, or 10; for shade/sun: 3 or 8; for the sun and cheapest seats: 4, 5, 6, or 7. Note these key words: *corrida*—a real fight with professionals; *novillada*—rookie matadors and younger bulls. Getting tickets through your hotel or a booking office is convenient, but they add 20 percent or more and don't sell the cheap seats. There are two booking offices; call both before you buy: at Plaza del Carmen 1 (Mon-Sat 9:30-13:00 & 16:30-19:00, Sun 9:30-14:00, tel. 915-319-131, or buy online at www.bullfightticketsmadrid.com; run by English-speaking José, who also sells soccer tickets) and at Calle Victoria 3 (Mon-Fri 10:00-14:00 & 17:00-19:00, Sat-Sun 10:00-14:00, tel. 915-211-213). To save money, you can stand in the ticket line at the bullring. Except for important bullfights—or during the San Isidro festival—there are generally plenty of seats available. About a thousand tickets are held back to be sold in the five days leading up to a fight, including the day of the fight. Scalpers hang out before the popular fights at the Calle Victoria booking office. Beware: Those buying scalped tickets are breaking the law and can lose the ticket with no recourse.

For a dose of the experience, you can buy a cheap ticket and just stay to see a couple of bullfights. Each fight takes about 20 minutes, and the event consists of six bulls over two hours. Or, to keep your distance but get a sense of the ritual and gore, tour the bull bar on Plaza Mayor (described on page 1367).

Madrid's **Bullfighting Museum** (Museo Taurino) is not as good as Sevilla's or Ronda's (free, Tue-Fri 9:30-14:30, Sun 10:00-13:00, closed Sat and Mon and early on fight days, at the back of bullring, tel. 917-251-857).

"Football" and Bernabéu Stadium—Madrid, like most of Europe, is enthusiastic about soccer (which they call *fútbol*). The Real Madrid team plays to a spirited crowd Saturdays and Sundays from September through May (tickets from €50—sold at bullfight box offices listed earlier). One of the most popular sightseeing activities among European visitors to Madrid is touring the 80,000-seat stadium. The €15 unguided visit includes the box seats, dressing rooms, technical zone, playing field, trophy room, and a big panoramic stadium view (daily 10:00-19:00, Metro: Santiago Bernabéu, www.realmadrid.com, tel. 913-984-300).

Nightlife in Madrid

Those into clubbing may have to wait until after midnight for the most popular places to even open, much less start hopping. Spain has a reputation for partying very late, not ending until offices open in the morning. If you're people-watching early in the morning, it's actually hard to know who is finishing their day and who's just starting it. Even if you're not a party animal after midnight, make a point to be out with the happy masses, luxuriating in the cool evening air between 22:00 and midnight. The scene is absolutely unforgettable.

▲▲▲**Paseo**—Just walking the streets of Madrid seems to be the way the Madrileños spend their evenings. Even past midnight on a hot summer night, entire families with little kids are strolling, enjoying tiny beers and tapas in a series of bars, licking ice cream, and greeting their neighbors. A good area to wander is along Gran Vía (from about Metro: Callao to Plaza de España). Or start at Puerta del Sol, and explore in the direction of Plaza Santa Ana. The pedestrianized Calle de las Huertas is also understandably popular with strollers.

▲**Zarzuela**—For a delightful look at Spanish light opera that even English-speakers can enjoy, try zarzuela. Guitar-strumming Napoleons in red capes; buxom women with masks, fans, and castanets; Spanish-speaking pharaohs; melodramatic spotlights; and aficionados clapping and singing along from the cheap seats, where the acoustics are best—this is zarzuela...the people's opera. Originating in Madrid, zarzuela is known for its satiric humor and surprisingly good music. You can buy tickets at Theater Zarzuela, which alternates between zarzuela, ballet, and opera throughout the year (€16-40, box office open 12:00-18:00 for advance tickets or until showtime for that day, Jovellanos 4, near the Prado, Metro: Sevilla or Banco de España, tel. 915-245-400, http://teatrodela zarzuela.mcu.es; to purchase tickets online, go to the theater section of www.servicaixa.com and choose the English version). The TI's monthly guide has a special zarzuela section.

▲▲Flamenco—Although Sevilla is the capital of flamenco, Madrid has three easy and affordable options. And on summer evenings, Madrid puts on live flamenco events in the Royal Palace gardens (ask TI for details).

Taberna Casa Patas attracts big-name flamenco artists. You'll quickly understand why this intimate (30 tables, 120 seats) and smoky venue is named "House of Feet." Since this is for locals as well as tour groups, the flamenco is contemporary and may be jazzier than your notion—it depends on who's performing (€31, Mon-Thu at 22:30, Fri-Sat at 21:00 and 24:00, closed Sun, 1.25-1.5 hours, price includes cover and first drink, reservations smart, no flash cameras, Cañizares 10, tel. 913-690-496, www.casapatas.com). Its restaurant is a logical spot for dinner before the show (€30 dinners, Mon-Sat from 20:00). Or, since it's three blocks south of the recommended Plaza Santa Ana tapas bars, this could be your post–tapas-crawl entertainment.

Las Carboneras, more downscale, is an easygoing, folksy little place a few steps from Plaza Mayor with a nightly hour-long flamenco show (€30 includes an entry and a drink, €58 gets you a table up front with dinner and unlimited cheap drinks if you reserve ahead, ask about discount when you book direct and show this book, Mon-Thu at 22:30 and often at 20:30, Fri-Sat at 20:30 and 23:00, closed Sun, reservations recommended, Plaza del Conde de Miranda 1, tel. 915-428-677, Enrique). And though Las Carboneras lacks the pretense of Casa Patas, Casa Patas has better-quality artists and a riveting seriousness. Considering that Las Carboneras raised its prices to essentially match Casa Patas, the "House of Feet" is the better value.

Las Tablas Flamenco offers a less expensive nightly show respecting the traditional art of flamenco. You'll sit in a plain room with a mix of tourists and Madrileños in a modern, nondescript office block just over the freeway from Plaza de España (€24 with drink, reasonable drink prices, Sun-Thu 22:30, Fri-Sat 20:00 & 22:00, 1.25-hour show, corner of Calle de Ferraz and Cuesta de San Vicente, tel. 915-420-520, www.lastablasmadrid.com).

Regardless of what your hotel receptionist may want to sell you, other flamenco places—such as Arco de Cuchilleros (Calle de los Cuchilleros 7), Café de Chinitas (Calle Torija 7, just off Plaza Mayor), Corral de la Morería (Calle de Morería 17), and Torres Bermejas (off Gran Vía)—are filled with tourists and pushy waiters.

Mesones—These long, skinny cave-like bars, famous for customers drinking and singing late into the night, line the lane called Cava de San Miguel, just west of Plaza Mayor. If you were to toss lowbrow barflies, Spanish karaoke, electric keyboards, crass tourists, cheap sangria, and greasy calamari into a late-night blender and turn it on, this is what you'd get. It's generally lively only on Friday and Saturday.

Late-Night and Jazz Bars—If you're just picking up speed at midnight, and looking for a place filled with old tiles and a Gen-X crowd, power into **Bar Viva Madrid** (daily 13:00-3:00 in the morning, downhill from Plaza Santa Ana on Calle Manuel Fernández y González, tel. 914-293-640). The same street has other late-night bars filled with music. Or hike on over to the recommended **Chocolatería San Ginés** (for a dessert of *churros con chocolate*).

For live jazz, **Café Central** is the old town favorite. Since 1982 it's been known as the place where rising stars get their start (€14, 22:00 nightly, cheap drinks, great scene, Plaza del Ángel 10, tel. 913-694-143, www.cafecentralmadrid.com).

Movies—During Franco's days, movies were always dubbed in Spanish. As a result, movies in Spain remain about the most often dubbed in Europe. Dubbing was encouraged by Franco's xenophobia and the need to censor popular entertainment during his rule. When dubbing a movie, you can change the meaning and almost no one knows. To see a movie with its original soundtrack, look for "V.O." (meaning "original version"). **Cine Ideal,** with nine screens, is a good place for the latest films in V.O. (€8, 5-minute walk south of Puerta del Sol at Calle del Dr. Cortezo 6, tel. 913-692-518 for info). For extensive listings, see the *Guía del Ocio* entertainment guide (described on page 1327) or a local newspaper.

Sleeping in Madrid

Madrid has plenty of centrally located budget hotels and *pensiones*. Most of the accommodations I've listed are within a few minutes' walk of Puerta del Sol.

You'll have no trouble finding a sleepable double for €40, a good double for €80, and a modern, air-conditioned double with all the comforts for €110. Prices vary throughout the year at bigger hotels, but remain about the same for the smaller hotels and *hostales*. It's almost always easy to find a place. Anticipate full hotels only during May (the San Isidro festival, celebrating Madrid's patron saint with bullfights and zarzuelas—especially around his feast day on May 15) and September (when conventions can clog the city). During the hot months of July and August, prices can be soft—always ask for a discount.

Given the economic downturn, hoteliers are willing and eager to make a deal. I'd suggest emailing several hotels (including business-class hotels) to ask for their best price. Comparison-shop and make your choice.

Sleep Code

(€1 = about $1.40, country code: 34)
S = Single, **D** = Double/Twin, **T** = Triple, **Q** = Quad, **b** = bathroom, **s** = shower only. Unless otherwise noted, credit cards are accepted, English is spoken, and breakfast is *not* included.

To help you easily sort through these listings, I've divided the rooms into three categories, based on the price for a standard double room with bath during high season:

$$$ Higher Priced—Most rooms €100 or more.
$$ Moderately Priced—Most rooms between €70-100.
$ Lower Priced—Most rooms €70 or less.

Prices can change without notice; verify the hotel's current rates online or by email. For other updates, see www.ricksteves.com/update.

With all of Madrid's street noise, I'd request the highest floor possible. Also, twin-bedded rooms are generally a bit larger than double-bedded rooms for the same price. During slow times, drop-ins can often score a room in business-class hotels for just a few euros more than the budget hotels (which don't have prices that fluctuate as wildly with demand).

Fancier Places in the Pedestrian Zone Between Puerta del Sol and Gran Vía

These business-class hotels are good values for those willing to spend a little more. Their formal prices may be inflated, but most offer weekend and summer discounts when it's slow. Drivers pay about €24 a day in garages. Use Metro: Sol for all but Hotel Ópera (Metro: Ópera).

$$$ Hotel Liabeny rents 220 plush, spacious, business-class rooms offering all the comforts (Sb-€110, Db-€125, Tb-€182, 10 percent cheaper mid-July-Aug and Fri-Sat, prices vary widely according to demand, breakfast-€16, air-con, sauna, gym, off Plaza del Carmen at Salud 3, tel. 915-319-000, fax 915-327-421, www.liabeny.es, info@liabeny.es).

$$$ Hotel Preciados, a four-star business hotel, has 73 welcoming, sleek, and modern rooms as well as elegant lounges. It's well-located and reasonably priced for the luxury it provides (Db-€125-160, prices are often soft, checking Web specials in advance or dropping in will likely enable you to snag a room for around €100, breakfast-€15, Wi-Fi, parking-€18, just off Plaza de Santo Domingo at Calle Preciados 37, tel. 914-544-400, fax 914-544-401, www.preciadoshotel.com, preciadoshotel@preciadoshotel.com).

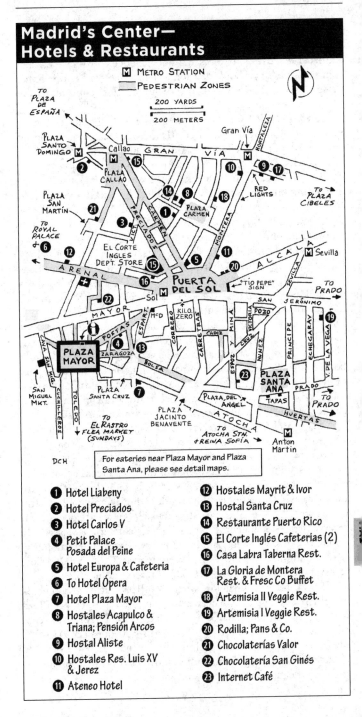

Madrid's Center— Hotels & Restaurants

M METRO STATION

PEDESTRIAN ZONES

200 YARDS

200 METERS

For eateries near Plaza Mayor and Plaza Santa Ana, please see detail maps.

DCH

① Hotel Liabeny

② Hotel Preciados

③ Hotel Carlos V

④ Petit Palace Posada del Peine

⑤ Hotel Europa & Cafeteria

⑥ To Hotel Ópera

⑦ Hotel Plaza Mayor

⑧ Hostales Acapulco & Triana; Pensión Arcos

⑨ Hostal Aliste

⑩ Hostales Res. Luis XV & Jerez

⑪ Ateneo Hotel

⑫ Hostales Mayrit & Ivor

⑬ Hostal Santa Cruz

⑭ Restaurante Puerto Rico

⑮ El Corte Inglés Cafeterias (2)

⑯ Casa Labra Taberna Rest.

⑰ La Gloria de Montera Rest. & Fresc Co Buffet

⑱ Artemisia II Veggie Rest.

⑲ Artemisia I Veggie Rest.

⑳ Rodilla; Pans & Co.

㉑ Chocolaterías Valor

㉒ Chocolatería San Ginés

㉓ Internet Café

$$$ Hotel Carlos V is a Best Western with 67 sharp high-ceilinged rooms, elegant breakfast, and a pleasant lounge (Sb-€95, standard Db-€115, Tb-€135, tax not included, breakfast-€9, air-con, non-smoking floors, elevator, Wi-Fi, Maestro Victoria 5, tel. 915-314-100, fax 915-313-761, www.hotelcarlosv.com, recepcion @hotelcarlosv.com).

$$$ Petit Palace Posada del Peine feels like part of a big modern chain (which it is), but fills its well-located old building with fresh, efficient character. Behind the ornate and sparkling Old World facade is a comfortable and modern business-class hotel with 67 rooms just a block from Plaza Mayor (Db-€100-160 depending on demand, tax not included, breakfast-€15, air-con, free use of laptops and Internet access in all rooms, Calle Postas 17, tel. 915-238-151, fax 915-232-993, www.hthoteles.com, pos @hthoteles.com).

$$ Hotel Europa, with sleek marble, red carpet runners along the halls, happy Muzak charm, and an attentive staff, is a tremendous value. It rents 102 squeaky-clean rooms, many with balconies overlooking the pedestrian zone or an inner courtyard. The hotel has an honest ethos, and offers a straight price (Sb-€74, Db-€92, Db with view-€110, Tb-€130, Qb-€155, Quint/b-€175, tax not included, breakfast extra, air-con, elevator, free Internet access, Wi-Fi in lobby and cafeteria, Calle del Carmen 4, tel. 915-212-900, fax 915-214-696, www.hoteleuropa.net, info@hoteleuropa.net, run by Antonio and Fernando Garaban and their helpful and jovial staff, Javi and Jim). The recommended Europa cafeteria-restaurant next door is a lively and convivial scene—fun for breakfast.

$$ Hotel Ópera, a serious and contemporary hotel with 79 classy rooms, is located just off Plaza Isabel II, a four-block walk from Puerta del Sol toward the Royal Palace (Db-€75-95 but prices spike wildly with demand, includes breakfast, air-con, elevator, free Internet access, ask for a higher floor—there are nine—to avoid street noise, Cuesta de Santo Domingo 2, Metro: Ópera, tel. 915-412-800, fax 915-416-923, www.hotelopera.com, reservas@hotelopera.com). Hotel Ópera's cafeteria is deservedly popular. Consider their "singing dinners"—great operetta music with a delightful dinner—offered nightly at 22:00 (around €65, reservations smart, call 915-426-382 or reserve at hotel).

$$ Hotel Plaza Mayor, with 34 solidly outfitted rooms, is tastefully decorated and beautifully situated a block off Plaza Mayor (Sb-€70, Db-€85-90, superior Db-€110, Tb-€120, air-con, elevator, Wi-Fi, Calle Atocha 2, tel. 913-600-606, fax 913-600-610, www.h-plazamayor.com, info@h-plazamayor.com, Lee). Ask about free breakfast when you book direct (by email, phone, or fax), pay the rates listed above, and show this book.

Cheaper Bets Near Puerta del Sol and Gran Vía

These three are all in the same building at Calle de la Salud 13, overlooking Plaza del Carmen—a little square with a sleepy, almost Parisian ambience.

$ Hostal Acapulco rents 16 bright rooms with air-conditioning and all the big hotel gear. The neighborhood is quiet enough that it's smart to request a room with a balcony (Sb-€49-54, Db-€59-64, Tb-€77-80, elevator, free Internet access and Wi-Fi, fourth floor, tel. 915-311-945, fax 915-322-329, www.hostal acapulco.com, hostal_acapulco@yahoo.es, Ana and Marco).

$ Hostal Triana, also a good deal, is bigger—with 40 rooms—and offers a little less charm for a little less money (Sb-€42, Db-€55, Tb-€75, includes taxes, rooms facing the square have air-con and cost €3 extra, other rooms have fans, elevator, free Wi-Fi, first floor, tel. 915-326-812, fax 915-229-729, www.hostaltriana.com, triana@hostaltriana.com, Victor González).

$ Pensión Arcos is tiny, granny-run, and old-fashioned—it's been in the Hernández family since 1936. You can reserve by phone—in Spanish, and you must pay in cash—but its five rooms are clean, quiet, and served by an elevator. You also have access to a tiny roof terrace and a nice little lounge. For cheap beds in a great locale, assuming you can communicate, this place is unbeatable (D-€36, Db-€40, fifth floor, air-con, closed Aug, tel. 915-324-994, Anuncia and Sabino).

More Cheap Sleeps at the Top of Calle de la Montera

These three places are a few minutes' walk from Puerta del Sol and a stone's throw from Gran Vía at the top of Calle de la Montera, which some dislike because of the young prostitutes who hang out here. They're legal, and the zone is otherwise safe and comfortable.

$ Hostal Aliste rents 11 decent rooms in a dreary-yet-secure building at a great price for readers of this book (Sb-€30, Db-€40, extra bed-€20, air-con, elevator, Internet access and Wi-Fi, Caballero de Gracia 6, third floor, tel. 915-215-979, www.hostalaliste.net, h.aliste@teleline.es, Rachael and Edward speak English).

$ Hostal Residencia Luis XV is a big, plain, well-run, and clean place offering a good value. It's on a quiet eighth floor (there's an elevator). It can be smoky. They also run the 36-room **Hostal Jerez**—similar in every way—on the sixth floor (Sb-€45, Db-€59, Tb-€75, includes tax, air-con, elevator, ask about free Wi-Fi with this book, Calle de la Montera 47, tel. 915-221-021, fax 915-221-350, www.hrluisxv.net, reservas@hrluisxv.net).

Other Budget Beds in the Center

$$ **Ateneo Hotel,** just steps off Puerta del Sol, lacks public spaces and character, but its 38 rooms are close to business-class (Db-€75-90, occasionally less or more, air-con, elevator, Internet access and free Wi-Fi, Calle de la Montera 22, tel. 915-212-012, fax 915-233-136, www.hotel-ateneo.com, info@hotel-ateneo.com).

$ **Hostal Mayrit** and **Hostal Ivor** rent 28 rooms with thoughtful touches on pedestrianized Calle del Arenal (Sb-€50, Db-€65, air-con, elevator, near Metro: Ópera at Calle del Arenal 24, third floor, tel. 915-480-403, www.hostalivor.com, reservas @hostalivor.com).

$ **Hostal Santa Cruz,** simple and well-located, has 16 rooms at a good price (Sb-€45, Db-€58, Tb-€85, air-con, elevator, a block off Plaza Mayor at Plaza de Santa Cruz 6, second floor, tel. 915-222-441, fax 915-237-088, www.hostalsantacruz.com, info@hostal santacruz.com).

$ **Madrid Municipal Youth Hostel** (Albergue Juvenil Madrid) is fairly new and decidedly big, with 132 beds. It has four to six beds per room with lockers, modern bathrooms, and lots of extras, such as a laundry room, billiards, and movies (dorm bed-about €25, breakfast included, co-ed rooms, Internet access, Metro: Tribunal, then walk two minutes down Calle de Barceló to Calle de Mejia Lequerica 21, tel. 915-939-688, fax 915-939-684, www.ajmadrid.es, info@ajmadrid.es).

Near the Prado

To locate the following three places, see "Madrid's Museum Neighborhood" map on page 1347.

$$$ **Hotel Lope de Vega** offers good business-class hotel value near the Prado. It is a "cultural-themed" hotel inspired by the 17th-century writer Lope de Vega. With 60 rooms, it feels cozy and friendly for a formal hotel (Sb-€105, Db-€115-135, Tb-€180, one child sleeps free, prices about 20 percent lower Fri-Sun and during most of the summer, air-con, elevator, Internet access, parking-€23/day, Calle Lope de Vega 49, tel. 913-600-011, fax 914-292-391, www.hotellopedevega.com, lopedevega@hotellope devega.com).

At Cervantes 34: Two fine budget *hostales* are at Cervantes 34 (Metro: Antón Martín—but not handy to Metro). Both are homey, with inviting lounge areas; neither serves breakfast. The building next door may be under construction during your stay, which could make for a noisy siesta. $ **Hostal Gonzalo** has 15 spotless, comfortable rooms on the third floor and is well-run by friendly and helpful Javier. It's deservedly in all the guidebooks, so reserve in advance (Sb-€45, Db-€55, Tb-€70, air-con, elevator, Wi-Fi, tel. 914-292-714, fax 914-202-007, www.hostalgonzalo.com, hostal

@hostalgonzalo.com). Downstairs, the nearly as polished **$ Hostal Cervantes** also has 15 rooms (Sb-€50, Db-€60, Tb-€75, includes tax, cheaper when slow and for longer stays, some rooms with air-con, Internet access and Wi-Fi, tel. 914-298-365, fax 914-292-745, www.hostal-cervantes.com, correo@hostal-cervantes.com, Fabio).

Eating in Madrid

In Spain, only Barcelona rivals Madrid for taste-bud thrills. You have three dining choices: a memorable, atmospheric sit-down meal in a well-chosen restaurant; a forgettable, basic sit-down meal; or a stand-up meal of tapas in a bar...or four. Unless otherwise noted, these places start serving lunch at 13:00 or 13:30 and dinner starting at 20:30. You'll often find the places nearly empty with a few forlorn early-bird tourists and then thriving with locals after 14:00 and 22:00. Many restaurants close in August. Madrid has famously good tap water, and waiters willingly serve it free—just ask for *agua del grifo*. A new ban on smoking in public places should clear the air in formerly notoriously smoky restaurants.

I've grouped the recommended restaurants by neighborhood—near Plaza Mayor, Plaza Santa Ana, the Royal Palace, the Prado, and Puerta del Sol. I've listed a range of eateries, from splurges to cheap eats to fun pub crawls and churros with chocolate. Enjoy!

Near Plaza Mayor
Fine Dining
Restaurante Casa Paco is a Madrid tradition. Check out its old walls plastered with autographed photos of Spanish celebrities who have enjoyed their signature dish—ox grilled over a coal fire. Though popular with tourists, the place is authentic, confident, and uncompromising. It's a worthwhile splurge if you want to dine out well and carnivorously (€15-25 plates, ox sold by weight, 200 grams—which is almost half a pound—is a hearty steak, Plaza de la Puerta Cerrada 11, tel. 913-663-166).

Sobrino del Botín is a hit with many Americans because "Hemingway ate here." It's grotesquely touristy, pricey, and the last place Papa would go now...but still, people love it, and go for the roast suckling pig, their specialty. If phoning to make a reservation, choose the upstairs for a still-traditional, but airier style over the downstairs, which has a dark, medieval-cellar ambience (€35 meals; €40 fixed-price meal includes wine, bread, gazpacho, pig, dessert; daily 13:00-16:00 & 20:00-24:00, a block downhill from Plaza Mayor at Cuchilleros 17, tel. 913-664-217).

Posada de la Villa serves Castilian cuisine in a 17th-century inn. This sprawling, multi-floor restaurant has open-beam ceilings, which give it a rustic flair. Peek into the big oven to see the baby

Eating near Plaza Mayor

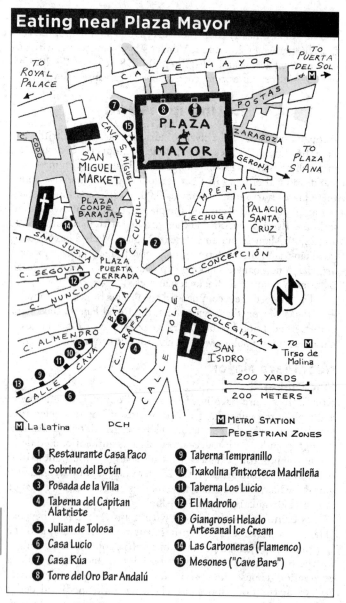

1. Restaurante Casa Paco
2. Sobrino del Botín
3. Posada de la Villa
4. Taberna del Capitan Alatriste
5. Julian de Tolosa
6. Casa Lucio
7. Casa Rúa
8. Torre del Oro Bar Andalú
9. Taberna Tempranillo
10. Txakolina Pintxoteca Madrileña
11. Taberna Los Lucio
12. El Madroño
13. Giangrossi Helado Artesanal Ice Cream
14. Las Carboneras (Flamenco)
15. Mesones ("Cave Bars")

pigs about to make some diner happy. If you're not going to Toledo or Sevilla, this is a good place to try roast lamb, the house specialty (€30 meals, closed Sun evening and Aug, Calle Cava Baja 9, tel. 913-661-860). Posada de la Villa's twin, **Taberna del Capitan Alatriste,** is more fresh and modern, a half-block away, and run by the same owners. They serve classic cuisine with lots of game under open beams in a stylish medieval vault (€25 plates, closed Mon, Grafal 7, tel. 913-661-883).

Julian de Tolosa is chic, pricey, elegantly simple, and popular with natives who know good food. They offer a small, quality menu of Navarra's regional cuisine, from T-bone steak *(chuletón)* to red *tolosa* beans, in a spacious, sane setting with nothing touristy (€45 meals, closed Sun, Calle Cava Baja 18, tel. 913-658-210).

Casa Lucio is a favorite splurge among power-dressing Madrileños. The king and queen of Spain eat in this formal place, but it's accessible to commoners. This is a good restaurant for a special night out and a full-blown meal, but you pay extra for this place's fame (€45 for dinner, nightly from 21:00, closed Aug, Calle Cava Baja 35; unless you're the king or queen, reserve several days in advance—and don't even bother on weekends; tel. 913-653-252).

Eating Cheap near Plaza Mayor

Madrileños enjoy a bite to eat on Plaza Mayor (without its high costs) by grabbing food to go from a nearby bar and just planting themselves somewhere on the square to eat (squid sandwiches are popular). But for many tourists, dinner at a sidewalk café right on Plaza Mayor is worth the premium price (consider Cervecería Pulpito, southwest corner of the square at #10).

Squid Sandwiches: Plaza Mayor is famous for its *bocadillos de calamares.* For a tasty €2.50 squid-ring sandwich, line up at **Casa Rúa** at Plaza Mayor's northwest corner, a few steps up Calle Ciudad Rodrigo (daily 11:00-23:00). Hanging up behind the bar is a photo-advertisement of Plaza Mayor from the 1950s, when the square contained a park.

Bullfighting Bar: The **Torre del Oro Bar Andalú** on Plaza Mayor has walls lined with grisly bullfight photos. This place is good for drinks, but you pay a premium for the tapas and food... the cost of munching amidst all that bullephenalia while enjoying their excellent Plaza Mayor outdoor seating (daily 8:00-15:00 & 18:00-24:00, closed in Jan).

Tapas on Calle Cava Baja, South of Plaza Mayor

Just three minutes south of Plaza Mayor, Calle Cava Baja fills each evening with mostly young, professional Madrileños prowling for chic tapas and social fun. Tapas are the toothpick appetizers, salads, and deep-fried foods traditionally served in Spanish bars. Come at night only and treat the entire street as a destination. I've listed a few standards, but excellent new eateries are always opening up. For a good, authentic Madrid dinner experience, take time to survey the many options along this street and then choose your favorites. Remember, it's easier and touristy early, jammed with locals later. (If you want a formal dining experience on this street, try Posada de la Villa, Julian de Tolosa, or Casa Lucio, recommended in "Fine Dining," earlier.) These Calle Cava Baja tapas bars are worth special consideration:

Taberna Tempranillo, ideal for hungry wine-lovers, offers fancy tapas and fine wine by the glass (see listing on the board). While there are a few tables, the bar is just right for hanging out. With a phrasebook in hand or a spirit of adventure, use their fascinating menu to assemble your dream meal. It's packed and full of commotion—the crowds can be overwhelming. Arrive by 20:00 or plan to wait (closed Aug, Calle Cava Baja 38, tel. 913-641-532).

Txakolina Pintxoteca Madrileña is a thriving bar serving Basque-style *pinchos* (tiny fancy sandwiches—*pintxo* in Basque) to a young crowd (€3/*pincho*, Calle Cava Baja 26, tel. 913-664-877).

Taberna Los Lucio is a jam-packed bar serving good tapas, salads, *huevos estrellados* (scrambled eggs with fried potatoes), and wine. If you'd like to make it a sit-down meal, head to the tables in the back. Their basement is much less atmospheric (Calle Cava Baja 30, tel. 913-662-984).

El Madroño ("The Berry Tree," a symbol of Madrid) is more of a cowboy bar, a block to the left off the top of Calle Cava Baja. (Their other bar with the same name, which you may see while heading toward Plaza Mayor, doesn't have the same ambience.) Preserving a bit of old Madrid, a tile copy of Velázquez's famous *Drinkers* grins from its facade. Inside, look above the stairs for photos of 1902 Madrid. Study the coats of arms of Madrid through the centuries as you try a *vermut* (vermouth) on tap and a €4 sandwich. Or ask to try the *licor de madroño;* a small glass *(chupito)* costs €2. Indoor seating is bright and colorful; the sidewalk tables come with great people-watching (which is why you pay more to eat the same food outside). Munch *raciones* at bar or front tables to be in the fun scene or have a quieter sit-down meal at the tables in the back (closed Mon, Plaza de la Puerta Cerrada 7, tel. 913-645-629).

Ice Cream Finale: **Giangrossi Helado Artesanal,** a popular chain, serves Argentinean-style ice cream, considered to be some of Madrid's best. With a plush white leather lounge and lots of great flavors, this hipster ice cream shop offers a sweet way to finish your dining experience in this area (at the end of Calle Cava Baja at #40, 50 yards from La Latina Metro stop, tel. 902-444-130).

Near Plaza Santa Ana

Fine Dining

El Caldero ("The Pot") is romantic and *the* place for paella and other rice dishes. A classy, in-the-know crowd appreciates the subdued elegance and crisp service of this place. The house specialty is *arroz caldero* (a variation on paella). Served with panache from a cauldron hanging from a tripod, it serves two for €28. Most of the formal rice dishes come in pots for two—like the €30-per-couple paella (closed Sun-Mon, Calle de las Huertas 15—for location see map on page 1370, tel. 914-295-044). Wash down your meal with the house sangria.

The Madrid Pub-Crawl Dinner (for Beginners)

For maximum fun, people, and atmosphere, go mobile for dinner: Do the *tapeo,* a local tradition of going from one bar to the next, munching, drinking, and socializing. While tiny €2 tapas plates are standard in Andalucía (and commonly served in Madrid's Calle Cava Baja area), these days most of Madrid's bars offer bigger €6 plates called *raciones,* ideal for a small group to share. The real action begins late (around 21:00). But for beginners, an earlier start, with less commotion, can be easier. The litter on the floor is normal; that's where people traditionally toss their trash and shells (it's unsanitary to put it back on the bar). Don't worry about paying until you're ready to go. Then ask for *la cuenta* (the bill).

If done properly, a pub crawl can be a highlight of your trip. Before embarking upon this culinary adventure, learn a little about tapas. Your ability to speak a little Spanish will get you a much better (and less expensive) experience.

Prowl the area between Puerta del Sol and Plaza Santa Ana. There's no ideal route, but the little streets between Puerta del Sol, San Jerónimo, and Plaza Santa Ana (see map) hold tasty surprises. Nearby, Calle de Jesús de Medinaceli is also lined with popular tapas bars. Here I've described a five-stop tapa crawl. These places are good, but don't be afraid to make some discoveries of your own. The more adventurous should read this crawl for ideas, and skip directly to the advanced zone (Lavapiés), described at the end of this section. For a more trendy pub crawl with designer tapas and finer wine, visit the bars on Calle Cava Baja (listed earlier).

• *From Puerta del Sol, walk east a block down Carrera de San Jerónimo to the corner of Calle Victoria.*

Museo del Jamón (Museum of Ham): This frenetic, cheap, stand-up bar (with famously rude service) is an assembly line of fast and simple *bocadillos* and *raciones.* It's tastefully decorated—unless you're a pig (or a vegetarian). Take advantage of the easy photo-illustrated menus that show various dishes and their prices. The best ham is the pricey *jamón ibérico*—from pigs who led

MADRID

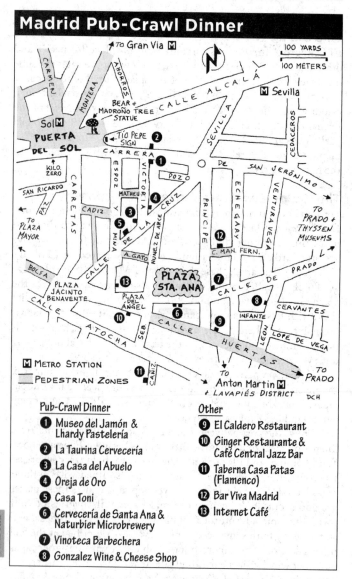

Madrid Pub-Crawl Dinner

Pub-Crawl Dinner

1. Museo del Jamón & Lhardy Pastelería
2. La Taurina Cervecería
3. La Casa del Abuelo
4. Oreja de Oro
5. Casa Toni
6. Cervecería de Santa Ana & Naturbier Microbrewery
7. Vinoteca Barbechera
8. Gonzalez Wine & Cheese Shop

Other

9. El Caldero Restaurant
10. Ginger Restaurante & Café Central Jazz Bar
11. Taberna Casa Patas (Flamenco)
12. Bar Viva Madrid
13. Internet Café

stress-free lives in acorn-strewn valleys. Point clearly to what you want, and be very specific to avoid being served a pricier meal than you intended: A plate of low-end *jamón blanco* costs only €2.50, whereas *jamón ibérico* costs €14. For a small sandwich, ask for a *chiquito* (€1, or €4 for *ibérico*). If you're on a budget, don't let them sell you the *ibérico* (daily 9:00-24:00, sit-down restaurant upstairs, air-con).

• Nearby are two options. Across the street is the touristy and over-priced bull bar, La Taurina. (I wouldn't eat here, but you're welcome to ponder the graphic photos that celebrate the gory art of bullfighting.) And next door take a detour from your pub crawl with something better for grandmothers:

Lhardy Pastelería: Offering a genteel taste of Old World charm in this district of rowdy pubs, this place has been a fixture since 1839 for Madrileños wanting to duck in for a cup of soup or a light snack. Step right in, and pretend you're an aristocrat back between the wars. Serve yourself. You'll pay as you leave (on the honor system). Help yourself to the silver water dispenser (free), a line of elegant bottles (each a different Iberian fortified wine: sherry, port, and so on, €2/glass), a revolving case of meaty little pastries (€1 each), and a fancy soup dispenser (chicken broth con-sommé–€2, or €2.50 with a splash of sherry...local style—bottles in the corner, help yourself; Mon-Sat 9:30-15:00 & 17:00-21:30, Sun 9:30-15:00 only, Carrera de San Jerónimo 8).

• Next, forage halfway up Calle Victoria to the tiny...

La Casa del Abuelo: This is where seafood-lovers savor siz-zling plates of tasty little *gambas* (shrimp) and *langostinos* (prawns), with bread to sop up the delightful juices. As drinks are cheap and dishes are pricey, you might want to share a *ración* or just try the wine. Try *gambas a la plancha* (grilled shrimp, €8.10) or *gambas al ajillo* (ah-HEE-yoh, shrimp version of escargot, cooked in oil and garlic, €8.80) and a €2 glass of sweet red house wine (daily 12:00-24:00, Calle Victoria 12).

• Across the street is...

Oreja de Oro: The "Golden Ear" is named for what it sells—sautéed pigs' ears (*oreja*, €5). While pig ears are a Madrid specialty, this place is Galician—they serve *pimientos de padrón* (sautéed miniature green peppers—quite possibly the tastiest plate of the entire crawl, €4.50), and the distinctive *ribeiro* (ree-BAY-roh) wine, served Galician-style, in characteristic little ceramic bowls to disguise its lack of clarity (closed Wed).

• For a finale, continue uphill and around the corner to...

Casa Toni: This memorable little spot is my favorite stop on this crawl. Run by Toni, it has a helpful English menu and several fun, classic dishes to try: *patatas bravas* (fried potatoes in a spicy sauce, €4), *berenjena* (deep-fried slices of eggplant, €5), *champiñones* (sautéed mushrooms, €5.50), and gazpacho—the cold tomato-and-garlic soup (€2.50) which is generally served only during the hot season, but available here year-round just for you (closed July, Calle Cruz 14).

More Options: If you're hungry for more, and want a trendy, up-to-date, pricier tapas scene, head for Plaza Santa Ana, with lively bars spilling out onto the square. Survey the entire scene.

Consider **Cervecería de Santa Ana** (tasty tapas with two zones: rowdy, circa-1900 beer-hall and classier sit-down) or **Naturbier,** a local microbrewery. **Vinoteca Barbechera,** at the downhill end of the square, has an inviting menu of tapas and fine wines by the glass (indoor and outdoor seating).

Gonzalez, a venerable gourmet cheese and wine shop with a circa-01930s interior, offers a genteel opportunity to enjoy a plate of first-class cheese and a fine glass of wine with friendly service and a fun setting. Their €13 assortment of five Spanish cheeses—more than enough for two—is a cheese-lover's treat (€10 lunch buffet, nice wines by the glass, closed Sun-Mon, three blocks past Plaza Santa Ana at Calle de León 12, tel. 914-295-618, Francisco).

Near the Royal Palace

Casa Ciriaco is popular with Madrileños who appreciate good traditional cooking—stews and partridge—with no affectation (€35 meals, €20 fixed-price lunch and dinner, closed Wed and Aug, Calle Mayor 84, tel. 915-480-620). It was from this building in 1906 that an anarchist bombed the royal couple on their wedding day (for details, see page 1344). Photos of the carnage are inside the front door.

La Bola Taberna, touristy but friendly and tastefully elegant, specializes in *cocido Madrileño*—Madrid stew. The €19 stew consists of various meats, carrots, and garbanzo beans in earthen jugs. This is a winter dish, prepared here for the tourists. The stew is served as two courses: First you enjoy the broth as a soup, then you dig into the meat and veggies (about €35/person for full meal, closed Sun, cash only, midway between Royal Palace and Gran Vía at Calle Bola 5, tel. 915-476-930).

Café de Oriente serves a great three-course lunch special (€14.50, Mon-Fri, 13:00-16:00 only) in fin-de-siècle elegance immediately across the park from the Royal Palace. While its cafeteria area is reasonable, its restaurant is pricey (Plaza de Oriente 2, tel. 915-413-974).

El Anciano Rey de los Vinos is a venerable, circa-1909 wine bar famous for its vermouth on tap. It's an expensive place to dine, but offers affordable tapas and drinks at its classic bar. A free small plate of tapas comes with each drink (closed Tue, across busy street from cathedral at Calle de Bailén 19, tel. 915-595-332).

Casual Dining near the Prado

Each of the three big art museums has a decent cafeteria. Or choose from these eateries, the first four within a block of the Prado and the last just steps from the Reina Sofía (for locations, see "Madrid's Museum Neighborhood" map on page 1347).

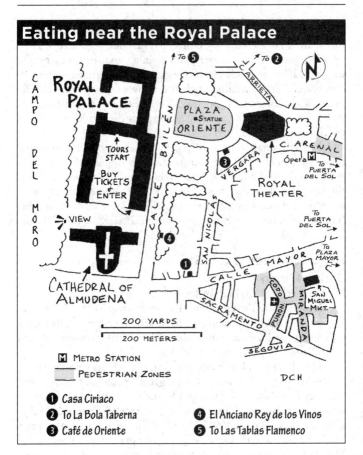

Eating near the Royal Palace

CAMPO DEL MORO

ROYAL PALACE

TOURS START

BUY TICKETS & ENTER

VIEW

CATHEDRAL OF ALMUDENA

CALLE BAILÉN

PLAZA ORIENTE
■STATUE

VERGARA

SAN NICOLÁS

CARRIETA

To ⑤   To ②

C. ARENAL

Ópera Ⓜ To PUERTA DEL SOL

ROYAL THEATER

To PUERTA DEL SOL

To PLAZA MAYOR

CALLE   MAYOR

SACRAMENTO

CODO NUNO

MIRANDA

SAN MIGUEL MKT.

SEGOVIA

200 YARDS

200 METERS

Ⓜ METRO STATION

▢ PEDESTRIAN ZONES

DCH

❶ Casa Ciriaco
❷ To La Bola Taberna
❸ Café de Oriente
❹ El Anciano Rey de los Vinos
❺ To Las Tablas Flamenco

Taberna de Dolores, a winning formula since 1908, is a commotion of locals enjoying €2.50 *canapés* (open-face sandwiches), tasty *raciones* of seafood, and *cañas* (small beers) at the bar or at a few tables in the back (daily 11:00-24:00, Plaza de Jesús 4, tel. 914-292-243).

Terra Mundi serves Galician cuisine to locals and tourists alike in a pleasant faux-rustic setting. Their €10-12 fixed-price meals are a good deal; the bar also serves a limited tapas menu. The *pimientos de Padrón* (grilled peppers, €7) are a highlight (Tue-Sun 13:00-16:30 & 20:30-1:00 in the morning, Mon 13:00-16:30 only, air-con, Calle Lope de Vega 32, tel. 914-295-280).

VIPS is a bright, popular chain restaurant, handy for a cheap and filling salad. Engulfed in a big bookstore, this is a high-energy, no-charm eatery (daily 9:00-24:00, across the boulevard from northern end of Prado, under Palace Hotel). In 2001 Spain's first Starbucks opened next door.

Viva la Vida Organic Market and Vegetarian Buffet, a tiny deli, offers a take-away buffet that delights vegetarians. Dish up what you like on a paper plate or in a paper box, pay by the weight (€2/100 grams, a plateful is generally 300 grams—about 10 ounces), and grab a nearby bench or hike over to the picnic-friendly Prado Museum grounds or Royal Botanical Garden (daily 11:00-24:00, a few blocks toward the center from the Prado at Calle de las Huertas 57, tel. 913-697-254).

El Brillante is a classic dive right on Plaza Sánchez Bustillo, the square in front of the Centro de Arte Reina Sofía. It offers pricey tapas and baguette sandwiches, but everyone comes for the fried squid sandwiches (evidenced by the older señoras with mouthfuls of *calamares)*. Sit at the simple bar or at an outdoor table (long hours daily, two entrances—one on Plaza Sánchez Bustillo, the other at Plaza del Emperador Carlos V 8, tel. 915-392-806).

North of Puerta del Sol
Eating Cheap
See the map on page 1361 for locations.

Restaurante Puerto Rico fills a long, congested hall by serving good meals for great prices to smart Madrileños (€10 three-course fixed-price meal, closed Sun, Chinchilla 2, between Puerta del Sol and Gran Vía, tel. 915-219-834).

Hotel Europa Cafetería is a fun, high-energy scene with a mile-long bar, old-school waiters, great people-watching, local cuisine, and a fine €11 fixed-price lunch (daily 7:00-24:00, next to the recommended Hotel Europa, 50 yards off Puerta del Sol at Calle del Carmen 4, tel. 915-212-900). The menu lists three price levels: bar (inexpensive), table (generally pricey), or terrace (sky-high but with good people-watching). Your best value is to stick to the lunch menu if you're sitting inside, or order off the plastic *barra* menu if you sit at the bar (the €3 ham-and-egg toast or the homemade *churros* make a nice breakfast).

El Corte Inglés' top-floor cafeterias (in both of its buildings) are fresh, modern, and popular, though not particularly cheap. One is just off Puerta del Sol at the intersection of Calle de Preciados and Calle de Tetuán, but the better one is near Plaza Callao. The lunch hour is busy, though it's worth the wait for its great views of Gran Vía and Plaza de España. Take a number for both the *terraza* and the cafeteria, and see which number comes up first (Mon-Sat 10:00-22:00, closed Sun even though rest of store is open).

Casa Labra Taberna Restaurante is famous as the birthplace of the Spanish Socialist Party in 1879...and as a spot for great cod. Packed with Madrileños, it manages to be both dainty and rustic. It's a wonderful scene with three distinct sections: the stand-up bar (cheapest, with two lines: one for munchies, the other for drinks), a peaceful little sit-down area in back (a little more expensive but still cheap; €6 salads), and a fancy restaurant (€20 lunches). Their tasty little €1.25 *tajada de bacalao* cod dishes put them on the map. The waiters are fun to joke around with (daily 11:00-15:30 & 18:00-23:00, a block off Puerta del Sol at Calle Tetuán 12, tel. 915-310-081).

La Gloria de Montera Restaurante, a hip Spanish bistro with white tablecloths and a minimalist-library ambience, serves mediocre food at a cheap price and with fast American-style table-turning—no long coffee klatches here (€8-12 fish and meat plates, daily, no reservations—arrive early or put your name on the list, a block from Gran Vía at Caballero de Gracia 10, tel. 915-234-407).

Ginger Restaurante, a twin with the same menu and formula and a little more comfortable seating, is just off Plaza Santa Ana (on Calle de las Huertas at Plaza del Ángel 12—see map on page 1370, tel. 913-691-059).

Fresc Co is the place for a cheap, modern, fast, and buffet-style meal. It's a chain with a winning plan: a long, appealing salad and buffet bar with one cheap price for all-you-can-eat, including dessert, a drink, and unlimited refills on everything (€9 lunch, €10 dinner, daily 12:30-24:00, air-con, Caballero de Gracia 8, tel. 915-216-052).

Vegetarian: **Artemisia II** is a hit with vegetarians who like good, healthy food without the typical hippie ambience that comes with most veggie places (great €12 three-course fixed-price lunch Mon-Fri only, open daily 13:30-16:00 & 21:00-24:00, 2 blocks north of Puerta del Sol at Tres Cruces 4, a few steps off Plaza del Carmen, tel. 915-218-721). **Artemisia I,** II's older sister, is located two blocks east of Plaza Santa Ana at Ventura de la Vega 4, off Carrera de San Jerónimo (same hours, tel. 914-295-092).

Fast Food and Picnics

For an easy, light, cheap meal, try **Rodilla**—a popular sandwich and salad chain with a shop on the northeast corner of Puerta del Sol at #13 (daily 9:30-23:00). **Pans & Company,** with shops throughout Madrid and Spain, offers healthy, tasty sandwiches and pre-packaged salads (daily 9:00-24:00, locations at Puerta del Sol, on Plaza Callao, at Gran Vía 30, and many more).

For a picnic, the department store **El Corte Inglés** has well-stocked meat and cheese counters downstairs (Mon-Sat 10:00-22:00, Sun 11:00-21:00, see "One-Stop Shopping" on page 1331).

Churros con Chocolate

Those not watching their cholesterol will want to try the deep-fried doughy treats called *churros* (or the thicker *porras*), best enjoyed by dipping them in pudding-like hot chocolate. Though many *chocolaterías* offer the dunkable fritters, *churros* are most delicious when consumed fresh out of the greasy cauldron at a place that actually fries them. See the map on page 1361 for locations.

Chocolaterías Valor is a modern chain that does *churros* with pride and gusto. A few minutes' walk from nearly all my hotel recommendations, it's a fine place for breakfast. With a website like www.amigosdelchocolate.com, you know where their heart is (€4 *churros con chocolate,* daily 8:00-22:30, Fri-Sat until 24:00, a half-block below Plaza Callao and Gran Vía at Postigo de San Martín 7, tel. 915-229-288).

Chocolatería San Ginés is a classy institution, much beloved by Madrileños for its *churros con chocolate* (€4). Dunk your *churros* into the chocolate pudding, as locals have done here for more than 100 years. Though quiet before midnight, it's packed with the disco crowd in the wee hours; the popular dance club Joy Eslava is next door (open 21 hours a day—it's only closed 6:30-9:30; from Puerta del Sol, take Calle del Arenal 2 blocks west, turn left on bookstore-lined Pasadizo de San Ginés, and you'll see the café—it's at #5; tel. 913-656-546).

Lavapiés District Tapas Crawl (for the Adventurous)

The neighborhood called Lavapiés is emerging as a colorful magnet for people-watching. This is where the multiethnic tapestry of Madrid society enjoys pithy, cheap, seedy-yet-fun-loving life on the streets. Neighborhoods like this typically experience the same familiar evolution: Initially they're so cheap that only the immigrants, downtrodden, and counter-culture types live there. The diversity and color they bring attracts those with more money. Businesses erupt to cater to those bohemian/trendy tastes. Rents go up. Those who gave the area the colorful liveliness in the first place can no longer afford to live there. They move out...and here comes Starbucks. For now, Lavapiés is still edgy, yet comfortable enough for most.

This district has almost no tourists. (It's too scary.) Old ladies with their tired bodies and busy fans hang out on their tiny balconies as they have for 40 years, watching the scene. Shady types lurk on side streets (don't venture off the main drag, don't show your wallet or money, and don't linger on Plaza Lavapiés).

For food, you'll find all the various kinds of tapas bars described earlier in "The Madrid Pub-Crawl Dinner," plus great Indian (almost all run by Bangladeshis) and Moroccan eateries. I've listed a couple of places that appealed to me...but explore your options. I'd recommend taking the entire walk once, then backtracking and eating at the place or places that appeal to you.

From the Antón Martín Metro stop (or Plaza Santa Ana),

MADRID

walk down Calle del Ave María (on its way to becoming Calle del Ave Allah) to Plaza Lavapiés (where old ladies hang out with the swarthy drunks and a mosaic of cultures treat this square as a communal living room; the Lavapiés Metro station is here), and then up Calle de Lavapiés to the recently remodeled square, Plaza Tirso de Molina (Metro stop). This square was once plagued by druggies. Now home to flower kiosks and a playground, it's homey and inviting. This is a good example of the new vision for Madrid's public spaces.

On Calle Ave María: **Bar Melos** is a thriving dive jammed with a hungry and nubile crowd. It's famous for its giant patty melts called *zapatillas de lacón y queso* (because they're the size and shape of a *zapatilla* or slipper, €7, feeds at least two, Ave María 44, smoky tables in back). **Nuevo Café Barbieri,** one of a dying breed of smoky mirrored cafés with a circa-1940 ambience, offers classical music in the afternoon and jazz in the evening (Calle del Ave María 45).

On Calle de Lavapiés: At Calle de Lavapiés 44, consider an Indian place or drop into **Montes Wine Bar** (countless wines open and served by the glass, good tapas, crawl under the bar to get to the WC).

Madrid Connections

By Train

Madrid has two main train stations: Chamartín and Atocha. At the Atocha Station, AVE and other long-distance trains depart from a different area than local *cercanías* trains (for more details, see "Arrival in Madrid" on page 1327).

AVE Trains: Spain's AVE (AH-vay) bullet train opens up some good itinerary options. You can now get from Madrid's Atocha Station to **Barcelona** in about three hours, with trains running almost hourly. The AVE train is generally faster (timed from downtown to downtown) and easier than flying, but not necessarily cheaper. Basic second-class tickets are €115 one-way for most departures and €135 for the fastest, peak-time departures. First-class tickets are €200. Advance purchase discounts (40-60 days ahead) are available through the national rail company (RENFE), but sell out quickly. Save by not traveling on holidays.

The AVE is also handy for visiting **Sevilla** (and, on the way, **Córdoba**). The basic Madrid-Sevilla second-class AVE fare is €70-80, depending upon departure time; first-class AVE costs €130 and comes with a meal). Consider this exciting day trip to Sevilla from Madrid: 7:00-depart Madrid, 8:45-12:40-in Córdoba, 13:30-20:45-in Sevilla, 23:30-back in Madrid.

Other AVE destinations include **Toledo** (10/day, 30 minutes,

€10, from Atocha) and **Segovia** (8/day, 35 minutes, €10, from Chamartín Station, take train going toward Valladolid). For the latest, pick up the AVE brochure at the station, or check www .renfe.com. Prices vary with times and class. Eurailpass-holders get a big discount (e.g., Madrid to Sevilla is €9 second-class, but only at RENFE ticket windows—discount not available at ticket machines). Reserve each AVE segment ahead (tel. 902-320-320 for Atocha AVE info).

Below I've listed both non-AVE and (where available) AVE trains, to help you compare your options.

From Madrid by Train to: Toledo (AVE: nearly hourly, 30 minutes, from Atocha), **Barcelona** (AVE: almost hourly, 3 hours from Atocha; plus 1 night train from Chamartín, 9 hours), **Lisbon** (1/day departing at 22:25, 9 hours, overnight Hotel Train from Chamartín), **Paris** (3/day, 13 hours, direct overnight—a €185 Hotel Train, reserve more than 15 days in advance and hope there are seats left in the €89 *tarifa promo* deals, from Chamartín). General train info: toll tel. 902-320-320, for international journeys: tel. 902-243-402, www.renfe.com.

Madrid's Barajas Airport

Ten miles east of downtown, Madrid's modern airport has four terminals. Terminals 1, 2, and 3 are connected by long indoor walkways (about an 8-minute walk apart), and serve airlines including Delta, United, US Airways, Air Canada, and Spanair. The newer Terminal 4 serves airlines including Iberia, Vueling, British, and American, and also has a separate satellite terminal called T4S. To transfer between Terminals 1-3 and Terminal 4, you can take a 10-minute shuttle bus (free, leaves every 10 minutes from departures level), or take the Metro (stops at Terminals 2 and 4). Make sure to allow enough time if you need to travel between terminals (and then for the long walk within Terminal 4 to the gates). For more information about navigating this massive airport, go to www.aena.es.

International flights typically use Terminals 1 and 4. At the Terminal 1 arrivals area, you'll find a helpful English-speaking **TI** (marked *Oficina de Información Turística*, Mon-Sat 8:00-20:00, Sun 9:00-14:00, tel. 913-058-656), **ATMs,** a **flight info office** (marked simply *Information* in airport lobby, open daily 24 hours, tel. 902-353-570), a **post-office** window, a **pharmacy,** lots of **phones** (buy a phone card from the nearby machine), a few scattered **Internet** terminals (small fee), **eateries,** a **RENFE office** (where you can get train info and buy long-distance train tickets, daily 8:00-21:00, tel. 902-320-320), and on-the-spot **car-rental agencies.** The super-modern Terminal 4 offers essentially the same services. The **luggage storage** *(consigna)* is in Terminal 2, near the Metro exit.

Iberia, Spanair, and Air Europa are Spain's airlines, connecting a reasonable number of cities in Spain, as well as international destinations (ask for best rates at travel agencies). Vueling is the most popular discount airline in Iberia (e.g., Madrid-Barcelona flight as cheap as €30 if booked in advance, tel. 902-333-933, www.vueling.com).

Getting Between the Airport and Downtown

By Public Bus: Bus #200 shuttles travelers between airport Terminals 1, 2, and 3 (departing from arrivals level every 10 minutes, runs 6:00-24:00) and the Metro stop Avenida de América (northeast of the historical center) in about 20 minutes. From that Metro stop, you can connect to your hotel by taking the Metro or hopping a taxi. Bus #204 serves Terminal 4 the same way. The trip costs only €1 (buy ticket from driver; or get a shareable 10-ride Metrobus ticket for €9 at a tobacco shop). Another public bus runs between the airport (all terminals) and Atocha Station (€2, runs 24 hours a day).

By Metro: The subway involves two transfers to reach the city center (€2; or add a €1 supplement to your €9 10-ride Metrobus ticket). The airport's futuristic "Aeropuerto T-1, T-2, T-3" Metro stop (notice the ATMs, subway info booth, and huge lighted map of Madrid) is in Terminal 2. Access the Metro at the check-in level; to reach the Metro from Terminal 1's arrivals level, stand with your back to the baggage claim, then go to your far right, up the stairs, and follow red-and-blue Metro diamond signs to the station (8-minute walk). The Terminal 4 stop is the end of the line. To get to Puerta del Sol, take line 8 for 12 minutes to Nuevos Ministerios, then continue on line 10 to Tribunal, then line 1 to Puerta del Sol (30 minutes more total); or exit at Nuevos Ministerios and take a €5 taxi or bus #150 straight to Puerta del Sol.

By Minibus Shuttle: The AeroCity shuttle bus provides door-to-door transport in a seven-seat minibus with up to three hotel stops en route. It's promoted by hotels, but if you want door-to-door service, simply taking a taxi generally offers a better value.

By Taxi: Considering the speed, ease, and economy of riding the subway in from the airport, I'd opt for the Metro over taxis, keeping in mind that transferring lines probably involves climbing some stairs. If you take a taxi between the airport and downtown, allow about €30 during the day *(Tarifa 1)* or €35-40 at night and on Sundays *(Tarifa 2)*. For Terminal 4, add about €10. Insist on the meter. The €5.50 airport supplement is legal. There is no charge for luggage. Plan on getting stalled in traffic.

SWITZERLAND

GIMMELWALD
and the BERNER OBERLAND

Interlaken • Lauterbrunnen • Gimmelwald •
Mürren • Wengen

Frolic and hike high above the stress and clouds of the real world. Take a vacation from your busy vacation. Recharge your touristic batteries high in the Alps, where distant avalanches, cowbells, the fluff of a down comforter, the whistle of marmots, and the crunchy footsteps of happy hikers are the dominant sounds. If the weather's good (and your budget's healthy), ride a cable car from the traffic-free village of Gimmelwald to a hearty breakfast at Schilthorn's 10,000-foot-elevation, revolving Piz Gloria restaurant. Linger among alpine whitecaps before riding, hiking, or paragliding down 5,000 feet to Mürren and home to Gimmelwald.

Your gateway to the rugged Berner Oberland is the grand old resort town of Interlaken. Near Interlaken is Switzerland's open-air folk museum, Ballenberg, where you can climb through original traditional houses gathered from every corner of this diverse country.

Ah, but the weather's fine and the Alps beckon. Head deep into the heart of the Alps, and ride the cable car to the stop just this side of heaven—Gimmelwald.

Planning Your Time

Rather than tackle a checklist of famous Swiss mountains and resorts, choose one region to savor: the Berner Oberland.

Interlaken is the region's administrative headquarters and transportation hub. Use it for business—banking, post office, laundry, shopping—and as a springboard for alpine thrills.

With decent weather, explore the two areas that tower above either side of the **Lauterbrunnen Valley,** south of Interlaken: On one side is the **Jungfrau** (and beneath it, the towns of Wengen and

Kleine Scheidegg), and on the other is the **Schilthorn** (overlooking the villages of Gimmelwald and Mürren).

For accommodations without the expense and headache of mountain lifts, consider the valley-floor village of **Lauterbrunnen.** But for the best overnight options, I'd stay on the scenic ridge high above the valley, in the rustic hamlet of **Gimmelwald** or the resort town of **Mürren.** I've also listed some options in the resort of **Wengen** and a few other mountain towns. Ideally, spend three nights in the region, with a day exploring each side of the valley.

For the fastest look, consider a night in Gimmelwald, breakfast at the Schilthorn, an afternoon doing the Männlichen-Wengen hike, and an evening or night train out. What? A nature-lover not spending the night high in the Alps? Alpus interruptus.

Getting Around the Berner Oberland

For more than a century, this region has been the target of nature-worshipping pilgrims. And Swiss engineers and visionaries have made the most exciting alpine perches accessible...

By Lifts and Trains: Part of the fun—and most of the expense—here is riding the many mountain trains and lifts (gondolas and cable cars).

Trains connect Interlaken to Wilderswil, Grindelwald, Lauterbrunnen, Wengen, Kleine Scheidegg, and the Jungfraujoch. Lifts connect Wengen to Männlichen and Grund (near Grindelwald); Grindelwald to First; Lauterbrunnen to Grütschalp (where a train connects to Mürren); and the cable-car station near Stechelberg to Gimmelwald, Mürren, and the Schilthorn.

For an overview of your many options, study the "Alpine Lifts in the Berner Oberland" map on page 1385. Lifts generally go at least twice hourly, from about 7:00 until about 20:00 (sneak preview: www.jungfraubahn.ch or www.schilthorn.ch).

Beyond Interlaken, trains and lifts into the Jungfrau region are only 25 percent covered by Eurailpasses, without using a flexiday; with the Swiss Pass, they're free up to Wengen or Mürren (uphill from there, Swiss Pass-holders pay half-price). Ask about discounts for early-morning and late-afternoon trips, youths, seniors, families, groups (assemble a party of 10 and you'll save about 25 percent), and those staying a while. Generally, round-trips are just double the one-way cost, though some high-up trains and lifts are 10-20 percent cheaper. It's possible to buy your entire package of lifts at once, but then you don't have the flexibility to change with the weather.

Popular local passes include the following:

The **Junior Card,** for families traveling with children, is a great deal, and pays for itself in the first hour of trains and lifts (30 SF/one child, 60 SF/two or more children, lets children under 16

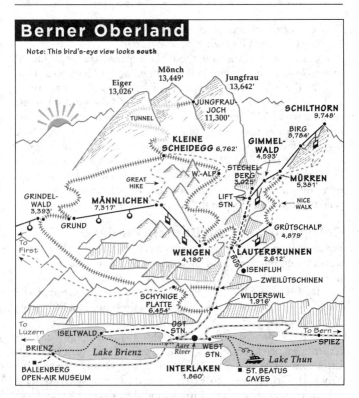

Berner Oberland

Note: This bird's-eye view looks **south**

Eiger 13,026'
Mönch 13,449'
Jungfrau 13,642'
JUNGFRAU JOCH 11,300'
TUNNEL
SCHILTHORN 9,748'
BIRG 8,784'
KLEINE SCHEIDEGG 6,762'
GIMMEL-WALD 4,593'
GREAT HIKE
W.-ALP
STECHEL-BERG 3,025'
MÜRREN 5,381'
GRINDEL-WALD 3,393'
MÄNNLICHEN 7,317'
LIFT STN.
NICE WALK
GRUND
GRÜTSCHALP 4,879'
To First
WENGEN 4,180'
LAUTERBRUNNEN 2,612'
ISENFLUH
ZWEILÜTSCHINEN
SCHYNIGE PLATTE 6,454'
WILDERSWIL 1,916'
To Luzern
OST STN.
ISELTWALD
To Bern
BRIENZ
Aare River
WEST STN.
Lake Thun
SPIEZ
Lake Brienz
BALLENBERG OPEN-AIR MUSEUM
INTERLAKEN 1,860'
ST. BEATUS CAVES

travel free with at least one parent, buy at Swiss train stations).

The **Berner Oberland Regional Pass** is a good idea for those staying a week and exploring the region extensively (7-day version-230 SF, discount with Swiss Pass, includes 3 days of unlimited travel and 4 days of half-price fares on all trains, buses, and lifts—even all the way south to Gstaad and Brig, valid May-Oct, 15-day version-277 SF, www.regiopass-berneroberland.ch).

The **Jungfraubahnen Pass** is more limited in scope, covering six consecutive days of unlimited transportation in just the Jungfrau region. This pass covers all the trains, lifts, buses, and funiculars, with one exception: you pay half-price for the train between Kleine Scheidegg and the Jungfraujoch (200 SF, or 150 SF with Swiss Pass, valid May-Oct, tel. 033-828-7233, www .jungfraubahn.ch).

By Car: Interlaken, Lauterbrunnen, Isenfluh, and Stechelberg are all accessible by car. You can't drive to Gimmelwald, Mürren, Wengen, or Kleine Scheidegg, but don't let that stop you from staying up in the mountains; park the car and zip up on a lift. To catch the lift to Gimmelwald, Mürren, and the Schilthorn, park at the cable-car station near Stechelberg (2 SF/2 hours, 6 SF/

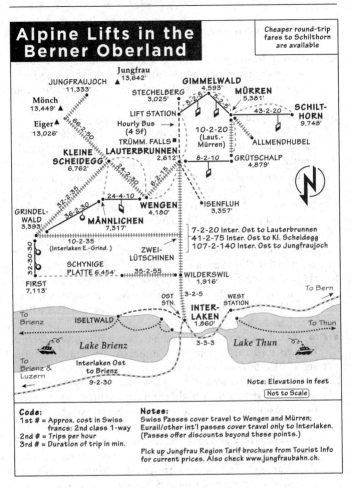

Alpine Lifts in the Berner Oberland

Cheaper round-trip fares to Schilthorn are available

JUNGFRAUJOCH 11,333'

Jungfrau ▲ 13,642'

GIMMELWALD 4,593'

STECHELBERG 3,025'

MÜRREN 5,381'

Mönch ▲ 13,449'

SCHILT-HORN 9,748'

LIFT STATION

43-2-20

Eiger ▲ 13,026'

Hourly Bus (4 Sf) →

10-2-20 (Laut.-Mürren)

ALLMENDHUBEL

TRÜMM. FALLS ■

KLEINE SCHEIDEGG 6,762'

LAUTERBRUNNEN 2,612'

8-2-10

GRÜTSCHALP 4,879'

24-4-10

WENGEN 4,180'

ISENFLUH 3,357'

32-2-35

36-2-30

GRINDEL-WALD 3,593'

MÄNNLICHEN 7,317'

10-2-35 (Interlaken E.-Grind.)

ZWEI-LÜTSCHINEN

7-2-20 Inter. Ost to Lauterbrunnen
41-2-75 Inter. Ost to Kl. Scheidegg
107-2-140 Inter. Ost to Jungfraujoch

32-30-30

SCHYNIGE PLATTE 6,454'

35-2-55

WILDERSWIL 1,916'

FIRST 7,113'

OST STN.

3-2-5

WEST STATION

To Bern

To Brienz

ISELTWALD

INTER-LAKEN 1,860'

To Thun

Lake Brienz

3-3-3

Lake Thun

To Brienz & Luzern

Interlaken Ost to Brienz
9-2-30

Note: Elevations in feet

Not to Scale

Code:
1st # = Approx. cost in Swiss francs; 2nd class 1-way
2nd # = Trips per hour
3rd # = Duration of trip in min.

Notes:
Swiss Passes cover travel to Wengen and Mürren; Eurail/other int'l passes cover travel only to Interlaken. (Passes offer discounts beyond these points.)

Pick up Jungfrau Region Tarif brochure from Tourist Info for current prices. Also check www.jungfraubahn.ch.

day, cash only; see page 1405 for more information). To catch the train to Wengen or Kleine Scheidegg, park at the train station in Lauterbrunnen (parking: 2 SF/2 hours, 10 SF/9-24 hours).

Helpful Hints in the Berner Oberland

Weather: The local economy lives by the weather. You're wise to be in touch. Ask at your hotel or the TI for the latest. A local TV station showing live video from the famous (and most expensive-to-reach) peaks plays just about wherever you go. For the latest weather, you can also check www.swisspanorama .com (entire area), www.jungfraubahn.ch (for Jungfraujoch), or www.schilthorn.ch (for Schilthorn peak).

Closed Days: On Sundays and holidays (including the lesser-known religious holidays), small-town Switzerland is quiet.

GIMMELWALD

Hotels are open, and lifts and trains run, but many stores are closed.

Off-Season Closures: Note that at higher altitudes, many hotels, restaurants, and shops are closed between the skiing and hiking seasons: from late April until late May, and again from mid-October to early December.

Rainy-Day Options: When it rains here, locals joke that they're washing the mountains. If clouds roll in, don't despair. They can roll out just as quickly. With good rain gear and the right choice of trail, a hike in the rain can be thoroughly enjoyable, with surprise views popping out all around you as the clouds break. Some good bad-weather options are the North Face Trail, the walk from Mürren or Allmendhubel to Grütschalp, the Sefinen Valley hike, and the Lauterbrunnen Valley walk. Also consider a visit to Trümmelbach Falls or the Lauterbrunnen Valley Folk Museum. All of these options are described in this chapter.

Local Guidebook: For an in-depth look at the area's history, folk life, flora, fauna, and for extensive hiking information, consider Don Chmura's *Exploring the Lauterbrunnen Valley* (sold throughout the valley, 8 SF).

Visitors Cards *(Gästekarten):* The hotels in various towns issue free visitor's cards that include measly discounts on some sights (ask for details at your hotel).

Skiing: The Berner Oberland is a great winter-sports destination, with good snow on its higher runs, incredible variety, relatively reasonable prices, and a sense of character that's missing in many swankier resort areas. You can even swish with the Swiss down the world's longest sledding run (9 miles long, out of Grindelwald, only open when snow's good). Three ski areas cluster around the Lauterbrunnen Valley: Mürren-Schilthorn (best for expert skiers), Kleine Scheidegg-Männlichen (busiest, best variety of runs), and Grindelwald-First (best for beginners and intermediate skiers, but lower elevation can make for iffier snowpack). Lift tickets cost around 60 SF a day, including the Sportspass Jungfrau, which covers all three areas (see www.jungfrauwinter.ch for prices and info).

Interlaken

When the 19th-century Romantics redefined mountains as something more than cold and troublesome obstacles, Interlaken became the original alpine resort. Ever since, tourists have flocked to the Alps "because they're there." Interlaken's glory days are long gone, its elegant old hotels eclipsed by the new, more swanky alpine resorts. Today, its shops are filled with chocolate bars, Swiss Army knives, and sunburned backpackers.

While European jet-setters are elsewhere, Interlaken is cashing in on a huge interest from India and the Arab world. Indians come to escape their monsoon season—especially in April and May—and to visit places they've seen in their movies. (The Alps often stand in for Kashmir, which is less accessible to film crews.) There's even a restaurant called "Bollywood" atop the Jungfraujoch. People from the hot and dry Arabian Peninsula come here just to photograph their children frolicking in the mist and fog.

Orientation to Interlaken

Efficient Interlaken (pop. 5,500) is a good administrative and shopping center. Take care of business, give the town a quick look, and view the live TV coverage of the weather higher up (at the TI)... then head for the hills.

Tourist Information

The TI has good information on the region (June Mon-Fri 8:00-18:00, Sat 8:00-16:00, closed Sun; July-Aug Mon-Fri 8:00-19:00, Sat 8:00-17:00, Sun 10:00-12:00 & 17:00-19:00; Sept Mon-Fri 8:00-18:00, Sat 9:00-13:00, closed Sun; shorter hours Oct-May; under the 18-story skyscraper on the main street between West and Ost train stations, a 10-minute stroll from either, Höheweg 37; tel. 033-826-5300, www.interlaken.ch). The *You Want It All* booklet is an almanac covering everything you need in Interlaken (except for some events, which are covered more thoroughly in the monthly entertainment guide). There's no point in buying a regional map, as good mini-versions of the map are included in various free transportation and hiking brochures.

Arrival in Interlaken

Interlaken has two train stations: Ost (East) and West. All trains stop at both stations. If heading for higher-altitude villages, get off at the Ost station. For hotels in Interlaken, get off at the West station. The West station also has a helpful and friendly information center for in-depth rail questions (Mon-Fri 9:00-12:00 & 13:30-18:30,

Sat 9:00-12:00 & 13:30-17:00, closed Sun, tel. 058-327-4750, www
.bls.ch; ticket windows open daily 6:40-19:00). Ask about discount
passes, special fares, railpass discounts, and schedules for the scenic mountain trains. There's an exchange booth next to the ticket
windows. A post office with a cluster of phone booths is a few
blocks away.

It's a pleasant 20-minute walk between the West and Ost stations, an easy, frequent train connection (2-3/hour, 3.40 SF), or a
quick trip on the bus (5/hour, 10 minutes, 3.40 SF, tel. 058-448-
2008, www.postauto.ch). From the Ost station, private trains take
you deep into the mountainous Jungfrau region (see "Interlaken
Connections," page 1398).

Helpful Hints

Laundry: Friendly Helen Schmocker's **Wäscherei** has a change
    machine, soap, English instructions, and a delightful river-
    side location (self-service daily 7:00-22:00—6 SF/load; full
    service Mon-Fri 8:00-12:00 & 13:30-18:00, Sat until 16:00,
    closed Sun, drop off in the morning and pick up that after-
    noon—12 SF/load; from the main street take Marktgasse over
    two bridges to Beatenbergstrasse 5, tel. 033-822-1566).

Bike Rental: You can rent bikes at either train station on week-
    days but not weekends (11.50 SF/2 hours, 25 SF/half-day,
    33 SF/day, 5 SF less with Eurailpass or Swiss Pass, Mon-Fri
    8:00-17:00, later drop-off possible, closed Sat-Sun, www.renta
    bike.ch).

Self-Guided Walk

Welcome to Interlaken

Most visitors use Interlaken as a springboard for high-altitude
thrills (and rightly so). But the town itself has history and scenic
charm and is worth a short walk. This 45-minute stroll circles from
the West train station down the main drag to the big meadow, past
the casino, along the river to the oldest part of town (historically a
neighboring town called Unterseen), and back to the station.

• *From the West train station, walk along...*

    Bahnhofstrasse: This main drag, which turns into Höheweg
as it continues east, cuts straight through the town center from
the West train station to the Ost station. The best Swiss souvenir
shopping is along this Bahnhofstrasse stretch (finer shops are on
the Höheweg stretch, near the fancy hotels). At the roundabout
is the handy post office (with free public WCs). Just behind the
post office on Marktgasse, the hardware store stocks real cowbells
(both ornate and plain). At Höheweg 2, the TV in the window of
the Schilthornbahn office shows the weather up top.

GIMMELWALD

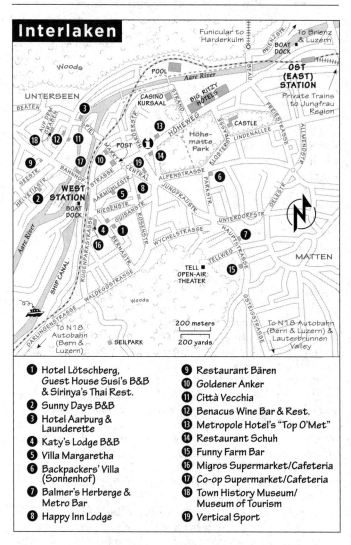

Interlaken

1. Hotel Lötschberg, Guest House Susi's B&B & Sirinya's Thai Rest.
2. Sunny Days B&B
3. Hotel Aarburg & Launderette
4. Katy's Lodge B&B
5. Villa Margaretha
6. Backpackers' Villa (Sonnenhof)
7. Balmer's Herberge & Metro Bar
8. Happy Inn Lodge
9. Restaurant Bären
10. Goldener Anker
11. Città Vecchia
12. Benacus Wine Bar & Rest.
13. Metropole Hotel's "Top O'Met"
14. Restaurant Schuh
15. Funny Farm Bar
16. Migros Supermarket/Cafeteria
17. Co-op Supermarket/Cafeteria
18. Town History Museum/ Museum of Tourism
19. Vertical Sport

The 18-story **Metropole Hotel** (a.k.a. the "concrete shame of Interlaken") is by far the town's tallest building. Step right into the lobby and ride the elevator to the top for a commanding view of the "inter-laken" area, and gaze deep into the Jungfrau region to the scenic south. A meal or drink here costs no more than one back on earth. Consider sipping a drink on its outdoor view terrace (or come back tonight—it's open very late).

• *On your right is...*

Höhematte Park: This "high meadow," or Höhematte (but generally referred to simply as "the park"), marks the beginning

GIMMELWALD

of Interlaken's fancy hotel row. Hotels like the Victoria-Jungfrau hearken back to the days when Interlaken was *the* top alpine resort (late 19th century). The first grand hotels were built here to enjoy the views of the Jungfrau in the distance. (Today, the *jung Fraus* getting the most attention are next door, at Hooters.)

The park originated as farmland of the monastery that pre-dated the town (marked today by the steeples of both the Catholic and Protestant churches—neither of any sightseeing interest). The actual **monastery site** is now home to the courthouse and county administration building. With the Reformation in 1528, the mon-astery was shut down, and its land was taken by the state. Later, when the land was being eyed by developers, the town's leading hotels and business families bought it and established that it would never be used for commercial buildings (a very early example of smart town planning). There was talk of building a parking lot under it, but the water table here, between the two lakes, is too high. (That's why the town cemetery is up on the hillside.) Today, this is a fine place to stroll, hang out on the park benches or at Restaurant Schuh, and watch the paragliders gracefully land.

From the park, turn left into the grounds of **Casino Kursaal,** where, at the top of each hour, dwarves ring the toadstools on the flower clock. The Kursaal, originally a kind of 19th-century fat farm, is now both a casino (passport but no tie required to enter) and a convention center.

• *Follow the path left of the Kursaal to the river (huge public swimming pool just over the river). Walk downstream under the train track and cross the pedestrian bridge, stopping in the middle to enjoy the view.*

Aare River: The Aare River is Switzerland's longest. It connects Lake Brienz and Lake Thun (with an 18-foot altitude difference—this short stretch has quite a flow). Then it tumbles out of Lake Thun, heading for Bern and ultimately into the Rhine. Its level is controlled by several sluices. In the distance, a church bell tower marks a different parish and the neighborhood of Unterseen, which shares the town's name, but in German: Like the word *Interlaken*, *Unterseen* means "between the lakes." Behind the spire is the pointy summit of the Niesen (like so many Swiss peaks, capped with a restaurant and accessible by a lift). Stroll downstream along the far side of the river to the church spire. The delightful riverside walk is lined by fine residences. Notice that your Jungfrau view now includes the Jungfraujoch observation deck (the little brown bump in the ridge just left of the peak).

• *At the next bridge, turn right to the town square lined with 17th cen-tury houses on one side and a modern strip on the other.*

Unterseen: This was a town when Interlaken was only a mon-astery. The church is not worth touring. A block away, the (gener-ally empty) **Town History Museum/Museum of Tourism** shows off classic posters, fascinating photos of the construction of the Jungfraujoch, and exhibits on folk life, crafts, and winter sports—all well-described in English (5 SF, May-mid-Oct Tue-Sun 14:00-17:00, closed Mon and mid-Oct-April, Obere Gasse 26).

Return to Station: From Unterseen, cross the river on Spielmatte, and you're a few minutes' walk from your starting point. On the second bridge, notice the border between the two towns, or parishes, marked by their respective heraldic emblems (each with an ibex, or wild mountain goat). A block or so later, on the left, is the Marktplatz. The river originally ran through this square. The town used to be called "Aaremühle" ("Aare mill") for the mill that was here. But in the 19th century, town fathers made a key marketing decision: Since "Aaremühle" was too difficult to pronounce for the English tourists who first flocked here, they changed the name to "Interlaken." Judging from the throngs of tourists on the main drag, it worked.

Sights near Interlaken

Swiss Open-Air Folk Museum at Ballenberg

Across Lake Brienz from Interlaken, the Swiss Open-Air Museum of Vernacular Architecture, Country Life, and Crafts in the Berner Oberland is a rich collection of more than 100 traditional and historic buildings brought here from every region of the country. All the houses are carefully furnished, and many feature traditional craftspeople at work. The sprawling 50-acre park, laid out roughly as a huge Swiss map (Italian Swiss in the south, Appenzell in the east, and so on), is a natural preserve providing a wonderful setting for this culture-on-a-lazy-Susan look at Switzerland.

The Thurgau house (#621) has an interesting wattle-and-daub (half-timbered construction) display, and house #331 has a fun bread museum and farmers' shop. There are daily events and demonstrations (near the east entry), hundreds of traditional farm animals (like very furry-legged roosters, near the merry-go-round in the center), and a chocolate shop (under the restaurant on the east side).

An outdoor cafeteria with reasonable prices is inside the west entrance, and fresh bread, sausage, mountain cheese, and other goodies are on sale in several houses. Picnic tables and grills with free firewood are scattered throughout the park.

The little wooden village of Brienzwiler (near the east entrance) is a museum in itself, with a lovely pint-size church.

Cost and Hours: 20 SF, covered by Swiss Pass. A RailAway combo-ticket, available at both Interlaken stations, includes transportation to and from Ballenberg and your admission (39 SF from Interlaken West station, 36 SF from Interlaken Ost, add 17.40 SF

GIMMELWALD

to return by boat instead). The houses are open daily mid-April-Oct 10:00-17:00, but the grounds and restaurants stay open until 18:00 (last bus to Brienz train station leaves Ballenberg east/west entrances at 18:00/18:07). Pick up a daily craft demonstration schedule at the entry, and buy the 2-SF map/guide so you'll know where you are. The more expensive picture book is a better souvenir than guide. Guided two-hour tours in English must be booked well in advance (11 SF, tel. 033-952-1030, www.ballenberg.ch).

Getting There from Interlaken: Take the train from either of Interlaken's train stations to Brienz (2/hour, 30 minutes, 9 SF one-way from West station or get the RailAway combo-ticket—described above). From the Brienz station, catch a bus to Ballenberg (10 minutes, 3.40 SF one-way; leaves Ballenberg east entrance on the hour, then picks up at west entrance at :07 after the hour). Consider returning from Brienz by boat (boat dock next to train station, one-way to Interlaken Ost-25 SF).

Boat Trips

"Interlaken" is literally "between the lakes" of Thun and Brienz. You can explore these lakes on a lazy boat trip, hopping on and off as the schedule allows (free with Swiss Pass or Eurailpass but uses a flexi-day, schedules at TI or at travel center in West station). The boats on Lake Thun (5/day in summer, 2/day spring and fall, 5-hour round-trip, 61 SF) stop at the St. Beatus caves (30 minutes away, described next) and two visit-worthy towns: Spiez and Thun. The boats on Lake Brienz (5/day July-Aug, 2-4/day off-season, 3-hour round-trip, 43 SF) stop at the super-cute village of Iseltwald and at Brienz (easy bus and train connections back to Interlaken from Brienz, near Ballenberg Open-Air Folk Museum—described on page 1391).

The **St. Beatus caves** on Lake Thun can be visited with a one-hour guided tour (18 SF, 2/hour, Easter-mid-Oct daily 10:30-17:00, closed mid-Oct-Easter, tel. 033-841-1643, www.beatushoehlen .ch). The best excursion plan: Ride the bus from Interlaken (1-2/hour, 20-minute ride, 4.80 SF, line #21—direction: Thun, departs West station at :19 past the hour); tour the caves; take the short, steep hike down to lake; and return by boat (12 SF one-way, 30 minutes to Interlaken).

Adventure Sports

For the thrill-seeker with money, several companies offer trips such as rafting, canyoning (rappelling down watery gorges), bungee jumping, and paragliding. Costs range from 150 SF to 190 SF. Interlaken's two dominant companies are **Alpin Raft** (tel. 033-823-4100, www.alpinraft.com) and **Outdoor Interlaken** (tel. 033-826-7719, www.outdoor-interlaken.ch). Other companies are generally just booking agents for these two outfits. For an overview of your options, visit www.interlakenadventure.com or study the racks of brochures at most TIs and hotels (everyone's getting a cut of this lucrative industry).

Several years ago, two fatal accidents jolted the adventure-sport business in the Berner Oberland, leading to a more professional respect for the risks involved. Companies have very high standards of safety. Statistically, the most dangerous sport is mountain biking. Enjoying nature up close comes with risks. Adventure sports increase those risks dramatically. Use good judgment.

Less-Risky Alternatives

Vertical Sport has a breathtaking indoor rock-climbing facility, where you can snack or enjoy a nice cup of hot chocolate while watching hotshots practice their gravity-defying skills (Tue-Fri and Sun 9:00-18:00, Sat 9:00-16:00 or until 22:00 in bad weather, closed Mon, private lessons for beginners by the hour, at the back of the park across from Hotel Savoy at Jungfraustrasse 44, tel. 033-823-5383, www.verticalsport.ch).

Outdoor Interlaken's Seilpark offers five rope courses of varying difficulty and height in a forest, giving you a tree-top adventure through a maze of rope bridges and zip lines (37 SF, family deals, must weigh between 44 and 264 pounds; June-Aug daily 10:00-18:00; April-May and Sept-Oct Mon-Fri 13:00-18:00, Sat-Sun 10:00-18:00; closed Nov-March; from Interlaken West station, it's a 15-minute walk—head right up Rugenparkstrasse and into the park, then look for signs; tel. 033-826-7719, www .outdoor-interlaken.ch).

Castles

A few impressively well-kept and welcoming old castles in the Interlaken area are worth considering for day trips by boat, bus, or car.

Thun Castle (Schloss Thun), built between 1180 and 1190 by the Dukes of Zähringen, has a five-floor historical museum offering insights into the cultural development of the region over a period of some 4,000 years. From the corner turrets of the castle, you are rewarded with a spectacular view of the city of Thun, the lake, and the Alps (8 SF, April-Oct daily 10:00-17:00, Nov-Jan Sun only 13:00-16:00, Feb-March daily 13:00-16:00, tel. 033-223-2001, www.schlossthun.ch).

Hünegg Castle (Schloss Hünegg), in Hilterfingen (farther along Lake Thun, toward Interlaken), contains a museum exhibiting furnished rooms from the second half of the 19th century. The castle is situated in a beautiful wooded park (9 SF, mid-May-mid-Oct Mon-Sat 14:00-17:00, Sun 11:00-17:00, closed off-season, tel.

GIMMELWALD

033-243-1982, www.schloshuenegg.ch).

Oberhofen Castle (Schloss Oberhofen), also on Lake Thun, is ideal for those interested in gardens. Its beautifully landscaped park with exotic trees is a delight (free, mid-May–mid-Oct daily from 10:00 until dusk, closed off-season). The museum in the castle depicts domestic life in the 16th through 19th centuries, including a Turkish smoking room and a medieval chapel (10 SF, mid-May–mid-Oct Mon 14:00–17:00, Tue–Sun 11:00–17:00, closed off-season, tel. 033-243-1235, www.schlossoberhofen.ch).

Nightlife in Interlaken

Youthful Night Scenes—For counterculture with a reggae beat, check out **Funny Farm** (past Balmer's Herberge hostel, in Matten). The young frat-party dance scene rages at the **Metro Bar** at Balmer's (bomb-shelter disco bar, with cheap drinks and a friendly if loud atmosphere). And if you're into **Hooters,** you won't have a hard time finding it.

Mellower After-Dark Hangouts—The first three options are also described later, under "Eating in Interlaken": For a stylish wine bar with local yuppies, check in at the **Benacus Piazza del Vino** on the square in Unterseen. To nurse a drink with a view of the park, the outdoor tables at **Restaurant Schuh** are the place to be. The **"Top O'Met"** bar and café has great indoor and outdoor view seating with reasonable prices, 18 floors above everything else in town (in the Metropole Hotel skyscraper, open nightly until late). **Hotel Oberland** (near the post office) often has live alpine music in its restaurant/bar.

Sleeping in Interlaken

I'd sleep in Gimmelwald, or at least Lauterbrunnen (20 minutes by train or car). Interlaken is not the Alps. But if you must stay here...

$$$ Hotel Lötschberg, with a sun terrace and 21 rooms, is run with lots of thoughtful touches by English-speaking Susi (Sb-135 SF, Db-178 SF, big Db-198 SF, extra bed-35 SF, family deals, closed Nov–mid-April, elevator, pay Internet access, free Wi-Fi, free laundry machines, free loaner bikes; lounge with microwave, fridge, and free tea and coffee; 3-minute walk from West station: leaving station, turn right, after Migros at the circle go left to General-Guisan-Strasse 31; tel. 033-822-2545, fax 033-822-2579, www.lotschberg.ch, hotel@lotschberg.ch).

$$ Guest House Susi's B&B is Hotel Lötschberg's no-frills, cash-only annex, offering three nicely furnished, cozy rooms and

Sleep Code

(1 SF = about $1, country code: 41)

S = Single, **D** = Double/Twin, **T** = Triple, **Q** = Quad, **b** = bathroom, **s** = shower only. Unless otherwise noted, credit cards are accepted, English is spoken, and breakfast is included.

To help you sort easily through these listings, I've divided the rooms into three categories, based on the price for a standard double room with bath:

$$$ Higher Priced—Most rooms 150 SF or more.
  $$ Moderately Priced—Most rooms between 90-150 SF.
    $ Lower Priced—Most rooms 90 SF or less.

Prices can change without notice; verify the hotel's current rates online or by email. For other updates, see www .ricksteves.com/update.

four apartments with kitchenettes (Sb-119 SF, Db-151 SF; apartment-140 SF/2 people, 250 SF/4-5 people; free Wi-Fi, hotel closed Nov-mid-April but apartments available with 5-night stay, same contact info as Hotel Lötschberg, above).

$$ Sunny Days B&B, a homey, nine-room place in a quiet residential neighborhood, is run by Dave from Britain (Sb-98-110 SF, Db-120-158 SF, prices vary with size of room and view, extra bed-about 40 SF, less in winter, 1-night stay-20 SF extra, pay Internet access in lobby, pay Wi-Fi; exit left out of West station and take first bridge to your left, after crossing two bridges turn left on Helvetiastrasse and go 3 blocks to #29; tel. 033-822-8343, www.sunnydays.ch, mail@sunnydays.ch).

$$ Hotel Aarburg offers 10 plain, peaceful rooms over a restaurant in a beautifully located but run-down old building a 10-minute walk from the West station (Sb-75 SF, Db-130 SF, 10 SF more in July-Aug, 2 doors down from launderette at Beatenbergstrasse 1, tel. 033-822-2615, fax 033-822-6397, hotel -aarburg@quicknet.ch).

$$ Katy's Lodge B&B is a funky old house in a quiet, handy location. While not cozy, it rents seven basic rooms at a good price (Db-90-108 SF, T-114-126 SF, Qb-140-160 SF, 6-bed room-228 SF; ask about 10 percent discount on 3-night stay with cash and this book, garden, playground, 3-minute walk from West station, across from Hotel Lötschberg at Bernastrasse 7, tel. 033-821-0963, www.katys-lodge.ch, katyslodge@bluewin.ch).

$$ Backpackers' Villa (Sonnenhof) Interlaken is a creative guest house run by a Methodist church group. It's fun, youthful, and great for families, without the frat-party scene of Balmer's Herberge (listed below). Travelers of any age feel comfortable here (dorm bed in 2- to 7-bed room with free locker, sheets, and towel-37-45 SF, S-79 SF, Sb-91 SF, D-98 SF, Db-118 SF, T-135-153 SF, Tb-165 SF, Q-164-180 SF, Qb-196 SF, includes breakfast, some Jungfrau-view balconies, kitchen, garden, movies, small game room, pay Internet access, free Wi-Fi, laundry, free admission to public swimming pool/spa, no curfew, no membership required, open all day, reception open 7:00-23:00, free use of public buses—bus #2 runs from hostel to either station, 10-15-minute walk from stations, across the park from the TI at Alpenstrasse 16, tel. 033-826-7171, fax 033-826-7172, www.villa.ch, mail@villa.ch).

$ **Villa Margaretha,** run by English-speaking Frau Kunz-Joerin, offers the best cheap beds in town. It's like Grandma's big Victorian house on a residential street. Keep your room tidy, and you'll have a friend for life (D-90 SF, T-135 SF, Q-180 SF, the three rooms share one big bathroom, 2-night minimum, apartment for 2-3 people-1,000 SF/week, closed Oct-April, cash only, no breakfast served but dishes and kitchenette available, lots of rules to abide by, go up small street directly in front of West station to Aarmühlestrasse 13, tel. 033-822-1813, www.villa-margaretha.com, info@villa-margaretha.com).

$ **Balmer's Herberge** is many people's idea of backpacker heaven. This Interlaken institution comes with movies, table tennis, a launderette, bar, restaurant, free Wi-Fi, pay Internet access, tiny grocery, kitchen, bike rental, swapping library, excursions, bus pass, a shuttle-bus service (which meets important arriving trains), and a friendly, hardworking staff. This little Nebraska, a hive of youthful fun and activities, is home for those who miss their fraternity. It can be a mob scene, especially on summer weekends (bunk in 6- to 12-bed dorm-29 SF, S-45 SF, D-77 SF, T-104 SF, Q-138 SF, includes sheets and breakfast, open year-round, emailed reservations recommended 5 days in advance for private rooms, Hauptstrasse 23, in Matten, 15-minute walk from either train station, tel. 033-822-1961, fax 033-823-3261, www.balmers.com, mail@balmers.ch). They also have private rooms in an adjacent guest house (Db-130 SF, Tb-165 SF, Qb-220 SF).

$ **Happy Inn Lodge,** above the lively, noisy Brasserie 17 restaurant, has 16 cheap backpacker rooms and two new doubles with private baths (bed with bedding in 4- to 8-bed dorm-22-24 SF, S-32-60 SF, D-64-80 SF, Db-84-104 SF, T-78-108 SF, Q-104-144 SF, breakfast-8 SF, no membership required, no curfew, pay Internet access, free Wi-Fi, bus pass, 5-minute walk from West station at Rosenstrasse 17, tel. 033-822-3225, fax 033-822-3268, www.brasserie17.ch, info@happyinn.com).

Eating in Interlaken

In Unterseen, the Old Town Across the River

Restaurant Bären, in a classic low-ceilinged building with cozy indoor and fine outdoor seating, is a great value for *Rösti*, fondue, raclette, fish, traditional sausage, and salads (20-30-SF plates including fondue for one, Cordon Bleu is popular, open daily 11:30-14:00 & 17:30-22:00, closed Mon for lunch and all day off-season; from West station, turn left on Bahnhofstrasse, cross the river, and go several blocks to Seestrasse 2; tel. 033-822-7526).

Goldener Anker is *the* local hangout—smoky, with a pool table and a few unsavory types. If you think Interlaken is sterile, you haven't been to the "Golden Anchor." Jeannette serves and René cooks, just as they have for 25 years. This place, with its "melody rock and blues" ambience, sometimes hosts small concerts, and has launched some of Switzerland's top bands (hearty 15-25-SF salads, fresh vegetables, 3 courses for 20 SF, daily from 16:00, Marktgasse 57, tel. 033-822-1672).

Città Vecchia serves decent Italian with seating indoors or out, on a leafy square (16-22-SF pizzas, 20-28-SF pastas, 30-40-SF plates, daily 11:30-14:00 & 17:30-23:30, closed Tue Oct-April, on main square in Unterseen at Untere Gasse 5, tel. 033-822-1754).

Benacus Wine Bar and Restaurant is a snooty, trendy spot serving Euro-Asian modern cuisine and tapas with a good list of open wines (28-38-SF plates, closed Sun-Mon, Stadthausplatz, tel. 033-821-2020).

On or near Interlaken's Main Drag (Höheweg)

Interlaken's main drag, Höheweg, is lined with eateries. Asian, American, and Middle Eastern group tourism cuts into the local ambience, but you do have plenty of options.

Sirinya's Thai Restaurant is run by charming Sirinya, who serves great Thai dishes and famous spring rolls at reasonable prices (19-24-SF plates, Tue-Sat 16:00-23:30, Sun 11:00-22:00, closed Mon, at the recommended Hotel Lötschberg, General-Guisan-Strasse 31, tel. 033-821-6535).

Metropole Hotel's "Top O'Met," capping Interlaken's 18-story aesthetic nightmare, is actually a decent café/restaurant serving traditional and modern food at down-to-earth prices. For just 6 SF, you can enjoy a glass of wine and awesome views from an indoor or outdoor table (25-SF lunch deals include 2 courses and a drink, daily 11:30-24:00, Höheweg 37, just step into the Metropole Hotel and go up the elevator as far as you can, tel. 033-828-6666).

Restaurant Schuh retains its grand-café ambience on the best real estate in town (at the corner of the park, across from

Metropole Hotel and TI). The interior is a big tour-group food fight, but there's no better place to nurse a drink or coffee and watch the paragliders float into the park (live schmaltzy music, newspapers, Höheweg 56, tel. 033-822-9441).

Cheap Eats

Interlaken's two big supermarkets sell picnic supplies and also have reasonable self-service restaurants: **Migros** is across the street from the West station (Mon-Thu 8:00-18:30, Fri 8:00-21:00, Sat 7:30-17:00, closed Sun), while the **Co-op** is across the river from the West station, on your right (same hours as Migros). The only grocery store open late at night is **Co-op Pronto** (daily 6:00-22:30, 30 yards west of TI on Höheweg).

Interlaken Connections

While there are a few long-distance trains from Interlaken, you'll generally transfer in **Bern**. Train info: toll tel. 0900-300-300 or www.rail.ch.

From Interlaken Ost by Train to: Lauterbrunnen (2/hour, 20 minutes), **Bern** (2/hour, 55 minutes, some with change in Spiez), **Spiez** (3/hour, 25 minutes), **Brienz** (1-2/hour, 20 minutes), **Zürich** and **Zürich Airport** (2/hour, 2-3 hours, most with transfer in Bern or Spiez), **Luzern** (hourly, 2-2.5 hours), **Lugano** (hourly, 4.75 hours, 1-2 changes), **Zermatt** (1-2/hour, 2.25 hours, transfer in Spiez and Visp), **Florence** (8/day, 6-7 hours, 2-3 changes), **Venice** (6/day, 6-8 hours, 2-4 changes, no decent overnight option), **Salzburg** (6/day, 7.5-8.5 hours, 2-3 changes), **Nice** (6/day, 9-11 hours, 2-5 transfers), **Paris** (nearly hourly, 6-6.5 hours).

From Interlaken to the Lauterbrunnen Valley

To reach the heart of the valley, drive or take the train to Lauterbrunnen (train leaves twice an hour from Interlaken Ost station, 20 minutes). You cannot drive to Gimmelwald (park at the cable-car station near Stechelberg and ride up on the lift; see "Getting to Gimmelwald," page 1406) or to Mürren, Wengen, or Kleine Scheidegg (park in Lauterbrunnen and take the cable car to Mürren or the train to Wengen/Kleine Scheidegg). For more details, see "Lauterbrunnen Valley Connections," page 1404.

Lauterbrunnen

Lauterbrunnen is the valley's commercial center and transportation hub. In addition to its train station and cable car, the one-street town is just big enough to have all the essential services (bank, post office, bike rental, launderette, and so on)—plus several hotels. It's idyllic, in spite of the busy road that slices it in two. Sitting under sheer cliffs at the base of the valley, with its signature waterfall spurting mightily out of the cliff (floodlit at night), Lauterbrunnen is a fine springboard for Jungfrau and Schilthorn adventures. But for spending the night, I still prefer Gimmelwald or Mürren, perched on the ledge above the valley.

Orientation to Lauterbrunnen

Tourist Information

Stop by the friendly TI to check the weather forecast, use the Internet (1 SF/6 minutes), find out about guided walks and events, and buy hiking maps or any regional train or lift tickets you need (June-mid-Sept daily 9:00-12:00 & 13:00-18:00, Sat-Sun until 18:00, shorter hours off-season, located near the Co-op grocery, tel. 033-856-8568, www.mylauterbrunnen.com).

Arrival in Lauterbrunnen

The slick, modern train station has lockers and is across the main street from the cable-car station. Go left as you exit the station to find the TI. Drivers can find parking in the large, multistory pay lot behind the station (2 SF/2 hours, 10 SF/9-24 hours, www.jungfraubahn.ch).

Helpful Hints

Medical Help: Dr. Bruno Durrer, who has a clinic near the Jungfrau Hotel (look for *Arzt* sign), is good. He and his associate both speak English (tel. 033-856-2626, answered 24/7).

Internet and Laundry: Two places within a short walk of each other in the town center compete for your coins: The **Valley Hostel** is automated (Internet access-2.50 SF/15 minutes, launderette-5 SF/load, includes soap, May-Oct daily 9:00-21:00, shorter hours Nov-April, don't open dryer door until machine is finished or you'll have to pay another 5 SF to start it again, tel. 033-855-2008), while **Airtime** is fully staffed (Internet access-10 SF/hour, pay Wi-Fi, self-service laundry-10 SF/load, full-service laundry-25 SF/load, May-Oct daily 9:00-19:00, shorter hours Nov-April, café sells homemade goodies and English-language paperbacks, also books

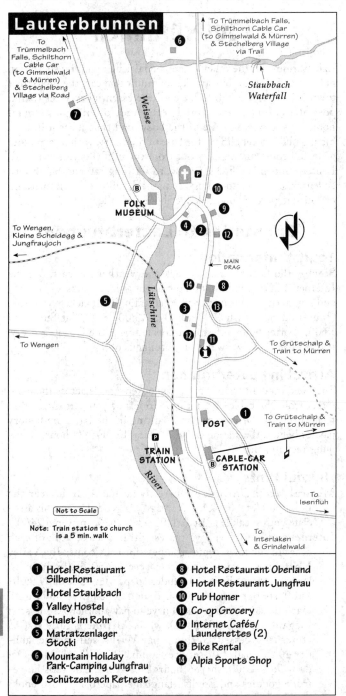

Lauterbrunnen

To Trümmelbach Falls, Schilthorn Cable Car (to Gimmelwald & Mürren) & Stechelberg Village via Road ⑦

To Trümmelbach Falls, Schilthorn Cable Car (to Gimmelwald & Mürren) & Stechelberg Village via Trail

⑥

Staubbach Waterfall

Weisse

P

🅱 FOLK MUSEUM

To Wengen, Kleine Scheidegg & Jungfraujoch

Lütschine

⑩
⑨
④ ②
⑫

MAIN DRAG

⑤

To Wengen

⑭ ⑧
③ ⑬
⑫ ⑪

To Grütschalp & Train to Mürren

POST ①

To Grütschalp & Train to Mürren

P

TRAIN STATION

🅱 CABLE-CAR STATION

River

To Isenfluh

Not to Scale

Note: Train station to church is a 5 min. walk

To Interlaken & Grindelwald

① Hotel Restaurant Silberhorn
② Hotel Staubbach
③ Valley Hostel
④ Chalet im Rohr
⑤ Matratzenlager Stocki
⑥ Mountain Holiday Park-Camping Jungfrau
⑦ Schützenbach Retreat
⑧ Hotel Restaurant Oberland
⑨ Hotel Restaurant Jungfrau
⑩ Pub Horner
⑪ Co-op Grocery
⑫ Internet Cafés/ Launderettes (2)
⑬ Bike Rental
⑭ Alpia Sports Shop

GIMMELWALD

adventure sports, tel. 033-855-1515, www.airtime.ch). The word's out on their aptly named "world-famous" brownies.

Grocery Store: The **Co-op** is on the main street (Mon-Fri 8:00-12:00 & 14:00-18:30, Sat 8:00-12:00 & 13:30-17:00, closed Sun).

Bike Rental: You can rent mountain bikes at **Imboden Bike** on the main street (25 SF/half-day, 35 SF/day; full-suspension—35 SF/half-day, 55 SF/day; daily July-Aug 8:30-20:00, Sept-June 9:00-18:30 except closed for lunch 12:00-13:00 Oct-May, tel. 033-855-2114, www.imboden-bike.ch).

Sports Gear: You can rent hiking boots, skis, and snowboards at the **Alpia Sports** shop (Mon-Fri 8:00-12:00 & 14:00-18:00, Sat-Sun 10:00-12:00 & 16:00-18:00, shorter hours in fall and closed in May, at Hotel Crystal, tel. 033-855-3292, www.alpiasport.ch).

Activities in and near Lauterbrunnen

Hikers' Loop from Lauterbrunnen—If you're staying in Lauterbrunnen, consider this ambitious but great day plan: Ride the cable car to Grütschalp, walk along the ridge to Mürren, take the cable car up to the Schilthorn and back down to Mürren, ride the funicular up to Allmendhubel, take the North Face Walk to Gimmelwald, take the lift down to the Stechelberg station, catch the PostBus to Trümmelbach Falls, and walk through the valley back into Lauterbrunnen. Make it more or less strenuous or time-consuming by swapping lifts and hikes (all described later in this chapter). Or rent a mountain bike and do a wheeled variation on this (parking your bike in Mürren for the Schilthorn trip).

▲**Trümmelbach Falls**—If all the waterfalls have you intrigued, sneak a behind-the-scenes look at the valley's most powerful, Trümmelbach Falls (11 SF, daily July-Aug 8:30-18:00, April-June and Sept-mid-Nov 9:00-17:00, closed mid-Nov-March, tel. 033-855-3232, www.truemmelbach.ch). It's about halfway between Lauterbrunnen and the Schilthornbahn station (about a 45-minute walk from either one, at a leisurely pace). To save time, you can take the PostBus to the falls from either place. Once there, you'll ride an elevator up through the mountain and climb through several caves (wet, with lots of stairs, and—for some—claustrophobic) to see the melt from the Eiger, Mönch, and Jungfrau grinding like God's band saw through the mountain at the rate of up to 5,200 gallons a second (that's 20,000 liters—nearly double the beer consumption at Oktoberfest). The upper area is the best; if your legs ache, skip the lower falls and ride down on the elevator.

▲▲**Cloudy-Day Lauterbrunnen Valley Walk**—Try the easy trails and pleasant walks along the floor of the Lauterbrunnen

GIMMELWALD

Valley. For a smell-the-cows-and-flowers lowland walk—ideal for a cloudy day, weary body, or tight budget—take the PostBus from Lauterbrunnen town to the Schilthornbahn station near Stechelberg (left of river) and follow the riverside trail back for three basically level miles to Staubbach Falls, near the town church (you can reverse the route, but it's a very gradual uphill to Stechelberg). A trail was recently cut into the cliff to take visitors up "behind" Staubbach Falls (at the uphill end of Lauterbrunnen town). But the trail stops short of the actual falls, and you'll feel betrayed after making the short climb—I'd skip it.

There's a fine, paved, car-free, riverside path all the way along the valley (popular with bikers). Detour to Trümmelbach Falls (described earlier) en route (it's about a 45-minute walk from the Schilthornbahn station to Trümmelbach Falls, and another 45 minutes to Lauterbrunnen). In this "Valley of Many Waterfalls" (literally), you'll see cone-like mounds piled against the sides of the cliffs, formed by centuries of rocks hurled by tumbling rivers.

If you're staying in Gimmelwald, try this plan: Take the Schilthornbahn lift down to the Stechelberg station (5 minutes), then walk to Trümmelbach Falls (45 minutes), then on to Lauterbrunnen (45 minutes). To return to Gimmelwald from Lauterbrunnen, take the cable car up to Grütschalp (10 minutes), then either walk to Gimmelwald (1.5 hours) or take the train to Mürren (10 minutes). From Mürren, it's a downhill walk (30 minutes) to Gimmelwald. (This loop trip can be reversed, or started in any point along the way—such as Lauterbrunnen or Mürren.)

Lauterbrunnen Valley Folk Museum (Talmuseum Lauterbrunnen)—This interesting museum shows off the local folk culture and two centuries of mountaineering from all the towns of this valley. You'll see lots of lace, exhibits on cheese and woodworking, cowbells, and classic old photos (free with "visitor's card" given by local hotels, 3 SF otherwise, mid-June-mid-Oct Tue and Thu-Sun 14:00-17:30; closed Mon, Wed, and off-season; English handout, just over bridge and below church at the far end of Lauterbrunnen town, tel. 033-855-3586 or 033-855-1388, www.talmuseumlauterbrunnen.ch).

Hang Out with Base-Jumpers—In recent years, the Lauterbrunnen Valley has become an El Dorado of base-jumping (parachuting off cliffs), and each season thrill-seekers hike to the top of a cliff, leap off—falling as long as they can (this provides the rush)—and then pull the ripcord to release a tiny parachute, hoping it will break their fall and a gust won't dash them against the walls of the valley.

Locals generally have little respect for the base-jumpers, whom they consider reckless. But to learn more, talk with the jumpers themselves, who congregate at the **Pub Horner,** at the upper end of town (near the waterfall). This is the grittiest place in Lauterbrunnen, providing cheap beds and meals for base-jumpers and the only real after-dark scene. Locals, base-jumpers, and stray tourists gather here in the pub each evening (9 rooms, bunks-32 SF, D-64-86 SF, cheaper apartments, no breakfast, free Wi-Fi and Internet access for customers, BBQ dinner in summer, dancing nightly from 22:00 upstairs, tel. 033-855-1673, www.hornerpub .ch, mail@hornerpub.ch, run by Gertsch Ferdinand). Their kitchen sells cheap pastas and raclette, and puts out a nightly salad bar (8-14-SF meals).

Sleeping in Lauterbrunnen

(2,612 feet, 1 SF = about $1, country code: 41)
$$$ Hotel Silberhorn is a big, formal, 32-room, three-star hotel that still manages to feel family-run. It has generous public spaces and a recommended, elegant-for-Lauterbrunnen restaurant just above the quiet lift station across from the train station. Almost every double room comes with a fine view and balcony. They're in the midst of remodeling their rooms, so ask for a newer room for the same price (Sb-89-109 SF, Db-159-179 SF, bigger "superior" Db-180-209 SF, pay Internet access, free Wi-Fi in lobby, tel. 033-856-2210, www.silberhorn.com, info@silberhorn.com).

$$ Hotel Staubbach, a big, Old World place—one of the first hotels in the valley (1890)—is being lovingly restored by hardworking American Craig and his Swiss wife, Corinne. The staff is friendly, and the hotel has the casual feel of a national park lodge, with 30 simple and comfortable rooms that are being updated. It's family-friendly, there's a kids' play area, and the parking is free. Rooms that face up the valley have incredible views, though you may hear the happy crowd across the meadow at Pub Horner or the church bells chiming on the hour. Guests can watch a DVD of my TV show on the region in the lounge (S-90-100 SF, Sb-120 SF, D-110-120 SF, Db-140 SF, Tb-190 SF, Qb-220-240 SF, 10 SF extra per room for 1-night stays, 20 SF extra for balcony rooms with valley view, closed Nov-mid-April, elevator, free Wi-Fi, 4 blocks up from station on the left, tel. 033-855-5454, fax 033-855-5484, www.staubbach.com, hotel @staubbach.com).

$ Valley Hostel is practical and comfortable, offering 70 inexpensive beds for quieter travelers of all ages, with a pleasant garden and the welcoming Abegglen family: Martha, Alfred, Stefan, and Fränzi (D with bunk beds-60 SF, twin D-70 SF, beds in larger family-friendly rooms-25 SF/person, breakfast-5 SF, most rooms have no sinks, kitchen, 16-SF cheese fondue on request for guests 18:00-20:00, Internet access, Wi-Fi, coin-op laundry, 2 blocks up from train station, tel. & fax 033-855-2008, www.valleyhostel.ch, info@valleyhostel.ch).

$ Chalet im Rohr—a creaky, old, woody firetrap of a place—has oodles of character (and lots of Asian groups and paragliders). It offers 50 beds in big one- to four-bed rooms that share six showers (27 SF/person, no breakfast, cash only, common kitchen, free Wi-Fi, across from church on main drag, tel. & fax 033-855-2182, www.chaletimrohr.ch, bookings@chaletimrohr.ch, Elsbeth von Allmen-Müller).

$ Matratzenlager Stocki is rustic and humble, with the cheapest beds in town (15 SF with sheets in easygoing little 25-bed co-ed dorm with kitchen, closed Nov-Dec, across river from station, tel. 033-855-1754, Frau Graf).

$ Camping: Two campgrounds just south of town provide 15-35-SF beds (in dorms and 2-, 4-, and 6-bed bungalows, sheets-5 SF, kitchen facilities, cash only, big English-speaking tour groups). **Mountain Holiday Park-Camping Jungfrau,** romantically situated beyond Staubbach Falls, is huge and well-organized by Hans. It also has fancy cabins and mobile homes by the week (tel. 033-856-2010, www.camping-jungfrau.ch). **Schützenbach Retreat,** on the left just past Lauterbrunnen toward Stechelberg, is a simpler campground (tel. 033-855-1268, www.schuetzenbach.ch).

Eating in Lauterbrunnen

At **Hotel Restaurant Oberland,** Mark (Aussie) and Ursula (Swiss) Nolan take pride in serving tasty, good-value meals from a fun menu. It's a high-energy place with lots of tourists and a huge front porch good for lingering into the evening (17-SF pizzas, 20-25-SF main courses, traditional Swiss dishes, daily 11:30-21:00, tel. 033-855-1241).

Hotel Restaurant Jungfrau, along the main street on the right-hand side, offers a wide range of specialties, including fondue and *Rösti,* served by a friendly staff. Their terrace has a great valley view (daily 12:00-14:00 & 18:00-21:00, tel. 033-855-3434, run by Brigitte Melliger).

Hotel Restaurant Silberhorn is the local choice for a fancy meal out. Call to reserve a view table (14-SF salad plate, 23-35-SF main dishes, daily from 18:00, classy indoor and outdoor seating, above the cable-car station, tel. 033-856-2210).

Lauterbrunnen Valley Connections

The valley-floor towns of Lauterbrunnen and Stechelberg have connections by mountain train, bus, and cable-car to the traffic-free villages, peaks, and hikes high above. Prices and trip durations given are per leg unless otherwise noted.

From Lauterbrunnen by Train to: Interlaken (2/hour, 20 minutes, 7.20 SF), **Wengen** (2/hour, 15 minutes, 6.40 SF), continues to **Kleine Scheidegg** (hourly, 30 minutes, 30 SF), where you change to a different train to reach the **Jungfraujoch** (2/hour, 50 minutes, 66 SF) or **Grindelwald** (2/hour, 30 minutes, 32 SF).

By Cable Car to: Grütschalp (2/hour, 10 minutes), where you can catch a train to **Mürren** (2/hour, 10 minutes); total trip time 30 minutes, total cost 10.40 SF.

By PostBus to: Schilthornbahn cable-car station (hourly, 15 minutes, 4 SF, covered by Swiss Pass), continues to **Stechelberg town** (hourly, 5 minutes, 4 SF).

By Car to: Schilthornbahn cable-car station (10-minute drive, parking lot: 2 SF/2 hours, 6 SF/day, cash only).

From Schilthornbahn Cable-Car Station near Stechelberg to: Gimmelwald (2/hour, 5 minutes, 5.80 SF), continues to **Mürren** (2/hour, 10 minutes, 5.80 SF) and the **Schilthorn** (2/hour, 20 minutes, 43 SF). The cable car runs up from the valley station—and down from Mürren—at :25 and :55 past the hour (5:55-19:55; after 19:55, runs only once an hour until 23:45, and until 24:55 Fri-Sat). From Gimmelwald to both Mürren and the valley station, the cable car runs at :00 and :30 (6:00-20:00; after 20:00 runs only once an hour until 23:50, and until 1:00 in the morning Fri-Sat).

Gimmelwald

Saved from developers by its "avalanche zone" classification, Gimmelwald was (before modern tourism) one of the poorest places in Switzerland. Its traditional economy was stuck in the hay, and its farmers—unable to make it in their disadvantaged trade—survived only on a trickle of visitors and on Swiss government subsidies (and working the ski lifts in the winter). For some travelers, there's little to see in the village. Others (like me) enjoy a fascinating day sitting on a bench and learning why they say, "If heaven isn't what it's cracked up to be, send me back to Gimmelwald."

Take a walk through the town. The huge, sheer cliff face that dominates your mountain views is the Schwarzmönch ("Black Monk"). The three peaks above (or behind) it are, left to right, the Eiger, Mönch, and Jungfrau. While Gimmelwald's population dropped in the last century from 300 to about 120 residents, traditions survive. Most Gimmelwalders have one of two last names: von Allmen or Feuz. They are tough and proud. Raising hay in this rugged terrain is labor-intensive. One family harvests enough to feed only about 15 cows. But they'd have it no other way, and,

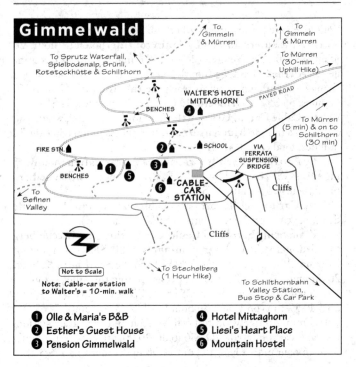

Gimmelwald

To Gimmeln & Mürren

To Gimmeln & Mürren

To Sprutz Waterfall, Spielbodenalp, Brünli, Rotstockhütte & Schilthorn

To Mürren (30-min. Uphill Hike)

PAVED ROAD

WALTER'S HOTEL MITTAGHORN ❹

BENCHES

To Mürren (5 min) & on to Schilthorn (30 min)

FIRE STN.

❷   ■ SCHOOL

VIA FERRATA SUSPENSION BRIDGE

BENCHES   ❶ ❺   ❸

Cliffs

To Sefinen Valley

❻   CABLE-CAR STATION

Cliffs

Not to Scale

Note: Cable-car station to Walter's = 10-min. walk

To Stechelberg (1 Hour Hike)

To Schilthornbahn Valley Station, Bus Stop & Car Park

❶ Olle & Maria's B&B
❷ Esther's Guest House
❸ Pension Gimmelwald

❹ Hotel Mittaghorn
❺ Liesi's Heart Place
❻ Mountain Hostel

unlike the absentee-landlord town of Mürren, Gimmelwald is locally owned. (When word got out that urban planners wished to develop Gimmelwald into a town of 1,000, locals pulled some strings to secure the town's bogus avalanche-zone building code. Today, unlike nearby resort towns, Gimmelwald's population is the same all year.) Those same folks are happy the masses go to touristy and commercialized Grindelwald, just over the Kleine Scheidegg ridge. Don't confuse Gimmelwald and Grindelwald—they couldn't be more different.

Thanks to the leadership of the village teachers (Olle and Maria) and their son (Sven), Gimmelwald now has a helpful little website (www.gimmelwald.ch). There you can check out photos of the town in different seasons, get directions for 11 of the best hikes out of town, and see all the latest on activities and rooms for rent.

Getting to Gimmelwald

To get from Lauterbrunnen to Gimmelwald, you have two options:

1. Schilthornbahn cable car: The faster, easier way—best in bad weather or at the end of a long day with lots of luggage—is to drive. It's 10 minutes from Lauterbrunnen (or 30 minutes from Interlaken) to the Schilthornbahn cable-car station near

Stechelberg (parking lot: 2 SF/2 hours, 6 SF/day, cash only).

If you don't have a car, ride the PostBus from Lauterbrunnen to the Schilthornbahn station (4 SF, 15 minutes, departs hourly—coordinated with arrival of train in Lauterbrunnen, www.postauto.ch).

From the Schilthornbahn station, the cable car whisks you in five thrilling minutes up to Gimmelwald (5.80 SF, 2/hour at :25 and :55 past the hour 5:55-19:55, at :55 only 19:55-23:45 and until 24:55 Fri-Sat; Gimmelwald is the first stop). Note that the Schilthornbahn cable car is closed for servicing for a week in early May and also from mid-November through early December. If you're here during this time, you'll ride the cargo cable car directly from the valley floor up to Mürren, where a small bus shuttles you down to Gimmelwald.

2. Grütschalp cable-car and Mürren train: The more scenic route is to catch the cable car from Lauterbrunnen to Grütschalp, where a special vintage train will roll you along the incredibly scenic cliffside to Mürren (total trip from Lauterbrunnen to Mürren: 30 minutes, 10.40 SF, www.jungfraubahn.ch). From there, either walk to the middle of Mürren and take a left down a moderately steep paved path 30 minutes to Gimmelwald, or walk 10 minutes across Mürren to catch the cable car down to Gimmelwald (5.80 SF).

Self-Guided Walk

Welcome to Gimmelwald

Gimmelwald, though tiny, with one zigzag street, offers a fine look at a traditional Swiss mountain community.

• *Start this quick walking tour at the...*

Cable-Car Station: When the lift came in the 1960s, the village's back end became its front door. Gimmelwald was, and still is, a farm village. Stepping off the cable car and starting up the path, you see a sweet little hut. Set on stilts to keep out mice, the hut was used for storing cheese (the rocks on the rooftop here and throughout the town are not decorative—they keep the shingles on through wild storms). Behind the cheese hut stands the village schoolhouse, long the biggest building in town (in Catholic Swiss towns, the biggest building is the church; in Protestant towns, it's the school). But in 2010, classes ceased. Gimmelwald's students now go to school in Lauterbrunnen; the building is used as a chapel when the Protestant pastor makes his monthly visit. Up and across from the station, just beyond the little playground, is the recommended Mountain Hostel.

• *Walk up the lane 50 yards, past the town's Dalí-esque art gallery (the shower in the phone booth), to Gimmelwald's...*

"Times Square": The yellow alpine "street sign" shows where you are, the altitude (1,370 meters—that's 4,470 feet), how many hours *(Std.)* and minutes it takes to walk to nearby points, and which tracks are serious hiking paths (marked with red and white, and further indicated along the way with red and white patches of paint on stones). You're surrounded by buildings that were built as duplexes—divided vertically right down the middle to house two separate families. The writing on the post office building is a folksy blessing: "Summer brings green, winter brings snow. The sun greets the day, the stars greet the night. This house will keep you warm. May God give us his blessings." The date indicates when it was built or rebuilt (1911). Gimmelwald has a strict building code. For instance, shutters can only be painted certain colors.

• *From this tiny intersection, we'll follow the town's main street (away from cable-car station).*

Main Street: Walk up the road. Notice the announcement board: one side for tourist news, the other for local news (e.g., deals on chainsaw sharpening, upcoming shooting competitions). Cross the street and peek into the big new barn, dated 1995. To the left of the door is a cow-scratcher. Swiss cows have legal rights (for example, in the winter, they must be taken out for exercise at least three times a week). This big barn is built in a modern style. Traditionally, barns were small (like those on the hillside high above) and closer to the hay. But with trucks and paved roads, hay can be moved more easily, and farm businesses need more cows to be viable. Still, even a well-run big farm hopes just to break even. The industry survives only with government subsidies. Small as Gimmelwald is, it still has daily mail service. The postman comes down from Mürren each day (by golf cart in summer, sled in winter) to deliver mail and to pick up letters at the communal mailbox (outside the recently shuttered post office). As you wander, notice private garden patches. Until recently, most locals grew their own vegetables—often enough to provide most of their family's needs.

• *Go just beyond the next barn. On your right is the...*

Water Fountain/Trough: This is the site of the town's historic water supply. Local kids love to bathe and wage water wars here when the cows aren't drinking from it. Detour left down a lane about 50 yards (along a wooden fence and then past pea-patch gardens) to the next trough and the oldest building in town, Husmättli, from 1658. (The town's 17th-century buildings are mostly on the road zigzagging below town.) Study the log-cabin construction. Many are built without nails. The wood was logged up the valley and cut on the water-powered village mill (also below town). Gimmelwald heats with wood, and since the wood needs to age a couple of years to burn well, it's stacked everywhere.

• *Back on the paved road, continue uphill.*

Twenty yards along, on the left, the first house has a bunch of scythes hanging above the sharpening stone. Farmers pound, rather than grind, the blade to get it razor-sharp for efficient cutting. Feel a blade...carefully.

A few steps further, notice the cute cheese hut on the right (with alpine cheese for sale). Its front is an alpine art gallery with nail shoes for flower pots. Nail shoes grip the steep, wet fields—this is critical for safety, especially if you're carrying a sharp scythe. Even today, farmers buy metal tacks and fasten them to boots. The hut is full of strong cheese—up to three years old.

Look up. In the summer, a few goats are kept here (rather than in the high alp) to provide families with fresh milk (about a half-gallon per day per goat). The farmers fence off the fields, letting the goats eat only the grass that's most difficult to harvest.

On the left (at the *B&B* sign) is the home of Olle and Maria, the village schoolteachers. Maria runs the Lilliput shop (the "smallest shop with the greatest gifts"—handmade delights from the town and region, just ring the bell and meet Maria). Her children—Sven, Sara, and Carina—do a booming trade in sugar-coated almonds.

• *Fifty yards farther along is the...*

Alpenrose: At the old schoolhouse, you might see big ceremonial cowbells hanging under the uphill eave. These swing from the necks of cows during the procession from the town to the high Alps (mid-June) and back down (mid-Sept). If the cows are gone, so are the bells—hanging from similar posts under the eaves of mountain huts in the high meadows.

• *At the end of town, pause where a lane branches off to the left, leading into the dramatic...*

Sefinen Valley: All the old homes in town are made from local wood cut from the left-hand side of this valley (shady side, slow-growing, better timber).

• *A few steps ahead, the road switches back at the...*

Gimmelwald Fire Station: The *Föhnwacht Reglement* sheet, posted on the fire station building, explains rules to keep the village from burning down during the fierce dry wind of the Föhn season. During this time, there's a 24-hour fire watch, and even smoking cigarettes outdoors is forbidden. Mürren was devastated by a Föhn-caused fire in the 1920s. Because villagers in Gimmelwald—mindful of the quality of their volunteer fire department—are particularly careful with fire, the town has not had a terrible fire in its history (a rare feat among alpine villages).

Check out the other posted notices. This year's Swiss Army calendar tells reservists when and where to go (in all four official Swiss languages). Every Swiss male does a 22-week stint in the military, then a few days a year in the reserves until about age 30.

GIMMELWALD

The *Schiessübungen* poster details the shooting exercises required this year. In keeping with the William Tell heritage, each Swiss man does shooting practice annually for the military (or spends three days in jail).

• *Take the...*

High Road to Hotel Mittaghorn: The resort town of Mürren hovers in the distance. And high on the left, notice the hay field with terraces. These are from WWII days, when Switzerland, wanting self-sufficiency, required all farmers to grow potatoes. Today, this field is a festival of alpine flowers in season (best at this altitude in May and June).

• *Our walk is over. From Hotel Mittaghorn, you can return to Gimmelwald's "Times Square" via the path with the steps cutting downhill.*

Nightlife in Gimmelwald

Evening fun in Gimmelwald is found at the **Mountain Hostel** (offering a pool table, Internet access, lots of young Alp-aholics, and a good chance to share information on the surrounding mountains) or Walter's bar at the **Hotel Mittaghorn.** From almost anywhere in Gimmelwald, you can watch the sun tuck the mountaintops into bed as the moon rises over the Jungfrau. If this isn't your idea of nightlife, stay in Interlaken.

Sleeping in Gimmelwald

(4,593 feet, 1 SF = about $1, country code: 41)
Gimmelwald is my home base in the Berner Oberland. To inhale the Alps and really hold them in, you'll sleep high in Gimmelwald, too. Poor and pleasantly stuck in the past, the village has only a few accommodations options—all of them quirky and memorable. Rates include entry to the public swimming pool in nearby Mürren (at the Sportzentrum, described on page 1413). Factor the cable-car cost (5.80 SF per ride from Stechelberg or Mürren) into your accommodation costs. The cable car goes up and down twice an hour (up from the valley floor and down from Mürren at :25 and :55 past the hour 5:55-19:55, at :55 only 19:55-22:45, last trip at 23:45 Sun-Thu and at 24:55 Fri-Sat; from Gimmelwald to both Mürren and the valley runs 6:00-20:00 at :00 and :30, on the hour 20:00-23:00, last trip at 23:50 Sun-Thu and at 1:00 in the morning Fri-Sat). Be warned: You'll meet a lot of my readers in this town. This is a disappointment to some; others enjoy the chance to be part of a fun extended family.

$$ At Olle and Maria's B&B, the Eggimanns rent two rooms—Gimmelwald's most comfortable—in their quirky but alpine-sleek chalet. Maria and Olle, who job-share the village's only teaching position and raise three kids of their own, offer visitors a rare and intimate peek at this community (D-130 SF, Db with kitchenette-190 SF for 2 or 200 SF for 3 people, optional breakfast-20 SF, 3-night minimum, cash only, guarantee your reservation in advance with a check or PayPal, last check-in preferred at 21:00, free Wi-Fi, laundry service; from cable car, continue straight for 200 yards along the town's only road, B&B on left; tel. 033-855-3575, oeggimann@bluewin.ch).

$$ Esther's Guest House, overlooking the village's main intersection, rents seven clean, basic, and comfortable rooms, three of which have private bathrooms (S-50-70 SF, big D-120 SF, Db-120 SF, big T-140 SF, Tb-170-180 SF, Q-180 SF, Qb-190-200 SF, family room with private bath for up to 5 people-230 SF, cash preferred, breakfast-15 SF, 2-night minimum, pay Internet access, free Wi-Fi, low ceilings, fine guests' kitchen, tel. 033-855-5488, fax 033-855-5492, www.esthersguesthouse.ch, info@esthersguest house.ch). Esther also rents two four-person **apartments** with kitchenettes next door (150-160 SF for 2 people, 210-220 SF for 4 people, extra bed-30 SF, 3-night minimum, check website for details).

$$ Pension Gimmelwald is an old farmhouse converted into a family-style inn, with 12 simple rooms, a six-bed dorm, and the town's only restaurant. Its terrace, overlooking the Mountain Hostel, has gorgeous views across the valley (bed in 6-bed dorm-25 SF, S-60 SF, D-100 SF, T-150 SF, Q-185 SF, less in winter, open June-Oct and mid-Dec-mid-April, breakfast-12 SF, 2-minute walk up from cable-car station, tel. 033-855-1730, www.pension gimmelwald.com, twnewark@yahoo.com, Englishman David).

$ Hotel Mittaghorn is a classic, creaky, thin-walled, alpine-style place with a superb view of the Jungfrau Alps. It's run by Walter Mittler, a Swiss gentleman in his late 80s, with help from trusty Tim. The hotel has three rooms with private showers (first-come, first-served) and four rooms that share a coin-operated shower (open April-Oct, S-54 SF, D-86 SF, T-129 SF, 6-SF surcharge per person for 1-night stays, cash only, simple but hearty 15-SF dinner at 19:30 by reservation only, free Internet access, a five-minute climb up the path from the village center, tel. 033-855-1658, www.ricksteves.com/mittaghorn, mittaghorn@gmail.com). Please don't contact the hotel when it's closed (Nov-March). To make a reservation, wait until April 1 (or later) to book by phone or email; it's also necessary to reconfirm by phone the day before your arrival. If no one's there when you arrive, look for a card in the hallway directing you to your room.

$ Liesi's Heart Place is run by the former proprietor of Pension Gimmelwald, who now rents a little suite in her home with a view and terrace. Liesi loves to help guests celebrate special occasions (Db-80-110 SF, Tb-110-150 SF, Qb-150-180 SF with 2-night stay, laundry, pleasant garden with grill, reserve by email and reconfirm 2-3 days before arrival, credit card number required to reserve but cash only to pay, located near Chalet Huusmätteli, tel. 033-855-1662, www.liesisheartplace.ch).

$ Mountain Hostel is a beehive of activity, as clean as its guests, cheap, and friendly. The hostel has low ceilings, a self-service kitchen, a mini-grocery, a bar, free pool table, laundry, free Internet access and Wi-Fi, and healthy plumbing. It's mostly a college-age crowd; families and older travelers will probably feel more comfortable elsewhere. Petra Brunner has lined the porch with flowers. This relaxed hostel survives with the help of its guests. Read the signs, respect Petra's rules, and leave it tidier than you found it—bus your plates and clean the kitchen. This is one of those rare spots where a congenial atmosphere spontaneously combusts as the piano plays, and spaghetti becomes communal as it cooks. If you've shown up without a reservation, check the front desk for Petra's sign-up sheet, where she lists any available beds for tonight. This is not the place for your own private kegger; there is a fun bar on the premises, but brining your own alcohol is discouraged (28 SF/bed in 6- to 15-bed rooms, includes sheets, showers-1 SF, no breakfast, free Wi-Fi, laundry, good pizzas sold in the evening, open mid-April–mid-Nov, 20 yards up the trail from lift station, reserve with credit card through website or by phone after 18:00, tel. 033-855-1704, www.mountainhostel.com, info@mountainhostel.com).

Eating in Gimmelwald

The only restaurant in town is at **Pension Gimmelwald,** dishing up good food indoors or out on its glorious view terrace. They serve local, organically farmed meat and cheese, salads, and even make their own *Rösti* (13-22-SF main dishes, Tue-Sat 12:00-15:00 & 18:00-21:00, Sun 12:00-18:00, closed Mon). The **Mountain Hostel** has a decent members' kitchen and makes great pizzas in the evenings (14 SF, non-guests welcome). **Hotel Mittaghorn** serves dinner only to its guests (15 SF).

Consider packing in a **picnic** meal from the larger towns. Mürren, a five-minute cable-car ride or a 30-minute hike up the hill, has good restaurants and a grocery (described later, under "Eating in Mürren"). If you need a few groceries and want to skip the hike to Mürren, you can buy the essentials—noodles, spaghetti sauce, and candy bars—at the Mountain Hostel's reception desk, or check out the little store at Pension Gimmelwald. Local farmers post signs to sell their produce.

Mürren

Mürren—pleasant as an alpine resort can be—is traffic-free and filled with bakeries, cafés, souvenirs, old-timers with walking sticks, employees enjoying incentive trips, and Japanese tourists making movies of each other. Its chalets are prefab-rustic. With help from a cliffside train, funicular, and cable car, hiking options are endless from Mürren. Sitting on a ledge 2,000 feet above the Lauterbrunnen Valley, surrounded by a fortissimo chorus of mountains, the town has all the comforts of home (for a price) without the pretentiousness of more famous resorts.

Historic Mürren, which dates from 1384, has been overwhelmed by development. Still, it's a peaceful town. There's no full-time doctor, no police officer (they call Lauterbrunnen if there's a problem), and no resident priest or pastor. (The Protestant church—up by the TI—posts a sign showing where the region's roving pastor preaches each Sunday.) There's not even enough business to keep a bakery open year-round (Mürren's bakery is open mid-June-Sept and Dec-April)—a clear indication that this town is either lively or completely dead, depending on the season. (Holiday population: 4,000. Permanent residents: 400.) Keep an eye open for the "Milch Express," a tiny cart that delivers fresh milk and eggs to hotels and homes throughout town.

Orientation to Mürren

Mürren perches high on a ledge, overlooking the Lauterbrunnen Valley. You can walk from one end of town to the other in about 10 minutes.

There are two ways to get to Mürren: on the train from Grütschalp (10 minutes, connects via 10-minute cable car to Lauterbrunnen, 30-minute total trip) or on the Schilthornbahn cable car from near Stechelberg (in the valley), which stops at Gimmelwald, Mürren, and continues up to the Schilthorn. The train and cable-car stations (which both have WCs and lockers) are at opposite ends of town.

Tourist Information: Mürren's TI can help you find a room and gives hiking advice (July-mid-Sept Mon-Sat 8:30-19:00, Thu until 20:00, Sun 8:30-18:00, less off-season, above the village, follow signs to *Sportzentrum*, tel. 033-856-8686, www.mymuerren.ch).

Helpful Hints

R & R: The slick **Sportzentrum** (sports center) that houses the TI offers a world of indoor activities. The pool is free with the regional visitor's card given by local hotels (July-mid-Sept

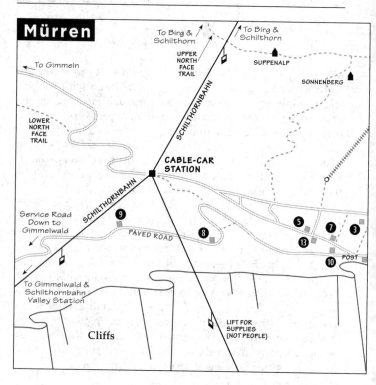

Mon-Sat 8:30-19:00, Thu until 20:00, Sun 8:30-18:00; pool and sauna generally opens at 10:00 Tue-Wed and Fri, otherwise at 13:00; shorter hours off-season, closed May and Nov-mid-Dec, www.muerren.ch/sportzentrum). In season, they offer squash, mini-golf, table tennis, and a fitness room.

Money: There's an ATM by the Co-op grocery in the middle of town. You can change money at the TI.

Internet Access: Connect at the **TI** (5 SF/15 minutes), at the **cable-car station** inside an old gondola (5 SF/15 minutes), or at the **Eiger Guesthouse** (4 SF/20 minutes, daily 8:00-23:00, across from the train station).

Laundry: Hotel Bellevue has a slick and modern little self-service launderette in its basement (5 SF/wash, 5 SF/dry, open 24/7).

Bike Rental: You can rent mountain bikes at **Stäger Sport** (25 SF/half-day, 35 SF/day, includes helmet, daily 9:00-18:00, closed late Oct-mid-May, in middle of town, tel. 033-855-2355, www.staegersport.ch). There's a bigger bike-rental place in Lauterbrunnen (Imboden Bike, described on page 1401). Use caution on rough stretches.

Mürren Massage: Sabina Kulicka is very strong—and she knows how to iron out your back after a good hike (90 SF/hour, lots

To Birg & Schilthorn

ALLMENDHUBEL

To Grütschalp

FUNICULAR

SPORT-
ZENTRUM

To Grütschalp &
Lift Down to
Lauterbrunnen

TRAIN
STATION

Cliffs

Note:
Cable-car station to train
station = 10-min. walk

Not to Scale

❶ Alpin Palace Hotel
❷ Hotel Alpina &
   Edelweiss Cafeteria
❸ Hotel/Rest. Bellevue
   & Launderette
❹ Hotel/Restaurant
   Jungfrau
❺ Hotel/Restaurant
   Blumental
❻ Eiger Guesthouse
❼ Chalet Fontana
❽ Chalet Helvetia
❾ Chalet Böbs
❿ Stägerstübli
   Restaurant
⓫ Bar Bistro
⓬ Tham Chinese
   Restaurant
⓭ Co-op Grocery

of options, daily 8:00-21:00, in Hotel Alpenruh, tel. 033-855-4538, mobile 079-527-0832).

Skiing: The Mürren-Schilthorn ski area is the Berner Oberland's best place for experts, especially those eager to tackle the famous, nearly 10-mile-long Inferno run. The runs on top, especially the Kanonenrohr, are quite steep and have predictably good snow; lower areas cater to all levels, but can be icier. For rental gear, try the friendly, convenient **Ed Abegglen** shop (best prices, next to recommended Chalet Fontana, tel. 033-855-1245), **Alfred's Sporthaus** (good selection and decent prices, between ski school and Sportzentrum, tel. 033-855-3030), or **Stäger Sport** (one shop in Sportzentrum and another on the lower road near cable-car station, tel. 033-855-2330).

Self-Guided Walk

Welcome to Mürren

Mürren has long been a top ski resort, but a walk across town offers a glimpse into its past. This stroll takes you through town on the main drag, from the train station (where you'll arrive if coming from Lauterbrunnen) to the cable-car station, then back up to the

Allmendhubel funicular station.

• *Start at the...*

Train Station: The first trains pulled into Mürren in 1891. (A circa-1911 car is permanently parked at the Grütschalp station.) A display case inside the station shows an original car from the narrow-gauge, horse-powered line that rolled fancy visitors from here into town. The current station, built in 1964, comes with impressive engineering for heavy cargo. Look out back, where a small truck can be loaded up, attached to the train, and driven away.

• *Wander into town along the main road (take the lower, left fork).*

Stroll Under the Alpin Palace Hotel: The towering Alpin Palace Hotel was the "Grand Palace Hotel" until it burned in 1928. Its Jugendstil Hall is the finest room in Mürren. The small wooden platform on the left—looking like a suicide springboard—is the place where snow-removal trucks dump their loads over the cliff in the winter. Look back at the meadow below the station: This is a favorite grazing spot for chamois (the animals, not the rags for washing cars). Ahead, at Edelweiss Hotel, step to the far corner of the restaurant terrace for a breathtaking view stretching from the big three (Eiger, Mönch, and Jungfrau) on the left to the lonely cattle farm in the high alp on the right. Then look down.

Haus Montana is the spot where Kandahar ski boots were first made in 1933 (to give the necessary support to daredevils racing from the Schilthorn to the valley floor in Mürren's infamous Inferno race). Today, the still-respected Kandahar boots are made in nearby Thun.

• *Continue toward...*

"Downtown" Mürren: You'll pass the main intersection (where the small service road leads down to Gimmelwald) and the only grocery store in town (Co-op). The tiny fire barn (labeled *Feuerwehr*) has a list showing the leaders of the volunteer force and their responsibilities. The old barn behind it on the right evokes the time, not so long ago, when the town's barns housed cows. Imagine Mürren with more cows than people, rather than with more visitors than residents.

• *Reaching the far end of Mürren, you come to the...*

Cable-Car Station: The first cable car (goes directly to the valley floor) is for cargo, garbage, and the (reputedly) longest bungee jump in the world. The other takes hikers and skiers up to the Schilthorn and down to the valley via Gimmelwald.

• *Hiking back along the high road, you'll enter...*

Upper Mürren: You'll pass Mürren's two churches, the Allmendhubel funicular station, and the Sportzentrum (with swimming pool and TI).

• *Consider riding the...*

Allmendhubel Funicular: A quaint-looking but surprisingly rewarding funicular (from 1912, renovated in 1999) carries nature-lovers from Mürren to Allmendhubel, a perch offering a Jungfrau view that (while much lower) rivals the Schilthorn. At the station, notice the 1920s bobsled. The restaurants here (full- and self-service) have awesome views. Allmendhubel is particularly good for families. At 7.40 SF one-way (12 SF round-trip, 6 SF with Swiss Pass), it's cheaper than the Schilthorn (mid-June-mid-Oct runs every 20 minutes, daily 9:00-17:00, tel. 033-855-2042 or 033-856-2141, www.schilthorn.ch). The restaurant overlooks a great playground. And the entertaining children's hike—with rough and thrilling, kid-friendly alpine rides along the way—departs from here. This is also the departure point for the North Face hike and walks to Grütschalp (see "Hiking and Biking," page 1424).

• *Our walk is finished. Enjoy the town and the views.*

Activities in Mürren

During ski season and the height of summer, the Mürren area offers plenty of activities for those willing to seek them out. In July and August, you can enjoy occasional folkloric evenings (some Wednesdays, at the Sportzentrum), morning tours of flowers and wildlife (Sun at 9:00, meet at Allmendhubel station, 12 SF includes funicular ride up, 1.5 hours, led by Othmar from Hotel Bellevue—call him at 078-604-1401), and weekly yoga lessons by Denise (of Chalet Fontana, mobile 078-642-3485). Ask at your hotel or the TI for the latest. In spring and fall, Mürren is pretty dead.

If you have a bit of climbing experience—and want to get your heart pumping—**Klettersteig Via Ferrata** provides licensed guides to lead you down a vertigo-inducing *via ferrata* course (mountain climbing via an iron cable) from Mürren to Gimmelwald. Climbers are attached to a 1.4-mile-long steel cable as they traverse sheer cliffs, swinging rope bridges, and impossibly steep ladders. Reservations are smart (95 SF includes equipment, minimum 4 people, mid-June-Oct, takes 3 hours, tel. 033-821-6100, www.klettersteig-muerren.ch, info@be-je.ch).

Nightlife in Mürren

Eiger Guesthouse is a popular sports bar–type hangout with pool tables, games, Internet stations, and a fine stock of whiskies. **Stägerstübli** is another good place to congregate. **Hotel Bellevue,** with its elegant alpine-lounge ambience, is also good for a drink. (All of these places are further described later, under "Sleeping in Mürren" or "Eating in Mürren.")

Sleeping in Mürren

(5,381 feet, 1 SF = about $1, country code: 41)

Prices for accommodations are often higher during the ski season. Many hotels and restaurants close in spring, roughly from Easter to early June, and may also shut down any time between late September and mid-December.

$$$ Hotel Alpina is a simple place with 24 comfortable rooms and a concrete feeling—a good thing, given its cliff-edge position (Sb-85 SF, Db-160 SF, Tb-200 SF, Qb-220 SF, most rooms with awesome Jungfrau views and balconies, prices less off-season and without a view, outside of mid-June–mid-Aug ask about Rick Steves discount, family rooms, pay Internet access, free Wi-Fi, homey lounge, exit left from train station and walk 2 minutes, tel. 033-855-1361, fax 033-855-1049, www.muerren.ch/alpina, alpina@muerren.ch; Cecilia, her cheerful son Roger, and his wife Agripina).

$$$ Hotel Bellevue has a homey lounge, solid woodsy furniture, a great view terrace, the hunter-themed Jägerstübli restaurant, and 17 great rooms at fair rates—most with balconies and views (Sb-105-145 SF, Db-170-190 SF, ask about special deals with this book in June, Db-150 SF if staying 2 nights or more in Sept-Oct, free Internet access and Wi-Fi, tel. 033-855-1401, fax 033-855-1490, www.muerren.ch/bellevue, bellevue-crystal@bluewin.ch, Ruth and Othmar Suter).

$$$ Hotel Jungfrau offers 29 modern and comfortable rooms and an apartment for up to 6 people (Sb-95-120 SF, Db-180-220 SF, lower prices are for non-view rooms, elevator, laundry service-15 SF, pay Wi-Fi, downhill from TI/Sportzentrum, tel. 033-856-6464, fax 033-856-6465, www.hoteljungfrau.ch, mail @hoteljungfrau.ch, Alan and Veronique).

$$$ Hotel Blumental has 16 older but nicely furnished rooms and a fun game/TV lounge (Sb-75-80 SF, Db-150-170 SF, 10 percent cheaper in Sept-Oct, higher prices are for July-Aug, outside of July-Aug book direct and ask about Rick Steves discount, pay cable Internet, attached restaurant listed under "Eating in Mürren," tel. 033-855-1826, fax 033-855-3686, www.muerren.ch/blumental, blumental@muerren.ch; Ralph and Heidi, fourth generation in the von Allmen family). Their modern little chalet out back rents six rooms (Db-130-160 SF, includes breakfast in the hotel).

$$ Eiger Guesthouse is a friendly, creaky, easygoing home-away-from-home that offers 12 good budget rooms (S-70 SF, Sb-80-95 SF, D-100-120 SF, Db-130-160 SF, bunk Q-160-180 SF, Qb-200-240 SF; closed late Oct-Nov and for one month after Easter, free Wi-Fi, game room, terrace, across from train station, tel. 033-856-5460, fax 033-856-5461, www.eigerguesthouse.com, info@eigerguesthouse.com). The restaurant serves good, reasonably priced dinners (18-25 SF).

$ Chalet Fontana, run by charming Englishwoman Denise Fussell, is a rare budget option in Mürren, with simple, crispy-clean, and comfortable rooms (S-45-55 SF, D-75-85 SF, large D-95 SF, T-125 SF, price varies with size of room, 5 SF cheaper without breakfast, cash only, closed Nov-April, fridge in common kitchen, across street from Stägerstübli restaurant in town center, mobile 078-642-3485, www.chaletfontana.ch, chaletfontana@muerren .ch). If no one's home, check at the Ed Abegglen shop next door (tel. 033-855-1245, off-season only). Denise also rents a family apartment with kitchen, bathroom, and breakfast (two bedrooms with 3 beds each, 130 SF/2 people, 160 SF/3 people, 200 SF/4 people, 260 SF/6 people).

$ Chalet Helvetia, run by Edmée Hunziker, offers a homey, clean, two-bedroom apartment with bathroom, kitchen, separate entrance, and balcony from 40 SF per person (up to 4 people, no breakfast, 2-night minimum, laundry service-10 SF/load, 200 yards below cable-car station on path to Gimmelwald on right, tel. 033-855-4169, mobile 079-234-7867, www.chalet-helvetia.com, chalet.helvetia@quicknet.ch).

$ Chalet Böbs, with terrific views, is the last house in Mürren on the road to Gimmelwald (at the sign, walk up the path to the right, and it's on the left). Kitty and Albert, an alphorn player, rent three apartments with kitchens: one that sleeps two people and two that sleep up to five people—each with a double bed, bunk bed, and a twin bed (Sb-70 SF, Db-90 SF, Tb-130 SF, Quad or 5b-150 SF, 3-night minimum, tel. 033-855-1463, mobile 078-633-6091, boebs@quicknet.ch, www.boebs.ch).

Eating in Mürren

Many of these restaurants are in or near my recommended hotels. Outside of summer and ski season, it can be hard to find any place that's open (ask around).

Stägerstübli is everyone's favorite Mürren diner. It's the only real restaurant not associated with a hotel. Located in the town center, this 1902 building was once a tearoom for rich tourists, while locals were limited to the room in the back—which is now the nicer area to eat. Sitting on its terrace, you know just who's out and about in town (18-35-SF lunches and dinners, big portions, lovely lamb, daily 11:30-21:00, closed first week of Sept, Lydia).

Bar Bistro has inexpensive light meals and impressive views (Mon-Wed 9:00-19:00, Thu-Sat 9:00-20:00, closed Sun, at the Sportzentrum, overlooking the ice rink).

GIMMELWALD

Tham Chinese Restaurant is a humble place with good food that brings spice to the local eating scene (Thai and Chinese dishes, daily 12:00-20:00, near the train-station end of town on the lower road, tel. 033-856-0110).

Hotel Blumental specializes in typical Swiss cuisine, but also serves fish, international, and vegetarian dishes in a stony and woody dining area (15-29-SF specials, 21-31-SF fondue served for one or more, 14-SF pastas, daily from 16:30, tel. 033-855-1826).

Restaurant Hotel Jungfrau is a dressy ski lodge with a modern octagonal dining room and a fine view terrace. The salad bar (11 SF per plate or 17 SF all-you-can-eat) is always excellent, and 45 SF buys you a four-course meal (23-SF cheese fondue—minimum 2 people, veggie options, nightly 18:00-21:30, on upper road downhill from TI/Sportzentrum, tel. 033-856-6464).

Edelweiss cafeteria offers self-serve lunches and restaurant dinners with the most cliff-hanging dining in town—the views are incredible (pizzas, hearty salads, sandwiches; self-service until 17:00, then full service; next to the recommended Hotel Alpina).

Hotel Bellevue's restaurant is atmospheric, with three dining zones: view terrace, elegant indoor area, and the Jägerstübli—a cozy, well-antlered hunters' room guaranteed to disgust vegetarians. This is a good bet for game, as they buy chamois and deer direct from local hunters (lamb or game-34-44 SF, cheaper options as low as 15 SF, mid-June-Oct daily 11:30-14:00 & 18:00-21:00, closed off-season, tel. 033-855-1401).

The **Co-op** is the only grocery store in town, with good picnic fixings and sandwiches (Mon-Fri 8:00-12:00 & 13:45-18:30, Sat until 17:00, closed Sun). Given restaurant prices, this place is a godsend for those on a tight budget.

Wengen

Wengen—a bigger, fancier Mürren on the east side of the valley—has plenty of grand hotels, many shops, tennis courts, mini-golf, and terrific views. This traffic-free resort is an easy train ride above Lauterbrunnen and halfway up to Kleine Scheidegg and Männlichen, and offers more activities for those needing distraction from the scenery. (But hiking is better from Mürren and Gimmelwald.) Many Wengen shops take lunch very seriously, and close down for at least an hour around noon.

The **TI** is two blocks from the station: Go up to the main drag, turn left, and it's on the left. They have info on guided walks, short hikes, and local Internet cafés and Wi-Fi hotspots, and they sell hiking maps (daily in summer 9:00-18:00 except closed Sun

12:30-13:30, closed Sat-Sun mid-Oct-mid-Dec, coin-op Internet access-1 SF/3 minutes, tel. 033-855-1414, www.mywengen.ch).

If you're here in the winter to ski the Keine Scheidegg-Männlichen slopes, Wengen makes the best home base. Rent your gear from **Molitor Sport + Mode,** still run by the family of founder and famous ski racer Karl Molitor (who's now 92). Even if you're not renting a thing, stop in to see the cool old photos, gear, and Karl's medals on display, which add up to a mini–ski-racing museum (on Wengen's main drag, on the left past Männlichen cable-car station, tel. 033-855-2131). Other rental shops include **Alpia Sport** (right above train station, tel. 033-855-2626) and **Central-Sport** (on the main drag, past post office, tel. 033-855-2323).

The **Co-op grocery** here is great for picnic fixings—it's larger than most groceries in the area (Mon-Sat 8:00-18:30, closed Sun).

Sleeping and Eating in Wengen

(4,180 feet, 1 SF = about $1, country code: 41)

Above the Train Station

$$$ Hotel Berghaus, in a quiet area a five-minute walk from the main street, offers 19 rooms above a fine restaurant specializing in fish (Sb-92-125 SF, Db-184-250 SF, ask about discount with this book and cash, elevator, pay Internet access, pay Wi-Fi, open June-Sept and late Dec-Easter, tel. 033-855-2151, fax 033-855-3820, www.berghaus-wengen.ch, info@berghaus-wengen.ch, Fontana family). At the train station, you can dial #114 on the hotel phone to request a free pickup. Or, to walk to the hotel from the main drag, head up the street across from Hotel Bernerhof, bear right at the fork, go 200 yards more past the church, and it's on the left.

$$$ Hotel Schönegg, on Wengen's main drag, is a centrally located splurge, decorated with antiques and old wood (Sb-120-140 SF, Db-240-280 SF; all rooms have balconies and great views, cozy family room with fireplace, free Wi-Fi, good restaurant with big terrace, look for big light-yellow hotel above main drag one block past TI, tel. 033-855-3422, fax 033-855-4233, www.hotel-schoenegg.ch, mail@hotel-schoenegg.ch, Herr Berthod und Frau Steiner).

Below the Train Station

$$ Bären Hotel, run by friendly Therese and Willy Brunner, offers 14 tidy rooms, some with perky, bright-orange bathrooms. Their restaurant is bright and inviting, offering garden-fresh Swiss cuisine (daily specials for 16.50 SF; Sb-70-90 SF, Db-140-150 SF, Tb-180-240 SF, pricier in winter, dinner-20 SF more, family rooms, free Internet access and Wi-Fi, kids' playroom, tel. 033-855-1419, fax 033-855-1525, www.baeren-wengen.ch, info @baeren-wengen.ch). From the station, cross the street to the Co-op grocery, turn right and go under the rail bridge, and follow the road down the hill—the hotel will be on your right.

$$ Clare and Andy's Chalet (Trogihalten) offers three rustic, low-ceilinged rooms (1-room studio: Sb-56 SF, Db-90 SF; 2-room suite: Sb/Db-106 SF, Tb-149 SF, Qb-188 SF; 4-room flat: Tb-159 SF, Qb-192 SF, 5 people-240 SF, 6 people-294 SF, 7 people-327 SF; breakfast-15 SF, no restaurant but dinner by request-35 SF, 4-night minimum preferred, prices higher for shorter stays, cash only, all rooms with balconies, tel. & fax 033-855-1712, mobile 079-423-7813, www.chaletwengen.ch, info@chaletwengen .ch, Clare is English, Andy is Swiss). From the station, follow the main street until Hotel Bernerhof, then turn left and follow the paved downhill path. Stay straight on the gravel path where the pavement curves, and look for the British flag up on the right.

More in the Berner Oberland

Lifts and Trains

Doing at least one of the two high-altitude thrill rides described here is an essential Berner Oberland experience.

▲▲▲The Schilthorn and a 10,000-Foot Breakfast

The Schilthornbahn cable car carries skiers, hikers, and sightseers effortlessly to the 10,000-foot summit of the Schilthorn, where the Piz Gloria station awaits, with a solar-powered revolving restaurant, shop, and panorama terrace. At the top, you have a spectacular panoramic view of the Eiger, Mönch, and Jungfrau mountains, lined up on the horizon.

As you ascend in the cable car, keep an eye on the altitude meter. Ask at the Schilthorn station for a cable-car souvenir decal.

Linger on top. Head out to the terrace, where information boards identify each peak. The names of the hard-to-miss big three hint at local folklore: The cowled Mönch (monk—note the shape of its peak) fends off the Eiger (ogre) to protect the Jungfrau (maiden—though she hardly seems to need the help). Directional signs point hikers toward some seriously steep downhill climbs. Watch paragliders set up, psych up, and take off, flying 45 minutes with the birds to distant Interlaken. Walk along the ridge out back. This is a great place for a photo of the mountain-climber you.

GIMMELWALD

Youth hostelers—not realizing that rocks may hide just under the snow—scream down the ice fields on plastic-bag sleds from the Schilthorn mountaintop. (There's an English-speaking doctor in Lauterbrunnen—see page 1399.)

Inside, Piz Gloria has a free "touristorama" film room with a "Multi-Vision" slide show that includes some explosive highlights from the James Bond thriller that featured the Schilthorn, *On Her Majesty's Secret Service*. (To start the video clip, press the button on the column in the middle of the room).

You can ride up to the Schilthorn and hike down, but it's tough. (Hiking *up* from Gimmelwald or Mürren is easier on your knees...if you don't mind a 5,000-foot altitude gain.) For information on **hikes** from lift stations along the Schilthorn cable-car line, see "Hiking and Biking," page 1424. My favorite "hike" from the Schilthorn is simply along the ridge out back, to get away from the station and be all alone on top of an Alp.

Cost and Hours: You can ride to the Schilthorn and back from the Stechelberg station on the valley floor (95 SF), Gimmelwald (84 SF), or Mürren (74 SF). Snare a 25 percent discount for early and late rides (roughly before 9:00 and after 15:30) and in spring and fall (roughly May and Oct). Travelers with a Swiss Pass (who get half off) or with a Eurailpass (25 percent discount) might as well go whenever they like, because you can't double up discounts. Lifts go twice hourly, and the ride from Gimmelwald (including two transfers) to the Schilthorn takes 30 minutes. Park your car at the valley station near Stechelberg (2 SF/2 hours, 6 SF/day, cash only). For more information, including current weather conditions, see www.schilthorn.ch or call 033-826-0007.

Breakfast at 10,000 Feet: The "007 Breakfast Buffet" is huge (27.50 SF, 8:00-11:00, save a little money by buying the combo cable-car ticket—92 SF, 59 SF with Swiss Pass, but you must leave from the Stechelberg station by 8:55). The restaurant also serves hot dishes all day at prices that don't rise with the altitude (around 20 SF).

▲▲▲Jungfraujoch

The literal high point of any trip to the Swiss Alps is a train ride through the Eiger to the Jungfraujoch. At 11,300 feet, it's Europe's highest train station. (If you have a heart or lung condition, you may want to check with your doctor before making this ascent.) The ride from Kleine Scheidegg takes about an hour (sit on the right side for better views), including two five-minute stops at stations actually halfway up the notorious North Face of the Eiger. You have time to look out windows and marvel at how people could climb the Eiger—and how the Swiss built this train track more than a hundred years ago. The second half of the ride takes

you through a tunnel inside the Eiger (some newer train cars run multilingual videos about the history of the train line).

Once you reach the top, study the Jungfraujoch chart to see your options (many of them are weather-dependent). There's a restaurant, history exhibit, "ice palace" (a cavern with a gallery of ice statues), and a 20-minute video that plays continuously. A tunnel leads outside, where you can summer ski (33 SF for gear and lift ticket), sled (free loaner discs with a 5-SF deposit), or hike an hour across the ice to Mönchsjochhütte (a mountain hut with a small restaurant). An elevator leads to the Sphinx observatory for the highest viewing point, from which you can see the Aletsch Glacier—Europe's longest, at nearly 11 miles—stretch to the south. Remember that your body isn't used to such high altitudes. Signs posted at the top remind you to take it easy.

One of the best hikes in the region—from Männlichen to Kleine Scheidegg—could be combined with your trip up to the Jungfraujoch (see page 1429).

Cost and Hours: The first trip of the day to the Jungfraujoch is discounted; ask for a Good Morning Ticket, and leave the top by 12:30 (Nov-April you can get Good Morning rates for the first or second train and return any time that day; train runs all year; round-trip fares to Jungfraujoch: from Lauterbrunnen-166 SF, or 130 SF for first trip—about 7:00; from Kleine Scheidegg-112 SF, or 90 SF for first trip—about 8:00; confirm times and price, 25 percent discount with Swiss Pass and Eurailpass, railpass holders get a better deal than Good Morning Ticket and can't combine discounts). Pick up a leaflet on the lifts at a local TI (www.jungfraubahn.ch). If it's cloudy, skip the trip; for a terse and trilingual weather forecast from the Jungfraujoch, call 033-828-7931.

Hiking and Biking

This area offers days of possible hikes. Many are a fun combination of trails, mountain trains, and cable-car rides. I've listed them based on which side of the Lauterbrunnen Valley they're on: west (the Gimmelwald/Mürren/Schilthorn side) or east (the Jungfrau side).

On the Gimmelwald (West) Side of the Lauterbrunnen Valley
Hikes from the Schilthorn
Several tough trails lead down from the Schilthorn, but most visitors take the cable car round-trip simply for the views (see "Lifts and Trains," earlier). If you're a serious hiker, consider walking all the way down (first hike) or part of the way down (second hike) back into Gimmelwald. Don't attempt to hike down from the

Schilthorn unless the trail is clear of snow. Adequate shoes and clothing (weather can change quickly) and good knees are required. You can visit the Sprutz Waterfall on your way to Gimmelwald.

From the Top of the Schilthorn (very difficult)—To hike downhill from the Piz Gloria revolving restaurant at the peak, start at the steps to the right of the cable, which lead along a ridge between a cliff and the bowl. As you pass huge rocks and shale fields, keep an eye out for the painted rocks that mark the scant trail. Eventually, you'll hit the service road (a ski run in the winter), which is steep and not very pleasant. Passing a memorial to a woman killed by lightning in 1865, you come to the small lake called Grauseeli. Leave the gravel road and hike along the lake. From there, follow the trail (with the help of cables when necessary) to scamper along the shale in the direction of Rotstockhütte (to Gimmelwald, see next hike) or Schilttal (the valley leading directly to Mürren; follow *Mürren/Rotstockhütte* sign painted on the rock at the junction).

▲▲Birg to Gimmelwald via Brünli (moderately difficult)—Rather than doing the very long hike all the way back down into Gimmelwald, I prefer walking the easier (but still strenuous) hike from the intermediate cable-car station at Birg. This is efficiently combined with a visit to the Schilthorn (from Schilthorn summit, ride cable car halfway down, get off at Birg, and hike down from there; buy the round-trip excursion early-bird fare—which is cheaper than the Gimmelwald-Schilthorn-Birg ticket—and decide at Birg if you want to hike or ride down).

The most interesting trail from Birg to Gimmelwald is the high one via Grauseeli lake and Wasenegg Ridge to Brünli, then down to Spielbodenalp and the Sprutz Waterfall. Warning: This trail is quite steep and slippery in places, and can take four hours. Locals take their kindergartners on this hike, but it can seem dangerous to Americans unused to alpine hikes. Do not attempt this hike in snow, which you might find at this altitude, even in the peak of summer. (Get local advice.)

From the Birg lift station, hike toward the Schilthorn, taking your first left down and passing along the left side of the little Grauseeli lake. From the lake, a gravelly trail leads down rough switchbacks (including a stretch where the path narrows and you can hang onto a guide cable against the cliff face) until it levels out. When you see a rock painted with arrows pointing to Mürren and Rotstockhütte, follow the path to Rotstockhütte (traditional old farm with light meals and drinks, mattress loft with cheap beds), traversing the cow-grazed mountainside.

For a thrill, follow Wasenegg Ridge. It's more scary than dangerous if you're sure-footed and can handle the 50-foot-long "tightrope-with-handrail" section along an extremely narrow ledge

GIMMELWALD

Gimmelwald Area Hikes

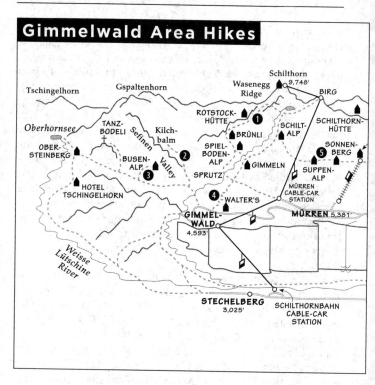

with a thousand-foot drop. This trail gets you to Brünli with the least altitude drop. (The safer, well-signposted approach to Brünli is to drop down to Rotstockhütte, then climb back up to Brünli.) The barbed-wire fence leads to the knobby little summit, where you'll enjoy an incredible 360-degree view and a chance to sign your name on the register stored in the little wooden box.

A steep trail winds directly down from Brünli toward Gimmelwald and soon hits a bigger, easy trail. The trail bends right (just before the farm/restaurant at Spielbodenalp), leading to Sprutz. Walk under the Sprutz Waterfall, then follow a steep, wooded trail that deposits you in a meadow of flowers at the top side of Gimmelwald.

Hikes from Gimmelwald

▲**Up Sefinen Valley to Kilchbalm (very easy)**—An easy trail from Gimmelwald is up the Sefinen Valley (Sefinental). This is a good rainy-weather hike, as you can go as far as you like. After two hours and a gain of only 800 feet, you hit the end of the trail and Kilchbalm, a dramatic bowl of glacier fields. Snow can make this trail unsafe, even into the summer (ask locally for information), and there's no food or drink along the way.

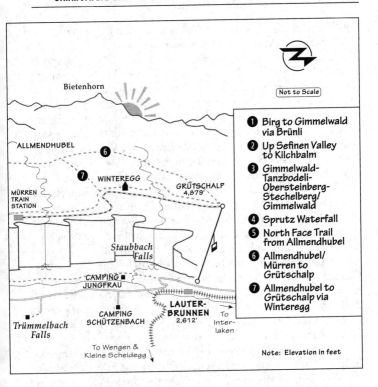

Bietenhorn

Not to Scale

ALLMENDHUBEL

6

7 WINTEREGG

MÜRREN
TRAIN
STATION

GRÜTSCHALP
4,879'

*Staubbach
Falls*

CAMPING
JUNGFRAU

■ *Trümmelbach
Falls*

CAMPING
SCHÜTZENBACH

LAUTER-
BRUNNEN
2,612'

To Inter-
laken

To Wengen &
Kleine Scheidegg

**❶ Birg to Gimmelwald
via Brünli**

**❷ Up Sefinen Valley
to Kilchbalm**

**❸ Gimmelwald-
Tanzbodeli-
Obersteinberg-
Stechelberg/
Gimmelwald**

❹ Sprutz Waterfall

**❺ North Face Trail
from Allmendhubel**

**❻ Allmendhubel/
Mürren to
Grütschalp**

**❼ Allmendhubel to
Grütschalp via
Winteregg**

Note: Elevation in feet

From the Gimmelwald fire station, walk about 100 yards down the paved Stechelberg road. Leave it on the dirt Sefinental road, which becomes a lane, then a trail. You'll cross a raging river and pass a firing range where locals practice their marksmanship (Fri and Sat evenings; the *danger of fire* sign refers to live bullets). Follow signs to Kilchbalm into a forest, along a river, and finally to the glacier fields.

▲**Gimmelwald-Tanzbodeli-Obersteinberg-Stechelberg/ Gimmelwald (more difficult, for good hikers)**—This eight-hour, 11-mile hike is extremely rewarding, offering perfect peace, very few people, traditional alpine culture, and spectacular views. (There's no food or drink for five hours, so pack accordingly.) As the trail can be a bit confusing, this is best done with a good, locally purchased map.

About 100 yards below the Gimmelwald firehouse, take the Sefinental dirt road (described in previous listing). As the dirt road switches back after about 30 minutes, take the right turn across the river and start your ascent, following signs to *Obersteinberg*. After 1.5 hours of hard climbing, you have the option of a side-trip to Busenalp. This is fun if the goat-and-cow herder is there, as you can watch traditional cheesemaking in action. (He appreciates a bottle of wine from hikers.) Trail markers are painted onto rocks—watch carefully. After visiting Busenalp, return to the main path.

At the *Obersteinberg 50 Min/Tanzbodeli 20 Min* signpost, head for Tanzbodeli ("Dancing Floor"). This is everyone's favorite alpine perch—great for a little romance, or a picnic with breath-taking views of the Obersteinberg valley. From here, you enter a natural reserve, so you're likely to see chamois and other alpine critters. From Tanzbodeli, you return to the main trail (there's no other way out) and continue to Obersteinberg. You'll eventually hit the Mountain Hotel Obersteinberg (see listing on page 1434; American expat Vickie will serve you a meal or drink).

From there, the trail leads to Mountain Hotel Tschingelhorn (see "Sleeping in Obersteinberg," later). About an hour later, you hit a fork in the trail and choose where you'd like your hike to end: back to Gimmelwald (2 hours total) or Stechelberg (near the bottom of the Schilthornbahn cable car, 1.5 hours total).

▲**Sprutz Waterfall (moderately difficult)**—The forest above Gimmelwald hides a powerful waterfall with a trail snaking behind it, offering a fun gorge experience. While the waterfall itself is not well-signed, it's on the Gimmelwald-Spielbodenalp trail. It's steep, through a forest, and can be very slippery when wet, but the actual crossing under the waterfall is just misty.

The hike up to Sprutz from Gimmelwald isn't worth the trip in itself, but it's handy when combined with the hike down from Birg and Brünli (described earlier) or the North Face Trail (see next listing). As you descend on either of these two hikes, the trail down to Gimmelwald splits at Spielbodenalp—to the right for the forest and the waterfall; to the left for more meadows, the hamlet of Gimmeln, and more gracefully back into Gimmelwald.

Hikes from Mürren/Allmendhubel
▲▲**North Face Trail from Allmendhubel (easy and family-friendly)**—For a pleasant, mainly downhill, two-hour hike (4 miles, from 6,385 feet to 5,375 feet)—with some stretches that can be challenging if you're not in shape—ride the Allmendhubel funicular up from Mürren (much cheaper than Schilthorn, good restaurant at top, see page 1417). From there, follow the well-signed route, which loops counterclockwise around to Mürren (or cut off at Spielbodenalp, near the end, and descend into Gimmelwald via the Sprutz Waterfall). As this trail doesn't technically start at Allmendhubel, you'll start by following signs to *Sonnenberg.* Then just follow the blue signs. You'll enjoy great views, flowery mead-ows, mountain huts, and a dozen information boards along the way, describing the fascinating climbing history of the great peaks around you.

Along the trail, you'll pass four farms (technically "alps," as they are only open in the summer) that serve meals and drinks. Sonnenberg was allowed to break the all-wood building code with concrete for protection against avalanches. Suppenalp is quainter. Lean against the house with a salad, soup, or sandwich and enjoy the view. Just below Suppenalp is a new little adventure park with zip lines and other kid-pleasing activities.

Notice how older huts are built into the protected side of rocks and outcroppings, in anticipation of avalanches. Above Suppenalp, Blumental ("Flower Valley") is hopping with marmots. Because hunters are not allowed near lifts, animals have learned that these are safe places to hang out—giving tourists a better chance of spotting them.

The trail leads up and over to a group of huts called Schiltalp (good food, drink, and service, and a romantic farm setting). If the poles under the eaves have bells, the cows are up here. If not, the cows are still at the lower farms. Half the cows in Gimmelwald (about 100) spend their summers here. In July, August, and September, you can watch cheese being made and have a snack or drink. Thirty years ago, each family had its own hut. Labor was cheap and available. Today, it's a communal thing, with several families sharing the expense of a single cow herder. Cow herders are master cheesemakers and have veterinary skills, too.

From Schiltalp, the trail winds gracefully down toward Spielbodenalp. From there, you can finish the North Face Trail (continuing down and left through meadows and the hamlet of Gimmeln, then back to Mürren, with more historic signposts); or cut off right (descending steeply through a thick forest and under the dramatic Sprutz Waterfall into Gimmelwald).

▲**Allmendhubel/Mürren to Grütschalp (fairly easy)**—For a not-too-tough, two-hour walk with great Jungfrau views, ride the funicular from Mürren to Allmendhubel (6,344 feet) and walk to Grütschalp (a drop of about 1,500 feet), where you can catch the train back to Mürren. An easier version is the lower Bergweg from Allmendhubel to Grütschalp via Winteregg and its cheese farm. For a super-easy family stroll with grand views, walk from Mürren just above the train tracks either to Winteregg (40 minutes, restaurant, playground, train station) or through even better scenery on to Grütschalp (1 hour, train station), then catch the train back to Mürren.

Hikes on the Jungfrau (East) Side of the Lauterbrunnen Valley

▲▲▲**Männlichen-Kleine Scheidegg (easy and with dramatic views)**—This is my favorite easy alpine hike (2.5 miles, 1.5 hours, 900-foot altitude drop to Kleine Scheidegg). It's entertaining all the way, with glorious Jungfrau, Eiger, and Mönch views.

(Remember, that's the Young Maiden being protected from the Ogre by the Monk.) Trails may be snowbound into June; ask about conditions at the lift stations or local TIs (see Jungfraujoch information under "Lifts and Trains," page 1423).

If the weather's good, start off bright and early. From the Lauterbrunnen train station, take the little mountain train up to Wengen. Sit on the right side of the train for great valley and waterfall views on your way up to Wengen. In Wengen, buy a picnic at the Co-op grocery across from the station, walk across town, and catch the lift to Männlichen, located on the top of the ridge high above you. The lift can be open even if the trail is closed; if the weather is questionable, confirm that the Männlichen-Kleine Scheidegg trail is open before ascending. Don't waste time in Wengen if it's sunny—you can linger back here after your hike.

Riding the gondola from Wengen to Männlichen, you'll go over the old lift station (inundated by a 1978 avalanche that buried a good part of Wengen—notice there's no development in the "red zone" above the tennis courts). Farms are built with earthen ramps on the uphill side in anticipation of the next slide. The forest of avalanche fences near the top was built after that 1978 avalanche. As you ascend you can also survey Wengen—the bright red roofs mark vacation condos, mostly English-owned and used only a few weeks a year.

For a detour that'll give you an easy king- or queen-of-the-mountain feeling, turn left from the top of the Wengen-Männlichen lift station, and hike uphill 10 minutes to the little peak (Männlichen Gipfel, 7,500 feet).

Then go back to the lift station (which has a great kids' area) and enjoy an hour's walk—facing spectacular alpine panorama views—to Kleine Scheidegg for a picnic or restaurant lunch. To start the hike, leave the Wengen-Männlichen lift station to the right. Walk past the second Männlichen lift station (this one leads to Grindelwald, the touristy town in the valley to your left). Ahead of you in the distance, left to right, are the north faces of the Eiger, Mönch, and Jungfrau; in the foreground is the Tschuggen peak, and just behind it, the Lauberhorn. This hike takes you around the left (east) side of this ridge. Simply follow the signs for Kleine Scheidegg, and you'll be there in about an hour—a little more for gawkers, picnickers, and photographers. You might have to tiptoe through streams of melted snow—or some small snow banks, even well into the summer—but the path is well-marked, well-maintained, and mostly level all the way to Kleine Scheidegg.

About 35 minutes into the hike, you'll reach a bunch of benches and a shelter with incredible unobstructed views of all three peaks—the perfect picnic spot. Fifteen minutes later on the left, you'll see the first sign of civilization: Restaurant

Grindelwaldblick (the best lunch stop up here, open daily, closed Dec and May). Hike to the restaurant's fun mountain lookout to survey the Eiger and look down on the Kleine Scheidegg action. After 10 more minutes, you'll be at the Kleine Scheidegg train station, with plenty of lesser lunch options (including Restaurant Bahnhof).

From Kleine Scheidegg, you can catch the train up to "the top of Europe" (see Jungfraujoch information, page 1423), take the train back down to Wengen, or hike downhill (gorgeous 30-minute hike to Wengernalp station, a little farther to the Allmend stop; 60 more steep minutes from there into Wengen). The alpine views might be accompanied by the valley-filling mellow sound of alphorns and distant avalanches. If the weather turns bad or you run out of steam, catch the train at any of the stations along the way. After Wengernalp, the trail to Wengen is steep and, though not dangerous, requires a good set of knees. The boring final descent from Wengen to Lauterbrunnen is knee-killer steep—catch the train instead.

▲▲**Schynige Platte to First (more difficult)**—The best day I've had hiking in the Berner Oberland was when I made this demanding six-hour ridge walk, with Lake Brienz on one side and all that Jungfrau beauty on the other. Start at Wilderswil train station (just outside Interlaken) and catch the little train up to Schynige Platte (6,560 feet; 2/hour, 55 minutes, 35 SF). The high point is Faulhorn (8,790 feet, with its famous mountaintop hotel). Hike to a small mini-gondola called "First" (7,110 feet), then ride down to Grindelwald and catch a train back to your starting point, Wilderswil. Or, if you have a regional train pass (or no car but endless money), take the long, scenic return trip: From Grindelwald, take the lift up to Männlichen (2/hour, 30 minutes, 32 SF), do the hike to Kleine Scheidegg and down to Wengen (described above), then head down into Lauterbrunnen.

For a shorter (3-hour) ridge walk, consider the well-signposted Panoramaweg, a loop from Schynige Platte to Daub Peak.

The alpine flower park at the Schynige Platte station offers a delightful stroll through several hundred alpine flowers (free, June-Sept daily 8:30-18:00, www.alpengarten.ch), including a chance to see edelweiss growing in the wild.

Lowa, a leading local manufacturer of top-end hiking boots, has a promotional booth at the Schynige Platte station that provides free loaner boots to hikers who'd like to give their boots a try. They're already broken in, but bring thick socks (or buy them there).

If hiking here, be mindful of the last lifts (which can be as early as 16:30). Climbing from First (7,113 feet) to Schynige Platte (6,454 feet) gives you a later departure down and less climbing. The

TI produces a great Schynige Platte map/guide narrating the train ride up and describing various hiking options from there (available at Wilderswil station).

Mountain Biking

Mountain biking is popular and accepted, as long as you stay on the clearly marked mountain-bike paths. You can rent bikes in Mürren (Stäger Sport, see page 1414) or in Lauterbrunnen (Imboden Bike, see page 1401). The Lauterbrunnen shop is bigger, has a wider selection of bikes, and is likely to be open when the Mürren one isn't. On trains and cable cars, bikes require a separate ticket.

The most popular bike rides include the following:

Lauterbrunnen to Interlaken: This is a gentle downhill ride via a peaceful bike path across the river from the road (don't bike on the road itself). You can return to Lauterbrunnen by train (13 SF total for bike and you). Or rent a bike at either Interlaken station, take the train to Lauterbrunnen, and ride back.

Lauterbrunnen Valley (between Stechelberg and Lauterbrunnen town): This delightful, easy bike path features plenty of diversions along the way (several listed under "Activities in and near Lauterbrunnen" on page 1401).

Mürren to Winteregg to Grütschalp and Back: This fairly level route takes you through high country, with awesome mountain views.

Mürren to Winteregg to Lauterbrunnen: This scenic descent, on a service road with loose gravel, takes you to the Lauterbrunnen Valley floor.

Mürren-Gimmelwald-Sefinen Valley-Stechelberg-Lauterbrunnen-Grütschalp-Mürren: This is the best ride, but it's demanding—with one very difficult stretch where you'll likely walk your bike down a steep gulley for 500 yards. You'll take the cable car from Lauterbrunnen up to Grütschalp.

More Sleeping and Eating in the Berner Oberland

I'd sleep in Gimmelwald, Mürren, or Lauterbrunnen. But you could also consider the following places.

Sleeping and Eating at or near Kleine Scheidegg
(6,762 feet)

This high settlement above the timberline is where you catch the train up to the Jungfrau. All of these places serve meals. Confirm prices and availability before ascending. Note that the last train down to Wengen leaves Kleine Scheidegg at 18:30.

$$$ Hotel Bellevue des Alpes, lovingly maintaining a 1930s elegance, is a worthwhile splurge. Since the 1840s, five generations of von Allmens (subsidized by the family income from Trümmelbach Falls) have run this classic old alpine hotel. The hallway is like a museum, with old photos (Sb-220-260 SF, Db-370-530 SF, includes breakfast and sumptuous 5-course dinner, open only mid-June–mid-Sept, tel. 033-855-1212, fax 033-855-1294, www .scheidegg-hotels.ch, welcome@scheidegg-hotels.ch).

$$ Restaurant Bahnhof invites you to sleep face-to-face with the Eiger (dorm bed-51 SF with breakfast, 70 SF also includes dinner; D-170 SF with breakfast and dinner; in the train station building, tel. 033-828-7828, www.bahnhof-scheidegg.ch, info @bahnhof-scheidegg.ch).

$ Restaurant Grindelwaldblick, a 10-minute hike from the train station, is more charming, romantic, and remote than Restaurant Bahnhof (38 SF/bed in 8- to 20-bed rooms, includes sheets and breakfast, closed Nov and May, tel. 033-855-1374, fax 033-855-4205, www.grindelwaldblick.ch). The restaurant, with a great sun terrace and a cozy interior, sells good three-course lunches (14-25 SF) and 25-SF dinners.

Sleeping in Stechelberg
(3,025 feet)

Stechelberg is the hamlet at the end of the road up the Lauterbrunnen Valley; it's about a mile beyond the Schilthornbahn lift that goes up to Gimmelwald, Mürren, and the Schilthorn (it's a five-minute PostBus ride or a 20-minute trail walk between the lift station and the village). Beyond Stechelberg lies the rugged Rear Lauterbrunnen Valley, the edge of the Jungfrau-Aletsch-Bietschhorn nature reserve—the most glaciated part of the Alps.

$$ Hotel Stechelberg, at road's end, is surrounded by waterfalls and vertical rock, with a garden terrace, good restaurant, and 16 quiet rooms—half in a creaky old building, half in a concrete, no-character new building (D-86-110 SF, Db-130, Db with balcony-168 SF, T-147 SF, Tb-186 SF, Q-180 SF, Qb-234 SF, bus stops here 1-2/hour, free Wi-Fi, tel. 033-855-2921, fax 033-855-4438, www.hotel-stechelberg.ch, hotel@stechelberg.ch, Marianne and Otto).

$ The Alpenhof fills a former "Nature Friends' Hut" with cheap beds. Creaking like a wooden chalet built in 1926 should, and surrounded by a broad lawn, it provides a fine, inexpensive base for drivers and families (28 SF/bed in 2- to 6-bed rooms, each group gets a private room, breakfast-12 SF, tel. 033-855-1202, www.alpenhof-stechelberg.ch, alpenhof@stechelberg.ch, Diane and Marc). From the Hotel Stechelberg, go up the paved path, go right at the fork, and cross the river; it's on your left.

Sleeping in Obersteinberg
(5,900 feet)

Here's a wild idea: **$$ Mountain Hotel Obersteinberg** is a working alpine farm with cheese, cows, a mule shuttling up food once a day, and an American (Vickie) who fell in love with a mountain man. It's a 2.5-hour hike from either Stechelberg or Gimmelwald. They rent 12 primitive rooms and a bunch of loft beds. There's no shower, no hot water, and only meager solar-panel electricity. Candles light up the night, and you can take a hot-water bottle to bed if necessary (S-85 SF, D-166 SF, includes linen, sheetless dorm beds-68 SF; these prices include breakfast and dinner, without meals S-37 SF, D-74 SF, dorm beds-20 SF; closed Oct-May, tel. 033-855-2033). The place is filled with locals and Germans on weekends, but it's all yours on weekdays. Why not hike here from Gimmelwald and leave the Alps a day later?

If you like the idea of a hut on this hike—but also like electricity—try **$$ Mountain Hotel Tschingelhorn,** 15 minutes closer to Stechelberg (similar prices, tel. 033-855-1343, www.tschingelhorn.ch).

Sleeping in Isenfluh
(3,560 feet)

The PostBus takes you up on a spectacular road, through a long and narrow tunnel to the tiny hamlet of Isenfluh, which is even smaller than Gimmelwald and offers better views (bus departs from Lauterbrunnen train station almost hourly—times posted at stop, 15 minutes, 4 SF one-way).

$$$ Hotel Restaurant Waldrand has a decent restaurant (including great fresh salads) and five reasonably priced rooms (Sb-85 SF, Db-170 SF, Tb-190 SF, cash only, includes breakfast, tel. 033-855-1227, fax 033-855-1392, www.hotel-waldrand.ch, info@hotel-waldrand.ch, Vreni and Urs Werthmüller).

APPENDIX

Embassies and Consulates

Austria: US Embassy, Boltzmanngasse 16, Vienna, tel. 01/313-390, embassy@usembassy.at; consular services at Parkring 12a, daily 8:00-11:30, tel. 01/313-397-535, www.usembassy.at, consulate vienna@state.gov

Belgium: US Embassy, 27 Boulevard du Régent/Regentlaan, Brussels, tel. 02-811-4300, Mon-Fri 9:00-18:00, closed Sat-Sun, after-hours emergency call and ask to be connected to the duty officer, http://belgium.usembassy.gov; US Consulate, next door to embassy at 25 Boulevard du Régent/Regentlaan, passport services Mon-Thu 13:30-15:30, Fri 9:00-11:00, closed Sat-Sun

Czech Republic: US Embassy, Tržiště 15, Prague, in the Little Quarter below the castle, tel. 257-022-000, passport services Mon-Fri 8:30-11:30, http://czech.prague.usembassy.gov, ACSPrg @state.gov

France: US Embassy, 4 avenue Gabriel, to the left as you face Hôtel Crillon, Paris, Mo: Concorde, tel. 01 43 12 22 22, passport services open Mon-Fri 9:00-11:00, online appointments possible, closed Sat-Sun, http://france.usembassy.gov

Germany: US Embassy, Pariser Platz 2, Berlin, tel. 030/83050; consular services at Clayallee 170, Mon-Fri 8:30-12:00 by appointment only, closed Sat-Sun, tel. 030/8305-1200—calls answered Mon-Fri 14:00-16:00 only, after-hours emergency call and ask to be connected to the duty officer, www.usembassy.de, acsberlin@state.gov

Great Britain: US Embassy, 24 Grosvenor Square, London, Tube: Bond Street, tel. 020/7499-9000, passport services available Mon-Fri 8:30-12:00 & 14:00-16:00, www.usembassy.org.uk, SCSLondon@state.gov

European Calling Chart

Just smile and dial, using this key:
AC = Area Code, LN = Local Number.

European Country	Calling long distance within ...	Calling from the US or Canada to ...	Calling from a European country to ...
Austria	AC + LN	011 + 43 + AC (without the initial zero) + LN	00 + 43 + AC (without the initial zero) + LN
Belgium	LN	011 + 32 + LN (without initial zero)	00 + 32 + LN (without initial zero)
Bosnia-Herzegovina	AC + LN	011 + 387 + AC (without initial zero) + LN	00 + 387 + AC (without initial zero) + LN
Britain	AC + LN	011 + 44 + AC (without initial zero) + LN	00 + 44 + AC (without initial zero) + LN
Croatia	AC + LN	011 + 385 + AC (without initial zero) + LN	00 + 385 + AC (without initial zero) + LN
Czech Republic	LN	011 + 420 + LN	00 + 420 + LN
Denmark	LN	011 + 45 + LN	00 + 45 + LN
Estonia	LN	011 + 372 + LN	00 + 372 + LN
Finland	AC + LN	011 + 358 + AC (without initial zero) + LN	999 (or other 900 number) + 358 + AC (without initial zero) + LN
France	LN	011 + 33 + LN (without initial zero)	00 + 33 + LN (without initial zero)
Germany	AC + LN	011 + 49 + AC (without initial zero) + LN	00 + 49 + AC (without initial zero) + LN
Gibraltar	LN	011 + 350 + LN	00 + 350 + LN
Greece	LN	011 + 30 + LN	00 + 30 + LN
Hungary	06 + AC + LN	011 + 36 + AC + LN	00 + 36 + AC + LN
Ireland	AC + LN	011 + 353 + AC (without initial zero) + LN	00 + 353 + AC (without initial zero) + LN

European Country	Calling long distance within ...	Calling from the US or Canada to ...	Calling from a European country to ...
Italy	LN	011 + 39 + LN	00 + 39 + LN
Montenegro	AC + LN	011 + 382 + AC (without initial zero) + LN	00 + 382 + AC (without initial zero) + LN
Morocco	LN	011 + 212 + LN (without initial zero)	00 + 212 + LN (without initial zero)
Netherlands	AC + LN	011 + 31 + AC (without initial zero) + LN	00 + 31 + AC (without initial zero) + LN
Norway	LN	011 + 47 + LN	00 + 47 + LN
Poland	LN	011 + 48 + LN (without initial zero)	00 + 48 + LN (without initial zero)
Portugal	LN	011 + 351 + LN	00 + 351 + LN
Slovakia	AC + LN	011 + 421 + AC (without initial zero) + LN	00 + 421 + AC (without initial zero) + LN
Slovenia	AC + LN	011 + 386 + AC (without initial zero) + LN	00 + 386 + AC (without initial zero) + LN
Spain	LN	011 + 34 + LN	00 + 34 + LN
Sweden	AC + LN	011 + 46 + AC (without initial zero) + LN	00 + 46 + AC (without initial zero) + LN
Switzerland	LN	011 + 41 + LN (without initial zero)	00 + 41 + LN (without initial zero)
Turkey	AC (if there's no initial zero, add one) + LN	011 + 90 + AC (without initial zero) + LN	00 + 90 + AC (without initial zero) + LN

- The instructions above apply whether you're calling a land line or mobile phone.
- The international access codes (the first numbers you dial when making an international call) are 011 if you're calling from the US or Canada, or 00 if you're calling from virtually anywhere in Europe (except Finland, where it's 999 or another 900 number, depending on the phone service you're using).
- To call the US or Canada from Europe, dial 00, then 1 (the country code for the US and Canada), then the area code and number. In short, 00 + 1 + AC + LN = Hi, Mom!

Italy: US Embassy, Via Vittorio Veneto 119/A, Rome, 24-hour emergency line—tel. 06-46741, non-emergency—tel. 06-4674-2420, Mon-Fri 8:30-12:00, closed Sat-Sun, http://rome.usembassy.gov, uscitizensrome@state.gov; US Consulate, Lungarno Vespucci 38, Florence, tel. 055-266-951, http://florence.usconsulate.gov

The Netherlands: US Embassy, Lange Voorhout 102, The Hague, tel. 070/310-2209, visits by appointment only, http://netherlands.usembassy.gov; US Consulate, Museumplein 19, Amsterdam, general services Mon-Fri 13:30-16:30, emergency visits Mon-Fri 8:30-11:30, closed Sat-Sun; tel. 020/575-5309 during office hours, after-hours emergency call officer at tel. 070/310-2209, http://amsterdam.usconsulate.gov, USCitizenServicesAms@state.gov

Spain: US Embassy, Calle Serrano 75, Madrid, tel. 915-872-240, Mon-Fri 8:30-13:00, emergency tel. 915-872-200, http://madrid.usembassy.gov

Switzerland: US Embassy, Sulgeneckstrasse 19, Bern, tel. 031-357-7011, Mon-Fri 9:00-11:30, closed Sat-Sun, emergency tel. 031-357-7777, http://bern.usembassy.gov, bernacs@state.gov

Transportation

This section contains basic information on trains, driving, and flights.

Trains

A major mistake Americans make is relating public transportation in Europe to the pathetic public transportation they're used to at home. By rail, you'll have Europe by the tail. While many people simply buy tickets as they go ("point to point"), the various train passes give you the simplicity of ticket-free, unlimited travel, and depending on how many trips you do, often offer a savings over regular point-to-point tickets. Fast, long-distance, international, or overnight trains are more likely to require reservations at some point before boarding; you can make your more critical reservations from home.

For a summary of railpass deals and point-to-point ticket options (available in the US and in Europe), check out our free, annually updated *Guide to Eurail Passes* at www.ricksteves.com/rail. If you decide to get a railpass, this guide will help you know you're getting the right one for your trip. To study train schedules in advance on the Web, look up http://bahn.hafas.de/bin/query.exe/en (Germany's excellent all-Europe timetable).

Eurail Global Pass and Eurail Selectpass

Eurail Global passes offer you unlimited first-class travel on all public railways in 22 European countries. These popular passes

Point-to-Point Rail Tickets: Cost & Time

This chart shows the cost of second-class train tickets. Connect the dots of your itinerary, add up the cost, compare it with a railpass, and see what is better for your trip.

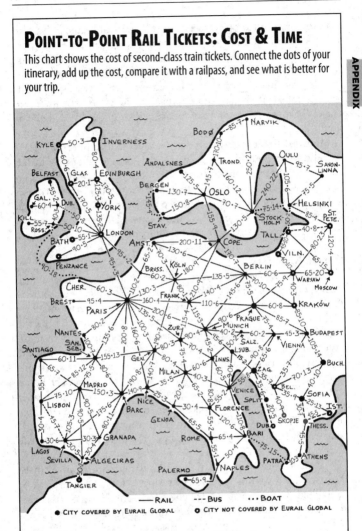

RAIL — — — BUS · · · BOAT

● CITY COVERED BY EURAIL GLOBAL   ○ CITY NOT COVERED BY EURAIL GLOBAL

First number between cities = Approximate cost in US dollars for a one-way, second class ticket. **Second number** = Number of hours the trip takes.

Important: These fares and times are based on European web sources. Actual prices may vary due to currency fluctuations and local promotions. Local competition can cut the actual price of some boat crossings (from Italy to Greece, for example) by 50 percent or more. For approximate first-class rail prices, add 50 percent. Travel times and fares are for express trains where applicable.

give you most of Europe (except Great Britain and some of Eastern Europe) by the tail. Choose between the consecutive-day pass (ranging from 15 days to three months) or the cheaper flexipass (any 10 or 15 individual days in two months). Travel partners (2-5 people traveling together) save 15 percent with Saverpasses, available in consecutive-day and flexipass versions. Youths under 26 travel cheaper with second-class passes. Kids under 12 pay half the adult rate.

Eurail Selectpasses give you a selected number of "flexi" travel days in your choice of three, four, or five adjoining Eurail countries, whether connected by rail or ferry (e.g., a three-country Selectpass could cover France, Italy, and Switzerland). Selectpasses are fine for a focused trip, but to see the Best of Europe, you'd do best with a Eurail Global pass. These passes also give a 15 percent Saverpass discount to two or more companions traveling together.

Eurail Analysis

For an at-a-glance break-even point, remember that a one-month Eurail Global pass is a good value if, for example, your route is Amsterdam-Rome-Madrid-Paris. Passes pay for themselves quicker in the north, where the cost per mile is higher. Check the Rail Tickets map in this chapter to see if your planned travels merit purchasing a train pass. If it's about even, go with the pass for the convenience of not having to wait in line to buy tickets (on trains that don't require paid reservations) and for the fun and freedom to travel "free." Even if second-class tickets work out a bit cheaper than a first-class pass for travelers over 26, consider the added value of a first-class pass: On a crowded train, your chances of getting a seat are much better if your pass allows you to sit anywhere on the train.

Rail-and-drive passes are popular varieties of many of these passes. Along with a railpass (Eurailpass, Eurail Selectpass, or individual country), you get vouchers for a few Hertz or Avis car-rental days. These allow travelers to do long trips by train and enjoy a car where they need the freedom to explore. Great areas for a day of joyriding include Germany's Rhine Valley or Bavaria, France's Provence, and the Alps (for "car hiking"). When comparing prices, remember that each day of car rental comes with about $50 of extra expenses (CDW insurance, gas, parking), which you can divide among the people in your party.

Renting a Car

You'll need to bring your US driver's license. In some countries—including Austria, Italy, and Spain—you'll also need an International Driving Permit (available at your local AAA office for $15 plus the cost of two passport-type photos; see www

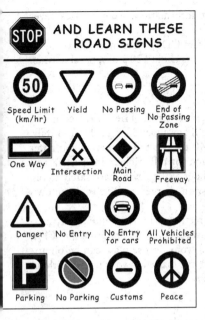

STOP AND LEARN THESE ROAD SIGNS

Speed Limit (km/hr)

Yield

No Passing

End of No Passing Zone

One Way

Intersection

Main Road

Freeway

Danger

No Entry

No Entry for cars

All Vehicles Prohibited

Parking

No Parking

Customs

Peace

.aaa.com). In other countries, it's recommended, though not required, that you carry an International Driving Permit.

As Europe's internal borders fade, your car comes with the paperwork you need to drive wherever you like in Western and most of Eastern Europe (always check when booking). But if you're heading to a country in far-eastern or southeastern Europe that still has closed borders, state your travel plans up front to the rental company when making your reservation. Some companies have limits on eastward excursions (for example, you can only take cheaper cars, and you may have to pay extra insurance fees). When you cross these borders, you may be asked to show proof of insurance (called a "green card"). Ask your car-rental company if you need any other documentation for crossing the borders on your itinerary.

For trips of at least three weeks, leasing—which includes taxes and insurance—is the best way to go (for more information, see www.ricksteves.com/driving).

Car Insurance Options

When you rent a car, you are liable for a very high deductible, sometimes equal to the entire value of the car. Limit your financial risk in case of an accident by choosing one of these three options: Buy Collision Damage Waiver (CDW) coverage from the car-rental company, get coverage through your credit card (free, if your card automatically includes zero-deductible coverage), or buy coverage through Travel Guard (tel. 800-826-4919, www.travelguard.com).

Buying CDW insurance is the easiest but priciest option. Using the coverage that comes with your credit card is cheaper, but can involve more hassle. If you're taking a short trip, the cheapest solution is to buy Travel Guard's CDW insurance. It's valid everywhere in Europe except the Republic of Ireland, and some Italian car-rental companies refuse to honor it. Residents of some states (Washington, Texas, New Hampshire, and Kansas) aren't allowed to buy this coverage. For more information, see www.ricksteves.com/cdw.

Theft insurance (separate from CDW insurance) is mandatory in Italy. The insurance usually costs about $20 a day, payable when you pick up the car.

Driving

I use the freeways whenever possible. They're free in the Netherlands and Germany; you'll pay about $4-9 per hour in Italy, France, and Spain; roughly $40 for the toll sticker as you enter Switzerland; and about $10 each for toll stickers in Austria and the Czech Republic. It costs about $20 a day to park safely in big cities, and there's a $13 "congestion charge" to drive in downtown London.

Be warned that driving is restricted in many Italian city centers. If you drive in an area marked *Zona Traffico Limitato* (ZTL, often shown above a red circle), your license plate can be photographed and a hefty (€150-plus) fine mailed to your home, without your ever being stopped by a cop.

Cheap Flights

Connecting your itinerary by air is cheaper than you might think. Thanks to Europe's budget airlines, you can get between many European cities for about $100 one-way. Some amazing promotional deals can even bring fares down into the single digits. The best deals are from major hub cities.

One of the best websites for comparing inexpensive flights is www.skyscanner.net. Other comparison search engines include www.wegolo.com and www.whichbudget.com. Airlines offering inexpensive flights include easyJet (www.easyjet.com) and Ryanair (www.ryanair.com).

Be aware of the potential drawbacks of flying on the cheap: nonrefundable and nonchangeable tickets, rigid baggage restrictions (and fees if you have more than what's officially allowed), airports far outside of town, tight schedules that can mean more delays, little in the way of customer assistance if problems arise, and, of course, no frills. Read the small print—especially baggage policies—before you book.

Resources

Resources from Rick Steves

Rick Steves' Best of Europe 2012 is one of many books in my series on European travel, which includes country guidebooks, city and regional guidebooks, Snapshot guides (excerpted chapters from my

Begin Your Trip at www.ricksteves.com

At our travel website, you'll find a wealth of free information on European destinations, including fresh monthly news and helpful tips from thousands of fellow travelers. You'll also find my latest guidebook updates (www.ricksteves.com/update) and my travel blog.

Our **online Travel Store** offers travel bags and accessories specially designed to help you travel smarter and lighter. These include my popular carry-on bags (roll-aboard and rucksack versions), money belts, totes, toiletries kits, adapters, other accessories, and a wide selection of guidebooks, planning maps, and DVDs.

Choosing the right **railpass** for your trip—amidst hundreds of options—can drive you nutty. We'll help you choose the best pass for your needs and ship it to you for free, plus give you a bunch of free extras.

Rick Steves' Europe Through the Back Door travel company offers **tours** with more than three dozen itineraries and about 400 departures reaching the best destinations in this book...and beyond. You'll enjoy great guides, a fun bunch of travel partners (with small groups of generally around 24-28), and plenty of room to spread out in a big, comfy bus. You'll find European adventures to fit every vacation length. For all the details, and to get our Tour Catalog and a free Rick Steves Tour Experience DVD (filmed on location during an actual tour), visit www.ricksteves.com or call our Tour Department at 425/608-4217.

country guides), Pocket Guides (full-color little books on big cities), and my budget-travel skills handbook, *Rick Steves' Europe Through the Back Door*. Many of my books are available in electronic format. My phrase books—for Italian, French, German, Spanish, and Portuguese—are practical and budget-oriented. My other books include *Europe 101* (a crash course on art and history), *Mediterranean Cruise Ports* (how to make the most of your time in port), and *Travel as a Political Act* (a travelogue sprinkled with tips for bringing home a global perspective). For a list of my major titles, see the inside of the last page of this book.

Video: My TV series, *Rick Steves' Europe,* covers European destinations in 100 shows. To watch episodes, visit www.hulu .com/rick-steves-europe; for scripts and other details, see www .ricksteves.com/tv.

Audio: My weekly public radio show, *Travel with Rick Steves,* features interviews with travel experts from around the world. I've also produced free, self-guided audio tours of the top sights in London, Paris, Florence, Rome, and Venice. All of this audio content is available for free at Rick Steves Audio Europe, an extensive online library organized by destination. Choose whatever interests you, and download it for free to your computer or mobile device at www.ricksteves.com/audio europe, iTunes, or the Rick Steves Audio Europe smartphone app.

Conversions and Climate

Numbers and Stumblers

- Europeans write a few of their numbers differently than we do: 1 = 1, 4 = 4, 7 = 7. Learn the difference or miss your train.
- Europeans write dates as day/month/year (Christmas is 25/12/12).
- Except in Great Britain, commas are decimal points, and decimals are commas. A dollar and a half is 1,50. There are 5.280 feet in a mile.
- When counting with fingers, start with your thumb. If you hold up your first finger to request one item, you'll probably get two.

- What we Americans call the second floor of a building is the first floor in Europe.
- Europeans keep the left "lane" open for passing on escalators and moving sidewalks. Keep to the right.

Metric Conversions (approximate)

A kilogram is 2.2 pounds, and 1 liter is about a quart, or almost four to a gallon. A kilometer is six-tenths of a mile. I figure kilometers to miles by cutting them in half and adding back 10 percent of the original (120 km: 60 + 12 = 72 miles, 300 km: 150 + 30 = 180 miles).

1 foot = 0.3 meter	1 square yard = 0.8 square meter
1 yard = 0.9 meter	1 square mile = 2.6 square kilometers
1 mile = 1.6 kilometers	1 ounce = 28 grams
1 centimeter = 0.4 inch	1 quart = 0.95 liter
1 meter = 39.4 inches	1 kilogram = 2.2 pounds
1 kilometer = 0.62 mile	32°F = 0°C

Climate

Here is a list of average temperatures (first line—average daily high; second line—average daily low; third line—days of no rain). This can be helpful in planning your itinerary, but I have never found European weather to be particularly predictable, and these charts ignore humidity. For more details, check www.world climate.com.

J	F	M	A	M	J	J	A	S	O	N	D
AUSTRIA • Vienna											
34°	38°	47°	58°	67°	73°	76°	75°	68°	56°	45°	37°
25°	28°	30°	42°	50°	56°	60°	59°	53°	44°	37°	30°
16	17	18	17	18	16	18	18	20	18	16	16
BELGIUM • Brussels											
40°	44°	51°	58°	65°	72°	73°	72°	69°	60°	48°	42°
30°	32°	36°	41°	46°	52°	54°	54°	51°	45°	38°	32°
10	11	14	12	15	15	14	13	17	14	10	12
CZECH REPUBLIC • Prague											
31°	34°	44°	54°	64°	70°	73°	72°	65°	53°	42°	34°
23°	24°	30°	38°	46°	52°	55°	55°	49°	41°	33°	27°
18	17	21	19	18	18	18	19	20	18	18	18
FRANCE • Paris											
43°	45°	54°	60°	68°	73°	76°	75°	70°	60°	50°	44°
34°	34°	39°	43°	49°	55°	58°	58°	53°	46°	40°	36°
14	14	19	17	19	18	19	18	17	18	15	15

	J	F	M	A	M	J	J	A	S	O	N	D

GERMANY • Berlin

35°	38°	48°	56°	64°	70°	74°	73°	67°	56°	44°	36°
23°	23°	30°	38°	45°	51°	55°	54°	48°	40°	33°	26°
15	12	18	15	16	13	15	15	17	18	15	16

GREAT BRITAIN • London

43°	44°	50°	56°	62°	69°	71°	71°	65°	58°	50°	45°
36°	36°	38°	42°	47°	53°	56°	56°	52°	46°	42°	38°
16	15	20	18	19	19	19	20	17	18	15	16

ITALY • Rome

52°	55°	59°	66°	74°	82°	87°	86°	79°	71°	61°	55°
40°	42°	45°	50°	56°	63°	67°	67°	62°	55°	49°	44°
13	19	23	24	26	26	30	29	25	23	19	21

NETHERLANDS • Amsterdam

40°	42°	49°	56°	64°	70°	72°	71°	67°	57°	48°	42°
31°	31°	34°	40°	46°	51°	55°	55°	50°	44°	38°	33°
9	9	15	14	17	16	14	13	11	11	9	10

SPAIN • Madrid

47°	52°	59°	65°	70°	80°	87°	85°	77°	65°	55°	48°
35°	36°	41°	45°	50°	58°	63°	63°	57°	49°	42°	36°
23	21	21	21	21	25	29	28	24	23	21	21

SWITZERLAND • Bern

38°	42°	51°	59°	66°	73°	77°	76°	69°	58°	47°	40°
29°	30°	36°	42°	49°	55°	58°	58°	53°	44°	37°	31°
20	19	22	21	20	19	22	20	20	21	19	21

Temperature Conversion: Fahrenheit and Celsius

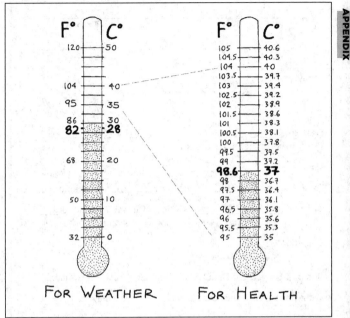

Europe takes its temperature using the Celsius scale, while we opt for Fahrenheit. For a rough conversion from Celsius to Fahrenheit, double the number and add 30. For weather, remember that 28°C is 82°F—perfect. For health, 37°C is just right.

Hotel Reservation

To: _____   _____
                hotel   *email or fax*

From: _____   _____
                name   *email or fax*

Today's date: _____ / _____ / _____
                        day   *month*   *year*

Dear Hotel _____ ,

Please make this reservation for me:

Name: _____

Total # of people: _____   # of rooms: _____   # of nights: _____

Arriving: _____ / _____ / _____   My time of arrival (24-hr clock): _____
                day   *month*   *year*   (I will telephone if I will be late)

Departing: ____ / ____ / ____
                 day   *month*   *year*

Room(s): Single____   Double ____   Twin____   Triple ____   Quad____

With: Toilet ____   Shower____   Bath ____   Sink only____

Special needs: View____ Quiet____ Cheapest ____ Ground Floor____

Please email or fax confirmation of my reservation, along with the type of room reserved and the price. Please also inform me of your cancellation policy. After I hear from you, I will quickly send my credit-card information as a deposit to hold the room. Thank you.

_____
Name

_____
Address

_____
City   *State*   *Zip Code*   *Country*

Before hoteliers can make your reservation, they want to know the information listed above. You can use this form as the basis for your email, or you can photocopy this page, fill in the information, and send it as a fax (also available online at www.ricksteves.com/reservation).

Packing Checklist

Whether you're traveling for five days or five weeks, here's what you'll need to bring. Pack light to enjoy the sweet freedom of true mobility. Happy travels!

- ❑ 5 shirts: long- and short-sleeve
- ❑ 1 sweater or lightweight fleece
- ❑ 2 pairs pants
- ❑ 1 pair shorts
- ❑ 1 swimsuit
- ❑ 5 pairs underwear and socks
- ❑ 1 pair shoes
- ❑ 1 rainproof jacket with hood
- ❑ Tie or scarf
- ❑ Money belt
- ❑ Money—your mix of:
  - ❑ Debit card (for ATM withdrawals)
  - ❑ Credit card
  - ❑ Hard cash (in easy-to-exchange $20 bills)
- ❑ Documents plus photocopies:
  - ❑ Passport
  - ❑ Printout of airline eticket
  - ❑ Driver's license
  - ❑ Student ID and hostel card
  - ❑ Railpass/car rental voucher
  - ❑ Insurance details
- ❑ Daypack
- ❑ Electronics—your choice of:
  - ❑ Camera (and related gear)
  - ❑ Mobile phone or smartphone
  - ❑ iPod (or other MP3 player)
  - ❑ Laptop/netbook
  - ❑ ebook reader
  - ❑ Chargers for each of the above
  - ❑ Plug adapter

- ❑ Empty water bottle
- ❑ Wristwatch and alarm clock
- ❑ Earplugs
- ❑ Toiletries kit
  - ❑ Toiletries
  - ❑ Medicines and vitamins
  - ❑ First-aid kit
  - ❑ Glasses/contacts/sunglasses (with prescriptions)
- ❑ Sealable plastic baggies
- ❑ Laundry soap
- ❑ Clothesline
- ❑ Small towel
- ❑ Sewing kit
- ❑ Travel information (guidebooks and maps)
- ❑ Address list (for sending postcards)
- ❑ Postcards and photos from home
- ❑ Notepad and pen
- ❑ Journal

If you plan to carry on your luggage, note that all liquids must be in 3.4-ounce or smaller containers and fit within a single quart-size sealable baggie. For details, see www.tsa.gov/travelers.

INDEX

INDEX

INDEX

INDEX

MAP INDEX

Rick's free app and podcasts

The FREE **Rick Steves Audio Europe**™ app for iPhone, iPad and iPod Touch gives you 29 self-guided audio tours of Europe's top museums, sights and historic walks—plus more than 200 tracks filled with cultural insights and sightseeing tips from Rick's radio interviews—all organized into geographic-specific playlists.

Let **Rick Steves Audio Europe**™ amplify your guidebook.

With Rick whispering in your ear Europe gets even better.

Thanks Facebook fans for submitting photos while on location! From top: John Kuijper in Florence, Brenda Mamer with her mother in Rome, Angel Capobianco in London, and Alyssa Passey with her friend in Paris.

Find out more at ricksteves.com

Join a Rick Steves tour

Enjoy Europe's warmest welcome... with the flexibility and friendship of a small group getting to know Rick's favorite places and people. It all starts with our free tour catalog and DVD.

Great guides, small groups, no grumps.

See more than three dozen itineraries throughout Europe

▸ Plan Your Trip

Browse thousands of articles and a wealth of money-saving tips for planning your dream trip. You'll find up-to-date information on Europe's best destinations, packing smart, getting around, finding rooms, staying healthy, avoiding scams and more.

▸ Eurail Passes

Find out, step-by-step, if a railpass makes sense for your trip—and how to avoid buying more than you need. Get free shipping on online orders

▸ Graffiti Wall & Travelers Helpline

Learn, ask, share—our online community of savvy travelers is a great resource for first-time travelers to Europe, as well as seasoned pros.

Rick Steves' Europe Through the Back Door, Inc

NOW AVAILABLE:
eBOOKS, APPS & BLU-RAY

eBOOKS

Most guides are available as eBooks from Amazon, Barnes & Noble, Borders, Apple, and Sony. Free apps for eBook reading are available in the Apple App Store and Android Market, and eBook readers such as Kindle, Nook, and Kobo all have free apps that work on smartphones.

RICK STEVES' EUROPE DVDs

10 New Shows 2011–2012
Austria & the Alps
Eastern Europe
England & Wales
European Christmas
European Travel Skills & Specials
France
Germany, BeNeLux & More
Greece & Turkey
Iran
Ireland & Scotland
Italy's Cities
Italy's Countryside
Scandinavia
Spain
Travel Extras

BLU-RAY

Celtic Charms
Eastern Europe Favorites
European Christmas
Italy Through the Back Door
Mediterranean Mosaic
Surprising Cities of Europe

PHRASE BOOKS & DICTIONARIES

French
French, Italian & German
German
Italian
Portuguese
Spanish

JOURNALS

Rick Steves' Pocket Travel Journal
Rick Steves' Travel Journal

APPS

Select Rick Steves guides are available as apps in the Apple App Store.

PLANNING MAPS

Britain, Ireland & London
Europe
France & Paris
Germany, Austria & Switzerland
Ireland
Italy
Spain & Portugal

Rick Steves books and DVDs are available at bookstores and through online booksellers.

Credits

Contributors
Gene Openshaw

Gene is a writer, composer, and lecturer on art and history. Specializing in writing walking tours of Europe's cultural sights, Gene has co-authored 10 of Rick's books. When not traveling, Gene enjoys composing music, recovering from his 1973 trip to Europe with Rick, and living everyday life with his daughter.

Steve Smith

Steve manages tour planning for Rick Steves' Europe Through the Back Door and co-authors the France guidebooks with Rick. Fluent in French, he's lived in France on several occasions, starting when he was seven, and has traveled there annually since 1986.

Honza Vihan

Honza, co-author of Rick's book on Prague & the Czech Republic, grew up roaming the Czech countryside in search of the Wild West. Once the borders opened, he set off for South Dakota. His journey took him to China, Honduras, India, and Iran. Honza, who now leads Rick Steves' tours through Eastern Europe, lives in Prague with his wife and son.

Researchers
Amanda Buttinger

Amanda moved to Madrid in 1998, thinking she'd be there a year. Since then she's found many reasons to stay, from learning more Spanish to guiding and travel writing to the best of all—sunny city walks with her dog and her boys.

Ben Cameron

Ben experienced his first taste of European travel when he was three, exploring medieval castles with his parents. Returning after graduation, he was hooked and has spent much of his time since exploring Europe independently and leading tours for Rick Steves. When not living out of his backpack, Ben splits his time between Rome and Seattle.

Lee Evans

Lee Evans left his Eastern Washington home on a Congress-Bundestag Scholarship and never looked back. After completing his studies in Florence and Prague, he finally found his home in the greatest city on the planet: Berlin. His beautiful wife and daughter tolerate his historical ranting and frequent absences as a tour guide.

Cameron Hewitt

Cameron writes and edits guidebooks for Rick Steves, specializing in Eastern Europe. For this book, Cameron updated the chapters on Vienna, London, and Bath. He lives in Seattle with his wife Shawna.

Helen Inman

After graduating with a law degree, Helen left England for the Mediterranean, finding sunshine, vibrant energy, and Latin culture and languages. Before working as a guide for Rick Steves tours and as a guidebook researcher, she enjoyed five years in Italy. She now lives in Spain, where she thrives on a diet of dancing, laughter, *cava,* and seafood.

Cathy McDonald

Cathy, a guidebook editor and researcher for Rick Steves, brings a naturalist's perspective to Europe's landscapes. She lives in Seattle, where she has written about the Pacific Northwest for more than 15 years as a freelance travel writer for *The Seattle Times.*

Amanda Scotese

Amanda Scotese freelances as a journalist and editor in Chicago. Her travels in Italy include a stint selling leather jackets in Florence's San Lorenzo Market, basking in the Sicilian sun, and helping out with Rick Steves' guidebooks and tours.

Gretchen Strauch

Before Gretchen became a guidebook editor for Rick Steves, she lived in Europe for four years: studying in Scotland, teaching in Germany, and traveling constantly. She gladly attempts Dutch pronunciation in return for the tulips, pancakes, and canals, and she'd do just about anything for a fresh Liège waffle.

Ian Watson

Ian has worked with Rick's guidebooks since 1993, after starting out with other guidebook series. Originally from upstate New York, Ian speaks several European languages, including German, and makes his home in Reykjavík, Iceland.

Images

Location	Photographer
Front Color Matter	
Full-page image: Arnhem Open-Air Museum, Netherlands	Dominic Bonuccelli
Table of Contents	
Golden Hinde, London	Dominic Bonuccelli
Hallstatt, Austria	Rick Steves
Bruges, Belgium	Dominic Bonuccelli
Dolomites, Italy	Dominic Bonuccelli
Introduction	
Gondolas in Venice	Dominic Bonuccelli
Austria	
Full-page image: Vienna—St. Peter's Church	Cameron Hewitt
Vienna—Schönbrunn Palace	Cameron Hewitt
Salzburg	Rick Steves
Hallstatt	David C. Hoerlein
Belgium	
Full-page image: Bruges Canal	Rick Steves
Bruges	David C. Hoerlein

Czech Republic
Full-page image:
    Prague—Charles Bridge   Cameron Hewitt
Prague—View of Prague Castle   Cameron Hewitt

France
Full-page image: Paris—
    Venus de Milo, Louvre Museum   Rob Unck
Paris—Louvre Museum   Rick Steves
Provence—Pont du Gard   Rick Steves
The French Riviera—Nice   David C. Hoerlein

Germany
Full-page image: Munich—Marienplatz Dominic Bonuccelli
Bavaria—Neuschwanstein Castle   Dominic Bonuccelli
Rothenburg   David C. Hoerlein
Rhine River   Dominic Bonuccelli
Berlin—Gendarmenmarkt   Cameron Hewitt

Great Britain
Full-page image:
    London's British Museum   Rick Steves
London—Houses of Parliament   Rick Steves
Bath—Pulteney Bridge   Lauren Mills

Italy
Full-page image: Florence—
    Michelangelo's *David*   Rick Steves
Rome—Piazza Navona   Rick Steves
Venice—Church of
    San Giorgio Maggiore   David C. Hoerlein
Florence—Piazzale Michelangelo Rick Steves
The Cinque Terre—Corniglia   Rick Steves

Netherlands
Full-page image: Amsterdam   Rick Steves
Amsterdam   Rick Steves
Haarlem—Market Square   Rick Steves

Spain
Full-page image: Moorish Arches   David C. Hoerlein
Barcelona—Montjuïc   David C. Hoerlein
Madrid—Retiro Park   David C. Hoerlein

Switzerland
Full-page image: Gimmelwald   Dominic Bonuccelli
Gimmelwald   Cameron Hewitt

Rick Steves' Guidebook Series

City, Regional, and Country Guides

Rick Steves' Amsterdam,
Bruges & Brussels
Rick Steves' Best of Europe
Rick Steves' Budapest
Rick Steves' Croatia
& Slovenia
Rick Steves' Eastern Europe
Rick Steves' England
Rick Steves' Florence
& Tuscany
Rick Steves' France
Rick Steves' Germany
Rick Steves' Great Britain
Rick Steves' Greece: Athens
& the Peloponnese
Rick Steves' Ireland

Rick Steves' Istanbul
Rick Steves' Italy
Rick Steves' London
Rick Steves' Paris
Rick Steves' Portugal
Rick Steves' Prague
& the Czech Republic
Rick Steves' Provence
& the French Riviera
Rick Steves' Rome
Rick Steves' Scandinavia
Rick Steves' Spain
Rick Steves' Switzerland
Rick Steves' Venice
Rick Steves' Vienna,
Salzburg & Tirol

Snapshot Guides

Excerpted from country guidebooks, the Snapshots Guides
cover many of my favorite destinations, such as *Rick Steves'
Snapshot Barcelona, Rick Steves' Snapshot Scotland,* and
Rick Steves' Snapshot Hill Towns of Central Italy.

Pocket Guides

My new Pocket Guides are condensed, colorful guides to
Europe's top cities, including Paris, London, Rome, and more.
These combine the top self-guided walks and tours from my
city guides with vibrant full-color photos, and are sized to slip
easily into your pocket.

Rick Steves' Phrase Books

French
French/Italian/German
German
Italian
Portuguese
Spanish

ore Books

eves' Europe 101: History and Art for the Traveler
es' Europe Through the Back Door
' European Christmas
editerranean Cruise Ports
cards from Europe
as a Political Act

Avalon Travel
a member of the Perseus Books Group
1700 Fourth Street
Berkeley, CA 94710, USA

Printed in Canada by Friesens
First printing August 2011

For the latest on Rick Steves' lectures, guidebooks, tours, public television series, and public radio show, contact Europe Through the Back Door, Box 2009, Edmonds, WA 98020, 425/771-8303, fax 425/771-0833, www.ricksteves.com, rick@ricksteves.com.

ISBN: 978-1-59880-979-4
ISSN: 1096-7702

Europe Through the Back Door Reviewing Editor: Jennifer Madison Davis
ETBD Editors: Gretchen Strauch, Tom Griffin, Suzanne Kotz
ETBD Managing Editor: Risa Laib
Avalon Travel Senior Editor and Series Manager: Madhu Prasher
Avalon Travel Project Editor: Kelly Lydick
Proofreader: Jamie Andrade
Indexer: Stephen Callahan
Production & Typesetting: McGuire Barber Design
Cover Design: Kimberly Glyder Design
Graphic Content Director: Laura VanDeventer
Maps and Graphics: David C. Hoerlein, Laura VanDeventer, Lauren Mills, Barb Geisler, Mike Morgenfeld, Brice Ticen, Kat Bennett, Chris Markiewicz
Front Matter Color Photos: Page i: Reichstag Dome, Berlin © Laura VanDeventer; Page xiv: Arnhem Open-Air Museum in the Netherlands © Dominic Bonuccelli, page xvi: Salzburg Cathedral, Germany © Dominic Bonuccelli
Cover Photo: Palais de Justice and River Seine, Paris, France © BL Images Ltd/Alamy

ABOUT THE AUTHOR

RICK STEVES

 Since 1973, Rick Steves has spent 100 days every year exploring Europe. Rick produces a public television series (*Rick Steves' Europe*), a public radio show (*Travel with Rick Steves*), and a podcast (*Rick Steves Audio Europe*); writes a bestselling series of guidebooks and a nationally syndicated newspaper column; organizes guided tours that take thousands of travelers to Europe annually; and offers an information-packed website (www.ricksteves.com). With the help of his hardworking staff of 70 at Europe Through the Back Door—in Edmonds, Washington, just north of Seattle—Rick's mission is to make European travel fun, affordable, and culturally enlightening for Americans.